Electromagnetic Horn Antennas

Edited by
A. W. Love
Member of the Technical Staff
Space Division
Rockwell International

A volume in the IEEE PRESS Selected Reprint Series,
prepared under the sponsorship of the
IEEE Antennas and Propagation Society.

IEEE PRESS

The Institute of Electrical and Electronics Engineers, Inc. New York

International Standard Book Numbers: Clothbound: 0-87942-075-8
Paperbound: 0-87942-076-6

Library of Congress Catalog Card Number 75-44649

PRINTED IN THE UNITED STATES OF AMERICA

Hayser

ML

Electromagnetic Horn Antennas

OTHER IEEE PRESS BOOKS

Waveform Quantization and Coding, *Edited by N. S. Jayant*
Solar Cells, *Edited by C. E. Backus*
Computer Networking, *Edited by R. P. Blanc and I. W. Cotton*
Communications Channels: Characterization and Behavior, *Edited by B. Goldberg*
Large-Scale Networks: Theory and Design, *Edited by F. T. Boesch*
Optical Fiber Technology, *Edited by D. Gloge*
Selected Papers in Digital Signal Processing, II, *Edited by the Digital Signal Processing Committee*
A Guide for Better Technical Presentations, *Edited by R. M. Woelfle*
Career Management: A Guide to Combating Obsolescence, *Edited by H. G. Kaufman*
Energy and Man: Technical and Social Aspects of Energy, *Edited by M. G. Morgan*
Magnetic Bubble Technology: Integrated-Circuit Magnetics for Digital Storage and Processing, *Edited by H. Chang*
Frequency Synthesis: Techniques and Applications, *Edited by J. Gorski-Popiel*
Literature in Digital Processing: Author and Permuted Title Index (Revised and Expanded Edition), *Edited by H. D. Helms, J. F. Kaiser, and L. R. Rabiner*
Data Communications via Fading Channels, *Edited by K. Brayer*
Nonlinear Networks: Theory and Analysis, *Edited by A. N. Wilson, Jr.*
Computer Communications, *Edited by P. E. Green, Jr. and R. W. Lucky*
Stability of Large Electric Power Systems, *Edited by R. T. Byerly and E. W. Kimbark*
Automatic Test Equipment: Hardware, Software, and Management, *Edited by F. Liguori*
Key Papers in the Development of Coding Theory, *Edited by E. R. Berlekamp*
Technology and Social Institutions, *Edited by K. Chen*
Key Papers in the Development of Information Theory, *Edited by D. Slepian*
Computer-Aided Filter Design, *Edited by G. Szentirmai*
Laser Devices and Applications, *Edited by I. P. Kaminow and A. E. Siegman*
Integrated Optics, *Edited by D. Marcuse*
Laser Theory, *Edited by F. S. Barnes*
Digital Signal Processing, *Edited by L. R. Rabiner and C. M. Rader*
Minicomputers: Hardware, Software, and Applications, *Edited by J. D. Schoeffler and R. H. Temple*
Semiconductor Memories, *Edited by D. A. Hodges*
Power Semiconductor Applications, Volume II: Equipment and Systems, *Edited by J. D. Harnden, Jr. and F. B. Golden*
Power Semiconductor Applications, Volume I: General Considerations, *Edited by J. D. Harnden and F. B. Golden*
A Practical Guide to Minicomputer Applications, *Edited by F. F. Coury*
Active Inductorless Filters, *Edited by S. K. Mitra*
Clearing the Air: The Impact of the Clean Air Act on Technology, *Edited by J. C. Redmond, J. C. Cook, and A. A. J. Hoffman*

Contents

"I conceive that these things, King Gelon, will appear incredible to the great majority of people who have not studied mathematics, but that to those who are conversant therewith and have given thought to the question of the distances and sizes of the earth, the sun and moon and the whole universe, the proof will carry conviction. And it was for this reason that I thought the subject would not be inappropriate for your consideration."

—Archimedes,
The Sand Reckoner

Introduction

As an acoustical instrument, the horn has been used for thousands of years to amplify sound waves. Indeed, it performs this function so well that Joshua's only weapons, when he secured the fall of Jericho, were seven trumpets fashioned from ram's horns. As an electromagnetic device, the horn cannot lay claim to any such longevity, but it is perhaps not quite such a newcomer on the scene as many of us think. There is a justifiable tendency to regard the horn antenna synonymously with microwaves, but the impression that the latter came into being just in time to be exploited in World War II is incorrect. In fact, both microwaves and horn antennas were in use in the late nineteenth century.

Only 15 years elapsed between James Clerk Maxwell's theoretical prediction of the existence of electromagnetic waves in 1873 and Heinrich Hertz's experimental verification in 1888. In that year, Hertz generated, radiated, and detected microwaves (the wavelength was about 66 cm) using dipole-fed parabolic cylinder antennas for both transmission and reception. A great amount of scientific interest was shown in microwaves during the next 12 or so years, and one of the devices that was used in investigating their properties was the electromagnetic horn. It is true that interest dwindled after 1900 when it became apparent, as a result of the work of Marconi, that much longer wavelengths were to be preferred for long range radio communication. Interest in microwaves did not then revive until the late 1930's after which, of course, the exigencies of World War II produced a veritable explosion in the development of the art.

The forerunner of the horn, namely, the hollow pipe radiator, seems first to have been used by Sir Oliver Lodge; he demonstrated such a device for radiating and receiving microwaves in London in June 1894. In 1897 the Indian physicist, Professor J. Chunder Bose, visited London and lectured at the Royal Institution. His lecture included a demonstration of a millimeter-wave spectrometer operating at a frequency of 60 GHz! Among the components comprising the spectrometer were plane and cylindrical mirrors, dielectric prisms, and a true pyramidal horn which Bose referred to as a "collecting funnel." With such a spectrometer, he was able to determine the value 1.734 for the refractive index of sulphur. An excellent account of these early researches has been given by J. F. Ramsay [1], to whom I am indebted for bringing to my attention this fascinating prehistory.

Coincidentally, 1897 was the year in which Lord Rayleigh published his famous paper on waveguide transmission, the existence of which was anticipated, as Ramsay notes, by the experimental work of Lodge. Nor were microwave investigations being neglected in the United States, for in that same year, 1897, a 9-cm wavelength interferometer was in use in Professor A. A. Michelson's laboratory in Chicago; it was capable of 1 percent accuracy in the measurement of wavelength and index of refraction. Although their equipment may be thought crude by modern standards, these early researchers showed remarkable insight, ingenuity, and inventiveness. They were familiar with, and used, polarizers, "cutoff" metal plate gratings, quarter and half-wave plates, artificial dielectrics, lenses, and even dual-prism directional couplers. Their detectors were insensitive, but their spark gap sources were relatively powerful; about the only thing lacking was monochromaticity. It was, indeed, a notable era, that decade of the 1890's, but we must leave it in favor of things more current.

The need for a volume of collected papers is generally greatest in a new and rapidly expanding field of scientific or engineering endeavor in which textbooks and reference works have not yet become available. As we have seen, horn antennas can hardly be said to be new, but they certainly represent a field which has been anything but dormant in recent years. The impetus for activity in electromagnetic horn radiator design has stemmed, of course, from the need to wring out every last fraction of a decibel in gain from the large satellite communications and radio astronomy reflector antennas that are in use all over the world today. The fact that fully 60 percent of the papers in Parts V, VI, and VII of this book, all of which deal with the design of high-efficiency feed horns, have been published since 1970 attests to this activity. This alone might well justify the preparation of a volume of reprints on the subject. An equally compelling reason, perhaps, is to be found in the surprising fact that there is no single reference work or textbook available today that deals solely with electromagnetic horn radiators. Consequently, the interested engineer must often undertake a search of the literature in order to obtain up-to-date information for his design needs. This can be a time-consuming effort, for relevant articles are scattered throughout the journals and periodicals of a number of countries. Thus, no fewer than 15 different publications are represented in the present volume.

The horn has, of course, much greater utility than merely that of a feed for reflectors and lenses. It is a common element in phased array antennas. It is a reliable and accurate gain standard and, finally, it is a useful radiator in its own right, easy to excite and simple to build. These attributes make the horn invaluable to engineers and scientists in a number of fields, and it is to these workers that this book is addressed. The emphasis in selection of papers has been twofold: to present those papers that establish fundamental theory and operating principles upon which the engineer/scientist may build to suit his own needs, and to include articles containing useful and pertinent information that will permit him, when faced with the need to use a horn antenna, to rest secure in the knowledge that the design he selects is at least close to optimum for the intended application.

The reader should be aware that the book is a collection of reprinted papers only, and does not contain other new or original material. Company reports, laboratory notes, technical memoranda, and the like have been excluded; all included material has been selected strictly from among published papers that had originally been subjected to editorial and technical review by competent referees. It therefore is reasonable to claim that the volume represents the state of the art in electromagnetic horn radiator development as it exists today.

The book has been organized into eight parts. The first part contains papers of historical significance that first appeared in the approximate decade between 1939 and 1950. The second covers general topics associated with radiation by horns and open waveguides. Part III is devoted to the theoretical calculation and experimental measurement of the gain of horn radiators, given the aperture dimensions and slant length, while Part IV deals with the use of simple horns as feeds for paraboloidal reflectors. In contrast, the next three parts are concerned with the more complex kinds of horns whose development has been stimulated by the need to maximize either the gain or the gain/temperature ratio (*G/T*) of large reflector antennas. These more sophisticated versions are the multimode, corrugated, and dielectric-loaded horn radiators; they are treated in Parts V, VI, and VII, respectively. The last part, VIII, is given over to the horn/reflector antenna. The papers within each of the parts are largely, but not entirely, arranged in chronological order.

Introductory comments have been provided for each part in an effort to tie the various parts together and to form some semblance of a cohesive whole. These comments include references to articles that could not be included for reasons of space, and to papers on related topics that did not quite fit within the framework of this volume. A bibliography of these and other papers is to be found at the end of each introductory section.

References

[1] J. F. Ramsay, "Microwave antenna and waveguide techniques before 1900," *Proc. IRE*, vol. 46, pp. 405–415, Feb. 1958.

Part I
Historical

With the revival of interest in microwaves and waveguide transmission lines in the 1930's, it was to be expected that horn antennas would again come into use. We find suggestions to this effect in papers by Southworth [1] and Barrow [2] that appeared in 1936. Radiation from the open end of a rectangular waveguide was studied theoretically and experimentally and reported on by Barrow and Greene [3] in 1938. They gave the now familiar expressions for the *E*- and *H*-plane patterns due to $TE_{0,n}$ modes and showed comparisons between theory and experiment. They also correctly conjectured that unexpected radiation appearing in the rear hemisphere was due to diffraction at the mouth of the guide, especially at the *E*-plane edges.

The first analysis of radiation by a true horn, however, was given by Barrow and Chu. Their paper of January 1939 is the first in the present volume. In Part I of their work, a clear description of the radially propagating modes in a sectoral, radial waveguide is given. In their terminology, *H* modes have no component of electric field in the radial direction ($E_\rho \equiv 0$). In Part II they apply Huyghens' principle to the waveguide field that would occur in the horn mouth if the sides were of infinite extent, and they proceed to calculate what we now call the *H*-plane pattern of an *H*-plane sectoral horn. This is done both for the H_{01} and H_{03} modes that are analogous to the same modes in a rectangular guide. They observe that the radiation patterns of a sectoral and rectangular guide behave similarly when the flare angle is small and the radial length not too long. But for fixed radial length and increasing flare angle, they show that the beam first begins to sharpen, reaches a minimum width, and then broadens again. Today we know that the use of a lens in the mouth of the horn (to correct the "phase error") would yield narrower and narrower patterns as the flare angle is increased. A companion paper (not included here) by Barrow and Lewis [4] offers experimental evidence to corroborate the theory.

The next two papers are of practical importance. That of Southworth and King gives experimental patterns for a number of open-ended round waveguides and conical horns of varying flare angle. The one by Chu and Barrow complements their theoretical paper, and gives detailed design data applicable to both *E*- and *H*-plane sectoral horns. They make brief reference to the pyramidal horn.

In the fourth paper, Chu discusses difficulties in applying the Kirchhoff formulation of Huyghens' principle to the calculation of horn radiation patterns (see also Schelkunoff [5] and Stratton and Chu [6]). Accordingly, Chu introduces a modified Kirchhoff formula with which he calculates the radiation patterns of open circular and rectangular waveguides and of sectoral horns. He observes that open waveguide radiators tend to suffer problems arising from higher modes that adversely affect the patterns and power gain when large apertures are used, and he proposes to avoid these difficulties by flaring the guide to form an electromagnetic horn. However, he analyzes only the sectoral horn.

In his paper on phase correction, Rust seems to have been among the first (see also Kock [7]) to recognize that loss in directivity of the sectoral horn can be thought of as being due to curvature of the phase front in the aperture or, equivalently, to phase error. Rust calls it "phase slip" and suggests that horn length should be great enough to limit the slip to 90°. He devised the metal plate lens as a means for correction.

The next two papers are analytical. Horton uses the method of Schelkunoff [5] to calculate the patterns of TE modes in rectangular, circular, and semicircular waveguides. He observes that the results will apply to horns of similar shape if the flare angle is small. Schorr and Beck use Schelkunoff's formalism in what appears to be the first attempt at a rigorous treatment of the radiation from conical horns. They begin with the field expressions for outward-going spherical waves in a conical waveguide (both TE and TM waves are treated), and a clear discussion of the nature of these waves is given in a manner analogous to that in Barrow and Chu's paper concerning cylindrical waves in a sectoral guide. The radiation field is calculated only for the dominant TE_{11} mode on the assumption of small horn flare angle. Comparisons are made with the experimental results of Southworth and King (the second paper in this part).

The last paper in this part is by King, and presents a considerable body of experimental data on both the pattern shape and the gain of conical horns of varying length and aperture diameter. As far as I am aware, King introduces, for the first time, the notion of an optimum gain horn, that is, a horn that has maximum gain for a given length. It will be apparent to the reader that this paper could just as well have been placed in Part III as in this part.

Two papers that are not included in this volume are nevertheless worthy of mention. One, by Rhodes [8], contains a large body of experimental pattern data on pyramidal horns. The other, by Woonton, Hay, and Vogan [9], has a good discussion of the shortcomings of the Kirchhoff–Huyghens formulation, and presents a number of measured patterns on rectangular horns.

References

[1] G. C. Southworth, "Hyper frequency wave guides—General considerations and experimental results," *Bell Syst. Tech. J.*, vol. 15, pp. 284–309, Apr. 1936.

[2] W. L. Barrow, "Transmission of electromagnetic waves in hollow tubes of metal," *Proc. IRE*, vol. 24, pp. 1298–1328, Oct. 1936.
[3] W. L. Barrow and F. M. Greene, "Rectangular hollow pipe radiators," *Proc. IRE*, vol. 26, pp. 1498–1519, Dec. 1938.
[4] W. L. Barrow and F. D. Lewis, "The sectoral electromagnetic horn," *Proc. IRE*, vol. 27, pp. 41–50, Jan. 1939.
[5] S. A. Schelkunoff, "On diffraction and radiation of electromagnetic waves," *Phys. Rev.*, vol. 56, pp. 308–316, Aug. 15, 1939.
[6] J. A. Stratton and L. J. Chu, "Diffraction theory of electromagnetic waves," *Phys. Rev.*, vol. 56, pp. 99–107, 1939.
[7] W. E. Kock, "Metal lens antennas," *Proc. IRE*, vol. 34, pp. 828–836, Nov. 1946.
[8] D. R. Rhodes, "An experimental investigation of the radiation patterns of electromagnetic horn antennas," *Proc. IRE*, vol. 36, pp. 1101–1105, Sept. 1948.
[9] G. A. Woonton, D. R. Hay, and E. L. Vogan, "An experimental investigation of formulas for the prediction of horn radiation patterns," *J. Appl. Phys.*, vol. 20, pp. 71–78, Jan. 1949.

Theory of the Electromagnetic Horn*

W. L. BARROW†, ASSOCIATE MEMBER, I.R.E., AND L. J. CHU†, NONMEMBER, I.R.E.

Summary—*A theoretical analysis of the operation of the electromagnetic horn "antenna" is derived from Maxwell's equations. The details apply to a horn of sectoral shape. The analysis also applies to a tapered hollow-pipe transmission line. Certain transmission quantities, like the phase constant, attenuation constant, velocity of propagation, etc., are calculated for horns of any angle of flare and the field configuration within the horn is plotted. One result is a clear understanding of the propagation of waves within the horn. Another result is that design specifications for horns may be established. Calculations of radiation patterns made in this analysis agree satisfactorily with experiments reported in a companion paper.*

Introduction

In a companion paper,[1] the radiation of electromagnetic waves from a horn of sectoral shape is discussed from experimental and practical viewpoints, particularly with respect to the realization of a straight-line landing-path system for the blind landing of airplanes.

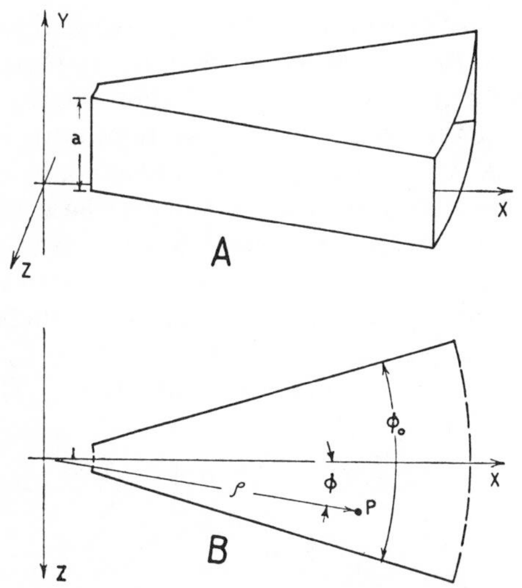

Fig. 1—View of sectoral horn A and the cylindrical co-ordinate system B.

In this paper, we shall present the theory of the transmission of waves through the inside of the horn and into the outer free space. Although the analysis applies specifically to the sectoral horn, it provides a clear physical picture of the operation of electromagnetic horns of any shape. The method may be applied to a number of specific shapes, such as conical and hyperbolic, for which the boundary-value problem can be solved.

Although in this paper the emphasis will be on the electromagnetic horn, the problem that we solve is of much broader import. For example, the analysis applies directly to the transmission of waves in a hollow-pipe line with constants that change uniformly along its length, that is, to a "tapered" hollow-pipe line. The similar problem has been solved for conventional transmission lines. The analysis also bears on the operation of a tapered section of hollow pipe used as a connection between two uniform hollow-pipe lines of unequal cross sections. Such tapered sections may be used to reduce the electrical discontinuity when joining two pipes of unequal dimensions, for an aid in matching their impedances, and for other purposes. The strong similarity between the internal aspects of the electromagnetic horn and the hollow-pipe line makes it helpful to carry over into the horn problem certain of the conceptions and terminology of hollow-pipe transmission theory.

The analysis falls naturally into two parts. In the first part, the boundary conditions for a horn of perfect conductivity and of infinite length will be imposed on the appropriate solutions of Maxwell's equations to obtain the expressions for the electric and magnetic fields within the horn and to derive the more important transmission properties of these internal waves. In the second part, Huygens' principle will be invoked to calculate the shape of the radiation field at a great distance from the mouth of the horn by assuming the distribution across the mouth to be the same as would exist there if the sides of the horn extended to infinity. General discussions of electromagnetic-horn radiators will be given throughout the paper.

Part I. Waves Inside the Sectoral Horn

The Field Inside the Horn

The shape of the sectoral horn is shown in Fig. 1, which also shows the cylindrical co-ordinate system y, ρ, and ϕ. The horn is bounded by perfectly conducting surfaces at $\phi = \pm\phi_o/2$ and at $y = 0, a$. The interior space is assumed to be nonconducting and of dielectric constant ϵ and permeability μ; in the horn, this space will usually be air, but in the hollow-pipe applications of this analysis it might be another gas or a vacuum. In other cases, it might be a liquid or even a solid dielectric.

* Decimal classification: R111.2. Original manuscript received by the Institute, June 10, 1938. Presented in part before the joint meeting of the I.R.E. and the U.R.S.I., Washington, D. C., April 30, 1938. Many of the calculations contained in this paper were made as a part of a Doctor's thesis in the Department of Electrical Engineering at Massachusetts Institute of Technology by L. J. Chu.

† Massachusetts Institute of Technology, Cambridge, Massachusetts.

[1] W. L. Barrow and F. D. Lewis, "The sectoral electromagnetic horn," Proc. I.R.E., this issue, pp. 41–50.

Reprinted from *Proc. IRE*, vol. 27, pp. 51–64, Jan. 1939.

In this section, the sides of the horn are assumed to extend to infinity in the ρ direction, or at least so far in that direction that the field in the region under consideration is not disturbed by end effects. The origin will be left out of explicit formulation, as will the exact configuration of the exciting system. As discussed in the companion paper,[1] excitation may take place either by means of a section of hollow pipe opening into the horn near the apex, or origin of the co-ordinate system, by means of an exciting rod or antenna located within the horn near the apex, or by means of a suitable high-frequency energy-converting device disposed in the throat. In the latter cases, a suitable reflector is desirable, and the distance between the antenna and reflector should be adjusted or adjustable. In any case, waves of the same type may be excited inside the horn.

Maxwell's equations in a form suitable for our problem with an assumed time variation $e^{i\omega t}$, where $i=\sqrt{-1}$, $\omega=2\pi\times$ frequency, and $t=$ time in seconds, are as follows:

$$
\begin{aligned}
i\omega\epsilon\rho E_y &= \frac{\partial}{\partial\rho}(\rho H_\phi) - \frac{\partial}{\partial\phi}H_\rho \\
i\omega\epsilon\rho E_\rho &= \frac{\partial}{\partial\phi}H_y - \frac{\partial}{\partial y}(\rho H_\phi) \\
i\omega\epsilon E_\phi &= \frac{\partial}{\partial y}H_\rho - \frac{\partial}{\partial\rho}H_y \\
-i\omega\mu\rho H_y &= \frac{\partial}{\partial\rho}(\rho E_\phi) - \frac{\partial}{\partial\phi}E_\rho \\
-i\omega\mu\rho H_\rho &= \frac{\partial}{\partial\phi}E_y - \frac{\partial}{\partial y}(\rho E_\phi) \\
-i\omega\mu H_\phi &= \frac{\partial}{\partial y}E_\rho - \frac{\partial}{\partial\rho}E_y.
\end{aligned}
\qquad (1)
$$

The components E_y, E_ρ, E_ϕ, H_y, H_ρ, and H_ϕ of electric field E and magnetic field H, respectively, in these expressions are complex quantities independent of the time and depend on the space variables only. The actual field is the real part of $Ee^{i\omega t}$ and of $He^{i\omega t}$. A practical system of units is used in which

$E=$ electric intensity in volts per centimeter

$H=$ magnetic intensity in amperes per centimeter

$\mu=$ permeability in mhos per centimeter (for air $\mu_o=4\pi\cdot 10^{-9}$)

$\epsilon=$ dielectric constant in farads per centimeter (for air $\epsilon_o=10^{-11}/36\pi$)

$c=1/\sqrt{\mu\epsilon}=$ velocity of light in a medium with constants μ, ϵ (for air, $c=$ velocity of light in vacuum $=3\times 10^{10}$ centimeters per second).

A great number of solutions may be obtained for (1) and the choice of any particular solution or group of solutions depends on the conditions of the problem. It is possible to choose solutions that lead to fields varying with all three of the co-ordinates y, ρ, ϕ or with any two of them. We may also classify all possible waves into two broad types, the E waves and the H waves, corresponding to similar types of waves in hollow metal pipes. The E wave has no *radial* component of magnetic intensity ($H_\rho=0$) and the H wave has no *radial* component of electric intensity ($E_\rho=0$). The several lowest-order waves of each type may be excited readily by an appropriate disposition of antennas near the throat or by means of a corresponding wave from a hollow pipe opening into the throat.

For the moment, we limit our attention to one type of wave, namely, that corresponding to the $H_{0,m}$ wave, m an odd integer, in a hollow pipe of rectangular cross section.[2] This wave is the one used in the sectoral horn of the companion paper to produce a single sharp beam of radiant energy and will be called the $H_{0,m}$ wave in a sectoral horn hereafter. In this wave, all components of field are independent of y, the electric intensity is everywhere parallel to the y axis, i.e., perpendicular to the top and bottom surfaces, and the magnetic field lies in planes perpendicular to the y axis. The problem, therefore, reduces to a two-dimensional one in which E_ρ, E_ϕ, and H_y are all zero. Under these conditions, (1) reduces to

$$
\begin{aligned}
i\omega\epsilon\rho E_y &= \frac{\partial}{\partial\rho}(\rho H_\phi) - \frac{\partial}{\partial\phi}H_\rho \\
-i\omega\mu\rho H_\rho &= \frac{\partial}{\partial\phi}E_y \\
i\omega\mu H_\phi &= \frac{\partial}{\partial\rho}E_y.
\end{aligned}
\qquad (2)
$$

By eliminating H_ϕ and H_ρ from (2), we obtain the following equation for E_y:

$$\left[\frac{\partial^2}{\partial\rho^2} + \frac{1}{\rho}\frac{\partial}{\partial\rho} + \frac{1}{\rho^2}\frac{\partial^2}{\partial\phi^2} + \left(\frac{\omega}{c}\right)^2\right]E_y = 0. \qquad (3)$$

The general solution of this equation is

$$E_y = [A\sin(m\nu\phi) + B\cos(m\nu\phi)] \cdot\left[CJ_{m\nu}\left(\frac{\omega}{c}\rho\right) + DY_{m\nu}\left(\frac{\omega}{c}\rho\right)\right] \qquad (4)$$

where A, B, C, and D are complex constants, $J_{m\nu}$ and $Y_{m\nu}$ are Bessel functions of the first and second kinds,

[2] L. J. Chu and W. L. Barrow, "Electromagnetic waves in hollow metal tubes of rectangular cross section," Proc. I.R.E., vol. 26, pp. 1520–1555; December, (1938).

respectively, of the $m\nu$ *th* order, and the positive integer m and the real constant ν are both to be determined from the boundary conditions.

There is a correspondence between the expression for E_y from (4) for the horn and the corresponding expression for the $H_{0,m}$ wave in a hollow pipe of rectangular cross section. First, in the hollow pipe there is a sinusoidal space variation in the z direction transverse to the direction of propagation, but in the horn there is a sinusoidal space variation in the ϕ direction along an arc of a circle with its center at the apex of the horn, which is also at right angles to the propagation direction. Second, in the pipe the waves travel along the axis in the x direction with an exponential form of propagation, but in the horn they travel outward in the radial direction with a Bessel function form of propagation. Only those $H_{0,m}$ waves which have an electric field of even symmetry about the center of the pipe radiate beams with a central lobe. For this reason, only the cosine term in (4) will be retained. As a practical matter, the sine term cannot exist if the horn is excited by an antenna placed vertically in the $\phi=0$ plane, as it is in the normal operation of the horn. A wave propagated in the radial direction may be conveniently represented by the Bessel function of the third kind, or Hankel function,

$$K_{m\nu} = J_{m\nu} - iY_{m\nu}. \tag{5}$$

Hence, we put the constants C and D in (4) equal to 1 and $-i$, respectively. With these modifications, we obtain from (4) and (2) the following solutions for the field within the horn:

$$\left.\begin{aligned} E_y &= B\cos(m\nu\phi)K_{m\nu}\left(2\pi\frac{\rho}{\lambda}\right)\\ H_\rho &= B\frac{m\nu}{i\omega\mu\rho}\sin(m\nu\phi)K_{m\nu}\left(2\pi\frac{\rho}{\lambda}\right)\\ H_\phi &= -Bi\sqrt{\frac{\epsilon}{\mu}}\cos(m\nu\phi)K_{m\nu}'\left(2\pi\frac{\rho}{\lambda}\right)\end{aligned}\right\} \tag{6}$$

where $K_{m\nu}'$ is the derivative of $K_{m\nu}$ with respect to its argument $(2\pi\rho/\lambda)$ and λ is the wavelength of a plane wave in an unbounded medium of constants μ and ϵ. The remaining components of field are zero, i.e., $H_y=E_\rho=E_\phi=0$.

The metal is assumed to have an infinitely high conductivity.[3] The boundary conditions require that the tangential component of the electric field vanish at the boundary. There is no electric field in our wave tangential to the top and bottom surfaces of the horn, hence, the boundary conditions are automatically satisfied for $y=0,a$. At the two sides, where $\phi=\pm\phi_o/2$, E_y must vanish, so we must have

$$\cos(m\nu\phi_o/2) = 0. \tag{7}$$

This equation can be satisfied by letting the integer m be odd (1, 3, 5, . . .) and

$$\nu = \frac{\pi}{\phi_o}. \tag{8}$$

The integer m specifies the order of the wave. Physically it indicates the number of half-period sinusoidal variations between the two sides of any component of the field along an arc $\rho=$constant. The constant ν depends only on the flare angle ϕ_o, as specified by (8). Since m is always associated with ν as a product, the product

$$m\nu = \frac{m\pi}{\phi_o} \tag{9}$$

determines the behavior of the wave inside the horn. Thus, as will be made clear later, the $H_{0,3}$ wave $(m=3)$, in a horn of $\phi_o=60$ degrees behaves in a way similar to the $H_{0,1}$ wave $(m=1)$ in a horn of $\phi_o=20$ degrees. In the preferred mode of operating the sectoral horn, $m=1$ and $m\nu=\pi/\phi_o$; this mode corresponds to a single half-period distribution around an arc connecting the two flared sides and a uniform distribution along lines perpendicular to the arc and the radii.

The field distribution of the $H_{0,1}$ wave for $\phi_o\cong 30$ degrees is sketched in an approximate way in Figs. 2 and 3, respectively. The field distributions of the third- and higher-order waves may be sketched in a similar manner. The rectangles shown at the right-hand end of the figures are developed views of the arctuate cross sections of the horn. Near the small end or "throat," the wavelength in the horn is very large and the crowding of the magnetic lines indicates the relatively large magnitudes of field intensities. As will be explained in a following paragraph, the waves are offered large opposition in passing through this part of the horn, hence we term it the "attenuation" region. Farther away from the throat the waves enter a part of the horn through which they pass with little or no opposition, which we term the "transmission" region. In the beginning of the transmission region, the magnetic lines form closed loops. It is observed from Figs. 2 and 3 that the wavelength in the horn, as well as the concentration of the lines of force, decreases gradually as the waves travel outward.

Near the throat the radial component of the magnetic field is still of considerable magnitude, but in

[3] The attenuation caused by finitely conducting walls will not be given in this paper. Its effect will generally be small, because of the short length of the structures used for horns.

the more distant parts of the horn this component becomes negligible compared to the other two components of field. However, both the magnetic and the electric lines of force are normal to each other and to the direction of propagation, and the waves inside the horn behave very much as do transverse electromagnetic waves in free space. If the sides of the horn are terminated to form a "mouth" in this distant region, and if we assume that the termination does not materially effect the wave near the mouth, these substantially transverse cylindrical waves may continue their propagation outward into the surrounding free space. Because there is no appreciable longitudinal field, they easily form a beam in space, but because of the limited dimensions of the mouth this beam has a definite angular spread.

Viewed in this way, the operation of the horn consists in guiding electromagnetic energy from a source disposed in the throat outward in such a way that a substantially transverse wave is produced over the bounded but relatively large surface of the mouth. If certain conditions are satisfied as to the nature of the source, the shape of the wave radiated from the horn depends primarily on the configuration of the horn.

Transmission Constants

The transmission properties of the waves in the horn may be expressed by a number of physical quantities, such as the phase constant, the phase

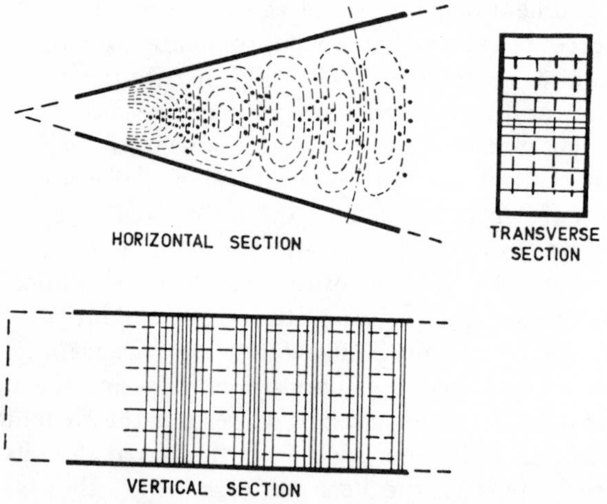

Fig. 2—Sketch of field distribution of the $H_{0,1}$ wave in a sectoral horn. Dotted lines represent magnetic field intensity and solid lines represent electric field intensity.

velocity, the wavelength, the attenuation, the density of flow of energy, the energy distribution, and the characteristic wave impedance.

For exponentially propagated waves, like waves on wires or in hollow pipes, the attenuation constant α and the phase constant β may be defined as the logarithmic rate of decrease of magnitude and of change of phase, respectively, in the direction of propagation x, and the expression results

$$\alpha + i\beta = -\frac{\partial}{\partial x}\log E = -\frac{1}{E}\frac{\partial E}{\partial x} \tag{10}$$

where E represents any component of the field. In the conventional cases, all components of the field have the same exponential variation with x and therefore $\alpha+i\beta$ is simply the coefficient of x in the exponent.

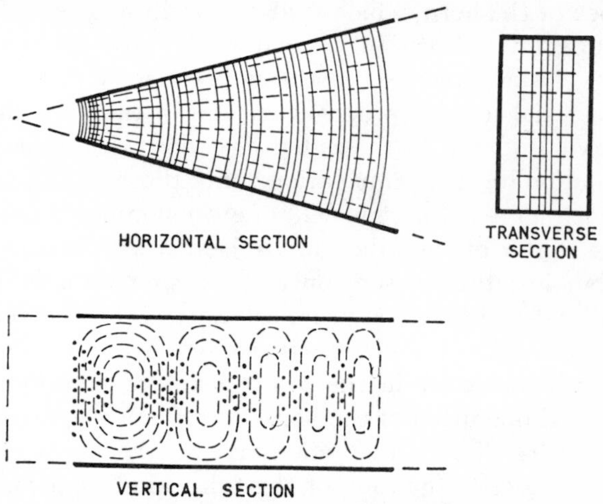

Fig. 3—Sketch of field distribution of the $H_{0,1}$ wave in a sectoral horn. Dotted lines represent magnetic field intensity and solid lines represent electric field intensity.

A more complicated situation exists in the horn. The waves are propagated in the radial direction ρ and the Hankel functions specify the variation with ρ. Furthermore, the three components E_y, H_ρ, and H_ϕ do not vary in the same functional way. Despite the above differences, we will use the definition (10) for the horn also, replacing x by ρ. Since our principal interest is in the electric field, which we can easily measure experimentally, we will deal with E_y alone. Using the value for E_y from (6), we get

$$\alpha + i\beta = -\frac{2\pi}{\lambda}\,\frac{K_{m\nu}'\left(2\pi\dfrac{\rho}{\lambda}\right)}{K_{m\nu}\left(2\pi\dfrac{\rho}{\lambda}\right)} \tag{11}$$

where the prime respresents differentation with respect to the argument.

The interpretation of these expressions for α and β will make definite the conceptions of the attenuation and the transmission regions described qualitatively in the last section. We define the attenuation region as that portion of the horn in which the phase constant β is very small compared to its value $2\pi/\lambda$ for a wave in free space. Similarly, we define the *trans-*

mission region as that portion of the horn in which the phase constant β is almost equal to $2\pi/\lambda$. The attenuation region involves small values of ρ and the

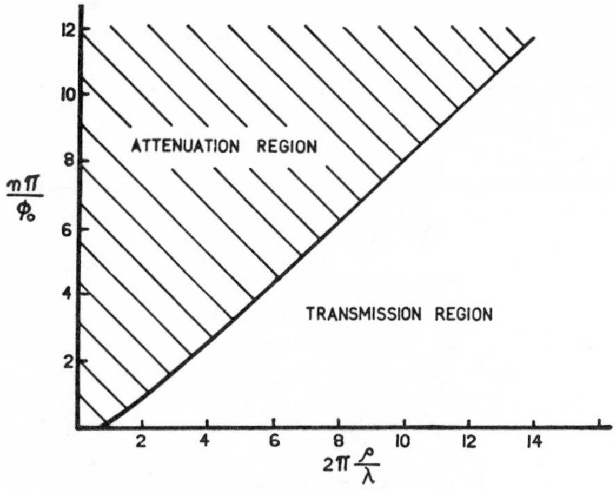

Fig. 4—Attenuation and transmission regions for a sectoral horn.

transmission region large values. By using the following asymptotic expressions for the Hankel function

$$K_{m\nu} \cong \begin{cases} \frac{1}{(m\nu)!}\left(\frac{2\pi\rho}{2\lambda}\right)^{m\nu} + i\,\frac{(m\nu-1)!}{\pi}\left(\frac{2\lambda}{2\pi\rho}\right)^{m\nu}, & \rho \text{ small} \\ \sqrt{\frac{2\lambda}{\pi 2\pi\rho}}\, e^{-i[2\pi(\rho/\lambda)-((2m\nu-1)/4)\pi]}, & \rho \text{ large} \end{cases} \quad (12)$$

we obtain the approximate expressions for α and β in the two regions

$$\text{attenuation region} \begin{cases} \alpha \cong \frac{m\pi}{\phi_o\rho} \\ \beta \cong \frac{2\pi}{\lambda} \cdot \frac{\pi}{\left[\left(\frac{m\pi}{\phi_o} - 1\right)!\right]^2 \cdot \left(\frac{\pi\rho}{\lambda}\right)^{(2\pi m/\phi_o)-1}} \end{cases} \quad (13)$$

$$\text{transmission region} \begin{cases} \alpha \cong \frac{1}{2\rho} \\ \beta \cong \frac{2\pi}{\lambda}. \end{cases} \quad (14)$$

The boundary between these two regions is not definite, as should be evident from the way in which they were defined. For convenience alone we may say that the values of $2\pi\rho/\lambda$ for which $Y_{m\pi/\phi_o}(2\pi\rho/\lambda)$ passes through its lowest root represent the dividing line. With this reservation, the attenuation and transmission regions are shown in Fig. 4 (computed from values from Jahnke and Emde, *Tables of Functions*). For small flare angles ϕ_o, the attenuation region extends over large distances from the apex. As the flare angle is increased, the attenuation region shrinks and is confined substantially to the throat. This region occupies a progressively longer portion of the horn for the successively higher-order waves.

The phase constant β is small compared to $2\pi/\lambda$ in the attenuation region, but it increases as the wave progresses outward, i.e., with increasing ρ, and approaches the value $2\pi/\lambda$ for a free-space wave when the transmission region is reached. This behavior is illustrated by the curves of Fig. 5, which have been computed from the exact expression of (11). The dotted line marks the transition between attenuation and transmission regions. The similarity between these curves and the corresponding ones for a hollow pipe is worthy of note.

The phase velocity v_p and the wavelength of the waves within the horn λ_h (not to be confused with the free-space wavelength of the exciting current, which is denoted throughout the paper by λ) are given by $v_p = \omega/\beta$ and $\lambda_h = 2\pi/\beta$, respectively. Curves of these two quantities are reproduced in Fig. 6. The dotted line again separates the attenuation region (above the line) from the transmission region (below the line). For a horn of given flare angle, the phase velocity is substantially infinite for distances ρ/λ up to a certain range, which range is greater the smaller is the flare angle ϕ_o. Within this range, the group velocity $v_g = d\omega/d\beta$ is almost zero and a signal will be propagated with very small velocity. The waves in this

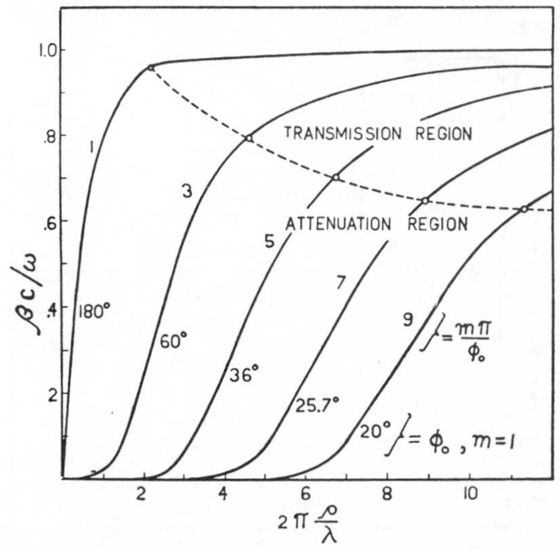

Fig. 5—Phase constant $\beta c/\omega$) versus the radial distance from the apex in wavelengths $2\pi\rho/\lambda$ for different values of flare angle ϕ_o and for waves of different orders m.

part of the horn have a hybrid character halfway between standing waves and traveling waves. In the region of transition, the velocity of a signal increases as it propagates outward, rapidly approaching the velocity of light as it enters the transmission region. In the transmission region, the waves are clearly of the traveling-wave type. The phase velocity becomes smaller during this course and also approaches the value for light.

The curves also show the way in which the several higher-order waves behave. For example, the curve for $m\pi/\phi_o = 3$ applies to the $H_{0,1}$– wave in a horn of 60-degree flare angle, but the $H_{0,3}$ wave in the same horn is governed by the curve for $m\pi/\phi_o = 9$. For distances $2\pi\rho/\lambda$ above three in magnitude, the $H_{0,1}$ wave in this horn has emerged from its "frozen" or quasi-stationary condition, while the $H_{0,3}$ wave must travel to a distance $2\pi\rho/\lambda$ equal to about eleven before it is released to be freely transmitted.

We have assumed the horn to have a perfectly conducting boundary, and the dielectric inside it to be a perfect insulator. Since there can be no loss of energy as Joule heat in either medium, the same amount of total power must be transmitted through any cylindrical cross section of the horn. The density of the transmitted power, i.e., the real part of the Poynting vector in the radial direction, must be proportional to $1/\rho$ and consequently the field should be proportional to $1/\sqrt{\rho}$. We observe that in the transmission region the field does behave in this way. The expression for the attenuation constant, $\alpha = 1/2\rho$, is a natural consequence of the diverging shape of the horn. In the attenuation region, the attenuation constant is given approximately by mv/ρ, but only the small part $1/2\rho$ is caused by the divergence. This fact does not mean that there is dissipation of energy; it indicates simply that a small fraction only of the energy in this region is transmitted through the horn in the radial direction.

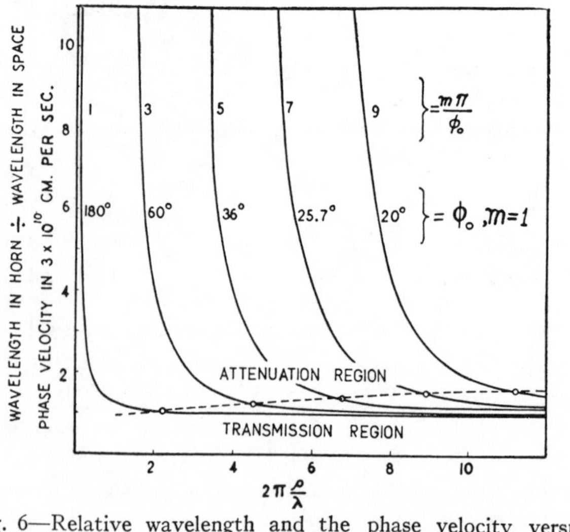

Fig. 6—Relative wavelength and the phase velocity versus $2\pi\rho/\lambda$ for different values of $m\pi/\phi_o$.

The attenuation curves of Fig. 7 are based upon the exact formula (11). The dotted line has the same significance as does the dotted line in Fig. 5. The dashed line represents the asymptotic value $1/2\rho$ which is caused by the spreading of energy over the cylindrical cross section, whose area increases constantly with the radius ρ. This figure again shows definitely the cutoff effect in the horns of different flare angles, and for waves of different orders in a horn of given flare angle.

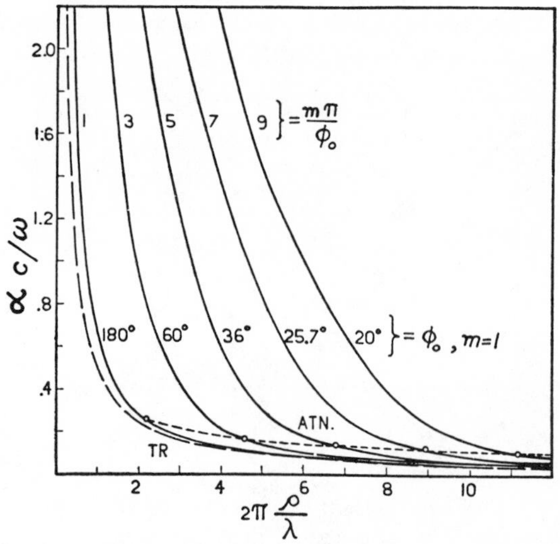

Fig. 7—Attenuation constant $\alpha c/\omega$) versus radial distance in wavelengths $2\pi\rho/\lambda$ for different values of $m\pi/\phi_o$.

As discussed above, these horn waves degenerate into the $H_{0,m}$ wave in a rectangular hollow pipe as the flare angle is reduced indefinitely. For this case, if we let $\rho = \rho_1 + x$ and $x \ll \rho_1$, $\phi_o\rho_1$ becomes the linear dimension b of the rectangular pipe. In the hollow pipe, the transmission characteristics α, β, etc., are no longer dependent upon the longitudinal co-ordinate x, and there is a definite ratio of b/λ which separates the transmission and attenuation regions. Since b is a constant, the two regions mentioned depend only on the frequency and lose the spatial meaning that they have in the horn. When $\lambda = \lambda_o = 2b/m$, the critical wavelength of the $H_{0,m}$ wave, both α and β are zero. For $\lambda < \lambda_o$, the attenuation constant only is zero, and for $\lambda > \lambda_o$, the phase constant only is zero.

The effect of finite conductivity is greater in the attenuation region than in the transmission region, as may be seen from the following argument. The power dissipated in the walls is roughly proportional to the square of the magnitude of the tangential magnetic field at the boundary. Since, for the same amount of transmitted power, this field is relatively large in the attenuation region, the power loss in this region is also comparatively large. As a consequence, the curves of the attenuation constant will be steeper for actual horns than are the curves for the ideal horns of perfect conductivity as shown in Fig. 7.

Energy Flow and Characteristic Impedance

Another useful physical quantity is the density of flow of energy, as given by the Poynting vector P. Its time-average value is as follows:

$$P = \tfrac{1}{2}(E \times H^*) \tag{15}$$

where P, E, and H^* are complex vector quantities, and H^* is the conjugate of H. By using (6), the three components of P are obtained as follows:

$$\left.\begin{aligned} P_y &= 0 \\ P_\rho &= -i\,|B|^2 \frac{1}{2}\sqrt{\frac{\epsilon}{\mu}} \\ &\qquad \cos^2(m\nu\phi) K_{m\nu}(2\pi\rho/\lambda) K_{m\nu}'^*(2\pi\rho/\lambda) \\ P_\phi &= i\,|B|^2 \frac{m\nu}{2\omega\mu\rho} \\ &\qquad \sin(m\nu\phi)\cos(m\nu\phi)\,|K_{m\nu}(2\pi\rho/\lambda)|^2 \end{aligned}\right\}. \tag{16}$$

There is no flow of energy in the y direction. The Poynting vector in the ϕ direction is a pure imaginary quantity, hence there is no net energy transfer in that direction either. An imaginary flow of energy is equivalent to reactive power[4] in electric-circuit analysis. Since P_ϕ is the product of E_y and the component of H_ρ that is out of time phase with E_y, it gives a direct measure of the amount of energy that oscillates with respect to time back and forth in the horn without getting out. In the attenuation region, P_ϕ is proportional to $(2\pi\rho/\lambda)\mu^{-2m\nu-1}$, and in the transmission region it is proportional to $(2\pi\rho/\lambda)^{-2}$.

The only direction in which energy is transmitted is the radial one. The integral of P_ρ over a cylindrical surface ρ = constant from $-\phi_o/2$ to $+\phi_o/2$ and from 0 to a, is given by

$$S = -i\,|B|^2 \sqrt{\frac{\epsilon}{\mu}}\,\frac{\phi_o a\rho}{4} K_{m\nu}(2\pi\rho/\lambda) K_{m\nu}'^*(2\pi\rho/\lambda). \tag{17}$$

The real part of S is

$$S_{\text{real}} = |B|^2 \sqrt{\frac{\epsilon}{\mu}}\,\frac{\phi_o a\rho}{4} \big[J_{m\nu}(2\pi\rho/\lambda) Y_{m\nu}'(2\pi\rho/\lambda) - Y_{m\nu}(2\pi\rho/\lambda) J_{m\nu}'(2\pi\rho/\lambda)\big]. \tag{18a}$$

The factor in the square brackets is known as the Wronskian of $J_{m\nu}$ and $Y_{m\nu}$. It is equal to $\lambda/\rho\pi^2$ as given by Watson.[5] Therefore the total power transmitted in the radial direction is

$$S_{\text{real}} = |B|^2 \sqrt{\frac{\epsilon}{\mu}}\,\frac{\phi_o a\lambda}{4\pi^2}. \tag{18b}$$

[4] W. V. Lyon, "Reactive power and power factor," *Trans. A.I.E.E.*, vol. 52, pp. 763–770; September–December, (1933).

[5] Watson "Treatise on the Theory of Bessel Functions," equation 1, p. 76, Cambridge University Press, (1922).

It is independent of ρ. That is, the power transmitted through any one cylindrical section of the horn is the same as that transmitted through any other such section, as required by the law of conservation of energy.

The imaginary part of S is the reactive power in the radial direction,

$$S_i = -|B|^2 \sqrt{\frac{\epsilon}{\mu}}\,\frac{\phi_o a\rho}{4}\,\frac{\partial}{\partial(2\pi\rho/\lambda)}|K_{m\nu}(2\pi\rho/\lambda)|^2. \tag{19}$$

In the attenuation region, the reactive power is large compared to the transmitted power. In the transmission region, the reactive power is inversely proportional to the radial distance from the apex. When ρ/λ is sufficiently large, it is negligibly small compared to the transmitted power.

The time average of the stored energy densities may be computed from the expressions

$$\begin{aligned} &\text{electric energy density} = \tfrac{1}{4}\epsilon\,|E_y|^2 \\ &\text{magnetic energy density} = \tfrac{1}{4}\mu\big[|H_\rho|^2 + |H_\phi|^2\big]. \end{aligned} \tag{20}$$

We wish to compute the energy stored in a small volume of the horn contained between the bounding walls and two cylindrical surfaces $\rho = \rho_1$ and $\rho = \rho_1 + \delta\rho$ where $\delta\rho$ is arbitrarily small. To this end, we integrate (20) over the volume just described, using the values from (19), and obtain the total electric and magnetic energies stored in this volume

$$\begin{aligned} U_E &= \tfrac{1}{8}|B|^2 \epsilon\phi_o\rho_1 a\,|K_{m\nu}|^2 \cdot \delta\rho \\ U_H &= \tfrac{1}{8}|B|^2 \epsilon\phi_o\rho_1 a \left[|K_{m\nu}'^2| + \left(\frac{m\nu\lambda}{2\pi}\right)^2 |K_{m\nu}|^2 \right] \cdot \delta\rho. \end{aligned} \tag{21a}$$

With the aid of the approximations (12), we find that both U_E and U_H are relatively large in the attenuation region, decrease rapidly as ρ_1/λ increases, and approach the limiting value

$$\lim_{\rho_1/\lambda\to\infty} U_E = \lim_{\rho_1/\lambda\to\infty} U_H = \frac{1}{8\pi^2}|B|^2 \epsilon\phi_o a\lambda \cdot \delta\rho. \tag{21b}$$

If we take twice the value from (21b) with $\delta\rho = 1$, we obtain the limiting value for the total stored energy per centimeter length in the horn. Comparing this quantity with (19), we find that the ratio of the power transmitted through a cross section to the total energy stored per centimeter is exactly $1/\sqrt{\epsilon\mu}$, i.e., this ratio is equal to the velocity of light in a medium like that within the horn. The same situation exists in a plane wave in free space.

In both the attenuation region and the transmission region, the magnetic energy is always greater than the electric energy; the two energies approach each other in value only when ρ/λ is very large. The predominance of magnetic energy allows us to consider the field of this type of wave as inductive rather than capacitive. The large energy densities near the throat are caused by the proximity to the source. At greater distances from the source, the above-described inductive effect becomes less, and consequently the energy densities decrease. At large distances from the source, the only energy present is that coming from the source as radiation in the ρ direction and the wave then behaves almost like a plane wave.

The characteristic wave impedance[6] in the radial direction is given by

$$Z_o = -\frac{E_y}{H_\phi} = -i\sqrt{\mu/\epsilon}\,\frac{K_{m\nu}}{K_{m\nu}'}\cdot \tag{22a}$$

By separating the real and imaginary parts, we obtain the characteristic resistance R_o and the characteristic reactance X_o,

$$R_o = \frac{\omega}{c}\sqrt{\frac{\mu}{\epsilon}}\,\frac{\beta}{\alpha^2+\beta^2};\qquad X_o = \frac{\omega}{c}\sqrt{\frac{\mu}{\epsilon}}\,\frac{\alpha}{\alpha^2+\beta^2} \tag{22b}$$

where α and β are the attenuation constant and the phase constant respectively, given by (11). The reactance is always positive; therefore in agreement with the preceding paragraph, it represents an inductive field. Figs. 8 and 9 show the curves of R_o and X_o as a function of $2\pi\rho/\lambda$ for several values of $m\pi/\phi_o$. The resistance approaches $\sqrt{\mu/\epsilon}=377$ ohms for large values of $2\pi\rho/\lambda$, and the reactance approaches zero. Thus, the characteristic impedance of the horn is the same as that of free space when the wave is well into the transmission region.

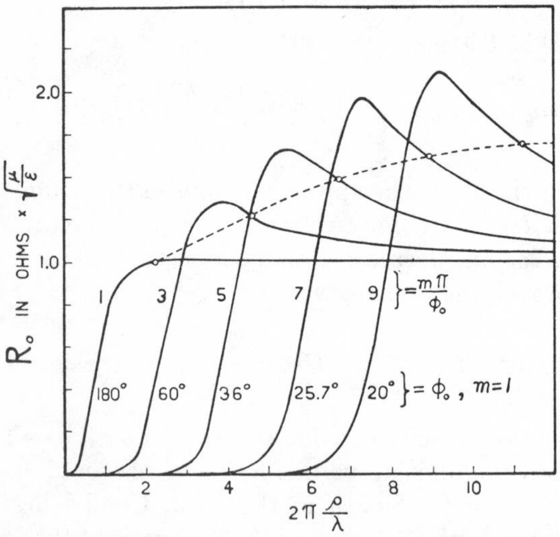

Fig. 8—Resistive component R_0 of characteristic impedance versus radial distance in wavelengths ρ/λ for different values of $m\pi/\phi_o$.

We have now formed a rather complete picture of the behavior of the energy inside the horn that may be summarized as follows: We may consider that the field is composed of two parts, the "induction" field and the "radiation" field. The energy associated with the induction field is not propagated away but is stored in the field. Its amplitude decreases rapidly as the distance from the source is increased. The radiation field represents the actual traveling wave with which the transmitted energy is associated. In our particular case, the components of this field are transverse to the radial direction, and the Poynting vector is a pure real quantity. The magnitude of the radiation field is proportional to $1/\sqrt{\rho}$, hence, the total energy transmitted through any cylindrical cross section is constant. In the attenuation region, the induction field predominates. In the transmission region, the induction field is negligible and the radiation field predominates.

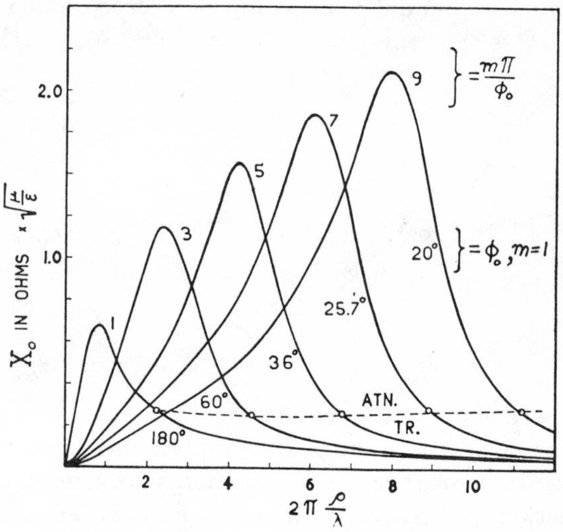

Fig. 9—Reactive component X_0 of characteristic impedance versus radial distance in wavelengths ρ/λ for different values of $m\pi/\phi_o$.

What is the significance of the two fields on the performance of the horn? Let us assume that a certain feeding system generating one only of the first- or higher-order waves is disposed in the throat of the horn. The field at the throat is fixed by the feeding system, and the sum of the induction and the radiation fields at the throat must be equal to the field at the feeding system. If the induction field at the throat is large compared to the radiation field, only a small amount of energy may be derived from the feeding system, as the voltage of the feeding system

[6] S. A. Schelkunoff, "The impedance concept and its application to problems of reflection, refraction, shielding and power absorption," *Bell Sys. Tech. Jour.*, vol. 17, pp. 17–49; January, (1938).

is fixed, and the active power is small compared to the reactive power. On the other hand, if the conditions are such that the induction field is small compared to the radiation field at the exciter, the power derived from the feeding system will be relatively large. It is primarily the radiation field in the horn that is useful in most practical instances.

The attenuation property of the horn provides an effective means for eliminating higher-order waves. To make this point clear, let us assume that a horn is excited for the $H_{0,1}$ wave by a small antenna in its throat. As the current oscillates in the antenna, not only the $H_{0,1}$ wave but also the higher-order waves or spatial harmonics are produced, which tend to propagate in the radial direction of the horn. In the vicinity of the throat, the field distribution along an arc of the horn is nonsinusoidal because of the presence of these $H_{0,m}$ waves, and is so configured that the boundary conditions at the surface of the antenna are satisfied. The magnitude of the fields of the higher-order waves are less than that of the $H_{0,1}$ wave at the throat. We observe from Fig. 3 that, for a given value of flare angle ϕ_o, the range of the attenuation region is approximately proportional to the order of the wave. If the throat is appropriately near the apex, it may be in the transmission region of the $H_{0,1}$ wave but deep in the attenuation region of the third- and higher-order $(m=3, \ldots)$ waves. The $H_{0,1}$ wave is transmitted freely in this case but the higher-order waves are "inductive" and very little of their fields can penetrate the attenuation region. That is, most of the energy associated with the $H_{0,1}$ wave is transmitted out through the horn, but only a small fraction of the energy associated with the higher-order waves is able to get out as far as the mouth. Consequently, the field distribution across the mouth will be substantially free from the third- and higher-order waves and will be a half-period sinusoid.

$H_{n,0}$ Waves in the Sectoral Horn

The discussion up to this point has concerned electromagnetic-horn waves whose electric field is vertically polarized, i.e., parallel to the y axis of Fig. 1. These waves correspond closely to the $H_{0,m}$ waves in a rectangular hollow pipe. Another simple type of horn wave of interest is that in which the electric field is polarized along the arc, or ϕ coordinate, of the same figure. This second type of wave corresponds to the $H_{n,0}$ wave in the rectangular pipe. In this section, we present without discussion the essentials of the analysis for this type of wave in the sectoral horn.

When $E_y=0$ and $E_\rho=0$ in (1), the Maxwell equations are reduced to the following groups of three equations, involving E_ϕ, H_ρ, and H_y:

$$\left.\begin{aligned} i\omega\epsilon E_\phi &= \frac{\partial}{\partial y}H_\rho - \frac{\partial}{\partial \rho}H_y \\ i\omega\mu\rho H_y &= -\frac{\partial}{\partial \rho}(\rho E_\phi) \\ i\omega\mu\rho H_\rho &= \frac{\partial}{\partial y}(\rho E_\phi) \end{aligned}\right\}. \tag{23}$$

The wave equation for E_ϕ is as follows:

$$\frac{\partial^2 E_\phi}{\partial \rho^2} + \frac{1}{\rho}\frac{\partial E_\phi}{\partial \rho} + \left(\frac{\omega}{c}\right)^2 E_\phi + \frac{\partial^2 E_\phi}{\partial y^2} - \frac{1}{\rho^2}E_\phi = 0. \tag{24}$$

After separation of variables, the solution is found to be simply

$$E_\phi = B \begin{Bmatrix}\sin\\ \cos\end{Bmatrix}(\gamma y) K_1\left(\sqrt{\left(\frac{\omega}{c}\right)^2 - \gamma^2}\,\rho\right). \tag{25}$$

The boundary conditions require that E_ϕ vanish at the top and bottom surfaces of the horn, $y=0,a$. At $y=0$, the cosine term vanishes. At $y=a$, $\sin \gamma y=0$, which condition provides the values for γ,

$$\gamma = n\pi/a, \quad n = 1, 2, 3, \cdots. \tag{26}$$

Therefore, the three components of fields are given by

$$\begin{aligned} E_\phi &= B \sin\left(\frac{n\pi}{a}y\right) K_1\left(\sqrt{\left(\frac{\omega}{c}\right)^2 - \left(\frac{n\pi}{a}\right)^2}\,\rho\right) \\ H_y &= -B\frac{\sqrt{\left(\frac{\omega}{c}\right)^2 - \left(\frac{n\pi}{a}\right)^2}}{i\omega\mu} \sin\left(\frac{n\pi}{a}y\right) K_0\left(\sqrt{\left(\frac{\omega}{c}\right)^2 - \left(\frac{n\pi}{a}\right)^2}\,\rho\right) \\ H_\rho &= B\frac{n\pi/a}{i\omega\mu\rho}\cos\left(\frac{n\pi}{a}y\right) K_1\left(\sqrt{\left(\frac{\omega}{c}\right)^2 - \left(\frac{n\pi}{a}\right)^2}\,\rho\right). \end{aligned} \tag{27}$$

This wave is independent of the flare angle of the horn, and has a sinusoidal variation in the y direction. The field distribution of the $H_{0,1}$ wave for $\phi_o = 30$ degrees is sketched in Fig. 3.

The transmission properties of the $H_{n,0}$ waves in the sectoral horn depend mainly upon the distance between the top and bottom surfaces. The Hankel functions represent a traveling wave only when their argument is a real quantity. In our case, since ρ is always real, the condition is that

$$\frac{n\pi}{a} < \frac{\omega}{c}. \tag{28}$$

By setting the two terms equal to each other, we obtain a definite cutoff frequency f_o,

$$f_o = \frac{nc}{2a}\cdot \tag{29}$$

This cutoff frequency is exactly the same as that of the $H_{n,0}$ wave in a rectangular hollow pipe if the values of a in both cases are equal.

Using (9), the attenuation constant α and the phase constant β for $f>f_o$ are given by

$$\alpha + i\beta = -\sqrt{(2\pi/\lambda)^2 - (n\pi/a)^2}\cdot\frac{K_1'(\sqrt{(2\pi/\lambda)^2 - (n\pi/a)^2}\,\rho)}{K_1(\sqrt{(2\pi/\lambda)^2 - (n\pi/a)^2}\,\rho)}\cdot \tag{30}$$

When $2\pi/\lambda$ is replaced by $\sqrt{(2\pi/\lambda)^2-(n\pi/a)^2}$ in Figs. 5 and 7, the curves for $n\pi/\phi_o=1$ illustrate the variations of α and β with the radial distance ρ. The attenuation is caused solely by the decreasing of energy density as the area of the cylindrical surface increases with ρ.

Part II. Waves Radiated Into Space

Calculation of Radiation Patterns

The transmission theory of waves inside horns developed in the foregoing section apply, strictly, only to horns that extend to infinity in the radial direction. Although we are not able to treat rigorously a horn of finite length, we have obtained an approximate solution suitable for most cases of practical interest. In this solution, the assumption is made that the field distribution across the mouth is the same that would exist at this distance from the apex if the sides of the horn extended to infinity. Thus, the end effects are neglected. The radiation characteristic is then calculated from this distribution by means of Huygens' principle. It is feasible to carry out this process under the following conditions: (a) the mouth of the horn is several wavelengths beyond the attenuation region of the wave; (b) the flare angle is not too large, say less than 90 degrees; (c) the radial length of the horn is greater than several wavelengths; and (d) the radiation comes from the mouth of the horn only.

We shall now investigate the radiation characteristics of the $H_{0,m}$ wave in the sectoral horn. As has been shown in a previous paper,[7] the radiation pattern in the x,y plane for the $H_{0,m}$ wave in a rectangular pipe depends roughly only upon the dimension a of the rectangular pipe. The field distribution of the $H_{0,m}$ wave in a sectoral horn in the x,y plane is similar to that of the $H_{0,m}$ wave in the rectangular pipe, and we may, therefore, expect the radiation pattern in the x,y plane to be approximately the same in form as the $H_{0,m}$ wave in the rectangular pipe. For this reason, our interest lies mainly in the radiation patterns in the x,z plane, and only these patterns will be calculated. A spherical co-ordinate system r, θ, ζ will be employed, but calculations are limited to the plane $\zeta=\pi/2$ in which our interest principally resides.

The radiation field is best obtained from the Hertzian vector Π for the field within the horn. Although such a representation gives no additional information inside the horn, it is more convenient to

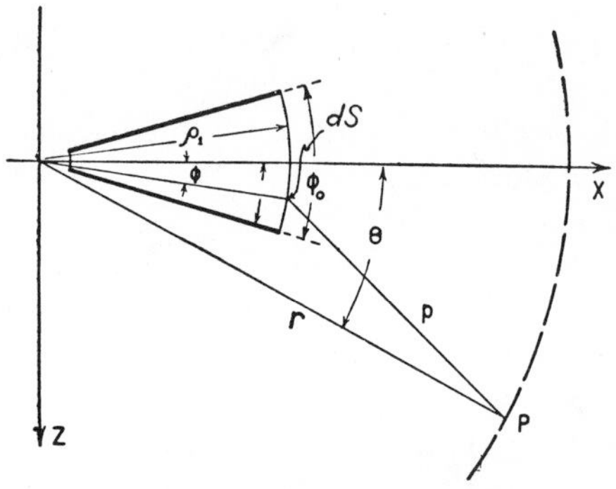

Fig. 10—Spherical co-ordinate system used in calculating radiation patterns.

use than is the electric or the magnetic intensity in securing the complex field of the radiation in the wave zone. The relations between H, E, and Π are as follows:

$$H = i\omega\epsilon \operatorname{curl} \Pi$$
$$E = \left(\frac{\omega}{c}\right)^2 \Pi + \operatorname{grad}\operatorname{div}\Pi. \tag{31}$$

The values of H and E have been determined in Part I. The determination of Π from H and E is not unique. However, if we let div Π be equal to zero, the Hertzian vector for the sectoral-horn waves discussed here may be written as

$$\Pi = i_y\Pi_y = i_y\left(\frac{c}{\omega}\right)^2 E_y \tag{32}$$

where i_y is a unit vector in the positive y direction and Π_y is the component of Π in the same direction. The value of E_y is that given in (6); consequently, Π_y also has this same form. Although the horn terminates along the cylindrical surface ρ, as shown in Fig. 10, we assume that (32) and (6) represent the field along this surface without appreciable distortion. We shall consider the case in which only one of the $H_{0,m}$ waves exists in the horn.

The Hertzian vector Π_y' in the outside space at a

[7] W. L. Barrow and F. M. Greene, "Rectangular hollow-pipe radiators," Proc. I.R.E., vol. 26, pp. 1498–1519; December, (1938).

point P at a distance large compared with the wavelength and the dimensions of the horn may be calculated by Huygens' principle, which may be written in the form[8]

$$\Pi_y' = \frac{1}{4\pi}\iint \frac{1}{p}\left[\frac{i\omega}{c}\Pi_y \cos(n', p) + \frac{\partial \Pi_y}{\partial p}\right] e^{-i(\omega/c)p} dS \quad (33)$$

The inner normal to the surface element dS is n' and p is the distance between this element and point of observation P. The integration is to be taken over the cylindrical surface of the mouth. It should also be extended over the outer metallic surface of the horn, but that is out of the question, since the field distribution is not known there.

Substituting the value for Π_y into (33) gives

$$\Pi_y' = \frac{B}{4\pi}\left(\frac{c}{\omega}\right)^2 \int_0^a \int_{-\phi_0/2}^{\phi_0/2} \frac{i\omega}{pc}\left[K_{m\nu}\left(\frac{\omega}{c}\rho_1\right)\cos(\phi-\theta)\right. \quad (34)$$
$$\left. + K_{m\nu}'\left(\frac{\omega}{c}\rho_1\right)\right] \cos(m\nu\phi) e^{-(i\omega/c)p} \rho_1 d\phi dy.$$

If the angle of flare is small, the factor in the bracket is slowly varying compared to the remaining factors. We shall use the mean value θ of $(\phi-\theta)$ over the surface and bring the bracketed factor outside the integral. Further, we shall approximate $K_{m\nu}$ and $K_{m\nu}'$ by their asymptotic forms. The point P lies in the x,y plane, hence p may be approximated, for large values of r, by

$$p = \sqrt{r^2 + \rho_1^2 - 2r\rho_1 \cos(\phi-\theta)} = r - \rho_1 \cos(\phi-\theta). \quad (35)$$

Making these modifications in (34), we obtain

$$\Pi_y' = \frac{iB}{4\pi}\frac{c}{\omega}\frac{a}{r}\frac{1}{\pi}\sqrt{\rho_1\lambda}(1+\cos\theta)e^{-(i\omega/c)(r+\rho_1)} \quad (36)$$
$$\cdot \int_{-\phi_0/2}^{\phi_0/2} \cos(m\nu\phi) e^{i(\omega/c)\rho_1\cos(\phi-\theta)} d\phi.$$

The evaluation of the integral in (36) is rather involved and will not be given here. The result, valid for the x,z plane at large distances from the mouth, is given by

$$\Pi_y' = \frac{iB}{4\pi}\frac{3\lambda^2}{16\pi}\frac{a}{R\sqrt{10}}(1+\cos\theta)e^{i[-2\pi(r/\lambda)+9\pi\lambda(m\nu)^2/320\rho_1]}$$
$$\cdot\left[e^{im\nu\theta}\int_{u_1}^{u_2}\tfrac{1}{2}\{J_{-1/2}(u) - iJ_{1/2}(u)\}du \right. \quad (37)$$
$$\left. + e^{-im\nu\theta}\int_{u_3}^{u_4}\tfrac{1}{2}\{J_{-1/2}(u) - iJ_{1/2}(u)\}du\right]$$

where

$$u_1 = \left[-\frac{\phi_0}{2} - \theta - m\nu\frac{9\pi\lambda}{160\rho_1}\right]^2 \frac{80\rho_1}{9\pi\lambda}$$

$$u_2 = \left[\frac{\phi_0}{2} - \theta - m\nu\frac{9\pi\lambda}{160\rho_1}\right]^2 \frac{80\rho_1}{9\pi\lambda}$$

$$u_3 = \left[-\frac{\phi_0}{2} - \theta + m\nu\frac{9\pi\lambda}{160\rho_1}\right]^2 \frac{80\rho_1}{9\pi\lambda}$$

$$u_4 = \left[\frac{\phi_0}{2} - \theta + m\nu\frac{9\pi\lambda}{160\rho_1}\right]^2 \frac{80\rho_1}{9\pi\lambda}.$$

Each term of the integral is known as Fresnel's integral, for which numerical tables are available.

The component Π_y' is the resultant Hertzian vector for the radiation field. It is convenient to resolve it into the spherical co-ordinate components, as follows:

$$\Pi_r' = \Pi_y' \cos\zeta \sin\theta$$
$$\Pi_\theta' = \Pi_y' \cos\zeta \cos\theta \quad (38)$$
$$\Pi_\zeta' = \Pi_y' \sin\zeta$$

where Π_r', Π_θ', and Π_ζ' are the components of Π_y' in the r, θ, and ζ directions, respectively. In the x,z plane ζ is equal to $\pi/2$, consequently, Π_r' and Π_θ' vanish, and Π_ζ' is equal to Π_y'.

Applying (31) to (37) and neglecting terms involving powers of $1/r$ greater than the first, we find that the radial components of field vanish and a transverse electromagnetic wave propagated in the radial direction results with components

$$H_\theta' = \left(\frac{\omega}{c}\right)^2\sqrt{\frac{\epsilon}{\mu}}\Pi_y' \quad (39)$$
$$E_\zeta' = -\left(\frac{\omega}{c}\right)^2\Pi_y'.$$

A plot in polar co-ordinates of the absolute magnitude of $E_\zeta(\theta)$ supplies the radiation characteristic or pattern of the horn. The numerical evaluation of these patterns, which involves the integral of (37), is quite lengthy, but evaluations have been made for a series of different conditions. These calculations are all for lengths ρ_1/λ equal to or greater than 8. In such horns, the $H_{0,1}$ wave has traveled a distance of five or six wavelengths beyond the attenuation region. Calculations are made for $u < 50$, corresponding to values of θ from -60 to $+60$ degrees. Because of the insufficiency of available numerical tables, the pattern beyond that angle is not readily calculated, but the amplitudes of the secondary lobes have been estimated at less than ten per cent of that of the principal lobe.

Since the $H_{0,1}$ wave is of greatest practical importance the following radiation patterns for this wave have been calculated: (1) the variation of radiation

[8] Slater and Frank, "Introduction to Theoretical Physics," Chapters XXVI and XXVII. McGraw-Hill Book Company, New York, N.Y. (1933).

pattern with the flare angle of the horn; (2) the variation of radiation pattern with the length of the horn; and (3) the effect of the simultaneous presence of an $H_{0,3}$ wave.

Discussion of Patterns

Fig. 11 illustrates the radiation patterns from horns having equal ratios of $\rho_1/\lambda=8$ but different flare angles ϕ_o. The dotted, solid, and dashed lines are for horns having $\phi_o=30$, 40, and 50 degrees, respectively. These curves show that on increasing the

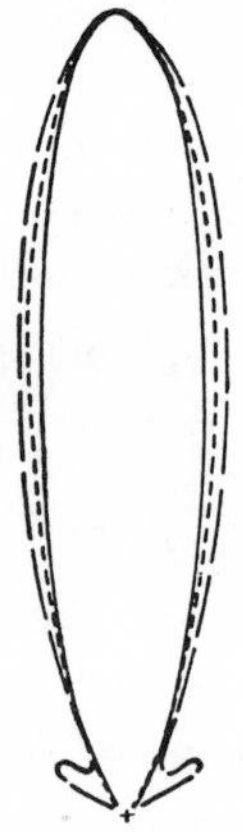

Fig. 11—Calculated radiation pattern of electric intensity in the x,z plane for a sectoral horn of length $\rho_1/\lambda=8$ for the following flare angles: 30 degrees (dotted curve); 40 degrees (solid curve); and 50 degrees (dashed curve).

flare angle from a small value, the beam is first sharpened and then broadened again. The flare angle giving a minimum beam angle is about 40 degrees, which is very close to the value for the experimental horn, as reported in the companion paper.[1]

The broadening of the radiation patterns that accompanies either an increase or a decrease of the flare angle from the optimum value was discussed to some extent in the companion paper. In connection with the radiation from rectangular hollow pipes,[7] it was shown that the sharpness of the beam depends only on the dimension b of the pipe. When the flare angle of the horn is small the sides are almost parallel to each other and the radial direction ρ along which the wave is propagated is not greatly different from the longitudinal direction x. Consequently, waves from horns of small flare angles behave very much like those from rectangular pipes. When the arc length $\phi_o\rho_1$ at the mouth of the horn, which is equivalent to the dimension b of the rectangular pipe, is decreased by decreasing the flare angle the beam is broadened. On the other hand, if the flare angle is made too large, it is evident that the wave will be propagated over a wide angle even inside the horn. It may be recalled that a sectoral horn of $\phi_o=180$ degrees is nothing other than a plane surface, or baffle, which is obviously not very effective for directional radiation.

With the value of flare angle of 40 degrees, calculation shows that there is no detectable variation in the shapes of the patterns for variations of the radial length ρ_1/λ within the range from 8 to 12. This range of ρ_1/λ is practically important. Horns of this length are neither too short to hinder the formation of horn waves, nor too long to make the mechanical construction impracticable.

Let us see what happens if the radial length of the horn is made very large. In this case the arc at the mouth of the horn is a great number of wavelengths long, and we may perform the integration of Π_y' in an approximate way using Fresnel zones.[9] The radiation field in the x,z plane of such a horn can thus be shown to have the form

$$|E| = \text{const.}\left|\frac{1}{r}\cos\left(\frac{\pi\theta}{\phi_o}\right)e^{i\omega r/c}\right|. \qquad (40)$$

That is, the radiation pattern is the same as the field distribution along an arc inside the long horn and the beam angle is equal numerically to the flare angle.

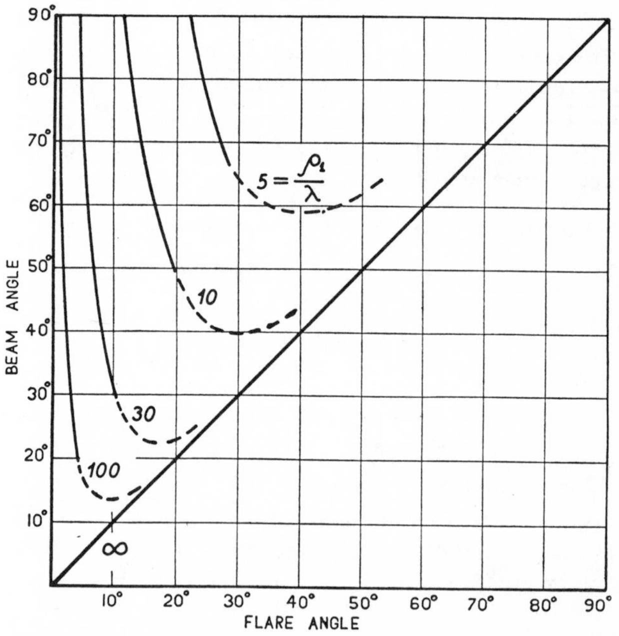

Fig. 12—Theoretical curves of beam angle versus flare angle for horns of several radial lengths ρ_1/λ. The dotted portions of the curves are estimated; the solid portions are calculated.

Naturally, the limiting expression (40) does not include the case of zero flare angle; because this case reverts to the hollow-pipe radiator. The beam angle, therefore, does not become zero for $\phi_o=0$ but assumes a value that depends on the width b of the pipe.

We see that there are two important factors which

[9] See page 308 of footnote reference (8).

play vital but opposite rôles in determining the radiation pattern of a sectoral horn. These factors are the arc length at the mouth of the horn and the divergence of the waves inside the horn. Consider a short horn several wavelengths long. If the flare angle is small, the beam angle of the radiation pattern is essentially controlled by the arc length or aperture at the mouth of the horn and larger apertures produce sharper beams. If the flare angle is large, on the other hand, the beam angle is essentially controlled by the direction of propagation in the horn, i.e., by the angle of flare. The smaller the flare angle, the less divergent will be the directions of propagation in the horn, and the sharper is the radiated beam. If the flare angle is neither too large nor too small, the opposite effects of the two factors compensate each other and the beam angle has its sharpest value.

The more or less complicated way in which the beam angle is affected by the several factors may be

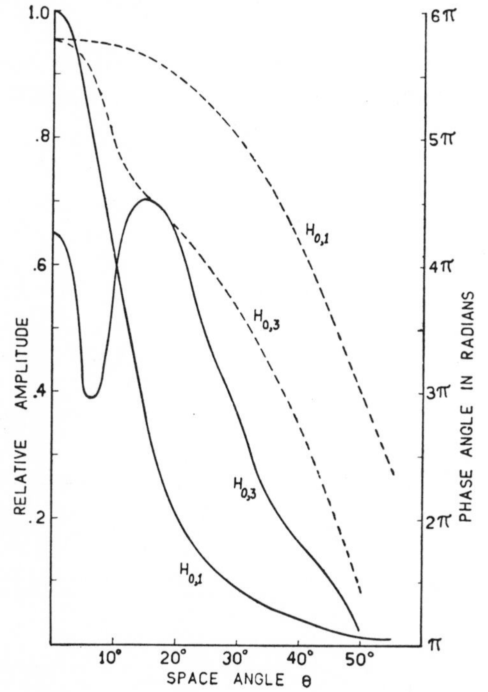

Fig. 13—Relative amplitudes and phases of the two separate components of radiated electric intensity from $H_{0,1}$ and $H_{0,3}$ waves, respectively, of equal amplitudes and phases at the mouth of a sectoral horn of length $\rho_1/\lambda = 8$ and flare angle of 40 degrees. Solid curves show relative amplitudes and dotted curves show relative phases.

shown clearly by a set of curves of beam angle versus flare angle for horns of different radial lengths. Such a family of curves is reproduced in Fig. 12. In this figure, the asymptotic curve for infinite length and the steeply descending solid curves for finite lengths are accurate. The dotted portions are approximate and are only intended to indicate general behavior. A study of these curves brings out the following general facts:

1. For a constant flare angle, the beam angle decreases with an increase of the length.
2. For a constant flare angle, there is a corresponding length beyond which the beam angle does not decrease appreciably with further increase in length.
3. For a constant length, there is always an optimum flare angle for which the beam angle is a minimum.

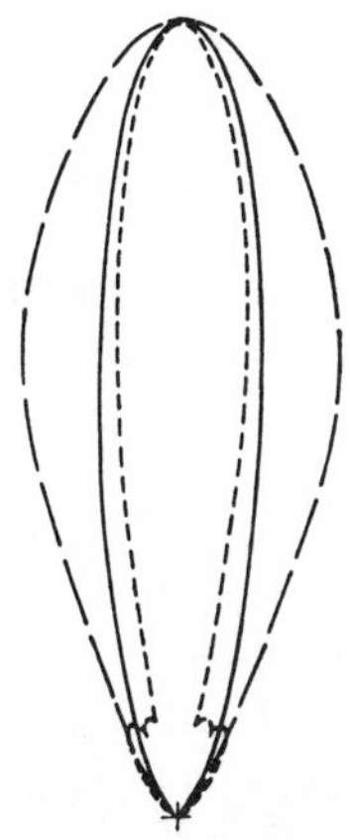

Fig. 14—Radiation patterns of electric intensity from sectoral horn in x,z plane with $\rho_1/\lambda = 8$ and $\phi_o = 40$ degrees when both $H_{0,1}$ and $H_{0,3}$ waves are present simultaneously. Dashed curve for a distribution across the mouth of E_y=const. [cos $(\pi\phi/2\phi_0) - \frac{1}{3}$ cos $(3\pi\phi/2\phi_0)$]. Dotted curve for a distribution E_y=const. [cos $(\pi\phi/2\phi_0) + \frac{1}{3}$ cos $(3\pi\phi/2\phi_0)$]. Solid curve for a distribution E_y=const. [cos $(\pi\phi/2\phi_0)$].

4. The optimum flare angle decreases with increasing length, as does also the corresponding minimum beam angle.
5. For a constant aperture, the beam angle decreases with decreasing flare angle and is a minimum for zero flare angle, (viz., for a hollow-pipe radiator).

In some cases, the $H_{0,1}$ wave will not exist alone inside the horn. For example, in a horn with $\phi_o = 40$ degrees but a relatively wide throat, it is possible to have an appreciable amount of the $H_{0,3}$ wave at the mouth. Higher-order $H_{0,m}$ waves also may be present in certain cases.

To determine the effect of the presence of an $H_{0,3}$ wave, we just plot separately in Fig. 13 the relative amplitude and the phase angles of the radiated electric field intensity for the $H_{0,1}$ and the $H_{0,3}$ waves. The horn is 8 wavelengths long from apex to mouth and has $\phi_o = 40$ degrees. The amplitudes and phases of the electric field intensities for the two waves are taken as equal; that is, $B_1K_v(2\pi\rho_1/\lambda) = B_3K_{3v}(2\pi\rho_1/\lambda)$. The figure shows that the amplitude of the central lobe of the $H_{0,3}$ wave is only 64 per cent of that of the $H_{0,1}$ wave. There is a secondary lobe of larger amplitude than the central one. Furthermore, the phase difference between the radiated fields of the $H_{0,1}$ wave and the $H_{0,3}$ wave is almost zero within the central lobe of the $H_{0,3}$ pattern, and is approximately π radians apart within the second lobe of this wave.

Since the fields are linearly superposable, we are able to construct a composite pattern from Fig. 13 when the $H_{0,1}$ and the $H_{0,3}$ waves exist at the same time. The resultant radiation field in space is the complex sum of the fields radiated by the two waves independently. Let

$$w = \frac{B_3K_{3v}(2\pi\rho_1/\lambda)}{B_1K_v(2\pi\rho_1/\lambda)}.$$

This quantity is complex and indicates the ratio of the amplitudes and the phase difference between the electric fields of the two mentioned waves. The three radiation patterns of Fig. 14 are for ratios of $w=-1/3$ (dashed curve) and $w=+1/3$ (dotted curve), respectively; while the solid curve is the radiation pattern of the $H_{0,1}$ wave alone, drawn for sake of comparison. Thus, when the two waves are simultaneously present at the mouth of the horn, the radiation pattern may be broader or narrower than that for the $H_{0,1}$ wave alone, depending on the relative phase of the two component waves at the mouth of the horn. The larger the amplitude of the $H_{0,3}$ wave, the more prominent is this effect. In either case, however, the secondary-lobe size is increased. In terms of the resultant electric field distribution at the mouth of the horn, a peaked distribution produces a sharp beam with secondary lobes of appreciable amplitude, and a flattened distribution produces a broad beam. For a sharp, clean-cut beam without appreciable side lobes, an undistorted sinusoidal distribution at the mouth of the horn appears to be essential.

Conclusion

The analysis presented here provides an adequate explanation of the way in which the electromagnetic horn functions as a radio "antenna," and gives quantitative expressions and results from which the design of horns of sectoral shape can be carried out. The very satisfactory accord between the theory developed here and the experiments reported in the companion paper is convincing evidence that we are able to design horns for various applications in a thoroughly engineering manner.

Metal Horns as Directive Receivers of Ultra-Short Waves*

G. C. SOUTHWORTH†, MEMBER I.R.E., AND A. P. KING†, ASSOCIATE MEMBER, I.R.E.

Summary—*The following paper describes some experiments made to determine the directive properties of metal pipes and horns when used as receivers of electromagnetic waves. The experiments were of two kinds. One consisted of measurements of received power, with and without the horn in place, and the other of the determination of the directional patterns of the horns in two perpendicular planes. The results indicate that electromagnetic horns of this kind provide a simple and convenient way of obtaining effective power ratios of a hundred or more (20 decibels). The effects of varying the several horn parameters are investigated. It is shown that there is an optimum angle of flare. The possibility of forming arrays of pipes or horns is mentioned.*

Introduction

An experimental study of electrical transmission through dielectric wires and through hollow metal pipes has been in progress at the Bell Telephone Laboratories for some time. Results of this work have been reported from time to time in the technical literature.§ The first of these reports[1] dealt with the more general aspects of the problem and stated that "discontinuities in wave guides, particularly those in which no shield is present, tend toward losses by radiation. In the case of a hollow conducting pipe, radiation issues from the open end much the same as sound waves from a hollow tube. It has been possible to expand the ends of these pipes into horns, thereby obtaining effects very similar to those common in acoustics. Such an electrical horn not only possesses considerable directivity but it may also provide a moderately good termination for the pipe to which it is connected. In so doing its function is probably quite analogous to that of a true acoustic horn which provides an efficient radiating load for its sound motor." The present paper extends this earlier work by giving more detailed information about the directivities of the open ends of hollow pipes and of simple horns as their several dimensions are varied. It will be noted that the data were taken with horns of circular cross section. Data taken on horns of rectangular cross section appear in a recent paper by Barrow.[6]

The results below show that even with relatively simple horns it is possible to obtain power improvements of some hundred times (20-decibel gain) that of an ordinary simple half-wave antenna. Although this is no more than the gain of the best transoceanic antenna arrays it should be borne in mind that it relates to a single unit and that it should be possible to obtain added gain by placing two or more horns in an array or possibly by changing the nature of the horn itself. However, these are matters outside of the scope of the present paper and of a kind that can best be considered after the properties of the individual elements are better known.

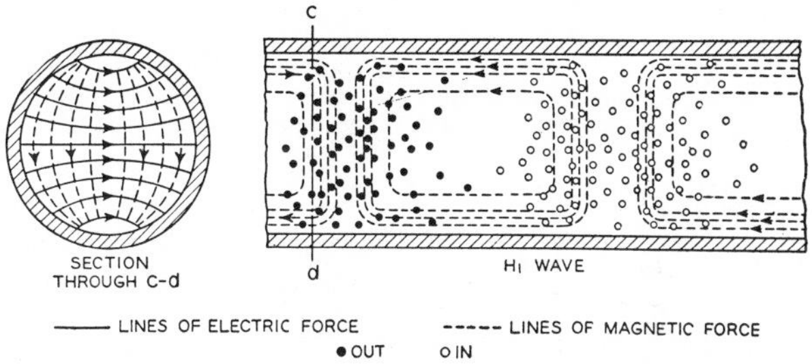

Fig. 1—Configuration of the H_1 type of wave. This wave was used throughout this particular study of horns.

There are many forms of electric waves that may be propagated through pipes and projected from horns. Superficially at least they differ materially from the acoustic waves with which we are generally familiar. This paper will be concerned with the so-called H_1 configuration shown as Fig. 1. The properties of the other forms of waves are, of course, also of interest and will most likely be the subjects of later papers.

The experiments and results described below are necessarily of a preliminary and an exploratory kind. It will be readily appreciated that in order to disentangle the many variables that prevail in a problem of this kind and accordingly to obtain anything like a complete picture of the properties of horns requires experiments made over a wide range of circumstances. This paper is therefore of the nature of an early progress report.

Experimental Apparatus

The apparatus used in these experiments consisted of a generator of continuous electric waves 10 or 15 centimeters in length, together with an appropriate receiver located 30 or more wavelengths away. Both the transmitter and the receiver were mounted about a meter above the floor. The horns or pipes under test could have been affixed to either the transmitter or the receiver. However, it seemed more expedient

* Decimal classification: R116.6. Original manuscript received by the Institute, June 15, 1938.
† Bell Telephone Laboratories, Inc., New York, New York.
§ See Bibliography attached.
[1] Numbers refer to Bibliography.

Reprinted from *Proc. IRE*, vol. 27, pp. 95–102, Feb. 1939.

in these tests to make them a part of the receiver. The relative merits of these horns were determined both from an intercomparison of the received power with and without the horn attached and from the sharpness of the directional patterns plotted from measurements made as the horns were pointed at various angles relative to the incoming signal. Together, these two kinds of information supply a fairly complete specification of their properties.

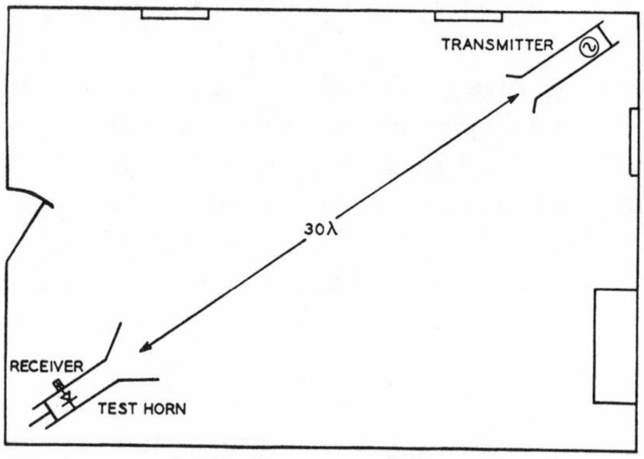

Fig. 2—Arrangement of apparatus used in obtaining directional characteristics of pipes and horns.

In some cases the transmitter and receiver were located at opposite corners of a room about 20 feet square. In others the test signals were transmitted out of an upstairs window to the receiver located on the ground a 100 or so wavelengths away. Results from the two methods were in general agreement. Fig. 2 shows the general arrangement of the apparatus when the indoor experiments were in progress.

It should be possible to use as the transmitter any of the conventional forms of generators such as, for instance, the Barkhausen, magnetron, or negative-grid types. The one actually used was a wave-guide adaptation of the Barkhausen oscillator. It has already been described.[1] The corresponding receiver is shown in schematic form by Fig. 3. A photograph is shown in Fig. 4. It will be observed that protractors are provided on the two principal axes so that both the angles of azimuth and elevation may be measured.

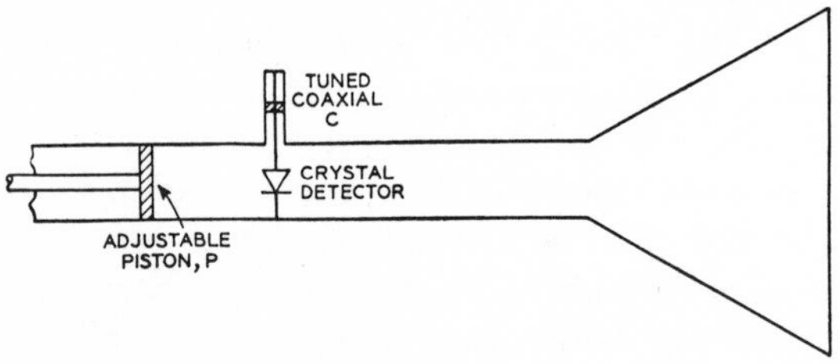

Fig. 3—Schematic of the component parts of the receiver consisting of a conical horn and a cylindrical pipe with tuned detector and adjustable piston.

The receiver proper is of the resonant-cavity type and is made up of a short section of tuned wave guide bounded at one end by a movable piston and at the other by a diametral conductor of adjustable length. This conductor carries a calibrated silicon-crystal rectifier of special construction whose direct-current response, measured either on a potentiometer or a microammeter, enables relative gains to be measured. The construction of the detector and the arrangement of its associated tuned wires are both shown in Fig. 5 for each of two alternate arrangements. This tuning together with the piston adjustment may be regarded as part of the process of matching the detector to the horn pickup device. When this matched condition has been obtained there is not only approximately an optimum of received power but there is also a minimum of standing wave in the space between the horn and the detector. Under this condition the receiver as a whole approximates a perfect absorber.

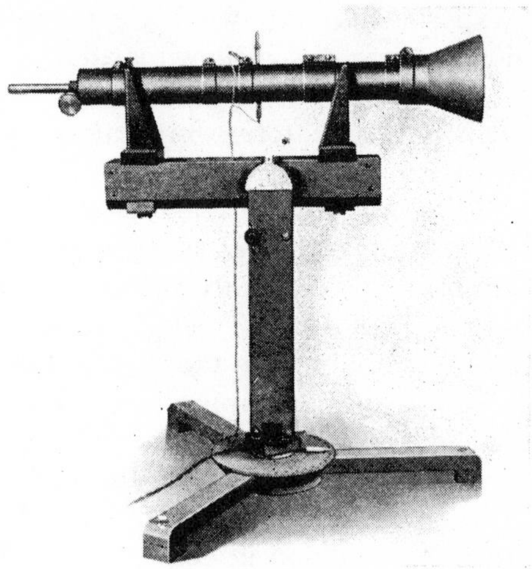

Fig. 4—The complete receiver and mounting.

The condition of minimum reflection may, if necessary, be verified by measurements with a small traveling detector which samples the wave power in the pipe between the cavity and the horn. The construction of the latter device is shown by Fig. 6. It consists of a crystal detector preferably of the form shown as Fig. 5(b) provided with an extremely short pickup wire extending through a narrow slot cut in the top of the pipe. A rack-and-pinion drive permits smooth motion along the slot. A centimeter scale is useful in measuring the position of the detector. The pickup wire on the detector is made just long enough to give a readable deflection on the direct-current microammeter to which the detector is connected and when properly adjusted it offers no appreciable discontinuity to the passing waves and consequently does not materially alter the conditions prevailing in the pipe below. A slot cut in a pipe of this kind does not materially affect the behavior of a traveling H_1 wave provided the slot is not too wide and provided it lies in a plane perpendicular to the lines of electric force.

The process of matching a receiver to a horn is largely manual and consists simply of successive approximations obtained by adjusting the coaxial C and the piston P of Fig. 3 until the levels of the peaks approximate those of the valleys. Ratios of maxima to minima in the standing wave as low as 1.1 may be obtained. A ratio of 1.5 would be regarded as unsatisfactory. It may be observed that these values are

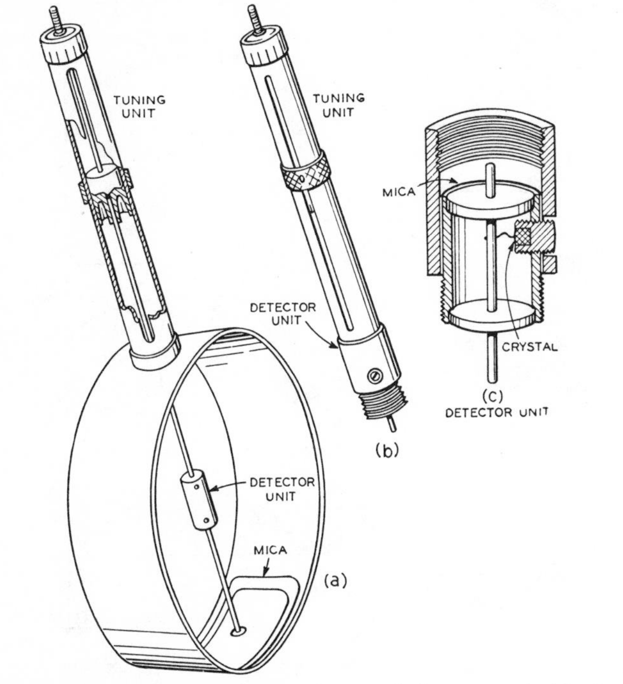

Fig. 5—Two alternate forms of crystal detector suitable for measurement work at extremely high frequencies.

comparable in magnitude with those obtained in high-frequency wire-line practice.

The technique of rectifying high-frequency currents by means of crystal detectors is almost as old as radio itself. Many materials exhibit the necessary asymmetric conductivity as for example carborundum, iron pyrites, galena, silicon, and molybdenite. Some are sensitive but lack stability of adjustment. Others require cumbersome associated apparatus such as biasing batteries and voltage dividers. Silicon was chosen for this work as a compromise of sensitivity and stability as well as simplicity of apparatus. No biasing battery is needed. A very small piece of the crystal is sufficient. This may conveniently be ground into a cylinder 1 millimeter in diameter by 1 millimeter long and pressed into a hole bored into the screw mounting shown in Fig. 5(c) above. Rectification takes place at or near the point of contact between the crystal and the fine spring wire. The surface of the crystal is carefully polished first with emery and later with rouge so that the contact point may slide freely over the smooth surface in seeking a sensitive point.

The contact wires used were either of 8-mil tungsten or 10-mil phosphor bronze wire having a length before bending of about 2 millimeters. It is believed that almost any material having a reasonable amount of stiffness can be used. The required contact pressure between the wire and crystal can best be determined by experiment. This adjustment can easily be carried out by connecting the assembled detector to an ohmmeter, and turning the adjusting screw and tapping the detector tube lightly until no change in contact is noted on the meter. This should then be repeated

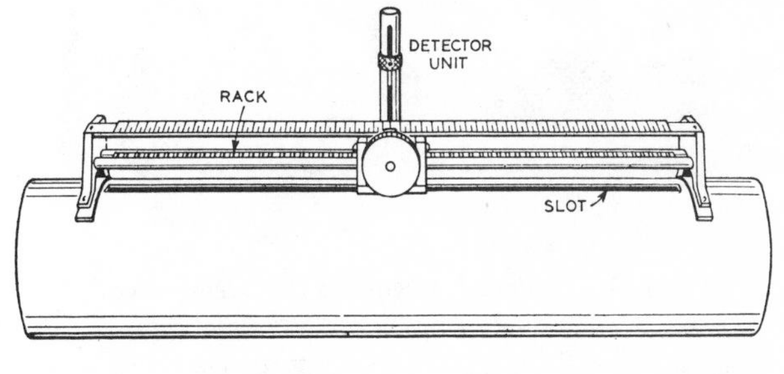

Fig. 6—Form of traveling detector used in determining the condition of standing waves in the terminated receiver.

with the terminals reversed. Representative resistances in the two directions are 500 and 2000 ohms. Although these may vary over rather wide limits with adjustment, their ratios should remain fairly constant in the range of 2–5. With moderate care, an adjustment can be maintained fairly constant for several weeks.

Calibration

In order to calibrate the rectifier we invoked the special property of the so-called H_1 wave by virtue of which the lines of electric force are roughly parallel chords across the circular wave guide. The assembled receiver operating under the same conditions that prevailed during the measurements was rotated relative to the incident field. The deflection was, of course, a maximum when the pickup was parallel to the lines of force and was essentially zero when at right angles thereto. In the latter case the detector was lying along a line of zero electric intensity. The resulting calibration assumes that the applied high-frequency voltage was proportional to the cosine of the angle between the lines of electric force and the conductor carrying the detector.

Horns and Pipes Under Test

For the most part the pipes and horns were made of 22-gauge galvanized iron riveted and soldered at the joints and were attached to short sections of brass pipe 12.4 centimeters in diameter. Representative samples are shown in Fig. 7. So far as had been possible the dimensions of the various horns have been included on the illustrations below along with the experimental results and need not be given at this time. The work here reported was done with horns of circular cross section. However, experiments have been made on horns of rectangular cross section and also some work has been done on exponential and parabolic horns.

Fig. 7—Representative horns that were tested.

Experimental Results

As already explained the experimental tests were of two kinds. In one case the relative wave amplitudes received from various angles in each of two mutually perpendicular planes were observed. In the other, relative received powers were observed along the preferred direction both with and without the directive device attached. In Figs. 8, 10, 11, and 12, both of these results are given. The former is expressed in the usual polar co-ordinate form and conveys at a glance the more essential properties of the horns. The other result is designated on the figures as G and represents a measured gain in decibels above the signal level that would have prevailed if a nondirectional receiver had been used.* The latter is a convenient single figure of merit useful where comparisons are desired.

In the polar diagrams shown, the solid curves represent measurements made in the plane containing the electric force while the dotted curves represent measurements taken in the plane of the magnetic force. The complete directional figure can therefore be regarded as roughly an ellipsoid of which these two plane figures are respectively orthogonal sections. The diagrams here shown are faithful reproductions of curves plotted from the original data on standard polar co-ordinate paper. These data were taken each at various angles as dictated by the need for accuracy ranging from $2\frac{1}{2}$ degrees for the more critical portions to 10 degrees for the least critical portions. The freedom from irregularities here shown is real and is a general characteristic of the radiation patterns of electromagnetic horns of this kind.

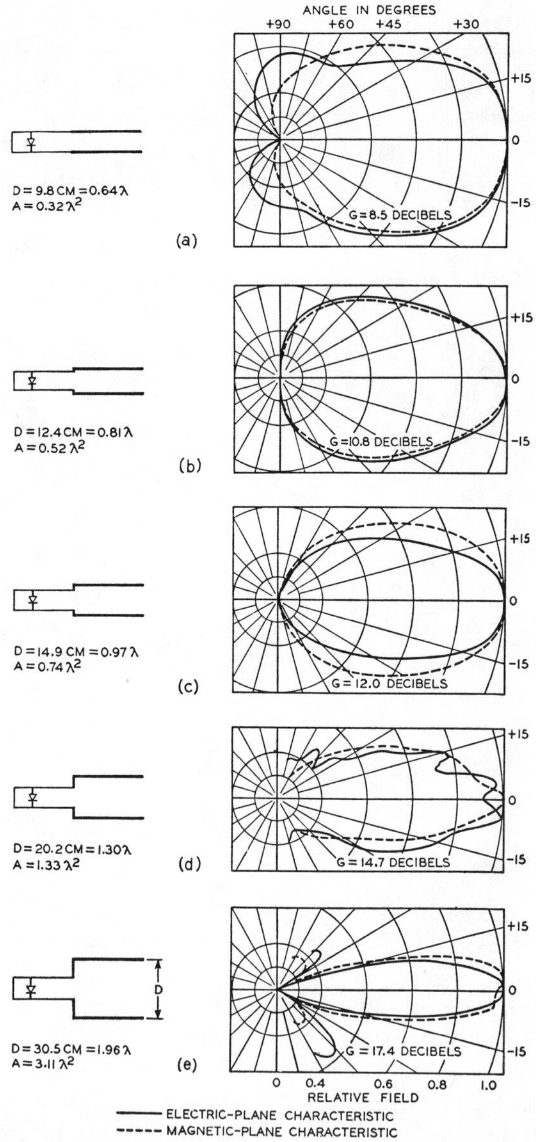

Fig. 8—Directional properties of the open ends of metal pipes of various diameters. Measurements were taken at a wavelength of 15.3 centimeters.

Circular Pipes

The directivities obtained from ordinary circular pipes of various diameters are shown in Fig. 8. The diameters of these pipes ranged from about 10 to 25 centimeters. These dimensions may be more signifi-

* The method by which these gains were fixed relative to the rather fundamental datum level, corresponding to a nondirectional source, is given in the attached Appendix. If gains relative to a half-wave antenna are desired one should deduct 2.15 decibels from the values here given.

cant when expressed in wavelengths for they are then directly comparable with the cutoff limit of 0.585 λ. Below this limit no appreciable power may be propagated through a wave guide.

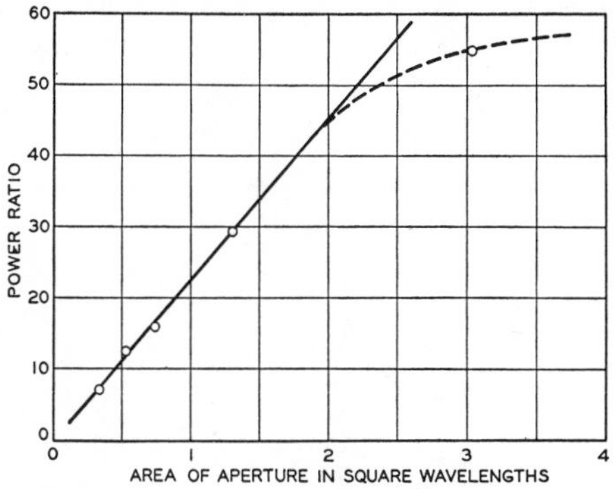

Fig. 9—Measured power improvements of metal pipe radiators, as a function of aperture. Data taken from Fig. 8.

It will be observed that the pattern in the plane of the electric force is in general somewhat sharper than that in the magnetic plane. The rather irregular pattern shown in Fig. 8(d) is probably due to experimental error. It has not been feasible to repeat this experiment under the conditions prevailing for the other sizes of pipe. In the last figure there are the beginnings of some secondary lobes similar in form to those often observed with ordinary antenna arrays when the spacings between their elements are large. In the case at hand the difficulty may have been due to the substantial discontinuity that exists at the point in the receiver where the 10-centimeter pipe and the 25-centimeter pipe join.

Fig. 9 shows the measured power improvements from these various pipes plotted against the areas of aperture in square wavelengths. The resulting curve turns out to be linear except for the larger diameters. If the function of a receiving device were merely that of cutting out a section from an advancing wave front and conveying the same, without reflection, back to a completely absorbing detector, then we should expect the power improvement to vary directly with the area of aperture. If, however, there are partial reflections or other effects tending to alter the phase relations between the various components then this optimum gain may not be fully realized. There are evidences of out-of-phase components of this kind in the secondary lobes of Fig. 8(e) and perhaps also in Fig. 8(d). These may account in part for the nonlinearity of Fig. 9.

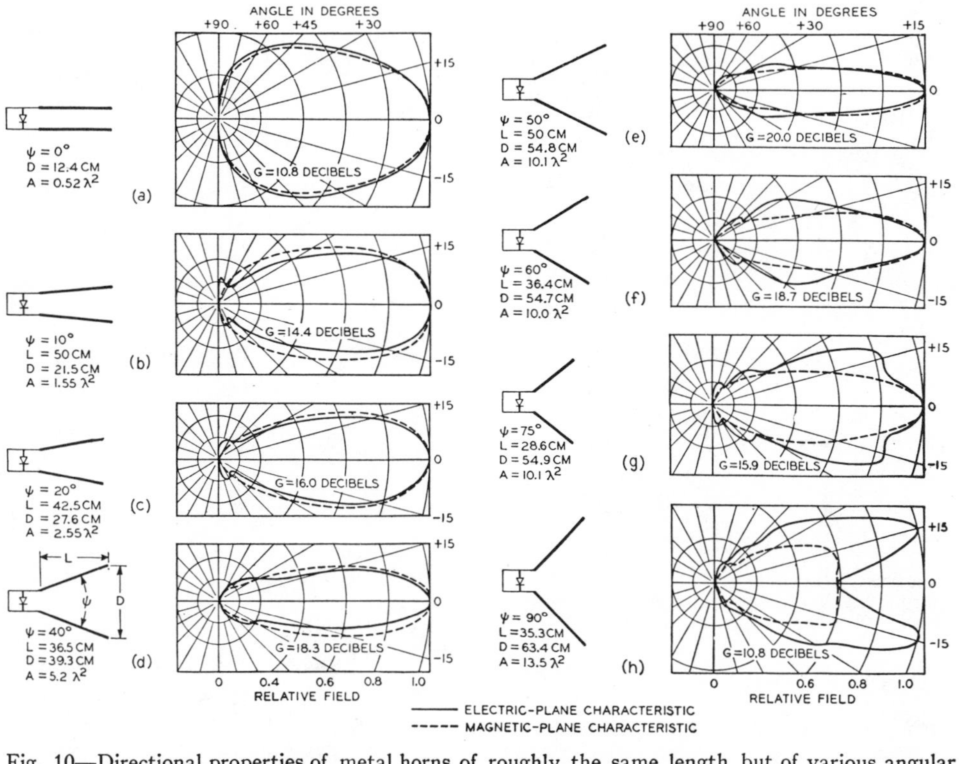

Fig. 10—Directional properties of metal horns of roughly the same length but of various angular openings. Measurements were taken at a wavelength of 15.3 centimeters.

Conical Horns

The work with horns of circular sections proceeded along several different directions. In one case it was desirable to know how the directive properties varied as the angle of flare was increased. In another case we were interested to see how these properties varied as the area of opening increased keeping the angle fixed at some value which the previous experiment had found to be favorable. Other variations will be evident from the paragraphs that follow.

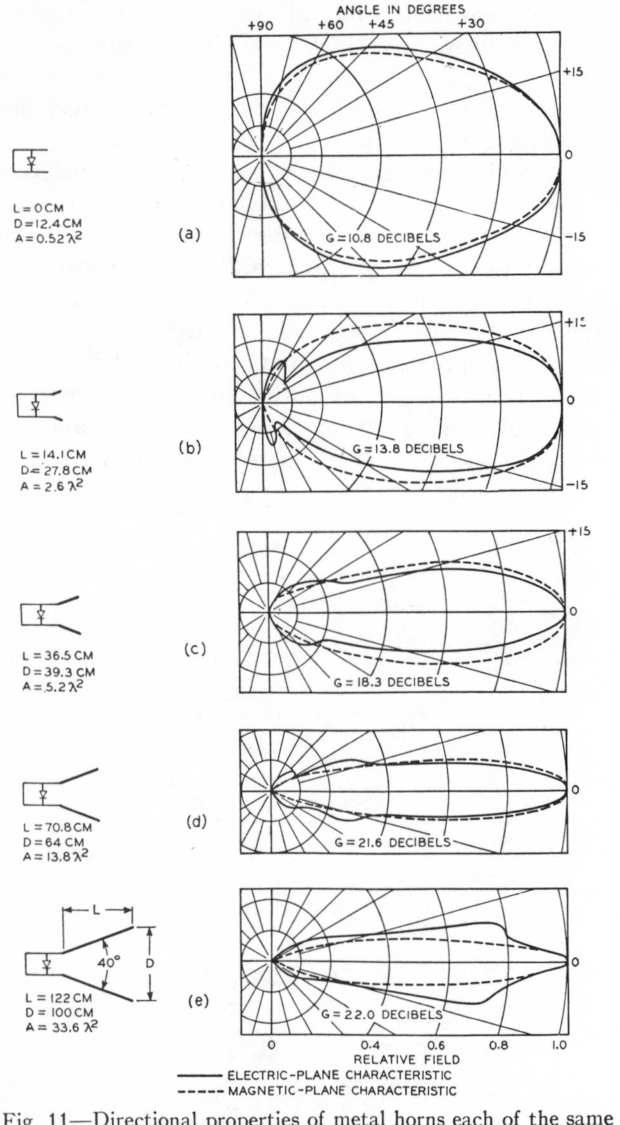

Fig. 11—Directional properties of metal horns each of the same angular opening but of different lengths. Measurements were taken at a wavelength of 15.3 centimeters.

Effect of Varying Angle

The results of the experiments with straight pipes naturally led to work on horns where the angle of flare was increased. It is convenient to regard the straight pipe as a horn of zero angle. Accordingly, measurements were made beginning with zero and continuing in small steps up to 90 degrees. Results were obtained as shown in Fig. 10.

It was not feasible to make the several horns of exactly comparable dimensions. The extent to which this desirable condition has been approximated will be noted from the dimensions given in the figure. It is fairly conclusive, however, that the gain has increased progressively with the angle of flare up to an angle about 50 degrees, after which spurious effects have become evident. This observed optimum holds only for the range of lengths noted above. In general longer horns call for smaller optimum angles.

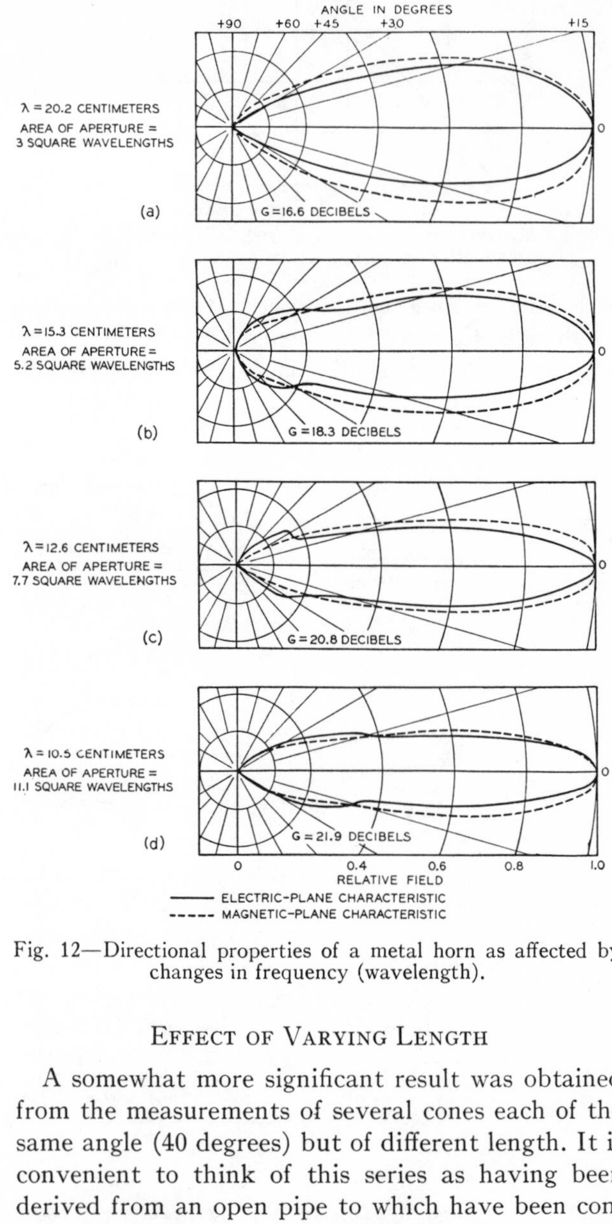

Fig. 12—Directional properties of a metal horn as affected by changes in frequency (wavelength).

Effect of Varying Length

A somewhat more significant result was obtained from the measurements of several cones each of the same angle (40 degrees) but of different length. It is convenient to think of this series as having been derived from an open pipe to which have been connected 40-degree horns of various lengths. It is apparent from Fig. 11 that, at first, directivity increased progressively with length but that little or no advantage was gained by increasing the size of the horn beyond that shown in the fourth figure. This result was to be expected, for we have not maintained the conditions for optimum angle.

Effect of Varying Wavelength

From considerations of similitude it would be expected that the most significant features of a directive system would be its dimensions measured in wavelengths. This means that two horns similar in form but differing in absolute dimensions would have identical directive properties provided they are operated on wavelengths proportional to their respective dimensions. As a consequence one should expect, from what has gone before, that the gain of a given horn should, in general, increase as the wavelength is reduced, for, in effect, we have increased the virtual dimensions of the horn by decreasing the operating wavelength. Tests were made on a single horn at each of 4 wavelengths with results as shown in Fig. 12.

Summary of Results With Simple Conical Horns

In order to reduce further the data above, the measured gains, expressed as power ratios, have been plotted against certain significant variables. The curves shown should be regarded as convenient lines of reference for comparing experimental points rather than graphs justified by data.

Fig. 13 shows how the power ratios of the various 40-degree horns increased with the area of the aperture. The results are comparable with those indicated by Fig. 8 for ordinary pipes. As before, the linear relation holds only for the smaller horns. This has already been explained. Fig. 14 shows how the power ratio of one of the 40-degree horns varied with wavelength.

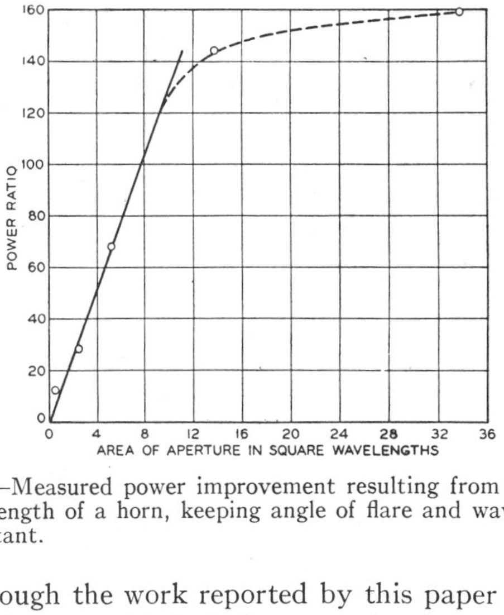

Fig. 13—Measured power improvement resulting from varying the length of a horn, keeping angle of flare and wavelength constant.

Although the work reported by this paper was of an exploratory kind, it has permitted two rather definite conclusions. (1) Radiating pipes and horns constitute simple and convenient means for obtaining directive gains amounting to 20 decibels or more. There is no reason to believe that this is the upper limit. (2) Both in the case of straight pipes and in the case of conical horns this gain, expressed as a power ratio, is within limits roughly proportional to area of

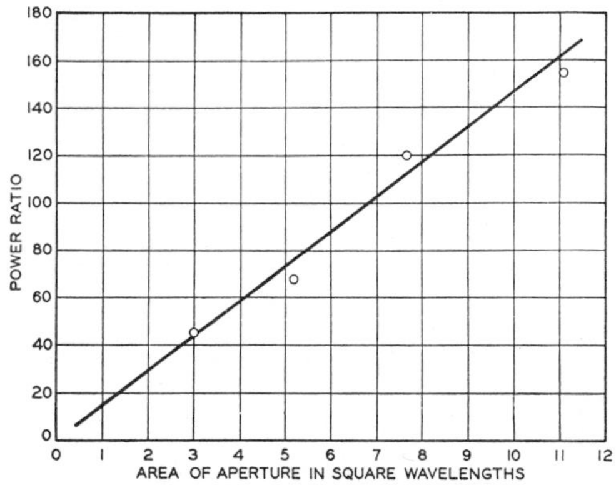

Fig. 14—Measured power improvement resulting from changing wavelength.

aperture. Presumably it holds in a more general way if we make appropriate changes in flare. This is more or less in keeping with experience with ordinary antenna arrays such as for instance those used in transoceanic communication.

The inherent simplicity of the horn antenna makes it particularly useful at ultra-radio frequencies where difficulties are often encountered in maintaining the proper amplitude and phase relations between the various elements of an array. Horns have been operated satisfactorily at frequencies of more than 3000 megacycles ($\lambda = 10$ centimeters) with results that seem to indicate that they should be even better at still higher frequencies. The lower limit of operation appears to be dictated mainly by convenience and economic considerations and consequently is not well established at this time. Electromagnetic horns possess an interesting and possibly a very important characteristic. Unlike tuned antenna arrays, these devices do not have critically sharp frequency characteristics. This principle should permit both easy changes in operating frequency and also the simultaneous transmission of a wide frequency band without serious distortion.

Appendix

As explained above the gains reported in this paper refer to a hypothetical nondirectional radiator. Such gains may therefore be regarded as absolute. According to this *primary reference standard*, a short doublet radiator such as is sometimes used as a standard in radio work has an absolute gain of 1.76 decibels. Similarly a half-wave antenna in free space has a gain of 2.15 decibels.

Three important steps were taken in referring the gains of these horns back to the primary reference standard. They are as follows: First, the various directional patterns shown above were related quantitatively to Figs. 8(a) and 8(b) by means of a very large number of measurements. Next their power ratios were compared with the areas of their respective directional patterns and a proportionality established. An excellent agreement between these factors was obtained.

It will be noted that the patterns of Figs. 8(a) and 8(b) are not too removed from an ellipsoid and appear almost to have resulted from a progressive sharpening beginning from a sphere. It therefore seemed reasonable to consider a sphere of this kind as an arbitrary *secondary reference standard* and also to assume that the proportionality factor derived above should extend also to the sphere. Such a sphere may be regarded as one of the two spheres generated by $r = A \cos \phi \sin \theta$ where the origin is located at the mouth of the radiating pipe with the conventional x axis coincident with the principal axis of the cylinder.

When the proportionality factor obtained above was extended from Fig. 8(a) to the secondary reference standard, a differential of 0.77 decibel was obtained. It is this quantity that is open to question for ordinarily it is not regarded as good radio practice to assume that the power ratios of directive systems are proportional to the areas of their respective patterns.

The final step consisted in relating the secondary reference standard to the primary standard. This step was mathematical and was based on the following reasoning. The power at a nondirective source necessary to produce a given field intensity at a given point in space is given by

$$P_1 = \frac{c}{4\pi}\int_0^{2\pi}\int_0^{\pi} E^2 \sin\theta \, d\theta \, d\phi \tag{1}$$

so

$$P_1 = cE^2. \tag{2}$$

The power at the source, necessary for the *secondary reference standard* to produce the same field intensity at the same point in the preferred direction is

$$P_2 = \frac{c}{4\pi}\int_0^{\pi}\int_0^{\pi} E^2 \cos^2\phi \sin^3\theta \, d\phi \, d\theta \tag{3}$$

$$P_2 = \frac{cE^2}{6}.$$

The ratio of the two powers necessary to produce the same field intensity by the two methods is, therefore,

$$\frac{P_1}{P_2} = 6.$$

This corresponds to a gain of 7.78 decibels. It represents the differential between the primary and secondary reference standards. Adding this figure to the relative gain of say Fig. 8(a) which in this case is 0.77 decibel we obtain 8.55 decibels as the absolute directivity of the latter. Other horns covered by this paper were related to Figs. 8(a) and 8(b) by measurement and accordingly their directivities were expressed absolutely. The errors involved by the approximations made above are not believed to be greater than a tenth of a decibel.

Bibliography

(1) G. C. Southworth, "Hyper-frequency wave guides—general considerations." *Bell Sys. Tech. Jour.*, vol. 15, pp. 284–309; April, (1936).
(2) Carson, Mead, and Schelkunoff, "Hyper-frequency wave guides—mathematical theory," *Bell Sys. Tech. Jour.*, vol. 15, pp. 310–333; April, (1936).
(3) W. L. Barrow, "Transmission of electromagnetic waves in hollow tubes of metal," Proc. I.R.E., vol. 24, pp. 1298–1328; October, (1936).
(4) G. C. Southworth, "Some fundamental experiments with wave guides," Proc. I.R.E., vol. 25, pp. 807–822, July, (1937).
(5) G. C. Southworth, "New experimental methods applicable to ultra-short waves," *Jour. App. Phys.*, vol. 8, pp. 660–665, October, (1937).
(6) W. L. Barrow and F. M. Greene, "Rectangular hollow-pipe radiators," Proc. I.R.E., vol. 26, pp. 1498–1519; December, (1938).
(7) L. J. Chu and W. L. Barrow, "Electromagnetic waves in hollow metal tubes of rectangular cross section," Proc. I.R.E., vol. 26, pp. 1520–1555; December, 1938.
(8) W. L. Barrow and F. D. Lewis, "The sectoral electromagnetic horn," Proc. I.R.E., vol. 27, pp. 41–50; January, (1939).
(9) W. L. Barrow and L. J. Chu, "Theory of the electromagnetic horn," Proc. I.R.E., vol. 27, pp. 51–64; January, (1939).

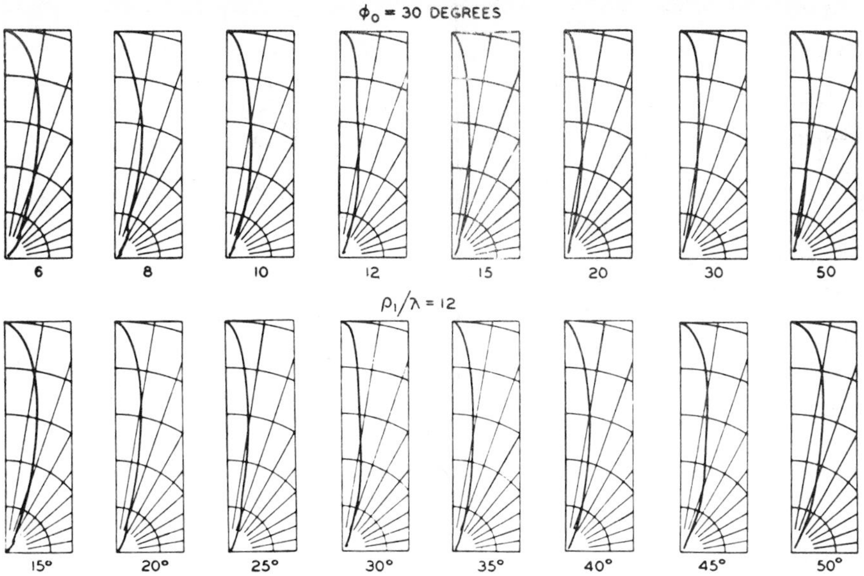

Figure 5. Two typical series of horizontal radiation patterns for the $H_{0,1}$ wave

Upper series for constant flare angle of 30 degrees and variable radial length. Lower series for constant radial length of 12 and variable flare angle

tenuation or filtration of higher order waves. This value of ρ_0 will be referred to as the "optimum cut-off length." Horns for the production of single-lobe smooth beams should have their cut-off lengths not too different from this optimum value. Figure 3 shows graphically the relation between the optimum cut-off length and the flare angle for the $H_{0,1}$ wave. For comparison, the radial extent of the high-attenuation region for the $H_{0,3}$ wave is given by the curve $n = 3$. The vertical dimension a affects neither the transmission characteristics of the $H_{0,1}$ waves nor the filtration of higher order waves except when $a >> \lambda$.

When radiation by means of the $H_{1,0}$ wave is desired, the $H_{3,0}$, $H_{5,0}$, . . . waves must be eliminated or filtered, which may be achieved by adjusting the dimension a. The $H_{1,0}$ wave is able to travel freely in the radial direction when $a > \pi/2$, but the $H_{3,0}$ wave requires $a > (3\lambda)/2$ for free transmission, etc. Therefore, to eliminate the higher order waves, the dimension a must be slightly greater than one-half wave length but less than three-halves wave lengths. The $H_{2,0}$ and $H_{4,0}$ waves can be prevented by constructing the exciting system with even symmetry about the plane $y = a/2$ equidistant from the two parallel sides of the horn.

Special cases may arise wherein several wave-types may be used simultaneously. It will be assumed in the remainder of this paper, however, that the construction of throat-and exciting means is such that either an $H_{0,1}$ or an $H_{1,0}$ wave alone exists in the horn.

Radiation Characteristics

When the horn waves reach the mouth, they become free from the guiding surfaces and spread out as radiant energy. The relative amplitude of the electric field intensity on a sphere of fixed radius large compared to wave length and aperture comprises the space radiation pattern. The radiation pattern along the intersection of this sphere and the x, y plane will be referred to as the vertical pattern and that along the x, z plane as the horizontal pattern. The discussions of this paper are confined to these two plane radiation characteristics.

In evaluating the effectiveness of a given horn to produce a directed beam of radiation, recourse to the following knowledge is useful: (1) the detailed shape of the radiation pattern, such as the presence and relative amplitudes of secondary lobes; (2) the angular width of the beam, or the "beam angle," defined here as twice the angle measured from the forward axis of the radiation pattern to the nearest radial line in this pattern along which the magnitude of the electric field intensity is ten per cent of its value on this axis; and (3) the relative power gain, defined as the ratio of the power radiated from a dipole to that radiated from the horn to produce, in each case, the same magnitude of electric field intensity at a fixed remote point on the x axis.

The radiation patterns were computed by means of Huygens' principle from the distribution of the Hertzian vector at the mouth.[3] This distribution was assumed to be the same as that which would exist at the plane of the mouth were the horn infinitely long: experiments have justified this assumption for most practical cases. The radiation patterns were plotted both in rectangular and in polar co-ordinates, and the beam angle was measured from the rectangular plots. The power radiated by the horn was obtained by integrating the Poynting vector over the mouth with the field at the mouth adjusted to give unity power density at a fixed distance r on the x axis from the origin. The power radiated by the dipole for the same effect is $(8\pi r^2)/3$. Al-

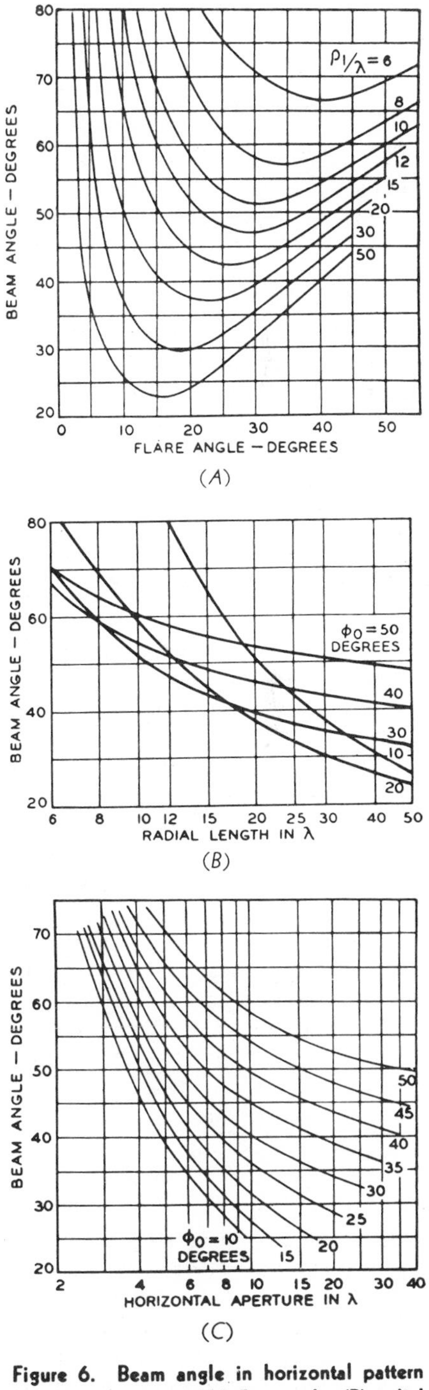

Figure 6. Beam angle in horizontal pattern for $H_{0,1}$ wave versus (A) flare angle, (B) radial length, and (C) horizontal aperture

though the power gain obtained in this way does not include copper losses in either horn or dipole, it is believed sufficiently accurate for most purposes.[6]

In the course of this research over a hundred radiation patterns were calcu-

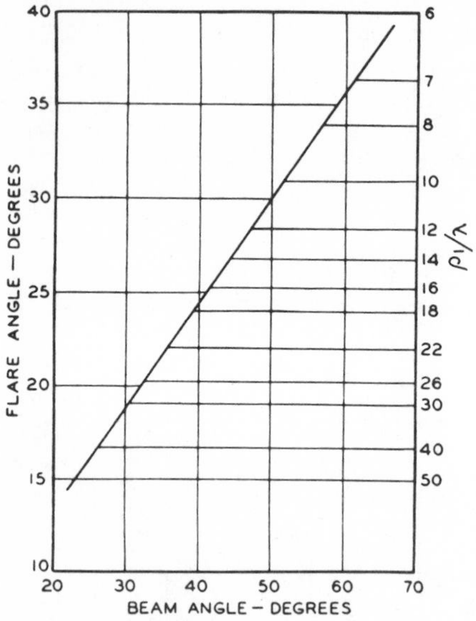

Figure 7. Optimum design curve for $H_{0,1}$ wave on beam-angle basis, giving shortest radial lengths and corresponding flare angles for a specified horizontal beam angle

lated for a wide range of horn parameters, plotted, and analyzed. Only a few of these patterns are reproduced here, but they show the same general shapes and trends possessed by all of the curves. A number of experimentally measured curves are on hand,[5] all of which agree satisfactorily with the calculated ones. Thus, the composite curves of beam angle, power gain, etc. are based on a considerable and, we believe, adequate amount of data.

The vertical patterns (in the x, y plane) have the same shapes as those of a rectangular hollow-pipe radiator. The explanation lies in the fact that the distributions of the horn waves in the y direction are similar to the distributions of the corresponding hollow-pipe waves in this direction. Patterns have been given elsewhere[3] and will not be reproduced here. The shape of the patterns comprises a principal lobe centered on the x axis and secondary lobes of relatively small amplitude. The sharpness of the principal lobe depends mainly on the vertical aperture a/λ. Figure 4 shows curves of beam angle versus vertical aperture for both $H_{0,1}$ and $H_{1,0}$ waves.

$H_{0,1}$ Wave

Two typical series of horizontal patterns for the $H_{0,1}$ waves are shown in figure 5. Only half of the beam is reproduced, but the opposite half is a mirror image of that which is given. Calculations for the back 180-degree sector cannot be made. The upper series for ϕ_0 = 30 degrees shows the variation with radial length ρ_1/λ, and the lower series for ρ_1/λ shows the effect of flare angle

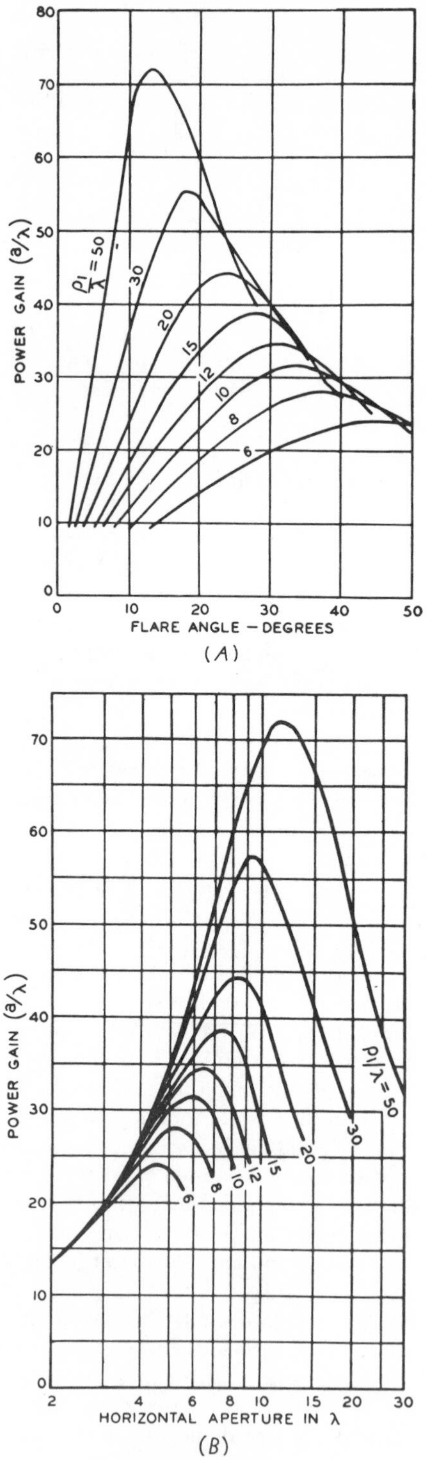

Figure 8. Power gain for $H_{0,1}$ wave versus (A) flare angle and (B) horizontal aperture

The values of power gain as read from the ordinate scale must be multiplied by the vertical aperture a/λ of the horn

ϕ_0. A glance at these patterns reveals that (1) for constant flare angle the sharpness of the beam is improved by increasing the length of the horn, up to a certain length, beyond which very little improvement occurs, and (2) for constant length there is a value of flare angle for which the beam angle is maximum. Although the radiation patterns show slight irregularities, secondary lobes are substantially absent from all of them. This fact, of considerable significance to some applications, is attributable to the half-sinusoid distribution of electric intensity at the mouth.

Curves are shown in figures 6*A*, *B*, and *C* relating the beam angle with the several design parameters. The trends (1) and (2) mentioned in the preceding paragraph may be traced in each of these curves. In particular, each curve in *A* has a minimum, and a line connecting these minima would be approximately a straight line through the origin. Such a straight line defines the shortest horns that may be employed to produce a beam of specified angle. A corresponding envelope line could be drawn in *B*.

Optimum conditions may be expressed numerically by plotting associated values of optimum flare angle and length versus the beam angle, as has been done in figure 7. This important design curve permits the ready specification of optimum horn dimensions for a beam of given angle.

Curves showing the variation of power

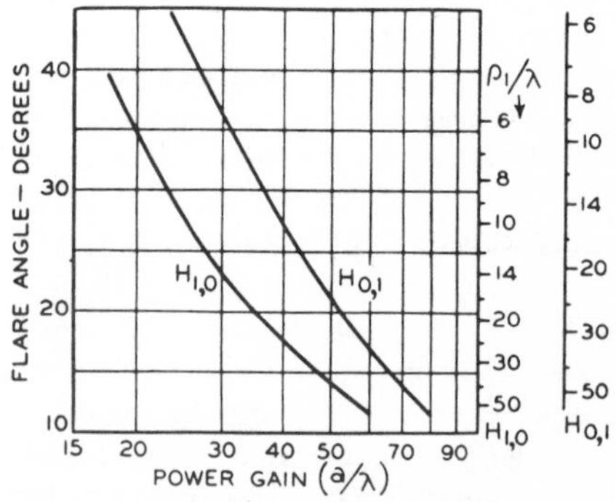

Figure 9. Optimum design curve for $H_{0,1}$ wave and $H_{1,0}$ wave on a power-gain basis, giving shortest radial lengths and corresponding flare angles for a specified power gain

The values of the power gain as read from the abscissa scale must be multiplied by the vertical aperture a/λ of the horn

gain with flare angle for a number of constant radial lengths are reproduced in figure 8*A*. Here, too, one finds that for a horn of any given length there is an optimum flare angle. In this case, it provides maximum power gain. The values of the maxima occur at smaller flare angles for increasing lengths of horn. The magnitude of the maximum power gain increases with increasing length. Figure 8*B* shows the variation of power gain with horizontal aperture. If the abscissas are multiplied by a/λ, this curve will show the variation of power gain with the transverse area of the mouth. Clearly, the gain is not a simple function of the mouth area.

The peaks of the curves in figure 8 provide optimum design conditions on a power gain basis. These optimum values of flare angle and length that provide maximum power gain are plotted in figure 9. This curve, as well as the accompanying one for the $H_{1,0}$ wave, allows the specification of optimum horn dimensions for a given power gain and supplements the curve of figure 7.

The absolute magnitude of the power gain is plotted for a vertical aperture a/λ = unity, but one should note that the power gain is directly proportional to the vertical aperture. Consequently, the values of power gain given in the curves are to be multiplied by the value of a/λ of the horn in question. Clearly, quite enormous power gains may be obtained. For example, for a horn of length $\rho_1/\lambda = 50$ having an optimum flare angle of 14° and a vertical aperture of a/λ of 10, the power gain is 720. A horn of these dimensions is entirely feasible and of moderate size at wave lengths of, say, ten centimeters. The power gain of the horn shown in the accompanying photograph is calculated to be 50.

$H_{1,0}$ Wave

Two representative series of horizontal radiation patterns (in the x, z plane) are shown in figure 10. The upper series is for horns of a constant flare angle of 35 degrees and the lower series for horns of a constant radial length of 15. The same general trends are found here that were noticed in figure 5 for the $H_{0,1}$ wave. However, the order of magnitude of the secondary peaks in the patterns is considerably greater with $H_{1,0}$ waves. For horns of equal length, increasing the flare angle from a small value at first will sharpen the principal part of the beam. It also increases the magnitude of the secondary peaks. For sufficiently large flare angles, these secondary peaks become larger than the principal beam. As a consequence, the beam becomes broader as the flare angle is increased. For horns of constant flare angle the tendency is also observed for the beam to broaden as the length of the horn is increased. However, for sufficiently great lengths, the width of the beam is substantially equal in magnitude to the flare angle.

The explanation of the exaggerated secondary peaks in the pattern of the $H_{1,0}$ wave lies in the uniform distribution of the field across the mouth in the horizontal direction and the abrupt discontinuity at the edges. The irregular shape of the horizontal patterns makes it impractical to define a beam angle and reference must be had to the actual radiation patterns.

Power gains for the $H_{1,0}$ wave are given by the curves of figure 11*A* and figure 11*B*. The general behavior of these curves is similar to those of the curves for the $H_{0,1}$ wave. The small oscillation of power gain at large flare angles is associated with the shift of the energy from principal lobe to secondary lobe, as described above. The power gain is a

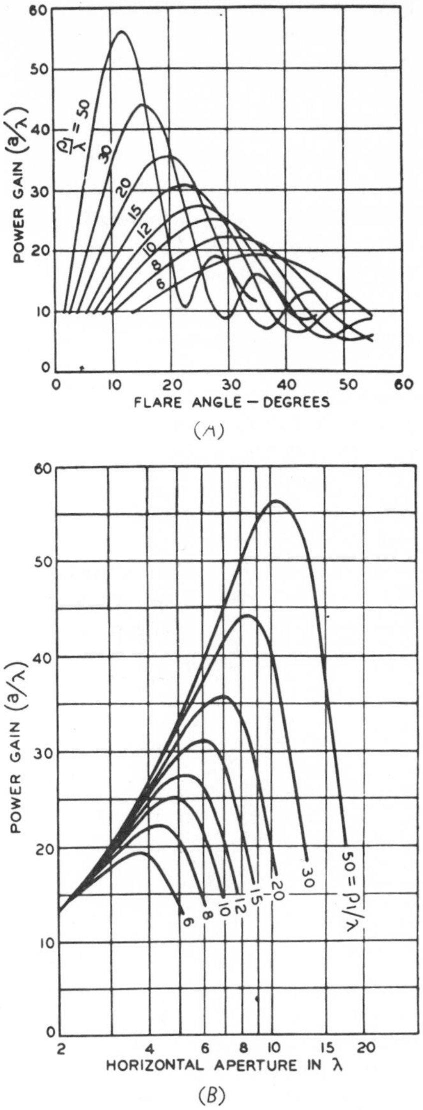

Figure 11. Power gain for $H_{1,0}$ wave versus (A) flare angle and (B) horizontal aperture

The values of power gain as read from the ordinate scale must be multiplied by the vertical aperture a/λ of the horn

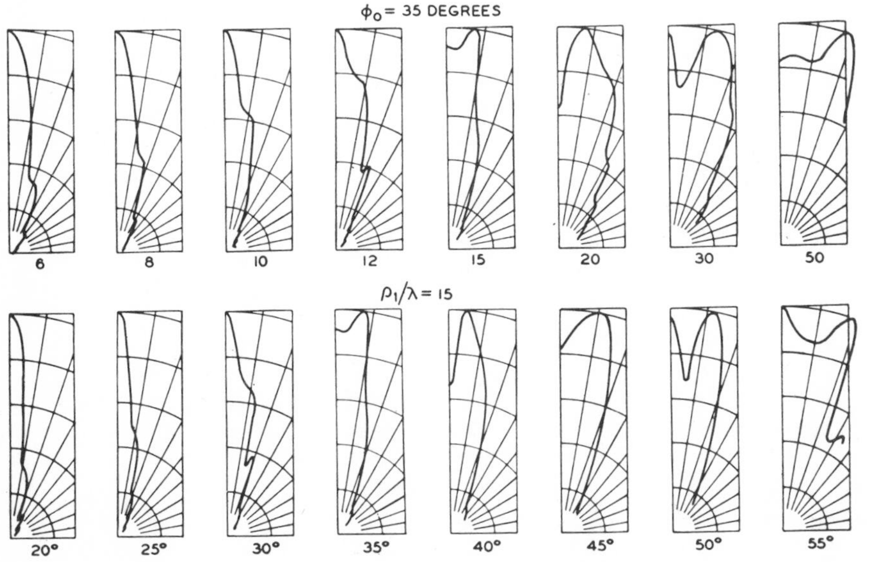

Figure 10. Two typical series of horizontal radiation patterns for the $H_{1,0}$ wave

Upper series for constant flare angle of 35 degrees and variable radial length. Lower series for constant radial length of 15 and variable flare angle

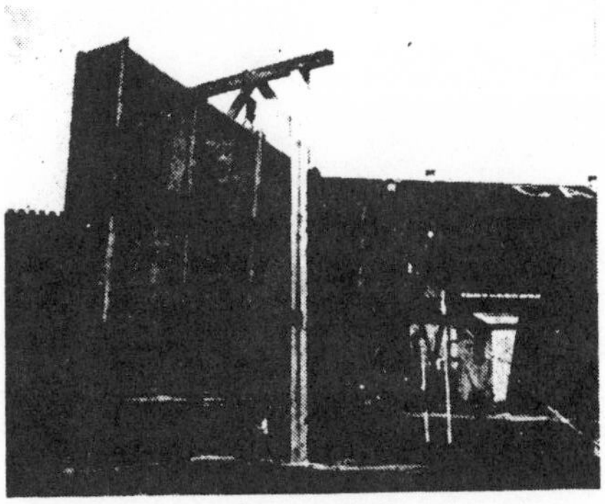

Figure 12

linear function of the vertical aperture a/λ for the $H_{1,0}$ wave also.

Optimum design for $H_{1,0}$ waves on a power gain basis is shown by the indicated curve of figure 9. Clearly, the power gain can be indefinitely increased by lengthening the horn and appropriately reducing the flare.

Concluding Remarks

Comparing the operation of the sectoral horn with the $H_{0,1}$ and the $H_{1,0}$ waves we arrive at the following conclusions. The $H_{0,1}$ wave gives a clean-cut beam comprising a principal lobe without appreciable secondary lobes, and the beam angle can be well controlled. The $H_{1,0}$ wave also gives a clean-cut beam for flare angles less than those required for maximum power gain, but an irregular beam for greater angles. On a power gain basis, there appears to be substantially no difference between the two waves.

Horns of pyramidal shape; that is, flaring in both transverse directions, may be designed on an approximate basis by means of the data presented in this paper. We may express the power gain $P_{0,1}'$ of a pyramidal horn operating with an $H_{1,0}$ wave roughly by the expression $P = kP_{0,1}\, a/\lambda$, where k is a numeric less than unity depending on the horizontal flare angle and the radial length. For small flare angles in the vertical plane, k will not differ greatly from unity, but for greater flares it will be substantially less than unity. When using an $H_{0,1}$ type of wave in a pyramidal horn, the vertical flare angle should be kept small if a clean-cut vertical radiation pattern is desired.

Bibliography

1. Hyper-Frequency Wave Guides—General Considerations and Experimental Results, **G. C. Southworth.** *Bell System Technical Journal,* volume 15, April 1936, pages 284–309.

2. Transmission of Electromagnetic Waves in Hollow Tubes of Metal, **W. L. Barrow.** *Proceedings* Institute of Radio Engineers, volume 24, number 10, October 1936, pages 1298–1328.

3. Rectangular Hollow-Pipe Radiators, **W. L. Barrow** and **F. M. Greene.** *Proceedings* Institute of Radio Engineers, volume 26, number 12, December 1938, pages 1498–1519.

4. Electromagnetic-Horn Radiators, **W. L. Barrow.** *Recueil des Travaux des Assemblees Generales de l' U. R. S. I.*

5. The Sectoral Electromagnetic Horn, **W. L. Barrow** and **F. D. Lewis.** *Proceedings* Institute of Radio Engineers, volume 27, January 1939, pages 41–50.

6. Theory of the Electromagnetic Horn, **W. L. Barrow** and **L. J. Chu.** *Proceedings* Institute of Radio Engineers, volume 27, January 1939, pages 51–64.

7. Metal Horns as Directive Receivers of Ultra-Short Waves, **G. C. Southworth** and **A. P. King.** *Proceedings* of the Institute of Radio Engineers, volume 27, February 1939, pages 95–102.

Calculation of the Radiation Properties of Hollow Pipes and Horns

L. J. Chu
Massachusetts Institute of Technology, Cambridge, Massachusetts
(Received March 18, 1940)

The radiation properties of hollow pipes and horns are analyzed. The vector Kirchhoff formula is employed. The radiation fields from the transverse electric wave in hollow pipes of circular and rectangular cross sections are derived. For the $TE_{1,1}$ wave in circular pipe and the $TE_{0,1}$ wave in the rectangular pipe, the directivities are analytically expressed in terms of beam angle and power gain. It is found that the two waves have substantially equal power gains on the basis of equal areas of openings. The formulae for the radiation fields of $TE_{0,1}$ and $TE_{1,0}$ waves in a sectoral horn are given, of which, curves illustrating the radiation properties have been published previously.

Introduction

Antenna arrays are ordinarily employed for directively radiating electromagnetic energy for wave-lengths of magnitudes down to a few meters. Near this lower limit, metallic reflectors of reasonable dimensions become feasible. At still shorter wave-lengths, say below a meter, hollow pipes and electromagnetic horns provide simple and convenient means for directing radiation.

Radiating hollow pipes and horns are usually at least several wave-lengths long and have one end open. Waves are excited near the closed end, they propagate along the pipe or horn surfaces, and finally they emerge from the open end as free radio waves. The properties of such waves in hollow pipes and horns have been discussed in a number of previous papers.[1–4] The purpose of the present paper is to discuss further theory of the radiation from the open ends.

For problems of this type, the usual procedure is as follows. First, we choose a closed surface with the opening as a part of it, and assume values of the field on this surface. For the opening these values may either be assumed to be such as would exist at the section, were the pipe or horn of infinite extent, or the resultant composed of the outcoming wave and the wave reflected back into the system from the opening. Over the remainder of the surface, the field is assumed to be zero. Then the radiation field in the free space is calculated from the assumed values of field at the opening.

The method frequently used is the application of Huygen's principle or Kirchhoff's formula, which is discussed in most standard textbooks on optics. It expresses the scalar wave function at a

[1] J. R. Carson, S. P. Mead and S. A. Schelkunoff, "Hyper-frequency wave guides—mathematical theory," Bell Sys. Tech. J. **15**, 310–333 (1936).

[2] W. L. Barrow, "Transmission of electromagnetic waves in hollow tubes of metal," Proc. I. R. E. **24**, 1298–1328 (1936).

[3] L. J. Chu and W. L. Barrow, "Electromagnetic waves in hollow metal tubes of rectangular cross section," Proc. I. R. E. **26**, 1520–1555 (1938).

[4] W. L. Barrow and L. J. Chu, "Theory of the electromagnetic horn," Proc. I. R. E. **27**, 51–64 (1939).

Reprinted with permission from *J. Appl. Phys.*, vol. 11, pp. 603–610, Sept. 1940.

point in free space in terms of the values of the wave function and its normal derivative on the surface. The scalar wave function on the closed surface *must be continuous and have continuous derivatives*. Extending this to vector wave functions, we take advantage of the fact that the rectangular components of a vector field or vector potential function are scalar wave functions. The correctness of this procedure can be verified by applying the formula to a known electromagnetic field of potential in a homogeneous medium. However, difficulty appears when the values on the surface of integration are not exactly known but are assumed, particularly if the assumed values are discontinuous. In this case, the applications of the Kirchhoff formula to the components of the electric and magnetic field vectors lead to a nontransverse radiation field which is physically impossible. By using the vector potential or Hertzian vector, this trouble can be eliminated, but the question of uniqueness arises since a given field on the surface of integration can be represented by a number of different vector potentials.

The failure of Kirchhoff's formula to give consistent or physically realizable results for the problem is the natural consequence of the misrepresentation of the field on the boundary surface, and is not the fault of the formula itself. We must recognize the fact that the assumed field is not continuous across the boundary of the opening, and such fields do not satisfy Maxwell's relations at the boundary. If we apply the Kirchhoff formula to the field vectors rather than the potentials, the calculated field cannot be expected to satisfy Maxwell's relations and possess the properties of a transverse wave.

The Kirchhoff formula for vector fields can be directly derived by means of the vector equivalent of Green's theorem.[5] For a source-free and homogeneous region, the vector Kirchhoff formula is exactly the same as the scalar one provided the vector wave function and its normal derivative on the surface are *continuous*. However, in order to apply the formula to diffraction problems, charges have to be introduced to take care of the discontinuity such that the assumed field satisfies Maxwell's equation.

[5] J. A. Stratton and L. J. Chu, "Diffraction theory of electromagnetic waves," Phys. Rev. **56**, 92–112 (1939).

The modified Kirchhoff formula for fields varying with time as $e^{i\omega t}$, is as follows:

$$\begin{aligned}4\pi\mathbf{E}'(x'y'z') &= \frac{1}{i\omega\epsilon}\oint \nabla\psi\mathbf{H}\cdot d\mathbf{s}\\ &\quad+\oint \psi\mathbf{E}\times d\mathbf{s}-\int_s\left[\mathbf{E}\frac{\partial\psi}{\partial n}-\psi\frac{\partial\mathbf{E}}{\partial n}\right]da,\\ 4\pi\mathbf{H}'(x'y'z') &= -\frac{1}{i\omega\mu}\oint \nabla\psi\mathbf{E}\cdot d\mathbf{s}\\ &\quad+\oint \psi\mathbf{H}\times d\mathbf{s}-\int_s\left[\mathbf{H}\frac{\partial\psi}{\partial n}-\psi\frac{\partial\mathbf{H}}{\partial n}\right]da,\end{aligned}\tag{1}$$

where $\psi=e^{-i\omega r}/r$,

$$r=[(x'-x)^2+(y'-y)^2+(z'-z)^2]^{\frac{1}{2}}$$

and $\mathbf{n}$ = normal to the surface, directed out of the region occupied by the observer. The surface integral is taken over the opening, if the rest of the surface is assumed to have zero field. The line integrals are taken along the contour across which the field is discontinuous. The positive direction of $d\mathbf{s}$ is determined by the right-hand rule with the thumb in the direction of $\mathbf{n}$. The fields $\mathbf{E}'$ and $\mathbf{H}'$ satisfy the Maxwell relations.

The accuracy of the modified Kirchhoff formula depends entirely upon how closely the assumed field approximates the actual field on the surface of integration. If the opening is large compared to the wave-length, the assumed value is a close approximation of the actual value, as shown in a number of experiments. Calculations have been made for the diffraction by a slit. The results checked closely with the exact solution even for a $1/\pi$ wave-length opening.

Another method, the equivalence theorem of electromagnetics, has been discussed by Schelkunoff and applied to calculate the radiation from the coaxial lines[6] and rectangular tubes.[7] The fields on the surface of integration are replaced by the equivalent electric and magnetic currents, from which the radiation fields are calculated. This method gives results identical with the modified Kirchhoff formula.

[6] S. A. Schelkunoff, "Some equivalence theorems of electromagnetics and their application to radiation problems," Bell Sys. Tech. J. **15**, 92–112 (1936).
[7] S. A. Schelkunoff, "On diffraction and radiation of electromagnetic waves," Phys. Rev. **56**, 308–316 (1939).

The field of the $TE_{l,m}$ wave ($H_{l,m}$ wave) inside an infinitely conducting hollow pipe of circular cross section of radius a is as follows:

$$\begin{aligned} H_z &= k_m^2 \cos l\phi J_l(k_m\rho)e^{-i\beta z}, \quad E_z = 0, \\ H_\rho &= -(\beta/\omega\mu)E_\phi = -i\beta k_m \cos l\phi J_l'(k_m\rho)e^{-i\beta z}, \\ H_\phi &= (\beta/\omega\mu)E_\rho = (i\beta l/\rho)\sin l\phi J_l(k_m\rho)e^{-i\beta z}, \end{aligned} \tag{2}$$

where $k_m = (k^2-\beta^2)^{\frac{1}{2}}$, $k_m a$ is the mth root of $J_l'(x)$, β is the phase constant, $k=\omega(\mu\epsilon)^{\frac{1}{2}}$, (z, ρ, ϕ) is the cylindrical coordinate system, and μ and ϵ are permeability and dielectric constant, respectively. The rationalized m.k.s. system of units is used. All the expressions have a $e^{i\omega t}$ variation with time.

To calculate the radiation from the open end, we assume that the field at the opening is such as would exist there, were the pipe infinitely extended. Both the distortion and reflection at the opening will be neglected. Set the opening of the pipe at $z=0$ as shown in Fig. 1. For $r \gg \rho$ and $r \gg 1/k$

$$r \simeq R - \rho \sin\theta \cos(\phi-\zeta), \quad \nabla\psi = \mathbf{i}_R ik\psi, \quad d\mathbf{s} = -\mathbf{i}_\phi a d\phi,$$

$$\mathbf{H}\cdot d\mathbf{s} = -H_\phi a d\phi, \quad \mathbf{E}\times d\mathbf{s} = -\mathbf{i}_z E_\rho a d\phi,$$

where $\mathbf{i}$ is a unit vector, the direction of which is indicated by the subscript. For the surface integral, it is best to resolve the electric field into Cartesian components.

$$\begin{aligned} E_x &= (i\omega\mu k_m/2)[J_{l-1}(k_m\rho)\sin(l-1)\phi + J_{l+1}(k_m\rho)\sin(l+1)\phi]e^{-i\beta z}, \\ E_y &= (i\omega\mu k_m/2)[J_{l-1}(k_m\rho)\cos(l-1)\phi - J_{l+1}(k_m\rho)\cos(l+1)\phi]e^{-i\beta z}. \end{aligned}$$

By substituting the appropriate terms into (1), we have,

$$\begin{aligned} 4\pi\mathbf{E}'(R,\theta,\zeta) = \Bigg[&-\{\mathbf{i}_r i\beta(\mu/\epsilon)^{\frac{1}{2}} + \mathbf{i}_z i\omega\mu\} l J_l(k_m a)\int_0^{2\pi} \sin l\phi e^{ika\sin\theta\cos(\phi-\zeta)}d\phi \\ &+ i(k\cos\theta+\beta)\int_0^a d\rho\int_0^{2\pi} d\phi\{\mathbf{i}_x E_x + \mathbf{i}_y E_y\}_{z=0}\rho^{-ik\rho\sin\theta\cos(\phi-\zeta)}\Bigg]\frac{e^{-ikR}}{R}. \end{aligned} \tag{3}$$

To evaluate the integral, we utilize the Bessel-Fourier series

$$e^{i\kappa\rho\cos(\phi-\zeta)} = J_0(\kappa\rho) + \sum_{n=1}^{\infty} 2i^n J_n(\kappa\rho)\cos n(\phi-\zeta)$$

and the Lommel integral

$$\int_0^a J_n(k_m\rho)J_n(\kappa\rho)\rho d\rho = \frac{1}{\kappa^2-k_m^2}[k_m a J_{n-1}(k_m a)J_n(\kappa a) - \kappa a J_{n-1}(\kappa a)J_n(k_m a)],$$

where $\kappa = k\sin\theta$.

After simplification and resolution into spherical components, we have

$$\begin{aligned} E_R' &= 0, \\ E_\theta' &= i^{l+1}\frac{l\omega\mu}{2R}\left(1+\frac{\beta}{k}\cos\theta\right)J_l(k_m a)\frac{J_l(ka\sin\theta)}{\sin\theta}\sin l\zeta\, e^{-ikR}, \\ E_\zeta' &= i^{l+1}\frac{ka\omega\mu}{2R}\left(\frac{\beta}{k}+\cos\theta\right)J_l(k_m a)\frac{J_l'(ka\sin\theta)}{1-(k\sin\theta/k_m)^2}\cos l\zeta\, e^{-ikR}. \end{aligned} \tag{4}$$

FIG. 1. Coordinate system for calculating the radiation from a circular hollow pipe.

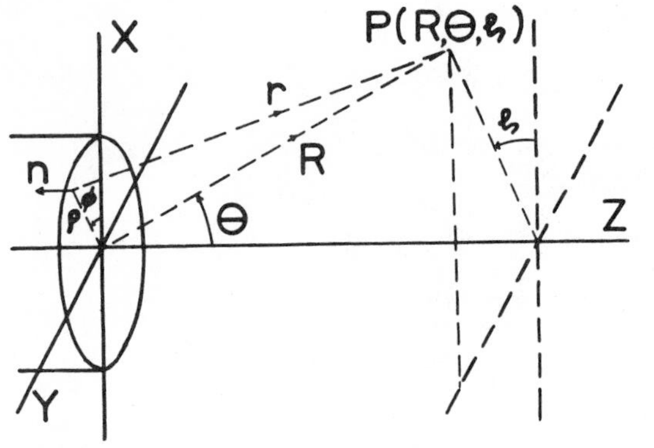

The $TE_{1,1}$ or $H_{1,1}$ wave corresponding to the first zero of $J_1'(x)$ has the lowest cut-off frequency and has low attenuation. As given by (2) for $l=1$, the wave is polarized in the y direction. Its radiation field can be obtained by putting $l=1$ in the above expressions. The radiation patterns in the ZX and YZ planes for $2a/\lambda=\frac{2}{3}$, 1, $\frac{3}{2}$ and 9/4 are plotted in Fig. 2. The open end of the circular pipe points toward the top of the paper. Only halves of the patterns are shown, the other halves being the mirror images. The cut-off wave-length of the wave inside the pipe is incidentally equal to $\lambda_1=2a/.585$. As the ratio of the diameter of the pipe to the wave-length is increased, the beam becomes sharper and the side lobes appear.

The sharpness of the beam can be described by the beam angle,[8] which may be defined as the angle measured from zero to zero including the main beam. This definition is particularly convenient for the present case. Thus in the YZ plane $\zeta=90°$, E_θ' is zero when $ka \sin\theta=3.83$ and the beam angle in the YZ plane,

$$2\theta=2\sin^{-1}(3.83\lambda/2\pi a).$$

Similarly, in the XZ plane, $E_\zeta'=0$ when $ka\sin\theta=5.33$ and the corresponding beam angle is $2\theta=2\sin^{-1}(5.33\lambda/2\pi a)$. These apply only for $2\theta<\pi$ radians. The beam is sharper in the YZ plane than in the XZ plane.

Another function which has practical significance, is the relative power gain. It is defined here as the ratio of the power radiated from a dipole to that radiated from the pipe to produce in each case, the same power per unit area at a fixed remote point on the Z axis. If the maximum power per unit area at a distance R from the dipole is unity, the total power radiated from the dipole will be $\frac{8}{3}\pi R^2$, the result of the integration of $\sin^2\theta$ over a sphere of radius R. The maximum power density radiated from the hollow pipe at the same distance is equal to the Poynting vector at $(x=0,\ y=0,\ z=R)$,

$$\frac{1}{32}\left(\frac{\epsilon}{\mu}\right)^{\frac{1}{2}}\frac{\omega^2\mu^2}{R^2}(ka)^2\left(1+\frac{\beta}{k}\right)^2[J_1(k_1a)]^2. \quad (5)$$

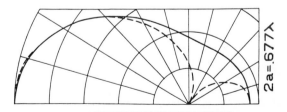

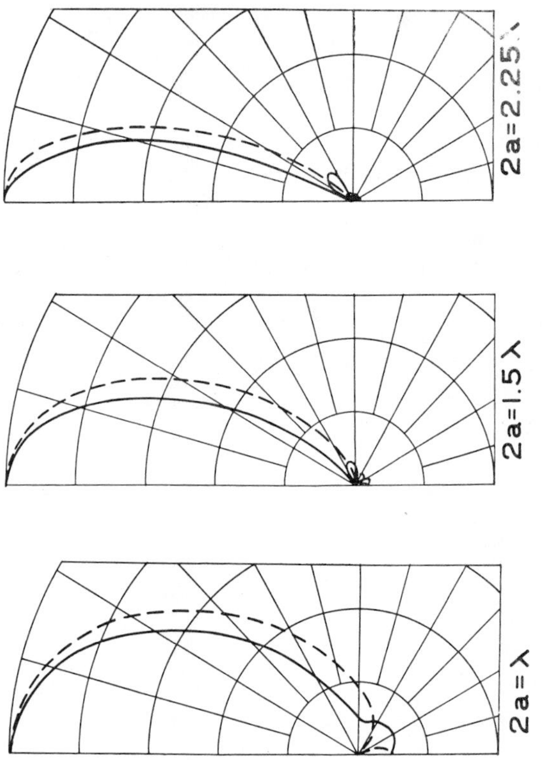

FIG. 2. The radiation patterns of $TE_{1,1}$ wave from a circular hollow pipe. The solid curves are patterns in YZ plane and dotted curves are patterns in XZ plane.

[8] W. L. Barrow and F. M. Greene, "Rectangular hollow pipe radiator," Proc. I. R. E. 26, 1498–1519 (1938).

We could integrate the Poynting vector, calculated from (4) over the sphere of radius R to obtain the total power radiated from the open end of the hollow pipe, but such procedure would involve tedious if not impossible computations and would not give more information than the one outlined below.

The exactness of the result calculated from the modified Kirchhoff formula increases as the ratios of the linear dimensions to the wave-length. In the neighborhood of the cut-off frequency, the power associated with the wave in the pipe is exceedingly small, and becomes zero in the limit on account of the vanishing of the transverse magnetic field. However, if such a wave did exist at the mouth of the pipe, the radiation field and therefore the power would not be zero and the result would be open to question. On the other hand, when the frequency is considerably above the critical value, the distortion of the field at the open end caused by scattering and reflection is negligible. Then, the total radiated power must be equal to that transmitted through the pipe. That the method used here does give the actual radiation field, is obvious since the assumed field on the surface of integration approaches the exact one.

The power transmitted through the tube associated with the $TE_{1,1}$ wave is the integral of the component of the Poynting vector along the axis over the cross section of the pipe.

$$\tfrac{1}{4}\pi\beta\omega\mu[(k_1a)^2-1][J_1(k_1a)]^2. \qquad (6)$$

The power gain as compared to a dipole is

$$\frac{k^3a^2}{3\beta}\left(1+\frac{\beta}{k}\right)^2 \Big/ [(k_1a)^2-1]$$

$$\cong 7.46\left[\frac{\text{area of opening}}{\lambda^2}\right], \qquad (7)$$

excluding the range of frequency at the neighborhood of cut-off value by setting β equal to k.

Thus the power gain of a circular hollow pipe is a linear function of the ratio of the opening to the square of the wave-length. The power gain as compared to some other system is the ratio of (7) and the power gain of the system as compared to a dipole. This is for the case for which only the $TE_{1,1}$ wave is present in the hollow pipe. Were other types of waves present at the same time, not only the radiation pattern but also the power gain would be changed. Higher order waves tend to appear in a circular pipe when the frequency is increased. Their effect is generally to decrease the power gain.

Southworth[9] has published some experimental results on a circular hollow pipe radiator. His power ratios are calculated on a different basis.

Radiation from Rectangular Hollow Pipes

The radiation from the open end of a rectangular hollow pipe is given below without much ado. The field of the $TE_{l,m}$ wave in a rectangular hollow pipe with four corners at $(0, 0, z)$, $(a, 0, z)$, (a, b, z) and $(0, b, z)$ can be expressed as follows:

$$H_z = k_{l,m}^2 \cos(xl\pi/a)\cos(ym\pi/b)e^{-i\beta z}, \quad E_z = 0,$$

$$H_x = -(\beta/\omega\mu)E_y = i\beta(l\pi/a)\sin(xl\pi/a)\cos(ym\pi/b)e^{-i\beta z}, \qquad (8)$$

$$H_y = (\beta/\omega\mu)E_x = i\beta(n\pi/b)\cos(xl\pi/a)\sin(ym\pi/b)e^{-i\beta z},$$

where $\quad k_{l,m} = [(l\pi/a)^2+(m\pi/b)^2]^{\frac{1}{2}}, \quad$ and $\quad \beta = (\omega^2\epsilon\mu - k_{l,m}^2)^{\frac{1}{2}}.$

Set the opening of the pipe at $z=0$. The radiation field at great distances from the open end is as

[9] G. C. Southworth and A. P. King, "Metal horns as directive receivers of ultra-short waves," Proc. I. R. E. **27**, 95–102 (1939).

follows:

$$\mathbf{E}' = \left(\frac{\mu}{\epsilon}\right)^{\frac{1}{2}} \frac{(\pi ab)^2}{2\lambda^3 R}\left[\mathbf{i}_\theta\left(1+\frac{\beta}{k}\cos\theta\right)\left\{\left(\frac{l\pi}{a}\sin\zeta\right)^2-\left(\frac{m\pi}{b}\cos\zeta\right)^2\right\}+\mathbf{i}_\zeta\left(\frac{\beta}{k}+\cos\theta\right)k^2_{l,m}\sin\zeta\cos\zeta\right]$$

$$\times\frac{\sin\left(\frac{a\pi}{\lambda}\sin\theta\cos\zeta+\frac{l\pi}{2}\right)}{\left(\frac{a\pi}{\lambda}\sin\theta\cos\zeta\right)^2-\left(\frac{l\pi}{2}\right)^2}\cdot\frac{\sin\left(\frac{b\pi}{\lambda}\sin\theta\sin\zeta+\frac{m\pi}{2}\right)}{\left(\frac{b\pi}{\lambda}\sin\theta\sin\zeta\right)^2-\left(\frac{m\pi}{2}\right)^2}\sin\theta$$

$$\times e^{-i\{kR-\pi/\lambda\sin\theta(a\cos\zeta+b\sin\zeta)-\pi/2(l+m+1)\}}. \quad (9)$$

The lowest order wave in a rectangular hollow pipe is the $TE_{0,1}$ wave. It is polarized in the X direction. Its radiation field is as follows:

$$\mathbf{E}' = -\left(\frac{\mu}{\epsilon}\right)^{\frac{1}{2}} \frac{\pi^3 a}{2\lambda^2 R}\left[\mathbf{i}_\theta\left(1+\frac{\beta}{k}\cos\theta\right)\cos\zeta+i_\zeta\left(\frac{\beta}{k}+\cos\theta\right)\sin\zeta\right]$$

$$\times\frac{\sin\left(\frac{\pi a}{\lambda}\sin\theta\cos\zeta\right)}{\frac{\pi a}{\lambda}\sin\theta\cos\zeta}\cdot\frac{\cos\left(\frac{\pi b}{\lambda}\sin\theta\sin\zeta\right)}{\left(\frac{\pi b}{\lambda}\sin\theta\sin\zeta\right)^2-\left(\frac{\pi}{2}\right)^2}e^{-i\{kR-\pi/\lambda\sin\theta(a\cos\zeta+b\sin\zeta)\}}. \quad (10)$$

An experimental and theoretical study has been made by Barrow and Greene[8] and discussed by Schelkunoff.[7] The above agrees with Schelkunoff's calculation and is slightly different from the calculation made by Barrow and Greene, using the scalar Kirchhoff formula applied to a Hertzian vector. The horizontal pattern (Fig. 9 of reference 8) from their calculation checks with the above ($\zeta=\pi/2$), but the vertical one differs roughly by a factor $\cos\theta$ from the author's ($\zeta=0$), (Fig. 10 of reference 8). The solid dots in their Fig. 10B, calculated by applying the scalar Kirchhoff formula directly to the electric field, check numerically with the above result, but the field has wrong polarization.

The beam angle in the XZ plane ($\zeta=0$) is

$$2\sin^{-1}(\lambda/a)$$

and that in the YZ plane ($\zeta=\pi/2$) is

$$2\sin^{-1}(3\lambda/2b).$$

With a rectangular hollow pipe radiator, the beam angles in the two planes can be controlled independently by adjusting the dimensions a and b. This is a definite advantage over the circular hollow pipe radiator, for which the beam angles are not independent, since there is only one dimension to be adjusted.

The relative power gain of a rectangular hollow-pipe radiator with $H_{0,1}$ wave, as compared to a dipole, can be proved to be

$$\frac{16}{3\pi}\frac{ab}{\lambda^2}\frac{k}{\beta}\left[1+\frac{\beta}{k}\right]^2 \cong 6.78\frac{\text{area of opening}}{\lambda^2}. \quad (11)$$

The phase constant β being set equal to k to exclude the range of frequency in the neighborhood of cut-off value.

On the basis of equal areas of openings the power gains of the circular hollow-pipe radiator and the rectangular one are substantially of equal magnitudes.

SECTORAL HORN RADIATOR

If other types of waves than the $TE_{0,1}$ wave in a rectangular hollow-pipe or the $TE_{1,1}$ wave in a circular one were absent, the hollow-pipe radiators would be an effective means of obtaining directivity and power gain. However, as the dimensions of the pipe increase, it is increasingly difficult to eliminate these other types of waves. The directivity will be out of control and the power gain will fall off from the expected value. This difficulty can be avoided by connecting the pipe to a flared horn whose relative dimensions are such that only the desired waves are allowed to propagate through it. This device has been called an *electromagnetic horn.*

Sectoral horns have been treated previously.[4,10,11] At this point we wlll give the calculations of the radiation field by means of the extension of the Kirchhoff formula. The sectoral horn is made with four conducting surfaces, forming a sector of a circular cylinder of finite depth a. The lowest order waves in this horn are the $TE_{0,1}$ and the $TE_{1,0}$ waves whose field inside the horn are as follows,

$TE_{0,1}$ *wave*

$$\begin{aligned} E_x &= \cos(\pi\phi/\phi_0)K_{\pi/\varphi_0}(k\rho), \\ H_\rho &= \frac{\pi}{i\omega\mu\rho\phi_0}\sin(\pi\phi/\phi_0)K_{\pi/\varphi_0}(k\rho), \\ H_\phi &= -i(\epsilon/\mu)^{\frac{1}{2}}\cos(\pi\phi/\phi_0)K'_{\pi/\varphi_0}(k\rho), \end{aligned} \tag{12}$$

$TE_{1,0}$ *wave*

$$\begin{aligned} E_\phi &= \sin(\pi x/a)K_1(k_0\rho), \\ H_x &= -\frac{k_0}{i\omega\mu}\sin(\pi x/a)K_0(k_0\rho), \\ H_\rho &= \frac{\pi}{i\omega\mu a}\cos(\pi x/a)K_1(k_0\rho). \end{aligned} \tag{13}$$

The cylindrical coordinates (x, ρ, ϕ) are used, the $\phi=0$ plane coinciding with the XZ plane. The horn is placed with the top and bottom surfaces at $x=a$ and $x=0$, and the flared sides at $\phi=\pm\phi_0/2$. The constant k is equal to $\omega(\epsilon\mu)^{\frac{1}{2}}$ and

$$k_0=(k^2-(\pi/a)^2)^{\frac{1}{2}}.$$

K indicates the Hankel function of the second kind.

We are mainly interested in the details of the radiation in the YZ plane, in which the sides of the horn are flared. Thus, we take a horn of finite length ρ_1, and assume the above fields to exist at the open mouth. The distance from any point (ρ_1, ϕ) on the mouth of the horn to the remote point of observation $(R, \theta, \zeta=\pm\pi/2$ on the YZ plane is approximately equal to

$$r=R-\rho_1\cos(\phi-\theta).$$

The asymptotic form of the Hankel functions can be used if $\rho_1 \gg \lambda$.

For the $TE_{0,1}$ wave, the two contour integrals in (1) vanish because both $\mathbf{H}\cdot d\mathbf{S}$ and $\mathbf{E}\times d\mathbf{s}$ are zero at the tips of the flared sides, and at the tips of the parallel sides they are oddly symmetrical about

[10] L. J. Chu and W. L. Barrow, "Electromagnetic horn design," Elect. Eng. **58**, 333–338 (1939).
[11] W. L. Barrow and F. D. Lewis, "The sectoral electromagnetic horn," Proc. I. R. E. **27**, 41–50 (1939).

the point of observation. The radiation field at $P(R, \theta, \zeta=\pm\pi/2)$

$$E_x' \cong \frac{i3a}{16(10)^{\frac{1}{2}}R}(1+\cos\ \theta)e^{i[-2\pi R/\lambda+9\pi^3\lambda/320\rho_1\phi_0{}^2]}\left[e^{i\pi\theta/\phi_0}F(u)\Big|_{u_1}^{u_2}+e^{-i\pi\theta/\phi_0}F(u)\Big|_{u_3}^{u_4}\right], \tag{14}$$

where $F(u)$ is the Fresnel integral

$$F(u)=\int \tfrac{1}{2}\{J_{-\frac{1}{2}}(u)-iJ_{\frac{1}{2}}(u)\}du \tag{15}$$

and

$$u_1=\left[-\frac{\phi_0}{2}-\theta-\frac{9\pi^2\lambda}{160\rho_1\phi_0}\right]^2\frac{80\rho_1}{9\pi\lambda}, \quad u_3=\left[-\frac{\phi_0}{2}-\theta+\frac{9\pi^2\lambda}{160\rho_1\phi_0}\right]^2\frac{80\rho_1}{9\pi\lambda},$$

$$u_2=\left[+\frac{\phi_0}{2}-\theta-\frac{9\pi^2\lambda}{160\rho_1\phi_0}\right]^2\frac{80\rho_1}{9\pi\lambda}, \quad u_4=\left[+\frac{\phi_0}{2}-\theta+\frac{9\pi^2\lambda}{160\rho_1\phi_0}\right]^2\frac{80\rho_1}{9\pi\lambda}.$$

This result is identical with the one given previously.[4]

For the $H_{1,0}$ wave, the radiation field in the YZ plane is found to be

$$E_\theta' = \frac{i3a}{8(10)^{\frac{1}{2}}\pi R}\left(\frac{k}{k_0}\right)^{\frac{1}{2}} e^{-i[kR-(k-k_0)\rho_1]}\left[e^{i(9\pi\lambda/320\rho_1)}\left\{F(u)\Big|_{u_5}^{u_6}+F(u)\Big|_{n_7}^{u_8}\right\}+2F(u)\Big|_{u_9}^{u_{10}}\right], \tag{16}$$

where

$$u_5=\frac{80\rho_1}{9\pi\lambda}\left[-\frac{\phi_0}{2}-\theta-\frac{9\pi\lambda}{160\rho_1}\right]^2, \quad u_8=\frac{80\rho_1}{9\pi\lambda}\left[\frac{\phi_0}{2}-\theta-\frac{9\pi\lambda}{160\rho_1}\right]^2,$$

$$u_6=\frac{80\rho_1}{9\pi\lambda}\left[\frac{\phi_0}{2}-\theta-\frac{9\pi\lambda}{160\rho_1}\right]^2, \quad u_9=\frac{80\rho_1}{9\pi\lambda}\left[-\frac{\phi_0}{2}-\theta\right]^2,$$

$$u_7=\frac{80\rho_1}{9\pi\lambda}\left[-\frac{\phi_0}{2}-\theta+\frac{9\pi\lambda}{160\rho_1}\right]^2, \quad u_{10}=\frac{80\rho_1}{9\pi\lambda}\left[\frac{\phi_0}{2}-\theta\right]^2.$$

More approximately,

$$E_\theta' = i\frac{3a}{4(10)^{\frac{1}{2}}\pi R}e^{-ikR}(1+\cos\ \theta)F(u)\Big|_{u_9}^{u_{10}}. \tag{17}$$

In calculating the radiation field from the sectoral horn, integrals of the following type occur.

$$\int \cos\ \phi e^{ik\rho\ \cos\ (\phi-\theta)}d\phi. \tag{18}$$

There seems no hope of finding the exact solution. The expansion of the exponential would give a slowly convergent series which is useless for numerical calculation. An approximate solution is obtained, however, by replacing the cos $(\phi-\theta)$ in the exponent by $1-(10/9\pi^2)(\phi-\theta)^2$. The factor cos ϕ is split into exponentials. By completing the square in the exponents, the result can be transformed into Fresnel's integral.

$$F(x^2)=\left(\frac{2}{\pi}\right)^{\frac{1}{2}}\int e^{ix^2}dx=\int \tfrac{1}{2}[J_{-\frac{1}{2}}(x^2)-iJ_{\frac{1}{2}}(x^2)]d(x^2) \tag{19}$$

for which a numerical table is available. Since this approximation of cos $(\phi-\theta)$ is good only for $(\phi-\theta)<\pi/2$, the calculation is limited to values of $|\theta|<(\pi-\phi_0)/2$.

The curves illustrating the radiation properties of horns have been published previously without mathematical expressions or analytical discussion;[10] the above material supplies this lack.

THE PHASE CORRECTION OF HORN RADIATORS

By N. M. Rust.*

(Abstract *of a lecture delivered at the* Radiolocation Convention *27th March*, 1946.)

The work described herein was for the most part carried out in the late summer of 1941, when the field was new to us and our technique of wave matching was not far advanced.

Very early in the development of microwave technique it was realized that by flaring out a wave guide into a horn, a useful radiator could very simply be produced. A 30° beam width with small side-lobes, easily obtained with a horn in the new region, was at first regarded as a good diagram on the basis of experience with longer waves, but it was soon realized that for most purposes much narrower beam widths and higher aerial gains were required than could be obtained with simple horns.

The directivity of a horn can be estimated in terms of the size of the aperture and the field distribution across it (as determined by the polarization of the feed). The polar diagram can never be sharper than that of the ideal aperture across which the phase of the field is uniform. In-phase distribution may be approximated to any required degree by using a horn of sufficient length. Large apertures, however, require impracticably long horns.

The directivity may be assessed in relation to the constancy of phase across the surface of the aperture. Fig. 1(*a*) pictures the problem. For simplicity, vertically-polarized horns, flared out horizontally only, are considered. Three horns of different lengths are shown, each of the same aperture—10 wavelengths. It has been found experimentally that if the aperture is large compared with the wavelength the equi-phase front is substantially circular in the horizontal plane, the centre of the circle being approximately at the virtual apex. It will be noticed that the maximum phase difference, that between centre and sides, depends upon the length of horn. This length must be at least 50 wavelengths (for the aperture chosen) to reduce this maximum phase difference, or "slip" as it may be termed, to less than 90°; whilst if the length is made equal to the aperture the slip becomes over a wavelength. One might expect the allowable limit to be that of the horn 25 wavelengths long, for which the phase slip is 180°, as the aperture then lies within the first Fresnel zone. However, polar diagram calculations have been made assuming cosine distribution of field strength across the aperture [Fig. 1(*b*)], and from these it will be seen that serious widening of the base occurs for the 180° case. If, on the other hand, the phase slip is limited to 90°, as for the horn 50 wavelengths long, a tolerable diagram is obtained. A rough rule based on these factors, and confirmed by practical tests, was therefore used:—The maximum phase slip should not be allowed to exceed 90°.

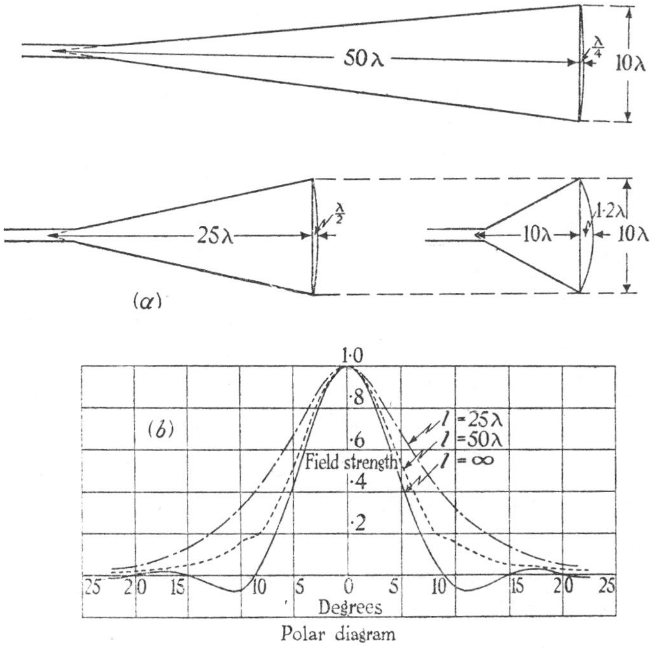

Fig. 1.—Illustrating the necessity for using long "simple" horns to reduce phase slip.

Thus a horn of large aperture and length comparable with the aperture should have some form of phase correction to conform to this rule. In considering possible methods of phase correction it occurred to us to use the well-known property of wave-guide propagation that the phase velocity of the field compounded by the waves reflected from the metal surfaces is greater than the free-space velocity. Thus metal partitions acting as sections of wave guides could be used to obtain the correction. Fig. 2(*a*) illustrates a method of applying this principle. The shortest horn of Fig. 1 (having a maximum phase slip of 425°) is shown in cross-section. The polarization is normal to the plane of the diagram; partitions are arranged radially, and the phase correction is effected by adjusting their length.

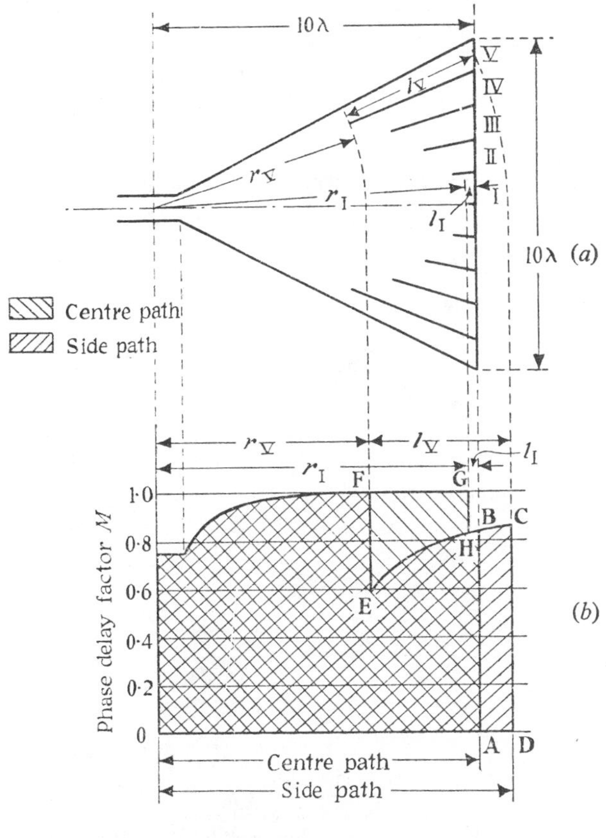

Fig. 2.—Method of designing plates.

* Marconi's Wireless Telegraph Co., Ltd.

Reprinted with permission from *J. Inst. Elec. Eng.*, vol. 93, pt. IIIA, pp. 50–51, Mar.–May 1946.

It will be clear that the phase delay from apex to aperture must be made the same for each path through the wave-guide sections, and that the longer paths, the outer ones, will require longer wave-guide sections than the central ones. (Equiangular spacing is assumed.) The correct lengths may be determined very simply by means of a graphical construction, illustrated in Fig. 2(*b*). Without entering into a detailed description of this, it will suffice to say that the factor *M* which relates the wave-guide phase velocity to the free-space velocity ($v_p = c/M$) may be interpreted as a phase delay factor. With radial disposition of plates, *M*, which is dependent upon the plate separation, varies with the distance from the apex. Integrating *M* against this distance for each path determines the phase delay, and the areas representing the respective phase delays are made equal by adjusting the lengths of the plates. It is desirable from several points of view to choose the partition spacing so that the factor *M* is never less than one-half.

Correct phasing is realized at only one frequency, but conditions are not critical. At frequencies higher than the correct frequency, the aperture size, as measured in wavelengths, increases, and this tends to compensate the loss due to phase slip, resulting in approximately constant gain over an appreciable waveband. In the example illustrated the maximum phase slip is only 73·5° for an increase of frequency of 10%, and the horn would actually work quite well over a ± 10% band-width.

It is usually required to flare out in both directions, and then the plates can be shaped to secure equi-phase conditions right over the aperture. This is done by making the phase delay for each path equal, along all radial lines from the apex.

It was found more convenient to correct the phase with a rectangular box extension, using parallel plates. Three methods may be used for arranging and adjusting the plates, namely:—

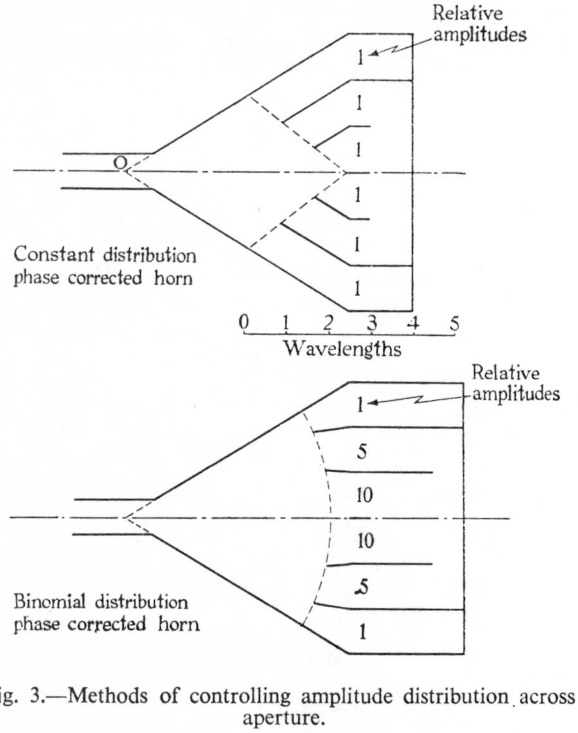

Fig. 3.—Methods of controlling amplitude distribution across aperture.

(*a*) Spacing constant; length varied

(*b*) Length constant; spacing varied, and

(*c*) Both length and spacing varied, to obtain section lengths acting as half-wavelength elements, in order to improve conditions for impedance matching. For small flaring in the E-plane the plates can be rectangular without appreciable loss of gain. When correction is required in all planes at least one boundary of the plates must be curved.

Fig. 3 shows how the amplitude distribution across the aperture can be controlled. Two extreme cases are illustrated, but results between these two can be obtained by suitable adjustments. In (*a*) the inclined outer plates are arranged to intercept a relatively large proportion of the field, in order to produce (approximately) equal field strength at each section centre. Such an arrangement gives a sharp diagram with high side-lobes. In (*b*) the inclined outer plates, which are steered towards the sides of the horn, restrict the amplitude at the edges, and a binomial distribution law is approached, resulting in a broader diagram but with small side-lobes. In both cases the final phase adjustment is made with the parallel plates.

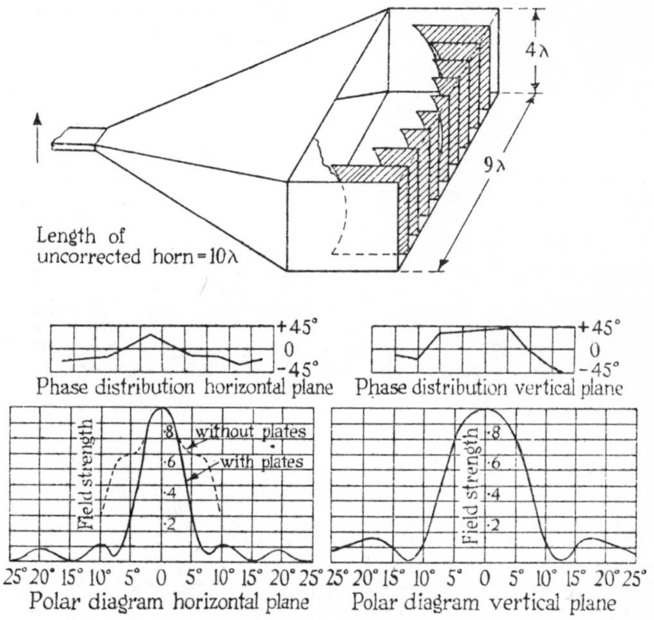

Fig. 4.—Practical results obtained with medium-sized horn using vertical polarization.

Fig. 4 illustrates some practical results obtained with a medium-sized horn corrected in both planes, using vertical polarization.

Acknowledgment

This lecture is published with the approval of the Board of Admiralty, the work described having been carried out under the auspices of the Admiralty Signal Establishment and Messrs. Marconi's Wireless Telegraph Co. Ltd. The author acknowledges his indebtedness to the many members of these and other establishments who, at one time or another, expressed interest or participated in the work.

On the Theory of the Radiation Patterns of Electromagnetic Horns of Moderate Flare Angles*

C. W. HORTON†

Summary—**A method attributed to Schelkunoff for the computation of radiation patterns is considered. For the case of transverse electric waves in a waveguide or horn of moderate flare angle, the problem of calculating the radiation pattern is reduced to that of evaluating two definite integrals. These integrals are evaluated for rectangular, circular, and semicircular horns for some common modes of vibration. A small amount of experimental data are presented to illustrate the agreement between theory and experiment.**

I. Introduction

A METHOD of computing radiation patterns from electromagnetic horns that is easy to apply and which leads to patterns that agree well with experimental patterns has been developed by Schelkunoff.[1,2] Schelkunoff's theorems may be formulated in several different ways of which the following is selected for the present purpose. When an electromagnetic wave is radiated from the open end of a semi-infinite waveguide, the radiation pattern is the same as the pattern of a suitable distribution of surface electric currents J, and of surface magnetic currents M, over the aperture Σ of the waveguide. These current distributions are determined by

$$\vec{J} = \vec{n} \times \vec{H}^\circ \tag{1}$$

$$\vec{M} = -\vec{n} \times \vec{E}^\circ. \tag{2}$$

$\vec{n}$ is the normal to the aperture pointing out into the space away from the waveguide. $\vec{E}^\circ$ and $\vec{H}^\circ$ are the values of the electric and magnetic fields that would exist across Σ if the waveguide had not been terminated. When computing the radiation pattern of the current distributions, it is necessary to allow for the presence of the metallic waveguide which acts as a baffle. If the waveguide is large, its effect is secondary and may be neglected. This approximation is made in the following analysis.

It can be shown that the modes of vibration in sectoral and conical horns approach the corresponding modes of vibration in rectangular and circular waveguides as the limiting case when the flare angle approaches zero. This means that the radiation patterns which are derived for an open waveguide may be applied directly to an electromagnetic horn, as long as the flare angle is not too large.

The values of $\vec{E}$ and $\vec{H}$ in the radiation field may be computed from

$$\vec{E} = i\omega\mu\vec{A} - (1/i\omega\epsilon) \text{ grad div } \vec{A} - \text{curl } \vec{F} \tag{3}$$

$$\vec{H} = i\omega\epsilon\vec{F} - (1/i\omega\mu) \text{ grad div } \vec{F} + \text{curl } \vec{A} \tag{4}$$

where $\vec{A}$ and $\vec{F}$ are a magnetic and an electric vector potential, respectively, which are given by

$$\vec{A} = (1/4\pi)\int_\Sigma (\vec{J}/r') \exp(ikr')d\Sigma \tag{5}$$

$$\vec{F} = (1/4\pi)\int_\Sigma (\vec{M}/r') \exp(ikr')d\Sigma. \tag{6}$$

Here r' is the distance from the surface element $d\Sigma$ to the field point. These equations are in mks units and are true for periodic fields with the time factor $\exp(-i\omega t)$.

In the next section the case of a transverse electric wave is considered, and (1) to (6) are reduced to a simple form suitable for the computation of the distant, or Fraunhofer, diffraction pattern.

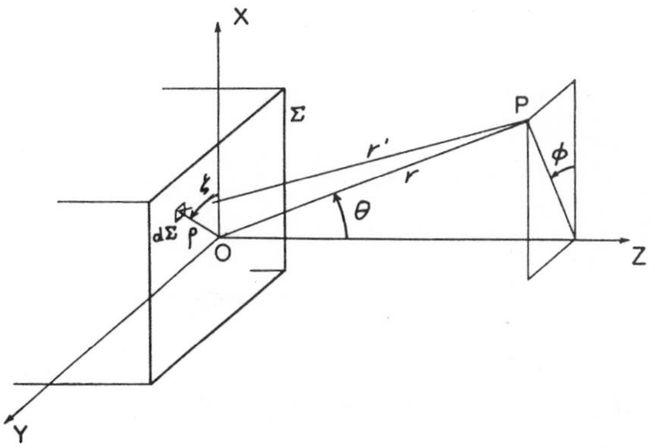

Fig. 1—The relations between the co-ordinate systems and the waveguide.

II. Application to the Transverse Electric Field

Consider the co-ordinate systems shown in Fig. 1. The location of the field point P is given in spherical co-ordinates (r, θ, ϕ), while the location of the apertural element $d\Sigma$ is given in polar co-ordinates (ρ, ζ). One has

$$r'^2 = \rho^2 + r^2 - 2r\rho\cos(\phi - \zeta)\sin\theta.$$

For large values of r, the ρ^2 may be neglected and the binomial expansion may be applied to give

* Decimal classification: R118×R120. Original manuscript received by the Institute, September 10, 1948; revised manuscript received, January 24, 1949.

This work has been done under sponsorship of the Bureau of Ordnance, Navy Department, Contract NOrd-9195, at The University of Texas, and has been extracted from "On the Theory of the Radiation Patterns of Electromagnetic Horns," Bumblebee Report No. 86, Defense Research Laboratory, The University of Texas.

† Defense Research Laboratory, The University of Texas, Austin, Tex.

[1] S. A. Schelkunoff, "Some equivalence theorems of electromagnetics and their application to radiation problems," *Bell Sys. Tech. Jour.*, vol. 15, pp. 92–112; January, 1936.

[2] S. A. Schelkunoff, "On diffraction and radiation of electromagnetic waves," *Phys. Rev.*, vol. 56, pp. 308–316; August 15, 1939.

Reprinted from *Proc. IRE*, vol. 37, pp. 744–749, July 1949.

$$r' \cong r - \rho \cos(\phi - \zeta) \sin\theta. \quad (7)$$

The r' in the denominator of (5) and (6) may be replaced directly by r, while the r' in the exponent must be replaced by the more accurate form of (7). Thus (5) and (6) become

$$\vec{A} = \{\exp(ikr)/4\pi r\} \cdot \int_\Sigma \vec{J} \exp\{-ik\rho\cos(\phi-\zeta)\sin\theta\} d\Sigma \quad (8)$$

$$\vec{F} = \{\exp(ikr)/4\pi r\} \cdot \int_\Sigma \vec{M} \exp\{-ik\rho\cos(\phi-\zeta)\sin\theta\} d\Sigma. \quad (9)$$

Although $\vec{A}$ and $\vec{F}$ are functions of θ and ϕ as well as r, if we confine our attention to distant field points so that powers of $(1/r)$ greater than the first are negligible, then $\vec{A}$ and $\vec{F}$ may be treated as a constant vector times a function of r in performing the vector operations indicated in (3) and (4).

A transverse electric wave in the waveguide may be represented by

$$\vec{E} = \{\vec{i} f(x, y) + \vec{j} g(x, y)\} \exp(ik'z - i\omega t) \quad (10)$$

where $k'(=2\pi/\lambda_{\text{guide}})$ need not equal the free-space value k. The magnetic field $\vec{H}$ associated with $\vec{E}$ has components given by

$$\left.\begin{aligned} H_x &= -(k'/\omega\mu) g(x, y) \exp(ik'z - i\omega t) \\ H_y &= (k'/\omega\mu) f(x, y) \exp(ik'z - i\omega t) \\ H_z &= (1/i\omega\mu)\{g_x(x, y) - f_y(x, y)\} \exp(ik'z - i\omega t) \end{aligned}\right\} . \quad (11)$$

When $\vec{E}$ is evaluated from (3), (8), (9), (10), and (11) and powers of $(1/r)$ higher than the first are neglected, one finds

$$\left.\begin{aligned} E_r &= 0 \\ E_\theta &= -i(k + k'\cos\theta)\{R_1(\theta, \phi)\cos\phi \\ &\quad + R_2(\theta, \phi)\sin\phi\}(1/r)\exp(ikr - i\omega t) \\ E_\phi &= +i(k' + k\cos\theta)\{R_1(\theta, \phi)\sin\phi \\ &\quad - R_2(\theta, \phi)\cos\phi\}(1/r)\exp(ikr - i\omega t) \end{aligned}\right\} \quad (12)$$

where

$$R_{\substack{1\\2}}(\theta, \phi) = (1/4\pi) \int_\Sigma \begin{matrix} f(x, y) \\ g(x, y) \end{matrix} \cdot \exp\{-ik\rho\cos(\phi - \zeta)\sin\theta\} d\Sigma. \quad (13)$$

This derivation is given in the Appendix. Since $\vec{E}$ is a transverse wave, the components of the magnetic field may be found from the relationships

$$\left.\begin{aligned} H_r &= 0 \\ H_\theta &= -(k/\omega\mu)E_\phi \\ H_\phi &= +(k/\omega\mu)E_\theta \end{aligned}\right\} . \quad (14)$$

It might be pointed out that, normally, in spherical co-ordinates, θ is required to be positive, so that two values of ϕ (say, ϕ_0 and $\phi_0+\pi$) are required to specify a full plane. However, it is equally permissible to specify a fixed value of ϕ and allow θ to take on both positive and negative values. This interpretation will be used in the discussion of patterns.

The problem of computing the radiation pattern of a semi-infinite waveguide for a transverse electric wave has been reduced to the problem of performing the integration of (13). This integration will be performed for various common waveguide sections.

III. Symmetry Considerations

It is possible to state certain general properties of the radiation pattern, provided the functions $f(x, y)$ and $g(x, y)$ are real. For example, the real parts of $R_1(\theta, \phi)$ and $R_2(\theta, \phi)$ are even functions of θ while the imaginary parts are odd functions of θ.

Consider the pattern in the plane $\phi=0$. If the waveguide is symmetric about the x axis, and if $g(x, y)$ is an odd function of y, the component $E_\phi=0$. Similarly, if $f(x, y)$ is an odd function of y, $E_\theta=0$. On the other hand, if the waveguide is symmetric about the y axis, then $R_1(\theta, \phi)$ is pure real or imaginary according as $f(x, y)$ is an even or odd function of x. Likewise, $R_2(\theta, \phi)$ is even or odd according as $g(x, y)$ is an even or odd function of x.

Consider next the plane $\phi=90°$. If the waveguide is symmetric about the y axis, and if $f(x, y)$ is an odd function of x, the component $E_\phi=0$. Similarly, if $g(x, y)$ is an odd function of x, $E_\theta=0$. On the other hand, if the waveguide is symmetric about the x axis, then $R_1(\theta, \phi)$ is pure real or imaginary according as $f(x, y)$ is an even or odd function of y. Likewise, $R_2(\theta, \phi)$ is even or odd according as $g(x, y)$ is an even or odd function of y.

IV. The Effect of a Perfectly Conducting Baffle

If the mouth of the waveguide or horn is mounted in a large, flat, perfectly conducting sheet, the pattern will be altered. The effect of these changes has been discussed by Schelkunoff.[3] When these changes are carried out, one has in place of (12)

$$\left.\begin{aligned} E_r &= 0 \\ E_\theta &= -2ik\{R_1(\theta, \phi)\cos\phi \\ &\quad + R_2(\theta, \phi)\sin\phi\}(1/r)\exp(ikr - i\omega t) \\ E_\phi &= +2ik\cos\theta\{R_1(\theta, \phi)\sin\phi \\ &\quad - R_2(\theta, \phi)\cos\phi\}(1/r)\exp(ikr - i\omega t) \end{aligned}\right\} . \quad (15)$$

V. Transverse Electric Waves in a Rectangular Waveguide

The radiation patterns of rectangular horns are well known,[4] and consequently they will be treated briefly

[3] See page 312 of footnote reference 2.
[4] S. A. Schelkunoff, "Electromagnetic Waves," p. 359, D. van Nostrand Co., New York, N. Y., 1945.

only in order to show the practicality of the present approach.

The transverse electric wave $TE_{m,n}$ has an electric field characterized by

$$f(x, y) = -(n\pi/b)\cos(m\pi/2 + m\pi x/a)\sin(n\pi/2 + n\pi y/b) \quad (16)$$

$$g(x, y) = +(m\pi/a)\sin(m\pi/2 + m\pi x/a)\cos(n\pi/2 + n\pi y/b) \quad (17)$$

where a is the dimension of the waveguide in the x direction and b is the dimension in the y direction.

In order to evaluate $R_1(\theta, \phi)$ and $R_2(\theta, \phi)$ simply, it is desirable to introduce two dimensionless parameters, α and β, defined as

$$\alpha = (ka/2)\cos\phi\sin\theta \quad (18)$$

$$\beta = (kb/2)\sin\phi\sin\theta. \quad (19)$$

Integration of (13) gives

$$R_1(\theta, \phi) = (\pi n^2 ab/8b)A\alpha/\{(m\pi/2)^2 - \alpha^2\}\{(n\pi/2)^2 - \beta^2\} \quad (20)$$

and

$$R_2(\theta, \phi) = -(m^2 b/n^2 a)R_1(\theta, \phi). \quad (21)$$

The constant A takes on the following four possible values:

m even, n even	$A = i\sin\alpha\sin\beta$
m even, n odd	$A = \sin\alpha\cos\beta$
m odd, n even	$A = \cos\alpha\sin\beta$
m odd, n odd	$A = -i\cos\alpha\cos\beta$.

In the particular case of the $TE_{0,1}$ mode the radiation patterns can be evaluated to give

$$\left.\begin{aligned} E_r &= 0 \\ E_\theta &= i(\pi a/8)(k + k'\cos\theta) \\ &\quad \cdot\cos\phi(\sin\alpha/\alpha)\cos\beta/\{(\pi/2)^2 - \beta^2\} \\ E_\phi &= -i(\pi a/8)(k' + k\cos\phi) \\ &\quad \cdot\sin\phi(\sin\alpha/\alpha)\cos\beta/\{(\pi/2)^2 - \beta^2\} \end{aligned}\right\} . \quad (22)$$

The spherical wave factor $(1/r)\exp(ikr - i\omega t)$ has been omitted in these and in the remainder of the equations. The various factors have simple physical explanations. In the $TE_{0,1}$ mode there is no variation in the electric field strength with the variable x. Thus there is no shading in the x direction, and the part of the pattern that results from integrating with respect to x is $(\sin\alpha/\alpha)$, which is the radiation pattern commonly associated with an unshaded rectangular opening. In the y direction the intensity of the electric vector varies cosinusoidally. This shading gives rise to the terms which are a function of β. The terms in ϕ represent the effects of the polarized source. The factors of the form $(1+\cos\theta)$ occur because of the flow of energy through the opening.

Figs. 2 and 3 show the experimental and theoretical patterns in the E and H planes, respectively, for a bisectoral horn. By the "E plane" is meant the plane containing the electric vector in the $TE_{0,1}$ mode. The dimensions of the horn are $1.82\lambda_0$ in the H plane and $1.47\lambda_0$ in the E plane. It may be seen that the agreement between theory and experiment is good.

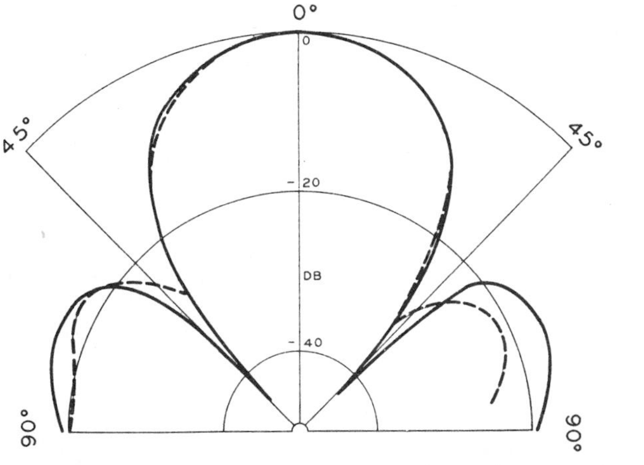

Fig. 2—The pattern in the E plane produced by a $TE_{0,1}$ wave in a bisectoral horn of dimensions $1.47\lambda_0$ and $1.82\lambda_0$ in the E and H planes, respectively. The solid line is theoretical and the dashed line is experimental.

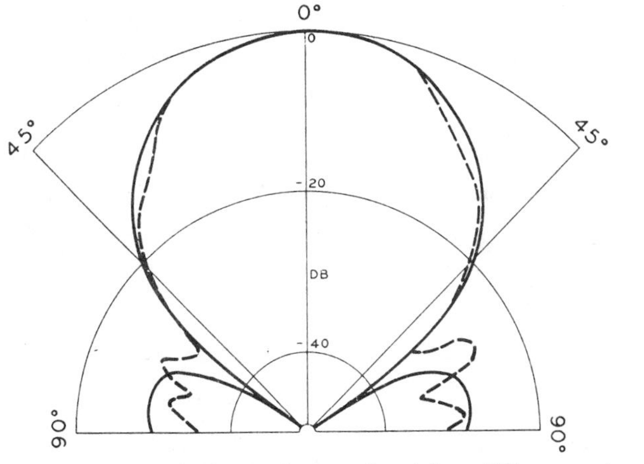

Fig. 3—The pattern in the H plane produced by a $TE_{0,1}$ wave in a bisectoral horn of dimensions $1.47\lambda_0$ and $1.82\lambda_0$ in the E and H planes, respectively. The solid line is theoretical and the dashed line is experimental.

VI. Transverse Waves in a Circular Waveguide

A. The $TE_{0,1}$ Mode of Vibration

The simplest mode of vibration in a circular waveguide is known as the $TE_{0,1}$ mode. For this mode, omitting an amplitude constant,

$$E_\rho = 0 \quad (23)$$

$$E_\zeta = J_1(q\rho/a)\exp(ik'z - i\omega t) \quad (24)$$

where

a = radius of the guide

$q = 3.832$ = first positive root of $J_1(x) = 0$.

For this mode of vibration, the functions $f(x, y)$ and $g(x, y)$ defined in (10) become

$$f(x, y) = -J_1(q\rho/a) \sin \zeta \quad (25)$$

$$g(x, y) = +J_1(q\rho/a) \cos \zeta. \quad (26)$$

Hence, one has

$$R_{\substack{1\\2}}(\theta, \phi) = \mp (1/4\pi) \int_0^a \int_0^{2\pi} J_1(q\rho/a) \begin{matrix}\sin\\ \cos\end{matrix} \xi \cdot \exp\{-ik\rho \cos(\phi - \zeta) \sin\theta\} \rho d\rho d\zeta. \quad (27)$$

This can be integrated in a straightforward manner to give

$$R_{\substack{1\\2}}(\theta, \phi) = \mp (ia^2 q J_0(q)/2) \begin{matrix}\sin\\ \cos\end{matrix} \phi J_1(\gamma)/(q^2 - \gamma^2) \quad (28)$$

where

$$\gamma = ka \sin\theta. \quad (29)$$

Thus (12) gives

$$\left.\begin{aligned} E_r &= 0\\ E_\theta &= 0\\ E_\phi &= (a^2 J_0(q)/2q)(k' + k\cos\theta) q^2 J_1(\gamma)/(q^2 - \gamma^2) \end{aligned}\right\} \quad (30)$$

as the pattern of a circular waveguide excited in the $TE_{0,1}$ mode.

The function $q^2 J_1(\gamma)/(q^2 - \gamma^2)$ is plotted in Fig. 4 as a function of the dimensionless angle γ. This is the pattern that one would observe in any plane through the $0z$ axis.

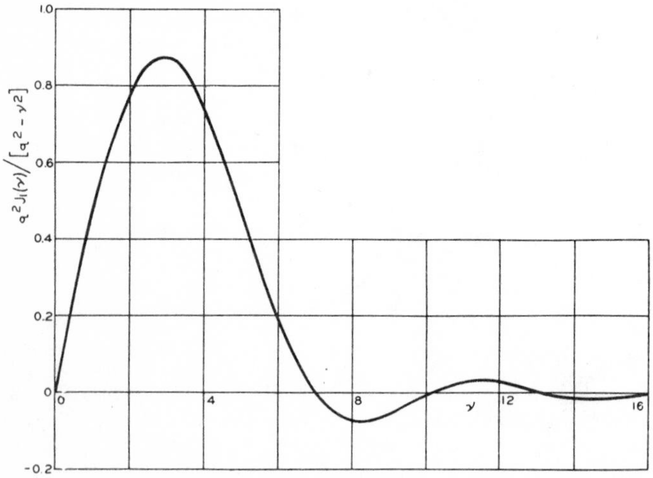

Fig. 4—The pattern in any plane of a $TE_{0,1}$ wave in a circular waveguide versus the dimensionless angle γ.

B. The $TE_{1,1}$ Mode of Vibration

The next most simple mode of vibration in a circular waveguide is known as the $TE_{1,1}$ mode in which the electric field components are

$$E_\rho = (a/p\rho) J_1(p\rho/a) \cos\zeta \exp(ik'z - i\omega t) \quad (31)$$

$$E_\zeta = -J_1'(p\rho/a) \sin\zeta \exp(ik'z - i\omega t) \quad (32)$$

where

a = radius of the waveguide

$p = 1.841$ = first positive root of $J_1'(x) = 0$.

Corresponding to these components, one has

$$f(x, y) = (a/p\rho) J_1(p\rho/a) \cos^2\zeta + J_1'(p\rho/a) \sin^2\zeta \quad (33)$$

$$g(x, y) = \{(a/p\rho) J_1(p\rho/a) - J_1'(p\rho/a)\} \sin\zeta \cos\zeta. \quad (34)$$

After some manipulation of Bessel functions, one arrives at the following expressions for the components of the electric field.

$$\left.\begin{aligned} E_r &= 0\\ E_\theta &= -i\{a^2 J_1(p)/4p\}(k + k'\cos\theta) \cos\phi P_1(\gamma)\\ E_\phi &= +i\{a^2 J_1(p)/4p\}(k' + k\cos\theta) \sin\phi P_2(\gamma) \end{aligned}\right\} \quad (35)$$

where

$$\gamma = ka \sin\theta \quad (29)$$

$$P_1(\gamma) = 2J_1(\gamma)/\gamma \quad (36)$$

$$P_2(\gamma) = 2p^2 J_1'(\gamma)/(p^2 - \gamma^2). \quad (37)$$

For the orientation under consideration, the planes $\phi = 0$ and $\phi = \pi/2$ will be denoted as the E and the H planes, respectively. Aside from the factor $(k + k'\cos\theta)$, $P_1(\gamma)$ is the pattern in the E plane of a circular waveguide or horn with $TE_{1,1}$ waves. Fig. 5 shows a plot of $P_1(\gamma)$ versus the dimensionless angle γ.

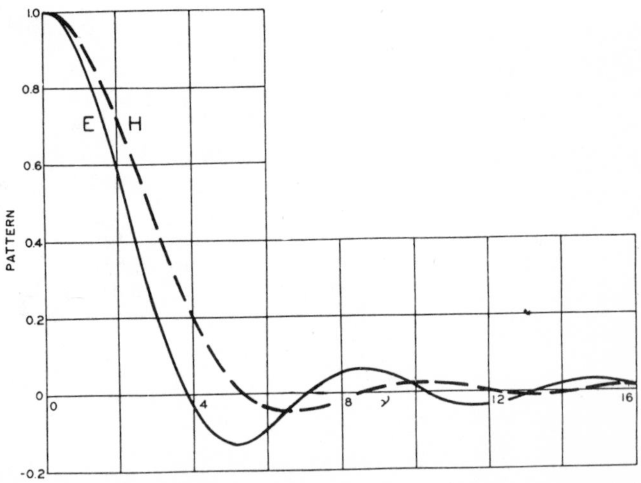

Fig. 5—The patterns in the E and H planes of a $TE_{1,1}$ wave in a circular horn versus the dimensionless angle γ. The solid curve E is a plot of $P_1(\gamma)$ of (36) and is the pattern in the E plane. The dashed curve H is a plot of $P_2(\gamma)$ of (37) and is the pattern in the H plane.

Aside from the factor $(k' + k\cos\theta)$, $P_2(\gamma)$ is the pattern in the H plane of a circular waveguide with $TE_{1,1}$ waves. Fig. 5 shows a plot of $P_2(\gamma)$ versus the dimensionless angle γ.

Figs. 6 and 7 show experimental and theoretical patterns in the E and H planes, respectively, for a circular horn whose diameter is $1.85\lambda_0$.

VII. The $TE_{1,1}$ Mode in a Semicircular Waveguide

The circular waveguide is frequently criticized because there is no physical restraint to prevent the rotation of the plane of the E vector. A possible solution of this difficulty would be to use a semicircular waveguide, although the writer has not seen this discussed. The field components given by (31) and (32) will satisfy the boundary conditions in a semicircular waveguide bounded by the plane $\phi = \pm\pi/2$. The writer has not been able to effect the integration for $R(\theta, \phi)$ except for the two principal planes, $\phi = 0$ and 90°.

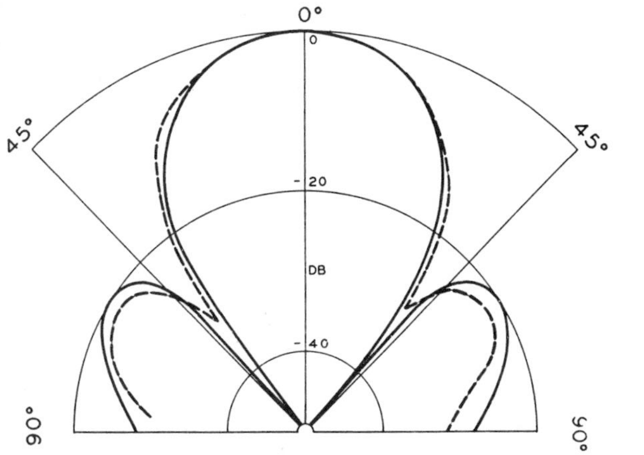

Fig. 6—The pattern in the E plane produced by a $TE_{1,1}$ wave in a conical horn whose largest diameter is $1.85\lambda_0$. The solid line is theoretical and the dashed line is experimental.

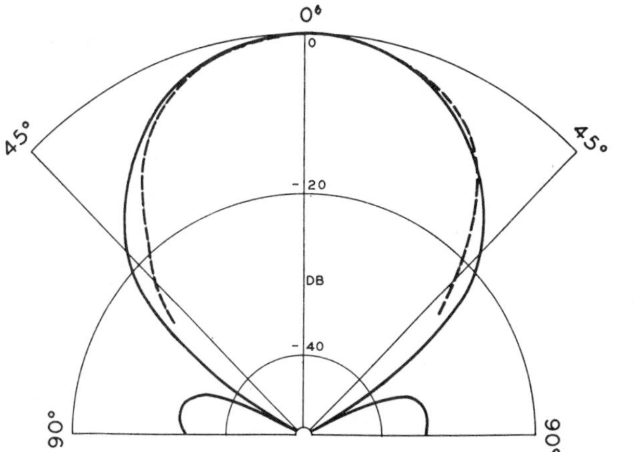

Fig. 7—The pattern in the H plane produced by a $TE_{1,1}$ wave in a conical horn whose largest diameter is $1.85\lambda_0$. The solid line is theoretical and the dashed line is experimental.

A. The Plane $\phi = 0$

It is possible to apply the arguments used in section III to show that $E_\phi = 0$; i.e., $R_2(\theta, 0) = 0$. After the integration with respect to ζ has been performed, one has

$$R_1(\theta, 0) = (a^2/8) \int_0^1 [J_0(ps)J_0(\gamma s) - J_2(ps)J_2(\gamma s)]s ds$$

$$- i(a^2/4) \int_0^1 [J_1(ps)\boldsymbol{H}_0(\gamma s)/ps - J_2(ps)\boldsymbol{H}_1(\gamma s)/\gamma s] s ds.$$

Obviously, the final pattern will be of the form $A(\gamma) - iB(\gamma)$, where $A(\gamma)$ is an even and $B(\gamma)$ is an odd function of γ. The integration can be performed to give the following pattern in the plane $\phi = 0$:

$$\left.\begin{aligned} &E_r = 0 \\ &E_\theta = -i\{a^2J_1(p)/4p\}(k + k' \cos\theta)\{A(\gamma) - iB(\gamma)\} \\ &E_\phi = 0 \end{aligned}\right\} \quad (38)$$

where

and $$\left.\begin{aligned} A(\gamma) &= P_1(\gamma)/2 = J_1(\gamma)/\gamma \\ B(\gamma) &= \boldsymbol{H}_1(\gamma)/\gamma \end{aligned}\right\}. \quad (39)$$

It will be noted that the real part of E_θ is equal to one-half the value of E_θ for a circular waveguide given in (35). That this must be true can be seen as follows. If two semicircular waveguides are matched together to form one circular waveguide, then the combined pattern is

$$A(\gamma) - iB(\gamma) + A(\gamma) + iB(\gamma) = 2A(\gamma).$$

A plot of $2A(\gamma)$ is shown in Fig. 5. The graph of $B(\gamma)$ is shown in Fig. 8.

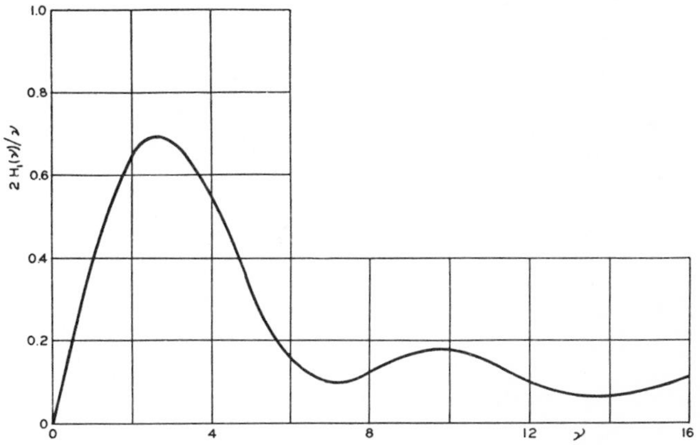

Fig. 8—A plot of the imaginary part of the pattern in the E plane of a $TE_{1,1}$ wave in a semicircular waveguide versus the dimensionless angle γ. A plot of twice the real part is given by the solid curve in Fig. 5.

B. The Plane $\phi = \pi/2$

It is obvious from considerations of symmetry that E_ϕ will have the same pattern in the case of the semicircular waveguide as it does in the circular waveguide. The exact expressions will differ by a factor 2 which arises from the fact that the area is doubled in the case of the full waveguide. Therefore, the pattern of E_ϕ in the present case is one-half of the value given in (35) and plotted in Fig. 5.

E_θ is zero in the plane $\phi = \pi/2$ for the full circular waveguide, but it is not zero in the case of the semicircular waveguide. When the integration with respect to θ is performed over the semicircle, one finds

$$R_2(\theta, \pi/2) = i(a^2/2\pi\gamma) \int_0^1 \{\cos(\gamma s) - \sin(\gamma s)/\gamma s\} \cdot \{J_1(ps)/ps - J_1'(ps)\} ds.$$

This can be integrated to give

$$R_2(\theta, \pi/2) = i(a^2/2\pi p^2)\{J_e(p, \gamma) + \cos\gamma J_0(p) - 1\}. \quad (40)$$

The function $J_s(p, x)$, which is defined as

$$J_s(p, x) = \int_0^x J_0(pu) \sin u du, \tag{41}$$

has been extensively studied by Schwartz,[5] who tabulates the function $J_s(p, x)$ to $8D$ for $p=0.1$ (0.1) 1 and $x=0$ (0.1) 5. Unfortunately, this range of values is not suitable for the application to the diffraction patterns.

Thus the pattern in the plane $\phi=\pi/2$ becomes

$$E_r=0$$

$$E_\theta=-i(a^2/2\pi p^2)(k+k'\cos\theta)\{J_s(p,\gamma)+\cos\gamma J_0(p)-1\}$$

$$E_\phi=+i\{a^2 J_1(p)/8p\}(k'+k\cos\theta)P_2(\gamma).$$

Figs. 9 and 10 show the patterns in the E and the H planes, respectively, of a semicircular horn whose diameter is $1.85\lambda_0$. The measurement in the H plane is for E_ϕ only.

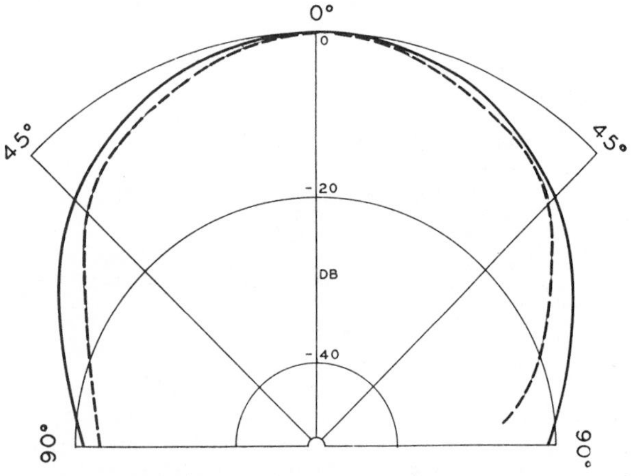

Fig. 9—The pattern in the E plane produced by a $TE_{1,1}$ wave in a semicircular horn whose largest diameter is $1.85\ \lambda_0$. The solid line is theoretical and the dashed line is experimental.

Acknowledgment

The writer wishes to thank R. B. Watson for the use of the experimental patterns that are shown in this paper.

Appendix

The derivation of (12) can best be done in two parts. First, let $g(x, y)\equiv 0$. Then

$$\vec{J} = \vec{n}\times\vec{H}^0 = -\vec{i}(k'/\omega\mu)f(x,y)\exp(ik'z-i\omega t)$$

$$\vec{M} = -\vec{n}\times\vec{E}^0 = -\vec{j}f(x,y)\exp(ik'z-i\omega t).$$

Neglecting powers of $(1/r)$ larger than the first, one has

$$\vec{A} = -\vec{i}(k'/\omega\mu r)R_1(\theta,\phi)\exp(ikr-i\omega t)$$

$$\vec{J} = -\vec{j}(1/r)R_1(\theta,\phi)\exp(ikr-i\omega t),$$

where $R_1(\theta, \phi)$ is defined in (13), and, consequently,

$$\text{curl}\,\vec{F} = \vec{i}R_1(\theta,\phi)(ik/r)(\partial r/\partial z)\exp(ikr-i\omega t)$$

$$-\vec{k}R_1(\theta,\phi)(ik/r)(\partial r/\partial x)\exp(ikr-i\omega t)$$

and

$$\text{grad div}\,\vec{A} = \vec{r}_0 R_1(\theta,\phi)(k'k^2/\omega\mu r)(x/r)\exp(ikr-i\omega t).$$

Upon converting $\vec{i}$, $\vec{k}$, and the cartesian components to polar form, one obtains

$$E_r = 0$$

$$E_\theta = -i(k+k'\cos\theta)\cos\phi\cdot R_1(\theta,\phi)(1/r)\exp(ikr-i\omega t)$$

$$E_\phi = +i(k+k'\cos\theta)\sin\phi\cdot R_1(\theta,\phi)(1/r)\exp(ikr-i\omega t).$$

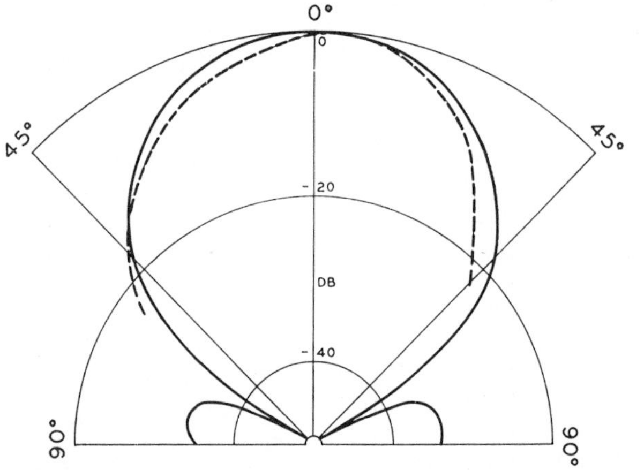

Fig. 10—The pattern in the H plane produced by a $TE_{1,1}$ wave in a semicircular horn whose largest diameter is $1.85\ \lambda_0$. The solid line is theoretical and the dashed line is experimental.

The second case of $f(x, y)\equiv 0$ can be derived as a special case of the preceding equations. If the electric vector in the waveguide is rotated 90° from $+\vec{i}$ to $+\vec{j}$, the electric and magnetic vectors in the radiation field must be rotated 90°. Hence the angle ϕ in the coefficients of the preceding equations must be replaced by $\phi-90°$, and $f(x, y)$ must be replaced by $g(x, y)$.

[5] L. Schwartz, "Investigations of some functions related to the cylindrical functions of zero order," *Luftfahrtforschung*, vol. 20, pp. 341–372; 1944. This paper has been translated by J. Lotsof for the Cornell Aeronautical Laboratory, May, 1946.

Electromagnetic Field of the Conical Horn*

MARVIN G. SCHORR** AND FRED J. BECK, JR.
Yale University, New Haven, Connecticut
(Received January 20, 1950)

Maxwell's equations are solved for a perfectly conducting conical wave guide and the propagation coefficients of this guide are discussed. The field at the mouth of a finite conical horn is estimated and the radiation therefrom is calculated in integral form. These integrals are solved in series form for horns of small flare angle and moderate length and the results compared with experiment.

INTRODUCTION

THE use of electromagnetic horns for both matching purposes and enhanced radiation directivity in high frequency antennae was suggested by Southworth[1] and Barrow[2] in 1936. Since that time many observers have verified these properties and several attempts have been made to attain a satisfactory agreement between theory and experiment. The early workers calculated radiation phenomena from the scalar Kirchhoff-Huygens principle, but it was soon recognized that this formalism was inadequate, the major defect being in the assumption of continuity of the fields at the aperture from which the radiation ensues. Two rigorously correct methods are available for computing radiation from horn structures. They are the vector diffraction theory of Stratton and Chu,[3] and the assumed field technique recently restated by Schelkunoff.[4] A recent paper by Woonton, Hay, and Vogan[5] gives a good discussion of some of these matters.

The great majority of the existent theoretical work has been done for propagation in and radiation from uniform wave guide and sectoral horns. Buchholz[6] gave a rather complete analysis of electromagnetic fields in conical wave guide and also commented on a method of exciting such a guide. However he treated only the special case of azimuthally symmetric guided waves. Excellent experimental work is available in the literature on both conical[7] and pyramidal horns[8] and it is the purpose of this paper to show that the rigorous assumed-field technique, when applied to the conical horn, yields good agreement with experiment over a range of cone angles for which the radiation integrals may be satisfactorily evaluated.

FIELDS IN CONICAL WAVE GUIDE

Let us first consider the permissible electromagnetic fields inside a perfectly conducting conical wave guide of semi-infinite extent, filled with a dielectric of permeability μ and permitivity ϵ, ϵ being complex if the dielectric is lossy. The choice of a spherical (r, θ, ϕ) coordinate system is clearly indicated, and if the apex of the cone coincides with the origin of coordinates and the polar axis is the longitudinal axis of symmetry of the cone, then conical surfaces will coincide with surfaces of constant colatitude and the flare angle of the cone will be measured by the colatitude of its surface. The flare angle, so defined and henceforth used, is then one-half the total angle subtended by the cone. The cone is assumed excited near the apex in such a manner that the fields propagate positively radially outward; also the azimuthal reference axis is chosen so that a single trigonometric function describes the azimuthal variations of the fields. The permissible fields are well known and are given by:

Transverse-Electric Waves

$$\begin{aligned}
&E_r=0\\
&E_\theta=Bj\omega\mu\cos m\phi\, h_n^{(2)}(kr)P_n^m(x)\\
&E_\phi=-Bj\omega\mu\sin\theta\sin m\phi\, h_n^{(2)}(kr)P_n^{m\prime}(x)\\
&H_r=B[n(n+1)/r]\sin m\phi\, h_n^{(2)}(kr)P_n^m(x)\\
&H_\theta=-B\sin\theta\sin m\phi[(1/r)h_n^{(2)}(kr)\\
&\qquad\qquad+kh_n^{(2)\prime}(kr)]P_n^{m\prime}(x)\\
&H_\phi=B[m/\sin\theta]\cos m\phi[(1/r)h_n^{(2)}(kr)\\
&\qquad\qquad+kh_n^{(2)\prime}(kr)]P_n^m(x);
\end{aligned}\qquad(1)$$

* This paper is an abstract of a dissertation presented by the first named author (Marvin G. Schorr) for the degree of Doctor of Philosophy in Yale University, May, 1949.
** Now at Tracerlab, Inc., Boston, Massachusetts.
[1] G. C. Southworth, Bell Sys. Tech. J. **15**, 284 (1936).
[2] W. L. Barrow, Proc. I.R.E. **24**, 1298 (1936).
[3] J. A. Stratton and L. J. Chu, Phys. Rev. **56**, 92 (1939).
[4] S. A. Schelkunoff, Phys. Rev. **56**, 308 (1939).
[5] Woonton, Hay, and Vogan, J. App. Phys. **20**, 71 (1949).
[6] H. Buchholz, Ann. d. Physik **37**, 173 (1940).
[7] G. C. Southworth and A. P. King, Proc. I.R.E. **27**, 95 (1939).
[8] D. R. Rhodes, Proc. I.R.E. **36**, 1101 (1948).

Reprinted with permission from *J. Appl. Phys.*, vol. 21, pp. 795–801, Aug. 1950.

Transverse-Magnetic Waves

$$\begin{aligned}
E_r &= B[n(n+1)/r]\sin m\phi h_n^{(2)}(kr)P_n^m(x)\\
E_\theta &= -B\sin\theta \sin m\phi[(1/r)h_n^{(2)}(kr)\\
&\qquad +kh_n^{(2)\prime}(kr)]P_n^{m\prime}(x)\\
E_\phi &= B[m/\sin\theta]\cos m\phi[(1/r)h_n^{(2)}(kr)\\
&\qquad +kh_n^{(2)\prime}(kr)]P_n^m(x)\\
H_r &= 0\\
H_\theta &= B(j\omega\epsilon m/\sin\theta)\cos m\phi h_n^{(2)}(kr)P_n^m(x)\\
H_\phi &= Bj\omega\epsilon\sin\theta\sin m\phi h_n^{(2)}(kr)P_n^{m\prime}(x),
\end{aligned} \tag{2}$$

where the primed function always denotes the derivative with respect to the argument, and the wave number $k=2\pi/\lambda$, λ being the free space wave-length and $\omega^2=\mu\epsilon$. The $h_n^{(2)}(kr)$ and $P_n^m(x)$ are the spherical Hankel function of the second kind and associated Legendre function of the first kind respectively, and $x=\cos\theta$. The spherical Hankel function of the first kind does not appear since it represents a wave traveling in the negative radial direction, contrary to hypothesis; the associated Legendre function of the second kind also does not appear since it has a singularity on the polar axis which is contained in the region considered. The spherical Hankel function of the second kind has a singularity at the origin but this is of no consequence since, as will be seen later, the neighborhood of the origin is very highly attenuating so that no energy ever reaches it. The single-valuedness of the solutions in azimuth requires that m be an integer which we may take as positive. The colatitude boundary condition, namely $E_r=E_\phi=H_\theta=0$ at $\theta=\theta_0$, requires for TE waves,

$$[-\sin\theta P_n^{m\prime}(\cos\theta)]_{\theta=\theta_0}=0, \tag{3}$$

and for TM waves,

$$P_n^m(\cos\theta_0)=P_n^m(x_0)=0. \tag{4}$$

Hence n must be a root of the multibranched transcendental Eqs. (3) or (4) considered as functions of the order n of the associated Legendre function. In general n will be non-integral and a function of the flare angle θ_0 of the cone; we may consider only the positive roots. For small integral values of n, $0<n\leqq 10$, excellent tables of associated Legendre functions are available for determining the zeros of Eqs. (3) and (4)[9] and reasonably accurate interpolation to non-integral orders is possible. For large orders the zeros may be determined from the asymptotic expansions of these functions.

The solutions of Eqs. (1) and (2) then form a doubly infinite set corresponding to all positive integral m and all positive n giving zeros of Eqs. (3) and (4). Those modes actually present in the guide will of course be determined by the source of excitation.

It is convenient in discussing conical wave guide to adopt the cylindrical wave guide terminology since if we allow a given cross section of the cone to remain constant and let the flare angle approach zero, then in the limit the cone goes over into a hollow cylinder. The permissible modes in conical guide are hence designated TE_{mp} or TM_{mp} having m field variations in one azimuthal circuit and p field variations from the polar axis to the cone wall. The designation of propagation constants for conical guide does not, however, follow in the usual sense. In conical wave guide the fields are not periodic functions of the propagation coordinate r and propagation constant loses much of its intuitive meaning. However, in lieu of a better definition, a complex propagation coefficient is defined for conical wave guide, in the manner used by Barrow and Chu for sectoral horns,[10] by

$$\gamma(Q,r)=-1/Q(\partial Q/\partial r)=-(\partial/\partial r)(\log Q), \tag{5}$$

where Q is any field component. In general γ will be a function of r and will be different for various field components. This definition, it may be observed, reduces directly to the usual definition of the propagation constant if Q is simple harmonic in r, and γ is then a true constant. For regions in which γ is not too rapid a function of radius useful information is still obtained.

In an entirely similar manner we may define a pseudo guide wave-length $\lambda_g(Q,r)=2\pi/Im\gamma$, and a pseudo phase velocity $v_p(Q,r)=\omega/Im\gamma$. From Eq. (1) for TE waves and the asymptotic expansions of the spherical Hankel function for large and small argument

$$h_n^{(2)}(kr)=\begin{cases}\left(\dfrac{\pi}{4}\right)^{\frac{1}{2}}\dfrac{1}{(n+\frac{1}{2})!}\left(\dfrac{kr}{2}\right)^n \\ \qquad +j\left(\dfrac{\pi}{4}\right)^{\frac{1}{2}}(n-\frac{1}{2})!\left(\dfrac{2}{kr}\right)^{n+1}, & kr\ll 1 \\ \dfrac{1}{kr}\exp\left[-j\left(kr-\dfrac{n+1}{2}\pi\right)\right], & kr\gg 1\end{cases} \tag{6}$$

where $(n+\frac{1}{2})!$ has been written for the gamma function $\Gamma(n+\frac{3}{2})$, we may obtain the parameters of Table I which gives the propagation coefficient, the pseudo guide wave-length, and the pseudo phase velocity for the E_θ and H_ϕ components. Following Barrow and Chu we designate $kr\gg 1$ as a transmission region and that for which $kr\ll 1$ an attenuation region. In the transmission region the waves behave asymptotically as spherical waves in a free medium while in the attenuation region the behavior is similar to that in a uniform cross section guide near the cut-off wave-length.

These results can be expected to have physical validity only if the propagation coefficient γ is not too severe a function of r, or in other words, if the radial space variation is almost periodic. In the region near the apex where this condition is not true two anomalies arise. First, the phase of $\gamma(H_\phi)$ in the attenuation region is negative, which in uniform guide indicates a wave traveling in the negative radial direction, contrary to

[9] Math. Tables Project, Columbia University Press, New York (1945).

[10] W. L. Barrow and L. J. Chu, Proc. I.R.E. 27, 51 (1939).

hypothesis. Second, the group velocity v_g, if computed from the usual relation $v_g=d\omega/d(I_m\gamma)$ turns out to be of the same form as the phase velocity and the product of group and phase velocities is not c^2, as is required for a dispersionless medium. These anomalies can be ascribed to the severe aperiodicity of the Hankel functions in the region near the apex. It should be emphasized that the physical significance of the propagation coefficients here developed should not be exaggerated; however the implications of the results are of value in understanding the phenomena occurring.

Additional light on the properties of conical wave guide may be obtained from the behavior of the Poynting vector and power flow in the guide. It is not difficult to show that the angular components of the Poynting vector S are always pure imaginaries whereas the radial component is in general complex. In the attenuating region the radial component is largely imaginary along with the angular components. These latter decrease as $1/r^3$ at large distances and soon reach a negligible value compared with the radial component which decreases only as $1/r^2$.

From Eqs. (1) and (2), and the asymptotic expansions of the Hankel functions, Eq. (6), it is readily observed that in the transmission region all transverse field components decrease with reciprocal radius while the radial components decrease as reciprocal radius squared. As the wave progresses down the guide it therefore becomes more nearly a TEM wave matched to free medium, as may be seen from the wave impedance. For TE and TM waves, respectively, the wave impedance is given asymptotically by

$$kr\gg 1,\quad \begin{cases} Z_E=(\mu/\epsilon)^{\frac{1}{2}} \\ Z_H=(\mu/\epsilon)^{\frac{1}{2}} \end{cases}$$

$$kr\ll 1,\quad \begin{cases} Z_E=(\mu/\epsilon)^{\frac{1}{2}}\left[\dfrac{\pi(2n+1)}{n(n-\frac{1}{2})!(n+\frac{1}{2})!}\times\left(\dfrac{kr}{2}\right)^{2n+2}+j\dfrac{4}{nkr}\right] \\ Z_H=(\mu/\epsilon)^{\frac{1}{2}}\left[\dfrac{\pi(2n+1)}{(n-\frac{1}{2})!(n+\frac{1}{2})!}\times\left(\dfrac{kr}{2}\right)^{2n}-j\dfrac{n}{kr}\right]. \end{cases} \tag{8}$$

In regions near the apex the wave impedances are largely reactive, inductive for TE and capacitive for TM waves. As the wave moves into the transmission region the reactive part decreases, the resistive part increases and approaches asymptotically the characteristic impedance $(\mu/\epsilon)^{\frac{1}{2}}$ of the free medium.

RADIATION FROM A CONICAL HORN

Let us consider a cylindrical wave guide feeding a concentric conical wave guide. We will assume the cylindrical guide is excited in its lowest mode, TE_{11}, as is usually the case. At the junction of the uniform guide with the cone there is a discontinuity in the slope of the conducting boundary and higher order modes are required to satisfy the boundary conditions, the fundamental mode being partially reflected and partially transmitted. In the cylindrical guide the higher order modes will be rapidly attenuated but the behavior in the conical guide depends on whether the waves are introduced in the attenuating or transmitting regions of the cone. Certainly the cone will be transmitting for the fundamental mode on purely physical grounds since the diameter of the cone cross section is always greater than that of the uniform guide. The higher order modes, however, may be in an attenuating region and we have seen that such modes have an attenuation coefficient linearly proportional to the mode order, n, of the wave. The distance that a given order mode travels in an attenuating region may be calculated in a strictly qualitative manner, if it is assumed that in conical guide any order wave is in an attenuating region until the cross-sectional diameter of the cone approximates the diameter of a cylindrical guide just permitting propagation of that order wave in the uniform guide. If the diameter of the uniform guide operating in its lowest mode is D_0, and if the diameter corresponding to the nth mode is D_n, then the distance of travel of the nth mode wave in an attenuating region of the conical guide of flare angle θ_0 may be taken as

$$d=(D_n-D_0)/(2\sin\theta_0).$$

Small flare angles result in long journeys through attenuating regions. Also small flare angles result in smaller discontinuities at the cylinder-cone junction and, hence, require less higher mode energy to satisfy the boundary conditions. These factors both markedly discriminate against higher order modes.

In the conical guide, then, there will be present TE and/or TM waves composed principally of a fundamental and contaminated with higher order modes whose magnitudes depend on the flare angle and length of the guide. As the wave propagates in the positive radial direction, Eqs. (1), (2), and (6) show that, asymptotically, the radial components decrease only as reciprocal radius. Hence, some distance down the conical guide the wave will be almost transverse electromagnetic with only a small radial component. As this occurs, the wave impedance approaches that of a wave in free medium. Cutting off the conical guide at this distance should not materially alter the fields anywhere inside the cone since it is essentially matched into free space; very little energy will be reflected from the mouth. The small radial component still present is just sufficient to close the loops of the field lines of the TEM wave in free medium. The open ended cone thus becomes a source of radiation.

The calculation of the radiation characteristics of such a source involves two approximations at the outset:

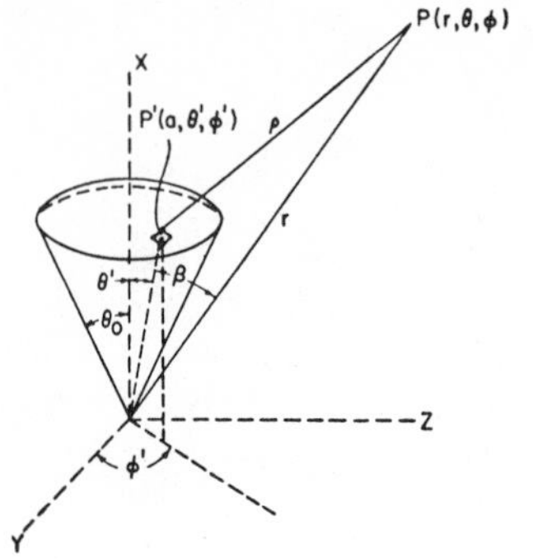

FIG. 1. Coordinate system for radiation calculations.

(1) the field at the mouth of the horn is assumed to be that which would exist at that cross section if the horn extended to infinity; and (2) there is assumed to be no field leakage around the rim of the mouth to the exterior surface of the horn. These matters have been discussed at length by others and will here be assumed valid provided the cone flare angle is not too great and its length is not too short.

The assumed field technique of Love,[11] MacDonald,[12] and later Schelkunoff[4] leads to the following expressions for the electric and magnetic intensities.

$$E=k^2A+\nabla\nabla\cdot A-j\omega\mu\nabla\times F,\qquad H=k^2F+\nabla\nabla\cdot F+j\omega\epsilon\nabla\times A, \tag{9}$$

where the vector potentials A and F are given by

$$F=-\frac{1}{j\omega\mu}\int_{S'}\frac{[n\times E']ds'}{4\pi\rho},\qquad A=\frac{1}{j\omega\epsilon}\int_{S'}\frac{[n\times H']ds'}{4\pi\rho}. \tag{10}$$

and E and H are the fields at any point in space distant ρ from a surface element ds' on which a field E' and H' exist, n being the unit vector normal to the surface and brackets indicating retardation in the Lorentz sense. The TE field at the mouth of the horn, S', is given by Eq. (1), and Fig. 1 shows the coordinate system used. Note that primed coordinates refer to the cone mouth while unprimed coordinates refer to the field point $P(r,\theta,\phi)$. Since the integrands are vector quantities the change in direction of the unit spherical vectors must be considered. This is most readily accomplished by expressing all vectors in rectangular coordinates. Noting that for the distant field

$$\rho\doteq r-a\cos\beta,$$

and

$$\cos\beta=\cos\theta\cos\theta'+\sin\theta\sin\theta'\cos(\phi-\phi');$$

and defining B_E and B_H by

$$B_E=B\frac{a^2}{4\pi r}e^{-jkr}h_n^{(2)}(ka)$$

$$B_H=B\frac{a^2}{j\omega\epsilon 4\pi r}e^{-jkr}\left[\frac{1}{a}h_n^{(2)}(ka)+kh_n^{(2)\prime}(ka)\right],$$

so that $B_H/B_E=-Z_H$ at the spherical cap $r=a$; then the rectangular components of F and A are given by:

$$\begin{aligned}
F_x&=-B_E\int_0^{\theta_0}\int_0^{2\pi}e^{jka\cos\beta}\sin m\phi'\times\sin^3\theta' P_n^{m\prime}(x')d\theta'd\phi',\\
F_y&=B_E\int_0^{\theta_0}\int_0^{2\pi}e^{jka\cos\beta}\{mP_n^m(x')\cos m\phi'\sin\phi'\\
&\qquad+P_n^{m\prime}(x')\sin m\phi'\cos\phi'\sin^2\theta'\cos\theta'\}d\theta'd\phi',\\
F_z&=-B_E\int_0^{\theta_0}\int_0^{2\pi}e^{jka\cos\beta}\{mP_n^m(x')\cos m\phi'\cos\phi'\\
&\qquad-P_n^{m\prime}(x')\sin m\phi'\sin\phi'\sin^2\theta'\cos\theta'\}d\theta'd\phi',\\
A_x&=B_H\int_0^{\theta_0}\int_0^{2\pi}e^{jka\cos\beta}mP_n^m(x')\times\cos m\phi'\sin\theta'd\theta'd\phi',\\
A_y&=-B_H\int_0^{\theta_0}\int_0^{2\pi}e^{jka\cos\beta}\times\{mP_n^m(x')\cos m\phi'\cos\phi'\cos\theta'\\
&\qquad-P_n^{m\prime}(x')\sin m\phi'\sin\phi'\sin^2\theta'\}d\theta'd\phi',\\
A_z&=-B_H\int_0^{\theta_0}\int_0^{2\pi}e^{jka\cos\beta}\times\{mP_n^m(x')\cos m\phi'\sin\phi'\cos\theta'\\
&\qquad+P_n^{m\prime}(x')\sin m\phi'\cos\phi'\sin^2\theta'\}d\theta'd\phi'.
\end{aligned} \tag{11}$$

The azimuthal integrations are over an orthogonal interval and present no difficulty, but the colatitude integrations are not over an orthogonal range and the evaluation of these integrals does not seem possible, analytically, in their present form. For small flare angles approximations may be made which permit the evaluation of the integrals in a sufficiently converging series.

The horn is assumed excited in the dominant TE mode used by Southworth and King in an experimental study of the radiation patterns of conical horns with which the calculated patterns are compared. We take

$$\begin{aligned}
\cos\beta&\doteq\cos\theta+\sin\theta\sin\theta'\cos(\phi-\phi')\\
P_n^1(\cos\theta')&\doteq\sin(\alpha\theta')P_n^1(\cos\theta_0)\\
P_n^{1\prime}(\cos\theta')&\doteq-\frac{\alpha\cos(\alpha\theta')}{\sin\theta'}P_n^1(\cos\theta_0),
\end{aligned} \tag{12}$$

where $\alpha=\pi/2\theta_0$. The Legendre function approximation may be checked against tabulated values for integral n and is very good except for a small range where θ' is nearly equal to θ_0. The approximation in $\cos\beta$ involves neglect of the variation of $\cos\theta'$ over the aperture of

[11] A. E. H. Love, Phil. Trans. **A197**, 1 (1901).

[12] H. M. MacDonald, Proc. London Math. Soc. **E10**, 91 (1911).

TABLE I. Propagation coefficients in conical wave guide.

		E_θ component	H_ϕ component
$kr\gg 1$	γ	$1/r+jk$	$1/r+jk$
	λ_g	λ	λ
	v_p	c	c
$kr\ll 1$	γ	$\frac{n+1}{r}+jk\frac{\pi}{2}\frac{2n+1}{(n-\frac{1}{2})!(n+\frac{1}{2})!}\left(\frac{kr}{2}\right)^{2n}$	$\frac{n+2}{r}-jk\frac{\pi}{2}\frac{(2n+1)(n+1)}{n(n-\frac{1}{2})!(n+\frac{1}{2})!}\left(\frac{kr}{2}\right)^{2n}$
	λ_g	$\lambda\cdot\frac{2}{\pi}\frac{(n-\frac{1}{2})!(n+\frac{1}{2})!}{2n+1}\left(\frac{2}{kr}\right)^{2n}$	$\lambda\cdot\frac{2}{\pi}\frac{n(n-\frac{1}{2})!(n+\frac{1}{2})!}{(2n+1)(n+1)}\left(\frac{2}{kr}\right)^{2n}$
	v_p	$c\cdot\frac{2}{\pi}\frac{(n-\frac{1}{2})!(n+\frac{1}{2})!}{2n+1}\left(\frac{2}{kr}\right)^{2n}$	$c\cdot\frac{2}{\pi}\frac{n(n-\frac{1}{2})!(n+\frac{1}{2})!}{(2n+1)(n+1)}\left(\frac{2}{kr}\right)^{2n}$

the horn. The phase factor may now be written as

$$e^{jka\cos\beta}=e^{jka\cos\theta}\cdot e^{j\frac{1}{2}ka\sin\theta\sin(\theta'+\phi-\phi')}\cdot e^{j\frac{1}{2}ka\sin\theta\sin(\theta'-\phi+\phi')},$$

and the last two factors expanded in a Fourier-Bessel series of the form

$$e^{jx\sin y}=\sum_{p=-\infty}^{\infty}J_p(\gamma)e^{jpy}.$$

Setting

$$\gamma=\tfrac{1}{2}ka\sin\theta,$$

$$e^{jka\cos\beta}=e^{jka\cos\theta}\sum_{p=-\infty}^{\infty}\sum_{s=-\infty}^{\infty}J_p(\gamma)J_s(\gamma)\cdot e^{j[(p+s)\theta'+(p-s)\phi-(p-s)\phi']}. \quad (13)$$

The neglect of the variation of $\cos\theta'$ over the mouth is thus seen to be a first order approximation in that terms of the second order and higher are neglected. It should be noted that the extent of the approximation is a function of the length, ka, of the horn and, for long horns, the neglected portion of the phase factor may have a considerable effect on the integrals, even though θ' varies over only a small range. The approximation is best for short horns and for co-latitudes far removed from the polar axis.

In the expansion, Eq. (13), the azimuthal coordinate ϕ' appears only in the trigometric form $e^{-j(p-s)\phi'}$ and this expansion when inserted in Eq. (11) is multiplied by other trigonometric functions of ϕ' and integrated over the orthogonal interval $(0, 2\pi)$. This will cause the vanishing of all terms of the double sum, Eq. (13), except those for which a definite constant relation exists between the indices p and s, and the double sum is reduced to a single sum over the index p. The vector potentials then become, from Eq. (11) with $m=1$,

$$F_x=-j\pi/2B_EP_n^1(x_0)e^{j(ka\cos\theta+\phi)}\times\sum_{p=-\infty}^{\infty}J_p(\gamma)J_{p-1}(\gamma)f_x(p,\theta_0),$$

$$F_y=-j\pi/2B_EP_n^1(x_0)e^{j(ka\cos\theta+2\phi)}\times\sum_{p=-\infty}^{\infty}J_p(\gamma)J_{p-2}(\gamma)f_y(p,\theta_0),$$

$$F_z=-\pi B_EP_n^1(x_0)e^{jka\cos\theta}\sum_{p=-\infty}^{\infty}\{\langle J_p(\gamma)\rangle_{\mathrm{Av}}^2f_z(p,\theta_0)+1/2e^{j2\phi}J_p(\gamma)J_{p-2}(\gamma)f_y(p,\theta_0)\},$$

$$A_x=\pi B_HP_n^1(x_0)e^{j(ka\cos\theta+\phi)}\times\sum_{p=-\infty}^{\infty}J_p(\gamma)J_{p-1}(\gamma)a_x(p,\theta_0),\quad (14)$$

$$A_y=-\pi B_HP_n^1(x_0)e^{jka\cos\theta}\sum_{p=-\infty}^{\infty}\{\langle J_p(\gamma)\rangle_{\mathrm{Av}}^2a_y(p,\theta_0)+1/2e^{j2\phi}J_p(\gamma)J_{p-2}(\gamma)a_z(p,\theta_0)\},$$

$$A_z=j\pi/2B_HP_n^1(x_0)e^{j(ka\cos\theta+2\phi)}\times\sum_{p=-\infty}^{\infty}J_p(\gamma)J_{p-2}(\gamma)a_z(p,\theta_0);$$

where the "f" and "a" functions are defined by

$$f_x(p,\theta_0)=(\alpha/2)\{g_1(2p+1,\theta_0)-2g_1(2p-1,\theta_0)+g_1(2p-3,\theta_0)\},$$

$$f_y(p,\theta_0)=-j(\alpha/4)\{g_1(2p,\theta_0)+g_2(2p-2,\theta_0)-g_1(2p-4,\theta_0)\},$$

$$f_z(p,\theta_0)=j(\alpha/4)\{g_1(2p+2,\theta_0)-g_2(2p,\theta_0)-g_1(2p-2,\theta_0)\},$$

$$a_x(p,\theta_0)=(\alpha/8)\{g_2(2p,\theta_0)-g_2(2p-2,\theta_0)\},\quad (15)$$

$$a_y(p,\theta_0)=-j(\alpha/2)\times\{\tfrac{1}{4}[g_2(2p+1,\theta_0)+g_2(2p-3,\theta_0)]-[g_1(2p+1,\theta_0)-g_1(2p-3,\theta_0)]\},$$

$$a_z(p,\theta_0)=-j(\alpha/2)\times\{\tfrac{1}{4}[g_2(2p-1,\theta_0)+g_2(2p-3,\theta_0)]+[g_1(2p-1,\theta_0)-g_1(2p-3,\theta_0)]\},$$

and the "g" functions are given by

$$g_1(K,\theta_0)=\frac{\alpha e^{jK\theta_0}-jK}{K^2-\alpha^2}$$

$$g_2(K,\theta_0)=-\frac{4}{\alpha}\frac{Ke^{jK\theta_0}-j\alpha}{K^2-\alpha^2}.\quad (16)$$

The "g" functions and hence "f" and "a" converge as reciprocal summation index provided $|K|$ is greater

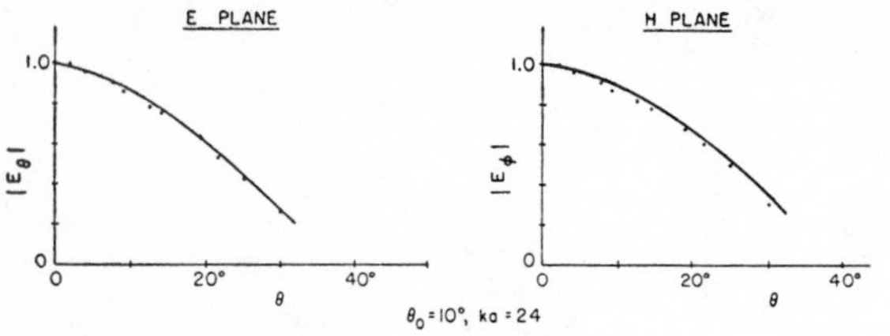

FIG. 2. Radiation pattern for conical horn of 10° flare angle. Solid curve is experimental and dotted points are calculated.

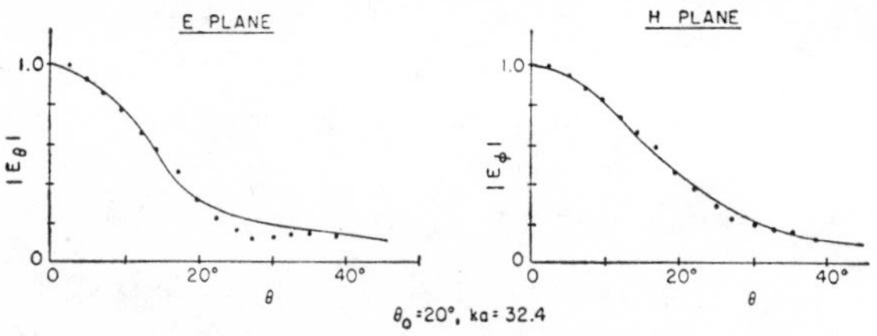

FIG. 3. Radiation pattern for conical horn of 20° flare angle. Solid curve is experimental and dotted points are calculated.

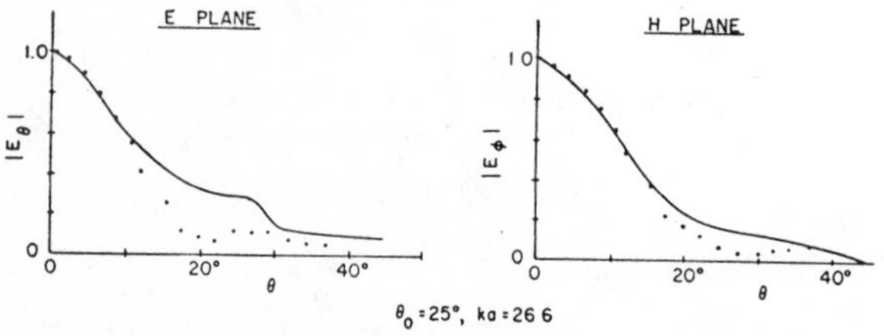

FIG. 4. Radiation pattern for conical horn of 25° flare angle. Solid curve is experimental and dotted points are calculated.

than α. The product of the two Bessel functions converges rapidly once the order p is greater than the argument γ. Hence the summations of Eq. (14) converge rapidly and, in general, only about γ terms must be included in the sum. These summations are over all integral values of p, positive and negative; however, the symmetry properties of the summands permits expression of the series as sums over only the positive integral indices. The only non-vanishing summations are those for which the total summand is an even function of the index of summation.

The vector potentials vary with radius as e^{-jkr}/r and thus if one ignores those radiation field components which vary faster than reciprocal radius, then Eq. (9) reduces to

$$E=k^2\frac{e^{-jkr}}{r}\{\theta_1[(\mu/\epsilon)^{\frac{1}{2}}F_\phi+A_\theta]-\phi_1[(\mu/\epsilon)^{\frac{1}{2}}F_\theta-A_\phi]\},$$

$$H=k^2\frac{e^{-jkr}}{r}\{\theta_1[F_\theta-(\epsilon/\mu)^{\frac{1}{2}}A_\phi]+\phi_1[F_\phi+(\epsilon/\mu)^{\frac{1}{2}}A_\theta]\},$$

where F and A are now the angular parts of the vector potentials, the radial parts being included in the e^{-jkr}/r factor. A receiving dipole oriented parallel to the E plane will then measure electric intensity patterns pro-

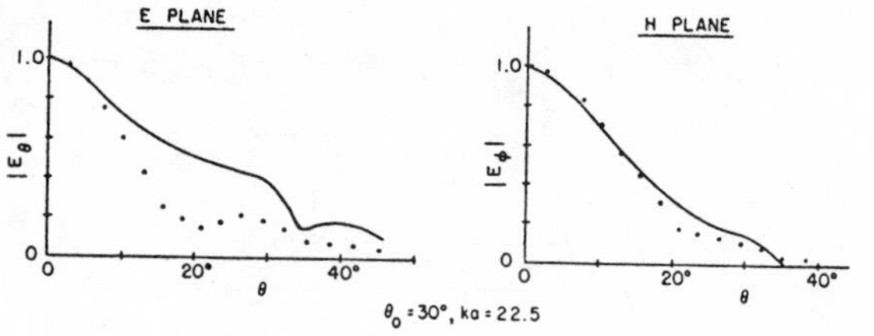

FIG. 5. Radiation pattern for conical horn of 30° flare angle. Solid curve is experimental and dotted points are calculated.

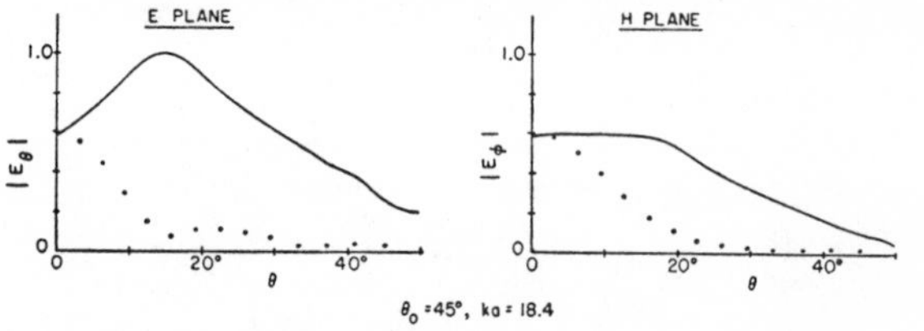

FIG. 6. Radiation pattern for conical horn of 45° flare angle. Solid curve is experimental and dotted points are calculated.

portional to

$$E_{\theta E}\propto F_z-A_x\sin\theta+A_y\cos\theta$$
$$E_{\phi H}\propto -F_x\sin\theta+F_z\cos\theta+A_y$$

in the $E(\phi=0)$ and $H(\phi=\pi/2)$ planes, respectively.

The "g," "f," and "a" functions have been tabulated for various flare angles up to 45 degrees. If γ is restricted to values less than eight, then ten terms of the series are adequate. The field point colatitude at which numerical information is obtained is $\theta=\arcsin 2\gamma/ka$ and will be a function of the length of the horn. In general, it is found that longer horns give sharper radiation patterns and the increased resolution and decreased maximum field angle is not undesirable. However, no information on the small scale radiation at large polar angles is predicted. The greatest contribution to the radiation arises from the F_z and A_y components; F_x and A_x are negligible in all horns up to about 30 degrees flare angle.

Radiation patterns were calculated for horn flare angles from 10 to 45 degrees and horn lengths, ka, from 18.4 to 32.4. Horn parameters were chosen to agree with those used by Southworth and King[7] in an experimental study of conical horns fed by cylindrical guide at 15.3 cm free space wave-length. The flare angles used by them are total flare angles and hence double the flare angle θ_0 used here; the lengths of their horns were determined from the diameter of the aperture D and the excitation wave-length λ by

$$ka=(\pi D)/(\lambda\sin\theta_0).$$

The resulting patterns are shown in Figs. 2 to 6 in which the magnitude of the electric field is plotted as a function of the field point polar angle in the E and H planes. The solid curves are replots of Southworth and King's Fig. 10,[7] while the dotted points are normalized values calculated by the assumed field method. Amplitude patterns are given here so as to compare directly with the experimental patterns. Only one-half the pattern is shown, since the theory is completely symmetrical, with respect to co-latitude, about the polar axis. There is little difference in the experimental curves between symmetrical halves but, where such differences exist, the average of the two halves was used to draw the solid curves.

The agreement between theory and experiment is seen to be good in the E plane for the 10° and 20° horns, poor at 25° and 30°, and very poor for the 45° horn. In the H plane the agreement is excellent for 10° and 20° horns, fair for 25° and 30°, and very bad for the 45° horn. The complete failure of the theory for the 45° horn is perhaps not surprising in the light of the small angle approximation made. Certainly it is not sound to neglect the variation of $\cos\theta'$ when the flare angle is as large as $\pi/4$. The possibility existed that the large discrepancy in the case of this 45° horn might be due to a considerable third harmonic excitation at the mouth because of the large discontinuities at the feed junction and the relative shortness of this horn. However, a qualitative calculation of the third harmonic contribution was unable to account for this behavior. The theory, in its present form, seems unable to yield a radiation pattern whose maximum amplitude is anywhere but on the polar axis, whereas experiment shows that it is quite possible to obtain maximum radiation in other directions. This effect has also been observed by Chu and Barrow[13] in the sectoral horn even after great care had been taken to eliminate all higher order modes. This peaking off the polar axis seems definitely to be a characteristic of large flare angle horns with which the present small angle theory is unable to cope.

Another anomaly in the theory is its prediction of varying horn length, at constant flare angle, on the pattern. The horn length, ka, enters only through γ, the argument of the Bessel functions, and hence the only effect of a change in ka is to alter the field point polar angle at which the calculation yields numerical results. An increase in length will sharpen the whole pattern, but no change should occur in the relative amplitudes of the side lobes and other structure. This prediction is not wholly confirmed by experiment in that, while the directivity tends to increase with length, lobes become more prevalent. This discrepancy again arises from the phase factor approximation where, it will be recalled, the neglect of the variation of $\cos\theta'$ can be justified only for small flare angles and moderate horn lengths. From the figures it is seen that the E plane directivity, i.e., that polar angle at which the amplitude falls to .707 of its maximum amplitude, is always somewhat greater than that in the H plane, the relation being approximately $E_{\theta E}=E_{\phi H}\cos\theta$. However, the H plane pattern is usually much smoother, with less side lobe, and falls to zero somewhat faster.

In conclusion it is perhaps worth while to point out that for pyramidal horns the same field Eqs. (1) and (2) apply provided only that the associated Legendre function of the first kind $P_n^m(x)$ is replaced wherever it occurs by

$$L_n^m(x)=aP_n^m(x)+bQ_n^m(x).$$

The radial part of these conical horn solutions apply directly to the pyramidal case and hence the various propagation factors computed for conical wave guide follow identically for pyramidal guide.

[13] L. J. Chu and W. L. Barrow, Trans. A.I.E.E. 58, 333 (1939).

The Radiation Characteristics of Conical Horn Antennas*

A. P. KING†, SENIOR MEMBER, IRE

Summary—**This paper reports the measured radiation characteristics of conical horns employing waveguide excitation. The experimentally derived gains are in excellent agreement with the theoretical results (unpublished) obtained by Gray and Schelkunoff.**

The gain and effective area is given for conical horns of arbitrary proportions and the radiation patterns are included for horns of optimum design. All dimensional data has been normalized in terms of wavelength, and are presented in convenient nomographic form.

I. Introduction

THIS PAPER reports the experimental results obtained with conical horn antennas having a linear rate of flare and employing waveguide excitation which is limited to the dominant mode. Some earlier experiments made in this field have been reported.[1] This study was conducted at the Holmdel Laboratory of the Bell Telephone Laboratories.

Conical horns probably comprise the most simple antenna structure, and in the range of moderate antenna gains, in the vicinity of 20 db, they are quite compact in size. Since the length of a conical horn increases directly with the power gain, the length of the horn may become objectionably long at high gains. In this respect, and in general, conical horns exhibit gain and directional characteristics which are quite similar to those of rectangular or pyramidal horns. Since the axial gain can readily be calculated from their physical dimensions, conical horns are especially useful as antenna gain standards.

Most of the conical horn measurements were made at a wavelength around 10 cm; a few in the 3-cm range. The measurement of antenna gain is in terms of absolute gain, i.e., relative to an isotropic radiator and the general measuring procedures closely follow the techniques reported in an earlier paper.[2] Since the radiation characteristics of a conical horn are determined by its dimensions in wavelengths, it has been convenient to normalize all dimensional data in terms of wavelength.

II. General

A conical horn is a section of a right circular cone and is usually connected to a cylindrical waveguide as shown in Fig. 1. An alternate form of excitation may comprise a rectangular waveguide which is gradually flared into the circular waveguide or into the horn directly. For either dominant wave (TE_{10}) excitation in rectangular waveguide or TE_{11} wave excitation in circular waveguide, the conical horn has been found to exhibit substantially the same behavior.

The performance of this class of antenna can be determined by specifying two dimensions. These are the axial length L and the diameter of the horn aperture d_m, as indicated in Fig. 1.

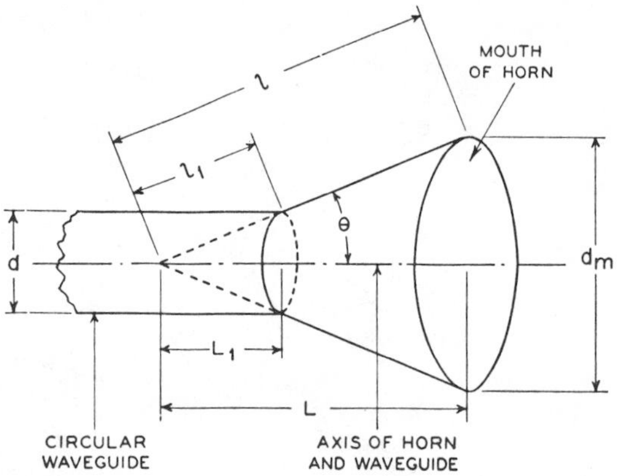

Fig. 1—Conical horn.

The absolute gain of a conical horn of arbitrary dimensions is given by the theoretical curves of Fig. 2 which were derived by Gray and Schelkunoff.[3] A number of horns measured over a wide range of values show excellent agreement with the calculated values of Fig. 2. Conical horns of a fixed length and varying aperture size exhibit a gain variation characteristic which is analogous to that of rectangular horns. For a conical horn whose axial length L is fixed, the axial gain increases as the aperture diameter d_m increases up to a certain optimum value. For all other values of d_m the gain will be less. The dimensions which correspond to a maximum gain for a given length are horns of optimum design. These proportions are indicated by the dashed line of Fig. 2. However, for the case of conical horns whose aperture (d_m) is fixed and the axial length is allowed to vary the gain varies in a different manner, the maximum gain now occurs when the length is infinite. The latter is, of course, equivalent to a circular waveguide radiator whose diameter is d_m.

The measured values of 6 conical horns, whose proportions vary over a wide range, are indicated by the points $a, b, \cdots, f$ in Fig. 2. Of these, horns a and b are

* Decimal classification: R325.8×R120. Original manuscript received by the Institute, June 8, 1949; revised manuscript received, October 11, 1949.

† Bell Telephone Laboratories, Inc., Holmdel, N. J.

[1] G. C. Southworth and A. P. King, "Metal horns as directive receivers of ultra-short waves," Proc. I.R.E., vol. 27, pp. 95–102, February, 1939.

[2] C. C. Cutler, A. P. King, and W. E. Kock, "Microwave antenna measurements," Proc. I.R.E., vol. 35, pp. 1462–1471; December, 1947.

[3] M. C. Gray and S. A. Schelkunoff, Bell Telephone Laboratories, from unpublished data.

Reprinted from *Proc. IRE*, vol. 38, pp. 249–251, Mar. 1950

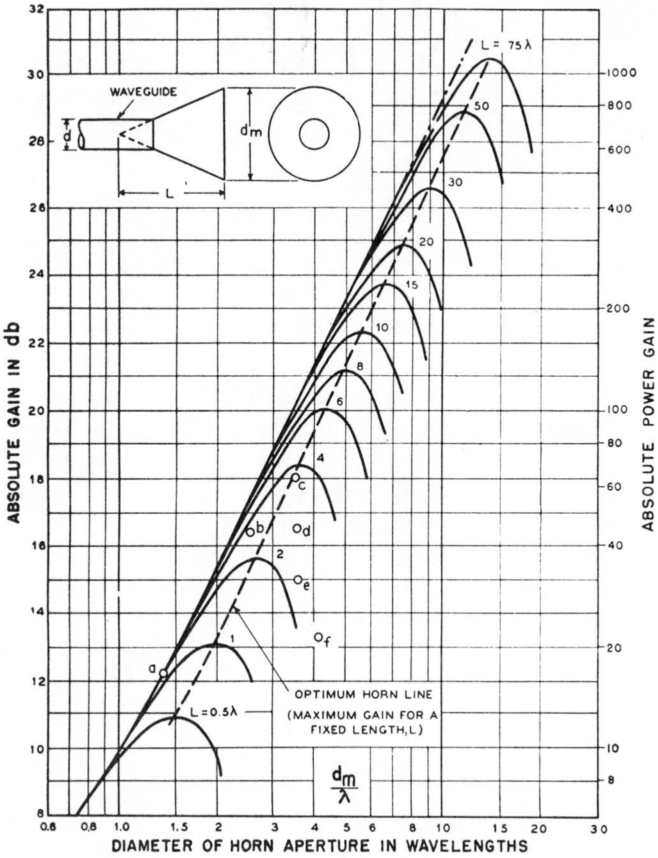

Fig. 2—The absolute gain of a conical horn as a function of aperture diameter (d_m/λ) for a series of axial lengths, L.

for values of aperture diameter d_m, less than optimum, point c corresponds very closely to optimum, and horns d, e, f are for horns whose diameter (d_m) exceeds optimum. The radiation characteristics of these particular horns are plotted in Fig. 3. These patterns indicate a typical behavior over this range of horn proportions, in that the magnetic plane patterns have a single major

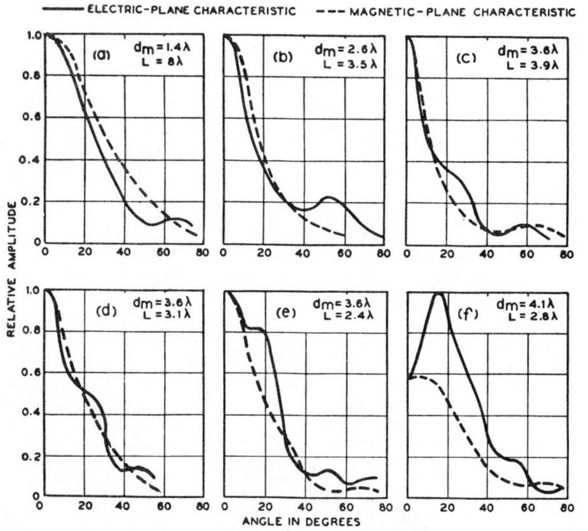

Fig. 3—Directional characteristics are shown of a series of conical horns of varying proportions. In Figs. (a) and (b) the apertures for horn length L are of less than optimum value, in (c) of optimum value, and in (d), (e), (f) of greater than optimum value.

lobe and are relatively free from minor lobes. In the electric plane, the minor lobe is separated from the major lobe for (a) and (b) where the values of d_m are appreciably less than optimum. However, as the value of d_m approaches the optimum value, the minor lobe moves toward the axis of the beam and merges with the major lobe, as shown in Fig. 3(c). As d_m increases beyond the optimum, the minor lobe continues to rise higher on the side of the major lobe as indicated in Fig. 3 by patterns (d) and (e). A still further increase in d_m to the proportions indicated in Fig. 3(f), produces a splitting of the major lobe with the result that radiation is no longer a maximum along the axis. To obtain good major lobe characteristics which are moderately free from minor lobe effects, it is preferable to operate in the range where the aperture diameter, d_m, does not exceed the optimum value.

III. Optimum Horns

The optimum horns considered throughout this paper are restricted to conical horns so proportioned that for a given axial length L, the antenna gain is a maximum. Optimum horns are generally most useful since they comprise the most compact antenna for a given gain.

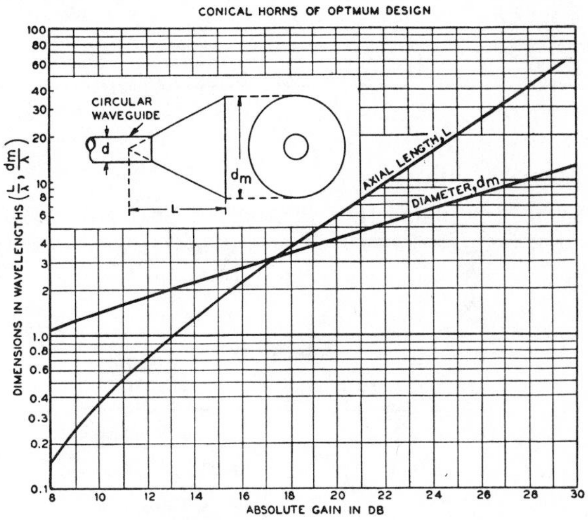

Fig. 4—Shows diameter d_m and axial length L as a function of axial gain for conical horns of optimum design.

The gain-dimensional data for optimum horns is given in Fig. 4. The geometrical relationships are

$$\frac{l}{\lambda} - \frac{L}{\lambda} = 0.3 \tag{1}$$

$$\frac{L}{\lambda} \approx 0.3\left(\frac{d_m}{\lambda}\right)^2, \tag{2}$$

where l, the radial length, is indicated in Fig. 1.

A typical measured radiation pattern for an optimum conical horn, whose absolute gain is 17.7 db, is shown in Fig. 5. Additional experimental data are presented in nomographic form in Fig. 6 for plotting the directional characteristics of optimum horns whose aper-

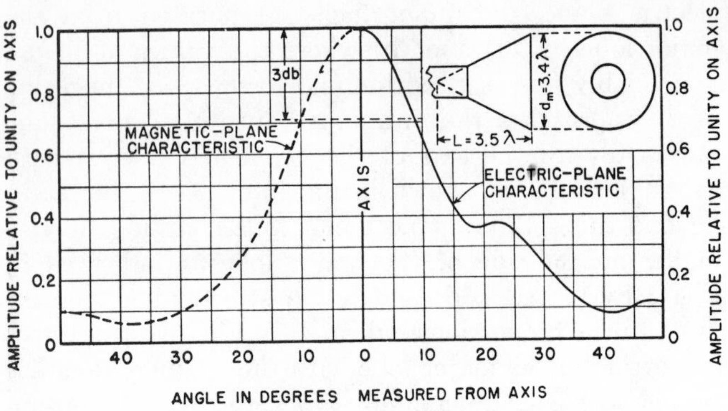

Fig. 5—Radiation pattern of a 17.7-db gain conical horn of optimum design.

ture diameter d_m/λ lies in the range of 1.5–15λ. In this nomogram the amplitude, relative to unity in the direction of maximum radiation intensity, is represented by the slant lines, the abscissa the value of aperture d_m/λ, and the ordinate gives the radiation angle relative to the axis of the beam. The beam angle ϕ, between points 3 db below the maximum radiation intensity, is

$$\phi_M \approx \frac{70}{\left(\frac{d_m}{\lambda}\right)} \text{ degrees (beam angle in the magnetic plane)} \quad (3)$$

$$\phi_E \approx \frac{60}{\left(\frac{d_m}{\lambda}\right)} \text{ degrees (beam angle in the electric plane).} \quad (4)$$

As indicated in (3) and (4) above, the beam angle is somewhat sharper in the electric plane than in the magnetic plane. These two beam angles can be made equal

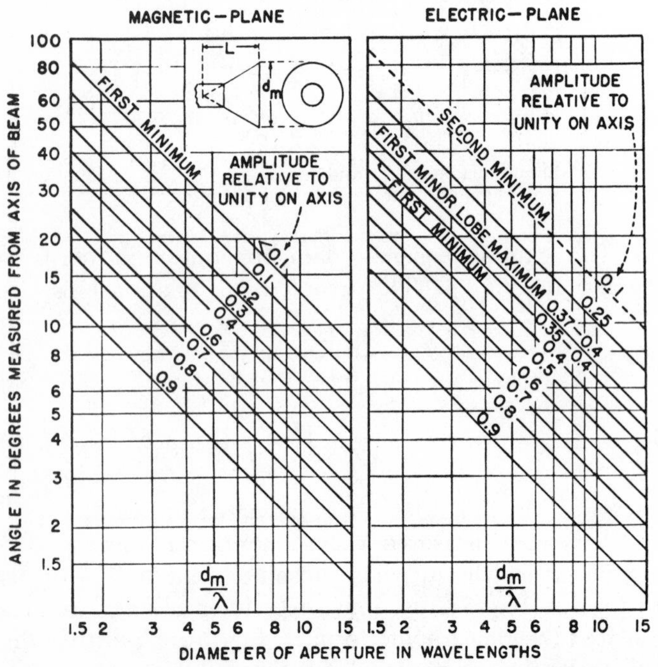

Fig. 6—Nomograph for plotting the radiation characteristic for conical horns of optimum design.

(at points 3 db below maximum radiation intensity) by deforming the circular aperture to an ellipse whose major to minor axis ratio is approximately 1.2, the minor axis being parallel to the electric plane.

IV. Effective Area of Conical Horns

The effective area A_{eff} of an antenna is

$$A_{eff} = \frac{g\lambda^2}{4\pi}, \quad (5)$$

where g is the absolute power gain and λ the free-space wavelength. For an antenna whose intensity distribution, polarization and phase are uniform across its aperture, the effective area is equivalent to the actual aperture area A. While it is difficult to realize this degree of perfection in practice, it serves as a criterion to indicate how closely the performance of an antenna approaches the ideal. Usually the effective area of an antenna is expressed relative to the actual area, as a ratio A_{eff}/A. The aperture area of a conical horn is

$$A = \frac{\pi}{4} d_m^2 \quad (6)$$

and the ratio

$$\frac{A_{eff}}{A} = \frac{g}{\pi^2\left(\frac{d_m}{\lambda}\right)^2}, \quad (7)$$

where g is the absolute power gain. The effective area for a conical horn of arbitrary proportions may be calculated from the values of g (after converting to power gain) and the corresponding values d_m/λ in Fig. 2. For a horn whose dimensions correspond to optimum design, the effective area is 0.52 or 52 per cent that of the actual area. When the aperture (d_m) of a conical horn is fixed, its effective area increases with the axial length (L) and reaches a maximum value of $A_{eff}/A = 0.84$ (84 per cent) for very long horns. The effective area as a function of the axial length, relative to the length at optimum, is shown in Table I.

TABLE I
Effective Area of Conical Horns

Length relative to optimum	Effective area A_{eff}/A
0.5	20%
0.75	39%
1.0	52%
1.5	69%
2.0	75%
3.0	80%
4.0	82%
∞	84%

As is indicated in this table, only a small increase in effective area or axial gain is realized by increasing the axial length beyond 2 or 3 times the value corresponding to optimum.

Part II
Papers of General Interest

In the first two papers in this part, edge diffraction theory [1] is introduced by Peters *et al.* for the purpose of calculating total *E*-plane patterns of horns, including radiation in the backlobe region. The method has since been applied to *H*-plane pattern calculation with some success [2].

The third paper, by Narasimhan and Rao, points out and corrects an error that occurred in Silver's text [3] concerning radiation by *E*-plane sectoral horns. The error arose through the unwitting use of a left-handed cylindrical coordinate system in figure 10.9(a) on page 351 of the text. As a result, equations 45(a) and (b) on pages 357 and 358 are incorrect. The authors show results of computations indicating that the incorrect formulas give rise to large errors in the sidelobe region of *E*-plane sectoral horn patterns.

The next four papers are all concerned with conical horns. Li and Turrin give results of computer calculations of the near zone fields of a TE_{11} mode conical horn that agree well with experiment. Hamid, in the second of the four, applies the geometrical theory of diffraction (GTD) to calculate the gain and patterns of a dominant mode conical horn (see also [4]). The last two of this quartet of papers are by Narasimhan and Rao; in one, a new approach to pattern calculations is presented, and in the second, they show how to treat horns with large flare angles. In each case, a simplified, asymptotic solution for the spherical mode fields in a conical horn is used and leads to closed form expressions for the radiation patterns and gain.

Three practical, applications-oriented papers follow. Epis describes aperture compensating techniques for equalizing the *E*- and *H*-plane patterns of horns. Walton and Sundberg give design information for constructing broad-band ridged horns and include useful information on lens design. Finally, Kerr describes short horns that are capable of covering a decade or more in frequency range. Other applications-oriented papers are found in [5]–[7].

In the final paper, Muehldorf presents a comprehensive discussion of the phase center of pyramidal, rectangular, and diagonal horn antennas. He shows that, in general, the *E*- and *H*-plane phase centers are not coincident for a pyramidal horn. Two articles, not included here, on the subject of the phase center in horn antennas are found in [8] and [9].

References

[1] B. Ye Kinber, "Diffraction at the open end of a sectoral horn," *Radio Eng. Electron. Phys.*, vol. 10, pp. 1620–1632, Oct. 1962.

[2] J. S. Yu and R. C. Rudduck, "*H*-plane pattern of a pyramidal horn," *IEEE Trans. Antennas Propagat.*, vol. AP-17, pp. 651–652, Sept. 1969.

[3] S. Silver, "Microwave antenna theory and design," ch. 10 by J. R. Risser, *MIT Radiation Laboratory Series*, vol. 12. New York: McGraw-Hill, 1949.

[4] M. A. K. Hamid, "Mutual coupling between sectoral horns side by side," *IEEE Trans. Antennas Propagat.*, vol. AP-15, pp. 475–477, May 1967.

[5] G. M. Peace and E. E. Swartz, "Amplitude compensated horn antenna," *Microwave J.*, vol. 7, pp. 66–68, Feb. 1964.

[6] A. H. LaGrone and G. F. Roberts, "Minor lobe suppression in a rectangular horn through the utilization of a high impedance choke flange," *IEEE Trans. Antennas Propagat.*, vol. AP-14, pp. 102–104, Jan. 1966.

[7] C. Ancona, "Wide-angle sectoral horns using leaky-wave wall structures," *IEEE Trans. Antennas Propagat.*, vol. AP-22, pp. 475–477, May 1974.

[8] Y. Hu, "A method of determining phase centers and its application to electromagnetic horns," *J. Franklin Inst.*, vol. 271, pp. 31–39, Jan. 1961.

[9] M. Teichman, "Precision phase center measurement of horn antennas," *IEEE Trans. Antennas Propagat.*, vol. AP-18, pp. 689–690, Sept. 1970.

A Method for Computing *E*-Plane Patterns of Horn Antennas

P. M. RUSSO, STUDENT MEMBER, IEEE, R. C. RUDDUCK, MEMBER, IEEE, AND L. PETERS, JR., SENIOR MEMBER, IEEE

***Abstract*—This paper introduces a method for calculating the total antenna pattern in the *E* plane, including the backlobe region, of a horn by applying diffraction theory. Treatment of diffraction by a thick edge permits horns of various edge thicknesses to be treated. The diffraction concepts developed by Sommerfeld and Pauli, which treated plane wave diffraction by a wedge, are extended so that diffraction of plane and cylindrical waves by thin or thick edges may be treated. The diffracted fields are obtained by applying the relations developed by Pauli in conjunction with reciprocity.**

When the theory is applied to the horn, the significant radiation mechanisms are direct radiation from the source at the horn apex and diffracted radiation due to the edges. The computed *E*-plane patterns of a horn antenna agree with measured patterns.

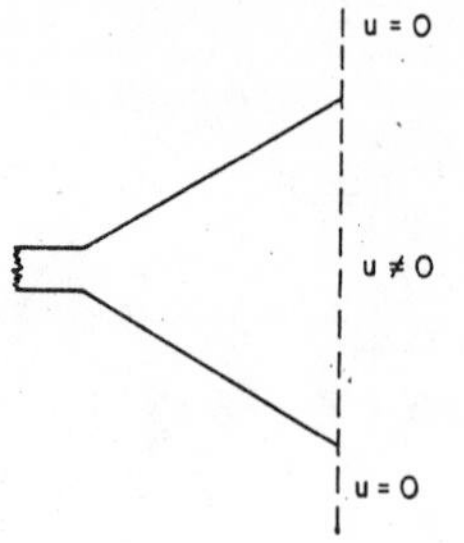

Fig. 1. Application of equivalence principle to horn.

Introduction

APERTURE methods for evaluating the fields of aperture antennas are restricted in the practical sense that the fields behind the aperture plane, or in the back direction of the antenna, are not easily obtained. Such formulations as Schelkunoff's equivalence principle could, in theory, be used to evaluate the fields of any antenna in all space. However, the electric and magnetic currents or fields must be known over the entire antenna surface, and then a difficult surface integral must be evaluated. Usually the exterior surface currents on antenna structures, exclusive of the antenna aperture, do not contribute significantly to the fields in the region of the antenna main beam. The radiation in this region is due to a distribution of Huygens sources in the antenna aperture. For example, by extending the aperture for the horn antenna (as in Fig. 1) and implicitly assuming that the fields are identically zero on this plane, except over the aperture, the equivaence principle can be applied to obtain the fields. It is common practice to determine the aperture distribution by geometrical optics or by experiment. The fields to the left of this infinite plane cannot be obtained because of the assumptions involved; but the fields to the right of the aperture can be computed with excellent results, provided the aperture distribution is accurately measured. The horn antenna represents a case for which this aperture method is used to obtain the forward fields, whereas the backlobe region must generally be obtained experimentally.

This paper introduces a method for calculating the total *E*-plane pattern, including the backlobe region, of a horn by applying diffraction theory. Initially, Keller's[1,2] geometrical theory of diffraction was applied to this problem; however, the diffraction coefficients used in this technique are not generally adequate for these computations, since the appropriate diffraction coefficients used in the geometrical theory of diffraction are for a plane wave incident on a perfectly conducting wedge whereas cylindrical wave incidence is applicable to the horn. Insofar as the diffraction in the *E* plane is concerned, the horn may be considered to have a cylindrical wave emanating from its throat.

Consequently, the diffraction for cylindrical wave incidence was determined through the use of Pauli's[3] equations for diffraction of a plane wave by a perfectly conducting wedge, together with the principle of reciprocity. This diffraction solution allows the *E*-plane patterns to be calculated with good accuracy for horns of various edge thicknesses. Previous treatment of antennas by half-plane diffraction methods have been introduced by Lysher[4] for paraboloid reflector antennas and Ohba[5] for corner reflector antennas.

Review of Edge Diffraction Theory

The problem of straight-edge diffraction by a perfectly conducting wedge was first solved by Sommerfeld.[6] He considered a plane electromagnetic wave normally incident on the wedge of an angle $(2-n)\pi$ (shown in Fig. 2). The azimuthal angle ψ and ψ_0 are associated with the angle of diffraction and the angle of incidence, respectively.

Manuscript received March 20, 1964; revised September 28, 1964. The work reported here was supported in part by Contract AF 30(602)-3269 between Rome Air Development Center, Griffiss Air Force Base, N. Y., and The Ohio State University Research Foundation, Columbus, Ohio.

P. M. Russo is with Systems Research Labs., Dayton, Ohio.
R. C. Rudduck and L. Peters, Jr. are with the Antenna Lab., Dept. of Electrical Engineering, The Ohio State University, Columbus, Ohio.

[1] Keller, J. B., Diffraction by an aperture, *J. Appl. Phys.*, vol 28, Apr 1957, pp 426–444.
[2] Keller, J. B., Geometrical theory of diffraction, *J. Opt. Soc. Am.*, vol 52, Feb 1962, pp 116–130.
[3] Pauli, W., On asymptotic series for functions in the theory of diffraction of light, *Phys. Rev.*, vol 54, Dec 1938, pp 924–931.
[4] Lysher, L., J., A study of the near-field behind a parabolic antenna, M.Sc., thesis, The Ohio State University, Columbus, Ohio, 1961.
[5] Ohba, Y., On the radiation pattern of a corner reflector finite in width, *IEEE Trans. on Antennas and Propagation*, vol AP-11, Mar 1963, pp 127–132.
[6] Sommerfeld, A., *Optics*, New York: Academic Press, Inc., 1954, pp 245–265.

Reprinted from *IEEE Trans. Antennas Propagat.*, vol. AP-13, pp. 219–224, Mar. 1965.

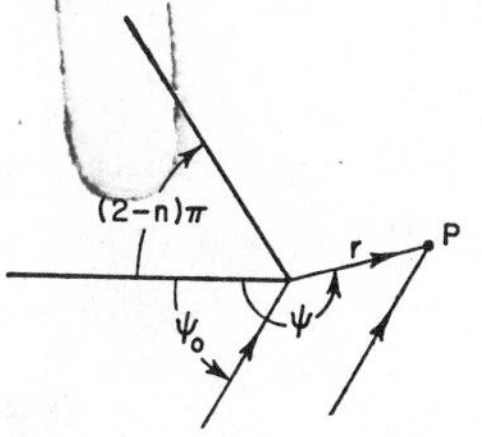

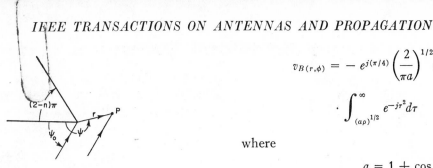

Fig. 2. Diffraction of plane wave by wedge.

The field u at point P is a solution to the scalar wave equation subject to the appropriate boundary conditions; the solution may be formulated as

$$u_{(r,\psi)} = v_{(r,\psi+\psi_0)} \pm v_{(r,\psi-\psi_0)} \tag{1}$$

Polarization determines the choice of sign such that, with the electric vector perpendicular (parallel) to the edge, the positive (negative) sign is chosen. It is convenient to represent the incident or reflected field in the form

$$v_{(r,\phi)} = v_{(r,\psi\pm\psi_0)} \tag{2}$$

such that the $(-)$ sign yields the incident fields and the $(+)$ sign yields the reflected fields. The component field is given by

$$v_{(r,\phi)} = v^* + v_B \tag{3}$$

where v^* is the geometrical optics field given by

$$v^* = \begin{cases} e^{j\rho\cos(\phi+2\pi nN)} & -\pi < \phi + 2\pi nN < \pi \\ & N = 0, \pm 1, \pm 2 \cdots \\ 0 & \text{otherwise} \end{cases} \tag{4}$$

and v_B is the diffracted field given by

$$v_B = \frac{1}{2\pi n}\int_C \frac{e^{j\rho\cos\beta}}{1 - e^{-j(\beta+\phi)/n}}\, d\beta \tag{5}$$

where

$$\rho = kr \tag{6}$$

Here C is the appropriate path in the plane of the complex variable.

An asymptotic expression for (5), obtained by Sommerfeld, is of the form

$$v_{B(r,\phi)} \approx (2\pi\rho)^{-1/2} e^{-j\left(\rho+\frac{\pi}{4}\right)} \frac{n^{-1}\sin\pi/n}{\cos\pi/n - \cos\phi/n} \tag{7}$$

This form yields infinite fields in the vicinity of the shadow boundary and is valid only if

$$\rho\left(\cos\frac{\pi}{n} - \cos\frac{\phi}{n}\right)^2 \gg 1 \tag{8}$$

However, for the special case of $n=2$, the diffracted field expression was obtained by Sommerfeld in terms of the Fresnel Integral as

$$v_{B(r,\phi)} = -e^{j(\pi/4)}\left(\frac{2}{\pi a}\right)^{1/2} e^{j\rho\cos\phi}\left|\cos\frac{\phi}{2}\right| \cdot \int_{(a\rho)^{1/2}}^{\infty} e^{-j\tau^2} d\tau \tag{9}$$

where

$$a = 1 + \cos\phi \tag{10}$$

It should be noted that the positive square root of $(a\rho)$ should always be taken. The sum $v^* + v_B$ can also be represented more compactly by

$$v_{(r,\phi)} = \frac{e^{j(\pi/4)}}{\sqrt{\pi}} e^{j\rho\cos\phi} \int_{-\infty}^{(2\rho)^{1/2}\cos\phi/2} e^{-j\tau^2} d\tau \tag{11}$$

It is seen that no discontinuities exist for $\phi=\pi$ in (11).

By making a transformation of variables and choosing an appropriate contour, Pauli[3] obtained an expression for Sommerfeld's solution (5) which is expressed in series form as

$$v_{B(r,\phi)} = \frac{2e^{j(\pi/4)}}{n\sqrt{\pi}} \frac{\sin\frac{\pi}{n}\left|\cos\frac{\phi}{2}\right|}{\cos\frac{\pi}{n} - \cos\frac{\phi}{n}} \cdot e^{jkr\cos\phi} \int_{(a\rho)^{1/2}}^{\infty} e^{-j\tau^2} d\tau + \cdots \tag{12}$$

where the higher order terms may be neglected for large kr. In the case of the thin half-plane $(n=2)$, the higher order terms are identically zero and (12) reduces to (9). If the higher order terms may be neglected, the value of v_B converges to one-half the incident field at the shadow boundary or at $\phi=\pi$.

If the assumption that $(a\rho)$ is large is valid, the asymptotic form of (12) which is given in (7) may be used to advantage as

$$v_{B(r,\phi)} = \frac{v_{(\phi)} e^{-j(\rho+\pi/4)}}{\sqrt{2\pi\rho}} \tag{13a}$$

where

$$v_{(\phi)} = \frac{\frac{1}{n}\sin\frac{\pi}{n}}{\cos\frac{\pi}{n} - \cos\frac{\phi}{n}} \tag{13b}$$

and higher order terms are neglected. It should be noted that (13) is valid provided the condition of (8) is satisfied.

The geometrical theory of diffraction developed by Keller[1,2] makes use of the form given in (13) to extend geometrical optics to include diffraction phenomena at edges.

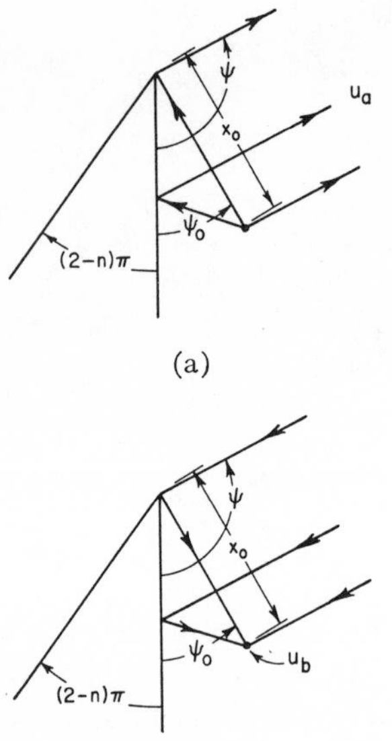

(a)

(b)

Fig. 3. Illustration of reciprocity.

Cylindrical Wave Incidence on a Wedge

Diffraction of a plane wave by a perfectly conducting wedge has been discussed in the preceding section. However, the more general situation of cylindrical wave diffraction by a wedge is of particular importance in the analysis of the horn antenna. The solution for these fields can also be obtained in the familiar formulation of plane wave diffraction theory.

The two-dimensional problem under consideration is illustrated in Fig. 3(a) with the line source located at (x_0, ψ_0). It is convenient to maintain the definitions of Fig. 2, i.e., ψ_0 equals the incident angle and ψ equals the diffraction angle in the direction of the desired field u_a.

Because of the cylindrical nature of the incident field, the plane wave diffraction theory discussed in the previous chapter cannot be directly applied to obtain u_a. However, the solution is obtained from the reciprocal example in Fig. 3(b). With the point of observation and source interchanged, the total fields u_a and u_b are equivalent by the reciprocity principle. The field u_b is now obtained from (1) for a plane wave incident on the wedge at an angle ψ

$$u_b = v_{(x_0,\psi_0-\psi)} \pm v_{(x_0,\psi_0+\psi)} \tag{14}$$

Using the property that

$$v_{(r,\phi)} = v_{(r,-\phi)} \tag{15}$$

the solution for u_a becomes

$$u_a = v_{(x_0,\psi-\psi_0)} \pm v_{(x_0,\psi+\psi_0)} \tag{16}$$

This is the solution for diffraction of a cylindrical wave by a wedge, which may be viewed as being directly obtained from (1) by substituting the radial distance x_0 to the line source for r of the observation point.

Equation (16) represents the field at an infinite distance from the edge but it gives a good angular representation of the field for moderate distances from the edge. The phase reference for (16) is at the edge; the superposition of diffraction from several edges requires the use of a common phase reference.

Plane wave diffraction is now a special case of (16). It is seen that when the line source recedes to infinity, (16) must be evaluated by the form of v_B given in (13). Moreover, the approximation of (13), large akr, may be valid for cylindrical wave diffraction. That is, the diffraction for cylindrical wave incidence is the same as that for plane wave incidence in regions sufficiently removed from any shadow boundary; the region about a shadow boundary in which the two are significantly different depends on the radial distance x_0 to the line source.

Diffraction by a Thick Edge

At higher microwave frequencies, all practical edges usually have significant thicknesses in terms of wavelength, i.e., thicknesses greater than $\lambda/10$. However, no exact solution has been obtained for an edge of finite thickness. Burke and Keller[7] have formulated a solution in which the thick edge is modeled by two 90° wedges as shown in Fig. 4. The first-order diffracted rays are illustrated in Fig. 5. The incident ray from some arbitrary line source is incident only on the visible corner A and is diffracted into the regions of space illustrated. One of these diffracted rays is directed toward corner B, which it illuminates, and is there diffracted into the regions of space as illustrated. One of these rays, diffracted at corner B, now illuminates corner A, and again rays emanate into space as shown. This sequence is then repeated; however, the amplitudes associated with these rays diminish rapidly and usually only the diffracted rays shown in Fig. 5 need be considered.

In the formulation of Burke and Keller, the diffraction coefficients for plane wave incidence were employed, and the value of the field at corner B which is diffracted from corner A was taken as the value of an equivalent plane wave incident on corner B. This method when applied for edge thicknesses on the order of a wavelength does not give good results because the illumination of corner B by the diffracted wave from corner A is that of a cylindrical wave rather than a plane wave. The distinction between cylindrical wave diffraction and plane wave diffraction is great for small edge thicknesses but decreases with increasing edge thickness. It should be noted that for any finite edge thickness, plane wave diffraction is not valid near a shadow boundary.

Morse[8] has introduced a technique in which the diffi-

[7] Burke, J. E., and J. B. Keller, Diffraction by a thick screen, a step and related axially symmetric objects, EDL-E48, Contract DA 36-039-sc-78281, Sylvania Electronic Systems, Mountain View, Calif., Mar 1960.

[8] Morse, B. J., Diffraction by polygonal cylinders, *J. Math. Phys.*. vol 5, Feb 1964, pp 199–214.

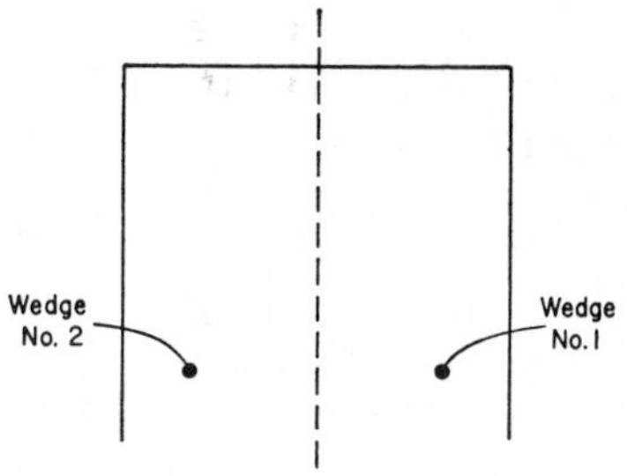

Fig. 4. Model of thick edge.

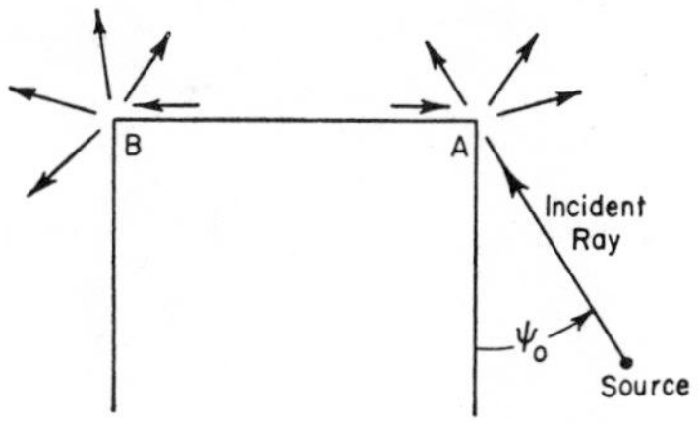

Fig. 5. Cylindrical wave diffraction by a thick edge.

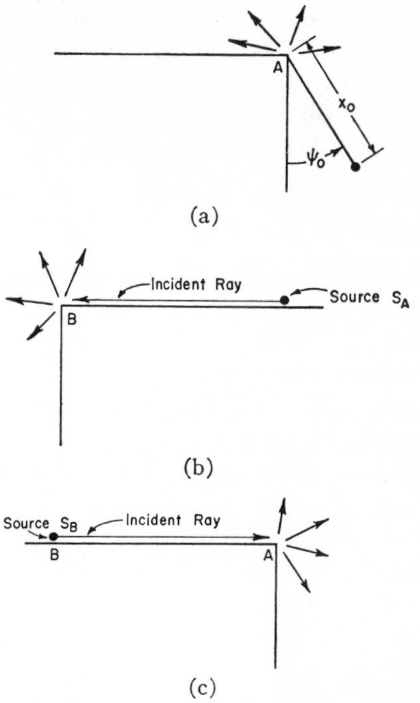

Fig. 6. Construction of diffracted fields by a thick edge.

culty of using plane wave diffraction coefficients for the double diffraction across the edge is overcome by asymptotic expansion of the Green's Theorem Integrals. Effectively, the total field on the edge surfaces is integrated to obtain the diffracted field in regions near multiple diffraction shadow boundaries. However, Morse's equations apply to thick edge diffraction for plane wave incidence but not for cylindrical wave incidence.

The steps employing the diffraction of a cylindrical wave by a 90° wedge to obtain the diffraction by a thick edge are illustrated in Fig. 6. Here a line source located at (x_0, ψ_0) illuminates corner A of a 90° wedge, and the diffracted fields are obtained as previously discussed. It is desired to locate an equivalent source s_A at corner A of such a magnitude that both the original and equivalent sources have identical far fields in the direction of the incident ray of Fig. 6(b). Now when s_A is located at corner A in Fig. 6, either the equivalent source or the original source illuminates corner B with the same field. Diffraction from corner B is readily obtained from Fig. 6(b) and (16). To obtain the next higher, multiple-diffracted field, the same process is applied to Fig. 6(c); that is, an equivalent source s_B is located at corner B such that the far diffracted field of s_A and the far field of the equivalent source are identical in the direction of the incident ray of Fig. 6(c). Now either source, s_B or the diffracted field from s_A, will illuminate corner A with the same intensity. Diffraction from corner A due to the source s_B shown in Fig. 6(c) is readily obtained in the same manner as before. This process is then repeated to obtain higher order, multiple diffracted fields, but usually they are negligible. By summing the appropriate fields, the total diffraction from corners A or B can be obtained in closed form. For instance, for the situation illustrated in Fig. 7, the total diffracted fields are

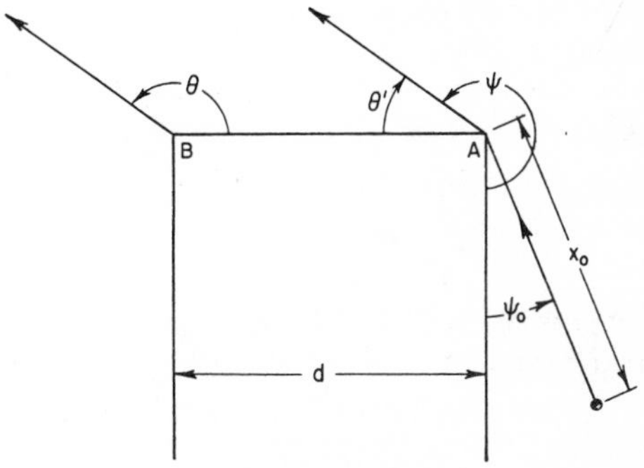

Fig. 7. Coordinate system for cylindrical wave diffracted by a thick edge.

$$v_B = \left(v_{B(x_0,270-\psi_0)} \pm v_{B(x_0,270+\psi_0)}\right) \frac{v_{B(d,\theta)}}{1 - v^2_{B(d,0)}} \cdot \exp(-jkd \cos \theta) \text{ corner } B \qquad (17a)$$

and

$$v_B = \left(v_{B(x_0,270-\psi_0)} \pm v_{B(x_0,270+\psi_0)}\right) \frac{v_{B(d,0)} v_{B(d,\theta')}}{1 - v^2_{B(d,0)}} + \left(v_{B(x_0,\psi-\psi_0)} \pm v_{B(x_0,\psi+\psi_0)}\right) \text{ corner } A \qquad (17b)$$

where the exponential factor in (17a) refers the phase to corner A.

In practical situations, especially for square edges of small thickness, i.e., $d < \lambda/2$, v_B must be evaluated carefully. It will be recalled that $v_{B(r,\phi)}$ is an infinite series given by (12) which converges very rapidly, provided r is sufficiently large. Then only the first term is significant, the higher order terms being negligible. Conversely, for small r, convergence is slower and higher order terms must be included in the computation of

$v_{B(r,\phi)}$. This becomes tedious work, if necessary; and to compound the difficulty, Pauli[3] gives only two higher order terms. Therefore, $v_{B(r,\phi)}$ has not been calculated for very small values of r, i.e., $v_{B(d,\theta')}$, $v_{B(d,\theta)}$, and $v_{B(d,0)}$ cannot be evaluated for $d<\lambda/2$. For the situation in which $d=0$, the solution for the total field in the presence of the infinitesimally thin edge is obtained from (16) with $n=2$.

Application of Theory to the Horn

In the case of the pyramidal horn, the dominant propagating mode within the horn may be approximated as having a spherical phase front with the phase center at the horn throat as shown in Fig. 8; this mode has uniform amplitude in the E plane and a sinusoidal amplitude distribution in the H plane in which the field vanishes at one pair of walls. Thus, only diffraction by the E-plane edges contributes significantly to the E- and H-plane diffraction patterns. This is clearly illustrated in Fig. 9. Here the edge diffraction obeys the extended form of Fermat's principle.[2] To obtain the E-plane pattern, the horn is rotated in a plane perpendicular to the diffracting edges, and only the diffraction from the midpoints contributes to the pattern. Diffraction occurring at all points along the edge contributes to the total H-plane pattern; and non-normal incidence of the incident wave, as in Fig. 9, must be taken into consideration.

Consequently, the E-plane patterns of a pyramidal horn may be treated as the diffraction by two edges illuminated by a line source as illustrated in Fig. 10 for a thin-walled horn and in Fig. 11 for a thick-walled horn.

In the case of the thin-walled horn, the illuminating cylindrical wave and the diffraction from one edge is given by (16) in which the phase is referred to that edge. The diffraction by the other edge may also be obtained from (16), but its phase must be referred to the former edge in order to superimpose these components of diffraction. The E-plane pattern for a horn of length x_0 and a half angle of α as shown in Fig. 10 is thus given by

$$\left\{\begin{matrix}\exp\left[jkx_0\cos(\pi-\alpha+\theta)\right] \\ 0\end{matrix}\right\} + v_{B(x_0,\pi-\alpha+\theta)} + \exp\left[-j2kx_0\sin\alpha\sin\theta\right]v_{B(x_0,\pi-\alpha-\theta)} \quad (18)$$

where the first term represents the geometrical optics rays in the region $|\theta|<\alpha$, and the exponential factors refer the phase to the upper edge. In the regions specified by $90°<|\theta|<180°-\alpha$, one of the diffracted terms drops out because the corresponding rays are shielded by the opposite horn wall.

The procedure for the thick-walled horn is the same as that mentioned previously except that each diffraction term in (18) is replaced by the diffraction by a thick edge as given by (17). In the backlobe regions, the diffraction from the inside corners of the edges do not contribute, and shielding of the outside corners occurs in the same regions as for the thin-walled horn.

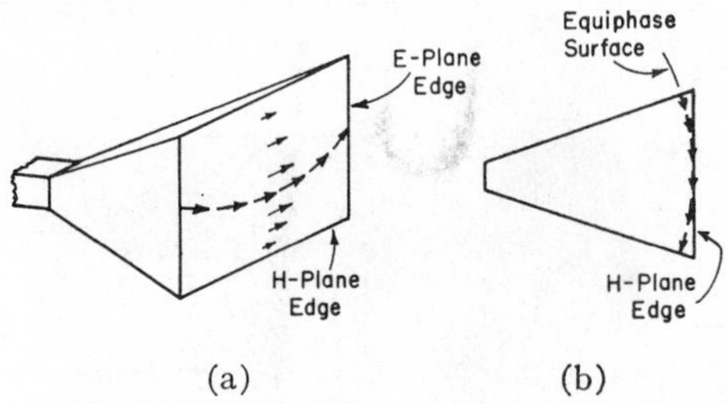

Fig. 8. Orientation of polarization vectors (E field) within horn.

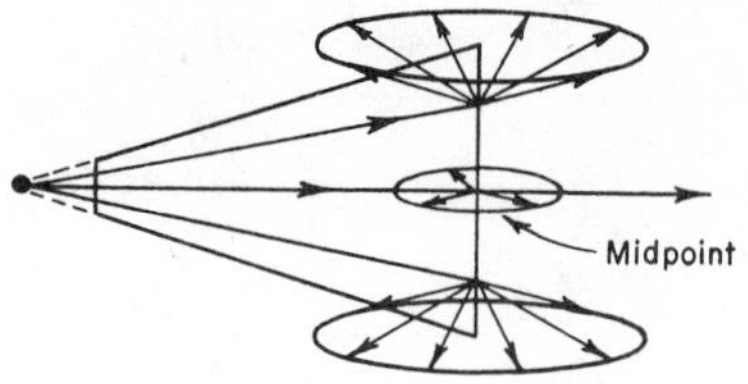

Fig. 9. Diffraction from E-plane edge.

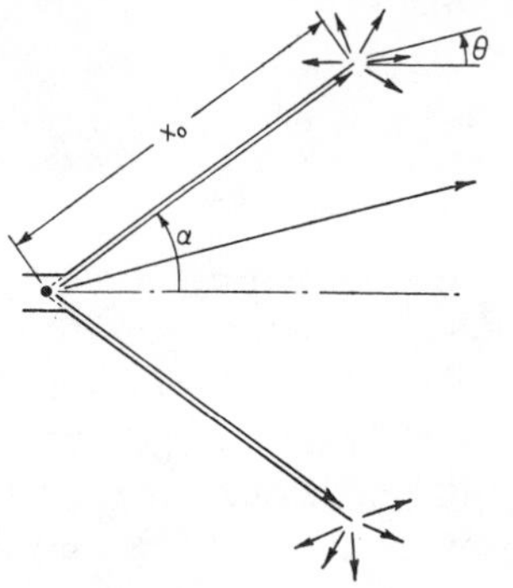

Fig. 10. E-plane cross section of thin-walled horn.

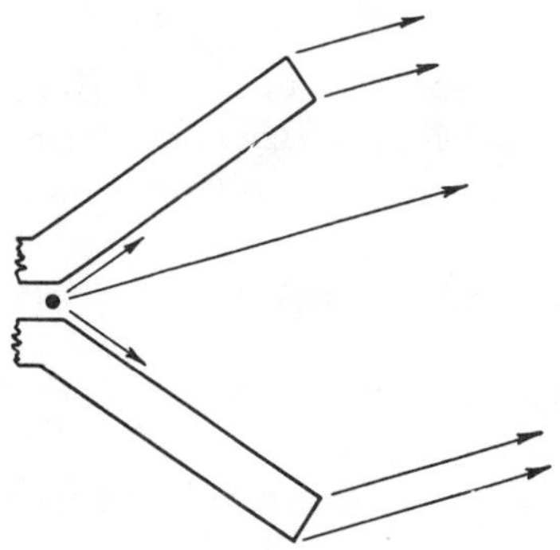

Fig. 11. E-plane cross section of thick-walled horn.

Results

The theory developed in the preceding sections has been applied to the horn antenna of length $x_0=17$ inches and angle $2\alpha=35°$ as shown in Fig. 12. The theoretical patterns are compared with experimental patterns which were measured at 10 Gc/s.

In order to facilitate experimentation, part of the E-plane faces were cut away and 0.015-inch brass sheets were permanently fastened to the horn to fill the cutouts. These brass sheets provide edges thin enough to be equivalent to the thin half-plane equations with $n=2$. Bolts were fastened to the horn edges so that

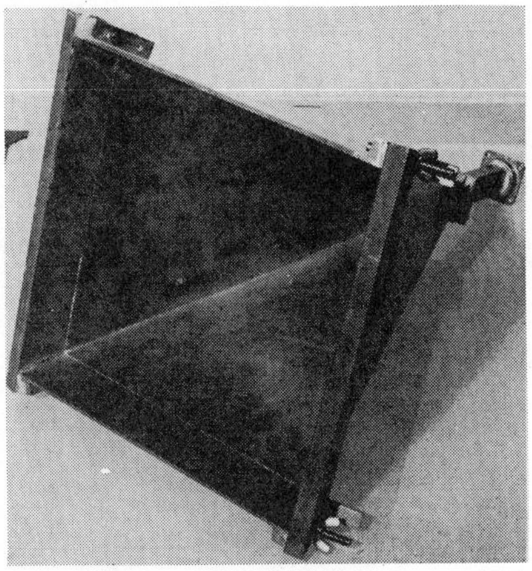

Fig. 12. Pyramidal horn adapted for experiment.

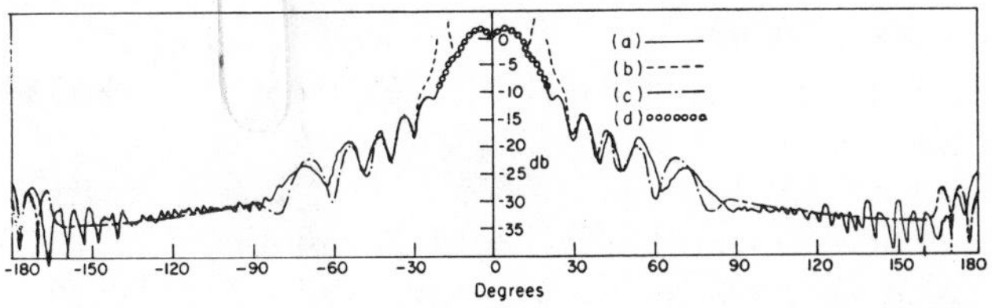

Fig. 13. E-plane pattern of thin-walled horn. (a) Measured pattern, (b) calculated using plane wave diffraction (13), (c) either method of calculation, and (d) calculated using cylindrical wave diffraction (18).

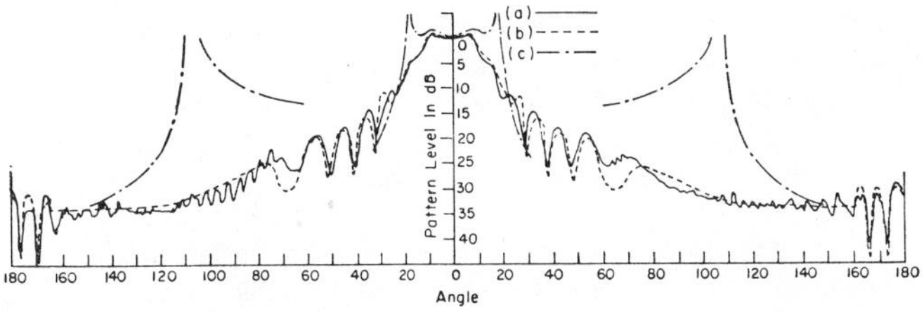

Fig. 14. E-plane pattern of a thick walled horn. (a) Measured pattern, (b) calculated using cylindrical wave diffraction (17), and (c) calculated using plane wave diffraction (13).

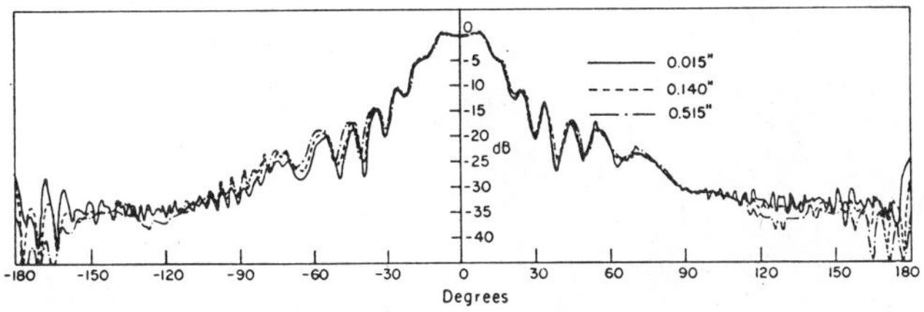

Fig. 15. Comparison of measured horn patterns for various wall thicknesses.

plates of varying thicknesses could be secured on top of the brass sheets, making it possible to vary the edge thickness as shown in Fig. 12.

Figures 13 and 14 compare the measured and calculated patterns for the horn with the thin edge and with an edge thickness of 0.5 inch, respectively. Remarkable agreement between theory and experiment is obtained. Figure 13 shows the results obtained when Keller's Geometrical Theory of Diffraction is employed for the thin edge, and there is very good agreement, except in the immediate regions of the shadow boundary. By this method, the diffraction at the edges is taken as plane wave diffraction. The diffraction at each edge is given by (13) if the incident wave is put in the form

$$\sqrt{x_0}\,\frac{e^{-jk(r'-x_0)}}{\sqrt{r'}} \tag{19}$$

where r' is measured from the horn throat. However, when the method is applied to the thick edge, the region of the shadow boundary dominates the pattern, shown in Fig. 14, rendering this otherwise valuable technique useless for this application.

It should be noted that Morse's[2] treatment of shadow boundaries is not valid for the shadow boundaries of the incident cylindrical wave from the horn throat. Along these boundary directions, which coincide with the horn walls, Morse's technique, as well as Keller's, yields a plane wave field as the diffracted field, i.e., a uniform field with amplitude independent of distance, whereas the technique of this paper gives the diffracted field for cylindrical wave incidence, i.e., proper cylindrical wave dependence.

However, it appears that Morse's technique should be valid for treating the horn if it is viewed as having its two walls formed by two rectangular cylinders. The horn would be viewed as receiving a plane wave from various directions, and the field at the point of contact between the two cylinders should be representative of the horn antenna pattern. The same viewpoint may be applied to the thin-walled horn in order to obtain its pattern by use of Sommerfeld's solution (9), but the concept of diffraction of a cylindrical wave is necessary to treat the thick edge in the manner employed in this paper. Morse's technique does appear to offer an alternate method for treating thick-walled horns.

A comparison of the measured patterns for several edge thicknesses is shown in Fig. 15. There is some distortion of the backlobes, due partly to the presence of the waveguide feed; otherwise, these lobes would have uniform level as predicted in the calculations.

Conclusions

Pauli's equations for diffraction of a plane wave by a perfectly conducting wedge are used in conjunction with the principle of reciprocity to obtain the diffraction of cylindrical waves by a wedge. This development allows the treatment of diffraction by thick edges.

The E-plane pattern of the pyramidal horn is computed by use of these extended diffraction concepts. It has been shown that the radiation of the horn is due to diffraction by the E-plane edges and by direct radiation from the source at the apex of the horn. Theoretical and experimental patterns are in excellent agreement, thus demonstrating that the method for treating diffraction by edges is valid.

The principles employed here are the same as those of Keller's geometrical theory of diffraction. However, application of the diffraction coefficients of this theory is inadequate for treatment of the horn antenna; the use of diffraction of cylindrical waves is necessary. Morse has developed a modification to the geometrical theory of diffraction which permits treatment of thick edges.

Comprehensive Analysis for *E*-Plane of Horn Antennas by Edge Diffraction Theory

J. S. YU, R. C. RUDDUCK, MEMBER, IEEE, AND L. PETERS, JR., SENIOR MEMBER, IEEE

Abstract—Edge diffraction theory is used in analyzing the radiation characteristics of typical horn antennas. The far-sidelobe and backlobe radiation has been solved without employing field equivalence principles which are impractical in the problem.

A corner reflector with a magnetic line source located at the vertex is proposed as a model for the principal *E*-plane radiation of horn antennas. A complete pattern, including multiple interactions and images of induced line sources, is obtained in infinite series form. Diffraction mechanisms are used for appropriate approximations in the computations. The computed patterns are in excellent agreement with measured patterns of typical horn antennas. Radiation intensity of the backlobe relative to mainlobe intensity is obtained as a back-to-front ratio and plotted as a function of antenna dimensions.

I. Introduction

Analytically, the descriptions of the propagating modes in a horn are summarized by Kraus [1]. In general, aperture techniques must be used to calculate the radiation pattern, and it is assumed that the aperture distribution is that of the incident wave and is zero outside the aperture. The patterns thus obtained give satisfactory main lobes and near sidelobes. As for far sidelobes and backlobes, Schelkunoff's equivalence principles could be applied if current distributions on the outer surfaces were known. For a horn antenna, extreme difficulty is involved in accurately describing the current distributions. Furthermore, difficulty would arise in evaluating the consequent surface integrals. The impracticality of the equivalence principles had left radiation problems of the far sidelobes and backlobes still unsolved until edge diffraction techniques were applied [5].

In 1962, Ye Kinber [2] derived horn patterns and the coefficient of coupling between two adjacent horns by diffraction theory. Examples are given for both *E*-plane and *H*-plane patterns, in which discontinuities are pointed out, and emphasis has not been made on side and backlobes. In 1963, Ohba [3] used diffraction theory to compute the radiation pattern in the *H*-plane of a corner reflector. Disagreement was noted as a result of neglecting contributions from the other edges of the corner reflector. Recently, Russo, Rudduck, and Peters [5] employed edge diffraction theory with proper assumptions to obtain *E*-plane patterns of a thin-edged and a thick-edged horn. Only the first-order diffraction terms were used to compute the thin-edged horn patterns. The results, with possible discontinuities left in the side and backlobes, are in good agreement with the measured pattern. Even though the higher-order diffraction terms and the reflections inside the horn are neglected, the combination of the employed concepts and assumptions constitutes a new method of analysis for horn antennas. We shall follow this new method to develop a more complete analysis by including the previously neglected higher-order diffractions and the reflections inside the horn antenna.

Manuscript received August 12, 1965; revised November 4, 1965. The research reported herein was supported in part by Contract AF 30(602)-3269 between Air Force Systems Command, Research and Technology Division, Rome Air Development Center, Griffiss Air Force Base, New York, and the Antenna Laboratory, The Ohio State University Research Foundation, Columbus, Ohio, Project No. 1767.

The authors are with the Antenna Laboratory, Dept. of Electrical Engineering, The Ohio State University, Columbus, Ohio.

II. Radiation Mechanisms

The proposed antenna model used in Russo, Rudduck, and Peters [5] was a corner reflector formed by two perfectly conducting plane walls intersecting at an angle $2\theta_E$ as shown in Fig. 1. If we let the corner reflector be infinite in extent along the z-direction, the problem is thus reduced to a two-dimensional one. The primary source is a magnetic line current assumed at the vertex S. This assumption considerably simplifies treatment in the principal E-plane of a horn antenna fed by a waveguide supporting the TE_{10} mode.

The angular coordinate θ, shown in Fig. 1, is the common reference angle. The angles ψ are the field angles referred to each individual wedge at which diffraction occurs. The angles α are called incident angles of illumination. All the first subscripts refer to the points at which diffraction occurs, while the second subscripts refer to the points of origin of incident rays. This notation will be used throughout the following discussions. There are four wedges (A, B, S, and W) to be treated by diffraction theory. Wedges A and B have zero wedge angle, while wedges S and W have wedge angles of $2\theta_E$ and $2(\pi-\theta_E)$, respectively. The property of symmetry of the reflector will be used to simplify the problem by considering only the upper half of the pattern.

From the assumed magnetic line source at S, a uniform cylindrical wave is radiated in the region $-\theta_E \leq \theta \leq \theta_E$. This uniform cylindrical wave is called the geometrical optics wave which illuminates wedges A and B. The diffractions at A and B caused by this illumination are the first-order diffractions, which are directional cylindrical waves radiated from the wedges. The geometrical optics rays from S and the first-order diffracted rays from A and B are shown in Fig. 2(a). The first-order radiation pattern in the far-field can now be

Reprinted from *IEEE Trans. Antennas Propagat.*, vol. AP-14, pp. 138–149, Mar. 1966.

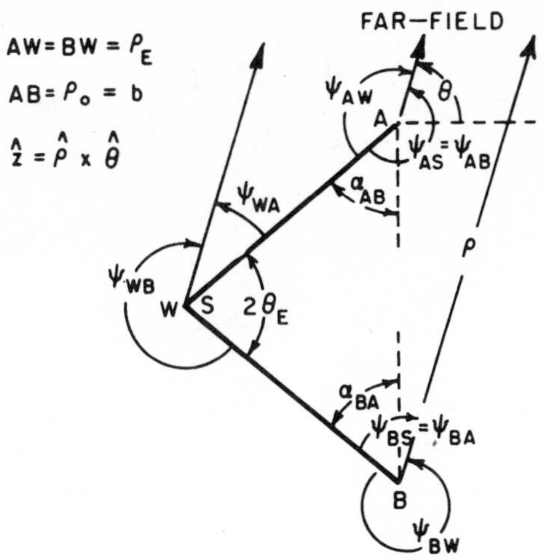

Fig. 1. Corner reflector.

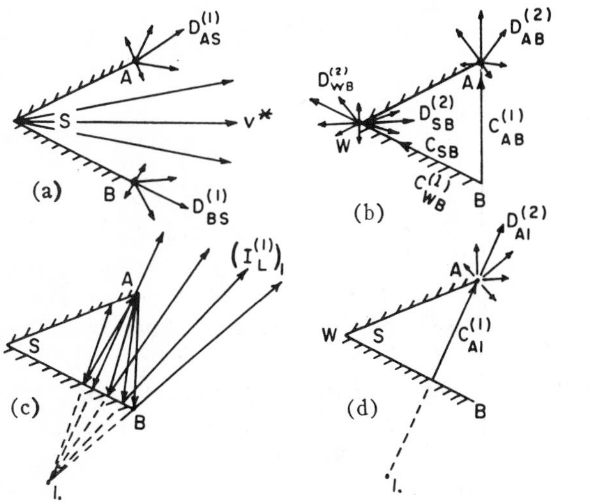

Fig. 2. Radiation mechanism of the antenna model. (a) Direct rays and the first-order diffracted rays due to illimination from primary source at *S*. (b) The second-order diffractions due to the first-order illumination from *B*. (c) The first image in the lower wall due to the first-order diffraction at *A*. (d) The second-order diffraction due to the first image in the lower wall.

obtained by superposition of the far-field intensities of the primary source and the two induced sources. The first-order analysis is presented in Russo, Rudduck, and Peters [5].

To consider the diffraction process further, one can observe from Fig. 2(b) that the induced source at *B* illuminates wedges *A*, *S*, and *W* to give three second-order diffraction terms. In the same manner, the first-order-induced source at *A* illuminates wedges *B*, *S*, and *W* to give three more second-order diffracted waves. These six second-order-induced sources will continue to give third- and higher-order diffraction. The induced intensity becomes smaller with increasing order, and the phase delay of successive illumination can be properly taken into account.

Since the reflector has perfectly conducting walls, the diffracted waves from *A* and *B* are partially reflected by the walls. Some of the first-order diffracted rays from *A* are reflected by the lower wall, as shown in Fig. 2(c). The reflected rays can be described by the method of images.

Figure 2(d) shows that wedge *A* is illuminated by one of the first-order images from the lower wall. The number of images is determined by the flare angle of the reflector. The effects of the reflector walls can then be taken into account by the images and the subsequent diffraction of the images.

When the process of diffraction and reflection described above is completed, the far-field patterns of the reflector antenna can be obtained by superimposing the contributions from the primary source at *S*; the induced sources at *A*, *B*, *S*, and *W*; and the images in both walls. Formulation of the pattern, including all orders of diffraction and reflection, is obtained in Section III.

III. Formulation of Solution in Infinite Series Form

In this formulation the diffraction of a cylindrical wave by a perfectly conducting wedge is employed [4], [5]. Pauli's formulation [6] of Sommerfeld's solution [7] to wedge diffraction of a plane wave permits the diffracted wave to be expressed in terms of Fresnel integrals. The far-zone diffracted waves, both the incident and reflected terms, induced by a uniform cylindrical wave of unit intensity from a line source, can be written as

$$v_B(\rho, \phi^{i,r}, n) = \frac{\operatorname{Exp}\left\{j\left(\frac{\pi}{4} + k\rho\cos\phi^{i,r}\right)\right\}}{\sqrt{\pi}} \cdot \left[\frac{2\left|\cos\frac{\phi^{i,r}}{2}\right|\sin\frac{\pi}{n}}{n\left(\cos\frac{\pi}{n} - \cos\frac{\phi^{i,r}}{n}\right)}\int_{\sqrt{ak\rho}}^{\infty} e^{-j\tau}\,d\tau + \begin{pmatrix}\text{higher-order terms negligible}\\ \text{for large } k\rho \text{ or } n \text{ very close to } 2\end{pmatrix}\right] \tag{1}$$

with

$$a = 1 + \cos\phi^{i,r}. \tag{2}$$

The propagation factor $R^{-1/2}$ Exp $(-jkR)$ where R is the distance of the far-field point from the edge is suppressed in (1). The quantity ρ is the distance from the edge to the source point. The angles $\phi^{i,r}$ are the diffraction-field angles of the incident and reflected terms, respectively. The value of n is obtained by setting the wedge angle equal to $(2-n)\pi$. The solution v_B is a directional cylindrical wave radiated from the edge of the wedge. It may, therefore, be considered that a directional line source is induced at the edge of the wedge. The concept of induced line source is good in general except when n is quite different from 2 and $k\rho$ is very small.

The method of images is also needed in the following formulation. For our antenna model, the reflection of waves by the walls can be described by image-waves [4]. The descriptions are strictly of geometrical considerations. We shall use only the results for this paper.

First, referring to Figs. 1 and 2(a), the geometrical optics wave radiated from the primary source S is a uniform cylindrical wave, normalized as

$$v^*(\theta) = 1, \qquad -\theta_E \le \theta \le +\theta_E, \tag{3}$$

where v^* has point S as phase-reference, and outside the defined region v^* is identically zero. The cylindrical-wave propagation factor $R^{-1/2}$ Exp $(-jkR)$ to the far-field is suppressed in (3) because only the angular dependence is of interest.

Wedges A and B are illuminated by the cylindrical wave from S with zero incident-angle. Since there is no reflection term, the diffracted waves from A and B have only one term.

Excluding the portion of waves diffracted into the corner reflector, the waves directly diffracted to the far-field can be written from (1) as

$$D_{AS}^{(1)} = v_B(\rho_E, \pi - \theta_E + \theta, 2), \; -\frac{\pi}{2} \le \theta \le (\pi + \theta_E), \tag{4a}$$

$$D_{BS}^{(1)} = v_B(\rho_E, \pi - \theta_E - \theta, 2), \; \frac{\pi}{2} \ge \theta \ge -(\pi + \theta_E), \tag{4b}$$

where D_{AS} and D_{BS} designate diffraction at A and B because of illumination from S. The superscript (1) means first-order diffraction. The expressions of ϕ's in terms of θ can be obtained from Fig. 1. The argument n is equal to 2 for both A and B because they have zero wedge angle. It should be noted that the notation v_B follows the form of the original solution and the subscript B has no connection with the wedge B.

The first-order radiation patterns, neglecting the reflections inside the corner reflector, can now be obtained by simply superimposing the terms in (3) and (4). The discontinuities in v^* at $\theta = \pm\theta_E$ in (3) are eliminated by $D_{AS}^{(1)}$ and $D_{BS}^{(1)}$, respectively. Although the pattern is continuous at $\theta = \pm\theta_E$, two sets of new discontinuities at $\theta = \pm\pi/2$ and $\pm(\pi+\theta_E)$ are observed in (4). Therefore, the first-order pattern, in general, has discontinuities at these directions.

Let us next examine the reflections of the first-order rays diffracted into the reflector. Since the diffracted waves from A and B are symmetrical with respect to $\theta=0$, as can be seen from (4), the treatment of the image-waves from the reflector can be simplified. The images are formed symmetrically in the lower and upper walls. The image waves from the two walls can be obtained by replacing θ of $D_{AS}^{(1)}$ and $D_{BS}^{(1)}$ in (4) by $(-2i\theta_E - \theta)$ and $(2i\theta_E - \theta)$, respectively, giving

$$(I_L^{(1)})_i = v_B(\rho_E, \pi - (2i+1)\theta_E - \theta, 2),$$

$$\frac{\pi}{2} - (i+1)\theta_E \le \theta \le \frac{\pi}{2} - i\theta_E; \tag{5a}$$

$$(I_U^{(1)})_i = v_B(\rho_E, \pi - (2i+1)\theta_E + \theta, 2),$$

$$-\left[\frac{\pi}{2} - (i+1)\theta_E\right] \ge \theta \ge -\left[\frac{\pi}{2} - i\theta_E\right];$$

$$i = 1, 2, 3 \cdots h; \tag{5b}$$

and

$$h(\text{the largest integer}) \le \frac{\pi}{2\theta_E},$$

where the subscripts L and U indicate that the image terms are from the lower and the upper walls, respectively. The number of images in each wall is equal to the largest integer h which is less than or equal to $\pi/2\theta_E$. When the ratio $\pi/2\theta_E$ is not an integer, the valid region for the last images should be modified to

$$\frac{\pi}{2} - (h+1)\theta_E \le \theta \le \pi - (2h+1)\theta_E \quad \text{for the lower wall,}$$

and

$$-\left[\frac{\pi}{2} - (h+1)\theta_E\right] \ge \theta \ge -[\pi - (2h+1)\theta_E]$$

for the upper wall.

Each term in (5) has its properly defined regions and is set zero outside the region. The first image in the lower wall, caused by the first-order-diffracted rays from A, is shown in Fig. 2(c). Figure 3 shows the images in the lower wall for $h=4$. It is noted that the true image waves of the diffracted waves from A are those with i odd in the lower wall and i even in the upper wall.

Descriptions of the first-order diffracted waves from A and B and their reflected waves have been completed above. The higher-order terms to be treated in the following discussion are necessary for cases in which small dimensions are encountered or high accuracy is desired. Physically, the higher-order terms describe the effects of illumination of edges by the lower-order-induced sources and their images. Mathematically, they are required to overcome the discontinuities of the lower-order terms in the radiation pattern. Taking the two first-order diffraction terms in (4), for instance, the discontinuities mentioned earlier can only be eliminated by taking into account the second-order diffraction in the specified directions.

At $\theta=\pi/2$, wedge A is illuminated by the first-order-induced source at B in (4b). This intensity of illumination from B to A is called the first-order coupling coefficient,

$$C_{AB}^{(1)} = D_{BS}^{(1)}\left(\theta = \frac{\pi}{2}\right),$$

as shown in Fig. 2(b). Because of symmetry, the first-order coupling coefficient from A to B in the direction $\theta = -\pi/2$ is equal to $C_{AB}^{(1)}$. Therefore, using (4), we have

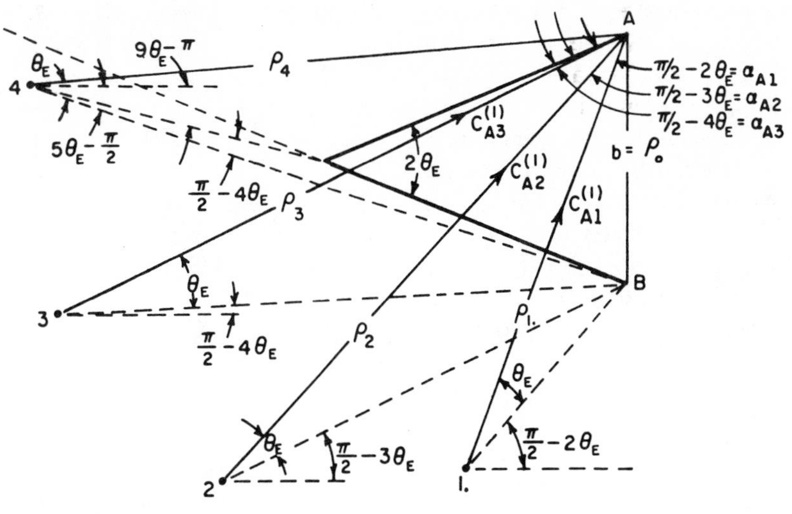

Fig. 3. Four images in the lower wall.

$$C_{AB}^{(1)} = C_{BA}^{(1)} = v_B\left(\rho_E, \frac{\pi}{2} - \theta_E, 2\right). \quad (6)$$

Similarly, wedge W is illuminated by both A and B at $\theta = \pm(\pi+\theta_E)$, respectively. The coupling coefficients can be obtained in the same manner as

$$C_{WA}^{(1)} = C_{WB}^{(1)} = v_B(\rho_E, 2\pi, 2). \quad (7)$$

Since the diffracted waves are slowly varying functions in the neighborhood of a certain angle, it is a good approximation that wedges A, B, and W are illuminated by uniform cylindrical waves of the intensities shown in (6) and (7). Under this assumption, the second-order diffracted waves can be obtained as

$$D_{AB}^{(2)} = C_{AB}^{(1)}\left[v_B\left(b, \frac{\pi}{2} + \theta, 2\right) + v_B\left(b, \frac{3\pi}{2} - 2\theta_E + \theta, 2\right)\right],$$
$$-\frac{\pi}{2} \leq \theta \leq \pi + \theta_E; \quad (8a)$$

$$D_{BA}^{(2)} = C_{BA}^{(1)}\left[v_B\left(b, \frac{\pi}{2} - \theta, 2\right) + v_B\left(b, \frac{3\pi}{2} - 2\theta_E - \theta, 2\right)\right],$$
$$\frac{\pi}{2} \geq \theta \geq -(\pi + \theta_E); \quad (8b)$$

$$D_{WA}^{(2)} = C_{WA}^{(1)}[v_B(\rho_E, -\theta_E + \theta, n_W],$$
$$\theta_E \leq \theta \leq 2\pi - \theta_E; \quad (8c)$$

$$D_{WB}^{(2)} = C_{WB}^{(1)}[v_B(\rho_E, 2\pi - \theta_E - \theta, n_W)],$$
$$-\theta_E \geq \theta \geq -(2\pi - \theta_E), \quad (8d)$$

and

$$n_W = 2 - \frac{2\theta_E}{\pi} \quad (8e)$$

where the arguments used can be obtained from Fig. 1.

Next, we note in (5) that the image waves are discontinuous at angles

$$\theta = \pm\left(\frac{\pi}{2} - i\theta_E\right), \qquad i = 1, 2, 3 \cdots (h-1),$$

at which the wedges A and B are illuminated by the rays from images of lower and upper walls, respectively. Figure 3 shows the geometry of the images with $h=4$ in the lower wall. The coupling coefficients from the images to wedge A can be obtained from (5) as

$$C_{A_i}^{(1)} = I_L^{(1)}\left(\theta = \frac{\pi}{2} - i\theta_E\right), \quad i = 1, 2, \cdots, (h-1).$$

By symmetry, the coupling coefficients from the images in the upper wall to wedge B are equal to $C_{A_i}^{(1)}$ as

$$C_{A_i}^{(1)} = C_{B_i}^{(1)} = v_B\left(\rho_E, \frac{\pi}{2} - (i+1)\theta_E, 2\right)$$
$$i = 1, 2, \cdots (h-1). \quad (9)$$

The second-order diffraction at A and B illuminated by the images can now be written as

$$D_{A_i}^{(2)} = C_{A_i}^{(1)}\left[v_B\left(\rho_i, \frac{\pi}{2} + i\theta_E + \theta, 2\right) + v_B\left(\rho_i, \frac{3\pi}{2} - (i+2)\theta_E + \theta, 2\right)\right]$$
$$-\frac{\pi}{2} \leq \theta \leq \pi + \theta_E, \quad (10a)$$

$$D_{B_i}^{(2)} = C_{B_i}^{(2)}\left[v_B\left(\rho_i, \frac{\pi}{2} + i\theta_E - \theta, 2\right) + v_B\left(\rho_i, \frac{3\pi}{2} - (i+2)\theta_E - \theta, 2\right)\right]$$
$$\frac{\pi}{2} \geq \theta \geq -(\pi + \theta_E), \quad (10b)$$

$$\rho_i = \rho_{i-1} \cos \theta_{E+\rho_0} \cos i\theta_E,$$

and

$$i = 1, 2, \cdots, (h-1), \tag{10c}$$

where the arguments can be obtained by using Fig. 3 as reference. The second-order diffraction terms obtained in (10) are appropriately arranged for each boundary of the defined regions in (5), except that the last boundary is given by $\theta = \pm(\pi/2-(h+1)\theta_E)$ if $\pi/2\theta_E$ is an integer, or $\theta = \pm(\pi-(2h+1)\theta_E)$ if $\pi/2\theta_E$ is not an integer. The boundaries, in either case, correspond to the directions in which wedge S is illuminated by the induced sources at A and B. Therefore, the coupling coefficients from A and B to S can be obtained from (5) by symmetry as

$$C_{SA}^{(1)} = C_{SB}^{(1)} = v_B(\rho_E, 0, 2), \tag{11}$$

which gives rise to the second-order diffraction at wedge S as

$$\left.\begin{aligned} D_{SA}^{(2)} &= C_{SA}^{(1)}[v_B(\rho_E, \theta_E-\theta, n_S)] \quad (12a)\\ D_{SB}^{(2)} &= C_{SB}^{(1)}[v_B(\rho_E, \theta_E+\theta, n_S)] \quad (12b)\end{aligned}\right\} -\theta_E \le \theta \le +\theta_E,$$

and

$$n_S = 2 - n_W = \frac{2\theta_E}{\pi}\cdot \tag{12c}$$

Now, we have completed the descriptions of all second-order diffractions which physically take into account the effects of illumination by the first-order-induced sources and mathematically eliminate all the first-order discontinuities. Summing up the second-order diffraction at A, B, W, and S gives

$$D_A^{(2)} = D_{AB}^{(2)} + \sum_{i=1}^{h-1} D_{A_i}^{(2)}, \qquad -\frac{\pi}{2} \le \theta \le \pi + \theta_E; \tag{13a}$$

$$D_B^{(2)} = D_{BA}^{(2)} + \sum_{i=1}^{h-1} D_{B_i}^{(2)}, \qquad \frac{\pi}{2} \ge \theta \ge -(\pi + \theta_E); \tag{13b}$$

$$D_W^{(2)} = D_{WA}^{(2)} + D_{WB}^{(2)}, \qquad \theta_E \le \theta \le -\theta_E; \tag{13c}$$

$$D_S^{(2)} = D_{SA}^{(2)} + D_{SB}^{(2)}, \qquad -\theta_E \le \theta \le \theta_E, \tag{13d}$$

where (8), (10), and (12) can be used for computation. Following the same procedure used to obtain (5), the second-order image waves from the lower and upper walls can be obtained as

$$\begin{aligned}(I_L^{(2)})i = C_{AB}^{(1)}\Big[&v_B\Big(b, \frac{\pi}{2} - 2i\theta_E - \theta, 2\Big) + v_B\Big(b, \frac{3\pi}{2} - 2(i+1)\theta_E - \theta, 2\Big)\Big]\\ &+ \sum_{k=1}^{h-1} C_{Ak}\Big[v_B\Big(\rho_k, \frac{\pi}{2} - i\theta_E - \theta, 2\Big) + v_B\Big(\rho_k, \frac{3\pi}{2} - (3i+2)\theta_E - \theta, 2\Big)\Big],\end{aligned}$$

$$\frac{\pi}{2} - (i+1)\theta_E \le \theta \le \frac{\pi}{2} - i\theta_E; \tag{14a}$$

$$\begin{aligned}(I_U^{(2)})i = C_{BA}^{(1)}\Big[&v_B\Big(b, \frac{\pi}{2} - 2i\theta_E + \theta, 2\Big) + v_B\Big(b, \frac{3\pi}{2} - 2(i+1)\theta_E + \theta, 2\Big)\Big]\\ &+ \sum_{k=1}^{h-1} C_{Bk}\Big[v_B\Big(\rho_k, \frac{\pi}{2} - i\theta_E + \theta, 2\Big) + v_B\Big(\rho_k, \frac{3\pi}{2} - (3i+2)\theta_E + \theta, 2\Big)\Big],\end{aligned}$$

$$-\Big[\frac{\pi}{2} - (i+1)\theta_E\Big] \ge \theta \ge -\Big[\frac{\pi}{2} - i\theta_E\Big]; \tag{14b}$$

and

$$i = 1, 2, 3 \cdots h,$$

where the θ of $D_A^{(2)}$ and $D_B^{(2)}$ in (13) have been replaced by $(\mp 2i\theta_E - \theta)$, respectively. Note that the boundary of the last image $i = h$ should follow (4), if $\pi/2\theta_E$ is not exactly an integer.

We have observed above that while the first-order discontinuities are eliminated by the inclusion of second-order diffractions, new discontinuities occur again at the boundaries of the regions defined in (13) and (14). These second-order discontinuities can be eliminated only by introducing third-order diffraction. The higher the order of diffraction the smaller will be the magnitude of discontinuities. It is theoretically possible to consider the order of diffraction as high as desired. In other words, the magnitude of each discontinuity can be made negligibly small if sufficient orders of diffraction are included. For completeness, the iterative formulas for all possible higher-order diffractions are presented in the Appendix.

The total far-field pattern of the corner reflector can now be obtained by superposition of all terms presented in the Appendix. Taking wedge A as a common phase reference, and considering only the upper-half region, $0 \le \theta \le \pi$, the total far-field $u(\theta)$ can be written from (23) as:

$$u(\theta) = \left[v^* + \sum_{m=2}^{\infty} D_S{}^{(m)}\right] y_{AS} + \left[\sum_{m=1}^{\infty} D_A{}^{(m)}\right]$$
$$+ \left[\sum_{m=1}^{\infty} D_B{}^{(m)}\right] y_{AB} + \left[\sum_{m=2}^{\infty} D_W{}^{(m)}\right] y_{AW}$$
$$+ \sum_{i=1}^{h}\left[\sum_{m=1}^{\infty} (I_L{}^{(m)})i\right] y_{Ai}$$
$$+ \left[\sum_{m=1}^{\infty} (I_U{}^{(m)})h\right] y_{Bh} y_{AB}, \qquad (15)$$

where the last images in the upper wall are included because in general they may contribute to the upper-half region. The local phase factors referred to A can be written from Figs. 1 and 3 as

$$y_{AS} = \text{Exp.}\,[-j2\pi\rho_E \cos(-\theta_E + \theta)],$$
$$y_{AB} = \text{Exp.}\,[-j2\pi b \sin\theta],$$
$$y_{AW} = \text{Exp.}\,[-j2\pi\rho_E \cos(\theta_E - \theta)] = y_{AS},$$
$$y_{Ai} = \text{Exp.}\,[-j2\pi\rho_i \sin(i\theta_E + \theta)], \qquad (16)$$

and

$$y_{Bh} = \text{Exp.}\,[-j2\pi\rho_i \sin(h\theta_E - \theta)].$$

IV. The Approximated Solutions

For the idealized corner reflector in Fig. 1, the pattern can generally be calculated by (15) as accurately as desired. The fundamental limitation of the edge diffraction method is the approximation of the multiple diffraction as omnidirectional line sources. However, this limitation will rarely be encountered for the symmetrical corner reflector of typical dimensions. Since the contributions of the higher-order terms to the pattern decrease with increasing order, computations may be made by including only those terms which are significant in their defined regions. The following approximations are made to obtain a pattern including only significant higher-order terms.

The total contribution from wedge S is given by the first term of (15) which contains diffraction terms equal or higher than the second-order. For typical dimensions, these diffraction terms are negligibly small as compared to v^* of unit intensity. Therefore, for all practical purposes, the first term of (15) may simply be approximated by v^* alone. In the following three terms in (15), the second-order diffraction should be retained for calculation because their regions include side- and backlobes in which v^* is absent. The image terms in (15) contribute both to the regions of main- and sidelobes. Therefore, approximation of images should, in theory, be made individually. We shall instead treat the images of the same order as a group and assume that only the first-order images have significant contribution to the pattern.

Based on the approximations mentioned above the pattern of the corner reflector can now be obtained approximately from (15) as:

$$u(\theta) \approx [v^*] y_{AS} + \left[D_{AS}{}^{(1)} + D_{AB}{}^{(2)} + \sum_{i=1}^{h-1} D_{Ai}{}^{(2)}\right]$$
$$+ \left[D_{BS}{}^{(1)} + D_{BA}{}^{(2)} + \sum_{i=1}^{h-1} D_{Bi}{}^{(2)}\right] y_{AB}$$
$$+ [D_{WA}{}^{(2)} + D_{WB}{}^{(2)}] y_{AW}$$
$$+ \sum_{i=1}^{h} [I_L{}^{(1)})_i] y_{Ai} + [(I_U{}^{(1)})_h] y_{Bh} y_{AB}. \qquad (17)$$

Since this is an approximated pattern, discontinuities are expected to be increasingly noticeable with decreasing size of the corner reflector. Let us examine, term by term, the continuity of (17) in the upper-half region $0 \leq \theta \leq \pi$. At $\theta = \theta_E$, the discontinuity of v^* is eliminated by $D_{AS}{}^{(1)}$. At $\theta = \pi/2$, the discontinuity of $D_{BS}{}^{(1)}$ is eliminated by $D_{AB}{}^{(2)}$, but there are no higher-order terms included in (17) to compensate for the discontinuities of $D_{BA}{}^{(2)}$ and $D_{Bi}{}^{(2)}$, with $i = 1, 2, \cdots, (h-1)$. Similarly, at $\theta = -(\pi + \theta_E)$, the discontinuity of $D_{BS}{}^{(1)}$ is eliminated by $D_{WB}{}^{(2)}$, but those of $D_{BA}{}^{(2)}$ and $D_{Bi}{}^{(2)}$, with $i = 1, 2, \cdots, (h-1)$, are left uncompensated. The discontinuities at $\theta = \pi/2 - i\theta_E$ of $(I_L{}^{(1)})i$ are all eliminated by $D_{Ai}{}^{(2)}$ and $D_{Bi}{}^{(2)}$, with $i = 1, 2, \cdots, (h-1)$. The discontinuity of $(I_U{}^{(1)})h$ takes place in the defined regions of v^* and is usually unnoticeably small. The discontinuities of $D_{WA}{}^{(2)}$ and $D_{WB}{}^{(2)}$ at $\theta = \theta_E$ are also unnoticeably small for a typical corner reflector.

Within the accuracy of the approximations made to obtain (17), it is desirable to have the pattern continuous in the entire region. To accomplish this, the second-order discontinuities at $\theta = \pi/2$ and $-(\pi + \theta_E)$ mentioned above need to be eliminated. The coupling coefficients from B to A resulting from the second-order-induced sources at B can be obtained from (13b) as:

$$C_{AB}{}^{(2)} = D_B{}^{(2)}\left(\theta = \frac{\pi}{2}\right)$$
$$= C_{BA}{}^{(1)} C_{ABA} + \sum_{i=1}^{h-1} C_{Bi}{}^{(1)} C_{ABi} \qquad (18a)$$

with

$$C_{ABA} = v_B(b, 0, 2) + v_B(b, \pi - 2\theta_E, 2) \qquad (18b)$$
$$C_{ABi} = v_B(\rho_i, i\theta_E, 2) + v_B(\rho_i, \pi - (i+2)\theta_E, 2), \qquad (18c)$$

where (8b) and (10b) are used. Because of the interaction between A and B by $C_{AB}{}^{(2)}$, a third-order difraction can be written for A and B with the same defined region in (13). If the process of interaction between A and B continues to infinite order, a coupling coefficient can be obtained [5] in closed form as

$$C_{AB} = \frac{C_{AB}^{(1)} + \sum_{i=1}^{h-1} C_{Ai}^{(1)} C_{ABi}}{1 - C_{ABA}}, \quad (19)$$

where the property of symmetry is used and C_{ABA} and C_{ABi} are given from (18). The continuity of the total pattern at $\theta=\pi/2$ is now ensured by using C_{AB} instead of $C_{AB}^{(1)}$ for $D_{AB}^{(2)}$ and $D_{BA}^{(2)}$ in (17) as

$$D_{AB} = C_{AB}\left[v_B\left(b, \frac{\pi}{2} + \theta, 2\right) + v_B\left(b, \frac{3\pi}{2} - 2\theta_E + \theta, 2\right)\right], \quad 0 \leq \theta \leq \pi, \quad (20a)$$

and

$$D_{BA} = C_{AB}\left[v_B\left(b, \frac{\pi}{2} - \theta, 2\right) + v_B\left(b, \frac{3\pi}{2} - 2\theta_E - \theta, 2\right)\right] \quad \begin{cases} 0 \leq \theta \leq \frac{\pi}{2} \\ -(\pi + \theta_E) \leq \theta \leq \pi, \end{cases} \quad (20b)$$

where the v_B terms in (8) are used and the regions are restricted to the upper-half region.

As a consequence of the modified equations in (20), the uncompensated terms at $\theta = -(\pi+\theta_E)$ are now D_{BA} and $D_{Bi}^{(2)}$, with $i=1, 2 \cdots (h-1)$. The coupling coefficient from B to W resulting from these terms can be written from (20) and (10) as

$$C_{WB}' = D_{BA}(\theta = -(\pi + \theta_E)) + \sum_{i=1}^{h-1} D_{Bi}^{(2)}(\theta = -(\pi+\theta_E)),$$

$$\begin{aligned} C_{WA}' &= D_{AB}(\theta = \pi + \theta_E) + \sum_{i=1}^{h-1} D_{Ai}^{(2)}(\theta = \pi + \theta_E) \\ &= C_{AB}\left[v_B\left(b, \frac{3\pi}{2} + \theta_E, 2\right) + v_B\left(b, \frac{5\pi}{2} - \theta_E, 2\right)\right] \\ &\quad + \sum_{i=1}^{h-1} C_{Ai}^{(1)}\left[v_B\left(\rho_i, \frac{3\pi}{2} + (i+1)\theta_E, 2\right) + v_B\left(\rho_i, \frac{5\pi}{2} - (i+1)\theta_E, 2\right)\right], \end{aligned}$$

which is a new coupling coefficient to ensure the continuity of the total pattern at $\theta = -(\pi+\theta_E)$ or $\pi - \theta_E$. Adding this new coupling coefficient to $C_{WA}^{(1)}$ in (8c), the diffracted fields at W are modified as

$$\left.\begin{aligned} D_{WA} &= C_{WA}[v_B(\rho_E, -\theta_E + \theta, n_W)] \\ D_{WB} &= C_{WA}[v_B(\rho_E, 2\pi - \theta_E - \theta, n_W)] \end{aligned}\right\}, \quad \theta_E \leq \theta \leq \pi, \quad (21)$$

where

$$C_{WA} = C_{WA(1)} + C_{WA}'.$$

Using (20) and (21), an approximated "continuous" pattern can be finally written from (17) as

$$\begin{aligned} u(\theta) &= [v^*]y_{AS} + \left[D_{AS}^{(1)} + D_{AB} + \sum_{i=1}^{h-1} D_{Ai}^{(2)}\right] \\ &\quad + \left[D_{BS}^{(1)} + D_{BA} + \sum_{i=1}^{h-1} D_{Bi}^{(2)}\right] y_{AB} \\ &\quad + [D_{AW} + D_{BW}]y_{AW} \\ &\quad + \sum_{i=1}^{h} [(I_L^{(1)})_i]y_{Ai} + [(I_U^{(1)})_i]y_{Bh}y_{AB}. \end{aligned} \quad (22)$$

For typical dimensions of a corner reflector (22), in general, gives excellent prediction of the radiation pattern. Examples are given in Section V.

V. Computed Patterns Compared with Measured Patterns of Horn Antennas

To illustrate the validity of the corner reflector as a model of the pyramidal horn antenna fed by a waveguide supporting TE_{10} mode, (22) is computed and compared with measured patterns. Figure 4 shows the experimental setup of a horn antenna in which the idealized model is the corner reflector ASB used to derive (22). The associated waveguide and the calibrated attenuator and diode detector are not considered in pattern prediction.

First, consider a horn antenna of $\rho_E = 41.3$ cm and $2\theta_E = 35°$ which is fed by a waveguide propagating the TE_{10} mode at 9.8 Gc/s. The horn length ρ_E, in terms of wavelength, is equal to 13.5λ. The measured far-field pattern is shown in Fig. 5. The pattern computed by (22) is shown displaced 5 dB below the measured pattern. Comparison of two patterns shows excellent agreement in the overall lobe structure. The small deviation of relative field intensity in the region $50° < \theta < 80°$ is primarily due to the approximation that the second- and higher-order images are negligible. The presence of the waveguide and the associated attenuator and detector shown in Fig. 4 is responsible for the interference in the region $80° < \theta < 180°$ of the measured pattern. For comparison, the pattern computed by only first-order diffraction, treated in Russo, Rudduck, and Peters [5], is plotted displaced 5 dB above the measured pattern. As mentioned earlier, the discontinuities at $\theta = 90°$ and $(180° - \theta_E)$ are expected in the first-order pattern.

When the frequency is increased corresponding to $\rho_E = 24.8\lambda$ for the same horn, the three patterns are as shown in Fig. 6. The same conclusions drawn for Fig. 5 remain true, except that the interference from the waveguide and the associated structure becomes larger because the physical size is larger in terms of wavelength. In Fig. 7, three patterns are shown for a small horn antenna of $\rho_E = 5.61\lambda$ and $2\theta_E = 21.2°$. Although the overall lobe structure is still in good agreement with the measured pattern, a larger deviation in intensity level is observed around $\theta = 80°$ of the pattern by (22). This disagreement results because the second-order image terms neglected are not negligibly small for small horns. Therefore, better patterns can be obtained for small horns by including the second-order image terms and their subsequent effects on the total pattern.

The three examples presented above have demonstrated the accuracy of (22) for pattern computations of typical horn antennas. The accuracy of the experimental measurements is assumed to have 1 dB fluctuation when the intensity is around 40 dB below the reference intensity. In view of this, (22) is sufficient for horn antennas of typical dimensions. When ρ_E and θ_E become smaller, it is easily observed from Fig. 7 that the second-order image terms in (14) should be included to ensure good prediction around the region $\theta = 90° - \theta_E$.

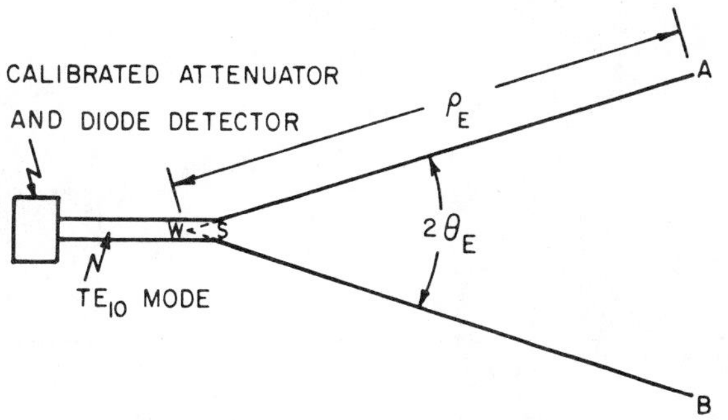

Fig. 4. The *E*-plane of a horn antenna.

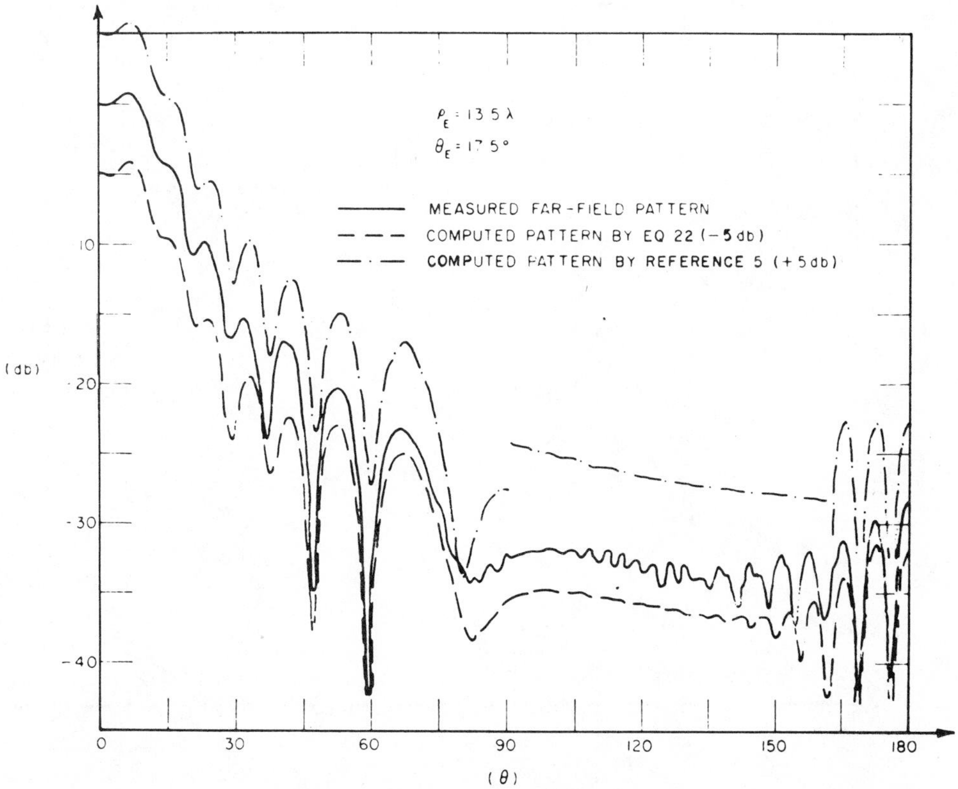

Fig. 5 A comparison of patterns.

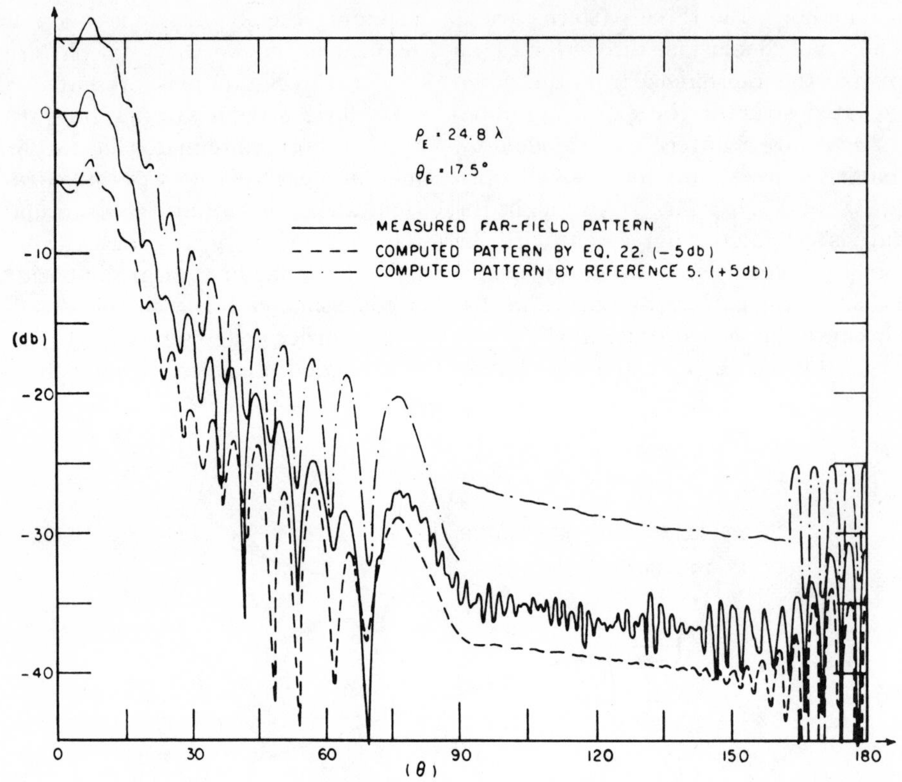

Fig. 6. A comparison of patterns.

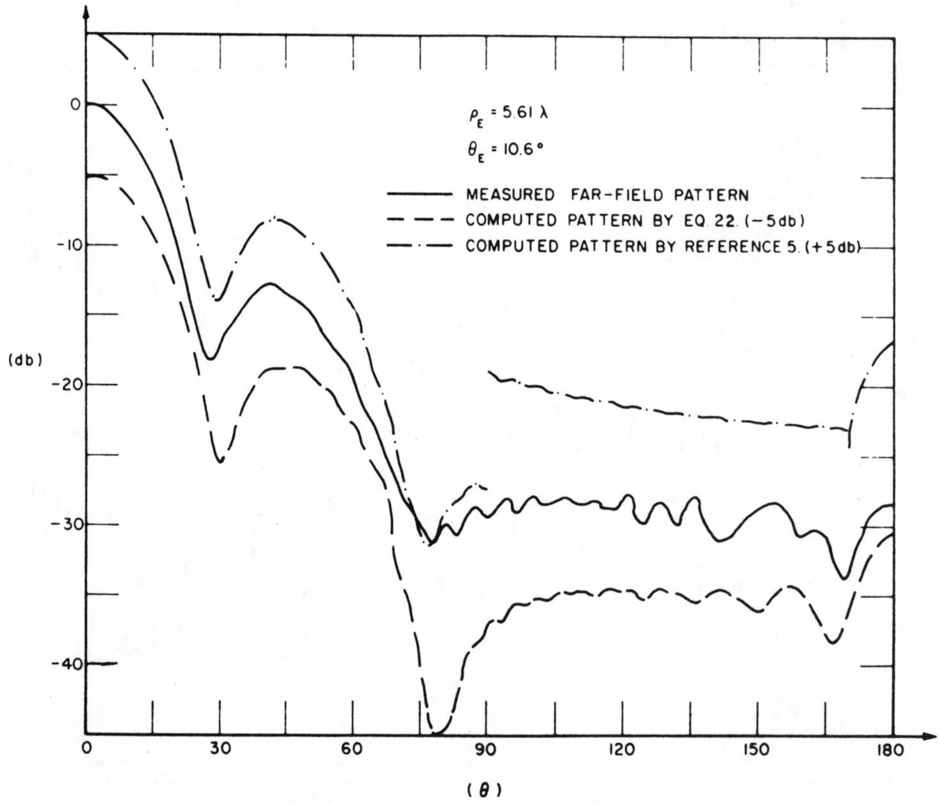

Fig. 7. A comparison of patterns.

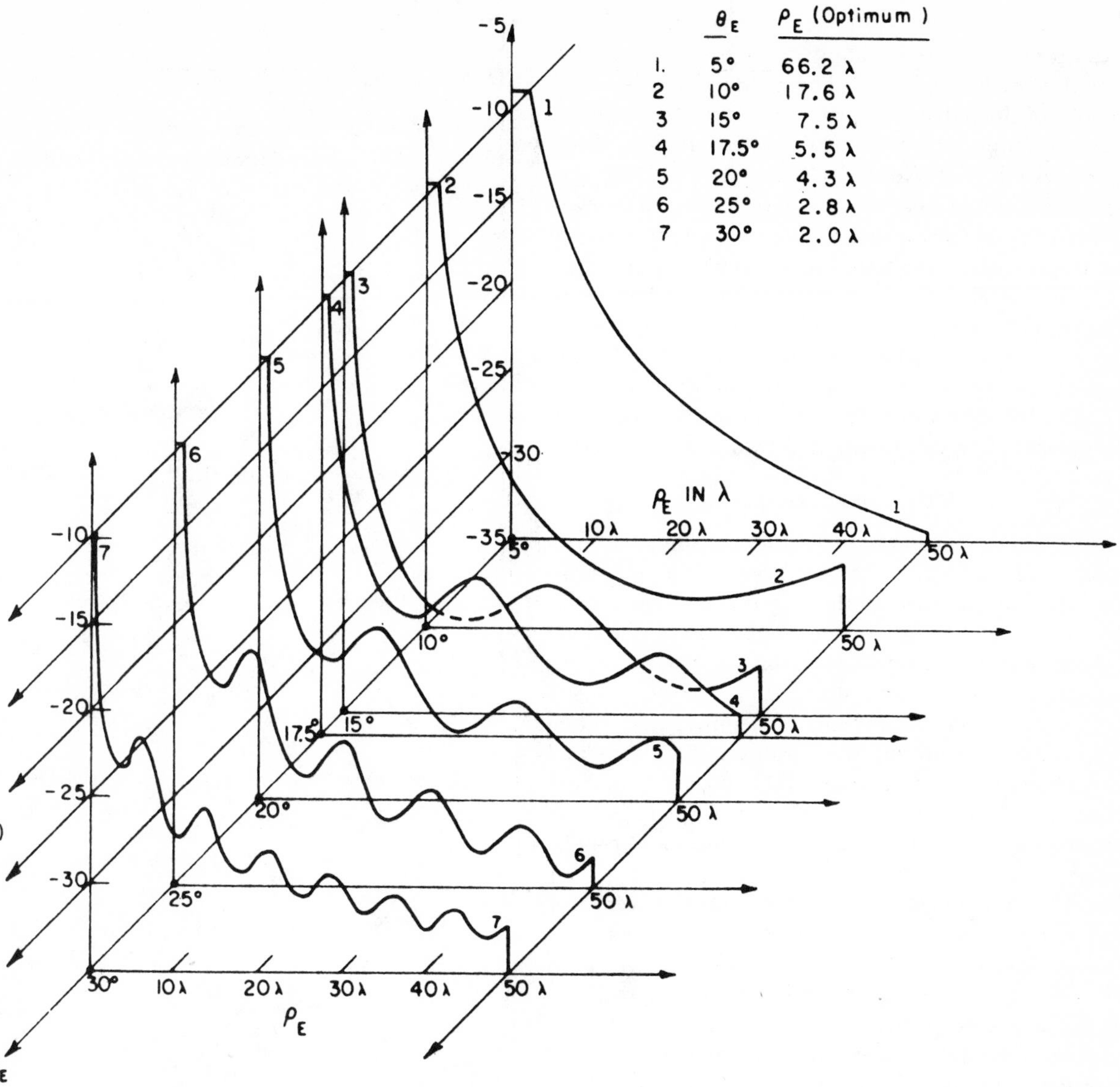

Fig. 8. Back-to-front ratios of the antenna model.

VI. Relative Back Levels

The radiation patterns, either measured or computed always have a backlobe maximum at $\theta=180°$, even though this maximum value is not necessarily the largest maximum in the region $180°-\theta_E<\theta<180°$. The difference between the value at $\theta=180°$ and that of the largest maximum is generally small. Therefore, the radiation intensity at $\theta=180°$ can be taken as a representative value for backlobe region. It is also observed that the radiation intensity in the region $90°<\theta<180°-\theta_E$ is, in general, smaller than the mentioned representative value.

The back-to-front ratios of the model are plotted in Fig. 8 as a function of length ρ_E for seven values of angle θ_E. A set of measured data is compared with a calculated curve in Fig. 9. All calculated back-to-front ratios are approximated by use of only the first-order diffraction terms, which are sufficiently accurate for this purpose.

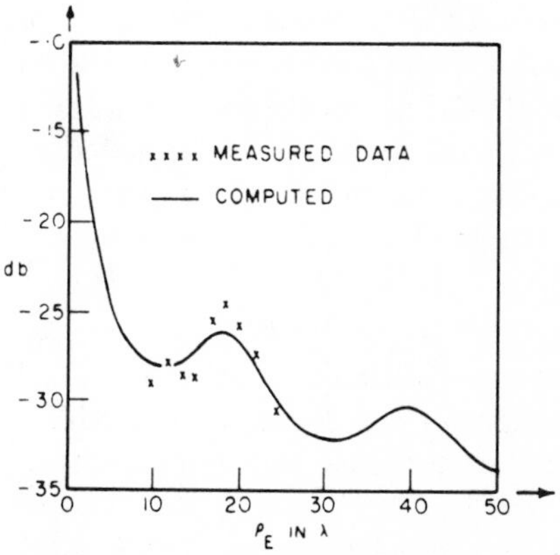

Fig. 9. Back-to-front ratio of $2\theta_E=35°$.

It is interesting to compare the first minimum points in Fig. 8 to the defined optimum [8] horn lengths. The values of optimum horn lengths are tabulated in Fig. 8 and are found to be one half of that of ρ_E, which give the first minimum back-to-front ratios.

The sets of ρ_E and θ_E giving rise to the minima in the curves do not necessarily imply that $u(0)$ is maximum and that $u(\pi)$ is minimum. The reason for this is the main lobe of the pattern begins to bifurcate at the points where minimum back-to-front ratios occur. For a horn antenna with $\theta_0=25°$, and $\rho_E=6.5\lambda$, 17λ, 27λ, 38λ, and 48λ, where minima take place in Fig. 8, the main beam of the pattern is split into two, four, six, eight, and ten lobes, respectively. However, Fig. 8 can be used to evaluate approximately the representative back-radiation intensity $u(\pi)$ relative to front-radiation intensity $u(0)$. If the horn antenna is large enough, it is generally safe to expect that the radiation intensity, on the average in the region $90°<\theta<180°-\theta_E$, is about 5 dB lower than the representative value $u(\pi)$ as shown in Figs. 8 and 9.

VII. Conclusions

The E-plane patterns, including far-sidelobes and backlobes, of horn antennas have been formulated without employing aperture methods and equivalence principles. The edge diffraction techniques employed here are those used in Russo, Rudduck, and Peters [5]. In this paper the higher-order diffraction at the edges and the reflection inside the antenna model have been taken into account. Considering the various assumptions and the mathematical difficulties inherent in aperture methods it is shown here that diffraction theory is more accurate and practical in analyzing radiation characteristics of typical horn antennas.

For typical dimensions of the proposed reflector model, the pattern may be computed by (15) as accurately as desired. The approximated pattern has been shown, in Figs. 5, 6, and 7 to be in excellent agreement with the measured patterns of horn antennas for which the reflector model is intended. Comparisons with the first-order patterns indicate that the improvements of (22) are mainly in the far-sidelobes and backlobes. As a consequence of the approximations made to obtain (22), the pattern level tends to deviate more and more in the region around $\theta=90°-\theta_E$, when horn dimensions become smaller. Figure 7 shows that the second-order image terms can no longer be assumed negligible for small horns. In conclusion, (22) is generally sufficient to predict patterns of typical horn antennas.

Appendix

The mth order diffraction at wedges A, B, W, and S and the images of the corner reflector in Fig. 1 may be written similar to the second-order terms as follows:

$$
\begin{aligned}
D_A^{(m)}(\theta) &= D_{AB}^{(m)} + D_{AW}^{(m)} + D_{AS}^{(m)} + \sum_{i=1}^{h-1} D_{Ai}^{(m)},\\
D_B^{(m)}(\theta) &= D_{BA}^{(m)} + D_{BW}^{(m)} + D_{BS}^{(m)} + \sum_{i=1}^{h-1} D_{Bi}^{(m)},\\
D_W^{(m)}(\theta) &= D_{WA}^{(m)} + D_{WB}^{(m)},\\
D_S^{(m)}(\theta) &= D_{SA}^{(m)} + D_{SB}^{(m)},\\
(I_L^{(m)})_i &= D_A^{(m)}(-2i\theta_E - \theta),
\end{aligned}
\tag{23}
$$

and

$$(I_U^{(m)})_i = D_B^{(m)}(+2i\theta_E - \theta),$$

where the valid regions are identical to those defined in (13) and (14). The components in (23) can be obtained analogous to (8), (10), and (12) as follows:

$$
\begin{aligned}
D_{AB}^{(m)}(\theta) &= C_{AB}^{(m-1)}\left[v_B\left(b, \frac{\pi}{2}+\theta, 2\right) + v_B\left(b, \frac{3\pi}{2} - 2\theta_E + \theta, 2\right)\right]\\
&\qquad -\frac{\pi}{2} \le \theta \le \pi + \theta_E;\\
D_{BA}^{(m)}(\theta) &= D_{AB}^{(m)}(-\theta),\\
&\qquad \frac{\pi}{2} \ge \theta \ge -(\pi+\theta_E);\\
D_{WA}^{(m)}(\theta) &= C_{WA}^{(m-1)}\left[v_B(\rho_E, -\theta_E+\theta, n_W)\right],\\
&\qquad \theta_E \le \theta \le 2\pi - \theta_E;\\
D_{WB}^{(m)}(\theta) &= C_{WA}^{(m-1)}\left[v_B(\rho_E, 2\pi - \theta_E - \theta, n_W)\right],\\
&\qquad -\theta_E \ge \theta \ge -(2\pi - \theta_E);\\
\left.\begin{aligned} D_{SA}^{(m)}(\theta) &= C_{SA}^{(m-1)}\left[v_B(\rho_E, \theta_E - \theta, n_S)\right]\\ D_{SB}^{(m)}(\theta) &= D_{SA}^{(m)}(-\theta)\end{aligned}\right\}&\\
&\qquad -\theta_E \le \theta \le \theta_E;\\
D_{Ai}^{(m)}(\theta) &= C_{Ai}^{(m-1)}\left[v_B\left(\rho_i, \frac{\pi}{2}+i\theta_E+\theta, 2\right) + v_B\left(\rho_i, \frac{3\pi}{2} - (i+2)\theta_E + \theta, 2\right)\right]\\
&\qquad -\frac{\pi}{2} \le \theta \le \pi + \theta_E;\\
D_{Bi}^{(m)}(\theta) &= D_{Ai}^{(m)}(-\theta),\\
&\qquad \frac{\pi}{2} \ge \theta \ge -(\pi+\theta_E);\\
D_{AW}^{(m)}(\theta) &= C_{AW}^{(m-1)}\left[v_B(\rho_E, \pi+\theta_E-\theta, 2)\right],\\
&\qquad \frac{\pi}{2} \le \theta \le \pi + \theta_E;\\
D_{BW}^{(m)}(\theta) &= D_{AW}^{(m)}(-\theta),\\
&\qquad -\frac{\pi}{2} \ge \theta \ge -(\pi+\theta_E);\\
D_{AS}^{(m)}(\theta) &= C_{AS}^{(m-1)}\left[v_B(\rho_E, \pi-\theta_E+\theta, 2)\right],\\
&\qquad -\frac{\pi}{2} \le \theta \le \pi + \theta_E;
\end{aligned}
\tag{24}
$$

and

$$D_{BS}^{(m)}(\theta) = D_{AS}^{(m)}(-\theta), \qquad \frac{\pi}{2} \ge \theta \ge -(\pi+\theta_E),$$

where the property of symmetry with respect to $\theta=0$ is used to obtain symmetrical terms. The coupling coefficients of different orders can also be formulated in infinite series form [4]. The coupling coefficients are obtained as

$$
\begin{aligned}
C_{AB}^{(m)} &= C_{BA}^{(m)} = D_A^{(m)}\left(\theta = \frac{-\pi}{2}\right) \\
C_{WA}^{(m)} &= D_A^{(m)} \qquad (\theta = \pi + \theta_E) \\
C_{SA}^{(m)} &= D_A^{(m)} \qquad (\theta = -\,\theta_E) \\
C_{Ai}^{(m)} &= D_A^{(m)} \qquad \left(\theta = -\frac{\pi}{2} - i\theta_E\right) \\
C_{AW}^{(m)} &= D_W^{(m)} \qquad (\theta = \theta_E) \\
C_{AS}^{(m)} &= D_S^{(m)} \qquad (\theta = \theta_E) \qquad (25)
\end{aligned}
$$

in which the process of iteration may be used to include as many orders of diffraction as desired. As soon as coupling coefficients are properly evaluated, the diffraction of any order can then be obtained by making use of (23) and (24).

Acknowledgment

Thanks are due to C. H. Davis for the measurements and M. L. Tripp for the computations.

References

[1] J. D. Kraus, *Antennas*. New York: McGraw-Hill, 1950, pp. 375–380.
[2] B. Ye Kinber, "Diffraction at the open end of a sectoral horn," *Radio Engrg. Electron. Phys.*, vol. 7–10, pp. 1620–1632, October 1962.
[3] Y. Ohba, "On the radiation pattern of a corner reflector finite in width," *IEEE Trans. on Antennas and Propagation*, vol. AP-11, pp. 127–132, March 1963.
[4] J. S. Yu and R. C. Rudduck, "The *E*-plane radiation pattern of an antenna model for horn antennas," Antenna Lab., The Ohio State University Research Foundation, Columbus, Rept. 1767–3, April 1, 1965, prepared under contract AF 30(602)-3269, Rome Air Development Center, Griffiss Air Force Base, N. Y.
[5] P. M. Russo, R. C. Rudduck, and L. Peters, Jr., "A method for computing *E*-plane pattern of horn antennas," *IEEE Trans. on Antennas and Propagation*, vol. AP-13, pp. 219–224, March 1965.
[6] W. Pauli, "On asymptotic series for functions in the theory of diffraction of light," *Phys. Rev.*, vol. 54, pp. 924–931, December 1938.
[7] A. Sommerfeld, *Optics*. New York: Academic, 1954, pp. 245–265.
[8] H. Jasik, *Antenna Engineering Handbook*. New York: McGraw-Hill, 1961, ch. 10, p. 8.

A Correction to the Available Radiation Formula for E-Plane Sectoral Horns

M. S. NARASIMHAN AND V. VENKATESWARA RAO

Abstract—**A correction to the available radiation formula [1] for E-plane sectoral horn has been proposed. Calculated radiation patterns based on the corrected formula, are shown to be in better agreement with the measured radiation patterns for several values of fiare-angles of the E-plane sectoral horns.**

Based on the vector diffraction formula, an expression has been derived for the radiated far-field in the principal planes of an E-plane sectoral horn [1]. It has been noticed by the present authors that the cylindrical coordinate system (r,θ,x) used in [1 p. 351 fig. 10.9(a)] for representing the horn-aperture fields is not right handed. Hence this requires correction. (However the coordinate system used for representing the aperture fields in an H-plane sectoral horn is right handed).

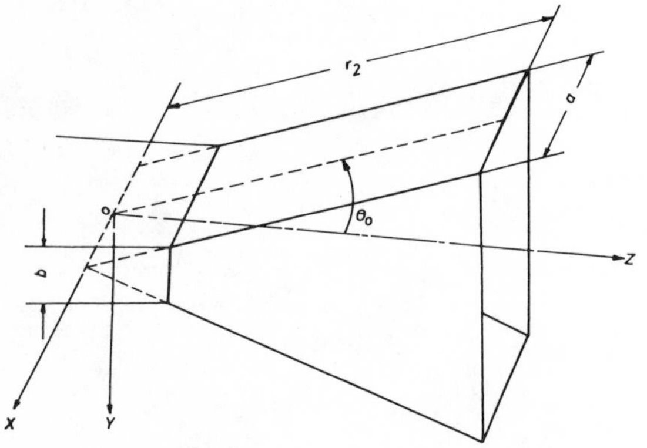

Fig. 1. Coordinate system for E-plane sectoral horn geometry.

Retaining all notations used in [1 sect. 10] a right-handed cylindrical coordinate system for the E-plane sectoral horn is shown in Fig. 1. With this system of coordinates (a typical point in this coordinate system being $P(r,\theta,x)$) an extensive manipulation yields the following expressions for the radiation formula.

E Plane ($\phi = 90°$):

$$\mathbf{E}_P = -\mathbf{i}_\Theta \frac{jkr_2 \exp(-jkR)}{4\pi R} \int_0^a dx \int_{-\theta_0}^{+\theta_0} \exp[jkr_2 \cos(\Theta - \theta)] \cdot [E_\theta + (\mu/\epsilon)^{1/2} H_x \cos(\Theta - \theta)]\, d\theta. \quad (1a)$$

H Plane ($\phi = 0$):

$$\mathbf{E}_P = +\mathbf{i}_\phi \frac{jkr_2 \exp(-jkR)}{4\pi R} \int_0^a dx \cdot \int_{-\theta_0}^{+\theta_0} \exp[jk(x \sin\Theta + r\ \cos\theta \cos\Theta)] \cdot [E_\theta \cos\Theta + (\mu/\epsilon)^{1/2} H_x \cos\theta]\, d\theta. \quad (1b)$$

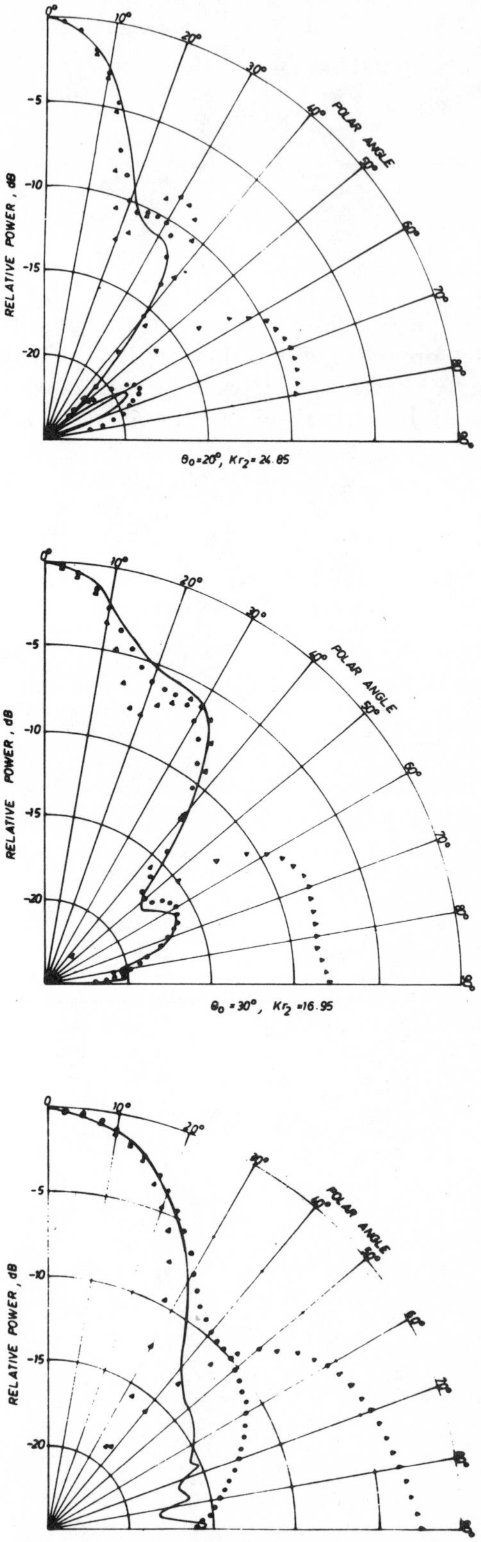

(a)

Fig. 2. Comparison of calculated and measured E-plane radiation pattern of E-plane sectoral horns. — measured pattern; △ calculated by [1, p. 357, eq. (45a)]; ○ calculated by (1a).

Manuscript received February 15, 1973; revised May 16, 1973.
The authors are with the Department of Electrical Engineering, Indian Institute of Technology, Madras 600036, India.

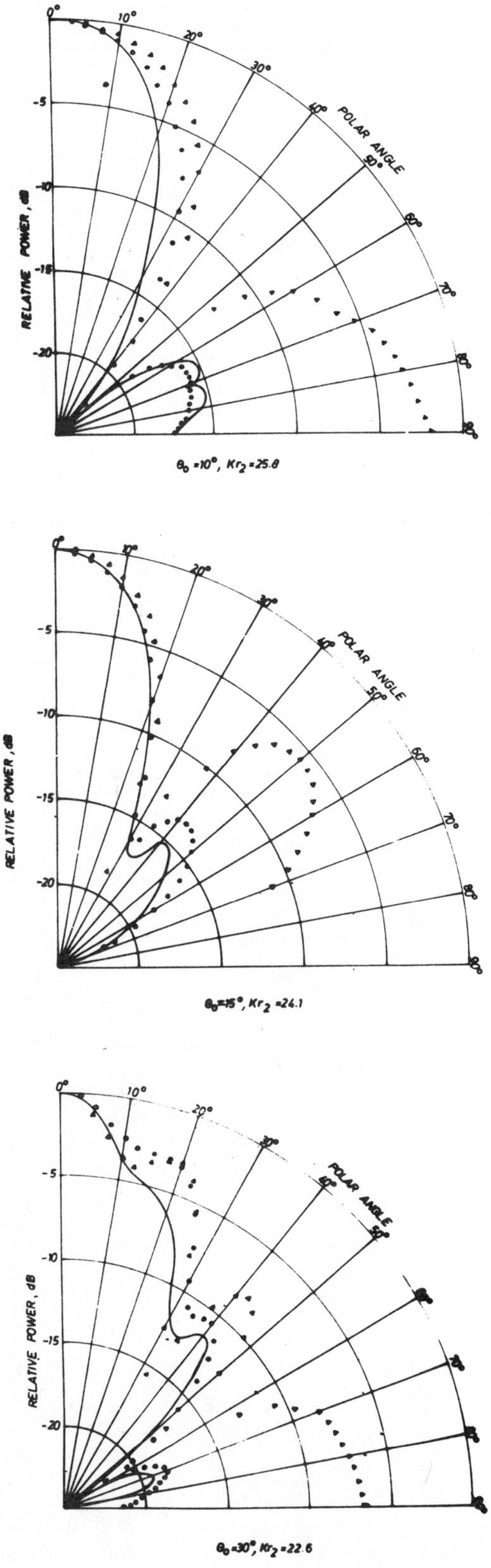

(b)

Fig. 2. *Continued.*

It may be noticed that (1a) and (1b) are identical to the formulas derived in [1, sect. 10] but for a sign change within the integrand. However this sign change significantly affects the radiation pattern in the near and far sidelobe regions. In order to emphasize the validity of (1) the E-plane radiation patterns of a few typical horns considered in [1 sect. 10] (for the TE_{10} to x mode) have been calculated numerically using (1a) as well as using the formula given by [1 sect. 10 eq. (45a)]. In Fig. 2(a) these computed values have been compared with the measured values furnished in [1 sect. 10]. Furthermore in Fig. 2(b) a similar comparison of calculated results has been made with the far-field pattern measurement data of a few E-plane sectoral horns of our own design. The comparison reveals the validity of the proposed correction.

It may be of interest to point out that computations for radiation patterns of wide-flare corrugated E-plane sectoral horns [2] for the HE_{11} mode of operation yield results in concordance with measured values only when the proposed correction in the available radiation formula is taken into account. Furthermore, instead of using the vector diffraction formulation, the E-plane radiation field has been represented as a sum of free-space cylindrical TE and TM wave functions. Based on this formulation, computed radiation patterns for a few typical corrugated E-plane sectoral horns (supporting the HE_{11} mode) closely follow the computations based on (1a).

Acknowledgment

Computing facilities of the Computer Center at A.C. College of Technology, Madras, India, have been made use of for numerical evaluation of radiation patterns.

References

[1] S. Silver, *Microwave Antenna Theory and Design.* New York: McGraw-Hill, 1949, sect. 10, pp. 350–365.
[2] M. S. Narasimhan and V. Venkateswara Rao, "Radiation characteristics of corrugated E-plane sectoral horns," *IEEE Trans. Antennas Propagat.*, vol. AP-21, pp. 320–327, May 1973.

Near-Zone Field of the Conical Horn

In predicting the performance of the near-field Cassegrainian antenna[1] it is necessary to know in detail the characteristics of the near-zone field of the primary feed. The conical horn can be used as the primary feed in a variation of the near-field Cassegrainian configuration. While the subject of the far-field of the conical horn has been treated rather extensively in the past,[2,3] there is a dearth of information on its near-field. Perhaps this is partially due to the difficulty in evaluating the necessary integrals analytically; but with the high speed digital computers presently available, it is now possible to obtain numerical results with relative ease. We have obtained some computed data on the near-field of the conical horn by numerical integration and have made measurements on a 50° horn at 11.166 kMc. Good agreement between theory and experiment was found.

In computing the near-field of the conical horn we assume that the field at the mouth of the horn is the same as that which exists at the same cross section of an infinite horn and that the field does not spill around the rim of its mouth. These assumptions are justified if the total flare angle of the horn is not too large and if the length of the horn is not too short in terms of wavelength. Therefore, we can write the near-field (which exists at a distance that is at least a few wavelengths from the mouth of horn) as the surface integral[4]

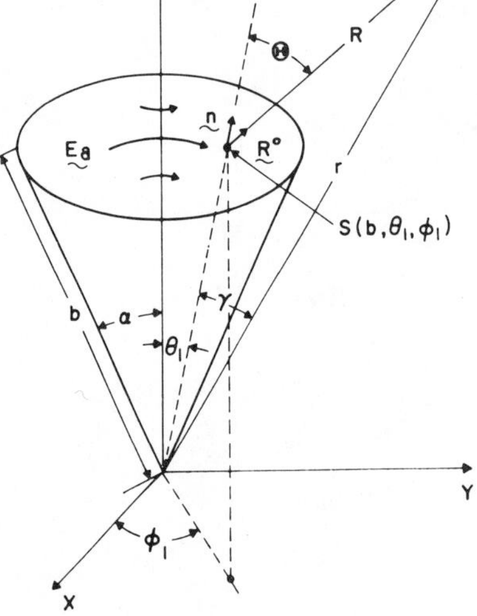

Fig. 1—The coordinate system for the conical horn.

$$E_p = \frac{-jk}{4\pi} \int_S R^0 \times [n \times E_a - \eta R^0 \times (n \times H_a)] \frac{e^{-jkR}}{R} dS, \quad (1)$$

where E_p is the near-field; E_a and H_a are the electric and magnetic fields over the aperture S; n is the unit vector normal to S; R is the distance from a source point on S to the field point P; R^0 is a unit vector along R; η is the impedance and k is the propagation constant of free space. (See Fig. 1.) For small flare angles and long horn lengths the aperture field is very nearly TEM and (1) can be reduced further.

$$E_p(r, \theta, \phi) = \frac{jk}{4\pi} \int_0^{2\pi} \int_0^{\alpha} [E_a(1 + \cos \Theta) - (E_a \cdot R^0)(n + R^0)] \cdot \frac{e^{-jkR}}{R} b^2 \sin \theta_1 d\theta_1 d\phi_1 \quad (2)$$

with

$$R = \sqrt{b^2 + r^2 - 2br \cos \gamma}$$
$$\cos \Theta = (r \cos \gamma - b)/R$$

and

$$\cos \gamma = \sin \theta \sin \theta_1 \cos (\phi - \phi_1) + \cos \theta \cos \theta_1.$$

As indicated in Fig. 1, the horn is of length b and of total flare angle 2α. The origin of the coordinate system is chosen to be coincident with the vertex of the horn and the polar axis coincident with the axis of symmetry of the cone. The field point is given by (r, θ, ϕ), while a source point on S is given by (b, θ_1, ϕ_1). The aperture surface S is taken to be a

Manuscript received May 25, 1964; revised July 6, 1964.

[1] D. C. Hogg and R. A. Semplak, "An experimental study of near-field Cassegrainian antennas," Submitted for publication *Bell Sys. Tech. J.*

[2] G. C. Southworth and A. P. King, "Metal horns as directive receivers of ultra-short waves," PROC. IRE, vol. 27, pp. 95–102; February, 1939.

[3] M. G. Schorr and F. J. Beck, Jr., "Electromagnetic field of the conical horn," *J. Appl. Phys.*, vol. 21, pp. 795–801; August, 1950.

[4] S. Silver, "Microwave Antenna Theory and Design," McGraw-Hill Book Co., Inc., New York, N. Y., pp. 158–160; 1949.

Reprinted from *IEEE Trans. Antennas Propagat.*, vol. AP-12, pp. 800–802, Nov. 1964.

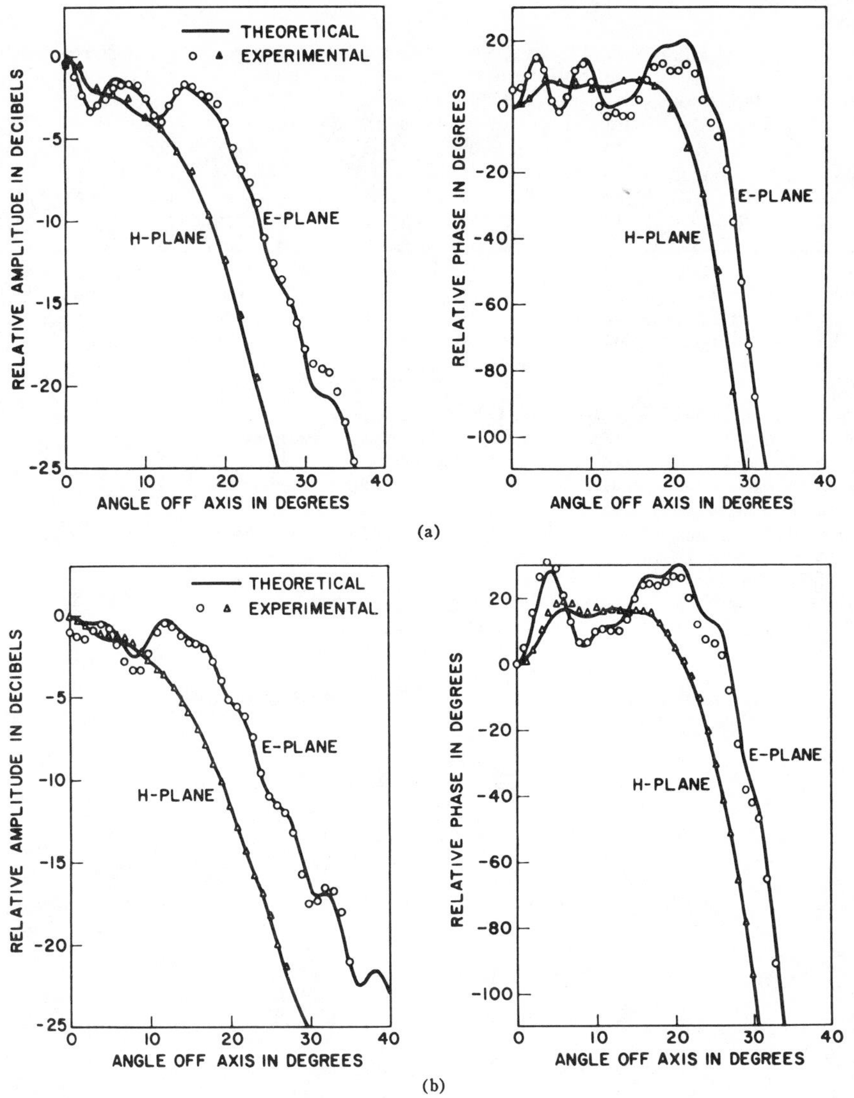

Fig. 2—Near-field patterns of the conical horn. Both amplitude and phase are normalized to their "on-axis" ($\theta = 0°$) values. (a) $r = 23.52\lambda$. (b) $r = 46.23\lambda$.

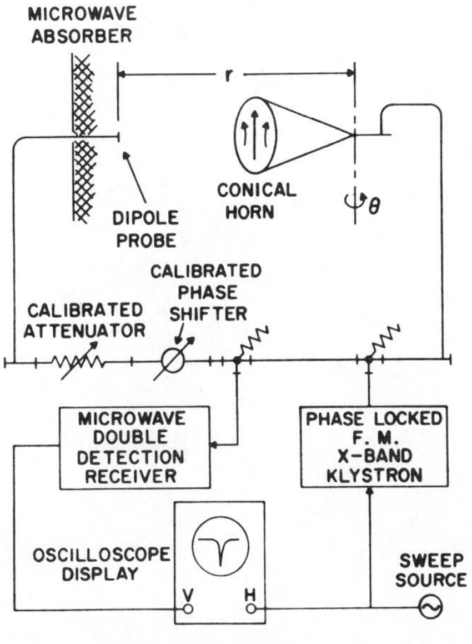

Fig. 3—The experimental set-up.

spherical surface of radius b over the mouth of the horn.

In our computation we assumed the horn to be excited in the dominant TE mode.[3] This mode of excitation is easily obtained in practice by feeding the horn with a circular waveguide excited in its dominant (TE_{11}) mode. The horn we used in our computation and experiment has a total flare angle of 50° and an aperture diameter of 11.34 wavelengths ($b = 13.42$ wavelengths and $\lambda = 2.685$ cm). Fig. 2 shows the computed curves and the measured points of the principal components of the near-field in the two principal planes of the horn (ϕ component in the H-plane and θ component in the E-plane). The computation was performed by means of numerical integration on an IBM 7094 computer. The aperture field $\boldsymbol{E}_a$ was taken to be the same as the TE_{11} mode of a circular waveguide but with a spherical phase front. The term involving $\boldsymbol{E}_a \cdot \boldsymbol{R}^0$ was neglected since its contribution to the components of the field actually computed is very small.

Experimental data were taken point by point in an anechoic chamber using a modified null method. The method involved an oscilloscope display of the null obtained by frequency modulating a phase-locked klystron source and by having different path lengths in the two arms of the null bridge (see Fig. 3). Phase and amplitude information were obtained from a calibrated phase shifter and a calibrated attenuator. The system has proven to be very stable with measurement errors limited by calibration and readout of the phase shifter and of the attenuator and by mechanical stability of the bridge arm components.

Measurements were made in the principal planes by rotating the conical horn about an axis through the projected apex of the cone and sampling the field with a coaxially fed dipole. The dipole was oriented such that it measured the θ component of the field in the E-plane of the horn and the ϕ component in the H-plane. The data shown in Fig. 2 are averages of pairs of measurements symmetrically taken on either side of $\theta = 0$. In general, the symmetric pair of measurements were in good agreement in the region of amplitude 10 db below reference. At lower amplitude levels the agreement degrades somewhat. Maximum measurement errors are estimated at $\pm 3°$ and ± 1 db in phase and in amplitude, respectively, in the region from reference to 10 db below reference. The accuracy in angular setting of the horn is $\pm 0.05°$.

In view of the good agreement between theory and experiment, we feel that the method of computation used is sufficiently accurate for predicting the near-field of conical horns having total flare angle up to 60° or 70° and aperture diameters of more than a few wavelengths.

The authors are grateful to A. B. Crawford for suggesting this work and for his encouragement and to Mrs. C. L. Beattie who programmed the computation.

TINGYE LI
R. H. TURRIN
Bell Telephone Labs., Inc.
Holmdel, N. J.

Diffraction by a Conical Horn

M. A. K. HAMID, MEMBER, IEEE

Abstract—The geometrical theory of diffraction is used to investigate the gain and radiation pattern of a conical horn excited by a circular waveguide operating in the TE_{11} mode. A simple expression for evaluating the eigenvalues in the horn is derived and a systematic procedure is given for converting the field of the dominant mode into a geometrical-optics ray form. It is shown that the dominant contribution due to these rays may be attributed, in the principal planes of diffraction, to a pair of Brillouin rays emanating from a spheroidal mode-caustic generator. The edge rays excited at the aperture plane are also taken into account and their contribution is obtained as an asymptotic series in terms of the horn dimensions. Finally, it is shown that the ray-optical technique gives a physical insight into the diffraction mechanisms of a conical horn and leads to an excellent agreement with experiment.

I. Introduction

THE METHODS commonly used in the radiation calculations of horn antennas are based on Fraunhofer diffraction [1] and are not sufficiently refined since they lead to patterns that are not in satisfactory agreement with experiment, particularly away from the main beam [2], [3]. These methods suffer from the lack of an accurate knowledge of the aperture field distribution in terms of the finite dimensions of the horn and the amplitude of modes excited at the feed junction.

The analytical background of the Fraunhofer diffraction is based on the scalar diffraction theory. The elements of this theory are contained in the approximate principle proposed by Huygens in 1690 [4]. However, the basic equations of the theory in a modern sense were derived by Fresnel [5], Kirchhoff [6], and Rayleigh [7]. These equations become invalid when the aperture dimensions and observation distance are of the same order of magnitude as the wavelength for reasons which have been amply discussed in the literature [8]–[11].

For problems of this type, a completely rigorous approach is too difficult and is probably of no practical importance. Nevertheless, by making suitable approximations, Schell [12], Ohba [13], Kinber [14], Russo, Rudduck, and Peters [15], and others [16]–[18] have shown that the ray-optical method is quite promising for solving horn problems.

The purpose of this investigation, therefore, is to apply the geometrical theory of diffraction by Keller [19], [20] in order to combine the mode and ray theories for a single horn and to apply the results for calculating the gain and radiation pattern. Thus the field at an observation point is obtained from the sum of the fields on all the excited geometrical-optics and edge rays passing through that point. The accuracy of the field on the edge rays is improved in order to deal with the near field and shadow boundary regions of the edges at the waveguide and aperture junctions of the horn. A simple expression for evaluating the eigenvalues in the horn is derived and a systematic procedure given for converting the dominant mode field into a geometrical-optics ray form. It is shown that the dominant contribution due to these rays may be attributed, in the principal planes of diffraction, to a pair of Brillouin rays emanating from a spheroidal mode-caustic generator. The edge rays excited at the aperture plane are also taken into account and their contribution is obtained as an asymptotic series in terms of the horn dimensions. The predictions for the gain and radiation pattern are finally established by an excellent agreement with experiment.

Manuscript received December 15, 1967; revised March 22, 1968. This research was supported by the National Research Council of Canada under Grant A-3326 and by the Defence Research Board of Canada under Grant 6801-37. This paper was presented at the 1967 International Symposium on Antennas and Propagation, Ann Arbor, Mich.

The author is with the Antenna Laboratory, Department of Electrical Engineering, University of Manitoba, Winnipeg, Canada.

II. Field Expansion in a Long Conical Horn

Consider a conical horn whose axial height and flare angle are denoted by h and α, respectively, where $Kh \gg 1$ and K is the wave number $2\pi/\lambda$. The horn is assumed fed by a circular waveguide of radius a operating in the dominant TE_{11} mode as shown in Fig. 1.

In general the electric field components in the horn due to transverse electric modes are given by

$$E_r = 0,\ E_\theta = \frac{-1}{r\sin\theta}\frac{\partial F_r}{\partial\theta},\ E_\phi = \frac{1}{r}\frac{\partial F_r}{\partial\theta} \tag{1}$$

where the potential F_r is given in spherical coordinates, with the origin at the apex as shown in Fig. 1, by the expression [21]

$$(F_r)_{m,\nu} = P_\nu{}^m(\cos\theta)\cos(m\phi)\hat{H}_\nu{}^{(1)}(Kr) \tag{2}$$

where

$$\hat{H}_\nu{}^{(1)}(Kr) = Krh_\nu(Kr) = \left[\frac{\pi Kr}{2}\right]^{1/2} H^{(1)}_{\nu+1/2}(Kr) \tag{3}$$

and $h_\nu(Kr)$ is the spherical Hankel function of order ν while $p_\nu{}^m(\cos\theta)$ are the associated Legendre functions of order ν and degree m.

In order to satisfy the boundary condition $E_\phi = 0$ at $\phi = \pm\alpha/2$, the parameter ν must be a solution of the equation

$$\left[\frac{d}{d\theta}p_\nu{}^m(\cos\theta)\right]_{\theta=\pm\alpha/2} = 0. \tag{4}$$

Since we are primarily interested in the first dipole mode, we set m equal to unity and (4) may hence be rewritten in the form

Reprinted from *IEEE Trans. Antennas Propagat.*, vol. AP-16, pp. 520–528, Sept. 1968.

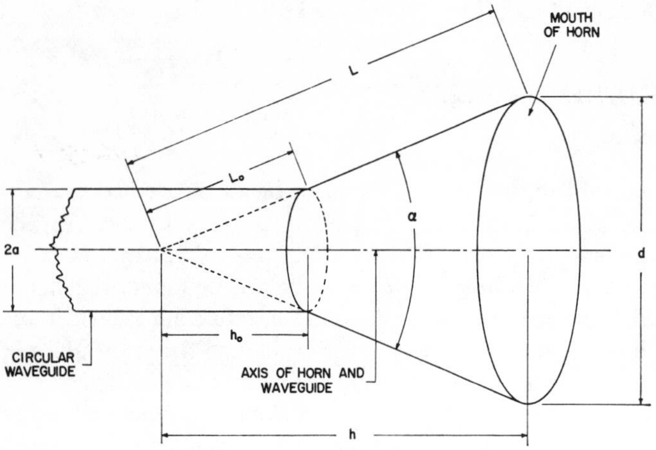

Fig. 1. Physical dimensions of the conical horn.

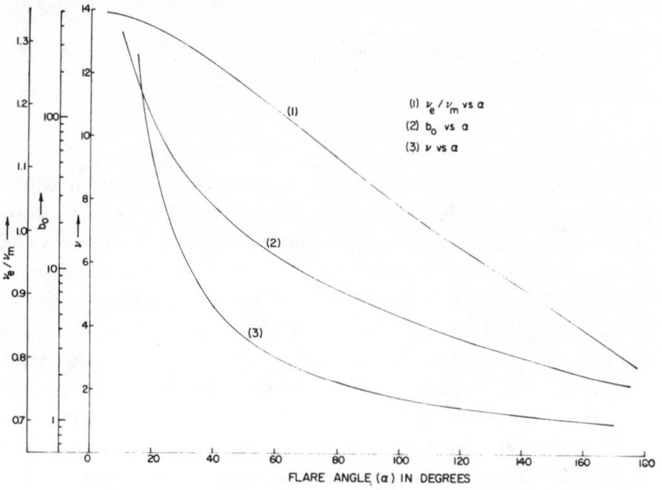

Fig. 2. b_0, ν and ν_e/ν_m versus flare angle (α).

$$\left[\frac{d^2}{d\theta^2} P_\nu(\cos\theta)\right]_{\theta=\pm\alpha/2} = 0 \tag{5}$$

where we use the relation

$$p_\nu{}^1(\cos\theta) = \frac{d}{d\theta}[P_\nu(\cos\theta)] \tag{6}$$

and the resulting solution for ν is given by

$$\nu = -0.5 + 0.5[1 + 4b_0]^{1/2} \tag{7}$$

where b_0 is given by (see Fig. 2)

$$b_0 = \frac{\log_{10}[(1-\alpha/\pi)/4]}{\log_{10}[\cos(\alpha/2)]} \tag{8}$$

as shown in Appendix I. A plot of ν versus α, based on (7), is shown in Fig. 2 and agrees with the numerical results of Kay [22] for the dominant TE_{11} mode. The components of the geometrical-optics field are hence given by

$$E_\theta{}^g = \left[\frac{\pi K r}{2}\right]^{1/2}\left[\frac{\sin\phi}{r\sin\theta}\right][P_\nu{}'(\cos\theta)]H^{(1)}_{\nu+1/2}(Kr) \tag{9}$$

$$E_\phi{}^g = \left[\frac{\pi K r}{2}\right]^{1/2}\left[\frac{\cos\phi}{r}\right][p_\nu{}''(\cos\theta)]H^{(1)}_{\nu+1/2}(Kr) \tag{10}$$

where the single and double prime notation denotes single and double derivatives with respect to θ.

III. Interpretation of the Geometrical-Optics Field in Terms of Brillouin Rays

In this section we obtain approximate expressions for $E_\theta{}^g$ and $E_\phi{}^g$ which are valid for small flare angles and represent the fields as Brillouin rays as already shown by Kinber [14] for the case of a sectoral horn. To do this we convert the right-hand sides of (9) and (10) to the exponential form of ray fields and we show that these are the usual Brillouin rays excited by a mode caustic.

For the propagation condition $Kr > \nu + \frac{1}{2}$, the Hankel function in (9) and (10) may be expressed, for large values of Kr, by the leading term of the Debye asymptotic expansion [23], [24], i.e.,

$$H_{\nu'}{}^{(1)}(Kr) \simeq \left[\frac{2}{\pi}\right]^{1/2} \frac{e^{j\{K[\sqrt{r^2-(\nu'/K)^2}-(\nu'/K)\cos^{-1}(\nu'/Kr)]-\pi/4\}}}{\{K[\sqrt{r^2-(\nu'/K)^2}]^{1/2}\}^{1/2}} \tag{11}$$

where

$$\nu' = \nu + 0.5 = 0.5(1+4b_0)^{1/2}. \tag{12}$$

The θ-dependence in (9) and (10) may also be expressed approximately in terms of exponentials as shown in (55) and (58) of Appendix II. The final results for $0 \leq \theta < \pi/3$ are given by

$$[p_\nu{}'(\cos\theta)]/\sin\theta \doteqdot 0.5b_1[1 + 0.5e^{j\nu_e\theta} + 0.5e^{-j\nu_e\theta}] \tag{13}$$

$$p_\nu{}''(\cos\theta) \doteqdot 0.91b_1[2 - 0.5e^{j\nu_m\theta} - 0.5e^{-j\nu_m\theta}] \tag{14}$$

where b_1, ν_e, and ν_m are defined in (51), (56), and (59), respectively. In particular, the ratio ν_e/ν_m is given by

$$\nu_e/\nu_m = 0.348\left[\frac{1+4b_0}{1+0.267b_0}\right]^{1/2} \tag{15}$$

which is also the inverse of the electric-to-magnetic beamwidths ratio due to the geometrical-optics field only. The validity of this ratio is supported by experimental evidence for optimum design conical horns whose physical dimensions correspond to minimum edge diffraction along the axis. Thus for the case of $\alpha = 52°$, this ratio is 1.22 or approximately 2 percent higher than the experimental value given by King [26]. A plot of ν_e/ν_m vs. α, based on (15), is given in Fig. 4.

In order to trace a ray diagram for the conical horn, we change the order ν' of the Hankel functions in (11) to ν_e for the electric plane and ν_m for the magnetic plane. This approximation is only valid for large values of K_r and employs the usual asymptotic expansion of the Hankel function for large arguments [21], i.e.,

$$H_{\nu'}{}^{(1)}(Kr) \sim \begin{cases} j^{\nu_e-\nu'}H_{\nu_e}{}^{(1)}(Kr) \\ j^{\nu_m-\nu'}H_{\nu_m}{}^{(1)}(Kr) \end{cases}. \tag{16}$$

The field components in the electric and magnetic planes,

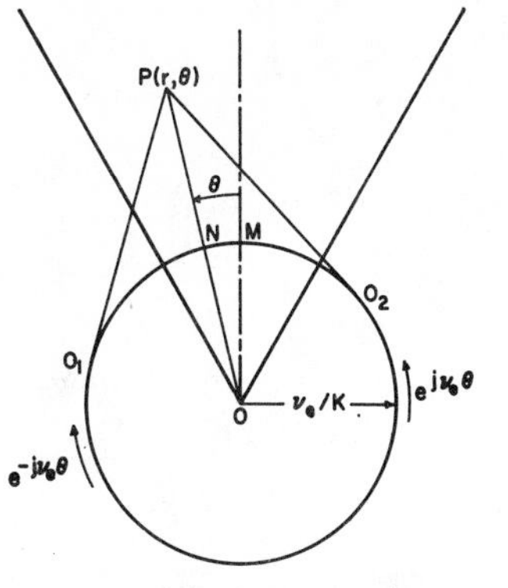

Fig. 3. Geometrical parameters used in tracing the E-plane Brillouin-ray diagram for a conical horn.

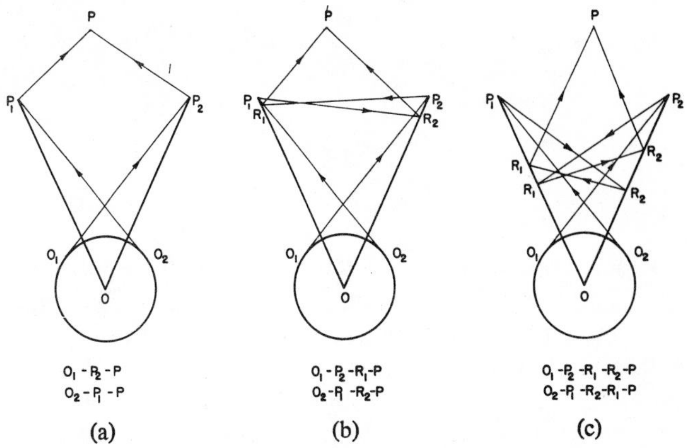

Fig. 4. Singly diffracted rays in the E-plane.

corresponding to $Kr \gg \nu'$, $\theta \leq \alpha/2$, are given by the following relations.

Electric plane ($\phi = \pi/2$):

$$E_{\theta}{}^{g} \doteqdot \frac{0.5b_1 j^{\nu_e - \nu'}}{r}\left[1 + 0.5e^{j\nu_e\theta} + 0.5e^{-j\nu_e\theta}\right] \cdot \left[\exp j\{K[\sqrt{r^2 - (\nu_e/K)^2} - (\nu_e/Kr)\cos^{-1}(\nu_e/K)] - \pi/4\}\right]. \quad (17)$$

Magnetic plane ($\phi = 0$):

$$E_{\theta}{}^{g} \doteqdot \left[\frac{0.91b_1 j^{\nu_m - \nu'}}{r}\{2 - 0.5e^{j\nu_m\theta} - 0.5e^{-j\nu_m\theta}\}\right] \cdot \left[\exp j\{K[\sqrt{r^2 - (\nu_m/K)^2} - (\nu_m/Kr)\cos^{-1}(\nu_m/K)] - \pi/4\}\right]. \quad (18)$$

Examination of (17) shows that the first term is independent of θ and may therefore be neglected in the derivation of the E-plane radiation pattern. The phase angles at the second and third terms, ψ_1 and ψ_2, are given by

$$\begin{bmatrix}\psi_1\\ \psi_2\end{bmatrix} = K[(r^2 - r_e{}^2)^{1/2} - r_e\cos^{-1}(r_e/r) \pm r_e\theta] + \psi_0 \quad (19)$$

where

$$r_e = \nu_e/K, \quad \psi_0 = (\nu_e - \nu')\pi/2 - \pi/4.$$

The first term in (19) represents the length of the tangents PO_1 and PO_2 from P to a circle of radius r_e centered at the apex 0 as shown in Fig. 3. Furthermore, since the arc of a circle is the radius times the subtended angle in radians, the second term in (19) is obviously O_1N or O_2N. Similarly, the third term in (19) represents the arc length MN while the last term, ψ_0, is a constant phase angle. Thus ψ_1 and ψ_2 are proportional to $PO_1 - O_1N + MN$ and $PO_2 - O_2N - MN$ and, consequently, the tangents PO_1 and PO_2 may be regarded as the rays that determine the geometrical-optics field at P. A similar pair of rays may also be derived from (18) for the H-plane following the same procedure with O_1, O_2, ν_e, and r_e replaced by O_3, O_4, ν_m and r_m, respectively.

The caustic of the Brillouin rays is a circle of radius r_e in the E-plane and a circle of radius r_m in the H-plane, while the resulting field amplitudes on these rays are proportional to the distances PO_1, PO_2 and PO_3, PO_4, respectively. The tangency points O_1 to O_4 are the new equivalent sources for the fundamental mode field since they are the stationary phase points with respect to the observation point P. Furthermore, each caustic circle supports two current waves traveling in opposite directions at the speed of light as shown in Fig. 3. For $\alpha < 112°$, these circles may be viewed as the projections of an oblate spheroid in the E-plane and a prolate spheroid in the H-plane and vice versa for $\alpha > 112°$. For $\alpha \doteqdot 112°$, the ratio $\nu_e/\nu_m = 1$, as shown in Fig. 2, and the two circles combine to form a single spherical caustic in three dimensions.

IV. The Edge-Ray Field

In order to calculate the contribution from the aperture edges we note that there are two singly diffracted rays passing through each observation point P off the axis in either principal plane. These rays come from the nearest and farthest points of the edge denoted by P_1, P_2 in the E-plane, as shown in Fig. 4(a), and P_3, P_4 in the H-plane. In addition, there are edge rays diffracted at P_1 and P_2 that suffer single or multiple wall reflections at R_1 and R_2 before reaching P, as shown in Fig. 4. The resulting contribution in each plane is the product of the field intensity at the source of the incident Brillouin rays times an appropriate diffraction function which takes into account the nature of the edge and orientation of the incident and diffracted rays [19], [27]. This function is given in the electromagnetic case of a spherical wave incident on the curved aperture edge of a conical horn by [19]

$$F_i[s_1, s_2, \delta_1, \delta_2] \sim -\frac{e^{jK(s_1+s_2)+j\pi/4}}{2(2\pi K)^{1/2}[s_1 s_2(s_1+s_2)]^{1/2}} \cdot \left[\sec\frac{\delta_2 - \delta_1}{2} \mp \sec\frac{\delta_2 + \delta_1}{2}\right] \cdot [1 + 2d^{-1}s_2\cos\delta_2]^{-1/2}, \quad Ks_1 \gg 1, \quad Ks_2 \gg 1 \quad (20)$$

while the edge-edge interaction across the aperture is calculated using the plane wave diffraction function [19]

$$F_i'[s_1, s_2, \delta_1, \delta_2] \sim -\frac{e^{jKs_2+j\pi/4}}{2(2\pi Ks_2)^{1/2}} \cdot \left[\sec\frac{\delta_2-\delta_1}{2} \mp \sec\frac{\delta_2+\delta_1}{2}\right] \cdot [1+2d^{-1}s_2\cos\delta_2]^{1/2}, \quad Ks_2 \gg 1 \tag{21}$$

where the subscript i denotes the edge number and ranges from 1 to 4 in the same manner as P_i in Fig. 4. The upper and lower signs in (20) and (21) correspond to the magnetic and electric planes of diffraction or to the cases when the scalar field (upper sign) or its normal derivative (lower sign) vanishes at the edge. The arguments of the diffraction functions are defined by

$s_{1,2}$ = magnitude of vectors joining the diffracting edge with the source and observation point, respectively.

$\delta_{1,2}$ = angles between the inner surface of the wall terminating in the diffracting edge and s_1 and s_2, respectively.

Using these definitions and normalizing the field intensity at $O_{1,2}$ to unity, we obtain from Fig. 4(a) the field on the singly diffracted rays:

$$E_1^d = F_1[r_0, r_1, \gamma_0, \gamma_1] + F_2[r_0, r_2, \gamma_0, \gamma_2] \tag{22}$$

where

$$r_0 = (L^2 - r_e^2)^{1/2}, \quad \gamma_0 = \sin^{-1}(r_e/L)$$

$$r_1 \sim r - L\cos(\alpha/2 - \theta), \quad r_2 \sim r - L\cos(\alpha/2 + \theta)$$

$$\gamma_1 = \sin^{-1}\left[\frac{r}{r_1}\sin(\alpha/2 - \theta)\right],$$

$$\gamma_2 = \sin^{-1}\left[\frac{r}{r_2}\sin(\alpha/2 + \theta)\right],$$

$$\gamma_{1,2} > \pi/2 - \alpha/2.$$

Similarly, the field on the singly diffracted, singly reflected edge rays, shown in Fig. 4(b), is given by

$$E_2^d \sim -F_1[r_0, r_3, \gamma_0, \gamma_3] - F_2[r_0, r_4, \gamma_0, \gamma_4] \tag{23}$$

where R_1 and R_2 are the points of reflection and

$$r_3 \sim r - L\cos(1.5\alpha + \theta), \quad r_4 \sim r - L\cos(1.5\alpha - \theta),$$

$$\gamma_3 = \sin^{-1}\left[\frac{r}{r_3}\sin(1.5\alpha + \theta)\right],$$

$$\gamma_4 = \sin^{-1}\left[\frac{r}{r_4}\sin(1.5\alpha - \theta)\right],$$

$$\gamma_{3,4} < \pi/2 - \alpha/2.$$

Finally, the contribution from the singly diffracted, doubly reflected rays, shown in Fig. 4(c), is given by

$$E_3^d \sim F_1[r_0, r_5, \gamma_0, \gamma_5] + F_2[r_0, r_6, \gamma_0, \gamma_6] \tag{24}$$

where

$$r_5 \sim r - L\cos(2.5\alpha - \theta), \quad r_6 \sim r - L\cos(2.5\alpha + \theta),$$

$$\gamma_5 = \sin^{-1}\left[\frac{r}{r_5}\sin(2.5\alpha - \theta)\right],$$

$$\gamma_6 = \sin^{-1}\left[\frac{r}{r_6}\sin(2.5\alpha + \theta)\right],$$

$$\gamma_{5,6} < \pi/2 - \alpha/2.$$

The total field contribution from the singly diffracted rays is hence given by the sum of (22) to (24), i.e.,

$$E_s^d = E_1^d + E_2^d + E_3^d \tag{25}$$

which is evaluated using the upper and lower signs in (20) for the magnetic and electric planes of diffraction, respectively.

The higher-order rays due to doubly and multiply diffracted rays at the aperture edges lead to field contributions that are lower in magnitude than the geometrical-optics and singly diffracted edge terms. In particular, only the doubly diffracted rays need to be taken into account when the diameter of the aperture is several wavelengths [17]–[19]. Thus, considering Fig. 5 for the E-plane, we note that (a) represents the rays diffracted at one point on the edge and diffracted again at the opposite point on the edge before reaching P. The corresponding contribution at P is given by

$$E_4^d \sim \{F_1[r_0, d, \gamma_0, \pi/2-\alpha/2]\}\{F_1'[d, r_1, \pi/2-\alpha/2, \gamma_1] + F_2'[d, r_2, \pi/2-\alpha/2, \gamma_2]\}. \tag{26}$$

Similarly, the contribution from (b) due to the rays diffracted at one point on the edge, reflected at the wall along the normal, and diffracted again at the same point on the edge, is given by

$$E_5^d \sim -\{F_1[r_0, 2L\sin\alpha, \gamma_0, \pi/2-\alpha]\} \cdot \{F_1'[2L\sin\alpha, r_1, \pi/2-\alpha, \gamma_1] + F_2'[2L\sin\alpha, r_2, \pi/2-\alpha, \gamma_2]\}. \tag{27}$$

The rays shown in (c) represent those diffracted at one point on the edge, diffracted again at the opposite point on the edge, and finally reflected at the wall before reaching P. The corresponding contribution at P is given by

$$E_6^d \sim -\{F_1[r_0, d, \gamma_0, \pi/2-\alpha/2]\} \cdot \{F_1'[d, r_3, \pi/2-\alpha/2, \gamma_3] + F_2'[d, r_4, \pi/2-\alpha/2, \gamma_4]\}. \tag{28}$$

Finally, (d) represents those rays diffracted at one point on the edge and reflected twice within the horn and reach P after suffering an additional diffraction at the opposite point on the edge. The corresponding field term at P is given by

$$E_7^d \sim \{F_1[r_0, r_7, \gamma_0, \pi/2-1.5\alpha]\} \cdot \{F_1'[r_7, r_1, \pi/2-1.5\alpha, \gamma_1] + F_2'[r_7, r_2, \pi/2-1.5\alpha, \gamma_2]\} \tag{29}$$

where

$$r_7 = \sqrt{2}\,L(1-\cos 3\alpha)^{1/2}.$$

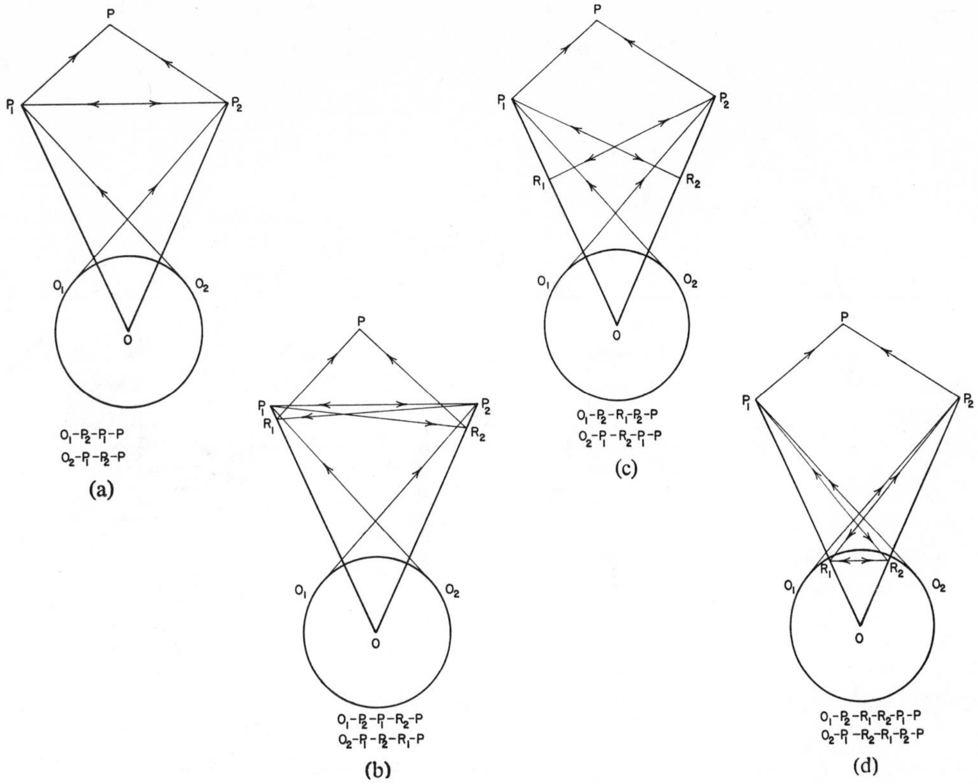

Fig. 5. Doubly diffracted rays in the E-plane.

The multiply diffracted edge field is hence given by

$$E_m{}^d = E_4{}^d + E_5{}^d + E_6{}^d + E_7{}^d \tag{30}$$

while the total edge field in the E-plane is the sum of the singly and multiply diffracted fields, i.e.,

$$E^d = E_s{}^d + E_m{}^d \tag{31}$$

which includes the contributions from both points on the edge (P_1 and P_2) as long as either of the angles γ_1 or γ_2 lies in the range $\pi/2-\alpha/2$ to $3\pi/2-\alpha/2$ or $2\pi-\alpha$ to 2π (back lobe region). In the shadow region, on the other hand, where γ_1 or γ_2 lies in the range $3\pi/2-\alpha/2$ to $2\pi-\alpha$, the contribution to E^d comes from either P_1 or P_2 only. The first exception to these rules corresponds to the shadow boundary regions of the edge where $\gamma_{1,2}=\pi\pm\gamma_0$ at the shadow lines and the secant terms in (20) and (21) become infinite. To improve the accuracy of the asymptotic approximation for such cases, the angles δ_1 and δ_2 in (20) and (21) are multiplied by the amplitude correction factor G which is evaluated in detail elsewhere [17], [28]. The second exception corresponds to the case where P, P_1, and P_2 lie on a straight line (i.e., γ_1 or γ_2 equal to $3\pi/2-\alpha/2$) and the field on the resulting ray (P_1-P_2-P or P_2-P_1-P) is multiplied by the factor 0.5. This factor is also derived elsewhere [17], [20], [29] and will not therefore be described any further.

The total edge field in the magnetic plane may also be expressed by (31) with $E_s{}^d$ obtained from (25) and $E_m{}^d$ from (30) with the upper sign in (20) and (21) and P_1, P_2, γ_1, γ_2, r_1, r_2, r_e replaced everywhere by P_3, P_4, r_3, r_4, r_m, respectively.

V. Gain and Radiation Pattern

The gain function may be calculated using the expression

$$g = \frac{4\pi P(0,0)}{P_t(\theta,\phi)} \tag{32}$$

which may also be written as

$$g = \frac{4\pi[\,|E_\theta|^2]_{\theta=\phi=0}}{\int_0^{2\pi}\int_0^{\pi}[\,|E_\theta|^2+|E_\phi|^2]r^2\sin\theta\, d\theta d\phi} \tag{33}$$

where $P_t(\theta, \phi)$ is the total power radiated and $P(0, 0)$ is the maximum power radiated per unit solid angle, which is in the direction $\theta=\phi=0$. The fields E_θ and E_ϕ in (33) are computed numerically using (9), (10), and (31) to include the contributions of the geometrical-optics as well as the edge rays to the far field.[1] The results for the absolute gain as a function of the aperture diameter d/λ are given in Fig. 6 for various values of the axial height h/λ. Since the gain

[1] Essentially the same results can be obtained for the gain when the absolute value of $P_t(\theta, \phi)$ is computed by integrating the Poynting vector in the circular waveguide over a transverse plane. Here the electric and magnetic fields in the waveguide are well known [30] and the integration may be carried out in the same manner as shown in chapter 10 of [1]. The throat reflection coefficient, which is needed in this case, is obtained from the approximate results of Leonard and Yen [31] for a long horn which are then modified to include the contribution from the aperture edge rays that travel toward the waveguide region. The ratio of this absolute value for $P_t(\theta, \phi)$ to the relative value given in the denominator of (33) is the normalization constant which must be multiplied by the numerator of (33) to give the absolute value of $P(0, 0)$.

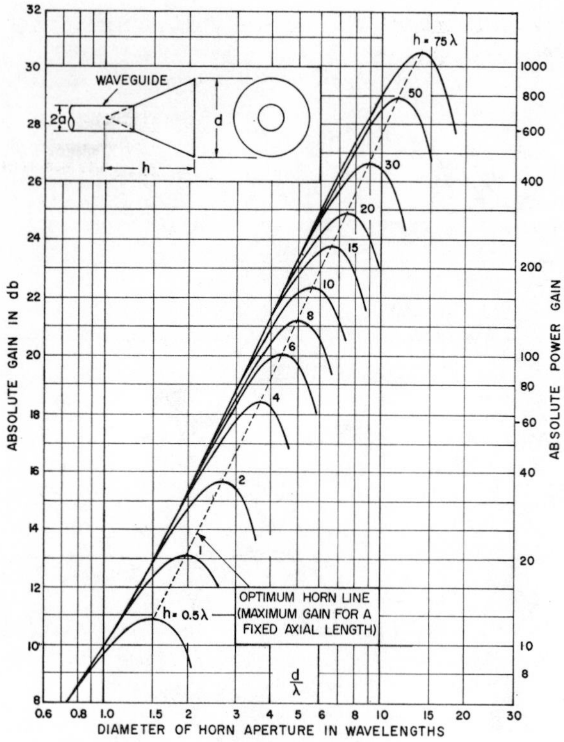

Fig. 6. Absolute gain of a conical horn as a function of physical dimensions.

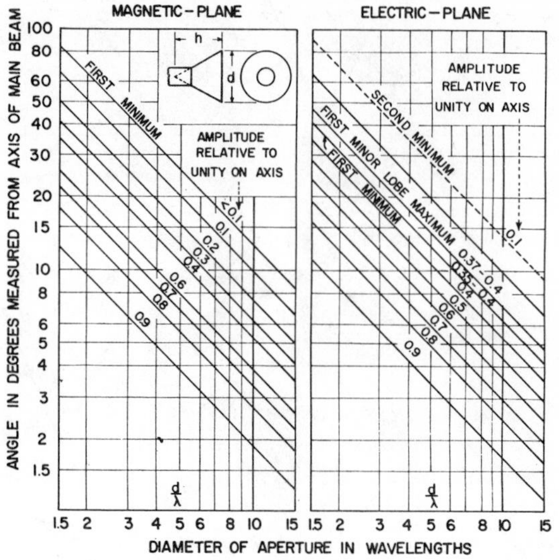

Fig. 8. Monograph for plotting the radiation characteristics for conical horns of optimum design.

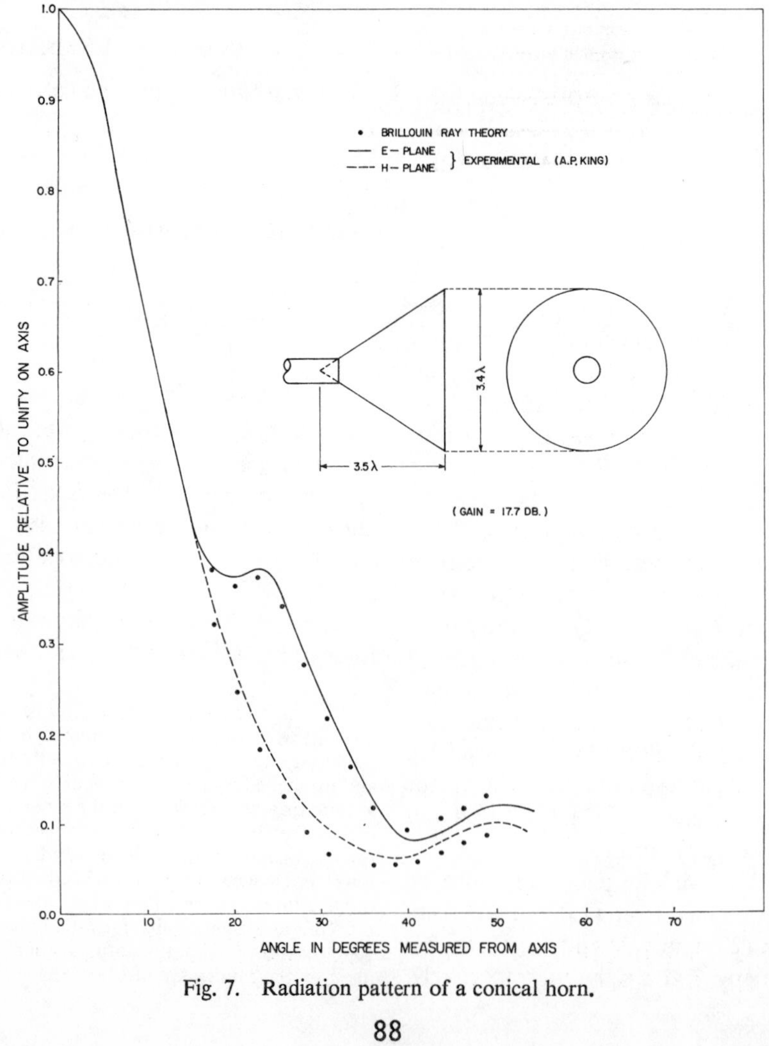

Fig. 7. Radiation pattern of a conical horn.

versus d/λ increases up to a certain maximum for each fixed value h/λ, the dashed line in this figure corresponds to horns of optimum design as shown by King [26].

In Fig. 7 a plot is given of the E- and H-plane radiation patterns of an optimum horn, whose dimensions approximately correspond to a gain of 17.7 dB as obtained from Fig. 6. These patterns, as well as the monograph of Fig. 8 for plotting the radiation patterns of optimum horns, are also based on a numerical computation using (9), (10), and (31).

VI. Discussion and Conclusions

Examination of our theoretical results shows that Kinber's two-dimensional Brillouin ray tracing technique has been extended for the fundamental horn mode to three dimensions. This has been achieved with the aid of an exact solution for the eigenvalues of the horn and correction factors to improve the accuracy of the fields on "transitional" rays in the near zone and along the shadow boundaries of the edge.

Comparison of our predicted results for the gain and radiation pattern of conical horns of various dimensions with the experimental results of King [26] shows an excellent agreement. The maximum deviation for the gain and the absolute pattern was found to be ± 0.09 dB and ± 3 percent, respectively. We have therefore provided a theoretical justification for King's experimental results using the ray-optical technique. In particular, the optimum horn line in Fig. 6 has been verified and may be calculated using the empirical formula

$$g \doteqdot 7 + 20.576 \log_{10} (d/\lambda)$$

which is only valid for the ranges of values for g, d/λ, and h/λ given in Fig. 6.

Appendix I

Evaluation of Eigenvalues ν

The functions $P_\nu(u)$ satisfy the Legendre differential equation

$$(1 - u^2)\frac{d^2y}{du^2} - 2u\frac{dy}{du} + [\nu(\nu + 1)]y = 0 \quad (34)$$

where $u = \cos\theta$ and $y = P_\nu(\cos\theta)$. Rewriting (34) in the alternative form,

$$\frac{d^2y}{d\theta^2} + (\cot\theta)\frac{dy}{d\theta} + \nu(\nu + 1) = 0 \quad (35)$$

and combining (5) and (35) we obtain the first-order differential equation

$$\frac{dy}{d\theta} + \nu(\nu + 1)y\tan\theta = 0, \qquad \theta = \pm\,\alpha/2 \quad (36)$$

and hence the solution

$$P_\nu[\cos(\alpha/2)] = a_0[\cos(\alpha/2)]^{\nu(\nu+1)} \quad (37)$$

where a_0 is a constant. An alternative solution of (5) may be simply expressed in the form

$$P_\nu[\cos(\alpha/2)] = a_1(\alpha/2) + a_2 \quad (38)$$

where a_1 and a_2 are constants. From (37) and (38) we obtain the result[2]

$$\nu = -\,0.5 \pm 0.5[1 + 4b_0]^{1/2} \quad (39)$$

where b_0 is given by

$$b_0 = \frac{\log_{10}\left(\dfrac{a_1\alpha/2 + a_2}{a_0}\right)}{\log_{10}(\cos\alpha/2)} \quad (40)$$

and the θ-dependence is hence described by the conical functions $P_{-0.5+0.5\sqrt{1+4b_0}}(\cos\theta)$. The constants a_0, a_1, and a_2 may be conveniently obtained from the properties of the Legendre functions $P_\nu(\cos\theta)$. Since these functions and their second derivatives vanish for $\nu=1$, $\theta=\pi/2$ and $\nu=2$, $\theta=\pi/4$, we obtain from (37), (38), and (39), without any loss of generality, the results

$$a_0 = 2, \quad a_1 = -\,1/\pi, \quad a_2 = 0.5 \quad (41)$$

and hence

$$b_0 = \frac{\log_{10}[(1 - \alpha/\pi)/4]}{\log_{10}[\cos(\alpha/2)]}\,. \quad (42)$$

Appendix II

Approximate Evaluation of $[P_\nu'(\cos\theta)]/\sin\theta$ and $P_\nu''(\cos\theta)$ in Terms of Exponential Functions

The Legendre functions $P_\nu^m(\cos\theta)$ may be approximated by exponential functions[3] using the integral representation [25]

$$\frac{\Gamma(\nu-m+1)}{\Gamma(\nu+m+1)}\left[(\cos m\pi)P_\nu^m(\cos\theta) - \frac{2}{\pi}(\sin m\pi)Q_\nu^m(\cos\theta)\right]$$
$$= \sqrt{\frac{2}{\pi}}\cdot\frac{(\sin\theta)^{-m}}{\Gamma(m+\frac{1}{2})}\int_0^\theta \frac{\cos(\nu+\frac{1}{2})\beta}{(\cos\beta - \cos\theta)^{1/2-m}}\,d\beta. \quad (43)$$

For $m=1$, we have

$$P_\nu^1(\cos\theta) = P_\nu'(\cos\theta) = -\frac{\sqrt{2/\pi}\,\Gamma(\nu+2)}{\Gamma(1.5)\Gamma(\nu)\sin\theta}[I] \quad (44)$$

where the integral I is given by

$$I = \int_0^\theta [\cos(\nu+\tfrac{1}{2})\beta][\cos\beta - \cos\theta]^{1/2}d\beta. \quad (45)$$

[2] Since $P^\mu_{-\nu-1}(z) = P_\nu^\mu(z)$, the two solutions for ν lead to identical results.

[3] There are more direct approximations for these functions in the literature [24]. However, these are not suitable for small values of θ.

An approximate value for the integral I may be obtained using the relation

$$\cos(\delta) \doteqdot 1 - \frac{\delta^2}{2.05}, \qquad 0 \leq \delta < \pi/3, \tag{46}$$

which is derived elsewhere [17] on the basis of the least-squares method. Hence

$$(\cos\beta - \cos\theta)^{1/2} \doteqdot \left(\frac{\theta^2 - \beta^2}{2.05}\right)^{1/2}, \quad 0 \leq \beta, \theta < \pi/3, \tag{47}$$

and

$$I \doteqdot \frac{\theta}{\sqrt{2.05}} \int_\theta^\theta (\cos \nu'\beta)[1 - (\beta/\theta)^2]^{1/2} d\beta. \tag{48}$$

Substituting (46) in (48) and neglecting the higher-order terms, we obtain

$$I \doteqdot \frac{5\theta^2}{6\sqrt{2.05}} [1 - 0.14\nu'^2\theta^2]. \tag{49}$$

The ratio $[P_\nu'(\cos\theta)]/\sin\theta$ is hence given approximately by

$$[P_\nu'(\cos\theta)]/\sin\theta \doteqdot \frac{b_1\theta^2(1 - 0.14\nu'^2\theta^2)}{\sin^2\theta} \tag{50}$$

where

$$b_1 = -\frac{5\Gamma(\nu+2)\sqrt{2/\pi}}{6\Gamma(1.5)\Gamma(\nu)\sqrt{2.05}} = -0.524b_0. \tag{51}$$

Using the relation

$$\sin\theta = \theta\left(1 - \frac{\theta^2}{\pi^2}\right)\left(1 - \frac{\theta^2}{2^2\pi^2}\right)\cdots \tag{52}$$

we find, after completing the squares in the right-hand side of (50) and neglecting small terms, that

$$[P_\nu'(\cos\theta)]/\sin\theta \doteqdot b_1[1 - 0.07\nu'^2\theta^2]^2. \tag{53}$$

The right-hand side of (53) may be expressed as a cosine function using (46), i.e.,

$$b_1[1 - 0.07\nu'^2\theta^2]^2 = b_1\left[1 - \left(\frac{\nu'\theta}{2.64}\right)^2 \Big/ 2.05\right]^2 \doteqdot b_1\cos^2(\nu'\theta/2.64) \tag{54}$$

and thus

$$[P_\nu'(\cos\theta)]/\sin\theta \doteqdot 0.5b_1[1 + \cos(\nu_e\theta)] \tag{55}$$

where

$$\nu_e = \nu'/1.32 = 0.379(1 + 4b_0)^{1/2} \tag{56}$$

and the subscript e denotes the electric plane.

The functions $P_\nu''(\cos\theta)$ may be expressed from (35), (12), and (55) by

$$P_\nu''(\cos\theta) = -b_0 - 0.5b_1\cos\theta[1 + \cos(\nu_e\theta)]. \tag{57}$$

Using (46) and (51) in (57) we obtain for $0 \leq \theta < \pi/3$

$$P_\nu''(\cos\theta) \doteqdot 0.91b_1[2 - \cos(\nu_m\theta)] \tag{58}$$

where

$$\nu_m = [(\nu_e^2 + 2)/1.82]^{1/2} = 1.09[1 + 0.267b_0]^{1/2} \tag{59}$$

and the subscript m denotes the magnetic plane. The final results are obtained by expressing the cosine terms in (55) and (58) in terms of exponential functions as shown in (13) and (14).

Acknowledgment

The author thanks Prof. J. L. Yen of the Department of Electrical Engineering, University of Toronto, for many profitable discussions during the early stages of this work.

References

[1] S. Silver, *Microwave Antenna Theory and Design*, M.I.T. Radiation Lab. Ser., vol. 12. New York: McGraw-Hill, 1949, pp. 166–170.

[2] W. L. Barrow and L. J. Chu, "Theory of the electromagnetic horn," *Proc. IRE*, vol. 27, pp. 51–64, January 1939.

[3] S. A. Schelkunoff and H. T. Friss, *Antennas, Theory and Practice*. New York: Wiley, 1952, ch. 16.

[4] C. Z. Huygens, *Treatise on Light*. Leyden, 1690. (Discussed by F. Whittaker in *A History of the Theories of Aether and Electricity*, vol. 1. London: Thomas Nelson and Son, Ltd., 1951, p. 23.)

[5] A. Fresnel, *Memoirs de l'Academie*, 1826, p. 339; *Oeuvres Completes*, vol. 1, p. 247. (Quoted by B. B. Baker and E. T. Copson, *The Mathematical Theory of Huygens' Principle*, 2nd ed. Oxford: Clarendon Press, 1949, p. 20.)

[6] G. Kirchhoff, *Berliner Sitzungsberichte*, 1882, p. 641; *Ann. Phys.*, vol. 18, 1883, p. 663; *Vorlesungen über Mathematische Physik* (*Optik*), p. 23. (Quoted by Baker and Copson [5], p. 37.)

[7] J. W. S. Rayleigh, *The Theory of Sound.* New York: Dover, 1945 (originally published in 1896).

[8] J. A. Stratton and L. J. Chu, "Diffraction theory of electromagnetic waves," *Phys. Rev.*, vol. 56, July 1939.

[9] S. A. Schelkunoff, "On diffraction and radiation of electromagnetic waves," *Phys. Rev.*, vol. 56, August 1939.

[10] C. J. Bowkamp, "Diffraction theory," *Rept. Progr. Phys.*, vol. 17, pp. 35–100, 1954.

[11] A. Sommerfeld, *Optics*, Lectures on Theoretical Physics, vol. 4. New York: Academic Press, 1954.

[12] A. C. Schell, "The corner array," USAF Cambridge Research Center, Bedford, Mass., AFCRC-TR-59-105, ASTIA Doc. AD209201, January 1959.

[13] Y. Ohba, "On the radiation pattern of a corner reflector finite in width," *IEEE Trans. Antennas and Propagation*, vol. AP-11, pp. 127–132, March 1963.

[14] B. Y. Kinber, "Diffraction at the open end of a sectoral horn," *Radio Engrg. Electronic Phys.*, vol. 7–10, pp. 1620–1632, October 1962.

[15] P. M. Russo, R. C. Rudduck, and L. Peters, Jr., "A method for computing *E*-plane patterns of horn antennas," *IEEE Trans. Antennas and Propagation*, vol. AP-13, pp. 219–224, March 1965.

[16] J. S. Yu, R. C. Rudduck, and L. Peters, Jr., "Comprehensive analysis for *E*-plane of horn antennas by edge diffraction theory," *IEEE Trans. Antennas and Propagation*, vol. AP-14, pp. 138–149, March 1966.

[17] M. A. K. Hamid, "Near field transmission between horn antennas," Antenna Lab., Dept. of Elec. Engrg., University of To-

ronto, Toronto, Canada, Research Rept. 43, April 1966; presented at Internat'l Symp. on Antennas and Propagation, Palo Alto, Calif., December 1966.

[18] ——, "Gain of electromagnetic horns" (*Abstracts*), Joint U. S.-Canadian URSI Spring Meeting, Commission 6, Session 1, Ottawa, Canada, May 1967.

[19] J. B. Keller, "Diffraction by an aperture," *J. Appl. Phys.*, vol. 28, pp. 426–444, April 1957.

[20] J. B. Keller, R. M. Lewis, and B. D. Seckler, "Diffraction by an aperture—II," *J. Appl. Phys.*, vol. 28, pp. 570–579, May 1957.

[21] R. F. Harrington, *Time-Harmonic Electromagnetic Fields.* New York: McGraw-Hill, 1961, ch. 6.

[22] A. F. Kay, "The wide flare horn—a novel feed for low noise broadband and high aperture efficiency antennas," TRG Inc., East Boston, Mass., Sci. Rept. 2, Contract AF19(604)-8057, Doc. AFCRL-62-757, p. 31, October 1962.

[23] P. M. Morse and H. Feshbach, *Methods of Theoretical Physics*, pt. 1. New York: McGraw-Hill, 1953, p. 630.

[24] *Handbook of Mathematical Functions*, Appl. Math. Ser. 55. Washington, D. C.: NBS, June 1964, pp. 366, 336.

[25] W. Magnus and F. Oberhettinger, *Formulas and Theorems for the Special Functions of Mathematical Physics.* New York: Chelsea Pub. Co., 1949, p. 67.

[26] A. P. King, "The radiation characteristics of conical horn antennas," *Proc. IRE*, vol. 38, pp. 249–251, March 1950.

[27] J. B. Keller, "Backscattering from a finite cone," Div. of Electromagnetic Research, Inst. of Math. Sci., New York University, New York, N. Y., Research Rept. EM-127, February 1959.

[28] M. A. K. Hamid, "Near field of a conducting edge," *IEEE Trans. Antennas and Propagation*, vol. AP-15, May 1967.

[29] ——, "Mutual coupling between sectoral horns side by side," *IEEE Trans. Antennas and Propagation* (*Communications*), vol. AP-15, pp. 475–477, May 1967.

[30] S. Ramo, J. R. Whinnery, and T. V. Duzer, *Fields and Waves in Communication Electronics.* New York: Wiley, 1965, p. 430.

[31] D. J. Leonard and J. L. Yen, "Junction of smooth flared waveguides," *J. Appl. Phys.*, vol. 28, pp. 1441–1448, December 1957. (See also, by the same authors, "Waveguide-horn junctions," Antenna Lab., Dept. of Elec. Engrg., University of Toronto, Toronto, Canada, Research Rept. 4, pp. 47–52, December 1954)

Modes in a conical horn: new approach

M. S. Narasimhan, M.Tech., and B. V. Rao, Ph.D.

Indexing terms: *Antenna radiation patterns, Waveguides*

Abstract

An analytically simple, sufficiently accurate, and self-consistent solution for modes in a conical horn is presented. The eigenfunctions and eigenvalues derived from the simpler solution for the TE and TM modes of different orders are close to the exact solution. Application of the simpler solution for obtaining the aperture field and, subsequently, the far-field-radiation patterns of conical horns of arbitrary flare angles excited in the TE_{11} mode, with the aid of a vector diffraction formula, yields results in close agreement with experiment. The new approach provides a simple and accurate solution for the balanced hybrid modes in corrugated conical horns with small and wide flare angles, emphasising the more general validity of the technique adopted.

List of principal symbols

α_0 = semivertical angle of cone
L = axial length of cone
a = aperture radius of cone
ρ', ϕ' = plane polar co-ordinates of point on aperture of cone
$r', \theta'\phi'$ = spherical polar co-ordinates of point on aperture
$\boldsymbol{a}'_r, \boldsymbol{a}'_\theta, \boldsymbol{a}'_\phi$ = unit vectors associated with (r', θ', ϕ')
$\boldsymbol{a}_x, \boldsymbol{a}_y, \boldsymbol{a}_z$ = unit vectors associated with Cartesian system of co-ordinates
R, θ, ϕ = spherical polar co-ordinates of point in far field
$\boldsymbol{a}_R, \boldsymbol{a}_\theta, \boldsymbol{a}_\phi$ = unit vectors associated with (R, θ, ϕ)
$\boldsymbol{E}'_t, \boldsymbol{H}'_t$ = aperture fields tangential to circularly plane aperture
$\boldsymbol{n}' = \boldsymbol{a}_z$
$J_m(x)$ = Bessel function of first kind, order m
$J'_m(x)$ = first derivative (with respect to the argument) of $J_m(x)$
p_{mn} = nth nonvanishing root of $J'_m(x)$
q_{mn} = nth nonvanishing root of $J_m(x)$
$H^2_y(x)$ = Hankel function of second kind
λ = free-space wavelength
Z_0 = intrinsic impedance of free space
$k = 2\pi/\lambda$
μ_0 = permeability of free space
ϵ_0 = permittivity of free space
$G(0, 0)$ = on-axis gain
Z = wave impedance at any point within conical waveguide, $Z = E_\theta/H_\phi = -E_\phi/H_\theta$

1 Introduction

The conical-horn antenna has assumed considerable importance in recent years because of its versatile role, as in polarisation-diversity applications,[1] in beam waveguides for launching Gaussian modes[2] and, sometimes, in omnidirectional television antenna systems.[3]

Theoretical study of the radiation characteristics of a conical horn requires an accurate knowledge of the aperture field expressed in terms of the amplitude of modes excited at the feed junction. The exact form of the modes in a conical horn is well known, but determination of the modes is, in general, complicated, and requires numerical solution of eigenvalues. An analytically simple and sufficiently accurate asymptotic solution for conical-horn modes is presented in this paper. A comparison with the exact solution for eigenfunctions and eigenvalues of modes of different orders shows that the asymptotic solution is valid for all values of flare (semivertical) angle α_0 of the cone (i.e. $0 \leqslant \alpha_0 \leqslant 90°$).

The simpler solution for horn modes is employed to obtain the aperture field of a conical horn with long axial length excited in the TE_{11} mode accurately. Applying a vector diffraction formula,[4] the radiation pattern and gain of conical horns with arbitrary flare angles have been derived. Close agreement between theory and experiment establishes the validity of the simpler solution assumed. The generality of the asymptotic solution adopted for horn modes is emphasised by the fact that a direct application of the same technique for obtaining the balanced hybrid modes in a corrugated conical horn yields results in close agreement with experiment.[5,6] Although only the TE_{11} mode is considered for calculating the radiation pattern and gain, the theory can be easily extended to other higher-order modes. Although, in the past, a few authors[7] have treated the radiation properties of conical horns, a simpler approach of more general validity correlated better with experiment than the method presented here does not seem to have been reported anywhere in the literature.

Paper 6351 E, first received 6th July and in revised form 22nd October 1970
Mr. Narasimhan and Dr. Rao are with the Department of Electrical Engineering, Indian Institute of Technology, Powai, Bombay 76, India

2 Asymptotic solutions for modes of a long conical horn

The electromagnetic-field components of a long conical horn ($kL \gg 1$ where L is the axial length) with a flare angle α_0 bounded by perfectly conducting walls are assumed to be identical to those in a conical waveguide of the same flare angle. The potentials conventionally used to generate modes of a conical horn are given by[8]

$$\begin{pmatrix} f^e \\ f^m \end{pmatrix} = \begin{pmatrix} A_{mn} \\ B_{mn} \end{pmatrix} P^m_s(\cos\theta)\cos m\phi\sqrt{(r)}H^2_{s+1/2}(kr) \quad . \quad . \quad . \quad . \quad (1)$$

where $H_y(x)$ is the Hankel function of the second kind. Given m, the eigenvalues s are evaluated from the characteristic equations

$$\frac{d}{d\theta}\{P^m_s(\cos\theta)\} = 0 \text{ at } \theta = \alpha_0 \quad . \quad . \quad . \quad . \quad . \quad . \quad (2)$$

and $$\{P^m_s(\cos\theta)\} = 0 \text{ at } \theta = \alpha_0 \quad . \quad . \quad . \quad . \quad . \quad . \quad (3)$$

corresponding to TE_{mn} and TM_{mn} modes, respectively. The asymptotic solutions for the potentials f^e and f^m (given by eqn. 1) are obtained by replacing $\sin\theta$ by θ in the $(H)(\theta)$ part of the Helmholtz equation* in spherical polar co-ordinates and solving the resulting Bessel's differential equation,[5] subject to the condition that $(H)(\theta)$ is finite at $\theta = 0$. Such a procedure leads to the following relationships:

$$\begin{pmatrix} u^e \\ u^m \end{pmatrix} = \begin{pmatrix} A_{mn} \\ B_{mn} \end{pmatrix} J_m(v\theta)\cos m\phi\sqrt{(r)}H^2_y(kr) \quad . \quad . \quad (4)$$

where $v = \sqrt{\{s(s+1)\}}$, $y = s + 0{\cdot}5$ and u^e and u^m represent the asymptotic solutions corresponding to f^e and f^m, respectively, given by eqn. 1. On applying the appropriate boundary conditions, the eigenvalue s is expressed in an explicit closed form given by

$$s = -0{\cdot}5 + (0{\cdot}25 + p^2_{mn}/\alpha^2_0)^{1/2} \quad . \quad . \quad . \quad . \quad . \quad (5)$$

$$s = -0{\cdot}5 + (0{\cdot}25 + q^2_{mn}/\alpha^2_0)^{1/2} \quad . \quad . \quad . \quad . \quad . \quad (6)$$

* The $(H)(\theta)$ part of the Helmholtz equation corresponds to the differential equation satisfying the $(H)(\theta)$ part of the solution for $u^{e,m}$ obtained from $\nabla^2 u^{e,m} + k^2 u^{e,m} = 0$ using the variables-separable method

Reprinted with permission from *Proc. Inst. Elec. Eng.*, vol. 118, pp. 287-292, Feb. 1971.

for TE_{mn} and TM_{mn} modes, respectively. The field vectors $\boldsymbol{E}$ and $\boldsymbol{H}$ representing the horn modes are obtained with the aid of the following relationships:[8]

$$\boldsymbol{E} = -\nabla \times \boldsymbol{F} \quad \boldsymbol{H} = \frac{1}{j\omega\mu_0} \nabla \times \nabla \times \boldsymbol{F} \quad . \quad . \quad . \quad . \quad (7)$$

for TE_{mn} modes

$$\boldsymbol{H} = \nabla \times \boldsymbol{A} \quad \boldsymbol{E} = \frac{1}{j\omega\epsilon_0} \nabla \times \nabla \times \boldsymbol{A} \quad . \quad . \quad . \quad . \quad (8)$$

for TM_{mn} modes

where $\boldsymbol{A} = \boldsymbol{a}_r u^e$ and $\boldsymbol{F} = \boldsymbol{a}_r u^m$.

In spite of the approximation $\sin\theta \simeq \theta$ made in solving the $(H)(\theta)$ part of the Helmholtz equation, the solution given by eqn. 4, after applying the boundary conditions, is accurate, even for large values of θ. Application of the boundary condition minimises the error that would be otherwise present at the boundary $\theta = \alpha_0$ because the solutions obtained from the approximate, as well as the exact, differential equation for $(H)(\theta)$ are equalised at $\theta = \alpha_0$. Since only those solutions which satisfy a set of boundary conditions are of concern, the technique adopted is justified. As a verification of the above, the normalised values of E_θ and E_ϕ obtained from the asymptotic and exact solutions are compared in Figs. 1A and 1B for a horn with $\alpha_0 = 90°$ excited in the dominant mode, and, in this case, the maximum deviation of the asymptotic solution from the exact solution is less than 2%. Calculation for a horn with $\alpha_0 = 45°$ shows the same result. In addition to the dominant mode, a similar comparison between the two solutions for the first few higher-order modes (E_{11}, E_{12} and H_{12} modes being considered) shows that the asymptotic solution is close to the exact solution to within 5% for horns with $\alpha_0 \leqslant 90°$.

The eigenvalue s associated with the asymptotic solution has been expressed in an explicit closed form by eqns. 5 and 6. For the dominant mode, the maximum deviation of s, calculated according to eqn. 5, from the exact value is less than 5% when $\alpha_0 \leqslant 45°$. However, for other higher-order modes (E_{11}, E_{12}, E_{13}, . . ., E_{1n}; H_{12}, H_{13} . . ., H_{1n}), the difference between the two is very small for any value of $\alpha_0 \leqslant 90°$, as shown in Table 1. It is inferred that the order of error in s obtained from eqns. 5 and 6 progressively diminishes as the mode number n increases, for a given α_0. A comparison between the asymptotic and exact solutions* for s as a function of α_0 has been made in Fig. 2 for the first ten modes.

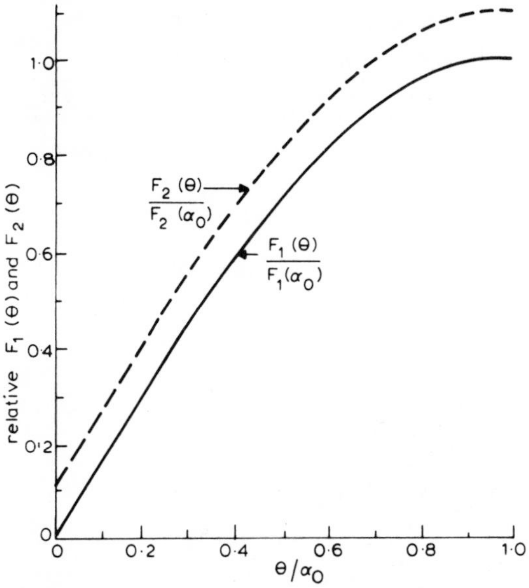

Fig. 1A
Comparison of $F_1(\theta)$ and $F_2(\theta)$ for the TE_{11} mode

$\alpha_0 = 90'$, $F_1(\theta) = P_1^1(\cos\theta)$ and $F_2(\theta) = J_1\left(\frac{1\cdot841}{\alpha_0}\theta\right)$. To facilitate comparison, $\frac{F_2(\theta)}{F_2(\alpha_0)}$ has been displaced from $\frac{F_1(\theta)}{F_1(\alpha_0)}$ by $+0\cdot1$

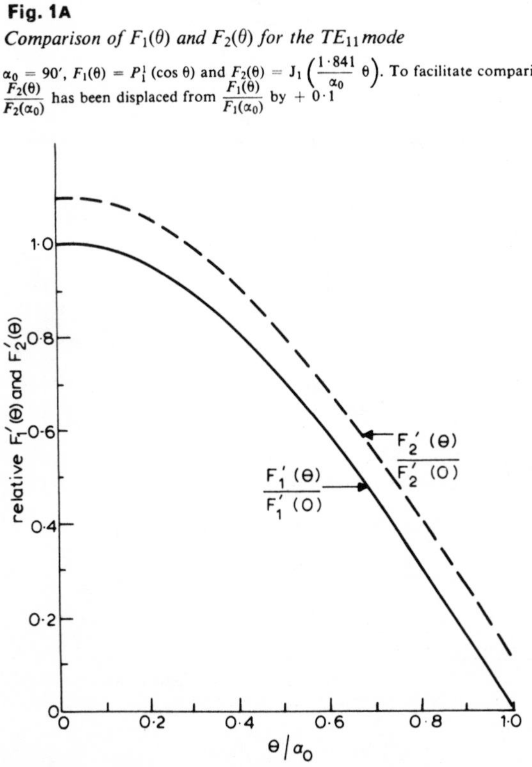

Fig. 1B
Comparison of $F_1'(\theta)$ and $F_2'(\theta)$

To facilitate comparison, $\frac{F_2'(\theta)}{F_2'(0)}$ has been displaced from $\frac{F_1'(\theta)}{F_1'(0)}$ by $+0\cdot1$

Table 1

ERROR IN EIGENVALUES (GIVEN BY EQNS. 5 AND 6) FOR FIRST FEW MODES (TE AND TM) AS FUNCTION OF FLARE ANGLE

Mode designation \ Flare angle α_0, deg	30	60	90
	%	%	%
TM_{11}	0·05	0·09	0·44
TM_{12}	0·02	0·03	0·13
TM_{13}	0·01	0·02	0·07
TM_{14}	<0·01	0·01	0·03
TM_{15}	<0·01	<0·01	0·02
TE_{12}	0·55	1·20	2·00
TE_{13}	0·24	0·45	0·78
TE_{14}	0·11	0·25	0·41
TE_{15}	0·07	0·12	0·26

A direct application of the technique presented here for obtaining the balanced hybrid modes in a corrugated conical horn yields good results. In particular, the maximum deviation of the asymptotic solution for E_θ and E_ϕ of a corrugated conical horn (with $\alpha_0 = 60°$) from the exact solution given by Clarricoats[9] for the HE_{11} mode is less than 2%. Details relating to this have been treated elsewhere.[5] Thus, the asymptotic technique presented results in an analytically simple self-consistent and sufficiently accurate description of the modes of a conical horn.

3 Study of radiation from conical horn excited in TE_{11} mode

In this Section, the asymptotic solution for horn modes is employed to study the far-field radiation patterns of a conical horn excited in the TE_{11} mode. There are different methods for calculating radiation patterns of horn antennas from a knowledge of the aperture distribution. One of the methods of determining accurately the radiation pattern uses the modal-function expansion of Potter.[10]

In this method, the field $\boldsymbol{E}_s'$ over the spherical cap $r = r_0$ ($r_0 = L\sec\alpha_0$) is expanded in terms of spherical TE and TM modes of free space (assuming $\boldsymbol{E}_s' = 0$ for $\alpha_0 < \theta < \pi - \alpha_0$) which are subsequently used to represent the diffracted far field at an observation point $P(R, \theta, \phi)$. The other method of calculating the far-field radiation pattern will be to integrate the aperture field over S' (Fig. 3) using the well known vector diffraction formula.[10] Recently, James and

* The exact solution for s was obtained by solving eqns. 2 and 3 numerically with the aid of a digital computer

Longdon[11] have established that these techniques are mathematically equivalent. However, for circular apertures (as with a conical horn), application of the vector diffraction formula involves fewer special functions and integrations than the modal-expansion method. Therefore the aperture-field method is used.

The assumptions inherent in the aperture-field method are described by Silver.[12] Further, it is assumed that the field over the aperture is the same as that which exists at the same cross-section of an infinite horn. The field does not spill around the rim of the horn mouth. The radiator is perfectly matched to free space.*

Subject to the assumptions stated above, the fictitious electric and magnetic current densities over the horn aperture are given by[13]

$$\boldsymbol{K} = \boldsymbol{n}' \times \boldsymbol{E}_t' \text{ and } \boldsymbol{J} = \boldsymbol{H}_t' \times \boldsymbol{n}' \quad . \quad . \quad . \quad . \quad . \quad (9)$$

where $\boldsymbol{E}_t'$ and $\boldsymbol{H}_t'$ are aperture fields at a point P' an S' (see Fig. 3). Radiation due to these fictitious sources at an observation point $P(R, \theta, \phi)$ is calculated with the aid of the following relationships:[12]

* It can be shown that the wave impedance over the aperture of a long conical horn ($kr_0 \gg 1$) is approximately equal to the intrinsic impedance of free space

$$\boldsymbol{E_P} = -\frac{1}{\epsilon_0}\nabla \times \boldsymbol{F} - \frac{j}{\omega\mu_0\epsilon_0}\nabla \times \nabla \times \boldsymbol{A} \quad . \quad . \quad (10)$$

$$\text{where } \boldsymbol{A} = \frac{\mu_0}{4\pi}\iint \boldsymbol{J}\frac{e^{-jk\eta}}{\eta}\,dS' \text{ and } \boldsymbol{F} = \frac{\epsilon_0}{4\pi}\iint \boldsymbol{K}\frac{e^{-jk\eta}}{\eta}\,dS' \quad . \quad . \quad . \quad . \quad (11)$$

Making the far-field approximations given by

$$k \gg \frac{1}{\eta},\ \boldsymbol{a}\eta \simeq \boldsymbol{a}_R \text{ and } \eta \simeq R - x'\cos\theta\cos\phi' - y'\sin\theta\sin\phi'$$

after extensive manipulations,† eqn. 10 reduces to a simpler form given by

$$E_P = \frac{-jk}{4\pi}\frac{e^{-jkR}}{R}(1+\cos\theta)\iint_{S'}\{\boldsymbol{a}_\theta(E_x'\cos\phi + E_y'\sin\phi) + \boldsymbol{a}_\phi(E_y'\cos\phi - E_x'\sin\phi)\} \times \exp\{jk(x'\sin\theta\cos\phi + y'\sin\theta\sin\phi)\}\,dS' \quad . \quad (12)$$

where $\boldsymbol{E}_t' = \boldsymbol{a}_x E_x' + \boldsymbol{a}_y E_y'$.

† In the course of the derivation, it has been taken that $E_\phi'/H_\theta' = -E_\theta'/H_\phi' = Z_0$ and $H_r' = 0$ over the horn aperture. This conforms with the initial assumptions

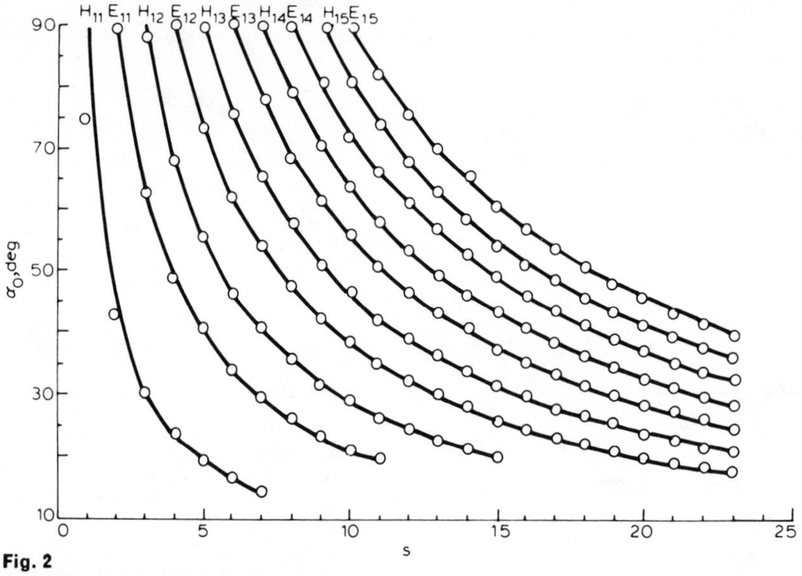

Fig. 2

Comparison of asymptotic values of s (given by eqns. 5 and 6) with the corresponding exact values

——— exact values
○○○ values corresponding to asymptotic solution

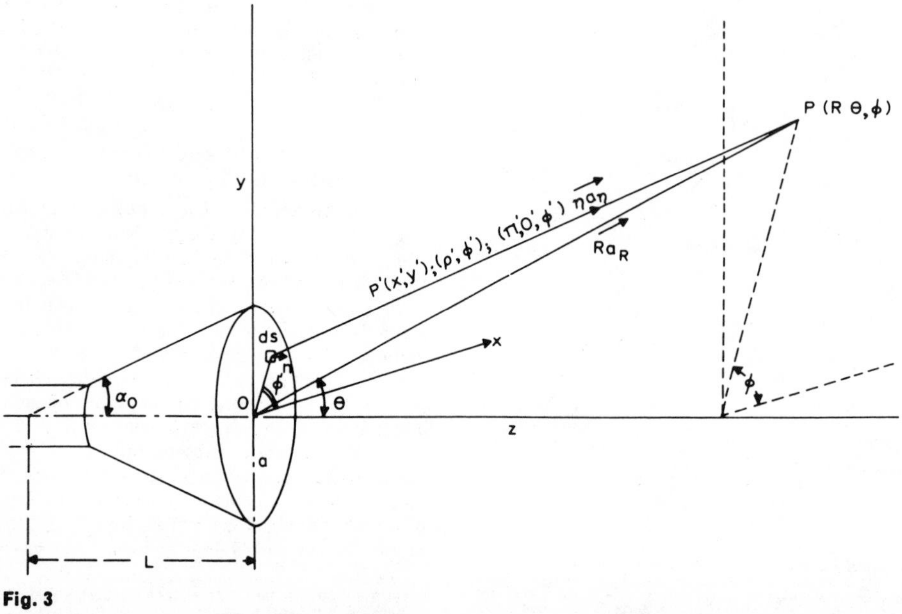

Fig. 3

Co-ordinate system for radiation-pattern calculations

For the TE_{11} mode, the electric field

$$E' = a'_\theta E'_\theta + a'_\phi E_\phi \quad . \quad . \quad . \quad . \quad . \quad . \quad . \quad . \quad . \quad (13)$$

at any point $P'(r', \theta', \phi')$ on S', obtained from eqns. 4 and 7, is given by

$$E'_\theta = \frac{A_{11}}{r' \sin\theta'} J_1\left(\frac{p_{11}}{\alpha_0}\theta'\right) \sin\phi' \sqrt{(r')} H_y^2(kr') \quad . \quad (14)$$

$$E'_\phi = \frac{A_{11}}{r'}\frac{p_{11}}{\alpha_0} J'_1\left(\frac{p_{11}}{\alpha_0}\theta'\right) \cos\phi' \sqrt{(r')} H_y^2(kr') \quad . \quad (15)$$

The time convention $e^{j\omega t}$ is implicit throughout, and the prime associated with $J_1(x)$ denotes differentiation with respect to the argument. Therefore,

$$a'_\theta E'_\theta = C_{11} f(r') \left\{ \frac{J_1(p_{11}\theta'/\alpha_0)}{p_{11}\tan\theta'/\alpha_0} \sin\phi'(a_x \cos\phi' + a_y \sin\phi') - a_z \frac{\alpha_0}{p_{11}} J_1\left(\frac{p_{11}\theta'}{\alpha_0}\right)\sin\phi' \right\} \quad . \quad (16)$$

$$a'_\phi E'_\phi = C_{11} f(r') \left\{ J_1\left(\frac{p_{11}\theta'}{\alpha_0}\right) \cos\phi'(-a_x \sin\phi' + a_y \cos\phi') \right\} \quad . \quad . \quad . \quad . \quad (17)$$

where $C_{11} = \frac{A_{11}p_{11}}{\alpha_0}$ and $f(r') = \frac{H_y^2(kr')}{\sqrt{r'}}$

Making the approximation* $\tan\theta' \simeq \theta'$, from eqns. 16 and 17, with some algebraic manipulation,

$$E'_t = a_x E'_x + a_y E'_y = \frac{C_{11} f(r')}{2} [a_x J_2(x) \sin 2\phi' + a_y \{J_0(x) - J_2(x)\cos 2\phi'\}] \quad . \quad . \quad . \quad . \quad (18)$$

where $x = p_{11}\theta'/\alpha_0$

$$\text{Let} \quad N = \iint_{S'} E'_t \exp\{jk\rho' \sin\theta \cos(\phi - \phi')\}\rho' d\rho' d\phi' \quad . \quad (19)$$

Making use of the relationship

$$\exp\{jh\cos(\phi - \phi')\} = J_0(h) + \sum_{n=1}^{\infty} 2(j)^n J_n(h) \cos n(\phi - \phi')$$

from eqns. 18 and 19,

$$N_x = -\pi C_{11} \sin 2\phi I_1 \quad . \quad . \quad . \quad . \quad . \quad . \quad . \quad . \quad (20)$$

$$N_y = \pi C_{11}(I_2 + \cos 2\phi I_1) \quad . \quad . \quad . \quad . \quad . \quad . \quad (21)$$

$$\text{where } I_1 = \int_0^a J_2(v) J_2(k\rho' \sin\theta) F(\rho')\rho' d\rho' \quad . \quad . \quad . \quad . \quad (22)$$

$$I_2 = \int_0^a J_0(v) J_0(k\rho' \sin\theta) F(\rho')\rho' d\rho' \quad . \quad . \quad . \quad . \quad (23)$$

$$v = (p_{11}/\alpha_0)\tan^{-1}(\rho'/L)$$

$$F(\rho') = H_y\{k\sqrt{(L^2 + \rho'^2)}\}/\sqrt{(L^2 + \rho'^2)^{1/2}}$$

and a is the aperture radius.

From eqns. 12, 19, 20 and 21, the following relationships are obtained:

$$(E_P)_\theta = \frac{-jk}{4\pi}\frac{e^{-jkR}}{R}(1 + \cos\theta)(N_x \cos\phi + N_y \sin\phi) = D_{11}\frac{e^{-jkR}}{R}\left(\frac{1 + \cos\theta}{2}\right)(I_2 - I_1)\sin\phi \quad . \quad (24)$$

$$(E_P)_\phi = \frac{-jk}{4\pi}\frac{e^{-jkR}}{R}(1 + \cos\theta)(N_x \sin\phi - N_y \cos\phi) = D_{11}\frac{e^{-jkr}}{R}\left(\frac{1 + \cos\theta}{2}\right)(I_2 + I_1)\cos\phi \quad . \quad (25)$$

$$\text{where} \quad D_{11} = \frac{-jkC_{11}}{2}$$

* The approximations $\sin\theta' \simeq \theta'$ and $\tan\theta' \simeq \theta'$ are made only in the amplitude of E', and no such approximation is made in $f(r')$ which represents the phase variation of E' over S'. Such a procedure is valid (for $\alpha_0 < 45°$), since, in diffraction calculations, one often approximates the amplitudes of the Huyghens's sources, keeping their phases accurate, however

Eqns. 24 and 25 represent the far-field radiation patterns† of a conical horn excited in the TE_{11} mode.

The experimental radiation patterns of conical horns with different flare angles[14] in the E and H planes have been compared with theoretical results in Figs. 4(i) and (ii). Close

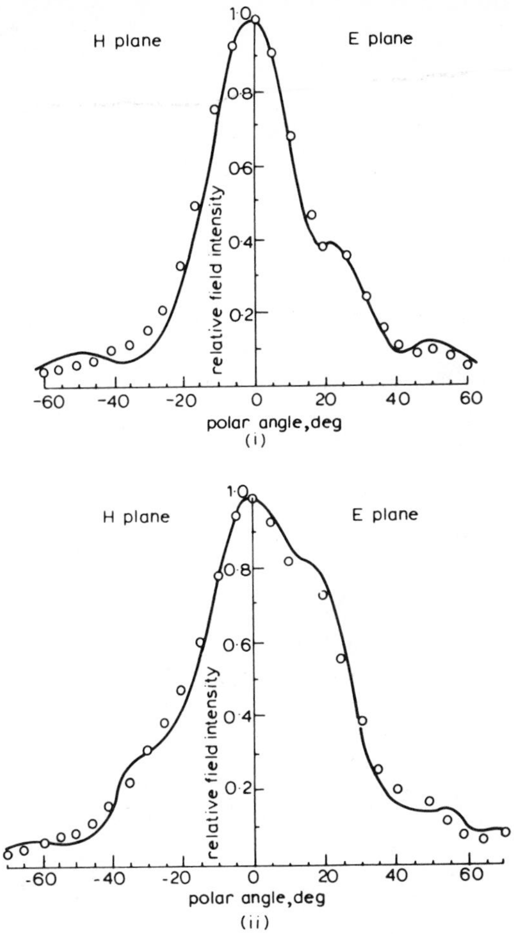

Fig. 4

Comparison of experimental E and H patterns with theory

——— experiment
○○○ calculated
(i) Horn with $a = 1{\cdot}7\lambda$, $L = 3{\cdot}5\lambda$ and $\alpha_0 = 25{\cdot}9°$
(ii) Horn with $a = 1{\cdot}8\lambda$, $L = 2{\cdot}4\lambda$ and $\alpha_0 = 36{\cdot}9°$

agreement between theory and experiment, in the geometrical optics as well as in the shadow region of the radiating horn establishes the validity of the assumed field expansion.

It is of interest to calculate the on-axis gain $G(0, 0)$ from the simpler solution (for a horn excited in the TE_{11} mode). For this, it is necessary to know the total power radiated by the horn, which is given by

$$P_t = \frac{1}{2}\text{Re}\int_{S'}(E' \times H'^*) . dS \quad . \quad . \quad . \quad . \quad . \quad . \quad (26)$$

where S' is a spherical cap of radius L located within the horn, E' is given by eqns. 13, 14 and 15 , and H' is given by

$$H' = a'_\theta H'_\theta + a'_\phi H'_\phi \quad . \quad . \quad . \quad . \quad . \quad . \quad . \quad . \quad (27)$$

where

$$H'_\theta = -E'_\phi/Z, \; H'_\phi = E'_\theta/Z \text{ and } Z = \frac{-j\omega\mu_0\sqrt{(r')}H_y^2(kr')}{d/dr\{\sqrt{(r')}H_y^2(kr')\}} \quad . \quad . \quad . \quad . \quad (28)$$

Making the approximation‡ $\sin\theta \simeq \theta$, with some algebra one

† For the radiation-pattern calculations, Schelkunoff's vector diffraction formula has been used instead of Silver's formula.[12] The reason for this is that, in Silver's formula, an approximate value for the phase error over the horn aperture [given by the asymptotic value of $H_y^2(kr')$] has been used. This is valid only for a long conical horn. Application of Schelkunoff's formula, on the other hand, enables one to preserve the exact value of phase error [as given by $H_y^2(kr')$] in radiation-pattern calculations

‡ The validity of the approximation $\sin\theta \simeq \theta$ has already been explained

obtains the following expression for the complex Poynting vector over the spherical cap S':

$$(1/2)\boldsymbol{E} \times \boldsymbol{H}'^{*} = -(A_{11}^2/2L)|H_y(kL)|^2|\boldsymbol{V}|^2(1/Z^{*}) \quad (29)$$

where

$$\boldsymbol{V} = \boldsymbol{a}'_\theta \left\{ \frac{p_{11}\cos\phi'}{\alpha_0} J'_1\left(\frac{p_{11}\theta'}{\alpha_0}\right)\right\} - \boldsymbol{a}'_\phi \left\{ \frac{\sin\phi'}{\theta'} J_1\left(\frac{p_{11}\theta'}{\alpha_0}\right)\right\}$$

The total power radiated by the horn is given by

$$P_t = \mathrm{Re}\left\{ \frac{A_{11}^2}{2L} \frac{|H_y^2(kL)|^2}{Z^{*}} \int_{S'} |\boldsymbol{V}|^2 dS' \right\} \quad . \quad . \quad . \quad (30)$$

It is shown in Appendix 6 that

$$\int_{S'} |\boldsymbol{V}| dS' = (\pi/2)L^2 p_{11}^2 \{J_1(p_{11})\}^2 (1 - 1/p_{11}^2) \quad . \quad . \quad (31)$$

for the TE_{11} mode and

$$\mathrm{Re}\left\{ \frac{|H_y^2(kL)|^2}{Z^{*}} \right\} = \frac{1}{Z_0} \frac{2}{\pi k L} \quad . \quad . \quad . \quad . \quad . \quad . \quad (31a)$$

It follows from eqns. 30, 31 and 31*a* that

$$P_t = \frac{p_{11}^2 A_{11}^2}{2kZ_0} \{J_1(p_{11})\}^2 \left(1 - \frac{1}{p_{11}^2}\right) \quad . \quad . \quad . \quad . \quad (32)$$

From eqns. 24 and 25,

$$P(0, 0) = \frac{A_{11}^2 p_{11}^2}{Z_0 \alpha_0^2} \frac{k^2}{8R^2} \left| I_2 \right|^2_{\theta=0} \quad . \quad . \quad . \quad . \quad . \quad . \quad (33)$$

Therefore

$$G(0, 0) = \frac{4\pi R^2 P(0, 0)}{P_t} = \frac{\pi k^3 \left| I_2 \right|^2_{\theta=0}}{\alpha_0^2 J_1^2(p_{11}) \left(1 - \frac{1}{p_{11}^2}\right)} \quad . \quad (34)$$

For a horn with a long axial length and $\alpha_0 < 45°$, the integral I_2 may be approximated† as

$$[I_2]_{\theta=0} \simeq \frac{1}{\pi L} \int_0^a J_0\left(\frac{p_{11}}{a}\rho'\right) \exp\left(\frac{-j\rho'^2\pi}{\lambda L}\right) \rho' d\rho' \quad . \quad . \quad (35)$$

$$= \frac{1}{\pi L}\left[\frac{\lambda L}{2\pi} e^{-jq} \{U_1(2q, p_{11}) + jU_2(2q, p_{11})\}\right] \quad . \quad (36)$$

where $q = (\pi a^2/\lambda L)$ and $U_n(w, z)$ is the Lommel's function of two variables defined by:[15]

$$U_n(w, z) = \sum_{m=0}^{\infty} (-1)^m (w/z)^{n+2m} J_{n+2m}(z)$$

One obtains, from eqns. 34 and 36,

$$G(0, 0) = \frac{2L^2}{a^2} \frac{\{U_1^2(2q, p_{11}) + U_2^2(2q, p_{11})\}}{\{J_1(p_{11})\}^2 \left(1 - \frac{1}{p_{11}^2}\right)} \quad . \quad . \quad (37)$$

In eqn. 37, the approximation $\alpha_0 \simeq a/L$ has been used. To test the validity of the formula for on-axis gain (eqn. 37), variation of $G(0, 0)$ with normalised aperture radius a/λ has been studied with L/λ as a parameter. The results of such a study are effectively presented by a family of curves shown in Fig. 5. These curves are practically the same as those given by King.[14] Further, in Table 2 the on-axis gain of conical horns with six different flare angles calculated according to eqns. 37 has been compared with the values obtained experimentally.[14] The close agreement between the two inspires further confidence in the asymptotic solution adopted for conical-horn modes.

Even though only the dominant mode has been considered for far-field radiation-pattern calculation, with a little modification it is possible to extend the theory to such other higher-order modes, as, for example, a horn excited in the TM_{01} mode.[3] As pointed out above, the simpler and accurate solution for the balanced hybrid modes (HE_{mn} or EH_{mn}) in corrugated conical horns provided by the asymptotic solution[5] emphasises its general validity. Further, theoretical results obtained for the far-field-radiation patterns of corrugated conical horns (with small and wide flare angles), based on the asymptotic solutions, show close agreement with the available experimental results for the HE_{11} mode. The details relating to this have been treated elsewhere.[6]

† The approximations used to simplify I_2 are given by $v = (p_{11}\theta'/\alpha_0) = (p_{11}\rho'/a)$ and $\{H_y(kr')\}/\sqrt{(r')} \simeq (1/\pi L)\exp(-j\pi\rho'^2/\lambda L)$. The second approximation implies that $kL \gg 1$ and $kL \gg y$ in a long conical horn

Table 2

COMPARISON BETWEEN THEORETICAL AND EXPERIMENTAL ON-AXIS GAIN

Axial length	Aperture diameter	Flare angle	Theoretical gain (eqn. 37)	Experimental gain (Ref. 14)
		deg	dB	dB
8λ	$1{\cdot}4\lambda$	5·0	12·1	12·2
$3{\cdot}5\lambda$	$2{\cdot}6\lambda$	20·3	16·7	16·5
$3{\cdot}9\lambda$	$3{\cdot}6\lambda$	24·8	17·9	18·0
$3{\cdot}1\lambda$	$3{\cdot}6\lambda$	30·1	16·4	16·6
$2{\cdot}8\lambda$	$4{\cdot}1\lambda$	36·2	12·8	13·2
$3{\cdot}5\lambda$	$3{\cdot}4\lambda$	25·9	17·5	17·7

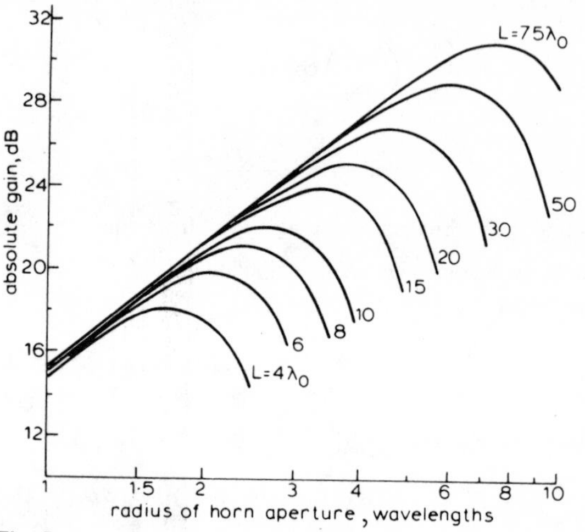

Fig. 5

Variation of on-axis gain with significant dimensions of cone

Computing facilities at the computer centre, Tata Institute of Fundamental Research, Bombay, were made use of for numerically calculating the radiation pattern and gain of conical horns.

4 Conclusions

The asymptotic solution used for studying the modes of a conical horn has a form simpler than the exact solution. In particular, the eigenvalues associated with the horn modes are expressed in explicit closed forms. The eigenfunctions and eigenvalues obtained from the asymptotic solution have only a small deviation from the exact solution for the first few modes of a conical horn, irrespective of the value of α_0. The simpler solution is used to derive the aperture field of a long conical horn excited in the TE_{11} mode. A vector diffraction formula has been applied to derive expressions for the radiation pattern and gain of a conical horn with an arbitrary flare angle excited in the TE_{11} mode. Close agreement between theory and experiment establishes the validity of the simpler solution adopted for studying horn modes. Application of the same technique for obtaining balanced hybrid modes (HE_{mn} or EH_{mn}) in corrugated conical horns, provides a simpler and accurate solution. This emphasises the more general validity of the method adopted for studying modes of a conical horn.

5 References

1 ALLEN, P. A., and TOMPKINS, R. D.: 'An instantaneous microwave polarimeter', *Proc. Inst. Radio Engrs.*, 1959, **47**, pp. 1231–1237

2 OKRESS, E. C.: 'Microwave power engineering—Vol. 1 (Academic Press, 1968), pp. 228–255

3 FELDMANN, J., REHFELD, B., ROSSELER, G. J., and SAKOWSKI, K. H.: 'A study of the technical feasibility of terrestrial omnidirectional t.v. transmission in the 12-GHz band', *IEEE Trans.*, 1969, **COM-17**, pp. 475–480

4 SCHELKUNOFF, S. A.: 'On diffraction and radiation of electromagnetic waves', *Phys. Rev.*, 1939, **56**, pp. 308–316
5 NARASIMHAN, M. S., and RAO, B. V.: 'Hybrid modes in corrugated conical horn', *Electron. Lett.*, 1970, **6**, pp. 32–34
6 NARASIMHAN, M. S., and RAO, B. V.: 'Diffraction by wide-flare-angle corrugated conical horns', *ibid.*, **6**, pp. 469–471
7 SCHORR, M. G., and BECK, F. J.: 'Electromagnetic field of a conical horn', *J. Appl. Phys.*, 1950, **21**, pp. 795–801
8 HARRINGTON, R. F.: 'Time harmonic electromagnetic fields' (McGraw-Hill, 1961), chap. 6
9 CLARRICOATS, P. J. B.: 'Analysis of spherical hybrid modes in a corrugated conical horn', *Electron. Lett.*, 1969, **5**, pp. 189–190
10 POTTER, P. D.: 'Application of spherical wave theory to Cassegrainian-fed paraboloids', *IEEE Trans.*, 1967, **AP-15**, pp. 727–735
11 JAMES, J. R., and LONGDON, L. W.: 'Calculation of radiation patterns' *Electron. Lett.*, 1969, **5**, pp. 567–569
12 SILVER, S.: 'Microwave antenna theory and design' (McGraw-Hill, 1949)
13 WALTER, C. H.: 'Travelling wave antennas' (McGraw-Hill, 1965), chap. 2, pp. 18–46
14 KING, A. P.: 'Radiation characteristics of horn antennas', *Proc. Inst. Radio Engrs.*, 1950, **38**, pp. 249–251
15 WATSON, G. N.: 'A treatise on the theory of Bessel functions' (Cambridge University Press, 1958), p. 537

6 Appendix

It is required to evaluate the integral

$$I = \int_{S'} \left[\left\{ \frac{p_{11}}{\alpha_0} \cos\phi' J_1'\left(\frac{p_{11}\theta'}{\alpha_0}\right) \right\}^2 + \left\{ \frac{\sin\phi'}{\theta'} J_1\left(\frac{p_{11}\theta'}{\alpha_0}\right)^2 \right\} \right] \times L^2\theta' d\theta' d\phi' \quad . \quad (38)$$

To do this, a more general form of I is considered to facilitate algebraical manipulations. Let

$$M = \int_0^{2\pi} \int_0^{\alpha_0} \left[\left\{ \frac{p_{mn}}{\alpha_0} \cos m\phi' J_m'\left(\frac{p_{mn}\theta'}{\alpha_0}\right) \right\}^2 + \left\{ \frac{m}{\theta'} \sin m\phi' J_m\left(\frac{p_{mn}\theta'}{\alpha_0}\right) \right\}^2 \right] \times L^2\theta' d\theta' d\phi' \quad . \quad (39)$$

Putting $x = (p_{mn}\theta'/\alpha_0)$ in eqn. 39, and making use of the recurrence relationships for Bessel's functions, with a little algebra, the following relationship can be obtained:

$$M = \frac{\pi L^2}{2} \int_0^{p_{11}} \{J_{m-1}^2(x) + J_{m+1}^2(x)\} x dx \quad . \quad . \quad . \quad (40)$$

The integral in eqn. 40 is evaluated with the aid of Lommel's relationships and subject to the conditions $J_m'(p_{mn}) = 0$. Finally, one obtains

$$M = \frac{\pi L^2}{2} p_{mn}^2 \{J_m^2(p_{mn})\} \left(1 - \frac{m^2}{p_{mn}^2}\right) \quad . \quad . \quad . \quad . \quad (41)$$

Further, it is required to simplify

$$g(kL) = \mathrm{Re}\left\{ \frac{|H_y^2(kL)|^2}{Z^*} \right\} \quad . \quad . \quad . \quad . \quad . \quad . \quad . \quad (42)$$

To do this, the wave impedance Z in eqn. 42 is expressed in a form given by:

$$\frac{1}{Z(kL)} = \frac{j}{Z_0} \left\{ \frac{H_y'^2(kL)}{H_y^2(kL)} + \frac{1}{2kL} \right\} \quad . \quad . \quad . \quad . \quad . \quad (43)$$

Simplification of eqn. 42 with the aid of eqn. 43 and the Wronskian formula given by

$$J_y(x)N_y'(x) - N_y(x)J_y'(x) = 2/\pi x \quad . \quad . \quad . \quad . \quad (44)$$

leads to $g(kL) = \dfrac{2}{\pi Z_0 kL}$ . . . . (45)

Radiation from Conical Horns with Large Flare Angles

Abstract—**Radiation patterns of conical horns with large flare angles excited in the TE_{11} mode are calculated from a simple solution for horn modes using the vector diffraction formula. Radiation patterns are expressed in closed form when the half-flare angle is less than 30°. Patterns obtained by experiment show close agreement with calculated results.**

Introduction

A conical horn finds several useful applications as in polarization diversity [1] and the launching of Gaussian modes in beam waveguides [2]. In this communication an accurate expression for the aperture field of a long conical horn is obtained from a simple solution for conical horn modes indicated in a previous paper [3]. From the expressions for the aperture field, the radiation patterns of conical horns with large flare angles (excited in the TE_{11} mode) are obtained using the vector diffraction formula. The radiation patterns calculated for a few typical horns are in close agreement with patterns obtained by experiment. This emphasizes the validity of the simpler expressions used to represent the modes in a conical horn.

Derivation of Aperture Field

The aperture fields of a long conical horn with half-flare angle α_0 may be assumed to be the same in a conical waveguide of which the horn forms a truncated section. An analytically simple sufficiently accurate and self-consistent solution for modes in a conical horn may be derived from the potential of the form [3]

$$u = A_{mn} J_m(v_1\theta) \cos m\phi (r)^{1/2} H_y^{(2)}(kr) \qquad (1)$$

where $v_1 = p_{mn}/\alpha_0$, p_{mn} is the nth nonvanishing root of $J_m'(x) = 0$ (for TE modes), $y = (0.25 + p_{mn}^2/\alpha_0^2)^{1/2}$, $H_y^{(2)}(x)$ is the Hankel function of the second kind and k is the propagation constant of a planar wave in free space. It has been verified that the eigenfunctions and eigenvalues derived from (1) for the first few modes (whether of TE or TM type) of a conical horn (with $0 < \alpha_0 \leq 90°$) are close to the exact solution. Further, application of (1) for obtaining the spherical hybrid-modes in corrugated conical horns yields simpler and accurate solutions [4]. This demonstrates the general validity of the solution given by (1).

Manuscript received December 29, 1970; revised April 19, 1971.

Reprinted from *IEEE Trans. Antennas Propagat.*, vol. AP-19, pp. 678–681, Sept. 1971.

For the TE_{11} mode of excitation, the electric-field components in the horn are given by

$$E_\theta = \frac{A_{11}}{r^{1/2}\sin\theta} J_1(v\theta)\sin\phi H_v^{(2)}(kr) \tag{2a}$$

$$E_\phi = \frac{A_{11}}{r^{1/2}} vJ_1'(v\theta)\cos\phi H_v^{(2)}(kr) \tag{2b}$$

where $v = p_{11}/\alpha_0$. When $\alpha_0 < 30°$, the aperture field of the horn may be approximated as

$$\boldsymbol{E}_t' = \boldsymbol{a}_y' A_0 \exp\left(\frac{-j\pi\rho'^2}{\lambda L}\right) \tag{3}$$

where L is the axial length of the horn, $P'(\rho',\phi')$ represents plane polar coordinates of a point over the circularly plane aperture, $\boldsymbol{a}_x',\boldsymbol{a}_y',\boldsymbol{a}_z'$ are unit vectors associated with the Cartesian system of coordinates, and $\lambda = 2\pi/k$. Variables relating to the aperture are primed and those of the far field are unprimed.

It may be mentioned that the values of $|E_x'|$, $|E_y'|$ (components of the aperture field) were numerically calculated along a number of ordinates over the circularly plane aperture S' for a few typical horns with $\alpha_0 < 30°$. The computed results showed that $|E_y'| \gg |E_x'|$ and that $|E_y'|$ is nearly a constant. Hence the approximation given by (3) is justified. Furthermore, a quadratic phase error over the aperture has been assumed.

Calculation of Radiation Patterns

Calculation of the radiation pattern of conical horns excited in the TE_{11} mode is carried out using the vector diffraction formula [5]. In the first place, long conical horns with $\alpha_0 < 30°$, are considered. In this case, the aperture field is given by (2). Assuming that the circularly plane aperture of the horn is terminated in a fictitious electric screen, infinite in extent, the far-field radiation pattern can be calculated from the following relation [6]:

$$\boldsymbol{E}_p = C_{11}\frac{\exp(-jkR)}{R}(\boldsymbol{a}_\theta \sin\phi + \boldsymbol{a}_\phi \cos\theta\cos\phi) \cdot \int_S \boldsymbol{E}_t' \exp[jk\rho'\sin\theta\cos(\phi-\phi')]\,dS \tag{4}$$

where $P(R,\theta,\phi)$ is the far-field point and C_{11} is a normalization constant. Using (3) in (4), one obtains with some algebra:

$$\boldsymbol{E}_p = C_{11}\frac{\exp(-jkR)}{R}(\boldsymbol{a}_\theta \sin\phi + \boldsymbol{a}_\phi \cos\theta\cos\phi) \cdot [U_1(2s,d) + jU_2(2s,d)] \tag{5}$$

where $s = \pi a^2/\lambda L$, a is the aperture radius, $d = ka\sin\theta$, and $U_n(w,z)$ is the Lommel function of two variables defined by [7]

$$U_n(w,z) = \sum_{m=0}^{\infty}(-1)^m\left(\frac{w}{z}\right)^{n+2m} J_{n+2m}(z).$$

The following expression is obtained for the on-axis gain

$$G(0,0) = \left(\frac{16L^2}{a^2}\right)\sin^2\left(\frac{\pi a^2}{2\lambda L}\right). \tag{6}$$

Normalized radiation patterns (shown in Fig. 1) were computed for two different values of α_0 and L. Radiation patterns were also measured experimentally for these two cases using a conventional pattern measurement setup. The experimental and calculated results of the E-plane radiation patterns closely agree, whereas a slight discrepancy exists between theory and experiment in the H-plane patterns (Fig. 1) for the two cases considered. The reason for this discrepancy is that the aperture field $\boldsymbol{E}_t'$ (3) was obtained by considering only the E_y' component of $\boldsymbol{E}' = \boldsymbol{a}_\theta' E_\theta + \boldsymbol{a}_\phi' E_\phi$ over S and the E_x' (cross polarization) component was neglected. The E_x' component also (though small in comparison with E_y') influences the H-plane pattern; the larger the value of θ, the greater is the influence of E_x'. The E_z' component, on the other hand, has no influence on the E-plane pattern, because contribution to the far field arising from the cross-polarization components over S that are symmetrically located with respect to the E plane are 180° out of phase. Values of on-axis gain calculated from (6) closely agree with the experimental values obtained by King [8] for several values of α_0. This is shown in Table I.

In order to calculate the radiation patterns of a wide-flare horn ($\alpha_0 > 30°$) with a long axial length and hence a large aperture area in terms of wavelengths it is appropriate to employ Silver's far-field

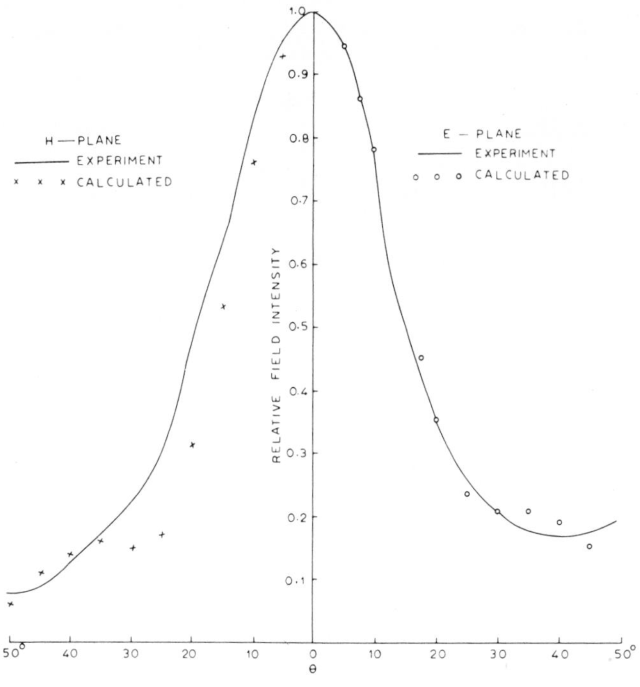

(a)

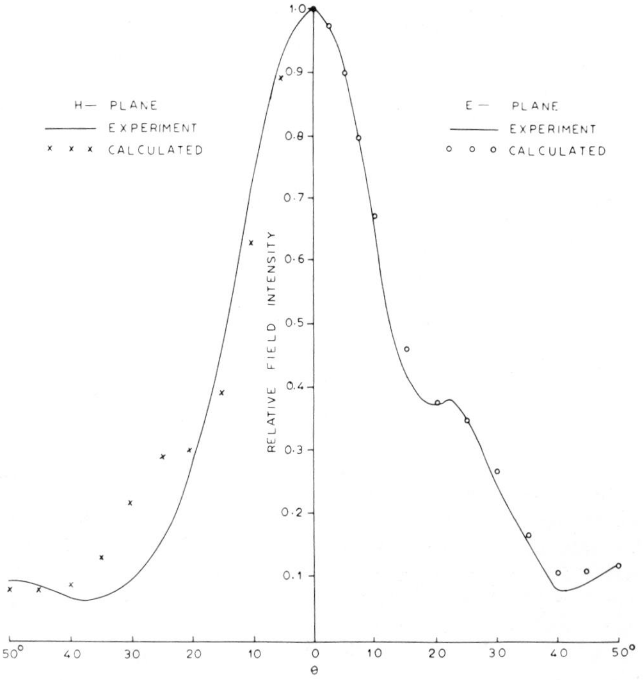

(b)

Fig. 1. Far-field radiation patterns of conical horn. (a) $\alpha_0 = 20°$, $a = 1.3\lambda$, and $L = 3.5\lambda$. (b) $\alpha_0 = 26°$, $a = 1.7\lambda$, and $L = 3.5\lambda$.

TABLE I

VALUES OF ON-AXIS GAIN: CALCULATED AND EXPERIMENTAL

Axial Length (λ)	Aperture Diameter (λ)	Flare Angle (degrees)	On-Axis Gain Calculated (dB)	On-Axis Gain Experimental (dB)
8.0	1.4	5.0	11.8	12.2
3.5	2.6	20.3	16.3	16.5
3.9	3.6	24.8	17.4	18.0
3.1	3.6	30.1	15.7	16.6
3.5	3.4	25.9	16.9	17.7

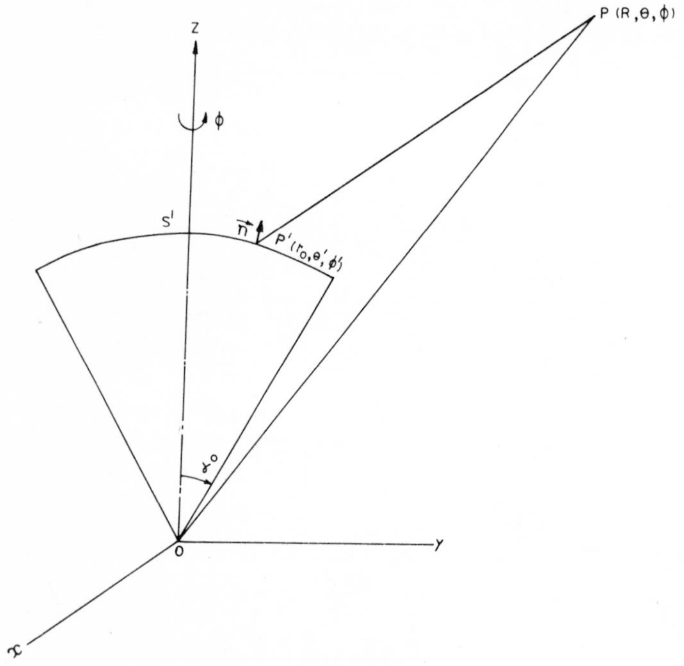

Fig. 2. Coordinate system for radiation pattern calculations of wide-flare conical horn.

formula given by

$$E_p = C_{11}\left(\frac{\exp(-jkR)}{R}\right) a_R \times \int_{S'} [n \times E_s' - Z_0 a_R \times (n \times H_s')] \times \exp(jk\varrho \cdot a_R) \cdot dS' \quad (7)$$

E_s' and H_s' appearing in (7) are the aperture fields defined over the spherical cap S' (Fig. 2). $\varrho = a_r' r_0$ and $n = a_r'$. Accurate expressions for E_s' and H_s' as given by (2) should be used in (7). Assuming that in a long conical horn [3]

$$\frac{E_\theta'}{H_\phi'} = \frac{-E_\phi'}{H_\theta'} = Z_0 \quad \text{and} \quad H_r \doteq 0 \text{ over } S' \quad (8)$$

the following expression is obtained for the far-field radiation pattern after considerable manipulation:

$$E_p = C_{11}\left(\frac{\exp(-jkR)}{R}\right)(a_\theta N_\theta^F \sin\phi + a_\phi N_\phi^F \cos\phi) \quad (9)$$

where

$$N_\theta^F = N_\theta^{Fr} + jN_\theta^{Fi}, \qquad N_\phi^F = N_\phi^{Fr} + jN_\phi^{Fi} \quad (10)$$

$$N_\theta^{Fr,Fi} = \int_0^{\alpha_0}\left[(p_1 + p_2)\begin{matrix}\cos\\ \sin\end{matrix}(u) \mp p_3 \begin{matrix}\sin\\ \cos\end{matrix}(u)\right] d\theta' \quad (11)$$

$$N_\phi^{Fr,Fi} = \int_0^{\alpha_0}\left[(p_1 + p_2)\begin{matrix}\cos\\ \sin\end{matrix}(u) \mp q_3 \begin{matrix}\sin\\ \cos\end{matrix}(u)\right] d\theta' \quad (12)$$

$$p_1 = F_1(\theta')(\cos\theta\cos\theta' + 1)[J_0(u_1) - J_2(u_1)]\sin\theta' \quad (13)$$

$$p_2 = F_2(\theta')(\cos\theta + \cos\theta')[J_0(u_1) + J_2(u_2)]\sin\theta' \quad (14)$$

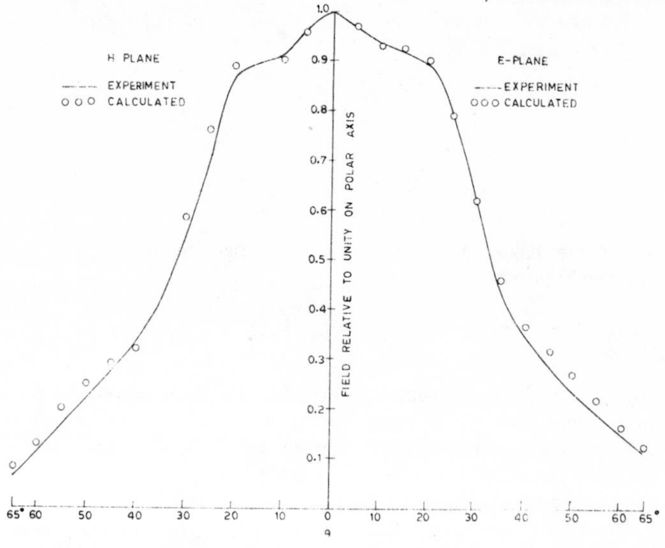

Fig. 3. Far-field radiation patterns of conical horn with $\alpha_0 = 45°$, and $kr_0 = 15$.

$$p_3 = 2F_1(\theta')\sin\theta\sin^2\theta' J_1(u_1) \quad (15a)$$

$$q_3 = 2F_2(\theta')\sin\theta\sin^2\theta' J_1(u_1) \quad (15b)$$

$$u = kr_0\cos\theta\cos\theta' \quad \text{and} \quad u_1 = kr_0\sin\theta\sin\theta' \quad (16)$$

$$F_1(\theta) = \frac{J_1(v\theta)}{\sin\theta}, \quad F_2(\theta) = vJ_1'(v\theta) \quad (17)$$

Far-field radiation patterns of a wide-flare conical horn with $\alpha_0 = 45°$ and $kr_0 = 15$ obtained by calculation using (9), as well as by experiment are compared in Fig. 3 and show close agreement. Similar comparisons were made for other horns with different values of α_0 and r_0 and close agreement was noticed between the calculated and experimental results.

CONCLUSIONS

It is possible to obtain the radiation pattern and on-axis gain of long conical horns with small flare angles (excited in the TE_{11} mode) in a closed form using an approximate expression for the aperture field derived from an analytically simple and sufficiently accurate solution for modes in a conical horn. For wide-flare conical horns with a long axial length, Silver's formula can be employed to derive accurately the far-field radiation patterns. Experimental results for the radiation patterns of conical horns are in close agreement with the results obtained numerically from the radiation formulas derived. The stated conclusions emphasize the validity of the assumed aperture fields and the technique adopted for radiation pattern calculations.

ACKNOWLEDGMENT

Computing facilities of the Computer Centre at Tata Institute of Fundamental Research, Bombay, India, were used for the numerical computation of radiation patterns.

M. S. NARASIMHAN
Dep. Elec. Eng.
Indian Inst. Technol.
Madras-36, India.

B. V. RAO
Dep. Elec. Eng.
Indian Inst. Technol.
Bombay-76, India

REFERENCES

[1] P. A. Allen and R. D. Tompkins, "An instantaneous microwave polarimeter," *Proc. IRE*, vol. 47, July 1959, pp. 1192–1201.
[2] E. C. Okress, *Microwave Power Engineering*, vol. 1. New York: Academic Press, 1968, pp. 228–240.
[3] M. S. Narasimhan and B. V. Rao, "Transmission properties of electromagnetic waves in conical waveguides," *Int. J. Electron.*, vol. 27, Aug. 1969, pp. 119–139.

[4] ——, "Hybrid modes in corrugated conical horns," *Electron. Lett.*, vol. 6, Jan. 1970, pp. 32–34.
[5] S. Silver, *Microwave Antenna Theory and Design*. New York: McGraw-Hill, 1949, ch. 5.
[6] R. E. Collin and F. J. Zucker, *Antenna Theory*—Part I. New York: McGraw-Hill, 1969, ch. 3.
[7] G. N. Watson, *A Treatise on the Theory of Bessel Functions*. Cambridge: Cambridge Univ. Press, 1958, pp. 537–550.
[8] A. P. King, "Radiation characteristics of horn antennas," *Proc. IRE*, vol. 38, Mar. 1950, pp. 249–251.

COMPENSATED ELECTROMAGNETIC HORNS†

JAMES J. EPIS
Sylvania Electric Products, Inc.
ELECTRONIC DEFENSE LABORATORIES
Mountain View • California

I. INTRODUCTION

The E- and H-plane radiation pattern beamwidths of the typical "aperture-type" antenna usually are unequal. Thus, the space radiation polar diagram generally is elliptical in cross section. In some applications, it is highly desirable to use an antenna whose polar diagram is circularly symmetric about its central axis. For the special case of linear polarization, it is evident that a necessary condition for a circularly symmetric polar diagram is attaining identical radiation patterns in the E- and H-planes. Thus, for the general case of elliptical polarization, this condition must be satisfied for both of the orthogonal, linearly polarized vector components of the polar diagram.

By using the aperture modification to be described, the desirable equalization of each pair of E- and H-plane patterns is accomplished almost precisely for one of the most important and useful aperture-type antennas, namely, electromagnetic horns. It should be appreciated that any attainment of these desirable results for horns is tantamount to an attainment of the same results for many cases of another of the most important and useful aperture-type antennas: parabolic reflectors. This statement can be made because horns are very often employed as feeds for parabolic reflectors, and the pencil beam collimated by a parabolic reflector will be circularly symmetric when its feed antenna polar diagram is circularly symmetric.

† *The work described in this paper has been supported by the Signal Corps under Contract DA 36-039 SC-73170.*

II. APERTURE COMPENSATION FOR CONICAL HORNS AND SQUARE-PYRAMIDAL HORNS

In this section, after presenting pertinent preliminary considerations, the aperture modification in question is described and its effects on radiation patterns and input VSWR are illustrated and discussed.

A. Preliminary Considerations

The radiation polar diagrams of typical conical and square-pyramidal horns have E-plane patterns which generally are appreciably narrower than their respective H-plane patterns. Two factors responsible for this condition are illustrated pictorially in Figure 1. These factors are:

(1) Because of dominant mode excitation provided by the waveguide transmission line, the E-plane aper-

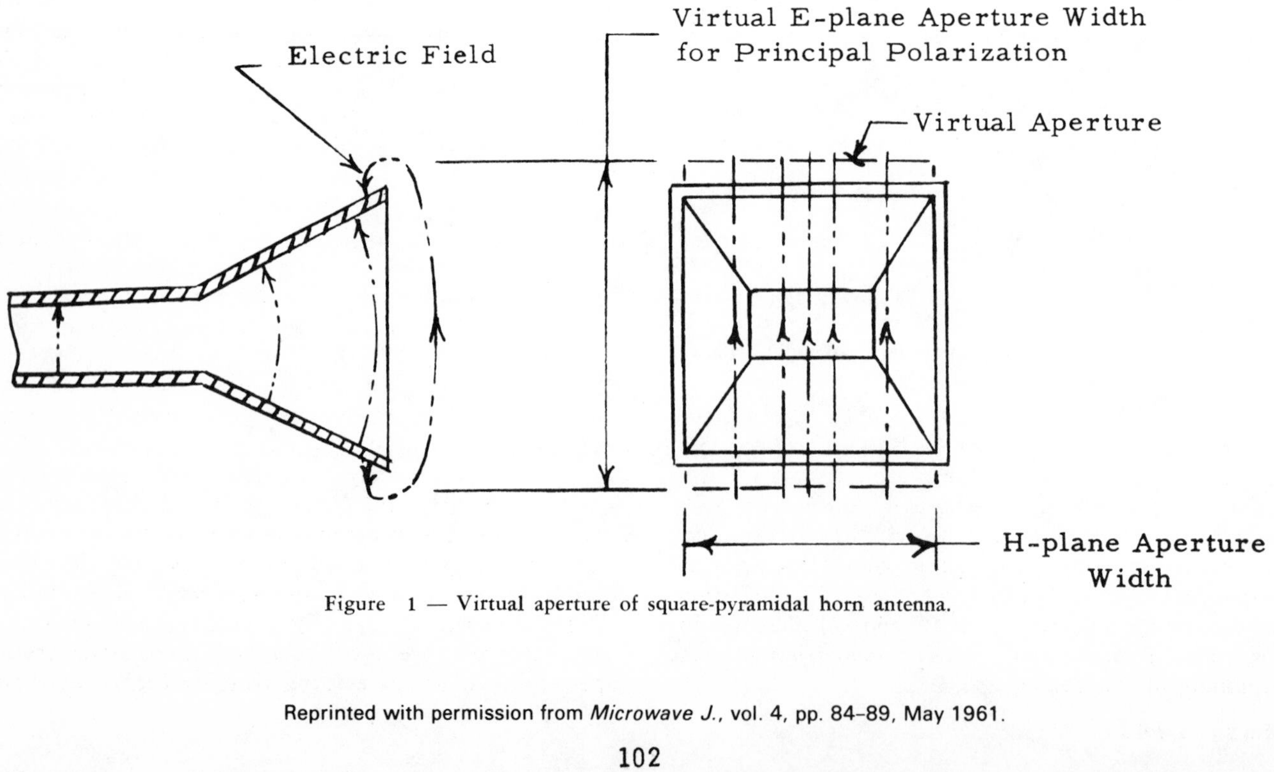

Figure 1 — Virtual aperture of square-pyramidal horn antenna.

Reprinted with permission from *Microwave J.*, vol. 4, pp. 84–89, May 1961.

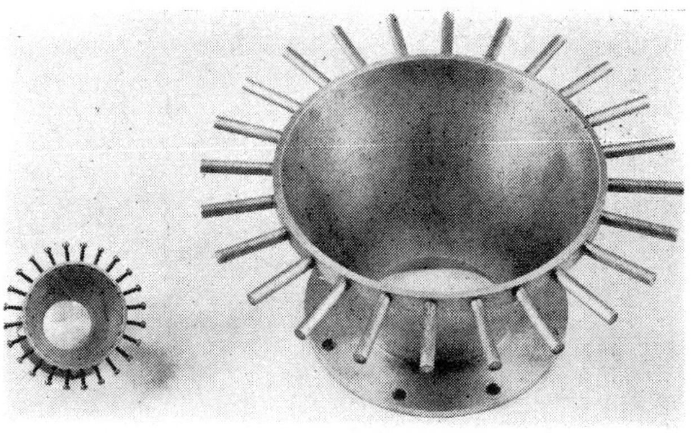

Figure 2 — Compensated horn antennas.

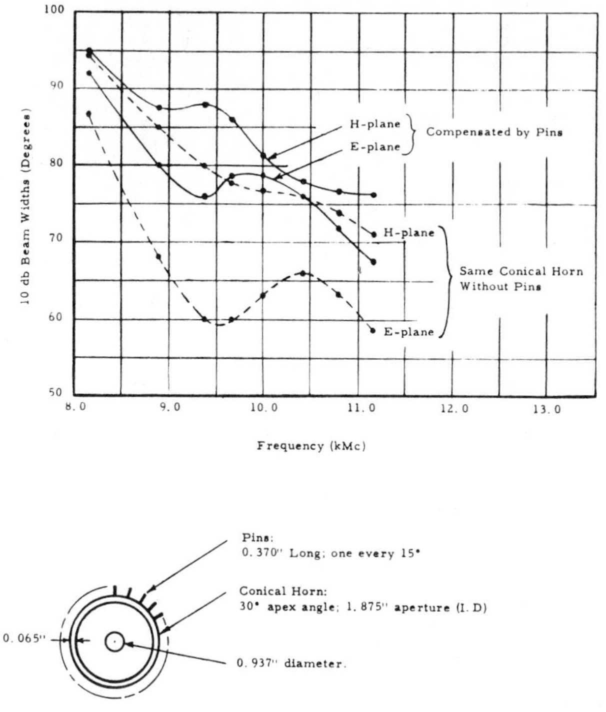

Figure 3 — E- and H- plane beam widths of compensated and standard conical horn -A.

ture illumination function is approximately constant, while in the H-plane the illumination is tapered approximately sinusoidally;

and

(2) In the E-plane, because of fringing electric fields exterior to the horn aperture, the effective or virtual E-plane aperture width is larger than the physical width. In contrast, the electric field in the H-plane is necessarily zero on the walls of the horn, so that the effective H-plane aperture width is the same as the physical width.

These factors are additive, each contributing to relatively narrow E-plane patterns. Although a square horn is used in the illustration, the same two statements apply to conical horns.

Any successful horn modification evidently should counteract either or both of the factors in (1) and (2). In this regard, no modification effective for both broadband operation and *all* polarizations is believed to be possible as far as counteracting the factor in (1) is concerned. Of course, for a very restricted mode of operation, the polar diagram of a pyramidal horn can be made almost circularly symmetric by using a rectangular aperture: the aperture width in the H-plane is increased until the H-plane pattern has the same full-beamwidth as that of the E-plane pattern. But it is clear that this procedure will work only for vertically polarized excitation, where the "vertical" direction is to be understood as the direction parallel to either narrow edge of the rectangular aperture. Thus, for the important cases of all elliptical and circular polarizations only the vertical component of the radiation polar diagram of a rectangular horn can be circularly symmetric. In fact, the long edge of the rectangular aperture is the E-plane aperture width for "horizontal" linear polarization, so that the polar diagram cross section for this component would necessarily be very much more elliptical than that of square-pyramidal horns and conical horns.

Over a broad frequency band, the horn aperture compensation technique to be described produces a nearly circularly symmetric beam for any arbitrary linear, circular, and elliptical polarization so that the resulting "compensated horn" overcomes the specific severe limitation of rectangular horns described in the foregoing paragraph, and also substantially decreases the limitations imposed by the intrinsic factors (1) and (2) presented for conventional conical and square-pyramidal horns at the beginning of this section.

B. Horn Aperture Modification and its Effect on E- and H-plane Ten db Beamwidths

Several aperture modifications of conical horns were investigated in conjunction with a broadband automatic tracking antenna project. The modification found to be the most successful for broadband operation is illustrated by the two modified horns shown in Figure 2. The modification is accomplished by simply fastening small diameter metallic pins or else machine screws on the exterior periphery of the horn aperture. Measured E- and H-plane 10 db beamwidths of two such horns are plotted in Figures 3 and 4 along with corresponding beamwidths of the same two horns measured before their apertures were modified. It is evident that the addition of the pins on the horn perimeter generally causes both the E- and H-plane patterns to become broader, but this effect is always much more pronounced in the E-plane. Radiation pattern 10 db beamwidths in the two mutually perpendicular planes are much closer to being similar for either compensated horn so that, as desired, the compensated polar diagram is appreciably more nearly circular in cross section. The results in Figures 3 and 4 are plotted for a 1.37:1 frequency band; the aperture modification yields similar pattern compensation over broader bands.

A qualitative explanation for this polar diagram compensation is simple to formulate. As illustrated in the bottom drawing in Figure 5, the metallic pins in and near the E-plane effectively diminish the tangential or principally polarized component of the fringing electric fields that exist (top drawing) in and near the E-plane of a simple horn. Thus, the pins cause the virtual or effective E-plane aperture to become smaller, so that the corresponding radiation pattern is broadened. On the other hand, the pins situated in and near the H-plane are adjacent to regions of relatively low incident field intensity, and these pins are also either perpendicular or nearly perpendicular to any existing fringing fields. For these

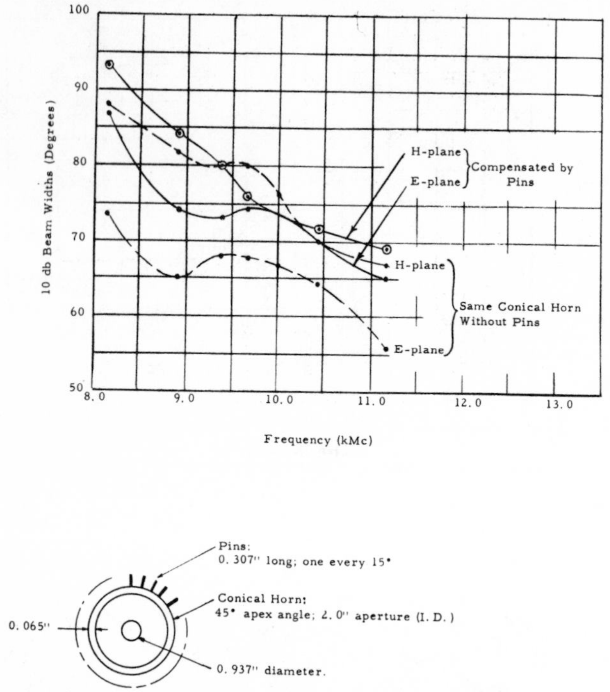

Figure 4 — E- and H- plane beam widths of compensated and standard conical horn -B.

reasons, the H-plane pattern should be changed only slightly. Since the E-plane pattern originally is appreciably narrower than the H-plane pattern, it follows that the addition of the pins should cause the two patterns to approach similarity. In summary, the factor presented in statement (2) at the beginning of Section II-A should be effectively counteracted by this horn-aperture modification.

C. Typical Radiation Patterns and Effect of the Aperture Modification on Input VSWR

Measured radiation patterns of corresponding conventional and compensated conical horns are plotted in Fig-

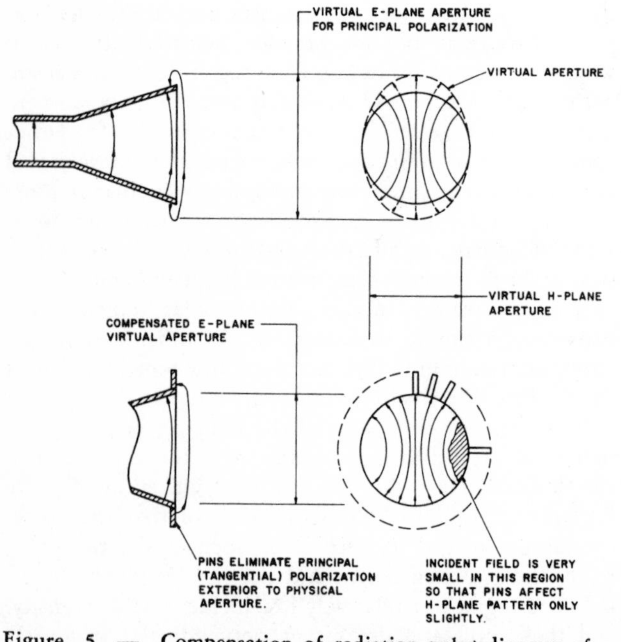

Figure 5 — Compensation of radiation polar diagram of a conical horn.

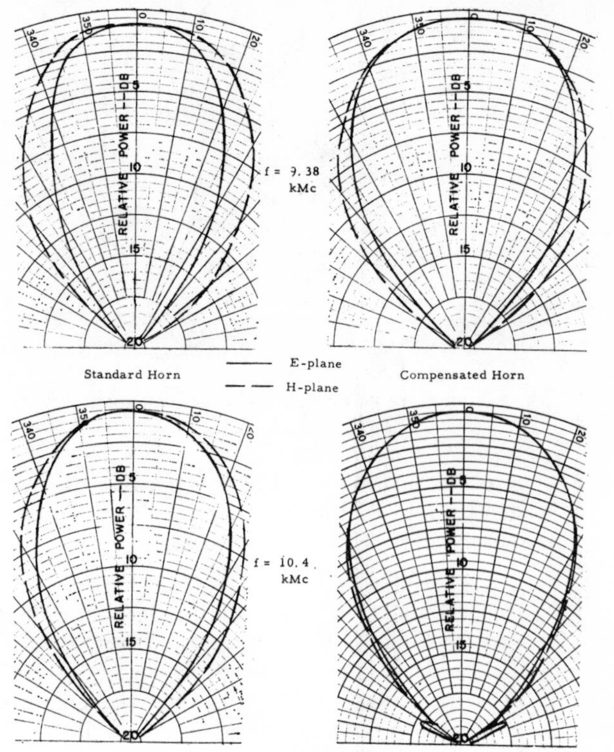

Figure 6 — E- and H- plane patterns of conical horn -A.

ures 6, 7, and 8. The results in the first two figures are for the horns A and B identified in Figures 3 and 4. A casual inspection of any set of E- and H-plane radiation patterns of corresponding conventional and compensated horns reveals a much higher degree of pattern similarity for the compensated version. Figure 8a shows typical results for a horn having the same flare angle as horn-A and a larger diameter, while Figure 8b is for a horn with a smaller flare angle but nearly the same diameter. These results together with those in Figures 6 and 7 indicate

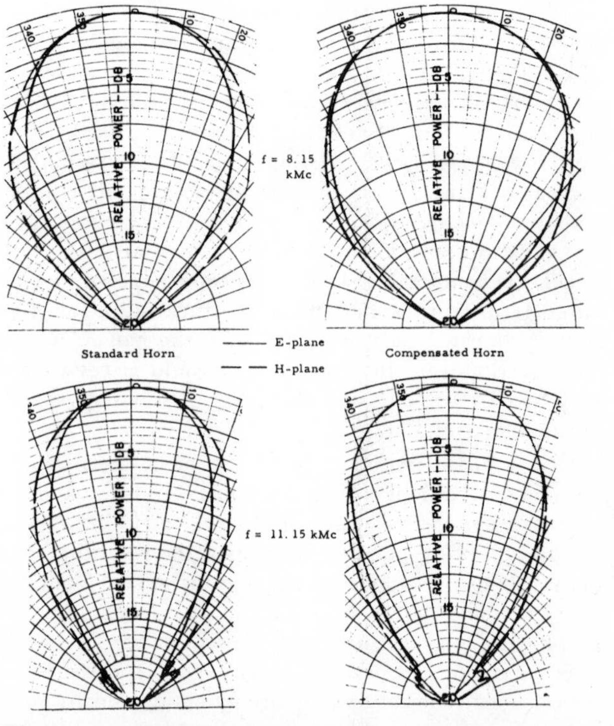

Figure 7 — E- and H- plane patterns of conical horn -B.

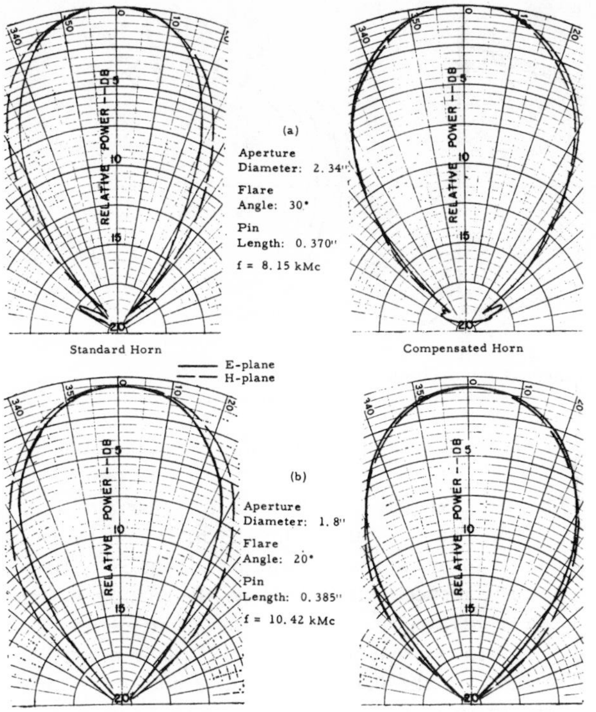

Figure 8 — E- and H- plane patterns of standard and compensated conical horns.

that the aperture compensation technique is effective for a wide range of horn parameters. This effectiveness was indeed observed from pattern measurements for a 1.4:1 bandwidth using conical horns of diameter sizes and flare angles suitable for feeding high gain, parabolic reflectors (reflector gain> 25 db).

Figure 9 illustrates the E-plane radiation pattern variation as a function of pin length for a constant signal frequency. Recall that this pattern is the one that is strongly affected by the pins. In measurements over

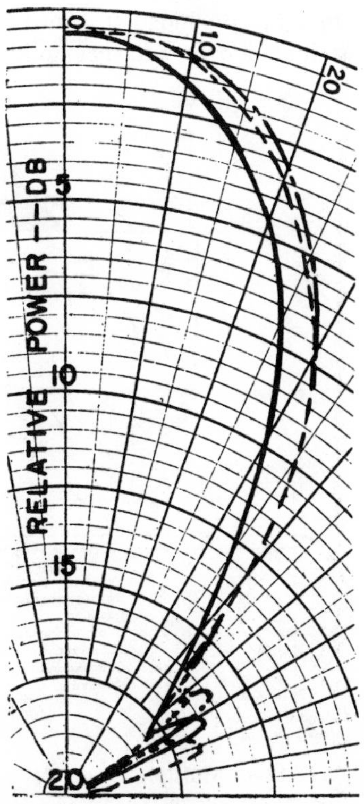

Figure 9 — E-plane radiation pattern versus pin length. (Conical horn -B, f = 10.4 kMc)

Pin Length:

———— 0.0
- - - - - 0.313''
- —— - —— 0.435'' and 0.470''

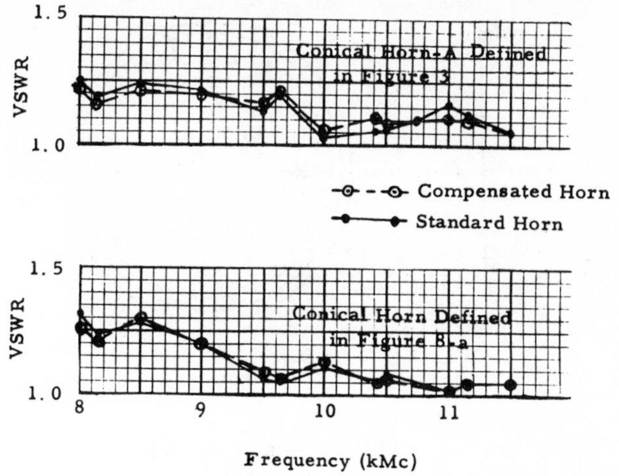

Figure 10 — Input VSWR of compensated and standard conical horns. (Including effect of input rectangular-to-circular waveguide tapered transition.)

broad frequency bands, it was found that pin length is not a critical parameter after a certain minimum length is reached. For the bandwidth frequency ratio of 1.4:1, an optimum interval of values for this length was often apparent, the interval depending on the horn flare angle and diameter, but selecting a precise pin length was never an important criterion for desirable broadband performance.

The same general behavior was observed as a function of the pin spacing, or the number of pins placed on the horn perimeter. Pin-to-pin spacing was not critical for angular spacings smaller than about 18 degrees. But use of too many pins, more than one about every 8 degrees, did not produce the desired results for a broad band. In particular, placing a continuous metallic rim on the horn — which corresponds to using a zero pin spacing — was found to be quite unfavorable for the polar diagram compensation of interest.

The effect of the aperture modification on the input VSWR of two of the conical horns investigated is shown by Figure 10. It is apparent that the average VSWR of either horn is not unfavorably affected. This result was observed for all horns tested, a total of five. Negligible effect on input VSWR should be expected because the "compensating pins" are placed in such a location where they can reflect only a very small amount of energy back into the horn.

While no measurements were made using square-aperture pyramidal horns, there can be little doubt that the described aperture modification is also effective for this type of horn for all possible polarizations. As already implied, the type of polar diagram improvement considered — equalization of E- and H-plane radiation patterns — is next to impossible to achieve for all polarizations in rectangular horns.

D. Construction Techniques for the Modified Horns

It is believed that two relatively simple methods of fastening the "compensating pins" to a horn should be indicated. In the case of brass horns, an economical technique is the following: tapped holes are made in the wall of the horn near its perimeter (small horn, Figure 2), and ordinary machine screws are soft-soldered in these tapped holes. The heads of the screws do not have

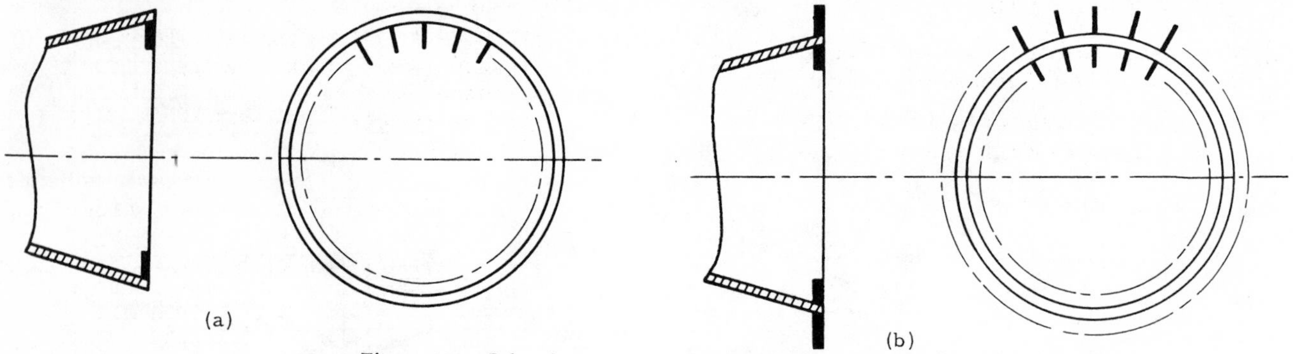

Figure 11 — Other horn aperture compensation techniques.

to be cut away. Press-fitting aluminum rods into holes drilled through a narrow rim on the horn perimeter is a relatively simple technique for aluminum horns. The pins on the large horn in Figure 2 are secured in this manner.

III. OTHER APERTURE MODIFICATIONS

Other aperture modifications that were investigated are illustrated in Figure 11. It was found that the modification on the left in Figure 11 is very effective in the desired manner but only for a relatively narrow frequency band. Results at other frequencies indicate that the pins are excited too strongly, appreciable radiation from the pins themselves generally causing the appearance of high side lobes in the E-plane. The horn aperture on the right in Figure 11 is modified by a combination of the other techniques. In general, no important advantage was obtained from this combination. For bandwidth frequency ratios larger than about 1.1:1, the originally described aperture modification always produced the best results by a wide margin.

IV. SPECIAL APPLICATIONS FOR THE COMPENSATED HORNS

The compensated horns can advantageously replace conventional horns in applications in which either circular polarization or else any elliptical polarization of relatively constant axial ratio is desired throughout as large a solid angle (within the radiation polar diagram) as possible. These applications include not only systems in which horn antennas are used by themselves, but also narrow pencil beam antenna systems employing parabolic reflectors. In the latter cases, the compensated horns would of course be used as the feed antennas.

To understand why the compensated horns will be better than conventional horns for these applications it is necessary to appreciate the general facts illustrated in Figure 12. These facts are:

(1) For any circularly and elliptically polarized antenna, two distinct polar diagrams may be considered to exist, one for each of two orthogonal electric fields E_1 and E_2 in the antenna aperture. Both of these linearly polarized polar diagrams have an E-plane and an H-plane;

(2) One of the two E-planes is the *same* plane P_1 in space as one of the H-planes. The same fact is true for the remaining E- and H-planes, except that these radiation pattern planes are in the space plane P_2 perpendicular to space plane P_1; and

(3) The two orthogonal, linearly polarized electric field components E_a and E_b in the plane P_1 are due to one E-plane pattern and one H-plane pattern, respectively. Similarly, the orthogonal electric field components E_c and E_d in plane P_2 are due to the remaining E- and H-plane patterns.

To illustrate the contention under consideration, let us suppose that circular polarization is desired and assume that an ideal quarter-wave plate is used in circular or square waveguide feeding any horn. An ideal quarter-wave plate will produce circular polarization in the direction of the polar diagram axis. At any angle off-axis in either plane P_1 or P_2 the smallest possible axial ratio is then equal to the difference between the E- and H-plane radiation patterns existing in those planes. This fact becomes evident after considering statement (3), above, and the orthogonally polarized radiation patterns illustrated in Figure 12. Unfortunately, measured axial ratios off-axis are seldom equal to the respective smallest possible values, the reason being that a single effective center-of-phase for both linearly polarized components of radiation for every spatial direction does not exist in any horn. But, if the defined ideal quarter-wave plate is always used, it may be concluded that smaller axial ratios should be distributed over a larger solid angle if a compensated

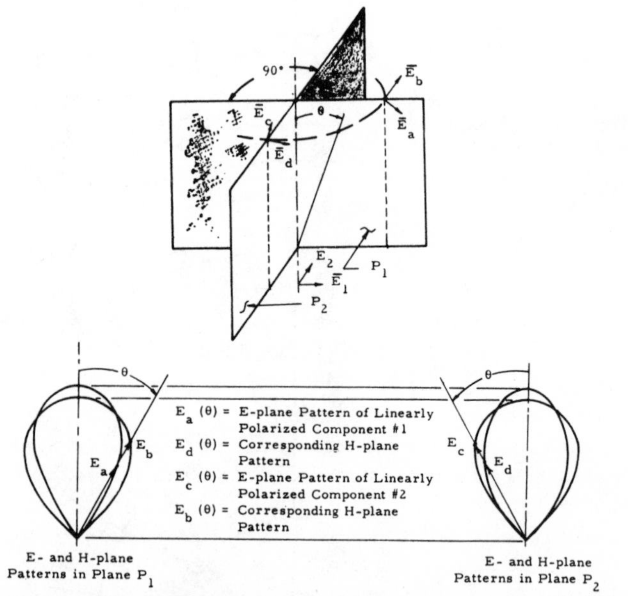

Figure 12 — Multiple E- and H- plane patterns for elliptically polarized antennas.

TABLE I

Measured Axial Ratios on Polar Diagrams of a Compensated and Conventional Conical Horn.

Data for Conical Horn-A
(Defined in Figure 3); f = 10.4 kMc

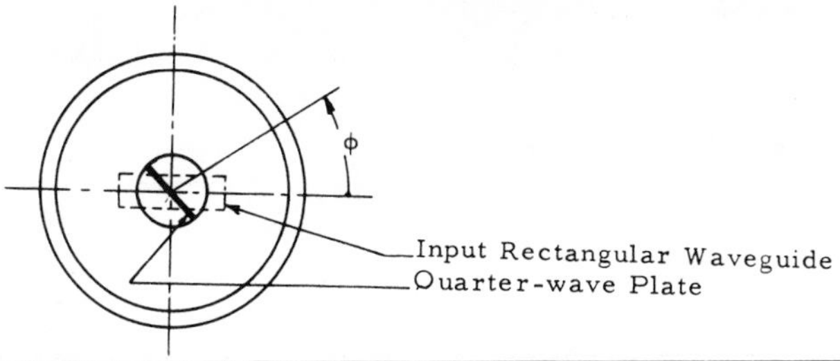

Angle φ (Degrees)	Angle from Horn Axis (Degrees)	Axial Ratio (db) Compensated Horn-A	Conventional Horn-A
	0	0.3	0.3
	10	0.3	0.4
Zero	20	0.8	1.2
and	30	1.7	3.7
180	35	3.4	5.8
	40	4.8	8.0
	45	7.7	13.4
	50	13.8	>23
	20	0.9	1.6
	30	2.3	4.1
45	35	2.9	5.1
and	40	4.3	7.5
225	45	8.0	13.1
	50	13.9	>23
	20	1.0	1.8
	30	2.5	4.2
90	35	3.1	5.2
and	40	4.7	8.7
270	45	8.5	14.8
	50	15.8	>23
	20	1.0	1.5
	30	2.1	3.6
135	35	3.1	5.5
and	40	5.3	8.7
315	45	7.9	14.7
	50	15.3	>23

horn is used in place of its conventional version. A good example is illustrated by the measured data presented in Table I. Corresponding axial ratios are significantly better (smaller) for the compensated horn. To conclude the present discussion, it is recalled that a quarter-wave plate in circular or square waveguide feeding a square or conical horn may be oriented to produce any desired or selected axial ratio on the polar diagram axis. For all cases, it can be argued that axial ratios off-axis should be appreciably closer to the selected value on-axis after the horn in use is compensated.

It is apparent that the compensated horns can be used to advantage in any system in which a nearly circularly symmetric radiation polar diagram is desired or required for all possible polarizations. The polarization characteristics in the most important applications of this type usually must be changed simply and very rapidly, specifically excluding mechanical re-orientation of either the horn or its transmission line. This tactically important requirement precludes the use of rectangular horns, even for the most simple case wherein only the orientation of linear polarization is varied. For this case employing the compensated horns, because they are fed using circular waveguide, only an input adaptor is rotated. In the most general system, in which arbitrary changes in elliptical polarization are made, a quarter wave plate in the circular waveguide is the only additional part re-oriented.

Using the compensated horns as feed antennas in passive automatic tracking antennas is perhaps the most important example of the special applications described in the preceding paragraph. In this regard, it may be intuitively obvious and it can be proved[1] that a circularly symmetric pencil beam is the optimum type for conically scanning, automatic tracking antennas. Every error-signal characteristic is optimum only for this type of scanning pencil beam; for example, the harmonic content in the error signal is minimized.[2,3] Other specific important characteristics in this class are described in the reference no. 3.

The compensated horns could also be used to improve the error-signal characteristics of certain monopulse tracking antenna systems because a circularly symmetric polar diagram is also the most favorable type for each of the four similar antenna beams generally used in these systems. However, the larger physical area required by the compensated horn-aperture represents a distinct disadvantage for the case of high gain monopulse systems wherein the horns are used as feeds for a single reflector. Thus, any significant advantage not offset by a significant disadvantage obtained by using the compensated horns in monopulse systems would probably be restricted to relatively low antenna gain applications in which the four horns are used without a parabolic reflector.

V. CONCLUSIONS

The radiation polar diagram of conical and square-pyramidal horns is substantially improved by the relatively simple aperture modification described. E- and H-plane radiation patterns are made nearly similar for a broad frequency band. Input VSWR is not affected unfavorably by the aperture modification. The most important advantage of these compensated horns over rectangular horns lies in the fact that the equalization of the E- and H-plane patterns is present for all polarizations in the compensated horns, while this pattern equalization is obtainable only for a single linear polarization in rectangular horns. For this basic reason and other reasons, the compensated horns can advantageously be used in place of conventional horns in several antenna systems.

References

1. James J. Epis, "Fourier Analysis of Error Signals of Conically Scanning Antennas and Applications to Monopulse," Technical Memorandum EDL-M273; Electronic Defense Laboratories, Mountain View, Calif.
2. Ibid.
3. James J. Epis, "Design and Performance Characteristics of a Broadband Automatic Tracking Antenna of Novel Design," Technical Memorandum EDL-M348; Electronic Defense Laboratories, Mountain View, Calif. To be submitted for publication in IRE Transactions of PGAP.

Broadband Ridged Horn Design

K. L. WALTON & V. C. SUNDBERG

INTRODUCTION

Antennas which make efficient use of the spatial volume they occupy are quite often highly desirable. When this high volume efficiency is required over a wide frequency range, it becomes a much more difficult task. Consideration of broadband antennas naturally leads to consideration of pseudo-infinite log-periodic antennas which have proven useful on so many applications. Log-periodic antennas, however, are limited to a gain of approximately 10 db independent of the frequency. This means that while the antenna may have a very high volume efficiency at the low frequencies, the efficiency at the higher frequencies may not be all that is desired.

Horn antennas have high aperture efficiencies but have been capable of operating over only limited bandwidths. In recent years ridges have been added to the waveguide and flared sections of the horns to increase their bandwidth. Since the ridges must be terminated within the flared section, the horn aperture must be half a wavelength or more in width (H-plane) at the lowest frequency to permit propagation of the TE_{10} mode.

However, when extremely wide bandwidths are considered, an aperture more than a half wavelength wide at the lowest frequency is many wavelengths wide at the highest frequency. This means that large phase errors will be present across the aperture unless the horn is extremely long. This has been the limiting factor at the high end of the frequency band of operation of ridged horns in the past. (With ridged horns it is doubtful that even lengthening of the horn would eliminate the phase error unless the aperture is very much greater than a half wavelength at the lowest frequency.) In the design discussed in this paper, a dielectric lens is used to reduce the phase error to a minimum.

RIDGED WAVEGUIDE PARAMETERS

The basic horn configuration (Figure 1) consists of ridged waveguide terminated at one end in a waveguide to coax transformer and at the other end in the flared horn section. Locating the transformer probe in the center of the waveguide and using a short straight section of ridged waveguide, as the wave launcher, precludes exciting the TE_{20} mode so that the maximum usable bandwidth (MUB) is the ratio of TE_{10} to TE_{30} mode cutoff wavelengths $\left(\frac{\lambda_c^{10}}{\lambda_c^{30}}\right)$ rather than $\left(\frac{\lambda_c^{10}}{\lambda_c^{20}}\right)$.

The equations for the cutoff wavelengths of the various modes in ridged waveguide have been derived[1,2,3] and as used here are as follows:

$$\frac{B}{D}\tan\theta_2 - \cot\theta_1 + \frac{B_c}{y_{01}} = 0 \quad (1)$$

$$\frac{B}{D}\cot\theta_2 + \cot\theta_1 - \frac{B_c}{y_{01}} = 0 \quad (2)$$

where

$$\theta_1 = \frac{360}{\lambda_c}\left(\frac{A-S}{2}\right)\text{degrees.}$$

$$\theta_2 = \frac{360}{\lambda_c}\left(\frac{S}{2}\right)\text{degrees.}$$

The value of the discontinuity susceptance term $\left(\frac{B_c}{y_{01}}\right)$ is derived in a paper by Whinnery and Jamieson,[4] and Equation (1) applies to TE_{M0} modes where M is odd while Equation (2) applies where M is even.

Hopfer[2] has derived an expression for the characteristic impedance of

Reprinted with permission from *Microwave J.*, vol. 7, pp. 96–101, Mar. 1964.

ridged waveguides for the TE_{10} mode at infinite frequency which is as follows:

$$Z_{0\infty} = 1/y_{0\infty}$$

where

$$y_{0\infty} = 2\sqrt{\frac{\epsilon_o}{\mu_o}}\frac{\lambda_c}{2\pi D}\left\{\frac{2D}{\lambda_c}\cos^2\left(\frac{\pi S}{\lambda_c}\right) \ln\csc\left(\frac{\pi D}{2B}\right) + \frac{\pi S}{2\lambda_c} + \frac{1}{4}\sin\left(\frac{2\pi S}{\lambda_c}\right) + \frac{D}{B}\frac{\cos^2\left(\frac{\pi S}{\lambda_c}\right)}{\sin^2\left(\frac{\pi}{\lambda_c}(A-S)\right)}\left[\frac{\pi(A-S)}{2\lambda_c} - \frac{1}{4}\sin\left(\frac{2\pi(A-S)}{\lambda_c}\right)\right]\right\} \quad (3)$$

The characteristic impedance at a frequency F is given by

$$Z_0 = Z_{0\infty}/\sqrt{1-\left(\frac{F_c}{F}\right)^2} \quad (4)$$

Previously published curves of λ_c^{10} and λ_c^{30} proved to be inadequate to provide the necessary range of waveguide design parameters so additional calculations were performed. This was done using an IBM 1620 computer. Equation (1) was programmed for the computer along with an expression which gave a rough estimate of the expected value of λ_c^{10}/A for the values of B/A, D/B, and S/A. The computer was then used to calculate the left-hand side of Equation (1), using Newton's method of successive approximations until the result was equal to zero, to the required number of places. The final value of λ_c^{10}/A was then printed out. This value of λ_c^{10}/A was also inserted into Hopfer's expression for the impedance of the waveguide and the result printed out. The cut-off wavelength of the TE_{30} mode was computed in a similar manner.

The results of this computer program are display in Figures 2-8, where λ_c^{10}/A and λ_c^{30}/A are plotted as functions of S/A for various values of B/A (.3 to .9) and D/B. Curves of λ_c^{30}/A are not plotted for all values of D/B in order to keep the graphs readable. It can be seen that λ_c^{30} is relatively insensitive to changes in D/B, but λ_c^{10} is markedly so, hence the maximum usable bandwidth increases very rapidly as the gap between the ridges becomes small.

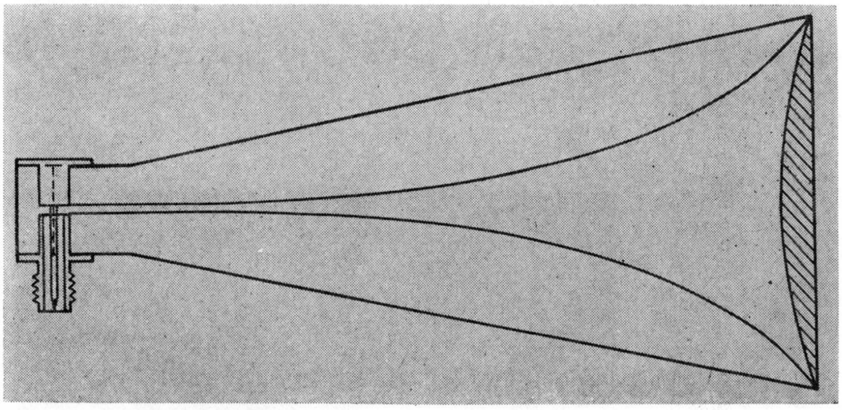

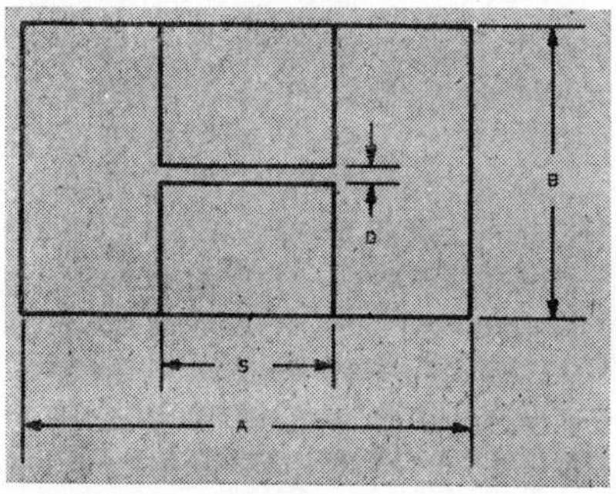

A = width of waveguide or horn cross-section
B = height of waveguide or horn cross-section
S = width of ridge
D = height of gap

Figure 1 — Ridged horn with lens.

DESIGN OF THE RIDGES IN THE FLARED SECTION

The ridges must be extended into the flared horn section past the point where the flared section becomes sufficiently wide to support the TE_{10} mode at the lowest operating frequency. The ridge height and width taper must also be such that the associated impedance taper is a smooth transition from the ridge impedance (50 ohms or less) to the impedance of free space (377 ohms). (If the ridges are terminated at the aperture, or at a point in the flared section, such that it is considerably wider than a half wavelength at the lowest operating frequency, 377 ohms is very close to the required impedance.)

Experimentally it has been found that an exponential impedance taper of the form

$$Z = Z_{0\infty} e^{KX}; \quad 0 \le X \le \frac{l}{2} \quad (5)$$

$$Z = 377 + Z_{0\infty}\left(1 - e^{K(l-X)}\right); \quad \frac{l}{2} \le X \le l \quad (6)$$

is quite satisfactory. Here $Z_{0\infty}$ is the characteristic impedance of the waveguide and K is a constant such that the impedance of the midpoint of the flared section is the average of the end point impedances.

If there are no severe restrictions on the horn length, the simplest ridge to fabricate has a constant width, and only D/B is a variable. In this case S/A is dictated at any cross section by the chosen horn aperture and axial length so that it is necessary only to choose the proper value of D/B in conformance with Equations (5) and (6) and Figures 2-8. The flared section should be kept reasonably long since the impedance transformation should be accomplished over an axial

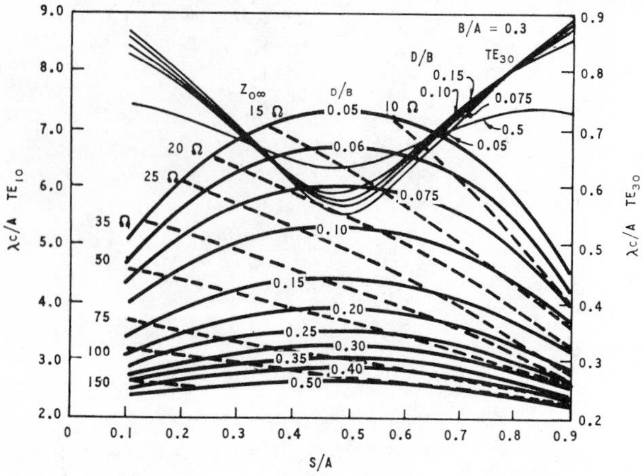

Figure 2 — TE_{10} and TE_{30} mode cutoff wavelengths in doubly-ridged waveguide. $Z_{0\infty}$ is also shown. B/A = 0.3.

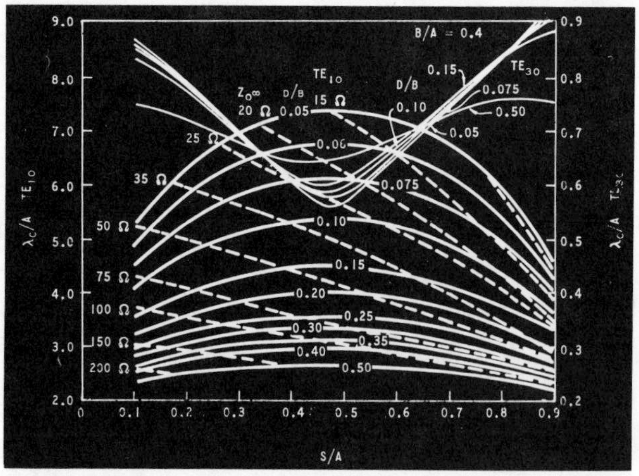

Figure 3 — TE_{10} and TE_{30} mode cutoff wavelengths in doubly-ridged waveguide. $Z_{0\infty}$ is also shown. B/A = 0.4.

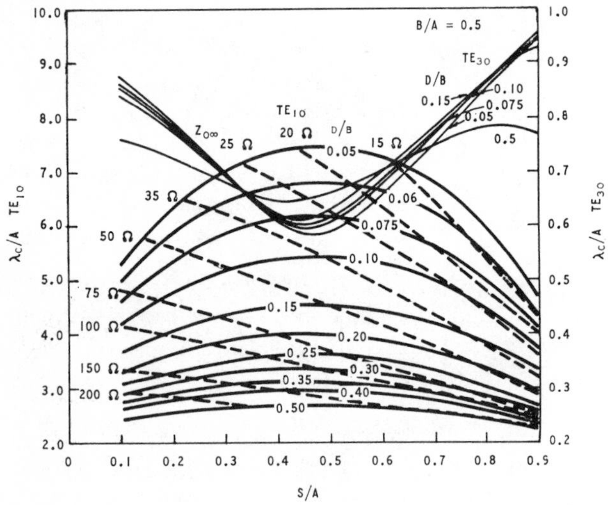

Figure 4 — TE_{10} and TE_{30} mode cutoff wavelengths in doubly-ridged waveguide. $Z_{0\infty}$ is also shown. B/A = 0.5.

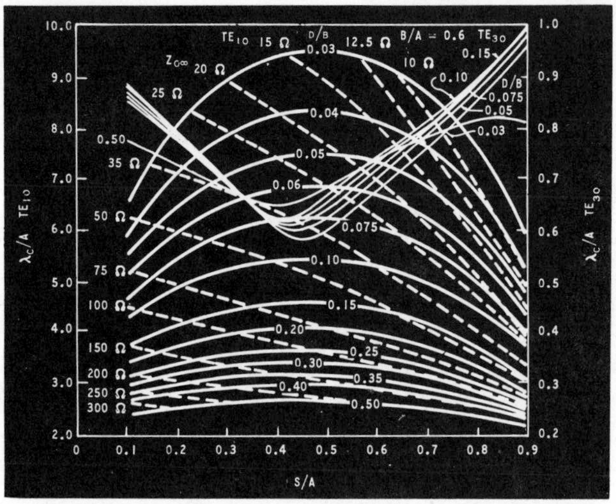

Figure 5 — TE_{10} and TE_{30} mode cutoff wavelengths in doubly-ridged waveguide. $Z_{0\infty}$ is also shown. B/A = 0.6.

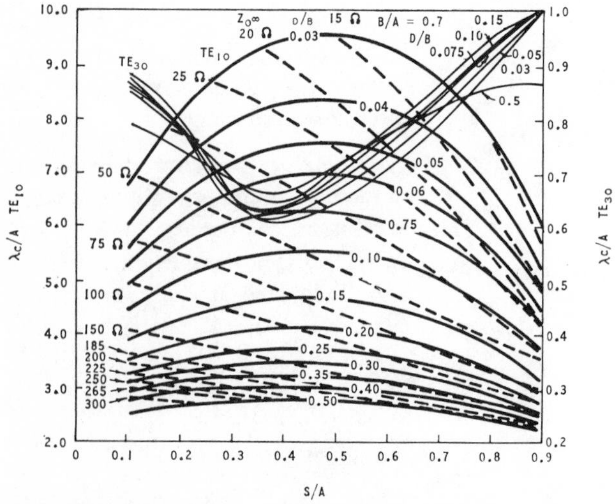

Figure 6 — TE_{10} and TE_{30} mode cutoff wavelengths in doubly-ridged waveguide. $Z_{0\infty}$ is also shown. B/A = 0.7.

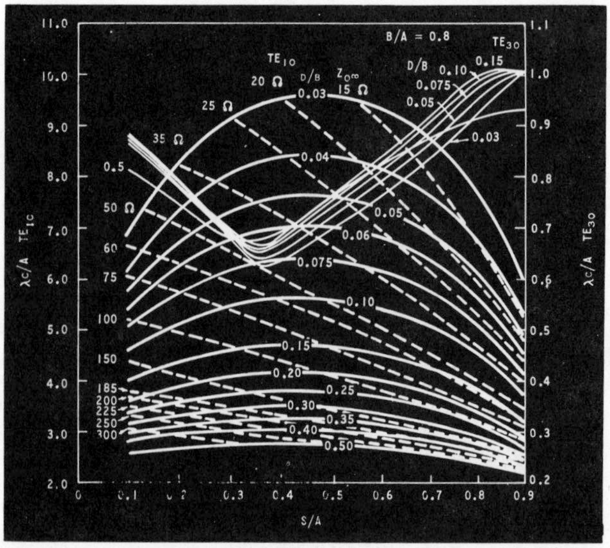

Figure 7 — TE_{10} and TE_{30} mode cutoff wavelengths in doubly-ridged waveguide. $Z_{0\infty}$ is also shown. B/A = 0.8.

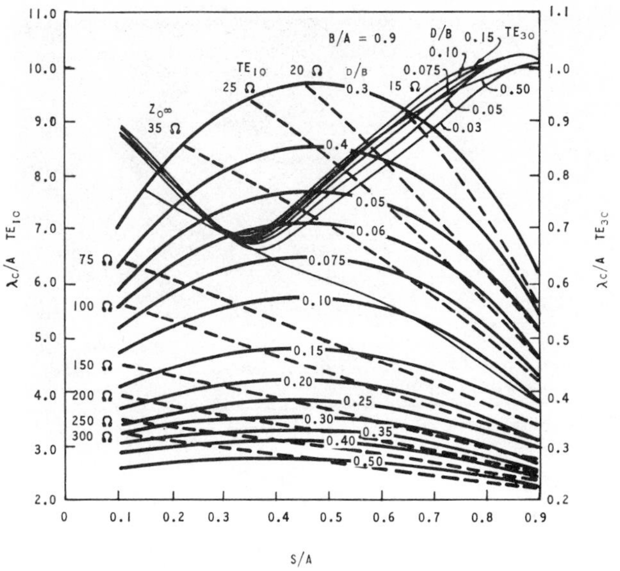

Figure 8 — TE_{10} and TE_{30} mode cutoff wavelengths in doubly - ridged waveguide. $Z_{0\infty}$ is also shown. B/A = 0.9.

length on the order of a half wavelength at the lowest operating frequency. However, if the length is restricted, maintaining a constant ridge width may result in a ridge which is very high near the aperture. This is undesirable since the H-plane amplitude distribution then becomes highly peaked in the center, and a large phase error occurs in the E plane, both of which result in a reduced gain for the horn.

This condition can be alleviated by allowing the width of the ridges to increase in the flared section. Care must be taken to keep the TE_{10} mode cutoff wavelength within the flared section equal to or longer than that in the ridged waveguide section. One approach is to let $[\lambda_c^{10}]^{\text{waveguide}} = [\lambda_c^{10}]^{\text{flared}}$ so that D/B and S/A are uniquely determined from the graphs. Such a constraint on the cutoff wavelength imposes a very nearly linear flare in the width of the ridges when a linear impedance taper is used.

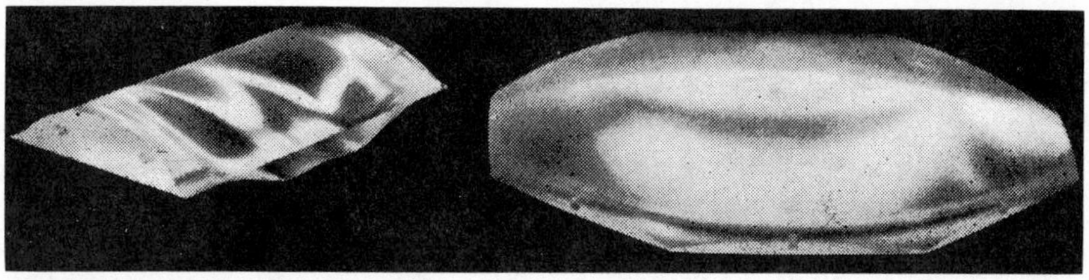

Figure 10 — Two forms of lenses.

DESIGN OF THE COAX TO RIDGED WAVEGUIDE TRANSFORMER

Figure 9 is a sketch of the transition in normalized dimensions. The design was arrived at experimentally by trial and error and the only critical dimension is the distance from the probe center to the shorting plate, which must be less than one half wavelength at the highest operating frequency.

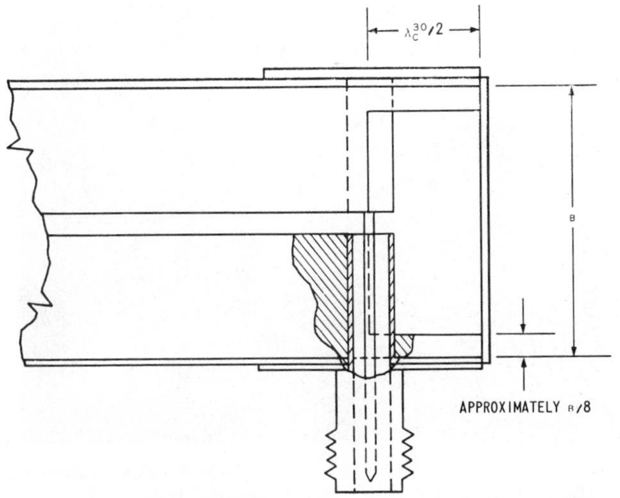

Figure 9 — Coaxial to ridged waveguide transformer.

DESIGN OF A PHASE CORRECTING LENS

Efficient utilization of the horn aperture requires that less than 90 degrees maximum phase error exist across the aperture at all operating frequencies. The aperture phase error at each point in a horn without ridges is approximately equal to the difference between the ray path length to that point and the shorter axial path length. Obviously, for a given axial length, the phase error is a quadratic function of the maximum aperture dimension so that a small increase in the electrical aperture dimension results in a large increase in phase error. To illustrate this point, a horn which is one wavelength (λ_0) in diameter at its lowest operating frequency must have an axial length of 5.0 wavelengths (λ_0), if it is to be operated over a 10:1 band with a maximum phase error of 90°. In general, horns of this length are impractical, so the dielectric phase correcting lens described below is a more desirable solution.

A plano-convex lens fed on the convex side has a very sharply tapered amplitude distribution.[6] Utilization of this type of lens in a horn aperture greatly reduces its radiation efficiency since both the E- and H-plane amplitude will be sharply tapered. It can be shown,[6] however, that a doubly-convex lens (Figure 10), designed so that half of the required refraction occurs at the first surface, has very little effect on the amplitude distribution of the source.

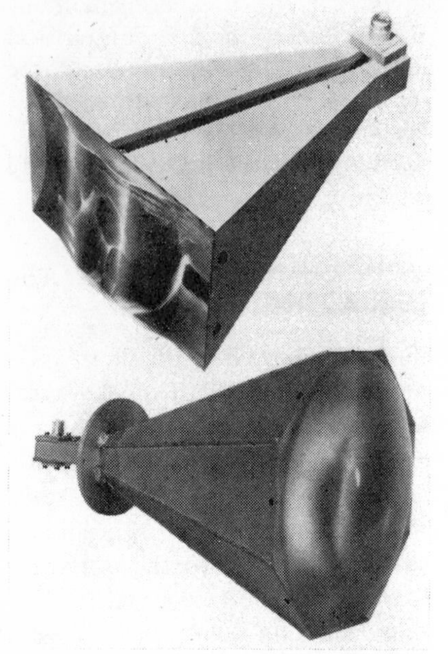

Figure 11 — Two types of doubly-ridged, lens-corrected horns.

The lens is designed by measuring the phase error in the E and H planes at the upper end of the frequency band, with an RF probe, and designing a compensating lens from this data. It has been found that the E- and H-plane contours of constant phase differ greatly due to the presence of the ridges in the horn. In general, the curvature of the phase front in the aperture is greater in the E plane than in the H plane. Furthermore, the phase front in the H plane may have a ripple in the center of the aperture. When the aperture is small in terms of wavelength at the lowest operating frequency, the ridges must be extended to the aperture (Figure 11). In this case the phase front becomes quite distorted by the ridges. Horns in which the ridges can be terminated a reasonable distance from the aperture have a phase front approximately spherical. For such horns a doubly-convex lens may be suitable; for others a more complicated lens is required.

For small phase errors the most satisfactory design is a composite lens (Figure 10) consisting of two cylindrical lenses — one for each plane. In this case the E-plane phase error is corrected by a plano-convex cylindrical lens, while the H plane is corrected by a cylindrical lens with both concave and convex surfaces (see Figure 10). For phase errors equal to or less than $\lambda/2$, these lenses are so thin that no appreciable amplitude perturbation is observable and by careful phase measurement, the final horn-lens combination will have only a few degrees phase error.

EXPERIMENTAL RESULTS

Figure 11 shows two quite different doubly-ridged, lens-corrected horns. (The photograph is a composite, and the relative size is not correct.) VSWR curves for these two horns are shown in Figure 12; gain characteristics in Figure 13. Numbers have been assigned to the horns for the sake of expedience. Horn No. 1 is shown at the bottom of the photograph and Horn No. 2 at the top.

Horn No. 1 was designed to be used from 2-11 Gc. Its waveguide parameters are $B/A=0.465$, $S/A=0.425$, $D/B=0.138$. The curves show this waveguide to have $Z_{0\infty}=50\Omega$. For the proper waveguide width (A) the cutoff frequency of the TE_{10} mode is 1.5 Gc; TE_{30} mode is cutoff at 11.8 Gc.

Horn No. 2 has parameters $B/A=0.70$, $S/A = 0.375$, $D/B = 0.045$, which yields a $Z_{0\infty}=26\Omega$ and, for the proper values of (A), a TE_{10} mode cutoff frequency of 910 Mc; TE_{30} mode cutoff frequency of 11.6 Gc.

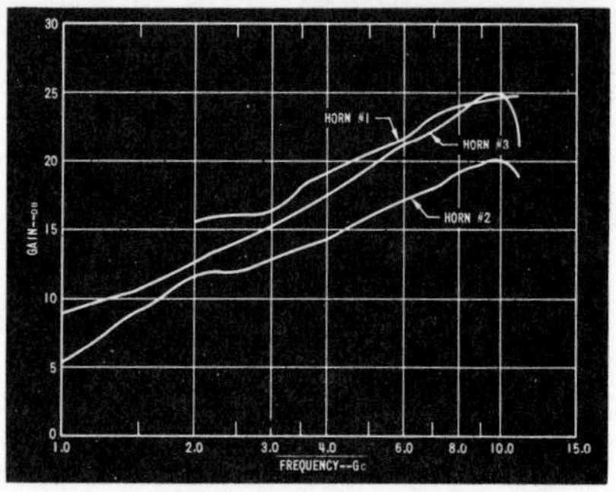

Figure 13 — Gain of three doubly-ridged, lens-corrected horns.

The characteristics of Horn No. 3 are also shown in Figures 12 and 13. This horn has very nearly the same physical appearance as Horn No. 1, but is designed to operate over the 1-11 Gc frequency range. The parameters of Horn No. 3 are $B/A=0.70$, $S/A=0.375$, $D/B=0.030$, which produce a ridged waveguide with $Z_{0\infty}=19\Omega$. The TE_{10} mode cutoff frequency is 755 Mc; TE_{30} mode cutoff frequency is 11.6 Gc. Horn No. 3 was also to be used over the 1-11 Gc frequency range, but in an effort to locate the VSWR peak outside of the operating frequency range, the horn was designed to have a 15.4:1 maximum usable bandwidth. However, as Figure 12 shows, as the bandwidth is extended, the VSWR peaks become higher, and there are more than one of significant height.

These peaks are not explained by any theory within our knowledge; however, at least one is present in all designs and they increase in magnitude and become narrower as the MUB is increased. For MUB's less than about 8:1, the spike amplitude is small (VSWR$<$2.5:1 Re $Z_{0\infty}$)

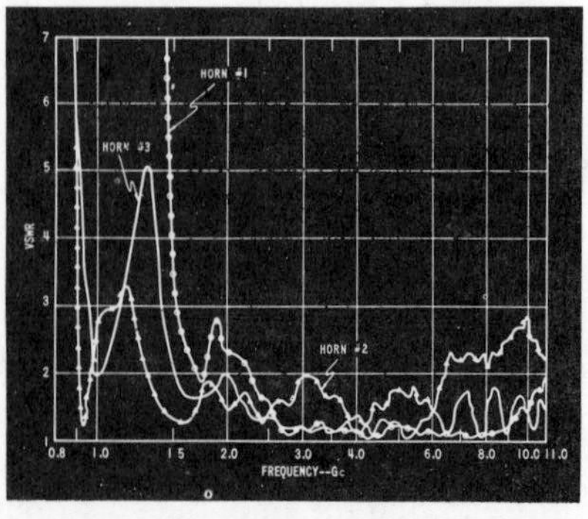

Figure 12 — VSWR of three doubly-ridged, lens-corrected horns.

Figure 14 — Horn No. 1.

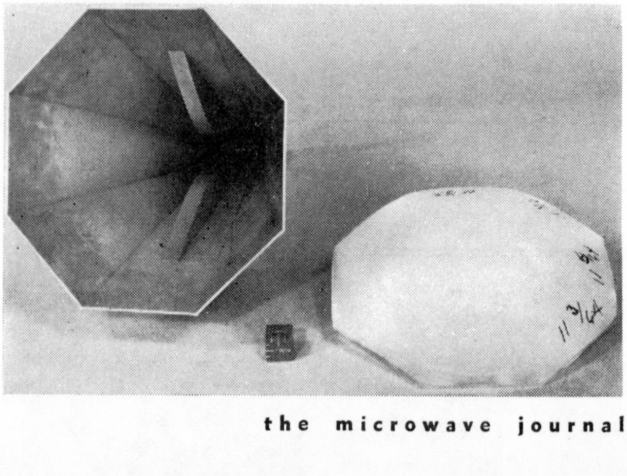

and can be ignored in most horn designs.

According to theory, the impedance, as a function of frequency, obeys Equation (4). The impedance remains relatively constant except near the TE_{10} mode cutoff frequency. Because of this a broadband impedance transformer[6] can be employed to transform the impedance of the ridged waveguide to 50 ohms. This was done on Horn No. 3 where the characteristic impedance of the ridged waveguide was 19 ohms. As Figure 12 shows, where the average VSWR without a transformer would be 2.6:1 over the major portion of the bandwidth, the average is much lower.

The dimension (B) must be kept less than a wavelength at the highest operating frequency to prevent propagation of the TE_{02} mode.

If all aspects of the horn design are carefully executed, the final antenna characteristics (beamwidth, gain, side-lobe levels, axial ratio, etc.) will closely approximate that of the conventional narrow band "optimum" waveguide horn. All of the previously mentioned design variations (impedance transformer, various lenses, etc.) have been tried with good results. However, extreme care must be taken in the horn fabrication and assembly or the final results can be most disappointing.

PARABOLIC REFLECTOR FEED

A ridged horn of this type is at present being employed as a feed for an offset-fed parabolic reflector. The assumption here is that when a parabolic reflector is illuminated by a feed whose beamwidth varies inverse-

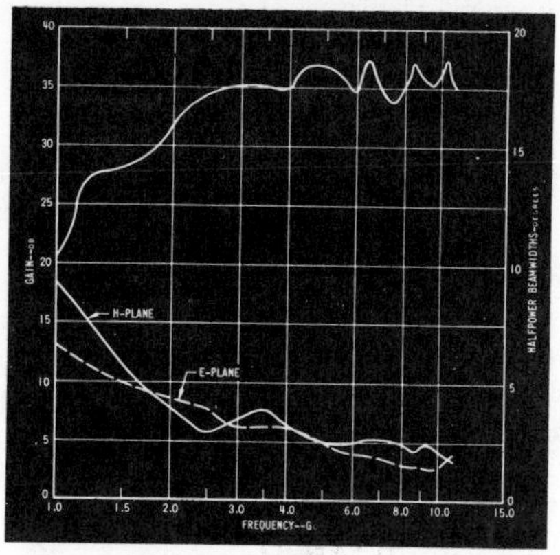

Figure 15 — Characteristics of the constant gain antenna.

ly with frequency, the gain and beamwidths of the secondary pattern will become nearly constant at frequencies above that at which the first feed pattern null illuminates the reflector edge.[7] This effect is quite useful in broadband antennas where a large reflector is required to obtain the desired gain at the lower frequencies. However, illuminated in the normal manner at the higher frequencies, this same reflector would produce secondary patterns with beamwidths much too narrow to be useful.

The ridged horn meets the requirements for the feed of such a system since its pattern beamwidths vary inversely with frequency, and it is capable of operating over a sufficiently wide bandwidth so that this effect becomes important.

Figure 15 shows the gain and beamwidth characteristics of an antenna system using the near-constant gain technique. In this case it was desired to obtain the gain shown at the upper end of the frequency band, and to restrict the reflector diameter to eight feet. The gain will remain relatively constant above the frequency at which the first null illuminates the reflector edge. An eight-foot parabolic reflector should have a gain of approximately 35 db at 3 Gc. The feed was therefore designed such that the first nulls were at the edge of the reflector at this frequency. The ridged horn feed, fitted at 3 Gc, had patterns at 1.0 Gc, which were excessively wide, resulting in a large amount of spillover at the frequencies near 1.0 Gc. This, of course, led to low aperture efficiencies at these frequencies. This could have been prevented by the use of a larger reflector if such had been permissible. A larger aperture feed would have resulted in better efficiencies near 1.0 Gc, but it would also have reduced the gain in the constant gain region.

REFERENCES

1. Cohn, S. B., "Properties of Ridge Wave Guide," *Proc. IRE,* pp. 783-788, August 1947.

2. Hopfer, S. W., "The Design of Ridged Waveguides," *Trans. PGMTT,* pp. 20-29, October 1955.

3. Chen, T. S., "Calculations of the Parameters of Ridge Waveguides," *Trans. PGMTT,* pp. 12-17, January 1957.

4. Whinnery, J. R. and H. W. Jamieson, "Equivalent Circuits for Discontinuities In Transmission Lines," *Proc. IRE,* Vol. 32, pp. 98-116, February 1944.

5. Silver, S., *Microwave Antenna Theory and Design,* MIT Rad. Lab. Series, pp. 389-395, McGraw-Hill Book Co., Inc., New York, N. Y., 1949.

6. Cohn, S. B., "Optimum Design of Stepped Transmission Line Transformer," *Trans. PGMTT,* pp. 16-21, April 1955.

7. Gillard, C. W. and R. E. Franks, "Frequency Independent Antennas — Several New and Undeveloped Ideas," *the microwave journal,* Vol. 4, pp. 67-72, February 1961.

Short Axial Length Broad-Band Horns

JOHN L. KERR

Abstract—**Ever-increasing antenna frequency bandwidth requirements for countermeasures applications and electromagnetic compatibility measurements have provided the impetus for the development of a series of very broad-band horns. In addition to the broad bandwidth, a substantial reduction in axial length over that of earlier models has been achieved for the two designs discussed in this communication. The first horn described covers the frequency range from 1.0–12.0 GHz with the flared portion of the horn having an axial length of 6 in as compared with 12 in for an earlier model. Although horn antennas are not commonly considered for use at frequencies as low as 0.2 GHz, the short axial length design appeared to be an attractive approach in developing a very reasonably sized antenna operating in the 0.2–2.0 GHz range. The technique of fabricating the *H* plane walls in the form of a grid was used in both designs as a means of maintaining the required *H*-plane half-power beamwidths. The grid for the 1.0–12.0 GHz horn is of printed circuit form while the grid elements of the lower frequency horn are made of aluminum tubing. Electrical characteristics of both designs are presented, as well as some additional data for recent advances which indicate that a further reduction in axial length or an increase in bandwidth can be achieved with only a moderate rise in VSWR in the lower portion of the frequency range.**

Introduction

A development program, based on ever-increasing bandwidth requirements, has resulted in a series of very broad-band horn designs utilizing double-ridged waveguide techniques [1]. The earliest models for countermeasures applications provided bandwidths of slightly more than 3:1 for two small feed horns. More recent efforts have extended the bandwidth to more than 12:1 for two horn designs [2] for radio frequency interference (RFI) measurements. These were a feed horn and a moderate-gain horn (about 15 dB) for operation over the 1.0–12.0 GHz frequency range. The latter two horns provided the background for the short axial length designs described in this communication.

Initially, in the 1.0–12.0 GHz feed-horn development, an attempt was made to limit the axial length of the flared portion of the horn to 6 in. Due to higher than desired VSWR at the low end of the frequency range, the length was gradually increased to the final design dimension of 12 in. Near the end of that development, it was determined that a small linear taper superimposed on the logarithmic curve of the ridges tended to give a substantial improvement in VSWR in the first octave of the band and had little effect elsewhere. It then appeared likely that the 12-in axial length of the horn flare could be significantly reduced. That was, indeed, found to be so in a model with an axial length of 6 in. The original short model is shown in Fig. 1.

Description (1.0–12.0 GHz Horn)

Recently, new requirements were presented for an antenna which would maintain wider beamwidths in the upper portion of the 1.0–12.0 GHz frequency range than was the case for either the feed horn or the moderate-gain horn. The specified minimum half-power beamwidth was 30° and with a goal of not less than 40°. Although the original 6-in model exhibited pattern deterioration above 10.0 GHz and produced half-power beamwidths of approximately 25° at some frequencies, it was, nevertheless, a likely starting point in developing the required antenna. Pattern degradation above 10.0 GHz had also been experienced during the development of the moderate-gain horn when using the feed-horn launcher, requiring a new design to cover the upper portion of the band. On that basis, it was felt that by combining the 6-in axial length horn flare design

Manuscript received January 15, 1973; revised April 4, 1973.
The author is with the Radar Technical Area, Combat Surveillance and Target Acquisition Laboratory, U. S. Army Electronics Command, Fort Monmouth, N. J.

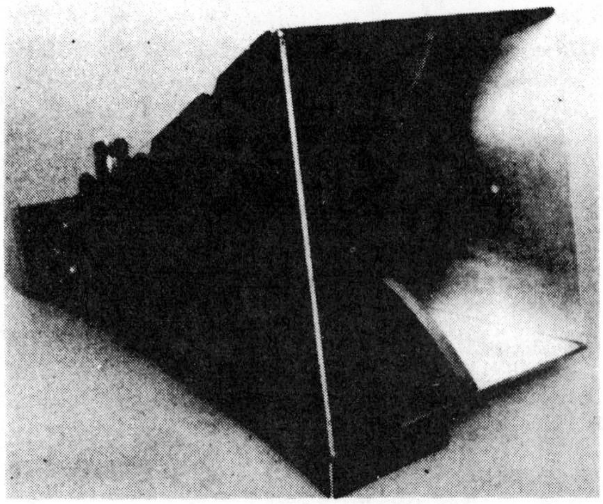

Fig. 1. Original 6 in axial length horn.

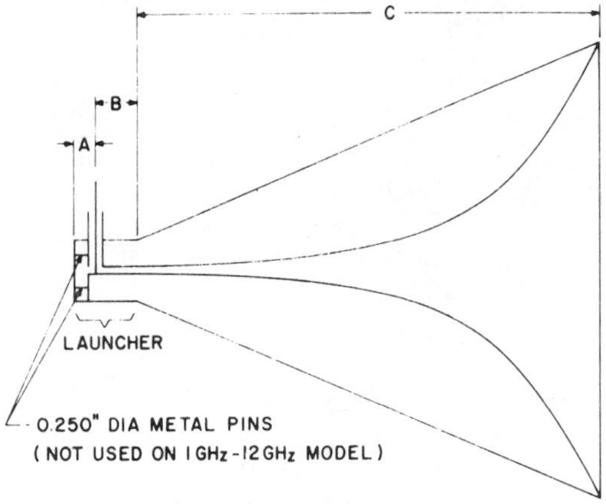

Fig. 2. Sketch of short axial length horn.

TABLE I
HORN DIMENSIONS

Internal Axial Dimensions[a]		
Dimension	1.0–12.0 GHz-Horn (in)	0.2–2.0 GHz Horn (in)
A	0.325	1.625
B	1.000	5.000
C	6.000	30.0000

Cross Section Dimensions				
Location	Width (in)	Height (in)	Width (in)	Height (in)
Back shorting plate	1.200	0.872	7.000	6.700
Feed point	1.200	0.872	7.000	6.700
Launcher-horn junction	3.400	2.616	14.200	6.700
Horn aperture	9.500	5.440	37.500	27.200

[a] Refer to Fig. 2.

Reprinted from *IEEE Trans. Antennas Propagat.*, vol. AP-21, pp. 710–715, Sept. 1973.

with the improved launcher, the performance of the short model could be extended up to 12.0 GHz.

A model combining those features was fabricated and a sketch is shown in Fig. 2. Table I summarizes the inner dimensions of the design. It is interesting to note that both the cross section of the launcher and the distance from the feed point to the back shorting plate are both extremely small, with the latter being an order of magnitude smaller than usual for operation at the low end of the frequency range. The small dimensions are, of course, necessary for proper operation at the higher frequencies. Also from Table I, it can be seen that both the height and width of the launcher increase from the feed point out to the launcher-horn junction. Fig. 3 is the graph from which the ridge curvature is determined. As indicated on the graph, the amount of additional linear taper required for best VSWR in the first octave of the band is 0.020× for the 6-in axial length horn. No attempt has, as yet, been made to determine

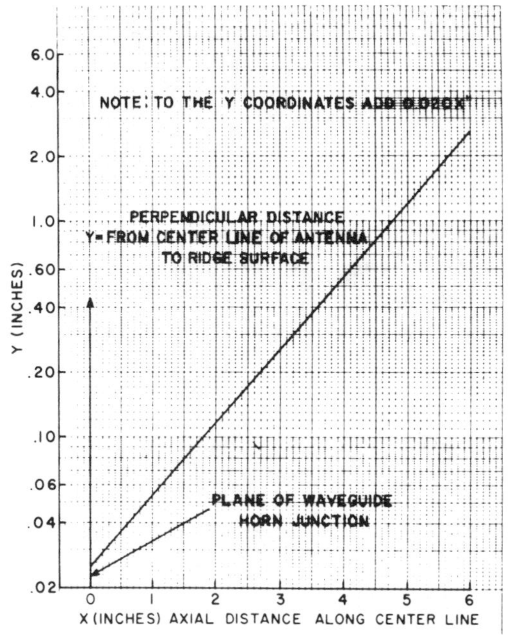

Fig. 3. Graph of ridge curve coordinates.

the reason for the beneficial effect of the additional linear taper. The spacing between the ridges increases from 0.050 in at the feed point to 5.44 in at the horn aperture. The ridge width is 0.375 in.

Measured Characteristics (1.0–12.0 GHz Horn)

Radiation patterns, VSWR, and gain measured over the frequency range of interest showed that the bandwidth of the short axial length horn had been extended to cover the entire 1.0–12.0 GHz band. The VSWR was quite satisfactory and the *E*-plane half-power beamwidth was less than 40° in only one instance. In the *H* plane, the half-power beamwidth was on the order of 25° in the range from 5.0–6.0 GHz. Marginal improvement in the narrow beamwidth region was achieved by increasing the *H*-plane flare angle. That also resulted in an increase in the *H*-plane aperture to 9.5 in as compared with 7.5 in on the initial model.

In an earlier development [3], it was shown that, at least for a longer axial length, the ridges have primary control of the radiation patterns in the upper portion of the band. In view of that finding, the sides which normally control the *H*-plane patterns were removed and a series of patterns recorded. These show that from 3.5–12.0 GHz the *H*-plane sides are not required and the *H*-plane half-power beamwidth remains at 30° or more. Below 3.5 GHz, the *H*-plane patterns tend to broaden too much with the sides removed. The preceding results suggest the use of a grid-type construction [4] for the *H*-plane walls. If the spacing between grid elements is on the order of 0.1 wavelength at the low end of the band, a plane reflector will be simulated. Over the very large bandwidth of this horn design, the spacing will then be greater than one wavelength at the upper end of the band and the grid should have very little effect there. The development model was modified to include grid construction of the *H*-plane sides. 0.093-in aluminum rods were used for the grid elements and were spaced slightly more than 0.1 wavelength at 1.0 GHz.

Although the electrical characteristics met the requirements, the soft aluminum grid elements were somewhat fragile. In addition, some thought was given to the problem of weatherproofing, if required, for other applications. For those reasons, a final modification was made which consisted of fabricating the *H*-plane sides in the form of a printed circuit grid. Fig. 4 is a photograph of the final version. The grid is composed of six strips, 0.030-in wide, which are equally spaced at 1.306-in intervals. The dielectric material used was 0.062-in thick aluminum-clad polyphenelene oxide or glass-reinforced Teflon.

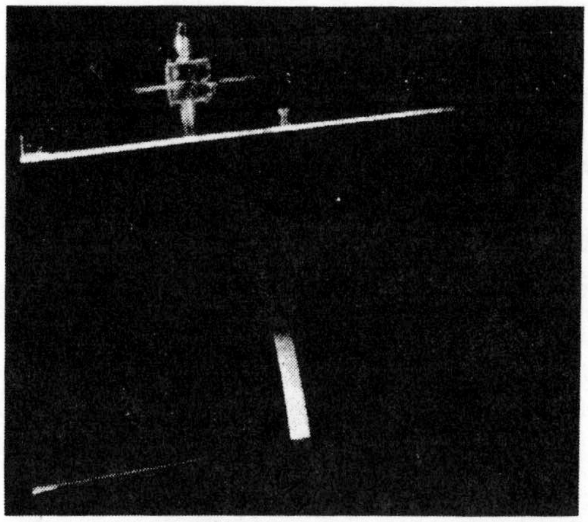

Fig. 4. Final development model (1.0–12.0 GHz horn).

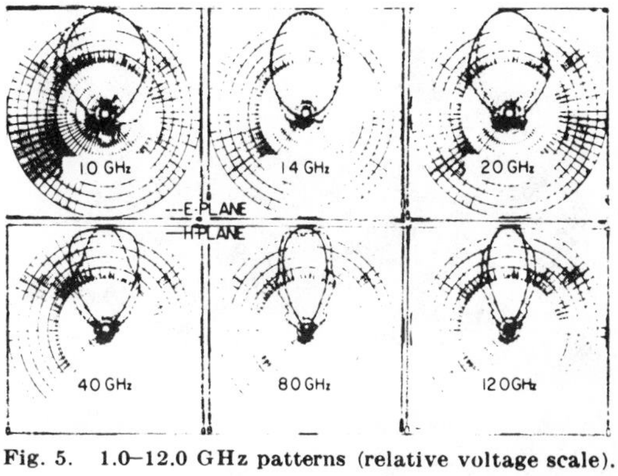

Fig. 5. 1.0–12.0 GHz patterns (relative voltage scale).

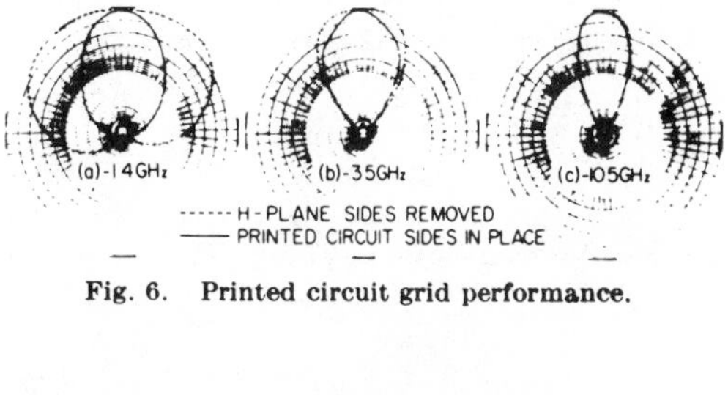

Fig. 6. Printed circuit grid performance.

Fig. 5 shows representative *E*- and *H*-plane patterns plotted on a relative voltage scale. The *H*-plane half-power beamwidth remains at 30° or more throughout the frequency range and the narrowest *E*-plane pattern, which was recorded at 3.5 GHz, is 36° wide. Fig. 6 indicates how the printed circuit *H*-plane sides affect the patterns over the band. Fig. 6(a) shows that at 1.4 GHz the grid construction gives essentially the same performance as that obtained with conventional metal sides. Fig. 6(b) indicates that the etched grid still has an effect at 3.5 GHz but much reduced from that at 1.4 GHz. Fig. 6(c) shows that the effect of the grid construction is negligible at 10.5 GHz. In fact, the effect is minor from approximately 4.0 GHz, where the grid spacing is approaching 0.5 wavelength.

Fig. 7 shows the VSWR and gain as measured on the final development model. The VSWR remains well under 2:1 over most of the 1.0–12.0 GHz band and to a limited extent below 1.0 GHz. It should be noted here that the VSWR has been measured using swept-frequency techniques. The format of Fig. 7 has been continued for reasons of easy comparison with large amounts of data recorded before the availability of the more modern equipment. The on-axis cross-polarized component has been measured to be down more than 40 dB.

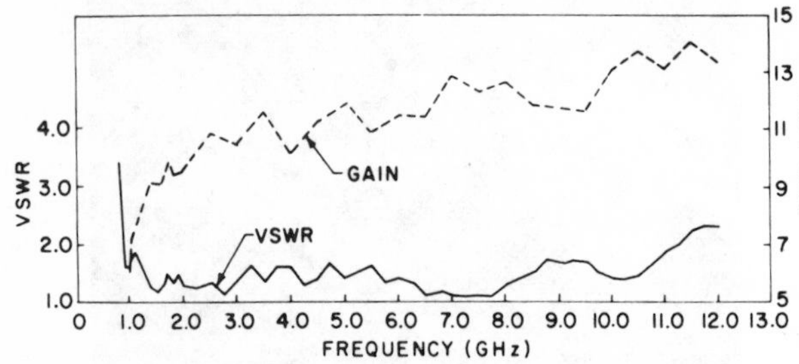

Fig. 7. VSWR and gain (1.0–12.0 GHz horn).

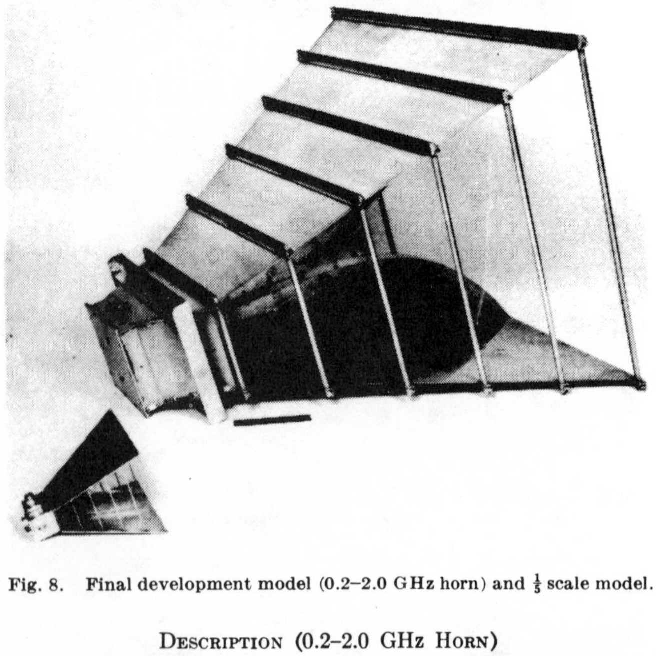

Fig. 8. Final development model (0.2–2.0 GHz horn) and $\frac{1}{5}$ scale model.

Description (0.2–2.0 GHz Horn)

Although horn antennas are not commonly considered for frequencies as low as 0.2 GHz, the short axial length design appeared to be an attractive approach to meet similar requirements in the 0.2–1.0 GHz range since scaling the original model by a factor of five results in a maximum dimension of 37.5 in. The reduced bandwidth also makes it possible to use the original feed-horn launcher design which is much easier to fabricate in sheet metal and has a considerable advantage in form-factor as compared with the version used on the 1.0–12.0-GHz horn. The use of a grid-type construction for the *H*-plane walls was again indicated for meeting the beamwidth requirement as well as for minimizing the weight; an important consideration because of the five-fold increase in size.

A 5:1 scale model of the antenna shown in Fig. 1, modified to include grid-type *H*-plane walls, was designed and fabricated. The configuration is outlined in Fig. 2 and shows the location of two metal rods which were required in this launcher design to suppress a very high VSWR (greater than 7:1) encountered in the upper portion of the band during the early stages of the 1.0–12.0 GHz feed-horn development. The end of the ridge just behind the feed point is a plate 3.225-in high by 1.875-in wide. The rods are directly connected at the point of intersection of the horizontal and vertical center lines of the plates and extend through the cavity to make contact with the back shorting plate. The horn dimensions are summarized in Table I. In this launcher design, only the width increases from the feed point out to the launcher-horn junction. The ridge curve is a scale version (×5) of that shown in Fig. 3, so that the spacing between the ridges increases from 0.250 inches at the feed point to 27.20 in. at the aperture.

Fig. 8 shows in some detail the method of construction of the horn and also shows the $\frac{1}{5}$ scale model which was used to establish the

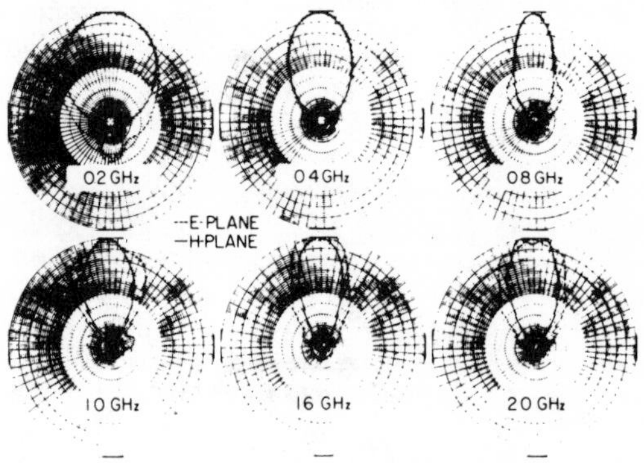

Fig. 9. 0.2- -2.0-GHz patterns (relative voltage scale).

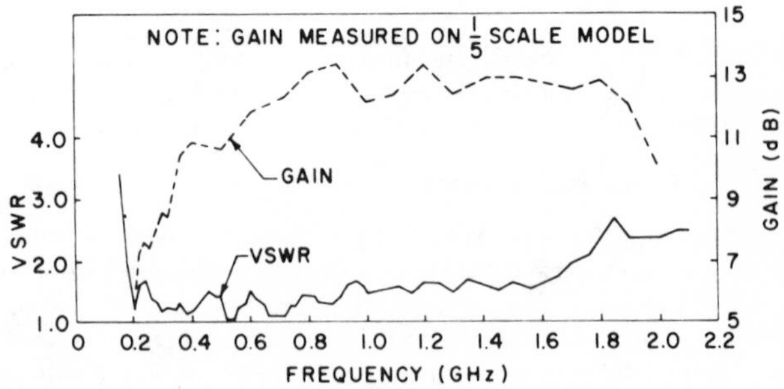

Fig. 10. VSWR and gain (0.2–2.0 GHz horn).

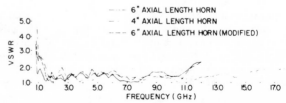

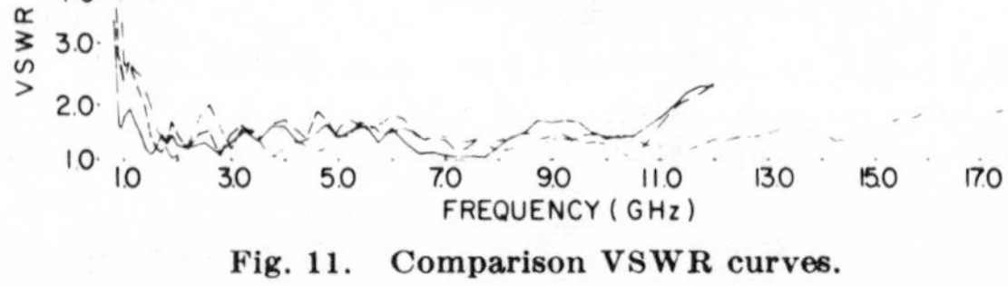

Fig. 11. Comparison VSWR curves.

design before going to the full-scale version. The grid elements on the larger horn are 0.500-in aluminum tubing spaced 6.140-in apart and the ridges are of hollow construction, 1.875-in wide. The weight is 21.25 lb.

Electrical Characteristics (0.2–2.0 GHz Horn)

Fig. 9 shows some typical radiation patterns plotted on a relative voltage scale. In this design, pattern degradation begins above 1.8 GHz and becomes severe above 2.0 GHz. Fig. 10 shows VSWR and gain. As indicated on the figure, the gain was measured on a scale-model basis because of the lack of good directive gain standards at the lower frequencies and the problem of strong ground reflections.

Additional Advances

At the conclusion of the two short axial length horn developments, the data were such as to suggest that perhaps the length could be further reduced or the bandwidth increased. A 4-in axial length model has been assembled and shows promising results. Pattern data are satisfactory over the 1.0–12.0 GHz band with a minimum beamwidth of 37° which more nearly approaches the original goal of not less than 40°. The VSWR is indicated by the dot–dash curve of Fig. 11. For comparison purposes, the solid curve repeats the results which were obtained on the 6-in model. One result of reducing the axial length is a rise in VSWR at the low end of the frequency range which is not too serious.

The 6-in axial length horn has been modified in an attempt to increase the bandwidth. The launcher cross section was reduced from 1.2 in by 0.872 in to 1.0 in by 0.625 in. That resulted in a moderate rise in VSWR at the lower frequencies and a reduction in VSWR at 12.0 GHz from 2.3:1 down to 1.6:1. The VSWR then increased gradually to a value of 3:1 at 15.0 GHz. Following that, the diameter of the cylindrical inserts which form the coaxial input was reduced from 0.276 in to 0.187 in and the input connector was changed from type N to type SMA. The result of the combination of changes is shown by the dashed curve of Fig. 11. The rise in VSWR at the low end of the band is due to the reduction in launcher cross section. However, a very substantial improvement over an extended bandwidth is obtained at the upper frequencies with a value of 2:1 being reached at 18.0 GHz.

Pattern data on the modified 6-in axial length model show that the bandwidth has been increased to 16.0 GHz or perhaps somewhat higher, depending on application. Serious pattern deterioration is encountered at approximately 18.0 GHz.

Conclusions

The two short axial length horn designs described in this communication met or exceeded the requirements and both are being used in increasing numbers for electromagnetic compatability measurements. Data on models designed to further reduce the axial length or to achieve an increase in bandwidth indicate that either result can be obtained with only a moderate rise in VSWR at the low end of the frequency range. The success with the 4-in axial length model translates to a very significant reduction of 10 in in axial length for the lower frequency horn described earlier. VSWR and pattern data on the modified version of the 6-in axial length horn now show a useful bandwidth approaching 18:1; covering the frequency range from 0.9–16.0 GHz or somewhat higher depending on application.

Acknowledgment

The author wishes to express his appreciation to W. Johnson and M. Timochko for their considerable efforts in accomplishing the several broadband horn designs and to thank Ms. J. Serwatka for her patience and diligence through the many typing chores. A special thanks is also due C. Eason, formerly of this Laboratory, who initiated the program many years ago.

References

[1] Radio Res. Lab. Staff, M.I.I. Lincoln Lab. *Very High Frequency Techniques*, vol. II. New York: McGraw-Hill, 1947, pp. 725–728.
[2] J. L. Kerr, "Broadband horns," Tech. Rep. ECOM-3319, AD714994 Aug. 1970.
[3] ——, "A very broadband low silhouette antenna," Tech. Rep. ECOM-3087, AD684915, Jan. 1969.
[4] J. D. Kraus, *Antennas*. New York: McGraw-Hill, 1950, p. 335.

The Phase Center of Horn Antennas

EUGEN I. MUEHLDORF, SENIOR MEMBER, IEEE

Abstract—The calculation of phase centers for rectangular and diagonal horns is presented. The calculation is based on a vector approach, by deriving the phase center from the expressions for the far field. Different expressions are derived for the phase center of the E and H planes. The phase center for an arbitrary plane is calculated from the E- and H-plane phase centers. Graphs are presented showing the dependence of the phase centers on horn dimensions.

I. Introduction

FOR CERTAIN applications, for example, a very precise interferometer, it is necessary to know the phase center of a horn antenna and the dependence of the phase center on the shape of the horn. The phase center is defined as the center of curvature of the intersection of a far-field phase surface with a plane containing the horn axis.

Previous work in this area has been done by Baur [1]. He bases his work on the Kirchhoff approximation [2], and he derives an elegant method for determining the phase center of the E plane. Because Kirchhoff's approximation is used as a starting point, the problem is basically treated as a scalar problem. The solution is therefore primarily applicable to sectoral horns.

A slightly different approach to the problem was taken by Hu [3], where a plot of the phase of the far field is used to determine the phase center. This method requires a suitable choice of coordinate system and phase constants; Hu evaluated the results for sectoral horns. Ujiie *et al.* [4] recognized that different phase centers will result for the E and H planes; they proceed to show only results for circular apertures with phase distributions which are a function of radius alone.

For many applications such as diagonal and rectangular horns, the problem must be treated as a vector problem. Consequently, the location of the phase center will be derived here from the general expressions for the far field.

To determine the phase center, it is necessary to use a second-order approximation to the field at the horn aperture. While the far-field equations for horns [2] are generally calculated by neglecting the fact that the horn aperture does not coincide with a phase front, such simplification cannot be afforded here. For square and diagonal horns discussed in this paper the integration is carried out over the horn aperture; however, a correction for the phase front is introduced. The phase front of the source is

Manuscript received November 17, 1969; revised April 15, 1970. This work was supported in part by NASA Goddard Space Flight Center under Contract NAS 5-11609.

The author is with IBM Federal Systems Division, Gaithersburg, Md. 20760.

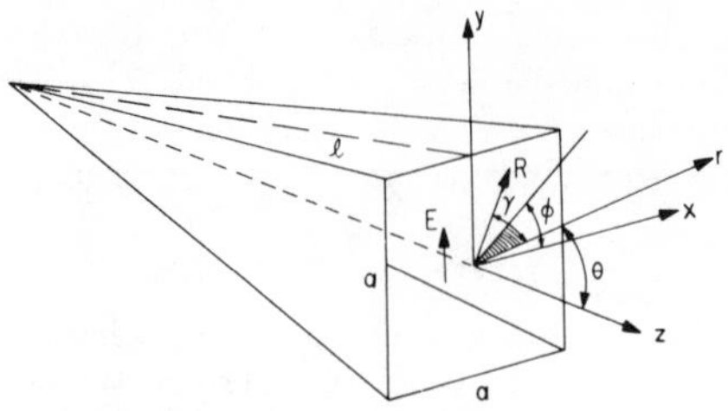

xyz	rectangular coordinate system
$r\theta\phi$	spherical coordinate system
θ	angle between r and z
ϕ	angle between x and projection of r on xy plane
γ	angle between r and R
R	distance from origin to a point in xy plane.

Fig. 1. Horn and coordinate systems.

approximated by a paraboloid of rotation

$$\delta = -\frac{x^2 + y^2}{2l} + \frac{a^2}{4l} \tag{1}$$

where

- l length of horn, as defined in Fig. 1
- a width of aperture
- δ deviation of the phase front from the aperture plane.

The coordinate systems used in this paper are a Cartesian x,y,z system for the source field and a spherical r,θ,ϕ system for the far field with the origins in the aperture plane (see Fig. 1).

II. Determination of the Phase Centers

Generally, the far field can be written as

$$\boldsymbol{E} = \begin{cases} 0 \\ \boldsymbol{a}_\theta \mid E_\theta \mid \exp j[kr - \psi_\theta(\theta,\phi)] \\ \boldsymbol{a}_\phi \mid E_\phi \mid \exp j[kr - \psi_\phi(\theta,\phi)]. \end{cases} \tag{2}$$

In (2) $\boldsymbol{a}_\theta$ and $\boldsymbol{a}_\phi$ are unit vectors in the coordinate directions θ and ϕ, while $k = 2\pi/\lambda$ is the wave constant.

A planar cut containing the axis is defined by letting $\phi = \phi_0$. Only for planar cuts which produce

$$\psi_\theta(\theta,\phi_0) = \psi_\phi(\theta,\phi_0) = \psi(\theta) \tag{3}$$

is a simple calculation possible. In this case the far field is linearly polarized, and both the θ and ϕ component have the same phase front. In cases where the condition expressed by (3) is not fulfilled, the far field is, in general, elliptically polarized, and the definition of a phase center may not be possible.

Reprinted from *IEEE Trans. Antennas Propagat.*, vol. AP-18, pp. 753–760, Nov. 1970.

Under the condition that a phase front exists for a linearly polarized far field, the planar cut through the phase front results in the equation

$$r = K + (1/k)\psi(\theta). \quad (4)$$

This represents an equiphase curve in the planar r,θ coordinate system, where K is a constant.

The radius of curvature ρ is given by

$$\rho = \frac{[r^2 + (r')^2]^{3/2}}{r^2 + 2(r')^2 - rr''} \quad (5)$$

where r' and r'' denote the first and second derivative with respect to θ. The case of interest, which will be computed here, is the phase center for the field near the z axis. For this case

$$\rho = \rho_0, \quad r = r(0), \quad r' = 0, \quad r'' = r''(0).$$

Then

$$\rho_0 = \frac{r^2(0)}{r(0) - r''(0)}. \quad (6)$$

The phase center location is defined as the distance Δ from the aperture into the horn, measured on the horn axis. Then

$$\Delta = \rho_0 - r(0). \quad (7)$$

Combining (6) and (7) and computing Δ, for $r(0) \rightarrow \infty$, leads to

$$\Delta = r''(0). \quad (8)$$

III. Phase Center for a Square Horn

The horn is assumed to have an aperture illumination described by

$$\boldsymbol{E}_{\text{ap}} = \begin{cases} 0 \\ \boldsymbol{a}_y E_0 \cos(\pi x/a) \exp jk\delta, \quad a/2 > y > a/2. \\ 0 \end{cases} \quad (9)$$

This type of illumination results when the horn is fed by a rectangular waveguide operating in the TE_{10} mode. The factor $\exp jk\delta$ compensates for deviation between phase front and aperture plane, as discussed in Section I.

For calculating the far field, the methodology described in Wolff [5] is used. The far-field components E_θ and E_ϕ can then be expressed as

$$E_\theta = -jk \frac{\exp(-jkr)}{4\pi r} (L_\phi + Z_0 N_\theta)$$

$$E_\phi = jk \frac{\exp(-jkr)}{4\pi r} (L_\theta - Z_0 N_\phi) \quad (10)$$

where Z_0 is the impedance of free space.

The far-field components are expressed in terms of an electric radiation vector $\boldsymbol{L}$ and a magnetic radiation vector $\boldsymbol{N}$, of which the θ and ϕ components are needed. The x and y components of the vectors $\boldsymbol{L}$ and $\boldsymbol{N}$ can be readily expressed as

$$N_y = -\frac{1}{Z_0} \int_{\text{ap}} E_y \exp jkR \cos\gamma \, ds$$

$$L_x = \int_{\text{ap}} E_y \exp jkR \cos\gamma \, ds \quad (11)$$

where R is the distance from the origin to a point in the aperture and γ is the angle between $\boldsymbol{R}$ and the vector $\boldsymbol{r}$ to the far-field point. The other components of the $\boldsymbol{L}$ and $\boldsymbol{N}$ are zero.

When the far-field components of $\boldsymbol{L}$ and $\boldsymbol{N}$ are properly converted into the r,θ,ϕ coordinate system, the following result is obtained:

$$E_\theta = jk \frac{\exp(-jkr)}{4\pi r} (1 + \cos\theta) \sin\phi \int E_y \exp jkR \cos\gamma \, ds$$

$$E_\phi = jk \frac{\exp(-jkr)}{4\pi r} (1 + \cos\theta) \cos\phi \int E_y \exp jkR \cos\gamma \, ds. \quad (12)$$

The expression $R \cos\gamma$ in the chosen coordinate system is

$$R\cos\gamma = x\cos\phi\sin\theta + y\sin\phi\sin\theta.$$

Then the electric radiation vector becomes

$$L_x = E_0 \exp jk \frac{a^2}{4l} \int_{-a/2}^{a/2} \cos\left(\frac{\pi x}{a}\right) \cdot \exp jk \left\{x\cos\phi\sin\theta - \frac{x^2}{2l}\right\} dx \cdot \int_{-a/2}^{a/2} \exp jk \left\{y\sin\phi\sin\theta - \frac{y^2}{2l}\right\} dy. \quad (13)$$

When the first integral is designated I_1 and the second I_2, then

$$I_1 = |I_1| \exp j \arctan \frac{f(\theta,\phi)}{g(\theta,\phi)} \quad (14a)$$

$$I_2 = |I_2| \exp j \left[\frac{\pi}{2}\frac{T^2}{v^2} + \arctan \frac{m(\theta,\phi)}{n(\theta,\phi)}\right] \quad (14b)$$

where

$$\frac{l\lambda}{2} = v^2, \quad \frac{v^2}{a} + l\cos\phi\sin\theta = P,$$

$$-\frac{v^2}{a} + l\cos\phi\sin\theta = Q, \quad l\sin\phi\sin\theta = T. \quad (15)$$

The expressions f, g, m, and n are complicated expressions in Fresnel cosine and Fresnel sine functions of P, Q, v, and a.

Finally one obtains for the far field

$$E_\theta = E_0 \frac{k}{4\pi r} |I_1||I_2| (1+\cos\theta) \sin\phi$$

$$\cdot \exp j \left\{ -kr + \frac{\pi}{2} + k\frac{a^2}{4l} + \frac{\pi}{2}\frac{T^2}{v^2} + \arctan\frac{m}{n} + \arctan\frac{f}{g} \right\}$$

$$E_\phi = E_0 \frac{k}{4\pi r} |I_1||I_2| (1+\cos\theta) \cos\phi$$

$$\cdot \exp j \left\{ -kr + \frac{\pi}{2} + k\frac{a^2}{4l} + \frac{\pi}{2}\frac{T^2}{v^2} + \arctan\frac{m}{n} + \arctan\frac{f}{g} \right\}. \tag{16}$$

Equation (16) shows that the field is linearly polarized; thus the phase front is

$$r = K_1 + \frac{\lambda}{4} + \frac{a^2}{4l} + \frac{\lambda T^2}{4v^2} + \frac{\lambda}{2\pi}\arctan\frac{m}{n} + \frac{\lambda}{2\pi}\arctan\frac{f}{g} \tag{17}$$

with K_1 a constant.

Planar cuts will be taken for two values of $\phi, \phi = 0$, representing the H plane, and $\phi = 90°$ representing the E plane.

For the H plane $\phi = 0$, $E_\theta = 0$, $T = 0$, and $m(\theta,\phi)/n(\theta,\phi) = 0$. Hence the expression for the phase front reduces to

$$r = K_2 + \frac{\lambda}{2\pi}\arctan\frac{f}{g}. \tag{18}$$

When differentiating it is observed that for points near the axis $\sin\theta \doteq \theta$ and, because of symmetry, $f'(0) = 0$ and $g'(0) = 0$. The result for $r''(0)$ is

$$r''(0) = \frac{\lambda}{2\pi}\frac{f''(0)g(0) - g''(0)f(0)}{f^2(0) + g^2(0)}. \tag{19}$$

Introducing the new abbreviations

$$U = \frac{v}{a} + \frac{a}{2v}, \quad W = \frac{v}{a} - \frac{a}{2v} \tag{20}$$

the final result for the phase center in the H plane is

$\Delta(\theta, \phi = 0)$

$$= l\left\{1 + \frac{\left[W\cos\frac{\pi}{2}U^2 - U\cos\frac{\pi}{2}W^2\right][C(U) - C(W)] + \left[U\sin\frac{\pi}{2}W^2 - W\sin\frac{\pi}{2}U^2\right][-S(U) + S(W)]}{[C(U) - C(W)]^2 + [-S(U) + S(W)]^2}\right\} \tag{21}$$

where $S(\cdot)$ indicates the Fresnel sine function and $C(\cdot)$ the Fresnel cosine function.

For the E plane $\phi = 90°$, $E_\phi = 0$, and $f(\theta,\phi)/g(\theta,\phi) = 0$. The phase front reduces to

$$r = K_3 + \frac{\lambda}{2\pi}\arctan\frac{m}{n} + \frac{l}{2}\sin^2\theta. \tag{22}$$

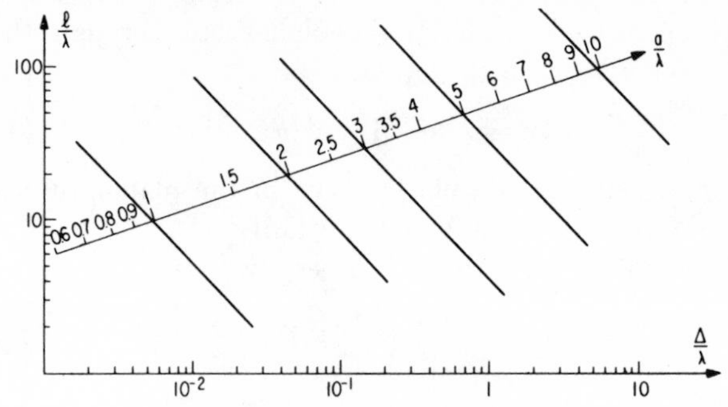

Fig. 2. Phase center for H-plane pattern of linearly polarized horn (21).

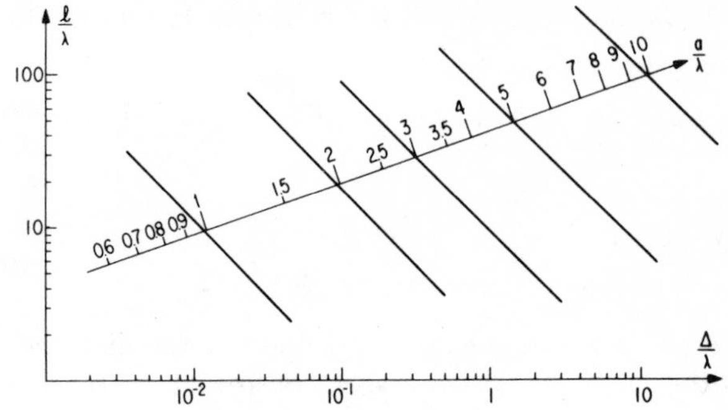

Fig. 3. Phase center for E-plane pattern of linearly polarized horn (24).

Observing that $\sin\theta \doteq \theta$ and $m'(0) = n'(0) = 0$ the result for $r''(0)$ becomes

$$r''(0) = \frac{\lambda}{2\pi}\frac{m''(0)n(0) - m(0)n''(0)}{m^2(0) + n^2(0)} + l. \tag{23}$$

Thus in the E plane the phase center is

$\Delta(\theta, \phi = 90°)$

$$= l\left\{1 - \frac{a}{2v}\frac{\cos\frac{\pi}{2}\left(\frac{a}{2v}\right)^2 C\left(\frac{a}{2v}\right) + \sin\frac{\pi}{2}\left(\frac{a}{2v}\right)^2 S\left(\frac{a}{2v}\right)}{C^2\left(\frac{a}{2v}\right) + S^2\left(\frac{a}{2v}\right)}\right\} \tag{24}$$

Equations (21) and (24) describe the relationship between horn parameters and phase center. They are valid in the region where $\theta \doteq \sin\theta$. These equations were evaluated numerically, and the resulting plots are shown in Figs. 2 and 3. In these figures, the normalized phase center Δ/λ is plotted versus l/λ with a/λ as parameter.

It can be seen, despite the complicated mathematical expressions, that in the chosen double logarithmic representation, the plots are basically straight parallel lines over the range of interest. The distance between the lines is logarithmically related to a/λ as indicated. Thus, for any desired a, a parallel line can be drawn through the a/λ scale.

Should it be desired to take a cut along an arbitrary plane, say $\phi = \phi_0$, then

$$r = K_4 + \frac{\lambda}{2\pi} \arctan \frac{m}{n} + \frac{\lambda}{2\pi} \arctan \frac{f}{g} + \frac{l}{2} \sin^2 \theta \sin^2 \phi_0. \tag{25}$$

For the derivative, it should be considered that for the term containing m/n one can approximate $\sin \theta \cos \phi_0 \doteq \theta \cos \phi_0$, while for the term containing f/g, the approximation is $\sin \theta \sin \phi_0 \doteq \theta \sin \phi_0$. Then one obtains

$$r''(0) = \sin^2 \phi_0 \frac{\lambda}{2\pi} \frac{f''(0)g(0) - g''(0)f(0)}{f^2(0) + g^2(0)} + l + \cos^2 \phi_0 \frac{\lambda}{2\pi} \frac{m''(0)n(0) - n''(0)m(0)}{m^2(0) + n^2(0)} \tag{26}$$

and the phase center becomes

$$\Delta(\theta,\phi = \phi_0) = l \left\{ 1 - \frac{a}{2v} \cos^2 \phi_0 \frac{\cos \frac{\pi}{2} \left(\frac{a}{2v}\right)^2 C\left(\frac{a}{2v}\right) + \sin \frac{\pi}{2} \left(\frac{a}{2v}\right)^2 S\left(\frac{a}{2v}\right)}{C^2\left(\frac{a}{2v}\right) + S^2\left(\frac{a}{2v}\right)} \right.$$
$$\left. + \sin^2 \phi_0 \frac{\left[W \cos \frac{\pi}{2} U^2 - U \cos \frac{\pi}{2} W^2\right][C(U) - C(W)] + \left[U \sin \frac{\pi}{2} W^2 - W \sin \frac{\pi}{2} U^2\right][-S(U) + S(W)]}{[C(U) - C(W)]^2 + [-S(U) + S(W)]^2} \right\}. \tag{27}$$

It is easily seen that this can also be expressed as

$$\Delta(\theta,\phi = \phi_0) = \cos^2 \phi_0 \Delta(\theta,\phi = 90°) + \sin^2 \phi_0 \Delta(\theta,\phi = 0). \tag{28}$$

Hence the phase center for an arbitrary planar cut can thus be calculated from the phase centers for $\phi = 0$ and $\phi = 90°$ by a process which resembles averaging.

IV. Phase Center for a Compensated Horn

The amplitude compensated horn [6] has a nonuniform aperture illumination along the y axis. The amplitude ratio 1:2:1 is achieved by introducing vanes into the horn, which split the energy entering from the feed. The field is given by

$$E_y = \boldsymbol{a}_y \begin{cases} 0, & y > a/2 \\ E_0 \cos(\pi x/a) \exp jk\delta, & a/2 \geq y > a/4 \\ 2E_0 \cos(\pi x/a) \exp jk\delta, & a/4 \geq y > -a/4 \\ E_0 \cos(\pi x/a) \exp jk\delta, & -a/4 \geq y > -a/2 \\ 0, & -a/2 \geq y. \end{cases} \tag{29}$$

The electric radiation vector $\boldsymbol{L}$ resulting from the field given by (29) is expressed by [compare (9) to (13)]

$$L_x = E_0 \exp jk \frac{a^2}{4l} \int_{-a/2}^{a/2} \cos\left(\frac{\pi x}{a}\right) \cdot \exp jk \left\{x \cos \phi \sin \theta - \frac{x^2}{2l}\right\} dx$$
$$\cdot \left[\int_{a/4}^{a/2} \exp jk \left\{y \sin \phi \sin \theta - \frac{y^2}{2l}\right\} dy + 2 \int_{-a/4}^{a/4} \exp jk \left\{y \sin \phi \sin \theta - \frac{y^2}{2l}\right\} dy + \int_{-a/2}^{-a/4} \exp jk \left\{y \sin \phi \sin \theta - \frac{y^2}{2l}\right\} dy\right]. \tag{30}$$

From (13) it can be seen that the only difference with respect to plain square horn is in the integral designated I_2.

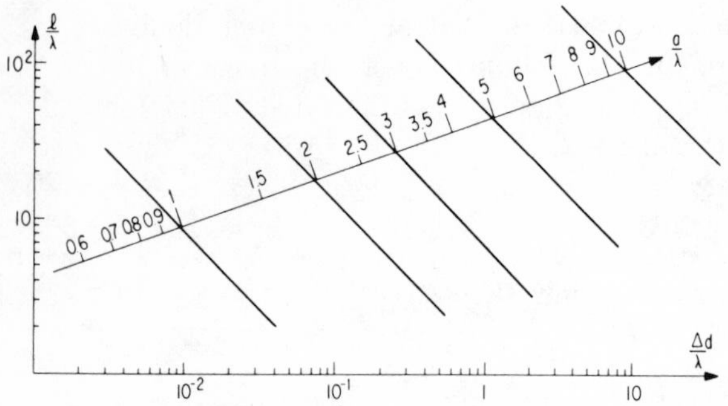

Fig. 4. Phase center for E-plane cut, compensated horn (31).

It can be found that the phase center Δ_c in the E plane of a compensated horn can be expressed by

$$\Delta_c(\theta,\phi = 90)$$

$$= l\left\{1 - \frac{a}{2v}\,\frac{\left[\cos\frac{\pi}{2}\left(\frac{a}{2v}\right)^2 + \frac{1}{2}\cos\frac{\pi}{2}\left(\frac{a}{4v}\right)^2\right]\left[C\left(\frac{a}{2v}\right) + C\left(\frac{a}{4v}\right)\right] + \left[\sin\frac{\pi}{2}\left(\frac{a}{2v}\right)^2 + \frac{1}{2}\sin\frac{\pi}{2}\left(\frac{a}{4v}\right)^2\right]\left[S\left(\frac{a}{2v}\right) + S\left(\frac{a}{4v}\right)\right]}{\left[C\left(\frac{a}{2v}\right) + C\left(\frac{a}{4v}\right)\right]^2 + \left[S\left(\frac{a}{2v}\right) + S\left(\frac{a}{4v}\right)\right]^2}\right\}. \tag{31}$$

The phase center in the H plane is the same as for the plain square horn and is given by (21).

Equation (31) is plotted in normalized form in Fig. 4. Fig. 4 has the same structure as Fig. 3, except for a slight shift to the left.

V. Phase Center of a Diagonal Horn

The diagonal horn [7] is obtained from the square horn shown in Fig. 1 by rotating the horn by 45°, but not the waveguide feed. The aperture field can be expressed by

$$\boldsymbol{E}_{\text{ap}} = \begin{cases} \boldsymbol{a}_x E_0 \cos\left[(\pi/a)y\right] \exp jk\delta \\ \boldsymbol{a}_y E_0 \cos\left[(\pi/a)x\right] \exp jk\delta \\ 0. \end{cases} \tag{32}$$

This field is obtained by feeding the horn with a waveguide in the TE_{10} mode.

From this the electric radiation, vector $\boldsymbol{L}$ can be expressed as

$$\boldsymbol{L} = \begin{cases} \boldsymbol{a}_x \exp jk\frac{a^2}{4l} E_0 \int_{-a/2}^{a/2} \cos\left(\frac{\pi}{a}x\right) \exp jk\left(-\frac{x^2}{2l} + x\cos\phi\sin\theta\right) dx \int_{-a/2}^{a/2} \exp jk\left(-\frac{y^2}{2l} + y\sin\phi\sin\theta\right) dy \\ -\boldsymbol{a}_y \exp jk\frac{a^2}{4l} E_0 \int_{-a/2}^{a/2} \exp jk\left(\frac{-x^2}{2l} + x\cos\phi\sin\theta\right) dx \int_{-a/2}^{a/2} \cos\left(\frac{\pi}{a}y\right) \exp\left(-\frac{y^2}{2l} + y\sin\phi\cos\theta\right) dy \\ 0. \end{cases} \tag{33}$$

By transforming $\boldsymbol{L}$ into the r,θ,ϕ coordinate system and observing that $Z_0N_x = L_y$, $Z_0N_y = -L_x$, $N_z = 0$, then from (10) the far field of the diagonal horn becomes

$$\boldsymbol{E} = \begin{cases} 0 \\ -\boldsymbol{a}_\theta(jk/4\pi r)\exp(-jkr)[1 + \cos\theta] \cdot[-L_x\sin\phi + L_y\cos\phi] \\ \boldsymbol{a}_\phi(jk/4\pi r)\exp(-jkr)[1 + \cos\theta] \cdot[L_x\cos\phi + L_y\sin\phi]. \end{cases} \tag{34}$$

Noting the similarity between (33) and (13), one sees that L_x takes the form of (13) while L_y takes a very similar form, except that $\cos\phi$ and $\sin\phi$ are interchanged. Hence

$$\boldsymbol{L} = \begin{cases} \boldsymbol{a}_x E_0 \exp j\,(a^2/4l) I_1 I_2 \\ -\boldsymbol{a}_y E_0 \exp j\,(a^2/4l) I_3 I_4 \\ 0 \end{cases} \tag{35}$$

where I_1 is given by (14a) and I_2 by (14b); I_3 and I_4 are the same as I_2 and I_1, except for interchanging $\sin\phi$ and $\cos\phi$.

For $\phi = 45°$ and 135°, $I_1 = I_4$ and $I_2 = I_3$. For $\phi = 45°$, $E_\phi = 0$, and this plane is the E plane, while for $\phi = 135°$, $E_\theta = 0$, and this plane is the H plane. The phase centers for both planes are the same.

The phase center of a diagonal horn can be calculated only for these two planes. For other values of ϕ the phase front of E_θ and E_ϕ are not the same, the field is elliptically polarized, and definition of a phase center meets with much difficulty.

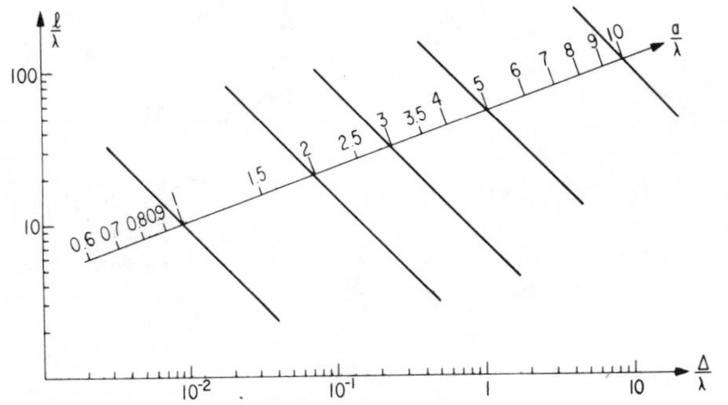

Fig. 5. Location of phase center versus horn parameters for diagonal horn (36).

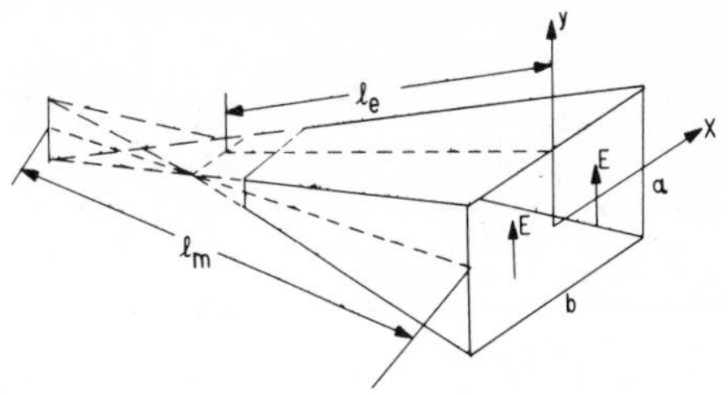

Fig. 6. Rectangular horn.

For calculation of the phase center (27) can be used, because for $\phi = 45°$ the far field depends only on I_1 and I_2. The phase center for a diagonal horn is therefore

$$\Delta_d(\theta,\phi = 45°) = l\left\{1 - \frac{a}{4v}\,\frac{\cos\left(\frac{\pi}{8}\frac{a^2}{v^2}\right)C\left(\frac{a}{2v}\right) + \sin\left(\frac{\pi}{8}\frac{a^2}{v^2}\right)S\left(\frac{a}{2v}\right)}{C^2\left(\frac{a}{2v}\right) + S^2\left(\frac{a}{2v}\right)}\right.$$

$$\left. + \frac{1}{2}\,\frac{[-S(U) + S(W)]\left[U \sin\frac{\pi}{2}W^2 - W\sin\frac{\pi}{2}U^2\right] + [C(U) - C(W)]\left[W\cos\frac{\pi}{2}U^2 - U\cos\frac{\pi}{2}W^2\right]}{[C(U) - C(W)]^2 + [-S(U) + S(W)]^2}\right\}. \quad (36)$$

A plot of Δ_d/λ versus l/λ with l/λ as parameters is shown in Fig. 5. This figure is basically the same as Figs. 2–4 except for the location of the curves in the graph.

VI. Rectangular Horns

The results derived in Sections III and IV can be easily modified for rectangular horns. Schelkunoff and Friis [8] show that the phase front for the rectangular horn is an elliptical paraboloid

$$\delta_1 = -(y^2/2l_m) - (y^2/2l_e) + \alpha. \quad (37)$$

In this expression α is a constant, which can be left unspecified for the calculation to follow, l_e is the length of the horn wall which is normal to the electric field, while l_m is the length of the wall parallel to the electric field. Fig. 6 shows the horn, the coordinate system, and how the horn walls must be extended for l_e and l_m to be measured. As it is seen, the walls of the horn must be extended until their planes intersect.

When (37) rather than (1) is used to determine the field

$$\boldsymbol{E}_{\text{ap}} = \boldsymbol{a}_y E_0 \cos[(\pi/a)x] \exp jk\delta_1$$

the expression for the electric radiation vector becomes [see (13)]

$$L_x = E_0 \exp jk\alpha \int_{-b/2}^{b/2} \cos\left(\frac{\pi}{b}x\right) \cdot \exp jk\left[x\cos\phi\sin\theta - \frac{x^2}{2l_m}\right]dx \cdot \int_{-a/2}^{a/2} \exp jk\left[y\sin\phi\sin\theta - \frac{y^2}{2l_e}\right]dy. \quad (38)$$

As it can be seen in integral I_1, a is replaced by b and l by l_m, while in integral I_2, l is replaced by l_e.

Then, because the resulting phase centers are calculated in essence independently from I_1 and I_2, we obtain

$$\Delta_r(\theta,\phi = 0) = l_m \left\{ 1 + \frac{\left[W_1 \cos\frac{\pi}{2} U_1^2 - U_1 \cos\frac{\pi}{2} W^2\right][C(U_1) - C(W_1)] + \left[U_1 \sin\frac{\pi}{2} W_1^2 - W_1 \sin\frac{\pi}{2} U_1^2\right][-S(U_1) + S(W_1)]}{[C(U_1) - C(W_1)]^2 + [-S(U_1) + S(W_1)]^2} \right\} \quad (39)$$

with

$$U_1 = \frac{v_m}{b} + \frac{b}{2v_m}, \quad W_1 = \frac{v_m}{b} - \frac{b}{2v_m}, \quad v_m = \left(\frac{l_m\lambda}{2}\right)^{1/2}$$

and

$$\Delta_r(\theta,\phi = 90°) = l_e \left\{ 1 - \frac{a}{2v_e} \frac{\cos\frac{\pi}{2}\left(\frac{a}{2v_e}\right)^2 C\left(\frac{a}{2v_e}\right) + \sin\frac{\pi}{2}\left(\frac{a}{2v_e}\right) S\left(\frac{a}{2v_e}\right)}{C^2\left(\frac{a}{2v_e}\right) + S^2\left(\frac{a}{2v_e}\right)} \right\} \quad (40)$$

with

$$v_e = \left(\frac{l_e\lambda}{2}\right)^{1/2}.$$

Figs. 2 and 3 can be used for rectangular horns, by appropriately replacing l by l_e or l_m, and Δ by Δ_r or Δ_{cr}, and furthermore, by replacing a by b in Fig. 2.

The phase center for an arbitrary plane with azimuth angle ϕ_0 can be found in the same fashion as derived for a square horn. Equation (28) is directly applicable, and

$$\Delta_r(\theta,\phi = \phi_0) = \cos^2 \phi_0 \Delta_r(\theta,\phi = 90) + \sin^2 \phi_0 \Delta_r(\theta,\phi = 0). \quad (41)$$

Relationships (39)–(41) can be used to construct horns with phase centers which are insensitive to the horn orientation. Of course, the insensitivity exists only for rays near the horn axis, since the formulas are derived for $\theta \doteq \sin\theta$.

To construct such a horn, Fig. 3 is taken and the l axis is labeled l_e, and from the knowledge of the aperture side a, Δ_r is determined. The determined Δ_r is then used in Fig. 2 for determining b from a given l_m.

For example assume $l_e = 4\lambda$, $l_m = 5\lambda$, and $a = 2\lambda$. From Fig. 3, $\Delta_r = 0.35\lambda$. From Fig. 2, it can be seen that for $\Delta_r = 0.35$ and $l_m = 5\lambda$ b must equal 2.4λ. Consequently, the sides of a rectangular horn with $l_e:l_m = 4:5$ which has a phase center insensitive to rotation and must have an aperture side ratio of 1:1:2.

Take as the next example a compensated horn for the same l_e, l_m, and a. Then from Fig. 4, $\Delta_{cr} = 0.37\lambda$ and from Fig. 2, $l_m = 5\lambda$, $b = 2.45\lambda$.

The approach described here yields only an approximation, since the horn parameters l_e, l_m, a, and b are not independent. The throat of the horn must fit to the waveguide cross section from which it is fed. Therefore, strictly speaking, when a, l_m, and l_e are chosen, then b will result from that. But the changes of l_m with a change in b will be so small that they can be neglected for practical applications. If the change of l_m should be excessive, a second and third iteration will yield sufficiently accurate design data.

VII. Conclusions

The phase centers of different horn antennas were treated as a vector problem. Consequently different expressions were derived for the phase center in the H plane and in the E plane. The phase center for an arbitrary plane can be computed from the E and H plane phase centers by an averaging process.

When the phase centers for the principal planes are plotted on a double logarithmic graph, the results are essentially straight lines. The spacing of the lines is logarithmic with respect to the aperture size. The exact location, however, depends on the distribution of the aperture illumination. Hence the E and H planes of a horn with a square aperture have different phase centers.

For a diagonal horn, the phase center can be defined only for the E and H plane, because the far field is elliptically polarized elsewhere. The phase center for the E and H plane of a diagonal horn is at the same location.

The phase centers were computed for square horns. However, since the computations for the E and H plane are independent of each other, the results are directly applicable to rectangular horns.

It is possible to construct rectangular horns with a phase center which is constant with respect to the horn orientation. This is achieved by giving the horn an aperture side ratio such that the E and H planes have the same phase center. Then it will also be the phase center for all other planar cuts.

Acknowledgment

The author wishes to thank F. Marek for carrying out the computations required for Figs. 2–5 and E. Kramer for his helpful discussions.

References

[1] K. Baur, "The phase center of aperture radiators," *Arch. Elek. Übertragung*, vol. 9, pp. 541–546, 1955.
[2] S. Silver, *Microwave Antenna Theory and Design.* Lexington, Mass.: Boston Technical Publishers, 1964.
[3] Y. Y. Hu, "A method of determining phase centers and its application to electro-magnetic horns," *J. Franklin Inst.*, pp. 31–39, January 1961.
[4] H. Ujiie, T. Yoneyama, and S. Nishida, "A consideration of the phase center of aperture antennas," *IEEE Trans. Antennas Propagat.* (Communications), vol. AP-15, pp. 478–480, May 1967.
[5] E. A. Wolff, *Antenna Analysis.* New York: Wiley, 1966.
[6] G. M. Peace and E. E. Swartz, "Aplitude compensated horn antenna," *Microwave J.*, vol. 7, pp. 66–68, February 1964.
[7] A. W. Love, "The diagonal horn," *Microwave J.*, vol. 5, pp. 117–122, March 1962.
[8] S. A. Schelkunoff and H. T. Friis, *Antennas: Theory and Practice.* New York: Wiley, and London: Chapman and Hall, 1952.

Part III
The Gain of Electromagnetic Horns

The gain of an antenna is almost always expressed with respect to an isotropic radiator. The latter is a very convenient mathematical reference, but is hardly of practical value since it does not exist, at least for a fixed state of polarization. The elementary half-wave dipole is sometimes an acceptable substitute, since its gain is accurately known (on the assumption of a sinusoidal current distribution), but its radiation pattern is bidirectional and the gain is inconveniently low. Consequently, the horn has become the universally accepted standard against which to measure the gain of other antennas. All the papers in this part are thus concerned with the accurate calculation of the gain of horn antennas.

The first two papers, by Jakes and by Braun, respectively, are concerned with refinements to the usual expression for the gain of a horn in terms of its aperture dimensions and slant length, and with the correction that must be applied at finite range. Following these is a practical paper by Braun in which all necessary information is given for the design of an optimum horn having a specified gain. The fourth paper, by Chu and Semplak, represents precision to a high degree. They use Lorentz reciprocity to calculate the power transfer between two identical antennas for arbitrary separation distance. With the aid of the Friis transmission formula, they then determine the appropriate correction factors to be applied in the determination of gain when the separation distance corresponds to the Fresnel region rather than the Fraunhofer. By this means, the gain of a pyramidal horn can be measured to an accuracy considerably better than 0.1 dB.

The part concludes with three papers by Jull. In the first, accurate horn gain measurements (with proximity corrections) are used to support the contention that edge diffraction effects are the principal source of error in using Schelkunoff's gain formula. In the second article, some very useful tables and graphs are given whereby gain correction factors for the Fresnel zone and for slant length of the horn may easily be determined. In the last paper, Jull uses the geometrical theory of diffraction to account for the hitherto unpredicted small oscillations that are observed to occur in the gain versus wavelength curve of horns. Additional papers relevant to the gain of horn antennas are listed in [1]–[3].

References

[1] E. V. Jull and E. P. DeLoli, "An accurate absolute gain calibration of an antenna for radio astronomy," *IEEE Trans. Antennas Propagat.*, vol. AP-12, pp. 439–447, July 1964.

[2] G. T. Wrixon and W. J. Welch, "Gain measurements of standard electromanetic horns in the K and K_a bands," *IEEE Trans. Antennas Propagat.*, vol. AP-20, pp. 136–142, Mar. 1972.

[3] E. V. Jull and L. E. Allan, "Gain of an *E*-plane sectoral horn—A failure of the Kirchhoff theory and a new proposal," *IEEE Trans. Antennas Propagat.*, vol. AP-22, pp. 221–226, Mar. 1974.

Gain of Electromagnetic Horns*

W. C. JAKES, JR.†, ASSOCIATE, IRE

Summary—An experimental investigation of the gain of pyramidal electromagnetic horns is described. For the horns tested it was found that (1) the "edge effects" are less than 0.2 db so that the gain of the horns may be computed to that accuracy from their physical dimensions and Schelkunoff's curves; and (2) for the transmission of power between two horns the ordinary transmission formula is valid, provided that the separation distance between the horns is measured between the proper reference points on the horns, rather than between their apertures.

I. Introduction

THE CUSTOMARY method of measuring the gain of large microwave antennas is by comparison with a small standard pyramidal horn. The gain of the standard horn is usually determined by calculation from the physical dimensions of the horn and use of curves given by Schelkunoff.[1] Since these curves are based on the assumption that the aperture field of the horn is the same as though the sides were continued indefinitely, it is apparent that the computed gain of the horn may be somewhat in error because of the doubtful validity of this assumption.

An experimental determination of the amount of error in the theoretically calculated gain due to this "edge effect" could be made by measuring the power transmitted between two identical horns at a separation distance r, measured between apertures, great enough so that the familiar transmission formula holds:

$$P_R = \left(\frac{G\lambda}{4\pi r}\right)^2 P_T \tag{1}$$

where

P_R = received power
P_T = transmitted power
G = gain of each individual horn
λ = free-space wavelength.

Any measurable difference between the gain computed from the horn dimensions and that given by (1) may be ascribed to edge effects.

Several considerations complicate the simple experiment described above. Ordinarily it is not practicable to make transmission measurements at extremely large values of r where it is reasonably certain that (1) holds. One condition, at least, that must be fulfilled is that the variation in phase of the transmitted wave over the aperture of the receiving horn should not exceed $\lambda/16$. If the transmitter were a point source, this would fix the minimum separation distance $r_{\min}$ between the two antennas as

$$r_{\min} = 2\frac{b^2}{\lambda}, \tag{2}$$

where b is the larger dimension of the horn aperture. Since the transmitting antenna is not a point source, there is some uncertainty about the point from which to measure $r_{\min}$; however if one measures from the aperture plane of the transmitter horn, it seems reasonable that the phase error will not exceed $\lambda/16$ at an $r_{\min}$ given by (2). It is not necessarily true, however, that if r is the distance between aperture planes the transmission formula (1) will be obeyed for the entire range of $r_{\min} < r < \infty$.

II. Experiments

The experimental part of this study was carried out at a wavelength of 1.25 cm, as the distances and physical dimensions of the horns involved become small and easily managed in this range. The variation of P_R with r (between apertures) for $40\lambda \leqq r \leqq 200\lambda$ was measured for a number of pyramidal horns of various dimensions. Fig. 1 shows the physical setup employed. To reduce the effect of reflections, no objects were allowed to come closer than 70λ to the center line of the horn.

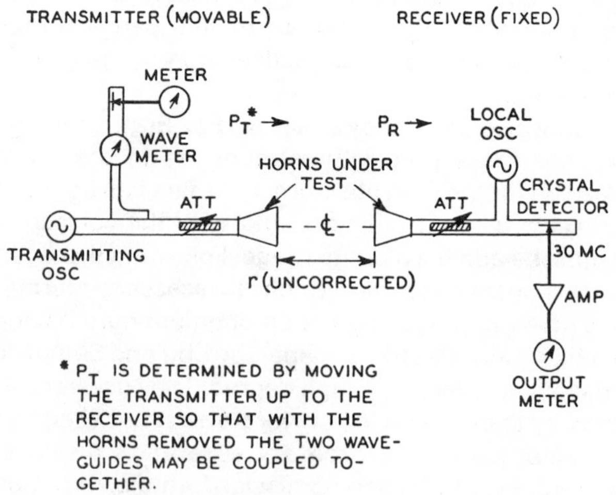

Fig. 1—Physical setup for measuring the variation with distance of the power transmission between two horn antennas.

Before listing the experimental results it will be helpful to give the horn nomenclature, as shown in Fig. 2. Note that in general the E-plane and H-plane slant lengths, l_E and l_H, are not necessarily equal. The "axial height" of the horn will be designated by h; if the horn

* Decimal classification: R325.82. Original manuscript received by the Institute, May 9, 1950; revised manuscript received, August 22, 1950.
† Bell Telephone Laboratories, Inc., Holmdel, N. J.
[1] S. A. Schelkunoff, "Electromagnetic Waves," D. Van Nostrand, Inc., New York, N. Y., pp. 363–365; 1943.

Reprinted from *Proc. IRE*, vol. 39 pp. 160–162, Feb. 1951.

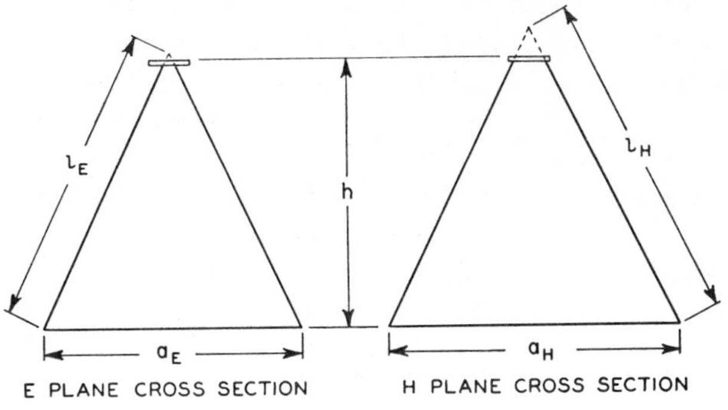

Fig. 2—Nomenclature for horn flared in both planes.

is optimum[2] the axial height will be designated by h_0.

In all, four pairs of horns were constructed and tested. They were made from sheet brass of 1/16 inch thickness; their physical dimensions are given in Table I. Note that horns 1 and 4 were optimum horns.

TABLE I

Horn	a_E	a_H	h
1	4.72λ	6.03λ	10λ $(=h_0)$
2	4.72λ	6.03λ	20λ $(>h_0)$
3	4.72λ	6.03λ	5λ $(<h_0)$
4	6.73λ	8.49λ	20λ $(=h_0)$

Curve *A* of Fig. 3 shows the experimental results for a pair of optimum horns (No. 1 in Table I); this is typical of the results obtained in general. It is to be noted that P_R does not vary as $1/r^2$, the departure being greater as r decreases. A distance d was found which, when added to the r co-ordinates of curve *A*, caused these points to lie on a straight line (curve *B*) whose slope corresponds to an inverse square variation of received power with distance. This indicates that if the separation distance is measured between the proper reference points on the horns, the inverse square relationship of (1) will be obeyed. The distance from the horn aperture back to this reference point will be called *D*.

Since the transmitting and receiving horns were identical in the above experiments, it follows that $D=d/2$. For the *optimum horns* (with $h=h_0$) D was found to be equal to the *axial height*. However, for the other horns the following was observed: if $h>h_0$, (horn 2) $D<h$; if $h<h_0$, (horn 3) $D>h$.

Since it has been experimentally demonstrated that (1) is valid for $r_{min}<r<\infty$ provided r is measured between the proper horn reference points, this equation may now be used with the proper r to compute the actual horn gain. Curve *B* of Fig. 4 shows the results of this computation for horn 1. For comparison, curve *A* of Fig. 4 was computed using for r in (1) the separation distance between horn apertures. Curve *C* is the gain calculated from the physical dimensions of the horn

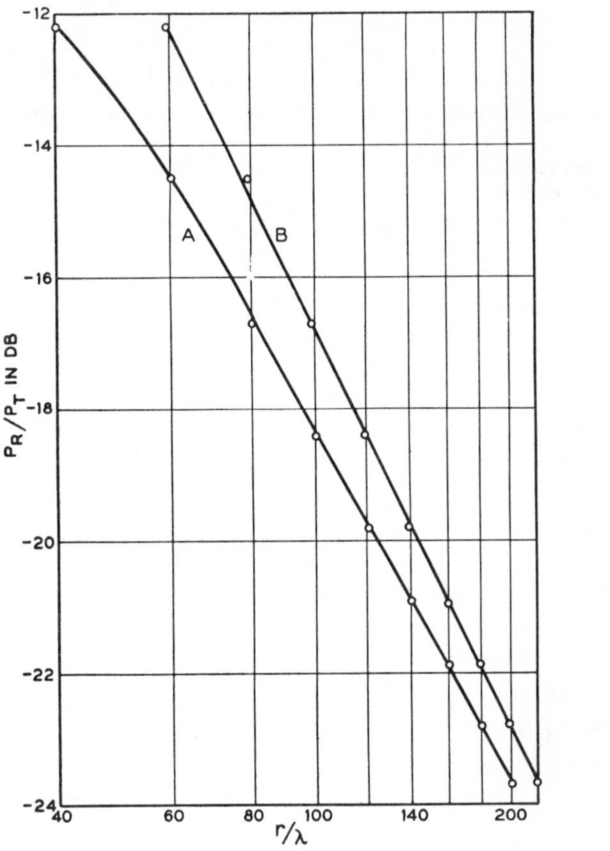

Fig. 3—Variation with distance of the power transmission between two horns. A. Experimental results. B. Experimental results corrected by adding a constant, d/λ, to the abscissae of the observed points.

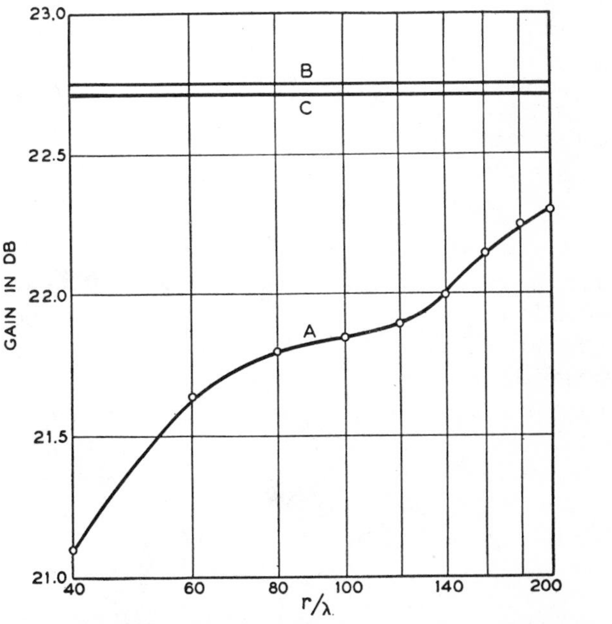

Fig. 4—Theoretical and experimentally observed horn gain. (Horn No. 1 in Table I.) A. Gain computed from (1) using for r the separation distance between apertures. B. Gain computed from (1) using for r the value r_0+d, where r_0 is the separation between apertures, d is a constant described in the text. C. Gain computed from the physical dimensions of the horn and Schelkunoff's curves.

[2] An optimum horn is one for which the flare angles in both planes are so chosen that, for a given length of horn, the gain is a maximum. This follows if:

$$a_E^2 \doteq 2l_E\lambda;\ a_H^2 \doteq 3l_H\lambda.$$

and Schelkunoff's curves. These three curves are representative of the results for the four pairs of horns; in general, the difference between curves B and C did not exceed 0.2 db, and for the optimum horns it was less than 0.1 db.

III. Conclusions

When computing the gain of pyramidal electromagnetic horns it is permissible to use their actual physical dimensions and Schelkunoff's curves. The error due to edge effects is less than 0.1 db for optimum horns, with aperture dimensions greater than 4λ.

If it is desired to compute the transmitted power between two identical horns, (1) is valid even in the transition zone between the Fraunhofer and Fresnel regions, provided r is replaced by r_0+2D. Here, r_0 is the separation between apertures and D is described above.

D for an optimum horn is equal to the axial height, but for horns shorter or longer than optimum, D is greater or less than the axial height and must be determined by experiment.

Gain of Electromagnetic Horns*

E. H. BRAUN†

Summary—**Recent experimental evidence indicates that the measured gain of pyramidal electromagnetic horns may be considerably in error if the measurements are carried out at short distances, and the aperture to aperture separation between horns is used in the gain formula $G=(4\pi R/\lambda)\sqrt{P_R/P_T}$.**

Further experimental verification of this effect has been obtained and a theory developed which is in good quantitative agreement with present experimental data and demonstrates the physical reasons why the previous "far field" criterion of $2D^2/\lambda$ is invalid.

Curves are presented from which the error in gain measured at any distance may be obtained and applied as a correction.

Introduction

RECENT EXPERIMENTS[1] have indicated that considerable error may be incurred in measuring the gain of electromagnetic horns at short distances if the aperture to aperture distance between the horns is used in the gain formula

$$G = \frac{4\pi R}{\lambda}\sqrt{\frac{P_R}{P_T}}. \tag{1}$$

Previously, an aperture to aperture separation (R) of about $2D^2/\lambda$ (D = larger horn dimension) was considered adequate, but the above experiments indicate that an error of the order of 1 db may occur at this distance, and that the true Fraunhofer gain may not be realized even at distances several times $2D^2/\lambda$.

The present work provides a theoretical explanation of the failure of the $2D^2/\lambda$ criterion, together with further experimental data in good quantitative agreement with the theory. The theory replaces the $2D^2/\lambda$ criterion with a new criterion, and in addition makes it possible to calculate the error incurred when this criterion is not satisfied.

Theory

Two assumptions are implicit in the gain formula: (a) The power arriving at the receiving aperture varies as $1/R^2$; (b) the wave striking the receiving horn is sensibly plane, so that the effective cross section of the receiving horn is $(\lambda^2/4\pi)G_\infty$, where G_∞ is the true Fraunhofer gain.

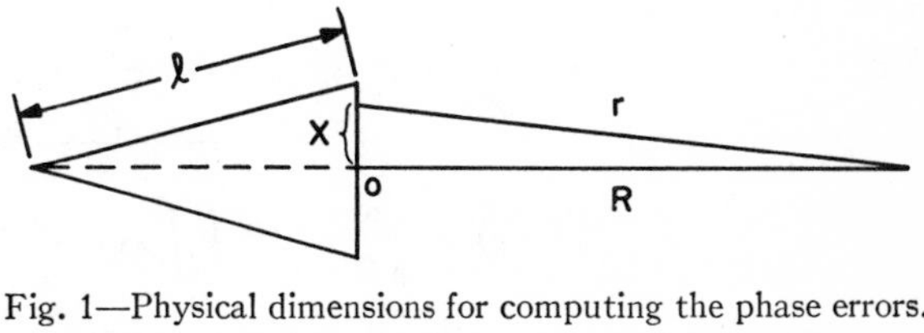

Fig. 1—Physical dimensions for computing the phase errors.

Actually, neither of these conditions is necessarily satisfied until the separation between the horn apertures is considerably greater than $2D^2/\lambda$. To show this qualitatively it should first be noted that the relative phases of contributions from different points in the aperture depend on the intrinsic phasing of the aperture and on the space phasing in exactly the same way; both are quadratic errors. Considering a sectoral horn for simplicity (Fig. 1), the intrinsic phase error can be shown[2] to be $-k(x^2/2l)$. The space phase error is $-k(r-R) = -k(\sqrt{R^2+x^2}-R) \cong -k(x^2/2R)$. The effect

* Decimal classification: R165×R265.2. Original manuscript received by the Institute September 29, 1952.

† Naval Research Laboratory, Washington, D. C.

[1] W. C. Jakes, Jr., "Gain of electromagnetic horns," Proc. I.R.E., vol. 39, pp. 160–162; February, 1951.

[2] S. A. Schelkunoff, "Electromagnetic Waves," D. Van Nostrand Book Co., New York, N. Y., p. 361, ff.; 1943.

Reprinted from *Proc. IRE*, vol. 41, pp. 109–115, Jan. 1953.

of phase error on gain can now be discussed, keeping in mind that the phase error may be due either to intrinsic phasing or to space phasing.

Let us first make a qualitative comparison of the gains of transmitting apertures having maximum phase errors of 0, $\lambda/8$, and $\lambda/4$, respectively. In the case of zero phase error contributions from the various points of the aperture add in phase as shown in Fig. 2(a). In going from zero phase error to a phase error of $\lambda/8$ the vectors are all rotated through small angles less than 40 degrees. The resultant would not be expected to differ materially from the in-phase case (Fig. 2(b)).

Going from a phase error of $\lambda/8$ to an error of $\lambda/4$, each vector is again rotated through an angle of less than about 40 degrees, but in addition to this rotation, the upper vectors are all rotated by the lower ones. This means that many of the vectors are rotated through large angles, and the resultant for $\lambda/4$ may differ considerably from the resultant for $\lambda/8$ (Fig. 2(c)).

Hence in going from a zero phase error to a $\lambda/8$ phase error, the gain changes by a very small amount, whereas in going from $\lambda/8$ to $\lambda/4$ (again a change of $\lambda/8$) the gain changes by a considerable amount.

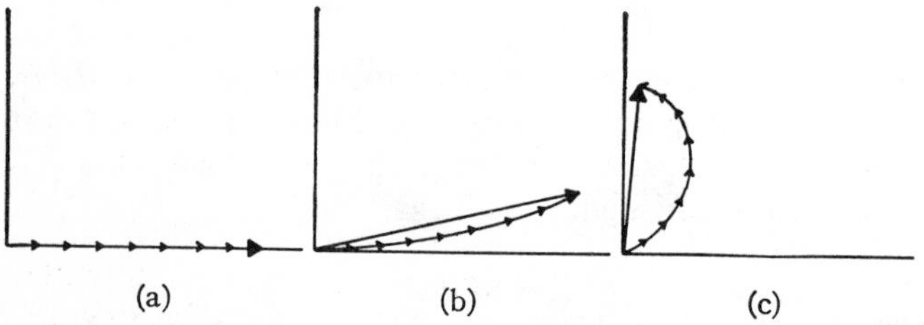

Fig. 2—Qualitative illustration of the effect of phase error on gain.

This may be seen more quantitatively from Schelkunoff's gain curves.[2] For a fixed aperture size "a," the phase error depends only on the slant height "l." For example, for $a/\lambda=6$, the slant height may be changed from $l=\infty$ (phase error $=0$) to $l=30\lambda$ (phase error $=0.15\lambda$), which represents a change in phase error of

$$\mathcal{E}(\xi, \eta) = \frac{E_0}{\lambda R} e^{-jkR} \iint \cos\frac{\pi y}{a}\, e^{-jk(x^2/2l_E+y^2/2l_H)} e^{-jk[(x-\xi)^2+(y-\eta)^2]/2R} dx\,dy$$

0.15λ, with only about 2 per cent loss in gain, whereas in going from $l=30\lambda$ (phase error $=0.15\lambda$) to $l=15\lambda$ (phase error $=0.30\lambda$), also a change in phase error of 0.15λ, the gain decreases by about 12 per cent. Thus the larger the initial phase error, the more sensitive the gain becomes to further variations in phase error.

In the case of an electromagnetic horn, as one moves in from the Fraunhofer region to the Fresnel region, the space phasing effectively adds a quadratic phase error to the intrinsic quadratic error of the aperture, that is to say, it makes the wave front appear more curved. On the basis of the preceding argument, one would expect the measured gain to decrease, the decrease being a function of the intrinsic phasing, as well as the space phasing. Hence the point at which the true Fraunhofer gain is realized cannot be specified by a simple expression involving the aperture dimensions alone, e.g., $2D^2/\lambda$.

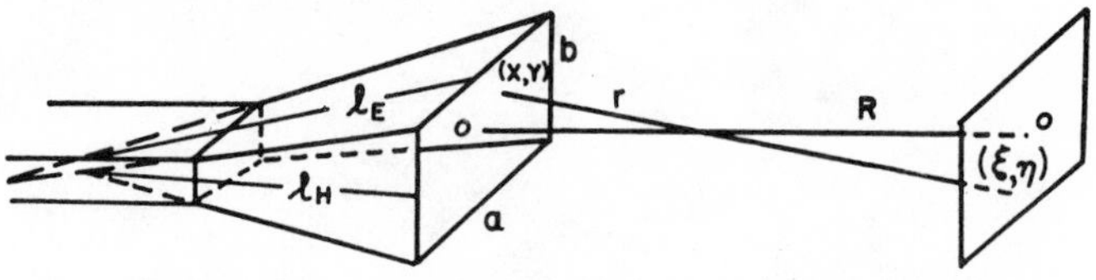

Fig. 3—Physical dimensions for calculating the gain.

To investigate the problem quantitatively, let us first calculate the amplitude of the field at any arbitrary point of the receiving aperture. The transmitting and receiving horn apertures are separated by a distance R, origins are chosen at the centers of the apertures, and points in the apertures are denoted by (x, y) and (ξ, η), respectively. The x and ξ axes are parallel to each other and to the E-vector, and the y and η axes are parallel to each other and to the H-vector. Pertinent dimensions are shown in Fig. 3.

Assuming the field at the aperture of the transmitting horn is the same as though the horn were continued,[2] the aperture distribution is given by

$$\mathcal{E}(x, y) = E_0 \cos\frac{\pi y}{a}\, e^{-jk(x^2/2l_E+y^2/2l_H)},$$

where l_E and l_H are the E and H plane slant heights, respectively.

From Fig. 3,

$$r = \sqrt{R^2+(x-\xi)^2+(y-\eta)^2} \cong R + \frac{(x-\xi)^2+(y-\eta)^2}{2R}.$$

Hence, in the Fresnel approximation,

Denoting $|\mathcal{E}(\xi, \eta)|$ by $E(\xi, \eta)$,

$$E(\xi, \eta) = \frac{E_0}{2\lambda R}\left| \int_{-a/2}^{+a/2} \left[e^{i(\pi y/a)} + e^{-i(\pi y/a)}\right] \cdot e^{-i(\pi/2)[(2/\lambda)(1/l_H+1/R)y^2-(4\eta/\lambda R)y]} dy \times \int_{-b/2}^{+b/2} e^{-i(\pi/2)[(2/\lambda)(1/l_E+1/R)x^2-(4\xi/\lambda R)x]} dx \right|$$

$$= \frac{E_0}{2\lambda R}\left| \int_{-a/2}^{+a/2} e^{-i(\pi/2)(Ay^2-By)} dy + \int_{-a/2}^{+a/2} e^{-i(\pi/2)(Ay^2-Cy)} dy \right|$$

$$\cdot\left|\int_{-b/2}^{+b/2} e^{-j(\pi/2)(Dx^2-Fx)}dx\right|,$$

where

$$A=\frac{2}{\lambda}\left(\frac{1}{l_H}+\frac{1}{R}\right),\qquad B=2\left(\frac{2\eta}{\lambda R}+\frac{1}{a}\right),$$

$$C=2\left(\frac{2\eta}{\lambda R}-\frac{1}{a}\right),\qquad D=\frac{2}{\lambda}\left(\frac{1}{l_E}+\frac{1}{R}\right),$$

$$F=\frac{4\xi}{\lambda R}\cdot$$

Completing the square in each exponent and factoring,

$$E(\xi,\eta)=\frac{E_0}{2\lambda R}\left|e^{j(\pi/2)(B^2/4A)}\int_{-a/2}^{+a/2}e^{-j(\pi/2)(\sqrt{A}\,y-B/2\sqrt{A})^2}dy\right.$$

$$\left.+\,e^{j(\pi/2)(C^2/4A)}\int_{-a/2}^{+a/2}e^{-j(\pi/2)(\sqrt{A}\,y-C/2\sqrt{A})^2}dy\right|$$

$$\times\left|e^{j(\pi/2)(F^2/4D)}\int_{-b/2}^{+b/2}e^{-j(\pi/2)(\sqrt{D}\,x-F/2\sqrt{D})^2}dx\right|.$$

Write

$$\frac{\pi}{2}(B^2/4A)=\epsilon+Q,$$

and

$$\frac{\pi}{2}(C^2/4A)=\epsilon-Q,$$

where

$$\epsilon=\frac{\pi\lambda}{4}\frac{Rl_H}{R+l_H}\left[\frac{4\eta^2}{\lambda^2R^2}+\frac{1}{a^2}\right],\qquad Q=\frac{\pi\eta}{a}\frac{l_H}{R+l_H}\cdot$$

Changing the variables, let

$$\alpha=\sqrt{A}\,y-B/2\sqrt{A},\qquad dy=d\alpha/\sqrt{A}$$

$$\beta=\sqrt{D}\,y-C/2\sqrt{A},\qquad dy=d\beta/\sqrt{A}$$

$$\psi=\sqrt{D}\,x-F/2\sqrt{D},\qquad dx=d\psi/\sqrt{D}.$$

$$E(\xi,\eta)=\frac{E_0}{2\lambda R\sqrt{AD}}\left|\left[\int_{\psi_1}^{\psi_2}e^{-j(\pi/2)\psi^2}d\psi\right]\right.$$

$$\left.\cdot\left[e^{jQ}\int_{\alpha_1}^{\alpha_2}e^{-j(\pi/2)\alpha^2}d\alpha+e^{-jQ}\int_{\beta_1}^{\beta_2}e^{-j(\pi/2)\beta^2}d\beta\right]\right|,\qquad(2)$$

where

$$\alpha_1=-\frac{1}{\sqrt{2}}\left[\frac{a}{\sqrt{\lambda}}\sqrt{\frac{R+l_H}{Rl_H}}+\left(\frac{\sqrt{\lambda}}{a}+\frac{2\eta}{R\sqrt{\lambda}}\right)\sqrt{\frac{Rl_H}{R+l_H}}\right]$$

$$\alpha_2=+\frac{1}{\sqrt{2}}\left[\frac{a}{\sqrt{\lambda}}\sqrt{\frac{R+l_H}{Rl_H}}-\left(\frac{\sqrt{\lambda}}{a}+\frac{2\eta}{R\sqrt{\lambda}}\right)\sqrt{\frac{Rl_H}{R+l_H}}\right]$$

$$\beta_1=-\frac{1}{\sqrt{2}}\left[\frac{a}{\sqrt{\lambda}}\sqrt{\frac{R+l_H}{Rl_H}}+\left(\frac{\sqrt{\lambda}}{a}-\frac{2\eta}{R\sqrt{\lambda}}\right)\sqrt{\frac{Rl_H}{R+l_H}}\right]$$

$$\beta_2=+\frac{1}{\sqrt{2}}\left[\frac{a}{\sqrt{\lambda}}\sqrt{\frac{R+l_H}{Rl_H}}-\left(\frac{\sqrt{\lambda}}{a}-\frac{2\eta}{R\sqrt{\lambda}}\right)\sqrt{\frac{Rl_H}{R+l_H}}\right]$$

$$\psi_1=-\frac{1}{\sqrt{2\lambda R}}\left[b\sqrt{\frac{R+l_E}{l_E}}+2\xi\sqrt{\frac{l_E}{R+l_E}}\right]$$

$$\psi_2=+\frac{1}{\sqrt{2\lambda R}}\left[b\sqrt{\frac{R+l_E}{l_E}}-2\xi\sqrt{\frac{l_E}{R+l_E}}\right].$$

These can be converted to Fresnel integrals

$$\int_{x_1}^{x_2}e^{-j(\pi/2)x^2}dx=\int_0^{x_2}e^{-j(\pi/2)x^2}dx-\int_0^{x_1}e^{-j(\pi/2)x^2}dx$$

$$=[C(x_2)-C(x_1)]-j[S(x_2)-S(x_1)].$$

Equation (2) then reads

$$E(\xi,\eta)=\frac{E_0\sqrt{l_El_H}}{4\sqrt{(R+l_E)(R+l_H)}}Y(\eta)X(\xi),\qquad(3a)$$

where

$$Y(\eta)=(\{\cos Q[C(\alpha_2)+C(\beta_2)-C(\alpha_1)-C(\beta_1)]$$
$$+\sin Q[S(\alpha_2)+S(\beta_1)-S(\alpha_1)-S(\beta_2)]\}^2$$
$$+\{\cos Q[S(\alpha_2)+S(\beta_2)-S(\alpha_1)-S(\beta_1)]$$
$$-\sin Q[C(\alpha_2)+C(\beta_1)-C(\alpha_1)-C(\beta_2)]\}^2)^{1/2}$$
$$X(\xi)=\{[C(\psi_2)-C(\psi_1)]^2+[S(\psi_2)-S(\psi_1)]^2\}^{1/2}.\qquad(3b)$$

To determine the average power per unit solid angle radiated by the transmitting horn in the direction of the receiving horn, the Poynting vector must be integrated over the receiving aperture. The expression for $|E(\xi,\eta)|^2$ obtained from (3) is unfortunately too complicated to integrate directly, but calculation of the aperture field for a number of different horns shows that $Y(\eta)$ and $X(\xi)$ can be approximated by

$$Y(\eta)=Y\left(\frac{a}{2}\right)+\left[Y(0)-Y\left(\frac{a}{2}\right)\right]\cos^{1/2}\left(\frac{\pi\eta}{a}\right)$$

$$X(\xi)=X\left(\frac{b}{2}\right)+\left[X(0)-X\left(\frac{b}{2}\right)\right]\cos^{1/2}\left(\frac{\pi\xi}{b}\right),$$

where $Y(0)$ and $Y(a/2)$, and $X(0)$ and $X(b/2)$ are the values of $Y(\eta)$ and $X(\xi)$ at the center and edges of the aperture, respectively. The cosinusoidal term is quite small, so that deviations in this term from exact $\cos^{1/2} x$ behavior are unimportant. Alternatively, (2) can be expanded in a Taylor series in ξ and η, thus obtaining an expression which can be averaged. The author has done this, but the present expressions are more symmetric and the numerical difference between the two methods is small.

Using these expressions for $Y(\eta)$ and $X(\xi)$, the average value of E^2 over the receiving aperture is

$$\overline{E_{ap}{}^2}=\frac{E_0{}^2l_El_H}{(R+l_E)(R+l_H)}\theta^2\omega^2,$$

where

$$\theta^2 = \frac{1}{4}\left\{Y^2\left(\frac{a}{2}\right) + 1.526\left[Y(0) - Y\left(\frac{a}{2}\right)\right]Y\left(\frac{a}{2}\right) + 0.636\left[Y(0) - Y\left(\frac{a}{2}\right)\right]^2\right\}$$

$$\omega^2 = \frac{1}{4}\left\{X^2\left(\frac{b}{2}\right) + 1.526\left[X(0) - X\left(\frac{b}{2}\right)\right]X\left(\frac{b}{2}\right) + 0.636\left[X(0) - X\left(\frac{b}{2}\right)\right]^2\right\}.$$

Taking the ratio of the receiving cross section to transmitting gain to be the same as that in the plane wave case, i.e., $A(R)/G(R) = \lambda^2/4\pi$, the power received is

$$P_R = \tfrac{1}{2}\sqrt{\epsilon/\mu}\,\overline{E_{ap}^2}\,(\lambda^2/4\pi)G(R).$$

Substituting this in the gain formula, (1), we have

$$G(R) = \frac{2\pi R^2\sqrt{\epsilon/\mu}\,\overline{E_{ap}^2}}{P_T} = \frac{2\pi R^2\sqrt{\epsilon/\mu}\,\overline{E_{ap}^2}}{(1/4)\sqrt{\epsilon/\mu}\,abE_0^2} = \frac{8\pi R^2\overline{E_{ap}^2}}{abE_0^2}. \qquad (4)$$

The ratio of this gain measured at a distance R to the gain which would be measured at infinity is given from (3) and (4) by

$$\frac{G(R)}{G(\infty)} = \frac{8\pi R^2\overline{E_{ap}^2}/abE_0^2}{(8\pi l_H l_E/ab)[C^2(r) + S^2(r)]\{[C(u) - C(v)]^2 + [S(u) - S(v)]^2\}}$$

$$\frac{G(R)}{G(\infty)} = \frac{\theta^2}{(1 + l_H/R)\{[C(u) - C(v)]^2 + [S(u) - S(v)]^2\}}\,\frac{\omega^2}{(1 + l_E/R)[C^2(r) + S^2(r)]},$$

where

$$r = \frac{b}{\sqrt{2\lambda l_E}}, \qquad u = \frac{1}{\sqrt{2}}\left(\frac{\sqrt{\lambda l_H}}{a} + \frac{a}{\sqrt{\lambda l_H}}\right), \qquad v = \frac{1}{\sqrt{2}}\left(\frac{\sqrt{\lambda l_H}}{a} - \frac{a}{\sqrt{\lambda l_H}}\right).$$

$G(R)/G(\infty)$ is thus a function of five independent variables, a, b, l_H, l_E, and R, and each of the two factors is a function of three independent variables, R being common to both. This makes it very difficult to express the results graphically, so that a separate calculation would have to be made for each set of horns to be tested. Since the calculation is tedious, it is fortunate that this expression can be re-written in terms of four new variables,

$$M = \frac{8\lambda R}{a^2}, \quad H = \frac{8\lambda l_H}{a^2}, \quad P = \frac{8\lambda R}{b^2}, \quad E = \frac{8\lambda l_E}{b^2}.$$

The first two depend on H plane dimensions only, and the second two on E plane dimensions only. M and P represent the reciprocals of the maximum phase errors across the aperture due to the space phasing, in the H and E planes, respectively. H and E represent the reciprocals of the maximum phase errors across the aperture due to intrinsic phasing, in the H and E planes, respectively.

In terms of these new variables, the final result becomes

$$\frac{G(R)}{G(\infty)} = \frac{\omega^2}{\left(1 + \frac{E}{P}\right)[C^2(r) + S^2(r)]} \cdot \frac{\theta^2}{\left(1 + \frac{H}{M}\right)\{[C(u) - C(v)]^2 + [S(u) - S(v)]^2\}},$$

where

$$r = 2/\sqrt{E}, \qquad u = \frac{\sqrt{H}}{4} + \frac{2}{\sqrt{H}}, \qquad v = \frac{\sqrt{H}}{4} - \frac{2}{\sqrt{H}}.$$

$$\theta^2 = \frac{1}{4}\left\{Y^2\left(\frac{a}{2}\right) + 1.526\left[Y(0) - Y\left(\frac{a}{2}\right)\right]Y\left(\frac{a}{2}\right) + 0.636\left[Y(0) - Y\left(\frac{a}{2}\right)\right]^2\right\}$$

$$\omega^2 = \frac{1}{4}\left\{X^2\left(\frac{b}{2}\right) + 1.526\left[X(0) - X\left(\frac{b}{2}\right)\right]X\left(\frac{b}{2}\right) + 0.636\left[X(0) - X\left(\frac{b}{2}\right)\right]^2\right\}$$

$$Y\left(\frac{a}{2}\right) = \Big(\{\cos Q[C(h) + C(l) - C(g) - C(k)] + \sin Q[S(h) + S(k) - S(l) - S(g)]\}^2 + \{\cos Q[S(h) + S(l) - S(g) - S(k)] - \sin Q[C(h) + C(k) - C(l) - C(g)]\}^2\Big)^{1/2}$$

$$Y(0) = \{[C(f) - C(e)]^2 + [S(f) - S(e)]^2\}^{1/2}$$

$$X\left(\frac{b}{2}\right) = \{[C(t) - C(p)]^2 + [S(t) - S(p)]^2\}^{1/2}$$

$$X(0) = [C^2(m) + S^2(m)]^{1/2}$$

$$h = +2\sqrt{\frac{H+M}{HM}} - \frac{1}{4}\sqrt{\frac{HM}{H+M}} - \frac{2}{M}\sqrt{\frac{HM}{H+M}},$$

$$l = +2\sqrt{\frac{H+M}{HM}} - \frac{1}{4}\sqrt{\frac{HM}{H+M}} + \frac{2}{M}\sqrt{\frac{HM}{H+M}},$$

$$g = -2\sqrt{\frac{H+M}{HM}} - \frac{1}{4}\sqrt{\frac{HM}{H+M}} - \frac{2}{M}\sqrt{\frac{HM}{H+M}},$$

$$k = -2\sqrt{\frac{H+M}{HM}} - \frac{1}{4}\sqrt{\frac{HM}{H+M}} + \frac{2}{M}\sqrt{\frac{HM}{H+M}},$$

$$f = +2\sqrt{\frac{H+M}{HM}} - \frac{1}{4}\sqrt{\frac{HM}{H+M}},$$

$$e = -2\sqrt{\frac{H+M}{HM}} - \frac{1}{4}\sqrt{\frac{HM}{H+M}},$$

$$p = -2\sqrt{\frac{E+P}{EP}} - 2\sqrt{\frac{E/P}{E+P}},$$

$$t = +2\sqrt{\frac{E+P}{EP}} - 2\sqrt{\frac{E/P}{E+P}},$$

$$m = +2\sqrt{\frac{E+P}{EP}},$$

$$Q = \frac{\pi}{2}\,\frac{H}{H+M},$$

$$M = \frac{8\lambda R}{a^2}, \quad H = \frac{8\lambda l_H}{a^2}, \quad P = \frac{8\lambda R}{b^2}, \quad E = \frac{8\lambda l_E}{b^2}.$$

(If all dimensions are given in wavelengths, set $\lambda = 1$ wherever it appears.)

Since the expression for $G(R)/G(\infty)$ has the form of a product of two factors, one depending on M and H alone, and one depending on P and E alone, each factor can be plotted separately in db as a one parameter family of curves, and the total correction to the gain will then be given by the sum of the corrections read off the two graphs (Figs. 4 and 5).

Since essentially the same assumptions are made in calculating $G(R)$ and $G(\infty)$, it might reasonably be expected that the percentage error is nearly the same for each, and hence the percentage error in the ratio is quite small. That this is so has been verified experimentally in a number of cases.

Use of Curves

In measuring the gain of a particular set of horns, one first wants to know the minimum aperture separation between horns which will give the correct far-field gain figure. Calculating H (and E) from the horn dimensions selects the proper curves on the two graphs for the particular horn in question. To find the minimum aperture separation for which the true Fraunhofer gain will be measured, one simply follows each curve out to the zero correction line, and arrives at two values of R, one for each plane. The larger value is the minimum aperture separation required.

In many cases this distance will be found to be prohibitively large, either because adequate space is not

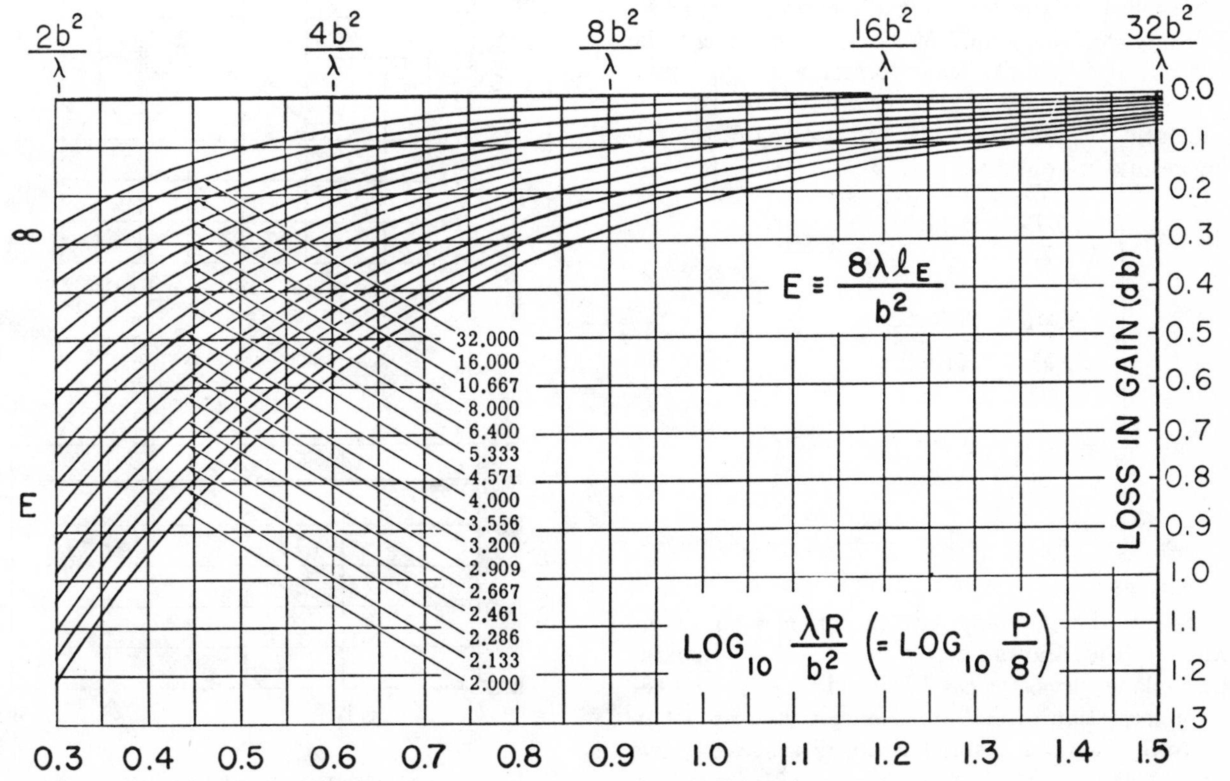

Fig. 4—*E*-plane correction curves.

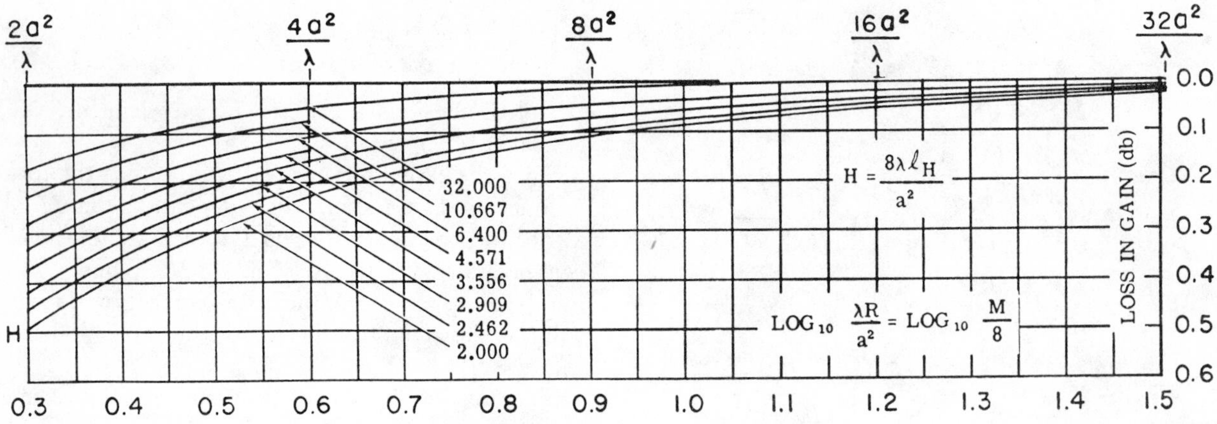

Fig. 5—*H*-plane correction curves.

available in which to perform the measurements, or because serious reflections are encountered when the distance to neighboring objects becomes comparable with the aperture to aperture separation. At some wavelengths, errors due to reflections may be appreciable even after considerable precautions have been taken to minimize them.

The alternative in this case is to make the measurements at shorter distances, and to then correct the measured values to obtain the true gain. This correction factor is obtained directly from the curves (by adding the corrections in db read off the two separate curves) for each distance at which measurements are carried out.

To afford the convenience and accuracy of linear interpolation, $\log M/8 = \log \lambda R/a^2$ and $\log P/8 = \log \lambda R/b^2$ are plotted on the H and E plane graphs, respectively, instead of M and P themselves.

For example, suppose one wishes to measure the gain of a horn having the following dimensions: $a = 4.69\lambda$, $b = 3.78\lambda$, $l_H = 6.52\lambda$, $l_E = 5.94\lambda$. A measurement is to be carried out at $R = 2a^2/\lambda$. What correction to the measured value is necessary to give the true gain?

Calculating E, H, $\log \lambda R/a^2$, and $\log \lambda R/b^2$, the following results are obtained.

$$E = \frac{8\lambda l_E}{b^2} = \frac{(8)(5.94)}{(3.78)^2} = 3.326,$$

$$H = \frac{8\lambda l_H}{a^2} = \frac{(8)(6.52)}{(4.69)^2} = 2.371,$$

$$\log \frac{\lambda R}{a^2} = \log 2 = 0.301,$$

$$\log \frac{\lambda R}{b^2} = \log \frac{2a^2}{b^2} = \log \frac{(2)(4.69)^2}{(3.78)^2} = 0.488.$$

Looking at the H-plane curves for $H = 2.371$ and $\log \lambda R/a^2 = 0.301$ shows a correction of 0.47 db. Looking at the E-plane curves for $E = 3.326$ and $\log \lambda R/b^2 = 0.488$ shows a correction of 0.49 db. Hence 0.96 db must be added to the "gain" measured at this distance to obtain the correct gain.

Experimental Results

Measurements have been carried out on a number of horns, and some of the results are given in Figs. 6 and 7. In each case the lower curve A is the uncorrected curve, and the upper curve B represents the average of the corrected points. The corrected points are also shown. The arrow is a "check point" obtained by comparing the horn with a small gain standard which was actually calibrated in the Fraunhofer region, or by actually measuring the gain of the horn in the Fraunhofer region when this was possible. All of the corrected points lie

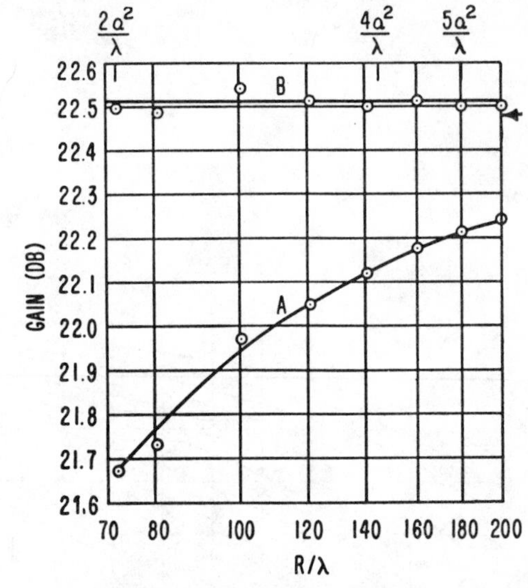

Fig. 6—Experimental results.

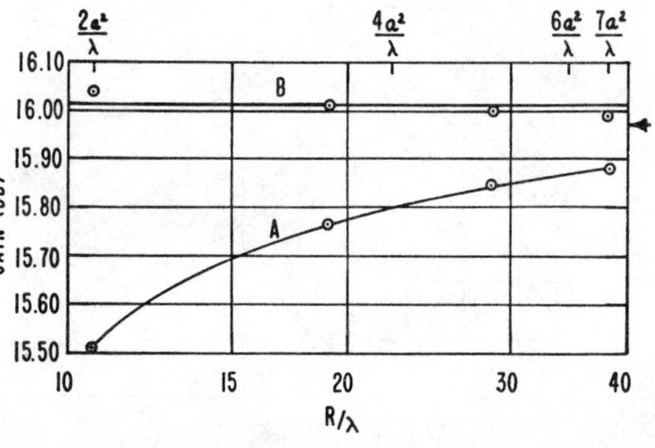

Fig. 7—Experimental results

within about 0.1 db of their average, and this average lies within about 0.1 db of the check point in every case. The horns tested represent phase errors ranging from about 1/16 to 1/2 wavelength. It can be seen that any attempt to use the uncorrected points to compute the gain will in general lead to large errors.

Considerable care was required in performing the experimental work, since the desired accuracy of measurement is very high. One of the principal difficulties was that encountered due to reflections from the walls of the room and from other objects. These were carefully minimized by the use of absorbing screens. Amplifiers and meters were calibrated, and each measurement was carried out at several different power levels. Bolometers were used as detectors. Whenever the ratio of P_R/P_T became too low (at large horn separations), P_T was measured by use of a calibrated directional coupler. It was felt that the calibration of the directional coupler would be less liable to change than that of a variable or fixed attenuator. It was found that the measurements could be repeated to better than ± 0.1 db on different days and using different pieces of equipment.

It has been suggested[1] that the correct gain figure may be obtained from the experimental data by measuring the distance "R" in the gain formula (1) between points located behind the apertures rather than between the apertures themselves. These points are located by the requirement that the received power fall off as $1/r^2$ when the separation "r" between the points, rather than between the apertures, is used.

However, if one attempts to locate these points experimentally one finds that the log P_R/P_T versus log r curve never becomes exactly a straight line with slope -2 for any location of the points, but that a set of curves is obtained, several of which approximate such a straight line over part of their length. Since one has no basis for choosing one curve above another, the location of these points, and hence the gain, remains indeterminate.

The author has also shown theoretically that such points are not fixed with respect to the horn apertures, but that their location is also a function of horn separation, and hence does not exist in the sense suggested above. This is the reason that experimental curves plotted with these points fixed are not straight lines.

The value of this method in determining the correct gain is therefore open to question.

Conclusions

Further experimental verification of the observed variation in measured gain with aperture separation for electromagnetic horns has been obtained. A theory has been developed which is in good quantitative agreement with the experimental data, and demonstrates the physical reasons why the previous "far field" criterion of $2D^2/\lambda$ is invalid. The $2D^2/\lambda$ criterion has been replaced by a generic set of curves from which the error in gain measured at any distance may be determined directly, and applied as a correction. The minimum aperture separation for which zero correction is required marks the beginning of the true Fraunhofer region.

Acknowledgment

The author would like to thank William T. Slayton of the Naval Research Laboratory for his assistance throughout the experimental part of this work, and C. H. Chrisman of the Operational Research Branch of the Naval Research Laboratory for arranging most of the numerical computation.

Some Data for the Design of Electromagnetic Horns*

E. H. BRAUN†

Summary—**Using an idea recently suggested by the author,[1] a table is presented from which the gain of all electromagnetic horns may be calculated with substantially the same accuracy obtainable using the gain formula.**

The exact parameters of an optimum horn are given, and a simple procedure for the design of optimum horns with a specified gain and other desirable properties is described.

RECENTLY the author described a method for extending the range and improving the accuracy of published curves for the gain of electromagnetic horns.[1] It has been found, however, that the curves which are available still leave something to be desired in the way of either accuracy or range, or both. Actually, the above method makes it unnecessary to plot a family of curves for various slant heights; only one curve is required to calculate the gain of all horns. Such a curve has recently been accurately computed by machine for l_E and $l_H = 50\lambda$, and gain figures obtained from it agree with those calculated from the formula within about 0.01 db. Such a curve obviates the necessity for ever using the formula.

Rather than reproduce this curve on a scale large enough to be read conveniently, it is felt that for publication purposes it would be simpler to present a table listing gain vs (adjusted) aperture dimensions (Tables I and II on the next page). Linear interpolation of the aperture dimension will result in negligible error.

The tables are used as indicated below.

For Pyramidal Horns

Let the H-plane and E-plane aperture dimensions and slant heights of the horn (*in wavelengths*) be a, b, l_H, and l_E, respectively. (See Fig. 1.)

1) Calculate

$$A = a\sqrt{\frac{50}{l_H}} \qquad B = b\sqrt{\frac{50}{l_E}}.$$

2) Look up G_H and G_E in the tables for these particular values of A and B, respectively.

3) Calculate

$$g = \frac{G_E G_H}{\frac{32}{\pi}\sqrt{\frac{50}{l_H}}\sqrt{\frac{50}{l_E}}} = \frac{G_E G_H}{10.1859\sqrt{\frac{50}{l_H}}\sqrt{\frac{50}{l_E}}}.$$

This is the actual gain of the horn.

If the values of either A or B or both come out smaller than 2, then simply substitute $(32/\pi)A$ and/or $(32/\pi)B$ for G_H and/or G_E, respectively, in the formula for g.

The gain of sectoral horns is obtained in a similar way.

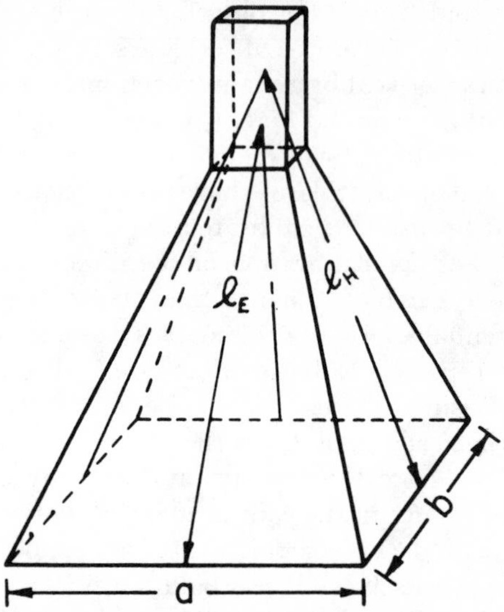

Fig. 1—Physical dimensions for calculating the gain.

For H-plane Sectoral Horns

1) Calculate

$$A = a\sqrt{\frac{50}{l_H}}.$$

2) Look up G_H in the H-plane table for this value of A.

3) Calculate

$$g = b\frac{G_H}{\sqrt{\frac{50}{l_H}}}.$$

This is the actual gain of the horn.

For E-plane Sectoral Horns

1) Calculate

$$B = b\sqrt{\frac{50}{l_E}}.$$

2) Look up G_E in the E-plane table for this value of B.

3) Calculate

$$g = a\frac{G_E}{\sqrt{\frac{50}{l_E}}}.$$

This is the actual gain of the horn.

* Manuscript received by the PGAP, August 2, 1955.

† Microwave Antennas and Components Branch, Electronics Div., Naval Research Lab., Washington 25, D. C.

[1] E. H. Braun, "Gain of electromagnetic horns," Proc. IRE, vol. 41, pp. 109–115; January, 1953.

Reprinted from *IEEE Trans. Antennas Propagat.*, vol. AP-4, pp. 29–31, Jan. 1956.

TABLE I

G_H AS A FUNCTION OF H-PLANE APERTURE DIMENSION "A"

A	G_H	A	G_H	A	G_H	A	G_H	A	G_H	A	G_H	A	G_H
2.0	20.370	4.6	46.635	7.2	71.291	9.8	90.633	12.4	99.019	15.0	92.591	17.6	75.416
2.1	21.387	4.7	47.628	7.3	72.164	9.9	91.195	12.5	99.052	15.1	92.066	17.7	74.701
2.2	22.402	4.8	48.619	7.4	73.031	10.0	91.740	12.6	99.062	15.2	91.528	17.8	73.991
2.3	23.422	4.9	49.609	7.5	73.889	10.1	92.270	12.7	99.051	15.3	90.972	17.9	73.282
2.4	24.439	5.0	50.595	7.6	74.739	10.2	92.781	12.8	99.012	15.4	90.400	18.0	72.581
2.5	25.452	5.1	51.578	7.7	75.580	10.3	93.274	12.9	98.953	15.5	89.822	18.1	71.886
2.6	26.471	5.2	52.559	7.8	76.413	10.4	93.751	13.0	98.871	15.6	89.214	18.2	71.199
2.7	27.488	5.3	53.536	7.9	77.236	10.5	94.208	13.1	98.763	15.7	88.601	18.3	70.516
2.8	28.501	5.4	54.512	8.0	78.049	10.6	94.646	13.2	98.638	15.8	87.976	18.4	69.847
2.9	29.518	5.5	55.475	8.1	78.854	10.7	95.067	13.3	98.486	15.9	87.337	18.5	69.183
3.0	30.532	5.6	56.449	8.2	79.644	10.8	95.470	13.4	98.309	16.0	86.688	18.6	68.534
3.1	31.545	5.7	57.418	8.3	80.427	10.9	95.848	13.5	98.114	16.1	86.026	18.7	67.891
3.2	32.560	5.8	58.377	8.4	81.196	11.0	96.207	13.6	97.894	16.2	85.355	18.8	67.262
3.3	33.573	5.9	59.334	8.5	81.956	11.1	96.547	13.7	97.654	16.3	84.677	18.9	66.643
3.4	34.579	6.0	60.286	8.6	82.703	11.2	96.869	13.8	97.387	16.4	83.990	19.0	66.038
3.5	35.595	6.1	61.232	8.7	83.440	11.3	97.168	13.9	97.101	16.5	83.319	19.1	65.447
3.6	36.605	6.2	62.176	8.8	84.164	11.4	97.446	14.0	96.793	16.6	82.594	19.2	64.871
3.7	37.612	6.3	63.115	8.9	84.875	11.5	97.702	14.1	96.464	16.7	81.888	19.3	64.305
3.8	38.622	6.4	64.046	9.0	85.567	11.6	97.938	14.2	96.113	16.8	81.179	19.4	63.758
3.9	39.629	6.5	64.975	9.1	86.250	11.7	98.149	14.3	95.740	16.9	80.461	19.5	63.222
4.0	40.633	6.6	65.896	9.2	86.923	11.8	98.342	14.4	95.348	17.0	79.742	19.6	62.703
4.1	41.637	6.7	66.810	9.3	87.579	11.9	98.510	14.5	94.936	17.1	79.023	19.7	62.201
4.2	42.645	6.8	67.720	9.4	88.221	12.0	98.658	14.6	94.504	17.2	78.301	19.8	61.714
4.3	43.639	6.9	68.623	9.5	88.844	12.1	98.783	14.7	94.054	17.3	77.578	19.9	61.243
4.4	44.641	7.0	69.518	9.6	89.460	12.2	98.882	14.8	93.586	17.4	76.854	20.0	60.788
4.5	45.639	7.1	70.407	9.7	90.053	12.3	98.965	14.9	93.095	17.5	76.134		

TABLE II

G_E AS A FUNCTION OF E-PLANE APERTURE DIMENSION "B"

B	G_E	B	G_E	B	G_E	B	G_E	B	G_E	B	G_E	B	G_E
2.0	20.362	4.6	46.397	7.2	69.123	9.8	81.301	12.4	73.784	15.0	46.499	17.6	19.910
2.1	21.381	4.7	47.362	7.3	69.847	9.9	81.426	12.5	73.041	15.1	45.268	17.7	19.316
2.2	22.395	4.8	48.326	7.4	70.555	10.0	81.518	12.6	72.265	15.2	44.040	17.8	18.767
2.3	23.410	4.9	49.283	7.5	71.248	10.1	81.581	12.7	71.459	15.3	42.813	17.9	18.264
2.4	24.425	5.0	50.233	7.6	71.923	10.2	81.611	12.8	70.621	15.4	41.593	18.0	17.805
2.5	25.440	5.1	51.181	7.7	72.586	10.3	81.609	12.9	69.753	15.5	40.379	18.1	17.395
2.6	26.456	5.2	52.123	7.8	73.219	10.4	81.575	13.0	68.856	15.6	39.174	18.2	17.030
2.7	27.472	5.3	53.057	7.9	73.841	10.5	81.510	13.1	67.931	15.7	37.982	18.3	16.714
2.8	28.481	5.4	53.985	8.0	74.441	10.6	81.408	13.2	66.980	15.8	36.801	18.4	16.445
2.9	29.490	5.5	54.908	8.1	75.025	10.7	81.277	13.3	66.001	15.9	35.636	18.5	16.223
3.0	30.503	5.6	55.821	8.2	75.585	10.8	81.110	13.4	64.997	16.0	34.488	18.6	16.048
3.1	31.511	5.7	56.728	8.3	76.127	10.9	80.909	13.5	63.969	16.1	33.359	18.7	15.921
3.2	32.518	5.8	57.626	8.4	76.645	11.0	80.676	13.6	62.917	16.2	32.250	18.8	15.839
3.3	33.527	5.9	58.517	8.5	77.142	11.1	80.405	13.7	61.844	16.3	31.164	18.9	15.804
3.4	34.530	6.0	59.401	8.6	77.616	11.2	80.104	13.8	60.748	16.4	30.104	19.0	15.814
3.5	35.534	6.1	60.272	8.7	78.065	11.3	79.765	13.9	59.635	16.5	29.069	19.1	15.870
3.6	36.534	6.2	61.134	8.8	78.492	11.4	79.393	14.0	58.501	16.6	28.063	19.2	15.967
3.7	37.531	6.3	61.987	8.9	78.892	11.5	78.987	14.1	57.351	16.7	27.086	19.3	16.108
3.8	38.530	6.4	62.828	9.0	79.269	11.6	78.545	14.2	56.188	16.8	26.142	19.4	16.289
3.9	39.524	6.5	63.659	9.1	79.619	11.7	78.068	14.3	55.008	16.9	25.232	19.5	16.521
4.0	40.515	6.6	64.477	9.2	79.944	11.8	77.559	14.4	53.816	17.0	24.355	19.6	16.769
4.1	41.504	6.7	65.285	9.3	80.240	11.9	77.014	14.5	52.614	17.1	23.515	19.7	17.064
4.2	42.490	6.8	66.080	9.4	80.510	12.0	76.435	14.6	51.402	17.2	22.713	19.8	17.394
4.3	43.472	6.9	66.862	9.5	80.752	12.1	75.822	14.7	50.183	17.3	21.951	18.9	17.755
4.4	44.450	7.0	67.630	9.6	80.964	12.2	75.176	14.8	48.959	17.4	21.228	20.0	18.147
4.5	45.425	7.1	68.385	9.7	81.146	12.3	74.497	14.9	47.731	17.5	20.548		

The following is a procedure for designing a horn having these four properties:

1) It is an optimum[2] horn.
2) It has approximately equal (half-power) E- and H-plane beamwidths.
3) It has a specified gain g.
4) It fits whatever waveguide is chosen in a simple butt joint.

[2] An optimum horn has aperture dimensions chosen to give maximum gain when the slant height is held fixed.

The exact dimensions fulfilling the first three conditions are (in wavelengths):[3]

$$a = 0.468\sqrt{g}$$

$$b = 0.346\sqrt{g}$$

$$l_E = 0.0576\, g$$

$$l_H = 0.0689\, g$$

where a and b, and l_H and l_E, are the H-plane and E-

[3] All dimensions in this paper are in wavelengths.

plane aperture dimensions and slant heights, respectively, all I.D. (See Fig. 1.)

However, if it is desired to have all sides of the horn meet the waveguide in a common plane, at least one dimension, say l_H, must be altered somewhat from the optimum value. This results in a horn having a gain which differs by a few tenths of a db from the original desired value. Hence two procedures are given, depending on whether or not the designer is willing to accept the few tenths of a db difference. In any case it should be emphasized that exact value of gain of final horn, as computed from Schelkunoff's curves, will be known. This theoretical gain should in turn be within about $\frac{1}{2}$ db of true gain, and in most cases, considerably closer.

Procedure (A): (Designer willing to accept small difference in gain)

1) Calculate

$$a = 0.468\sqrt{g}$$

$$b = 0.346\sqrt{g}$$

$$l_E = 0.0576g$$

$$l_H = \frac{a}{a - w_H}\sqrt{\left[l_E^2 - \left(\frac{b}{2}\right)^2\right]\left[\frac{b - w_E}{b}\right]^2 + \left(\frac{a - w_H}{2}\right)^2};$$

w_H and w_E are the H-plane and E-plane guide widths, respectively, both I.D. and in wavelengths.

2) Calculate gain of this horn using above method. Its gain will differ only slightly from original desired gain, and it will fit the waveguide accurately.

Procedure (B): (Designer desiring closer approximation to original gain)

1) Calculate

$$\bar{a} = 0.468\sqrt{g}$$

$$\bar{b} = 0.346\sqrt{g}$$

$$\bar{l}_E = 0.0576\, g$$

$$\bar{l}_H = \frac{\dfrac{\bar{b} - w_E}{\bar{b}}}{\dfrac{\bar{a} - w_H}{\bar{a}}}\,\bar{l}_E.$$

2) Compute the gain of this horn as above. Call this gain g_1.

3) Calculate

$$a = 0.468\sqrt{\frac{g^2}{g_1}}$$

$$b = 0.346\sqrt{\frac{g^2}{g_1}}$$

$$l_E = 0.0576\frac{g^2}{g_1}$$

$$l_H = \frac{a}{a - w_H}\sqrt{\left[l_E^2 - \left(\frac{b}{2}\right)^2\right]\left[\frac{b - w_E}{b}\right]^2 + \left(\frac{a - w_H}{2}\right)^2}.$$

4) Calculate the gain of this horn, which will now be extremely close to the original desired gain, and will fit the waveguide accurately.

Gain of Electromagnetic Horns

By T. S. CHU and R. A. SEMPLAK

(Manuscript received December 11, 1964)

The absolute gain of a standard horn is often measured by determining the transmission loss versus separation between two identical standard horns. Correction ratios are needed because the usual criterion for separation ($2a^2/\lambda$) may not justify the use of the far-zone power transmission formula. Using the near-field power transmission formula, the ratio between the Fraunhofer and Fresnel gain of a pyramidal electromagnetic horn has been computed as a function of horn dimensions and separation distance.

The calculated corrections have been applied in the absolute gain measurement of a standard horn which was used as a calibration reference in a recent 4080-mc gain measurement of a large horn-reflector antenna. The measured gain of the standard horn at 4080 mc is 20.11 db with an accuracy of ±0.035 db. The calculated gain is 20.15 db.

I. INTRODUCTION

Recently, a standard horn was used as a calibration reference in measuring the gain of a 400-square foot aperture horn-reflector antenna at 4080 mcs.[1] Since the horn-reflector antenna is currently being used for precision measurement of the absolute flux of stellar radio sources, it is desirable that the gain of the standard horn be known as accurately as possible. From previous work,[2] the calculated gain[7] of a standard horn was believed to be within ±0.1 db of its true gain. Our purpose was to measure the absolute gain of the standard horn to an accuracy better than that previously achieved.

The gain of a standard horn can be determined by measuring the transmission loss versus separation between two identical standard horns. In the technique of measurement commonly used, the separation distance is not large, and it is well known that the far-zone power transmission formula

$$P_R/P_T = (G\lambda/4\pi r)^2 \tag{1}$$

is not valid if the separation r between the apertures of the two horns

Reprinted with permission from *Bell Syst. Tech. J.*, vol. 44, pp. 527–537, Mar. 1965.

is not great enough. Therefore the gain formula

$$G = \frac{4\pi r}{\lambda} (P_R/P_T)^{\frac{1}{2}} \tag{2}$$

may introduce considerable error when the far-zone gain of pyramidal electromagnetic horns is measured at relatively short distances. Even an aperture-to-aperture separation r of about $2a^2/\lambda$ between two optimum horns, where a is the large dimension of the aperture, introduces an error of the order of 1 db. Jakes[2] suggested the junction of the horn with the feeding waveguide as the reference point for optimum horns. He demonstrated empirically that the error in gain may be reduced to about 0.1 db if r is measured between the reference points of two optimum horns. Braun[3] calculated the error in the gain of electromagnetic horns measured at short distances. However, his assumptions about the received power are questionable, since the power in the transmitted wave was averaged over the receiving aperture. Although the near-field power transmission formula appeared in the literature,[4] to our knowledge it has not been applied to the gain measurement of electromagnetic horns. With the aid of the digital computer, the near-field power transmission formula easily yields the required correction ratios for the far-zone gain of pyramidal electromagnetic horns measured at relatively short distances.

II. CALCULATION OF THE CORRECTIONS

Using the Lorentz reciprocity theorem, it has been shown[4] that the ratio of the received to transmitted power between two antennas at any separation is

$$\frac{P_R}{P_T} = \frac{1/4 \left| \int_s (\mathbf{H}_2 \times \mathbf{E}_1 + \mathbf{E}_2 \times \mathbf{H}_1) \cdot \hat{n} \, ds \right|^2}{\left\{ \mathrm{Re} \int_{s_1} (\mathbf{E}_1 \times \mathbf{H}_1^*) \cdot \hat{n}_1 ds \right\} \left\{ \mathrm{Re} \int_{s_2} (\mathbf{E}_2 \times \mathbf{H}_2^*) \cdot \hat{n}_2 ds \right\}} \tag{3}$$

where $\mathbf{E}_1$, $\mathbf{H}_1$ are the fields when antenna 1 is transmitting, $\mathbf{E}_2$, $\mathbf{H}_2$ are the fields when antenna 2 is transmitting; and $\hat{n}$, $\hat{n}_1$, and $\hat{n}_2$ are the unit normals of the surfaces. The surface S can be either one of the two antenna apertures. Equation (3) is an exact formula if all the field quantities are evaluated with both antennas in place and under matched conditions. In the following calculation the reflections between the antennas will be neglected; that is, in evaluating $\mathbf{E}_1$, $\mathbf{H}_1$ antenna 2 will be removed, and in evaluating $\mathbf{E}_2$, $\mathbf{H}_2$ antenna 1 will be removed. We also neglect any mismatch between antennas and their transmission lines.

Furthermore, we assume that the tangential components of **E** and **H** are related by the free-space impedance at each point:

$$\hat{n} \times \mathbf{E}^t = \sqrt{\frac{\mu}{\epsilon}}\, \mathbf{H}^t.$$

With these approximations, we can write down the power transmission formula between two electromagnetic horns at any separation.

$$\frac{P_R}{P_T} = \frac{\left| \int_{s_1} \int_{s_2} E_1^t(P) \frac{e^{-jkr}}{r} E_2^t(P') ds\, ds' \right|^2}{\lambda^2 \int_{s_1} | E_1^t(P) |^2 ds \int_{s_2} | E_2^t(P') |^2 ds'} \tag{5}$$

where P and P' are points on the aperture surfaces S_1 and S_2 respectively. Assuming the field at the aperture of the transmitting horn is the same as though the horn were continued (i.e., the usual Kirchhoff approximation), the tangential electric fields in the aperture are given by

$$E_1^t = E_1^0 \cos \frac{\pi y}{a} \exp - \left[jk \left(\frac{x^2}{2l_E} + \frac{y^2}{2l_H} \right) \right] \tag{6}$$

$$E_2^t = E_2^0 \cos \frac{\pi \eta}{a} \exp - \left[jk \left(\frac{\zeta^2}{2l_E} + \frac{\eta^2}{2l_H} \right) \right] \tag{7}$$

where l_E and l_H are the E- and H-plane slant heights respectively. The distance r may be approximated by

$$\begin{aligned} r &= [R^2 + (x - \zeta)^2 + (y - \eta)^2]^{\frac{1}{2}} \\ &\approx R + \frac{(x - \zeta)^2 + (y - \eta)^2}{2R}. \end{aligned} \tag{8}$$

All pertinent dimensions are illustrated in Fig. 1. Since the gain measurements usually involve two identical horns, $S_1 = S_2$, and substituting (6), (7), and (8) into (5), (2) reduces to the near-field gain in the Fresnel approximation:

$$G_N = \frac{4\pi \left| \int_s \int_{s'} \cos \frac{\pi y}{a} \cos \frac{\pi \eta}{a} \exp - \left[jk \left\{ \frac{x^2 + \zeta^2}{2l_E} + \frac{y^2 + \eta^2}{2l_H} + \frac{(x - \zeta)^2}{2R} + \frac{(y - \eta)^2}{2R} \right\} \right] ds\, ds' \right|}{\lambda^2 \int_s \cos^2 \frac{\pi y}{a}\, ds} \tag{9}$$

while the Fraunhofer gain is

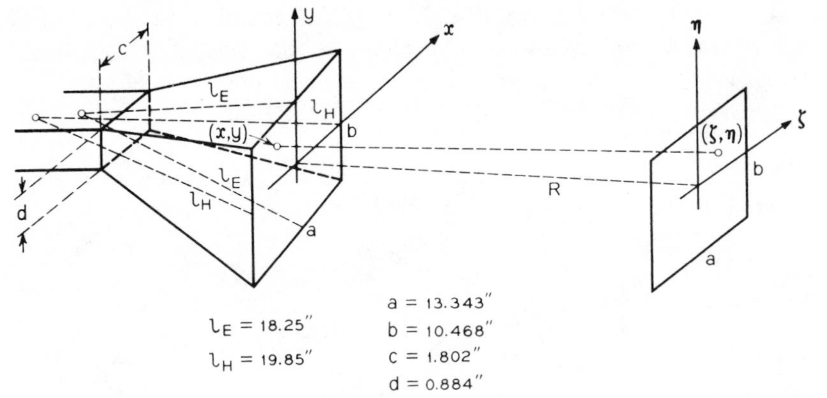

Fig. 1 — Physical dimensions for transmission between two electromagnetic horns.

$$G = \frac{4\pi \left| \int_s \int_{s'} \cos \frac{\pi y}{a} \cos \frac{\pi \eta}{a} \cdot \exp - \left[jk \left(\frac{x^2 + \zeta^2}{2l_E} + \frac{y^2 + \eta^2}{2l_H} \right) \right] ds\, ds' \right|}{\lambda^2 \int_s \cos^2 \frac{\pi y}{a}\, ds} . \quad (10)$$

Dividing (10) by (9) yields the required correction ratio. It is convenient to split this ratio into the E-plane correction and the H-plane correction

$$C = (G/G_N) = C_E C_H \quad (11)$$

where

$$C_E = \frac{\left| \int_{-b/2}^{b/2} \int_{-b/2}^{b/2} \exp - \left[jk \left(\frac{x^2 + \zeta^2}{2l_E} \right) \right] dx\, d\zeta \right|}{\left| \int_{-b/2}^{b/2} \int_{-b/2}^{b/2} \exp - \left[jk \left(\frac{x^2 + \zeta^2}{2l_E} \right) \right] \cdot \exp - \left[jk \frac{(x - \zeta)^2}{2R} \right] dx\, d\zeta \right|} \quad (12)$$

and

$$C_H = \frac{\left| \int_{-a/2}^{a/2} \int_{-a/2}^{a/2} \cos \frac{\pi y}{a} \cos \frac{\pi \eta}{a} \exp - \left[jk \left(\frac{y^2 + \eta^2}{2l_H} \right) \right] dy\, d\eta \right|}{\left| \int_{-a/2}^{a/2} \int_{-a/2}^{a/2} \cos \frac{\pi y}{a} \cos \frac{\pi \eta}{a} \exp - \left[jk \left(\frac{y^2 + \eta^2}{2l_H} \right) \right] \cdot \exp - \left[jk \frac{(y - \eta)^2}{2R} \right] dy\, d\eta \right|} . \quad (13)$$

The numerators in the above expressions may be identified as Fresnel integrals. After normalizing the parameters, we have

$$C_E = \frac{M\left[C^2\left(\frac{2}{\sqrt{M}}\right) + S^2\left(\frac{2}{\sqrt{M}}\right)\right]}{\left\{\left[\int_{-1}^{1}\int_{-1}^{1} \cos 2\pi\left(\frac{\omega^2 + \zeta^2}{M} + \frac{(\omega - \zeta)^2}{H}\right) d\omega\, d\zeta\right]^2 + \left[\int_{-1}^{1}\int_{-1}^{1} \sin 2\pi\left(\frac{\omega^2 + \zeta^2}{M} + \frac{(\omega - \zeta)^2}{H}\right) d\omega\, d\zeta\right]^2\right\}^{\frac{1}{2}}} \qquad (14)$$

and

$$C_H = \frac{\frac{N}{4}\{[C(f) - C(g)]^2 + [S(f) - S(g)]^2\}}{\left\{\left[\int_{-1}^{1}\int_{-1}^{1} \cos\frac{\pi}{2} u \cos\frac{\pi}{2} v \cos 2\pi\left(\frac{u^2 + v^2}{N} + \frac{(u - v)^2}{P}\right) du\, dv\right]^2 + \left[\int_{-1}^{1}\int_{-1}^{1} \cos\frac{\pi}{2} u \cos\frac{\pi}{2} v \sin 2\pi\left(\frac{u^2 + v^2}{N} + \frac{(u - v)^2}{P}\right) du\, dv\right]^2\right\}^{\frac{1}{2}}} \qquad (15)$$

where

$$M = 8\lambda l_E/b^2 \qquad H = 8\lambda R/b^2$$

$$N = 8\lambda l_H/a^2 \qquad P = 8\lambda R/a^2$$

$$f = \frac{1}{\sqrt{2}}\left(\sqrt{\frac{N}{8}} + \frac{1}{\sqrt{\frac{N}{8}}}\right) \qquad g = \frac{1}{\sqrt{2}}\left(\sqrt{\frac{N}{8}} - \frac{1}{\sqrt{\frac{N}{8}}}\right).$$

The Fresnel integrals are defined as

$$C(u) = \int_0^u \cos\frac{\pi}{2} t^2\, dt \qquad \text{and} \qquad S(u) = \int_0^u \sin\frac{\pi}{2} t^2\, dt$$

Equations (14) and (15) have been programmed for a digital computer; the results are summarized in Tables I and II.

It is interesting to notice that there exists substantial discrepancy between our correction ratios and those in Braun's article,[3] especially at short separations. In addition to the approximations made here, Braun employed an averaging process in which the power of the transmitted wave is integrated over the effective receiving aperture area $(\lambda^2/4\pi)G$. Therefore the correction ratios presented here are expected to be much more accurate than Braun's data and they should be useful for precision gain measurement of pyramidal electromagnetic horns.

TABLE I — E-PLANE CORRECTIONS (db)

M \ H	8	16	32	64	128	256
2.0	1.740	0.997	0.520	0.263	0.132	0.066
2.5	1.585	0.856	0.426	0.210	0.104	0.051
3.0	1.490	0.757	0.362	0.175	0.085	0.042
3.5	1.418	0.684	0.317	0.150	0.073	0.036
4.0	1.359	0.627	0.284	0.133	0.064	0.031
5.0	1.268	0.547	0.237	0.108	0.051	0.025
6.0	1.201	0.492	0.207	0.092	0.043	0.021
8.0	1.109	0.423	0.168	0.072	0.033	0.016
10.0	1.050	0.381	0.145	0.060	0.027	0.013
32.0	0.870	0.261	0.081	0.028	0.011	0.005
∞	0.779	0.205	0.052	0.010	0.003	0.001

$M = 8\lambda l_E/b^2$ $\qquad H = 8\lambda R/b^2$

III. MEASUREMENT TECHNIQUE

The standard horn was mounted in a wooden structure suitably covered with hairflex absorber; a sketch of the horn and its physical dimensions are shown in Fig. 1. A level monorail track was installed along the center line of the floor of an anechoic chamber. A stable, wooden equipment cart was designed to move smoothly along the monorail. One of two identical standard horns with hairflex baffle was mounted on the equipment cart (Fig. 2), the other being mounted in the end wall of the chamber. The equipment set-up is quite conventional and is shown schematically in Fig. 3.

The following procedure was used in the measurements: a reference level was set by removing the standard horns and connecting the waveguides directly (Fig. 3). With the standard horns in place and separated by $r \geqq 2a^2/\lambda$, a series of measurements of received power versus increas-

TABLE II — H-PLANE CORRECTIONS (db)

N \ P	8	16	32	64	128	256
2.0	0.833	0.422	0.209	0.104	0.052	0.026
2.5	0.772	0.376	0.181	0.089	0.044	0.022
3.0	0.717	0.336	0.159	0.077	0.038	0.019
3.5	0.671	0.304	0.141	0.067	0.033	0.016
4.0	0.633	0.279	0.127	0.060	0.029	0.014
5.0	0.575	0.242	0.107	0.049	0.024	0.012
6.0	0.533	0.216	0.093	0.042	0.020	0.010
8.0	0.478	0.183	0.075	0.033	0.015	0.007
10.0	0.443	0.162	0.064	0.027	0.013	0.006
32.0	0.340	0.103	0.033	0.012	0.005	0.002
∞	0.291	0.071	0.019	0.005	0.001	0.0002

$N = 8\lambda l_H/a^2$ $\qquad P = 8\lambda R/a^2$

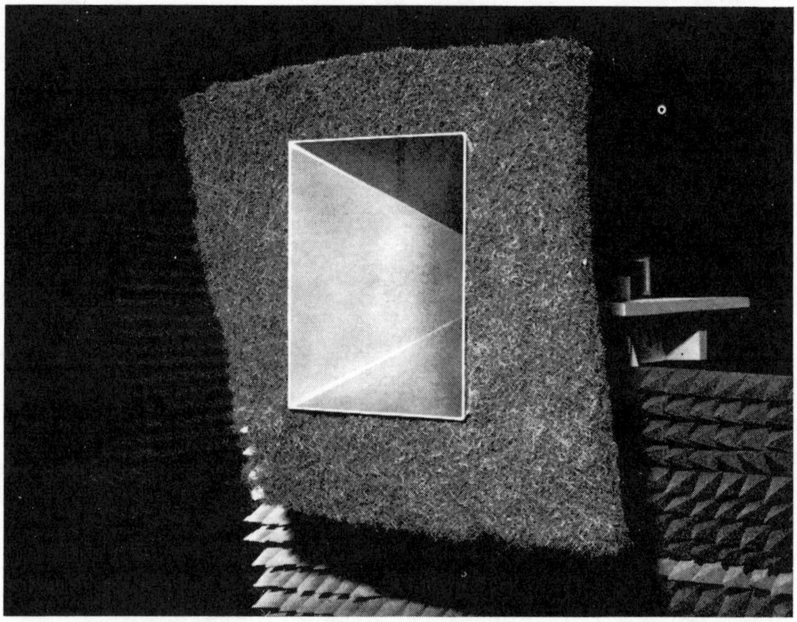

Fig. 2 — Standard horn mounted on equipment cart.

ing (r) were made. After completion of such a series, the reference level was rechecked by removing the standard horns and connecting the waveguides together. The above procedure was repeated several times for vertical and horizontal polarizations.

IV. RESULTS OF MEASUREMENT

The distribution of all of the measured gains at 4080 mc has been plotted as a histogram in Fig. 4. The near-field correction discussed above has been applied to these data. It should be pointed out that occurrences falling on the boundary lines of the columns have been evenly divided between the two neighboring columns; this accounts for the half occurrences which appear in the heights of some of the columns. The mean value of this sample distribution is 20.11 db, and its standard deviation is 0.05 db. The central limit theorem of probability theory indicates a 99.7 per cent confidence interval of $\bar{X} \pm (3\sigma/\sqrt{n})$ for the true mean, where $\bar{X}$ is the sample mean, n is the sample size, and σ is the population standard deviation.[5] Since the present sample size is 90, the population standard deviation should be close to the above sample standard devia-

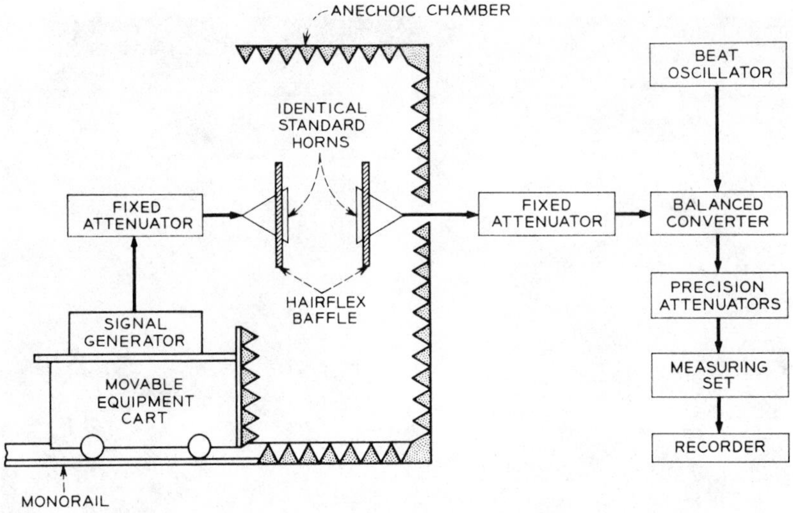

Fig. 3 — Equipment set-up.

tion, 0.05 db; therefore the random error in the mean value 20.11 db is of the order of ± 0.016 db $(3 \times 0.05/\sqrt{90})$.

The spread in the measured gain may be attributed to the following factors:

1. measuring system stability ± 0.01 db
2. precision attenuator readings ± 0.015 db
3. repeatability of electrical connections ± 0.015 db
4. imperfection of the anechoic chamber ± 0.02 db
5. interaction between the transmitting horn and the receiving horn ± 0.04 db.

The figures for the above factors are the estimates for one horn; they are half the probable random errors in the transmission between two horn antennas. Half of the measured gains were obtained when the horn apertures were vertically polarized, and half when horizontally polarized; when compared, the difference between the means of the two samples is only 0.01 db. This comparison implies only small errors due to the anechoic chamber.

The interaction effect is clearly demonstrated by the measured $(\lambda/2)$-period oscillation versus separation shown in Figs. 5(a) and 5(b). The amplitude of the oscillation is of the order of 0.05 db, and agrees fairly well with the qualitative calculation of Silver.[6]

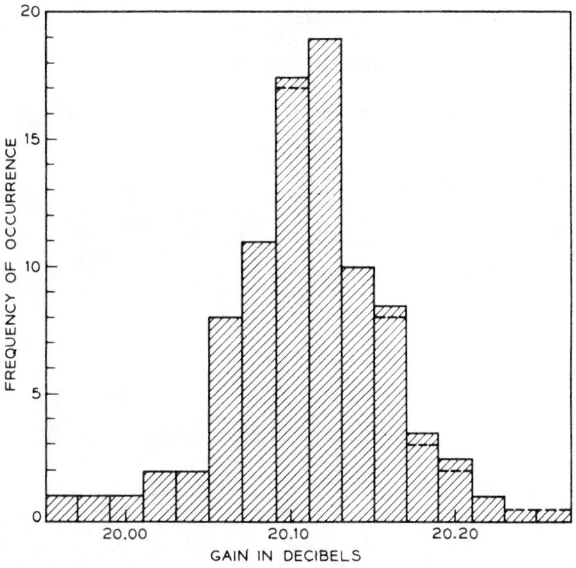

Fig. 4 — Histogram for the measured gains.

In addition to the random errors discussed above, the calibrated precision attenuators hide an absolute error which is constant for all measured gains. The probable value of this error is ± 0.04 db in the power transmission measurement, which contributes ± 0.02 db to the gain error. It follows that the total possible error of the measured gain (which includes the random error and the absolute attenuator error) is about ± 0.035 db. The calculated gain[7] of the standard horn is 20.15 db at 4080 mc. The discrepancy between the calculated value and the measured gain (20.11 db) is 0.04 db.

It should be pointed out that both transmitting and receiving horns in this gain measurement are isolated by 10-db fixed attenuators. However the mismatch at the horn-waveguide junction is not tuned out, because this same mismatch was not tuned out when the standard horn was used as a calibration reference for the gain measurement of the large horn-reflector antenna. A VSWR measurement revealed a reflection coefficient of -25 db, which represents a transmission loss of 0.015 db.

V. SUMMARY AND CONCLUSIONS

Using the near-field power transmission formula, the ratio between the Fraunhofer and Fresnel gain of a pyramidal electromagnetic horn

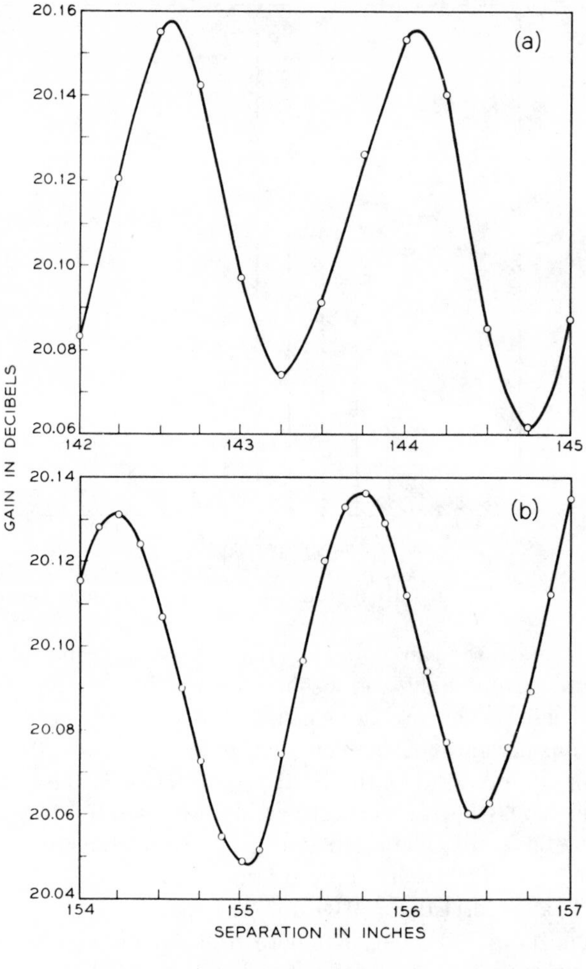

Fig. 5 — Measured gain variation due to interaction.

has been computed as a function of horn dimensions and separation distance. Our computations are expected to be much more accurate than previous data and should be very useful for precision gain measurement of pyramidal electromagnetic horns.

An application of the calculated corrections was made in the absolute gain measurement of a standard horn. The measured gain of the standard horn at 4080 mc is 20.11 db with an accuracy of ± 0.035 db; the calculated gain is 20.15 db. The interaction between two standard horns may introduce an error of the order of 0.05 db in the gain measurement at a separation distance of $2a^2/\lambda$; however, it is reduced considerably by taking the average of several measurements. The averaging procedure can also reduce other random errors due to environment, measuring system stability, attenuator readings, etc. Using the corrections presented above, together with other careful considerations, it is possible to achieve an accuracy well below 0.1 db in the gain measurement of pyramidal electromagnetic horns.

VI. ACKNOWLEDGMENT

The authors are indebted to Mrs. C. L. Beattie for programming the computations.

REFERENCES

1. Hogg, D. C., and Wilson, R. W., A Precise Measurement of the Gain of a Large Horn-Reflector Antenna, to be published.
2. Jakes, W. C., Gain of Electromagnetic Horns, Proc. IRE, *39*, Feb., 1951, pp. 160–162.
3. Braun, E. H., Gain of Electromagnetic Horns, Proc. IRE, *41*, Jan., 1953, pp. 109–115.
4. Hu, M. K., Near-Zone Power Transmission Formulas, IRE National Convention Record, *6*, Pt. 8, 1958, pp. 128–135.
5. Anderson, R. L., and Bancroft, T A., *Statistical Theory in Research*, McGraw-Hill, p. 71.
6. Silver, S., *Microwave Antenna Theory and Design*, McGraw-Hill, p. 592.
7. Schelkunoff, S. A., *Electromagnetic Waves*, D. Van Nostrand, p. 364.

On the Behavior of Electromagnetic Horns

***Abstract*—Some accurate microwave horn gain measurements with revised proximity corrections are presented. These experimental results indicate edge diffraction is the major source of error in Schelkunoff's gain expression and suggest a value for its accuracy.**

A few years ago some accurate gain measurements were made on microwave horns based on designs prepared long before by Slayton.[1] Only the final gain values were presented[2] and these included near-field or proximity corrections based on Braun's curves,[3] which have subsequently been improved upon by Chu and Semplak.[4] The revised results given here may be helpful to the still frequent users of Slayton's designs. In graphical form they illustrate an important feature of horn behavior from which an estimate of the accuracy of Schelkunoff's gain expression[5] may be made.

TABLE I

Gain of Microwave Horns, dB

λ, cm	Uncorrected Gain	Braun's Correction	Chu and Semplak's Correction	Antenna Gain
10.71	17.466	0.196	0.195	17.66
9.52	18.010	0.221	0.246	18.26
9.37	18.167	0.258	0.271	18.44
8.82	18.589	0.250	0.279	18.87
4.84	21.52	0.495	0.448	21.97
4.61	21.81	0.530	0.476	22.29
4.41	21.78	0.608	0.553	22.33
2.31	23.29	0.403	0.367	23.66
	23.17			23.54
2.22	23.46	0.449	0.410	23.87
	23.335			23.75
2.14	23.635	0.440	0.399	24.03
	23.52			23.92

In another letter[6] some details of the measurement procedure are mentioned and the remainder are described elsewhere.[7] The results shown in Table I include the effect of a matching slide screw tuner but aside from this the horns were those shown in Figs. A-14, A-12 and A-9 of Slayton.[1] Attenuation in a 40.6-cm waveguide extension is mainly responsible for the gain of one of the 1.8-cm band horns being about 0.12 dB lower than the other, but no measurable difference in gain was found between the horns of each pair for the 10-cm and 4.75-cm band horns, indicating that the gain values may be used with little error for carefully constructed horns based on their designs. The accuracy of these results, discussed in another letter,[6] is estimated at ± 0.03 dB probable error for the 1.8-cm band values and ± 0.02 dB probable error for the others. The results are plotted in Fig. 1, as are some of Slayton's experimental results.[1] Slayton's results include Braun's near-field correction[3] and, except for those in Fig. 1(a), are scaled from other horn measurements. An oscillation with frequency of the measured values about Schelkunoff's theoretical gain curve[5] appears to be present for the two lower-frequency horns but not for the higher-gain 1.8-cm band horn. Slayton also observed these oscillations and a similar trend is evident in his experimental results.[1]

Schelkunoff's expression for the gain of a horn accounts for neither the mismatch of the horn nor diffraction by its aperture edges. It also assumes an approximate form for the aperture field, but aperture-field fluctuations which could introduce these gain oscillations seem unlikely. If, as in these measurements, the horns are carefully matched, then the gain oscillations are probably caused by edge diffraction and ought to diminish in amplitude as the gain of the horn increases, for the same reason that Kirchhoff's diffraction theory is a better approximation with large apertures. This seems to be borne out by Fig. 1(a) and by Slayton's experimental results for the higher-gain horns. Further experimental support for this supposition is provided by Fig. 2, which shows the gain of a 7.44-meter^2 aperture horn-reflector antenna measured with the horn whose gain is shown in Fig. 1(b) as a comparison standard (see Jull and Deloli[2]). The probable error in these values is estimated at ± 0.04 dB. No oscillations are evident in this curve, indicating that, almost certainly, the oscillations of Fig. 1(b) are real and are not present for large apertures. Finally, it should be mentioned that geometrical diffraction theory has been used to include edge diffraction in the calculation of horn radiation patterns,[8],[9] with good experimental agreement.

How accurate is Schelkunoff's expression? From Fig. 1(c) its error limits appear to be about $\pm 2\frac{1}{2}$ percent (± 0.10 dB) for the gain of an 18.5-dB horn with aperture dimensions of about 3 to 4 wavelengths. For higher-gain horns the accuracy may be better, such as for the 22-dB horns of Fig. 1(b), where the limits seem to be about ± 0.06 dB with the attenuation of the tuner and waveguide feed (about 0.02 dB) accounted for, but for smaller horns it will probably be worse. The small discrepancy (0.04 dB in 20.11 dB) obtained at one frequency by Chu and Semplak may be fortuitous, as is that of 0.02 dB at $\lambda = 9.37$ cm in Fig. 1(c), and Findlay's estimate of one percent on this subject[10] might be considered optimistic if applied to small horns. The systematic discrepancy in Fig. 1(a) is a reminder that

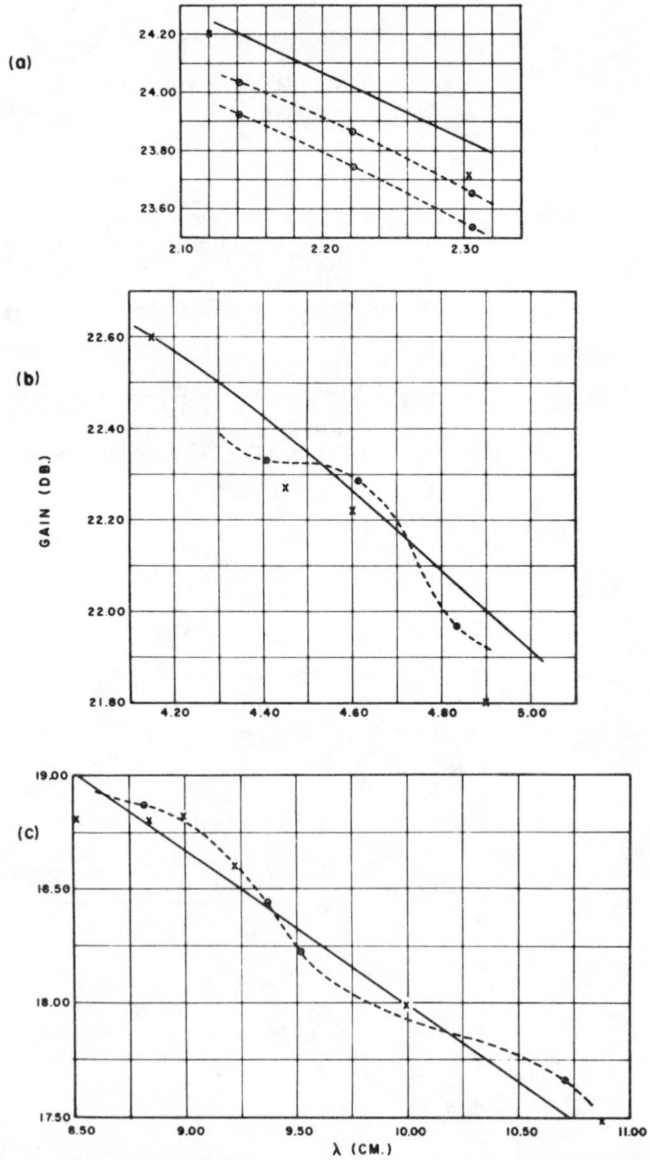

Fig. 1. Gain of Slayton's horns. (a) 1.8-cm band horn with 12.7-cm matching section. (b) 4.75-cm band horn with 21-cm matching section. (c) 10-cm band horn with 25.4-cm matching section.

-O- -O- measured values
× Slayton's values
——— calculated gain

Manuscript received August 7, 1967; revised August 21, 1967.

Reprinted from *Proc. IEEE*, vol. 56, pp. 106–108, Jan. 1968.

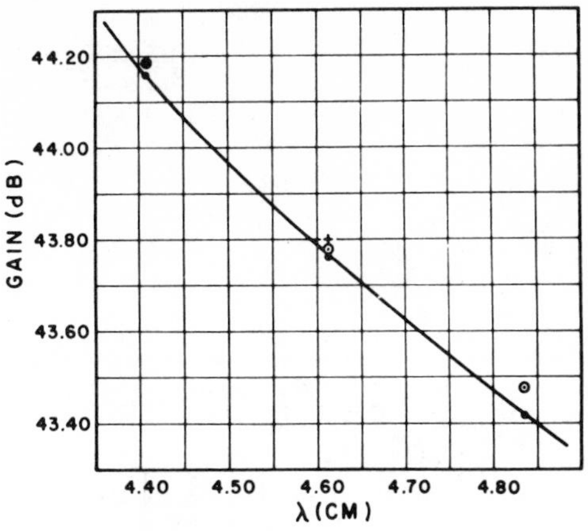

Fig. 2. Gain of a horn-reflector antenna.
+ measurements from 150.4-m range with near-field corrections
○ measurements from 301.6-m range with near-field corrections
● measurements with corrections for variations in the illuminating field.

less reliance can be placed on Schelkunoff's expression when it is applied to small horns at high frequencies for which construction tolerances are more critical, and that then the attenuation in the tuner and waveguide feed, in this case about 0.06 dB, definitely needs to be taken into account. This attenuation amounts to only about 0.01 dB in the 10-cm band measurements.

ACKNOWLEDGMENT

The measurements described here were made by E. P. Deloli assisted by W. W. Zuzak.

E. V. JULL
Radio and Elec. Engrg. Div.
National Research Council
Ottawa, Canada

REFERENCES

[1] W. T. Slayton, "Design and calibration of microwave antenna gain standards," U. S. Naval Research Lab., Washington, D. C., Rept. 4433, November 1954.

[2] E. V. Jull and E. P. Deloli, "An accurate absolute gain calibration of an antenna for radio astronomy," *IEEE Trans. Antennas and Propagation*, vol. AP-12, pp. 439-447, July 1964.

[3] E. H. Braun, "Gain of electromagnetic horns," *Proc. IRE*, vol. 41, pp. 109-115, January 1953.

[4] T. S. Chu and R. A. Semplak, "Gain of electromagnetic horns," *Bell Sys. Tech. J.*, vol. 44, pp. 527-537, March 1965.

[5] S. A. Schelkunoff and H. T. Friis, *Antennas—Theory and Practice*. New York: Wiley, 1952, p. 527.

[6] E. V. Jull and R. R. Bowman, "Electromagnetic horn gain measurements," to be published in *Proc. IEEE (Letters)*, vol. 56, February 1968.

[7] E. V. Jull and E. P. Deloli, "The precise calibration of a horn-reflector antenna for radio astronomy," National Research Council of Canada, Radio and Elec. Engrg. Div., Ottawa, Rept. ERB-637, June 1963.

[8] P. M. Russo, R. C. Rudduck, and L. Peters, Jr., "A method for computing *E*-plane patterns of horn antennas," *IEEE Trans. Antennas and Propagation*, vol. AP-13, pp. 219-224, March 1965.

[9] M. A. K. Hamid, "Near field transmission between horn antennas," University of Toronto, Dept. of Elec. Engrg. Rept. 43, April 1966.

[10] J. W. Findlay, "Absolute intensity calibrations in radio astronomy," *Ann. Rev. Astron. and Astrophys.*, vol. 4, pp. 77-94, 1966.

FINITE-RANGE GAIN OF SECTORAL AND PYRAMIDAL HORNS

Indexing term: Antenna theory

Finite-range effects are incorporated into Schelkunoff's pyramidal-horn gain formula, which is arranged as the product of in-phase aperture gain and E and H plane range and slant-length gain-reduction factors. These factors, readily computed, permit the on-axis gain of a horn to be obtained from two single-line curves.

In deriving the gain of a pyramidal horn by the Kirchhoff method, Schelkunoff[1] accounted for the effect of the horn flare by introducing a quadratic phase error in the dominant mode field along the aperture co-ordinates. Finite-range effects in the Fresnel zone can also be approximated to by a quadratic phase error in the aperture field. In combination, at a range r, the on-axis electric field of the pyramidal horn of Fig. 1 is approximately[2]

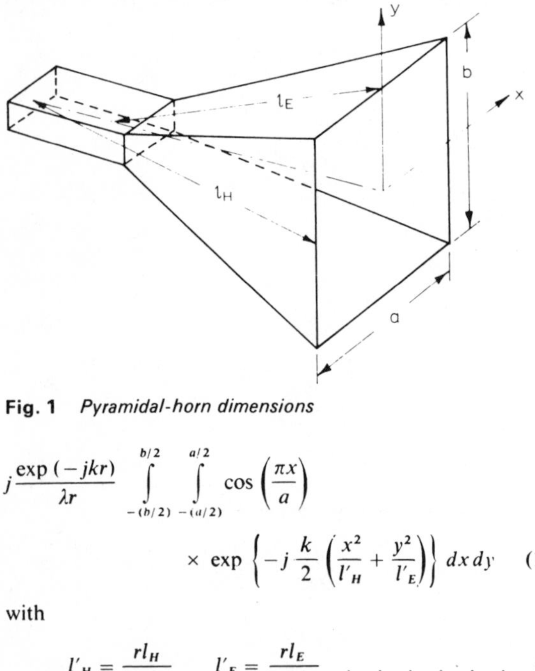

Fig. 1 *Pyramidal-horn dimensions*

$$j\frac{\exp(-jkr)}{\lambda r}\int_{-(b/2)}^{b/2}\int_{-(a/2)}^{a/2}\cos\left(\frac{\pi x}{a}\right)\times\exp\left\{-j\frac{k}{2}\left(\frac{x^2}{l'_H}+\frac{y^2}{l'_E}\right)\right\}dx\,dy \qquad (1)$$

with

$$l'_H = \frac{rl_H}{r+l_H} \qquad l'_E = \frac{rl_E}{r+l_E} \qquad (2)$$

and $k = 2\pi/\lambda$, where λ is the wavelength.

The usual procedures[1] can be used to reduce eqn. 1 to Fresnel integrals and subsequently to obtain the finite-range on-axis gain of a pyramidal horn. The result has the same form as Schelkunoff's gain expression, with l'_H and l'_E replacing l_H and l_E. The near-field pyramidal-horn gain can then be obtained from the product of the composite near-field E and H plane pyramidal-horn gains, which are available from parametric curves.[1]

A more accurate method of graphically obtaining numerical values is apparent if the finite-range gain formula is written

$$G = G_0 R_E R_H \qquad (3)$$

with

$$G_0 = \frac{32ab}{\pi\lambda^2} \qquad (4)$$

$$R_E = \frac{C^2(w)+S^2(w)}{w^2} \qquad (5)$$

and

$$R_H = \frac{\pi^2}{4}\frac{\{C(u)-C(v)\}^2+\{S(u)-S(v)\}^2}{(u-v)^2} \qquad (6)$$

$$C(w)-jS(w) = \int_0^w \exp\left(-j\frac{\pi}{2}t^2\right)dt \qquad (7)$$

are the Fresnel integrals and

$$w = \frac{b}{\sqrt{(2\lambda l'_E)}} \qquad (8)$$

$$\left.\begin{matrix}u\\v\end{matrix}\right\} = \pm\frac{a}{\sqrt{(2\lambda l'_H)}}+\sqrt{\left(\frac{\lambda l'_H}{2}\right)}\frac{1}{a} \qquad (9)$$

In eqn. 3, G_0 is the far-field gain of a rectangular aperture with

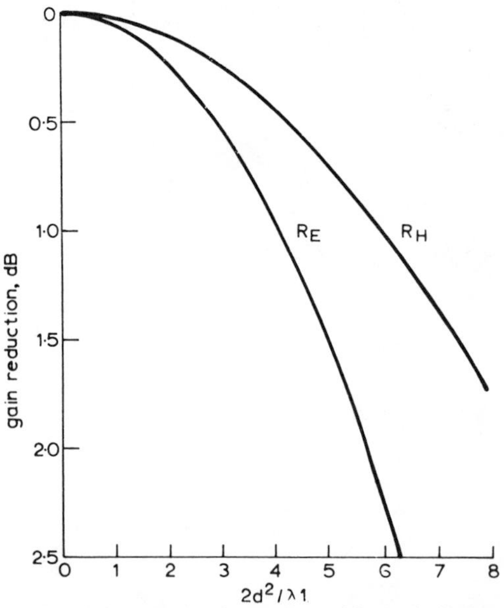

Fig. 2 *Gain-reduction factors R_E and R_H in decibels*

a uniform distribution in the y direction, a cosinusoidal variation in the x direction and uniform phase across the aperture. R_E and R_H include the gain reduction due to the E and H plane flare of the horn as well as the effect of finite range. As $r \to \infty$, eqn. 3 reduces to Schelkunoff's horn-gain formula, and as $l_E = l_H \to \infty$, one obtains the near-field on-axis gain of a rectangular aperture. If both range and slant lengths are much larger than the aperture dimensions, $R_E = R_H \simeq 1$, and the far-field in-phase gain of the horn aperture G_0 remains.

The gain of an E plane sectoral horn is obtained by letting $l'_H \to \infty$ in eqn. 3. Then $R_H \to 1$ and the gain is $G_E = G_0 E_E$. Similarly when $l'_H \to \infty$, $R_E \to 1$ and $G_H = G_0 R_H$ is the gain of an H plane sectoral horn.

In Table 1, R_E and R_H are tabulated as functions of the generalised parameter $s = 2d^2/\lambda l$, where d is the aperture

Reprinted with permission from *Electron. Lett.*, vol. 6, pp. 680–681, Oct. 15, 1970.

Table 1 GAIN-REDUCTION FACTORS R_E AND R_H

s	R_E	R_H
	dB	dB
0·5	0·015	0·007
1·0	0·060	0·029
1·5	0·134	0·064
2·0	0·239	0·114
2·5	0·374	0·179
3·0	0·541	0·257
3·5	0·738	0·349
4·0	0·967	0·454
4·5	1·229	0·573
5·0	1·525	0·705
5·5	1·854	0·850
6·0	2·218	1·007
6·5	2·618	1·176
7·0	3·054	1·357
7·5	3·527	1·547
8·0	4·037	1·748
9·0	5·166	2·175
10·0	6·427	2·630
11·0	7·769	3·101
12·0	9·081	3·577
13·0	10·163	4·043
14·0	10·783	4·486
15·0	10·849	4·892
16·0	10·502	5·252
18·0	9·474	5·819
20·0	8·847	6·210
22·0	8·901	6·504
24·0	9·637	6·785
26·0	10·938	7·102
28·0	12·430	7·460
30·0	13·312	7·831
32·0	13·052	8·175
34·0	12·251	8·460
36·0	11·666	8·684
38·0	11·607	8·869
40·0	12·121	9·047
42·0	13·104	9·243
44·0	14·221	9·462
46·0	14·851	9·692
48·0	14·619	9·911
50·0	13·937	10·101

The parameter $s = 2d^2/\lambda l$. Interpolation using second differences in the range $0 < s < 8$ will be in error by much less than 0·01 dB

dimension a or b, and l is l'_E or l'_H, respectively.* Graphs of R_E and R_H in decibels are shown in Fig. 2 for $0 < s < 8$, a range which suffices for most horns.†

The gain of a pyramidal horn in decibels is

$$G_{dB} = 10{\cdot}084 + 10\log_{10}(ab/\lambda^2) + 10\log_{10} R_E + 10\log_{10} R_H \quad . \quad . \quad . \quad . \quad (10)$$

from which the last, or second-to-last, terms, respectively, are omitted in the case of E and H plane sectoral horns.

* R_E and R^2_E, the near-field gain reduction of a uniform square aperature, have been previousy tabulated[3] as functions of w

† R_E and R_H for $1 < s < 100$ have been presented graphically as the near-field gain reduction of a rectangular aperture[4]

A major advantage of this approach is that the gain-reduction factors have been generalised so that the pyramidal-horn gain can be obtained from two single-line curves; inaccuracies introduced by reading between parametric curves are thereby avoided.

As an example, suppose that the gain of a standard horn[5] with the dimensions $a = 3{\cdot}241\lambda$, $b = 2{\cdot}400\lambda$, $l_H = 4{\cdot}745\lambda$, $l_E = 4{\cdot}215\lambda$ is required. $10\log_{10}(3{\cdot}241 \times 2{\cdot}400) = 8{\cdot}91$ and the gain of the in-phase aperture is 18·99 dB. Also

$$\frac{2a^2}{\lambda l_H} = \frac{2(3{\cdot}241)^2}{4{\cdot}745} = 4{\cdot}43$$

and

$$\frac{2b^2}{\lambda l_E} = \frac{2(2{\cdot}400)^2}{4{\cdot}215} = 2{\cdot}73$$

From Fig. 2, $R_E = -0{\cdot}56$ dB, $R_H = -0{\cdot}45$ dB and the horn gain is $18{\cdot}99 - 1{\cdot}01 = 17{\cdot}98$ dB. As a direct calculation from eqn. 3, 17·99 dB has uncertainty limits of about $\pm 0{\cdot}10$ dB, based on a comparison with measured values;[6] there is negligible error in calculating the gain by this method here.

If the gain of this horn is required at a range

$$r = 2a^2/\lambda = 21{\cdot}008\lambda$$

one uses

$$l'_H = \frac{21{\cdot}008 \times 4{\cdot}745}{21{\cdot}008 + 4{\cdot}745}\lambda = 3{\cdot}871\lambda$$

and

$$l'_E = \frac{21{\cdot}008 \times 4{\cdot}215}{21{\cdot}008 + 4{\cdot}215}\lambda = 3{\cdot}511\lambda$$

in place of l_H and l_E. Then

$$(2a^2)/(\lambda l'_H) = 5{\cdot}43 \qquad (2b^2)/(\lambda l'_E) = 3{\cdot}28$$

and the gain-reduction factors are $R_E = -0{\cdot}83$ dB and $R_H = -0{\cdot}65$ dB. The gain is $18{\cdot}99 - 1{\cdot}48 = 17{\cdot}51$ dB. This 0·47 dB finite-range gain reduction is much greater than the in-phase aperture reduction (0·05 dB) and also substantially more than one-half the reduction (0·53 dB) predicted for transmission between identical horns at this range under the same approximations.[7]

E. V. JULL *11th September 1970*

Radio & Electrical Engineering Division,
National Research Council
Ottawa 7, Ont., Canada

References

1 SCHELKUNOFF, S. A., and FRIIS, H. T.: 'Antennas—theory and practice (Wiley, 1952), p. 526

2 BRAUN, E. H.: 'Gain of electromagnetic horns', *Proc. Inst. Radio Engrs.*, 1953, **41**, pp. 109–115

3 POLK, C.: 'Optical Fresnel-zone gain of a rectangular aperture', *IRE Trans.*, 1956, **AP-4**, pp. 65–69

4 "The microwave engineers' technical and buyers' guide" (Horizon House, 1970), p. 65

5 SLAYTON, W. T.: 'Design and calibration of microwave antenna gain standards'. US Naval Research Laboratory, Washington, Report 4, 1954

6 JULL, E. V.: 'On the behavior of electromagnetic horns' *Proc. Inst. Elect. Electron. Engrs.*, 1968, **56**, pp. 106–108

7 CHU, T. S., and SEMPLAK, R. A.: 'Gain of electromagnetic horns' *Bell Syst. Tech. J.*, 1965, **44**, pp. 527–537

Errors in the Predicted Gain of Pyramidal Horns

EDWARD V. JULL

Abstract—**The concepts of the geometrical theory of diffraction are used to derive the on-axis gain of two-dimensional E plane sectoral horns. Geometrical optics and single (noninteraction) diffraction by the aperture edges yield essentially the Kirchhoff result—a monotonic gain versus wavelength curve. Reflection of diffracted fields from the horn interior and double diffraction at the aperture add an oscillation to this curve which is not significantly altered by further diffraction for moderate to large horns. Including these results approximately in Schelkunoff's equation for the pyramidal horn explains the gain variations observed in microwave gain standards and provides an error estimate in their predicted gain.**

I. Introduction

A SERIES of optimum pyramidal horns, designed and calibrated by Slayton [1], are widely used as microwave gain standards. Slayton reported "small, though definite, periodic wiggles" in his measured gain versus wavelength curves about the monotonic curve predicted by Schelkunoff's gain expression [2]. Later measurements on horns based on Slayton's designs have confirmed these observations [3], [4]. The object here is to account for the gain oscillations, at least qualitatively, by employing the concepts of the geometrical theory of diffraction [5]. An earlier attempt to do this [6] was incomplete.

It is impossible to analyze the pyramidal horn rigorously. Any modal field representation is at once approximate as the adjoining horn walls do not constitute a pair of orthogonal surfaces. This alone may not cause serious error, but if ray diffraction is used, and that appears to be the most promising approach, all but the rays at the center of the aperture are obliquely incident on the edges and, after reflection in the horn, the structure of the diffracted field is exceedingly complex. To avoid this impasse we observe that Schelkunoff's equation accurately represents the monotonic gain component, and that in it the effects of diffraction by the E- and H-plane edges of the horn are separable [2]. In the terminology of the geometrical theory of diffraction, Schelkunoff's expression includes the geometrical optics field of the horn and the singly diffracted fields from the aperture edges. It omits multiple diffraction and diffracted fields reflected from the horn interior. To a first approximation, diffraction by the E- and H-plane edges of the horn can be considered separately. Also, as excitation of the aperture edges parallel to the incident electric field is by rays first diffracted at the horn–waveguide junction, these diffracted fields are weaker than those of the edges parallel to the incident magnetic field. Consequently diffraction by only the latter is considered in detail here.

We are then led to consider the on-axis gain of a two-dimensional E-plane sectoral horn. This simpler structure yields to a ray diffraction analysis; previous studies have successfully predicted the radiation pattern [7] and reflection coefficient [8] of long horns.[1] The analysis reveals double diffraction in the horn produces gain oscillations similar to those observed in pyramidal horns of comparable dimensions. When this double diffraction by the H-plane edges is included in an approximate way in Schelkunoff's gain formula, there is some improvement in agreement with experiment at high frequencies and the gain oscillations are partially accounted for.

II. Far Fields of Magnetic Line Source Near Conducting Half-Plane

By using the exact solution for the far field of a magnetic line source near a conducting half plane, singularities on shadow boundaries occurring in a direct application of the geometrical theory of diffraction are avoided. In Fig. 1(a) the far field at r,θ of the source at r_0,θ_0 in isolation is

$$H_x^{\text{inc}}(r,\theta) = \left(\frac{\pi}{2}\right)^{1/2} \exp\left(-j\frac{\pi}{4}\right) H_0^{(2)}(k\rho)$$
$$\simeq \frac{\exp\{-jk[r - r_0\cos(\theta-\theta_0)]\}}{(kr)^{1/2}}, \qquad k\rho \gg 1 \tag{1}$$

where $k = 2\pi/\lambda$ is the free-space propagation constant. If this source is parallel to the edge of a conducting half-plane, there is a reflected far field in $0 < \theta < \pi - \theta_0$ given by (1) with $\theta + \theta_0$ replacing $\theta - \theta_0$, and in $0 < \theta < 2\pi$ a diffracted far field

$$H_x^{\text{diff}}(r,\theta) = \frac{\exp(-jkr)}{(kr)^{1/2}} f(r_0,\theta,\theta_0) \tag{2}$$

where

$$f(r_0,\theta,\theta_0) = v(r_0,\theta-\theta_0) + v(r_0,\theta+\theta_0) \tag{3}$$

[1] Gain calculations of conical horns by the geometrical theory of diffraction have also been described [9], but because the axis is a caustic of the diffracted rays of a circular aperture, it is impossible to calculate the on-axis gain from the expressions given. The numerical results which were presented seem to be identical with values obtained much earlier [10] by the Kirchhoff method.

Manuscript received May 16, 1972; revised August 14, 1972.
The author was with the Radio and Electrical Engineering Division, National Research Council of Canada, Ottawa, Ont., Canada. He is now with the Department of Electrical Engineering, University of British Columbia, Vancouver 8, B.C., Canada.

Reprinted from *IEEE Trans. Antennas Propagat.*, vol. AP-21, pp. 25–31, Jan. 1973.

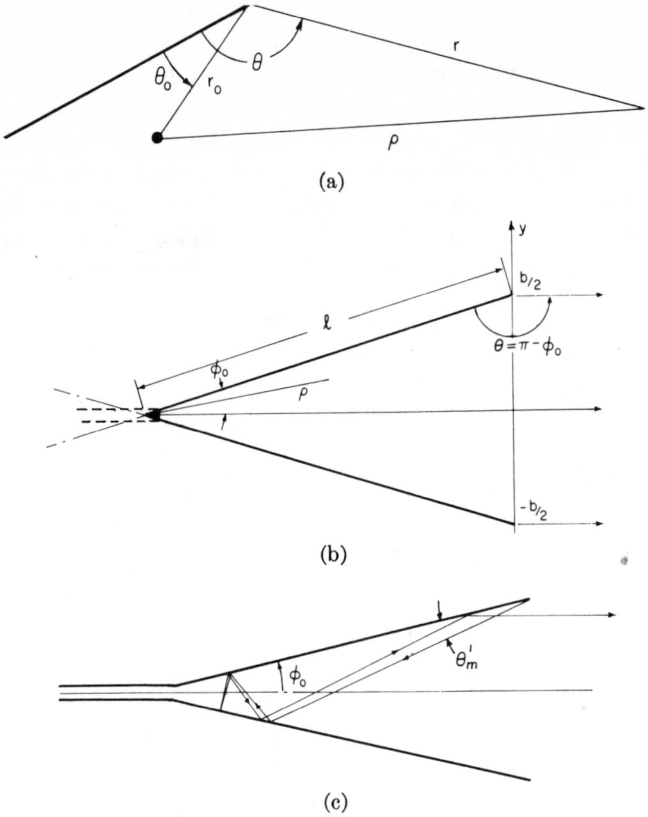

Fig. 1. (a) Coordinates for magnetic line source near a conducting half-plane. (b) Two-dimensional E-plane sectoral horn formed by conducting sector with magnetic line source at apex. Ray paths of on-axis geometrical optics and noninteraction aperture diffracted fields are shown. (c) Ray path of upper edge diffracted fields reflected in forward direction from horn interior.

with

$$v(r_0,\alpha) = -\frac{\exp(jkr_0\cos\alpha + j\pi/4)}{\sqrt{\pi}} \cdot \int_{(2kr_0)^{1/2}\cos\alpha/2}^{\infty} \exp(-j\tau^2)\,d\tau$$

$$= -\frac{\exp(jkr_0\cos\alpha)}{2}\left\{1-(1+j)\cdot\left[C\left(\left(\frac{4kr_0}{\pi}\right)^{1/2}\cos\frac{\alpha}{2}\right) - jS\left(\left(\frac{4kr_0}{\pi}\right)^{1/2}\cos\frac{\alpha}{2}\right)\right]\right\} \tag{4}$$

and

$$C(u) - jS(u) = \int_0^u \exp\left(-j\frac{\pi}{2}t^2\right) dt. \tag{5}$$

When this line source is on the conducting half-plane at $r_0 = l$ from the edge, the source field

$$H_x^{i}(r,\theta) = \frac{\exp[-jk(r - l\cos\theta)]}{(kr)^{1/2}} \tag{6}$$

produces a diffracted field

$$H_x^{d}(r,\theta) = \frac{\exp(-jkr)}{(kr)^{1/2}}\,v(l,\theta). \tag{7}$$

III. On-Axis Fields of Two-Dimensional Sectoral Horn

A. Noninteraction Fields

A simple model of a two-dimensional E-plane sectoral horn is a magnetic line source at the apex of a sector of finite length l, formed by two half-planes intersecting at an angle $2\phi_0$, as in Fig. 1(b). In addition to the source field of (6) and the diffracted field of the upper edge (7), there is a diffracted field from the lower edge identical in the forward direction $\theta = \pi - \phi_0$ because all fields are symmetrical about the horn axis. Neglecting interaction between the edges and walls of the horn, the on-axis far field is

$$H_1 = H_x^{i}(r,\pi-\phi_0) + 2H_x^{d}(r,\pi-\phi_0)$$

$$= \frac{\exp(-jkr)}{(kr)^{1/2}}\left[\exp(-jkl\cos\phi_0) + 2v(l,\pi-\phi_0)\right] \tag{8}$$

$$= \left(\frac{2}{kr}\right)^{1/2}\exp\left[-jk(r + l\cos\phi_0) + j\frac{\pi}{4}\right] \cdot [C(w) - jS(w)] \tag{9}$$

where

$$w = \frac{b}{(2\lambda l)^{1/2}\cos\phi_0/2}. \tag{10}$$

To compare (9) with the Kirchhoff result, the asymptotic form of (1), $(k\rho)^{-1/2}\exp(-jk\rho)$, $k\rho \gg 1$, is used with $\rho = (l^2\cos^2\phi_0 + y^2)^{1/2} \approx l\cos\phi_0 + y^2/(2l\cos\phi_0)$ for $y \ll l\cos\phi_0$, in

$$H_1 = \frac{\exp[-j(kr + \pi/4)]}{(r\lambda)^{1/2}}\int_{-b/2}^{b/2} H_x^{i}(y,0)\,dy$$

yielding, without further approximation, (9) with $w = b/(2\lambda l\cos\phi_0)^{1/2}$. For small ϕ_0 the two results are essentially the same, so the Kirchhoff solution contains geometrical optics and noninteraction singly diffracted fields of the aperture edges. Whereas with the Kirchhoff method, further improvement is not possible, the concepts of geometrical diffraction theory [5] may now be used to include interaction between the edges and walls of the horn.

B. Reflections from Horn Interior

The most significant interaction will arise from singly diffracted fields which reenter the horn and are reflected in the forward direction, as shown in Fig. 1(c). The path of edge diffracted rays reflected from the horn interior may be traced by locating the positions of the edge images. This was done by Yu *et al.* [7], who also determined the angular regions in which these image sources contribute. Each edge has m images, where m is the largest integer less than $\pi/(2\phi_0)$. The mth image source contributes to the on-axis far fields if $\theta_m' = \pi - (2m+1)\phi_0$ is positive. It can be shown from the geometry of Fig. 1(c) that this must be the direction for singly diffracted rays from the edge which proceed in the forward direction after m reflections in the horn interior. The distance along this ray path from the edge to the aperture plane is

$$s_m = 2l \sin \phi_0 \sum_{i=1}^{m} \sin (2i\phi_0).$$

Adding $2H_x^d(r + s_m, \theta_m')$ to (8), the on-axis far field becomes

$$H_1 = \frac{\exp(-jkr)}{(kr)^{1/2}} \{\exp(-jkl \cos \phi_0) + 2v(l, \pi - \phi_0) + 2 \exp(-jks_m) v[l, \pi - (2m+1)\phi_0]\}. \quad (11)$$

This reflection can occur for all orders of diffracted field, as discussed in the next section.

C. Multiple Diffraction

Doubly diffracted fields are produced by singly diffracted rays from the aperture edges which proceed in the directions $\theta_i = \pi/2 - i\phi_0$, $i = 1,2,\cdots,m$. For $i = 1$ these rays traverse the aperture and are doubly diffracted at the opposite edge, (see [8, fig. 6], where $i = n + 1$). For $i > 1$ the rays are reflected $i - 1$ times in the horn interior before being diffracted again at the same (i even) or opposite (i odd) edge. The ray-path length between single and double diffraction is $d_i = 2l \sin(i\phi_0)$ and the angle of incidence for double diffraction is θ_i. Assume the edges are now isotropic magnetic-line sources $H_x^d(r, \theta_i)$, defined by (7). Since the on-axis fields of the two edges are equal, their doubly diffracted fields in the $\theta = \pi - \phi_0$ direction are

$$H_2 = \frac{2 \exp(-jkr)}{(kr)^{1/2}} S_2 \quad (12)$$

where

$$S_2 = \sum_{i=1}^{m} v\left(l, \frac{\pi}{2} - i\phi_0\right) f\left(d_i, \pi - \phi_0, \frac{\pi}{2} - i\phi_0\right). \quad (13)$$

Double diffraction at the horn waveguide junction is not included here because its contribution to the on-axis field is very small, as discussed in Appendix I.

Doubly diffracted fields reflected from the interior of the horn without interruption into the forward direction under the conditions of Section III-B may be accounted for by adding to (13)

$$S_2^r = \exp(-jks_m) \sum_{i=1}^{m} v\left(l, \frac{\pi}{2} - i\phi_0\right) \cdot f\left(d_i, \pi - (2m+1)\phi_0, \frac{\pi}{2} - i\phi_0\right). \quad (14)$$

Triply diffracted fields are produced by doubly diffracted fields from the aperture edges which proceed in the directions θ_i. Again the ray-path length between double and triple diffraction is d_i and for triple diffraction the angle of incidence is θ_i and angle of diffraction $\pi - \phi_0$ for the on-axis far fields. The triply diffracted fields of the two edges in the forward direction may be written

$$H_3 = \frac{2 \exp(-jkr)}{(kr)^{1/2}} S_3 \quad (15)$$

where

$$S_3 = \sum_{i=1}^{m} v\left(l, \frac{\pi}{2} - i\phi_0\right) \sum_{j=1}^{m} f\left(d_i, \frac{\pi}{2} - j\phi_0, \frac{\pi}{2} - i\phi_0\right) \cdot f\left(d_j, \pi - \phi_0, \frac{\pi}{2} - j\phi_0\right). \quad (16)$$

To include triply diffracted fields reflected in the forward direction, when they occur,

$$S_3^r = \exp(-jks_m) \sum_{i=1}^{m} v\left(l, \frac{\pi}{2} - i\phi_0\right) \cdot \sum_{j=1}^{m} f\left(d_i, \frac{\pi}{2} - j\phi_0, \frac{\pi}{2} - i\phi_0\right) \cdot f\left(d_j, \pi - (2m+1)\phi_0, \frac{\pi}{2} - j\phi_0\right) \quad (17)$$

is added to (16).

Since $v(l,\alpha) \simeq 0\{[kl(1 + \cos\alpha)]^{-1/2}\}$, $kl(1 + \cos\alpha) \gg 1$, higher order diffracted fields will be successively smaller. The numerical results which follow indicate that single and double diffraction suffices for most horns.

IV. Gain of Two-Dimensional Horn

The ϕ component of incident electric field in the horn is

$$E_\phi^i = -\frac{1}{j\omega\epsilon_0} \frac{\partial H_x^i}{\partial \rho} = \frac{k}{\omega\epsilon_0} \left(\frac{\pi}{2}\right)^{1/2} \exp\left(-j\frac{3\pi}{4}\right) H_1^{(2)}(k\rho).$$

Power in the incident mode is obtained by integrating $\frac{1}{2}\,\mathrm{Re}\,(\bar{E}^i \times \bar{H}^{i*} \cdot \hat{\rho})$, where the asterisk denotes complex conjugate over a surface $\rho_0 < \rho < l$ in the horn. The incident power per unit length in the x direction of the horn is

$$P^i = \frac{1}{2} \mathrm{Re} \int_{-\phi_0}^{\phi_0} E_\phi^i H_x^{i*} \rho \, d\phi = \frac{\pi k \phi_0 \rho}{2\omega\epsilon_0} \mathrm{Re}\,\{-jH_1^{(2)}(k\rho) H_0^{(2)}(k\rho)\} = \frac{\phi_0}{\omega\epsilon_0}. \quad (18)$$

The on-axis gain per unit length in the x direction may be written

$$G = \frac{1}{2}\left(\frac{\mu_0}{\epsilon_0}\right)^{1/2} | H_x(r, \pi - \phi_0) |^2 \frac{2\pi r}{P^i} \quad (19)$$

where $H_x(r,\pi - \phi_0)$ is the sum of on-axis geometrical optics and all diffracted fields. This gain is $(1 - |\Gamma|^2)$ times the directivity, where Γ is the reflection coefficient of the aperture (see [8, eq. (18)]). If (9) and (18) are used in (19), the on-axis gain for single diffraction at the aperture is

$$G = \frac{2\pi}{\phi_0} [C^2(w) + S^2(w)] \tag{20}$$

where w is defined by (10). For small flare angles $\phi_0 \approx b/(2l)$, and (20) becomes

$$G = kbR_E \tag{21}$$

where

$$R_E = \frac{C^2(w) + S^2(w)}{w^2} \tag{22}$$

has been tabulated [11]. For long horns, as $l \to \infty$, $R_E \to 1$ and the gain of the resulting open-ended parallel-plate waveguide with a TEM mode incident is kb, which is exact [12]. Hence (21), which is also the Kirchhoff result, is an accurate approximation for long horns with small flare angles. However, if the conditions of Section III-B apply and singly diffracted fields are reflected in the forward direction from the horn interior, (11) rather than (9) in (19) gives for the on-axis gain

$$G = \frac{\pi}{\phi_0} | \exp(-jkl \cos \phi_0) + 2v(l,\pi - \phi_0) + 2v[l,\pi - (2m+1)\phi_0] |^2. \tag{23}$$

Double diffraction in most horns may be accounted for by including (12) with (8) in (19). Then the gain is

$$G = \frac{\pi}{\phi_0} | \exp(-jkl \cos \phi_0) + 2v(l,\pi - \phi_0) + 2S_2 |^2 \tag{24}$$

where S_2 is given by (13). If reflection in the forward direction can occur, $2(S_2 + S_2^r)$ are added within the absolute value bars of (23).

Triple diffraction within the horn is included by adding (15) to the on-axis fields and the gain is

$$G = \frac{\pi}{\phi_0} | \exp(-jkl \cos \phi_0) + 2v(l,\pi - \phi_0) + 2(S_2 + S_3) |^2 \tag{25}$$

where $v(l,\pi - \phi_0)$, S_2, and S_3 are defined by (4), (13), and (16), respectively. Triple diffraction with reflections in the forward direction is given by (23) with $2(S_2 + S_2^r + S_3 + S_3^r)$ within the absolute value bars.

In Fig. 2 the gain per unit length of a two-dimensional E-plane sectoral horn with a total flare angle $2\phi_0 = 32°$ and aperture $b = 24$ cm is shown. The monotonic curve, based on (20), includes geometrical optics and singly diffracted fields from the aperture and is essentially the Kirchhoff result. The solid oscillating curve, based on (24), includes double diffraction in the horn. Because the total doubly diffracted field consists of five components with progressively different amplitude and phase the gain oscillation varies cyclically in amplitude. Its period is slightly less than $2l/\lambda$. If triply diffracted fields are included by using (25), the dashed oscillating curve in Fig. 2 is obtained. Except at longer wavelengths, triple diffraction has little effect on the pattern of gain vs wavelength oscillation of this horn and higher order diffraction will have still less effect. Similar numerical results were obtained for a horn of different dimensions. Hence, for most horns, double diffraction suffices to account for the gain variations. To compare with gain variations observed in three-dimensional horns several assumptions must be made. These are discussed in the next section.

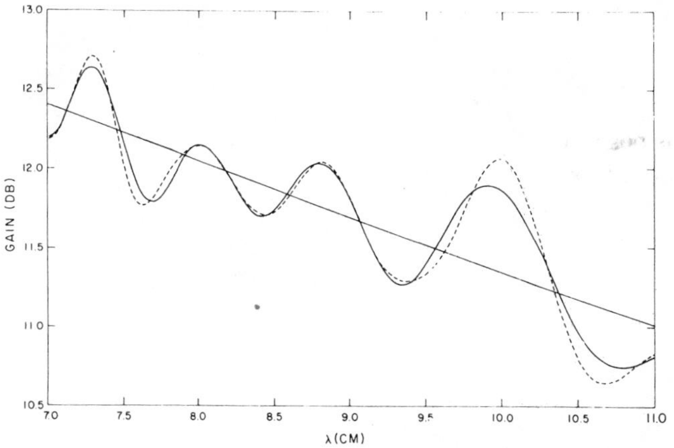

Fig. 2. On-axis gain per unit length of two-dimensional E-plane sectoral horn with $\phi_0 = 16°$, $l = 42.15$ cm, $b = 24.00$ cm, and $b' = 3.40$ cm. Noninteraction gain (20) is nearly linear here. Solid oscillating curve is (24) and dashed oscillation (25).

V. Pyramidal Horn Gain

Schelkunoff's equation for the on-axis gain of a pyramidal horn, based on Kirchhoff diffraction theory, may be written as

$$G = \frac{32ab}{\pi\lambda^2} R_E R_H \tag{26}$$

where $32ab/(\pi\lambda^2)$ is the gain of an in-phase field distribution uniform across one dimension of a rectangular aperture and cosinusoidal across the other (see Fig. 3). The E-plane flare R_E, defined by (22), with

$$w = \frac{b}{(2\lambda l_E)^{1/2}} \tag{27}$$

accounts for the phase variation in the aperture field due to the E-plane flare of the horn. The H-plane flare of the horn is represented by

$$R_H = \frac{\pi^2}{4} \frac{\{C(u) - C(v)\}^2 + \{S(u) - S(v)\}^2}{(u - v)^2} \tag{28}$$

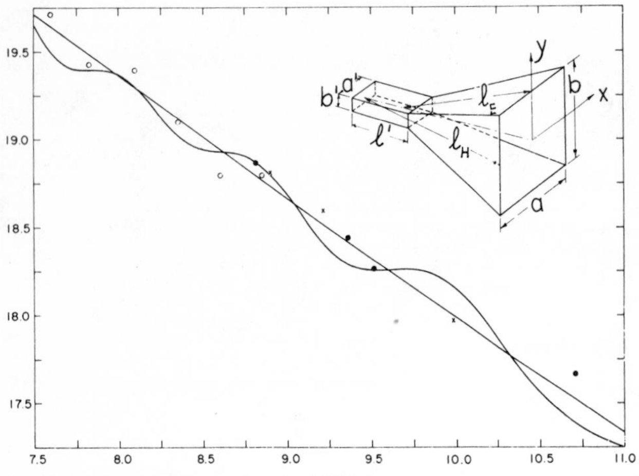

Fig. 3. Gain of 10-cm band pyramidal horn. $a = 32.41$ cm, $a' = 7.21$ cm, $b = 24.00$ cm, $b' = 3.40$ cm, $l_E = 42.15$ cm, $l_H = 47.45$ cm, $l' = 17.78$ cm. From [1]: × measured, ○ scaled. From [4]: ● measured. Monotonic curve: from (26). Oscillating curve: (26) with (30).

where the Fresnel integrals, defined by (5), have the arguments

$$\left.\begin{matrix} u \\ \\ v \end{matrix}\right\} = \pm \frac{a}{(2\lambda l_H)^{1/2}} + \frac{1}{a}\left(\frac{\lambda l_H}{2}\right)^{1/2}. \qquad (29)$$

Both R_E and R_H have been tabulated [11].

These expressions include a reliable approximation to the geometrical optics field and the singly diffracted fields of the aperture edges not reflected from the horn interior. R_E contains singly diffracted fields of the edges parallel to the incident magnetic field (H-polarized fields) and R_H the corresponding diffracted fields from the edges parallel to the incident electric field (E-polarized fields). With interaction between the edges and walls of the horn E- and H-polarized fields are inseparable, but a simple revision of these expressions based on physical considerations may be made. For the H-polarized fields the edge-wall interaction which affects the on-axis fields must occur primarily in that portion of the horn produced by flaring the waveguide in the E plane only, because of Fermat's principle for diffracted rays [5]. Only those fields from the waveguide normally or nearly normally incident upon the aperture edges will be diffracted in directions permitting reflection or double diffraction into the forward direction. Diffracted ray paths of the obliquely incident rays will lie on a cone with the edge as axis and very little of these fields will ultimately contribute to the on-axis radiation intensity. If all relevant reflection and double diffraction of the H-polarized horn fields is assumed to occur only in the region $|x| < a/2$ of Fig. 3, then these fields must be multiplied by

$$\frac{\pi}{2a}\int_{-a'/2}^{a'/2} \cos\left(\frac{\pi x}{a}\right) dx = \sin\left(\frac{\pi a'}{2a}\right) \approx \frac{\pi a'}{2a}.$$

Comparing (21) with (24) and taking into account the preceding considerations, a revised factor R_E to be used in (26) is

$$R_E = \frac{1 + \cos\phi_0}{4w^2} \cdot \left| \exp(-jkl\cos\phi_0) + 2v(l,\pi - \phi_0) + \frac{\pi a'}{a} S_2 \right|^2 \qquad (30)$$

in which $(1 + \cos\phi_0)/2$ appears from using (10) with $l = l_E$ for w, rather than (27). The final term in (30) accounts for double diffraction of the H-polarized fields. If diffracted fields are reflected in the forward direction then

$$R_E = \frac{1 + \cos\phi_0}{4w^2} \left| \exp(-jkl\cos\phi_0) + 2v(l,\pi - \phi_0) + \frac{\pi a'}{a}\left[v(l,\pi - (2m+1)\phi_0) + S_2 + S_2^r\right] \right|^2 \qquad (31)$$

is used where $v(l,\alpha)$, S_2, and S_2^r are defined by (4), (13), and (14), respectively.

Diffracted fields of the aperture edges parallel to the incident electric field (E-polarized fields) are initially diffracted at the horn-waveguide junction and consequently are weaker than the corresponding H-polarized fields. At the level of approximation considered here, reflection and double diffraction of these fields may be omitted. A pyramidal horn gain expression containing first-order edge-wall interaction of only the H-polarized fields is (26) with R_H defined by (28) and R_E by (30) or (31).

VI. Experimental and Numerical Results

The preceding expressions were used to calculate the gain of three of Slayton's horns [1]. Other horns in this series are scale models of these examples. Slayton presented experimental results for his horns and other results have since been reported [3], [4]. The measured gain values of Figs. 3–5 are for matched horns, whereas the calculated values include dominant mode mismatch at the aperture, but the reflection coefficients in Appendix II indicate this factor is negligibly small here. Equation (26) with (30) is represented by the oscillating curve for the 10 cm band horn of Fig. 3, while Schelkunoff's expression, (26) with (22), yields the curve which decreases monotonically with wavelength. This horn has the same E-plane dimensions as in Fig. 2 and the gain oscillation produced by doubly diffracted H-polarized fields in the horn is contained in (30). It does not accurately coincide with the observed gain oscillations for this horn, even allowing for experimental error in the measurements. The causes of this discrepancy are discussed later, but at least

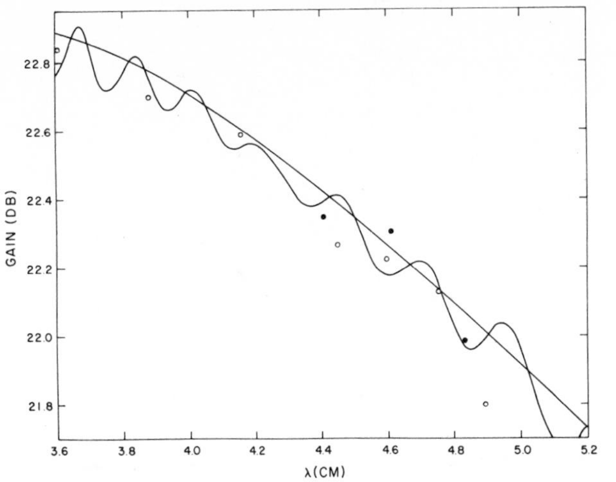

Fig. 4. Gain of 4.75-cm band pyramidal horn. $a = 28.85$ cm, $a' = 3.49$ cm, $b = 21.37$ cm, $b' = 1.58$ cm, $l_E = 47.50$ cm, $l_H = 50.84$ cm, $l' = 8.90$ cm. ○ from [1], ● from [4]. Monotonic curve: from (26). Oscillating curve: (26) with (31).

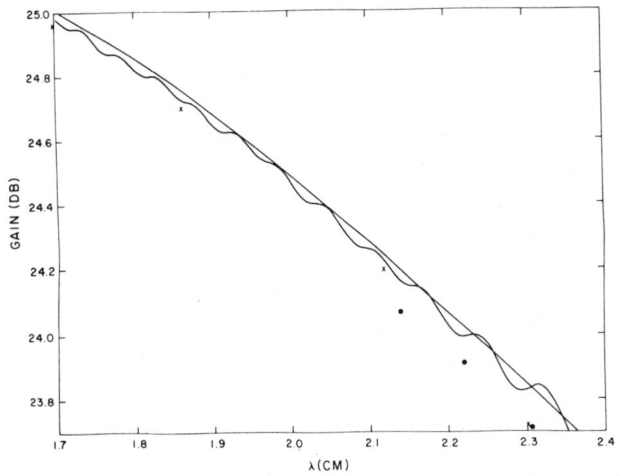

Fig. 5. Gain of a 1.80-cm band pyramidal horn. $a = 15.20$ cm, $a' = 1.58$ cm, $b = 12.47$ cm, $b' = 0.79$ cm, $l_E = 34.63$ cm, $l_H = 36.41$ cm, $l' = 7.62$. Measured values: × from [1], ● from [4]. Monotonic curve: from (26). Oscillating curve: (26) with (30).

an approximation to the gain oscillation appears to have been achieved.

Better agreement should appear at higher frequencies and this seems to be evident for the 4.75 cm band horn of Fig. 4. Here the conditions of section 3.2 apply and R_E defined by (31) has been used in (26). The singly diffracted fields reflected from the horn interior alone can produce a gain variation of about ± 0.06 dB at $\lambda = 4.4$ cm and are responsible for most of the observed gain oscillation, which is of larger magnitude than would otherwise be expected for a horn with this gain.

Gain oscillations are small for high gain horns [13] and the 1.8 cm band horn results in Fig. 5 clearly illustrate this reduction in oscillation. While many doubly diffracted fields contribute here ($m = 8$ in (30)), they are weak in high gain horns and, as reflection in the forward direction does not occur, the oscillation in gain is small. In this example ohmic losses in the waveguide feed and horn amount to about 0.03 dB at $\lambda = 2.0$ cm, according to the calculation in Appendix II, and this accounts in part for the discrepancy in Fig. 5. Ohmic losses amount to about 0.01 dB and 0.02 dB in the horns of Figs. 3 and 4, respectively.

VII. Conclusions and Discussion

In a two-dimensional E-plane sectoral horn singly diffracted fields of the aperture edges subsequently reflected from the interior and doubly diffracted produce oscillations in the on-axis gain versus wavelength curve. Higher order multiply diffracted and reflected fields have little effect on the gain of most horns. While the analysis is sufficiently complete and accurate for this two-dimensional horn, rather arbitrary assumptions are required to apply it to the pyramidal horn. The resulting expression predicts only approximately the amplitude, period and phase of oscillations observed in the gain versus wavelength curves of pyramidal horns.

Some improvement may be made through a similar analysis of the two-dimensional H-plane sectoral horn, leading to a revised R_H in (26), but it is probably more important to account for the differing propagation constants of modes reflected from the horn interior. This affects the period and phase of the varying gain component, especially at longer wavelengths, where the largest discrepancies with experiment appear. The estimate of the region of relevant edge-wall interaction, which affects the amplitude of the predicted gain oscillations, may also be adjusted, but it will not be easy to properly account for coupling between the E- and H-polarized fields at the aperture.

Clearly an accurate quantitative description of these gain variations in pyramidal horns is difficult, if not impossible, to achieve. A new design of antenna gain standard for microwave frequencies is perhaps a more practical objective. In the meantime, errors in the predicted gain of pyramidal horns may be reduced by ensuring, in their design, that diffracted fields from the aperture are not reflected in the forward direction. Equation (26) with (30) or (31) accounts approximately for the gain variations, providing an estimate of their magnitude for a particular horn and, at the higher frequencies for some horns, a more accurate value of the gain.

Appendix I

Diffraction at Horn-Waveguide Junction

A crude approximation to the horn-waveguide junction is the closed apex of a conducting wedge. This was used by Yu *et al.* [7], and may be adequate for pattern calculations, although their expression for the diffracted field is of doubtful validity for these wedge angles [7, eq. (1)]. These diffracted fields were omitted from their numerical calculations.

The tangential magnetic and electric dominant mode fields excited near the junction by singly diffracted fields from the aperture may be written

$$H_x = \alpha H_0^{(1)}(k\rho) + \beta H_0^{(2)}(k\rho) \tag{32}$$

$$E_\phi = \frac{-jk}{\omega\epsilon_0}\left[\alpha H_1^{(1)}(k\rho) + \beta H_1^{(2)}(k\rho)\right] \tag{33}$$

where

$$\alpha = \left(\frac{\pi}{2}\right)^{1/2} \frac{\exp\left[-j(2kl - 3\pi/4)\right]}{4\phi_0 kl} \tag{34}$$

is the dominant mode amplitude of singly diffracted fields excited at the aperture by (6), [8, eq. (13)]. β is the dominant mode amplitude of the fields diffracted at $\rho = \rho_0$, the horn-waveguide junction. Equating (32) and (33) there to the dominant (TEM) mode field produced in the waveguide gives

$$\beta = -\alpha \frac{H_1^{(1)}(k\rho_0) + jH_0^{(1)}(k\rho_0)}{H_1^{(2)}(k\rho_0) + jH_0^{(2)}(k\rho_0)}, \tag{35}$$

if ϕ_0 is not large. If $kl \gg 1$, α is small and $\beta \ll 1$. No significant change was observed in the numerical results of Fig. 2 when the on-axis field was multiplied by $1 + \beta$ and the incident power by $1 + 2\,\mathrm{Re}\,(\beta)$. Almost all the dominant mode field excited by aperture diffraction enters the waveguide. Higher order modes are nonpropagating in the waveguide and the junction region of the horn.

Appendix II

Reflection Coefficients and Ohmic Losses in Horns

The results of standing-wave measurements on the horns of Figs. 3–5 are shown in Fig. 6. These reflection coefficients consist of a component of about 0.012, 0.04, and 0.055, respectively, from the horn-waveguide junction and a component of about 0.01, 0.015, and 0.03, respectively, from the aperture. Minima in the reflection coefficient almost coincide with minima in the gain curve for the 10-cm band horns, but this is not apparent for the others. Fig. 6 shows that mismatch of the dominant mode in these horns cannot under any circumstances produce gain oscillations of magnitude comparable to that observed and that the aperture reflection coefficient has little effect on the gain. The largest gain reduction, about 0.01 dB, occurs for the 10-cm band horn.

Dominant (TE_{10}) mode ohmic loss in a rectangular brass waveguide of broad dimension a and a narrow dimension b is

$$\frac{2 \times 10^{-4}}{b[\lambda(1 - (\lambda/2a)^2]^{1/2}}\left[1 + \frac{2b}{a}\left(\frac{\lambda}{2a}\right)^2\right] \quad \mathrm{dB/m}. \tag{36}$$

Applying (36) at several cross-sections along the horn axis and integrating the resulting attenuation curve provides a simple calculation of ohmic loss. As attenuation falls rapidly beyond the horn-waveguide junction, errors in this approximation are unimportant. At $\lambda = 2.0$ cm the total attenuation in the horn of Fig. 5, including its waveguide feed, is 0.03 dB by this calculation, with a variation over the wavelength range shown of less than 0.01 dB. Attenuation in the 12.7-cm tuner attached to

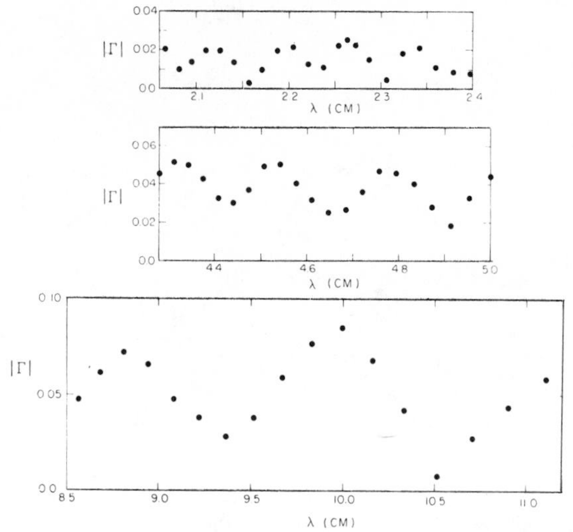

Fig. 6. Measured reflection coefficients of 1.8, 4.75, and 10-cm band horns.

the horn in calibration, also about 0.03 dB, was added to the measured values [4] which appear in Fig. 5. A similar calculation yields 0.02 dB for attenuation in the horn of Fig. 4 and the 21-cm tuner used in its calibration was accounted for by adding 0.02 dB to the measured values [4]. In Fig. 3 calculated ohmic losses in both horn and tuner amounted to only about 0.01 dB and no adjustment was made.

Acknowledgment

The author thanks Dr. A. L. VanKoughnett and Dr. G. C. McCormick for helpful discussions. B. Clark and Mrs. M. Steen assisted with the experimental and numerical results.

References

[1] W. T. Slayton, "Design and calibration of microwave antenna gain standards," U. S. Naval Res. Lab., Washington, D. C., Rep. 4433, Nov. 1954.
[2] S. A. Schelkunoff, *Electromagnetic Waves*. New York: Van Nostrand Rheinhold, 1943, pp. 360–364.
[3] R. R. Bowman, "Absolute gain measurements for horn antennas," Nat. Bur. Stand., Boulder, Colo., Tech. Rep. RADC-TR-68-349, p. 48, Nov. 1968.
[4] E. V. Jull, "On the behavior of electromagnetic horns," *Proc. IEEE* (Lett.), vol. 56, pp. 106–108, Jan. 1968.
[5] J. B. Keller, "Geometrical theory of diffraction," *J. Opt. Soc. Amer.*, vol. 52, pp. 116–130, 1962.
[6] E. V. Jull, "A revision of Schelkunoff's expression for the gain of a pyramidal horn," *Abstract G-AP Int. Symp.*, Austin, Tex., p. 286, Dec. 1969.
[7] J. S. Yu, R. C. Rudduck, and L. Peters, Jr., "Comprehensive analysis for *E*-plane of horn antennas by edge diffraction theory," *IEEE Trans. Antennas Propagat.*, vol. AP-14, pp. 138–149, Mar. 1966.
[8] E. V. Jull, "Reflection from the aperture of a long *E*-plane sectoral horn," *IEEE Trans. Antennas Propagat.*, vol. AP-20, pp. 62–68, Jan. 1972.
[9] M. A. K. Hamid, "Diffraction by a conical horn," *IEEE Trans. Antennas Propagat.*, vol. AP-16, pp. 520–528, Sept. 1968.
[10] G. C. Southworth, *Principles and Applications of Waveguide Transmission*. New York: Van Nostrand Rheinhold, 1950, p. 417.
[11] E. V. Jull, "Finite range gain of sectoral and pyramidal horns," *Electron. Lett.*, vol. 6, pp. 680–681, 1970.
[12] L. A. Wainstein, *The Theory of Diffraction and the Factorization Method*. Boulder, Colo.: Golem Press, 1969, p. 44.
[13] G. T. Wrixon and W. J. Welch, "Gain measurements of standard electromagnetic horns in the *K* and *Ka* bands," *IEEE Trans. Antennas Propagat.*, vol. AP-20, pp. 136–142, Mar. 1972.

Part IV
Simple Horn Feeds

A useful octave bandwidth feed for a paraboloidal reflector is described by Shimizu in the first paper. It employs a quadruply ridged horn and, in a reflector of focal ratio 0.42, it yields essentially constant and equal *E*- and *H*-plane beamwidths over an octave frequency range. This is followed by two papers dealing with the optimization of simple feed horns in parabolic reflectors. Herbison-Evans gives useful design graphs for round, square, and rectangular feed horns, while Rudge and Withers present a rather comprehensive analysis of the requirements for feeding reflectors, along with a tabulated horn design procedure. For further information on this topic, the reader should consult an early paper by Berkowitz [1] and one by Rudge [2].

A short paper by Ewell describes the use of dielectric slab transducers for transforming a fixed linear polarization into various states of linear and circular polarization at the feed horn aperture. Simultaneous dual polarization is possible with this technique (see Wong [3]). In the fifth paper, Wohlleben *et al.* describes a circular aperture horn feed that yields high aperture efficiency in reflectors of small focal ratio (i.e., < 0.35).

In the last paper of this section, Truman and Balanis present data for the design of optimum primary feed horns for reflectors. Their method is based on the analysis given by Rudge and Withers in the third paper in this part.

References

[1] B. Berkowitz, "Antennas fed by horns," *Proc. IRE*, vol. 41, pp. 1761–1765, Dec. 1953.

[2] A. W. Rudge, "Focal-plane field distribution of parabolic reflectors," *Electron. Lett.*, vol. 5, pp. 510–512, Oct. 16, 1969.

[3] J. Y. Wong, "A dual polarization feed horn for a parabolic reflector," *Microwave J.*, vol. 5, pp. 188–191, Sept. 1962.

Octave-Bandwidth Feed Horn for Paraboloid*

This note describes a broadband feed horn[1] which, when mounted at the focal point of a parabolic dish, yields equal E- and H-plane radiation patterns. The aperture of the feed horn (Fig. 1) is circular in cross section and operates on the fundamental TE_{11}-waveguide mode. Single-mode operation of the TE_{11} over a wide frequency range was obtained by quadruple-ridge loading of the circular waveguide feeding the horn.

An antenna consisting of a horn mounted at the focal point of a parabolic dish of $f/D = 0.42$ was constructed to check the radiation patterns of the complete antenna. The results of these tests showed that the E- and H-plane patterns taken at the frequencies of 15.1 and 30.2 kMc have identical half-power beamwidths of 1.2 degrees with the principal-plane sidelobes at least -23 db down from the main beam. The antenna, consisting of the feed horn mounted at the focal point of the parabolic dish, is shown in Fig. 2.

The secondary radiation patterns of the antenna were measured on a 1100-foot antenna range at the frequencies of 15.1 and 30.2 kMc, and are shown in Fig. 3. It can be seen from these patterns that, at both frequencies, the E- and H-plane patterns have

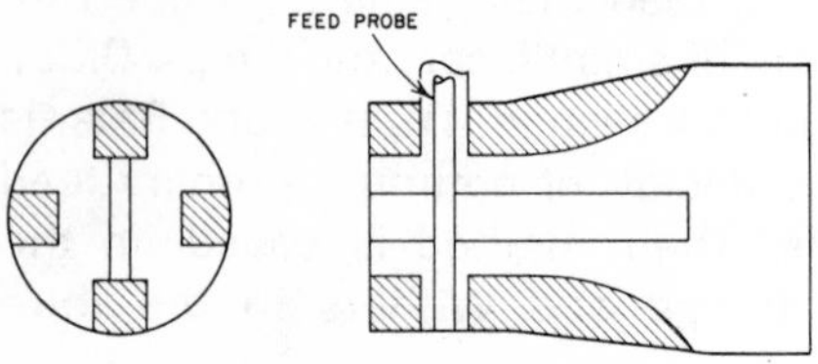

Fig. 1—Schematic diagram of the quadruply-ridged circular-waveguide antenna feed horn.

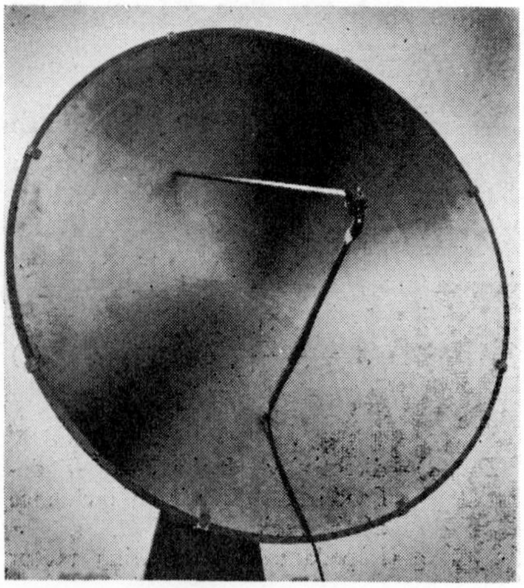

Fig. 2—Photograph of the parabolic antenna.

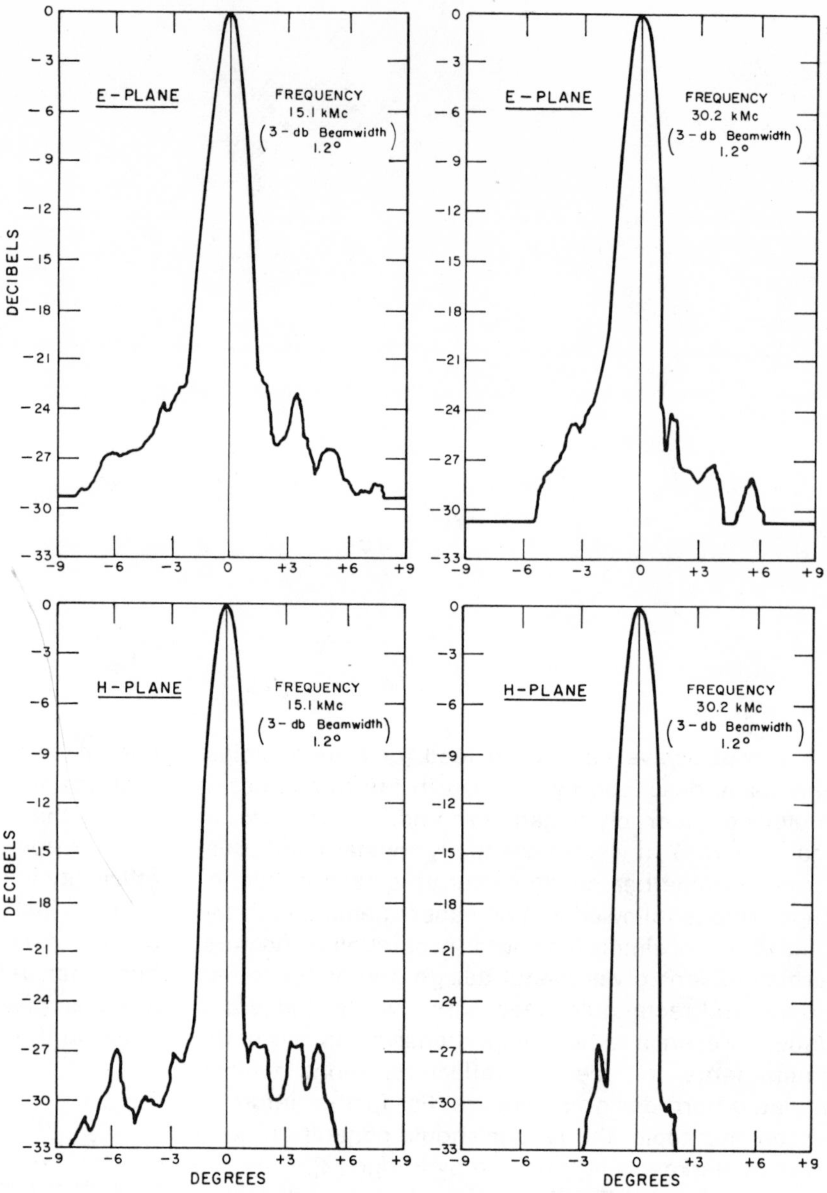

Fig. 3—E- and H-plane radiation patterns of the parabolic antenna.

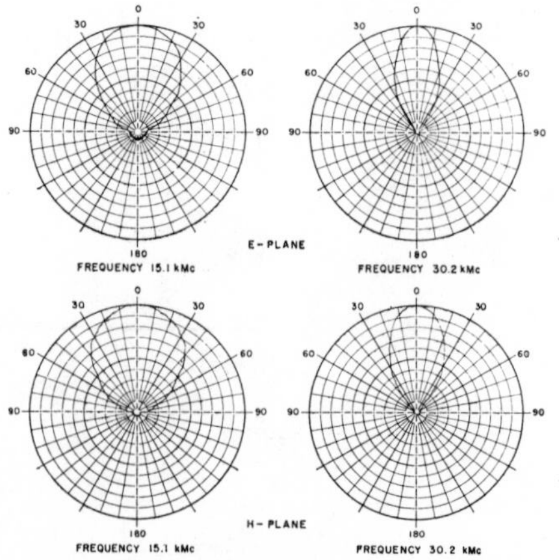

Fig. 4—E- and H-plane amplitude radiation patterns of the feed horn.

* Received by the PGAP, October 27, 1960.

[1] J. K. Shimizu, "Overseas Auroral Propagation Experiments," Final Rept., pt. 2, Stanford Res. Inst., Menlo Park, Calif., Contract AF30(602)-1871, SRI Project 2604; March 19, 1960.

Reprinted from *IRE Trans. Antennas Propagat.*, vol. AP-9, pp. 223–224, Mar. 1961.

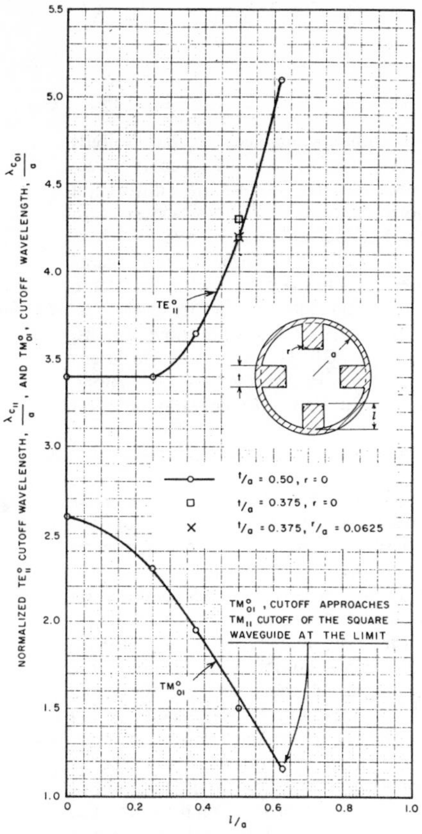

Fig. 5—Normalized quadruply-ridged circular waveguide TE_{11} and TM_{01}—cut-off wavelength (t/a=0.50).

equal half-power beamwidths of 1.2 degrees with all the sidelobes at least −23 db down from the main beam. These radiation patterns were produced with a quadruply-ridged primary feed horn having a cylindrical aperture 0.587 inch in diameter. This aperture corresponds to 0.75 λ_L, where λ_L is the free-space wavelength at the lower operating frequency.

The primary *E*- and *H*-plane radiation patterns of the feed horn alone, taken at 15.1 and 30.2 kMc, are shown in Fig. 4. The *E*- and *H*-plane patterns of the horn at 15.1 kKc show that the patterns are approximately 10 db down from the main beam at the angle of ±61.5 degrees. This angle corresponds to the edge of the parabolic dish with a focal-length-to-diameter ratio of f/d=0.42. At the frequency of 30.2 kMc, the aperture opening of the horn of 0.587-inch diameter corresponds to 1.50 λ_h, where λ_h is the free-space wavelength at the higher operating frequency. It can be seen from Fig. 4 that the pattern in the *E* plane is sharper than the *H*-plane pattern,[2] with the sidelobe levels at least −20 db down within the angle of ±61.5 degrees.

To be able to propagate a single TE_{11} mode over at least a 2:1 frequency range in a circular waveguide, some means of suppressing the higher-order modes is required.

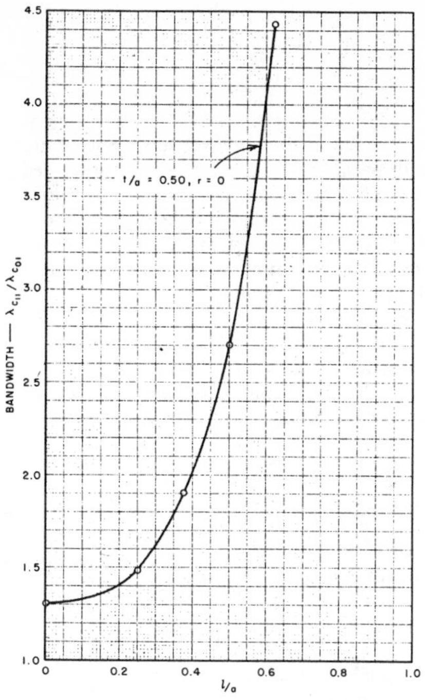

Fig. 6—Bandwidth of the quadruply-ridged circular waveguide (t/a=0.50).

When exciting the TE_{11} mode in a circular waveguide with the feed probes arranged as shown in Fig. 1, the first of these higher-order modes that will tend to destroy the desired feed-horn pattern will be the TM_{01}. The TM_{01} mode was suppressed by ridge-loading the circular waveguide.

In order to determine the effects on the cutoff frequencies of the TE_{11} and the TM_{01} modes as the ridge dimensions are varied, a quadruply ridged cavity was constructed and tested as a band-pass filter. The cross section of the cavity was constructed so that the length l and thickness t of the ridges could be varied. The results of these tests are shown in Fig. 5. In Fig. 6, the ratio of the two cutoff wavelengths is plotted as a function of the ratio l/a. This ratio corresponds to the bandwidth available between the cutoff of the TE_{11} mode and the cutoff of the TM_{01} mode. The data presented in Fig. 5 are for the case when t/a=0.50, and the TE_{11}-mode cutoff wavelengths for several other combinations of ridge thickness and length have been measured by Chait and Sakiotis.[3]

With a quadruple-ridge-loaded circular horn mounted at the focal point of a parabolic dish, it was possible to obtain equal beamwidth patterns at the two discrete frequencies, which are separated one full octave. Although the antenna described in this note was specifically designed to operate at 15.1 and 30.2 kMc, the feed horn for this antenna is capable of propagating a single TE_{11} mode over the frequency range from 12 to 36.2 kMc. The design data which are included in this paper show that it is possible to design a horn of this type to operage over a frequency band of more than 4:1.

A quadruple-ridge-loaded horn of this type may find many uses as a broad-band horn as well as a feed to yield a constant-beamwidth secondary pattern when mounted at the focal point of a parabolic dish.

ACKNOWLEDGMENT

The author wishes to acknowledge the help and advice received in the course of the work from Dr. E. M. T. Jones and Dr. R. C. Honey.

J. K. SHIMIZU
Stanford Res. Inst.
Menlo Park, Calif.

[2] G. C. Southworth, "Principles and Applications of Waveguide Transmission," D. Van Nostrand Co., Inc., New York, N. Y., pp. 404–407; 1960.

[3] H. N. Chait and N. G. Sakiotis, "Broad-band ferrite rotators using quadruply-ridged circular waveguide," IRE TRANS. ON MICROWAVE THEORY AND TECHNIQUES, vol. MTT-7, pp. 38–41; January, 1959.

Optimum paraboloid aerial and feed design

D. Herbison-Evans, M.A., D.Phil.

Synopsis

A computer study was made of the spillover, crosspolarisation and illumination efficiency of paraboloids of various focal-length/paraboloid-diameter (F/D) ratios, fed by rectangular, square and circular waveguides in their lowest-order modes. The feed radiation patterns used were those derived by simple diffraction theory from the incident waveguide-mode field distribution. The approximations made in this derivation give unnaturally low spillovers for very small aperture feeds, and thus favour short F/D systems, which would use such feeds. The feed dimensions were optimised to give a maximum figure of merit (gain/total noise temperature) for each combination of feed, receiver noise temperature and F/D ratio. Some of the optimum horn dimensions and resulting illumination tapers, excess aerial noise temperatures, gain efficiencies and figures of merit produced by the computations are presented. The results show, among other things, that the figure of merit of a low-F/D-ratio system is about 0·8 dB less than that of a large-F/D-ratio system. They also show that, if the system has a low receiver temperature, the feed dimensions should be larger than conventional design procedures indicate, to give up to 3 dB more edge-illumination taper.

List of symbols

a = Eplane halfwidth of rectangular feed aperture, radius of circular-feed aperture or halfwidth of square-feed aperture
b = Hplane halfwidth of rectangular-feed aperture
D = diameter of paraboloid reflector
E_θ, E_ϕ = components of electric field radiated by feed in spherical co-ordinates with origin at feed
E_x, E_y = components of electric field radiated by feed in rectangular co-ordinates with origin at feed
F = focal length of paraboloid reflector
G = gain of aerial relative to isotropic radiator
$J_1(x)$ = Bessel function of first kind and order one with argument x
$k = 2\pi/\lambda$
$M = 10\log\left(\frac{G}{T}\right) - 10\log\left(\frac{\pi^2 D^2}{\lambda^2 T_R}\right)$ = figure of merit relative to dish with 100% efficiency and undergraded receiver temperature
P_{00} = power radiated per unit solid angle by feed along its axis
P_t = total power radiated by feed
T = total equivalent noise temperature at aerial terminals
T_R = equivalent noise temperature due to receiver and aerial main beam
T_S = equivalent noise temperature of feed spillover past paraboloid
$\gamma = 2\pi$/guide wavelength
Γ = reflection coefficient at waveguide mouth
η_I = aperture illumination taper efficiency
η_p = efficiency factor due to crosspolarisation loss
η_s = efficiency factor due to spillover loss
θ = component of spherical co-ordinates about feed
λ = free-space wavelength
ρ = distance from point on paraboloid to focus
ϕ = component of spherical co-ordinates about feed
Φ = cone semiangle subtended by paraboloid at its focus

1 Introduction

One of the simplest methods of obtaining aerial gains in excess of 30 dB is the horn-fed paraboloid of revolution. The efficiency of this aerial depends on the focal-length/aperture-diameter (F/D) radio of the paraboloid and the noise temperature of the receiver, as well as the design and dimensions of its feed.

Paper 5428 E, first received 29th June and in revised form 11th August 1967. Crown copyright
Dr. Herbison-Evans was formerly with the Ministry of Technology Signals Research & Development Establishment, Christchurch, Hants., England, and is now with the School of Physics, University of New South Wales, N.S.W., Australia.

Previous general design procedures for optimising paraboloids have assumed either a long focal length[1,2] or approximations to the feed radiation pattern which lend themselves to integration.[3,4]

The optimum design of the feed–paraboloid combination for a maximum signal-power/noise-power ratio depends on the particular application. For radar, scatter and line-of-sight links and passive-satellite communication links, the received signal is proportional to the square of the aerial gain, so that the aerial may be designed for maximum G^2/total-noise-power ratio, where G is the gain above isotropic. For active-satellite communication ground systems, where the downlink is more critical than the uplink, as in the present generation of systems, the signal is proportional to the gain, and the aerial should give maximum G/total-noise-power ratio, i.e. figure of merit.

The total noise power can be conveniently expressed as an equivalent noise temperature and split into the sum of components due to the receiver, aerial mainbeam, diffraction sidelobes, defects in the paraboloidal surface, feed-support blockage and spillover by the feed outside the cone subtended by the dish at the feed. This last component is important in this study, as it is the one which is 'traded' for gain by altering the feed dimensions. Assuming the noises due to each component are relatively incoherent, their powers can simply be summed. In this study, all but the spillover will be lumped together and referred to as the 'receiver temperature'. The optimum feed–paraboloid configuration depends on this parameter.

2 Method

In this study, the effects of paraboloid F/D ratio and receiver noise temperature on the optimum design were investigated with more realistic approximations to the feed radiation patterns than previous investigations[3,4] using digital computers. The study was directed to the design of ground-terminal aerials for an active-satellite communication system. Thus the figure of merit or gain/total-noise temperature ratio was maximised with the aerial presumed to be directed at low elevation ($\simeq 10°$), when satellites tend to be at their maximum range and their signals weakest.

Three feeds which lend themselves to circular polarisation were investigated: rectangular, square and circular waveguides in their fundamental modes. The radiation patterns of the feeds were taken to be those derived by scalar diffraction theory from the transverse-field distribution of the modes.[5]

For the rectangular and square feeds,

$$E_\theta = \left\{1 + \left(\frac{\gamma}{k}\right)^2 \cos\theta\right\} \frac{\cos(ka\sin\theta\cos\phi)}{1 - \left(\frac{2ka\sin\theta\cos\phi}{2}\right)^2} \frac{\sin(kb\sin\theta\sin\phi)}{kb\sin\theta\sin\phi} \sin\phi \quad . \quad (1)$$

$$E_\phi = \left\{\left(\frac{\gamma}{k}\right)^2 + \cos\theta\right\} \frac{\cos(ka\sin\theta\cos\phi)}{1-\left(\frac{2ka\sin\theta\cos\phi}{\pi}\right)^2} \frac{\sin(kb\sin\theta\sin\phi)}{kb\sin\theta\sin\phi}\cos\phi \quad . \quad (2)$$

and for the circular feed,

$$E_\theta = \left\{1 + \left(\frac{\gamma}{k}\right)^2\cos\theta\right\} \frac{J_1(ka\sin\theta)}{ka\sin\theta}\sin\phi \quad . \quad . \quad (3)$$

$$E_\phi = \left\{\left(\frac{\gamma}{k}\right)^2 + \cos\theta\right\} \frac{J_1(ka\sin\theta)}{1-\left(\frac{ka\sin\theta}{1\cdot841}\right)^2}\cos\phi \quad (4)$$

In both cases, the reflection coefficient appearing in the equations in Reference 5 has been approximated by that due to the change in refractive index implied by the change in phase velocity. A more exact complex expression for the reflection coefficient is derived in Reference 5, but the extra complexity of its use was not considered to be justified at this stage. Thus the reflection coefficient was taken as

$$\Gamma = \frac{k-\gamma}{k+\gamma} \quad . \quad . \quad . \quad . \quad . \quad . \quad . \quad . \quad . \quad . \quad . \quad . \quad (5)$$

The calculation of the figure of merit of a particular combination of horn, paraboloid F/D ratio and receiver noise temperature, fell into three parts: spillover, crosspolarisation and illumination efficiency.

The spillover is the proportion of power radiated by the feed not intercepted by the paraboloid. It defines an efficiency factor η_s:

$$\eta_s = \frac{\int_0^\Phi \int_0^{2\pi} (E_\theta^2 + E_\phi^2)\sin\theta\, d\phi d\theta}{\int_0^\pi \int_0^{2\pi} (E_\theta^2 + E_\phi^2)\sin\theta\, d\phi d\theta} \quad . \quad . \quad . \quad . \quad (6)$$

where Φ is the semiangular aperture of the paraboloid. The denominator should be equal to the power leaving the waveguide aperture. So as to avoid the wiggly integral involved in its direct evaluation, the analytical formula for the gain was used to find it indirectly:

$$P_t = \frac{4\pi P_{00}}{G} \quad . \quad . \quad . \quad . \quad . \quad . \quad . \quad . \quad . \quad . \quad . \quad (7)$$

where

$$P_t = \int_0^\pi \int_0^{2\pi} (E_\theta^2 + E_\phi^2)\sin\theta d\phi d\theta \quad . \quad . \quad . \quad . \quad . \quad (8)$$

G = axial gain of feed over isotropic radiator

and $P_{00} = (E_\theta^2 + E_\phi^2)$ at $\theta = \phi = 0$ . . . . . . (9)

In our case,[6] for the rectangular and square feeds

$$P_{00} = \left\{1 + \left(\frac{\gamma}{k}\right)^2\right\}^2 \quad . \quad . \quad . \quad . \quad . \quad . \quad . \quad . \quad (10)$$

$$G = \frac{k^2 ab}{\pi}\frac{8}{\pi^2}\left\{1 + \left(\frac{\gamma}{k}\right)^2\right\}^2 \quad . \quad . \quad . \quad . \quad . \quad . \quad (11)$$

and for the circular feed

$$P_{00} = \frac{1}{4}\left\{1 + \left(\frac{\gamma}{k}\right)^2\right\}^2 \quad . \quad . \quad . \quad . \quad . \quad . \quad . \quad (12)$$

$$G = \frac{1}{4}(ka)^2 0\cdot8368\left\{1 + \left(\frac{\gamma}{k}\right)^2\right\}^2\left(\frac{k}{\gamma}\right)^2 \quad . \quad . \quad . \quad (13)$$

The crosspolarisation efficiency was found by integration across the focal plane of the wanted linear component:

$$\eta_p = \frac{\int_0^\Phi \int_0^{2\pi} E_x^2 \sin\theta\, d\phi d\theta}{\int_0^\Phi \int_0^{2\pi} (E_x^2 + E_y^2)\sin\theta\, d\phi d\theta} \quad . \quad . \quad . \quad . \quad (14)$$

where $E_x = E_\theta \sin\phi + E_\phi \cos\phi$ . . . . (15)

$E_y = E_\theta \cos\phi - E_\phi \sin\phi$ . . . . (16)

The aperture-illumination efficiency was found by using

$$\eta_I = \frac{\left|\int_0^\Phi \int_0^{2\pi} \frac{E_x}{\rho}\rho^2 \sin\theta\, d\phi d\theta\right|^2}{\int_0^\Phi \int_0^{2\pi} \rho^2 \sin\theta d\phi d\theta \int_0^\Phi \int_0^{2\pi} \left(\frac{E_x}{\rho}\right)^2 \rho^2 \sin\theta\, d\phi d\theta} \quad . \quad . \quad . \quad . \quad (17)$$

where

$$\rho = \frac{2F}{1+\cos\theta}$$

and F = focal length of paraboloid

The crosspolarisation was assumed to give rise to a final crosspolarisation pattern with most of its radiation near the axis. Hence it was assumed not to add to the noise temperature but only to diminish the gain. The total noise temperature was taken as

$$T = T_R + T_S(1 - \eta_s)$$

where T_R is the receiver temperature. Assuming that one half of the spillover is absorbed by a black ground at 300°K and that the other half sees the sky at 0°K, T_s was taken as 150°K. The results can be expressed simply for other dish orientations and sky and ground temperatures by linear scaling of T_R.

The figure of merit M of the combination was approximated to by

$$M = 10\log\left\{\eta_s\eta_p\eta_I \frac{T_R}{T_R + 150(1-\eta_s)}\right\} \quad . \quad . \quad (18)$$

giving a value relative to a uniformly illuminated aperture of the paraboloid diameter with no exess aerial noise. No account was taken of feed blocking, mismatching or other effects.

In the circular-feed case, the integrations were done analytically, and only single integrations were performed by the computer. For the rectangular and square feeds, the double integrations were done by computer. Integrations were done using an improved version of the adaptive Simpson procedure[6] to a relative accuracy of better than 0·001.

The approximations made in deriving the feed radiation patterns make them invalid in the range of feed dimensions used. This was brought out clearly by the spillover integration. This revealed that more energy was radiated into the cone subtended by the paraboloid than was transmitted through the waveguide aperture when the aperture transverse dimension dropped below about 0·9λ. Thus the results are biased in favour of low F/D ratios by having unnaturally low spillovers for small feed apertures.

The optimum horn dimensions were found by a golden-search procedure for each T_R and F/D. The golden search maximises a function of a variable over a limited range of that variable. This it does by examining the function at the golden points of the range; i.e. at $\frac{1}{2}(\sqrt{5} - 1)$ and $\frac{1}{2}(3 - \sqrt{5})$ of the range). Whichever is lower is taken as the boundary of a new range, and the procedure is recursively repeated. It brackets the maximum of the function more and more closely, until a desired accuracy is attained.

The results for a circular feed of the maximum figure of merit are shown in Fig. 1, with the Hplane illuminations required at the edge of the paraboloid relative to that at the apex (including space taper due to the different distances from the focus to the edge and the apex of the paraboloid) in Fig. 2, and the resulting aperture efficiencies and excess noise temperatures shown in Figs. 3 and 4. Similar curves were obtained with rectangular and square feeds. Figs. 5, 6 and 7 show the optimum feed dimensions for round, rectangular and square feeds. Fig. 8 shows figure of merit against T_R for $F/D = 0\cdot4$ and $1\cdot5$ for all three feeds.

The scatter on many of the graphs is probably spurious and the result of the finite accuracy of the integration and search procedures.

The asymptotic values obtained for a rectangular feed as F/D tends to infinity for 3000°K and 30°K were compared with the results of Milne and Raab[2] for a single-horn feed, optimising gain alone and gain/excess temperature, respectively. The efficiencies and temperatures (allowing for the

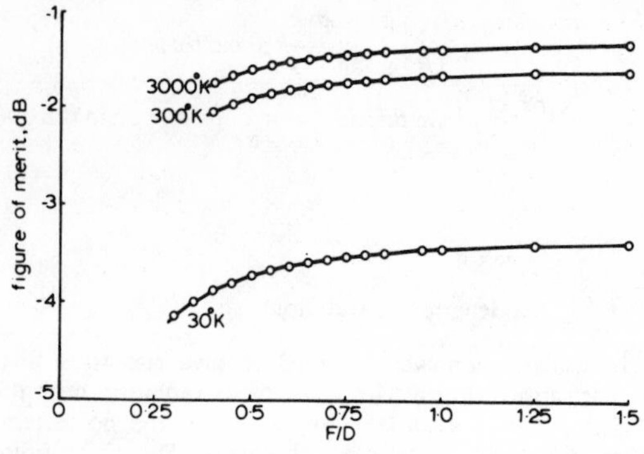

Fig. 1

Figure of merit against F/D for round feed

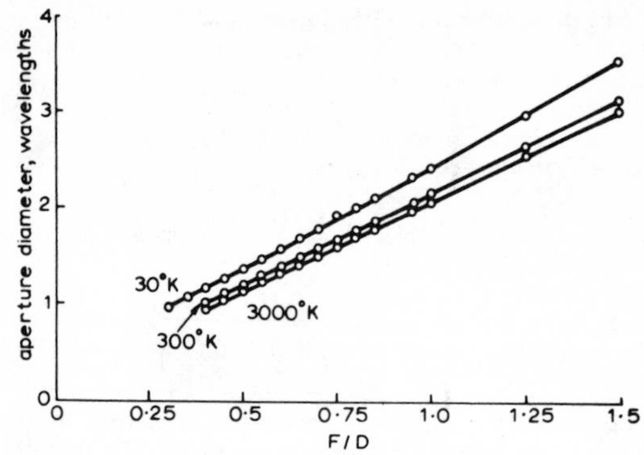

Fig. 5

Aperture diameter against F/D for round feed

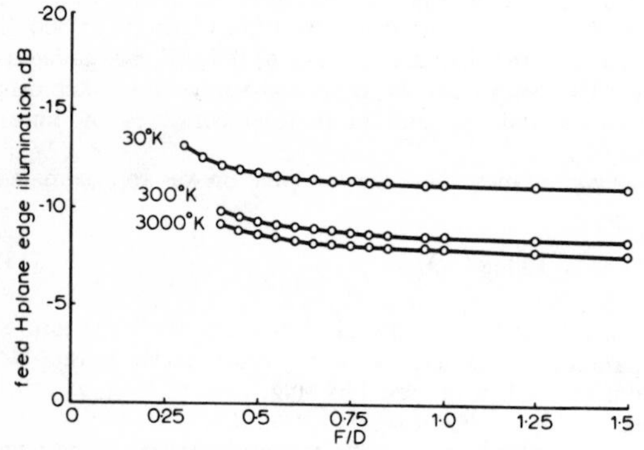

Fig. 2

Hplane edge illumination against F/D for round feed

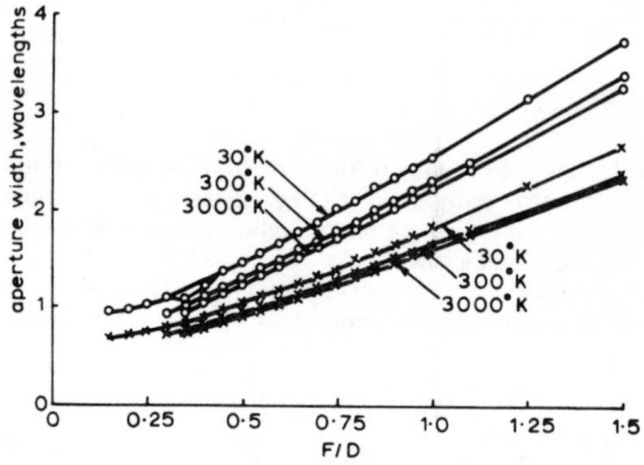

Fig. 6

Aperture width against F/D for rectangular feed

○ *Hplane*
× *Eplane*

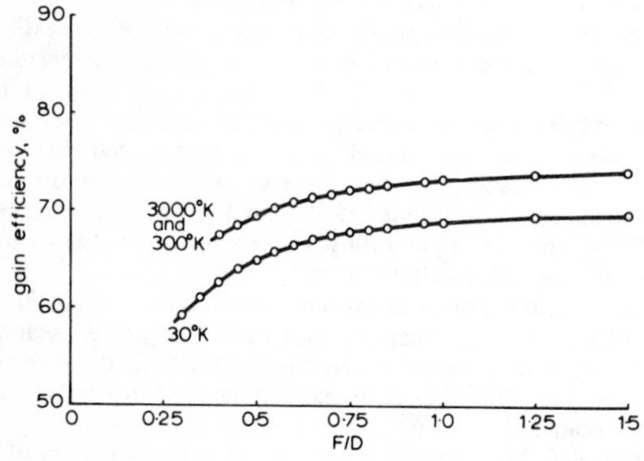

Fig. 3

Gain efficiency against F/D for round feed

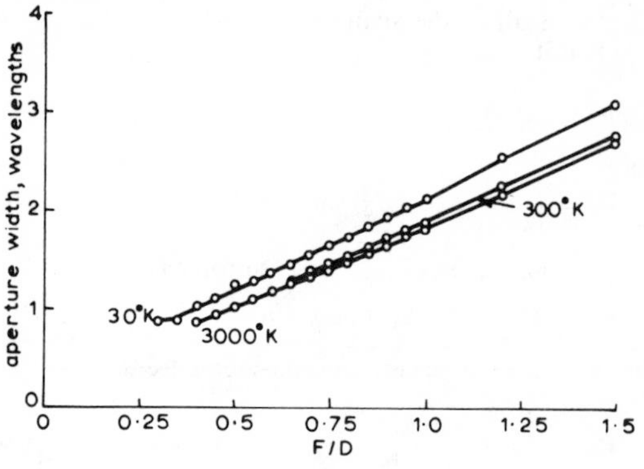

Fig. 7

Aperture width against F/D for square feed

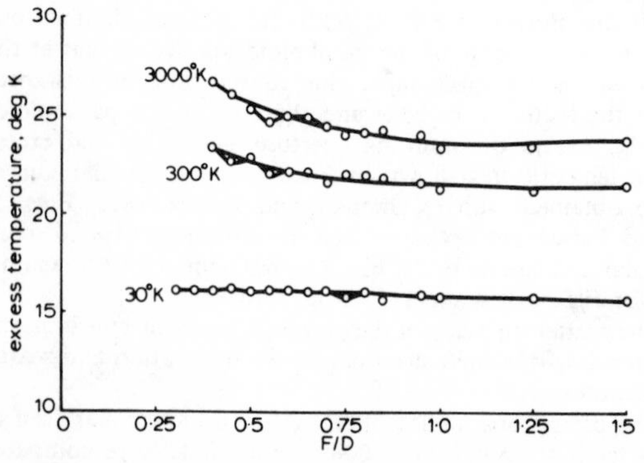

Fig. 4

Excess temperature against F/D for round feed

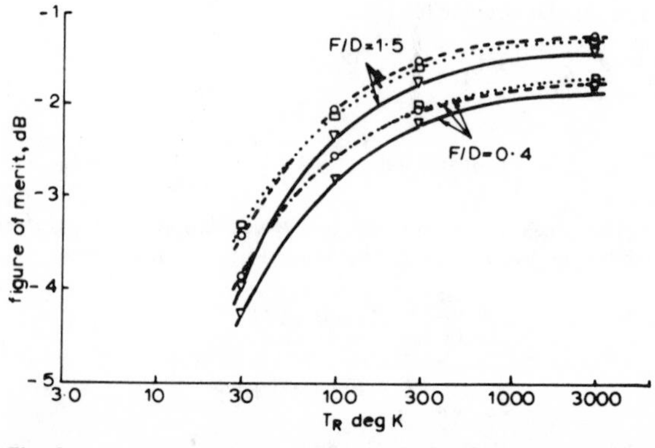

Fig. 8

Figures of merit compared

—▽— square, – – ○ – – rectangular, . . . □ . . . round

different environment models) agree closely, but the optimum horn dimensions derived here are slightly larger.

A point that arose in the calculations was that no optimum feed produced more than 2% of crosspolarised energy. This factor depends on the effective electric/magnetic dipole moment ratio at the feed aperture, and this is sensitive to the form taken for the reflection coefficient, since the mismatch at the feed aperture augments the electric field but diminishes the magnetic field there.[5]

3 Results

The following general conclusions can be made from the results:

(*a*) All three feeds give similarly shaped curves of figure of merit against F/D or T_R. However, the curves for rectangular and circular feeds are identical to within 0·1 dB and show an advantage over a square feed of 0·2–0·4dB. For circular polarisation, the square and circular feeds can be used directly, but a rectangular feed has to be synthetised from a square one, with internal fins at the edges of the aperture to constrict it for each linear-polarisation component separately. However, the difference in performance between the optimum circular and rectangular feeds is probably less than the excess conduction losses that this fin loading would entail for a rectangular feed, and so a conical horn is the indicated feed for circular polarisation.[8]

(*b*) The usual feed-design procedures specify the size of the feed by the illumination occurring in the direction of the edge of the paraboloid relative to that in the direction of the apex. The present work shows that, for most values of F/D and for all three types of feed, reducing the receiver temperature from 3000 to 300° K requires an increase in the optimum feed dimension to give an extra —0·7 dB edge illumination in the *H*plane. Reducing the receiver temperature from 3000 to 30° K requires an extra −3dB.

(*c*) Despite approximations leading to a bias in favour of low F/D ratios, the results show an advantage in gain of about 0·8dB for large over small F/D ratios for all receiver temperatures. This advantage would also hold for Cassegrain or Gregorian systems with a short-focus main dish but high magnification, as the spillover, crosspolarisation and aperture efficiency will be those apertaining to the long-focus equivalent paraboloid.[7] However, for these this advantage must be balance against extra losses due to blockage by the subreflector and diffraction effects due to its finite size.

(*d*) For all three feeds and over most F/D ratios, there is little change in the design for the optimum G/T ratio between receiver temperatures of 3000 and 300° K. Small changes in aerial temperature are swamped by the large receiver temperatures, and the resulting designs are virtually for maximum G alone. Thus the conclusions about optimum horn type and dimensions, and paraboloid F/D ratios are also true for applications requiring maximum G^2/T for this range of receiver temperature. The similar excess aerial noise temperatures in this range for rectangular and circular feeds indicates a spillover of about 15%. However, with a 30° K receiver temperature, the edge illumination should be tapered by a further 2–4dB. The rectangular and circular feeds give excess aerial noise temperatures of 18 and 16° K, respectively. These are nearly constant with respect to F/D and indicate a spillover for the optimum designs of approximately 12 and 10·5%, respectively.

4 Conclusions

The graphs of figure of merit against F/D enable a system designer who is intent on using a horn-fed paraboloid to choose an F/D ratio for the paraboloid he must use. He can trade the losses in the necessary waveguide run to a front feed, or the subreflector blocking and truncation losses of a Cassegrain feed, for the merit loss as the F/D ratio of the paraboloid is reduced. The curves presented here guide the choice of feed and give the optimum feed-aperture dimensions. A small point is that the designer must ensure that there is room for the length of the flare of the feed from normal waveguide dimensions to the required feed-aperture dimensions, giving less than a $\lambda/8$ phase error across the feed aperture.

He still has many other problems in the design of the aerial for the system. It is hoped that the results presented here can enable him to concentrate properly upon them.

5 Acknowledgments

Thanks are due to the Mathematical Services staff of SRDE and AAEE for their tolerance and understanding, and to K. Milne for illuminating discussions. Acknowledgment is due to the Controller of HM Stationery Office for permission to publish this paper.

6 References

1 CROMPTON, J. W.: 'On the optimum illumination taper for the objective of a microwave aerial', *Proc. IEE*, 1954, **101**, Pt. III, pp. 371–382
2 MILNE, K., and RAAB, A. R.: 'Optimum illumination tapers for four-horn and five-horn monopulse aerial systems' *in* 'Design and construction of large steerable aerials', *IEE Conf. Rep. Ser.* 21, 1966, pp. 12–16
3 SILVER, S.: 'Microwave antenna theory and design' (McGraw-Hill, 1949), p. 425
4 LIVINGSTON, M. L.: 'The effect of antenna characteristics on antenna noise temperature and system s.n.r.', *IRE Trans.*, 1961, **SET-7**, p. 71
5 FRADIN, A. Z.: 'Microwave antennas' (Pergamon, 1961), p. 147
6 KUNCIR, G. F.: Algorithm 103, *Commun. ACM*, 1962, **5**, p. 347
7 HANNAN, P. W.: 'Microwave antennas derived from the Cassegrain telescope', *IRE Trans.*, 1961, **AP-9**, pp. 140–153
8 REINTJES, J. F., and COATE, G. T.: 'Principles of radar' (McGraw-Hill, 1952, 3rd edn.), p. 955

Design of flared-horn primary feeds for parabolic reflector antennas

A. W. Rudge, Ph.D., Mem. I.E.E.E., and Prof. M. J. Withers, M.Sc., C.Eng., M.I.E.E.

Indexing terms: Antenna feeds, Waveguides

Abstract

The paper describes the derivation of a simple design procedure by which the dimensions of a rectangular flared-horn primary feed, operating in the TE_{10} mode, may be determined for parabolic reflectors, having any f/d ratio and with either a rectangular or circular contour, so that maximum aperture efficiency is obtained. The design technique is based on achieving a best match between the principal component of the reflector focal-plane electric field and that electric field existing in the horn mouth during transmission. In addition, the design procedure predicts the value of the spillover power, the reradiated power, the relative edge-field illumination, the resultant reflector aperture-field distribution and the value of the maximum aperture efficiency obtainable for the given combination of horn feed and reflector.

List of principal symbols

f = focal length of parabolic reflector
d = diameter of reflector
θ = halfangle subtended at focus by point on reflector
θ^* = maximum value of θ
$u = \sin\theta$
ρ, ϕ = aperture-plane polar co-ordinates
t, ϕ' = focal-plane polar co-ordinates
ϵ, η = aperture-plane rectangular co-ordinates
p, q = sines of rectangular aperture angular co-ordinates ($p = \sin\theta\cos\phi$; $q = \sin\theta\sin\phi$)
x, y = focal-plane rectangular co-ordinates
E = focal-plane field-distribution function
F = aperture-plane field-distribution function
T = transmission (or aperture) efficiency
T_c = reflector-curvature correction factor
W = principal focal-plane lobe width (between −10dB points)
T_0 = spillover power
R = reradiated power
Δ = relative edge-field illumination factor
λ = wavelength
$k = 2\pi/\lambda$

1 Introduction

The flared waveguide horn has been applied as a primary feed for parabolic-reflector antennas for many years, and, in this application, has been the subject of many publications.[1–7] Nevertheless, in the design of flared-horn primary feeds there is still a considerable dependence on empirical laws.[1,3,4] Although conventional diffraction theory can be applied when the reflector has a large focal-length/diameter (f/d) ratio,[6,7] the majority of the reflectors in present-day use have f/d ratios in the range 0·25–1·0, and in this region a comprehensive yet simple technique for the synthesis of the horn dimensions to achieve a desired overall antenna performance is lacking.

A much quoted empirical guide is that the feed horn should be designed so that its radiation pattern provides an illumination taper reaching approximately −10dB of the on-axis illumination at the reflector edges.[1] This figure can rarely be achieved with reflectors of small f/d ratio and it is often given as between −8 and −14dB.[1–4] While such a guide is not without its merits, the overall performance of a reflector antenna is dependent on a number of conflicting requirements which cannot easily be optimised for a specific application without more knowledge of the governing parameters. The relationships between the dimensions of the primary-feed horn and the reflector contour, the f/d ratio, the aperture efficiency, the spillover power, the reradiated power, the relative edge illumination and the radiation pattern are of particular importance.

This paper describes the derivation of a simple design procedure by means of which the dimensions of a rectangular-waveguide flared-horn primary feed, operating in the TE_{10} mode, may be determined for parabolic reflectors having any f/d ratio and with either a rectangular or circular contour, so that an optimum compromise may be obtained between the factors given above. The optimum compromise will be suggested as being that choice of primary-feed dimensions which will provide the maximum transmission of power to a matched load when the reflector aperture is uniformly illuminated from a distant electromagnetic source. Normalised to the total power incident on the reflector, this transmission is a definition of aperture efficiency.

The design procedure provides directly the value of the maximum aperture efficiency attainable for the combination of optimised horn and a given reflector profile. The relative levels of absorbed, overspilled and reradiated components of the total power intercepted by the given reflector are predicted, and, in addition, the electric-field distribution across the reflector aperture plane is defined in the transmission mode when the feed horn is employed to illuminate the reflector.

Although the design procedure is arranged to give the primary-feed-horn dimensions providing maximum aperture efficiency, the results given are such that a tradeoff of aperture efficiency for decreased sidelobe levels can be carried out. The necessary horn dimensions, and the other factors expressed above, can again be predicted with a little additional effort.

The procedure described does not account for reflector-profile errors, misalignment of the feed or aperture blocking. Methods of estimating the additional effects of profile errors, feed alignment and aperture blocking appear in the literature,[8,9,1] and, in general, require a knowledge of the errorfree antenna performance given here.

The scalar expressions used to represent the focal-plane electric fields are not exact; however, they have been found to provide a good approximation to the principal component of the reflector focal-plane electric field, and they have the advantage that their comparative simplicity permits the additional analytical manipulation required here.

Paper 6260 E, first received 21st April and in revised form 22nd June 1970
Dr. Rudge and Prof. Withers were formerly with the Department of Electrical Engineering, University of Birmingham, Birmingham, England. Dr. Rudge is now with IIT Research Institute, 10 West 35th Street, Chicago, Ill. 60616, USA, and Prof. Withers is a visiting professor of telecommunications at the Instituto Technologico de Aeronautica, Sao Jose dos Campos, Sao Paulo, Brazil

2 General theory

In a recent publication[10] it was shown that the principal components of the focal-plane electric-field distribution E of a parabolic reflector may be related to the reflector

Reprinted with permission from *Proc. Inst. Elec. Eng.*, vol. 117, pp. 1741–1749, Sept. 1970.

aperture-plane field distribution F by a scalar equation of the form

$$E(t, \phi') = j\frac{k}{2\pi}\int_0^{2\pi}\int_0^{\hat{u}} \frac{F(u, \phi)}{(1-u^2)^{1/2}} \exp\{jktu\cos(\phi - \phi')\}\, u\, du\, d\phi \quad . \quad (1)$$

with the nomenclature illustrated in Fig. 1 and $u = \sin\theta$, $\hat{u} = \sin\theta^*$, $k = 2\pi/\lambda$, and θ^* is the maximum value of θ.

If a rectangular flared horn is to be employed as a primary feed for one such reflector, it is of value to ascertain what percentage of the power collected by the reflector aperture will be absorbed by a matched load connected to the primary feed, assuming that the reflector aperture is uniformly illuminated from a far-field source. The transmission efficiency of the horn, in this respect, is a function of both its physical dimensions and its aperture electric-field distribution. It follows that, from a knowledge of the parameters governing the efficiency of the primary feed, horns may be designed having optimum dimensions with respect to transmission efficiency. Transmission efficiency T will be defined as the ratio of the power delivered to a matched load connected to the primary feed to the total power intercepted at the reflector aperture, when the reflector is exposed to a normally incident, linearly polarised, uniform electric field. In this sense, transmission efficiency is synonymous with the more usual term 'aperture efficiency'.

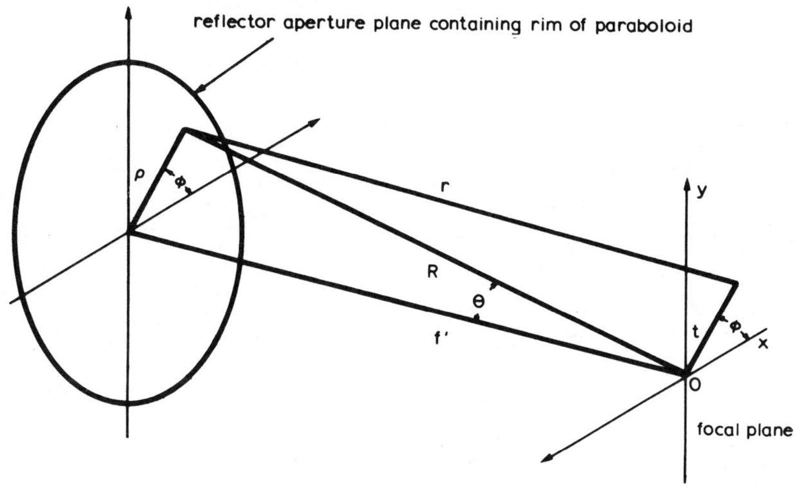

Fig. 1
Co-ordinate system employed

To carry out the analysis, a theorem expressed by Midgely[11] is suitable as an analytical tool. Consider the two antennas shown in Fig. 2 separated by a surface S which includes the aperture of B. With A radiating unit power and B terminated in a matched load, a vector field E_1, E_2 will exist on S. With B radiating unit power and A terminated in a matched load, a field E_2, H_2 will exist on S. It can be shown that[6, 11] the efficiency of the power transmission between the two antennas (which will, by the Lorentz reciprocity theorem, be the same in either direction) can be written quantitatively as

$$T = \iint_S (E_1 \times H_2 + H_1 \times E_2) \, . \, dS \quad . \quad . \quad . \quad (2)$$

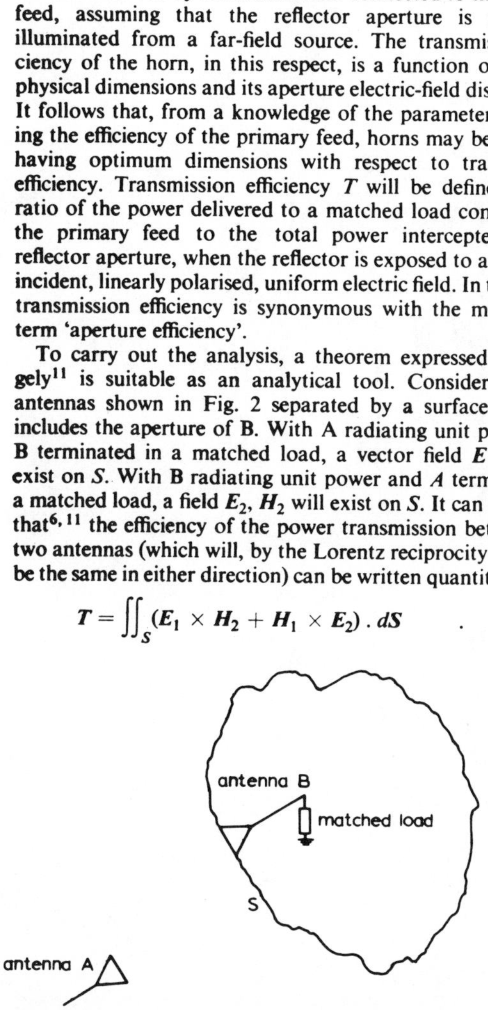

Fig. 2
Illustration of the transmission theory

For two linearly polarised antennas aligned so that their direction of polarisation is the same, eqn. 2 can be more simply expressed in scalar form as[6, 11]

$$T = K\iint_S E_1 E_2 dS \quad . \quad . \quad . \quad . \quad . \quad . \quad . \quad . \quad (3)$$

where K is a normalising constant.

In this form, determination of the transmission requires only a knowledge of the electric fields E_1 and E_2 over a common surface. Applied to the combination of primary feed and parabolic reflector, the surface of integration may be taken as the aperture plane of the primary feed situated in the focal plane of the parabolic reflector. The primary feed will comprise one antenna, the reflector aperture being the other. We will first examine the case of a rectangular flared horn used in conjunction with a parabolic reflector having a rectangular contour.

3 Rectangular parabolic reflector

It has been shown[10, 12] that the principal components of the focal-plane electric-field distribution resulting from a uniformly illuminated parabolic reflector may be obtained from eqn. 1 in the form

$$E(x) \propto \frac{2\hat{p}\sin kx\hat{p}}{kx_p} \qquad \hat{p} < 0{\cdot}5 \quad . \quad . \quad . \quad . \quad . \quad (4a)$$

$$E(x) \propto \pi J_0(kx) \quad \hat{p} = 1{\cdot}0 \quad . \quad . \quad . \quad . \quad . \quad (4b)$$

where $\hat{p} = \hat{u}\cos\phi$. Solutions for $E(y)$ are obtained by replacing $\hat{p}$ with $\hat{q}$, where $\hat{q} = \hat{u}\sin\phi$. $\hat{p}$ and $\hat{q}$ correspond to the sines of the maximum angles subtended in the principal planes by the rectangular parabolic reflector.

Consider, initially, a uniformly illuminated rectangular reflector having large f/d ratios. The focal-plane electric-field distribution will be given by

$$E_1(x, y) = j\frac{k}{\pi}(\hat{p}\hat{q})^{1/2}\frac{\sin k\hat{p}x}{k\hat{p}x}\frac{\sin k\hat{q}y}{k\hat{q}y} \quad . \quad . \quad . \quad (5)$$

The amplitude term is normalised to correspond to unity power collected at the reflector aperture. Provided the flare angle of the horn is kept small (i.e. preferably less than 10°), then, on transmission, the feed aperture having dimensions $2\hat{x}$ and $2\hat{y}$ will operate in the TE_{10} mode. The feed aperture distribution can then be expressed[1, 11] as

$$E_2(x, y) = \begin{cases} j\dfrac{1}{(2\hat{x}\hat{y})^{1/2}}\cos\left(\dfrac{\pi y}{2\hat{y}}\right) & |x| < \hat{x};\ |y| < \hat{y} \\ 0 & |x| > \hat{x};\ |y| > \hat{y} \end{cases} \quad . \quad . \quad . \quad . \quad (6)$$

Again, the amplitude term is normalised for unity power transmitted.

From eqns. 3, 5 and 6, the transmission efficiency will be given by

$$\Gamma = \frac{k}{\pi}\left(\frac{\hat{p}\hat{q}}{2\hat{x}\hat{y}}\right)^{1/2}\int_{-\hat{x}}^{\hat{x}}\int_{-\hat{y}}^{\hat{y}}\left\{\frac{\sin k\hat{p}x}{k\hat{p}x}\,\frac{\sin k\hat{q}y}{k\hat{q}y}\right\}\cos\left(\frac{\pi y}{2\hat{y}}\right)dxdy \quad . \; . \; . \; . \; (7)$$

which integrates to give

$$T = \frac{\sqrt{2}}{\pi}\left[\left\{\frac{S_i(\hat{X})}{\sqrt{\hat{X}}}\right\}\left\{\frac{S_i(\hat{Y}+\pi/2)+S_i(\hat{Y}-\pi/2)}{\sqrt{\hat{Y}}}\right\}\right] \quad (8)$$

where $\hat{X} = k\hat{p}\hat{x}$, $\hat{Y} = k\hat{q}\hat{y}$ and $S_i(z) = \int_0^z \frac{\sin z}{z}dz$ (a tabulated function).[17]

Eqn. 8 relates the transmission or aperture efficiency T to the aperture dimensions of the primary feed ($2\hat{x}$, $2\hat{y}$) and the angular dimensions of the reflector ($\hat{p}$, $\hat{q}$). Of the power intercepted by the reflector aperture, $100\,T\%$ will be absorbed in a matched load connected to the primary feed and $(1 - T)$ 100% will be lost as a result of spillover and reradiation from the horn mouth.

Fig. 3 shows the variation of the aperture efficiency with the variables $\hat{X}$ and $\hat{Y}$ from eqn. 8. In each case, the nonvarying parameter (i.e. either $\hat{X}$ or $\hat{Y}$) is set to its optimum value (i.e. that giving maximum transmission) while the other is varied. The relative magnitudes of the spillover and reradiated power are also shown. Spillover power constitutes that power which is intercepted by the reflector but is not incident on the horn mouth. The reradiated power comprises that power incident on the horn aperture which excites higher-order

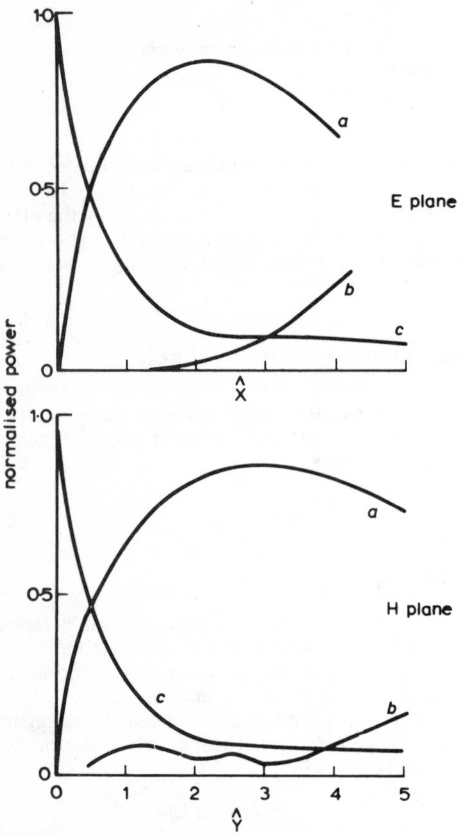

Fig. 3

Aperture characteristics

a Transmission efficiency
b Reflected (or reradiated) power
c Spillover power
For rectangular parabolic reflector with zero curvature ($T_c = 1 \cdot 0$)

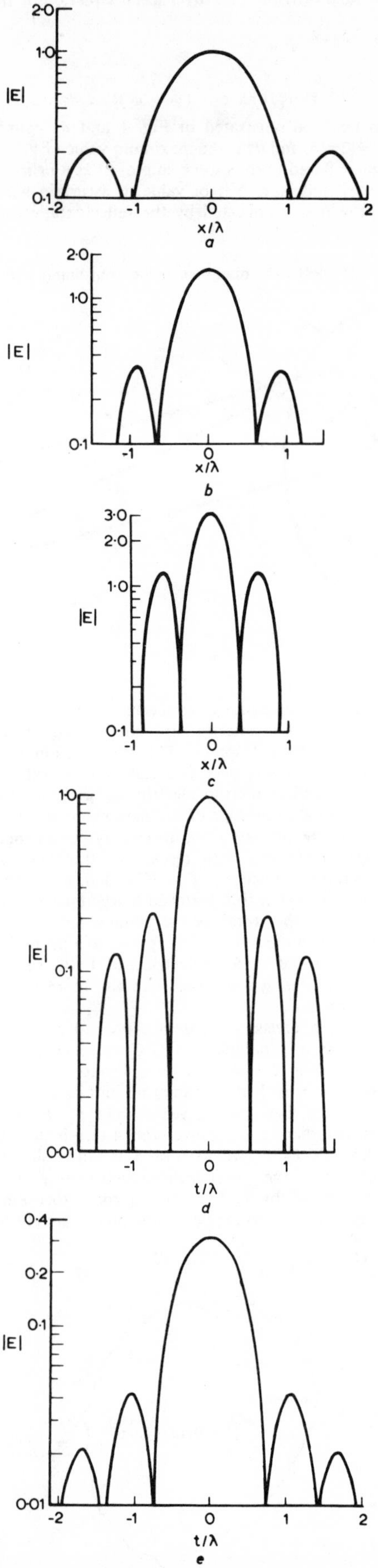

Fig. 4 *Principal component of focal-plane electric-field distribution*

For parabolic reflectors curved in one dimension
(*a*) $f/d = 1 \cdot 0$ (*b*) $f/d = 0 \cdot 5$ (*c*) $f/d = 0 \cdot 25$
For circular parabolic reflectors
(*d*) $f/d = 0 \cdot 25$ (*e*) $f/d = 0 \cdot 5$

modes in the horn and is subsequently reradiated back toward the main reflector. Similarly, considered in the transmission mode, spillover power corresponds to that power transmitted by the primary feed horn which is not intercepted by the reflector aperture, and the reradiated power is that which is incident on the reflector and reflected back into the primary feed. The derivation of the curves for these component powers is given in Appendix 12.1. For more details of the mechanism governing the reradiated power, see Reference 11.

From Fig. 3, the horn-aperture dimensions corresponding to maximum aperture efficiency are given by

$$2\hat{x} = \frac{2 \cdot 2\lambda}{\pi \hat{p}} \quad \text{(for the E plane width)} \qquad (9a)$$

$$2\hat{y} = \frac{3 \cdot 0\lambda}{\pi \hat{q}} \quad \text{(for the H plane width)} \qquad (9b)$$

From exprs. 4, it can be seen that the main lobe of the reflector focal-plane field distribution has widths between its -10dB points in the principal planes of $0 \cdot 74\ \lambda/\hat{p}$ and $0 \cdot 74\ \lambda/\hat{q}$. Designating these lobe widths by W_p and W_q, eqn. 9 may be written

$$2\hat{x} = 0 \cdot 95 W_p \text{ (E plane)} \qquad (10a)$$

$$2\hat{y} = 1 \cdot 29 W_q \text{ (H plane)} \qquad (10b)$$

From these equations, it can be seen that the primary-feed dimensions giving maximum aperture efficiency are of the same order as the -10dB lobe widths of the reflector focal-plane field distribution.

4 Small *f/d* ratios

Exprs. 4 indicate that, as the *f/d* ratio of the reflector becomes smaller, the effect on the focal-plane field distribution consists of a narrowing of the lobe widths and an increase in the level of the subsidiary lobes relative to the principal lobe. Fig. 4, reproduced from Reference 12, illustrates the effect.

From inspection of eqn. 7 and the results indicated in eqns. 10, it is evident that, for maximum transmission, we are concerned with an integation over a part of the main lobe of the reflector focal-plane electric-field distribution. Fig. 4 shows that the shape of the main lobe of this distribution at small *f/d* ratios is largely a scaled version of that at large *f/d* ratios, the scaling factor being the width of the main lobe, given by the function *W*. The variation of *W* with *f/d* ratio, which may be obtained from solutions to eqn. 1, is shown in Fig. 5 for both rectangular and circular parabolic reflectors.[12]

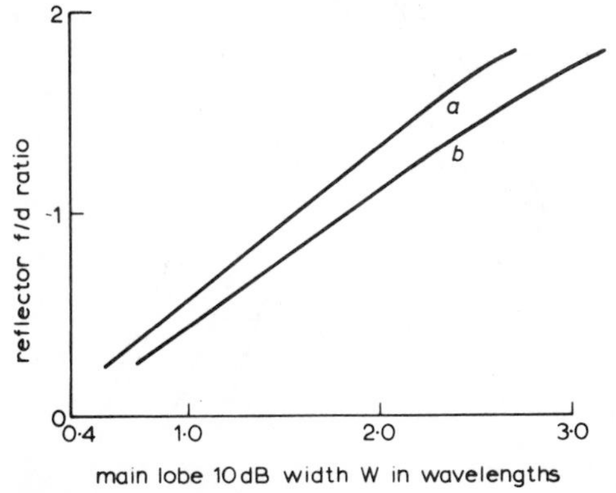

Fig. 5
Width of main focal-plane lobe between -10dB points for circular and rectangular parabolic reflectors having f/d ratios in the range 0·25–2·0
a Rectangular reflector
b Circular reflector

Conveniently, the variations are, to a good approximation, linear. Hence, by employing eqn. 1 and obtaining the values for W_p and W_q from Fig. 5, the primary-feed-horn dimensions providing maximum transmission may be obtained for any *f/d* ratio.

While the dimensions given by this technique will maintain a maximum-transmission condition, the peak value of the main lobe of the reflector focal-plane field is itself a function of the reflector *f/d* ratio. This is a consequence of the redistribution of power in the focal plane from the principal lobe to

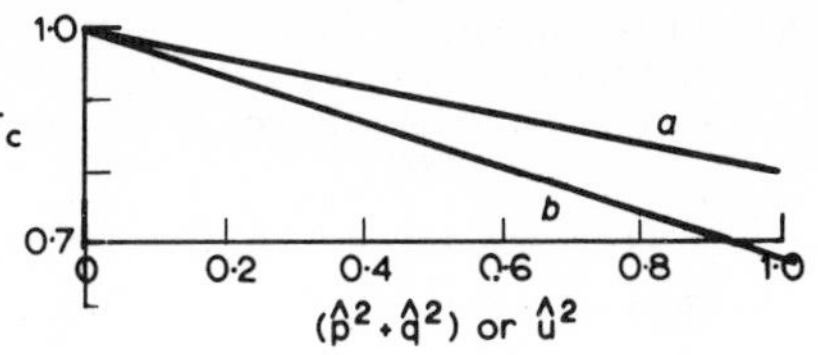

Fig. 6
Reflector-curvature correction factor T_c
a Rectangular reflectors
b Circular reflectors

the subsidiary lobes with increasing reflector curvature (see Fig. 4). Hence, the maximum aperture efficiency attainable with the optimised horn will be a function of the reflector *f/d* ratio. In Appendix 12.2, a curvature-correction factor T_c is derived. This factor, when multiplied by *T*, gives the aperture efficiency corrected for the specific *f/d* ratios involved. The curvature factor T_c is shown graphically in Fig. 6.

5 Circular parabolic reflector

For circular parabolic reflectors, expressions for the principal component of the focal-plane electric-field distribution may be obtained from eqn. 1 in the form[10]

$$E(t, \phi') \simeq jk\hat{u}^2 \frac{J_1(kt\hat{u})}{kt\hat{u}} \qquad \hat{u} < 0 \cdot 5 \qquad (11a)$$

$$E(t, \phi') = jk \frac{\sin kt}{kt} \qquad \hat{u} = 1 \cdot 0 \qquad (11b)$$

The functions are very similar in character to those obtained for a square rectangular reflector subtending the same maximum halfangles in the principal planes, i.e. $\hat{p} = \hat{q} = \hat{u}$. The chief differences are in the dimensions of the focal-plane lobe structure. Hence, with a suitable adjustment of the peak value and the positions of the first zeros, the rectangular-reflector focal-plane electric-field distribution given by eqn. 5 can be modified so that, over the principal lobe of the focal distribution, it closely approximates the circular reflector fields given in exprs. 11.

The zero shift is implemented very simply. Noting that $\hat{p} = \hat{q} = \hat{u}$, we see that $X = k\hat{u}x$ and $Y = k\hat{u}y$; eqn. 5 can be modified to provide a good approximation to the significant portion of the main lobe of the circular-reflector focal-plane field by scaling *X* and *Y* by factors of W_p/W_u and W_q/W_u, respectively, where W_u is the circular -10dB lobewidth factor illustrated in Fig. 5. The rectangular-horn aperture dimensions for maximum transmission are then given by eqns. 10 using the circular lobewidth factor W_u rather than the rectangular factors W_p and W_q. Effectively, we are scaling the horn dimensions in the ratio W_u/W_p and W_u/W_q.

To normalise the approximate focal-plane field distribution for unity power intercepted at the circular aperture, eqn. 5 must be multiplied by a normalising factor given by the square root of the ratio of the total power contained under the true circular-reflector focal-plane distribution, normalised for unity total power intercepted, to that contained in the approximate focal-plane power distribution. With the zero shift described, this factor can be expressed as

$$C = \left(\frac{W_u^2}{W_p W_q}\right)^{1/2} C_0 \qquad (12)$$

where C_0 is dependent on the maximum radius of the true circular focal field over which the normalisation is carried out. However, over the range of radii containing the limits of the optimised rectangular feed (i.e. $-8 \cdot 6$dB to -22dB radii on the main lobe of the circular focal-plane field distribution). The value of C_0 varies less than 1%, and thus the normalisation has been carried out at an arbitrary radius corresponding to the -10dB level on the circular distribution. C_0 is then found to be $0 \cdot 996$.

Following the procedure employed for the rectangular

reflector of large f/d ratio, the modified form of eqn. 5 is inserted into the transmission formula, and, after the integration has been carried out, the resultant transmission is given by eqn. 8 multiplied by C_0, with the variables $\hat{X}$ and $\hat{Y}$ replaced by scaled variables $\hat{X}_s$ and $\hat{Y}_s$ (where $\hat{X}_s = W_p/W_u\ \hat{X}$ and $\hat{Y}_s = W_q/W_u\ \hat{Y}$). For the f/d considered, $W_u/W_p = W_u/W_q = 1{\cdot}17$, and the maximum transmission condition occurs when

$$\hat{X} = k\hat{x}\hat{u} = 1{\cdot}17(2{\cdot}2) = 2{\cdot}58 \quad . \quad . \quad . \quad . \quad (13a)$$

$$\hat{Y} = k\hat{y}\hat{u} = 1{\cdot}17(3{\cdot}0) = 3{\cdot}51 \quad . \quad . \quad . \quad . \quad . \quad . \quad (13b)$$

providing a maximum transmission of $0{\cdot}996(0{\cdot}867) = 0{\cdot}865$.

As for the rectangular reflector, it is necessary to determine a curvature factor to correct this value of transmission at small f/d ratios. The derivation of this factor is similar to that of the rectangular case given in Appendix 12.2, and, for brevity, only the salient points will be given here.

The curvature correction is defined by eqn. 26 with a change to circular co-ordinates (u, ϕ) to fit the geometry of the circular reflector. To simplify the integration, it is taken that, with the feed dimensions given by eqns. 10, the Fourier transform of the horn-aperture field distribution will be close to circular symmetry over the range of angles subtended by the reflector. In this case, the horn-transform characteristics given in eqn. 29 can be written approximately as

$$G(U) = \frac{\sin U}{U} \quad . \quad . \quad . \quad . \quad . \quad . \quad . \quad . \quad . \quad . \quad (14)$$

where $\quad U = k\hat{x}u$

On carrying out the necessary integrations, the curvature factor T_c' for the circular reflector is given by

$$T_c' = 1 - \frac{\hat{u}^2}{2}\left\{\frac{\left(1 - \left(\frac{\sin 2\hat{X}}{\hat{X}}\right)\right) + \left(\frac{\sin^2\hat{X}}{1\hat{X}^2}\right)}{C_{in}(2\hat{X})}\right\} \quad . \quad (15)$$

where

$$\hat{X} = k\hat{x}\hat{u}$$

$$C_{in} = \int_0^V \frac{1 - \cos V}{V}\, dV \text{ (a tabulated function[17])}$$

For the maximum-transmission condition $\hat{X} = k\hat{x}\hat{u}$ (see eqn. 13a), and the curvature correction factor is illustrated in Fig. 6 for this condition.

6 Reflector edge-field illumination

The combination of the primary-feed-horn radiation characteristics and the f/d ratio of a particular reflector will culminate in an illumination taper across the reflector aperture plane. The effect of such illumination tapering in broadening the main beam of the antenna radiation pattern and reducing the sidelobe levels is well known.[1-4] In Appendix 12.3 the edge-field illumination factor Δ is derived for rectangular flared horns feeding parabolic reflectors of any f/d ratio. The edge-field illumination factor indicates the field strength at the reflector rim normalised to unity at the centre of the aperture. A graph of this function against the maximum angle subtended by the reflector from the focus is shown in Fig. 7 for values of $\hat{X}$ and $\hat{Y}$ corresponding to feed-horn dimensions providing maximum aperture efficiency for rectangular and circular parabolic reflectors.

The edge-field illumination corresponding to maximum aperture efficiency is shown to be a function of the reflector f/d ratio. The arbitrary -10dB illumination referred to in Section 1 can be seen to produce maximum aperture efficiency only for a rectangular reflector having $\hat{p}$ and $\hat{q}$ less than $0{\cdot}6$, corresponding to f/d ratios of greater than $0{\cdot}75$.

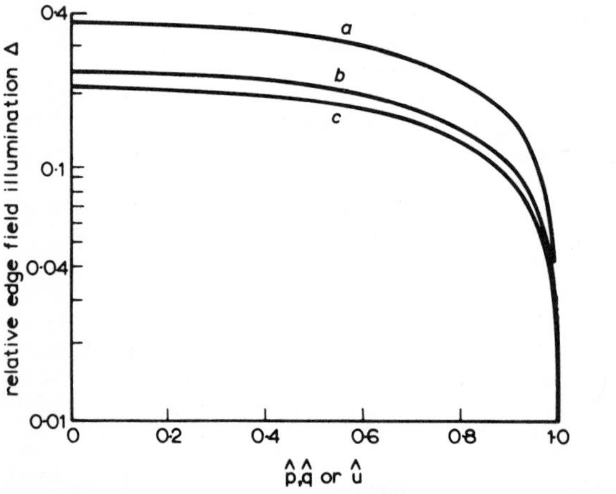

Fig. 7

Reflector edge-field illumination factor Δ for optimum transmission

a Rectangular reflectors, E and H planes
b Circular reflector, E plane
c Circular reflector, H plane

7 Reflector aperture-plane electric-field distribution

A necessary step in the prediction of the far-field radiation characteristics of the combination of primary feed and parabolic reflector is the determination of the electric

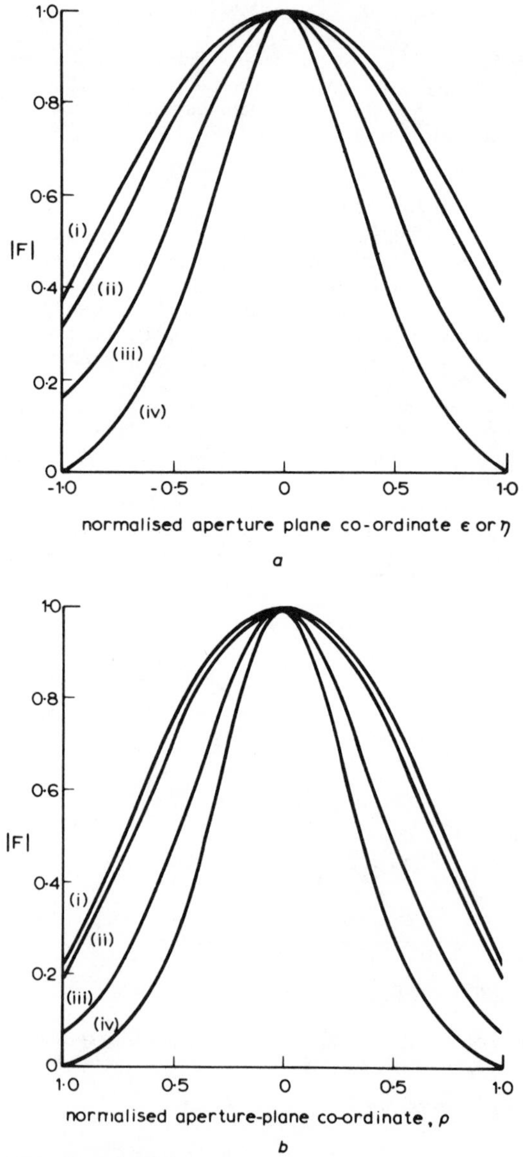

Fig. 8

Reflector aperture-plane electric-field distribution in the principal planes for various f/d ratios

a Rectangular reflectors, E or H plane
b Circular reflectors, E plane only
(i) $f/d \gg 1{\cdot}0$
(ii) $f/d = 1{\cdot}0$
(iii) $f/d = 0{\cdot}4$
(iv) $f/d = 0{\cdot}25$

field distribution in the aperture plane of the parabolic mirror when the primary feed is acting as a transmitting source. The reflector aperture plane is normally taken to be that containing the reflector rim for a circular reflector or a projection onto a plane immediately in front of the reflector for other mirror contours.[1,4] The overall antenna-radiation characteristics are then obtained by carrying out either Fourier or Hankel transformations on the projected aperture distribution.[1]

The reflector aperture electric-field distribution F may be obtained as a function of the subtended halfangle θ from eqns. 25 and 29 in Appendix 12.2. The reflector aperture-plane co-ordinates, originating at the centre of the aperture, normalised to a maximum value of unity at the reflector rim, and designated ρ and ϕ for the circular aperture and $\epsilon = \rho \cos\phi$, $\eta = \rho \sin\phi$ for the rectangular aperture, are related to the halfangle θ by

$$\rho = \tan\theta/2(\tan\theta^*/2)^{-1} \quad \ldots\ldots \quad (16)$$

On using simple trigonometric relationships, the aperture-plane co-ordinates can be related to the variable $u = (p^2 + q^2)^{1/2}$ by

$$u/\hat{u} = \rho(\cos^2\theta^*/2 + \rho^2 \sin^2\theta^*/2)^{-1} \quad \ldots \quad (17)$$

Similarly, in the principal planes of the rectangular aperture,

$$p/\hat{p} = \epsilon(\cos^2\theta^*/2 + \epsilon^2\sin^2\theta^*/2)^{-1} \text{ when } q = 0 \quad \ldots \quad (18a)$$

$$q/\hat{q} = \eta(\cos^2\theta^*/2 + \eta^2\sin^2\theta^*/2)^{-1} \text{ when } p = 0 \quad \ldots \quad (18b)$$

It can be seen from these equations that, for large f/d ratios (i.e. $\theta^* \ll \pi/2$), the reflector aperture-plane co-ordinates are effectively equal to the normalised u and p, q co-ordinates. Under these conditions, the reflector aperture-field distribution is identical to the far-field radiation pattern of the rectangular horn given by eqn. 29 between the limits $0 < u < \hat{u}$. For small f/d ratios, however, this approximation is not valid, and the resultant reflector aperture-plane field distribution, which will be given by substitution of eqn. 29 and eqn. 16 in eqn. 25, differs significantly from the horn radiation pattern. In Fig. 8 the reflector-aperture electric-field distribution in the principal planes is shown for various f/d ratios. The curves were obtained by carrying out the substitutions indicated above and using feed-horn dimensions which provide maximum aperture efficiency in each case.

8 Design procedure

A design procedure will now be established to determine the aperture dimensions of a rectangular-waveguide flared-horn primary feed operating in the TE_{10} mode so that maximum aperture efficiency is obtained when the feed is used in conjunction with a parabolic reflector of any f/d ratio. All the relevant performance characteristics discussed in Section 1 will be predicted directly. The design procedure is given in Table 1. The tabular form is employed to allow for the design differences incurred because of the reflector shape. The only input information required is the shape of the reflector and the f/d ratio or ratios in the principal planes.

The flare angle of the horn should be kept as small as is

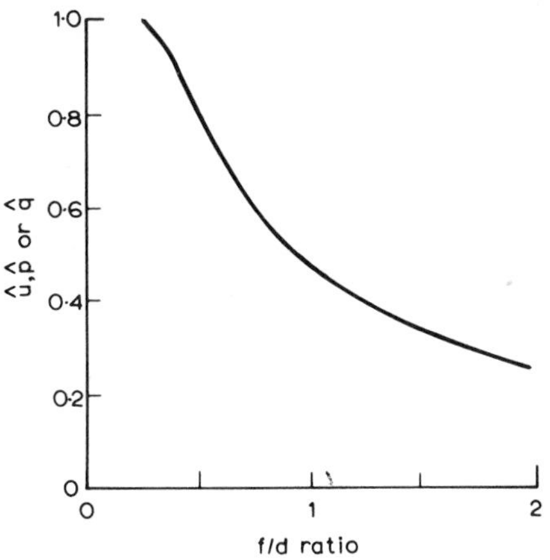

Fig. 9

Variation of $\hat{u}$, $\hat{p}$ or $\hat{q}$ with f/d ratio measured in the principal plane of the reflector

practicable. A flare angle of less than 10° is desirable, in that more rapid flaring may introduce phase variations or mode changes which were not allowed for in eqn. 6. See Reference 1 for further details.

Note that this analysis has been based on the assumption that the reflector has a true parabolic surface profile, and that aperture-blocking effects are negligible. Methods of estimating the additional effects caused by profile errors, aperture blocking and feed misalignment appear in the literature.[1,3,8,9]

Rectangular-aperture illuminations which are nonoptimum

Table 1

TABULATED DESIGN PROCEDURE

Operation	Circular-reflector diameter d	Rectangular aperature dimensions a (E plane) b (H plane)	Relevant area in text
1 Given the f/d ratios of the reflector in the horizontal and vertical planes, use Fig. 9 to determine the sines of the maximum angles subtended	$\hat{u}$	$\hat{p}$ (E plane) $\hat{q}$ (H plane)	
2 Obtain lobewidth factors from Fig. 5	W_u	W_p, W_q	Sections 3, 4 and 5
3 Horn-aperture dimensions may now be obtained by using the lobewidth factors from eqn. 10, $2\hat{x}$ = E plane width $2\hat{y}$ = H plane width	$2\hat{x} = 0{\cdot}95\,W_u$ $2\hat{y} = 1{\cdot}29\,W_u$	$2\hat{x} = 0{\cdot}95\,W_p$ $2\hat{y} = 1{\cdot}29\,W_q$	Sections 3, 4 and 5
4 From Fig. 6, obtain the value of curvature correction T_c . .	Use $\hat{u}^2$	Use $(\hat{p}^2 + \hat{q}^2)$	Sections 4, 5 and 12.2
5 Aperture efficiency T is then given by	$86{\cdot}5\,T_c\%$	$86{\cdot}7\,T_c\%$	Fig. 6 and Sections 4 and 5
6 Power intercepted by the reflector and reradiated by the primary feed horn R is given by	$2{\cdot}6\,T_c\%$	$2{\cdot}6\,T_c\%$	Section 12.1 and Fig. 6
7 Power intercepted by the reflector and lost as spillover T_0 . .	$(1-0{\cdot}891\,T_c)\ 100\%$	$(1-0{\cdot}893\,T_c)\ 100\%$	Sections 5 and 12.1 and Fig. 6
8 Obtain edge-field illumination factor Δ from Fig. 7 . . .	use $\hat{u}$ to obtain Δ_p and Δ_q	Use $\hat{p}$ to obtain Δ_p, $\hat{q}$ to obtain Δ_q	Sections 6 and 12.3
9 Reflector aperture-plane field distribution may be determined from Fig. 8			Section 7

with respect to aperture efficiency may be desired to reduce the level of the peak sidelobes in the antenna radiation pattern. To reduce the peak sidelobes, the values of $\hat{X}$ and $\hat{Y}$ can be increased from the optimum values of 2·2 and 3·0, with a resultant decrease in aperture efficiency, as illustrated in Fig. 3. The new efficiency may be obtained from eqn. 8, and the new curvature-correction factor T_c from eqn. 32. The effect on horn reradiation and spillover power can be seen in Fig. 3, and the levels are calculated by means of eqns. 19 and 20. The horn dimensions can be obtained via eqns. 9 and 10 on replacing the values of 2·2 and 3·0 with the new values of $\hat{X}$ and $\hat{Y}$. The edge-field illumination factors Δ can be derived from eqn. 34, and the resultant reflector aperture-plane field distribution can be determined by carrying out the substitutions described in Section 7.

Decreasing $\hat{X}$ and $\hat{Y}$ below the optimum values will result in higher sidelobe levels, less aperture efficiency, increased spillover and a decrease in the antenna 3dB beamwidth. If such a performance modification is required, the procedure will be as described for an increase in $\hat{X}$ and $\hat{Y}$.

The case is similar for circular reflector apertures. Then the new curvature correction can be obtained from eqn. 15, and $\hat{X}$ and $\hat{Y}$ will be varied around their optimum values of 2·58 and 3·41, respectively.

9 Conclusions

This paper has described the derivation of a comprehensive design procedure for determining the dimensions of rectangular flared horns operating in the TE_{10} mode and providing maximum aperture efficiency when the horns are used as primary feeds for parabolic reflectors of any f/d ratio. The reflectors may have either circular or rectangular contours. The derivation is based on an electric-field-matching theorem due to Midgely,[11] and uses a recently reported scalar approximation to carry out the field matching in the focal plane of the parabolic reflectors.[10]

From a knowledge of the reflector f/d ratio or ratios, the design procedure specifies the dimensions of the rectangular horn providing maximum reflector-aperture efficiency for this type of primary feed. In addition, the values of aperture efficiency, spillover power, reradiated power, reflector edge-field illumination and the reflector aperture-plane electric-field distribution are predicted directly for the given reflector–horn combination.

For reflectors having f/d radios greater than 0·75, the results given here are not in marked disagreement with the accepted empirical design guides; e.g. that the reflector edge illumination should be 8–14dB below that at the centre of the aperture.[3] However, at smaller f/d ratios, the maximum-transmission criterion indicates lower levels of relative edge illumination than −14dB. Although the optimisation process described here does not directly use the value of relative edge-field illumination, the results reveal that, for maximum aperture efficiency with this type of primary feed, there is a unique value for the relative edge illumination depending on the f/d ratio of the reflector. For example, the use of an arbitrary edge illumination of −10dB for rectangular reflectors having f/d ratios of less than 0·72 constitutes a rather undesirable tradeoff in aperture efficiency for increased edge illumination, and hence higher sidelobes in the antenna-radiation pattern, to gain a decrease in the antenna beamwidth. The edge-illumination factor given in this analysis includes the 'space-attenuation factor' employed in horn-design techniques using the edge-field illumination as the main parameter.[3]

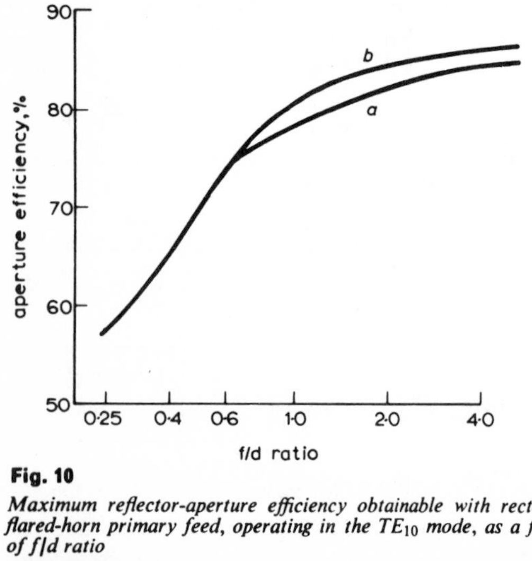

Fig. 10
Maximum reflector-aperture efficiency obtainable with rectangular flared-horn primary feed, operating in the TE_{10} mode, as a function of f/d ratio
a Square reflector
b Circular reflector

Fig. 10 illustrates, as a function of f/d ratio, the maximum aperture efficiency which can be obtained with rectangular flared-horn primary feeds operating in the TE_{10} mode. These values are those predicted by the design procedure of Table 1 and, allowing for additional losses due to reflector imperfections, are quite representative of such experimental evidence as is available.[3, 13]

The design procedure described here has been extrapolated and applied to an elliptical parabolic reflector having dimensions 125ft × 83ft with a focal length of 40ft. Using a rectangular horn feed with dimensions given by this procedure, a gain improvement of more than 1dB was reported over a similar rectangular horn designed on the basis of a direct application of diffraction theory.

The general theory has also been applied in the development of electrically controllable primary feeds for profile-error compensation, and beam steering of large parabolic reflectors.[14, 15, 16]

10 Acknowledgments

The authors wish to thank the University of Birmingham, England, and IIT Research Institute, Chicago, Ill., USA, for facilities to undertake the work.

11 References

1 SILVER, S.: 'Microwave antenna theory and design' (McGraw-Hill, 1949)
2 CUTLER, C. C.: 'Parabolic antenna design for microwaves', *Proc. Inst. Radio Engrs.*, 1947, **35**, pp. 1284–1294
3 JASIK, H.: 'Antenna engineering handbook' (McGraw-Hill, 1961)
4 SKOLNIK, M. I.: 'Introduction to radar systems' (McGraw-Hill, 1962)
5 McKEE, K. E., HOLTUM, A. G., *et. al.*: 'Optimising gain of parabolic antennas', *Microwaves*, 1967, **11**, 3rd March, pp. 34–38
6 VISOCEKAS, R.: 'NonCassegrainian indirect system for aerial illumination', *Proc. IEE*, 1964, **111**, (12), pp. 1969–1975
7 MILNE, K., and RAAB, A. R.: 'Optimum illumination tapers for four-horn and five-horn monopulse aerial systems', *in* 'Design & construction of large steerable aerials', *IEE Conf. Publ.* 21, 1966, pp. 12–16
8 RUZE, J.: 'Antenna tolerance theory—a review', *Proc. Inst. Elect. Electron. Engrs.*, 1966, **54**, pp. 633–640
9 HANSEN, R. C.: 'Microwave scanning antennas' (Academic Press, 1964), Vol. 1
10 RUDGE, A. W.: 'Focal-plane field distribution of parabolic reflectors', *Electron. Lett.*, 1969, **5**, pp. 510–512
11 MIDGELY, D.: 'A theory of receiving aerials applied to the reradiation of an electromagnetic horn', *Proc. IEE*, 1961, **108B**, pp. 645–650
12 RUDGE, A. W.: 'Adaptive primary feeds for phase error compensation in parabolic reflector antennae'. Ph.D. thesis, University of Birmingham, England, 1968
13 'Design & construction of large steerable aerials', *IEE Conf. Publ.* 21, 1966
14 DAVIES, D. E. N., and RUDGE, A. W.: 'Some results of electronic compensation for surface profile errors in parabolic reflectors', *Electron. Lett.*, 1968, **4**, pp. 433–434
15 RUDGE, A. W., and WITHERS, M. J.: 'Beam-scanning primary feed for parabolic reflectors', *ibid.*, 1969, **5**, pp. 39–41
16 RUDGE, A. W., and DAVIES, D. E. N.: 'Electronically controllable primary feed for profile-error compensation of large parabolic reflectors', *Proc. IEE*, 1970, **117**, (2), pp. 351–358
17 ABRAMOWITZ, M., and STEGUN, I. A.: 'Handbook of mathematical functions' (Dover, 1965)

12 Appendixes

12.1 Reradiation and spillover power

The factor $(1 - T)$ of the total power which, on reception, is intercepted by the reflector aperture yet is not absorbed by the primary-feed horn, has two components. The first is that power which falls on the horn aperture, but, not finding a complementary field distribution,[11] is reradiated back towards the reflector. The second component is that power which is not intercepted by the horn aperture, and it thus constitutes the spillover power. These components may be separated out by deriving the transmission efficiency T_i of a model horn having the same dimensions as the TE_{10}-mode horn but providing a perfect match to the reflector focal-field distribution, and thus absorbing all the power incident on its aperture.

The reradiated factor R of the TE_{10}-mode horn will then be given by

$$R = (T_i - T)T_c \quad (19)$$

and the spillover factor T_0 will be given by

$$T_0 = 1 - T_i T_c \quad (20)$$

where T_c is the curvature factor derived in Appendix 12.2.

The ideal aperture-field characteristic E_i for the model horn will be that which provides the best match (over $\pm\hat{x}$, $\pm\hat{y}$) to the incident field given by eqn. 5. Hence

$$E_i = jK_i\left(\frac{\sin k\hat{p}x}{k\hat{p}x}\frac{\sin k\hat{q}y}{k\hat{q}y}\right) \quad (21)$$

where K_i is a factor normalising for unity power over $\pm\hat{x}$, $\pm\hat{y}$.

$$K_i = \left[\frac{k^2\hat{p}\hat{q}}{4\left\{Si(2\hat{X}) - \frac{\sin^2\hat{X}}{\hat{X}}\right\}\left\{Si(2\hat{Y}) - \frac{\sin^2\hat{Y}}{\hat{Y}}\right\}}\right]^{1/2} \quad (22)$$

Then

$$T_i = \int_{-\hat{x}}^{\hat{x}}\int_{-\hat{y}}^{\hat{y}} E_1 E_i dx dy \quad (23)$$

giving, finally,

$$T_i = \frac{2}{\pi}\left[\left\{Si(2\hat{X}) - \frac{\sin^2\hat{X}}{\hat{X}}\right\}\left\{Si(2\hat{Y}) - \frac{\sin^2\hat{Y}}{\hat{Y}}\right\}\right]^{1/2}. \quad (24)$$

The reradiated and spillover factors are shown graphically in Fig. 3 for zero curvature ($T_c = 1\cdot 0$). Additional effects due to curvature will modify the reradiation and spillover, as indicated by eqns. 19 and 20.

12.2 Curvature factor T_c

The design procedure established in Section 8 employs the variation of the main-lobewidth function W with decreasing f/d ratio to extend the theory derived on the basis of large f/d ratios to the region of small f/d ratios. However, while this will maintain a maximum aperture efficiency, this maximum is itself a function of f/d ratio. The aperture distribution F for a rectangular reflector of any f/d ratio may be expressed in scalar form as[10, 12]

$$F(p,q)\begin{cases} = (1 - p^2 - q^2)^{1/2}G(p,q) & \begin{cases}|p| < \hat{p}\\ |q| < \hat{q}\end{cases}\\ = 0 & \begin{cases}|p| > \hat{p}\\ |q| > \hat{q}\end{cases}\end{cases} \quad (25)$$

where G is the 2-dimensional Fourier transform of the feed-horn aperture distribution.

In the derivation of the efficiency factor T, the curvature term $(1 - p^2 - q^2)$ in eqn. 1 was neglected. The effect of the term is to reduce the aperture efficiency with increasing values of $\hat{p}$ and $\hat{q}$ by creating a redistribution of power from the main lobe of the focal-plane distribution to the subsidiary lobes. A curvature factor will be defined as

$$T_c = \frac{\int_{-\hat{p}}^{\hat{p}}\int_{-\hat{q}}^{\hat{q}} F^2(p,q)dpdq}{\int_{-\hat{p}}^{\hat{p}}\int_{-\hat{q}}^{\hat{q}} G^2(p,q)dpdq} \quad (26)$$

We will examine this ratio when the rectangular reflector is fed by a flared rectangular horn operating in the TE_{10} mode. In this instance, the Fourier transform of the horn aperture distribution is separable, and we may write

$$G(p,q) = G_1(p)G_2(q) \quad (27)$$

On incorporating this change, and rearranging, eqn. 26 can be more usefully written in terms of the variables X and Y as

$$1 - T_c = \frac{\frac{\hat{p}^2}{\hat{X}^2}\int_{-\hat{X}}^{\hat{X}}\int_{-\hat{Y}}^{\hat{Y}} G_1^2(X)G_2^2(Y)X^2 dXdY + \frac{\hat{q}^2}{\hat{Y}^2}\int_{-\hat{X}}^{\hat{X}}\int_{\hat{Y}}^{\hat{Y}} G_1^2(X)G_2^2(Y)Y^2 dXdY}{\int_{-\hat{X}}^{\hat{X}}\int_{-\hat{Y}}^{\hat{Y}} G_1^2(X)\,G_2^2(Y)dXdY} \quad (28)$$

where $X = k\hat{x}p$ and $Y = k\hat{y}q$.

The Fourier transform of the aperture distribution of the rectangular horn operating in the TE_{10} mode may be expressed in terms of variables X and Y as[1]

$$G_1(X)G_2(Y) = \frac{\pi^2}{4}\left(\frac{\sin X}{X}\right)\left\{\frac{\cos Y}{\left(\frac{\pi^2}{4} - Y^2\right)}\right\} \quad (29)$$

where $2\hat{x}$ and $2\hat{y}$ correspond to the horn dimensions in the E and H planes, respectively.

Over the range of X and Y for which the integrals will be concerned, the distributions produced by G_1 and G_2 are similar. Hence, to simplify the mathematics, with only a small loss in accuracy, let

$$G_2(Y) = \frac{\sin aY}{aY} \quad (30)$$

where a is a scaling factor given by $\hat{X}_0/\hat{Y}_0$, and $\hat{X}_0$ and $\hat{Y}_0$ correspond to the values of the variable giving maximum transmission. Eqn. 28 now may be written

$$1 - T_c = \frac{1}{2}\frac{\frac{\hat{p}^2}{\hat{X}^2}\int_{-\hat{X}}^{\hat{X}}\int_{-\hat{Y}}^{\hat{Y}} \sin^2 X\frac{\sin^2 aY}{(aY)^2}dXdY + \frac{\hat{q}^2}{\hat{Y}^2}\int_{-\hat{X}}^{\hat{X}}\int_{-\hat{Y}}^{\hat{Y}}\frac{\sin^2 X}{X^2}\sin^2 aY dXdY}{\int_{-\hat{X}}^{\hat{X}}\int_{-\hat{Y}}^{\hat{Y}}\frac{\sin^2 X}{X^2}\frac{\sin^2 aY}{(aY)^2}dXdY} \quad (31)$$

where $\hat{X} = k\hat{x}\hat{p}$ and $\hat{Y} = k\hat{y}\hat{q}$.

Carrying out the integration, we obtain

$$1 - T_c = \frac{1}{2}\left[\frac{\left(1 - \frac{\sin 2\hat{X}}{2\hat{X}}\right)\hat{p}^2}{\hat{X}\left\{Si(2\hat{X}) - \frac{\sin^2\hat{X}}{\hat{X}}\right\}} + \frac{\left\{1 - \frac{\sin(2a\hat{Y})}{2a\hat{Y}}\right\}\hat{q}^2}{a\hat{Y}\left\{Si(2a\hat{Y}) - \frac{\sin^2 a\hat{Y}}{a\hat{Y}}\right\}}\right] \quad (32)$$

For a design incorporating maximum aperture efficiency, $\hat{X} = \hat{X}_0$ and $\hat{Y} = \hat{Y}_0$, and, therefore, noting that $a = \hat{X}_0/\hat{Y}_0$, we obtain

$$T_c = 1 - \frac{1}{2}\left[\frac{\left(1 - \frac{\sin 2\hat{X}_0}{2\hat{X}_0}\right)}{\hat{X}_0\left\{Si(2\hat{X}_0) - \frac{\sin^2\hat{X}_0}{\hat{X}_0}\right\}}\right](\hat{p}^2 + \hat{q}^2) \quad (33)$$

A graph of this function against $(\hat{p}^2 + \hat{q}^2)$ is shown in Fig. 6.

12.3 Edge-field illumination factor Δ

The aperture field distribution F of a parabolic reflector fed by a primary feed situated at its focus may be expressed by eqn. 25. The 2-dimensional Fourier transform G of the aperture distribution of a rectangular horn operating in the TE_{10} mode is given by eqn. 29. Thus, at the reflector edges in the horizontal and vertical planes, the amplitude of the field distribution, normalised for a unity value at the centre of the reflector, will be given by

$$\left.\begin{aligned} \Delta p &= \frac{\sin \hat{X}}{\hat{X}}(1-\hat{p}^2)^{1/2} && \text{(E plane)} \\ \Delta q &= \frac{\pi^2}{4}\left\{\frac{\cos \hat{Y}}{\left(\frac{\pi^2}{4}-\hat{Y}^2\right)}\right\}(1-\hat{q}^2)^{1/2} && \text{(H plane)} \end{aligned}\right\} \quad . \quad . \quad . \quad (34)$$

If $\hat{X}$ and $\hat{Y}$ are chosen to maintain a specific illumination condition (e.g., $\hat{X} = 2{\cdot}2$, $\hat{Y} = 3{\cdot}0$ for maximum transmission for the rectangular reflector and $\hat{X} = 2{\cdot}58$, $\hat{Y} = 3{\cdot}51$ for the circular reflector), Δ will vary only with the sine of the maximum halfangle subtended in the principal planes ($\hat{p}$, $\hat{q}$). Fig. 7 shows the function plotted against either $\hat{p}$ or $\hat{q}$.

Polarization-Transforming Antenna Feed Horns

Abstract—**A set of polarization-transforming antenna feed horns has been developed for an X-band radar antenna. Use of the proper feed horn permits transmission of horizontal, vertical, 45° linear, 135° linear, right circular or left circular polarization, and reception of both the parallel- (same sense as transmitted) and orthogonal-polarized return.**

A set of interchangeable polarization-transforming feed horns has been developed for a rapid-scan X-band radar antenna [1]. The antenna consists of four paraboloidal dishes arranged back-to-back on a vertical spindle; these dishes are sequentially energized as they pass through a given angular sector. A dual-mode coupler [2] is used to excite a square waveguide feed horn for each dish. If an empty square waveguide feed horn is used, a single linear polarization (e.g., horizontal) will be radiated by the antenna. Substitution of one of the polarization-transforming antenna feed horns described later for the empty square waveguide feed permits transmission of vertical, 45° linear, 135° linear, right circular or left circular polarization with the same horizontally polarized input. Simultaneous reception of both the parallel- (same sense as transmitted) and cross- (orthogonal) polarized returns is attained using the same feed horn and dual-mode coupler which were used for transmission. In addition, use of different feed horns on the four dishes of the antenna allows nearly simultaneous measurements (0.1-s separation) to be performed using up to four of the available polarizations.

The basic polarization-transforming element in the feed horn is a dielectric slab (polarization transducer) having wedge tapers at each end for matching and placed diagonally in the square waveguide feed horn. Fig. 1 shows the dielectric-slab polarization transducer in square waveguide. If a single TE_{01} waveguide mode is incident on such a polarization transducer, energy is coupled from the incident TE_{01} mode into the orthogonal TE_{10} mode, the amount of coupling being dependent upon the length of the dielectric slab. This behavior is shown in Fig. 2, where the power in each of the two orthogonal waveguide modes at the output of the polarization transducer, called parallel (TE_{01}) and orthogonal (TE_{10}) modes, is plotted as a function of length of the dielectric slab. As predicted by coupled-mode theory [3], there is a sinusoidal dependence of the amplitude of these modes on the length of the dielectric slab, and the relative time phase between the two modes remains constant at 90° until the first amplitude null is reached. This behavior is not critically dependent upon frequency, remaining essentially the same from 9.2 to 9.6 GHz.

If the length of the dielectric-slab polarization transducer is such that all of the energy is transformed into the orthogonal mode (this length is approximately 4.5 in for the slab of Fig. 2), an input which is horizontally polarized will produce an output which is vertically polarized, and vice versa. As can be seen from Fig. 2, the parallel component at a length of 4.5 in is more than 40 dB below the orthogonal component, resulting in almost pure linear polarization at the output.

If the length of the dielectric-slab polarization transducer is such that the two output modes are equal in amplitude (for the slab of Fig. 2, this length is approximately 2.6 in, including 1-in wedge tapers at each end for matching), a single linearly polarized input produces two equal-amplitude, orthogonal, linearly polarized output components, differing in time phase by 90°. Therefore, such a slab changes a linearly polarized input into a circularly polarized output. If the orientation of the dielectric slab is rotated 90°, the sense of circularity of the output polarization is reversed. The circularly polarized feed horn which was fabricated [4] utilized a Teflon slab 0.25 in thick and 3.75 in long, (including 1-in wedge tapers at each end for matching) rather than the polystyrene slab discussed previously.

Manuscript received January 4, 1971; revised March 29, 1971. This work was supported in part by the Department of the Navy, Naval Ship Systems Command, under Contract N00024-68-C-1125.

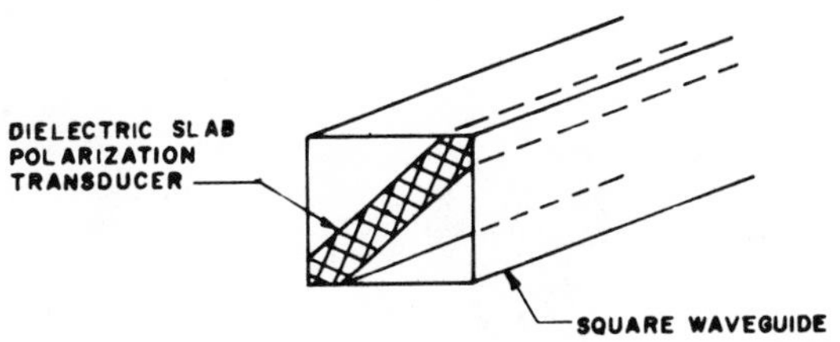

Fig. 1. Dielectric slab polarization transducer in square waveguide.

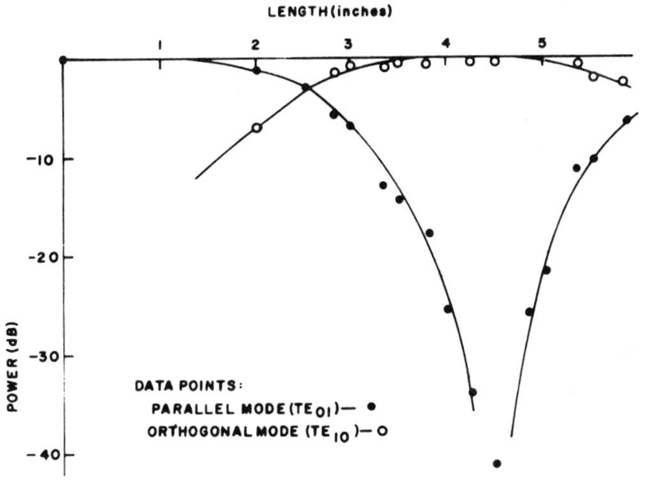

Fig. 2. Power in two orthogonal output modes of dielectric slab polarization transducer as function of length. (Input to transducer was only parallel (TE_{01}) mode. Transducer was polystyrene, 0.25 in thick. Length includes 1-in wedge tapers at each end for matching. Inside dimensions of square waveguide were 0.840 in by 0.840 in and frequency was 9.4 GHz.)

If the relative time phase between the output components of the linear-to-circular polarization transducer is adjusted so that the two equal-amplitude, orthogonal (horizontal and vertical) components are in time phase, the conditions for 45° linear polarization will be realized. A dielectric-slab quarter-wave plate placed parallel to one of the waveguide walls may be utilized to retard one of the orthogonal linear output components of the linear-to-circular polarization transducer 90° with respect to the other component, thus producing 45° linear output polarization. A horn was fabricated using a 0.25-in thick, 2.6-in long (including 1-in wedge tapers at each end for matching), polystyrene, linear-to-circular polarization transducer, followed by a quarter-wave plate consisting of a Teflon slab 0.25 in thick and 1.9 in long (including 0.5-in wedge tapers at each end for matching) centered upright in the square waveguide. These particular materials and dimensional ratios were selected so that the entire assembly would be short enough to fit into an existing feed horn, and the feed performed well from 9.2 to 9.6 GHz. However, if extremely broad-band performance is desired, the quarter-wave plate may be designed using techniques described by Ayres [5]. If the orientation of both slabs is rotated by 90°, the output polarization will also be rotated by 90°.

Fig. 3 shows the four types of feed horns which were developed. The ends of the tapered dielectric slabs are clearly visible; the diagonal tapers are ends of the dielectric-slab polarization transducers. The taper which is parallel to the bottom of the waveguide is the end of the quarter-wave plate; in this horn, the dielec-

Reprinted from *IEEE Trans. Antennas Propagat.*, vol. AP-19, pp. 681-682, Sept. 1971.

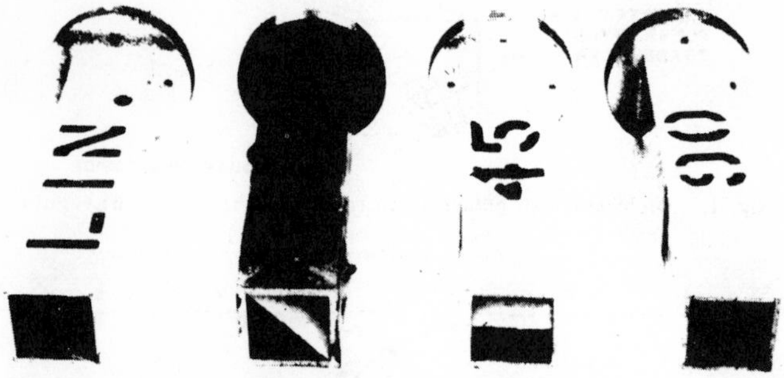

Fig. 3. Polarization-transforming antenna feed horns. For horizontally polarized input, output polarization will be, from left to right, horizontal (this horn contains no dielectric inserts), circular, 45° linear, and vertical.

tric-slab polarization transducer is located immediately behind this quarter-wave plate. The threaded rings on the rear of the polarization-transforming feed horns are used to attach the feeds to the dual-mode coupler. The protrusions visible on the sides of the square waveguides are where dielectric pins were inserted to secure the dielectric slabs.

The mock-up of one of the rapid-scan radar antennas was mounted on the antenna range for testing. Antenna patterns were recorded, and the gain and polarization of the antenna when fed by each of the four feed horns was measured at frequencies of 9.2, 9.4, and 9.6 GHz, and all feeds performed well over this frequency range. While none of the other feed horns produced as low sidelobes as the empty square waveguide feed for which the antenna was originally designed, the main lobe shape and 3-dB beamwidths were very similar for all of the feed horns over the frequencies of interest. Sidelobe levels were more than 22 dB down from the peak of the main beam in all cases. The gains of the antenna using various feed horns were compared, and, within experimental error (approximately 1/4 dB), the gains were the same for the different types of feed horns and for various feed horns of the same type.

The VSWR of each of these feeds was 1.3:1 or less over the frequency range 9.2 to 9.6 GHz. All of the feeds were high-power tested in the laboratory and radiated a 400-kW, 0.5-μs pulse with no indication of breakdown or deterioration due to the high power levels.

George W. Ewell
Eng. Exp. Stn.
Georgia Inst. Technol
Atlanta, Ga 30332

References

[1] E. R. Flynt *et al.*, "Appendices to A-725 final report," Eng. Exp. Stn., Georgia Inst. Technol., Atlanta, Contract NObsr-91024, Appendix A, Dec. 31, 1967.
[2] R. C. Johnson, F. L. Cain, and E. N. Bone, "Dual-mode coupler," *IEEE Trans. Microwave Theory Tech.* (Corresp.), vol. MTT-15, Nov. 1967, pp. 651–652.
[3] D. A. Watkins, *Topics in Electromagnetic Theory*. New York: Wiley, 1958, ch. 3.
[4] R. P. Zimmer, "Appendix B" in "Appendices to A-725 final report," E. R. Flynt *et al.*, Eds., Eng. Exp. Stn., Georgia Inst. Technol., Atlanta, Contract NObsr-91024, Dec. 31, 1967.
[5] W. P. Ayres, "Broad-band quarter-wave plates," *IRE Trans. Microwave Theory Tech.*, vol. MTT-5, Oct. 1957, pp. 258–261.

SIMPLE SMALL PRIMARY FEED FOR LARGE OPENING ANGLES AND HIGH APERTURE EFFICIENCY

Indexing terms: Antenna feeders, Reflector antennas, Circular waveguides, Antenna-radiation patterns

The most important characteristics of a waveguide feed with four $\lambda/4$ chokes offset from the waveguide aperture are discussed. This feed is useful for illumination of deep paraboloidal reflectors ($F/D < 0{\cdot}35$) and shows very good E–H plane equality and broad pattern bandwidth.

There exist only a few simple feed configurations based on a circular waveguide which are suitable for feeding deep paraboloid reflectors with focal-length/diameter ratios F/D less than 0·35. We have developed a feed,[1] derived from circular waveguide,[1, 2] which has a disc at the aperture[3] for the purpose of efficiency feeding the 100 m radiotelescope in Effelsberg from its primary focus. This telescope has an F/D ratio of 0·3, corresponding to a half-opening angle of $\theta_0 = 79{\cdot}8°$. One of the disadvantages of a single-mode circular waveguide is that the front/back ratio is poor ($F/B = -13$ dB).[1] Chokes can be introduced which suppress the current distribution on the outside of the waveguide walls, and therefore produce F/B values of better than 32 dB, as seen in the patterns shown in Figs. 2*a* and *b*. They also improve the axial symmetry of the radiation pattern.

Amplitude pattern: Lagrone and Roberts[4] achieved an F/B ratio greater than 38 dB and a sidelobe level greater than 16 dB by applying such $\lambda/4$ chokes at a rectangular pyramidal horn. In addition, experiments by Geyer[5] showed that circular patterns resulted from adding choke rings around a conical horn. We investigated experimentally the possibility of extending the multichoke concept on feeds for illumination of deep dishes ($65° < \theta_0 < 83°$). Optimisation experiments produced the feed configuration shown in Fig. 1. All values given in Fig. 1 are relative to the free-space wavelength λ_0. The position of the chokes, well behind the waveguide aperture, enabled a breakthrough in the ability to produce a broad 10 dB beamwidth and also a steep taper. The electrical length of this waveguide feed is of the order of $0{\cdot}631\lambda_0$ (Fig. 1), which seems to be extremely short.

We found two dominating facts from these experiments: first, the 10 dB beamwidth $\Delta\theta_{10dB}$ for large opening angles θ_0 ($100° < \Delta\theta_{10dB} < 156°$) is limited by the TE_{11} waveguide diameter if *no* matching devices (irises, screwtuners) are employed. Here, if rather large waveguide diameters are chosen ($0{\cdot}744 < d/\lambda_0 < 0{\cdot}900$), the dispersion remains low and there are practically no broadband ($\pm 3\%$) matching problems. Secondly, if broader 10 dB beamwidths are desired ($156° < \Delta\theta_{10dB} < 174°$), the waveguide diameter *must* be diminished to about $d/\lambda_0 \leqslant 0{\cdot}744$. This increases the dispersion and introduces matching problems. To circumvent

Reprinted with permission from *Electron. Lett.*, vol. 8, pp. 474–476, Sept. 21, 1972.

these difficulties, it is advisable, for simplicity, to introduce a conical junction at a distance of more than $1{\cdot}0\lambda_g$ behind the feeder aperture which forms a transition to a larger-diameter waveguide. Two examples are shown in Figs. 2*a* and *b* to demonstrate the behaviour discussed above. The amplitude pattern of Fig. 2*a* belongs to a scaled 2·8 cm model of an 11 cm original feed, with a waveguide diameter of $d/\lambda = 0{\cdot}744$ ($\Delta\theta_{10dB} = 159{\cdot}3^\circ$ in the *H*, *E* and 45° planes).

Fig. 2*b* refers to a model of an optimum 6 cm original feed (Fig. 1) of $d/\lambda = 0{\cdot}846$ ($\Delta\theta_{10dB} = 143{\cdot}6^\circ$ in the *H*, *E* and 45° planes) which has a ±10% pattern bandwidth (*E*–*H* plane deviation $\delta\theta_{10dB} \leq 0{\cdot}4^\circ$). Further, in Table 1, computed values for the feed efficiency of the two feeds are given. These computed values take no account of losses, aperture blockage (which, for the 100 m telescope, is significant), or the reductions due to phase variations across the reflecting surface. At 11 cm, the overall telescope aperture efficiency derived from radio source measurements is 55%±5%.

Phase pattern: Fig. 3 shows the phase pattern for the three phase-centre positions of the *H*, *E* and 45° planes for the 11 cm model. The maximum phase deviation at the opening angle θ_0 of the whole reflector (*E* plane) of $\Delta\phi = 27{\cdot}3^\circ$ fulfils approximately the well known Silver[3] phase condition ($\Delta\phi_{bound} \leq \lambda_0/16 = 22{\cdot}5^\circ$). The *E*, *H* and 45° plane phase centres are at 16·1, 7·6 and 17·3 mm, respectively, behind the waveguide aperture of the 11 cm original.

Impedance behaviour: The feeds for 11 and 6 cm wavelengths were made for radioastronomical measurements. The bandwidth required at the frequency of 2695 MHz was 60 MHz. This bandwidth was, in fact, achieved (v.s.w.r. < 1·06) with a 2-step circular-to-rectangular transducer. At the wavelength of 6 cm, operation from 4550 to 5050 MHz is required. Although the diameter of the feeding waveguide was increased from $0{\cdot}744\lambda_0$ to $0{\cdot}846\lambda_0$, a maximum matching bandwidth

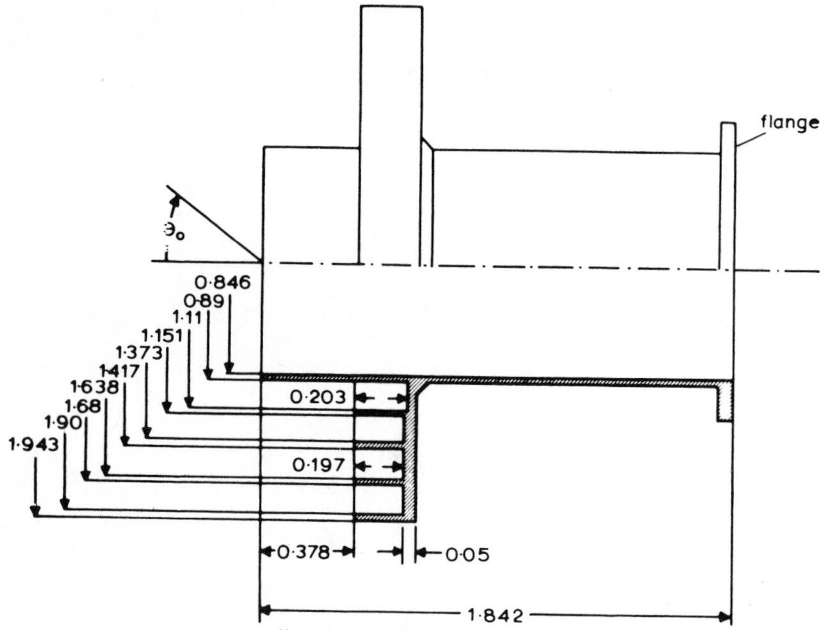

Fig. 1 *Primary-focus feed optimised for a 51·5 mm circular waveguide for 6·1 cm wavelength with four chokes*

Table 1 AVERAGE 10 dB BEAMWIDTH ($\Delta\theta_{10av}$), FRONT/BACK RATIO F/B, PATTERN BANDWIDTH Δf_{pat}, SPILLOVER POWER P_{sp}, FEED EFFICIENCY η_F, APERTURE EFFICIENCY η_{ap} AND DIRECTIVITY OF THE 100 m TELESCOPE FED BY THIS FEEDER

Feeder type	Figure	d_{TE11}/λ_0	$\Delta\theta_{10av}$	F/B	Δf_{pat}	P_{sp}	D_F	η_F	η_{ap}	D_{EF}
cm			deg	dB	%	%	dB	%	%	dB
11·1	2a	0·744	159·3	32	±3	4·5	6·25	95·5	78·4	67·76
6·1	2b	0·846	143·6	36	±10	3·6	7·4	96·4	73·7	72·76

All calculated values are from the measured feed pattern in the *E*, *H* and 45 planes

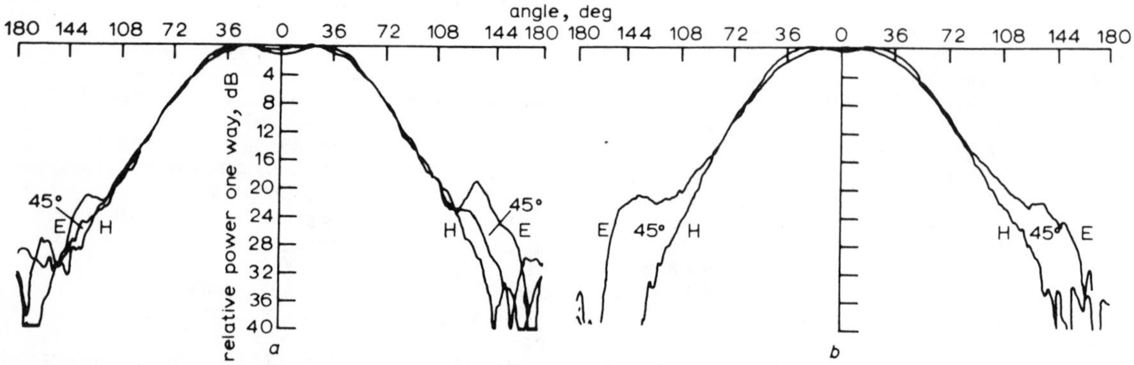

Fig. 2 *Amplitude pattern of a scaled 2·8 cm model of an original*

a 11 cm feed (waveguide diameter = $0{\cdot}744\lambda$)
b 6 cm feed (waveguide diameter $0{\cdot}846\lambda$, see Fig. 1)
Azimuth = ±180°, power: $0 < P < -40$ dB

Table 2 COMPARISON OF DATA OF SEVERAL FEEDERS FOR WIDE OPENING ANGLE (ALL FEEDERS GENERATE ONLY ONE MODE)

Value	Koch *et al.*[6]	McInnes and Booker	Wohlleben and Mattes
D_0/λ_0	1·95	7·38	1·943
L_0/λ_0	4·30	1·90	0·631*
Δf_{pat}, %	±3·0	±10·0	±10·0
$\Delta_{10dB\,max}$, deg	150·0	100·0	146·0
η_{ap}, %	71·0	68·0	74·0

* At this small diameter, a simultaneous operation with dipoles[8] is possible

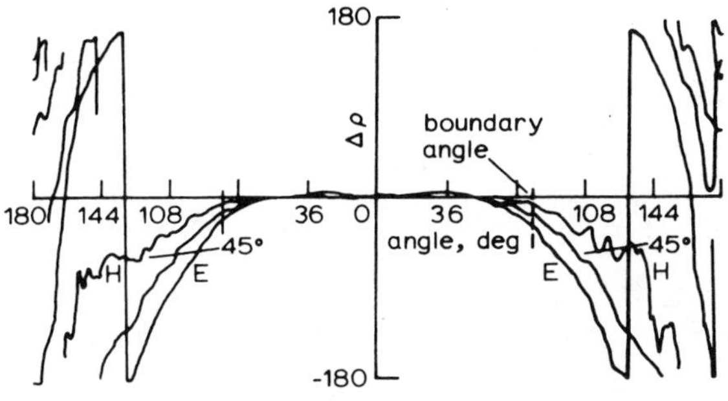

Fig. 3 *Phase pattern of the scaled 2·8 cm model of an 11 cm original for the E, 45° and H planes phase centre*
Azimuth = ±180°, phase: −180 < Δf < +180°

(v.s.w.r. < 1·06) of 250 MHz was achieved. A 3-step transducer was developed to achieve this 5% bandwidth. Further work is proceeding to match over as wide a frequency band as the polar patterns remain constant.

Comparison with other feeds: Feeds for reflecting telescopes of *F/D* ratios of 0·3 have been manufactured in a number of antenna laboratories. All attempt to illuminate the antennas efficiently. Comparisons give a guide to the relative merits of each type of feed, for which purpose published data[6, 7] have been compiled in Table 2. The great advantage of the feed described in this letter is its compact physical size. As a result, multifrequency operation will be possible.

Acknowledgments: The authors gratefully thank Prof. R. Wielebinski for helpful discussions, and Prof. P. J. B. Clarricoats, Queen Mary College, London, for the stimulation to write this letter.

R. WOHLLEBEN
H. MATTES
O. LOCHNER

Max-Planck-Institut für Radioastronomie
Argelanderstrasse 3
D-53 Bonn, W. Germany

30th August 1972

References

1 WOHLLEBEN, R., WIELEBINSKI, R., and MATTES, H.: 'Feeds for the 100 m Effelsberg telescope'. Proceedings of 2nd European microwave conference, Stockholm, Aug. 1971, paper B5/5
2 LANDECKER, T. L., and WIELEBINSKI, R.: 'Radiation pattern measurements of open circular and coaxial waveguides'. Proceedings of the ANZASS Congress (Australia), Hobart, 1965, pp. 1–20
3 SILVER, S.: 'Microwave antenna theory and design—Vol. 12' (MIT series, Dover-ISE, 1965), pp. 336–340
4 LAGRONE, A. H., and ROBERTS, G. F.: 'Minor lobe suppression in a rectangular horn antenna through the utilization of a high impedance choke flange', *IEEE Trans.*, 1966, **AP-14**, pp. 102–104
5 GEYER, H.: 'Runder Hornstrahler mit ringförmigen Sperrtöpfen zur gleichzeitigen Übertragung zweier polarisationsentkoppelter Wellen', *Frequenz*, 1966, **20**, pp. 22–28 (especially p. 27)
6 MCINNES, P. A., and BOOKER, D. D.: 'Corrugated conical horns with very wide flare angle'. Proceedings of the 2nd European microwave conference, Stockholm, Aug. 1971, paper B7/2
7 KOCH, F. G., SCHEFFER, H., and THIELEN, H.: 'Koaxialerreger für Parabolantennen mit hohem Flächenwirkungsgrad und geringer Überstrahlung', *Nachrichtentech. Fachber.*, 1972, **45**, pp. 70–75
8 WOHLLEBEN, R., and MATTES, H.: 'Doppeldipol-Erreger für den Primärfokus des 100 m Radioteleskops Effelsberg', *Nachrichtentech. Fachber.*, 1972, **45**, pp. 95–97

Optimum Design of Horn Feeds for Reflector Antennas

WILLIAM M. TRUMAN AND CONSTANTINE A. BALANIS

Abstract—A method of determining the optimum dimensions of a horn feed for a parabolic reflector using the power transferred to the feed as a criterion is described. To reduce the computation time, the focal plane and feed-horn aperture field distributions were expanded into finite power series whose coefficients were determined using collocation techniques. The paper extends previous work to include horns with flare angles greater than 10° and contains useful design curves.

INTRODUCTION

Although horns have been used as feeds for reflectors for many years, it was not until recently that a technique to determine the horn dimensions that produced maximum power transmission to the feed or to maximize the aperture efficiency was reported. Rudge and Withers [1] developed the technique by utilizing a theorem reported by Midgely [2]. The equation developed gives a measure of the power transferred to the feed as a function of the reflector focal plane field and the feed-horn aperture field. Rudge [3] found an integral equation for the focal plane field of the reflector for any f/d ratio. However, his approximations leading to the integration of the focal plane field expression are not very accurate for the more practical arrangements of reflector systems ($0.25 < f/d < 1.0$, or $90° > \theta_{max} > 30°$). Also, his assumed feed aperture field does not take into account the divergent phase front of the horn field. In this paper techniques are presented to eliminate the above shortcomings, reduce the computation time, and present useful design curves.

THEORY

For two antennas with linearly polarized fields in the same direction, the power transmission is given [2] by

$$P_r = K \int_S E_1 E_2 \, ds \tag{1}$$

where E_1, E_2 are the scalar fields created by each antenna individually on a common surface S, and K is a constant of proportionality. The expression is derived using the Lorentz reciprocity theorem [2]. In a reflector system arrangement, E_1 represents the reflector focal plane field, E_2 the feed-horn aperture field, and S the horn aperture used as the common surface of integration. To find the optimum dimensions of the horn for a given reflector, the power transmitted by the horn is kept constant while the dimensions are varied until P_r is maximized.

Referring to [4, fig. 2], Rudge [3] expressed the reflector focal plane field as

$$E_1(\psi) = G_1 \int_0^{\hat{u}} \frac{u}{(1-u^2)^{1/2}} J_0(\psi u) \, du \tag{2}$$

where, using the coordinate system of Fig. 1, $u = \sin\theta$, $\hat{u} = \sin\theta_{max}$, $\psi = kt = k(x^2+y^2)^{1/2}$, and G_1 is a constant.

In order to integrate (2), $J_0(\psi u)$ was expanded in a finite power series of the form

$$J_0(\psi u) = 1 + A_1(\psi u)^2 + B_1(\psi u)^4 + C_1(\psi u)^6 + D_1(\psi u)^8 + E_1(\psi u)^{10} + F_1(\psi u)^{12} \tag{3}$$

where

$$\begin{aligned} A_1 &= -0.2499275 \\ B_1 &= 0.1557649 \times 10^{-1} \\ C_1 &= -0.4255879 \times 10^{-3} \\ D_1 &= 0.6194299 \times 10^{-5} \\ E_1 &= -0.4867434 \times 10^{-7} \\ F_1 &= 0.1635705 \times 10^{-9}. \end{aligned} \tag{4}$$

Manuscript received May 29, 1973; revised January 17, 1974.
The authors are with the Department of Electrical Engineering, West Virginia University, Morgantown, W. Va. 26506.

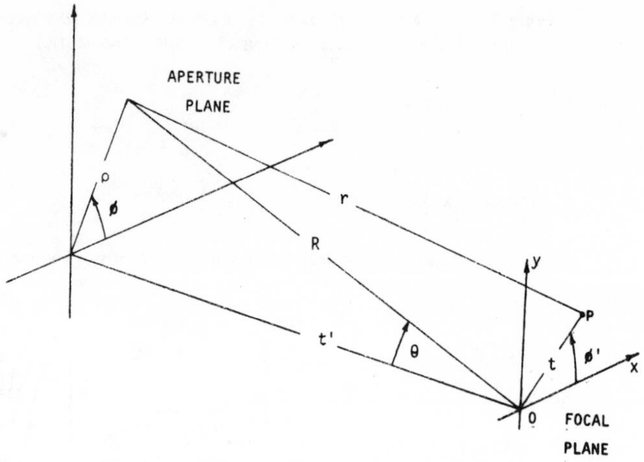

Fig. 1. Reflector and feed system coordinates.

The coefficients were determined using collocation and are valid in the range $0 \le \psi u \le 9$. With this expression for $J_0(\psi u)$, (2) can be integrated in a closed form, the accuracy of which will be discussed later.

In the horn aperture, a TE_{10} mode field is assumed of the form

$$E_2(X,Y) = G_2 \exp\left(-j\frac{X^2}{4\pi\rho_x}\right)\exp\left(-j\frac{Y^2}{4\pi\rho_y}\right)\cos\left(\frac{\pi}{2\hat{Y}}Y\right) \tag{5}$$

where $X = kx$, $Y = ky$, $\hat{X} = k\hat{x}$, $\hat{Y} = k\hat{y}$, $\hat{x}$ is half the horn height, $\hat{y}$ is half the horn width, ρ_x and ρ_y are the horn lengths (in wavelengths) in the E- and H-planes, respectively, and $G_2 = G_2'/(\hat{X}\hat{Y})^{1/2}$ is a normalization factor.

To perform the integration of (1) using (2) and (5), with reduced computation time, it was decided to expand the exponential and cosine terms of (5) into finite series and evaluate the coefficients as was done for (3). A detailed description of the expansions is given in [5].

RESULTS AND CONCLUSIONS

When $\hat{u} = 1$, (2) can be integrated into a closed form solution, and when $\hat{u}$ is small the approximate closed form solution used by Rudge and Withers [1] can be obtained as discussed in [5]. To check the validity of the collocation method used in the computations presented in this paper, we compared the series expansion technique against numerical integration and the special closed form solutions mentioned above.

For $\hat{u} = 1$, the numerical integration and collocation methods agreed with the exact closed form solution to within one percent over the needed range of ψ. For small $\hat{u}$ ($\hat{u} = 0.4$), the collocation method agreed with the numerical integration to within one percent where the approximate closed form solution, used by Rudge and Withers [1] in their design, agreed only to within 15 percent with the results of numerical integration. An expanded discussion of the accuracy of the results is presented in [5]. The performed comparisons gave a degree of confidence in our series expansion method employed for our computations.

In Fig. 2 we plotted the optimum horn dimensions versus f/d ratio for various horn lengths. The stars on the plots are the dimensions calculated using the method of Rudge and Withers [1], which apply for horns of infinite length. With the curves shown in Fig. 2, one can find the optimum dimensions of a horn for a reflector of any practical f/d ratio and, by interpolation, for any practical horn length.

To find the optimum dimensions shown in Fig. 2, the horn height and width were varied until P_r of (1) was maximized. A typical variation of P_r as a function of the horn dimensions is shown in Fig. 3 for $\hat{u} = 0.25$. This figure gives an indication of the sensitivity of P_r to a change in the horn dimensions.

It should also be pointed out that although the techniques were applied to a pyramidal feed-horn with a TE_{10} field distribution, the

Reprinted from *IEEE Trans. Antennas Propagat.*, vol. AP-22, pp. 585–586, July 1974.

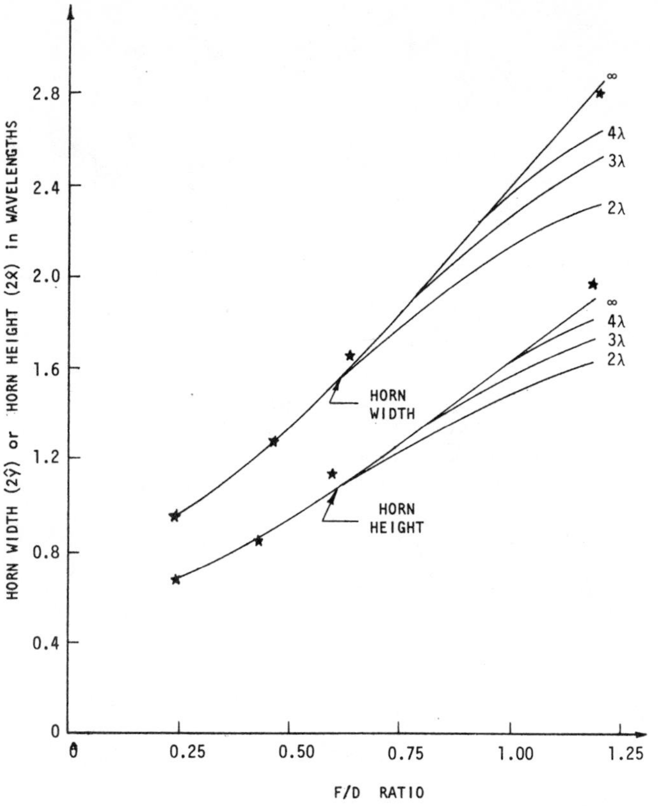

Fig. 2. Optimum horn dimensions versus f/d ratio for various horn lengths.

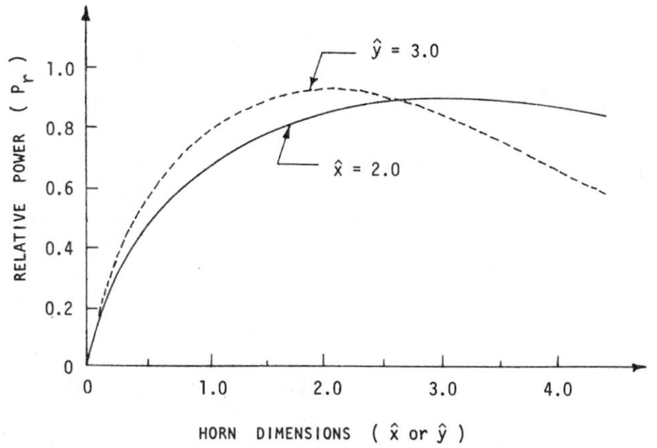

Fig. 3. Relative magnitude of power transfer as function of horn dimensions.

methods can be used for any other feed with any desired field variation.

REFERENCES

[1] A. W. Rudge and M. J. Withers, "Design of flared-horn primary feeds for parabolic reflector antennas," *Proc. IEE*, 108B, pp. 1741–1749, 1961.

[2] D. Midgely, "A theory of receiving aerials applied to the reradiation of an electromagnetic horn," *Proc. IEEE*, 108B, pp. 645–650, 1961.

[3] A. W. Rudge, "Focal-plane field distribution of parabolic reflectors," *Electron. Lett.*, vol. 5, pp. 510–512, 1969.

[4] P. A. Matthews and A. L. Cullen, "A study of the field distribution at an axial focus of a square microwave lens," *Proc. IEE*, 103C, pp. 449–456, 1956.

[5] W. M. Truman, "Optimization design methods of feeds for reflector antennas," MSEE thesis, Dep. Elec. Eng., West Virginia University, Morgantown, W. Va., Dec. 1973.

Part V
Multimode Horns

This part begins with a paper on the diagonal horn that is sometimes arbitrarily classified as "multimode" on the basis that its internal fields consist of a superposition of the orthogonal TE_{01} and TE_{10} modes in square waveguide. It is not a multimode horn in the sense that it makes use of higher order TE or TM modes. Consequently, it possesses only some of the desirable features of the usual multimode horn. Thus, it radiates a pattern with equal E- and H-plane beamwidths, suppressed E-plane sidelobes and beamwidths in the intercardinal planes that are nearly, but not quite, equal to those in the principal planes. These properties, however, are achieved only at the expense of pairs of cross-polarized lobes in the intercardinal planes that render it unsuitable for applications in which a high degree of polarization purity is required. The principle of the diagonal horn seems to have been known in Germany and to Ohio State University researchers in the 1950's. A low frequency version, called TAHA, was described in 1960 [1].

The original concept of using both dominant and higher order modes in a radiating horn appears to have been due to Potter. In the second paper in this part, he describes a technique for generating and combining a TM_{11} mode field with that of the dominant TE_{11} field in a conical horn in such a way as to create a high degree of axial symmetry, along with E-plane sidelobe suppression, in the radiated beam. There follow two short papers, given at the Northeast Radio Engineering Meeting (NEREM) in 1963, in the first of which Potter and Ludwig analyze the possibilities of beam shaping through superposition of higher modes in conical horns. In the second of these short papers, Jensen describes the extension of the multimode technique to pyramidal horns. In this case, the dominant mode, of course, is the TE_{10}, while the appropriate higher mode (and hence the counterpart of the TM_{11} mode in the conical horn) is a mixture of the TE_{12} and TM_{12} modes. This single, hybrid mode was called EM_{12} by Drabowitz [2] in recognition of the fact that the TE_{12} and TM_{12} modes have the same cutoff frequency and hence propagate with the same phase velocity. A useful discussion of higher order modes in large, square apertures will be found in Lenzing [3].

A definitive development of pattern synthesis for circular aperture horns is given by Ludwig in the fifth paper. He shows that the θ and $\emptyset$ components of the radiated field may be synthesized, respectively, from TM and TE round waveguide modes, and gives examples in which up to four modes are used. A short paper by Turrin follows, in which a very compact TM_{11} mode transducer and round horn are combined to form a small prime-focus feed possessing all the attributes of a multimode horn. Generation of the TM_{11} mode occurs due to an abrupt flare angle change in the guide. Cohn, in the next paper, shows how to apply flare angle changes to generate the hybrid $TE_{12} + TM_{12}$ mode in a pyramidal horn and gives an example of a feed for a large Cassegrain system. The same techniques are applied by Han and Wickert in their paper describing a multimode rectangular aperture horn. It radiates a circularly polarized beam of elliptical cross section that is useful for continental area coverage from a high altitude spacecraft.

A short article by Gruner describes a prime-focus multimode feed horn capable of operating in two frequency bands, at 4 and 6 GHz. This is followed by a longer paper by Koch who adopts a somewhat different approach toward obtaining a high aperture efficiency feed system for a paraboloid. He observes that a sector shaped beam, giving uniform illumination and low spillover over the reflector, can be generated by a $J_1(x)/x$ type of distribution over an infinitely large circular aperture. He approximates this distribution in a practical way by building up a feed aperture out of a central horn surrounded by coaxial annular rings in which appropriate amplitude tapers and field reversals take place.

The final three short papers in this part do not deal with horn radiators per se, but rather with means for converting dominant mode TE_{11} energy in a round guide into TM_{11} mode energy. Tomiyasu gives design data for a large diameter conical waveguide junction, while Agarwal and Nagelberg, and English treat the case of a step discontinuity at the junction of two round guides of unequal diameters. Loading by means of a dielectric ring at the step discontinuity, according to Agarwal and Nagelberg, appears to result in greater bandwidth compared to an unloaded step [4].

Since the dominant mode and the desired higher modes propagate with different velocities as they travel from the point of mode generation to the horn aperture, they will arrive in the correct phase relationship at only one frequency. For this reason, bandwidth is quite limited, and this appears to be the principal shortcoming of the multimode horn. An ingenious method for partially reducing this dispersion was devised by Ajioka and Harry [5] and yielded a 20 percent operating bandwidth.

References

[1] H. Brueckmann and B. Hagaman, "Horn antennas for HF long-range communication," *IEEE Trans. Antennas Propagat.*, vol. AP-8, pp. 523–526, Sept. 1960.

[2] S. Drabowitz, "Multimode antennas," *Microwave J.*, vol. 9, pp. 41–51, Jan. 1966.

[3] H. F. Lenzing, "Higher-order mode excitation in large-aperture receiving antennas," *Microwave J.*, vol. 12, pp. 61–65, Dec. 1969.

[4] E. Nagelberg and J. Shefer, "Mode conversion in circular waveguides," *Bell Syst. Tech. J.*, vol. 44, pp. 1321–1328, Sept. 1965.

[5] J. S. Ajioka and H. E. Harry, Jr., "Shaped beam antenna for earth coverage from a stabilized satellite," *IEEE Trans. Antennas Propagat.*, vol. AP-18, pp. 323–327, May 1970.

THE DIAGONAL HORN ANTENNA

A. W. LOVE
WILEY ELECTRONICS CO.
Phoenix • Arizona

Introduction

An unusual form of electromagnetic horn antenna has been investigated and found to have some very desirable properties. All cross-sections through the horn are square, including the aperture. For small flare angles, however, the mode of propagation within the horn is principally such that the electric vector is parallel to one of the diagonals. The resulting diagonal polarization of the aperture field has given rise to the name 'diagonal horn.'

The resulting radiation pattern in the far field possesses almost perfect circular symmetry so that the three, 10 and 20 db beamwidths are very closely equal, not only in the principal E and H planes, but also in the 45° and 135° planes. Side lobes in the principal planes are observed to be at least 30 db down, with a theoretical limit of 31.5 db. In the ±45° planes, first side lobes have been observed to lie between 23 and 27 db down, despite a theoretically predicted level of 19.2 db. Although cross-polarized lobes appear at about 16 db down in the ±45° planes, the horn efficiency remains high.

By contrast, a conventional pyramidal horn of square cross section will have an H-plane half power beamwidth about 35 per cent wider than that in the E-plane. Although its H-plane side lobe performance will be quite acceptable, in the E-plane, the first lobes usually appear at a 12 or 13 db level. The difference between the E and H-plane far field patterns is due to the nature of the aperture field. In the E-plane of the aperture, the field is constant, whereas in the H-plane, the field amplitude tapers in a cosine fashion, just as for the TE_{01} mode in rectangular waveguide.

To the best of the author's knowledge, this form of horn was first used by Tingye Li[1] as a feed for illuminating the paraxial region of a spherical reflecting surface. The horn's unusual properties have apparently escaped general notice, however, and have not been exploited until quite recently.

The Field in the Aperture

The wave which propagates in the slowly flaring diagonal horn is composed of two equal amplitude and equiphase conventional modes appropriate to square waveguide. One is a TE_{01} mode; the other is its orthogonal counterpart, a TE_{10} mode. Figure 1a indicates the two equal co-existing modes, while 1b shows the resulting electric field pattern at any particular cross-section at a suitable instant in time.

Confining attention to the electric vector only, it is apparent that only E_x exists for one mode, while only E_y exists for the orthogonal mode. Dropping the common propagating wave function, $e^{j(\omega t-\beta z)}$, the spatial variations of E_x and E_y are given by

$$E_x = \cos\frac{\pi y}{d} \quad (1)$$

$$E_y = \cos\frac{\pi x}{d} \quad (2)$$

In Equations 1 and 2 the field amplitude has been normalized to unity and the origin of coordinates has been taken at the center of the square cross-section.

Thus at any point (x, y) within the cross-section of Figure 1a, the resultant electric field is

$$E = \sqrt{\cos^2\left(\frac{\pi x}{d}\right) + \cos^2\left(\frac{\pi y}{d}\right)} \quad (3)$$

and its direction is inclined at the angle α to the x-axis, where

$$\tan\alpha = \frac{Ey}{Ex} \quad (4)$$

or

$$\tan\alpha = \frac{\cos\left(\frac{\pi x}{d}\right)}{\cos\left(\frac{\pi y}{d}\right)} \quad (5)$$

Since $\frac{dy}{dx} = \tan\alpha$, the differential equation for the lines of electric force is

Reprinted with permission from *Microwave J.*, vol. V, pp. 117–122, Mar. 1962.

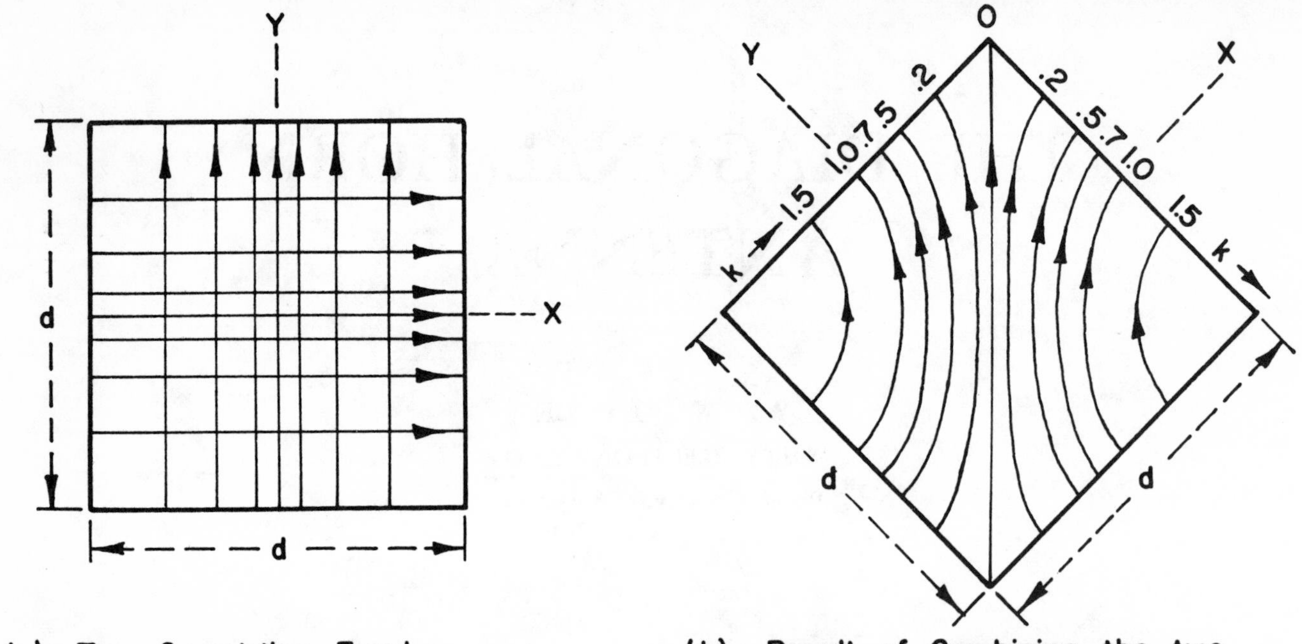

(a) Two Co-existing Equal Orthogonal Modes

(b) Result of Combining the two Modes Shown in (a)

Figure 1 — Electric field configuration inside square horn.

$$\cos\left(\frac{\pi y}{d}\right) \cdot dy = \cos\left(\frac{\pi x}{d}\right) \cdot dx \qquad (6)$$

The equation for the lines of force, obtained by integrating (6), is

$$\sin\left(\frac{\pi y}{d}\right) = \sin\left(\frac{\pi x}{d}\right) + k \; (-2 \leqq k \leqq 2) \qquad (7)$$

where k is constant for any one line of force.

The resultant field pattern, shown in Figure 1b, has been calculated on the basis of this analysis. Its resemblance to the dominant TE_{11} mode in circular guide is obvious and suggests a simple method for launching such a complex wave. As shown in Figure 2, standard rectangular guide carrying $TE^{\square}_{10}$ mode is gradually transformed to circular guide carrying the TE°_{11} mode. Another gradual transition carries the circular cross section into square and the horn then flares out to the desired aperture size.

We now make the usual approximations; namely that the effects of higher order modes and reflections can be neglected, and we take the aperture field to be identical with the one just described, and given by Equations 3 and 7 and Figure 1.

Calculation of Far-Field Radiation Patterns

The methods of diffraction theory[2] can now be applied to the aperture field to calculate radiation intensity in the Fraunhofer zone. By the superposition principle, we may decompose the aperture field into the two orthogonal components of Figure 1a. The far field intensities due to these two components will then be calculated separately and added vectorially to obtain the resultant far zone intensities. The coordinate system of Figure 3 will be used, with origin at the center of the aperture in the xy plane.

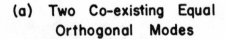

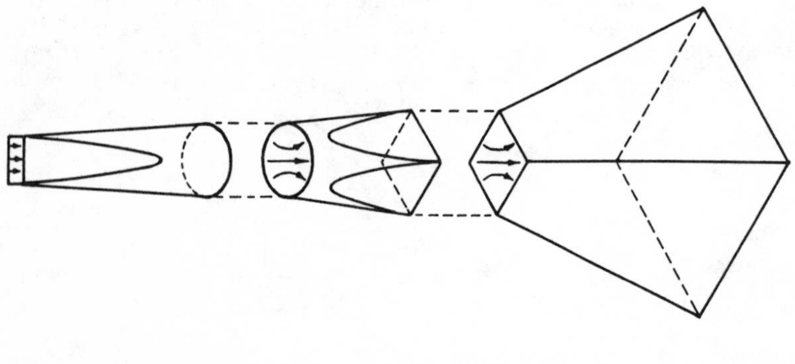

Figure 2 — Transition from rectangular guide to diagonally polarized horn.

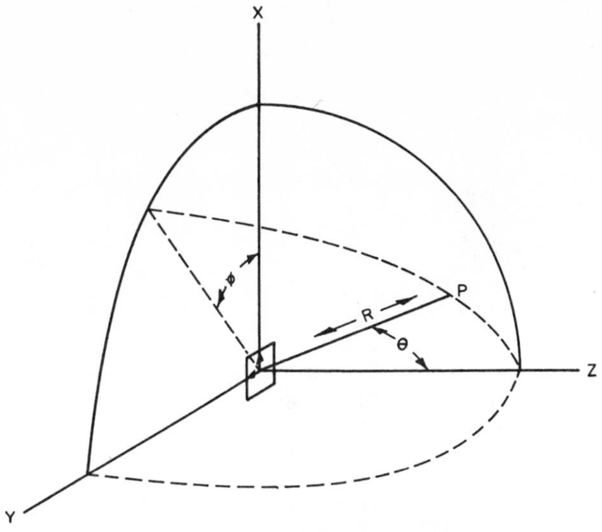

Figure 3 — Coordinate system used to relate far zone intensity to aperture field.

Following Silver[2], the amplitude at P in the far field, due to the aperture component E_y is

$$E^{(y)}(\theta,\phi) = \int_{-\frac{d}{2}}^{\frac{d}{2}} \int_{-\frac{d}{2}}^{\frac{d}{2}} \cos\left(\frac{\pi x}{d}\right) e^{\frac{2\pi j}{\lambda} \sin\theta\,(x\cos\phi + y\sin\phi)} \, dxdy \qquad (8)$$

Because this is a separable aperture distribution, the integrations over x and y may be carried out separately, and the following well known result is obtained:

$$E^{(y)}(\theta,\phi) = \frac{2d^2}{\pi} \frac{\sin(u\sin\phi)}{u\sin\phi} \cdot \frac{\cos(u\cos\phi)}{1 - \frac{4u^2}{\pi^2}\cos^2\phi} \qquad (9)$$

where $u = \frac{\pi d}{\lambda} \sin\theta$.

In similar fashion, the amplitude at P due to the aperture component E_x turns out to be,

$$E^{(x)}(\theta,\phi) = \frac{2d^2}{\pi} \frac{\sin(u\cos\phi)}{u\cos\phi} \cdot \frac{\cos(u\sin\phi)}{1 - \frac{4u^2}{\pi^2}\sin^2\phi} \qquad (10)$$

The far field electric vectors, $E^{(x)}$ and $E^{(y)}$, each have θ and ϕ components, but no radial (i.e., E_r) component. Regardless of the absolute directions of $E^{(x)}$ and $E^{(y)}$, however, these two vectors will always be at right angles to each other in the far field and their resultant will be a vector E (again having no E_r component), given by

$$E = \sqrt{[E^{(x)}]^2 + [E^{(y)}]^2} \qquad (11)$$

Reference to Figure 3 shows that the principal planes are given by $\phi=45°$ for the E-plane and $\phi=135°$ for the H-plane. But Equations 9 and 10 are identical, when $\phi=45°$ or $135°$, so that in either the E or H-plane (11) becomes

$$E = \frac{2\sqrt{2}d^2}{\pi} \cdot \frac{\sin\frac{u}{\sqrt{2}}}{\frac{u}{\sqrt{2}}} \cdot \frac{\cos\frac{u}{\sqrt{2}}}{1 - \frac{2u^2}{\pi^2}} \qquad (12)$$

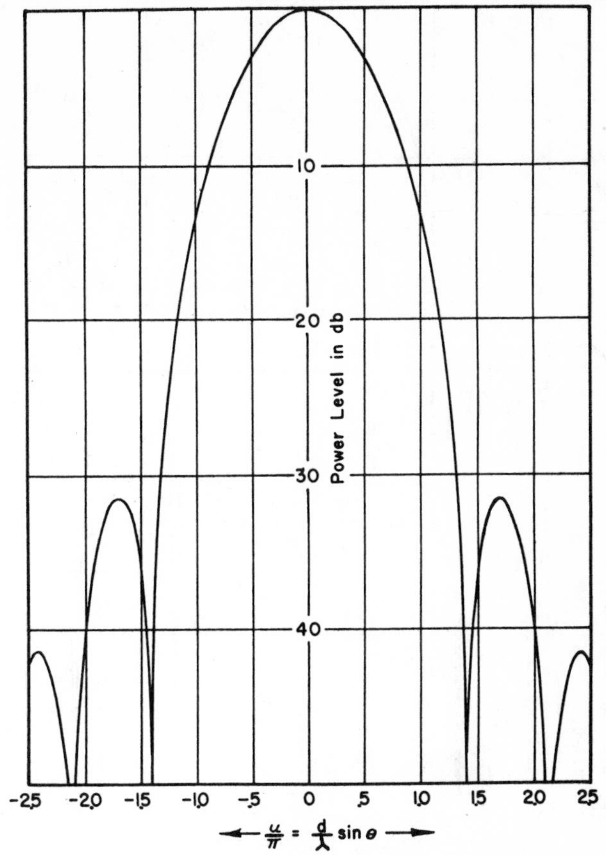

Figure 4 — E- and H-plane normal power patterns.

This equation determines the electric field amplitude in the far field in both principal planes. The direction of the electric vector is entirely in the E-plane and perpendicular to the H-plane, and there are no cross-polarized components.

Of interest also are the ± 45° planes lying between the principal planes, and these are investigated by setting $\phi=0$ and 180° in (9) and (10), obtaining

$$E^{(y)} = \frac{2d^2}{\pi} \frac{\cos u}{1 - \frac{4u^2}{\pi^2}} \qquad (9a)$$

$$E^{(x)} = \frac{2d^2}{\pi} \frac{\sin u}{u} \qquad (9b)$$

Substitution in (11) will give the resultant magnitude of the electric vector, but because (9a) and (9b) are in general unequal, this resultant vector will have a varying direction. However, its normal and cross-polarized components are easily found by vector resolution, and there results

$$E_{normal} = \frac{E^{(x)} + E^{(y)}}{\sqrt{2}} = \frac{\sqrt{2}\,d^2}{\pi}\left(\frac{\sin u}{u} + \frac{\cos u}{1 - \frac{4u^2}{\pi^2}}\right) \qquad (13)$$

$$E_{cross} = \frac{E^{(x)} - E^{(y)}}{\sqrt{2}} = \frac{\sqrt{2}\,d^2}{\pi}\left(\frac{\sin u}{u} - \frac{\cos u}{1 - \frac{4u^2}{\pi^2}}\right) \qquad (14)$$

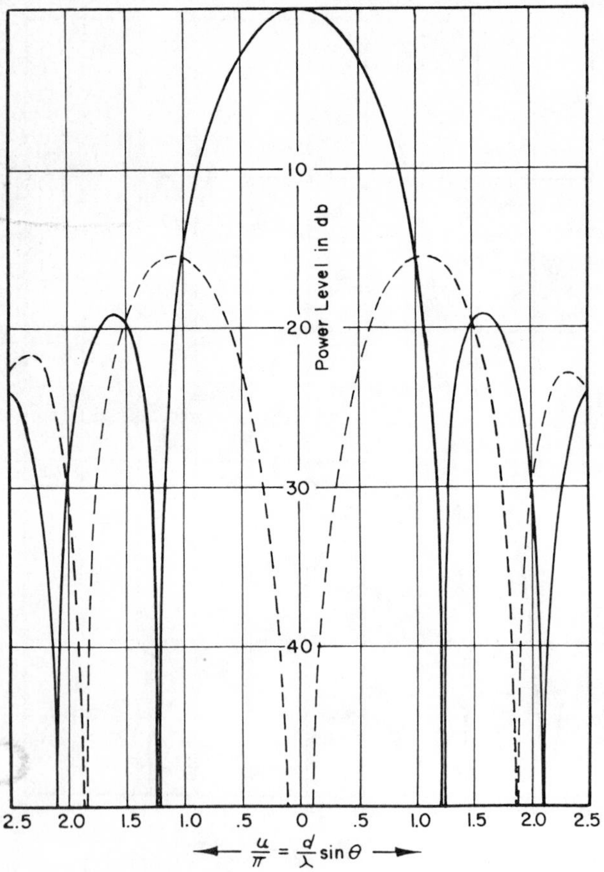

Figure 5 — 45° plane power patterns.

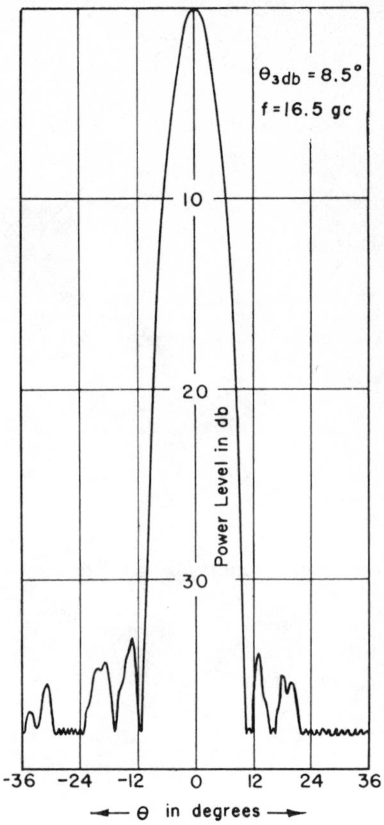

Figure 6 — E- and H-plane patterns; K_u-band horn.

The cross-polarized lobe, at a level of −16 db in the ±45° planes, occurs at the angular position $\theta = 61\lambda/d$ degrees.

To sum up, the far field principal plane patterns are given by Equation 12 and there is no cross-polarized component in these planes. The ±45° plane normal pattern is given by (13) and the cross-polarized pattern in these planes by (14).

For purposes of computing the secondary power spectra, shown in Figures 4 and 5, Equations 12, 13 and 14 are normalized by division by the factor $2\sqrt{2}\frac{d^2}{\pi}$. Salient features of the power spectra are given in the following table:

PARAMETER	PRINCIPAL PLANES	45° and 135° PLANES
3db Beamwidth, in degrees	58.5 λ/d	58.0 λ/d
10 db Beamwidth, in degrees	101 λ/d	98 λ/d
Angular Position First Null	81 λ/d	70 λ/d
Angular Position First Lobe	96 λ/d	92 λ/d
Level of First Side Lobe	31½ db	19 db
Angular Position Second Null	122 λ/d	122 λ/d
Angular Position Second Lobe	139 λ/d	147 λ/d
Level of Second Side Lobe	41½ db	24 db

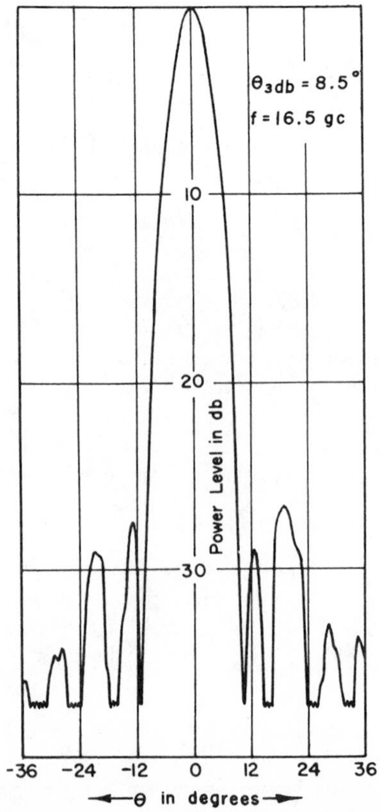

Figure 7 — 45 and 135° patterns; K_u-band horn.

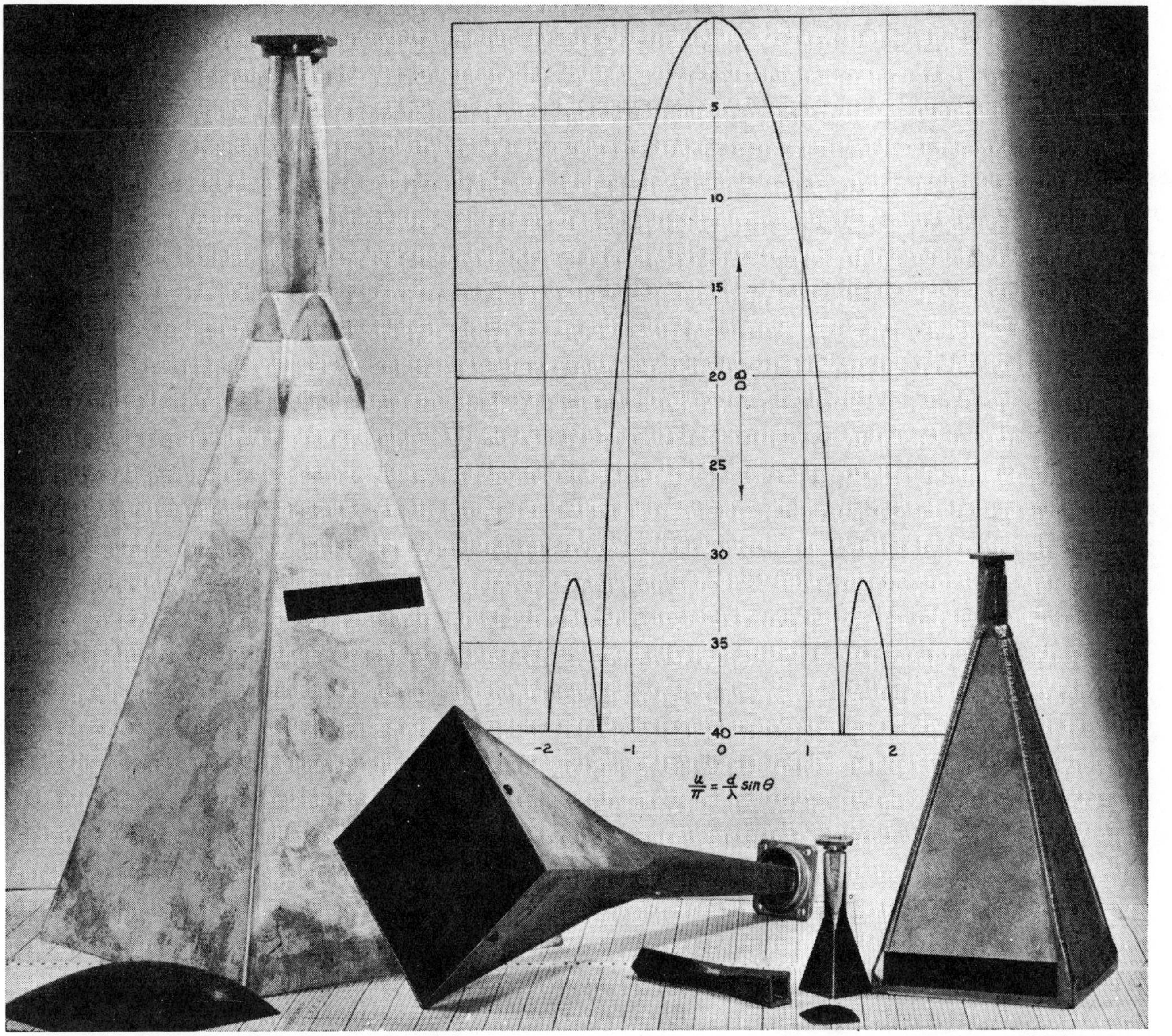

Various sizes of horns and some of the polystyrene dielectric lenses which are used with the larger horns are shown. The horns are used at X-band, Ku-band and Ka-band. All were made by the electroforming process whereby silver and/or copper is electrolytically deposited on a stainless steel mandrel. Because of the non-reentrant shape of the mandrel it can easily be pulled out after the deposition has built up the required wall thickness.

Gain and Aperture Efficiency

The gain of an aperture antenna is given by

$$G = \eta \frac{4\pi A}{\lambda^2} \qquad (15)$$

where A is the area of the aperture and η is the efficiency. It has been shown that $\eta = 81$ per cent for a rectangular aperture with uniform illumination in one plane and a cosine-squared power distribution in the orthogonal plane. This is just the type of illumination due to either of the orthogonal aperture field modes which characterize the diagonal horn. Thus, either mode by itself would produce an aperture efficiency of 81 per cent.

When the input power to the diagonal horn is divided equally between the two co-existing orthogonal modes, the gain due to either mode alone is reduced by one-half. However, the vector addition in the far field, as described by Equations 11 and 12 then doubles the power gain due to either mode alone. Hence, the gain remains unchanged and the efficiency of the diagonal horn is 81 per cent.

Experimental Results

A number of diagonal horn antennas has been constructed and experimental pattern measurements have confirmed the unique properties of these radiators.

Figures 6 and 7 are secondary patterns taken on a five inch square aperture K_u-band horn at 16.5 gc. Half-power beamwidth is 8.5° in all planes and agrees closely with the theoretical value given by $\triangle\theta_{1/2} = 58.5\ \lambda/d$. Side lobes in the principal planes are 33 db down compared with the theoretical 31.5 db. In the 45 and 135° planes, the first side lobes are 27 db down, which is considerably better than the predicted 19 db.

The half-power beamwidth for a four inch aperture K_a-band horn is 5.5° and agrees well with the predicted value. Again the highest side lobe in the principal planes is 33 db below the peak of the main beam. In the 45 and 135° planes, the highest lobes are 23 db down, which is still better than the predicted 19 db. Very satisfactory confirmation of the predictions given in the previous table has been obtained, with the puzzling exception of side lobe levels in the 45 and 135° planes. However, the K_u- and K_a-band horns described above were each fitted with polystyrene lenses in the aperture mouth in order to correct phase error over the aperture caused by horn flare angle, which is 15° in each case. The lenses are of the plano-convex type and produce a slight additional aperture illumination taper, which will cause a depression in side lobe levels.

Gain measurements, which are difficult to make to better than one db accuracy, yield efficiencies between 60 and 70 per cent for the above horns, so that lens losses are evidently small.

Conclusions

The properties of the diagonally polarized horn antenna have been derived theoretically and verified experimentally by pattern measurement. Although a lens is necessary for optimum performance when narrow beamwidth is required, the design and construction of the lens is simple and negligible loss results when low-loss polystyrene is used. A slight increase in VSWR occurs when a lens is used, but the lens itself is not frequently sensitive and the horn's desirable properties are retained over the whole bandwidth of the input waveguide.

This type of horn antenna can easily be converted to radiate circular polarization. All that is required is a differential phase shifter inserted in the guide where its cross-section is circular. The phase shifter is adjusted to produce phase quadrature between the two orthogonal modes. A properly designed differential phase shift section[3] will result in circular polarization over a considerable portion of the waveguide bandwidth.

Another use for the diagonal horn is as a feed horn for illuminating parabolic reflectors. For this application, the aperture to wavelength ratio of the horn (d/λ) approaches unity and the theory derived above is only very approximate. Nevertheless, the property of circular symmetry and low side lobes is preserved, making it possible to taper primary illumination over the reflector surface to 20 db down at the edge. The result is a pencil beam with very low side lobes and almost complete back lobe suppression, owing to the absence of spill-over.

References

1. Tingye Li, 'A Study of Spherical Reflectors as Wide-Angle Scanning Antennas,' *IRE Transactions on Antennas and Propagation*, vol. AP-7, No. 3, p. 223, July 1959.
2. S. Silver, 'Microwave Antenna Theory and Design,' M.I.T. Radiation Laboratory Series, vol. 12, pp. 180-186 and 334-347, McGraw Hill Book Co., 1949.
3. Alan J. Simmons, 'A Compact Broad-Band Microwave Quarter-Wave Plate,' *Proc. IRE*, Vol. 40, p. 1089, Sept. 1952.

A New Horn Antenna with Suppressed Sidelobes and Equal Beamwidths*

P. D. POTTER
JET PROPULSION LABORATORY
CALIFORNIA INSTITUTE OF TECHNOLOGY
Pasadena • California

Introduction and Previous Work

Pyramidal horns have been used for many years at UHF and microwave frequencies for applications requiring a simple type of antenna with medium gain (i.e., 10-30 db above isotropic), and are popular as antenna range illuminators, gain standards and reflector illuminators. Most of the large bulk of work done on pyramidal horns has been concerned with those of rectangular cross-section,[1-4] partly for historical reasons and also because of the attendant simple transition to standard rectangular waveguide. This work has been primarily concerned with the dominant $\overset{\square}{\mathrm{TE}}_{01}$ or $\overset{\square}{\mathrm{TE}}_{10}$ modes, although some effort has been applied to high-order rectangular modes,[1] notably for monopulse and beamshaping applications.

A relatively recent development, the diagonal-horn antenna,[5,6] appears to have somewhat superior sidelobe and beamwidth performance to the standard pyramidal horn. The aperture distribution in this horn, an in-phase superposition of the TE_{10} and TE_{01} modes, bears a strong physical resemblance to the aperture distribution in a conical horn, i.e., a pyramidal horn of circular cross-section.

It is well known that the conical horn, operating in the dominant $\overset{\circ}{\mathrm{TE}}_{11}$ mode, has effectively a tapered aperture distribution in the electric plane. For this reason its beamwidths in the electric and magnetic planes are more nearly equal than those with a square pyramidal horn — a valuable feature for polarization diversity applications. An additional result of this tapered electric-plane distribution is a more favorable sidelobe structure than with the square horn. The conical horn has received a reasonable amount of attention in the literature,[7-11] although it is not often used in practice because of its relative incompatibility with rectangular waveguide.

One of the important characteristics of horn radiators for most applications is the sidelobe level. It is important in antenna range, anechoic chamber and standard gain applications because of multipath considerations. In reflector illuminator applications, it is important because of main-beam efficiency and spurious wide-angle radiation effects. For the latter application, electric- and magnetic-plane phase center coincidence is also of importance. For many applications, equality of principal-plane beamwidths is an important third consideration.

In this report, a technique is presented[12] which simultaneously results in complete beamwidth equalization in all planes, complete phase center coincidence and at least 30-db sidelobe suppression in the electric plane. The magnetic-plane performance is unaffected. The technique, referred to as the "dual-mode conical horn," utilizes a conical horn excited at the throat region in both the dominant $\overset{\circ}{\mathrm{TE}}_{11}$ mode and the higher-order $\overset{\circ}{\mathrm{TM}}_{11}$ mode. These two modes are then excited in the horn aperture with the appropriate relative amplitude and phase to effect sidelobe suppression and beamwidth equalization. Phase center coincidence follows as a result. The predicted radiation pattern characteristics are easily derived, as is the technique for mode generation and control. Several experimental configurations were tested and were shown to have the predicted characteristics.

Although not yet investigated in detail, it should be pointed out that the same technique can be extended to use in horns of rectangular cross section.[23] Another recent dis-

---

* *This paper presents the results of one phase of research carried out at the Jet Propulsion Laboratory, California Institute of Technology, under Contract No. NAS 7-100, sponsored by the National Aeronautics and Space Administration.*

Reprinted with permission from *Microwave J.*, vol. VI, pp. 71–78, June 1963.

covery, also not yet investigated in detail, is that use of the TE_{12}° mode in addition to the TE_{11}° and TM_{11}° modes can provide H-plane sidelobe suppression in addition to the normal dual mode horn characteristics. In general, it is felt that the horn described in this article is only the first step in the technique of utilizing orthogonal waveguide modes to produce practical horn antennas with new radiation characteristics.

The Dual-Mode Conical Horn — Radiation Characteristics

Some effort has been expended toward use of the higher-order modes in pyramidal and sectorial horns to effect more desirable electric-plane radiation characteristics. Success has been only fair, however, since in general the associated radiation function argument varies with mode order. Certain pairs of these modes however, have radiation functions with the same argument, the only major difference being an additional envelope factor in one of the modes, varying rapidly in the main beam region and remaining relatively constant at larger angles. It is thus possible, by using this approach, to effect almost complete cancellation of radiation in all directions, except those within the main beam.

The radiation characteristics of the dominant TE_{11}° mode and the TM_{11}° mode in conical horns are worthy of detailed consideration. Based on work by Chu,[13] Silver[7] developed the radiation functions for open-end circular cross-section pipe, assumed to be equivalent to a conical horn. In this analysis the boundary problems arising due to the aperture discontinuity are neglected (Schorr and Beck make the same approximation in their conical analysis).[9] It is, of course, obvious that the boundary condition inside conical waveguide cannot be satisfied by cylindrical TE° modes, but must also utilize the cylindrical TM° modes.

This problem, not peculiar to conical horns, becomes progressively more severe with increasing horn flare angle. The effect is qualitatively described[4] as "aperture phase error," although this concept is incompatible with the cylindrical TE modes. (It is not, however, incompatible with the spherical TE modes used by Schorr and Beck.) It is reasonable to assume that all noncompensated conical horns radiate in both the TE_{11} and TM_{11} modes. It has previously been erroneously assumed that presence of the TM_{11} mode is always deleterious to the horn performance. The error in this assumption can easily be shown.

The polar and azimuthal component radiation patterns of the TE_{11} mode, respectively, are given by Silver[7] as follows: *

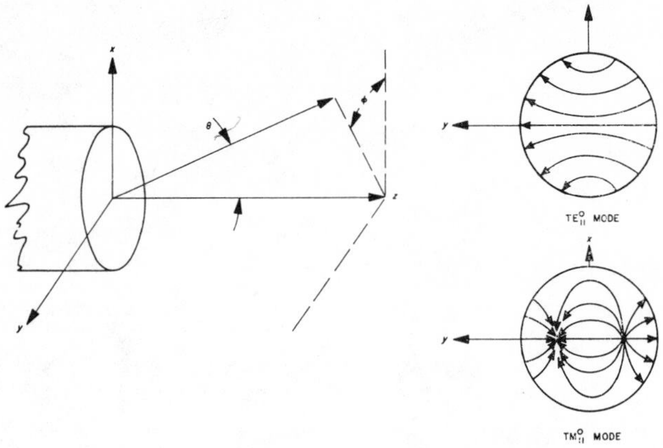

Figure 1 — Radiation coordinate system.

where

ω = radian frequency
μ = permeability
k = free-space propagation constant
a = aperture half diameter
J_1 = 1st-order Bessel function of the first kind
J'_1 = 1st derivative of J_1 with respect to its argument
$K_{11H}a$ = 1st root of J'_1 = 1.841
θ = polar angle
ϕ = azimuthal angle
R = distance from the aperture center to the observation point
$j = \sqrt{-1}$
$\beta_{11H} = \sqrt{k^2 - K^2_{11H}}$

The coordinate system, as well as the aperture electric-field distribution, is shown in Figure 1. In Figure 2 (a and b) the E- and H-plane calculated and measured patterns are shown for a particular example. As expected, Figure 2(a) indicates the results shown in the presence of spurious TM_{11}° energy. This energy cannot affect the radiation patterns shown in Figure 2(b), however, since TM° modes have no azimuthal electric field component in any direction.[7]

The polar radiation pattern for the TM_{11}° mode is given by Silver[7] as follows:

$$E_{\theta H} = -\frac{\omega\mu}{2R}\left(1+\frac{\beta_{11H}\cos\theta}{k}\right)J_1(K_{11H}a)\left[\frac{J_1(ka\sin\theta)}{\sin\theta}\right]\sin\phi e^{-jkR} \quad (1)$$

and

$$E\phi_H = -\frac{ka\omega\mu}{2R}\left(\frac{\beta_{11H}}{k}+\cos\theta\right)J_1(K_{11H}a)\left[\frac{J'_1(ka\sin\theta)}{1-\left(\frac{k\sin\theta}{K_{11H}}\right)^2}\right]\cos\phi e^{-jkR} \quad (2)$$

* *The aperture is assumed perfectly matched to space here.*

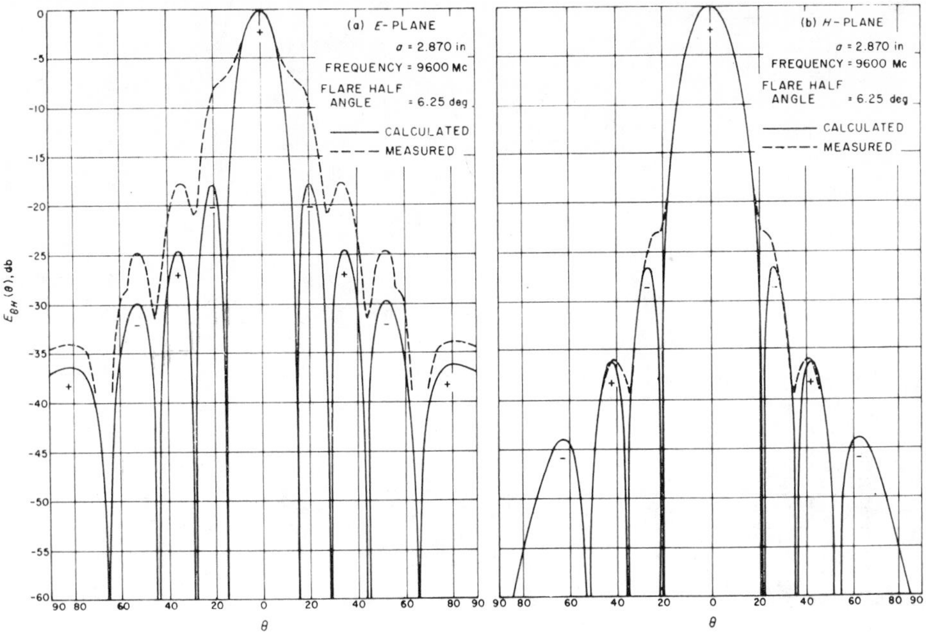

Figure 2 — Radiation patterns for the TE°_{11} mode.

$$E_{\theta E}=-\left(\frac{kaK_{11E}}{2R}\right)\left(\frac{\beta_{11E}}{k}+\cos\theta\right)\left[\frac{J'_1(K_{11E}a)}{1-\left(\frac{K_{11E}}{k\sin\theta}\right)^2}\right]\left[\frac{J_1(ka\sin\theta)}{\sin\theta}\right]\sin\phi e^{-jkR} \tag{3}$$

$$E_{\theta E}=0$$

where

$$K_{11E}a=\text{1st root of } J_1=3.832$$

$$\beta_{11E}=\sqrt{k^2-K^2_{11E}}$$

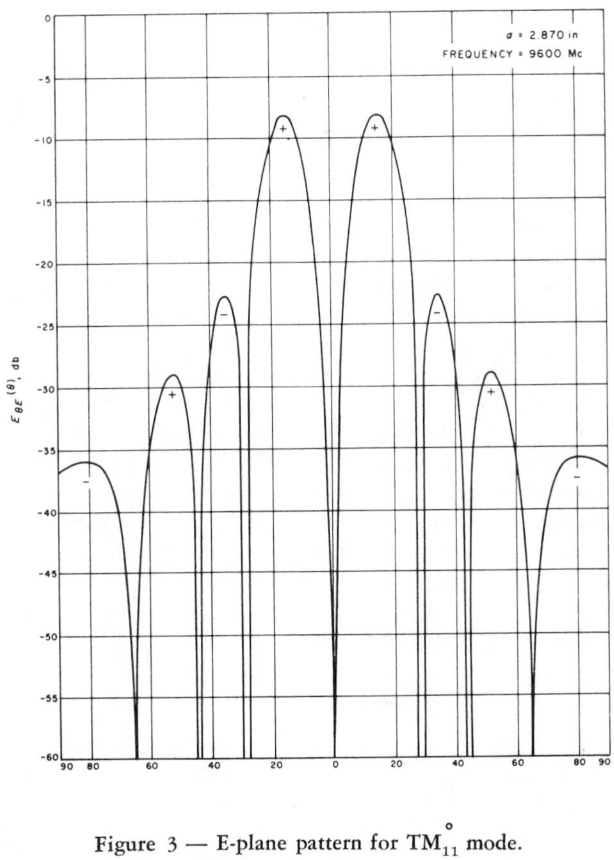

Figure 3 — E-plane pattern for TM°_{11} mode.

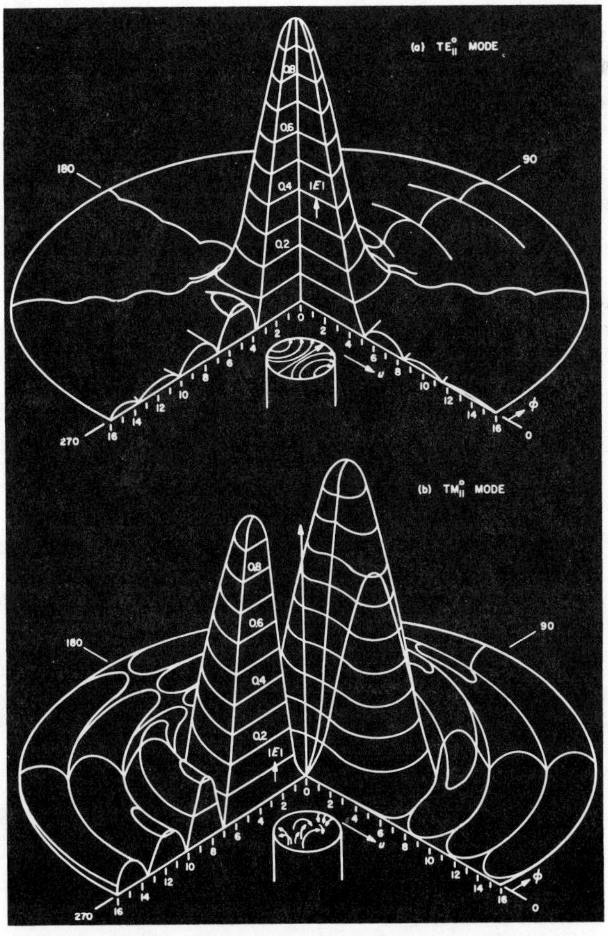

Figure 4 — Three-dimensional radiation patterns.

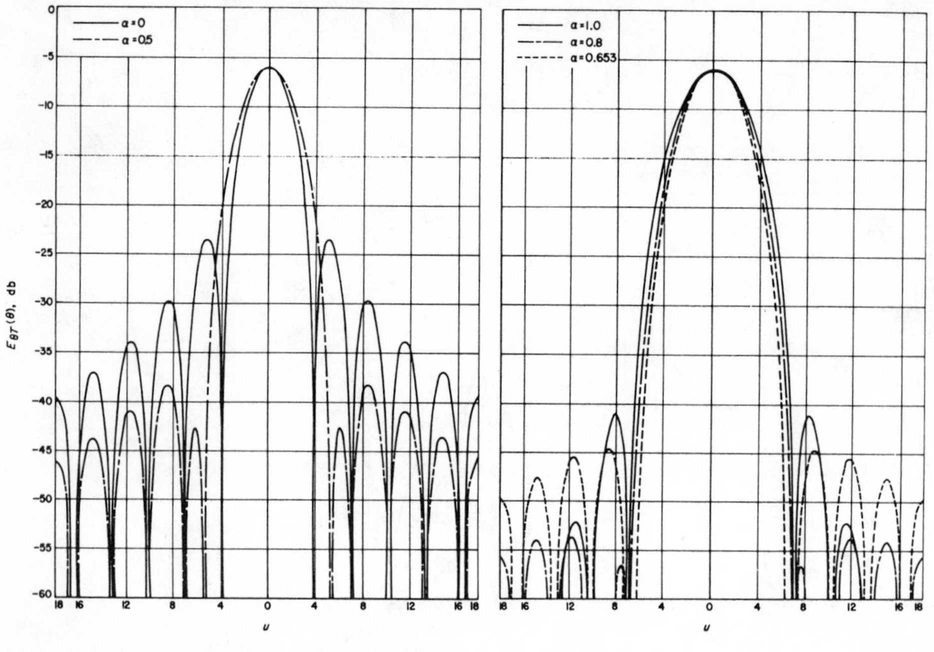

Figure 5 — Calculated dual-mode conical-horn patterns.

The aperture electric-field distribution is shown in Figure 1. The calculated $\overset{\circ}{\mathrm{TM}}_{11}$ radiation pattern in the plane of maximum radiation for the horn configuration used in Figure 2 (a and b) is shown in Figure 3.

A striking similarity in the E-plane $\overset{\circ}{\mathrm{TE}}_{11}$ and $\overset{\circ}{\mathrm{TM}}_{11}$ sidelobe structure is evident in Figures 2(a) and 3. This feature is also evident from a comparison of (1) and (3). By eliminating constants and assuming that cos θ is unity,

$$E_{\theta H} \approx \sin\phi \left[\frac{J_1(u)}{u}\right] \tag{4}$$

and

$$E_{\theta E} \approx \left[\frac{1}{1-\left(\frac{K_{11E}a}{u}\right)^2}\right] \sin\phi \left[\frac{J_1(u)}{u}\right] \tag{5}$$

where

$$u = ka \sin\theta \ . \tag{6}$$

For large u, the bracketed factor in (5) becomes very nearly unity, allowing the possibility of sidelobe cancellation. This factor becomes infinite and changes sign at the first zero of the $J_1(u)$ function. If, therefore, (4) and (5) are subtracted, partial cancellation occurs beyond the first root with electric-plane beam broadening in the main beam. The radiation characteristics of the $\overset{\circ}{\mathrm{TE}}_{11}$ and $\overset{\circ}{\mathrm{TM}}_{11}$ modes are more clearly seen in Figure 4 (a and b), which are three-dimensional representations similar to those used by Jahnke and Emde[14].

In order to predict the performance of the dual-mode conical horn in the electric plane, (1) and (3) may be simplified and combined as follows:

or, in approximate form,

$$E_{\theta T} \approx \left[1 - \frac{\alpha}{1-\left(\frac{K_{11E}a}{u}\right)^2}\right]\left[\frac{J_1(u)}{u}\right] \tag{8}$$

where α = arbitrary constant defining the relative power in the $\overset{\circ}{\mathrm{TE}}_{11}$ and $\overset{\circ}{\mathrm{TM}}_{11}$ modes.

Equation (8) is plotted in Figure 5 (a and b) for various values of α including $\alpha=0$, which corresponds to the dominant single-mode case. Although a range of α in the region of $\alpha=0.6$ is most interesting, particular applications will dictate the exact value chosen; for example, a value of $\alpha=0.653$ will equalize the E- and H-plane half-power beamwidths and make the phase centers coincident. This condition also results in the minimum possible backlobe.[15]

Measured data for the dual-mode conical horn are shown in Figure 6 (a—c) for the E-, 45-deg, and H-planes, respectively. The calculated E-plane data utilized (7). The 45-deg plane pattern is defined as the polarization component parallel to the $\phi=\pi/2$ plane, but measured in either the $\phi=\pi/4$ or $3\pi/4$ planes. Because of its redundancy, the 45-deg plane is more important than the E- or H-plane for many applications.[16] Two other aperture sizes were also tested in the dual-mode configuration; the associated E-plane radiation patterns are shown in Figures 7 and 8.

One other horn characteristic, the phase pattern, is of concern in reflector illumination applications[16]. The serrodyne[17] test setup used to measure this horn property is shown schematically in Figure 9. The measured E-plane phase pattern and the phase center position are shown in Figure 10 for the dual-mode horn with a=2.870 inches. Other planes are virtually identical.

A simple overall measure of horn performance is the

$$E_{\theta T} = \left[\left(1+\frac{\beta_{11H}}{k}\cos\theta\right) - \alpha\,\frac{\left(\frac{\beta_{11E}}{k}\right)+\cos\theta}{1-\left(\frac{K_{11E}}{k\sin\theta}\right)^2}\right]\left[\frac{J_1(ka\sin\theta)}{\sin\theta}\right] \tag{7}$$

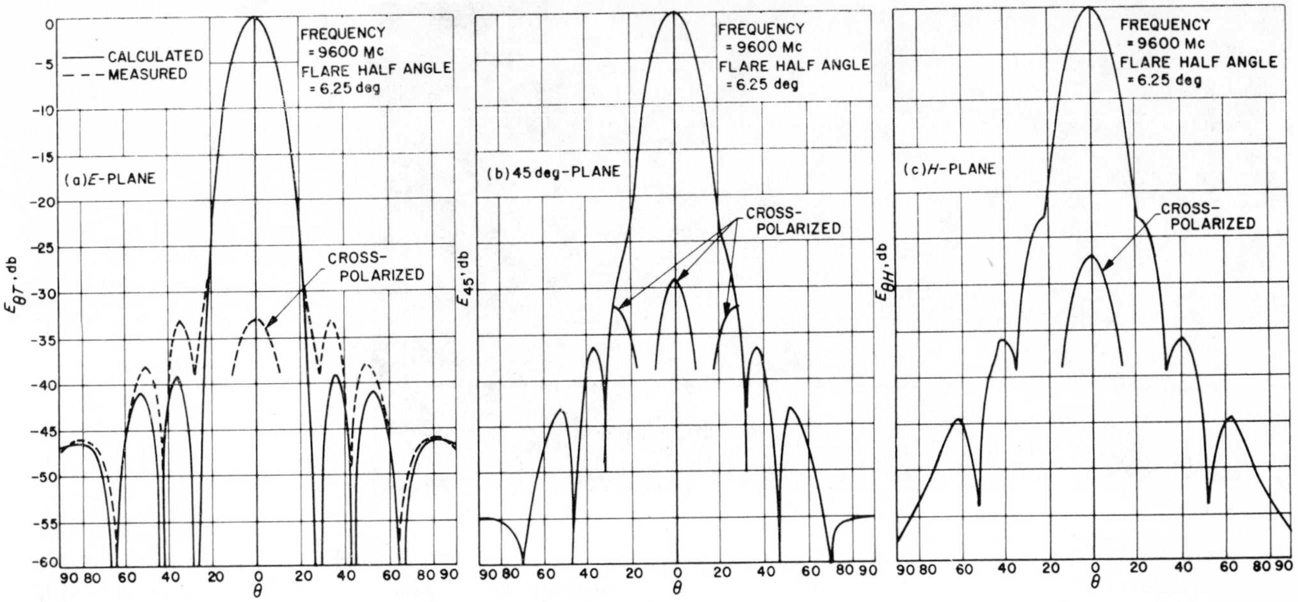

Figure 6 — Dual-mode patterns for a=2.870 inches.

beam efficiency, i.e., the fractional radiated power between $\theta=0$ and $\theta=\theta_1$, as a function of θ_1. Figure 11 (a–c) shows this factor in the E-, 45-deg and H-planes for dual-mode conical, square, single-mode conical and diagonal horn configurations. The latter is calculated from data published by Love.[5] All curves are normalized to the same half-power beamwidth, and all include cross-polarized energy. It can be seen that the popular diagonal horn would be a good competitor to the dual-mode conical horn if it were not for the 45- and 135-deg planes (unfortunately, the most important planes). It can also be seen that the dual mode conical horn is good in the H-plane, even though no sidelobe suppression is effected in that plane.

Mode Generation and Control

The technique of $\overset{\circ}{TM}_{11}$ mode generation is shown qualitatively in Figure 12, together with empirically determined parameters for the experimental horns. As can be seen in Figure 1, the step discontinuity boundary condition of zero tangential electric field on the step surface will be largely satisfied by the $\overset{\circ}{TE}_{11}$ and $\overset{\circ}{TM}_{11}$ modes. The two diameters are chosen to satisfy four conditions.

1. Only $\overset{\circ}{TE}_{11}$ (and possibly $\overset{\circ}{TM}_{01}$ and $\overset{\circ}{TE}_{21}$) can propagate to the left of the step.

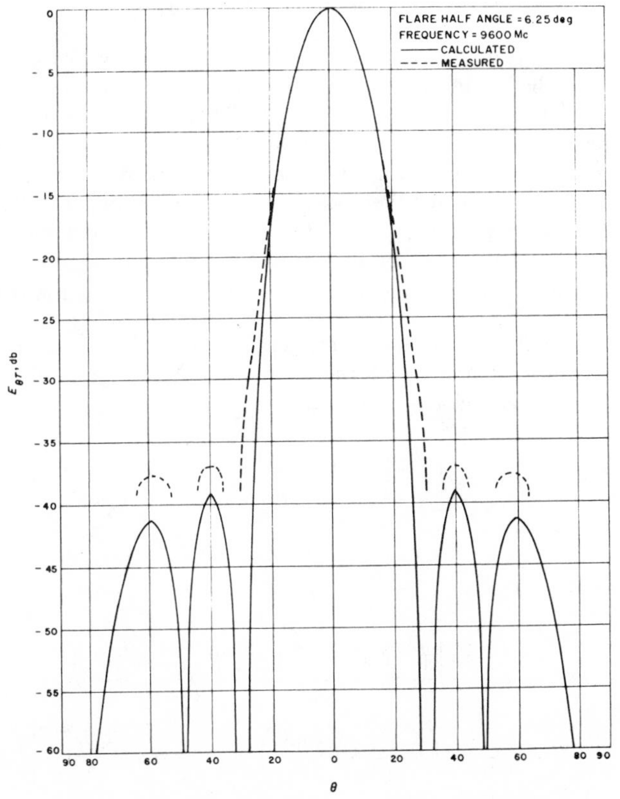

Figure 7 — E-plane dual-mode pattern for a=2.635 inches.

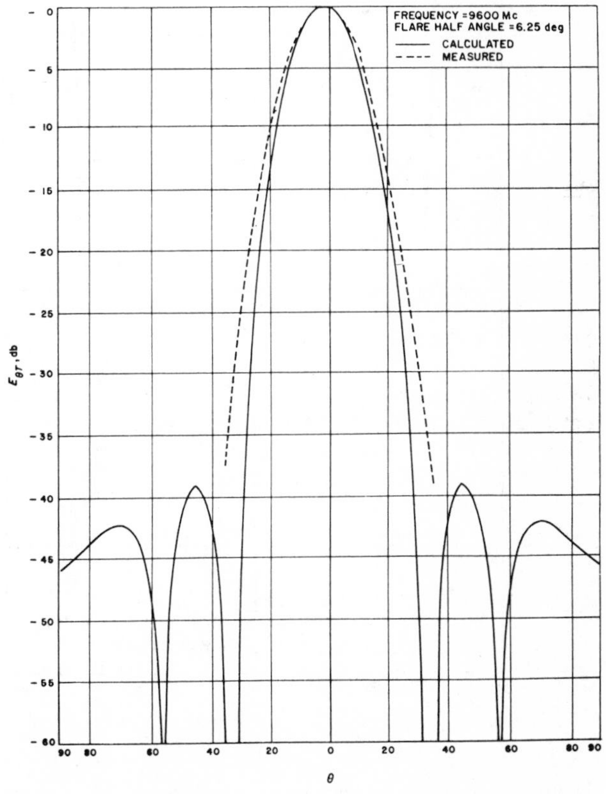

Figure 8 — E-plane dual-mode pattern for a=2.4000 inches.

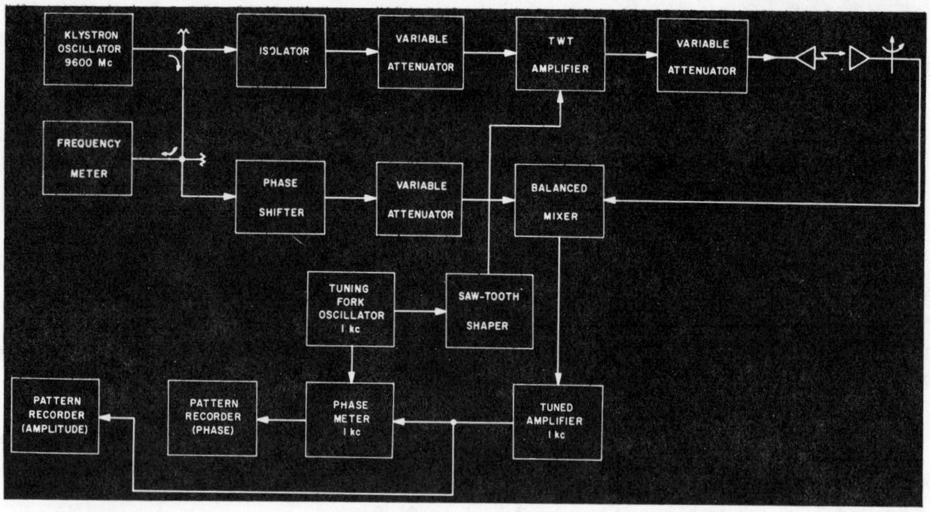

Figure 9 — Serrodyne phase measurement setup.

2. Only TE°_{11}, TM°_{01}, TE°_{21}, TE°_{01} and TM°_{11} can propagate to the right of the step.

3. TM°_{11} is generated in the correct power ratio relative to TE°_{11}.

4. TE°_{11} and TM°_{11} have significantly different phase velocities in the phase section to the right of the step.

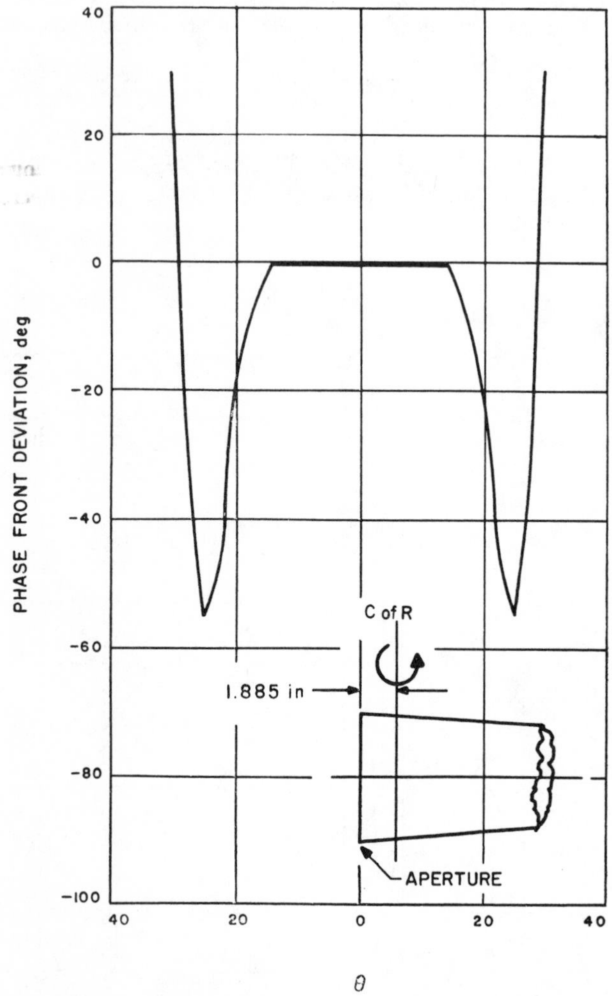

Figure 10 — Measured dual-mode conical-horn phase center characteristics.

The unwanted TM°_{01}, TE°_{21} and TE°_{01} modes are not excited because of symmetry in the mode generator and horn. In practice it was found that concentricity and circularity of the mode generator and horn components on the order of a few thousandths of a wavelength are necessary to make the effect of spurious modes negligible. This might pose a practical fabrication problem in the millimeter region, but is not otherwise serious.

The radial components of the assumed aperture field distributions for the TE°_{11} and TM°_{11} modes, respectively, are given by Silver[18] as

$$E_{rH} = j\omega\mu \frac{J_1(K_{11H}r)}{r} \sin\phi \tag{9}$$

$$E_{rE} = j\beta_{11E} K_{11E} J'_1(K_{11E}r) \sin\phi \tag{10}$$

From a careful comparison of (1), (3), (7), (9) and (10), it can be seen that the TE°_{11} and TM°_{11} modes must have their central fields in phase in the aperture to produce the desired radiation pattern. Thus, the length of the phasing section shown in Figure 12 must be chosen to account for the relative phase lengths of the horn for the two modes and also for the phase of mode generation. The latter has not yet been subjected to detailed analysis but is empirically established by the experimental data in Figure 12.

The differential phase length of the horn flare for the TE°_{11} and TM°_{11} modes can be easily calculated by straightforward integration of the standard formula[18] for waveguide phase velocity. The result is

$$\Delta\phi_H = \cot\gamma \left\{ \left[\left(\frac{a^2}{\lambda^2} - \frac{C^2_H}{4\pi^2} \right)^{\frac{1}{2}} - \left(\frac{a^2}{\lambda^2} - \frac{C^2_E}{4\pi^2} \right)^{\frac{1}{2}} - \left(\frac{C_H}{2\pi} \cos^{-1} \frac{C_H\lambda}{2\pi a} \right) + \left(\frac{C_E}{2\pi} \cos^{-1} \frac{C_E\lambda}{2\pi a} \right) \right] - \left[\left(\frac{a^2_1}{\lambda^2} - \frac{C^2_H}{4\pi^2} \right)^{\frac{1}{2}} - \left(\frac{a^2_1}{\lambda^2} - \frac{C^2_E}{4\pi^2} \right)^{\frac{1}{2}} - \left(\frac{C_H}{2\pi} \cos^{-1} \frac{C_H\lambda}{2\pi a_1} \right) + \left(\frac{C_E}{2\pi} \cos^{-1} \frac{C_E\lambda}{2\pi a_1} \right) \right] \right\} \tag{11}$$

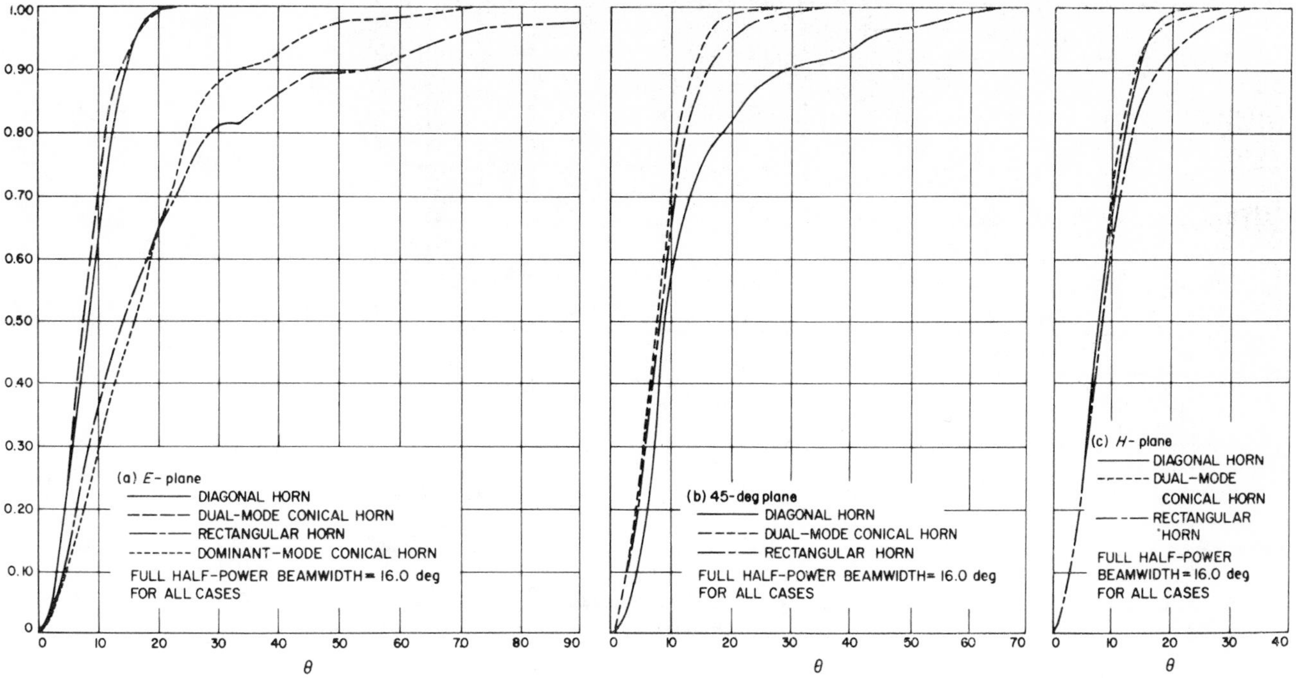

Figure 11 — Beam efficiency of various horns.

where

$\Delta\phi_H$ = differential phase in wavelengths

γ = horn-flare half angle

C_E = 1st root of $J_1 = 3.832$

C_H = 1st root of $J'_1 = 1.841$

λ = wavelength of operation

a_1 = horn-throat half diameter

Equation (11) is plotted in Figure 13(a) as a function of aperture size for various throat sizes.

The differential phase length of the phasing section in wavelengths per wavelength is given by

$$\Delta\phi_C = \frac{\lambda}{a_1}\left[\left(\frac{a_1^2}{\lambda^2} - \frac{C_H^2}{4\pi^2}\right)^{\frac{1}{2}} - \left(\frac{a_1^2}{\lambda^2} - \frac{C_E^2}{4\pi^2}\right)^{\frac{1}{2}}\right]. \quad (12)$$

Equation (12) is plotted in Figure 13(b) for the interesting range of a_1/λ. In the experimental work reported here, the phasing section length was determined empirically for the a = 2.870 inches configuration; (11) and (12) were then used to calculate the phasing section length change necessary for the 2.635- and 2.400 inches aperture configurations. The result, shown in Figures 7 and 8, indicates correct performance. The design procedure is thus adequately established with the use of Figures 5 (a and b), 12, and 13 (a and b).

One final point in the design should be considered — impedance matching. The VSWR of the unmatched horn for the configuration in Figure 12 was found to be 1.2:1, a value predicted by the TE_{11}°-mode wave impedance change at the step discontinuity. Data given in Marcuvitz[19] were successfully used to design a circular iris matching discontinuity. This matching device maintains circular symmetry, which not only helps mode control, but also allows complete polarization flexibility.

Applications

Since the TM_{11}° mode does not radiate axially, the dual-mode conical horn has less axial gain than a dominant-mode conical horn with the same aperture size. Its use, therefore, is not dictated in applications requiring maximum aperture efficiency; most horn applications, however.

Figure 12 — Dual-mode conical-horn configuration.

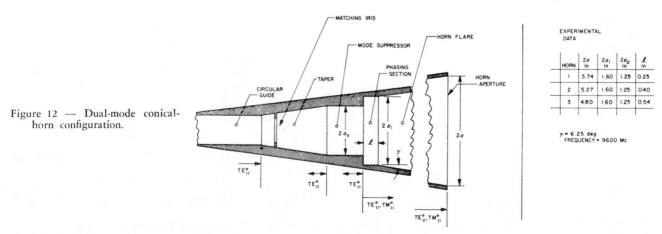

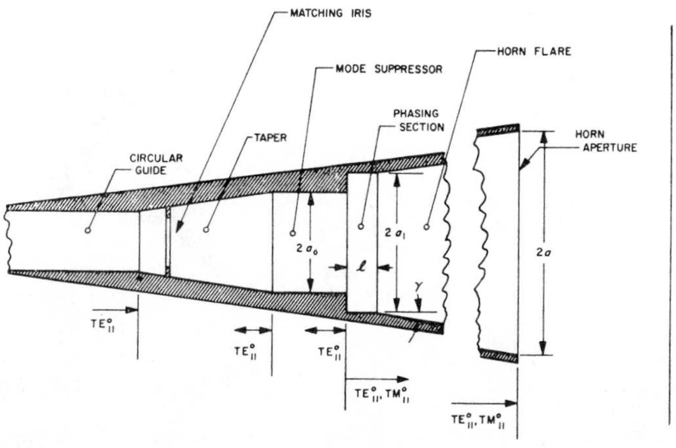

EXPERIMENTAL DATA

HORN	2a in	$2a_1$ in	$2a_0$ in	ℓ in
1	5.74	1.60	1.25	0.25
2	5.27	1.60	1.25	0.40
3	4.80	1.60	1.25	0.54

γ = 6.25 deg
FREQUENCY = 9600 Mc

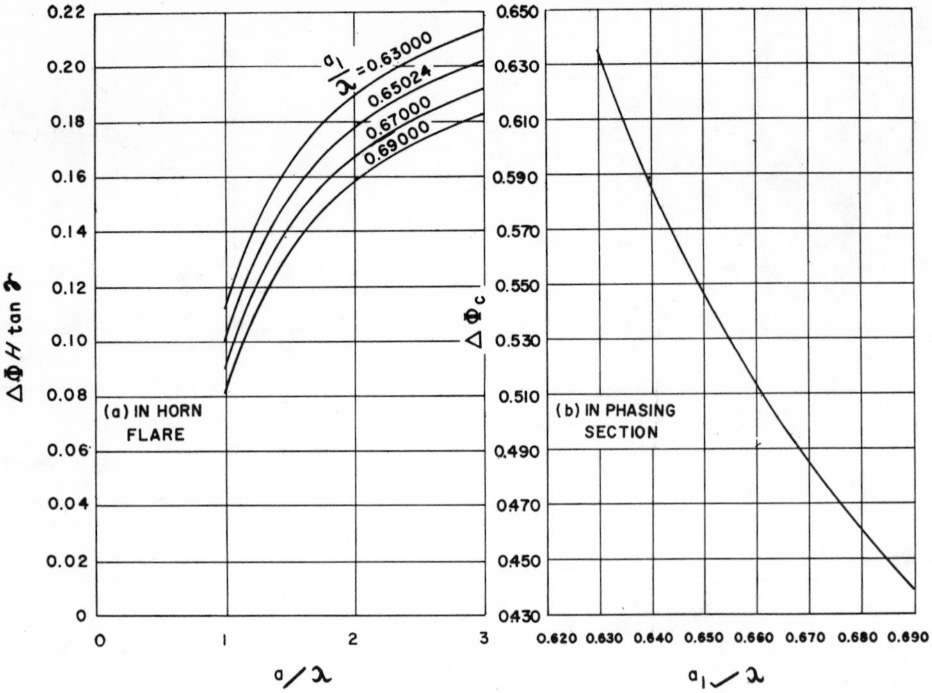

Figure 13 — Differential phase lengths.

are more concerned with pattern circularity and sidelobe performance. Obvious applications are for gain standards, anechoic chamber illuminators and pattern range illuminators. One of the most important applications for the dual-mode conical horn is in Cassegrainian feed systems. In such a system both the antenna aperture efficiency and the forward sidelobe level are critically dependent on the feedhorn beam efficiency characteristics.[20] The dual-mode horn was, in fact, developed for this application.

For some uses, a horn is an inconvenient structure because of its physical length in the direction of propagation. The popular horn reflector antenna[21] was developed as an excellent solution to this problem. More recently a conical-horn reflector antenna has been developed[22]. Although not yet experimentally investigated, it appears feasible to build a dual-mode conical-horn reflector antenna. Such an antenna would have the desirable sidelobe properties of the dual-mode conical horn combined with the physically convenient horn reflector configuration.

Acknowledgment

The author is grateful to Mr. Frank McCrea, who fabricated many of the horn components and performed all of the experimental tests, and to Mr. Arthur Ludwig, who suggested the three-dimensional representation for the TE°_{11} and TM°_{11} mode radiation patterns.

References

1. Silver, S., *Microwave Antenna Theory and Design,* McGraw-Hill Book Co., Inc., New York, 1949, Chapter 10.
2. Schelkunoff, S. A. and Friis, H. T., *Antennas Theory and Practice,* John Wiley and Sons, Inc., London, 1952, Chapter 16.
3. Jasik, H., ed., *Antenna Engineering Handbook,* McGraw-Hill Book Co., Inc., New York, 1961, Chapter 10.
4. Kraus, J. D., *Antennas,* McGraw-Hill Book Co., Inc., New York, 1950, Chapter 13.
5. Love, A. W., "The Diagonal Horn Antenna," *the microwave journal,* Vol. V, No. 3, March 1962, p. 117-122.
6. Brueckman, H., "Suppression of Undesired Radiation from Directional HF Antennas and Associated Feed Lines," *Proceedings of the IRE,* Vol. 46, August 1958, pp. 1510-1516.
7. Silver, op. cit., pp. 336-341.
8. Southworth, G. C., *Principles and Applications of Waveguide Transmission,* D. Van Nostrand Co., Inc., Princeton, N. J., 1950, pp. 415-419.
9. Schorr, M. G., and Beck, F. J., "Electromagnetic Field of the Conical Horn," *Journal of Applied Physics,* Vol. 21, August 1950, pp. 795-801.
10. King, A. P., "The Radiation Characteristics of Conical Horn Antennas," *Proceedings of the IRE,* Vol. 38, March 1950, pp. 249-251.
11. Horton, C. W., "On the Theory of the Radiation Patterns of Electromagnetic Horns of Moderate Flare Angles," *Proceedings of the IRE,* Vol. 37, 1949, pp. 744-749.
12. Potter, P. D., *Suppressed Sidelobe Horn Antenna,* Invention Report No. 30-133, Jet Propulsion Laboratory, Pasadena, Cal.
13. Chu, L. J., "Calculation of the Radiation Properties of Hollow Pipes and Horns," *Journal of Applied Physics,* Vol. 11, 1940, pp. 603-610.
14. Jahnke, E. and Emde, F., *Tables of Functions,* Dover Publications, New York, 1945, Fourth Ed.
15. Ajioka, J., private correspondence.
16. Potter, P. D., *The Aperture Efficiency of Large Paraboloidal Antennas as a Function of their Feed System Radiation Characteristics,* Technical Report No. 32-149, October 1961, Jet Propulsion Laboratory, Pasadena, Cal.
17. Cumming, R. C., "The Serrodyne Frequency Translator," *Proceedings of the IRE,* Vol. 45, February 1957, pp. 175-186.
18. Silver, op. cit., pp. 200-234.
19. Marcuvitz, N., *Waveguide Handbook,* MIT Radiation Laboratory Series, Vol. 10, McGraw-Hill Book Co., Inc., New York, 1951, Chapter 5.
20. Potter, P. D., "The Application of the Cassegrainian Principle to Ground Antennas for Space Communications," *IRE Transactions on Space Electronics and Telemetry,* Vol. 8, No. 2, June 1962.
21. Pippard, A. B., "The Hoghorn — An Electromagnetic Horn Radiator of Medium-Sized Aperture," *Journal of the IEE,* Pt. IIIA, Vol. 93, No. 10, 1946, pp. 1536-1538.
22. Leonard, M. V., "Bell Unveils Project Telstar Horn Antenna in Andover, Maine," *the microwave journal,* Vol. V., No. 5, May 1962.
23. Jensen, P. A., private correspondence.

SESSION 11: Antenna Feed Systems

MIT Lincoln Laboratory, Lexington, Mass.

TPM 11.1: Beamshaping by Use of Higher Order Modes in Conical Horns*

P. D. Potter and A. C. Ludwig

Jet Propulsion Laboratory, Calif. Inst. of Technology

Pasadena, Calif.

HORN ANTENNAS have been used for many years for applications requiring a single antenna of medium gain. The advent of large low-noise Cassegrainian antennas has focused additional attention on the importance of horn antenna design and performance[1].

Almost all of the work on horn antennas has been concerned with radiation by the associated dominant waveguide mode. In some cases this mode has been modified by structures in the aperture, or higher order modes have been utilized to synthesize desirable aperture distributions. A somewhat different approach is to consider the linear superposition of the radiation patterns of individual waveguide modes. By varying the relative amplitude of the modes, the resulting radiation pattern may be varied to best fit a preassigned pattern. It has been shown[2] that this approach can yield impressive results in sidelobe suppression, beam-width equalization, and cross polarization reduction.

An ideal horn antenna radiation pattern for many applications is one which has uniform radiation in the conical region of solid angle and has no radiation elsewhere. Such a *sector beam* antenna is, of course, physically unrealizable with a finite aperture size, but surprisingly close approximations to this ideal radiation pattern can be realized with physically simple antenna structures. What might be called a first order solution to this problem, using only the TE_{11} TM_{11} cylindrical waveguide modes, has been described earlier[2].

Calculated aperture field configurations for a conventional horn and the dual mode horn are shown in Figures *a* and *b*. It can be seen that the latter is very nearly linearly polarized throughout the aperture. In *a* and *b* of Figure 2 contours of the *y* component of the aperture distributions for the dominant and dual mode horn have been plotted, showing that almost perfect circular symmetry is achieved in the latter.

Figure 3 shows the aperture field as a function of the normalized radius, ρ, and also the optimized Taylor distribution[3] for the case of 40-db sidelobes and function order $(\bar{n})$ of 7. The near correspondence between this distribution and the *E*-plane dual mode distribution is striking in view of the fact that the dual mode distribution is so easily achieved physically.

Based on earlier work[4], the superposition of the radiation patterns of useful modes may be written as

$$E_{\theta T} = \sum_{n=0}^{N} B_n \frac{u J_1(u)}{u^2 - (\eta_{1nE} a)^2} \cos\phi \qquad (1)$$

$$E_{\phi T} = \sum_{n=1}^{N} A_n \frac{J_1'(u)}{u^2 - (\eta_{1nH} a)^2} \cos\phi \qquad (2)$$

Where

θ, ϕ = polar and azimuthal radiation angles.

$u = ka \sin\theta$.

a = aperture half-diameter.

k = free space propagation constant

$J_1(u)$, $J_1'(u)$ = Bessel function of the 1st kind and its derivative, with roots $\eta_{1nE}a$ and $\eta_{1nH}a$, respectively, and

A_n and B_n are arbitrary coefficients proportional to individual mode amplitudes

N is limited by the fact that for η_{1nE} or $\eta_{1nH} > \frac{2\pi a}{\lambda}$ the term represents *H* mode beyond cutoff.

At any root $u = \eta_{mnE}a$, the numerator of every term in equation (1) is zero; therefore the only non-zero term is the *n*th term in which the denominator is also zero. It is readily shown that

$$E_{\theta T}\Big|_{u = \eta_{1nE} a} = \frac{B_n}{2} J_1'(\eta_{1nE} a) \sin\phi \qquad (3)$$

and similarly

$$E_{\phi T}\Big|_{u = \eta_{1nH} a} = \frac{A_n}{2} \frac{J_1''(\eta_{1nH} a)}{\eta_{1nH} a} \cos\phi \qquad (4)$$

Coefficients may be uniquely determined using equations (3) and (4), to set the series (9) and (10) equal to a given function at all roots $u = \eta_{1n}a$.

The result is an approximate fit which may then be altered slightly to suit desired design goals. An approximation to uniform illumination, shown in Figure 4, was

* This paper presents the results of one phase of research carried out at the Jet Propulsion Laboratory, California Institute of Technology, under Contract No. NAS7-100, sponsored by the National Aeronautics and Space Administration.

[1] Potter, P. D., "The Application of the Cassegrainian Principle to Ground Antennas for Space Communications." *IRE Trans in Space Electronics and Telemetry;* June, 1962.

[2] Potter, P. D., "A New Horn Antenna with Suppressed Sidelobes and Equal Beamwidths," *The Microwave Journal;* June, 1963.

[3] Taylor, T. T., "Design of Circular Apertures for Narrow Beamwidth and Low Sidelobes," *AP-8;* Jan., 1960.

[4] Chu, L. J., "Calculation of the Radiation Properties of Hollow Pipes and Horns," *Journal Applied Phys,* Vol. 11, p. 603-610; 1940.

obtained with the above method in which the first 3 terms in each series are used, representing the TE_{11}, TE_{12}, TE_{13}, TM_{11} and TM_{12} modes. The last coefficient in each series was adjusted to equalize more nearly E- and H- plane beamwidths. The maximum overall antenna efficiency of a paraboloidal antenna using the curve shown in Figure 4 as a feed pattern has been calculated to be slightly over 90%, versus 76% for a conventional dominant-mode horn feed pattern. The actual gain in efficiency obtainable in practice will be determined by the number of modes which can be used, and the degree of control over relative mode phase and amplitudes which can be achieved.

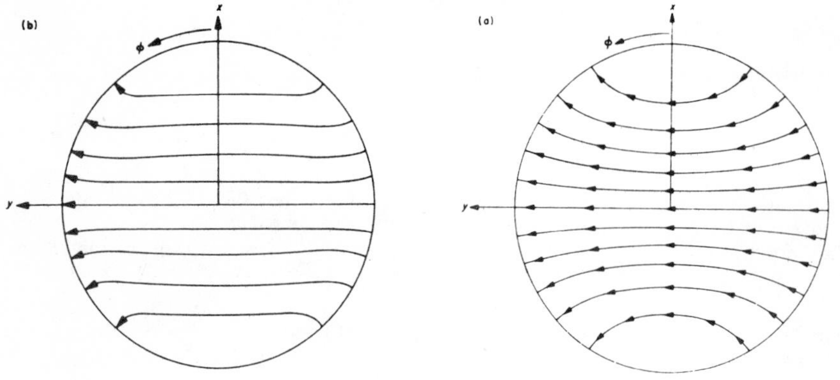

(Above)

FIGURE 1—**Aperture field configuration: (a) dominant mode horn and *(b)* dual mode horn.**

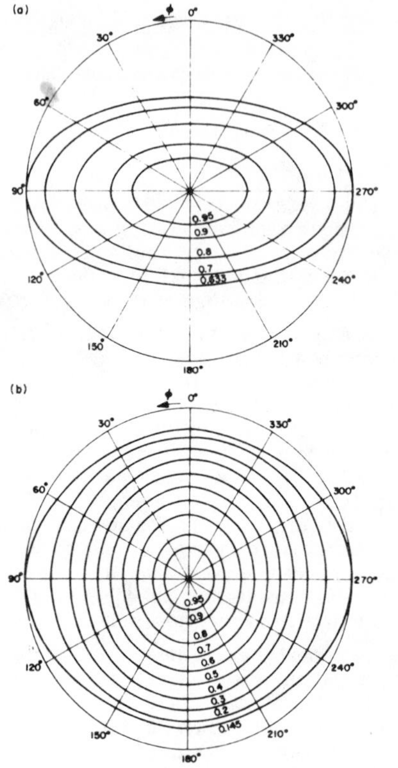

(Right)

FIGURE 2—**Aperture field contour diagrams; (a) dominant mode horn and *(b)* dual mode horn.**

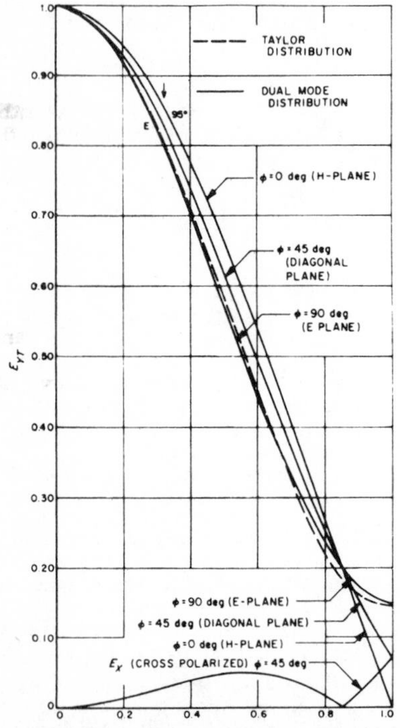

FIGURE 3—**Aperture field distributions: dual mode horn.**

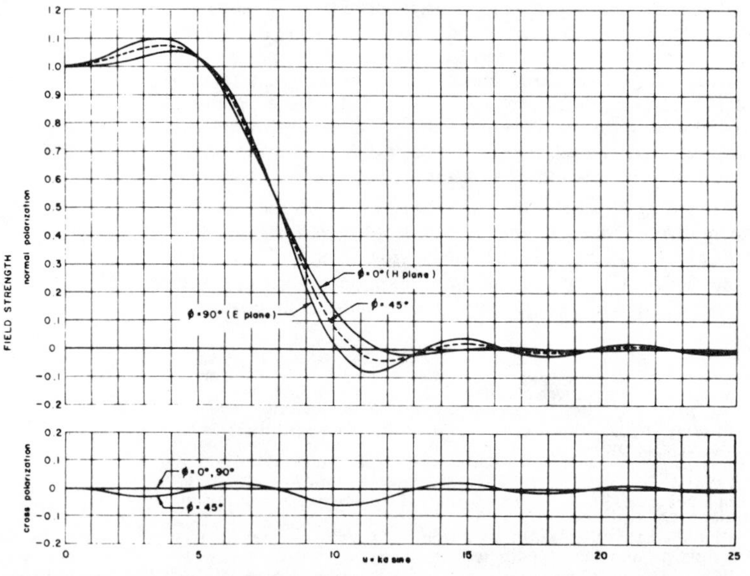

FIGURE 4—**Theoretical multimode radiation pattern.**

SESSION 11: Antenna Feed Systems

TPM 11.2: A Low-Noise Multimode Cassegrain Monopulse Feed with Polarization Diversity

P. A. Jensen

Hughes Aircraft Company

Fullerton, Calif.

RECENTLY there has been an increased interest in the use of multimode horns for microwave applications, especially in the field of low-noise Cassegrain antennas. The multimode horns utilized to date have been either of the type to provide monopulse capability with a single horn[1], or to provide pattern shaping on a single channel feed to obtain low spillover from the antenna[2]. Operational units of the foregoing feeds are currently used at the NASA-JPL Goldstone site. The multimode monopulse feed utilizes the TE_{10} mode in a rectangular crosssection horn for reference channel operation, and the TE_{20} and $TE_{11} + TM_{11}$ modes to form the dual plane monopulse patterns. The suppressed sidelobe feed consists of a conical horn using the TE_{11} mode for the basic radiation pattern, and adds the TM_{11} mode for sidelobe suppression in the E-plane. A convenient consequence of the mode phasing for low sidelobes is equalization of the radiation pattern beamwidths.

As an extension of the multimode monopulse horn mentioned, it has been discovered that the use of additional modes in the rectangular pyramidal horn will also result in sidelobe suppression in both the E and H plane, along with the additional benefit of beamwidth equalization, while still providing monopulse capability[3]. Such a horn has been designed and tested.

The multimode monopulse horn utilizes the basic TE_{10} mode to provide a reference channel radiation pattern. By examining the field distributions of the various modes possible it is easy to deduce that the probable modes necessary for suppressed sidelobe operation are the TE_{30} mode for H-plane suppression and a combination of the TE_{12} and TM_{12} modes for E-plane suppression; Figure 1. The latter two modes propagate at the same phase velocity, and also the cross-polarized components of the two modes exactly cancel[4] yielding the distribution shown in Figure 1. This degeneracy of mode propagation velocities, a property only of rectangular modes, is very useful in multimode design as it simplifies the mode control problem.

The radiation patterns of the general TE and TM modes are given by Silver[5]. For the modes used to obtain the suppressed sidelobe sum pattern, these radiation patterns are given by the following, after simplification and dropping constants

TE_{10} mode

$$E_\theta \simeq (1+\cos\theta)\,\frac{\sin\frac{u}{2}}{\frac{u}{2}} \qquad \phi=\frac{\pi}{2} \qquad \text{E-plane}$$

$$E_\phi \simeq -(1+\cos\theta)\,\frac{\cos\frac{u}{2}}{\left(\frac{u}{2}\right)^2-\left(\frac{\pi}{2}\right)^2} \qquad \phi=0 \ \text{H-plane}$$

TE_{12} and TM_{12} modes

$$E_\theta \simeq -u(1+\cos\theta)\,\frac{\sin\left(\frac{u}{2}+\pi\right)}{\left(\frac{u}{2}\right)^2-\pi^2} \qquad \phi=\frac{\pi}{2} \qquad \text{E-plane}$$

$$E_\phi = 0$$

TE_{30} mode

$$E_\theta \simeq -(1+\cos\theta)\,\frac{\sin\frac{u}{2}}{\frac{u}{2}} \qquad \phi=\frac{\pi}{2} \qquad \text{E-plane}$$

$$E_\phi \simeq (1+\cos\theta)\,\frac{\cos\frac{u}{2}}{\left(\frac{u}{2}\right)^2-\left(\frac{3\pi}{2}\right)^2} \qquad \phi=0 \ \text{H-plane}$$

The components described are plotted in Figure 2. The magnitudes of the TE_{12} and TM_{12} and TE_{30} radiation are adjusted to provide sidelobe cancellation at the second sidelobe of the TE_{10} radiation pattern. The sidelobe suppression effect of adding the components in each plane is shown by the resultant pattern. Also, it may be seen that although the E and H plane patterns do not have the same zeros, the beamwidths are quite close to being equal at least down to the 0.1 power point.

The additional modes necessary are the TE_{20} for H-plane monopulse, and the TE_{11} and TM_{11} mode combination for E-plane monopulse. These mode configurations are also shown in Figure 1, and their radiation patterns in Figure 3. It should be noticed that the difference pattern envelope to the first nulls in each plane lies within the corresponding sum envelope, thus giving near optimum illumination of both sum and difference simultaneously.

A crosssection of the multimode horn is shown in Figure 4. The monopulse bridge feeding the common aperture section is a standard four guide monopulse circuit providing dual polarization capability.

The matching section provides a match for all modes from the bridge input to the multimode horn. Along with the basic modes desired, additional higher order modes are excited to meet the boundary conditions. These modes are below cutoff in the matching section, thus causing a large reactive mismatch which must be compensated for by the matching section.

The difference mode phasing section is required to ensure the proper phasing between the TE_{20} and the

---

[1] *JPL Space Programs Summary No. 37-19*, Vol. III, p. 8-11, Deep Space Instrumentation Facility, JPL California Institute of Technology; Jan. 31, 1963.

[2] Potter, P. D., "A New Horn Antenna with Suppressed Sidelobes and Equal Beamwidths," *Microwave Journal*, p. 71-78; June, 1963.

[3] Jensen, P. A., "Low Noise Single Aperture Cassegrain Monopulse Feed," *Invention Disclosure PD 5462*, Hughes Aircraft Co.

[4] Silver, S., "Microwave Antenna Theory and Design," *McGraw-Hill Book Co.*, Chap. 7; 1949.

[5] Ibid, Chapter 10.

* This work was performed for the Jet Propulsion Laboratory, California Institute of Technology, sponsored by the National Aeronautics and Space Administration under Contract NAS7-100.

composite $TE_{11} + TM_{11}$ mode. This is necessary because of the difference in propagation velocity between the modes through the length of the horn. The length of this section is chosen to provide the additional differential phase shift between the modes to result in the correct phase relationship at the aperture.

The sum mode excitation and control section is the most critical portion of the horn. The step between region *C* and *D* is chosen such that in addition to the TE_{10} mode, the $TE_{12} + TM_{12}$ and TE_{30} modes are excited from the incident TE_{10} mode with the correct amplitude. The field configurations of these modes were shown in Figure 1. The size of this section *a* must be large enough to support all modes up to the TE_{30} mode. However, it must not permit propagation of any higher modes excited by the incident $TE_{11} + TM_{11}$ and TE_{20} modes. The next higher mode which would be excited is the $TE_{13} + TM_{13}$ mode combination from the $TE_{11} + TM_{11}$ incident modes. Therefore, the *a* dimension must be chosen above cutoff for the TE_{30} mode and below cutoff for the TE_{13} mode. This is a basic design consideration.

The length of this section must be chosen to provide the correct phasing of the TE_{10}, TE_{30}, TE_{12} and TM_{12} modes at the aperture. As three separate propagation velocities are involved, there is a unique length which must be determined for a given *a* dimension of the control section. This length is also a function of the aperture size *A* and the horn flare angle.

The design of the horn section requires consideration of both the aperture phase error and phasing between the sum pattern modes. The flare angle should be such that the phase error across the aperture is not excessive as in any horn design. However, the choice of flare angle determines the required horn length for a given aperture and given *a* dimension of control section. Since the phasing between the modes is a function of length, i.e.,

$$\Delta\phi = \int_0^L (\beta_1 - \beta_2)\, dl$$

where

$\Delta\phi$ = differential phase shift between modes.
β_1 = propagation constant of mode 1, etc.
l = length along horn

the flare angle must be chosen carefully to be sure that it is possible to find a design which will result in the correct phasing of all the modes at the aperture.

A design technique based on this discussion has been developed to result in a systematic design approach.

The low noise feed system is shown in Figure 5.

Further investigation and study of the use of multimodes are being carried out to realize other pattern shaping techniques and additional types of pattern control using higher modes in an aperture. The application of multimodes to sidelobe suppression is only one of many possible uses.

The author is grateful to *J. S. Ajioka* and *P. D. Potter* for many enlightening discussions; also to *W. A. Leeper* who performed much of the experimental work.

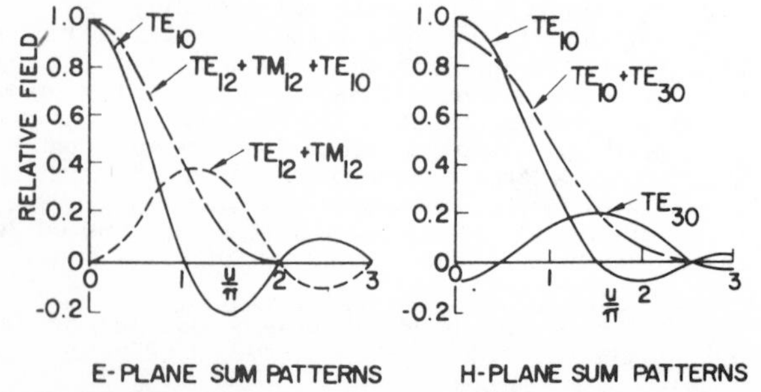

FIGURE 2—**Sum radiation patterns—theoretical.**

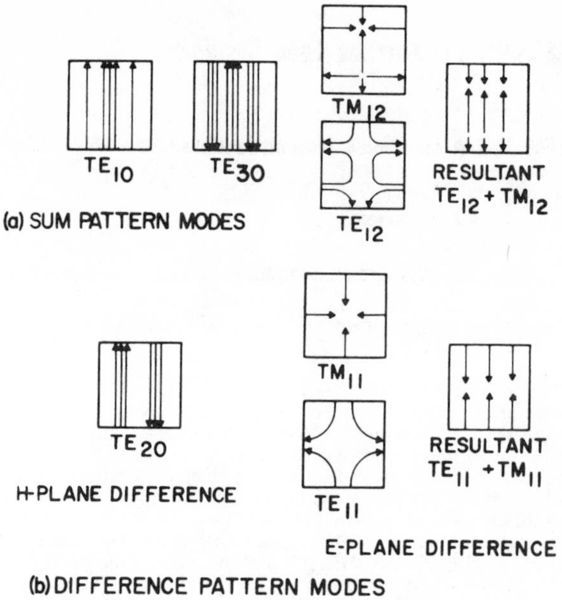

FIGURE 1—**Multimode horn field configurations.**

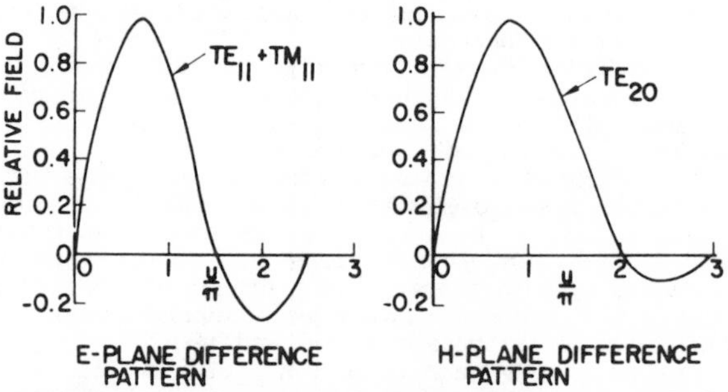

FIGURE 3—**Difference radiation patterns—theoretical.**

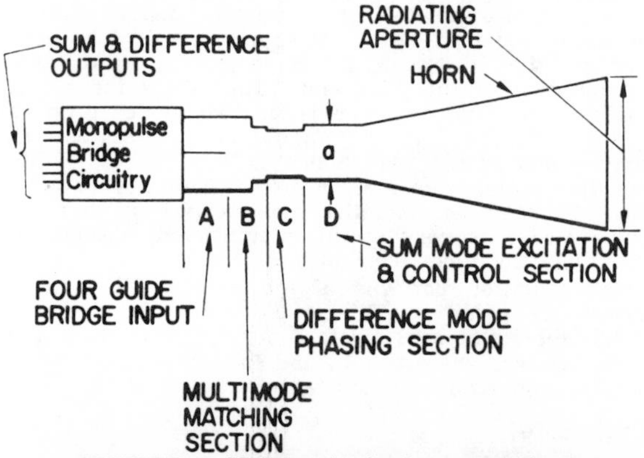

FIGURE 4—**Multimode feed crosssection.**

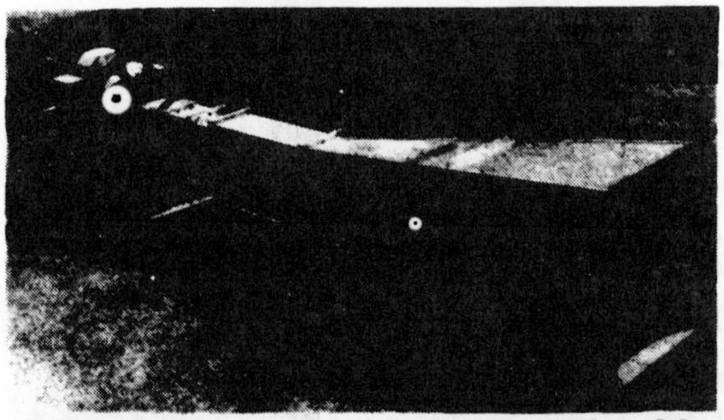

FIGURE 5—**Low noise feed—experimental model.**

Radiation Pattern Synthesis for Circular Aperture Horn Antennas

ARTHUR C. LUDWIG MEMBER, IEEE

Abstract—**A set of radiation pattern functions, suitable for synthesis of radiation patterns from circular aperture horn antennas, is obtained by assuming an aperture distribution consisting of the fields of cylindrical waveguide modes. A technique is presented for using a linear combination of the radiation pattern functions to approximate a desired radiation pattern. Linear combinations of the radiation pattern functions resulting in maximum secondary gain, when used to illuminate a paraboloidal antenna, are obtained empirically. Using spherical wave theory, maximum performance theoretically obtainable from an antenna is derived as a function of the aperture size of the feed system; the feed efficiency resulting from these theoretical limits on performance is compared to the feed efficiency of patterns obtainable from circular aperture horn antennas, and to experimental results of attempts to realize optimum circular aperture horn patterns.**

I. Introduction

SYNTHESIS OF radiation patterns from circular apertures has been the subject of several excellent papers [1]–[3] all using a method related to that advanced by Woodward [4]. The synthesis procedure involves the following steps: 1) choice of a source function describing the field distribution over the aperture, 2) calculation of the radiation patterns resulting from the source functions, and 3) expansion of a desired radiation pattern in terms of the source function patterns, thereby determining the required aperture distribution in terms of the source functions.

The choice of source function is dictated by the following criteria. 1) The source function must be amenable to closed-form integration over the aperture, and 2) the source function must give rise to radiation pattern functions amenable to some optimization procedure.

II. Choice of Source Functions

In references [1]–[3] a source function of the form

$$f(\rho) = \sum a_n J_0(\epsilon_n' \rho) \tag{1}$$

is assumed where J_0 is the Bessel function of order zero

$$\rho = r/a \text{ (see coordinate system, Fig. 1)}$$

$$J_0'(\epsilon_n') = \frac{d}{dz} J_0(z)\bigg|_{z=\epsilon_n'} = 0 \qquad n = 1, 2, 3, \cdots$$

$$a_n = \text{source function coefficient.}$$

Ruze [3] also includes a more general form of the above which has azimuthal dependence.

Manuscript received September 20, 1965; revised January 18, 1966. This paper presents one phase of research carried out at the Jet Propulsion Laboratory under Contract NAS 7-100, sponsored by the National Aeronautics and Space Administration.

The author is with the Jet Propulsion Laboratory, California Institute of Technology, Pasadena, Calif.

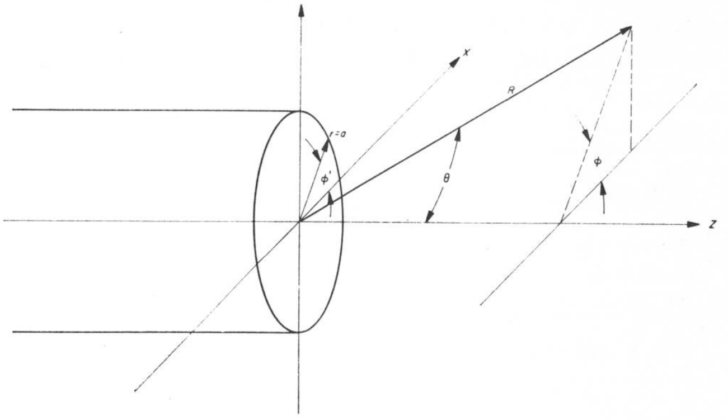

Fig. 1. Coordinate system.

Another choice of source functions, particularly suitable to synthesis of patterns from horn antennas, is simply the fields of cylindrical waveguide modes.

For TE modes

$$\boldsymbol{E}_{\mathrm{TE}_{mn}} = m \frac{J_m(\epsilon_{mn}'\rho)}{\rho} \sin m\phi' \boldsymbol{i}_r + \epsilon_{mn}' J_m'(\epsilon_{mn}'\rho) \cos m\phi' \boldsymbol{i}_\phi. \tag{2}$$

For TM modes

$$\boldsymbol{E}_{\mathrm{TM}_{mn}} = \epsilon_{mn} J_m'(\epsilon_{mn}\rho) \sin m\phi' \boldsymbol{i}_r + m \frac{J_m(\epsilon_{mn}\rho)}{\rho} \cos m\phi' \boldsymbol{i}_\phi - \frac{\epsilon_{mn}^2}{\gamma_{mn} a} J_m(\epsilon_{mn}\rho) \sin m\phi' \boldsymbol{i}_z; \tag{3}$$

where the coordinate system is shown in Fig. 1

$$\rho = r/a, \ a \text{ being the radius of the aperture}$$

$$\gamma_{mn}^2 = (\epsilon_{mn}/a)^2 - \left(\frac{2\pi}{\lambda}\right)^2$$

$$J_m(\epsilon_{mn}) = 0 \qquad n = 1, 2, 3, \cdots$$

$$J_m'(\epsilon_{mn}') = 0 \qquad n = 1, 2, 3, \cdots.$$

$\boldsymbol{i}_r$, $\boldsymbol{i}_\phi$, and $\boldsymbol{i}_z$ are unit vectors in the r, ϕ, and z directions, respectively, and all the terms have sinusoidal time variation.

We then choose the source functions to be

$$\boldsymbol{f}(\rho, \phi) = \begin{cases} \displaystyle\sum_{\substack{m=0\\n=1}}^{M,N} a_{mn}\boldsymbol{E}_{\mathrm{TE}_{mn}} + b_{mn}\boldsymbol{E}_{\mathrm{TM}_{mn}} & 0 \le r \le a \\ 0 & r > a \end{cases}. \tag{4}$$

Since the TE_{mn} and TM_{mn} fields form a complete orthogonal set in cylindrical waveguide, the set of pat-

Reprinted from *IEEE Trans. Antennas Propagat.*, vol. AP-14, pp. 434–440, July 1966.

terns resulting from these fields will represent all possible patterns obtainable from a circular horn antenna. Actually, another set of functions with $\sin m\phi$ and $\cos m\phi$ replaced with $-\cos m\phi$ and $\sin m\phi$, respectively, is necessary for completeness; a similar change of azimuthal dependence in the results to follow would provide a second set of possible patterns that are required for the general case of polar and azimuthal synthesis. This second set of patterns is not required (i.e., the coefficients are zero for proper coordinate rotation) for the synthesis of the optimum pattern to be defined later, and will not be considered further. The azimuthal dependence of (2) and (3) has been chosen such that the direction of principal polarization is the same for both TE and TM modes. This is necessary for the synthesis technique, and also reflects reality, since most types of mode generators would generate modes with this relative orientation.

III. Resulting Radiation Pattern Functions

The radiation patterns of the above source functions have been calculated by Chu [5] and are also given by Silver [6]. The derivation is based on the aperture field method, where the far-field pattern is given by

$$\mathbf{g}(R,\theta,\phi) = \frac{jke^{-jkR}}{4\pi R}(1+\cos\theta)a^2\int_0^1\int_0^{2\pi} f(\rho,\phi') \cdot e^{jka\rho\sin\theta\cos(\phi-\phi')}\rho\, d\rho d\phi \tag{5}$$

where the k = the free-space propagation constant $2\pi/\lambda$. The assumptions inherent in the aperture field method are discussed in the above references. In addition, it is assumed here that the guide wavelength at the aperture is nearly the free-space wavelength, and that reflection at the aperture may be neglected. These second-order effects, omitted here for simplicity, are considered by Silver and may be added as simple corrections to the results to follow.

The integration of (5), as outlined by Silver, is tedious, and will be omitted. The result is

$$\begin{aligned}\mathbf{g}(R,\theta,\phi) = {} & \frac{ke^{-jkR}}{2R}(1+\cos\theta)a^2 \\ & \cdot \sum_{\substack{m=0\\n=1}}^{M,N}\Bigg[a_{mn}j^m mJ_m(\epsilon_{mn}')\frac{J_m(ka\sin\theta)}{ka\sin\theta} \\ & - b_{mn}j^m\epsilon_{mn}J_m'(\epsilon_{mn})\frac{ka\sin\theta J_m(ka\sin\theta)}{\epsilon_{mn}^2-(ka\sin\theta)^2}\Bigg]\sin m\phi\, \mathbf{i}_\theta \\ & + \left[a_{mn}j^m\epsilon_{mn}'^2 J_m(\epsilon_{mn}')\frac{J_m'(ka\sin\theta)}{\epsilon_{mn}'^2-(ka\sin\theta)^2}\right]\cos m\phi\, \mathbf{i}_\phi. \end{aligned}\tag{6}$$

For radiation patterns $\mathbf{g}(R, \theta, \phi)$ consisting of $m=1$ terms only, at $\phi=0$, $g_\theta=0$, and $g_\phi=g_y$; at $\phi=90°$, $g_\phi=0$ and $g_\theta=g_y$. Thus for the case of $m=1$ only (the importance of this case will be brought out in a later section) g_θ and g_ϕ represent the E-Plane and H-Plane patterns of $\mathbf{g}(R, \theta, \phi)$, respectively, as conventionally defined. (For $m\neq 1$ the nomenclature of E- and H-Planes becomes somewhat ambiguous.) From (6) it is seen that TM modes (represented by the coefficient b_{mn}) have no ϕ component of electric field in their radiation patterns. It is also seen that the shape of the θ component of the radiation patterns from TE modes (represented by the coefficients a_{mn}) is determined by the function $J_m(ka \sin\theta)/ka \sin\theta$ which is a function of m but not a function of n. Therefore, for a given m, the ϕ component of $\mathbf{g}(R, \theta, \phi)$ may be synthesized as a function of a_{mn}, without affecting the θ component (which will be a linear combination of n patterns, all with the same θ dependence), and then the θ component may be synthesized as a function of b_{mn} without affecting the ϕ component. Equation (6) can be reformulated to express this independence.

First, to express (6) in more compact form, define

$$\begin{aligned} A_{mn} &\equiv -a_{mn}j^m kJ_m(\epsilon_{mn}')\epsilon_{mn}'^2a^2 \\ B_{mn} &\equiv b_{mn}j^m kJ_m'(\epsilon_{mn})\epsilon_{mn}a^2 \\ u &\equiv ka\sin\theta. \end{aligned}\tag{7}$$

Supressing the e^{-jkR}/R term, (6) becomes

$$\begin{aligned}\mathbf{g}(u,\phi) = {} & \frac{1+\sqrt{1-\left(\frac{u}{ka}\right)^2}}{2} \\ & \cdot\sum_{\substack{m=0\\n=1}}^{M,N}\left[-A_{mn}\frac{mJ_m(u)}{\epsilon_{mn}'^2u}+B_{mn}\frac{uJ_m(u)}{u^2-\epsilon_{mn}^2}\right]\sin m\phi\,\mathbf{i}_\theta \\ & + \left[A_{mn}\frac{J_m'(u)}{u^2-\epsilon_{mn}'^2}\right]\cos m\phi\,\mathbf{i}_\phi. \end{aligned}\tag{8}$$

Then, defining

$$B_{m0} \equiv \sum_{n=1}^{N} -A_{mn}\frac{m}{\epsilon_{mn}'^2} \tag{9}$$

and

$$\epsilon_{m0} \equiv 0,$$

equation (8) may be written as

$$\begin{aligned}\mathbf{g}(u,\phi) = {} & \frac{1+\sqrt{1-\left(\frac{u}{ka}\right)^2}}{2}\sum_{\substack{m=1\\n=0}}^{M,N}B_{mn}\frac{uJ_m(u)}{u^2-\epsilon_{mn}^2}\sin m\phi\,\mathbf{i}_\theta \\ & + \frac{1+\sqrt{1-\left(\frac{u}{ka}\right)^2}}{2}\sum_{\substack{m=0\\n=1}}^{M,N}A_{mn}\frac{J_m'(u)}{u^2-\epsilon_{mn}'^2}\cos m\phi\,\mathbf{i}_\phi. \end{aligned}\tag{10}$$

This form then reflects the fact that the ϕ component is synthesized with TE modes, and the θ component with TM modes, as discussed above.

The form of (10) is very similar to those obtained in [1]–[3]. The functions also possess the same general properties as the one given in the above references except for the added complications of the ϕ dependence, and the vector nature of (10) rather than the scalar form found by the previous authors. The scalar form is

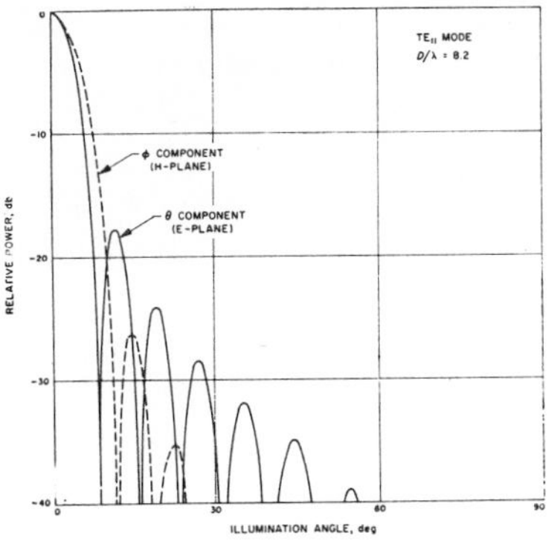

(a)

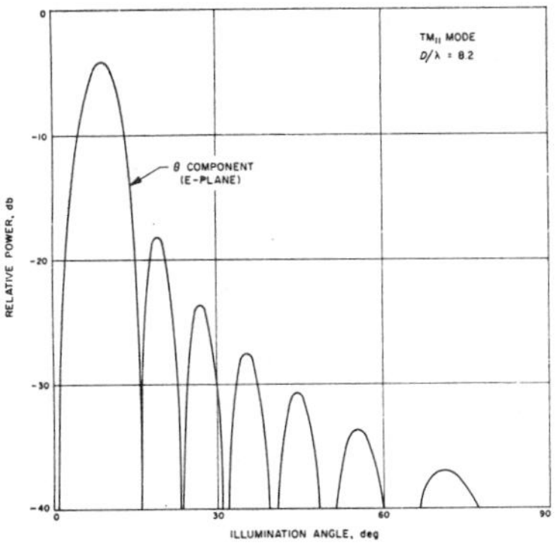

(b)

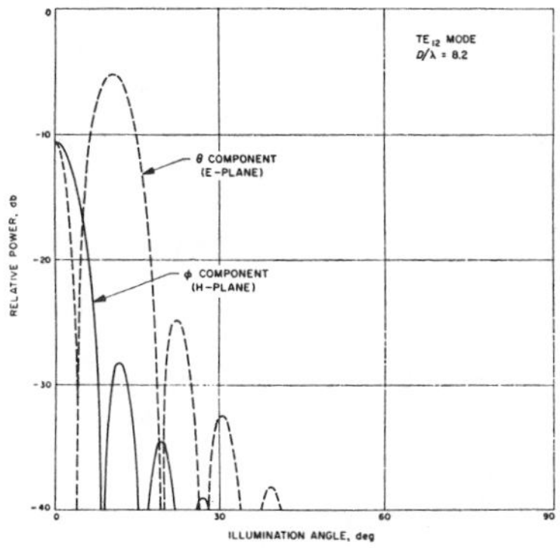

(c)

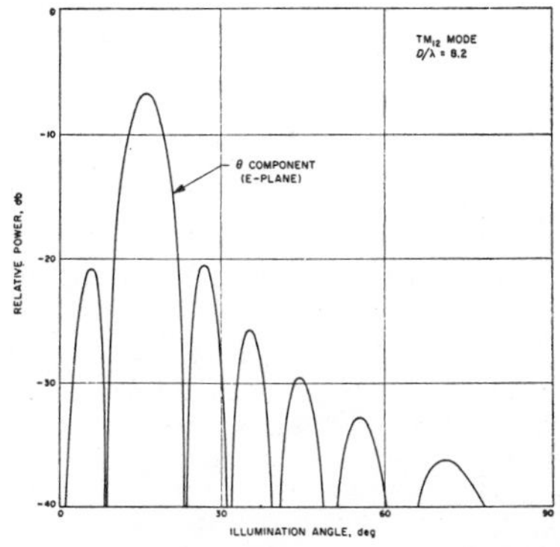

(d)

Fig. 2. Single-mode radiation patterns.

compatible with uniform polarization in the aperture, which is not the case in this development.

The principal plane patterns resulting from the excitation of each of several cylindrical waveguide modes, as given by (10), are shown in Fig. 2. The total radiated power is the same for each mode. The patterns reach a maxima near the points $u=\epsilon_{mn}$, or $u=\epsilon_{mn}'$ for the TM_{mn} and TE_{mn} modes, respectively, and have nulls at all of the remaining roots. It is important to note that for a given m, all TE_{mn} ϕ-component patterns have the same null points, except at the principal maxima. The same is true for θ-component patterns of TM_{mn} modes and the TE_{mn} θ-component pattern. Thus, again for a specific m, the value of the ϕ-component field strength at a root $u=\epsilon_{mn}'$ is determined solely by the value of the TE_{mn} mode at that point. The same is true of the TM modes for the θ component. (The TE_{1n} modes determine the value at $u=0$.)[1] This fact is the basis of the synthesis technique to be developed shortly.

The radiation patterns of the TE_{11} and TE_{12} modes for an aperture of $D/\lambda=4.7$ have been determined experimentally, and check very well with the patterns given by (10) [7]. It has also been experimentally verified that the excitation of the TM_{11} mode does not affect the ϕ-component pattern, and that its effect on the θ-component pattern agrees with the theoretical pattern [8].

IV. Synthesis of Desired Pattern

We will now consider an expansion of a desired radiation pattern $\boldsymbol{E}(u, \phi)$. Multiplying both sides of (10) by $\cos p\phi$ and integrating from 0 to 2π we obtain

$$\int_0^{2\pi} \boldsymbol{g}(u, \phi) \cos p\phi d\phi = \frac{1+\sqrt{1-\left(\frac{u}{ka}\right)^2}}{2} \pi \sum_{n=1}^{N} A_{pn} \frac{J_p'(u)}{u^2-\epsilon_{pn}'^2} \boldsymbol{i}_\phi. \quad (11)$$

At a root $u=\epsilon_{pq}'$, all terms in the sum are zero except for the $n=q$ term:

$$\int_0^{2\pi} \boldsymbol{g}(\epsilon_{pq}', \phi) \cos p\phi d\phi = \frac{1+\sqrt{1-\left(\frac{\epsilon_{pq}'}{ka}\right)^2}}{2} \pi A_{pq} \lim_{u\to\epsilon_{pq}'} \frac{J_p'(u)}{u^2-\epsilon_{pq}'^2} \boldsymbol{i}_\phi = \frac{1+\sqrt{1-\left(\frac{\epsilon_{pq}'}{ka}\right)^2}}{2} \pi A_{pq} \frac{J_p''(\epsilon_{pq}')}{2\epsilon_{pq}'} \boldsymbol{i}_\phi. \quad (12)$$

By substituting $\boldsymbol{E}(\epsilon_{pq}', \phi)$ for $\boldsymbol{g}(\epsilon_{pq}, \phi)$ in (12), the coefficients A_{pq} are uniquely defined

[1] At $u=0$ (10) reduces to $\boldsymbol{g}(0, \phi) = \sum_{n=1}^{N} - A_{1n} \frac{1}{2\epsilon_{1n}'^2} \boldsymbol{i}_y$.

$$A_{pq} = \frac{2}{1+\sqrt{1-\left(\frac{\epsilon_{pq}'}{ka}\right)^2}} \frac{2\epsilon_{pq}'}{\pi J_p''(\epsilon_{pq}')} \cdot \int_0^{2\pi} E_\phi(\epsilon_{pq}', \phi) \cos p\phi d\phi. \quad (13)$$

A similar expression is obtained for B_{pq} by using sin $p\phi$ in (11), and $u=\epsilon_{pq}$ in (12). It has been assumed that a suitable coordinate rotation has been performed such that the direction of principal polarization is the same for $\boldsymbol{E}(u, \phi)$ and $\boldsymbol{g}(u, \phi)$. Equation (13), and a similar equation for B_{pq} define an approximate fit such that the component of order m of $\boldsymbol{g}(u, \phi)$ equals the component of order m of $\boldsymbol{E}(u, \phi)$ at a discrete set of points $u=\epsilon_{m1}, \epsilon_{m2}, \epsilon_{m3}, \cdots$ for the θ component, and $u=\epsilon_{m1}'$, ϵ_{m2}', ϵ_{m3}', $\cdots$ for the ϕ component.

The azimuthal fit is similar to an ordinary Fourier expansion except for the fact that the coefficients are perturbed slightly due to the approximate nature of the fit in the polar planes. The accuracy of the fit obtainable by this technique is limited by a practical consideration. For a mode to be present in the aperture it must normally be above cutoff. Using asymptotic expansions for Bessel functions, the approximate condition for propagation is obtained as

$$2n + m < 4\frac{a}{\lambda} + \frac{1}{2} \quad \text{for TM Modes}$$

$$2n + m < 4\frac{a}{\lambda} + \frac{3}{2} \quad \text{for TE Modes.} \quad (14)$$

Thus the series expansion is finite except for the limiting cases of infinite aperture size, or zero wavelength. Another facet of this same problem is that for a fixed aperture size, adding modes broadens the radiation pattern. Thus the more modes used, the larger the aperture must be to provide a constant beamwidth. This can become very serious in terms of phase errors in the horn aperture, and also antenna aperture blockage in feed applications, for only a few additional higher order modes.

V. Synthesis of Optimum Pattern

With the above limitations in mind, (13) and a similar equation for B_{pq} may be used to develop approximate fits to a desired "optimum" pattern $\boldsymbol{E}(u, \phi)$. Ishimaru and Held [1] and Taylor [2] both define optimum as minimum beamwidth for a given sidelobe level. Ruze [3] considers an optimum pattern a flat top beam. Another possible choice for "optimum" is the pattern which provides maximum secondary gain when illuminating a paraboloidal reflector. It may be shown [9] that the illumination providing maximum gain is

$$\boldsymbol{E}(u, \phi) = \frac{2}{1+\sqrt{1-\left(\frac{u}{ka}\right)^2}} [\sin \phi \boldsymbol{i}_\theta + \cos \phi \boldsymbol{i}_\phi] \quad (15)$$

where we have used the relationship

$$\frac{2}{1+\sqrt{1-\left(\frac{u}{ka}\right)^2}} = \frac{2}{1+\cos\theta} = \sec^2\frac{\theta}{2}. \quad (16)$$

Since the optimum pattern has azimuthal dependence of the $m=1$ type only,[2] (13) for this case reduces to

$$A_{1q} = \frac{2\epsilon_{1q}'}{J_1''(\epsilon_{1q}')}\left[\frac{2}{1+\sqrt{1-\left(\frac{\epsilon_{1q}'}{ka}\right)^2}}\right]^2$$

$$A_{pq} = 0 \qquad p \neq 1. \quad (17)$$

The expression for B_{pq} is found to be

$$B_{1q} = \frac{2}{J_1'(\epsilon_{1q})}\left[\frac{2}{1+\sqrt{1-\left(\frac{\epsilon_{1q}}{ka}\right)^2}}\right]^2 \quad q > 0$$

$$B_{pq} = 0 \qquad p \neq 1. \quad (18)$$

B_{10} is not independent, and is given by (9). (This arises from the fact that the θ component and the ϕ component must be equal at $u=0$.) The pattern $\boldsymbol{g}(u, \phi)$ defined by these coefficients is not in fact the optimum pattern. That is, the approximate fit defined by this synthesis technique (see [3] for examples of this type of fit) is not the "best-fit" in the sense of a fit which minimizes gain loss.[3] Numerical evaluation of optimum coefficients was obtained by evaluating the secondary gain of a paraboloid illuminated by a pattern of the form given by (10) (with $m=1$ only), and varying the coefficients until a maximum gain was obtained. Gain losses due to spillover, cross polarization, and nonuniform illumination were considered. (The exact formulation used for efficiency is given in [9], and applies to the evaluation of all theoretical and experimental results in this article.) The case numerically evaluated assumed optical reflection from a hyperboloid subtending an approximately 14° half angle. By varying the eccentricity, the hyperboloid could in principle illuminate a paraboloid of arbitrary F/D, so that the optimum horn pattern is only a function of the angle the primary pattern subtends. (Although it would be interesting to know the dependence of the coefficients with respect to this parameter, only one case was evaluated due to the laborious nature of the optimization procedure.)

Optimum two-, three-, and four-mode patterns for this case are shown in Fig. 3. Principle polarization patterns (ξy) cut at ϕ values other than 0° or 90° lie be-

[2] It is interesting to note that while the $m=1$ type of illumination function is easily obtainable with feeds of circular symmetry, it is not in general obtained with rectangular feeds. This may be seen in the theoretical radiation patterns of rectangular horns as given by Silver [6], p. 242. However, rectangular horns utilizing suitable mode addition do approach this condition very closely.

[3] Gain loss is chosen as an error criteria in lieu of rms error, for example, because gain is of primary importance in the intended application for these patterns. This criteria also has the advantage of evaluating the effect of many errors (amplitude, phase, polarization, etc.) simultaneously.

tween the E- and H-plane patterns. Cross polarization (ξx) is equal to one-half the difference between the E- and H-plane patterns times sin z_4. This is true in general for $m=1$ modes with uniform phase patterns [9]. Mode powers and coefficients for these patterns are shown in Table I. Mode coefficients are given as the ratio of the empirically determined optimum coefficients to the coefficients defined in (17) and (18). A scaling ambiguity was resolved by setting this normalized value equal to 1.0 for the TE_{11} mode. It is seen that the empirically optimized coefficients vary considerably from those given by (17) and (18). Therefore, the primary value of the approximate fit defined by setting $g(u, \phi)$ equal to the desired pattern $E(u, \phi)$ at the roots ϵ_{mn} and ϵ_{mn}' is as a first approximation, and as a means to develop insight into the problem, in terms of what can and cannot be synthesized.[4]

VI. Theoretical Limitations on Performance

The question of optimum performance may also be approached using spherical wave theory. Any radiation pattern may be expanded in a series of spherical wave functions given by Stratton [10]. It may be shown that the maximum order n of spherical wave which may eminate from a given object which can be enclosed in a sphere of radius R, is given approximately by $n<kR$ [11], [19]. Figure 4 shows the maximum efficiency (the ratio of gain to gain in the case of uniform illumination) available from this limited number of spherical waves vs. D/λ, the diameter of the source in free-space wavelengths.[5]

The fact stated earlier that use of more modes (higher efficiency) requires larger apertures, appears to have fundamental significance as shown by Fig. 4. The combinations of spherical modes yielding maximum efficiency for an illumination half angle of 15° are shown in Fig. 5 for $n=15$ and $n=25$, corresponding to D/λ of 4.7 and 8.0 (approximately the aperture sizes for optimum dual mode and four mode patterns, respectively). The spherical wave patterns have total circular symmetry. The resemblance between the spherical mode patterns and the optimum circular horn patterns is striking, and illustrates the fact that a circular horn is an excellent means of realizing the theoretical maxima predicted by spherical wave theory.

[4] The basic principle involved is also very useful as a tool for analysis; for example, the determination of which modes are present in a waveguide may be made by taking a radiation pattern and observing the field strength at the roots $u=\epsilon_{mn}$ and ϵ_{mn}'.

[5] Figure 4 also reflects the fact that small diameter feeds are compatible with focal-point fed antennas, and that a large diameter feed is necessary to achieve the equivalent performance in a Cassegrainian antenna system. In order to achieve the maximum potential in a Cassegrainian antenna, one may move from the limiting curve for the primary illumination angle to the limiting curve for the secondary illumination angle by using a shaped subreflector and/or main reflector. This points out part of the potential of reflector synthesis techniques such as those developed by Potter (Jet Propulsion Lab., Pasadena, Calif., JPL Space Programs Summary 37-31, vol. IV, pp. 285–287, 1965) and Galindo ("Synthesis of dual reflector antennas," Electronics Research Lab., University of California, Berkeley, Rept. 64-22, July 1964)

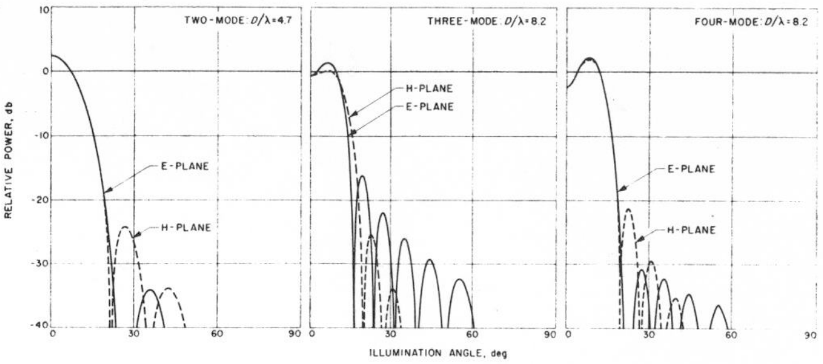

Fig. 3. Optimum theoretical patterns, multimode circular horn.

TABLE I
MODE COEFFICIENTS FOR OPTIMUM CIRCULAR HORN PATTERNS

Parameter	Mode			
	TE_{11}	TM_{11}	TE_{12}	TM_{12}
Optimum Two Mode:				
Normalized mode coefficient	1.000	0.307		
% Power in Mode	87.5%	12.5%		
Optimum Three Mode:				
Normalized mode coefficient	1.000	1.091	0.687	
% Power in Mode	26.5%	46.5%	27.0%	
Optimum Four Mode:				
Normalized Mode coefficient	1.000	1.289	0.981	0.381
% Power in Mode	16.8%	41.3%	35.0%	6.9%

VII. Experimental Results

Perhaps the most valuable aspect of the pattern synthesis approach described in this paper is the relationship between the desired far-field pattern, and the means of realization of the necessary aperture distribution. First of all, the patterns given by (10) are realizable with a circular horn antenna. The realization procedure is then to excite and control the required higher order waveguide modes. Some techniques for dealing with this problem have been developed [8], [12], [13], [14]. An existing feed utilizing two modes has been previously described in the literature [8]. A feed has been recently developed by the author utilizing four modes. Amplitude and phase patterns of this feed are shown in Fig. 6. The efficiency of this feed, including phase loss, but not including aperture blockage, is over 83 percent, evaluated on the basis of optical reflection. A scattered pattern from a 50-wavelength diameter hyperboloid illuminated by the four mode feed has been calculated numerically [15]. Efficiency of the secondary pattern, illuminating a paraboloid subtending a 60° half angle, was over 82 percent, including phase, cross polarization, illumination, and spillover losses, and loss due to 7° aperture blockage at the vertex.

VIII. Summary of Multimode Circular Horn Performance

The efficiency of experimentally realized multimode horn patterns is compared to the efficiency of optimum multimode horn patterns in Fig. 7. Also shown are the theoretical limitations on efficiency for the same size aperture. The computations are based on optical reflection from a hyperbola, and include losses due to phase

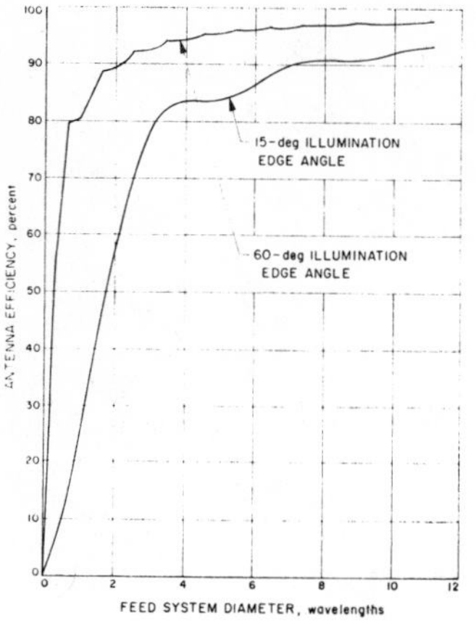

Fig. 4. Theoretical limitation on efficiency vs. feed system diameter.

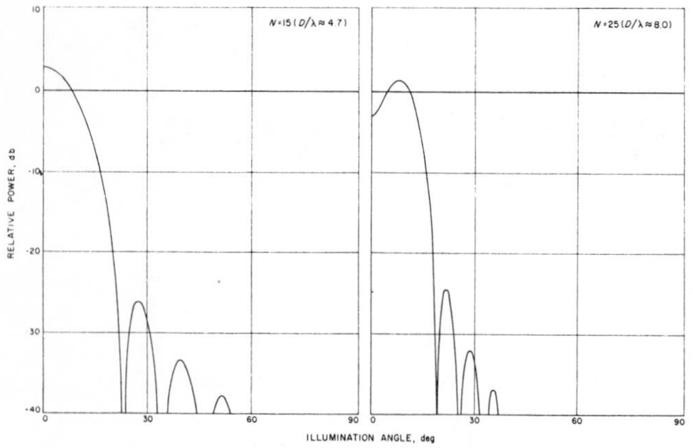

Fig. 5. Spherical wave functions; best N-term fit to uniform illumination.

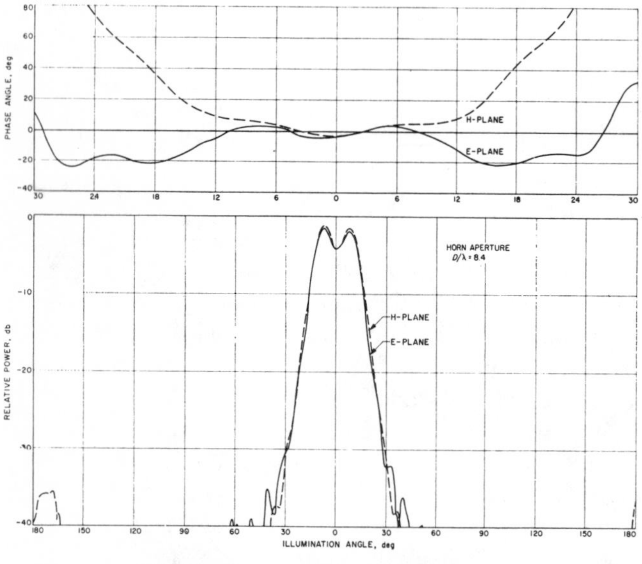

Fig. 6. Four-mode horn experimental amplitude and phase patterns.

errors, cross polarization, nonuniform amplitude illumination, and spillover. Aperture blockage is not included. It is evident from Fig. 7 that optimum multimode conical horn patterns are very near the theoretical maximum obtainable from any device of comparable aperture size. The optimum patterns appear to converge towards zero gain loss, but the author has not attempted

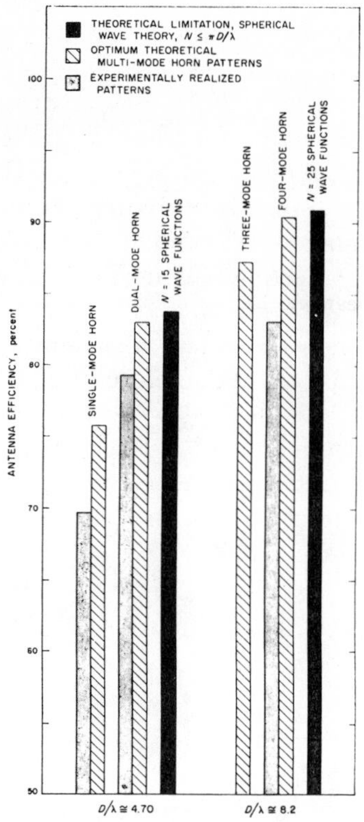

Fig. 7. Comparative efficiency of radiation patterns, 15-degree illumination edge angle (approximately).

a proof of this. The difference between the optimum patterns and the experimentally realized patterns is largely due to excess spillover, very probably due to phase errors in the horn aperture. Phase error in the patterns themselves is also appreciable in the four-mode case (negligible in the dual-mode case). The performance levels achieved by this technique are fairly high; the problem of mode generation and control is difficult, but improvements in this technology could result in even higher levels of performance.

The multimode synthesis technique is also applicable to rectangular horn antennas, and there has been considerable study with regard to that application [16], [17], [18].

Acknowledgment

The author is particularly indebted to P. D. Potter, who originally conceived the multimode approach to pattern synthesis, and encouraged and provided many of the ideas for the subsequent development of multimode technology presented in this article. The help of W. Marquez and F. McCrea in the experimental development of the four-mode horn is also greatly appreciated.

References

[1] A. Ishimaru and G. Held, "Analysis and synthesis of radiation patterns from circular apertures," *Canad. J. Phys.*, vol. 38, pp. 78–99, 1960.
[2] T. T. Taylor, "Design of circular apertures for narrow beamwidth and low sidelobes," *IRE Trans. on Antennas and Propagation*, vol. AP-8, pp. 17–22, January 1960.
[3] J. Ruze, "Circular aperture synthesis," *IEEE Trans. on Antennas and Propagation*, vol. AP-12, pp. 691–694, November 1964.

[4] P. M. Woodward, "A method of calculating the field over a plane aperture required to produce a given polar diagram," *J. IEE (London)*, vol. 93, pt. III-A, pp. 1554–1558, 1946.
[5] L. J. Chu, "Calculation of the radiation properties of hollow pipes and horns," *J. Appl. Phys.*, vol. II, pp. 603–610, September 1940.
[6] S. Silver, *Microwave Antenna Theory and Design*, Rad. Lab. ser., vol. 12, New York: McGraw-Hill, 1949, pp. 336–338.
[7] A. Ludwig, "Multimode horn feeds," Jet Propulsion Lab., Pasadena, Calif., JPL Space Programs Summary 37-20, vol. IV, pp. 126–130, April 1963.
[8] P. D. Potter, "A new horn antenna with suppressed sidelobes and equal beamwidths," *Microwave J.*, vol. VI, pp. 71–78, June 1963.
[9] A. Ludwig, "Antenna feed efficiency," Jet Propulsion Lab., Pasadena, Calif., JPL Space Programs Summary 37-26, vol. IV, pp. 200–208, April 1964.
[10] J. A. Stratton, *Electromagnetic Theory*. New York: McGraw-Hill, 1941, p. 416.
[11] P. D. Potter, "Spherical wave functions," Jet Propulsion Lab., Pasadena, Calif., JPL Space Programs Summary 37-24, vol. IV, pp. 150–154, December 1963.
[12] E. R. Nagelberg and J. Shefer, "Mode conversion in circular waveguides," *Bell Sys. Tech. J.*, pp. 1321–1338, September 1965.
[13] A. Ludwig, "Multimode horn research," Jet Propulsion Lab., Pasadena, Calif., JPL Space Programs Summary 37-24, vol. IV, pp. 154–156, December 1963.
[14] C. Yeh, "Excitation of higher-order modes by a step discontinuity of a circular waveguide," Jet Propulsion Lab., Pasadena, Calif., JPL Tech. Rept., 32-496, February 1964.
[15] W. V. T. Rusch, "Scattering from a hyperboloidal reflector in a Cassegrainian feed system," *IEEE Trans. on Antennas and Propagation*, vol. AP-11, pp. 414–421, July 1963.
[16] P. A. Jensen, "A low-noise multimode Cassegrain monopulse feed with polarization diversity," *NEREM Rec.*, pp. 94–95, November 1963.
[17] "Final Report for modification of DSIF SCM feeds," prepared by Hughes Aircraft, Company Ground Systems Group, Fullerton, Calif., for Jet Propulsion Lab., Pasadena, Calif., Re-order 64-52, January 1964.
[18] S. W. Drabowitch, "Multimode antennas," *Microwave J.*, pp. 41–51, January 1966.
[19] R. F. Harrington, "Effect of antenna size on gain, bandwidth, and efficiency," *J. Res. NBS*, vol. 64D, no. 1, pp. 1–12, 1960.

Dual Mode Small-Aperture Antennas

Potter,[1] in his original work on dual-mode excitation, investigated conical horns of aperture diameter four to five wavelengths to serve as feeds for Cassegrainian antennas. In this communication, measurement and theory of two modes in apertures one to two wavelengths in diameter are discussed. Such apertures have characteristics suitable for prime-focus feeds and other applications.

The basic notion involved is to excite a circular aperture with both the TE_{11}° and TM_{11}° modes with their relative phases and amplitudes adjusted to cancel the electric field at the aperture boundary. The ratio of mode powers required to produce this cancellation is

$$\frac{W_{M_{11}}}{W_{E_{11}}} = \frac{0.4191}{\sqrt{\left(1-\left(\frac{\lambda}{\lambda_{COE}}\right)^2\right)\left(1-\left(\frac{\lambda}{\lambda_{COM}}\right)^2\right)}}.$$

The resulting aperture field distribution for the princiapl planes is shown in Fig. 1. This highly tapered distribution over the aperture provides the following desirable features:

1) no edge currents to cause radiation from outside the aperture boundary with subsequent suppression of all side-lobes to at least -30 dB
2) wide beamwidths
3) improved impedance match compared with single dominant mode excitation
4) nearly circularly symmetric radiation patterns and coincident phase centers in the principal planes.

An undesirable feature is differential dispersion between the modes which results in narrowing the bandwidth.

The design structure employed to investigate these properties is shown in axial cross section by Fig. 2. Due to circular symmetry, only modes of even order can be excited. By restricting $\lambda_{CO}(TM_{11}^{\circ}) < d_2 < \lambda_{CO}(TM_{12}^{\circ})$, only $TE_{11}^{\circ} + TM_{11}^{\circ}$ energy will appear at the aperture. Length l is adjusted to provide the desired aperture boundary field cancellation. Obviously, cancellation occurs periodically with l which should be of minimum length in order to achieve maximum bandwidth. The conic section of half flare angle β provides the mode amplitude ratio control.

Figure 3 shows measured E plane radiation patterns for two aperture sizes. The corresponding ratios of computed mode powers ($W_{M_{11}}/W_{E_{11}}$) are 1.34 and 0.59, respectively. The measured H-plane patterns (not shown) are nearly identical for either the TE_{11} mode alone or the dual mode aperture excitation, as they should be; also the E and H plane patterns for dual mode excitation are nearly identical for a dynamic range of 15 dB from maximum. An improvement of impedance match is obtained using the dual mode, namely a VSWR of 1.1 as opposed to 1.4 for the single mode case. The bandwidth is typically less than 10% for side-lobe levels at 90° no worse than for the single mode case.

Potter gives the far field radiation pattern equations for the dual-mode circular aperture which were developed directly from Silver.[2] Perhaps the most significant aspect of this note is that the computed patterns shown on the figures are in good agreement with those measured for the small aperture sizes. This agreement might be expected since the approximations used by Silver in deriving the radiation patterns neglect the edge currents which are the primary source of radiation in the region behind the aperture.

It is also interesting to note that the ratio of field intensities (TE_{11} to TM_{11} mode) at the center of the aperture for aperture boundary field cancellation is a constant, independent of aperture size and equal to 0.784. Potter's α, defined by him as the ratio of the relative powers in the modes, is actually the ratio of the fields at one point, the aperture center, and is not the true propagating mode power ratio.

R. H. TURRIN
Crawford Hill Lab.
Bell Telephone Labs., Inc.
Holmdel, N. J.

Manuscript received August 30, 1966.

[1] P. D. Potter, "A new horn antenna with suppressed sidelobes and equal beamwidths," *Microwave J.*, vol. 6. pp. 71–78, June 1963.

[2] S. Silver, *Microwave Antenna Theory and Design.* New York: McGraw-Hill, 1949, pp. 337–338.

Reprinted from *IEEE Trans. Antennas Propagat.*, vol. AP-15, pp. 307–308, Mar. 1967.

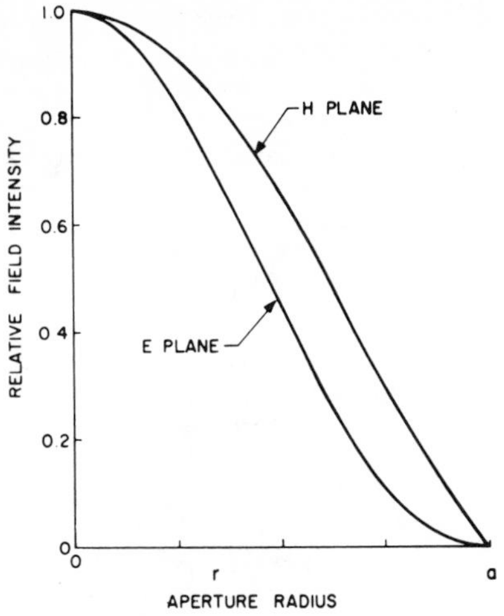

Fig. 1. Aperture field distributions in the principal planes for dual-mode excitation with field cancellation at the guide wall.

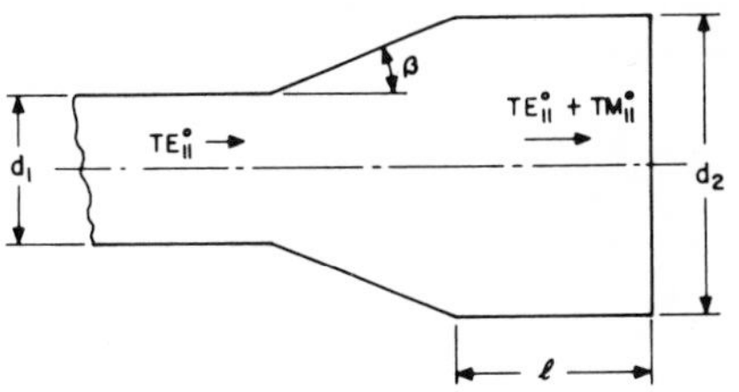

Fig. 2. Mode converter and aperture geometry for the dual-mode antenna.

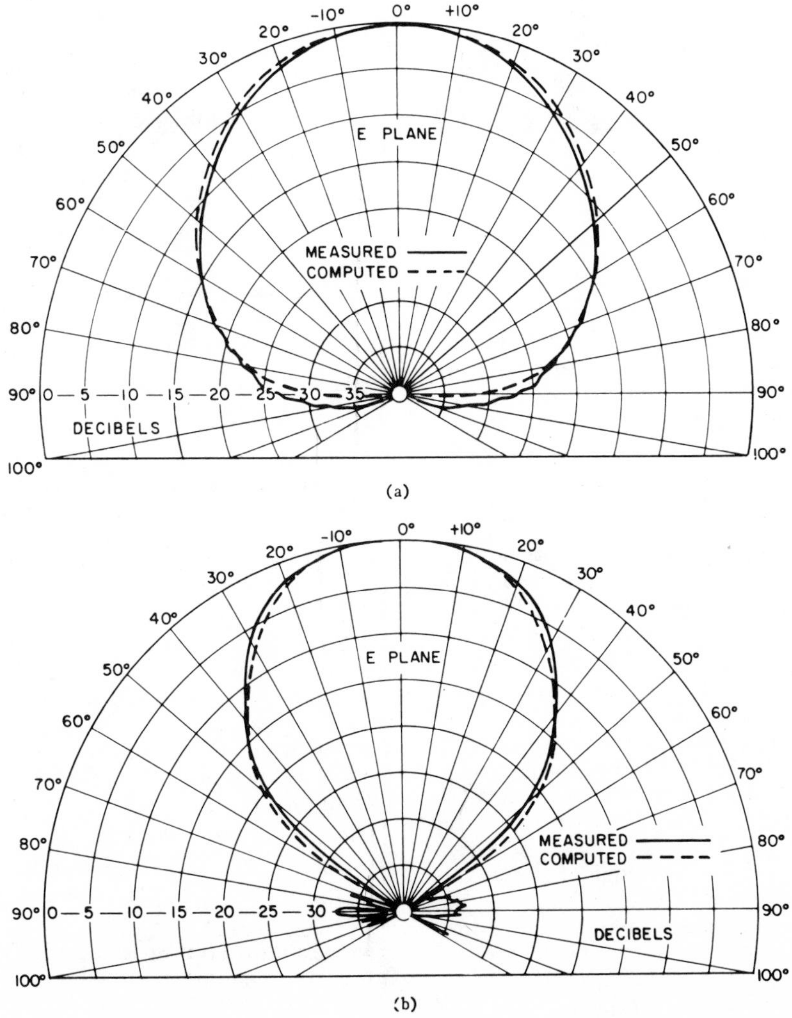

Fig. 3. *E*-plane far field radiation patterns for aperture diameters ($\lambda = 1.05''$), (a) 1.38 inches and (b) 1.95 inches.

Flare-Angle Changes in a Horn as a Means of Pattern Control*

DR. SEYMOUR B. COHN,

Consultant, Tarzana, California

A new technique is described for controlling the E-plane aperture distribution and radiation pattern of a pyramidal or conical horn. Small variations of flare angle at one or more points along the horn are used to produce a tapered aperture field in the E plane. Equal E- and H-plane beamwidths with low sidelobes are obtained. The structure is simple and economical to fabricate, and offers inherently low VSWR and minimum dissipation loss. A first-order design theory is applied successfully to a pyramidal feed horn for a low-noise Cassegrain antenna system.

Seymour B. Cohn received the B.E. degree from Yale University in 1942 and Ph.D. degree from Harvard University in 1948. He was employed by the Radio Research Laboratory at Harvard from 1942 to 1945, Sperry Gyroscope Co. from 1948 to 1953, Stanford Research Institute from 1953 to 1960, and Rantec from 1960 to 1967. Since 1967 he has worked as an independent consultant. Dr. Cohn is a former chairman of the G-MTT Administration Committee, and is an Associate Editor of the "microwave journal."

INTRODUCTION

This paper presents a new horn-radiator design particularly well suited as a feed for a Cassegrain-type antenna. Features of this design are: (1) equal E- and H-plane beamwidths; (2) low sidelobes in both E- and H-plane; (3) symmetrical structure permitting circular or any linear polarization; (4) simple, clean configuration providing economical fabrication, minimum dissipation loss, and low VSWR. Although attention is concentrated on square-cross-section pyramidal horns, the same technique may be applied to conical horns.

A pyramidal horn with square aperture has a theoretical ratio of H-plane to E-plane 3-dB beamwidth equal to 1.35. (This assumes TE_{10} aperture fields with half-sine-wave H-plane distribution and constant E-plane distribution.) The respective sidelobe levels are 23 and 13 dB below the peak of the main beam. For use as a high-gain, low-noise feed the E- and H-plane beamwidths should be equal, and the sidelobes should be down by at least 20 dB. Since the H-plane pattern is already satisfactory, a means was sought for introducing E-plane aperture taper in order to increase the beamwidth and reduce the sidelobes of the E-plane pattern. The technique adopted is conversion of part of the TE_{10} energy in the horn to TE_{12} and TM_{12} energy with proper amplitude and phase to yield the desired taper. This mode conversion is accomplished by one or more small changes of flare angle within the horn.

*The work described in this paper was performed for Rantec Division, Emerson Electric Co., Calabasas, California. The author is a consultant to Rantec and several other clients.

Generation of higher modes for equalizing E- and H-plane patterns has been used before in both pyramidal and conical structures. Examples are: (1) the "box" horn of S. J. Mason having an abrupt step in cross-section to generate TE_{10} and TE_{30} modes phased to reduce the H-plane beamwidth;[1] (2) a cluster of horns exciting proper TE_{10} plus TE_{12} and TM_{12} amplitudes in a rectangular aperture;[2] (3) a conical horn with abrupt cross-section step at the throat yielding E-plane aperture taper by addition of TE_{11} and TM_{11} modes;[3] (4) two in-phase rectangular waveguides opening abruptly into a larger rectangular waveguide with proportions yielding proper ratio of TE_{10}, TE_{12}, and TM_{12} amplitudes;[4] (5) probes and cavities in a waveguide section exciting the throat of the horn;[5] (6) transverse corrugations on the inside walls of the horn.[6,7,8]

Phase velocity of the TE_{10} mode differs from that of the TE_{12} and TM_{12} modes (which have equal velocity). A length of uniform waveguide or horn introduces a differential phase shift between the TE_{10} mode and the pair of TE_{12} and TM_{12} modes; therefore, proper phasing of the modes occurs only in a limited frequency band. Differential phase shift per unit length is especially great near the throat of the horn. One advantage of flare-angle changes within the horn compared to mode exciters at the throat of the horn is decreased differential phase shift between the point of mode excitation and the aperture. Hence the flare-change technique yields generally greater bandwidth. Good performance is at present limited to about 30 percent, but may be widened in the future.

APPROXIMATE ANALYSIS

Mode conversion at a flare-angle change is analyzed in an approximate manner to yield formulas adequate for design purposes. In Fig. 1a a horn of flare angle θ_1 is joined to a horn of flare angle $\theta_2 = 0$. Consider the phase fronts 1 and 2 applying to the two horn sections and intersecting at the flare-angle discontinuity points. The maximum separation between these phase fronts is

$$\Delta z = R - l = \frac{a_1}{2}\left[\csc\theta_1 - \cot\theta_1\right] = \frac{a_1}{2}\tan\frac{\theta_1}{2} \quad (1)$$

If θ_1 is less than about 0.4 radius (23°), Δz may be approximated by

$$\Delta z = \frac{a_1\,\theta_1}{4},\ (\theta_1 \text{ in radians}) \quad (2)$$

Similarly, if θ_1 and θ_2 both differ from zero, as shown in Fig. 1b and c, the phase-front separation is

$$\Delta z = \frac{a_1}{4}(\theta_1 - \theta_2) \quad (3)$$

The TE_{10}-mode phase difference corresponding to Δz is $\phi_m = 2\pi\Delta z/\lambda_g$, or

$$\phi_m = \frac{\pi\,a_1}{2\,\lambda_g}(\theta_1 - \theta_2) \quad (4)$$

where λ_g is guide wavelength of the TE_{10} horn mode and a_1 is the E-plane height at the flare-change point. For θ_1 and θ_2 small,

$$\lambda_g \approx \frac{\lambda}{\sqrt{1 - \left(\frac{\lambda}{2a}\right)^2}} \approx \lambda \text{ for } a > 2\lambda \quad (5)$$

where a is the H-plane width at the flare change point.

Assume now that the horn is sectoral with E-plane flare and constant H-plane width. Then with a small flare-angle change, an incident TE_{10} wave arriving from

Reprinted with permission from *Microwave J.*, vol. 13, pp. 41, 42, 44, 46, Oct. 1970.

the left yields predominately TE_{10} on the right plus small amplitudes of TE/TM_{12}, TE/TM_{14}, etc., where TE/TM denotes TE, TM pairs superimposed in amplitude and phase such that $E_x = 0$ at all points. Reflected waves in the various modes are relatively much smaller and will be ignored. In Fig. 2 the y axis lies in a phase

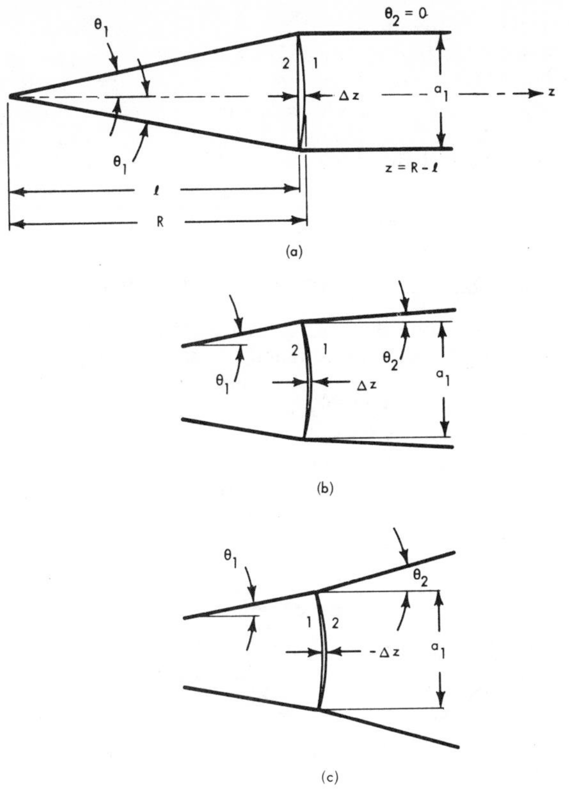

Fig. 1 — Flare-angle changes. In (a) and (b), $\theta_1 - \theta_2 > 0$; in (c), $\theta_1 - \theta_2 < 0$.

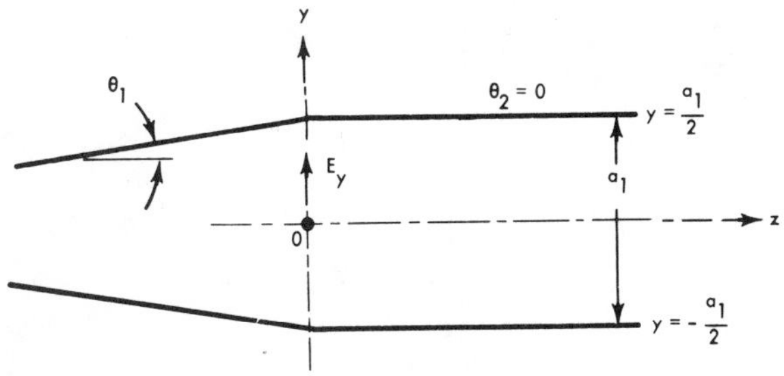

Fig. 2 — Flare change in E plane.

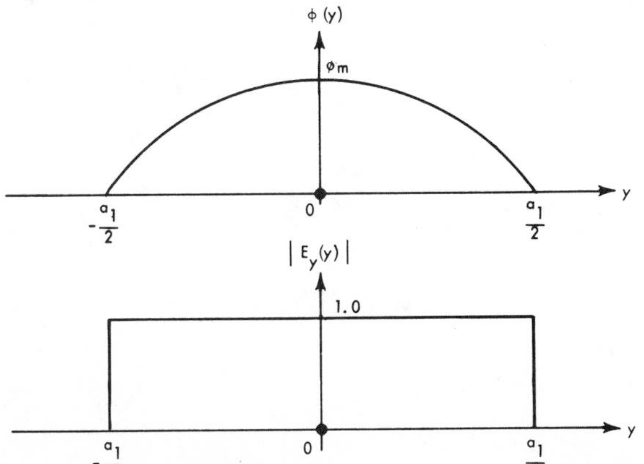

Fig. 3. — Assumed $\phi(y)$ and $|E_y(y)|$ in plane $z = 0$, $y = -a_1/2$ to $a_1/2$.

front of the $\theta_2 = 0$ horn section. This case is sufficiently general for analysis, since Eq. 4 shows that $\theta_1 - \theta_2$ defines the phase-front discontinuity, rather than θ_1 and θ_2 individually. The phase difference ϕ as a function of y is shown in Fig. 3.

As a first-order approximation subject to θ_1 being small, the sum of the TE_{10} and higher-order waves to the right of the discontinuity will match the incident TE_{10} wave in both amplitude and phase. For θ_1 small, incident $|E_y|$ is constant from $y = -a_1/2$ to $a_1/2$, and E_z may be neglected. Therefore, the sum of the waves on the right should match the $\phi(y)$ and $|E_y(y)|$ functions shown in Fig. 3:

$$\sum_{n=0}^{\infty} A_{2n} \cos \frac{2\pi n y}{a_1} = e^{j\phi(y)} \approx 1 + j\,\phi\,(y) \qquad (6)$$

where A_{2n} represents complex amplitudes of the TE_{10}, TE/TM_{12}, TE/TM_{14}, etc., modes. To a first order with $A_2, A_4, \ldots << A_0$, Eq. 6 can be satisfied by

$$A_0 = 1 \qquad (7)$$

$$\sum_{n=1}^{\infty} A_{2n} \cos \frac{2\pi n y}{a_1} = j\,\phi\,(y) \qquad (8)$$

Thus, the TE/TM_{12}, TE/TM_{14}, . . . components are imaginary and are in phase quadrature with respect to the transmitted TE_{10} component.

Equation (8) is a Fourier series in the period $y = -a_1/2$ to $a_1/2$. To simplify the result, let $\phi\,(y)$ be approximated by a half sine wave. Then the Fourier coefficients yield[9] the following $TE/TM_{1,2n}$ — mode amplitudes relative to $A_0 = 1$ for the TE_{10} mode:

$$A_2 = j\,\frac{4\phi_m}{3\pi},\quad A_4 = -j\,\frac{4\phi_m}{15\pi},\quad A_6 = j\,\frac{4\phi_m}{35\pi},$$

$$A_{2n} = -\frac{(-1)^n}{\pi}\cdot\frac{j4\phi_m}{(2n)^2-1} \qquad (9)$$

These amplitudes apply in the region just to the right of the discontinuity. By substituting Eq. 4 we obtain the following approximate relations for the mode amplitudes.

$$A_0 = 1$$

$$A_2 = j\,\frac{2a_1(\theta_1 - \theta_2)}{3\lambda},\quad A_4 = -\frac{1}{5}A_2,$$

$$A_6 = \frac{3}{35}A_2,\qquad A_{2n} = \frac{-3\,(-1)^n}{(2n)^2 - 1}A_2 \qquad (10)$$

If a pyramidal rather than sectoral horn is considered, the phase fronts will be spherical; hence TE_{30}, TE_{50}, TE/TM_{32}, etc., modes will be needed to satisfy $E_y(x) \propto \sin(\pi x/a)$ and $\phi = \phi\,(x)$. However, the half-sine-wave variation of $E_y(x)$ results in extremely rapid convergence of the Fourier expansion for $[\sin(\pi x/a_1)]\,.\,e^{j\phi(x)}$, and modes of higher order than unity in the H-plane may be neglected in practical design.

The formula for the amplitude A_2 of the TE/TM_{12} mode as given by Eq. 10 may be used to design the flare-angle change that yields a desired ratio of TE/TM_{12} amplitude to TE_{10} amplitude.* Note that the phase angle of A_2 lags A_0 by 90° when $\theta_1 - \theta_2 < 0$. Therefore, if the length of horn between the flare change and the

*Equation (10) applies to rectangular cross sections. A similar set of formulas for circular cross sections has been derived by K. Tomiyasu[10] (although not for an antenna application). The circular TE_{11} and TM_{11} modes are analogous to the rectangular TE_{10} and TE/TM_{12} modes as far as pattern improvement is concerned. Tomiyasu's coupling factor corresponding to A_2 is $j1.008\,(D/\lambda)\Delta\theta$, where D is the diameter at the flare-angle change $\Delta\theta$ radians.

aperture has 90° differential phase shift between the TE_{10} and TE/TM_{12} modes, these modes will be in phase at the center of the aperture. Similarly, when $\theta_1 - \theta_2 > 0$, 270° differential phase shift is required. Thus, the decrease in flare angle in Figs. 1a and b should be followed by 270° differential phase shift, and the increase in flare angle in Fig. 1c by 90°.

The phase shift ϕ_n of TE_{1n} and TM_{1n} modes in a square pyramidal horn is given in radians by

$$\phi_n = \frac{\pi}{\tan\theta}\left\{\frac{a_2}{\lambda}\sqrt{1-(1+n^2)\left(\frac{\lambda}{2a_2}\right)^2} - \frac{a_1}{\lambda}\sqrt{1-(1+n^2)\left(\frac{\lambda}{2a_1}\right)^2} + \frac{1}{2}\sqrt{1+n^2}\left[\sin^{-1}\left(\frac{\lambda}{2a_2}\sqrt{1+n^2}\right) - \sin^{-1}\left(\frac{\lambda}{2a_1}\sqrt{1+n^2}\right)\right]\right\} \qquad (11)$$

where a_1 is the aperture height and width at the left, a_2 is the same at the right, and θ is the flare angle. This formula is an approximation valid for small and moderate flare angles. The axial length is

$$l = \left(\frac{a_2 - a_1}{2}\right)\cot\theta \qquad (12)$$

When $\theta = 0$ and $a_1 = a_2$, ϕ_n is simply

$$\phi_n = \frac{2\pi l}{\lambda}\sqrt{1-\left(\frac{\lambda}{2a}\right)^2(1+n^2)} \qquad (13)$$

Equation 11 or 13 with n set equal to 0 and 2 is used to calculate the differential phase shift $\phi_0 - \phi_2$ for the TE_{10} and TE/TM_{12} modes.

The parameters a_1, a_2, θ and l should be adjusted by successive trials to provide the desired A_2 values, with required 90° or 270° differential phase shifts and reasonable dimensions. If sufficient A_2 cannot be produced by a single flare change, two flare changes may be used as in Fig. 4. Small A_2 values are directly additive to first order at the aperture.** Frequency sensitivity is greater, however, than in the case of a single flare change at 90° differential phase spacing from the aperture.

At the aperture of the horn, the phase front is desired to be plane, but is actually a circular arc as shown in Fig. 5. The phase-curvature error is the same as in the case of a flare-angle change in a horn from $\theta > 0$ to $\theta = 0$. Therefore, the phase curvature at the aperture is approximately equivalent to an additional TE/TM_{12} amplitude component A_2 given by Eq. 10. Because of the j factor in A_2, this TE/TM_{12} component leads the TE_{10} aperture component by 90 degrees. The amplitude of this TE/TM_{12} component can be minimized by making θ small. Also, it can be canceled by making the differential phase shift from flare-angle changes within the horn sufficiently different from 90 or 270 degrees to produce an equal but opposite TE/TM_{12} quadrature component at the aperture.

Equation 10 shows that the amplitudes A_2, A_4, A_6, ... are a rapidly decreasing progression. Therefore, the presence in the aperture of components of order greater than A_2 will affect the radiation pattern only in a minor way. However, these mode amplitudes may be canceled by the technique shown in Fig. 6, where the flare-angle change $\theta_1 - \theta_2$ is taken in two approximately equal steps separated by axial distance l. The length l is chosen so that the differential phase shift $\phi_0 - \phi_4$ between the TE_{10} and the TE/TM_{14} modes is 180 degrees. Then the small TE/TM_{14} component excited at the first discontinuity will be canceled by that at the second. A typical calculation shows that this length yields $\phi_0 - \phi_2$ about 42°; hence the total amplitude of the two equal TE/TM_{12}-mode phasors is reduced by the factor cos (42°/2) = 0.935 compared to the case $l = 0$. This reduction is minor enough to be neglected. If desired, the flare angle change may be divided into more than two parts in order to cancel modes of still higher order than TE/TM_{14}; however, this additional complication is not ordinarily necessary.

PERFORMANCE OF EXPERIMENTAL HORN

Figure 7 shows a horn constructed for use in a Cassegrain antenna system designed for optimum aperture and pattern control in the 3.7 - 4.2 GHz band.

A ratio of TE/TM_{12} to TE_{10} amplitude of 0.66 at the aperture would yield equal E- and H-plane beamwidths at the 10-dB points, while a ratio of 0.84 would yield best suppression of sidelobes. The flare-angle

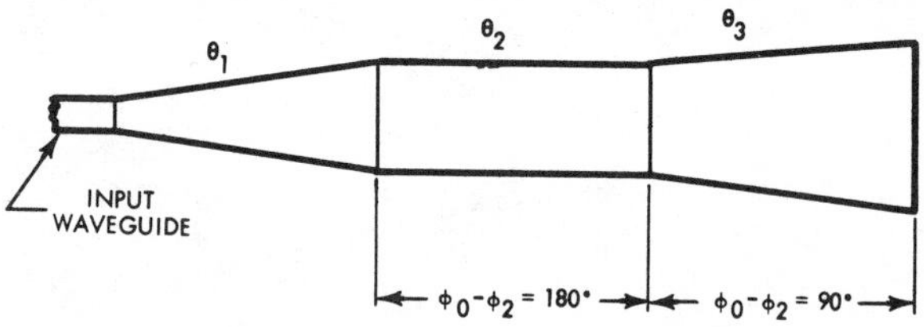

Fig. 4 — Use of two flare changes within the horn.

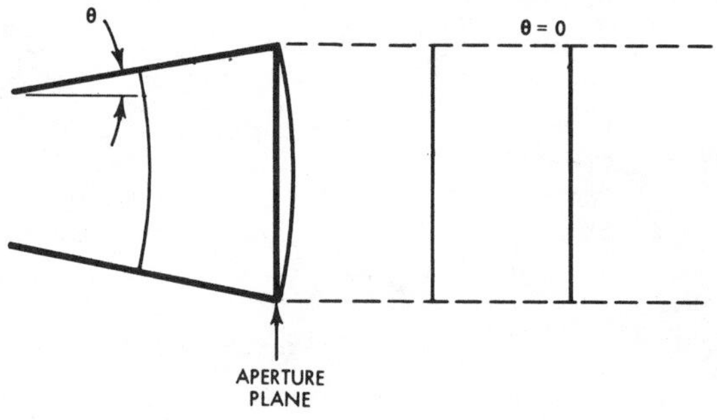

Fig. 5 — Radiation at aperture into effective $\theta = 0$ extension.

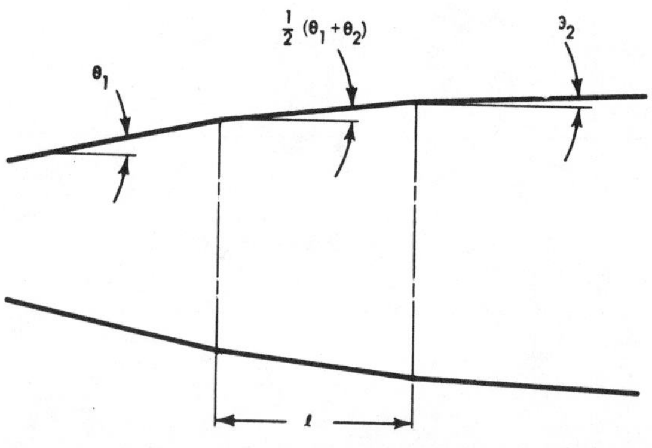

Fig. 6 — Double flare change to cancel TE/TM_{14} components.

**For A_2 values not sufficiently small for direct addition to be valid, each flare change may be considered equivalent to a directional coupler between TE_{10} and TE/TM_{12} transmission lines. The coupled-line amplitude factor is simply A_2, while the main-line amplitude factor is $\sqrt{1 - |A_2|^2}$.

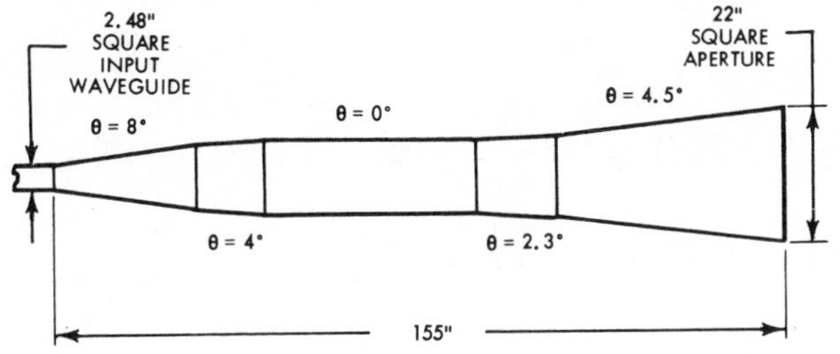

Fig. 7 — Outline drawing of feed horn for 97-ft. diameter Cassegrain antenna.

changes were designed by means of Eq. 10 to provide a ratio near the first of these values. The lengths were computed to give a good approximation to a plane phase front in the aperture, and to suppress TE/TM_{14} components.

After the prototype horn was constructed, the length of the $\theta = 0$ section was varied to yield the best compromise of E-plane patterns in the 3.7- to 4.2-GHz band. The final change in this length was about 10 percent from the design value. Figure 8 gives E- and H-plane patterns at three frequencies across the 3.7- to 4.2-GHz band. These patterns show that the design yields its intended objectives: (1) the E- and H-plane beamwidths are closely equal; (2) the H-plane patterns are scarcely affected by the flare changes; (3) both the E- and H-plane sidelobes are highly suppressed. For comparison, the theoretical beamwidths of the H-plane and E-plane patterns of an aperture containing a pure, plane TE_{10} field is 1.35:1, while the theoretical sidelobe levels are 23 and 13 dB, respectively. The maximum input VSWR measured 1.02 or less in the 3.7-to-4.2-GHz band.

Experimental verification has confirmed the concept and design method for synthesizing a tapered E-plane illumination in the aperture of a horn by means of small variations in flare angle. This new technique yields closely equal E- and H-plane beamwidths and low sidelobes. The horn's simple boundary, free of abrupt discontinuities, provides inherently low VSWR, minimum dissipation loss, and economical fabrication. Symmetry allows use of any polarization.

ACKNOWLEDGMENT

The feed subsystem utilizing the flare-change horn design was developed at Rantec Division of Emerson Electric Co. under the direction of Mr. K. C. Kelly. Experimental evaluation was performed by Mr. F. Lauriente.

REFERENCES

1) Silver, S., "Microwave Antenna Theory and Design," *Radiation Laboratory Series*, Vol. 12, McGraw-Hill Book Co., 1949; p. 377.
2) Hannan, P. W., "Optimum Feed for All Three Modes of a Monopulse Antenna; Part II, Practice," *IRE Trans. on Antennas and Propagation*, Vol. AP-9, Sept. 1961, pp. 454-461.
3) Potter, P. D., "A New Horn Antenna with Suppressed Sidelobes and Equal Beamwidths," *Microwave Journal*, Vol. 6, June 1963, pp. 71-78.
4) Drabowitch, S. W., "Multimode Antennas," *Microwave Journal*, Vol. 9, Jan. 1966, pp. 41-51.
5) Kelly, K. C., unpublished techniques used in several different feeds manufactured by Rantec Division, Emerson Electric Co.
6) Lawrie, R. E., and L. Peters, Jr., "Modifications of Horn Antennas for Low Sidelobe Levels," *IEEE Trans. on Antennas and Propagation*, Vol. AP-14, Sept. 1966, pp. 605-610.
7) Minnett, H. C., and B. MacA. Thomas, "A Method of Synthesizing Radiation Patterns with Axial Symmetry," *IEEE Trans. on Antennas and Propagation (Correspondence)*, Vol. AP-14, Sept. 1966, pp. 654-656.
8) Rumsey, V. H., "Horn Antennas with Uniform Power Patterns Around Their Axes," *IEEE Trans. on Antennas and Propagation (Correspondence)*, Vol. AP-14, Sept. 1966, pp. 656-658.
9) Terman, F. E., *Radio Engineers' Handbook*, McGraw-Hill Book Co., 1943; p. 23.
10) Tomiyasu, K., "Conversion of $TE_{11}{}^0$ Mode by a Large Diameter Conical Junction," *IEEE Trans. on Microwave Theory and Techniques (Correspondence)*, Vol. MTT-17, May 1969, pp. 277-279.

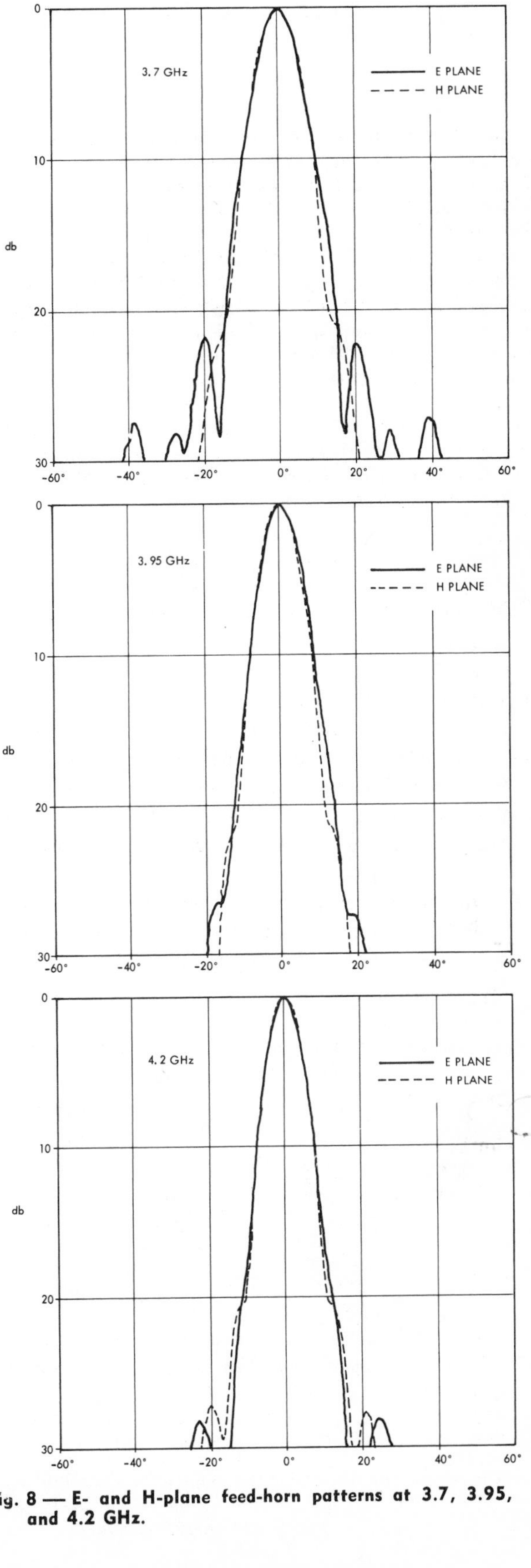

Fig. 8 — E- and H-plane feed-horn patterns at 3.7, 3.95, and 4.2 GHz.

A New Multimode Rectangular Horn Antenna Generating a Circularly Polarized Elliptical Beam

CHING C. HAN, MEMBER, IEEE, AND ADAM N. WICKERT, MEMBER, IEEE

***Abstract*—A multimode circularly polarized rectangular horn antenna generating an elliptical shaped beam is described. This antenna operates in two orthogonal mode sets, namely the TE_{10} + TE/TM_{12} and TE_{01} + TE/TM_{21} modes. By virtue of the higher order TE/TM modes, the aperture *E*-field distribution can be tapered such that the effective *E*-plane far-field beam width is approximately equal to the *H*-plane beam width of the other orthogonal set of modes, resulting in low off-axis polarization axial ratio. Because of the tapered aperture distribution, the radiation patterns also have low sidelobes. The elliptical cross section beam is a direct result of the rectangular shaped aperture. This antenna, used in conjunction with a spacecraft to illuminate an elliptical zone on the earth surface, offers high edge-of-coverage gain, low sidelobes, low edge-of-coverage (EOC) axial ratio, less RF sensitivity to the space environment, and low cost. The performance of this antenna has been evaluated experimentally.**

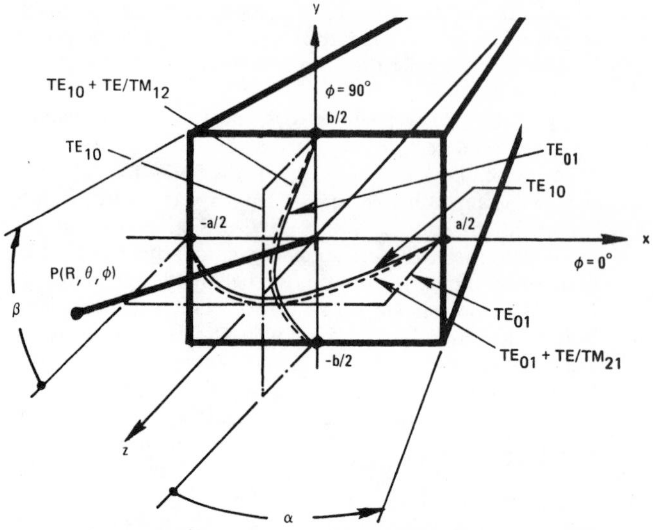

Fig. 1. Aperture *E*-field distributions.

I. INTRODUCTION

COMMUNICATION satelite antennas are often required to radiate circularly polarized signals and to illuminate earth surface regions that are not of circular shape; hence the need for an elliptical cross section beam antenna. A rectangular horn antenna has an elliptical shaped beam; however, if it is designed to propagate only the TE_{10} and TE_{01} modes (dominant modes), signals radiated off the axis of the beam will not be circularly polarized nor will the polarization axial ratio be near unity. This paper describes a new concept which enables a rectangular horn to radiate a circularly polarized elliptical beam with good off-axis axial ratio by employing higher order TE/TM_{12} and TE/TM_{21} modes together with the dominant modes.

The following discussion will show the operational principle of this antenna and that the wanted higher order modes can be generated by a symmetric discontinuity in an oversized waveguide. The aperture field method will then be used to derive the radiation patterns and the design criteria will be presented. Experimental results are shown to be in conformity with the theory.

II. THEORY OF OPERATION

To effectively radiate a circularly polarized wave from an aperature, the two orthogonal far-field spherical components, E_θ and E_ϕ, must have equal amplitude and proper phase. For illustration, consider only the two principal orthogonal planes of a conventional rectangular horn simultaneously propagating only the TE_{10} and TE_{01} modes. The E_θ and E_ϕ components do not have equal amplitude off the horn axis. If a portion of the TE_{10} and TE_{01} mode energy is now converted to the higher order TE/TM_{12} and TE/TM_{21} modes (beam shaping modes) with proper amplitude and phase, the *E*-plane aperture field distributions can be tapered as shown in Fig. 1. Thus the effective *E*-plane far-field beam width is broadened to closely match the *H*-plane beam width of the other orthogonal set of modes as depicted in Fig. 2. Because of the tapered aperture distribution, the sidelobe levels of the *E*-plane pattern also show significant reduction. Generating the elliptical cross section beam is a result of using the rectangular shape aperture.

If the tangential electric field $\boldsymbol{E}_r$ is known over the horn apperture, the far-field at a point P is then given by [1]:

$$\boldsymbol{E}_s(P) = \frac{-jk}{4\pi R} \exp(-jkR)\hat{R} \cdot \int_{-a/2}^{a/2}\int_{-b/2}^{b/2} \boldsymbol{E}_r(\cos\theta + \hat{z}\cdot\hat{s}) \cdot \exp[jk(x\sin\theta\cos\phi + y\sin\theta\sin\phi)]\, dx\, dy \quad (1)$$

where

- r position vector of differential radiating element $dx\, dy$
- $\hat{R}$ unit position vector of P
- $\hat{n}$ unit normal vector of $dx\, dy$
- $\hat{s}$ unit vector along a ray through the aperture
- k free space propagation constant

and the coordinate system is shown in Fig. 1.

Manuscript received August 8, 1973; revised June 28, 1974.

The authors are with the Philco-Ford Corporation, Western Development Laboratories, Palo Alto, Calif. 94303.

Reprinted from *IEEE Trans. Antennas Propagat.*, vol. AP-22, pp. 746–751, Nov. 1974.

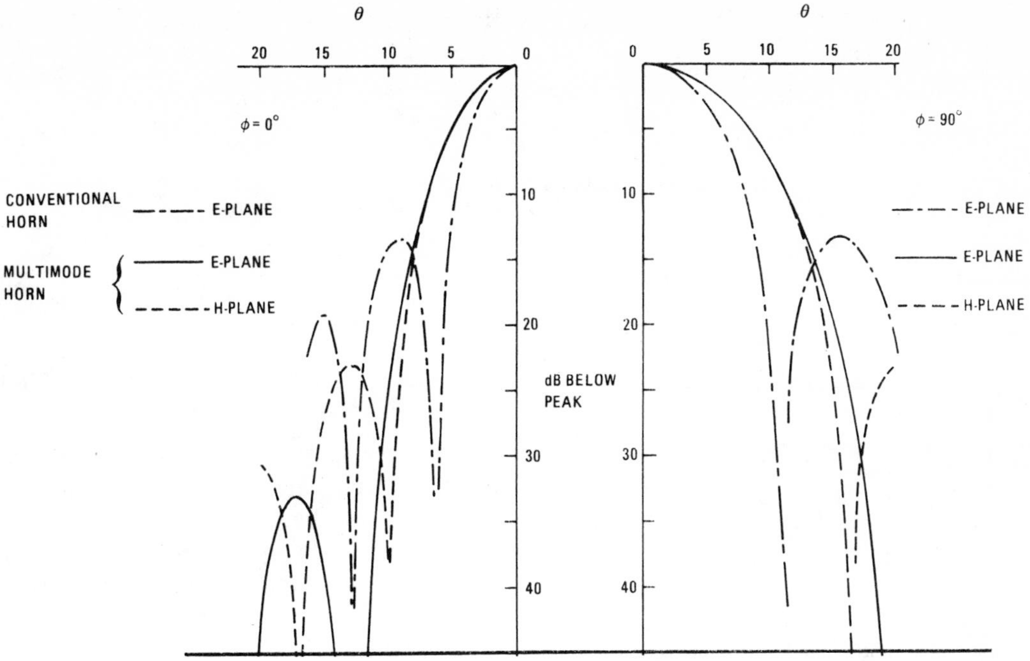

Fig. 2. Multimode horn computed radiation patterns.

The TE_{12} and TM_{12} modes can be excited by a dominant TE_{10} mode incident on a symmetric discontinuity in an oversized waveguide. The discontinuity used in this paper is a symmetric step. The unwanted TE_{20} and TE_{11} modes are not excited because of the even symmetry of the step discontinuity [2]. The size of the oversized waveguide is so chosen that only TE_{12} and TM_{12} modes can propagate. If we assume that the transverse field at the discontinuity plane is the same as the TE_{10} incident field which contains only a $\hat{y}$ component, then boundary conditions require that the summation of the modes at the boundary in the oversized waveguide contains only a $\hat{y}$ component. Since we have discussed that only TE_{12} and TM_{12} higher order modes will propagate, the implication is that the x components of these modes cancel at the boundary. Thus when two orthogonal linear components of a circularly polarized wave enter an oversized square guide through a square discontinuity and propagate toward a rectangular radiating aperture, the $\hat{x}$ and $\hat{y}$ components of the aperture field $\boldsymbol{E}_r$ can be written as [3]

$$E_x = \cos\left(\frac{\pi y}{b}\right) + C_x \cos\left(\frac{2\pi x}{a}\right) \cos\left(\frac{\pi y}{b}\right) \cdot \exp\left[+j(2\pi + \psi_x)\right] \quad (2)$$

and

$$E_y = p\left\{\cos\left(\frac{\pi x}{a}\right) + C_y \cos\left(\frac{\pi x}{a}\right) \cos\left(\frac{2\pi y}{b}\right) \cdot \exp\left[+j(2\pi - \psi_y)\right]\right. \quad (3)$$

where the C and ψ are the amplitude and phase of the mode conversion factor (a complex amplitude ratio of higher order mode to dominant mode), respectively. The term $(2\pi + \psi_x)$ is the phase difference between the TE_{01} and TE/TM_{21} modes, and $(2\pi - \psi_y)$ is the phase difference between the TE_{10} and TE/TM_{12} modes. The ratio of the complex amplitude of TE_{10} mode to that of TE_{01} mode is defined as p.

A general design would yield a $2n\pi$ rad phase difference between the dominant and the higher order mode. Because of the rectangular horn section, this may result in an impractically long horn length. Therefore, this differential phase difference may be made approximately equal to $2n\pi$ rad, as will be discussed in a later section.

If the phase distribution across the aperture has a small deviation, the term $\hat{z}\cdot\hat{s}$ may be set equal to unity. Invoking this in (1) and resolving E_r into x and y components

$$\boldsymbol{E}_r = E_x\hat{x} + E_y\hat{y} \quad (4)$$

the θ and ϕ component of $E_s(p)$ can be expressed as

$$E_\theta = \frac{-jk}{4R} \exp(-jkR)\,(1 + \cos\theta)(g_x \cos\phi + g_y \sin\phi) \quad (5)$$

and

$$E_\phi = \frac{-jk}{4R} \exp(-jkR)\,(1 + \cos\theta)(g_x \sin\phi - g_y \cos\phi) \quad (6)$$

where

$$g_x = \int_{-a/2}^{a/2} \int_{-b/2}^{b/2} E_x \cdot \exp\left[jk(x \sin\theta\cos\phi + y\sin\theta\sin\phi)\right] dx\,dy \quad (7)$$

and

$$g_y = \int_{-a/2}^{a/2} \int_{-b/2}^{b/2} E_y \cdot \exp jk(x \sin\theta\cos\phi + y\sin\theta\sin\phi)]\, dx\,dy. \quad (8)$$

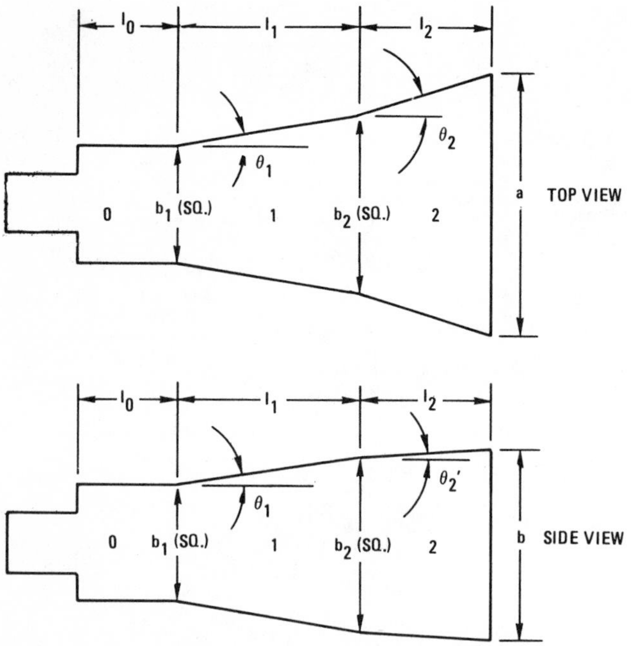

Fig. 3. Double-flare multimode horn configuration.

When the radiating aperture is a horn aperture, the phase of the field in the aperture varies with position in the aperture. If we assume that the horn has a small flare angle and long length, it can be shown that we may approximate the phase at a point (x,y) on the aperture relative to the center $(0,0)$, by the quadratic terms

$$\Delta(x,y) = \left(\frac{\sin(\alpha/2)}{a}\right)x^2 + \left(\frac{\sin(\beta/2)}{b}\right)y^2. \quad (9)$$

Also, we shall assume the amplitude of the electric field across the aperture is not affected appreciably by the fact that the aperture does not coincide with a wave front. Hence the aperture electric field in (2) and (3) is modified by taking into account the aperture phase variation and is given by

$$E_x = \left[\cos\left(\frac{\pi y}{b}\right) + C_x \cos\left(\frac{2\pi x}{a}\right)\cos\left(\frac{\pi y}{b}\right)\exp(j\psi)\right] \cdot \exp\left\{jk\left[\left(\frac{\sin(\alpha/2)}{a}\right)x^2 + \left(\frac{\sin(\beta/2)}{b}\right)y^2\right]\right\} \quad (10)$$

$$E_y = p\left[\cos\left(\frac{\pi x}{a}\right) + C_y \cos\left(\frac{\pi x}{a}\right)\cos\left(\frac{2\pi y}{b}\right)\exp(-j\phi)\right] \cdot \exp\left\{jk\left[\left(\frac{\sin(\alpha/2)}{a}\right)x^2 + \left(\frac{\sin(\beta/2)}{b}\right)y^2\right]\right\}. \quad (11)$$

If we assume left-hand circular polarization (LCP) is the principal polarization and right-hand circular polarization (RCP) is the cross polarization, the resolution of the far-field into LCP and RCP can be easily obtained according to

LCP (principal polarization

$$= \frac{1}{\sqrt{2}}(-jE_\theta + E_\phi)\exp(-j\phi) \quad (12)$$

RCP (cross polarization)

$$= \frac{1}{\sqrt{2}}(E_\theta - jE_\phi)\exp(j\phi). \quad (13)$$

III. DESIGN CONSIDERATIONS

The multimode rectangular horn can assume many forms including single-flare, double-flare, or multiple-flares. Fig. 3 shows a typical diagram of the double-flare horn. The first flare section has a square cross section. The second flare section ends at a rectangular aperture whose dimensions may be determined by the required edge-of-coverage (EOC) gain.

The wanted higher-order modes are generated at the step discontinuity in an oversized square waveguide in which odd modes (mode number $m + n$ is an odd number) above the TE/TM_{12} and TE/TM_{21} modes can not propagate. The mode conversion factor of a step discontinuity is derived in the Appendix. It is worthwhile noting that the higher order modes are also generated at junctions where the flare angle changes. Since higher order modes so generated have an amplitude proportional to the change in the flare [4], it is usually kept small to prevent these modes from being strongly excited. Thus the magnitude of the beam shaping modes is primarily controlled by the size of the step.

The most important and significant differential phase shifts are between the dominant mode and beam shaping mode of each set and between the two sets. In general, the former is kept as small as possible to enable the wanted higher order modes to efficiently shape the beam. This phase slip can be adjusted to a certain degree by adjusting the length of both the oversized guide section and the horn flare sections. The latter differential phase is principally chosen to obtain CP. Because axial ratio over the entire EOC angle is of interest, this latter phase shift is not necessarily 90°. Since the second horn flare section has a rectangular cross section, it also introduces phase displacement between the two perpendicular dominant modes. Thus if enough length is allowed in the design, the rectangular flare section can be designed to act as a polarizer. This has the advantage of eliminating the use of a separate polarizer.

As discussed previously, the overall length of the horn is primarily governed by the differential phase differences between TE_{10} and TE/TM_{12} modes, $\Delta\phi^{(10-12)}$, and between TE_{01} and TE/TM_{21} modes, $\Delta\phi^{(10-12)}$, which are given by

$$\Delta\phi^{(10-12)} = \Delta\phi_{l0}^{(10-12)} + \Delta\phi_{l1}^{(10-12)} + \Delta\phi_{l2}^{(10-12)} + \text{contribution from discontinuities} \quad (14)$$

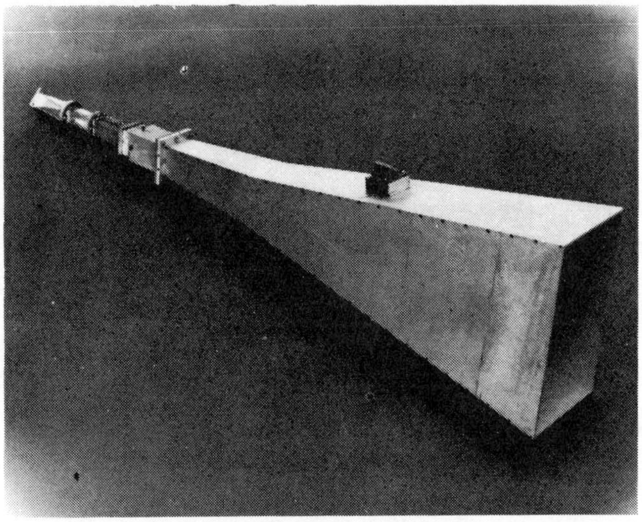

Fig. 4. Double-flare multimode horn test model.

and

$$\Delta\phi^{(01-21)} = \Delta\phi_{l0}{}^{(01-21)} + \Delta\phi_{l1}{}^{(01-21)} + \Delta\phi_{l2}{}^{(01-21)} + \text{contribution from discontinuities} \quad (15)$$

where subscripts $l0$, $l1$, and $l2$ denote contributions from different horn sections. The phase of each mode ϕ^{mn} can be calculated by

$$\phi^{mn} = \frac{2\pi}{\lambda}\int_0^l \beta_{mn}(z)\, dz$$

$$\frac{2\pi}{\lambda}\int_0^l \left(1 - \frac{\lambda^2}{4}\left(\left(\frac{m}{a(z)}\right)^2 + \left(\frac{n}{b(z)}\right)^2\right)\right)^{1/2} dz \quad (16)$$

where

β_{mn}	phase constant of TE_{mn} (or TM_{mn}) mode
l	axial length of horn section
$a(z), b(z)$	A and B dimensions at cross section location shown in Fig. 3
λ	free space wavelength.

Ideally, $\phi^{(10-12)}$ and $\phi^{(01-21)}$ should be a multiple of 360°. Unfortunately, for some applications this may result in an unacceptably long horn length. In this case, the phase differences can only be made approximately equal to 360°. How close they can be adjusted to 360° depends primarily on the difference of the differential phase in the rectangular flare section as can be seen by

$$\Delta\phi^{(10-12)} - \Delta\phi^{(01-21)} = \Delta\phi_{l2}{}^{(10-12)} - \Delta\phi_{l2}{}^{(01-21)}. \quad (17)$$

Note that phase contributions from discontinuities produce approximately equal phase differentials in both planes [5].

Although the foregoing design criterion is developed for a double-flare horn configuration, the principle applies equally well to single-flare or multiple-flare horn designs. For some applications such as in a communication satellite, the length of the antenna is limited. In such cases, the choice of the number of horn flare sections is determined by the required axial ratio and the tolerable aperture phase error. It was found exprerimentally that the main lobe of the antenna pattern will not be deteriorated if the flare angle change is kept within 5°.

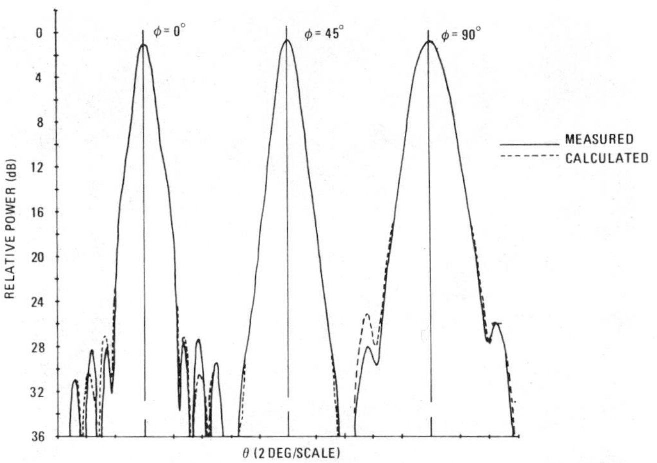

Fig. 5. Calculated and measured circular polarization radiation patterns.

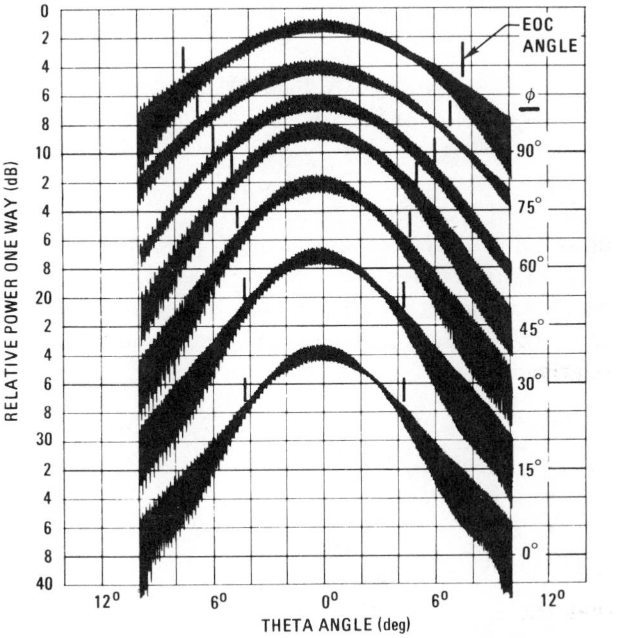

Fig. 6. Axial ratios of various pattern plane of double-flare test horn.

IV. COMPUTED AND EXPERIMENTAL RESULTS

An experimental X band double-flare multimode rectangular horn antenna, shown in Fig. 4, was designed and fabricated to provide maximum gain over an elliptical EOC angle of 8.8° × 15.2°. Typical computed and measured CP radiation patterns are shown in Fig. 5 for the 0°, 45°, and 90° pattern planes, respectively. It can be seen that the computed and measured patterns agree very well to the first sidelobe region. The sidelobe levels are typically 25 dB below the peak of the beam. If one took the desired beamwidth at two principal planes (in this case 8.8° × 15.2°) as the mathematical major and minor axis and plotted a true elliptical contour, the deviation of the measured beam shape from this true ellipse is neglibibly small.

Axial ratio patterns are shown in Fig. 6 for every 15°

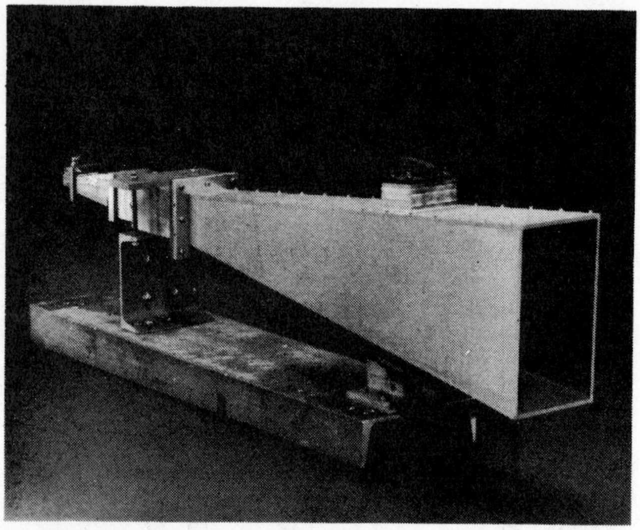

Fig. 7. Single-flare multimode horn test model.

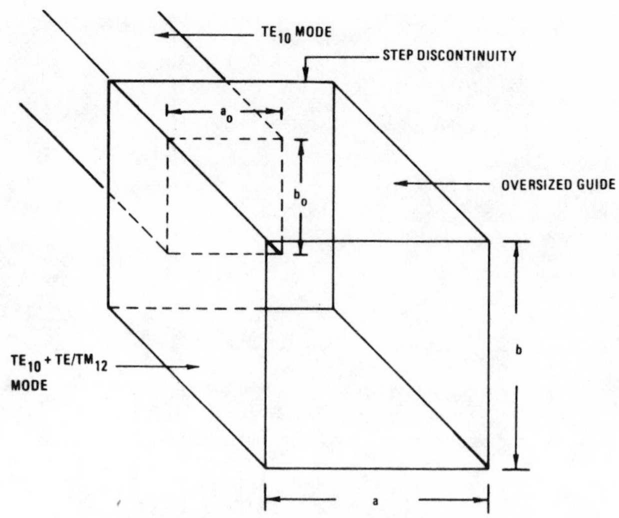

Fig. 8. Rectangular step discontinuity.

pattern plane cut. These patterns are obtained by continously rotating a linearly polarized source antenna and monitoring the signal response of the circularly polarized test antenna.

To verify that the rectangular flare section can be designed to act as a polarizer for a multimode retangular horn, a single-flare horn was fabricated and tested, as shown in Fig. 7. The axial ratio over the desired EOC angle, 9.2° × 16.0°, for every 15° pattern plane was found to be less than 1.5 dB.

V. CONCLUSION

In this paper a new concept, which utilizes a multimode rectangular horn antenna to generate a circularly polarized elliptical shaped beam, has been discussed. Experimental results show that the computed radiation patterns are in excellent agreement with the measured patterns. Test results show that an axial ratio of less than 2 dB can be achieved over an EOC angle of approximately 9° × 16°. The results indicate the applicability of this class of antenna for use in a communication satellite system to efficiently illuminate an elliptical shape zone on the surface of the earth.

APPENDIX

MODE CONVERSION IN A RECTANGULAR WAVEGUIDE BY A STEP DISCONTINUITY

The conversion of a portion of the TE_{10} mode energy to TE/TM_{12} mode in a rectangular waveguide can be achieved by introducing a symmetric discontinuity in an oversized guide as shown in Fig. 8. This oversized rectangular (or square) guide must be capable of supporting propagation of the TE/TM_{12} mode and be evanescent for other unwanted higher order modes. The TE_{11} and TE_{20} mode will not be excited because of the symmetry of the discontinuity.

For a first-order approximation, we may assume the TE_{10} electric field has a perfect match[1] at the step discontinuity junction and let the transverse field E_t at the discontinuity plane ($z = 0$) be the same as the TE_{10} incident field, i.e.,

$$E_t = \begin{cases} \hat{y}E_0 \cos \dfrac{\pi x}{a_0}, \text{ for } -\dfrac{a_0}{2} \le x \le \dfrac{a_0}{2}, \; -\dfrac{b_0}{2} \le y \le \dfrac{b_0}{2}. \\ 0, \qquad \text{elsewhere.} \end{cases} \tag{A1}$$

The electric field of the TE_{10} mode, $E^{TE_{10}}$, in the oversized guide can be written as

$$E_t^{TE_{10}} = \hat{y}E \cos \frac{\pi x}{a}. \tag{A2}$$

The transverse electric field of the TE/TM_{12} mode $E_t^{TE/TM_{12}}$ in the oversized guide is given by

$$E_t^{TE/TM_{10}} = \hat{x}A_x \sin \frac{\pi x}{a} \sin \frac{2\pi y}{b} + \hat{y}A_y \cos \frac{\pi x}{a} \cos \frac{2\pi y}{b}. \tag{A3}$$

At the left side of the junction, only TE_{10} mode can propagate. At the junction plane, however, an infinite number of modes are excited to match the boundary condition such that the transverse field of these modes satisfy the following equation:

$$E_t = E_t^{TE_{10}} + E_t^{TE/TM_{12}} + \text{other higher order modes.} \tag{A4}$$

From there we obtain

$$A_x^2 + A_y^2 = \left(\frac{8E_0A_y}{2\pi}\right) \frac{\cos[(\pi a_0/2a)]}{[(a/a_0) - (a_0/a)]} \sin\left(\frac{b_0\pi}{b}\right) \tag{A5}$$

[1] Mismatch VSWR has been measured for various small step sizes, which justifies the soundness of the assumption made here.

and

$$E = \left(\frac{4E_0 b_0}{b}\right) \frac{\cos[(a_0/2a)]}{[(a/a_0) - (a_0/a)]}. \qquad (A6)$$

Because the transverse electric field E_t at the junction plane has only a $\hat{y}$ component, from (A4) we find

$$A_x \sin\frac{\pi x}{a} \sin\frac{2\pi y}{b} + \text{other higher order modes' component} \equiv 0$$

which leads to $A_x = 0$. Thus (A5) becomes

$$A_y = \left(\frac{8E_0}{\pi}\right) \frac{\cos[(\pi a_0/2a)]}{[(a/a_0) - (a_0/a)]} \sin[(b_0\pi/b)].$$

Next, the conversion factor C is defined as the ratio of the magnitude of the TE/TM_{12} mode to the TE_{10} mode at the center of the top wall. That is,

$$C = \left| \frac{E_t^{TE/TM_{12}}}{E_t^{TE_{10}}} \right|_{\text{at } x=0;\, y=b/2} = \frac{A_y}{E} = \frac{2\sin(b_0\pi/b)}{(b_0\pi/b)}. \qquad (A7)$$

ACKNOWLEDGMENT

The authors wish to thank Dr. A. E. Smoll for his suggestions and many helpful discussions and H. W. Bilenko for programming the computed results.

REFERENCES

[1] S. Silver, *Microwave Antenna Theory and Design.* New York: McGraw-Hill, 1949, p. 158.

[2] G. C. Southworth, *Principles and Applications of Waveguide Transmission.* Canada: Van Nostrand, 1950, p. 356.

[3] Ramo, Whinnery, and Van Duzer, *Fields and Waves in Communication Electronics.* New York: Wiley, 1965, p. 241.

[4] R. E. Collin and F. J. Zucker, *Antenna Theory, Part 1.* New York: McGraw-Hill, 1969, p. 72.

[5] S. B. Cohn, "Flare-angle changes in a horn as a means of pattern control," *Microwave J.*, p. 41, Oct. 1970.

A 4- AND 6-GHz, PRIME FOCUS, CP FEED WITH CIRCULAR PATTERN SYMMETRY

Robert W. Gruner
COMSAT Laboratories
Clarksburg, Maryland 20734

A circularly polarized feed assembly providing efficient prime focus illumination of reflector antennas has been designed. Near-perfect complex pattern symmetry over the 4- and 6-GHz satellite communications bands (3700 to 4200 and 5925 to 6425 MHz) is achieved by using a multimode feed horn. The two bands are separately optimized by adding corrugations on the outside of the waveguide which are effectual only in the 4-GHz band and a radial step inside the waveguide which is effectual only in the 6-GHz band. The broadband polarizer in conjunction with the orthogonal mode transducer provides circularly polarized signals of opposing sense in the respective transmit and receive bands. The feed can also be used to provide orthogonal linear polarizations. Each of the three components in the feed assembly, the feed horn, polarizer, and orthomode transducer (OMT), will be briefly discussed.

Feed Horn

The feed horn design (Figure 1) utilizes two different techniques for circular pattern symmetry. In the 4-GHz band a corrugated section is used to equalize the E- and H-plane beamwidths [1]. For a given ratio of waveguide diameter to corrugated section diameter (d/D), a position of the corrugated section (L_1) to equalize the E- and H-plane beamwidths may be found. The position of the corrugated section is experimentally optimized by first observing the complex radiation response on a network analyzer in the H-plane at a -10-dB off-axis angle. The polarizations are then rotated 90°, and an E-plane measurement is made at the same off-axis angle. Finally, the E-plane complex radiation response is best matched in amplitude and phase to the previously noted H-plane response across the 500-MHz band. The H-plane response is chosen as the reference, since it is essentially independent of the position of the corrugations. As noted previously, the radial step has no effect in the 4-GHz band. The E- and H-plane amplitude and phase patterns are shown in Figure 2. The difference in E- and H-plane phase centers is less than 0.1 wavelength.

At 6 GHz a step discontinuity is introduced to launch the TM_{11} mode. The waveguide diameter ratio (d/2.125) is chosen to launch the correct amount of TM_{11} mode to equalize the E- and H-plane beamwidths [2]. The waveguide length (L_2) is adjusted to bring the TE_{11} and TM_{11} modes into proper phase relationship in the aperture plane of the horn. The position of the corrugated rings has a negligible effect in this band. Again the complex optimization procedure is performed with a network analyzer.

The E- and H-plane amplitude and phase patterns at the mid-band frequency are shown in Figure 3. The phase centers are essentially coexistent. For achieving the maximum gain in both bands, a frequency-independent illumination function would be optimum. The resultant illumination in this design approaches an $f^{1/2}$ relationship. It has been found experimentally that some improvement in the amplitude equality of the illumination functions in the two bands can be accomplished at the expense of degradation of the phase center characteristics. Impedance matching in the 6-GHz band is straightforward, since neither the radial step nor the waveguide to free space junction has any appreciable mismatch [3]. At 4 GHz the length (L_2) of waveguide serves as a 3/4 λg impedance transformer from the high-impedance, 2 1/8-inch waveguide to the lower impedance of free space. The horn has been matched to a VSWR ≤ 1.10 across both 500-MHz bands.

Polarizer

The basic design of the polarizer or quarter-wave plate consists of circular waveguide loaded with sequentially placed reactive irises. The polarizer functions by providing a 90° differential phase shift to two orthogonal TE_{11} modes launched in the circular waveguide. The differential phase may be adjusted to a near-constant 90 electrical degrees over a large frequency band through optimization of the inductive-capacitive susceptance ratio of the reactive irises by shaping the individual reactive irises. Broadband impedance matching is accomplished by varying the iris heights to create a prescribed reflection coefficient taper.

Several simplifying assumptions result in a technique for easily calculating the VSWR and phase shift characteristics vs frequency. These simplifying assumptions are predicated on a large number of reactive irises, each having a small reflection coefficient. This allows the phase shift of a single reactive iris to be simply calculated and makes it possible to neglect the second-order reflection effects between irises. The measured VSWR is ≤ 1.02 and the axial ratio is ≤ 1.65 dB from 3700 to 4200 and 5925 to 6425 MHz, as shown in Figure 4.

This paper is based upon work performed in COMSAT Laboratories under the sponsorship of the Communications Satellite Corporation.

Reprinted from *Int. IEEE/AP-S Symp. Program and Dig.*, June 10–12, 1974, pp. 72–74.

Orthomode Transducer

The OMT combines 4- and 6-GHz orthogonally polarized signals into a common 2 1/8-inch-diameter waveguide. The 6- to 4-GHz isolation is in excess of 55 dB. The VSWR is ≤1.10 in the 4-GHz band and ≤1.08 in the 6-GHz band.

Feed Assembly

Measurements were also made on the complete feed assembly. The radiated on-axis axial ratio is ≤2 dB for both frequency bands. The radiated axial ratio is slightly degraded from the polarizer data given in Figure 4. In a circularly polarized system the unterminated post polarizer mismatches appear as a degradation of the axial ratio. The VSWR of the feed is ≤1.07 in the 6-GHz band and ≤1.10 in the 4-GHz band. Dissipative loss of the feed in the 4-GHz receive band is less than 0.04 dB, resulting in a noise temperature contribution of less than 3 K. Based on measurements using a 10-ft parabolic antenna with f/D = 0.4, the overall efficiency is between 65 and 70 percent in the 4-GHz band and 60 to 65 percent in the 6-GHz band.

Acknowledgment

The author would like to acknowledge the contributions of B. Alderfer to the design and testing of the feed horn.

References

1. R. Wohlleban, H. Mattes, and O. Lochner (Electronics Letters, September 1972, p. 474).

2. W. J. English (private communication).

3. W. J. English (Microwave Theory and Techniques, October 1973, p. 633).

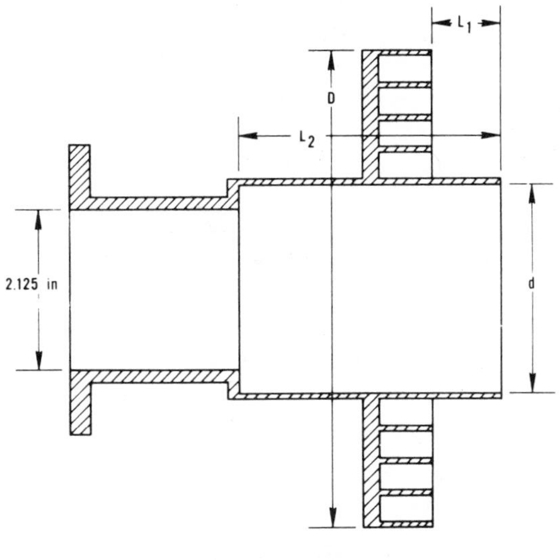

Figure 1. Feed Horn

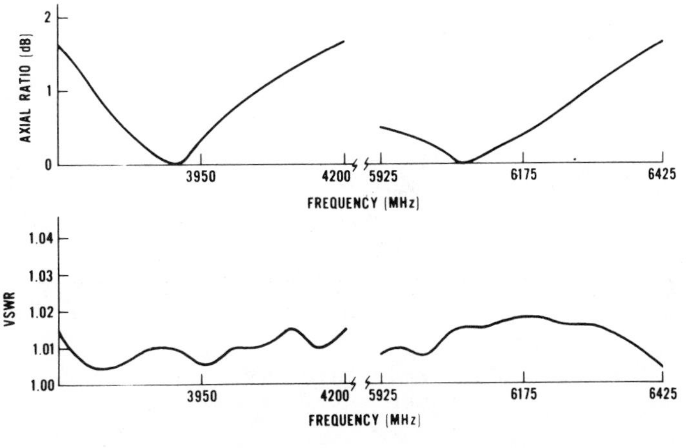

Figure 4. Axial Ratio and V.S.W.R. of Broadband Polarizer

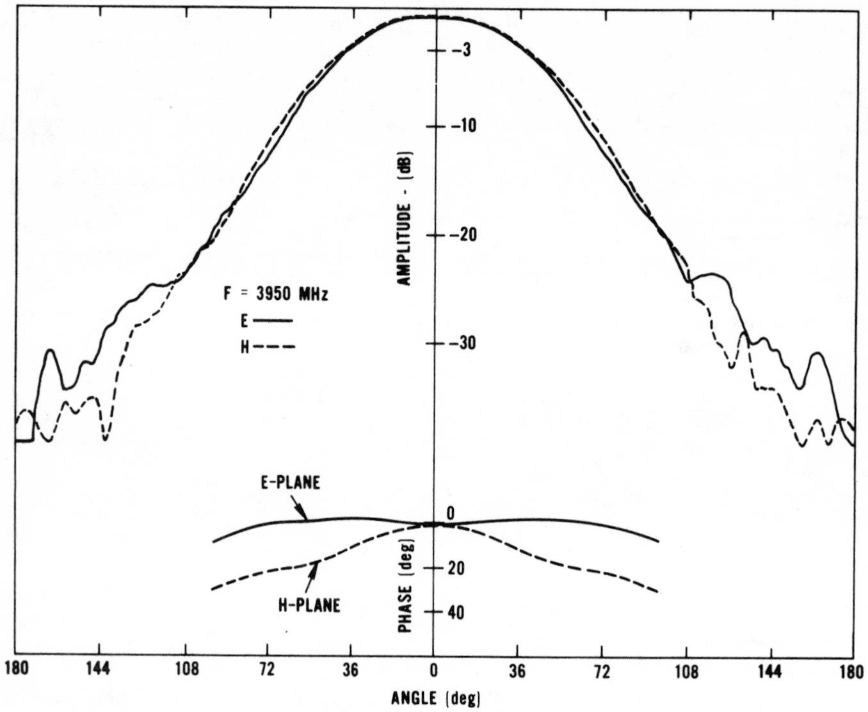

Figure 2. Feed Horn Amplitude and Phase Patterns at F = 3950 MHz

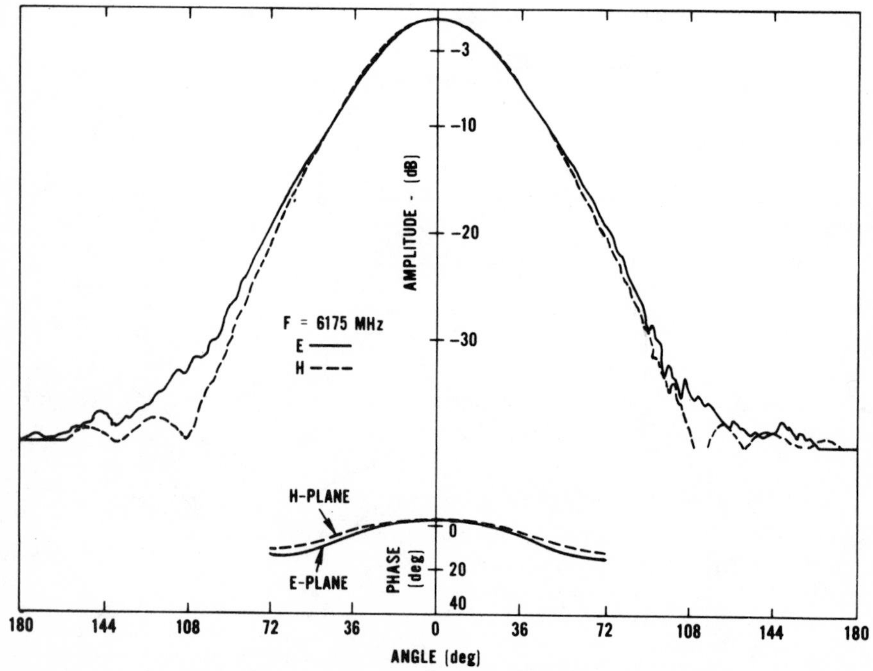

Figure 3. Feed Horn Amplitude and Phase Patterns at F = 6175 MHz

Coaxial Feeds for High Aperture Efficiency and Low Spillover of Paraboloidal Reflector Antennas

GERHARD F. KOCH

Abstract—Coaxial feeds produce an approximate sector-shaped pattern, an almost optimum pattern of a feed for high aperture efficiency and low spillover of paraboloid antennas. Such a coaxial feed consists of a central circular waveguide which is surrounded by one or more conductors with circular cross sections. Theoretical and experimental investigations on coaxial feeds excited by H_{11} modes have shown that the first ring yields the highest increase in the aperture efficiency of paraboloid antennas illuminated by them. Measurements performed on paraboloid antennas illuminated by a coaxial feed with only one ring yielded aperture efficiencies of 68 to 75 percent for angular apertures of the paraboloidal reflector of 100° to 160°. Circularly symmetric patterns in conjunction with almost linearly polarized aperture fields can be achieved by multimode coaxial feeds. The values for the aperture efficiency, which are calculated for paraboloid antennas illuminated by multimode coaxial feeds, nearly reach the theoretical optimum. The measured values are 68 to 80 percent. In addition, the multimode feeds produce very little cross polarization.

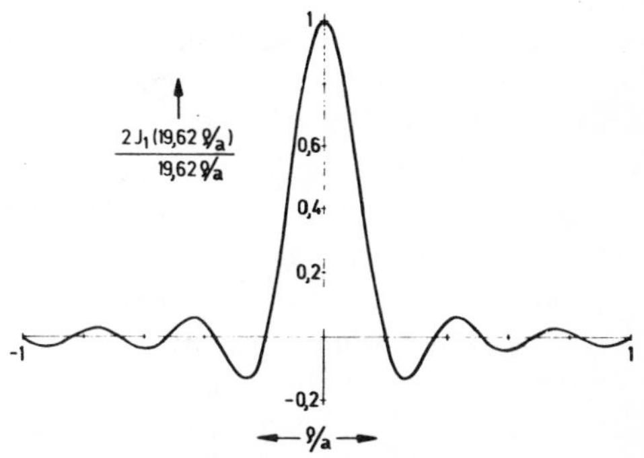

Fig. 1. Theoretical illumination of circular aperture for producing sector-shaped pattern.

I. Introduction

THE ALMOST optimum solution for high aperture efficiency and low spillover of a paraboloidal reflector antenna is a sector-shaped feed pattern. In theory [1], it requires an infinitely large circular feed aperture which is illuminated according to the function $J_1(x)/x$ (Fig. 1). Such a feed pattern can practically be approximated by a coaxial radiator [2] consisting of a central circular waveguide surrounded by one or several conductors with circular cross sections (Fig. 2).

In the light of the theory, the field distribution in the different aperture sections must be in accordance with the $J_1(x)/x$ function (i.e., corresponding amplitude and alternating phase), and the field must be linearly polar-

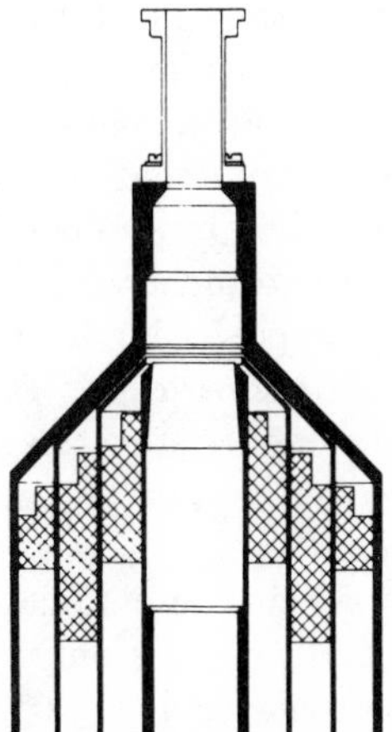

Fig. 2. Multiring coaxial feed for producing sector-shaped pattern.

Manuscript received August 18, 1972; revised September 22, 1972. This paper was presented in part at the 1971 International Symposium on Antennas and Propagation, Sendai, Japan.
The author is with the Fernmeldetechnisches Zentralamt, Deutsche Bundespost, Darmstadt, Germany.

Reprinted from *IEEE Trans. Antennas Propagat.*, vol. AP-21, pp. 164–169, Mar. 1973.

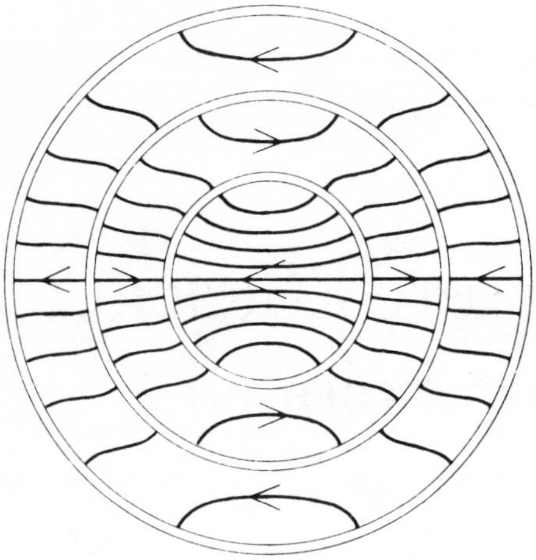

Fig. 3. Field distribution in aperture of 3-ring-coaxial-feed excited by H_{11} mode.

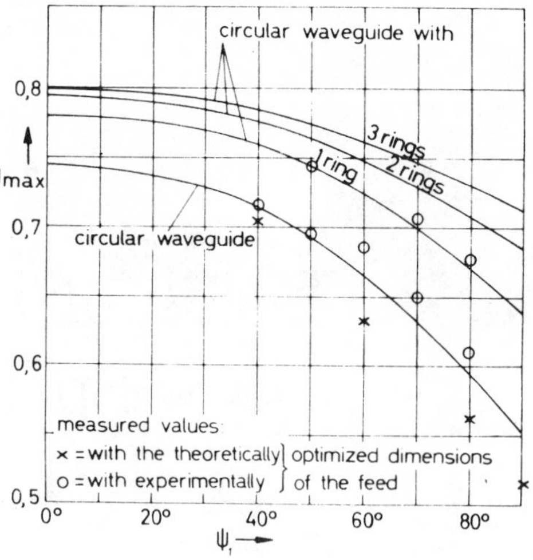

Fig. 4. Maximum obtainable aperture efficiency of paraboloid antennas with H_{11} excited coaxial feed (aperture blocking neglected in calculation).

ized. Using waveguides excited by the H_{11} mode [3], [4], (Fig. 3), experimental results have largely confirmed the theory.

II. Coaxial Feeds Excited by H_{11} Modes

In order to optimize the dimensions of the coaxial feed to obtain maximum aperture efficiency of a paraboloid antenna illuminated by it, theoretical investigations of the diameters of the waveguides and the relative amplitude of their excitation by the H_{11} mode [5] were made. When using Kirchhoff's boundary values in the aperture [6], [7], good results were obtained for the radiated field, provided the aperture dimensions are not considerably smaller than the wavelength [7], [8]. Therefore, the calculations of the field radiated by the coaxial feed were performed on this basis [5], [9]. The aperture efficiency of a paraboloid antenna illuminated by this feed was then determined by means of the calculated feed pattern (for details see [5] and [9]). The optimizing calculation yields the optimum diameters of the coaxial feed conductors and the optimum intensity ratios in the waveguides excited in alternating phase. Fig. 4 shows the maximum possible aperture efficiency q_{max} as a function of the angle $2\psi_1$ subtended by the paraboloid at its focus for simple circular waveguide feeds (in practice represented by long-horn-type feeds) as well as for coaxial feeds with one, two, or three rings. The maximum aperture efficiency is the higher, the smaller is the angular aperture $2\psi_1$. Moreover, it can be seen that there is a particularly high increase of q_{max} when changing over from the simple waveguide to a radiator consisting of a central waveguide and one ring only, for example from $q_{max} = 67$ to 72 percent for $\psi_1 = 60°$. For a feed with two or three rings, q_{max} rises but slightly to 75 and 76 percent, respectively. Hence, a radiator with only one ring has been constructed (Fig. 5). The coaxial waveguide of this feed is coupled to the central waveguide in such a manner that a bandwidth of about 10 percent is achieved. The calculated patterns agree quite well with the measured patterns of feeds determined for ψ_1 values

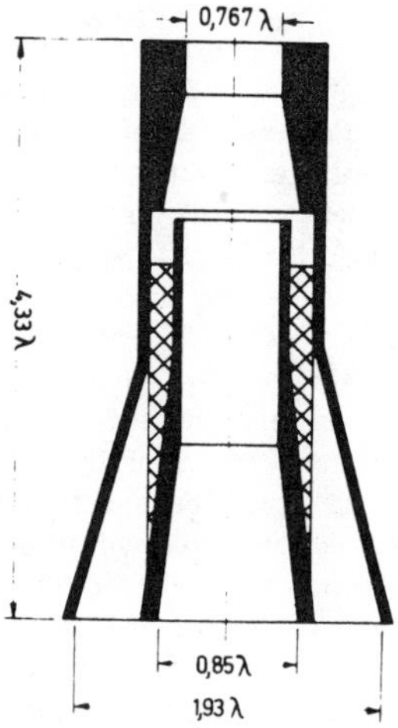

Fig. 5. Coaxial feed excited by H_{11} modes (experimentally optimized for $\psi_1 = 70°$).

up to 60°. Agreement is the worse as ψ_1 approaches 90°, since the calculation was performed on the basis of Kirchhoff's boundary values in the aperture, a condition which is not valid for small apertures. Therefore, the theoretically determined optimum diameters of the coaxial radiator must be corrected experimentally in such a manner that the pattern averaged from the measured values in the E- and H-planes approximates the mean calculated pattern as closely as possible. In Fig. 6, the narrow curves indicate the optimum dimensions according to theory, the bold curves indicate the experimentally determined dimensions. Since feeds of these dimensions have nearly the same average pattern in the approximate theory and in the experiment (Fig. 7), they also yield nearly the same values for q_{max} (circles in Fig. 4). If the phase in the aperture of the central radiator is not exactly opposite to that in the aperture of the ring radiator, the radiation produced by the coaxial feed has no longer the shape of a spherical wave and the amplitude pattern approximates the wanted sector shape not as well as in the case of antiphase excitation.

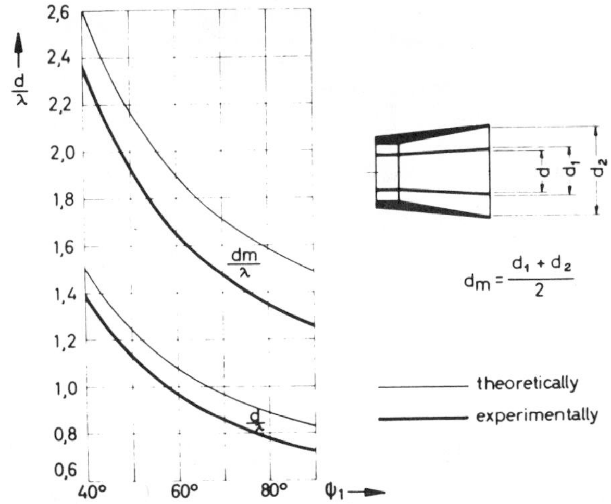

Fig. 6. Optimum diameter of waveguide and coaxial feeds excited by H_{11} mode.

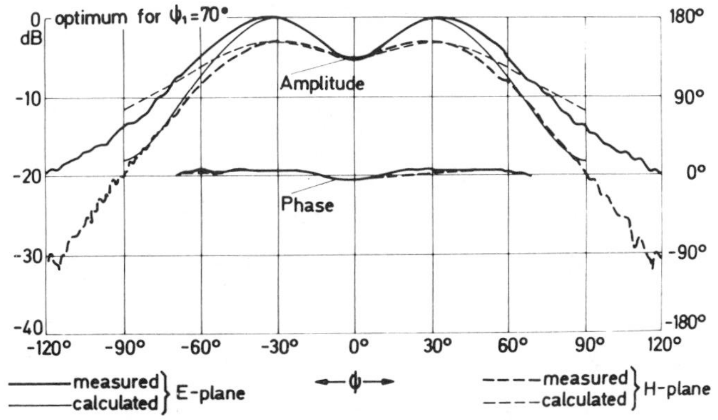

Fig. 7. Radiation patterns of H_{11} excited coaxial feed calculated by means of approximation theory using Kirchhoff's boundary values and measured on feed whose dimensions are corrected experimentally.

In summary, it can be said that this coaxial feed with one ring provides the following practical values of aperture efficiency of the paraboloid antenna:

$$\psi_1 = \begin{cases} 50° \\ 70° \\ 80° \end{cases} \quad q_{\max} = \begin{cases} 75 \text{ percent} \\ 71 \text{ percent} \\ 68 \text{ percent} \end{cases} \text{ (measured values).}$$

The edge illumination of the paraboloidal reflector does not decrease substantially with respect to that obtained with the optimum circular waveguide. If the coaxial radiator is so dimensioned that it yields the same aperture efficiency of the paraboloid antenna as an optimum circular waveguide, there is a 10-dB decrease of the edge illumination in the electric plane with respect to that of the circular waveguide. The radiation properties remain practically unchanged over an $\approx$10 percent frequency band.

III. Multimode Coaxial Feeds

The coaxial feeds excited by the H_{11} mode have different patterns in the E-plane and in the H-plane, i.e., they are not the optimum solution for the illumination of a paraboloidal reflector with circular aperture. A circularly symmetric pattern, in conjunction with an almost linearly polarized field in the aperture of the coaxial feed, however, can be obtained by adequate superposition of the H_{11} and E_{11} modes [10] in the central waveguide and of the H_{11} and H_{12} modes [2] in the ring-type waveguide (Fig. 8). The field strength in the aperture is approximately linearly polarized, and the amplitude of the field strength is approximately independent of the azimuth angle. But in the ring-type waveguide, 12 other modes are possible. These unwanted modes could be avoided by an appropriate excitation system. It consists of 12 probes (for the excitation of the H_{11} mode) and 12 longitudinal slots (for the excitation of the H_{12} mode) in the wall of the central radiator (Fig. 9). Because of the high degree of symmetry of this excitation system, all $H_{m,n}$ and all $E_{m,n}$ modes with $m = 0,2,3,4,5,6$ are suppressed [11]. The relative phase of the H_{11} mode to that of the E_{11} mode in the central radiator, as well as the relative phase of the H_{11} mode to that of the H_{12} mode in the ring radiator, must be set in such a way that the electric fields of the two superimposed modes have the same phase in the magnetic plane of the aperture. The intensity ratio of the H_{11} mode to the E_{11} mode and that of the H_{11} mode to the H_{12} mode were first determined theoretically in such a manner that the best approximation to the circular symmetry of the aperture field is obtained [11]. This was checked and corrected by means of an aperture field test setup [12].

With such a feed, we obtain a main lobe of the pattern with a very high degree of circular symmetry (Fig. 10). The E- and H-patterns coincide completely far beyond the angular aperture. The phase pattern is very good. It has the shape of a spherical wave in the illumination region. With this feed the cross-polarization intensity is reduced by about 10 dB with respect to that of a coaxial radiator or of a circular waveguide, both of which being excited by the H_{11} mode. This is shown by a theoretical investigation and is proved by measurements of the feed aperture field.

The multimode coaxial feed for deep reflectors differs from that for flat reflectors described above in two points [13]:

1) It is not necessary to excite an E_{11} mode in the central waveguide because the diameter is so small ($<$1 wavelength) that the waveguide produces a circularly symmetrical pattern by excitation with the H_{11} mode only.

2) The radiation coupling between central waveguide and ring waveguide is so strong that the H_{11} mode is excited in the ring-type waveguide. A special exciting system of probes is not required.

The advantage of this design is a larger bandwidth ($\approx$6 percent) since the differences in the lengths of the path to the aperture for the H_{11} and H_{12} modes are smaller (see Fig. 11). Fig. 12 shows the pattern of such a feed which is the optimum for half an angular aperture of 75°. According to [6], [14], the aperture efficiency of a

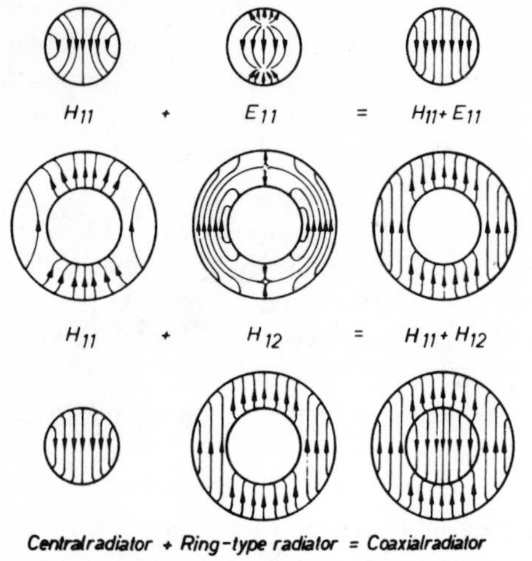

Fig. 8. Superposition of H_{11} and E_{11} modes in central radiator and of H_{11} and H_{12} modes in ring-type radiator.

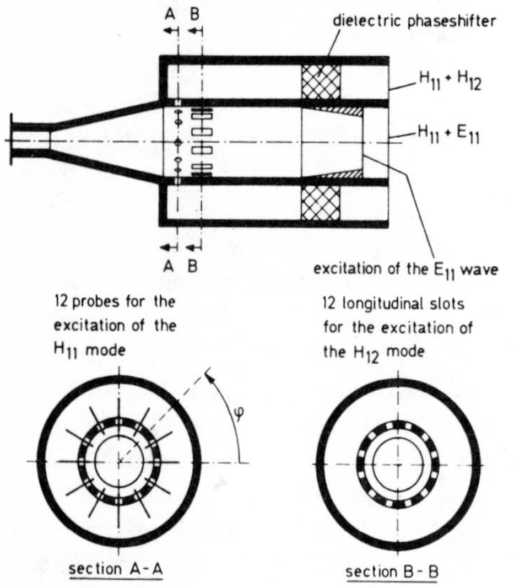

Fig. 9. Multimode coaxial feed for flat paraboloid antennas.

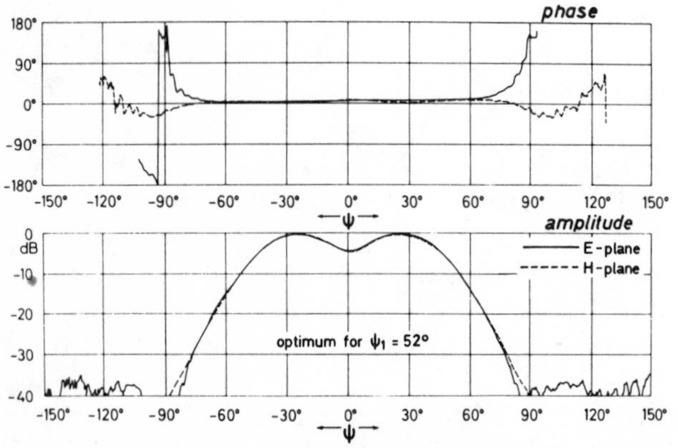

Fig. 10. Radiation patterns of multimode coaxial feeds optimized according to calculations of Fig. 13.

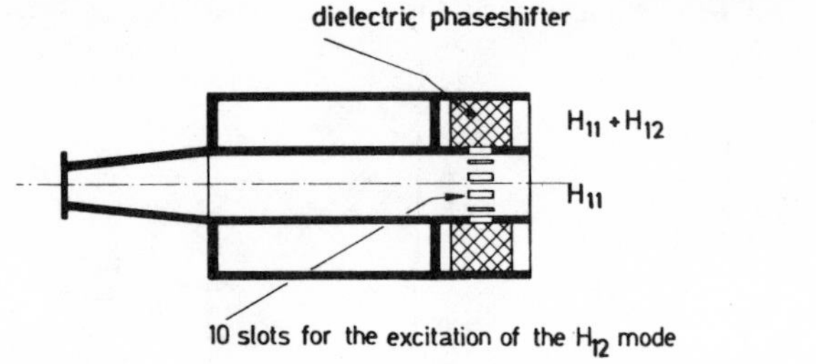

Fig. 11. Multimode coaxial feed for shallow paraboloid antennas.

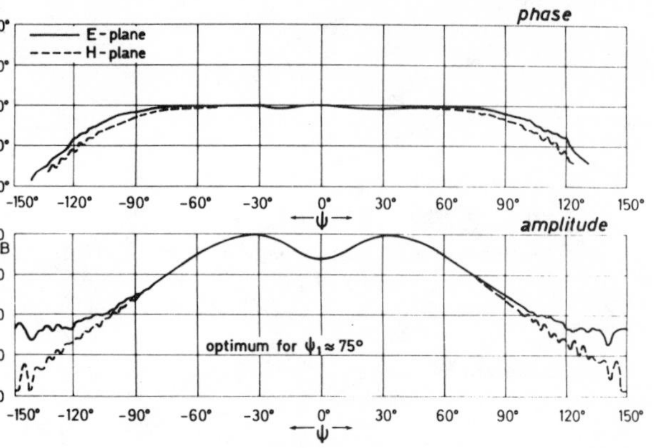

Fig. 12. Radiation patterns of multimode coaxial feeds optimized according to calculations of Fig. 13.

paraboloid antenna with a circular aperture is

$$q = \frac{f^2 \cot^2(\psi_1/2)}{\pi} \frac{\left[\int_{\psi=0}^{\psi_1}\int_{\varphi=-\pi}^{\pi} E_{pr}(\varphi,\psi)\frac{\tan(\psi/2)}{\cos^2(\psi/2)}\,d\varphi\,d\psi\right]^2}{Z_0 P_t} \tag{1}$$

where f is the focal length of the paraboloidal reflector, $E_{pr}(\varphi,\psi)$ the principal polarization component of the electric field in the aperture of the paraboloid antenna, Z_0 the intrinsic impedance of free space, P_t the total power radiated by the paraboloid antenna. If the electric far field radiated by the feed is given in terms of the spherical coordinates R,φ,ψ with their origin in the focus by

$$\boldsymbol{E}_{\text{feed}}(R,\varphi,\psi) = \boldsymbol{e}_\varphi E_\varphi(R,\varphi,\psi) + \boldsymbol{e}_\psi E_\psi(R,\varphi,\psi) \tag{2}$$

then the electric field in the aperture of the paraboloid antenna becomes

$$\boldsymbol{E}_{\text{aperture}}(\varphi,\psi) = \frac{R\cos^2(\psi/2)}{f} \cdot \{\boldsymbol{e}_x[-E_\varphi(R,\varphi,\psi)\sin\varphi + E_\psi(R,\varphi,\psi)\cos\varphi] - \boldsymbol{e}_y[E_\varphi(R,\varphi,\psi)\cos\varphi + E_\psi(R,\varphi,\psi)\sin\varphi]\} \tag{3}$$

where the y component is the principal polarization component. (x,y) are the Cartesian coordinates in the aperture plane and $\boldsymbol{e}_\varphi,\boldsymbol{e}_\psi,\boldsymbol{e}_x,\boldsymbol{e}_y$ are unit vectors. Using the expression for $E_{pr}(\varphi,\psi)$ in (3), the following is ob-

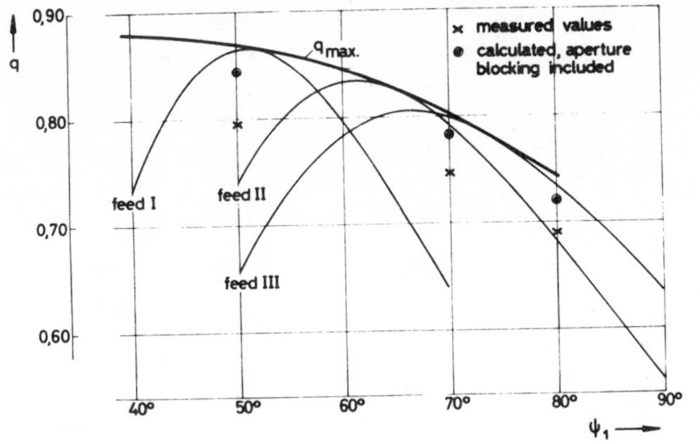

Fig. 13. Aperture efficiency of paraboloid antennas illuminated by multimode coaxial feed.

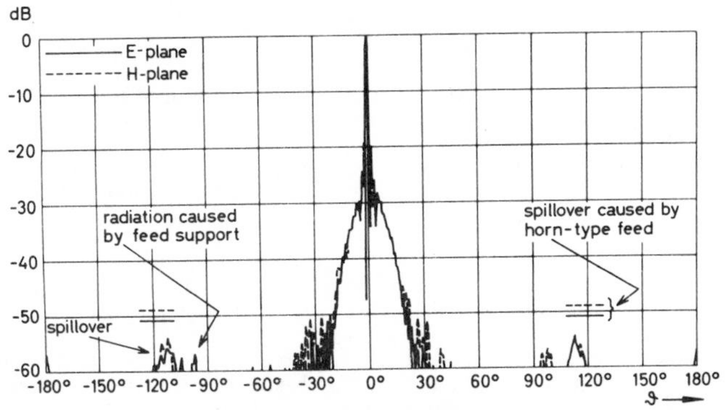

Fig. 14. Pattern of 2-m paraboloid antenna ($\psi_1 = 60°$) illuminated by multimode coaxial feed.

tained from (1)

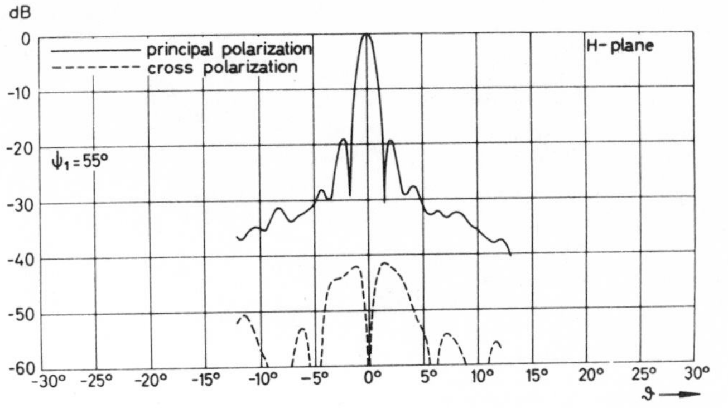

Fig. 15. Patterns of 1.5-m paraboloid antenna ($\psi_1 = 55°$) illuminated by multimode coaxial feed.

maximum aperture efficiency for a reflector of a certain ψ_1 is then determined by the envelope of these curves. The measured values indicated by the crosses give the following real values for q_{max}:

$$\psi_1 = \begin{cases} 50° \\ 70° \\ 80° \end{cases} \qquad q_{max} = \begin{cases} 80 \text{ percent} \\ 75 \text{ percent} \\ 68 \text{ percent} \end{cases} \text{(measured values).}$$

If the feed is not dimensioned for q_{max}, but for the same aperture efficiency as produced by an optimum circular waveguide feed, the edge illumination of the paraboloidal reflector and thus the spillover decrease by about 5 dB in the *E*-plane and by about 7 dB in the *H*-plane.

The pattern of a paraboloid antenna ($\psi_1 = 60°$) illuminated by a multimode coaxial feed is shown in Fig. 14. Since the feed is the optimum for $\psi_1 = 50°$, the spillover

$$q = \frac{\cot^2(\psi_1/2)}{\pi} \frac{\left[\int_{\psi=0}^{\psi_1}\int_{\varphi=-\pi}^{\pi} [E_\varphi(R,\varphi,\psi)\cos\varphi + E_\psi(R,\varphi,\psi)\sin\psi]\tan\left(\frac{\psi}{2}\right) d\varphi\, d\psi\right]^2}{\int_{\psi=0}^{\pi}\int_{\varphi=0}^{2\pi} [E_\varphi^2(R,\varphi,\psi) + E_\psi^2(R,\varphi,\psi)]\sin\psi\, d\varphi\, d\psi} \tag{4}$$

For a circularly symmetric distribution of a linearly polarized field in the feed aperture the field radiated by the feed is given by

$$E_\varphi(R,\varphi,\psi) = E_{feed}(R,\psi)\cos\varphi \tag{5a}$$

$$E_\psi(R,\varphi,\psi) = E_{feed}(R,\psi)\sin\varphi. \tag{5b}$$

Since these conditions are largely satisfied by the multimode coaxial feed, (4) can be reduced to

$$q = 2\cot^2\left(\frac{\psi_1}{2}\right) \frac{\left[\int_0^{\psi_1} C(\psi)\tan\left(\frac{\psi}{2}\right) d\psi\right]^2}{\int_0^{\pi} C^2(\psi)\sin\psi\, d\psi} \tag{6}$$

where $C(\psi)$ is the relative feed pattern. By means of this equation q is calculated on the basis of the measured feed pattern. This is done for three feeds (Fig. 13). The

in the electric plane is reduced by 5 dB and in the magnetic plane by 4.5 dB. An important advantage of this feed is the fact that a paraboloid antenna illuminated by it produces only very little cross-polarization. The maximum is −40 dB in the *E*- or *H*-plane (Fig. 15) and −35 dB in the 45° plane.

Fig. 16 shows the maximum obtainable aperture efficiency of paraboloid antennas illuminated by theoretically optimum feeds (according to calculations of Minnett and Mac A. Thomas [15]), by waveguide feeds or by coaxial feeds. This comparison shows that the aperture efficiency achieved by waveguide feeds which are excited by the H_{11} and E_{11} modes and especially by multimode coaxial feeds easily reaches the theoretical maximum. The reason that the values for the theoretical aperture efficiency of paraboloid antennas illuminated by multimode coaxial feeds are located on or even above the curve for the theoretical maximum is to be seen in the following: The aperture efficiency is calculated on the basis of the meas-

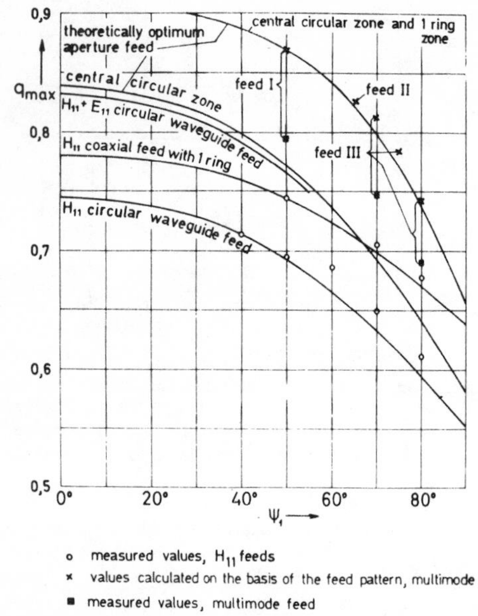

Fig. 16. Maximum obtainable aperture efficiencies of paraboloid antennas.

ured principal polarization of the feed pattern only, but the amount of the cross polarization is about 0.5 percent in case of feed I and about 5 percent in case of feed III. This would reduce the calculated values by ≈0.5 and 5 percent, respectively.

References

[1] G. F. Koch, "Paraboloid antennas with a low noise temperature," *Nachrichtentech Z. Commun. J.*, vol. 5, no. 3, pp. 125–131, 1966.

[2] ——, "A radiator for low-noise paraboloid antennas and also other possibilities of realizing a A_1-distribution," *Nachrichtentech Z. Commun. J.*, vol. 5, no. 4, pp. 153–158, 1966.

[3] ——, "A new feed for low-noise paraboloid antennas," in *Design and Construction of Large Steerable Aerials*, Inst. Elec. Eng. Conf. Publ. no. 21, pp. 163–167, 1966.

[4] G. F. Koch and H. Scheffer, "Coaxial radiator as feed for low noise paraboloid antennas," *Nachrichtentech. Z.*, vol. 22, no. 3, pp. 166–173, 1969.

[5] H. Scheffer, "Optimale Dimensionierung von Koaxialerregern für Parabolantennen," *Nachrichtentech. Z.*, vol. 24, no. 3, pp. 137–142, 1971.

[6] S. Silver, *Microwave Antenna Theory and Design.* New York: McGraw-Hill, 1949.

[7] G. F. Koch, "Die verschiedenen Ansätze des Kirchhoffschen Prinzips und ihre Anwendung auf die Beugungsdiagramme bei elektromagnetischen Wellen," *Arch. Elek. Übertragung*, vol. 14, pp. 77–98, 132–153, 1960.

[8] G. F. Koch and K. P. Dombek, "Einfluss der Aperturreflexion auf die Berechnung der Richtcharakteristiken von Hohlleiterstrahlern," *Arch. Elek. Ubertragung*, vol. 23, no. 11, pp. 553–560, 1969.

[9] H. Scheffer, "Die Strahlung der mit H-Wellen angeregten, offenen Koaxialleitung," *Arch. Elek. Ubertragung*, vol. 22, no. 11, pp. 514–518, 1968.

[10] P. D. Potter, "A new horn antenna with suppressed sidelobes and equal beamwidths," *Microwave J.*, vol. 6, no. 6, pp. 71–78, 1963.

[11] H. Thielen, "Ein Mehrmoden-Koaxialerreger für Parabolantennen mit hohem Flächenwirkungsgrad und geringer Überstrahlung," *Nachrichtentech. Z.*, vol. 24, no. 6, pp. 307–313, 1971.

[12] G. F. Koch and O. Loos, "Messplatz für die Ausmessung der Aperturfeldverteilung von Flächenstrahlern," Tech. Bericht des Fernmeldetech. Zentralamtes der Deutschen Bundespost 5051, März 1967.

[13] K. Seher, "Mehrmoden-Koaxialerreger für Parabolantennen mit grossem Öffnungswinkel," Tech. Bericht des Fernmeldetech. Zentralamtes der Deutschen Bundespost, A 454 TBr 14, Aug. 1972.

[14] G. F. Koch, "Gewinn, Wirkfläche und Flächenausnutzung von Richtantennen und die Methoden ihrer Bestimmung," *Telefunken J.*, vol. 26, no. 101, pp. 292–309, Aug. 1953.

[15] H. C. Minett and B. Mac A. Thomas, "Fields in the image space of symmetrical focusing reflectors," *Proc. Inst. Elec. Eng.*, vol. 115, no. 10, pp. 1419–1430, Oct. 1968.

Conversion of TE$_{11}$° Mode by a Large Diameter Conical Junction

Abstract—**If a TE$_{11}$° mode is incident on a large diameter conical junction, the first-order forward scattered modes required to match the curved phase front of the TE$_{11}$° mode are the TM$_{11}$° and TE$_{12}$° modes, and the second-order modes are the TM$_{12}$° and TE$_{13}$° modes. All of the higher order modes have transverse electric fields that are in phase quadrature with that of the TE$_{11}$° mode at the junction.**

A time-shared computer was employed to determine the relative amplitudes of the higher order modes required to match the TE$_{11}$°-mode curved phase front. It is assumed that 1) the change in cone angle is small, and 2) the cone diameter is much larger than the wavelength. After matching the curved phase front by the four higher order modes, the residual error was found to be negligible. Finally, the mode amplitudes are converted into mode power levels.

Introduction

If a TE$_{11}$° mode is incident on a conical junction with a small change in cone angle, the first-order effect is a negligible change in TE$_{11}$°-mode amplitude distribution but a detectable change in phase distribution across the cross section. The first-order forward scattered modes required to match the distorted, curved phase front of the TE$_{11}$° mode at the junction are the TM$_{11}$° and TE$_{12}$° modes. The electric fields of these three modes at the center of the waveguide are oriented in the same direction. The phases of the electric fields of the TM$_{11}$° and TE$_{12}$° modes are in quadrature with that of the TE$_{11}$° mode in order to satisfy the assumed boundary conditions of a distorted phase front and negligible amplitude distortion. The quadrature phase has been measured on a rectangular waveguide taper [1] and therefore it is considered to be a valid assumption for the present problem. For the second-order correction of the phase curvature of the TE$_{11}$° mode at the junction, TM$_{12}$° and TE$_{13}$° modes are required [2]. It is assumed that the backward scattered modes are negligible. If the diameter at the conical junction is sufficiently large relative to the wavelength, all of these four higher order modes will propagate. The magnitudes of the higher order modes generated by the conical junction were determined by using a time-shared computer.

The reflection and transmission of a TE$_{11}$° mode by a conical junction has been reported by Piefke [3]. He has also calculated the conversion to only the first higher order TM$_{11}$° mode by a small diameter junction.

Manuscript received June 12, 1968; revised December 11, 1968. The work was supported by the Rome Air Development Center under Contract AF 30(602)-3810.

Field Matching

The distorted phase front occurring at a conical junction in the taper can be represented by a spherical segment as shown in Fig. 1. The change in half-angle of the junction is $\Delta\theta$, the junction diameter is $D=2a$, and the displacement in phase front is $F(r)$. The displacement can also be given in terms of a radian phase shift by $F(r)2\pi/\lambda$ where λ is the wavelength. For a wave progressing from left to right, the phase is advanced at the center relative to the outer edge of the cross section.

As stated earlier, it will be assumed that the amplitude distribution of the incident TE$_{11}$° mode over the cross section will be negligibly altered by the junction, but that the phase will be altered measurable. This assumption is valid provided the phase displacement $F(0)$ at the center is small relative to λ. For small $\Delta\theta$ in radians,

$$F(0) \doteq \tfrac{1}{2}D\Delta\theta.$$

The field-matching procedure employed involves the electric fields of the modes, and in principle it should be possible to consider alternatively the magnetic fields. In order to match the distorted phase front at a junction, the TM$_{11}$°, TE$_{12}$°, TM$_{12}$°, and TE$_{13}$° modes are added in phase quadrature to the TE$_{11}$° mode as stated earlier. The relative amounts of the higher order modes are determined by the shape and magnitude of the distorted phase front. Further, there is a discontinuous shift in the phase of the TE$_{11}$° mode due to the change in the shape of the phase front at the conical junction. For conservation of power, the total amount of power in the higher order modes is subtracted from that of the TE$_{11}$° mode.

A rigorous analysis of the field matching problem requires consideration of the entire cross section at the junction. Analytically this is considerably more difficult than matching the phase along two radial directions that are along the planes of symmetry of the modes as is done in this analysis. In one direction, designated $\phi=0°$, only $E_\phi(r)$ of all the modes is considered; in the other direction designated $\phi=90°$, only $E_r(r)$ is considered. Both directions or axes are considered simultaneously, and the problem is to minimize the amount of mismatch along each axis between the distorted phase front and the resultant phase front synthesized by mode addition.

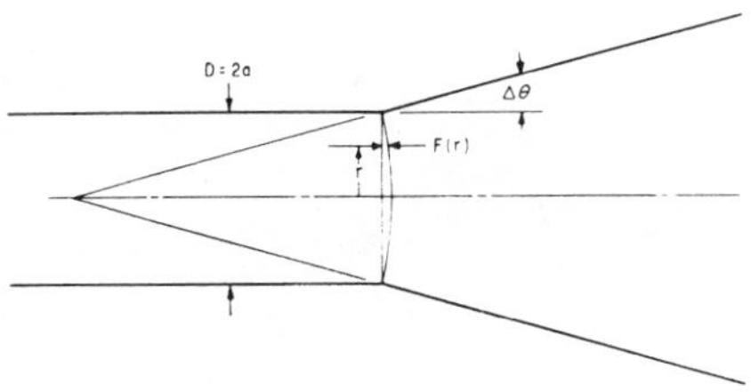

Fig. 1. Distorted phase front at a conical junction.

The particular electric field components of the various modes that are considered are given below [4].

TM Modes	TE Modes
$(J_n = 0)$	$(J_n' = 0)$
$E_r = -j\dfrac{\lambda_c}{\lambda_g}AJ_n'(k_cr')\sin n\phi$	$E_r = jn\eta\dfrac{\lambda_c}{\lambda}B\dfrac{J_n(k_cr')}{k_cr'}\sin n\phi$
$E_\phi = -jn\dfrac{\lambda_c}{\lambda_g}\dfrac{AJ_n(k_cr')}{k_cr'}\cos n\phi$	$E_\phi = j\eta\dfrac{\lambda_c}{\lambda}BJ_n'(k_cr')\cos n\phi$

where

A and B = constants
n = circumferential index
η = wave impedance
$r'=r/a$ = normalized radius
λ_c = cutoff wavelength
λ_g = guide wavelength
λ = free-space wavelength.

The field components of the modes to be considered have distributions as a function of r:

Mode	$\phi = 0°$	$\phi = 90°$
TE$_{11}$°	$J_1'(1.841r')$	$\dfrac{J_1(1.841r')}{1.841r'}$
TM$_{11}$°	$\dfrac{J_1(3.832r')}{3.832r'}$	$J_1'(3.832r')$
TE$_{12}$°	$J_1'(5.331r')$	$\dfrac{J_1(5.331r')}{5.331r'}$
TM$_{12}$°	$\dfrac{J_1(7.016r')}{7.016r'}$	$J_1'(7.016r')$
TE$_{13}$°	$J_1'(8.536r')$	$\dfrac{J_1(8.536r')}{8.536r'}$

Numerical values of these distribution functions with $r'=r/15$ are given in Tables I and II and plotted in Fig. 2. Also in Fig. 2, numerical values of $F(r)$ from Fig. 1 are plotted for an example of $\Delta\theta=2°$ and $D=2a$

TABLE I

ELECTRIC FIELD DISTRIBUTIONS

$E_\phi(r)$, $\phi=0°$

r	$TE_{11}°$	$TM_{11}°$	$TE_{12}°$	$TM_{12}°$	$TE_{13}°$	F (inches)
0	0.5000	0.5000	0.5000	0.5000	0.5000	0.262
1	0.4962	0.4971	0.4771	0.4869	0.4408	0.261
2	0.4877	0.4840	0.4084	0.4475	0.2783	0.257
3	0.4751	0.4640	0.3003	0.3866	0.0552	0.252
4	0.4555	0.4369	0.1721	0.3109	−0.1705	0.243
5	0.4309	0.4047	0.0265	0.2277	−0.3418	0.233
6	0.4025	0.3668	−0.1169	0.1453	−0.4176	0.220
7	0.3687	0.3251	−0.2434	0.0706	−0.3832	0.205
8	0.3310	0.2806	−0.3413	0.0098	−0.2541	0.188
9	0.2905	0.2349	−0.4017	−0.0338	−0.0708	0.168
10	0.2440	0.1891	−0.4192	−0.0586	0.1141	0.146
11	0.1993	0.1446	−0.3935	−0.0661	0.2502	0.121
12	0.1524	0.1025	−0.3292	−0.0594	0.3032	0.094
13	0.0983	0.0638	−0.2341	−0.0428	0.2641	0.065
14	0.0496	0.0294	−0.1201	−0.0214	0.1505	0.034
15	0	0	0	0	0	0

TABLE II

ELECTRIC FIELD DISTRIBUTIONS

$E_r(r)$, $\phi=90°$

r	$TE_{11}°$	$TM_{11}°$	$TE_{12}°$	$TM_{12}°$	$TE_{13}°$
0	0.5000	0.5000	0.5000	0.5000	0.5000
1	0.5000	0.4866	0.4916	0.4591	0.4799
2	0.4973	0.4518	0.4692	0.3452	0.4232
3	0.4913	0.3946	0.4333	0.1786	0.3387
4	0.4851	0.3194	0.3839	−0.0122	0.2390
5	0.4770	0.2273	0.3269	−0.1931	0.1387
6	0.4666	0.1265	0.2648	−0.3328	0.0507
7	0.4552	0.0219	0.2010	−0.4090	−0.0150
8	0.4421	−0.0820	0.1390	−0.4109	−0.0538
9	0.4291	−0.1788	0.0818	−0.3414	−0.0661
10	0.4121	−0.2644	0.0323	−0.2171	−0.0571
11	0.3944	−0.3337	−0.0080	−0.0630	−0.0349
12	0.3761	−0.3841	−0.0376	0.0907	−0.0083
13	0.3571	−0.4126	−0.0566	0.2149	0.0147
14	0.3368	−0.4189	−0.0653	0.2886	0.0288
15	0.3160	−0.4028	−0.0649	0.3000	0.0320

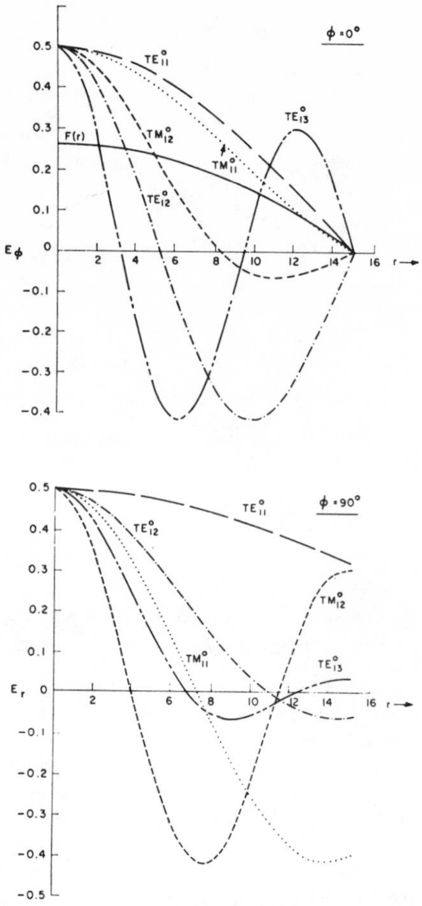

Fig. 2. Electric field distribution functions for $\phi=0°$ and 90°.

$=30$ inches. The value of $F(0)$ is 0.262 inches.

The radian phase-shift distribution $\alpha(r')$ is synthesized by adding proper amounts of the higher order mode fields and dividing by the corresponding component of the $TE_{11}°$ mode. The two equations for $\alpha(r')$ are given below where the C's are arbitrary scalar coefficients. For $\phi=0°$:

$$\alpha_0(r') = \frac{C_1\dfrac{J_1(3.832r')}{3.832r'} + C_2J_1'(5.331r') + C_3\dfrac{J_1(7.016r')}{7.016r'} + C_4J_1'(8.536r')}{J_1'(1.841r')}.$$

For $\phi=90°$:

$$\alpha_{90}(r') = \frac{C_1J_1'(3.832r') + C_2\dfrac{J_1(5.331r')}{5.331r'} + C_3J_1'(7.016r') + C_4\dfrac{J_1(8.536r')}{8.536r'}}{\dfrac{J_1(1.841r')}{1.841r'}}.$$

The range and shape (or curvature) of $\alpha(r)$ should match those of $F(r)2\pi/\lambda$, so that $\alpha(r)-F(r)2\pi/\lambda$ should be as close to a constant for all values of r and the two values of ϕ. If this constant value is designated as $K2\pi/\lambda$, the desired condition is to attain a minimum value of the sum of the absolute values at each radial position:

$$\sum_r \left| \alpha(r) - F(r)2\pi/\lambda + K2\pi/\lambda \right|.$$

This summation is to be taken for $\phi=0°$ and 90°, and the minimum should be equal for the two values of ϕ. The value of $K2\pi/\lambda$ is a discontinuous radian phase shift of the $TE_{11}°$ mode introduced to match the boundary condition at the junction.

A time-shared computer was employed to determine the C's and K that would minimize the summations over $r=0$ to $r=15$ in one-inch steps with $\lambda=3.523$ inches (3350 MHz). The results are

Mode	Coefficient	Value
$TM_{11}°$	C_1	0.30
$TE_{12}°$	C_2	0.23
$TM_{12}°$	C_3	−0.08
$TE_{13}°$	C_4	−0.05
$TE_{11}°$	K	0.17

The phases of the $TM_{11}°$ and $TE_{12}°$ modes are 90° ahead of that of the $TE_{11}°$ mode, whereas the negative signs of C_3 and C_4 mean that the phases of the $TM_{12}°$ and $TE_{13}°$ modes are 90° behind that of the $TE_{11}°$ mode.

As an indication of the fit of $\alpha(r)+K2\pi/\lambda$ to $F(r)2\pi/\lambda$, a tabulation of $\alpha(r)+K2\pi/\lambda-F(r)2\pi/\lambda$ is given in Table III for the two values of ϕ. Also given is the sum of the absolute differences $\sum||$ that has been minimized. This method of fitting was chosen over the least squares method so that the relatively large misfits at large radii (r near 15), where there is relatively less power density, would not exert disproportionate influence on the solution.

In order to assess the fit of the resultant function, the area under the $F(r)$ curve was taken, i.e.,

TABLE III

DISTRIBUTION OF DIFFERENCES

Radius	$\alpha(r)+K2\pi/\lambda-F(r)2\pi/\lambda$	
	$\phi=0°$	$\phi=90°$
0	2.04×10^{-3}	2.04×10^{-3}
1	1.32×10^{-3}	1.80×10^{-3}
2	-0.34×10^{-3}	-1.04×10^{-3}
3	-0.64×10^{-3}	-3.51×10^{-3}
4	-3.18×10^{-3}	-7.27×10^{-3}
5	-2.96×10^{-3}	-8.61×10^{-3}
6	-1.63×10^{-3}	-9.25×10^{-3}
7	1.42×10^{-3}	-7.62×10^{-3}
8	6.04×10^{-3}	-3.83×10^{-3}
9	10.14×10^{-3}	0.21×10^{-3}
10	13.51×10^{-3}	4.20×10^{-3}
11	12.32×10^{-3}	5.26×10^{-3}
12	5.71×10^{-3}	2.16×10^{-3}
13	-3.23×10^{-3}	-7.56×10^{-3}
14	-24.39×10^{-3}	-25.68×10^{-3}
15	-56.95×10^{-3}	-55.16×10^{-3}
$\Sigma\|\|$	0.146	0.145

$$\sum_r F(r) = 2.749.$$

Thus the summations of $\sum||$ indicate that the residual values are 5.34 percent and 5.31 percent of $\sum_r F(r)$ for $\phi=0°$ and 90°, respectively. It is deemed that these values of the residue are satisfactorily low to provide useful engineering results. Other values of ϕ should be checked for curve fitting and residual summations, but this was beyond the scope of the present investigation.

The foregoing numerical calculations have been made for a specific case of $\Delta\theta=2°$, $D=30$ inches, and $\lambda=3.523$ inches. The results can be translated into generalized equations provided $D\Delta\theta$ is small compared to λ. The ratios of the electric fields of the higher order modes at the center of the conical junction plane relative to that of the $TE_{11}°$ mode are equal to the C's tabulated above. These ratios are proportional to D/λ and to $\Delta\theta°$. Thus,

$$C = \frac{E_0}{E_{0TE_{11}}} \propto \frac{D}{\lambda}\Delta\theta°$$

where E_0 = mode electric field at the waveguide center, and $\Delta\theta°$ is in degrees. The generalized mode field conversion equations can be readily obtained, and these are

$$\frac{E_0\ TM_{11}}{E_0\ TE_{11}} = j\,1.76\times10^{-2}\frac{D}{\lambda}\Delta\theta°$$

$$\frac{E_0\ TE_{12}}{E_0\ TE_{11}} = j\,1.35\times10^{-2}\frac{D}{\lambda}\Delta\theta°$$

$$\frac{E_0\ TM_{12}}{E_0\ TE_{11}} = -j\,4.69\times10^{-3}\frac{D}{\lambda}\Delta\theta°$$

$$\frac{E_0\ TE_{13}}{E_0\ TE_{11}} = -j\,2.94\times10^{-3}\frac{D}{\lambda}\Delta\theta°.$$

MODE POWER

After determining the relative magnitudes of the electric fields of the converted modes, the power levels W of these modes can be calculated relative to that of the $TE_{11}°$ mode. By using standard formulas for mode power [4], the following mode power equations have been derived for air dielectric within the waveguide where a is the waveguide radius.

Mode	Power
$TE_{11}°$	$W_{TE_{11}} = 1.98912\times10^{-3}\,E_{0TE_{11}}{}^2a^2\left(\frac{\lambda}{\lambda_g}\right)$
$TM_{11}°$	$W_{TM_{11}} = 1.35157\times10^{-3}\,E_{0TM_{11}}{}^2a^2\left(\frac{\lambda_g}{\lambda}\right)$
$TE_{12}°$	$W_{TE_{12}} = 0.963236\times10^{-3}\,E_{0TE_{12}}{}^2a^2\left(\frac{\lambda}{\lambda_g}\right)$
$TM_{12}°$	$W_{TM_{12}} = 0.75049\times10^{-3}\,E_{0TM_{12}}{}^2a^2\left(\frac{\lambda_g}{\lambda}\right)$
$TE_{13}°$	$W_{TE_{13}} = 0.613898\times10^{-3}\,E_{0TE_{13}}{}^2a^2\left(\frac{\lambda}{\lambda_g}\right)$

The mode powers converted by the conical junction relative to that of the $TE_{11}°$ mode are

$$\frac{W_{TM_{11}}}{W_{TE_{11}}} = 2.11\times10^{-4}\left(\frac{D}{\lambda}\Delta\theta°\right)^2 \cdot \frac{\lambda_g\ TM_{11}\lambda_g\ TE_{11}}{\lambda^2}$$

$$\frac{W_{TE_{12}}}{W_{TE_{11}}} = 8.83\times10^{-5}\left(\frac{D}{\lambda}\Delta\theta°\right)^2 \cdot \frac{\lambda_g\ TE_{11}}{\lambda_g\ TE_{12}}$$

$$\frac{W_{TM_{12}}}{W_{TE_{11}}} = 8.30\times10^{-6}\left(\frac{D}{\lambda}\Delta\theta°\right)^2 \cdot \frac{\lambda_g\ TM_{12}\lambda_g\ TE_{11}}{\lambda^2}$$

$$\frac{W_{TE_{13}}}{W_{TE_{11}}} = 2.67\times10^{-6}\left(\frac{D}{\lambda}\Delta\theta°\right)^2 \cdot \frac{\lambda_g\ TE_{11}}{\lambda_g\ TE_{13}}.$$

ACKNOWLEDGMENT

The time-shared computations were skillfully performed by J. W. Maurer, and helpful criticisms were made by T. W. Dietze.

K. TOMIYASU
General Electric Co.
Research and Development Center
Schenectady, N. Y. 12301

REFERENCES

[1] K. Tomiyasu, "Mode conversion in short conical and asymmetrical-rectangular waveguide tapers," *IEEE Trans. Microwave Theory and Techniques* (Correspondence), vol. MTT-16, pp. 197–199, March 1968.

[2] C. C. H. Tang, "Mode conversion in tapered waveguides at and near cutoff," *IEEE Trans. Microwave Theory and Techniques*, vol. MTT-14, pp. 233–239, May 1966.

[3] G. Piefke, "Reflection at incidence of an H_{mn}-wave at junction of circular waveguide and conical horn," in *Electromagnetic Theory and Antennas*, vol. 6, pt. 1, E. C. Jordan, Ed., New York: Pergamon, 1963, pp. 209–234.

[4] S. Ramo, J. R. Whinnery, and T. Van Duzer, *Fields and Waves in Communication Electronics.* New York: Wiley, 1965.

Phase Characteristics of a Circularly Symmetric Dual-Mode Transducer

***Abstract*—This correspondence deals with the analysis and measurement of $TE_{11}^{\circ} \rightarrow TM_{11}^{\circ}$ mode conversion by circularly symmetric transducers in a circular waveguide. Two types are considered, the simple step change in radius and a discontinuity covered by a dielectric ring. For the first type, experimental results for both amplitude and phase are compared with predictions made on the basis of a computer program, with excellent agreement. The dielectric loaded transducer is of great interest since measurements have shown that such a device can be designed to launch the two modes with a relative amplitude and phase which is essentially independent of frequency over a very wide range. This configuration is therefore an excellent candidate for use in low-noise microwave antenna systems.**

I. Introduction

The use of multimode waveguides as feeds [1], [2] for low-noise antennas, e.g., in satellite communication systems, has stimulated interest in the properties of transducers which will launch higher order modes in correct relative amplitude and phase. One technique for achieving a dual-mode (TE_{11}° and TM_{11}°) excitation is by using a simple circularly symmetric discontinuity formed by joining two circular waveguides of diameters $2a$ and $2b$, as shown in Fig. 1. The radii a and b are chosen such that the smaller waveguide supports only the TE_{11}° mode, whereas the larger waveguide can support both the TE_{11}° and TM_{11}° modes. Although very simple, this configuration suffers from the fact that the relative phase of these two modes is a strong function of frequency.

On the other hand, measurements have shown that a very simple way of overcoming this phase dispersion is to load the step with a dielectric ring. It will be shown that the properties of this type of transducer are essentially independent of frequency for both amplitude and phase.

II. Properties of the Step Discontinuity

The mode conversion properties of a simple step discontinuity have been considered by other investigators [3]. One contribution of this correspondence consists of presenting a comparison between a particular set of experimental data and the results of an accurate computational analysis.

The relative phase of the radial electric fields at the wall of the larger waveguide at any location $z = d$ can be expressed as

$$\phi = \phi_0 + (\beta_{TM} - \beta_{TE})d \qquad (1)$$

Manuscript received June 16, 1969; revised July 30, 1969.

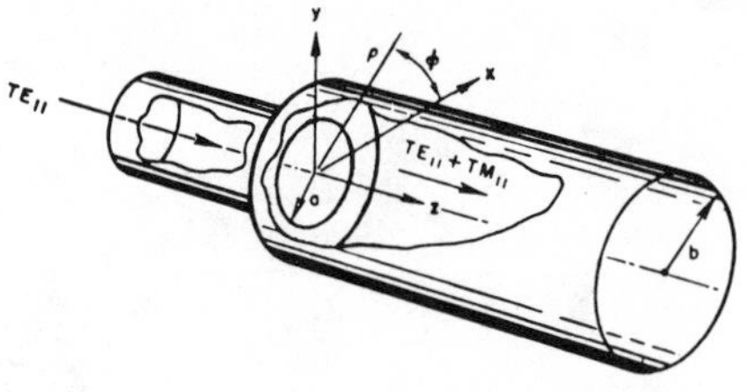

Fig. 1. $TE_{11} \rightarrow TM_{11}$ mode conversion at a discontinuity in a circular waveguide.

where ϕ_0 equals the relative phase at the step $z = 0$, and β_{TM}, β_{TE} represents the propagation constants. The quantity ϕ_0 can be determined theoretically by analyzing the waveguide discontinuity in terms of normal modes [4]. Applying the necessary boundary conditions at the connecting aperture leads to an integral equation which can then be solved numerically for the modal amplitudes in each waveguide [4]. Fig. 2, for example, shows the conversion coefficient C, defined as

$$C = 20 \log_{10} \left| \frac{E_p^{TM}}{E_p^{TE}} \right|_{p=b} \text{dB} \qquad (2)$$

plotted as a function of frequency. Fig. 3 gives the corresponding results for the relative phase.

Slotted line and probe measurements of the interference pattern caused by spatial beating of the propagating modes in the larger waveguides provide the necessary information to determine C and ϕ_0 experimentally. The measured results, indicated in Fig. 4 for a frequency band of 5.2 to 6.8 GHz, show good agreement with the computed values.

Except near TE_{11}° mode cutoff, the mode conversion over the frequency band is fairly constant, whereas the relative phase varies from 110 to 180°, showing a strong frequency dependence.

If this mode transducer is used as a feed to a dual-mode conical horn, the performance differs substantially from an optimum where it is required for a low sidelobe level that the radial components of electric field for the TE_{11} and TM_{11} modes be 180° out of phase at the edge, but this could only be achieved at a single frequency. It is therefore desirable to minimize the aperture phase dispersion over a frequency band.

III. Properties of the Dielectric Loaded Transducer

In order to overcome the inherent frequency dispersion of the simple step transducer, experiments were performed on the effects of dielectric loading as shown in Fig. 5. Although a precise theoretical explanation is very complicated, the improvement in performance which was noted can be attributed to

1) the effect of the dielectric loading on the relative phase at the step, and
2) the delay characteristics of the ring itself.

Reprinted from *IEEE Trans. Microwave Theory Tech.*, vol. MTT-18, pp. 69–71, Jan. 1970.

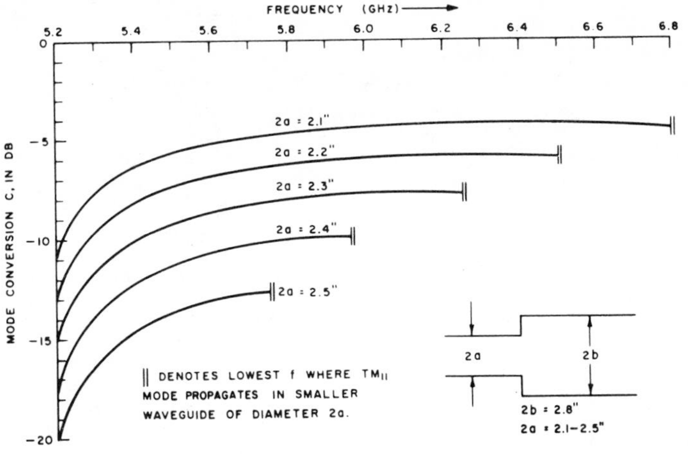

Fig. 2. $TE_{11} \rightarrow TM_{11}$ mode conversion coefficient of a step discontinutiy.

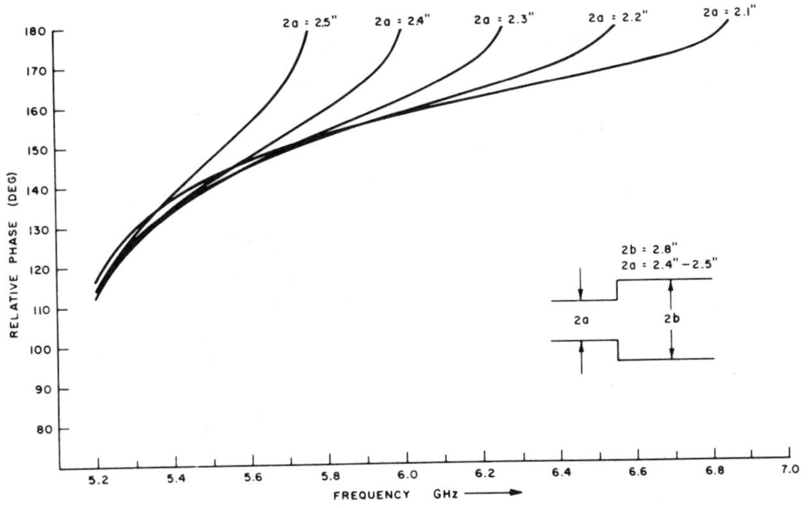

Fig. 3. Phase of TM_{11} mode relative to TE_{11} mode at the step discontinuity. TM_{11} lags TE_{11} in time.

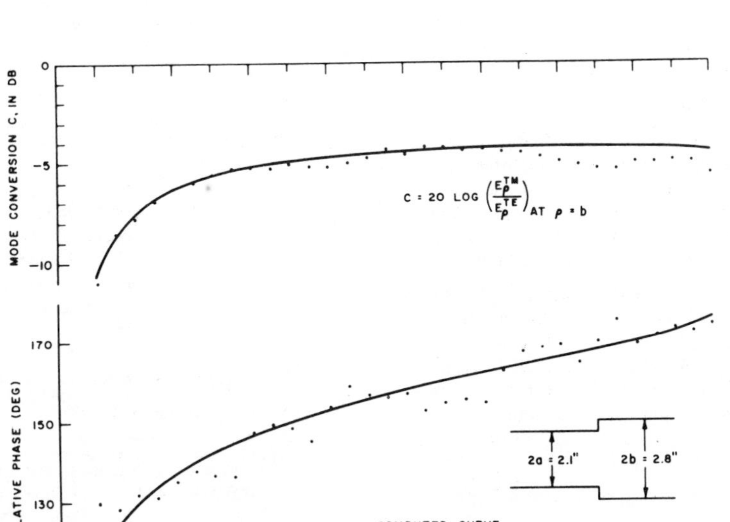

Fig. 4. Measured results.

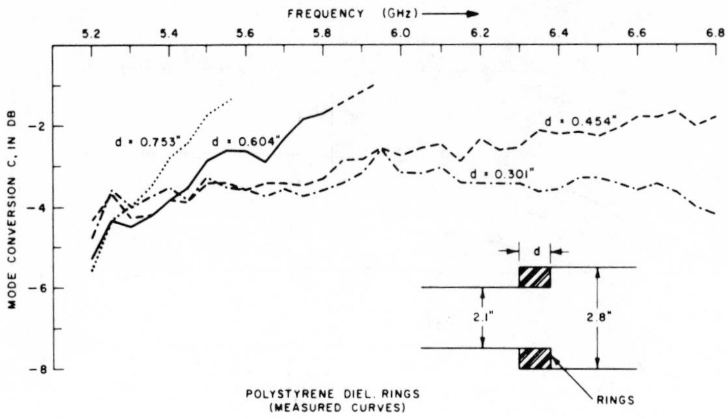

Fig. 5. $TE_{11} \rightarrow TM_{11}$ mode conversion of a dielectric loaded step discontinuity.

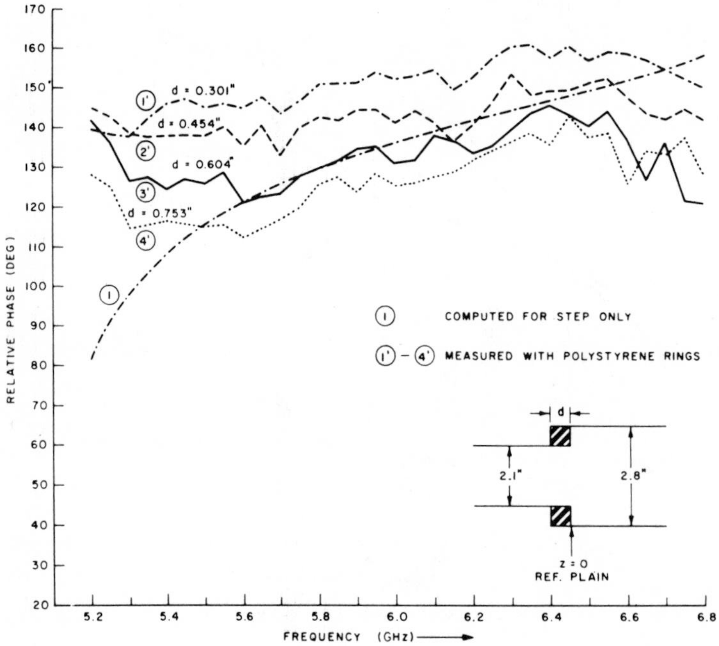

Fig. 6. Phase of TM_{11} relative to TE_{11} in a dielectric loaded step discontinuity.

On the basis of these results, it is concluded that such a configuration shows promise as a

Measured results using polystyrene rings of various thicknesses are shown in Figs. 5 and 6, from which the following observations on the effects of dielectric loading are made.

1) The mode conversion increases slightly as the thickness of the dielectric ring is increased and so does its frequency dependence. However, the frequency sensitivity of the relative phase is reduced appreciably by dielectric loading.
2) With increased dielectric loading, the relative phase shows a tendency to reverse its slope in the 5.2 to 6.8 GHz region.
3) The dielectric loading has very little or no effect on the relative phase characteristics at high frequencies.

nondispersive transducer for multimode waveguide applications.

K. K. Agarwal
Bell Telephone Labs., Inc.
North Andover, Mass.
E. R. Nagelberg
Bell Telephone Labs., Inc.
Whippany, N. J.

References

[1] P. D. Potter, "A new horn antenna with suppressed sidelobes and equal beamwidth," *Microwave J.*, vol. 6, pp. 71–78, 1963.
[2] J. S. Cook *et al.*, "The open Cassegrain antenna: pt. I. Electromagnetic design and analysis," *Bell Sys. Tech. J.*, vol. 44, pp. 1255–1300, 1965.
[3] E. R. Nagelberg and J. Shefer, "Mode-conversion in circular waveguides," *Bell Sys. Tech. J.*, vol. 44, pp. 1321–1338, 1965.
[4] W. J. Cole *et al.*, "Iterative solution of waveguide discontinuity problems," *Bell Sys. Tech. J.*, vol. 46, pp. 649–672, 1967.

The Circular Waveguide Step-Discontinuity Mode Transducer

WILLIAM J. ENGLISH

***Abstract*—Power conversion coefficients and the launch phase of propagating modes excited by a symmetric step-discontinuity in circular waveguide are accurately predicted by a modal analysis of the discontinuity which includes only a few evanescent modes. The relative power in transmitted and reflected propagating modes is presented as a function of normalized frequency for two step-discontinuity ratios to indicate typical solution results.**

I. Introduction

The use of higher order waveguide modes in a circular radiating aperture for beam shaping and sidelobe control has received attention in recent years [1]–[3]. The inclusion of TM_{11} and TE_{12} modes, along with the fundamental TE_{11} mode, in the radiating aperture permits: a) symmetric radiation patterns; b) low E- and H-plane sidelobes; and c) improved polarization characteristics.

Wexler [4] and Clarricoats [5], [6] have developed a modal analysis approach to waveguide discontinuity problems in which the transverse electromagnetic fields in the discontinuity aperture are expanded in terms of the normal modes of the two connected waveguides, and two simultaneous sets of equations for the complex reflection and transmission coefficients are formed by invoking continuity and zero-field conditions on the transverse components. This short paper summarizes the results of applying this approach to a circular waveguide step-discontinuity mode transducer which is ideally terminated at the source and load.

Manuscript received July 26, 1971; revised May 23, 1973. This short paper is based upon work performed in COMSAT Laboratories under corporate sponsorship.
The author is with COMSAT Laboratories, Clarksburg, Md. 20734.

II. Step-Discontinuity Properties

Fig. 1 illustrates typical mode transducing properties of the step-discontinuity illuminated with a fundamental TE_{11} mode. The relative power in transmitted and reflected propagating modes is presented as a function of normalized frequency for a given step size b/a. The launch phase of the TM_{11} and TE_{12} modes relative to the TE_{11} mode is also shown. The calculated results are in excellent agreement with experimental data previously reported by Agarwal and Nagelberg [7]. In addition, experimentally measured reflection coefficients are shown to confirm that the analysis predicts the high reflection coefficients encountered when the frequency is close to TM_{11} cutoff in the larger output guide. This feature is one of the distinct advantages of the rigorous modal analysis approach which includes reflected wave components in the input waveguide.

Fig. 2 illustrates the mode transducing properties of the junction when it is illuminated with a TM_{11} mode. These properties are informative for the design of multistep transducers. An incident TM_{11} mode only couples strongly to other TM_{1n} modes for the symmetric step-up junction and a large reflected power exists until the TM_{12} mode propagates.

In-phase radial electric field components on each side of the discontinuity aperture are compared in Fig. 3. Ideally, the tangential electric field is continuous across the common aperture area and zero on the metallic portion of the discontinuity aperture. As the number of modes considered in the analysis procedure increases from 10 to 20, the fine structure of the field components continues to change and the ideal boundary and continuity conditions are approached. The radial electric component experiences a singularity at the 90° corner in the smaller guide which is evident in the Fourier series summation.

Reprinted from *IEEE Trans. Microwave Theory Tech.*, vol. MTT-21, pp. 633–636, Oct. 1973.

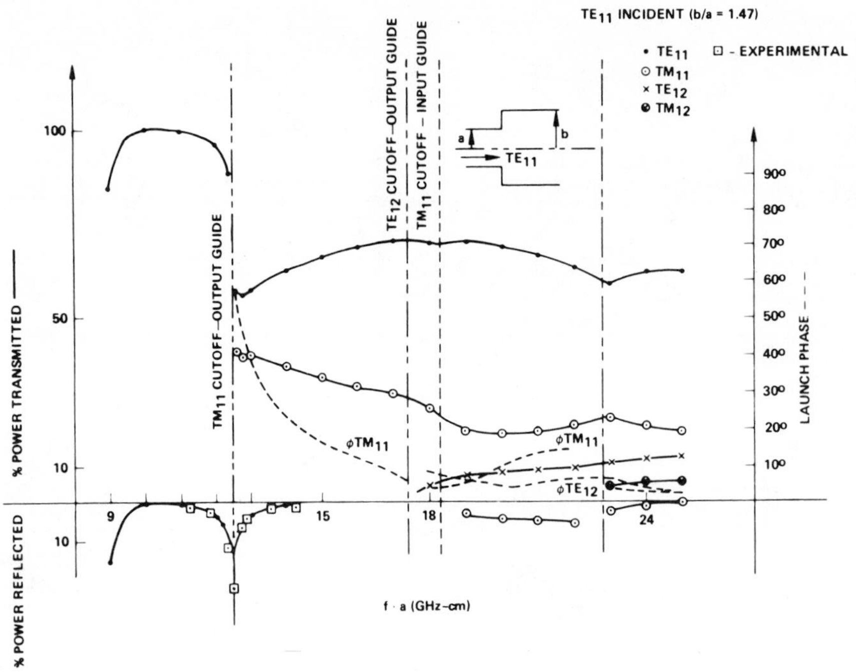

Fig. 1. Mode transducing properties (relative power and launch phase) of a symmetric step-discontinuity waveguide junction illuminated with an incident fundamental TE_{11} mode.

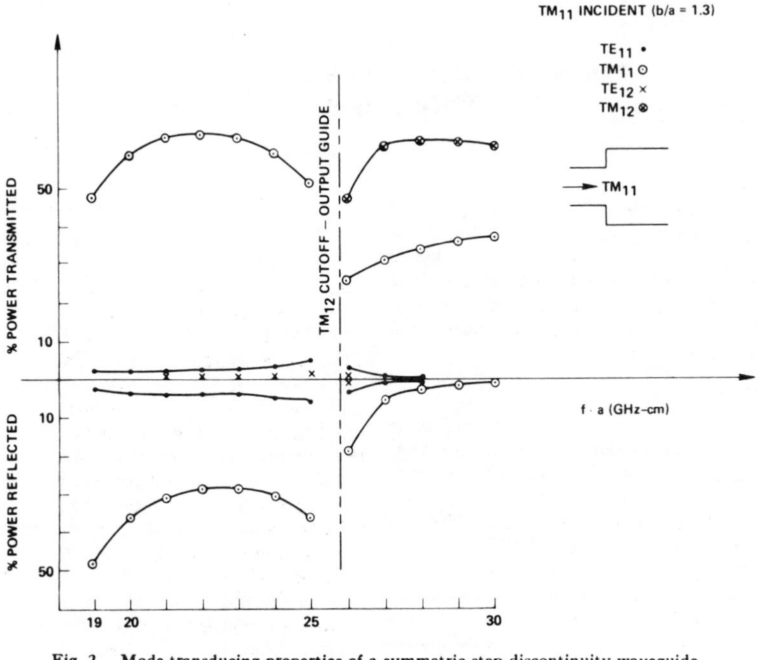

Fig. 2. Mode transducing properties of a symmetric step-discontinuity waveguide junction illuminated with an incident TM_{11} mode.

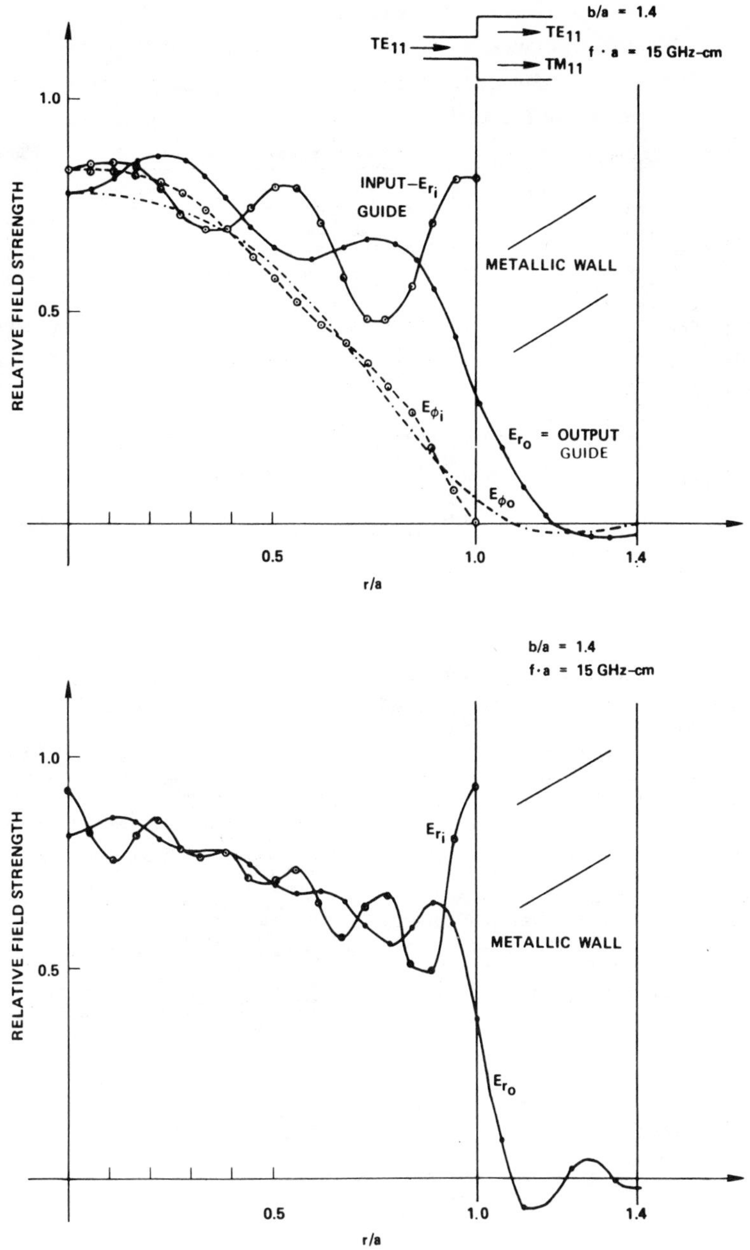

Fig. 3. Comparison of the input and output waveguide transverse aperture fields at the discontinuity junction—in-phase electric components (10 and 20 output guide modes).

TABLE I

JUNCTION PARAMETERS AS A FUNCTION OF THE NUMBER OF NORMAL MODES[a]

Number of Output Guide Modes MT	TE_{11} Transmission Coefficient	Relative TE_{11} Power	TM_{11} Transmission Coefficient	Relative TM_{11} Power
3	0.809 @ -1.88°	0.733	0.386 @ 22.99°	0.265
4	0.790 @ -3.05°	0.699	0.408 @ 20.70°	0.297
5	0.792 @ -2.34°	0.702	0.407 @ 21.42°	0.295
10	0.787 @ -2.48°	0.695	0.411 @ 20.74°	0.302
20	0.785 @ -2.35°	0.691	0.414 @ 20.57°	0.305

[a] *Note:* $b/a = 1.4$, $f \cdot a = 15$ GHz·cm.

TABLE II

RELATIVE POWER IN PROPAGATING AND EVANESCENT MODES[a]

No. of Mode	Reflected Power		Transmitted Power	
	PROPAGATING	REACTIVE	PROPAGATING	REACTIVE
M= 1	PM/P INPUT= 0.003516	+J 0.0	PM/P OUTPUT= 0.591403	+J 0.0
M= 2	PM/P INPUT= 0.0	+J-0.080699	PM/P OUTPUT= 0.305081	+J 0.0
M= 3	PM/P INPUT= 0.0	+J 0.010024	PM/P OUTPUT= 0.0	+J 0.070690
M= 4	PM/P INPUT= 0.0	+J-0.009721	PM/P OUTPUT= 0.0	+J-0.045942
M= 5	PM/P INPUT= 0.0	+J 0.003003	PM/P OUTPUT= 0.0	+J 0.018121
M= 6	PM/P INPUT= 0.0	+J-0.003332	PM/P OUTPUT= 0.0	+J-0.009543
M= 7	PM/P INPUT= 0.0	+J 0.001491	PM/P OUTPUT= 0.0	+J 0.001279
M= 8	PM/P INPUT= 0.0	+J-0.001792	PM/P OUTPUT= 0.0	+J-0.000572
M= 9	PM/P INPUT= 0.0	+J 0.000925	PM/P OUTPUT= 0.0	+J 0.002257
M=10	PM/P INPUT= 0.0	+J-0.001161	PM/P OUTPUT= 0.0	+J-0.003982
M=11	PM/P INPUT= 0.0	+J 0.000667	PM/P OUTPUT= 0.0	+J 0.003604
M=12	PM/P INPUT= 0.0	+J-0.000963	PM/P OUTPUT= 0.0	+J-0.003352
M=13	PM/P INPUT= 0.0	+J 0.000547	PM/P OUTPUT= 0.0	+J 0.001207
M=14	PM/P INPUT= 0.0	+J-0.000738	PM/P OUTPUT= 0.0	+J-0.000402
M=15	PM/P INPUT= 0.0	+J 0.001301	PM/P OUTPUT= 0.0	+J 0.000073
M=16	PM/P INPUT= 0.0	+J-0.001295	PM/P OUTPUT= 0.0	+J-0.000492
M=17	PM/P INPUT= 0.0	+J 0.000658	PM/P OUTPUT= 0.0	+J 0.000926
M=18	PM/P INPUT= 0.0	+J-0.000767	PM/P OUTPUT= 0.0	+J-0.001510
M=19	PM/P INPUT= 0.0	+J 0.000419	PM/P OUTPUT= 0.0	+J 0.000943
M=20	PM/P INPUT= 0.0	+J-0.000517	PM/P OUTPUT= 0.0	+J-0.000815

[a] *Note:* $b/a = 1.4$, $f \cdot a = 15$ GHz·cm.

Convergence results as a function of the number of normal modes considered are presented in Table I for a frequency where TE_{11} and TM_{11} modes both propagate in the output guide. Mode power conversion and launch phase coefficients converge rapidly and are essentially constant after six to eight evanescent modes on each side of the discontinuity are included. The ratio of the number of input to output waveguide modes considered is not significant if more than six evanescent modes are included; this supports a similar conclusion by Clarricoats [6].

The relative reactive power in the evanescent modes is shown in Table II, in which 20 modes are considered. The modes are numbered in terms of increasing cutoff frequencies. The reactive power quickly diminishes as the mode order increases and the inductive or capacitive nature of the discontinuity is provided by the total reactive power.

ACKNOWLEDGMENT

The author wishes to thank R. W. Gruner for his helpful discussions and his assistance with the measurement apparatus.

REFERENCES

[1] P. D. Potter, "A new horn antenna with suppressed sidelobes and equal beamwidths," *Microwave J.*, pp. 71–78, June 1963.
[2] J. S. Ajioka and H. Harry, Jr., "Shaped beam antenna for earth coverage from a stabilized satellite," *IEEE Trans. Antennas Propagat.*, vol. AP-18, pp. 323–327, May 1970.
[3] S. Drabowitch, "Multimode antennas," *Microwave J.*, pp. 46–51, Jan. 1966.
[4] A. Wexler, "Solution of waveguide discontinuities by modal analysis," *IEEE Trans. Microwave Theory Tech.*, vol. MTT-15, pp. 508–517, Sept. 1967.
[5] P. J. B. Clarricoats and K. R. Slinn, "Numerical solution of waveguide discontinuity problems," *Proc. Inst. Elec. Eng.*, vol. 114, pp. 878–885, July 1967.
[6] P. H. Masterman and P. J. B. Clarricoats, "Computer field-matching solution of waveguide transverse discontinuities," *Proc. Inst. Elec. Eng.*, vol. 118, pp. 51–63, Jan. 1971.
[7] K. K. Agarwal and E. R. Nagelberg, "Phase characteristics of a circularly symmetric dual-mode transducer," *IEEE Trans. Microwave Theory Tech.* (Corresp.), vol. MTT-18, pp. 69–71, Jan. 1970.

Part VI
Corrugated Horns

Because of the large number of papers in this part, it has seemed expedient to refrain from detailed comments on each one individually. Instead, I have chosen to group the papers regionally, and have confined my remarks to the making of general observations about the contributions of researchers in the several regions. First, however, a brief discussion of the history and the general background of the development of corrugated horns appears to be appropriate.

There can be little doubt that horn antenna research in the early 1960's was inspired by the need for improved feed systems for large radio astronomy and satellite tracking dishes. Feed horns were needed that would reduce spillover and cross-polarization losses and increase aperture efficiency from the area of 50–60 percent to the level of 75–80 percent. Thus, it is not surprising that the concept of the corrugated horn should arise independently, at about the same time, in two widely separated regions. In the United States, Kay [1] came to the realization that grooved walls in a horn would present the same boundary conditions to all polarizations and would therefore create a tapered aperture field distribution in all planes. This, in turn, would eliminate the spurious sources at the *E*-plane edges caused by diffraction and would result in equal *E*- and *H*-plane beamwidths. When appropriate grooved corrugations were cut into a wide-flare-angle feed horn, Kay had what he called the "scalar feed."

At about this same time, research at the Commonwealth Scientific and Industrial Research Organisation in Australia showed that the focal region fields of a paraboloidal reflector consisted of a superposition of cylindrical hybrid modes. Furthermore, it became clear that these hybrid modes were the natural propagating modes for a round waveguide whose internal walls were grooved with resonant slots. It was realized that such walls were anisotropic in the sense that they imposed exactly the same boundary conditions on both the electric and magnetic fields. Somewhat later, Rumsey was able to show that such a boundary condition at the walls of a horn would lead to axially symmetric radiation patterns. These events are recounted in two included short papers (the sixth and seventh papers in this part): "Propagation and Radiation Behaviour of Corrugated Feeds" by Minnett and Thomas, and "Horn Antennas with Uniform Power Patterns Around Their Axes" by Rumsey.

Thus was the corrugated horn born of the Australian work at the very time that the grooved scalar feed had its birth in the United States. If that is not coincidence enough, then consider that the multimode horn also came into being at the same time!

At first glance, it might seem that the multimode and corrugated horns accomplish similar results, namely, axisymmetric radiation patterns, by quite different means. In reality, the modal contents of the fields in the two cases are, with one important difference, the same. The difference can be understood by comparing the original multimode horn of Potter with a one-hybrid mode horn of Minnett and Thomas. In the former, the TE_{11} and TM_{11} modes have different phase velocities by virtue of the fact that the modes have different cutoffs because the boundary conditions on *E* and *H* are not the same. In the latter case, a hybrid mixture of TE_{11} and TM_{11} waves behaves as a single mode, called HE_{11}, in which both components propagate with the same velocity. The advantage of the corrugated horn, in terms of operating bandwidth, can easily be appreciated.

The first group of five papers in this part represents work done in the United States, beginning with that of Kay and Simmons. Following this are three papers by Ohio State University workers, including one in which the properties of corrugated surfaces are investigated in order to determine requirements on corrugation density and tooth thickness. Useful insight into corrugated horn operation when groove depth is a quarter wavelength is given in the final paper of this group, that by Knop and Wiesenfarth. The authors of this paper have noted an error in column 5 of Table I. The last five values of *D*, the *E* plane edge taper, should read 37.93, 45.02, 49.85, 53.66, and 57.41 dB, respectively. Additional papers relating to work carried out in the United States will be found in [2]–[8].

Eight articles contributed by workers in Australia make up the second group of regional papers. I have taken the liberty of including Rumsey's paper in this group because of its relevance to, and Professor Rumsey's close association with, the Australian work in 1965. Following the Minnett and Thomas paper (the eighth in this part) describing the synthesis of cylindrical hybrid modes that match the focal plane fields of a paraboloidal reflector are three papers describing practical applications of hybrid mode corrugated feeds (Vu and Vu, Thomas, and Vu and Hien). The last two of the eight papers are by Thomas, and deal with bandwidth and mode generation in corrugated cylindrical guide. Comprehensive analyses of focal region fields and of the performance of hybrid mode feeds in paraboloids are given in [9]–[11].

A great deal of research into corrugated horns has been done in the United Kingdom by Clarricoats and his colleagues at Queen Mary College. It is represented here by the next group of six papers. The first two are brief analyses of cylindrical and spherical hybrid modes in, respectively, a corrugated round waveguide and a corrugated conical horn. Radiation by a wide-flare scalar horn and by a lens-corrected scalar horn are treated in the next two papers, and are followed by a short article discussing near field radiation characteristics. The last of the six is a long, two-part paper by Clarricoats and Saha in which a comprehensive theoretical treatment of propagation and radiation by corrugated feeds is given. The authors point out the similarity between the balanced hybrid modes in a corrugated feed and those in optical fiber waveguides. They make the interesting comment that vertebrates and insects evolved a balanced hybrid mode of operation in their retinal receptor system many millions of years ago! Additional relevant material will be found in [12]–[18].

The fourth regional group comprises three papers by workers at the Technological University of Eindhoven in The Netherlands. The first two, by Jeuken and by Jeuken and Lambrechtse, compare experimental results with theory for narrow- and wide-flare-angle corrugated horns, respectively. The third consists of a detailed analysis of the operation of Kay's scalar feed by Jensen *et al.* Other Dutch work is reported in [19]–[22].

The final regional grouping consists of four papers by Narasimhan and his co-workers at the Indian Institute of Technology, Madras, India. In the first two, the authors again make use of a simplified, asymptotic solution (see Part II) for the spherical mode fields in a conical horn to obtain the gain and radiation patterns of corrugated horns, including those with wide flare angle. The third paper, by Narasimhan, is an analytical treatment of radiation from conical horns having arbitrary corrugation depth, provided only that this depth lies between one quarter and one half wavelength. The last paper describes a corrugated horn for phased array illumination. It contains closed form expressions for the gain and radiation patterns of such horns that are accurate enough for most engineering applications. Papers by the Indian researchers not included in this volume are listed in [23]–[26].

Supplemental articles of a miscellaneous nature will be found in [27]–[34].

References

[1] A. F. Kay, "The scalar feed," AFCRL Rep. 64-347, AD601609, Mar. 1964.

[2] W. F. Bahret and L. Peters, Jr., "Small-aperture, small-flare-angle corrugated horns," *IEEE Trans. Antennas Propagat.*, vol. AP-16, pp. 494–495, July 1968.

[3] G. W. Collins, "Multimode horns using corrugated surfaces," *IEEE G-AP Symp. Dig.*, pp. 125–127, 1971.

[4] D. Davis, "Corrugations improve monopulse feed horns," *Microwaves*, vol. 11, pp. 58–63, Apr. 1972.

[5] S. K. Buchmeyer, "Corrugations lock horns with poor beamshapes," *Microwaves*, vol. 12, pp. 44–49, Jan. 1973.

[6] T. Manwarren and A. Farrar, "Pattern shaping with hybrid mode corrugated horns," *IEEE Trans, Antennas Propagat.*, vol. AP-22, pp. 484–487, May 1974.

[7] R. Price, "High performance corrugated feed horn for the unattended earth terminal," *Comsat Tech. Rev.*, vol. 4, no. 2, pp. 283–302, Fall 1974.

[8] C. A. Mentzer, L. Peters, Jr., and F. B. Beck, "A corrugated horn antenna using *V*-shape corrugations," *IEEE Trans. Antennas Propagat.*, vol. AP-23, pp. 93–97, Jan. 1975.

[9] H. C. Minnett and B. MacA. Thomas, "Fields in the image space of symmetrical focussing reflectors," *Proc. Inst. Elec. Eng.*, vol. 115, pp. 1419–1430, Oct. 1968.

[10] B. MacA. Thomas, "Matching focal region fields with hybrid modes," *IEEE Trans. Antennas Propagat.*, vol. AP-18, pp. 404–405, May 1970.

[11] ——, "Theoretical performance of prime-focus paraboloids using cylindrical hybrid-mode feeds," *Proc. Inst. Elec. Eng.*, vol. 118, pp. 1539–1549, Nov. 1971.

[12] P. J. B. Clarricoats, "Similarities in the electromagnetic behavior of optical waveguides and corrugated feeds," *Electron. Lett.*, vol. 6, pp. 178–180, Mar. 19, 1970.

[13] H. K. Au, "Hybrid modes in corrugated conical horns with narrow flare angle and arbitrary length," *Electron. Lett.*, vol. 6, pp. 769–771, Nov. 26, 1970.

[14] P. J. B. Clarricoats and L. M. Seng, "Propagation and radiation characteristics of corrugated horns," *Electron. Lett.*, vol. 9, pp. 7–8, Jan. 11, 1973.

[15] ——, "Influence of horn length on radiation pattern of oblique-flare-angle corrugated horn," *Electron. Lett.*, vol. 9, pp. 15–16, Jan. 11, 1973.

[16] P. J. B. Clarricoats and A. D. Olver, "Low attenuation in corrugated circular waveguides," *Electron. Lett.*, vol. 9, pp. 376–377, Aug. 9, 1973.

[17] A. D. Olver, P. J. B. Clarricoats, and S. L. Chong, "Experimental determination of attenuation in corrugated circular waveguides," *Electron. Lett.*, vol. 9, pp. 424–426, Sept. 6, 1973.

[18] A. M. B. Al-Hariri, A. D. Olver, and P. J. B. Clarricoats, "Low attenuation properties of corrugated rectangular waveguide," *Electron. Lett.*, vol. 10, pp. 304–305, July 25, 1974.

[19] M. E. J. Jeuken and J. S. Kikkert, "A broadband aperture antenna with a narrow beam," *Alta Frequenza*, vol. 38, pp. 270–276, Mar. 1969.

[20] M. E. J. Jeuken and H. P. J. M. Roumen, "Broadband conical horn antennas with small flare angles," presented at the URSI Symp. on Electromagnetic Wave Theory, Tbilisi, USSR, Sept. 1971.

[21] J. K. M. Jansen and M. E. J. Jeuken, "Surface waves in the corrugated conical horn," *Electron. Lett.*, vol. 8, pp. 342–344, June 29, 1972.

[22] M. E. J. Jeuken, "Corrugated conical horn antennas with small flare angles," *De Ingenieur*, vol. 84, pp. ET88–ET94, Aug. 1972.

[23] M. S. Narasimhan, "Eigenvalues of a class of spherical wave functions," *IEEE Trans. Antennas Propagat.*, vol. AP-21, pp. 8–14, Jan. 1973.

[24] M. S. Narasimhan and V. V. Rao, "Radiation characteristics of corrugated *E*-plane sectoral horns," *IEEE Trans. Antennas Propagat.*, vol. AP-21, pp. 320–327, May 1973.

[25] M. S. Narasimhan, "Eigenvalues of a class of spherical surface-wave modes in corrugated conical horns," *IEEE Trans. Antennas Propagat.*, vol. AP-22, pp. 122–123, Jan. 1974.

[26] M. S. Narasimhan and V. V. Rao, "Radiation from wide-flare corrugated *E*-plane sectoral horns," *IEEE Trans. Antennas Propagat.*, vol. AP-22, pp. 603–608, July 1974.

[27] G. H. Bryant, "Propagation in corrugated waveguides," *Proc. Inst. Elec. Eng.*, vol. 116, pp. 203–213, Feb. 1969.
[28] D. B. Booker and P. A. McInnes, "Computer-predicted performance of corrugated conical feeds using experimental primary radiation patterns," *Electron. Lett.*, vol. 6, pp. 18–20, Jan. 8, 1970.
[29] M .J. Al-Hakkak and Y. T. Lo, "Circular waveguides with anistropic walls," *Electron. Lett.*, vol. 6, pp. 786–789, Nov. 26, 1970.
[30] R. Baldwin and P. A. McInnes, "Attenuation in corrugated rectangular waveguides," *Electron. Lett.*, vol. 7, pp. 771–772, Dec. 30, 1971.
[31] Z. Frank, "Very wideband corrugated horns," *Electron. Lett.*, vol. 11, pp. 131–133, Mar. 20, 1975.
[32] M. S. Narasimhan and Y. B. Malla, "Paraboloidal-reflector illumination with conical scalar horns," *Electron. Lett.*, vol. 8, pp. 111–112, Mar. 9, 1972.
[33] M. J. Al-Hakkak, "Dielectric loading of corrugated waveguide," *Electron. Lett.*, vol. 8, pp. 179–180, Apr. 6, 1972.
[34] Y. Takeichi, T. Hashimoto, and F. Takeda, "The ring-loaded corrugated waveguide," *IEEE Trans. Microwave Theory Tech.*, vol. MTT-19, pp. 947–950, Dec. 1971.

THE SCALAR FEED - A HIGH-PERFORMANCE FEED FOR LARGE PARABOLOID REFLECTORS

By A. J. Simmons and A. F. Kay

An ideal feed horn for paraboloid reflectors for many applications is one which combines low spillover, nearly uniform aperture illumination, equal E and H plane patterns, and wide frequency bandwidth, as well as providing a well defined center of phase. This paper describes a feed which is closer to these ideal characteristics than is the simple feed horn so often used.

In an attempt to first reduce spillover, we started, some years ago, by adding large conical shields about the aperture of small horns. While these shields had the desired effect in the H-plane, the beam in the E-plane was much wider than in the H-plane and had high sidelobes. These effects were attributed to the excitation of the rim of the horn in the E-plane because the amplitude taper in this plane is very slight. The apparent spurious sources at the edge of the aperture distort the desired main beam and cause the high sidelobes.

It was reasoned that if the same boundary conditions could be obtained inside the horn in the E and H planes, the field would have the same pattern in both planes. A metallic surface corrugated with many closely-spaced parallel, transverse grooves presents a reactive boundary which approaches the same boundary condition for TM (Transverse Magnetic) and TE (Transverse Electric) waves at grazing incidence. If the grooves are made deep enough so that the surface reactance is capacitive, surface waves cannot be supported. A wide-flare horn lined with such a reactive surface thus has the same boundary conditions for both polarizations. (Thus the name "Scalar" feed). We have studied many versions of such horns and have found that they do indeed have essentially the same pattern for both E and H planes. Such a horn is shown in Figure 1.

The characteristics of these large horns is that the radiated energy is confined to the angular sector determined by the horn flare angle rather than by the aperture size in wavelengths, as is the case for a conventional diffraction-limited horn, and the beamwidth is constant over a wide frequency band. The frequency limitation at present appears to be the waveguide excitation at the throat. By use of ridge-waveguide excitation, bandwidths approaching 2:1 have been obtained.

Another desirable feature, nearly uniform illumination, may also be approached with the scalar feed, although only at the expense of making the horn very large. The larger the shield, the more rapidly does the field drop off at the edges of the horn pattern, and the more nearly uniform is the illumination for a given amount of spillover. Phase center measurements over a 2:1 band have been performed on several scalar feeds. These horns were found to have a true center of phase, located near the throat, to within

---

A. J. Simmons and A. F. Kay are with TRG, Incorporated, a Subsidiary of Control Data Corporation, East Boston, Massachusetts, U. S. A.

Reprinted with permission from *Design and Construction of Large Steerable Aerials*, IEE Conf. Publ. 21, 1966, pp. 213–217.

the accuracy of measurement (approximately $\pm 10^o$). Furthermore, phase centers for E and H planes coincided.

Scalar feeds may be characterized by the angle of the conical shield, θ_f, which is defined as the total included angle of the cone, and by the slant length of the corrugated shield. The grooves in the latter are spaced approximately one-half wavelength apart at the highest frequency of operation, and we usually express the slant length in terms of the number of grooves. Typical beamwidth data versus frequency for various flare angles and for 5-groove feeds are shown in Figure 2, for various values of the cone angle. Note that for values of θ_f of 140° and less, the 10db width is quite constant with frequency and is approximately three-fourths of the flare angle. For θ_f greater than 140° the control of the beamwidth by the cone is not as great as for $\theta_f \leq 140^o$.

Also shown on Figure 2 is the variation in beamwidth of a typical diffraction-limited aperture chosen to have the same 10db width as the $\theta_f = 140^o$ horn in midband. The relative constancy of beamwidth for the Scalar feed may be observed.

A typical pattern for a 5-groove, $\theta_f = 140^o$ feed is shown in Figure 3, compared with a conventional horn pattern. This pattern shows the typical rapid drop-off at wide angles and absence of measurable sidelobes (sidelobes at least 30db down). The same pattern is obtained for both polarizations, in both E and H planes, and over the band of the horn, making the horn suitable for operation with dual polarization. The feed shown in Figure 1 for example is dual-polarized operating over a 1.3:1 band with voltage-standing-wave-ratio less than 1.2:1 for both polarizations and isolation between polarizations in excess of 40db.

Because of the difficulty of making accurate and meaningful measurements of antenna efficiency and noise temperature, particularly for large antennas with which the Scalar feed is useful, we have calculated these quantities, and have compared results using a typical diffraction-limited feed at a single frequency with a typical Scalar feed. The Scalar feed performance may of course be optimized over a wide band, because of the relative invariance with frequency of its performance. The results of two calculations are shown in Table 1, one being for a 10db taper (high-efficiency case) and the other for a 20db taper (low noise temperature case).

The results indicate that because of the lower spillover and slightly more optimum illumination, the gain with the Scalar feed should be 0.6 to 0.8db higher than that obtained with a standard feed, and the noise temperature may be improved by a factor of 3 in some cases.

Measurements to support these theoretical results are sparse. A 5GHz low-noise feed installed in the 85 foot diameter steerable paraboloid at the National Radio Astronomy Observatory in West Virginia, U.S.A. was estimated to give 60% aperture efficiency, when the data was corrected for dish surface tolerance errors, which were about 6mm rms. The antenna excess noise temperature was 12^oK, with about one-half of this contribution estimated to be attributable to feed spillover. These measurements agree reasonably well with the low-noise calculation in Table 1.

A number of these feeds have been built for application to radio-astronomy and tropospheric scatter communication. The design procedure is to pick the flare angle, θ_f to give the desired illumination taper and then to use as large a shield as is economically feasible, without excessive aperture blocking. Because of the large size of the feed, it is useful only for illuminating large paraboloids (greater than 30λ diameter). Scalar feeds have been built with aperture dimensions ranging from 2.5 to 10 wavelengths, and over the frequency range from 500MHz to 300GHz.

The design of these feeds has evolved over a period of several years on an empirical basis. In that time, optimization of throat diameter for best bandwidth and VSWR, optimization of groove depth and spacing, the effects of increasing or decreasing the number of grooves, and matching and pressurizing techniques have been studied. In addition, the design of dual-mode feeders to operate with the Scalar feed has been carried out. We are at present engaged in a theoretical study of the fields within the feed horn and hope to have a better theoretical understanding of its operation shortly.

We would like to acknowledge with gratitude the support of the United States Air Force Cambridge Research Laboratory in the early stages of this development under contract AF19(604)-8057.

TABLE 1
Comparison of Standard and Scalar Feed

	A		B	
	10db Taper (high efficiency)		20db Taper (low noise)	
	Scalar Feed	Standard Feed	Scalar Feed	Standard Feed
Spillover loss, including back lobe	4.7%	16.65%	0.7%	6.0%
Ohmic loss and feed support scattering	1.0%	1.0%	1.0%	1.0%
Illumination efficiency, compared to uniform illumination	81.0%	77.3%	63.5%	58.7%
Net aperture efficiency assuming a perfect reflector	76.5%	63.5%	62.5%	54.5%
Antenna excess noise temperature				
a) at zenith	16°K	28°K	4.7°K	5.7°K
b) near horizon	9.7°K	25°K	4.0°K	12°K

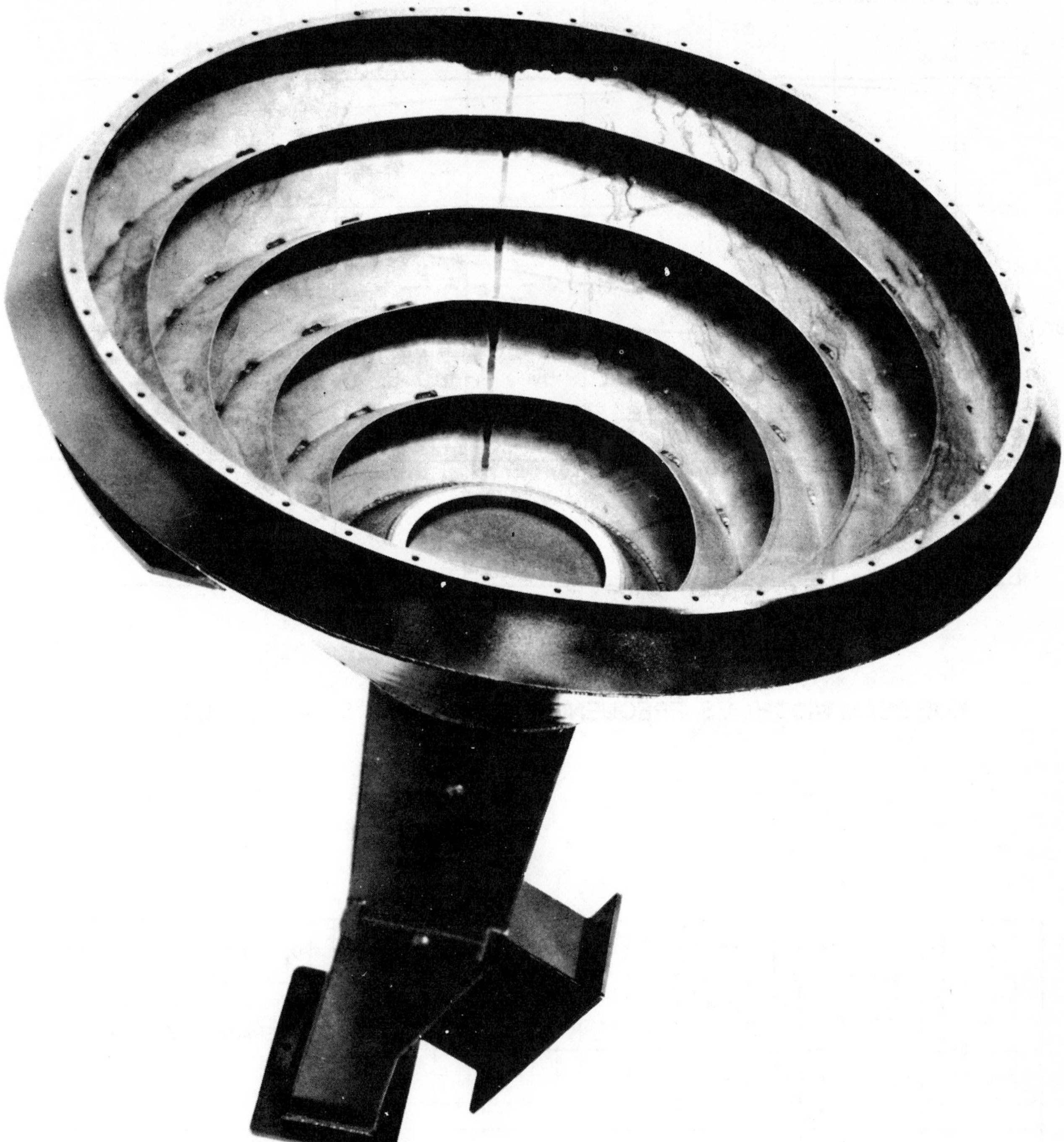

FIGURE 1

TYPICAL SCALAR FEED

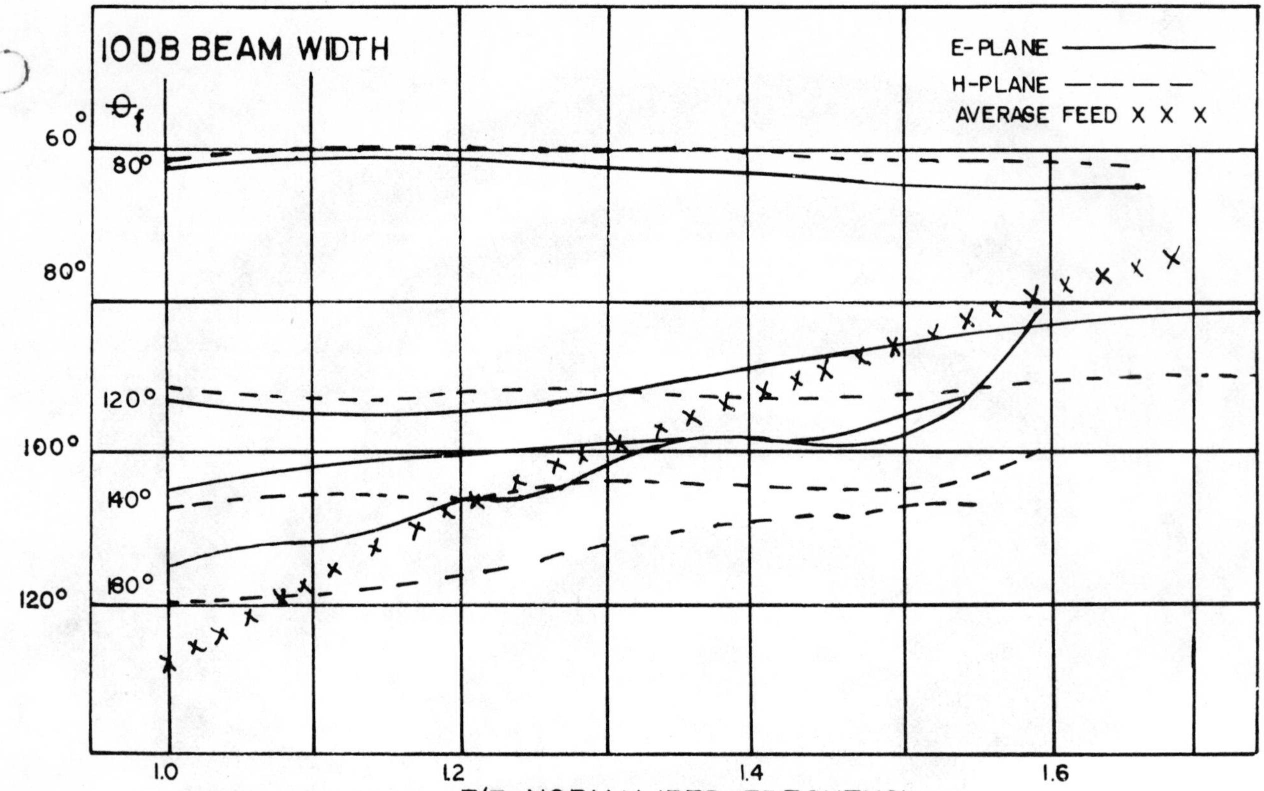

F/F$_L$ NORMALIZED FREQUENCY

FIG 2

10DB BEAM WIDTH VS FREQUENCY FOR VARIOUS SCALAR FEEDS

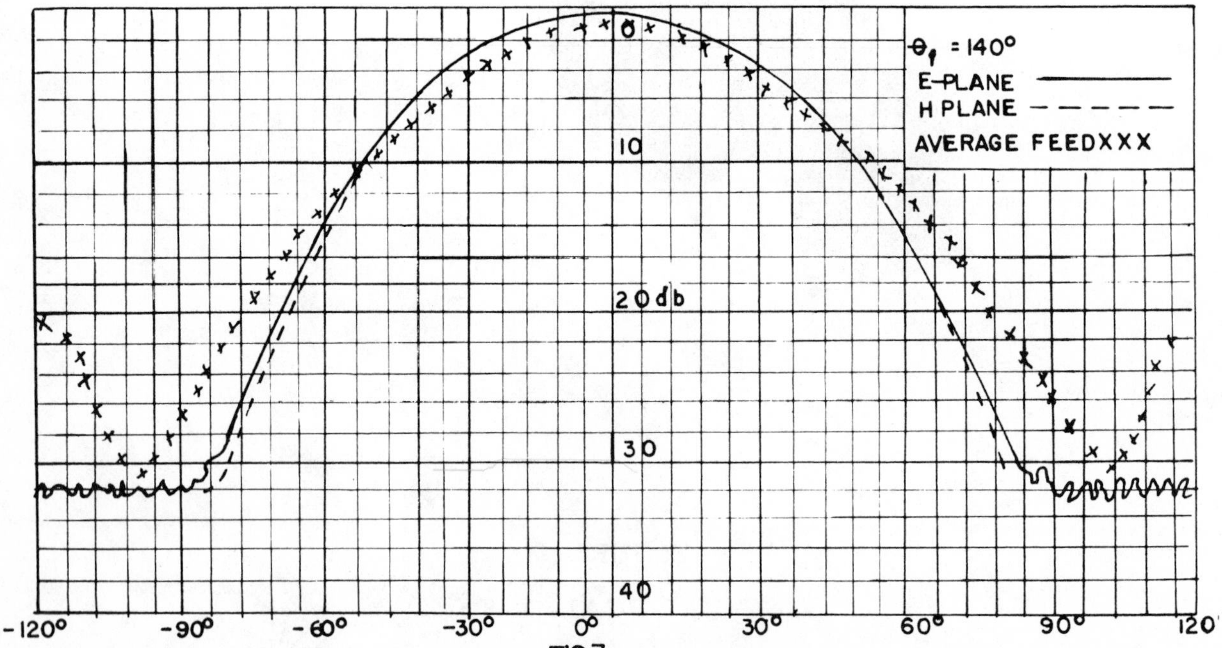

FIG3

TYPICAL PATTERN OF SCALAR FEED COMPARED TO AVERAGE FEED

Modifications of Horn Antennas for Low Sidelobe Levels

R. E. LAWRIE AND L. PETERS, JR., SENIOR MEMBER, IEEE

Abstract—**A modified horn antenna with significantly reduced backlobes over nearly a two-to-one frequency band is discussed. This horn has a well-defined phase center at its apex, and the E- and H-plane patterns are nearly identical over the frequency band if the horn has a square (or circular) aperture. Horns considered cover a wide range of flare angles and include one which fits the criterion for the optimum horn at the lower end of the operating frequency band. The VSWR is less than 1.2 over most of the frequency band.**

INTRODUCTION

IT IS WELL KNOWN that in the region of the main beam and first few sidelobes the radiation pattern of a horn antenna may be computed from its aperture distribution. However, outside this region energy diffracted at the edges of the horn determines the radiated field [1] and the radiation pattern can be computed with more accuracy by other means. First-order edge diffraction calculations, which are adequate for almost any horn for aspect angles within the included horn angle, are easy to make, requiring at most an adequate table of Fresnel Integrals.

Manuscript received March 1, 1966; revised May 15, 1966. The work reported here was supported in part by Contract AF 30(602)-3269 between Air Force Systems Command, Griffiss Air Force Base, New York, and The Ohio State University Research Foundation, Columbus, Ohio.

The authors are with the Antenna Laboratory, The Ohio State University, Columbus, Ohio.

In a pyramidal horn antenna the electric field vector is perpendicular to one pair of aperture edges, designated as E-plane edges. It has been shown that most of the backlobe structure of a pyramidal horn results from energy diffracted by these edges. In fact, the entire E-plane pattern of a particular horn antenna has been calculated accurately by treating the diffraction from such edges as well as the geometrical optics field [2].

The pertinent first-order radiating mechanisms [2], [3] for the E- and H-plane horn geometries are illustrated in Fig. 1. Higher order mechanisms [4] caused by multiple reflections of energy diffracted by the edge toward the opposite horn wall become significant for aspects outside the included angle of the horn when the horn has a small aperture. The far-field patterns of the

Reprinted from *IEEE Trans. Antennas Propagat.*, vol. AP-14, pp. 605–610, Sept. 1966.

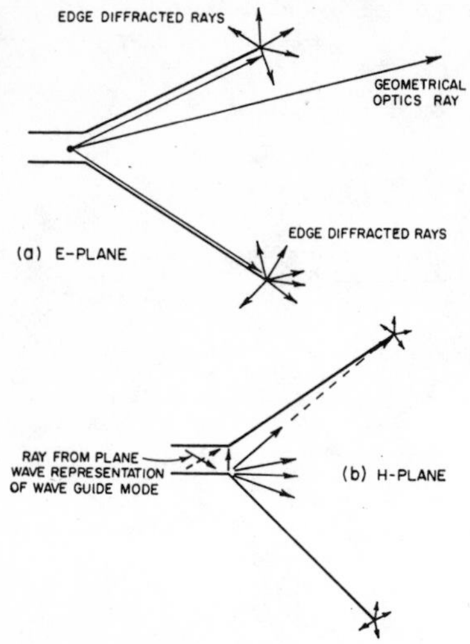

Fig. 1. Radiating mechanisms for horn antennas.

horn antenna can be obtained by summing the computed fields of these individual radiating mechanisms.

Studies of this type have shown that the principal source of backlobes is the field caused by edge diffraction in the E-plane. Furthermore, the fields caused by diffractions at the E-plane edges are the source of the irregularities often noted in the E-plane patterns of horn antennas. Diffracted fields of the H-plane walls do not yield a significant contribution to the E-plane radiation pattern of horn antennas. Consequently the reduction of the E-plane edge illumination would simultaneously reduce the backlobes and eliminate the irregularities in the E-plane pattern. The entire E- and H-plane patterns [2], [3], [4] of horn antennas have been calculated accurately without the intermediate step of determining an aperture distribution.

This paper describes two methods of reducing the sidelobes and backlobe levels of a horn by controlling the illumination of the E-plane edges. The basic approach is to prevent illumination of the E-plane edges by electrically modifying the walls of the horn having an E-plane edge as an element. The first modification is achieved by introducing a series of quarter-wavelength-deep choke slots into the walls of the horn near the aperture. The second modification is achieved by introducing a reactive surface in the form of a cutoff corrugated surface at the walls of the horn. Of course the horn walls must be thick enough initially to accept these modifications. The second modification may also be used to radiate a circularly polarized wave by placing corrugations in the orthogonal walls. When such a horn is excited with a circularly polarized signal, it would yield an antenna with a good axial ratio for angles equal to or less than the horn angle. The same principle may be applied to the circular horn simply by extending the corrugations around the wall of the horn.

The Choke-Slot Horn

Sciambi and Foldes [5] have suggested the use of choke slots to shield edges and thus reduce radiation leakage around these edges. This technique has been applied by Peters and Rudduck [6] who obtained a backlobe reduction of 24 dB using a 6-slot frame and by Kritikos et al. [7] who obtained a reduction of 21 dB using 2 slots. Kay [8] developed a circular horn with bent-choke slots separated by approximately 0.31λ (which he designated as the scalar feed) with backlobes more than 30 dB below pattern maximum.

The choke-slot horn described in this paper was constructed with an aperture 3.5 inches square and with a flare angle of 92°. At 10 GHz the slots are $\frac{3}{8}$-wavelength-deep with a spacing of 6 slots per wavelength. Six slots were used with the spacing between slots the same as the width of the slots. It is necessary to have an unmodified antenna for comparative measurements. With the choke-slot horn this is easily and accurately obtained by placing strips of aluminum tape over the slots and painting the tape with silver paint. The behavior of the backlobe level of the antenna relative to the maximum is of primary interest. These data, plotted as a function of frequency in Fig. 2, are compared to the relative backlobe level of the control horn. The lowest frequency used was 6.6 GHz; the choke depth at that frequency is $\lambda/4$.

The effect of the chokes on the main lobe is compared with the control antenna in Fig. 3, where beamwidth is plotted vs. frequency. It is felt that due to irregularities in the pattern of the control horn at the higher frequencies, the 6-dB beamwidth is a more representative parameter than the 3-dB beamwidth. It has been shown [2], [3] that the irregularities in the E-plane patterns of horn antennas are caused by the radiating mechanisms illustrated in Fig. 1.

Within its included angle the magnitude of the radiation field of a horn antenna depends upon the relative phase of the far fields of the different radiating mechanisms. Thus, the introduction of choke slots can result in a decrease or an increase in the axial radiation field and, consequently, the on-axis gain depending on whether the edge diffracted fields are more nearly in-phase or out of phase with the geometrical optics field. Furthermore, any loss due to currents flowing on the walls of the horn is probably reduced since the fields are now detached from the surface, resulting in increased efficiency.

The effectiveness of the chokes in rejecting energy from the E-plane walls can also be seen by probing the 3.5 inch aperture in both the E- and H-planes. The aperture distribution for the control horn is shown in Fig. 4 and may be compared with that of the choked horn shown in Fig. 5. The aperture distributions shown were obtained at 7.1 GHz. The chokes produce a symmetrical distribution in the E- and H-planes; this is substantially

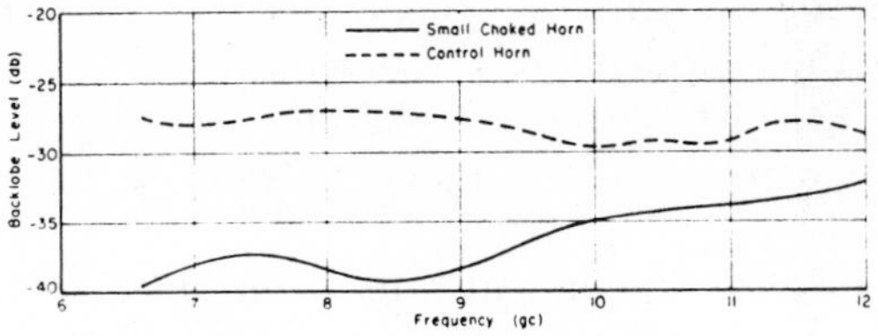

Fig. 2. Ratio of backlobe to mainlobe level of the choke slot horn and the control horn.

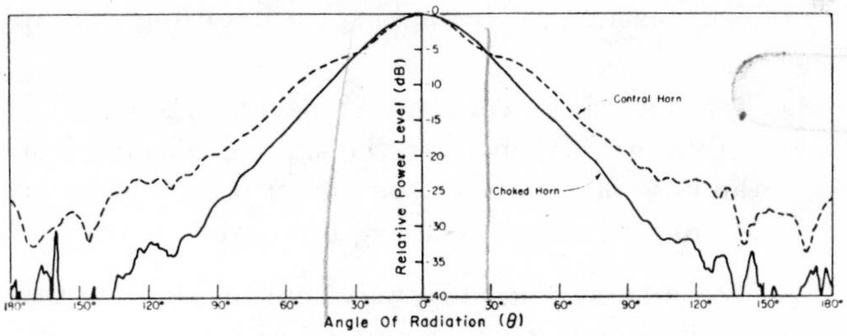

Fig. 6. Normalized E-plane patterns of the control horn and the choke slot horn at 6.6 GHz.

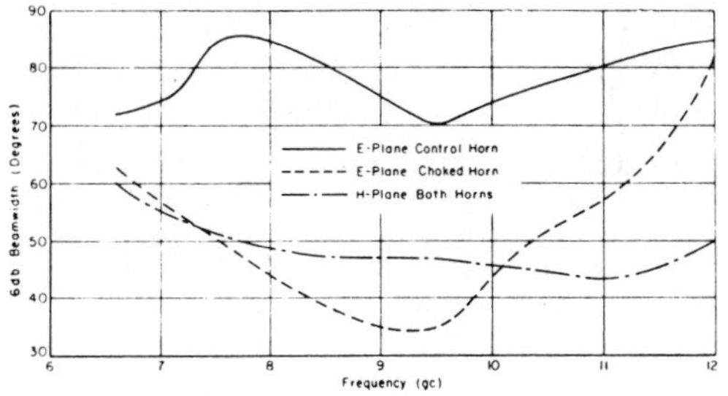

Fig. 3. 6-dB beamwidths of the choke slot horn and control horn.

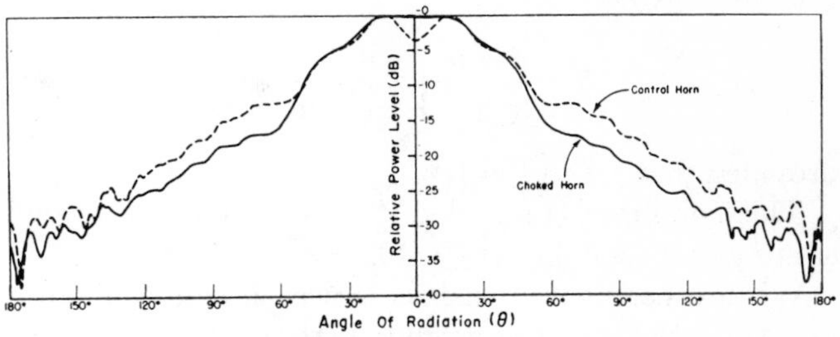

Fig. 7. Normalized E-plane patterns of the control horn and the choke slot horn at 12.0 GHz.

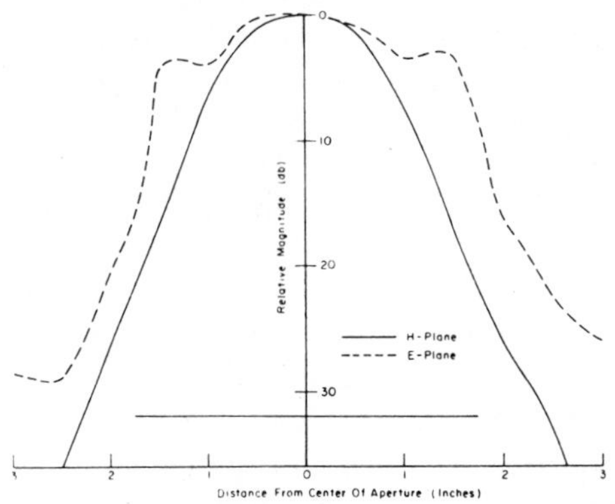

Fig. 4. Aperture field distribution of the control horn at 7.1 GHz.

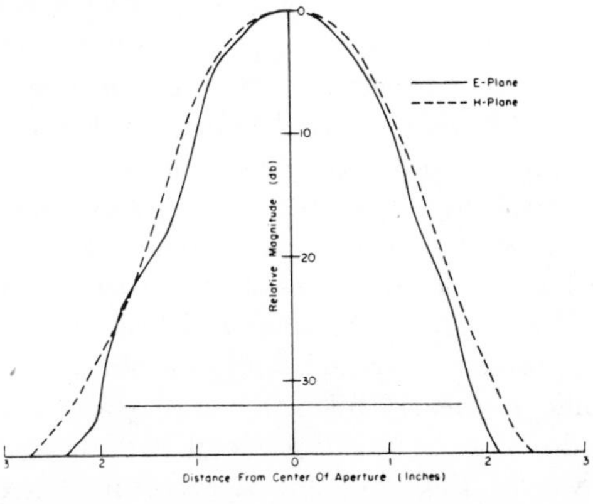

Fig. 5. Aperture field distribution of the choke slot horn at 7.1 GHz.

the same as the H-plane distribution of the control horn.

Figures 6 and 7 compare the E-plane pattern of the control horn and the choked horn at 6.6 GHz and 12.0 GHz, respectively. Note that at 12.0 GHz the main beam of the control horn has begun to split into two lobes. This splitting represents a limitation on the bandwidth of the horn. Splitting of the main beam of the choked horn does not occur at 12.0 GHz. Thus the splitting may be attributed to edge effects which have been eliminated by the choke slots.

The Corrugated Horn

Widely spaced choke slots as used in the choke-slot antenna yield results which are frequency sensitive. Consider two such slots in a planar surface which are separated by a distance S and which are illuminated by a wave propagating over the surface. The phase of the signal scattered by one slot relative to the phase of the signal scattered by the other slot is

$$kS \cos \theta \equiv \frac{\omega}{v} S \cos \theta$$

where ω is the angular frequency. This frequency dependent mechanism may be avoided by reducing the spacing between the slots.

If the spacing between choke slots is reduced until there are 10 or more slots per wavelength these yield a surface that may be defined as a corrugated surface. A horn with such a surface is shown in Fig. 8.

The analysis of an infinite corrugated surface may be

simplified considerably by making the following assumptions.

1) The slot walls (teeth) are vanishingly thin.
2) Only the TEM mode in the slots is reflected from the base of the slots. The higher order modes are attenuated before reaching the base.

The second assumption is equivalent to requiring that the slot width, g, be small compared with both the free-space wavelength and the slot depth d. For such a surface, results obtained by Elliott [9] can be used to show that the reactance of the surface is given to a good approximation by

$$X = \frac{g}{g+t}\sqrt{\frac{\mu}{\epsilon}} \tan k_0 d \tag{1}$$

provided that $g/(g+t) \approx 1$.

This condition is satisfied if $t \leq g/10$ and the second assumption is valid for $g \leq \lambda/10$.

When a corrugated surface is used in the walls of a horn in order to prevent illumination of the E-plane edges the surface reactance must be capacitive so that the surface will not support a surface wave. Thus, from (1), we require $\lambda/4 < d < \lambda/2$. Hurd [10] has shown that the cutoff depth d_c depends to some extent on the slot width g. However, curves given by Hurd indicate that for $g \leq \lambda/10$ the cutoff region is approximately $\lambda/4 < d < \lambda/2$.

A small corrugated horn was constructed with a 3.5 inch square aperture and a flare angle of 50° having an internal E-plane wall structure of many slots per wavelength (about 2.5 times that of the choked horn, or 15 per wavelength at 10 GHz). This particular horn satisfies the optimum horn condition at the lower end of its frequency range, namely at 8.0 GHz.

The comparison antenna for this horn is again the prototype covered with aluminum tape and paint. The curves of backlobe level vs. frequency for both antennas are shown in Fig. 9.

Figure 10 shows the 3-dB beamwidth vs. frequency curves of the corrugated horn and the control horn. The two are similar but displaced by about 4.2°. In contrast with the choked horn, the corrugations have resulted in an increase in beamwidth. The reason for this increased beamwidth has been discussed previously in this paper and this reason may be emphasized by considering the patterns of Fig. 11. The on-axis far fields of the geometrical ray and the edge rays are nearly in-phase as may be seen from the pronounced on-axis maximum of the control horn E-plane pattern for this geometry. The corrugations shield the edges and reduce the on-axis contribution from edge diffraction and consequently lower the axial radiated field resulting in a lower directivity and an increase in beamwidth. If the 10-dB beamwidth has been plotted in Fig. 11 the corrugated horn would have the lower beamwidth, since the edge diffracted fields which are lower for the corrugated horn are the sole contributors to the portion of the pattern outside the included angle of the horn.

The E-plane pattern of the small corrugated horn superimposed on the E-plane pattern of the control horn is shown in Fig. 11.

The E- and H-plane patterns of the small corrugated horn are nearly identical to that of Fig. 11 over the frequency band from 8 to 14 GHz. Thus it is suggested that the main beam in the E-plane can be obtained from known H-plane patterns of horn antennas [11]. This is further confirmed by the patterns of the large corrugated horn discussed below. Furthermore, there is a significant increase in the bandwidth of the corrugated horn in comparison to the bandwidth of the choked horn as may be seen by comparing Figs. 3 and 10.

A larger corrugated horn was constructed having a flare angle of 34°, a slant height of 15.85 inches, and a 9.7 inch square aperture. The corrugated surface is machined into the proper walls from within 1 inch of the throat to the mouth. The large control horn is a thick-edged horn having the same interior dimensions. The E-plane pattern of the large control horn and the large corrugated horn are shown in Fig. 12. The H-plane patterns of the large corrugated horn are nearly identical to that of the large control horn and are not shown.

Since the fields of the edge diffracted rays in the H-plane shown in Fig. 1(b) are small compared to the fields of the rays diffracted by the wedge at the throat of the horn, the phase center in the H-plane is near the throat of the horn. The presence of the cutoff corrugated surface reduces the direct illumination of the edges in the E-plane and, consequently, radiating mechanisms are quite similar to those of the H-plane horn of Fig. 1(b). Consequently, it is suggested that the phase centers in the E- and H-planes coincide.

In order to demonstrate that the E-plane phase center is at the same point, a lens was designed for the mouth of the large horn based on the assumption of coincident phase centers. The measured E-plane pattern for the horn-lens system is shown in Fig. 13. With the lens in place, the aperture distribution should have a cosine amplitude variation and uniform phase distribution.

The measured first null is at least 12 dB below the maximum of the first sidelobe. If the phase center had been at any point other than the assumed one, the uniform phase distribution would not have been obtained and the nulls would have been filled due to such a "phase error." For example, if the phase center had been displaced one wavelength along the axis toward the mouth of the horn (corresponding to a displacement of about 7 percent of the length of the horn), a phase error of approximately 30° would be obtained and the nulls would be nearly filled. Several points have been calculated for a uniform phase distribution and are also shown in Fig. 13. The agreement between the measured pattern and calculated points demonstrates that the phase centers for the E- and H-plane

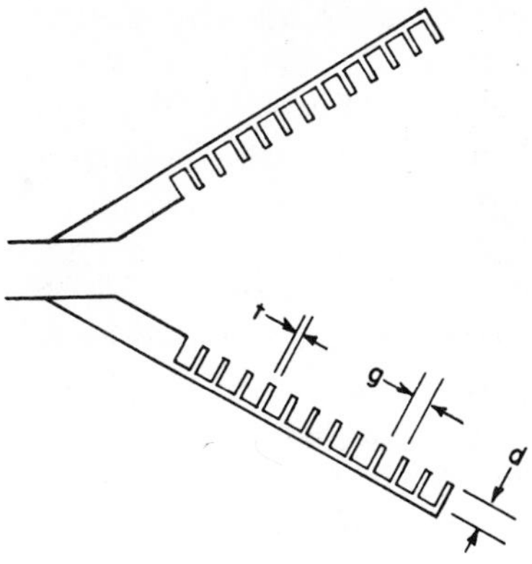

Fig. 8. The corrugated horn geometry.

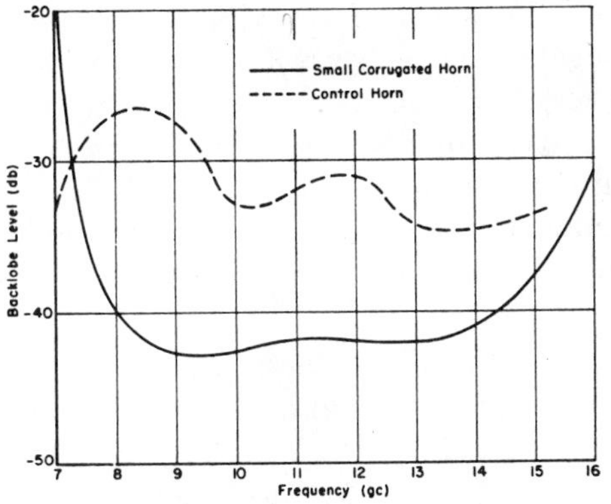

Fig. 9. Ratio of backlobe to mainlobe levels of the small corrugated horn and the control horn.

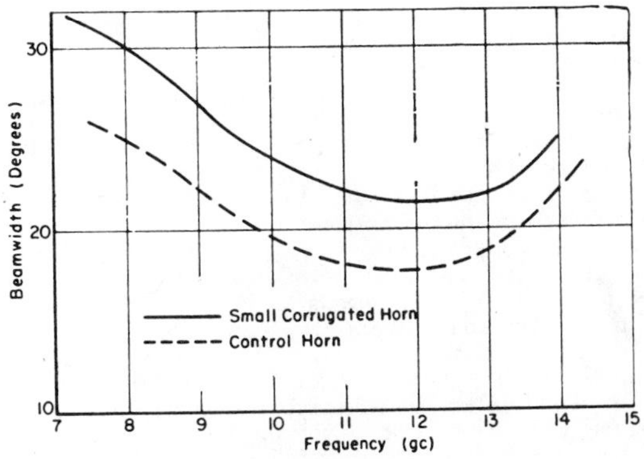

Fig. 10. 3-dB beamwidth of the small corrugated horn and the control horn.

D=3.5"

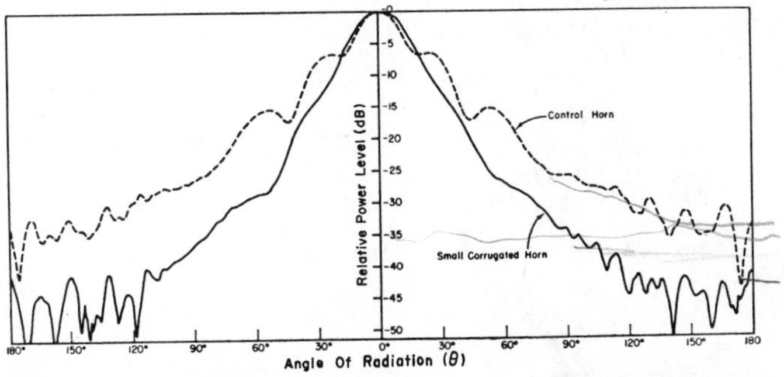

Fig. 11. Normalized E-plane patterns of the small corrugated horn and the control horn at 10 GHz.

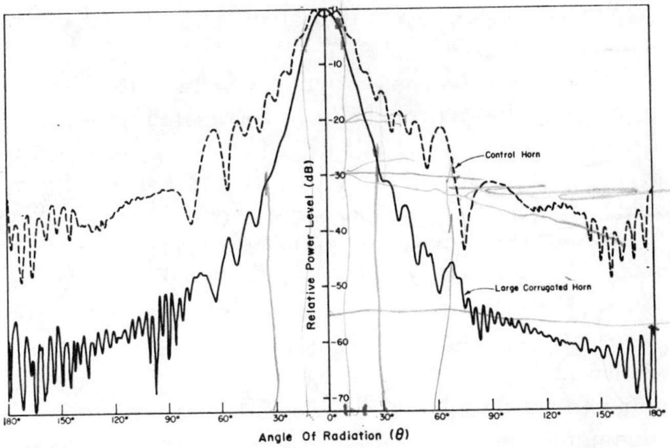

Fig. 12. Normalized E-plane patterns of the large corrugated horn and the control horn at 10 GHz.

9.7" aperture = D/λ = 12.32

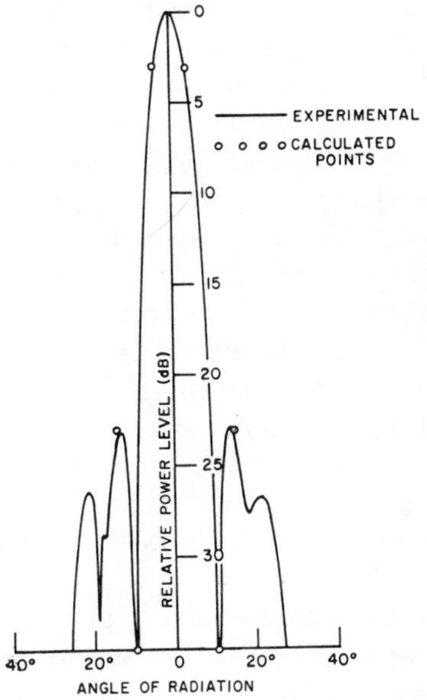

Fig. 13. E-plane pattern of the large corrugated horn with lens.

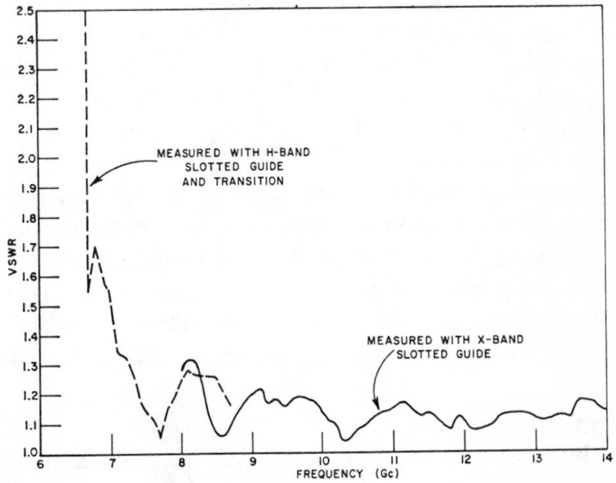

Fig. 14. VSWR of the large corrugated horn.

patterns coincide and are located at the throat of the horn.

The calculated directivity of the large control horn is 21.5 dB, while that of the large corrugated horn is 22.5 dB (measured gain = 22.35 dB). The change in directivity is caused by the reduction of the E-plane beamwidth and by the removal of the saddle in the E-plane pattern of the control horn. The saddle is attributed to edge effects. In other words, the fields diffracted by the edges of the control horn are not in-phase with the geometrical optics field resulting in the on-axis minimum shown in Fig. 12. These edge diffracted fields are significantly reduced and consequently the minimum is eliminated and the axial far field is increased by the use of the corrugated surface.

The backlobe of the large corrugated horn is 57 dB below the main beam. Thus it is 27 dB better than the control horn.

The presence of the corrugations close to the waveguide feed can affect the impedance of the horn. However, a low VSWR can be obtained over a broadband provided the corrugations are introduced at a small distance away from the waveguide feed. The measured VSWR of the large corrugated horn, with the corrugations beginning 2.5 inches from the waveguide feed, is shown in Fig. 14. Since the VSWR over the frequency band is reasonably low, the corrugated horn may be used in high power systems. It is conceivable that the narrow gaps of the corrugated surface might cause corona or other breakdown phenomena. However, the large corrugated horn described here has been energized by a source with 20 kW of peak power at 10 GHz and no evidence of any such breakdown phenomena has been noted.

Initial measurements of the E-plane pattern of the large corrugated horn indicated severe interference effects throughout the back hemisphere. It was found that the primary source of the interfering signals was leakage through the waveguide joints and components, i.e., detector, attenuator. A rearrangement of components and the judicious application of aluminum tape and metallic paint greatly reduced the interference. The remaining interference is attributed to scattering from various structures in the vicinity of the pattern range.

Conclusions

The use of choke slots or a corrugated structure in the walls of a horn antenna have been demonstrated to be effective methods of reducing the backlobe level of the horn. The use of corrugated surfaces produces a greater improvement than the choke slots. The attainable reduction in backlobe level is limited by diffraction from the wedge formed by the waveguide and the wall of the horn to the edge of the opposite wall, similar to the diffraction illustrated in Fig. 1(b) for the H-plane. It was found that the useable bandwidth of the modified horns is at least as great as the bandwidth of the transmission line feeding the horn.

The type of modified horns discussed in this paper may find applications such as use in pattern ranges and radar cross section ranges. As Kay [8] notes, the application of this type of antenna as a feed will result in the good low-temperature performance required in many modern systems, and will also be useful in the reduction of interference between various systems. Since its phase center is a well defined single point, the corrugated horn should also find application for lens and reflector antenna systems. One can envision further uses for cut-off corrugated surfaces, such as application to screening fences, for the reduction of interference and ground clutter in radar systems. Furthermore, corrugated surfaces might find application in the isolation of an antenna from surrounding surfaces, such as an air frame; however, such applications require further study.

References

[1] L. Peters, Jr., and R. C. Rudduck, "RFI reduction by control of antenna sidelobes," *IEEE Trans. on Electromagnetic Compatibility*, vol. EMC-6, pp. 1–11, January 1964.

[2] P. M. Russo, R. C. Rudduck, and L. Peters, Jr., "A method for computing *E*-plane patterns of horn antennas," *IEEE Trans. on Antennas and Propagation*, vol. AP-13, pp. 219–229, March 1965.

[3] J. S. Yu and R. C. Rudduck, "The H-plane radiation pattern of horn antennas," Antenna Laboratory, The Ohio State University Research Foundation, Columbus, Rept. 1767-5, May 1965, prepared under Contract AF 30(602)-2711 for Rome Air Development Center, New York.

[4] J. S. Yu, R. C. Rudduck, and L. Peters, Jr., "Comprehensive analysis for *E*-plane horn antennas by edge diffraction theory," *IEEE Trans. on Antennas and Propagation*, vol. AP-14, pp. 138–149, March 1966.

[5] A. F. Sciambi and P. Foldes, "A critique of advanced high performance antenna feed systems," RCA Missile and Surface Radar Division, Moorestown, N. J., 1964 (discussed in [7]).

[6] L. Peters, Jr., and R. C. Ruddick, "Application of electromagnetic absorbing materials as interference reduction techniques," Antenna Laboratory, The Ohio State University Research Foundation, Columbus, Rept. 1423-7, November 1963; prepared under Contract AF 30(602)-2711 for Rome Air Development Center, Air Research and Development Command, Griffiss AFB, New York.

[7] H. Kritikos, R. Dresp, and K. C. Lang, "Studies of antenna sidelobe reduction," Rome Air Development Center, Griffiss AFB, New York, Rept. RADC-TDR-64-355, vol. 1, October 1964.

[8] A. F. Kay, "The scalar feed," TRG Inc., East Boston, Mass., March 30, 1964, Sci. Rept. 5, prepared under Contract AF 19(604)-8057, Air Force Cambridge Research Laboratories, Office of Aerospace Research, USAF, Bedford, Mass.

[9] R. S. Elliott, "On the theory of corrugated plane surfaces," *IRE Trans. on Antennas and Propagation*, vol. AP-2, pp. 71–81, April 1954.

[10] R. A. Hurd, "The propagation of an electromagnetic wave along an infinite corrugated surface," *Canad. J. Phys.*, vol. 32, pp. 727–734, December 1954.

[11] D. R. Rhodes, "An experimental investigation of the radiation patterns of electromagnetic horn antennas," *Proc. IRE*, vol. 36, pp. 1101–1105, September 1948.

The Corrugated Horn as an Antenna Range Standard

ROSS CALDECOTT, C. A. MENTZER, AND
LEON PETERS, JR.

Abstract—**The corrugated horn discussed here is a valuable tool for use in microwave pattern ranges. It has the properties of concentrated energy in the main beam, low backlobes, high efficiency and almost monotonic amplitude, and phase radiation patterns which make the corrugated horn useful for a source antenna in a pattern range and also as a possible standard antenna for calibration purposes. A sample of the references that have dealt with the corrugated horn is given for the benefit of the reader [1]–[7].**

I. Properties of Corrugated Horn

Useful properties of the corrugated horn for an antenna range standard include: 1) nearly axially symmetric radiation patterns for a square or circular horn, 2) exceptionally low backlobe and sidelobes, 3) a well defined phase center, 4) nearly constant beamwidth over an octave bandwidth (with proper design), 5) circular polarization is obtainable over the main beam, 6) low loss, and 7) low VSWR. All of these properties have been experimentally verified.

The corrugated horn can be used to illuminate the region of space where the antenna (or scatterer) being studied is placed while producing minimal illumination in other directions. This is best illustrated by the concept of beam efficiency. Beam efficiency is defined here as

$$B = \frac{\left[\int_0^{2\pi}\int_0^{\theta} f(\theta,\phi)\,\sin\theta\,d\theta\,d\phi\right]}{\left[\int_0^{2\pi}\int_0^{\pi} f(\theta,\phi)\,\sin\theta\,d\theta\,d\phi\right]} \tag{1}$$

where $f(\theta,\phi)$ is the radiated power density and θ is the angle measured from the horn axis. The measured conical corrugated horn patterns for the E plane and the H plane are shown in Fig. 1(a). This horn is the "optimum" design [8] with a diameter of 3.4λ and a slant length of 3.9λ. Note the similarity of the two patterns to levels of below -25 dB and that the pattern is a monotonic function of the look angle. A series of additional patterns in planes 22.5°, 45°, and 67.5° from the E plane were measured and stored on the digital computer which is an integral part of our pattern range. The results of the integrations indicated in (1) are shown in Fig. 2. The measured cross polarized power is less than 1 percent of the total power. Similar measurements for a pyramidal horn gave the cross polarized power to be 3.17 percent. This lower cross polarized power is the principal advantage of the conical horn. The pyramidal corrugated horn is, however, easier to mass produce and can be fed by common rectangular waveguide components. The other parameters in Fig. 2 include the directivity, half-power beamwidth, and the (beam)

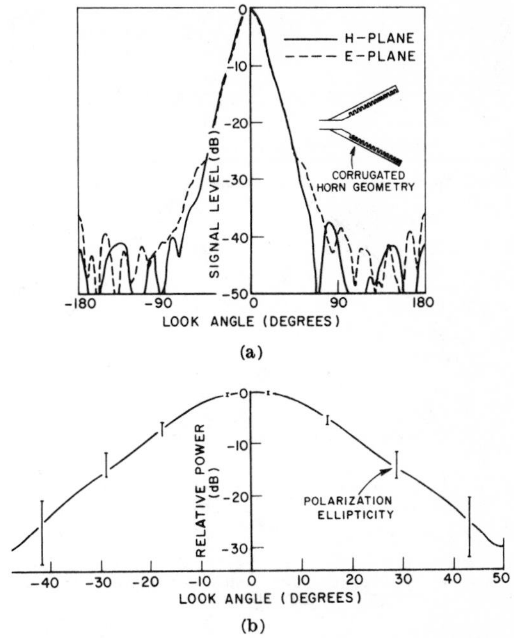

Fig. 1. Radiation patterns of conical corrugated horn. (a) Excited with linear polarization (3.7 GHz). (b) Excited with circular polarization (3.9 GHz).

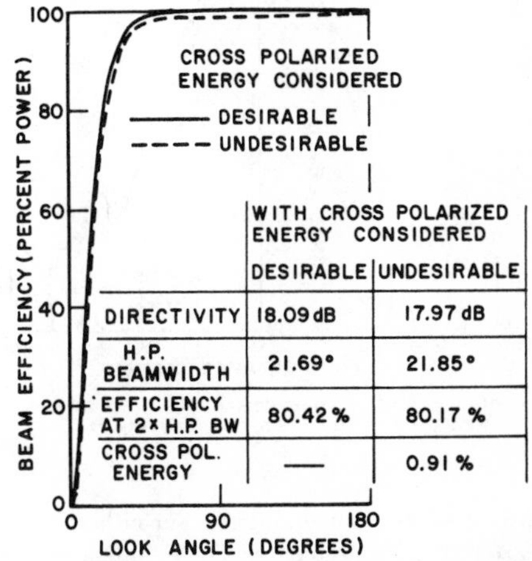

Fig. 2. Beam efficiency of conical corrugated horn (3.7 GHz).

efficiency at twice the half-power beamwidth.[1] It should be emphasized that the cross polarized power is radiated in the direction of the main beam. Any far-field scatterer removed 45° from the beam axis would have little influence on the results obtained when

Manuscript received October 4, 1972; revised January 29, 1973. This work was supported in part by Contract NAS1-10040 between National Aeronautics and Space Administration, Langley Research Center, and the Ohio State University Research Foundation.
The authors are with the ElectroScience Laboratory, Department of Electrical Engineering, Ohio State University, Columbus, Ohio 43212.

[1] The numbers shown on Fig. 2 indicate an accuracy to the second decimal. Even though the pattern measurements on which these numbers are based were made very carefully, these values should be rounded to the first decimal. The accuracy of the patterns in the vicinity of the main beam maximum are well within 0.1 dB accuracy. Larger errors could be tolerated at lower pattern levels because of the weighting introduced by the pattern in the various integrations. The integration process would tend to average out random errors and since the patterns were measured and recorded under control of a digital computer, smoothing procedures could be introduced and were used to further improve the accuracy.

Reprinted from *IEEE Trans. Antennas Propagat.*, vol. AP-21, pp. 562–564, July 1973.

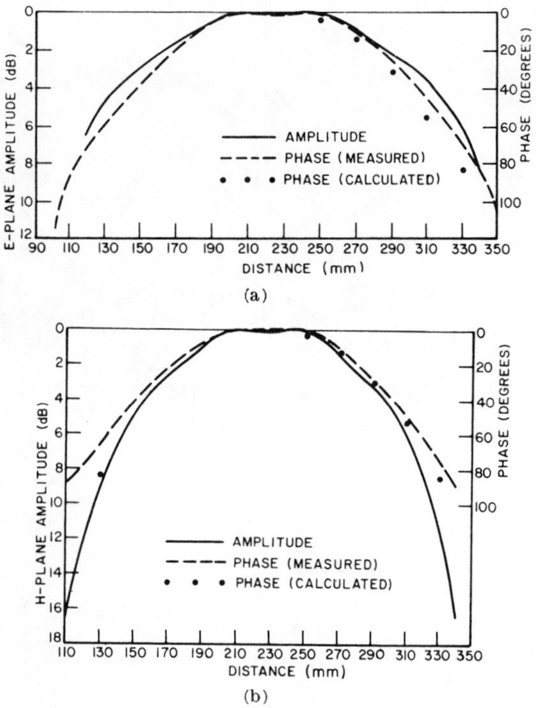

Fig. 3. Aperture distribution for conical corrugated horn. (a) E plane. (b) H Plane.

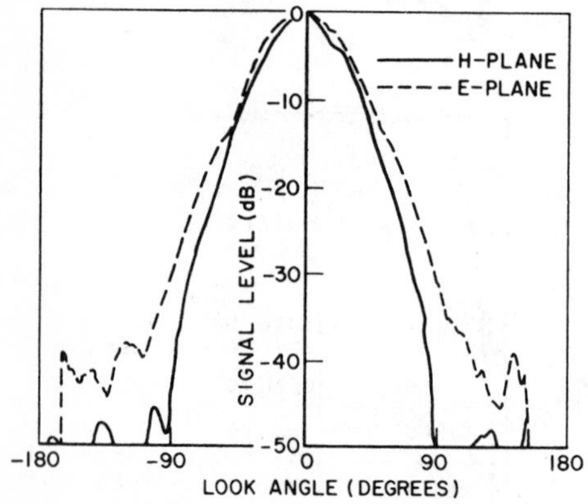

Fig. 4. Near-field radiation patterns of 10-in diameter conical corrugated horn (10-in range, 3.7 GHz).

this antenna is used as a range antenna for either antenna pattern or radar scattering measurements. These antennas should prove useful in reducing multipath effects and also in reducing absorber requirements in anechoic chambers. The low backlobes of Fig. 1(a) also ensure that the pattern range operator can work freely in back of the antenna. This conical corrugated horn has backlobes that are only of the order of 40 dB below the pattern maximum. A previously reported pyramidal corrugated horn had backlobes of the order of −60 dB [1].

Because of the reduced edge diffracted fields, the corrugated horn has a well defined phase center located at the apex of the horn. This has been demonstrated by direct measurement of the aperture distribution of both the conical and the pyramidal corrugated horns [1], [7]. Both the amplitude and phase distribution occurring in the conical horn are shown in Fig. 3(a) and (b) for the E plane and the H plane, respectively. The computed points represent the phase distribution of a point source located at the apex.

Perhaps the most important implication of a common phase center is that the corrugated horn with its similar amplitude patterns should produce, over the main beam, the same polarization with which it is excited. An experimental circularly polarized pattern of the conical horn is shown in Fig. 1(b). The vertical lines are the axial ratio obtained by rotating a linear antenna. The axial ratio over the main beam is good, particularly if the test volume of space is restricted to the 1-dB regions as should be done for accurate pattern measurements [9].

Measurements of the parameters of antennas and scatterers can also be made in the near zone of the corrugated horn. The phase distribution over the object under test can be determined since the phase center has been established. However, the amplitude distribution [9] over the object under test may deviate too far from the required uniform distribution and this represents a limiting factor. Both the amplitude and phase patterns of the corrugated horn have been measured at various ranges. A typical near zone amplitude pattern is shown in Fig. 4.

The loss measurement reported by Caldecott [7], [10] in this issue was used to obtain the loss in the conical corrugated horn and a one way loss on the order of 0.015 dB was measured. Used in conjunction with the directivity computation, it appears practical to evaluate the gain of a properly designed corrugated horn with a 0.1 dB accuracy.

II. Conclusions

Because of the properties presented here, the corrugated horn antenna should be established as a "standard" antenna. As a standard gain horn, it offers several advantages: 1) its low backlobe radiation makes gain comparison measurements more accurate (elimination of multipath signals), 2) it can be designed for nearly constant gain, 3) its low VSWR minimizes the effects of mismatch loss, and 4) it is possible to evaluate the gain of the corrugated horn without resorting to either theoretical analysis or the gain comparison procedure to less than a 0.1 dB accuracy.

Another potential use of the corrugated horn is that of an antenna range standard. The question of antenna range fidelity is almost always asked when an unusual phenomena is noted. The simple monotonically decaying pencil beam of the corrugated horn with a 40–60 dB dynamic range is a natural for checking the entire system by simply measuring its pattern and comparing it with one that has been carefully measured previously.

The corrugated horn is also useful as the source antenna of either a radar scattering range or an antenna pattern range. When it is used in a cw scattering range, it is much easier to null the system and to maintain a null since the fields radiated in the back direction are down several orders of magnitude. Its low VSWR ensures that the corrugated horn can easily be matched to the system. The clean pencil beam antenna ensures that most of the energy is radiated toward the target (scattering range) or antenna under test (antenna range) and that the multipath effects from nearby scattering objects or ground reflections are minimized. This corrugated horn may also be designed to radiate circularly polarized fields with an axial ratio of the order of 1 dB over the 3 dB half-power beamwidth since the corrugated horn has reasonably good axial symmetry and a well defined phase center.

Measurement of phase patterns is becoming more prevalent. A corrugated horn with a well established phase center (for observation points from which the horn apex is visible) and slowly changing phase pattern would represent a natural standard for phase measurements.

References

[1] R. E. Lawrie and L. Peters, Jr., "Modifications of horn antennas for low sidelobe levels," *IEEE Trans. Antennas Propagat.*, vol. AP-14, pp. 605–610, Sept. 1966, and U.S. Patent 3,631,502.
[2] V. H. Rumsey, "Horn antennas with uniform power patterns around their axes," *IEEE Trans. Antennas Propagat.*, vol. AP-14, No. 5, pp. 656–658, Sept. 1966.
[3] A. J. Simmons and A. F. Kay, "The scalar feed—a high performance feed for large paraboloid reflectors," in *1966 IEEE Conf. Publ.* 21, pp. 213–217.
[4] M. E. J. Jeuken and H. P. J. M. Roumen, "Broadband corrugated conical horn antennas with small flare angles," presented at 1971

URSI Int. Symp. Electromagnetic Wave Theory, Tbilisi, USSR, Sept. 9–15.

[5] P. J. B. Clarricoats, "Analysis of spherical hybrid modes in a corrugated conical horn," *Electron. Lett.*, vol. 5, no. 9, p. 189, 1969.

[6] W. F. Bahret and L. Peters, Jr., "Small aperture small-flare-angle corrugated horns," *IEEE Trans. Antennas Propagat.* (Commun.), vol. AP-16, pp. 494–495, July 1968.

[7] R. Caldecott, C. A. Mentzer, L. Peters, Jr., and J. Toth, "High performance *S*-band horn antennas for radiometer use," Ohio State Univ. ElectroScience Lab., Tech. Rep. 3033-1 NASA CR-2133, (prepared for NASA Langley Research Center), May 1972.

[8] H. Jasik, Ed., *Antenna Engineering Handbook.* New York: McGraw-Hill, 1961.

[9] R. G. Kouyoumjian and L. Peters, Jr., "Range requirements in radar cross section measurements," *Proc. IEEE*, vol. 53, pp. 920–928, Aug. 1965.

[10] R. Caldecott, "The generalized multiprobe reflectometer and its application to automated transmission line measurements," this issue, pp. 550–554.

Properties of Cutoff Corrugated Surfaces for Corrugated Horn Design

CARL A. MENTZER, MEMBER, IEEE, AND LEON PETERS, JR., SENIOR MEMBER, IEEE

***Abstract*—Corrugated horns involve a junction between the corrugated surface and a conducting groundplane. Proper horn design requires an understanding of the electromagnetic properties of the corrugated surface and this junction. An integral equation solution has been used to study the influence of corrugation density and tooth thickness on the power loss, surface current, and the scattering from a groundplane–corrugated surface junction.**

I. INTRODUCTION

THE CORRUGATED horn has been established as an antenna with low side lobes and backlobes, rotationally symmetric patterns (for square pyramidal and conical horn shapes), and broad-band performance [1]–[9].[1] These properties make this horn useful for many applications; including the one presently under study, i.e., as a radiometer antenna. A ray-optics model of the dominant radiation mechanisms of conventional horn antennas is shown in Fig. 1(a). In the corrugated horn (shown in profile in Fig. 1(b)) the corrugated surface (with capacitive surface impedance in the E-plane of the horn) serves to reduce or eliminate the fields associated with ray "a" of Fig. 1(a). This reduces or eliminates the usual high E-plane sidelobes.

Attention is focussed in this paper on 1) the effectiveness with which the fields of ray a of Fig. 1(a) are reduced, 2) the loss associated with these fields, and 3) the fields of new rays (b and c) generated at the junction where the corrugations are introduced. Ray analysis is applicable because of the local nature of diffracted fields and has been shown to be accurate for many antenna applications.

The influence of the corrugation shape and density on the scattering from the onset of the corrugations and on the losses in the horn has been ignored in previous work. The parametric study reported differs from previous corrugated horn studies in that it does not assume an impedance representation of the surface but focusses attention on the physical structure of this capacitive surface to generate further understanding of the operating principles of the corrugated horn. The goal is to establish design criteria for the construction of practical corrugated horn geometries through a detailed analysis of the groundplane–corrugated surface junction. The analysis includes studying the surface currents flowing on the corrugations and the loss in the corrugations as well as the scattering from the onset of the corrugations. The usual corrugated horn requirements are for 8 or more corrugations per wavelength and a corrugation depth "d" between 0.25λ and 0.5λ.[2] In addition, it is usually specified that the tooth thickness (t in Fig. 1(b)) should be much less than the corrugation width (W in Fig. 1(b)). In order to study the effects of varying these parameters, an integral equation solution was used to find the radiated fields and the surface currents associated with the groundplane-corrugated surface model of Fig. 2(a). This model was chosen for its similarity to one wall of a sectoral corrugated horn (i.e., the lower wall of Fig. 1(b)). In the corrugated horn, the illumination of the corrugations is by a cylindrical wave due to the diffraction from the horn–waveguide junction. In the model used, the magnetic line sources provide a similar cylindrical wave while at the same time place a null in the far field in the direction of the adjacent edge of the groundplane. Hence, it is not necessary to match over the entire groundplane but only over the illuminated part. This model is a valid representation of the diffracted fields and the fields on the corrugations. In performing the calculations, one requires the field to be matched at points on the illuminated portion of the groundplane and over the 20 corrugations. For all corrugation depths where cut-off operation is obtained (i.e., $0.25 \leq d/\lambda < 0.5$), the energy is forced away from the corrugated surface. Since the energy is forced off the corrugations, the fields over the corrugated surface need to be matched only over the corrugations which have significant surface currents flowing on the walls. Thus the surface model need not be closed. This conclusion was verified by computations using the open model shown and a similar model and observing no significant differences.

II. METHOD OF SOLUTION

Surface currents on the corrugations and scattering by the groundplane–corrugated surface junction of Fig. 2(a) were found using an H-field formulation for the TE field case discussed by Harrington. For this case, there is only a z component of magnetic field $\bar{H}$ and a tangential com-

Manuscript received April 17; revised July 25, 1973. This work was supported in part by Contract NAS1-10040 between NASA, Langley Research Center, Langley Station, Hampton, Va., and the Ohio State University Research Foundation.

The authors are with the ElectroScience Laboratory, Department of Electrical Engineering, Ohio State University, Columbus, Ohio 43212.

[1] A more complete list of references is given in [7].

[2] This depth would be in free space wavelengths for the parallel plate waveguide geometry of the corrugations. If the sides of the slot are terminated in conducting planes, then these electrical lengths would correspond to those of the TE_{10} waveguide mode.

Reprinted from *IEEE Trans. Antennas Propagat.*, vol. AP-22, pp. 191–196, Mar. 1974.

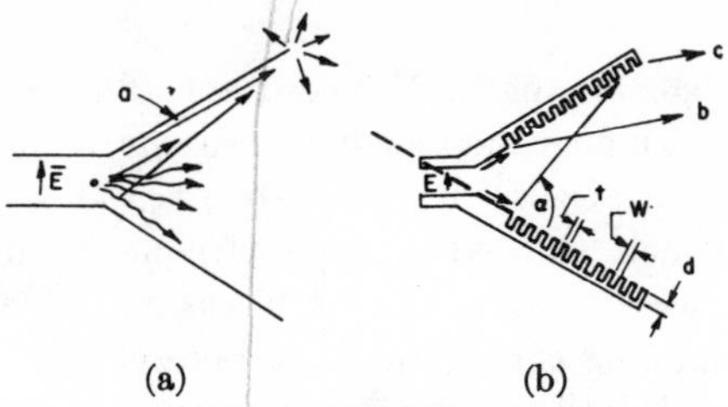

Fig. 1. (a) Conventional horn geometry. (b) Corrugated horn geometry.

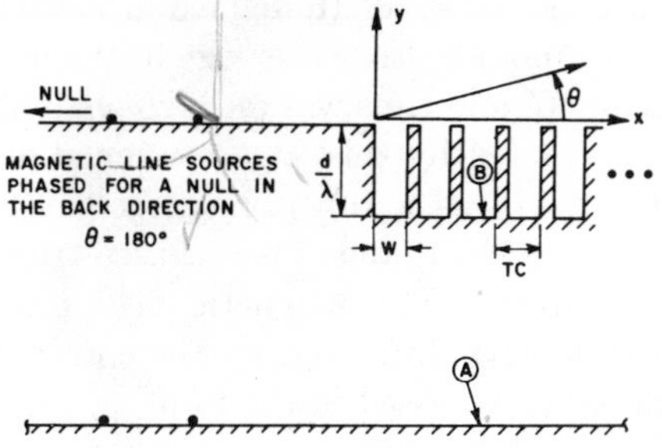

Fig. 2. Geometry for corrugated surface analysis.

ponent of surface current $\bar{J}$ ($\bar{J} = \hat{n} \times \bar{H}$, where $\hat{n}$ is the unit normal). At any point, the total magnetic field H_z is the sum of the incident and scattered magnetic fields H_z^i and H_z^s, respectively. The scattered field is related to its source, the surface current, by

$$H_z^s = \hat{U}_z \cdot \nabla \times \int JG\, d\bar{l}' \qquad (1)$$

where $\bar{J} = J\, d\bar{l}' = -[H_z]_{c^+}\, d\bar{l}'$ when H_z is evaluated on C^+ (just outside the contour C where the surface current $\bar{J}$ flows; the interior of C on the left side of $d\bar{l}'$) and G is the two-dimensional Green's function $G(\bar{\rho},\bar{\rho}') = 1/(4j)H_0^{(2)}(k\,|\,\bar{\rho} - \bar{\rho}'\,|)$. The resulting integral equation

$$J = -[H_z^i + \hat{U}_z \cdot \nabla \times \int JG\, d\bar{l}']_{c^+} \qquad (2)$$

is solved for the surface current J by the moment method using pulses as the basis function. This integral equation reduces to the matrix equation

$$[l_{mn}][f_n] = [g_m] \qquad (3)$$

where

$$[l_{mn}] = (j/4k)\,\Delta C_n(\hat{n}\cdot\bar{R})H_1^{(2)}(k\,|\,\bar{\rho}_m - \bar{\rho}_n\,|) \qquad (4)$$

matrix of coupling coefficients between the mth and the nth segments at $\bar{\rho}_m$ and $\bar{\rho}_n$ on the surface contour;

$\bar{R}$ = $(\bar{\rho}_m - \bar{\rho}_n)/(|\,\bar{\rho}_m - \bar{\rho}_n\,|)$ = unit vector between nth and mth points;

ΔC_n = $J_n\, dl$ = current moment at the nth point;

$[f_n]$ column vector of unknown surface current density on nth segment at the points (x_n,y_n) on the surface contour;

$[g_m]$ column vector of incident field ($= -H_z^i$) at the points (x_m,y_m) on the surface contour.

TABLE I
PARAMETERS CONSIDERED IN STUDY OF SQUARE CORRUGATIONS

Parameter	Notation in in Fig. 2	Values Considered
Corrugation depth (in wavelengths)	d/λ	0.25, 0.3125, 0.375, 0.4375, 0.5
Corrugation density (in corrugations per wavelength)	NCOR = $1/TC$ or N/λ	4, 6, 8, 10, 12
Corrugation shape (ratio of corrugation gap width to corrugation period)	W/TC	0.5, 0.6, 0.7, 0.75, 0.8, 0.9

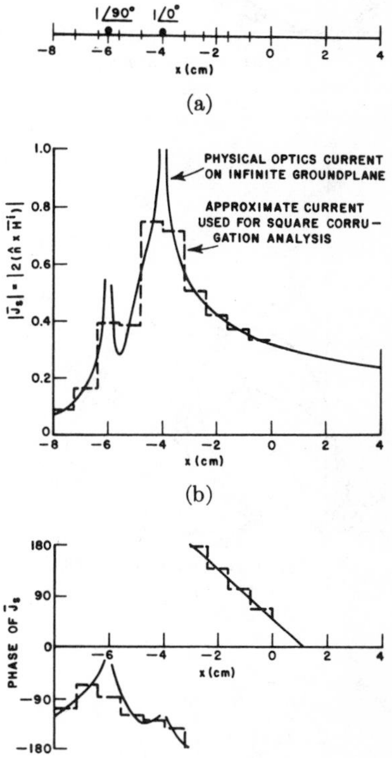

(c)

Fig. 3. Surface currents near line sources used to model groundplane–corrugated surface junction. (a) Matching points on groundplane side. (b) Surface current magnitude. (c) Surface current phase.

This matrix equation was solved using a Crout [11] matrix inversion subroutine.

III. Results for Square Corrugations

The parameters of the square corrugations of Fig. 2(a) which were varied in this study are shown in Table I. Many combinations of these parameters were studied to ascertain the influence of each on properties such as the scattering from the groundplane-corrugated surface junction, the surface current flowing on the corrugations and also the power loss in the corrugations.

The location of the matching segments on the groundplane near the line source pair is shown in Fig. 3(a). The physical optics currents on a finite segment of an infinite groundplane (shown in Fig. 2(b)) and the point matching approximate currents for the matching points selected are shown in amplitude and phase in Figs. 3(b) and 3(c).

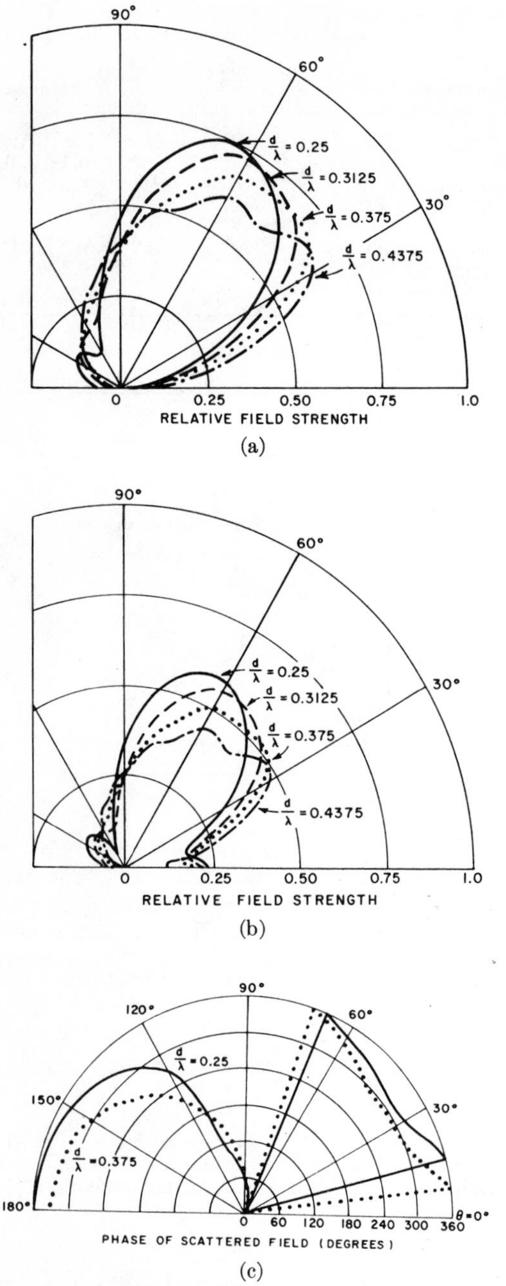

Fig. 4. Radiation pattern associated with groundplane–corrugated surface junction illuminated by cylindrical wave. (a) Total fields. (b) Scattered field amplitude. (c) Scattered field phase.

The fields associated with the groundplane-corrugated surface junction are shown in Fig. 4 for corrugation depths from 0.25λ to 0.4375λ for a corrugation density of 8 corrugations per wavelength (i.e., corrugation period = $TC = \lambda/8$) and for a corrugation shape ratio (ratio of corrugation gap width to corrugation period) of $W/TC = 0.75$. The scattered field phase is shown in Fig. 4(c). All of the other corrugation densities and corrugation profiles showed essentially the same patterns at the same corrugation depths and are therefore not included. The smoothly varying phase pattern indicates that the phase center of the scattered field is nearly at the origin of the coordinate system (the junction between the groundplane and the corrugations).

The range of angles observed for the scattered field maximum explains the peculiar behavior of the small corrugated horn discussed previously [1]. This horn had a pattern which showed a slight frequency dependence. However, as the end of this horn was cut off, the pattern of the remaining corrugated horn became quite frequency dependent. For the original corrugated horn, the scattered field maximum illuminated the opposite wall of the horn and weakly illuminated the aperture edge (the aperture edge was at about $\alpha = 43°$ (α defined in Fig. 1(b)). However, after the modification, the edge of the horn occurred at an angle of 50° and thus was more strongly illuminated. The fields diffracted by this edge combined destructively and constructively as a function of frequency with the desired radiated field and thus caused the frequency dependent patterns. The magnetic field intensity associated with the rays diffracted by the corrugated surface junction may be expressed in the form

$$H^D = H^i \frac{\exp(-jkr)}{r^{1/2}} F(\theta) \tag{5}$$

where H^i is the magnetic field incident on the junction, r is the range as measured from the junction, θ is the angle shown in Fig. 2, and $F(\theta)$ is the complex pattern factor shown in Figs. 4(b) and (c). The phase of $F(\theta)$ is a slowly varying function of θ and presents no difficulty for the application of geometrical theory of diffraction techniques (GTD). This information is sufficient to compute the diffracted fields associated with ray "b" of Fig. 1(b). While these computations have not been carried to completion at this time, they represent a straightforward implementation of accepted GTD practices similar to previous analyses of horn antennas [12]. The major goal at this time is to establish the condition for which this edge diffraction is negligible and this would occur when the angle to the opposite edge (α in Fig. 1(b)) is less than 20°–25° (or greater than 90°).

Another property of the corrugated surface is the rate of decay of the surface current flowing on the corrugation walls. The decay in the amplitude of the surface current is due to the energy being forced away from the corrugations and not caused by power loss in the conductor. Figs. 5–7 show the normalized surface current densities versus corrugation parameters. The surface current plotted is the current which exists at the bottom of each of the 20 corrugations (point "B" in Fig. 2(a)) normalized with respect to the surface current which exists at the same X coordinate on an infinite groundplane with the same sources acting (point "A" in Fig. 2(b)). This normalization removes the range dependence of the incident cylindrical fields and also selects the maximum current which exists on the surface of the corrugations.

Since to a good approximation only a TEM mode exists in the corrugation, the currents on the teeth at any point are

$$|J_y| = J_s \cos \beta(d + y) \tag{6}$$

where y assumes negative values and $\beta = 2\pi/\lambda_0$ is the

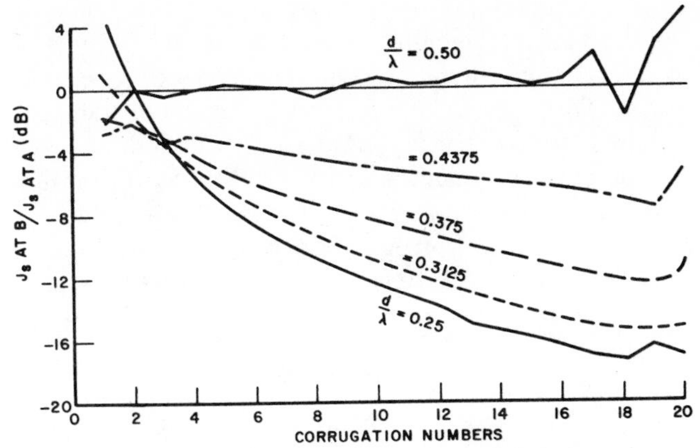

Fig. 5. Decay of surface current on corrugated surface due to energy being forced away from corrugation.

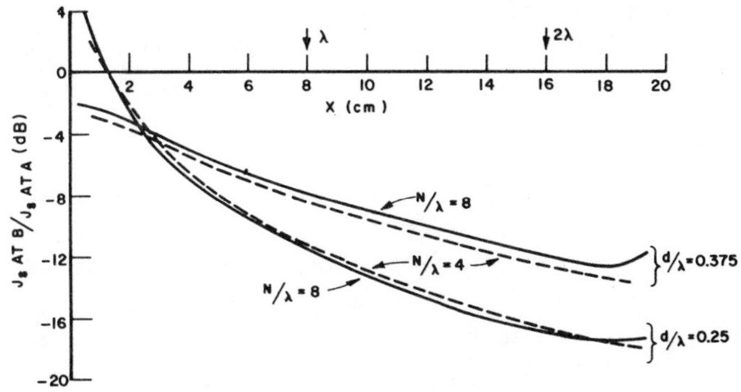

Fig. 6. Decay of surface currents on corrugations as function of corrugation density.

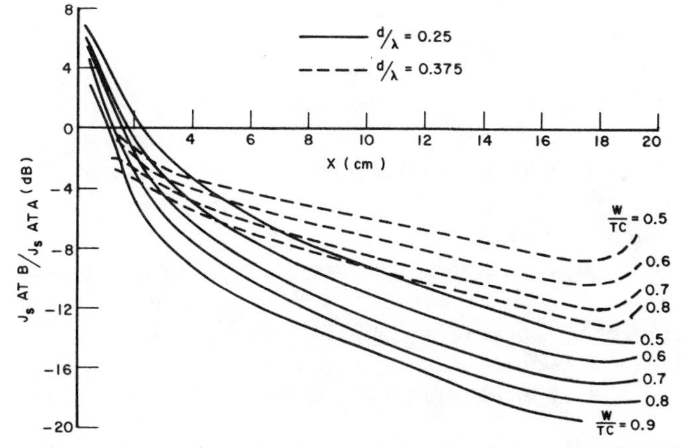

Fig. 7. Decay of surface currents on corrugations as function of corrugation shape.

propagation constant of a TEM wave in the parallel-plate waveguide region.

The most rapid decay is obtained for the $d/\lambda = 0.25$ case and as expected no decay occurs for the 0.5 case. The variations of the current near the end of the surface are caused by fields reflected from the termination of the structure and may be ignored. This property (the decay of the surface current) has been examined for other corrugation densities and profiles. Fig. 6 shows that the surface current decay is almost independent of the corrugation density. These results are plotted as a function of the

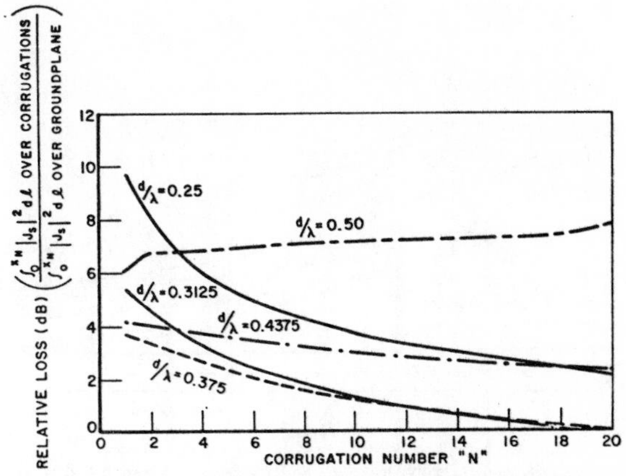

Fig. 8. Power loss in corrugated surface for various corrugation depths.

distance from the onset of the corrugations. The dependence of the surface current on the corrugation profile was also investigated and the results are shown in Fig. 7. The range of W/TC ratios considered was from 0.5 (thick metal vane between corrugations) to 0.9 (very thin metal vane). Beyond approximately $1/2\lambda$ from the onset of the corrugations (i.e., $x > 4$ cm for the $\lambda = 8$ cm case shown), the decay of the surface current per wavelength is nearly constant (~ 6 dB/λ at $d/\lambda = 0.25$ and ~ 4 dB/λ at $d/\lambda = 0.375$). Thus in a practical situation, one could use very thin vanes near the onset of the corrugations and thicker vanes (which are easier to construct) further from the onset of the corrugations. These curves then establish the length of corrugated horn required to reduce the edge diffracted fields. Since the current density at the top of the teeth is almost zero for $d = \lambda/4$ only a few teeth would be required here. For the $3/8\lambda$ depth, the currents at the top of the tooth would be 3 dB below those at the bottom. Thus the fields of the diffracted ray (a of Fig. 1(a)) that combine constructively and destructively with the geometrical optics fields are reduced to a negligible value with a surface that is two wavelengths in extent.

Another property of the corrugated surface which was investigated is the power loss in the corrugations. In an effort to make the results more general, the corrugated surface loss is normalized with respect to the loss in an equal size segment of an infinite groundplane of the same material (shown in Fig. 2(b)). This eliminates the need to assume a surface resistivity for the material. Figs. 8–10 show the normalized loss in dB. The loss shown in Fig. 8 is the sum of the loss in each corrugation from the onset of the corrugations (at the origin of the coordinate system) up to and including the loss in the Nth corrugation. The loss in the groundplane (used for normalization) is the loss in the region from the origin up to the X coordinate of the end of the Nth corrugation. Notice that most of the loss occurs in the first few corrugations and also that it appears that all of the curves (except the 0.5λ deep case) would cross the 0 dB line (eqial loss in corrugations and groundplane) after a reasonable number of corrugations (the 0.3125λ and 0.375λ deep cases cross in fewer than 20

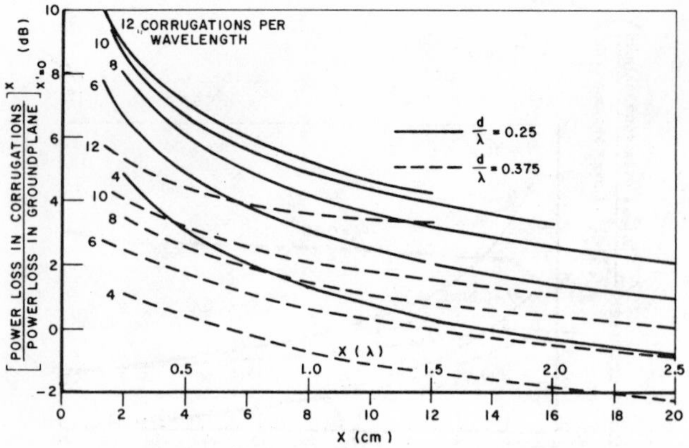

Fig. 9. Power loss in corrugations as function of corrugation density.

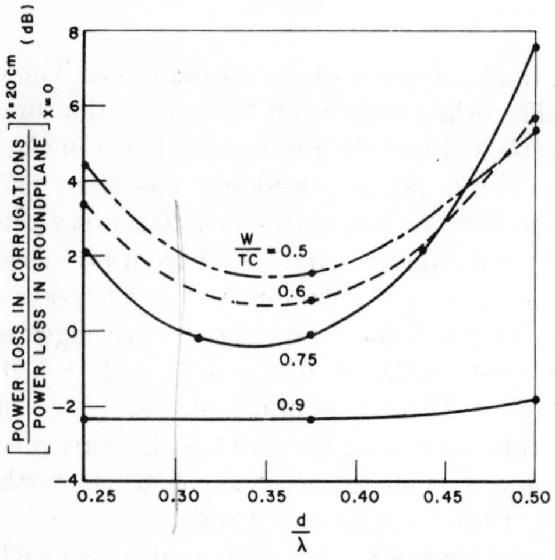

Fig. 10. Power loss in corrugated surface with 8 corrugations per wavelength for various corrugation shapes versus corrugation depth.

corrugations). The power loss is also dependent upon the corrugation density and shape. Fig. 9 shows the power loss in 0.25λ and 0.375λ deep corrugations for various corrugation densities. This loss is the loss in the corrugations from the origin to X normalized with respect to the loss in the same length segment of an infinite groundplane. Notice that the lower densities are less lossy than the high density surfaces. This result is reasonable in view of the fact that the surface current decay per wavelength is nearly independent of the corrugation density (c.f., Fig. 6). Thus the higher corrugation density with its greater surface area should be more lossy. The influence of the corrugation shape on the power loss may be seen in Fig. 10. Shown here is the loss in 20 corrugations (from $x = 0$ to $x = 20$ cm) versus the corrugation depth (D/λ) for various W/TC ratios. The $W/TC = 0.5$ case corresponds to a thick metal vane between corrugations while the $W/TC = 0.9$ case corresponds to a very thin vane. Notice that the thin vanes have lower loss than the thick vanes and that there exists a range of depths over which the loss is minimized.

The impedance of the horn is related to the magnitude of the wave reflected back toward the source. The computer programs developed here are not well designed to evaluate this reflection coefficient but can be used to obtain an indication of this parameter. The reflection coefficient of the groundplane–corrugated surface junction has a maximum at $d/\lambda = 0.25$ and decreases as d/λ increases. This agrees with previously measured values of corrugated horn VSWR. [2], [8] The VSWR also is a function of the corrugation density and shape. The results indicated a decreasing reflection from the onset of the corrugations as the corrugation density increases and an increasing reflection as the metal tooth between the corrugations became thinner.

IV. Conclusions

A parametric study of square corrugations has shown that this shape operates as a cut-off corrugated surface over a substantial bandwidth with relatively low loss. The study has also shown that the rate of decay of surface current is nearly independent of the corrugation density (the number of corrugations per wavelength) and that the lower corrugation densities (4 or 6 corrugations per wavelength) are desirable because of the lower loss. A significant part of the loss is confined to the first few corrugations and should allow one to treat this region with special care such as silver plating or special polishing of the surface when using corrugated surfaces in situations where low loss is important. In any event, the loss in the walls for most practical corrugated horns would be as low as (if not lower than) the loss in the same shape and size conducting wall of the same material with the same surface finish. The results also indicate that the VSWR of the horn will depend on the corrugation shape. For the groundplane-corrugated surface junction considered, the VSWR decreased with increasing corrugation density and increased with thinner teeth between the corrugations. Since the loss increases with increased corrugation density, some compromise is required. Six to eight corrugations per wavelength near the onset of the corrugations and then decreasing the density to two to four per wavelength should be adequate. Again, since the loss was lower and the VSWR higher for the very thin teeth, some compromise is also indicated. A corrugation width to period ratio of $W/TC = 0.75$ should be a good compromise value if one wants to avoid the complexity of changing the corrugation shape along the corrugated wall.

References

[1] R. Caldecott, C. A. Mentzer, L. Peters, Jr., and J. Toth, "High performance S-band horn antennas for radiometer use," Electro-Science Lab., Ohio State Univ., Columbus, Ohio, NASA Contractor Rep. CR-2133, Jan. 1973.
[2] R. E. Lawrie and L. Peters, Jr., "Modification of horn antennas for low sidelobe levels," *IEEE Trans. Antennas Propagat.*, vol. AP-14, pp. 605–610, Sept. 1966.
[3] W. F. Bahret and L. Peters, Jr., "Small-aperture small-flare angle corrugated horns," *IEEE Trans. Antennas Propagat.* (Commun.), vol. AP-16, pp. 494–495, July 1968.
[4] S. K. Buchmeyer, "Corrugations lock horns with poor beam-shapes," *Microwaves*, vol. 12, no. 1, pp. 44–49, Jan. 1973.
[5] H. C. Minnet and B. MacA. Thomas, "A method of synthesizing radiation patterns with axial symmetry," *IEEE Trans. Antennas Propagat.*, vol. AP-14, pp. 654–656, Sept. 1966.
[6] V. H. Rumsey, "Horn antennas with uniform power patterns around their axis," *IEEE Trans. Antennas Propagat.*, vol. AP-14, pp. 656–658, Sept. 1966.
[7] P. J. Clarricoats and P. K. Saha, "Propagation and radiation

behaviour of corrugated feeds, Parts I and II," *Proc. Inst. Elec. Eng.*, vol. 118, no. 9, pp. 1167–1186, Sept. 1971.
[8] M. E. J. Jeuken, "Frequency independence and symmetry properties of corrugated conical horn antennas with small flare angles," Theoretical Eng. Group, Eindhoven Univ. Tech., Eindhoven, The Netherlands, Dec. 1970.
[9] M. S. Narasimham and B. V. Rao, "Hybrid modes in conical corrugated horns," *Electron. Lett.*, vol. 6, pp. 32–34, 1970.
[10] R. F. Harrington, *Field Computation by Moment Methods.* New York: Macmillan, 1968, pp. 50–55.
[11] J. Westlake, *A Handbook of Numerical Matrix Inversion and Solution of Linear Equations.* New York: Wiley, 1968, pp. 10–14.
[12] P. M. Russo, R. C. Rudduck, and L. Peters, Jr., "A method for computing *E*-plane patterns of horn antennas," *IEEE Trans. Antennas Propagat.*, vol. AP-13, pp. 219–224, Mar. 1965.

On the Radiation from an Open-Ended Corrugated Pipe Carrying the HE_{11} Mode

CHARLES M. KNOP AND HANS J. WIESENFARTH

Abstract—The fields radiated by an HE_{11} mode in an aperture of a corrugated pipe with quarter-wave teeth are derived by considering the pipe to be situated in an infinite perfectly conducting ground plane. Unlike the case for a smooth wall pipe, this model is reasonable since the corrugations force the edge taper in the E plane of the pipe's aperture to be significantly increased from its smooth wall value of 4 dB. This considerably reduces the usual E-plane edge diffraction effects (those in the H plane are even less significant, being essentially the same as with no corrugations since the H-plane taper is is infinite in either case). This model reveals that the E-plane pattern of the pipe approaches the H-plane pattern (with its wider main beam and lower sidelobes) and that the radiation is nearly linearly polarized only if the aperture is sufficiently large ($C \equiv 2\pi a/\lambda_v \gtrsim 2\pi$, where λ_v is the free-space wavelength and a is the radius of the aperture). This is in agreement with experimental results given. (Existing solutions of Minnet–Thomas and Clarricoats–Saha based on the Silver formulation predict beam symmetry and zero cross polarization despite aperture size.) The radiation characteristics: beam efficiency, aperture efficiency, gain, and cross-polarization ratio are computed for typical horn aperture sizes (i.e., horn diameters of about one to ten free-space wavelengths). Recognition of the fact that the main beam radiation can be described by the universal horn pattern of Kelleher facilitates reflector feed design procedure for arbitrary reflector edge illumination levels.

Manuscript received December 1, 1971; revised March 10, 1972.
The authors are with the Andrew Corporation, Orland Park, Ill. 60462.

Reprinted from *IEEE Trans. Antennas Propagat.*, vol. AP-20, pp. 644–648, Sept. 1972.

I. Introduction

Derivations of the radiation from an open-ended corrugated pipe in free space have been reported [1]–[3] and follow the development of Silver [4]. However, as well be shown here, since the corrugations can greatly diminish the E-plane edge taper and hence the surface currents induced on the metallic pipe's rim, the presence of a large metallic ground plane will have little influence on the forward radiated fields (zero influence for vanishing surface currents). As a result, it is justified to adopt the model of the pipe terminated in a ground plane, as depicted in Fig. 1, to determine the radiated fields in the forward direction. This model will give increasingly accurate predictions as the size of the pipe increases since this increases the edge taper; hence it is adopted here and concisely shows that for quarter-wave operation the radiation is essentially linearly polarized and axially symmetric only if the aperture is sufficiently large. This is in agreement with experimental results given and is to be contrasted with the aforementioned solutions which predict zero cross polarization and exact beam symmetry despite aperture size.

II. Analysis

The pertinent pipe fields in a corrugated pipe (the internal geometry of which is also shown in Fig. 1) carrying the HE_{11} mode are [3]

$$E_\rho = \mathcal{E}_0\left[C_0J_1'(C_0)J_1'\left(C_0\frac{\rho_s}{a}\right) - J_1(C_0)J_1\left(C_0\frac{\rho_s}{a}\right)\right]\cos\phi_s$$

$$E_\phi = \mathcal{E}_0\left\{-C_0J_1'(C_0)\frac{J_1[C_0(\rho_s/a)]}{[C_0(\rho_s/a)]} + J_1(C_0)J_1'\left(C_0\frac{\rho_s}{a}\right)\right\}\sin\phi_s \tag{1}$$

where $\mathcal{E}_0$ is the driving field in the pipe, $\mathcal{E}_0 \equiv j\eta_v H_1 C/C_0 J_1(C_0)$, where propagation in the pipe such as $\exp[+j(\omega t - \beta z)]$ is understood throughout, and where $\beta = 2\pi/\lambda_g$, $\lambda_v/\lambda_g = +(1 - C_0^2/C^2)^{1/2}$, $C = \beta_v a = 2\pi a/\lambda_v = \omega/c$, $\eta_v = (\mu_v/\epsilon_v)^{1/2} = 120\pi\ \Omega$, and λ_v is the wavelength in unbounded vacuum or free space, λ_g is the guide wavelength, c is the speed of light in vacuum, β is the phase factor in the guide, β_v is the phase factor in vacuum, C is the circumference of the pipe's inner diameter expressed in free-space wavelengths, C_0 is the cutoff or eigenvalue, i.e., is C at cutoff, and H_1 is the maximum value of the driving axial magnetic field, H_{z1}, where $H_{z1} \equiv H_1 J_1[C_0(\rho_s/a)]\sin\phi_s$.

Using Bessel identities and expressing (1) in Cartesian coordinates,

$$E_x = -j\frac{\mathcal{E}_0C_0}{2}\left\{\cos(2\phi_s)\left[J_2\left(C_0\frac{\rho_s}{a}\right)J_0(C_0)\right] + J_0\left(C_0\frac{\rho_s}{a}\right)J_2(C_0)\right\}$$

$$E_y = -j\frac{\mathcal{E}_0C_0}{2}\sin(2\phi_s)J_0(C_0)J_2\left(C_0\frac{\rho_s}{a}\right). \tag{2}$$

The far-field Fourier transforms of these fields, i.e.,

$$\bar{E}_{x,y} = \frac{1}{(2\pi)^2}\iint_{\text{aperture}} E_{x,y}(\rho_s,\phi_s)\exp[+j\beta_v\rho_s\sin\theta\cos(\phi-\phi_s)]\,d\phi_s\rho_s d\rho_s \tag{3}$$

are then

$$\bar{E}_x = -j\frac{a^2\mathcal{E}_0C_0}{4\pi}f_0(\theta)\left[1 - \frac{f_2(\theta)}{f_0(\theta)}\cos(2\phi)\right]$$

$$\bar{E}_y = +j\frac{a^2\mathcal{E}_0C_0}{4\pi}f_2(\theta)\sin 2\phi \tag{4}$$

where use has been made of the orthogonality integrals

$$\int_0^{2\pi}\begin{pmatrix}\cos n\phi_s\\ \sin n\phi_s\end{pmatrix}\cdot\exp[+ju\cos(\phi-\phi_s)]\,d\phi_s = \begin{pmatrix}\cos n\phi\\ \sin n\phi\end{pmatrix}j^nJ_n(u)\cdot 2\pi \tag{5}$$

$$\int_0^1 xJ_n(lx)J_n(px)\,dx = \frac{1}{(l^2-p^2)}[pJ_n(l)J_n'(p) - lJ_n(p)J_n'(l)] \tag{6}$$

and where

$$f_0(\theta) = \begin{cases}\dfrac{-J_2(C_0)[C_0J_0(C\sin\theta)J_1(C_0) - C\sin\theta J_0(C_0)J_1(C\sin\theta)]}{C^2\sin^2\theta - C_0^2}, & \sin\theta \neq \dfrac{C_0}{C}\\[2ex] \dfrac{J_1(C_0)}{2}[J_1^2(C_0) + J_2^2(C_0)], & \sin\theta = \dfrac{C_0}{C}\end{cases} \tag{7}$$

$$f_2(\theta) = \begin{cases}\dfrac{J_0(C_0)[C_0J_2(C\sin\theta)J_1(C_0) - C\sin\theta J_2(C_0)J_1(C\sin\theta)]}{C^2\sin^2\theta - C_0^2}, & \sin\theta \neq \dfrac{C_0}{C}\\[2ex] \dfrac{J_0(C_0)}{4}\left[2J_1^2(C_0) - 6\dfrac{J_1(C_0)J_2(C_0)}{C_0} - J_2^2(C_0) - J_0(C_0)J_2(C_0)\right], & \sin\theta = \dfrac{C_0}{C}\\[2ex] 0. & \theta = 0.\end{cases} \tag{8}$$

Now, the far-zone fields from a pipe situated in an infinite ground plane are [5]

$$E_\theta = \eta_v H_\phi = A[\bar{E}_x \cos\phi + \bar{E}_y \sin\phi] \tag{9}$$

$$E_\phi = -\eta_v H_\theta = A[-\bar{E}_x \sin\phi + \bar{E}_y \cos\phi]\cos\theta \tag{10}$$

(where $A = +j2\pi\beta_v[\exp(-j\beta_v r)/r]$, which become

$$E_\theta = -jAa^2 \frac{\mathcal{E}_0 C_0}{4\pi} f_0(\theta)\left[1 - \frac{f_2(\theta)}{f_0(\theta)}\right]\cos\phi$$

$$E_\phi = +jAa^2 \frac{\mathcal{E}_0 C_0}{4\pi} \cos\theta f_0(\theta)\left[1 + \frac{f_2(\theta)}{f_0(\theta)}\right]\sin\phi. \tag{11}$$

TABLE I

QUARTER-WAVE OPERATION

C	a/b	C_0	λ_v/λ_g	D (dB)	d/λ_v
1.84	0.4810	1.84117	0.0000	4.0	0.3161
2.00	0.5066	1.9687	0.1763	6.301	0.3102
3.00	0.6254	2.2504	0.6613	15.648	0.2861
4.00	0.6981	2.3236	0.8140	21.336	0.2754
5.00	0.7470	2.3542	0.8822	25.514	0.2696
6.00	0.7824	2.3704	0.9187	28.848	0.2657
7.00	0.8089	2.3797	0.9404	31.611	0.2633
8.00	0.8295	2.3857	0.9545	33.998	0.2618
9.00	0.8474	2.3897	0.9641	36.085	0.2581
10.00	0.8610	2.3926	0.9710	37.959	0.2571
15.00	0.9032	2.3994	0.9871	37.959	0.2560
20.00	0.9260	2.4017	0.9928	37.9594	0.2545
25.00	0.9401	2.4028	0.9954	37.9594	0.2536
30.00	0.9497	2.4035	0.9968	37.9594	0.2530

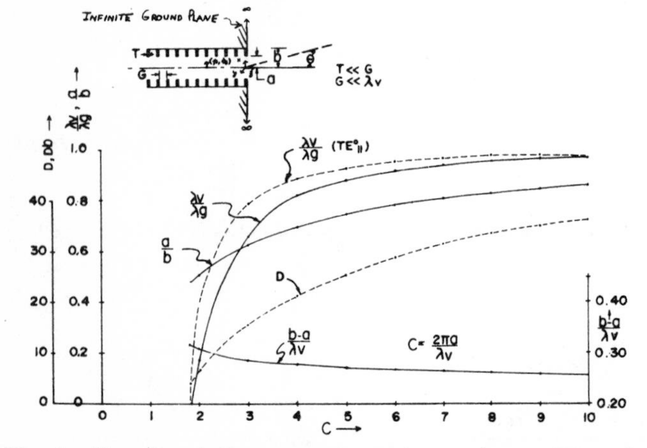

Fig. 1. Pipe–ground plane geometry and operating conditions for quarter-wave teeth.

In the preceding the dependence of C_0 on C and tooth depth, or a/b, is obtained by solving the transcendental equation for the $N = 1$ mode, namely,

$$\frac{CJ_1'(C_0)}{C_0 J_1(C_0)} - \frac{(C^2 - C_0^2)J_1(C_0)}{CC_0^3 J_1'(C_0)} = +\frac{J_1'(C)Y_1(CW) - Y_1'(C)J_1(CW)]}{J_1(C)Y_1(CW) - Y_1(C)J_1(CW)]} \tag{12}$$

One specifies a value of C and solves (13a) for W and (13b) for C_0. The results are shown in Table I and Fig. 1. The operation satisfying (13) is here referred to as the quarter-wave operation.

The normalized electrical tooth depth, $d/\lambda_v = (b-a)/\lambda_v$, is also plotted, which reveals that as the pipe becomes electrically larger (C increasing), this latter ratio approaches $\frac{1}{4}$, i.e., the wavelength in the radial gap approaches the free-space wavelength.

Also plotted is the normalized guide wavelength of the TE^0_{11} mode in an uncorrugated pipe of inner radius a for comparison, as where $W = b/a$. (It is noted that (1) and (14) are based on a surface impedance model valid for a sufficient number of teeth per free-space wavelength, $\lambda_v/G \gtrsim 5$, say, and also for thin teeth, i.e., $T/G \lesssim 0.10$, say.)

Of particular interest is the case for which the H_ϕ field vanishes at $\rho = a$, causing the right-hand side of (12) to vanish; (12) then reduces to

$$J_1^1(C)Y_1(CW) - Y_1^1(C)J_1(CW) = 0 \tag{13a}$$

$$\left[1 - \frac{C_0^2}{C^2}\right]J_1^2(C_0) - C_0^2\, J_1^1(C_0)]^2 = 0. \tag{13b}$$

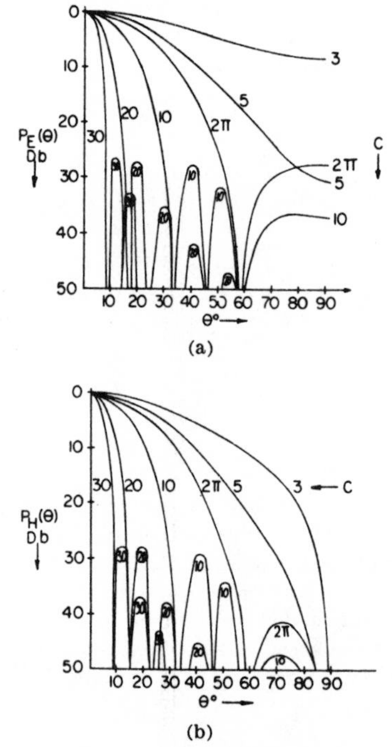

Fig. 2. Theoretical radiation patterns of corrugated HE_{11} pipe for quarter-wave teeth. (a) E plane. (b) H plane.

well as the edge taper D,

$$20\log_{10}\left|\frac{E_\rho(0,0)}{E_\rho(a,0)}\right|$$

in dB, of the radial field in the HE_{11} pipe at $\phi_s = 0$. This taper is seen to increase rapidly (from 4 dB for $C \approx 2$ to 30 dB for $C \approx 6$), as C increases and should be contrasted with that of the TE^0_{11} pipe which is always about 4 dB,

$$20\log_{10}\left|\frac{0.500}{J_1(X)/X}\right|$$

where $X = 1.841$. Thus the edge currents have a significantly lower value than the smooth counterpart for increasing pipe size. This greatly diminishes the E-plane diffraction effects. As will be seen, this leads to much lower (about 27.6 dB) E-plane first sidelobe levels contrasted to that for the uncorrugated pipe (about 17.6 dB) and to a broader E-plane main beam. It is noted, however, that the E-plane edge taper never becomes infinite for finite apertures, and hence the surface currents on the pipe are never zero; this leads to finite cross-polarized fields and slight beam asymmetry for finite apertures.

III. Radiation Patterns—Beam Efficiency

Computation of the E-plane ($\phi = 0$) and H-plane ($\phi = \pi/2$) patterns are shown in Fig. 2. The first sidelobe levels in *both* these planes are at least 27.5 dB down, and the E-plane patterns approach those of the H plane of the uncorrugated pipe. This indicates that with a corrugated pipe a higher percentage of the radiated power is concentrated in the main beam as compared to an uncorrugated pipe of the same size which has much lower (approximately 17.6 dB) E-plane first sidelobe levels. The beam efficiency η_B is of great importance to feed applications and is defined as the power radiated in the cone of angle θ_R divided by the power radiated throughout the entire space [6].

Computations of $\eta_B(C,\theta_R)$ are shown in Fig. 3 for the parameter $4 \leq C \leq 20$. (Note that for $C < 4$ the dB edge taper is probably inadequate to use the ground plane solutions, and the corresponding beam efficiencies calculated will be too high; hence these are not shown.) The range of θ_R in Fig. 3 for a given C corresponds to a range in the H-plane power density of 0 dB at $\theta_R = 0$ to approximately -20 dB at the maximum θ_R shown. Although a direct comparison of these beam efficiencies with those for an uncorrugated pipe are not presently possible, it can be seen from inspecting the work of Ruze [6] (for the conical horn case) that higher beam efficiencies result with quarter-wave corrugations due to suppression of the E-plane sidelobes and broadening of the E-plane main beam. Preliminary measurements made indicate this increase lies between 3–7 percent for $4 \lesssim C \lesssim 8$, for $\theta_R \approx 40°$.

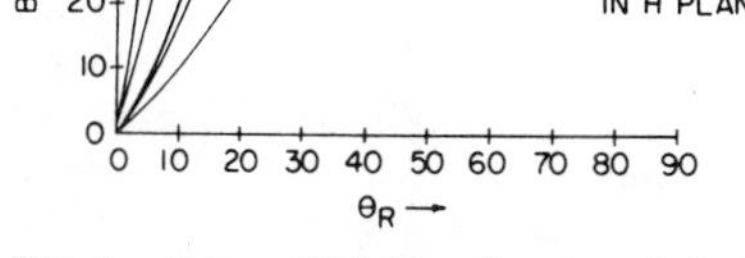

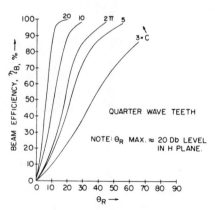

Fig. 3. Beam efficiency of corrugated pipe.

IV. Gain–Aperture Efficiency

Computations of gain, along with the aperture efficiency η_A as usually defined [6], were made and are shown in Fig. 4. It is noted that the aperture efficiency asymptotically approaches a constant value of approximately 68.8 percent as the antenna increases in size without limit.

V. Universal Horn Patterns

It is also of interest to note that from the computed patterns of Fig. 2 it is possible to describe the main beam by Kelleher's [7] universal horn patterns:

$$P_{dB}(\theta) \approx 10\left(\frac{\theta}{\theta_{10}}\right)^2 \tag{14}$$

as plotted in Fig. 5, where θ_{10} is the angle off axis at which power is 10 dB down from power on axis and where from Fig. 3 one obtains the dependence of θ_{10} on C, as shown in Fig. 5, and (14) then holds in both the E and H planes with θ_{10} chosen accordingly. A comparison of the Kelleher patterns so obtained with the exact patterns over the main beam region is not shown here but agrees within a fraction of a dB.

VI. Cross Polarization

From (11) the pertinent radiated fields expressed in terms of Cartesian coordinates are:

$$\begin{pmatrix} E_x(\theta,\phi) \\ E_y(\theta,\phi) \end{pmatrix} = +j\frac{Aa^2\mathcal{E}_0C_0}{4\pi}\cos\theta \begin{pmatrix} -f_0(\theta)[1 - f_2(\theta)/[f_0(\theta)]\cos 2\phi] \\ +f_2(\theta)\sin^2\phi \end{pmatrix} \tag{15}$$

It is convenient to define the cross-polarization ratio,

$$R(\theta,\phi) = 20\log_{10}\left|\frac{E_x(\theta,\phi)}{E_y(\theta,\phi)}\right|.$$

Examination of (15) shows that either in the E plane ($\phi = 0$) or the H plane ($\phi = \pi/2$), $E_y = 0$ ($R = \infty$), i.e., the field radiated has a single vector component for all θ (hence the term scalar feed). This, of course, is similar to the dual-mode Potter horn [8], the diagonal horn of Love [9], and the Ajioka [10] horn which also have no predicted cross polarization in the E and H planes. However, it is also noted from Table I that as $C \to \infty$, $C_0 \to 2.40$, i.e., $J_0(C_0) \to 0$ so $f_2(\theta) \to 0$, and hence $R \to \infty$, for all θ and ϕ. Also,

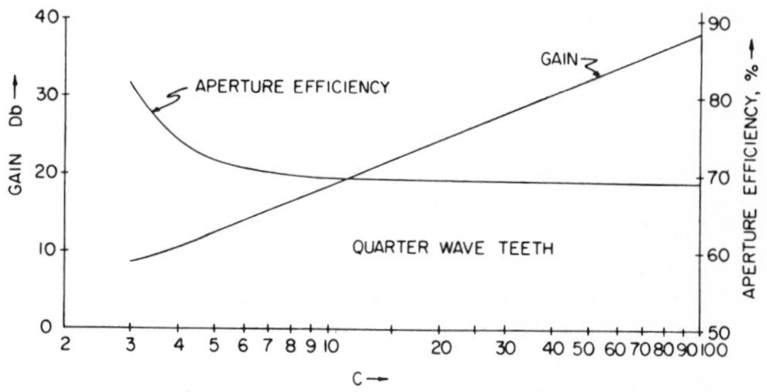

Fig. 4. Gain and aperture efficiency of corrugated pipe.

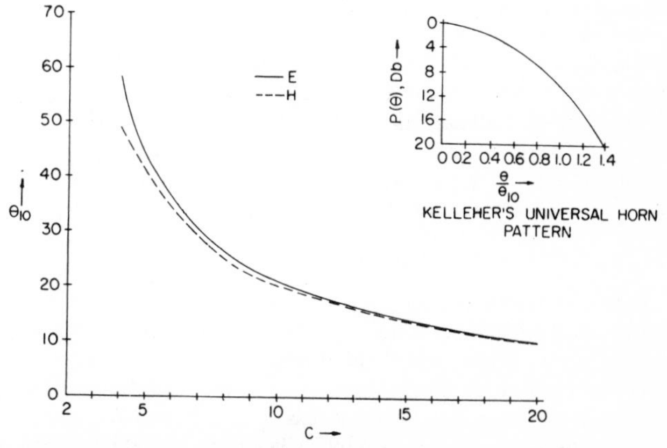

Fig. 5. Universal horn patterns of corrugated pipe.

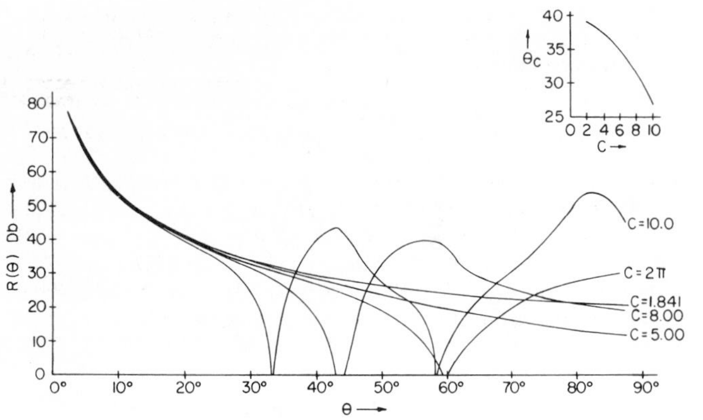

Fig. 6. Cross-polarization ratio (ϕ = 45°, 135°, 225°, 315° planes).

for C finite, it is seen that the worse cross-polarization case (R minimum) occurs for the diagonal planes (ϕ = 45°, etc.) for which

$$R(\theta) = 20 \log_{10} \left| \frac{f_0(\theta)}{f_2(\theta)} \right| .$$

This is plotted in Fig. 6 for the range of $1.841 \leq C \leq 10$ and $0 \leq \theta \leq 90°$. The diagonal horn of Love has $R(\theta,\phi)$ max ≈ 15 dB, and hence the corrugated horn's cross polarization is lower in these planes.

VII. Experimental Results

Fig. 7 shows some experimental results for the specific cases of a corrugated pipe with quarter-wave teeth and with apertures of $C = 2.26$, $C = 4.89$, and $C = 6.29$. The corresponding E-plane aperture edge tapers are (Fig. 1) approximately 8, 25, and 29 dB, respectively. A photo of the antennas is given in Fig. 8. These measurements substantiate the E-plane predictions of Fig. 2. Namely, that for small pipes, $1.84 \lesssim C \lesssim 3$, (Fig. 7(a)) the corrugations have little effect since the edge taper is small, and the E-plane patterns are essentially the same as with no corrugations For medium pipe sizes (Fig. 7(b), $4 \lesssim C \lesssim 6$) the edge taper increases significantly so that the E-plane patterns begin to broaden, and the sidelobes drop and approach those of the H plane (with or without corrugations). Finally, for large pipes (Fig. 7(c), $C \gtrsim 2\pi$) the E- and H-plane patterns are essentially identical over the main beam region with the E plane having the same low sidelobes as the H plane for $C \gtrsim 10$ as predicted by Fig. 2.

Other patterns taken were also in excellent agreement with theory in the main lobe vicinity, but only fair in the far sidelobe region. To accurately predict the radiation in the latter region, account of the currents on the edges and the back of the finite ground plane and the outer pipe walls must be considered. This is a much more difficult task, but it presumably can be done using edge diffraction theory [11] in conjunction with superposition of the preceding infinite ground plane solutions, and/or Weiner–Hopf techniques [12], [13]. Also, based on the good impedance predictions [14], [15] of apertures (excited with uncorrugated pipes) on finite ground planes utilizing the infinite plane model, the percentage of total radiated power in the far sidelobe region can be estimated to be a few percent. Thus for corrugated pipe with quarter-wave operation this power will be even smaller.

VIII. Conclusions

It has been shown that the HE_{11} mode in a corrugated pipe of sufficiently large diameter ($C \gtrsim 2\pi$) with quarter-wave teeth radiates as a "scalar feed;" the E-plane pattern is similar to the H-plane pattern of the uncorrugated pipe, with its associated broader main beam and lower sidelobes. The E- and H-plane main beam patterns can be described by Kelleher's universal horn pattern,

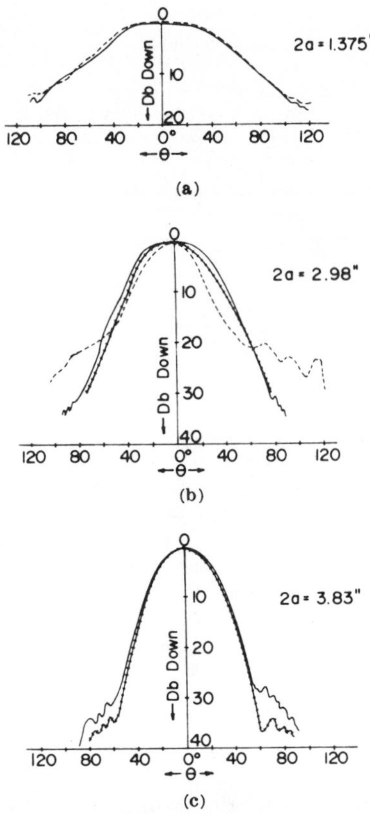

Fig. 7. Measured pattern as function of pipe size. All patterns taken at 6.175 GHz. ——E plane (corrugated); – – – –E plane (noncorrugated); –|–|–|–H plane (corrugated or noncorrugated). (a) Small pipe (C = 2.26). (b) Medium Pipe (C = 4.89). (c) Large pipe (C = 6.29).

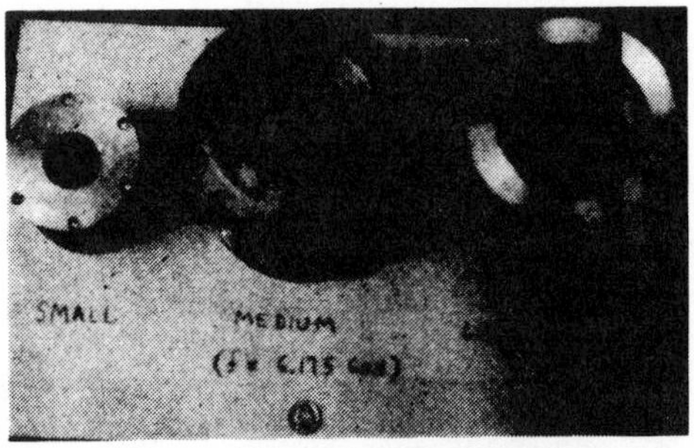

Fig. 8. Photo of antennas tested.

and these begin to coincide for $C \gtrsim 2\pi$. The beam efficiency is higher than that of the same size pipe uncorrugated, and the aperture efficiency has an upper bound of about 69 percent. The cross-polarized energy in the diagonal planes is less than that for known dual-mode horns.

For the purposes of design one can use Fig. 5 to determine the antenna size for a specified dB level at a specified angle off axis in either the E or H plane, and Fig. 1 will give the required tooth depth. The corresponding beam efficiency and gain are then predicted as Figs. 3 and 4, and the radiation patterns are given by Fig. 2.

Acknowledgment

The authors are indebted to T. Charlton of the Andrew Corporation for suggesting the formulation of the corrugated pipe radiation problem in terms of the E-plane edge taper in the aperture of the pipe, leading to the consequent ground plane model adopted.

References

[1] H. C. Minnet and B. MacA. Thomas, "A method of synthesizing radiation patterns with axial symmetry," *IEEE Trans Antennas Propagat.* (Commun.), vol. AP-14, pp. 654–656, Sept. 1966.
[2] P. J. B. Clarricoats and C. J. E. Phillips, "Optimum design of Gregorian corrected spherical-reflector antenna," *Proc. Inst. Elec. Eng.*, vol. I.E.E., 117, pp. 718–734, Apr. 1970.
[3] P. J. B. Clarricoats and P. K. Saha, "Propagation and radiation behavior of corrugated feeds," Pt. 1—Corrugated-waveguide feed," *Proc. Inst. Elec. Eng.*, vol. 118, pp. 1167–1176, Sept. 1971.
[4] S. Silver, *Microwave Antenna Theory and Design*, (M.I.T. Radiation Lab. Series, vol. 12). Cambridge, Mass.: Boston Technical Publishers, 1947, p. 161.
[5] C. M. Knop and G. I. Cohn, "Radiation from an aperture in a coated plane," *Radio Sci.*, vol. 68D, pp. 363–378, Apr. 1964.
[6] J. Ruze, "Antennas for radar astronomy," in *Radar Astronomy*, J. V. Evans and T. Hagfors, Eds. New York: McGraw Hill, 1968.
[7] K. S. Kelleher, *The Microwave Engineer's Handbook and Buyer's Guide*. New York: Horizon Press, 1964, p. 128; see also *Reference Data for Radio Engineers*, 5th ed. Indianapolis, Ind.: Howard W. Sams & Co., 1968, pp. 25–39.
[8] P. D. Potter, "A new horn antenna with suppressed side lobes and equal beam width," *Microwave J.*, vol. 6, pp. 71–78, June 1963.
[9] A. W. Love, "The diagonal horn antenna," *Microwave J.*, vol. 5, pp. 117–122, Mar. 1962.
[10] J. S. Ajioka and H. E. Harry, Jr., "Shaped beam antenna for earth coverage from a stabilized satellite," *IEEE Trans. Antennas Propagat.*, vol. AP-18, pp. 323–327, May 1970.
[11] C. A. Balanis, "Pattern distortion due to edge diffractions," *IEEE Trans. Antennas Propagat.* (Commun.) vol. AP-18, pp. 561–563, July 1970.
[12] D. S. Jones, *The Theory of Electromagnetism*. New York: Pergamon, 1964, ch. 9.
[13] R. Mittra and S. W. Lee, *Analytical Techniques in the Theory of Guided Waves*. New York: Macmillan, 1971.
[14] W. F. Croswell, R. C. Rudduck, and D. M. Hatcher, "The admittance of a rectangular waveguide radiating into a dielectric slab," *IEEE Trans. Antennas Propagat.*, vol. AP-15, pp. 627–633, Sept. 1967.
[15] M. C. Bailey and C. T. Swift, "Input admittance of a circular waveguide aperture covered by a dielectric slab," *IEEE Trans. Antennas Propagat.*, vol. AP-16, pp. 386–391 July 1968.

PROPAGATION AND RADIATION BEHAVIOUR OF CORRUGATED FEEDS

Clarricoats and Saha have recently published a comprehensive account of corrugated waveguide feeds, which have been studied extensively in a number of countries in the past few years [Proc. IEE, 1971, **118**, (9), pp. 1167-1176, 1177-1186]. However, two points in their interpretation of the original Australian work in this field are incorrect and, because of the definitive nature of their papers, warrant clarification.

The first of these repeats a misconception in a previous letter by Al-Hakkak and Lo.[A] Cylindrical corrugated structures for guiding fast, hybrid modes were not originated by V. H. Rumsey. The concept was first proposed at the CSIRO, and both the theory and an experimental model of the waveguide were well advanced by the time of Prof. Rumsey's stimulating visit towards the end of 1965. Prior to this visit, Prof. Rumsey had formulated certain theoretical conditions that must be satisfied by axially symmetric fields, and it was the realisation that our corrugated structures generated such fields that attracted his interest.

The work at CSIRO evolved directly from the discovery, during research on feed efficiency under NASA grant NsG-240-62, that the focused fields of a paraboloid can be represented by a series of cylindrical hybrid waves.* A study of the **E** and **H** field structure also led to the hypothesis that the waves could be confined in a cylindrical metal tube, provided that the walls were corrugated either circumferentially or longitudinally with resonant slots. As far as we are aware, this was the first time that multimode corrugated waveguides had been proposed for synthetising high-efficiency feeds.

These concepts were subsequently refined and elaborated by the present authors in collaboration. An important result of the focal-region analysis (published later in generalised form[B]) was that a uniform, linearly polarised wave, incident normally on the aperture of a paraboloid, produces 'balanced' hybrid modes at the focal plane. In these modes, the **E** and **H** fields were found to be identical in form and to satisfy the relation $\mathbf{E} = jZ_0\mathbf{H}$ (in complex notation), where Z_0 is the intrinsic impedance of space. A second result followed immediately by reciprocity: balanced hybrid modes radiating from the focal plane must illuminate the paraboloid aperture without crosspolarisation. Consequently, the radiation fields of these modes had to possess axial symmetry of polarisation.

A detailed study of boundary conditions, formulated in terms of anisotropic surface reactances and assuming only the lowest slot mode, confirmed the original hypothesis that balanced hybrid modes would propagate in a cylindrical corrugated tube with the slots tuned to resonance. An experimental waveguide with circumferential corrugations was therefore constructed to check the predicted propagation characteristics of the lowest (HE_{11}) mode. This structure was also designed so that measurements could be made on the fields radiated from one end, to test the prediction of radiation symmetry noted above.

These developments and, in particular, the successful results of the propagation measurements[C] were discussed with Prof. Rumsey during October 1965. He pointed out their relevance to previous theoretical studies[D] of fields, which everywhere satisfy the relationship $\mathbf{E} = \pm\, jZ_0\mathbf{H}$. These fields had been found to be characteristic of propagation over anisotropic surfaces, for which the boundary conditions on **E** and **H** are the same. Subsequently, he had deduced, by general electromagnetic arguments, that axially-symmetric fields were of the same type. As a result, the required fields could be expressed in terms of a single scalar function, so that the problem became one of discovering an appropriate function for the purpose.[E]

In practice, the determination of explicit solutions and, in particular, specific boundary structures is still difficult. This problem had not been solved prior to Prof. Rumsey's visit to CSIRO, where, as outlined above, a solution in terms of plane hybrid modes excited by cylindrical corrugated structures had already been achieved by a completely different approach. It is of interest to note that a related structure, exciting symmetric spherical modes, had been developed empirically in the USA by Kay and his associates. His report[F] on corrugated conical horns in March 1964 was unknown here at the time of our investigations.

Although our propagation measurements had accurately confirmed the expected characteristics of the HE_{11} mode, the measured radiation patterns were not at first quite symmetrical. Prof. Rumsey suggested that this was because the metal surface surrounding the aperture was smooth, and therefore did not have the same effect on both **E** and **H** fields. Consequently, the external fields did not satisfy the balance condition applying in the interior. When the corrugations were extended to this outside surface, the expected symmetry was achieved. Thus, Prof. Rumsey's contribution to the work here was twofold: first in emphasising the importance of the symmetry properties of the balanced, hybrid modes excited by our corrugated structures, and then in showing that his general formulation of the symmetry problem gave an added insight into these properties.

Subsequently, the original concept of using multi-hybrid-mode feeds for the high-efficiency illumination of paraboloidal and spherical reflectors was studied in some detail at CSIRO. The statement by Clarricoats and Saha that a 2-hybrid-mode feed described by Vu in 1970[G] represents the first investigation of multi-hybrid-mode feeds is therefore not correct. Two-hybrid-mode feeds of this type have been used extensively on the Parkes 64 m radiotelescope since 1967, and were fully described in a paper in 1968.[H]

13th June 1972

Division of Radiophysics — H. C. MINNETT
CSIRO — B. MacA. THOMAS
Sydney, NSW, Australia

References

A AL-HAKKAK, M. J., and LO, Y. T.: 'Circular waveguides with anisotropic walls', Electron. Lett., 1970, **6**, pp. 786-789

B MINNETT, H. C., and THOMAS, B. MacA.: 'Fields in the image space of symmetrical focusing reflectors', Proc. IEE, 1968, **115**, (10), pp. 1419-1430

C MINNETT, H. C., and THOMAS, B. MacA.: 'A method of synthesizing radiation patterns with axial symmetry', IEEE Trans., 1966, **AP-14**, pp. 654-656

D RUMSEY, V. H.: 'A new way of solving Maxwell's equations', ibid., 1961, **AP-9**, pp. 461-465

E RUMSEY, V. H.: 'Horn antennas with uniform power patterns around their axes', ibid., 1966, **AP-14**, pp. 656-658

F KAY, A. F.: 'The scalar feed'. US Air Force Cambridge Research Laboratory report 64-347, March 1964

G VU, T. B., and VU, Q. H.: 'Optimum feed for large radio telescopes: experimental results', Electron. Lett., 1970, **6**, pp. 159-160

H THOMAS, B. MacA.: 'Hybrid waveguide mode feeds for the illumination of large focusing reflectors'. Proceedings of Radio Research Board symposium on antenna research, Melbourne, Australia, 1968

We are naturally sorry that, owing to our misinterpretation of statements contained in References C and G, which originated in Australia, we failed to recognise fully the important original contribution of Minnett and Thomas in the development of the corrugated circular waveguide feed for reflector antennas. We are very grateful to them for explaining so clearly the history of this development in Australia and the valuable role played by Prof. Victor Rumsey during his 1965 visit.

Department of Electrical & Electronic Engineering — P. J. B. CLARRICOATS
Queen Mary College
Mile End Road
London E1 4NS, England

Institute of Radio Physics & Electronics — P. K. SAHA
Calcutta 9, India

* *MINNETT, H. C.: Internal memorandum, CSIRO, 1963*

Reprinted with permission from *Proc. Inst. Elec. Eng.*, vol. 119, p. 1280, Sept. 1972.

Horn Antennas with Uniform Power Patterns Around Their Axes

Summary

It is shown that a linearly polarized horn that has the same power pattern in all planes through the axis can be made from a synthetic material for which the boundary conditions on *E* and *H* are the same. An arbitrarily close approximation to this requirement can be realized by means of a grooved circular horn.

Introduction

For many purposes one needs a horn antenna having equal E and H plane patterns. Here we shall be concerned with the more general problem of making the power patterns equal in *all* planes through the axis. The efficient illumination of a parabolic antenna is one application of this kind of antenna, and the accompanying paper by H. C. Minnett and B. MacA. Thomas describes the development of this approach. Another important application occurs in connection with polarization measurements in radio astronomy. We measure polarization by measuring the powers $\langle E_x \overset{*}{E}_x \rangle$ $\langle E_y \overset{*}{E}_y \rangle$ and the correlation factor $\langle E_x \overset{*}{E}_y \rangle$, or in some equivalent way. In the case of a paraboloidal radio telescope, the complex signals E_x and E_y represent two orthogonal components received at the focus. Suppose the x- and y-axes are chosen as the E and H planes of the focal feed horn, so that the horn measures E_x. The measurement of E_y requires that the feed horn effectively or actually be turned through 90°. Now consider the cross section of the antenna beam on the celestial sphere. Ideally we should like it to be circular, but if the E and H patterns of the horn are not equal, it is clear that the beam will not have this circular symmetry. Consequently, when the horn is turned through 90° to measure E_y, the telescope sees a different area of the sky. For example, in an extreme case it might happen that a randomly polarized source was picked up when the horn was oriented to measure E_x but not when it was oriented to measure E_y. The "measured polarization" of the randomly polarized source would then be 100 percent linear in the E_x direction. It will be seen from this example that precise uniformity of the power pattern around the axis is essential in polarization measurements of the celestial source distribution.

Manuscript received May 15, 1966. The research reported here was supported in part by the National Science Foundation under Grant GK-676.

Thus if E_θ and E_ϕ represent the field transmitted by the horn, θ and ϕ being the usual spherical coordinates for colatitude and longitude, we want to make $|E_\theta|^2+|E_\phi|^2$ independent of ϕ. Starting from this requirement it will be shown that the walls of the horn have to be such that the boundary conditions on $\boldsymbol{E}$ are the same as those on $\boldsymbol{H}$. This condition can be synthesized in practice over a limited band by using a circular waveguide and horn with a ridged surface, as described in the accompanying paper by Minnett and Thomas. To see how polarization measurements would be made with such a horn, suppose we measure E_x by placing an electric dipole parallel to the x-axis in the waveguide. We can measure E_y by replacing the electric dipole by a magnetic dipole, also along the x-axis. Since the entire structure affects E and H in the same way, it is clear that $\boldsymbol{E}$ in the first measurement is equal to $\boldsymbol{H}$ in the second. The power patterns in the two measurements are therefore equal, and so we have a true measure of polarization.

Theory

At the outset it is clear that if we want the power pattern to be independent of ϕ, we need an antenna that is also independent of ϕ: in other words, a circular waveguide and circular horn at the focus of a circular

Reprinted from *IEEE Trans. Antennas Propagat.*, vol. AP-14, pp. 656–658, Sept. 1966.

paraboloid. In practice, the cross section of the waveguide is chosen to cut off all except the modes that vary as $\exp(\pm j\phi)$. Therefore the field radiated by the horn can be expressed as

$$\boldsymbol{E} = \boldsymbol{a} \exp(j\phi) + \boldsymbol{b} \exp(-j\phi) \qquad (1)$$

where $\boldsymbol{a}$ and $\boldsymbol{b}$ depend on θ but are independent of ϕ. The linearly polarized modes in the waveguide are represented by the functions cos ϕ and sin ϕ: they consist of equal amounts of the exp $(\pm j\phi)$ modes. Thus the linearly polarized patterns of the circular horn are represented by (1) when $\boldsymbol{a}$ and $\boldsymbol{b}$ represent equal powers. The condition for this is

$$\boldsymbol{a}\cdot\overset{*}{\boldsymbol{a}} = |\boldsymbol{a}|^2 = |\boldsymbol{b}|^2 = \boldsymbol{b}\cdot\overset{*}{\boldsymbol{b}}. \qquad (2)$$

We see from (1) that $\boldsymbol{a}$ and $\boldsymbol{b}$ represent the electric fields for the exp $(\pm j\phi)$ modes. Because the structure is independent of ϕ it is reasonably clear that, apart from a constant, $\boldsymbol{a}$ and $\boldsymbol{b}$ will be the same functions of θ except that the phase of b_ϕ relative to b_θ will differ from that for $\boldsymbol{a}$ by 180°, i.e.,

$$\frac{a_\phi}{a_\theta} = -\frac{b_\phi}{b_\theta}. \qquad (3)$$

This can be derived rigorously by expressing $\boldsymbol{a}$ and $\boldsymbol{b}$ as general combinations of TE and TM fields. Thus the TE part of $\boldsymbol{a}$ exp $j\phi$ is expressed in terms of a scalar $f(\theta)$ exp $j\phi$, and that of $\boldsymbol{b}$ $\exp(-j\phi)$ by $Cf(\theta)$ $\exp(-j\phi)$, C being constant. The standard formulas then show that (3) applies to the TE parts, and to the TM parts as well. So (3) holds in the general case.

Combining (2) and (3) we see that

$$|a_\theta|^2 = |b_\theta|^2 \qquad (4)$$

or

$$a_\theta = b_\theta \exp j\psi'.$$

On referring to the definition (1) of $\boldsymbol{a}$ and $\boldsymbol{b}$ we see that the position of the plane $\phi=0$ can be chosen to make $\psi'=0$. Thus

$$a_\theta = b_\theta \quad \text{and} \quad a_\phi = -b_\phi. \qquad (5)$$

Substitution in (1) gives

$$E_\theta = a_\theta \cos\phi \qquad (6)$$

$$E_\phi = ja_\phi \sin\phi. \qquad (7)$$

These, then, are the general formulas for the linearly polarized case with a_θ and a_ϕ independent of ϕ.

We now put in the requirement that the power pattern be independent of ϕ: $|E_\theta|^2 + |E_\phi|^2$ must be independent of ϕ. Substitution from (6) and (7) shows that this requires

$$|a_\theta|^2 = |a_\phi|^2. \qquad (8)$$

Stated as a formula: for the exp $j\phi$ excitation, E_θ and E_ϕ must have the same magnitude for all θ.

Now $\boldsymbol{a}$ represents a certain state of elliptical polarization. From (8) we have

$$a_\theta = a_\phi \exp j\psi.$$

It will be found that this means the polarization ellipse is inclined at 45° to the θ, ϕ directions or, in case $\psi=90°$, the polarization is circular. It will also be found that the polarization on axis $\theta=0$ is circular in any case, as is well known for the exp $j\phi$ excitation. It seems reasonably clear that the first case, that of elliptical polarization inclined at 45° to the coordinate directions, can be ruled out as impractical. Actually it could be generated by structures like the "sheath helix," i.e., cylindrical structures that are independent of ϕ but have anisotropically transparent walls. But such structures are not useful as feeds for parabolic antennas, and a more general consideration of the focusing problem does indeed rule out the elliptically polarized case. Therefore the far field of the horn must be circularly polarized everywhere when excited in the exp $j\phi$ mode.

The properties of such fields have already been worked out: they are basic to the theory of frequency-independent antennas.[1] They are such that the field vectors $\boldsymbol{E}$ and $\boldsymbol{H}$ are, apart from a constant, the same everywhere, in the near field as well as at infinity. Specifically,

$$\boldsymbol{E} = \pm jZ_0\boldsymbol{H} \qquad (9)$$

with Z_0 the intrinsic impedance of space (377 ohms approximately). Any solution of Maxwell's equations can be expressed as a combination of the two types. The elementary source for such fields is the combination of an electric and a magnetic dipole aligned in the same direction at the same point with moments related by the factor jZ_0. Any field of type (9) can be expressed in terms of a single scalar function f by the formula

$$\pm jZ_0\boldsymbol{H} = \boldsymbol{E} = \nabla\left(\frac{\partial f}{\partial z}\right) + k^2\boldsymbol{z}f \pm k\nabla x\boldsymbol{z}f \qquad (10)$$

with

$$k^2 = \omega^2\mu\epsilon = \left(\frac{2\pi}{\lambda}\right)^2 \quad \text{and} \quad Z_0^2 = \frac{\mu}{\epsilon} \qquad (11)$$

and $\boldsymbol{z}$=unit vector in fixed direction. The first two terms can be interpreted as the electric dipole component and the last as the magnetic dipole component.

[1] V. H. Rumsey, "A new way of solving Maxwell's equations," *IRE Trans. on Antennas and Propagation*, vol. AP-9, pp. 461–465, September 1961.

We see from (9) that such fields are supported by any structure that has the same effect on $\boldsymbol{E}$ as on $\boldsymbol{H}$. An ordinary metal surface does not have this effect: it forces the normal component of $\boldsymbol{H}$ to zero but the normal component of $\boldsymbol{E}$ is then maximum. Thus a synthetic surface is needed. Consider a grooved metal surface in the z, x plane, the width of the grooves being equal to the width of the metal ridge between them. When the width of the groove, denoted by a, is infinitesimal compared with the wavelength λ, the field within the groove must have $\boldsymbol{E}$ perpendicular to the sides of the groove. In other words, if the grooves are parallel to the z-axis, E_x is the only component of $\boldsymbol{E}$, and it is independent of x. Consequently, H_y and H_z are the only components of $\boldsymbol{H}$ in the groove and they depend only on y and z. If the varitaion with z is as $e^{jkz\cos\psi''}$, where ψ'' is a fixed parameter, the variation with y is as $e^{+jky\sin\psi''}$. It follows that if the depth of the groove, d, fits $4d \sin\psi''=\lambda$, $H_z=0$ at the top of the groove. Also, $E_z=0$ at the edge of the groove, so as $a\rightarrow 0$, E_z and H_z vanish at the surface formed by the edges of the sheets that form the sides of the grooves. Thus the effect of this surface on $\boldsymbol{E}$ is the same as on $\boldsymbol{H}$ for all incident fields with the same ψ'', i.e., the same variation along the grooves. This applies to a circular waveguide with the grooves cut perpendicular to the axis for all waveguide modes with a common $e^{j\phi}$ variation, but not if the grooves are parallel to the axis. The formula for d in this case, is however, different. It is expressed in terms of Bessel functions J_1 and N_1:

$$J_1{}^1(k[b-d])N_1(kb) = N_1{}^1(k[b-d])J_1(kb) \qquad (12)$$

where b is the radius of the bottom of the grooves. Thus a circular waveguide and horn fabricated of such a synthetic material will support the kind of field required to give a power pattern independent of ϕ with linear polarization.

The tests described by Minnett and Thomas indicate excellent performance from such a model, but a considerable amount of work remains to be done to determine the bandwidth and effect of groove width.

ACKNOWLEDGMENT

It is a pleasure to acknowledge the help of the CSIRO, Division of Radiophysics, Australia, and particularly the cordial cooperation of H. C. Minnett and B. MacA. Thomas.

V. H. Rumsey
Dept. of Elec. Engrg.
University of California
Berkeley, Calif.

A Method of Synthesizing Radiation Patterns with Axial Symmetry

Introduction

The cost of very large aperture antennas using accurate paraboloid reflectors has emphasized the need for improved feed systems to make optimum use of the received energy. A theory of feed pattern synthesis has been developed from a study of the fields at the focus of a circular-aperture paraboloid. These fields may be decomposed into components, termed hybrid modes, which possess symmetrical radiation properties and satisfy anisotropic boundary conditions.

This study has led to the concept of a feed consisting of the open end of a cylindrical corrugated waveguide in which hybrid modes can propagate. The pattern of such a feed is axially symmetric with zero cross-polarization response and may be shaped for high-efficiency, low-noise operation by a suitable choice of the hybrid-mode amplitudes. This technique needs only half the number of independently generated modes required by existing multimode methods giving nonsymmetrical patterns.

Manuscript received May 15, 1966; revised June 20, 1966. This work was part of a study of the performance of the CSIRO 210-foot radio telescope at Parkes, N.S.W., and was supported by NASA Research Grant NsG-240-62.

Feeds with symmetrical radiation patterns are also important for polarization measurements in radio astronomy. The symmetry of the feed patterns to be described are a consequence of the specific form of the hybrid-mode fields as disclosed by the focal-plane analysis. In an accompanying paper by V. H. Rumsey, in which the polarization application is emphasized, it is shown that the form of the fields required may also be deduced from the general conditions for exact uniformity of the power pattern about the axis.

Focal-Plane Fields

The fields in the focal region were calculated from the sources excited on the paraboloid surface by a linearly polarized, uniform plane-wave incident normally on the circular aperture. An important simplification, valid for large dishes and short wavelengths, is that the wave scattered by each element of surface is very nearly plane in the vicinity of the focus. For the Parkes dish, with a focal length of 26.2 meters, this assumption results in a phase error of less than $\lambda/16$ within an 11λ-diameter area of the focal plane at $\lambda = 10$ cm.

The plane-wave electric field arriving at the focal plane from an element of surface can be resolved into two components. One component is polarized in the plane of incidence, and has a component of E normal to the focal plane. The other is polarized normal to the plane of incidence and therefore E lies entirely in the focal plane. The fields in the first group, generated by an annular ring of the dish subtending an angle 2θ at the focus, combine near the focus to form an equiphase TM pattern in any plane parallel to the focal plane [Fig. 1(a)]. The fields of the second group form the TE pattern of Fig. 1(b).

Both patterns propagate along the dish axis with a velocity near the focal plane of $1/\cos\theta$ times the free-space velocity. The patterns in Fig. 1 are the TM_{1n} and TE_{1n} plane-wave solutions of Maxwell's equations appropriate for cylindrical waveguides. However, since the circles on which tangential E vanishes do not coincide, the two patterns cannot be simultaneously bounded by the same conducting tube.

The total field generated by the annular ring of the dish is the sum of the TM_{1n} and TE_{1n} mode patterns and may be termed the HE_{1n} hybrid mode. The transverse fields are linearly polarized for a paraboloid with a large focal length to diameter ratio (f/D), [Fig. 1(c)], but are curved for the values of f/D usual in radio telescopes.

Omitting the common phase factor, the expressions for the HE_{1n} fields at a point ρ, ξ in the focal plane are

$$\left.\begin{aligned} E_\rho &= E_\rho(\rho)\sin\xi \\ E_\xi &= E_\xi(\rho)\cos\xi \\ E_z &= E_z(\rho)\sin\xi \end{aligned}\right\} \qquad (1)$$

and

$$\left.\begin{aligned} H_\rho &= H_\rho(\rho)\cos\xi \\ H_\xi &= H_\xi(\rho)\sin\xi \\ H_z &= H_z(\rho)\cos\xi \end{aligned}\right\} \qquad (2)$$

Reprinted from *IEEE Trans. Antennas Propagat.*, vol. AP-14, pp. 654–656, Sept. 1966.

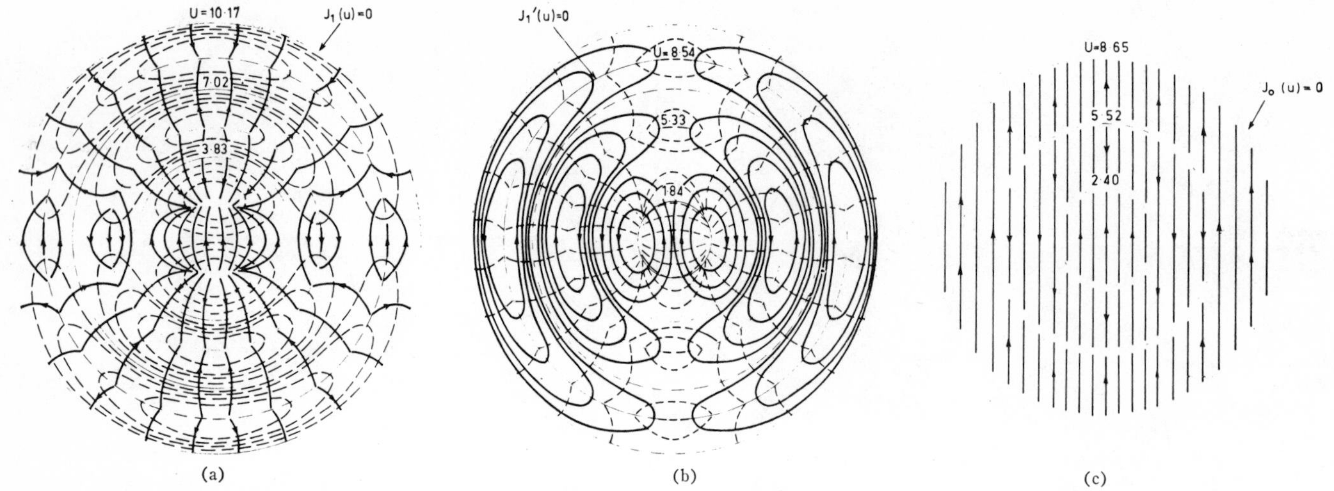

Fig. 1. Field patterns in focal plane (a) TM_{1n} component. (b) TE_{1n} component. (c) HE_{1n} hybrid mode.

where

$$\left.\begin{aligned} E_\rho(\rho) &= -jk\sin\bar{\theta}\Big\{\cos\bar{\theta}J_0(u) + (1-\cos\bar{\theta})\frac{J_1(u)}{u}\Big\} \\ E_\xi(\rho) &= -jk\sin\bar{\theta}\Big\{J_0(u) - (1-\cos\bar{\theta})\frac{J_1(u)}{u}\Big\} \\ E_z(\rho) &= -k\sin^2\bar{\theta}J_1(u) \end{aligned}\right\} \quad (3)$$

and

$$H_\rho(\rho) = -\frac{E_\rho(\rho)}{Z_0},\quad H_\xi(\rho) = \frac{E_\xi(\rho)}{Z_0},\quad H_z(\rho) = -\frac{E_z(\rho)}{Z_0}. \quad (4)$$

In the equations, $k=2\pi/\lambda$, $u=k\rho\sin\bar{\theta}$ ohms. The E and H fields of the hybrid mode are thus *identical* in form, except for a rotation of 90° in ξ, and at corresponding points are related by Z_0 as shown in (4).

The total focal-plane field is the sum of the hybrid-modes generated by all the elementary annular rings of the dish. The axial velocities of the modes range from 1 to $1/\cos\theta_0$ times the free-space velocity, where θ_0 is the semi-angle of the dish. All modes arrive at the focal plane in phase. For a paraboloid with a large f/D, the field is linearly-polarized and the amplitude distribution reduces to the well-known Airy pattern

$$\frac{J_1(k\rho\theta_0)}{(k\rho\theta_0)}.$$

This is the Fourier transform of the uniform amplitude distribution produced in the dish aperture by the incident wave. For small f/D values these simple relationships no longer hold. The focal-plane polarization is more complex and the amplitude varies circumferentially.

Hybrid-Mode Guides

By reciprocity, a feed which synthesized the entire focal-plane field distribution would radiate a symmetrical pattern producing uniform fields over the dish aperture and 100 percent aperture efficiency. In practice, of course, the feed aperture must be restricted. Appropriate boundaries for hybrid-modes can be developed by considering the circumferential and longitudinal surface reactances, defined, respectively, as

$$X_\xi = -jE_\xi/H_z;\quad X_z = jE_z/H_\xi \quad (5)$$

where the z-coordinate is directed from the focus to the vertex. By substituting (3) and (4) into (5), it is readily shown that the required surface must satisfy $X_\xi X_z = -Z_0^2$. Thus to match X_ξ and X_z at every point the boundary must be anisotropic.

This requirement may be realized in practice with corrugated metal surfaces. For example, a cylindrical surface with circumferential slots may be designed so that $H_\xi=0$ at the surface (zero longitudinal current). Also the edges of flanges between slots require $E_\xi=0$. With sufficient slots per wavelength the structure approximates a continuous anisotropic surface with $X_\xi=0$ and $X_z=\infty$. Similarly, a structure with longitudinal slots can be designed to simulate a continuous surface with $X_\xi=\infty (H_z=0)$ and $X_z=0 (E_z=0)$. This structure appears less attractive, however, because the normal TM_{1n} modes can also propagate.

It will be noted that these boundaries affect E and H fields in the same way in agreement with the fact that the fields are identical [see (3) and (4)]. We are indebted to V. H. Rumsey for this point of view, which he has developed in the accompanying contribution.

The hybrid-modes which can propagate in a circumferentially-slotted guide have values of $\bar{\theta}$ defined by

$$1-\cos\bar{\theta}_n = \frac{\bar{u}_n J_0(\bar{u}_n)}{J_1(\bar{u}_n)} \quad (6)$$

derived from (3). Here $\bar{u}_n = ka\sin\bar{\theta}_n$ where a is the internal radius of the guide.

Radiation from Hybrid-Mode Guide

Consider the radiation from the open end of a cylindrical hybrid-mode guide. The far-field components in a direction θ, ϕ due to all the annular rings of width $d\rho$ in the aperture are found to be

$$E_\theta = \frac{jk}{2R}e^{-jkR}\int_0^a \Big\{[E_\rho(\rho)+Z_0H_\xi(\rho)\cos\theta]J_1'(v) + [E_\xi(\rho)-Z_0H_\rho(\rho)\cos\theta]\frac{J_1(v)}{v}\Big\}\cdot\sin\phi\cdot\rho\cdot d\rho \quad (7)$$

$$E_\phi = \frac{jk}{2R}e^{-jkR}\int_0^a \Big\{[E_\xi(\rho)\cos\theta-Z_0H_\rho(\rho)]J_1'(v) + [E_\rho(\rho)\cos\theta+Z_0H_\xi(\rho)]\frac{J_1(v)}{v}\Big\}\cdot\cos\phi\cdot\rho\cdot d\rho \quad (8)$$

where $v=k\rho\sin\theta$. For zero cross polarization and symmetry of the paraboloid aperture fields, it can be shown that the radiated field of a feed must have the form

$$E_\theta = F(\theta)\sin\phi,\quad E_\phi = F(\theta)\cos\phi. \quad (9)$$

These conditions will be satisfied by (7) if

$$E_\rho(\rho) = -Z_0H_\rho(\rho),\quad E_\xi(\rho) = Z_0H_\xi(\rho). \quad (10)$$

Since (10) is identical with (4), the polarization and symmetry requirements are satisfied by the radiation from hybrid-mode fields.[1]

Substituting (3) and (4) into (7) we find

$$F(\theta) = \frac{jk}{2R}e^{-jkR}\Big\{J_1(\bar{u})\frac{J_1(\bar{v})}{\bar{v}}(1+\cos\theta\cos\bar{\theta}) + \frac{1}{1-\left(\frac{\bar{v}}{\bar{u}}\right)^2}\Big[J_1(\bar{u})J_1'(\bar{v}) - \frac{\bar{v}}{\bar{u}}J_1(\bar{v})J_1'(\bar{u})\Big](\cos\theta+\cos\bar{\theta})\Big\} \quad (11)$$

where $\bar{u}=ka\sin\bar{\theta}$ and $\bar{v}=ka\sin\theta$. Combined with (9), this equation gives the far-field pattern of a hybrid-mode (specified by $\bar{\theta}$) radiating from the open end of the guide. In general, the pattern is in the form of a symmetrical hollow cone of semi-angle $\bar{\theta}$.

[1] In the special case when $E_\xi(\rho)=E_\rho(\rho)=E(\rho)$, so that $-H_\rho(\rho)=H_\xi(\rho)=H(\rho)$ from (10), the hybrid-mode fields are linearly polarized with $E(\rho)=Z_0H(\rho)$ and can be represented by a distribution of Huygens sources. This is the case when f/D is large.

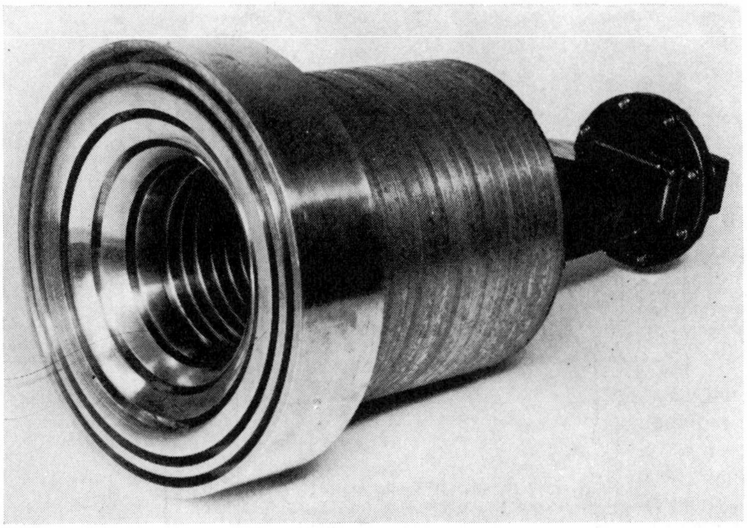

Fig. 2. HE_{11} feed for $\lambda = 11.3$ cm.

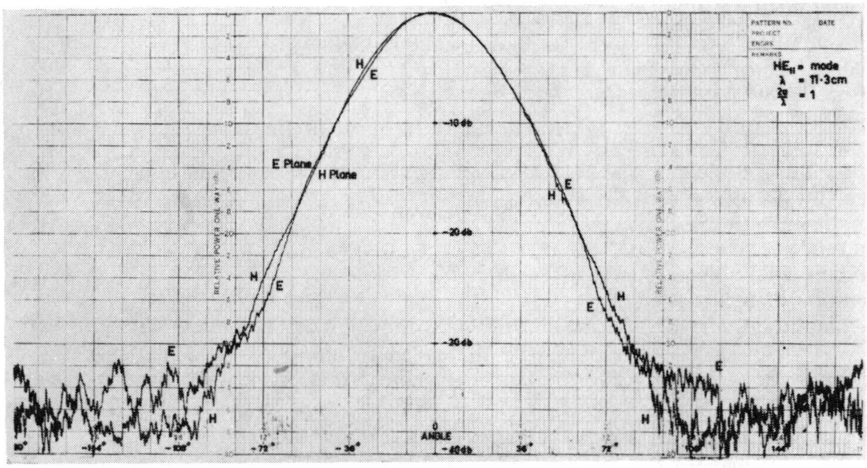

Fig. 3. E and H plane radiation patterns for HE_{11} feed.

The beamwidth decreases with aperture size a and in the limit each mode illuminates one elementary annular ring on the dish.

By superimposing a number of hybrid modes with appropriate relative amplitudes it is possible to synthesize the radial distribution desired in the paraboloid aperture. Five modes are sufficient, with $a/\lambda = 3.5$, to produce a very good approximation to a flat-topped distribution for maximum efficiency or a tapered one for reduced side lobes. In each case the distribution cuts off rapidly at the dish rim so that spillover (and hence antenna noise temperature) is minimized. Loss of efficiency due to restriction of the feed diameter is negligible. Each hybrid mode is equivalent to a pair of the modes (TE_{1n}, TM_{1n}) used in the existing method of synthesis with normal circular waveguides.[2] Thus with the corrugated waveguide technique only half the number of modes have to be independently generated.

In practice, the aperture of a corrugated structure is inevitably surrounded by a metal flange, equal in width to the slot depth, which forces tangential E, but not tangential H, to zero. In accordance with the concept stated by Rumsey, this difference in the treatment of E and H can upset the essential form of the exterior fields required for symmetry. To ensure the preservation of this form, the external surfaces of the feed must be constructed with the same anisotropic properties as the interior surface of the guide.

Experimentally, it has been found sufficient to curve the circumferentially-slotted guide surface gradually as shown in Fig. 2, so the aperture is surrounded by a number of concentric slots lying in the aperture plane. Similarly, a longitudinally-slotted guide would have a series of radial slots surrounding the aperture. The exterior slots in the first case permit only E_ρ and H_ρ fields on the surface. Calculations similar to (7) show that the external sources will radiate symmetrically provided the first equation of (10) is satisfied. In the second case only E_ξ and H_ξ are allowed on the surface and these must be related by the second equation of (10).

Experimental Work

Figure 2 shows a circumferentially-slotted structure for $\lambda = 11$ cm in which only the HE_{11} mode can propagate. The structure was made by bolting together rings with different internal diameters. Various combinations of ring thickness allowed the effect of slot/flange ratio and pitch of the structure to be studied.

The guide wavelength was determined over a range of wavelengths by cavity-type measurements with a plunger in one end. Over a 1.5 to 1 range in which the HE_{11} mode alone was propagated, agreement with values computed from the slot reactances was better than 2 percent, except near cutoff where the discrepancy increased to about 5 percent. In the reactance computation, a mode TE_{11} to ρ in the slots was assumed. The effect of different slot/flange ratios and pitches on the guide wavelength was small except near cutoff, when the predicted trend was observed.

Measurements on the feed have shown that the radiation pattern is virtually independent of the slot/flange ratio and pitch of the structure, and that the pattern is symmetrical at the resonant frequency of the slots (see Fig. 3). The beamwidth of the radiation pattern is less than the value deduced from (11) because the flaring of the aperture increases its effective diameter. Experiments on guides capable of carrying two and three hybrid modes are in progress.

Acknowledgment

It is a pleasure to acknowledge the contribution made by V. H. Rumsey to our work on hybrid-mode systems through his development of a general theory of symmetrical radiation fields.

H. C. Minnett
B. MacA. Thomas
CSIRO Division of Radiophysics
Sydney, Australia

[2] P. D. Potter and A. C. Ludwig, "Beam shaping by the use of higher-order modes in conical horns," *1963 NEREM Rec.*, p. 92.

OPTIMUM FEED FOR LARGE RADIO-TELESCOPES: EXPERIMENTAL RESULTS

Indexing terms: Radiotelescopes, Antenna feeders, Waveguides

Corrugated waveguide structures can be used to design highly efficient aperture-type feeds for both spherical and paraboloidal reflector antennas. The letter presents a brief account of experimental results obtained with a 2-hybrid-mode horn. It is shown that theoretical and experimental results agree closely.

It has been shown by Minnett *et al.*[1] that corrugated waveguide structures can support hybrid modes whose radiation patterns are cylindrically symmetrical. This type of waveguide can therefore be used to design efficient primary-feed horns for large radiotelescopes. The main advantage is that electric- and magnetic-plane phase-centre coincidence can be achieved, and crossover polarisation loss can be eliminated. In addition, radiation-pattern synthesis can easily be effected. For efficient illumination of the reflector, a multimode feed horn must be designed. This requires the determination of the relative amplitudes and phases of the hybrid modes needed to give optimum antenna performance. In this way, a highly efficient aperture-type feed horn can be designed for both spherical and paraboloidal reflector antennas.[2,3] In a more or less noise-free environment, one can aim for a uniform illumination, so that the antenna gain is a maximum. In other applications where the ambient temperature is significant, the effect of spillover on the system signal/noise ratio must be taken into account. A different mode composition must therefore be used to obtain a maximum signal/noise ratio.[4] The final problem involves the generation of hybrid modes in such a way that both their relative amplitudes and their phases can be readily controlled.

This letter briefly describes a corrugated feed horn designed to support two hybrid modes; i.e. HE_{11} and HE_{12}. The relative amplitudes of the modes are controlled by varying the degree of discontinuity at the junction of two corrugated waveguides of different diameter. A sketch of the junction is shown in Fig. 1. The relative phases are varied simply by varying the length of the larger section of the horn.

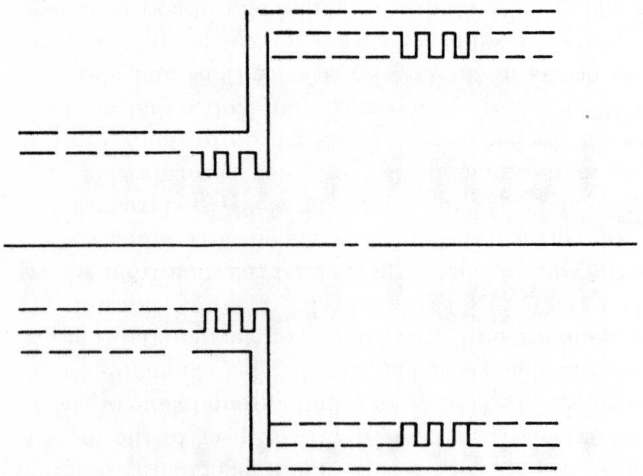

Fig. 1 *Mode generation by step discontinuity*

The radiation pattern of the *n*th hybrid mode is given by

$$F_n(\theta) = \frac{ka}{2R}\left[J_1(u_n)\frac{J_1(v)}{v}(1+\cos\theta\cos\theta_n) + \frac{(\cos\theta+\cos\theta_n)}{1-\left(\frac{v}{u_n}\right)^2}\left\{J_1(u_n)J_1'(v) - \frac{v}{u_n}J_1(v)J_1'(u_n)\right\}\right] \quad (1)$$

where θ_n satisfies the equation

$$1-\cos\theta_n = \frac{u_n J_0(u_n)}{J_1(u_n)} \quad (2)$$

where

$u_n = ka\sin\theta_n$

a = waveguide radius

$k = 2\pi/\lambda$

R = distance from the origin to the far-field point

J_n = Bessel function of the first kind, order n

J_n' = first derivative of J_n

θ = angle measured from the feed axis

As an illustration, consider a paraboloidal reflector where the halfangle subtended by the paraboloid at the focus is $\theta_0 = 63°$. It can be shown[4] that, if the ambient temperature is 240 K and the receiver noise temperature is 20 K, the best signal/noise ratio is obtained when $ka = 8{\cdot}17$. Fig. 2

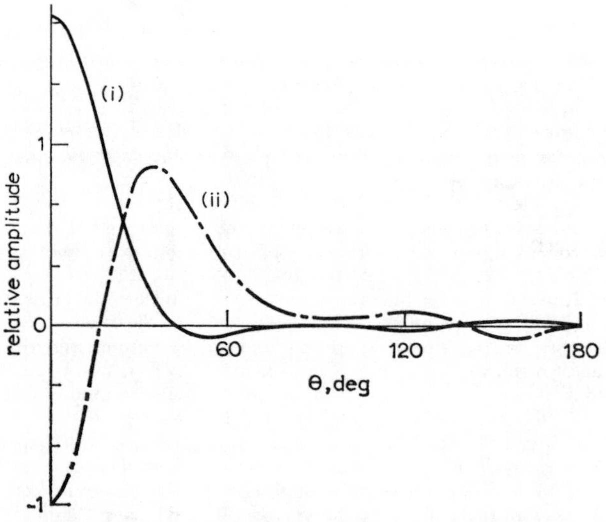

Fig. 2 *Radiation pattern of hybrid modes for ka = 8·17*
(i) HE_{11}
(ii) HE_{12}

Reprinted with permission from *Electron. Lett.*, vol. 6, pp. 159–160, Mar. 19, 1970.

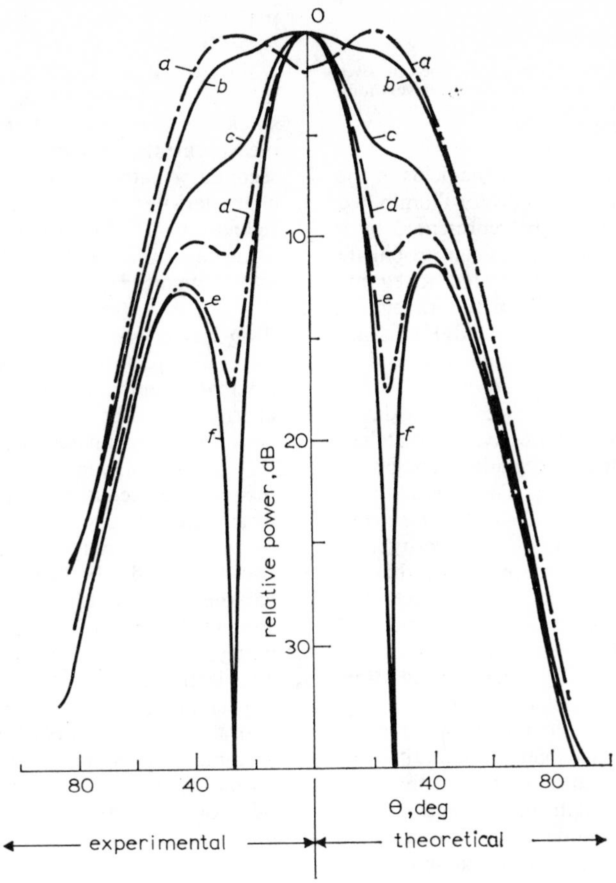

Fig. 3 *Theoretical and experimental patterns of a corrugated feed horn with ka = 8·17*

Phase differences:
a 0
b 36
c 72
d 108
e 144
f 180

shows the theoretical radiation patterns of the HE_{11} and HE_{12} modes supported by a corrugated waveguide of this dimension. The theoretical pattern required to give the optimum signal/noise ratio is given in Fig. 3 (right-hand half, part *a*) where the two hybrid modes are added in phase and in the correct amplitude ratio. For easy comparison, the corresponding experimental pattern is shown on the left-hand half of Fig. 3. Although not shown in Fig. 3, the experimental E and H plane patterns are almost identical.

For the spherical case, the two hybrid modes would have to be added out of phase, so as to compensate for spherical aberration.[2] To illustrate the case with which the relative phase can be controlled, Fig. 3 also shows the resultant patterns for various phase combinations. It is seen that the experimental curves agree closely with the corresponding theoretical curves.

In conclusion, this letter, together with previous work, demonstrates the feasibility of designing efficient aperture-type feeds for both spherical and paraboloidal reflector antennas.

T. B. VU
Q. H. VU

School of Electrical Engineering
University of New South Wales
PO Box 1, Kensington 2033, NSW, Australia

16th February 1970

References

1 MINNETT, H. C., and THOMAS, B. MACA.: 'A method of synthesizing radiation patterns with axial symmetry', *IEEE Trans.*, 1966, **AP-14,** pp. 654–656
2 VU, T. B.: 'Optimisation of efficiency of deep reflectors', *ibid.*, 1969, **AP-17** (to be published)
3 VU THE BAO: 'Optimisation of efficiency of reflector antennas: approximate method', *Proc. IEE*, 1970, **117,** pp. 30–34
4 VU, T. B.: 'Optimisation of performance of corrugated feed for paraboloidal antennas' (to be published)

PRIME-FOCUS ONE- AND TWO-HYBRID-MODE FEEDS

Indexing terms: Antenna feeders, Radiotelescopes

The design of prime-focus feeds, using either one- or two-hybrid modes in circumferentially corrugated waveguides, and their performances when used to illuminate the Parkes 210 ft radiotelescope, are briefly described.

In previous papers[1,2] it has been shown that the fields in the focusing region of a circularly symmetric reflector illuminated by a linearly polarised plane wave can be represented by a spectrum of axial hybrid waves. These waves can propagate as discrete modes in a circumferentially corrugated waveguide where both circumferential ***E*** and ***H*** fields at the waveguide boundary are zero.[3-6] The modes, designated HE_{1n}, are composed of in-phase TM_{1n} and TE_{1n} components, and at slot resonance the mode-content factor γ is unity.

It has also been shown that the focal-region fields of paraboloidal and spherical reflectors can be closely matched over the open end of a corrugated waveguide propagating only a small number of HE_{1n} modes.[7,8] For a paraboloid where the semiangle θ_0 is 63° ($f/D = 0{\cdot}41$) the resulting aperture efficiencies* η_a for the ideal one- and two-hybrid-mode feeds having the optimum normalised radii kb ($k = 2\pi/\lambda_0$) of 3·65 and 7·4 are 0·724 and 0·827, respectively.

The corresponding efficiencies can also be calculated by considering the radiation from the open end of cylindrical hybrid-mode guides. It has been shown[3,9] that the radiation pattern of the HE_{1n} mode is linearly polarised and circularly symmetric. In general, each mode illuminates an annular ring of the reflector, the highest-order mode illuminating the outer section. In particular, the radiation pattern of the two-mode feed has maximum field strength off axis and steeper sides than the pattern of the single-mode feed. Consequently it is a better approximation to the maximum-efficiency $\sec^2 \theta/2$ pattern.

However, when the figure of merit (f.m.) for a given receiver noise temperature T_R and not η_a is to be maximised, the relative mode powers and kb must be readjusted. When $T_R = 100$ K, then $kb = 4{\cdot}2$, f.m. $= 0{\cdot}64$, $\eta_a = 0{\cdot}69$ for the optimum one-mode feed, and $kb = 8{\cdot}0$, f.m. $= 0{\cdot}77$, $\eta_a = 0{\cdot}80$ for the optimum two-mode feed.

The performances of one- and two-hybrid-mode feeds designed for use on the Parkes 210 ft radiotelescope will now be briefly discussed.

One-hybrid-mode feeds: An experimental single-hybrid-mode feed with a normalised waveguide radius $ka = \pi$ and its radiation pattern have been discussed by Minnett and Thomas.[3] The curvature at the mouth of the horn which is essential for pattern symmetry over the band results in an effective aperture kb greater than ka. Detailed experiments have been carried out to evaluate the effect of the shape of the horn mouth on the radiation-pattern beamwidth, symmetry and bandwidth. These aspects will be considered in a later paper. In addition, the need to convert the TE_{11} mode in circular pipe to the HE_{11} mode over a relatively short length with negligible reflection has led to detailed theoretical[5] and experimental[6] studies of mode convertors.

Single-hybrid-mode prime-focus feeds based on the above work have been in use on the Parkes radiotelescope since 1967 at centre frequencies of 2·7 GHz (Reference 10) and 1·4 GHz, with bandwidths of 400 and 200 MHz, respectively. At the centre frequencies where $ka = 2{\cdot}5$, the intensity of the radiation patterns at ±63° is −15 dB, $\eta_a = 0{\cdot}69$ and f.m. $= 0{\cdot}66$ for $T_R = 100$ K.

Because these feeds have excellent polarisation characteristics and low spillover, they have been most suitable for single-reflector polarisation measurements, and also for the measurement of extended radio sources where a symmetrical secondary pattern with low side lobes is desirable. The characteristics of the 21 cm feed have also allowed a significant reduction in the instrumental polarisation in measurements using the Parkes 210 ft and 60 ft telescopes as a two-element interferometer.[11]

Two-hybrid-mode feeds: The two-hybrid-mode feed gives increased aperture efficiency for paraboloids and allows more efficient illumination of spherical reflectors where spherical aberration can be controlled by the correct adjustment of the amplitudes and phases of the two modes.

A factor which must be considered with two-mode feeds is the possible excitation of spurious modes. The slow wave,[4,5] which theoretically can propagate at frequencies below slot resonance, has not yet been detected in either the one- or two-mode feeds. In the two-mode feed, the EH_{12} mode, which has the TM_{12} and TE_{12} components out of phase (a mode-content factor γ of −1 at slot resonance), can exist. The pattern of this mode has a null along the axis, and the polarisation angle of the field vector is given by $(90° - 2\phi)$.[12] The simultaneous excitation of this mode is therefore undesirable, since its polarisation characteristic will introduce asymmetry into the desired radiation pattern. Near slot resonance, the radiation patterns of the EH_{12} mode, and of the combined HE_{11} and HE_{12} modes, can be measured independently in the $\phi = \pm 45°$ planes.

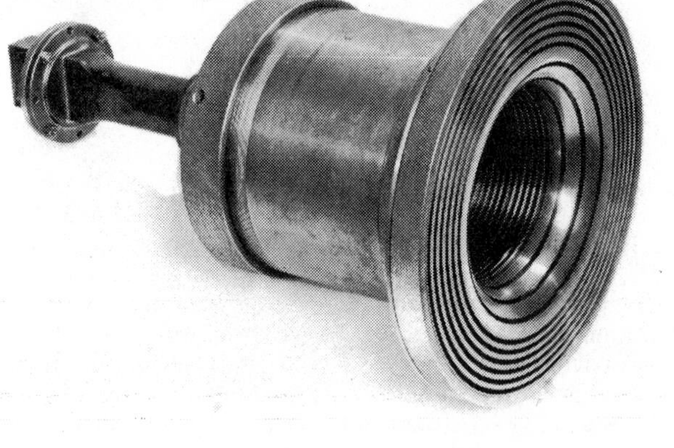

Fig. 1 *5 GHz two-hybrid-mode feed*

The HE_{11} and HE_{12} modes are most readily excited by a TE_{11} mode at a step discontinuity between the smooth pipe and corrugated waveguide. It has been found that a significant improvement in the match near cutoff can be obtained by gradually tapering the input waveguide near the step. This increased bandwidth is achieved with a slight reduction in the HE_{12} power for a given corrugated waveguide diameter. The hybrid modes at the step can also be excited by the HE_{11} mode,[13] but for a given step size this has the disadvantage that the resultant power in the unwanted EH_{12} mode at slot resonance is almost twice that when a TE_{11} mode is used for excitation.

The bandwidth of the feed is determined by the waveguide length L necessary to achieve the correct phasing of the

* Throughout the letter the efficiency calculations assume a perfect reflector with no aperture blockage

Reprinted with permission from *Electron. Lett.*, vol. 6, pp. 460–461, July 23, 1970.

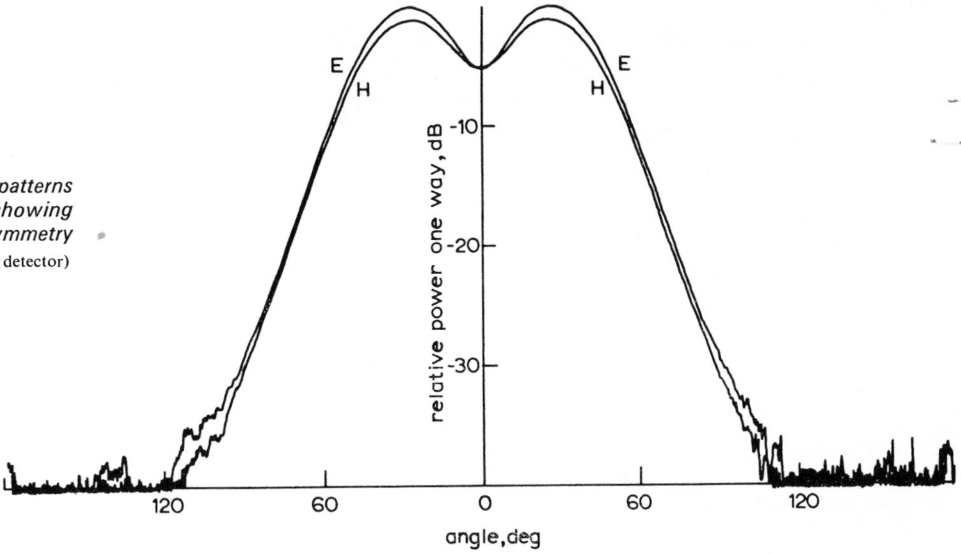

Fig. 2 *E and H plane radiation patterns of the feed in Fig. 1 at 5·0 GHz showing effect of EH_{12} mode on pattern symmetry*
(Noise level near −40 dB is caused by crystal detector)

modes at the aperture:

$$L = \Delta\Phi \Big/ k\left(\frac{k_z^{11}}{k} - \frac{k_z^{12}}{k}\right)$$

where k_z^{11} and k_z^{12} are the axial propagation coefficients of the two modes and $\Delta\Phi$ is the overall phase difference between the two modes over the length L. Since the denominator of the above equation decreases with increased frequency:

(i) the length required for a given phase difference and waveguide size increases with frequency

(ii) the change in phase $\Delta\Phi$ for a given bandwidth and waveguide size decreases as the centre frequency is increased. However, as ka increases, the reduced-feed beamwidth may result in a lowered aperture efficiency.

The principles outlined above have been used to design two feeds for Parkes: one, installed in May 1968 (see Fig. 1), has a centre frequency of 5·0 GHz with a bandwidth of 300 MHz; the other, installed in July 1969 for the Apollo 11 lunar landing, required a bandwidth of 30 MHz centred on 2·285 GHz. At the centre frequency of the 5 GHz feed $ka = 6{\cdot}65$, which ensures that the mean phase difference between the two modes at the band edges is only 23°. Because of the limited bandwidth required, ka for the Apollo feed was reduced to 6·08. This gives a wider beamwidth and ensures that the weight is kept to a minimum, since both the waveguide radius (5 in) and length are less than that required for wideband radioastronomy applications.

For both feeds the power in the HE_{12} mode was approximately 90% of the HE_{11} mode power. At the centre frequencies the average intensities of the radiation patterns at $\pm 63°$ were approximately $-13\frac{1}{2}$ dB for the 5 GHz feed (see Fig. 2) and −11 dB for the 2·3 GHz feed. The values for η_a, assuming no EH_{12} mode, were 0·78 and 0·815, respectively. The effect of this unwanted mode is to reduce η_a by 0·025. At 5·0 GHz, for $T_R = 100$ K, f.m. is 0·735 (0·755 if the EH_{12} mode is absent). At the band edges the reduction in η_a is 0·02.

The Parkes radiotelescope was used to compare the performance of the 5 GHz two-mode feed with that of a single-mode feed with characteristics similar to the lower-frequency feeds described above. Accurate measurements on an unpolarised radio source showed that the two-mode feed gave an increased efficiency of 12%, which is in close agreement with the predicted improvement.

The author wishes to acknowledge valuable discussions with H. C. Minnett, who originated the focal-region hybrid-wave research.

B. MACA. THOMAS

Division of Radiophysics
CSIRO
Sydney, Australia

19th June 1970

References

1 MINNETT, H. C., and THOMAS, B. MACA.: 'Fields in the image space of symmetrical focusing reflectors', *Proc. IEE*, 1968, **115**, pp. 1419–1430
2 THOMAS, B. MACA., MINNETT, H. C., and VU, T. B.: 'Fields in the focal region of a spherical reflector', *IEEE Trans.*, 1969, **AP-17**, pp. 229–232
3 MINNETT, H. C., and THOMAS, B. MACA.: 'A method of synthesizing radiation patterns with axial symmetry', *ibid.*, 1966, **AP-14**, pp. 654–656
4 CLARRICOATS, P. J. B., and SAHA, P. K.: 'Theoretical analysis of cylindrical hybrid modes in a corrugated horn', *Electron. Lett.*, 1969, **5**, pp. 187–189
5 MINNETT, H. C., and THOMAS, B. MACA.: 'Propagation in circular waveguides with anisotropic walls' (to be published)
6 THOMAS, B. MACA., and MINNETT, H. C.: 'Properties of hybrid modes in circular corrugated waveguides' (to be published)
7 THOMAS, B. MACA.: 'Matching focal-region fields with hybrid modes', *IEEE Trans.*, 1970, **AP-18**, pp. 404–405
8 VU, T. B.: 'Optimization of efficiency of deep reflectors', *ibid.*, 1969 **AP-17**, pp. 811–813
9 THOMAS, B. MACA.: 'Hybrid waveguide-mode feeds for the illumination of large focusing reflectors'. Proceedings of the Radio Research Board symposium on antenna research, Melbourne, Aug. 1968
10 BATCHELOR, R. A., BROOKS, J. W., and COOPER, B. F. C.: 'Eleven-centimeter broadband correlation radiometer', *IEEE Trans.*, 1968, **AP-16**, pp. 228–234
11 MORRIS, D., and WHITEOAK, J. B.: 'The distribution of linear polarization over 13 extended sources at 21·2 cm wavelength', *Austral. J. Phys.*, 1968, **21**, pp. 475–492
12 THOMAS, B. MACA.: 'Bandwidth properties of corrugated conical horns', *Electron. Lett.*, 1969, **5**, pp. 561–563
13 VU, T. B., and VU, Q. H.: 'Optimum feed for large radiotelescopes: experimental results', *ibid.*, 1970, **6**, pp. 159–160

A New Type of High-Performance Monopulse Feed

T. B. VU AND N. V. HIEN

Abstract—A circular corrugated waveguide can be used to design single-horn monopulse feeds with relatively wide bandwidth. The dominant hybrid mode in the corrugated structure provides the reference signal, whereas the error signal for the servodrive is derived from the TM_{01} mode in the usual manner.

Introduction

The use of rectangular corrugated waveguide for monopulse feed horns has been discussed in the literature [1]. This communication briefly discusses an experimental *X*-band model using a corrugated circular waveguide. The design is based on conventional tracking systems used for satellite communication, where a smooth-walled conical horn is used [2]. This is a single-horn multimode monopulse feed, and when a conventional circular waveguide is used, the TE_{11} mode and TM_{01} mode will provide the reference and error signal, respectively. Since the radiation patterns of the TE_{11} and TM_{01} modes resemble the "sum" and "difference" patterns of the classical monopulse feed, it is convenient to refer to the TE_{11} and TM_{01} as the "sum" and "difference" modes, respectively.

Manuscript received August 17, 1972; revised May 11, 1973. This work was supported in part by the Radio Research Board, Australia.
The authors are with the School of Electrical Engineering, University of New South Wales, Kensington, Australia.

It is noted that the TE_{11} pattern has relatively high sidelobes. In addition, its pattern symmetry is poor. One way of improving the sum mode performance is to excite both the TE_{11} and the higher order TM_{11} mode. As shown by Potter [3], a complete beam-width equalization in all planes and at least a 30-dB sidelobe suppression can be achieved in this way, provided that these two modes maintain their correct relative amplitude and phase in the horn aperture. However, with a conventional waveguide, the great difference between the phase velocities of these modes means that the desired phase relationship cannot be maintained as the frequency changes. In other words, a higher sum performance can be achieved, but only at the expense of the bandwidth.

To overcome these difficulties, a corrugated waveguide can be used. The corrugated boundary makes it possible for the waveguide to support modes having both E_z and H_z components (the so-called hybrid modes [4], [5]). These hybrid modes can be looked upon as linear combinations of conventional TE and TM modes which propagate in a smooth waveguide. The important thing is that the TE and TM components of a hybrid mode propagate with the same velocity in a corrugated waveguide. As a result, the dominant hybrid mode HE_{11} has all the desired properties of a TE_{11}–TM_{11} combination. In addition to this, its frequency characteristic is that of a single mode, i.e., the HE_{11} pattern is less frequency sensitive than the corresponding TE_{11}–TM_{11} combination in a smooth waveguide.

Reprinted from *IEEE Trans. Antennas Propagat.*, vol. AP-21, pp. 855–857, Nov. 1973.

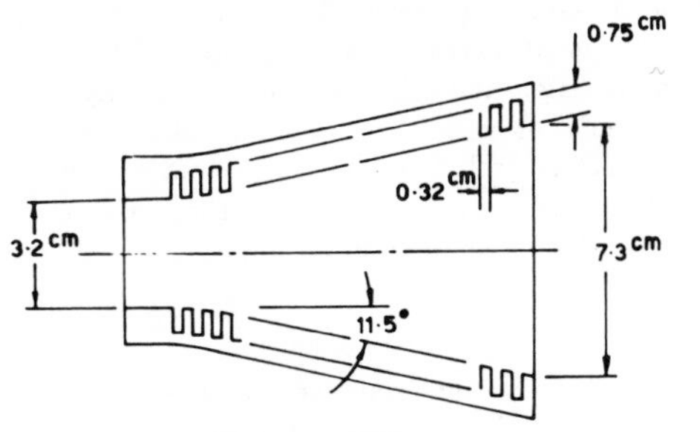

Fig. 1. Experimental horn.

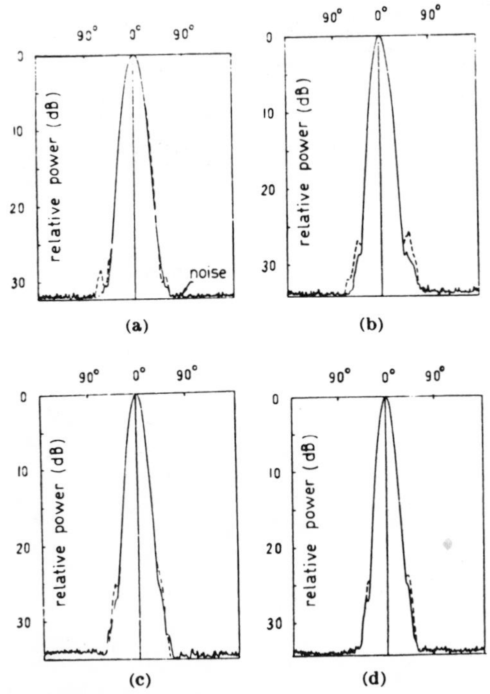

Fig. 2. Sum patterns at four frequencies. — H plane; - - - E plane. (a) 9.50 GHz. (b) 10.92 Ghz. (c) 11.5 GHz. (d) 11.9 GHz.

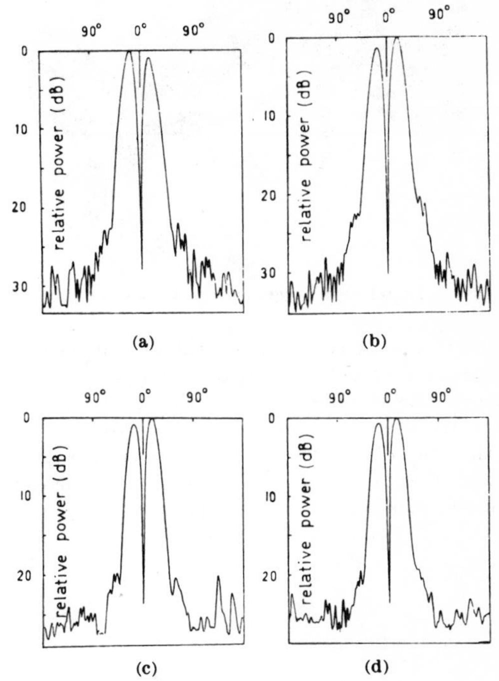

Fig. 3. Difference patterns at four frequencies. (a) 10.95 GHz. (b) 11.32 GHz. (c) 11.62 GHz. (d) 11.90 GHz.

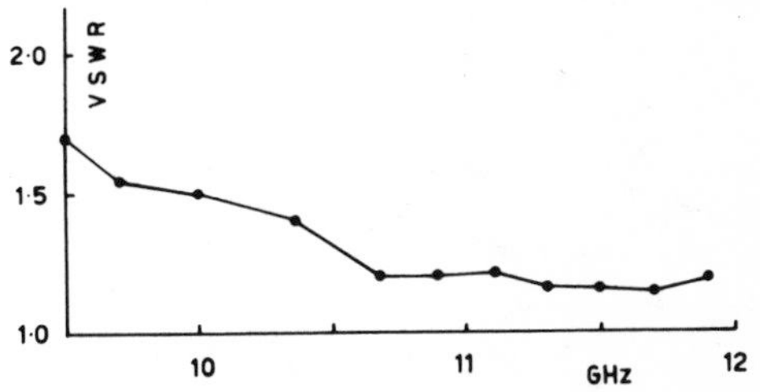

Fig. 4. VSWR measured at point in front of mode-coupling network.

Discussion of the Experimental Model

An X-band model was built to test the preceding properties. As mentioned before, this is a single-horn multimode monopulse feed, where the dominant hybrid mode HE_{11} provides the reference signal and the TM_{01} mode provides the error signal. Fig. 1 shows a detailed drawing of the model which was designed to operate at the nominal frequency of 10 GHz. Strictly speaking, the corrugation teeth must be at a right angle to the wall of the conical horn. However, experience has shown that a slight modification of the type shown in Fig. 1 does not significantly affect the results. This modified tooth configuration also simplifies the machining of the horn. The sum patterns for both E and H planes are shown in Fig. 2, and the difference patterns are shown in Fig. 3. It is seen that the pattern symmetry of the sum mode is maintained over the bandwidth concerned. The width of the main beam is also frequency insensitive. In addition, a satisfactory sidelobe suppression is achieved in this band. These characteristics are desirable for applications where the sum gain must be maintained over a wide frequency band. A typical example is the earth station antennas for present commercial satellite communication networks, where the same feed is used for both the transmit and receive band. The voltage standing-wave ratio (VSWR) measured at a point before the mode-coupling network is shown in Fig. 4. This is relatively high, but an improved VSWR can be obtained by having a smoother transition from a conventional to a corrugated waveguide.

A photo of the complete structure of the experimental model is shown in Fig. 5, where the mode-coupling network is also shown.

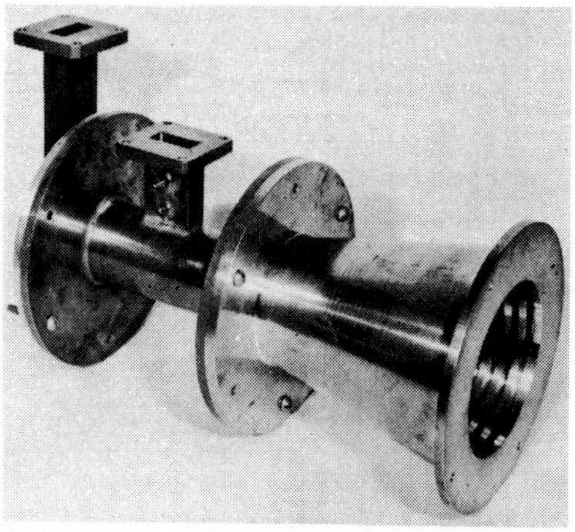

Fig. 5. Experimental model together with mode-coupling network.

This network consists of a conventional circular waveguide with two rectangular waveguide ports. In the receiving case, the dominant hybrid mode HE_{11} is converted to the TE_{11} in the smooth circular waveguide. The reference signal is then coupled to the first rectangular port through slots cut in the wall of this circular waveguide. A thin cylindrical metallic ring is used to match the reference port to the circular waveguide. This ring also prevents the sum mode from reaching the difference port, while it leaves the TM_{01} mode undisturbed. Thus the TM_{01} from the corrugated horn is allowed to propagate down the smooth circular waveguide, and is finally coupled to the second rectangular waveguide port through a circular waveguide-to-coaxial-to-rectangular waveguide adapter. It is noted in passing that the sum pattern is much narrower than the corresponding difference pattern. To obtain a near-optimum performance, one must increase the beamwidth of the sum pattern by using both the HE_{11} and the next higher order hybrid mode HE_{12}. The main disadvantage is that the sum pattern will then be more frequency sensitive [6]. It is also important to note that the corrugations raise the cutoff frequency of the TM_{01} mode; this must be taken into account in designing the horn.

References

[1] D. Davis, "Corrugations improve monopulse feed horns," *Microwaves*, pp. 58–63, Apr. 1972.

[2] G. V. Trentini, K. P. Romeiser, and W. Jatsch, "Dimensionierung und electrische Eigenschaften den 25m Antenne der Erdefunkstelle Raisting für Nachrichtenverbindungen über Satelliten," *Frequenz*, vol. 19, pp. 402–421, 1965.

[3] P. D. Potter, "A new horn antenna with suppressed sidelobes and equal beamwidths," *Microwave J.*, vol. VI, pp. 781–784, June 1963.

[4] P. J. B. Clarricoats and P. K. Saba, "Propagation and radiation behaviour of corrugated feeds," *Proc. Inst. Elec. Eng.*, vol. 118, pp. 1167–1186, Sept. 1971.

[5] B. M. Thomas, "Theoretical performance of prime-focus paraboloids using cylindrical hybrid-modes feeds," *Proc. Inst. Elec. Eng.*, vol. 118, pp. 1539–1549, Nov. 1971.

[6] T. B. Vu, "Corrugated horn as high-performance monopulse feed," *Int. J. Electron.*, vol. 34, pp. 433–444, Apr. 1973.

BANDWIDTH PROPERTIES OF CORRUGATED CONICAL HORNS

It is shown that the aperture fields of circumferentially corrugated conical horns remain virtually unchanged over a very wide frequency range, and that the bandwidth improves as the length of the horn is increased. The theory is applicable over a large range of flare angles.

Clarricoats[1] has considered the form of the fields in a conical horn with circumferential corrugations. Similar work has also been carried out in the CSIRO Division of Radiophysics during the past few years in an effort to achieve optimum illumination of paraboloidal and spherical reflectors. The work has mostly centred on the synthesis of the focal-region fields[2,3] by means of hybrid waves excited in cylindrical corrugated waveguides.[4] However, corrugated conical horns with different flare angles have also been studied theoretically and experimentally to establish the basic relationships with the cylindrical case.

Clarricoats has restricted the application of his analysis of circumferentially corrugated conical horns to the case where the longitudinal-surface reactance X_R is infinite, i.e. when pattern symmetry is achieved. For this particular case, the form of the field distribution across the phase fronts in the horn is independent of normalised radius kR, where $k = 2\pi/\lambda$. It was also shown that, for other constant nonzero values of X_R, the field distribution will be a function of kR. However, provided that the change is not too rapid, the excitation of higher-order modes will be negligible, and calculations can proceed on the assumption that the field distribution at any kR is determined by the value of X_R at that position.

The effect of frequency on the symmetry properties of the balanced-hybrid-mode fields propagating in conical horns with semiangles $\theta_1 \leqslant 90°$ will now be considered. The basic notation of previous papers has been retained, but otherwise Clarricoats's symbols have been used.

The field components of the HE_1 spherical mode are given by

$$\left.\begin{aligned} E_\theta &= E_\theta(\theta,R)\sin\phi \qquad & H_\theta &= H_\theta(\theta,R)\cos\phi \\ E_\phi &= E_\phi(\theta,R)\cos\phi \qquad & H_\phi &= H_\phi(\theta,R)\sin\phi \\ E_R &= E_R(\theta,R)\sin\phi \qquad & H_R &= H_R(\theta,R)\cos\phi \end{aligned}\right\} \quad (1a)$$

where

$$\left.\begin{aligned} E_\theta(\theta,R) &= -\frac{j\hat{H}}{kR}\left(\frac{\gamma P}{\sin\theta} - j\frac{\hat{H}'}{\hat{H}}P'\sin\theta\right) \\ E_\phi(\theta,R) &= \frac{j\hat{H}}{kR}\left(\gamma P'\sin\theta - j\frac{\hat{H}'}{\hat{H}}\frac{P}{\sin\theta}\right) \\ E_R(\theta,R) &= \frac{\hat{H}}{(kR)^2}\nu(\nu+1)P \\ Z_0H_\theta(\theta,R) &= \frac{j\hat{H}}{kR}\left(\frac{P}{\sin\theta} - j\frac{\hat{H}'}{\hat{H}}\gamma P'\sin\theta\right) \\ Z_0H_\phi(\theta,R) &= \frac{j\hat{H}}{kR}\left(P'\sin\theta - j\frac{\hat{H}'}{\hat{H}}\frac{\gamma P}{\sin\theta}\right) \\ Z_0H_R(\theta,R) &= -\gamma E_R(\theta,R) \end{aligned}\right\} \quad (1b)$$

and

$$\hat{H} = (kR)h_\nu^{(2)}(kR) \qquad \hat{H}' = d\hat{H}(kR)$$

$$P = \frac{P_\nu^{1}(\cos\theta)}{d(kR)} \qquad P' = \frac{dP_\nu^{1}(\cos\theta)}{d(\cos\theta)}$$

The mode-content factor* γ determines the field distribution of the spherical wave, so that, for the balanced hybrid with $\gamma = 1$ (designated HE_{1n})

$$E_\theta(\theta,R) = -Z_0H_\theta(\theta,R) \qquad \text{and } E_\phi(\theta,R) = Z_0H_\phi(\theta,R)$$

In the far-field (large kR), $\hat{H}'/\hat{H} = -j$ and eqns. 1*b* reduce to:

$$\left.\begin{aligned} E_\theta(\theta,R) &= \frac{j\hat{H}}{kR}\left(P'\sin\theta - \frac{\gamma P}{\sin\theta}\right) \\ E_\phi(\theta,R) &= \frac{j\hat{H}}{kR}\left(\gamma P'\sin\theta - \frac{P}{\sin\theta}\right) \\ E_R(\theta,R) &= \frac{\hat{H}}{(kR)^2}\nu(\nu+1)P \\ Z_0H_\theta(\theta,R) &= -E_\phi(\theta,R) \qquad Z_0H_\phi(\theta,R) = E_\theta(\theta,R) \end{aligned}\right\} \quad (2)$$

* In eqns. 3 and 4 of Reference 1, the symbol $\bar{\Lambda}$ is identical to $-j\gamma$. However, the definition given for $\bar{\Lambda}$ should read

$$\mathrm{T} = j\frac{b_\nu^{m}}{a_\nu^{m}}\left(\frac{\epsilon_0}{\mu_0}\right)^{1/2}$$

Reprinted with permission from *Electron. Lett.*, vol. 5, pp. 561–563, Oct. 30, 1969.

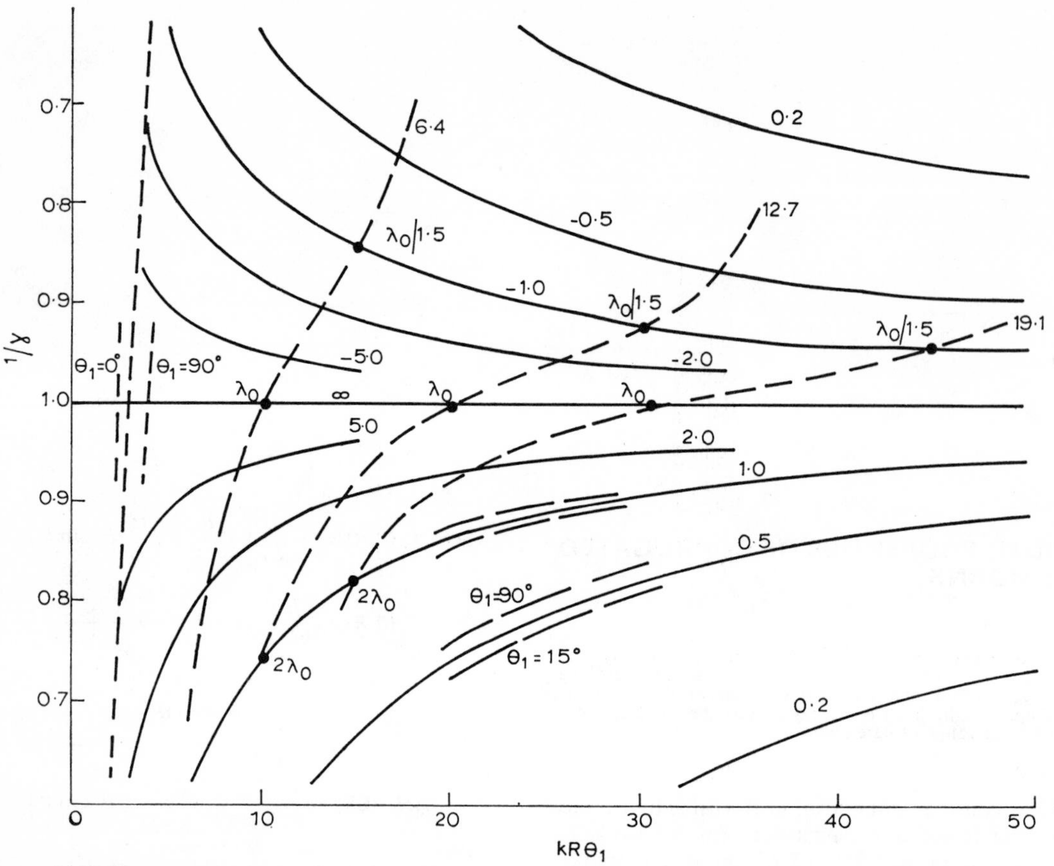

Fig. 1 *Variation of γ with normalised horn radius $kR\theta_1$ for the HE_1 mode where $\theta_1 = 60°$*

——— X_R/Z_0 constant (sections of the curves for $\theta_1 = 15°$ and 90° are also shown for various values of X_R/Z_0

— — — — $R\theta_1/d$ constant, for various values of $R\theta_1/d$

- - - - - $kR\theta_1$ for $\theta_1 = 0°$, 60° and 90° at junction of cylindrical waveguide, $ka = 2 \cdot 5$

For the balanced-mode, the field distribution is symmetrical about the axis and is linearly polarised. Where $\gamma = -1$, there is a null along the axis and because $E_\theta(\theta,R) = -E_\phi(\theta,R)$, the polarisation angle of the resultant field vector is given by $(90° - 2\phi)$. The simultaneous excitation of this latter mode is therefore undesirable, since its polarisation characteristic will introduce asymmetry into the radiation pattern of the $\gamma = 1$ mode.

In the circumferentially corrugated horn, the edges of the flanges separating the slots force $E_\phi(\theta_1,R)$ to be zero and hence

$$\gamma = \frac{P}{P' \sin^2\theta_1}$$

γ is dependent on the longitudinal surface reactance:

$$\frac{X_R}{Z_0} = \frac{jE_R(\theta_1,R)}{Z_0 H_\phi(\theta_1,R)} = \frac{-\nu(\nu+1)\sin\theta_1/kR}{\gamma - \frac{P'}{P}\sin^2\theta_1} \quad . \quad . \quad (3)$$

Elimination of P'/P from eqn. 3 gives

$$\frac{X_R}{Z_0} = -\frac{\nu(\nu+1)\theta_1 \sin\theta_1}{(kR\theta_1)(\gamma - 1/\gamma)} \quad . \quad . \quad . \quad . \quad . \quad . \quad . \quad . \quad (4)$$

When $\theta_1 \leqslant 90°$, calculations show that the numerator is, for a given mode, nearly constant. Hence, a single set of curves showing γ plotted against $kR\theta_1$ with X_R/Z_0 as parameter will suffice for all θ_1. The quantity $kR\theta_1$ is half the phase front at a distance kR from the origin or apex of the horn. In the limit when $\theta_1 = 0°$, $kR\theta_1$ is the normalised radius ka of a cylindrical waveguide. Eqn. 4 has been plotted in Fig. 1 for the HE_{11} mode when $\theta_1 = 60°$.

The dashed lines† at the left of Fig. 1 give the values of $kR\theta_1$ at the junction between the conical horn and a cylindrical waveguide with ka (or $kR\theta_1$) $= 2 \cdot 5$ and $X_R = \infty$ carrying the HE_{11} mode. If θ_1 is not small, there will be a relatively large change in the form of the fields at this discontinuity, and, because γ changes rapidly in this region, the effect becomes greater as X_R departs from infinity. To minimise the resultant excitation of higher-order modes at this point and their degrading effects on the match, it has been found desirable to increase the flare angle smoothly from zero in the cylindrical waveguide to the required flare angle θ_1.

† These lines also represent the lower limit (assuming $a/b \simeq 0 \cdot 1$) for which the far-field approximation holds

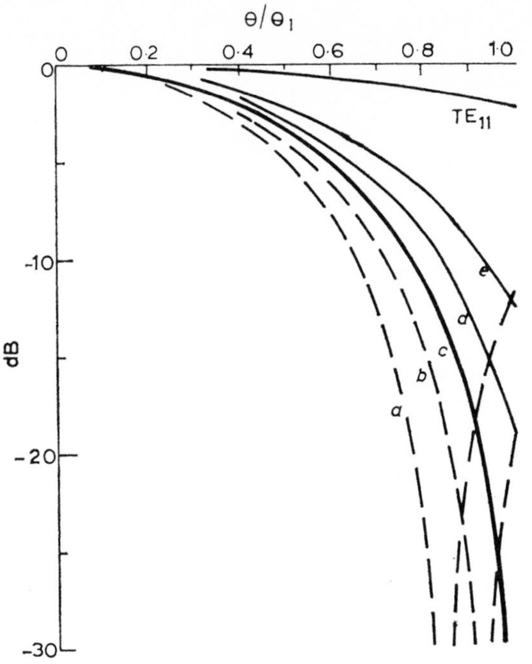

Fig. 2 *Far-field E plane distributions for the HE_1 mode where $\theta_1 = 60°$*
Also shown is the corresponding TE_{11} mode ($1/\gamma = 0$) distribution
a $\gamma = 0{\cdot}6$ d $1/\gamma = 0{\cdot}8$
b $\gamma = 0{\cdot}8$ e $1/\gamma = 0{\cdot}6$
c $\gamma = 1{\cdot}0$

Superimposed on Fig. 1 is a family of curves showing the variation of γ with $kR\theta_1$ for a circumferentially slotted boundary with slot depth d. The parameter of each curve is $R\theta_1/d$ and the slot reactance X_R, is $\delta Z_0 \tan kd$, where the slot/pitch ratio δ is here taken to be unity (i.e. infinitely thin flanges). The effect of reducing δ is to increase slightly the slopes of the curves. The slots resonate at a wavelength $\lambda_0 = 4d$ where the curves intersect the abscissa ($\gamma = 1$) and, for given horn dimensions, the curves show the variation of γ with λ. Operation at wavelengths lower than resonance ensures minimum change in γ with wavelength, besides being in the cutoff region of the hybrid slow waves. In addition, the aperture distribution becomes less frequency dependent as the length of the horn $kR_0\theta_1$ increases.

The effect of γ on the transverse-field components of the hybrid mode in a conical horn (see eqn. 2) is shown in Fig. 2, in which the $E_\theta(\theta)$ (or Eplane) component is plotted for $\theta_1 = 60°$. When $\gamma = 1$, the $E_\theta(\theta)$ and $E_\phi(\theta)$ components are identical and for other values of γ the $E_\phi(\theta)$ (or Hplane) component remains virtually unchanged. Also shown for comparison is the $E_\theta(\theta)$ component of the TE_{11} mode ($1/\gamma = 0$). The curves of $E_\theta(\theta)$ for $\theta_1 = 15°$ and $90°$ are in very close agreement with those shown for $\theta_1 = 60°$ when $\gamma < 1$. For $\gamma > 1$, however, the normalised 10dB beamwidth increases with θ_1, so that, for $1/\gamma = 0{\cdot}8$, it is -2% and $+2\%$ of the value for $\theta_1 = 60°$ when $\theta_1 = 15°$ and $90°$, respectively, and for $1/\gamma = 0{\cdot}6$ it is -4% and $+5\%$.

Figs. 1 and 2 show that, if the frequency of a conical horn of normalised length $kR_0\theta_1 = 20$ supporting the balanced HE_{11} mode is increased by 50%, then the 10dB beamwidth of the Eplane field across the aperture will increase by only 3% when $\theta_1 = 60°$. For $kR_0\theta_1 = 10$, the corresponding change would be approximately 7%. By comparison, the field distribution of the TE_{11} mode in a metal horn is unaffected by frequency. However, edge effects make the Eplane radiation pattern of this mode more sensitive to frequency[6] than the balanced hybrid mode where the field strength is low at the edge of the aperture.

Although radiation-pattern calculations taking into account these edge effects have not been attempted and any higher-order modes have been neglected, the theory developed here helps to explain the experimental results of Kay,[7] who found that the radiation patterns of corrugated conical horns remain virtually frequency independent over 1·5: 1 bandwidths.

The author wishes to acknowledge valuable discussions with H. C. Minnett and also with D. N. Cooper, who made available the Legendre-function root-finding computer program.

B. MACA. THOMAS

6th October 1969

Division of Radiophysics
CSIRO
PO Box 76, Epping, NSW 2121, Australia

References

1 CLARRICOATS, P. J. B.: 'Analysis of spherical hybrid modes in a corrugated conical horn', *Electron. Lett.*, 1969, **5**, pp. 189–190
2 MINNETT, H. C., and THOMAS, B. MACA.: 'Fields in the image space of symmetrical focusing reflectors', *Proc. IEE*, 1968, **115**, pp. 1419–1430
3 THOMAS, B. MACA., MINNETT, H. C., and VU THE BAO: 'Fields in the focal region of a spherical reflector', *IEEE Trans.*, 1969, **AP-17**, pp. 229–232
4 MINNETT, H. C., and THOMAS, B. MACA: 'A method of synthesising radiation patterns with axial symmetry', *ibid.*, 1966, **AP-14**, pp. 654–656
5 HARRINGTON, R. F.: 'Time-harmonic electromagnetic fields' (McGraw-Hill, 1961), pp. 85–86, and 264–266
6 KAY, A. F.: 'The wide flare horn', TRG report, contract AF 19(604)–8057, No. 2, Oct. 1962
7 KAY, A. F.: 'The scalar feed', TRG report, contract AF 19(604)–8057, No. 5, March 1964

MODE CONVERSION USING CIRCUMFERENTIALLY CORRUGATED CYLINDRICAL WAVEGUIDE

Indexing term: Circular waveguides

The principle of mode conversion using a tapered-reactance cylindrical waveguide surface is summarised. Experimental results are given for a multistage convertor which converts a TE_{11} mode into the HE_{11}, TM_{11} and EH_{12} modes in successive stages.

Introduction: Cylindrical circumferentially corrugated waveguides, which propagate the balanced HE_{11} hybrid mode, have been used extensively for prime-focus feeds on the Parkes 64 m radiotelescope since 1967.[1, 2] The HE_{11}-mode feed has a radiation pattern which is axially symmetrical and produces a linearly polarised distribution across the paraboloid aperture.[3, 4]

When reflector illumination over a large angle is desired, the corrugated-waveguide diameter must be close to cutoff.* Matching this waveguide to a TE_{11}-mode circular pipe over a wide band can be achieved in a corrugated convertor section in which the magnitude of the longitudinal surface reactance X_z increases from zero at the input smooth-walled pipe to a high value near the feed aperture.

In principle, this method of mode conversion can be extended to the excitation of the TM_{11} and higher-order HE_{1n}, TE_{1n} and TM_{1n} modes. The higher-order HE_{1n} modes have application to the efficient illumination of paraboloidal,[4] and especially spherical, reflectors.[5]

Principle of mode conversion: The characteristic equation[4] for a waveguide of radius a having an anisotropic surface with zero circumferential reactance is plotted in Fig. 1*a* for $ka = 6$. When X_z departs from zero, the TE_{1n} and TM_{1n} modes become hybrid, and when $X_z = \pm\infty$ the balanced HE_{1n} ($\gamma = 1$)† and the EH_{1n} ($\gamma = -1$) modes can propagate.

Figs 1A and 1B show the change in X_z along the guide required to convert from one mode to another. For example, to convert the TE_{11} mode to the HE_{11} mode, the slot depth must be gradually reduced from one-half to one-quarter of a wavelength. This requirement is in agreement with that deduced by Bryant[6, 7] for a rectangular corrugated-waveguide hybrid-mode convertor. A further gradual reduction in the slot depth from one-quarter of a wavelength to zero produces the TM_{11} mode. Alternatively, by gradually increasing the initial slot depth from zero, the TE_{11} mode can be converted into an EH_{11} slow-wave mode.

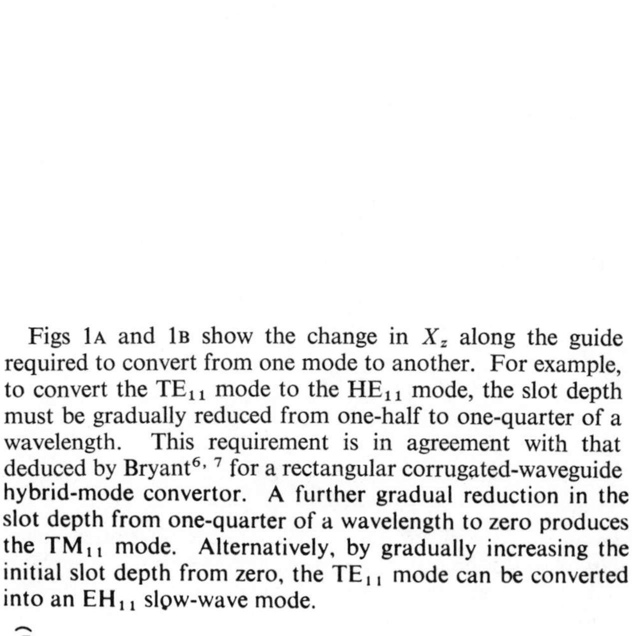

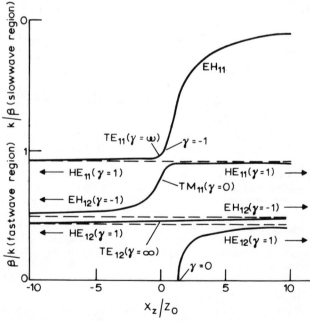

Fig. 1A *Longitudinal propagation coefficient β as a function of the longitudinal surface reactance X_z in a circular waveguide with zero circumferential surface reactance and normalised radius $ka = 6$*

The ordinate parameter β/k has been inverted in the slow-wave region

*The HE_{11}-mode feeds used on the Parkes reflector (semiangle 63°) have a minimum normalised waveguide radius ka of 2·3 ($k = 2\pi/\lambda$) at the lower edge of the band

† The mode-content factor[4] γ equals $-Z_0 H_z(u)/E_z(u)$, where $H_z(u)$ and $E_z(u)$ are the longitudinal components of waveguide field

In the design of a mode convertor, the waveguide diameter at any position along the convertor should be chosen so that any higher-order modes which are excited are beyond cutoff. In practice, this requirement is difficult to meet in the convertor section producing the $EH_{1n}(n > 1)$ mode, since the phase velocity of this mode is very close to the corresponding HE_{1n} mode. This may result in excessive coupling between the two modes, unless the convertor parameters change very slowly.

It is also necessary to minimise the excitation of lower-order modes. Only the wanted mode can propagate in the first section of the convertor, where the TE_{11} mode is transformed into the HE_{11} mode. In the second conversion process where the TM_{11} mode is obtained, the EH_{11} slow wave can propagate and, if excited, would convert to the TE_{11} mode. Consequently, the conversion process should be carried out gradually in this and later sections of the convertor.

Experimental mode convertors:

(*a*) *Technique:* To evaluate the performance of mode convertors, experiments at a centre frequency f_0 of 9·0 GHz were carried out with the three successive stages of conversion shown in Fig. 1B and Table 1. The corrugations, which were clamped together in a pipe, were each machined from metal

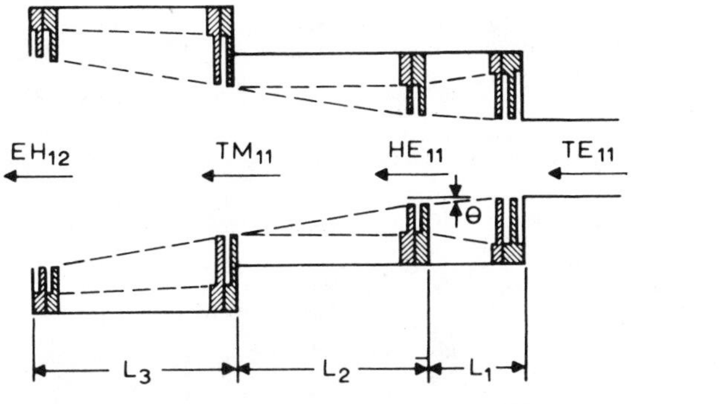

Fig. 1B *TE_{11} to EH_{12} mode convertor using circumferentially corrugated cylindrical waveguide*
Only a few of the slots are drawn

plate. To ensure good contact between the corrugations, one side of each corrugation was relieved to leave a rim of metal near the base of the slot. The inside diameter of each convertor section was gradually increased along its length so that β remained approximately constant.

The input voltage standing-wave ratios (v.s.w.r.s) of the convertors were measured using a slotted circular waveguide section. In each case, the output energy was absorbed by a well matched tapered wooden load in a uniform section of guide. To measure the TM_{11} to TE_{11} power ratio at the output of the TE_{11} to TM_{11} mode convertor, a circular waveguide slotted section was inserted between the convertor

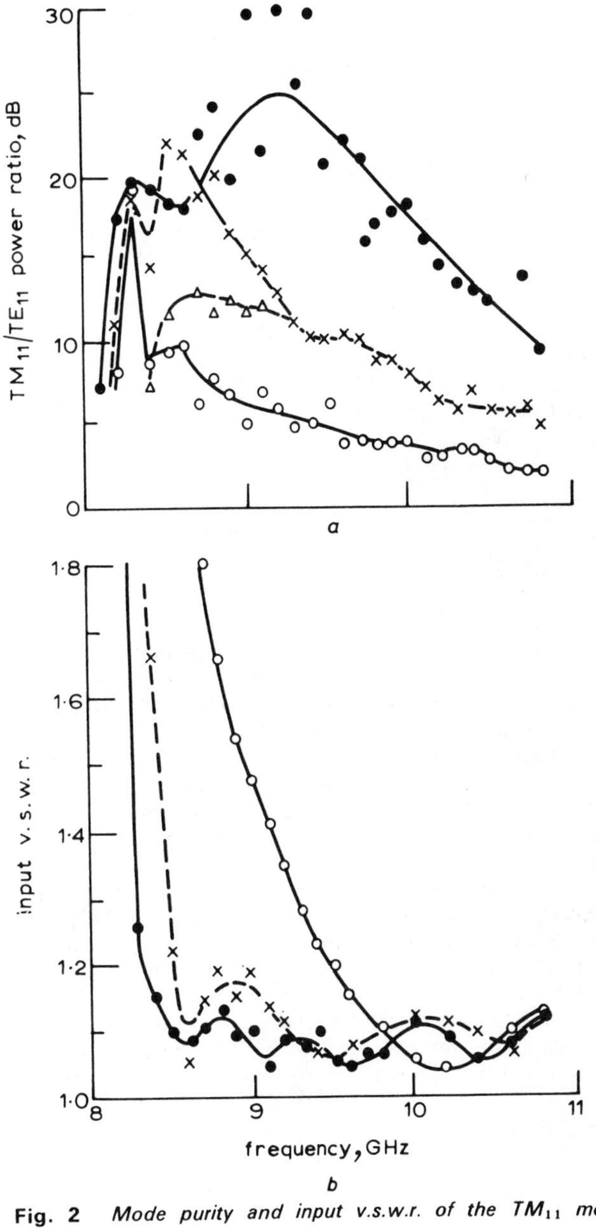

Fig. 2 *Mode purity and input v.s.w.r. of the TM_{11} mode convertor*

a Mode purity as a function of frequency
b Input v.s.w.r. $L_1 = 0·9\lambda_0$
●●● $L_2 = 3·6\lambda_0$ } number of slots / λ_0 $N = 22$
××× $L_2 = 1·8\lambda_0$ } slotwidth / pitch $\delta = 0·67$
○○○ $L_2 = 0·9\lambda_0$ } (type 1 corrugations)
□□□ $L_2 = 1·9\lambda_0$ $N = 10, \delta = 0·5$ (type-2 corrugations)

and the load. The residual v.s.w.r. of the line and load was approximately 1·04, which corresponds to a TM_{11} to TE_{11} power ratio of 34 dB at 9·0 GHz. Consequently, power ratios greater than approximately 26 dB (corresponding to a v.s.w.r. indication of 1·10) are relatively inaccurate.

The mode purity of the TE_{11} to EH_{12} mode convertor was deduced from the radiation patterns in the $\phi = \pm 45$ planes, where the HE_{1n} and EH_{1n} patterns are orthogonally polarised,[4, 8] The corrugated waveguide near the radiating aperture and the form of the corrugations surrounding the aperture were similar to the 2-hybrid-mode feed shown in Reference 2.

Table 1 CONVERTOR DETAILS

Section	Mode parameters			Typical convertor parameters	
	$k_0 a$	β/k_0	f_c*	L/λ_0	θ
			GHz		deg
TE_{11}	2·24	0·56	7·5		
TE_{11} to HE_{11}				0·9	4·2
HE_{11}	2·64	0·56	8·0 ($\delta = 0·67$) / 8·2 ($\delta = 0·5$)		
HE_{11} to TM_{11}				3·6	4·6
TM_{11}	4·47	0·52	7·7		
TM_{11} to EH_{11}				3·8	4·8
EH_{12}	6·50	0·60	7·4 ($\delta = 0·5$)		
HE_{12}†	6·50	0·55	8·0 ($\delta = 0·5$)		

* f_c = cutoff frequency
† Unwanted mode
$f_0 = 9·0$ GHz

(*b*) *Experimental results:* Radiation patterns of HE_{11}-mode feeds using TE_{11} to HE_{11} convertors show no crosspolarisation in the $\phi = -45°$ plane down to a level of 40 dB below the peak of the energy in the $\phi = 45°$ plane. Input v.s.w.r. measurements, made on the convertor when terminated in a wooden load and also when used with a feed, show that the v.s.w.r. deteriorates significantly if $L_1 < 0·9\,\lambda_0$, and that there is little improvement on making L_1 much greater than this value.

In Fig. 2, the performance of the TE_{11} to TM_{11} mode convertors is shown for various lengths L_2 of the HE_{11} to TM_{11} section. The power ratio is virtually independent of L_1, provided that $L_1 > 0·5\,\lambda_0$, but the v.s.w.r. deteriorates if $L_1 < 0·9\,\lambda_0$.

The results in Fig. 2 are for type-1 corrugations ($N = 22$, $\delta = 0·67$), except for one case in Fig. 2*a*, where the results with type-2 corrugations ($N = 10$, $\delta = 0·5$) are also shown. The latter produce a lower TM_{11} to TE_{11} power ratio at frequencies below f_0, an effect which was evident for all the lengths tested. The low-frequency v.s.w.r. 'cutoff' of the convertors using the type-2 corrugations occurs at a frequency about 0·3 GHz higher than that shown in Fig. 2*b* for the type-1 corrugations. The better low-frequency performance of the convertor using type-1 corrugations is most likely due to the lower cutoff frequency with these corrugations. In addition, the most important factor affecting the purity of the output TM_{11} mode over the frequency range is the length of the convertor, and not the number N of slots per wavelength. The lower limit of N has not yet been investigated fully.

Radiation patterns of the TE_{11} to EH_{12} convertor over a wide frequency range with $L_2 = L_3 = 3·8\lambda_0$ (type-2 corrugations) showed that the power in the EH_{12} and the unwanted HE_{12} mode were approximately equal, and that any HE_{11} mode present was insignificant. With a much longer TM_{11} to EH_{12} convertor section, it is probable that the purity of the EH_{12} output could be improved.

A mode generator capable of producing a relatively pure HE_{12} mode-power content has practical applications in feed design. A multistage convertor required to produce this mode from a TE_{11} mode input may need to be tens of wavelengths long. A better approach may be to excite a TM_{12} mode by some other method and to follow this by a single-stage corrugated convertor.

Acknowledgments: The author wishes to acknowledge the assistance of A. K. Falson and F. T. Watts in making the measurements.

B. MACA. THOMAS

21st June 1972

Division of Radiophysics
Commonwealth Scientific & Industrial Research Organisation
PO Box 76, Epping, NSW 2121, Australia

References

1 BATCHELOR, R. A., BROOKS, J. W., and COOPER, B. F. C.: 'Eleven-centimeter broadband correlation radiometer', *IEEE Trans.*, 1968, **AP-16**, pp. 228–234
2 THOMAS, B. MACA.: 'Prime-focus one- and two-hybrid-mode feeds', *Electron. Lett.*, 1970, **6**, pp. 460–461
3 MINNETT, H. C., and THOMAS, B.MACA.: 'A method of synthesizing radiation patterns with axial symmetry', *IEEE Trans.*, 1966, **AP-14**, pp. 654–656
4 THOMAS, B. MACA.: 'Theoretical performance of prime-focus paraboloids using cylindrical hybrid-mode feeds', *Proc IEE*, 1971, **118**, (11), pp. 1539–1549
5 THOMAS, B. MACA.: 'Matching focal-region fields with hybrid modes', *IEEE Trans.*, 1970, **AP-18**, pp. 404–405
6 BRYANT, G. H.: 'Propagation in corrugated waveguides', *Proc. IEE*, 1969, **116**, (2), pp. 203–213
7 BRYANT, G. H.: 'Monopulse multimode feed for military terminals' *in* 'Earth station technology'. *IEE Conf. Publ.* 72, 1970, pp. 245–249
8 THOMAS, B. MACA., and COOPER, D. N.: 'Two-hybrid-mode feeds for radio telescopes'. Paper presented at the antenna meeting held by the Nachrichtentechnische Gesellschaft at Darmstadt, W. Germany, Feb. 1972 (to be published in *Nachrichtentech. Fachber.*)

THEORETICAL ANALYSIS OF CYLINDRICAL HYBRID MODES IN A CORRUGATED HORN

The propagation behaviour of a corrugated cylinder is considered with particular reference to the application of such structures to hybrid-mode feeds for large reflector antennas. Results are presented which relate to the design of narrow-flare-angle horns of circular cross-section. These include the parametric dependence of a number of special points on the propagation curves. A procedure for achieving a balanced hybrid condition in the horn aperture is discussed following the proposal made by Bryant.

The use of a corrugated waveguide as a feed for a large reflector antenna has been considered by several authors.[1,2] Recently Minett and Thomas[3] have shown that the field in the focal region of a paraboloid reflector, which is illuminated by an axially directed plane wave, can be synthetised from cylindrical hybrid waves, and one structure known to support such waves is the corrugated circular waveguide of Fig. 1*a*. These waveguides have been the subject of considerable investigation in the past because of their application as slow-wave structures[4,5] and, in particular, in linear accelerators.[6] However, the fast-wave characteristics of azimuthally dependent modes have not been so extensively investigated, and here we present results which enable a wideband narrow-flare-angle corrugated horn to be designed.

In a previous study by one of the authors,[7] the general form of the characteristic equation for the phase-change coefficient β was given, and a transverse-network representation was described. For the present analysis, the corrugations are assumed to be infinitely thin and sufficiently closely spaced so that space harmonics may be neglected and the outward directed impedance of the H mode radial line $\vec{Z}$ may be assumed zero at $r = r_1$. The characteristic equation for hybrid-modes with field dependence $e^{-j\beta z}\, e^{jm\theta}$ then becomes

$$\overleftarrow{Z}(\overleftarrow{Y} + \vec{Y}) = M^2$$

where $\overleftarrow{Z} = -\dfrac{j\omega\mu_0}{K^2} F_m(Kr_1)$ $\quad \overleftarrow{Y} = -\dfrac{j\omega\epsilon_0}{K^2} F_m(Kr_1)$

$$F_m(x) = x\frac{J'_m(x)}{J_m(x)}$$

$$\vec{Y} = \frac{j\omega\epsilon_0}{k^2} S_m(k, r_1, r_0)$$

$$S_m(y_1, y_0) = y_1 \frac{J'_m(y_1)Y_m(y_0) - Y'_m(y_1)J_m(y_0)}{J_m(y_1)Y_m(y_0) - Y_m(y_1)J_m(y_0)}$$

$$M^2 = -\frac{m^2\beta^2}{K^4},$$

$$K^2 = \omega^2\epsilon_0\mu_0 - \beta^2 \qquad k^2 = \omega^2\epsilon_0\mu_0$$

$J_m(x)$ and $Y_m(x)$ are Bessel functions of the first and second kinds and of order m. Figs. 1*b* and *c* show, for $m = 1$ and for the first two modes, dispersion characteristics for two values of r_1/r_0. A number of special points are identified and their parametric dependence is illustrated in Fig. 1*d*.

As several authors have previously remarked,[1,8] an optimum-feed radiation pattern occurs when the admittance $\vec{Y} = 0$, i.e. when $S_1(k, r_1, r_0) = 0$ (see Fig. 1*d*, curve 5). In this circumstance, the longitudinal components of electric and magnetic field are in the ratio $\dfrac{E_z}{H_z} = \pm j\left(\dfrac{\mu_0}{\epsilon_0}\right)^{1/2}$. We shall refer to this as the balanced hybrid condition. For solutions corresponding to a negative sign of j, the radiation patterns have a null on the feed axis, whereas, for the positive sign, the radiation patterns have a maximum on axis. It is this latter class of modes which are of significance in antennas. Under the balanced hybrid condition, the radiation patterns in both E and H planes are identical, a feature which renders this type of feed particularly attractive for the efficient illumination of large reflectors.

Fig. 2 shows theoretical E and H plane patterns, derived by a Kirchhoff–Huygen's integration over the aperture field, for two values of kr_1, one of which (ω_1) corresponds to the balanced hybrid condition. It can be observed that, although

Reprinted with permission from *Electron. Lett.*, vol. 5, pp. 187–189, May 1, 1969.

the diffraction-limited beamwidth of the aperture is narrower at the upper frequency $\omega_2 = 1{\cdot}5\omega_1$, the E and H plane patterns are substantially the same, although not identical, as at ω_1.

In a practical design, the hybrid mode in the horn would be launched from the TE_{11} mode of circular waveguide. Following the proposal made by Bryant (p. 211, Reference ∞. The lowest operating frequency is chosen so that the balanced-hybrid condition exists in the aperture. Operation below this frequency is precluded because of the existence of the slow-wave mode shown in Figs. 1*b* and *c*. The stopband for this mode lies above ω_1. The highest operating frequency is chosen to be just below the cutoff frequency of the EH_{12} mode at the launcher.

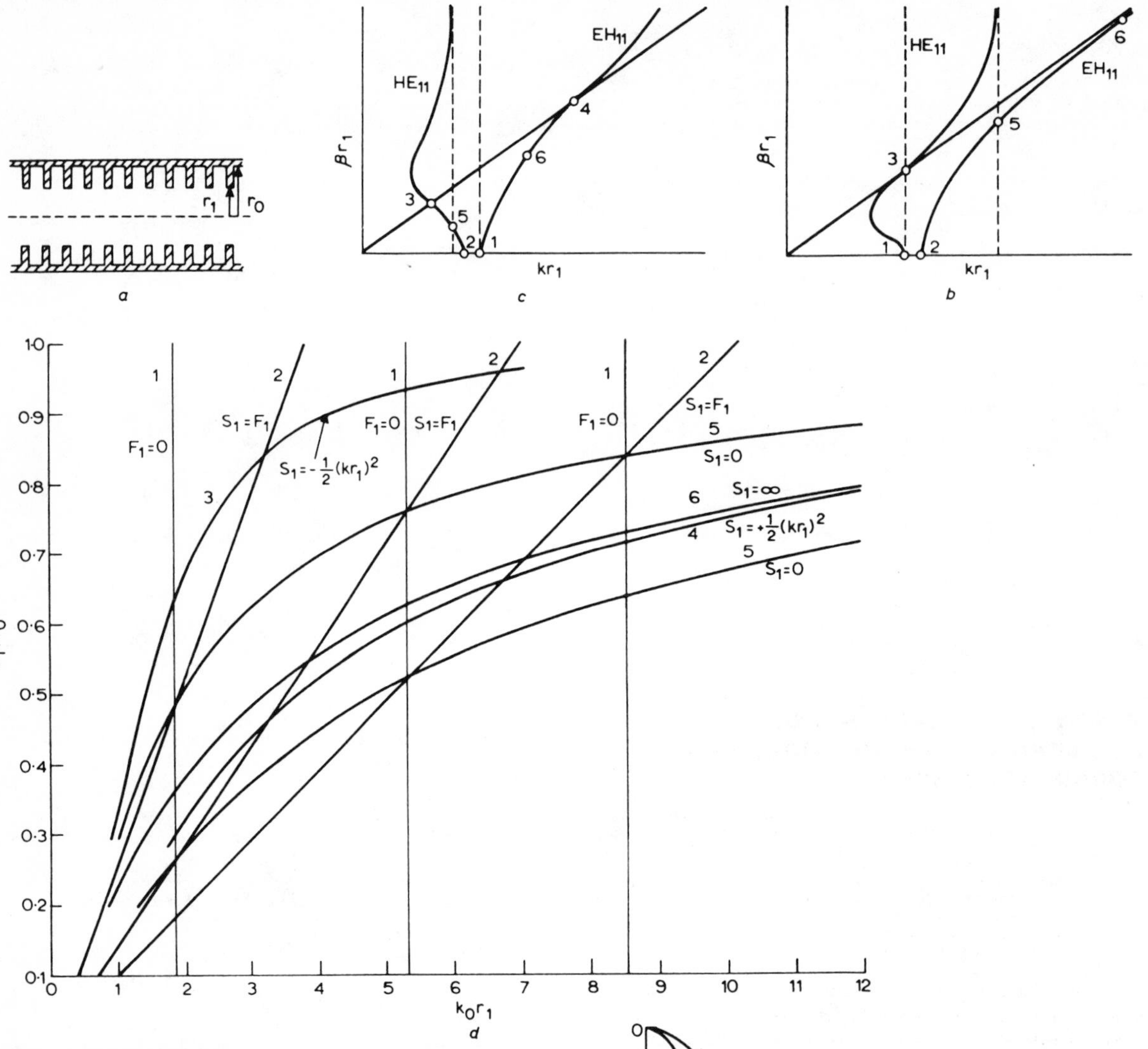

Fig. 1 *Corrugated circular waveguide and propagation characteristics*

a Corrugated circular waveguide, sectional view
b and *c* Dispersion diagrams for $r_1/r_0 = 0{\cdot}63$ and $r_1/r_0 = 0{\cdot}40$, respectively. Results refer to the first pair of modes with $m = 1$
d Parametric dependence of special points
1, 2: Cutoff for modes with $E_z = 0$ and $Q_z = 0$, respectively, at $\beta = 0$
3, 4: Condition $\bar{\beta} = \beta/k = 1$ corresponding to $S_1(k, r_1, r_0) = -\frac{1}{2}(kr_1)^2$
5: Balanced hybrid or 'open-circuit' boundary condition corresponding to $S_1(k, r_1, r_0) = 0$
6: Short-circuit boundary condition corresponding to $S_1(k, r_1, r_0) = \infty$

2), the ratio r_1/r_0 at the junction between the waveguide and the horn should be chosen so that, at the design frequency ω_1, $\vec{Y} = \infty$. Then $S_1(k_1, r_1, r_0) = \infty$ (see Fig. 1*d*, curve 6). As r_1 is gradually increased towards the horn aperture, the ratio r_1/r_0 is also increased, so that, in the aperture $\vec{Y} = S_1(k, r_1, r_0) = 0$ and at the design frequency, the balanced hybrid condition is realised. It can be seen from Fig. 1*d* that it is possible to design a horn so as to preclude surface-wave propagation.

We have also examined theoretically, using a computer method previously described,[9] the reflection at the junction between smooth and corrugated waveguides of the same radius r_1, as occurs at the launcher. Over a 2 : 1 bandwidth, the reflection coefficient does not exceed 0·11 and is zero at the frequency corresponding to the condition $S_1(k, r_1, r_0) =$

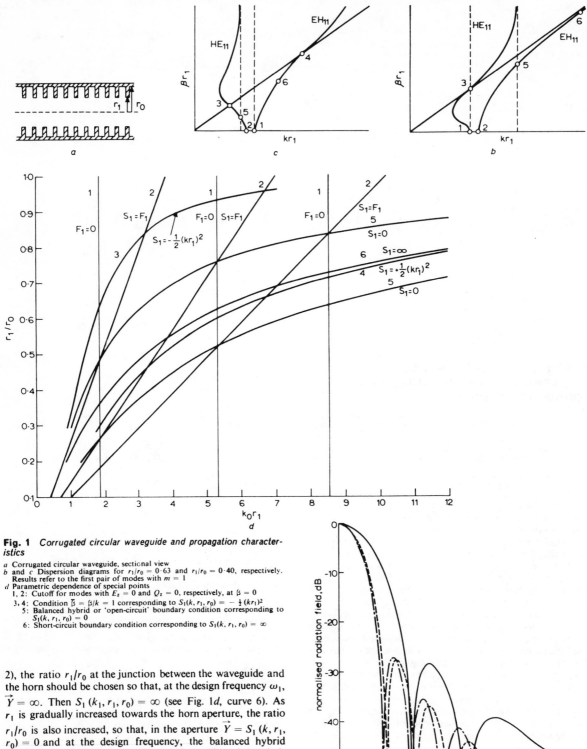

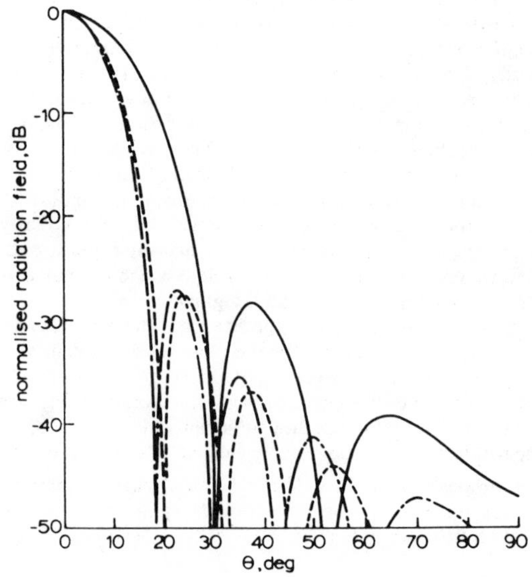

Fig. 2 *Theoretical far-field radiation pattern for EH_{11} mode with $r_1/r_0 = 0{\cdot}87$*

——— $kr_1 = 10{\cdot}85$, (balanced hybrid condition) E and H plane patterns identical
–·–·–· E plane pattern } $kr_1 = 16{\cdot}28$
– – – – H plane pattern }

The authors gratefully acknowledge a number of helpful discussions with G. Bryant.

P. J. B. CLARRICOATS *28th March 1969*

P. K. SAHA

Department of Electrical & Electronic Engineering
Queen Mary College
Mile End Road, London E1, England

References

1 MINNETT H. C., and THOMAS, B. MAC. A.: 'A method of synthesizing radiation patterns with axial symmetry', *IEEE Trans.*, 1966, **AP-14**, pp. 654–656

2 BRYANT, G. H.: 'Propagation in corrugated waveguides', *Proc. IEE*, 1969, **116**, pp. 203–213

3 MINNETT, H. C., and THOMAS, B. MAC. A.: 'Fields in the image space of symmetrical focusing reflectors', *ibid.*, 1968, **115**, pp. 1419–1340

4 FIELD, L. M.: 'Some slow-wave structures for travelling-wave tubes', *Proc. Inst. Radio Engrs.*, 1949, **37**, pp. 34–40

5 HENOCH, B. T.: 'Investigations of the disc-loaded and helical waveguide', *Trans. Roy. Ins . Technol. (Stockholm)*, 1958, (129)

6 WALKINSHAW, W.: 'Theoretical design of linear accelerators for electrons', *Proc. Phys. Soc.*, 1948, **61**, pp. 246–254

7 CLARRICOATS, P. J. B., and SOBHY, M. I.: 'Propagation behaviour of periodically loaded waveguides', *Proc. IEE*, 1968, **115**, pp. 652–661

8 SIMMONS, A. J., and KAY, A. F.: 'The scalar feed—a high performance feed for large paraboloid antenna', *IEE Conf. Publ. 21*, 1968, pp. 213–217

9 CLARRICOATS, P. J. B., and SLINN, K. R.: 'Numerical solution of waveguide-discontinuity problems', *Proc. IEE*, 1967, **114**, pp. 878–886

ANALYSIS OF SPHERICAL HYBRID MODES IN A CORRUGATED CONICAL HORN

An approximate analysis of fields in a corrugated horn is considered using spherical hybrid modes. Under the special condition where the slots are about a quarter-wavelength deep, the approximations are slight in the far-field region of the horn. Solutions are presented for the lowest-order spherical hybrid modes, and a procedure is described for the determination of the horn radiation pattern. A first step in the procedure involves the calculation of the hybrid-mode field in the horn aperture. Because diffraction will be minimal in wide-angle corrugated horns, the aperture and radiation patterns should be similar when the far-field approximation applies. This feature is verified for a 120° horn making use of experimental results due to Kay.

The demonstration by Kay[1] of the unique properties of a conical horn with corrugated walls has led to a considerable interest in the use of such devices as feeds for large reflector antennas. If the flare angle of the horn is sufficiently small, an analysis of the modes in the horn and their associated radiation patterns can be undertaken using cylindrical-mode functions.[2-4] However, when the flare angle exceeds about 10°, it is necessary to utilise spherical-mode functions if an accurate formulation is required. This will be the case for the wide-angle 'scalar' feeds investigated by Kay and others.[1,6]

In the present analysis, the field in the horn of Fig. 1*a* is represented in terms of a single spherical hybrid mode. The characteristic equation for the unknown separation constant ν is then obtained on matching the boundary conditions at the surface $\theta = \theta_1$. The corrugations are assumed sufficiently closely spaced that only a cutoff cylindrical E type mode exists within the slots thus when $\theta = \theta_1$, $\frac{E_\phi}{H_R} = Z_1 = 0$ and $\frac{H_\phi}{E_R} = Y_1$. In general, the boundary conditions cannot be satisfied with a single spherical hybrid mode, and, in an exact formulation, an infinite sum of spherical modes would be required. An exception occurs when $Y_1 = 0$, which is a case of particular importance in relation to antenna feeds. Then, provided that a far-field approximation holds at $R = R_0$, the aperture field can be determined quite accurately when the characteristic equation is solved subject to the above assumption. When the aperture field is known, the radiation pattern can be determined from a field expansion over $R = R_0$ in terms of a suitable combination of spherical TE and TM modes. The characteristic equation for ν is derived first, and results are presented for the case $Y_1 = 0$.

In region 1, a solution of the wave equations in spherical co-ordinates gives

$$E_R = a_\nu^m \frac{\nu(\nu+1)}{j\omega\epsilon_0 R}\hat{H}_\nu^{(2)}(kR)P_\nu^m(\cos\theta)\,e^{jm\phi} \quad . \quad . \quad (1)$$

$$H_R = b_\nu^m \frac{\nu(\nu+1)}{j\omega\mu_0 R}\hat{H}_\nu^{(2)}(kR)P_\nu^m(\cos\theta)\,e^{jm\phi} \quad . \quad . \quad (2)$$

where $\hat{H}_\nu^{(2)}(kR) = (kR)h_\nu^{(2)}(kR)$. $h_\nu^{(2)}(X)$ is a spherical Hankel function and $P_\nu^m(u)$ is an associated Legendre function of the first kind.

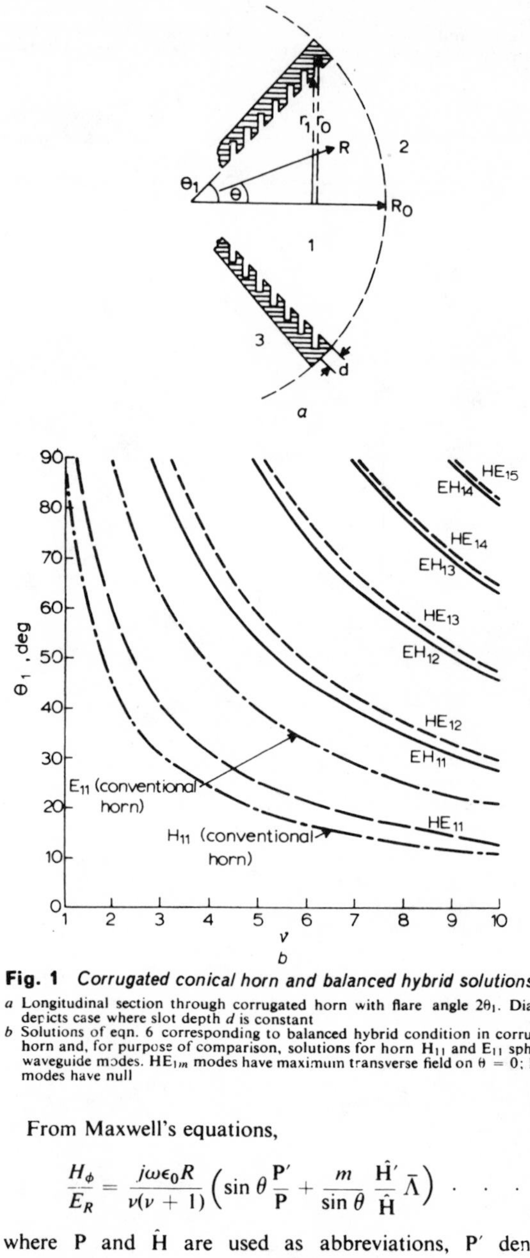

Fig. 1 *Corrugated conical horn and balanced hybrid solutions*

a Longitudinal section through corrugated horn with flare angle $2\theta_1$. Diagram depicts case where slot depth *d* is constant
b Solutions of eqn. 6 corresponding to balanced hybrid condition in corrugated horn and, for purpose of comparison, solutions for horn H_{11} and E_{11} spherical waveguide modes. HE_{1m} modes have maximum transverse field on $\theta = 0$; EH_{1m} modes have null

From Maxwell's equations,

$$\frac{H_\phi}{E_R} = \frac{j\omega\epsilon_0 R}{\nu(\nu+1)}\left(\sin\theta\frac{P'}{P} + \frac{m}{\sin\theta}\frac{\hat{H}'}{\hat{H}}\bar{\Lambda}\right) \quad . \quad . \quad . \quad (3)$$

where P and $\hat{H}$ are used as abbreviations, P′ denotes $\frac{dP_\nu^m(\cos\theta)}{d(\cos\theta)}$ and $\hat{H}'$ denotes $\frac{d\hat{H}(kR)}{d(kR)}$,

$$\frac{E_\phi}{H_R} = \frac{j\omega\mu_0 R}{\nu(\nu+1)}\left(-\sin\theta\frac{P'}{P} + \frac{m}{\sin\theta}\frac{\hat{H}'}{\hat{H}}\frac{1}{\bar{\Lambda}}\right) \quad . \quad . \quad (4)$$

$\bar{\Lambda} = \frac{b_\nu^m}{a_\nu^m}\left(\frac{\epsilon_0}{\mu_0}\right)^{1/2}$ and in the far field $\bar{\Lambda}$ is pure imaginary, as is $\frac{\hat{H}'}{\hat{H}}$, which tends to $-j$ in the limit when $kR \gg \nu$.[2]

Reprinted with permission from *Electron. Lett.*, vol. 5, pp. 189–190, May 1, 1969.

On matching the boundary conditions at $\theta = \theta_1$ and eliminating $\bar{\Lambda}$, the following characteristic equation for ν is obtained in the far-field limit:

$$f_\nu^m(\cos\theta_1)\{f_\nu^m(\cos\theta_1) + \hat{y}\} = m^2 \quad . \quad . \quad . \quad . \quad (5)$$

where $f_\nu^m(\cos\theta_1) = -\sin^2\theta_1 \dfrac{P'}{P}$

and $$\hat{y} = -\frac{\nu(\nu+1)\cos\theta_1}{kR}\,\frac{J_m'(kr_1)Y_m(kr_0) - J_m(kr_0)Y_m'(kr_1)}{J_m(kr_1)Y_m(kr_0) - J_m(kr_0)Y_m(kr_1)}$$

$$\doteq \frac{\nu(\nu+1)\cos\theta_1 \cot kd}{kR}$$

when $kr_1 \gg 1$ and $d = r_0 - r_1$

Now unless the slot depth d varies with R so that the normalised admittance $\hat{y}$ is independent of R, eqn. 5 is inconsistent with the separation-of-variables assumption, used in the derivation of eqns. 1 and 2. $\hat{y} = 0$ is an important special case which satisfies this requirement. Also, if kR_0 is sufficiently large so that $\hat{y}$ does not change appreciably with R over several wavelengths near $R = R_0$, eqn. 5 should yield useful general results for scalar feeds. Attention will now be confined to the special case $\hat{y} = 0$ and $m = 1$. This is of particular importance, since it may be shown that, under this condition, a spherical hybrid mode in the horn will excite TE and TM spherical modes in the space $R > R_0$ which, in combination, produce identical far-field E and H plane patterns with zero crosspolarisation.

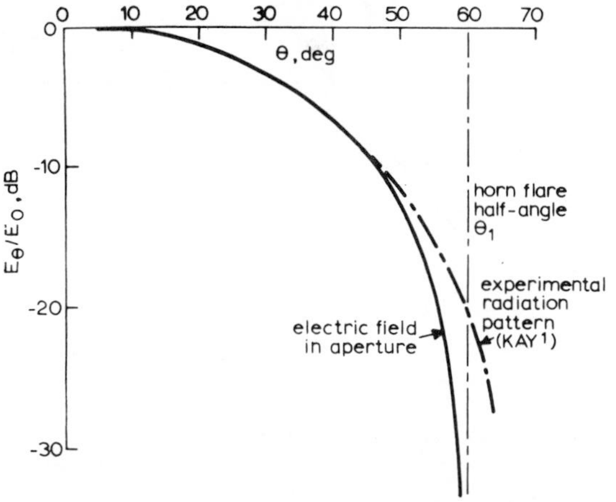

Fig. 2 *Normalised transverse electric field of balanced-hybrid HE_{11} spherical hybrid mode as a function of θ within corrugated horn for which $\theta_1 = 60°$; also experimentally measured radiation pattern for scalar feed of same θ_1 due to Kay*[1]

Eqn. 5 simplifies to

$$f_\nu^1(\cos\theta_1) = \pm 1 \quad . \quad . \quad . \quad . \quad . \quad . \quad . \quad . \quad . \quad (6)$$

and, from eqns. 3 and 4,

$$\bar{\Lambda} = \pm j \quad . \quad . \quad . \quad . \quad . \quad . \quad . \quad . \quad . \quad . \quad . \quad (7)$$

where the signs in eqns. 6 and 7 correspond. Eqn. 7 shows that $\left|\dfrac{E_R}{H_R}\right| = \left(\dfrac{\mu_0}{\epsilon_0}\right)^{1/2}$; therefore the condition is referred to as balanced hybrid. Solutions of eqn. 6 are shown in Fig. 1*b* for the first nine spherical hybrid modes. Only those modes corresponding to the minus-sign solution (shown by broken lines) yield transverse (to R) fields with a maximum on the horn axis. Positive-sign solutions correspond to fields with a null on axis. This behaviour is similar to that observed with radiation from hybrid modes at an aperture in a corrugated cylinder or dielectric rod. The transverse electric field $\bar{E}_T$ under balanced hybrid conditions is given below subject to a far-field approximation:

$$\bar{E}_T = -j^{n+1}a_\nu^1\left(\frac{\mu_0}{\epsilon_0}\right)^{1/2}\left\{\pm\frac{dP_\nu^1\cos\theta)}{d\theta} + \frac{P_\nu^1(\cos\theta)}{\sin\theta}\right\} \times (\mp \hat{i}_\theta + j\hat{i}_\phi)e^{-jkR}e^{j\phi} \quad . \quad (8)$$

where $\hat{i}_\theta$ and $\hat{i}_\phi$ are unit vectors.

It is evident that the field intensity is invariant with ϕ. In order to determine an accurate radiation pattern for the horn, the field over the surface $R = R_0$ may be expanded in terms of TE and TM spherical modes, which may be used to represent an arbitrary field in a spherical region. The pattern factor $F(\theta)$ may then be shown to be[9]

$$F(\theta) = \sum_{n=1}^{N} c_n\left(\frac{dP_n^1}{d\theta} + \frac{P_n^1}{\sin\theta}\right) \quad . \quad . \quad . \quad . \quad . \quad . \quad (9)$$

where

$$c_n = \frac{(-1)^n(2n+1)}{2n^2(n+1)^2}\int_0^{\theta_1}\left(\frac{dP_n^1}{d\theta} + \frac{P_n^1}{\sin\theta}\right)\left(\frac{dP_\nu^1}{d\theta} + \frac{P_\nu^1}{\sin\theta}\right)\sin\theta d\theta \quad . \quad . \quad . \quad . \quad (10)$$

A computer program is in preparation for the determination of $F(\theta)$ as a function of θ, with θ_1 and R_0 as parameters, although, when kR_0 is large compared with ν^2, $F(\theta)$ will be nearly independent of R_0. Eqn. 10 is derived on the assumption that $\bar{E}_T = 0$ for $\theta_1 < \theta < 2\pi - \theta_1$. In a more accurate derivation of $F(\theta)$, it would be necessary to represent the field in region 3 in terms of a summation of spherical TE and TM modes, although James and Longdon[5] have shown that, for a conventional horn, the assumption made in deriving eqn. 9 is well justified.

Under balanced-hybrid conditions, $\bar{E}_T = 0$ at $\theta = \theta_1$ within the horn, and it is to be expected that, for wide-angle horns, diffraction at the horn aperture will be minimal. In Fig. 2 is plotted $\left|\dfrac{E_T(\theta)}{E_T(0)}\right|$, from eqn. 8, for $\theta_1 = 60°$. Comparison is made with experimentally determined radiation-pattern measurements due to Kay[1] for a corrugated horn of the same flare angle. It is evident that there is close agreement between the patterns, provided that $\theta < 50°$. This agreement inspires confidence in the method used in the derivation of eqns. 6 and 8. Also, as it is well known[1,6] that the radiation patterns of wide-angle scalar feeds are frequency-independent over a wide range, it is to be expected that Fig. 1*b* can therefore be used for more general design purposes. In order to determine the aperture field pattern for an $m = 1$ mode, ν must first be determined from Fig. 1*b* for given θ_1, and the pattern $\dfrac{dP_\nu^1(\cos\theta)}{d\theta} + \dfrac{P_\nu^1(\cos\theta)}{\sin\theta}$ is then obtained using tables of the functions $\dfrac{P_\nu^1(\cos\theta)}{\sin\theta}$ and $\dfrac{dP_\nu^1(\cos\theta)}{d\theta}$. Tables of these functions exist for integer ν,[7] and these have been supplemented by tables for noninteger values appropriate to horns with θ_1 in the range 20°–90°.[8] Copies of these tables may be obtained on application to the author.

Acknowledgment is made to P. K. Saha for his help in preparing Fig. 1*b* and the table referred to above.

P. J. B. CLARRICOATS

28th March 1969

Department of Electrical & Electronic Engineering
Queen Mary College
Mile End Road, London E1, England

References

1 KAY, A. F.: 'The scalar feed', TRG report, contract AF19(604)-8057, March 1964
2 MINNETT, H., and THOMAS, B. MAC. A.: 'A method of synthesizing radiation patterns with axial symmetry', *IEEE Trans.*, 1966, **AP-14**, pp. 654–656
3 BRYANT, G.: 'Propagation in corrugated waveguides', *Proc. IEE*, 1969, **116**, pp. 203–213
4 CLARRICOATS, P. J. B., and SAHA, P. K.: 'Theoretical analysis of cylindrical hybrid modes in a corrugated horn', see pp. 187–189
5 JAMES, J., and LONGDON, L.: 'Predication of arbitrary electromagnetic fields from measured data', URSI symposium on electromagnetic theory, Stresa, Italy, 1968; to be published in *Alta Frequenza* symposium issue, April 1969
6 SIMMONS, A. J., and KAY, A. F.: 'The scalar feed—a high performance feed for large paraboloid antenna', *IEE Conf. Publ. 21*, 1968, pp. 213–217
7 Tables of associated Legendre functions (Columbia University Press, 1945)
8 SAHA, P. K.: 'Tables of associated Legendre functions for scalar feed applications', research report, Department of Electrical & Electronic Engineering, Queen Mary College, April 1969
9 POTTER P. D.: 'Application of spherical wave theory to Cassegrainian-fed paraboloids', *IEEE Trans.*, 1967, **AP-15**, pp. 727–735

RADIATION FROM WIDE-FLARE-ANGLE SCALAR HORNS

The radiation pattern of a wide-flare-angle scalar horn is determined by a modal-expansion technique and also by the Kirchhoff–Huygen method. Both approaches lead to similar results which agree well with experimental patterns obtained previously by Kay.

Introduction: In a recent letter,[1] the field in the aperture of a wide-flare-angle conical scalar horn was determined from a solution of the wave equation in spherical co-ordinates. A comparison has been made between the normalised aperture field of the dominant hybrid mode and an experimentally determined radiation pattern due to Kay,[2] for a scalar horn of flare half-angle $\theta_1 = 60°$. For angles from boresight $\theta < 50°$, the agreement is very close, but, as might be expected, the correlation progressively deteriorates as θ_1 is approached. In this letter, the radiation pattern is determined by two methods, both of which furnish results in satisfactory agreement with experiment, well into the shadow region.

Modal-expansion method: The aperture field may be expanded in terms of a sum of the TE and TM spherical modes of free space as previously discussed. The normalised far-field radiation pattern is then given by

$$\frac{f(\theta)}{f(0)} = \left| \frac{\sum_{n=1}^{N} \frac{c_n j^{n+1}}{h_n^{(2)}(x_0)} F_n(\theta)}{\sum_{n=1}^{N} \frac{c_n j^{n+1}}{h_n^{(2)}(x_0)} F_n(0)} \right| \qquad (1)$$

$$c_n = \frac{2n+1}{2n^2(n+1)^2} \int_0^{\theta_1} F_n(\theta) F_\nu(\theta) \sin\theta d\theta \qquad (2)$$

where $x_0 = kR_0 = \dfrac{2\pi R_0}{\lambda_0}$ and

$$F_n(\theta) = \left\{ \frac{dP_n^1(\cos\theta)}{d\theta} + \frac{P_n^1(\cos\theta)}{\sin\theta} \right\}$$

$P_n^1(\cos\theta)$ is an associated Legendre function of the first kind.

In passing, we note that the term $(-1)^n$ in eqn. 10 of Reference 1 should be omitted. Also, the pattern factor given there, in eqn. 9, refers to the horn aperture. The normalised radiation-pattern factor is as given in eqn. 1 above.

The value of ν in eqn. 2 is obtained under balanced-hybrid conditions from eqn. 6 of Reference 1, which is reproduced below in the present notation:

$$F_\nu(\theta) = 0 \qquad (3)$$

when $\theta = \theta_1$.

We have computed the normalised radiation pattern for a scalar horn from eqn. 1, with $\theta_1 = 60°$, $x_0 = 20$ and $N = 20$. This pattern is shown in Fig. 2 (broken curve) together with the experimental data taken from the report by Kay,[2] for a horn of the same flare angle. The agreement between experimental and theoretical results almost certainly lies within experimental accuracy. It is to be noted that, in practical scalar horns, the E-plane and H-plane patterns differ slightly, as shown in Fig. 2.

Kirchhoff–Huygen method: As an alternative to the modal-expansion technique, we have investigated the radiation pattern predicted by the classic Kirchhoff–Huygen method, with the radiating aperture chosen to be the spherical cap

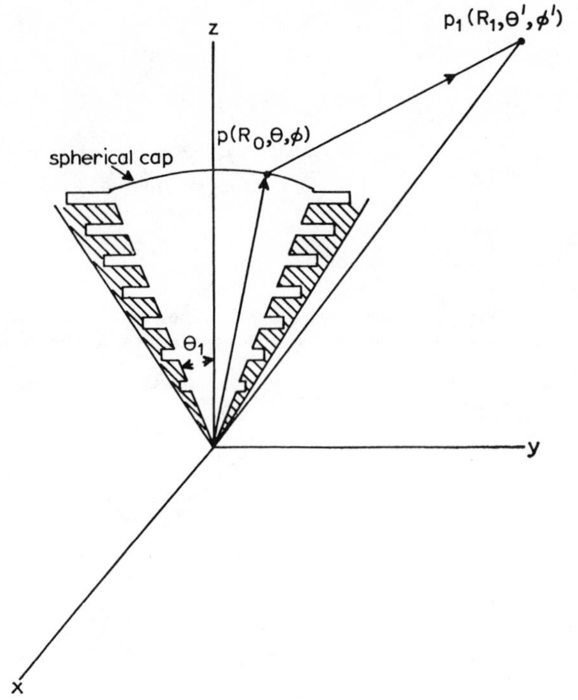

Fig. 1 *Scalar feed and co-ordinates*

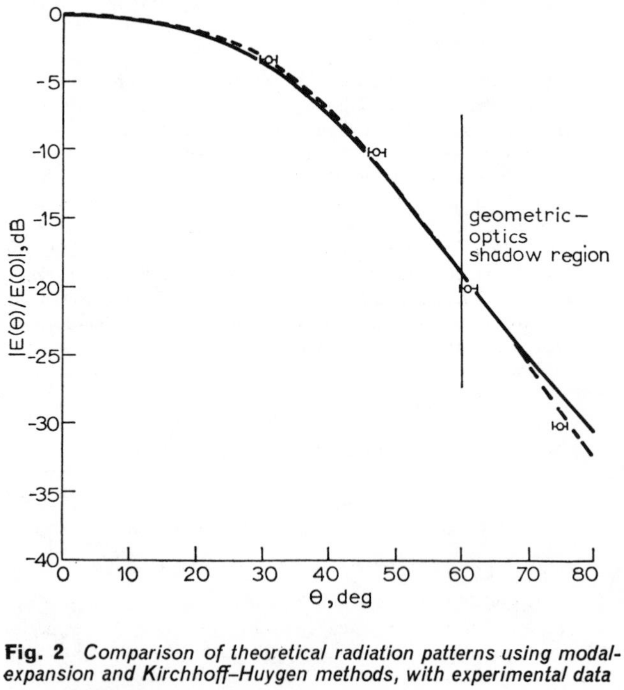

Fig. 2 *Comparison of theoretical radiation patterns using modal-expansion and Kirchhoff–Huygen methods, with experimental data*

Flare angle $\theta_1 = 60°$

———— by Kirchhoff–Huygen method for $kR_0 = 20$

- - - - - - - - by modal expansion method, $kR_0 = N = 20$

Experimental data due to Kay.[2] Points denote average of E- and H-plane beamwidths at midband; horizontal bar indicates difference

$R = R_0$, $-\theta_1 < \theta < \theta_1$. The aperture field is assumed to be that of the dominant mode of the scalar horn, subject to the far-field approximation discussed previously.[1] An outline of the analysis is given below, and results are presented in

Reprinted with permission from *Electron. Lett.*, vol. 5, pp. 376–378, Aug. 7, 1969.

Figs. 2 and 3 where the agreement with the experiments of Kay is again seen to be close over a very wide range of angles.

Fig. 1 shows the co-ordinates of field points p and p_1. From Reference 1*

$$E_p = F_y(\theta)(-\cos\phi \boldsymbol{i}_\theta - \sin\phi \boldsymbol{i}_\phi \quad \ldots \ldots \quad (4)$$

$$\left(\frac{\mu_0}{\epsilon_0}\right)^{1/2} H_p = -F_y(\theta)(\sin\phi \boldsymbol{i}_\theta - \cos\phi \boldsymbol{i}_\phi \quad \ldots \quad (5)$$

where $F_y(\theta)$ is given in eqn. 2.

From Silver,[3]

$$E_{p1} = \frac{-jk}{4\pi R_1} e^{-jkR_1}\boldsymbol{i}_{R1} \times \int_S \left\{\boldsymbol{i}_{R_0} \times E_p - \left(\frac{\mu_0}{\epsilon_0}\right)^{1/2} \boldsymbol{i}_{R_1} \times (\boldsymbol{i}_{R_0} \times H_p)\right\} e^{jkR_0 iR_1}\, dS \quad (6)$$

With extensive manipulation of intermediate equations, we obtain[4] from eqn. 6 the normalised θ and ϕ components of E_{p1}:

$$(E_{p1})_\theta = \{F_r(\theta') + jF_i(\theta')\}\cos\phi' \quad \ldots \ldots \quad (7)$$

$$(E_{p1})_\phi = -\{F_r(\theta') + jF_i(\theta')\}\sin\phi' \quad \ldots \quad (8)$$

$$\text{where } F_r(\theta') = \int_0^{\theta_1} G_r(\theta, \theta')F_y(\theta)d\theta \quad \ldots \ldots \quad (9)$$

$$F_i(\theta') = \int_0^{\theta_1} G_i(\theta, \theta')F_y(\theta)d\theta \quad \ldots \ldots \quad (10)$$

$$\text{and} \quad G_i^r(\theta, \theta') = \left\{(1 + \cos\theta)(1 - \cos\theta')\sin\theta \begin{matrix}\cos\\ \sin\end{matrix}(\alpha\cos\theta)\, J_0(\beta\sin\theta)\right\}$$
$$- \left\{(1 - \cos\theta)(1 - \cos\theta')\sin\theta \begin{matrix}\cos\\ \sin\end{matrix}(\alpha\cos\theta) \times J_2(\beta\sin\theta)\right\}$$
$$\mp \left\{2\sin\theta' \sin^2\theta \begin{matrix}\sin\\ \cos\end{matrix}(\alpha\cos\theta)J_1(\beta\sin\theta)\right\} \quad (11)$$

* In eqn. 8 of Reference 1, the ± signs associated with the i_θ term should be reversed

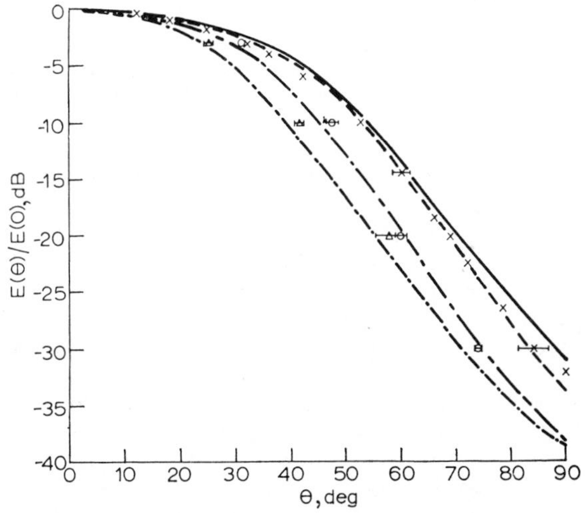

Fig. 3 *Comparison of theoretical radiation pattern using Kirchhoff–Huygen method with results due to Kay*

———— $\theta_1 = 70°$, $kR_0 = 20$
— — — $\theta_1 = 70°$, $kR_0 = 25$
- - - - - $\theta_1 = 60°$, $kR_0 = 25$
— - — - $\theta_1 = 50°$, $kR_0 = 20$

Experimental data due to Kay.[2] Points represent average of E-plane and H-plane beamwidths at midband frequency with indication of difference shown by horizontal bar

× $\theta_1 = 70°$, 10GHz ($kR_0 = 20$)
○ $\theta_1 = 60°$, 6GHz
△ $\theta_1 = 50°$, 15GHz

$\alpha = x_0\cos\theta'$, $\beta = x_0\sin\theta'$ and $J_0(x)$, $J_1(x)$, $J_2(x)$ are Bessel functions of first kind and of order 0, 1 and 2.

We note from eqns. 9 and 10 that the radiation pattern is circularly symmetric, and there is no cross-polarised component when the aperture field is linearly polarised.

By using the above equations, we have computed the normalised pattern factor $\frac{|E_{p_1}(\theta')|}{|E_{p_1}(0)|}$ for three values of θ_1 and for various values of x_0. These results are shown in Figs. 2 and 3 where further experimental results reported by Kay[2] are presented for comparison.

In Fig. 2, it can be seen that the Kirchhoff–Huygen method leads to a pattern which agrees very closely with the pattern derived from the modal-expansion method and the experimental results of Kay. In Fig. 3, further results are presented, and, for the 70° horn, the influence of the parameter x_0 is also investigated. A change in x_0 is equivalent to an alteration in horn length or phase centre. For the 60° and 50° horns, a value of x_0 has been assumed, as Kay does not give a value.

In summary, we have investigated two methods for the theoretical determination of the radiation pattern of wide-angle scalar feeds and have found them to be in excellent mutual agreement over a wide range of observation angles, and in quite close agreement with experimental results. The agreement observed inspires further confidence in the form chosen for the aperture field of a scalar horn. We have found that, in general, computer results can be obtained more rapidly with the Kirchhoff–Huygen method, although, when v is an integer, the time taken to obtain results of comparable accuracy is similar. However, we believe that the modal-expansion method can provide a greater physical insight and may prove of special value on pattern synthesis.

The authors gratefully acknowledge many helpful discussions with their colleague C. J. E. Phillips.

P. J. B. CLARRICOATS
P. K. SAHA

Department of Electrical & Electronic Engineering
Queen Mary College
Mile End Road, London E1, England

11th July 1969

References

1 CLARRICOATS, P. J. B.: 'Analysis of spherical hybrid modes in a corrugated conical horn', *Electron. Lett.*, 1969, **5**, pp. 189–190
2 KAY, A. F.: 'The scalar feed', TRG report, contract AF19(604)–8057, March 1964
3 SILVER, S.: 'Microwave antenna theory and design' (McGraw-Hill, 1949)
4 SAHA, P. K.: 'On the determination of the radiation pattern of a scalar horn using the Kirchhoff–Huygen method', report 002/1969, Department of Electrical & Electronic Engineering, Queen Mary College, June 1969

RADIATION PATTERN OF A LENS-CORRECTED CONICAL SCALAR HORN

An expression for the radiation pattern of a lens-corrected conical scalar horn is derived. Computed radiation patterns are presented for scalar-horns feeds containing planoconvex and meniscus lenses in their apertures. The patterns and beamwidths are compared with those of an uncorrected wide-angle scalar horn and an open-ended corrugated waveguide.

Introduction: It is well known that, to obtain a narrow beam from a large-aperture horn, the horn must be very long. Specifically, for a given flare length, the maximum flare angle has to be limited; otherwise quadratic phase error in the aperture causes directivity to decline.[1,2] Much larger flare angles, and hence a shorter horn length for a given aperture area, can be used if a lens is mounted in the horn aperture to correct the phase error. Although theoretical and experimental studies[3-5] of lens-corrected horns have been made in the past, the properties of lens-corrected scalar horns have not been reported previously, although it is known that they have been successfully employed in practice.* The conical scalar horn[6] possesses the useful feature of a circularly symmetric radiation pattern coupled with zero crosspolarisation if the aperture field is linearly polarised. Furthermore, scalar feeds exhibit very low side-lobe levels which make them attractive as feeds for communication-satellite antennas. However, the corrugated walls are difficult to fabricate, which is an added reason for examining the lens-corrected wide-angle feed as a possible device for the production of a narrow beam from a scalar horn of short flare length.

Radiation pattern of lens-corrected scalar horn: The design of a dielectric lens to transform a spherical wavefront into a plane phase front has been described by Silver.[7] Techniques for matching lenses by the introduction of ridges to simulate a homogeneous dielectric layer of variable permittivity have been discussed[8-10] and the zoning principle used to reduce the mass of a lens is also well known.[1,7] In the following analysis two simple lens types are considered: the planoconvex lens and the meniscus lens. The profiles of these lenses have been investigated previously and the results below may be found in the literature.[7]

Planoconvex lens: From Fig. 1*a*

$$f = r\frac{(1 - n\cos\theta)}{1 - n} \quad \ldots\ldots\ldots\ldots \quad (1)$$

where $n^2 = \epsilon/\epsilon_0$ = relative permittivity of the lens
and f = focal length of the lens.

Meniscus lens: From Fig. 1*b*

$$f = r\frac{(n - \cos\theta)}{n - 1} \quad \ldots\ldots\ldots\ldots \quad (2)$$

The pattern of the balanced hybrid mode in the corrugated

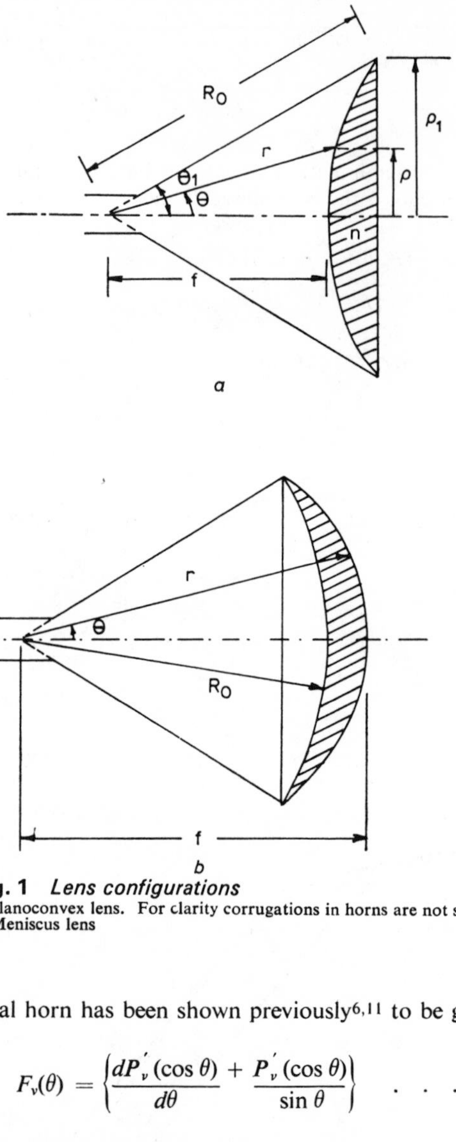

Fig. 1 *Lens configurations*
a Planoconvex lens. For clarity corrugations in horns are not shown
b Meniscus lens

conical horn has been shown previously[6,11] to be given by

$$F_\nu(\theta) = \left\{\frac{dP_\nu'(\cos\theta)}{d\theta} + \frac{P_\nu'(\cos\theta)}{\sin\theta}\right\} \quad \ldots\ldots \quad (3)$$

where ν is determined from

$$F_\nu(\theta_1) = 0 \quad \ldots\ldots\ldots\ldots\ldots \quad (4)$$

The field distribution at the point ρ,ϕ in the aperture plane is then

$$F(\rho) = F_\nu(\theta)\frac{N_{1,2}(\theta)}{f(n - 1)} \quad \ldots\ldots\ldots\ldots \quad (5)$$

where it may be readily shown that

$$N_1(\theta) = \left\{\frac{(n\cos\theta - 1)^3}{n - \cos\theta}\right\}^{\frac{1}{2}} \text{ for the planoconvex lens} \quad \ldots \quad (6)$$

* VIGGH, M.: Private communication

Reprinted with permission from *Electron. Lett.*, vol. 5, pp. 592–593, Nov. 13, 1969.

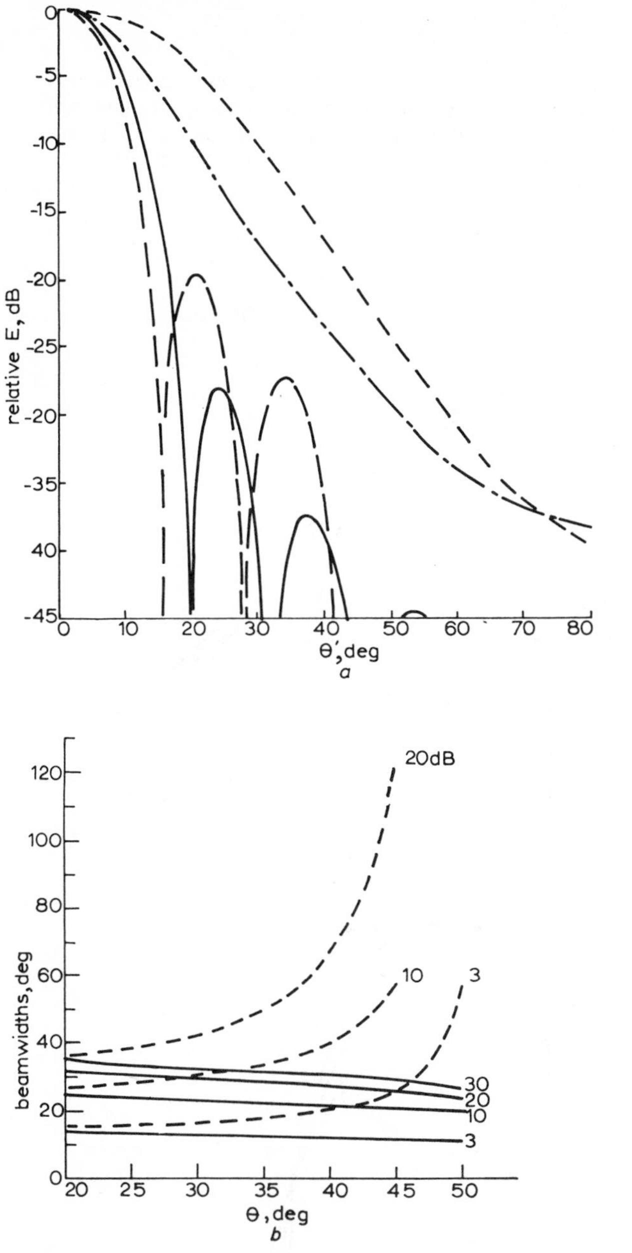

Fig. 2 *Radiation patterns and beamwidths of lens-corrected scalar feeds*

a Balanced hybrid radiation patterns for horns of normalised radius $2\pi\rho_1/\gamma = 16{\cdot}22$

———— open-ended waveguide $r_1/r_0 = 0{\cdot}91$
- - - - - - $\theta_1 = 40°$ uncorrected
–·–·–·–· $\theta_1 = 40°$ planoconvex lens, $n = 1{\cdot}6$
— — — $\theta_1 = 40°$ meniscus lens, $n = 1{\cdot}6$

b Beamwidths as a function of horn half flare angle for horns of aperture dimensions as in Fig. 2*a*

———— meniscus lens, $n = 1{\cdot}6$
- - - - - - planoconvex lens, $n = 1{\cdot}6$

while

$$N_2(\theta) = \left\{\frac{(n - \cos\theta)^3}{n\cos\theta - 1}\right\}^{\frac{1}{2}} \text{ for the meniscus lens} \quad . \ . \ . \ (7)$$

If $\quad n\cos\theta - 1 = n_1(\theta) \quad . \ . \ . \ . \ . \ . \ . \ . \ . \ . \ (8)$

and $\quad n - \cos\theta = n_2(\theta) \quad . \ . \ . \ . \ . \ . \ . \ . \ . \ . \ (9)$

the circularly symmetric radiation pattern is given by

$$g(\theta') = 2\pi f(n-1)\int_{\theta=0}^{\theta=\theta_1} \frac{F(\theta)}{N_{1,2}}(\theta)\, J_0\left\{kR_0 \sin\theta' \sin\theta \frac{n_{1,2}(\theta_1)}{n_{1,2}(\theta)}\right\} \times \sin\theta d\theta \quad . \ . \ . \ (10)$$

where the subscripts refer to the planoconvex and meniscus lens, respectively.

Fig. 2*a* shows computed radiation patterns $g(\theta')$ for scalar horns with aperture $2\pi\rho_1/\lambda = 16{\cdot}22$. Additional to the patterns for planoconvex and meniscus lenses, are shown patterns for an uncorrected 40° conical horn and for an open-ended corrugated circular waveguide with radius ratio 0·91. Parameters have been chosen so that the dominant hybrid mode is balanced in both conical and cylindrical feeds and all feeds have the same aperture. For the planoconvex lens the pattern of the uncorrected horn is compressed without any appreciable change in shape, as the lens only slightly modifies the aperture distribution. However, for the meniscus lens, the product $F_v(\theta)N_2(\theta)$ is almost constant with varying θ, as the radiation pattern suggests.

We have also investigated the dependence of the patterns on the horn flare angle as shown in Fig. 2*b*. As the meniscus lens produces a nearly uniform aperture distribution, the pattern varies only slightly with the flare angle, whereas, for the planoconvex lens, the width increases with increasing horn flare angle.

In summary, a planoconvex lens may be used to compress the radiation pattern of a wide-flare-angle scalar feed while preserving the characteristic pattern shape. A meniscus lens produces a pattern similar to an open-ended corrugated circular waveguide. Both lens systems are limited to use with horns whose flare angle θ_1 does not exceed $\cos^{-1}(1/n)$, as noted by Silver.[7]

P. J. B. CLARRICOATS *13th October 1969*
P. K. SAHA

Department of Electrical & Electronic Engineering
Queen Mary College
Mile End Road, London E1, England

References

1 COLLIN, R. E., and ZUCKER, F. J.: 'Antenna theory—Pt. 1' (McGraw-Hill, 1969), p. 632
2 SCHELKUNOFF, S., and FRIIS, H. T.: 'Antenna theory and practice' (Wiley, 1952), pp. 528–529
3 CUMMINS, J. A.: 'Side lobe reduction in the radiation field of lens corrected H-plane horns', M.Sc. thesis, Laval University, Aug. 1960
4 CUMMINS, J. A.: 'Two methods of improving the performance of lens corrected H-plane horns', IRE Canadian Convention Record, 1958, pp. 232–239
5 JONES, E. M. T., MORITA, T., and COHN, S. B.: 'Measured performance of matched dielectric lenses', *IRE Trans.*, 1956, **AP-4**, pp. 31–33
6 CLARRICOATS, P. J. B.: 'Analysis of spherical hybrid modes in a corrugated conical horn', *Electron. Lett.*, 1969, **5**, pp. 189–190
7 SILVER, S.: 'Microwave antenna theory and design' (McGraw-Hill, 1949)
8 MORITA, T., and COHN, S. B.: 'Microwave lens matching by simulated quarter-wave transformers', *IRE Trans.*, 1956, **AP-4**, pp. 33–39
9 JONES, E. M. T., and COHN, S. B.: 'Surface matching of dielectric lenses', *J. Appl. Phys.*, 1955, **26**, pp. 452–457
10 COLLIN, R. E.: 'Properties of slotted dielectric interfaces', *IRE Trans*, 1959, **AP-7**, pp. 62–73
11 CLARRICOATS, P. J. B., and SAHA, P. K.: 'Radiation from wide-flare-angle scalar horns', *Electron. Lett.*, 1969, **5**, pp. 376–378

NEAR-FIELD RADIATION CHARACTERISTICS OF CORRUGATED HORNS

Indexing terms: Antenna feeders, Waveguides, Guided electromagnetic-wave propagation

The amplitude and phase patterns of corrugated feed horns are predicted in the near-field region by means of a spherical-mode-expansion method which has been previously applied only in the far field. Excellent agreement has been observed with experimental patterns, and typical results for horns with flare semiangles of 12° and 70° are described.

Conical corrugated-horn feeds are in widespread use in high-efficiency microwave antennas, and their properties have been extensively investigated by many workers. Clarricoats and Saha[1, 2] have predicted their far-field radiation characteristics by the Kirchhoff–Huygens and spherical-mode-expansion methods and have obtained excellent agreement between the methods and with experimental results. In the near field, the latter method appears simpler to apply, and, in this letter, the method is explained, and the near-field phase and amplitude characteristics of horns with flare semiangles of 12° and 70° are predicted. The results are favourably compared with those obtained experimentally by the authors and by Masterman.* Since an important class of microwave antennas employ subreflectors which lie in the near field of a corrugated horn, the results of this letter permit the theoretical design of such antennas, details of which will be reported later.

The analysis follows closely on the far-field technique described previously.[1, 2] The electric field over a spherical cap in the aperture of the corrugated horn of Fig. 1A is expressed in terms of the dominant spherical hybrid mode:

$$E_a(R_0, \phi\theta) = a_1\, F_v{}^1(\theta)\, \frac{e^{-jkR_0}}{R_0}\, \varepsilon^{j\phi} \quad . \quad . \quad . \quad . \quad (1)$$

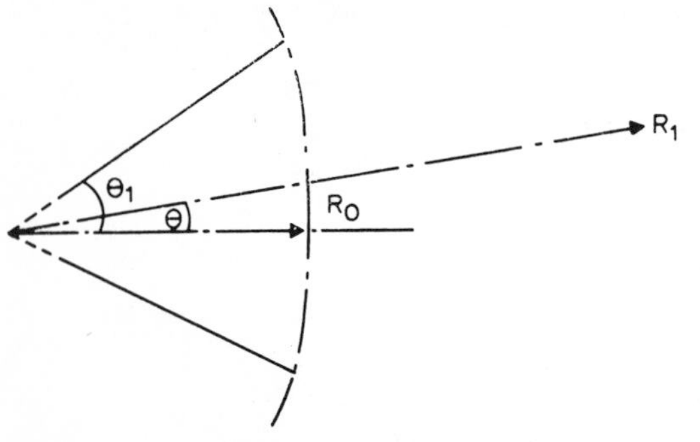

Fig. 1A *Co-ordinates of horn and point of observation*
For clarity, corrugations are omitted from horn

where

$$F_v{}^1(\theta) = \frac{dP_v{}^1(\cos\theta)}{d\theta} + \frac{P_v{}^1(\cos\theta)}{\sin\theta} \quad . \quad . \quad . \quad . \quad (2)$$

and $P_v{}^1(\cos\theta)$ is an associated Legendre function of the first kind and first order. We have assumed that the HE_{1m} spherical mode is present in the horn under balanced hybrid conditions, and in our subsequent calculations we consider only the dominant HE_{11} mode for which $m = 1$. The present method can be extended so as to apply at frequencies other than balanced hybrid[3] (for which the slots are approximately $\lambda/4$ in depth). However, we have found elsewhere,[2] that corrugated-horn feeds exhibit nearly perfect pattern symmetry over a very wide frequency band, and the above restriction is not serious.

* MASTERMAN, P. H.: Private communication

As in the far-field analysis, the aperture field is expanded in terms of a combination of spherical TE and TM modes so that, at $R = R_0$,

$$E_a(R_0, \theta) = \sum_{n=1}^{N} C_n\, h_n{}^{(2)}(kR_0)\, F_n{}^1(\theta) \quad . \quad . \quad . \quad . \quad (3)$$

where $h_n{}^{(2)}(kR_0)$ is a spherical Hankel function and the function $F_n{}^1(\theta)$ is obtained by replacing v by n in eqn. 2. By applying orthogonality relationships, we obtain the following expression for the nth coefficients in eqn. 3:

$$C_n = a_1 \frac{e^{-jkR_0}}{R_0} \; \frac{2n+1}{2n^2(n+1)^2\; h_n{}^{(2)}(kR_0)} \times \int_0^{\theta_1} F_v{}^1(\theta)\, F_n{}^1(\theta) \sin\theta\, d\theta \quad . \quad . \quad (4)$$

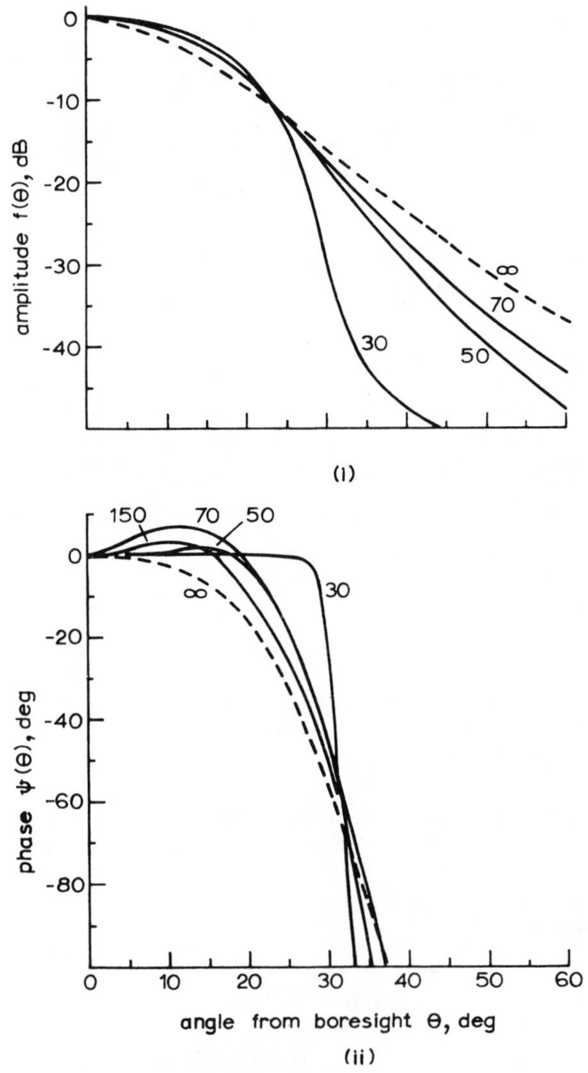

Fig. 1B *Theoretical amplitude (i) and phase (ii) patterns of conical corrugated feed horn*
$\theta_1 = 30°$, $KR_0 = 29{\cdot}05$, parameter KR_1

Finally, the electric field on a spherical surface at radius R_1 is given by

$$E_a(R_1, \theta) = \sum_{n=1}^{N} C_n\, h_n{}^{(2)}(kR_1)\, F_n{}^1(\theta) \quad . \quad . \quad . \quad . \quad (5)$$

$$= f(\theta)\, e^{j\psi(\theta)} \quad . \quad . \quad . \quad . \quad . \quad . \quad . \quad . \quad . \quad (6)$$

Reprinted with permission from *Electron. Lett.*, vol. 7, pp. 446–448, Aug. 12, 1971.

Since we have assumed balanced hybrid conditions in the horn aperture, the field will be linearly polarised throughout, provided that the horn excitation is linearly polarised. Previously, we obtained a form of eqn. 5 which was valid only in the far field.

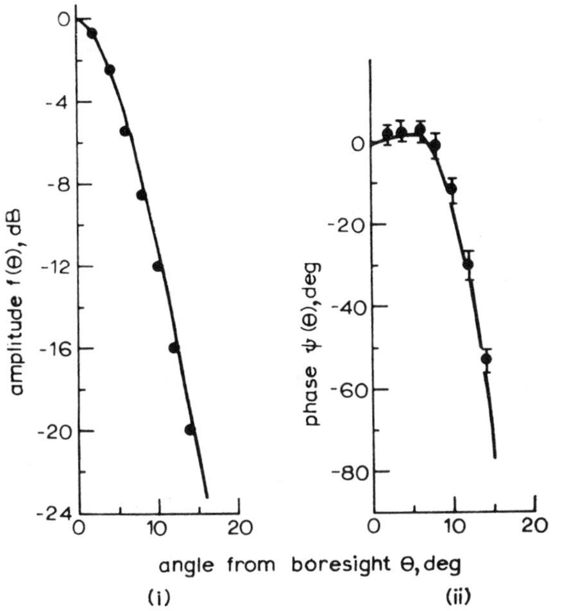

Fig. 2A *Amplitude (i) and phase (ii) patterns of conical corrugated feed horn*

$\theta_1 = 12°$, $KR_0 = 57{\cdot}5$, point of observation is such that $KR_1 = 71{\cdot}1$
Experimental points obtained at a frequency of 9 GHz

Fig. 1B shows computed amplitude and phase patterns for a 30° corrugated feed horn of normalised flare length $kR_0 = 29{\cdot}05$. In these computations, $N = 30$. When $kR_1 = 30$, i.e. for a surface very close to the horn aperture, the field-amplitude pattern closely resembles that of the function $F_\nu^1(\theta)$, as described elsewhere.[2,4] Likewise, in the range $0 < \theta < 30°$, the relative phase is nearly constant. With increasing values of kR_1, the amplitude pattern transforms, and, when $kR_1 > 200$, it has been found to resemble closely the far-field pattern. In the near field, the relative phase exhibits a shallow maximum which reaches a peak value when $kR_1 \simeq 100$. With increasing kR_1, the maximum then declines and moves closer to the axis. Finally, in the far field, the phase is a monotonic decreasing function of θ.

Fig. 2A shows a typical result obtained by us for a 12 feed horn for which $kR_0 = 57{\cdot}5$. The agreement between experiment and theory lies within experimental accuracy. We have obtained similar agreement for other values of kR_1.

Fig. 2B compares the results of the above theory with experimental measurements (broken lines) obtained by Masterman. The agreement again lies within the limits of experimental accuracy.

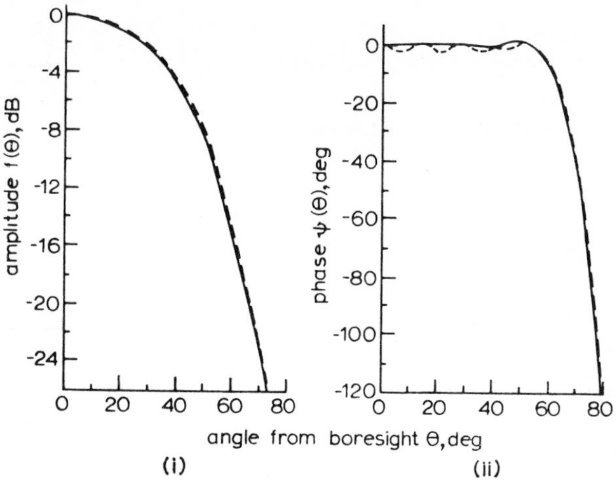

Fig. 2B *Amplitude (i) and phase (ii) patterns of conical corrugated feed horn*

$\theta_1 = 70°$, $KR_0 = 20$, point of observation is such that $KR_1 = 39{\cdot}8$
Experimental curves (broken lines) were obtained by Masterman at a frequency of 7·3 GHz

We have also made comparisons for a 9° horn and have obtained satisfactory agreement. We therefore believe that the spherical-mode-expansion method can be applied with confidence to the prediction of the phase and amplitude patterns of corrugated horns at distances from the aperture which range from within the near field through to the far field.

The authors gratefully acknowledge the assistance of their colleagues S. H. Lim, P. H. Masterman and C. E. R. C. Salema.

P. J. B. CLARRICOATS
A. D. OLVER

12th July 1971

Department of Electrical & Electronic Engineering
Queen Mary College
Mile End Road, London E1, England

P. K. SAHA

Institute of Radio Physics & Electronics
92 Acharya Prafulla Chandra Road, Calcutta 9, India

References

1 CLARRICOATS, P. J. B., and SAHA, P. K.: 'Radiation from wide-flare-angle scalar horns', *Electron. Lett.*, 1969, **5**, pp. 376–378
2 CLARRICOATS, P. J. B., and SAHA, P. K.: 'Propagation and radiation behaviour of corrugated feeds. Pt. 2—Corrugated-conical-horn-feed', *Proc. IEE*, 1971, **118** (to be published)
3 LUDWIG, A. C.: Near field far field transformations using spherical wave expansions', *IEEE Trans.*, 1971, **AP-19**, pp. 214–220
4 CLARRICOATS, P. J. B.: 'Analysis of spherical hybrid modes in a corrugated conical horn', *Electron. Lett.*, 1969, **5**, pp. 189–190

Propagation and radiation behaviour of corrugated feeds

Part 1—Corrugated-waveguide feed

Prof. P. J. B. Clarricoats, D.Sc.(Eng.), F.Inst.P., Fel.I.E.E.E., C.Eng., F.I.E.E., and P. K. Saha, B.Sc., M.Tech., Ph.D.

Indexing terms: *Antenna feeders, Waveguides, Guided electromagnetic-wave propagation, Waveguide junctions*

Abstract

An investigation of the propagation and radiation behaviour of circular corrugated waveguides is described. Particular attention is given to modes of unity azimuthal dependence because of their importance in antenna-feed applications. It is shown that the radiation pattern of a corrugated waveguide exhibits nearly perfect symmetry over a 1·5 : 1 frequency band, and, when the corrugations are approximately $\lambda/4$ deep, the pattern is symmetric and there is no crosspolarised component of radiated field. The attenuation of the dominant HE_{11} mode is investigated theoretically and is shown to be less than that of the H_{11} mode in a uniform waveguide over at least a 2 : 1 frequency bandwidth. An important similarity is described between the propagation behaviour of a corrugated waveguide and that of a dielectric rod of low relative permittivity, such as those used in fibre optics and optical waveguides. Finally, the determination of the input voltage standing-wave ratio (v.s.w.r.) at the junction between homogeneous and corrugated waveguides is theoretically and experimentally studied.

List of principal symbols

b = groove width
c = groove separation
d = slot depth
$F_m(x) = x \dfrac{J'_m(x)}{J_m(x)}$
$F(\theta)$ = pattern function defined by eqn. 56
$J_m(x)$ = Bessel function of 1st kind and order m
k = free-space wavenumber
K = transverse wavenumber
$K_m(y_1)$ = modified Bessel function of 3rd kind and order m
m = azimuthal wavenumber
$M_m(y_1) = y_1 \dfrac{K'_m(y_1)}{K_m(y_1)}$
r = radial co-ordinate
r_1, r_0 = internal radius of waveguide and radius of slot, respectively
R = radial distance in spherical co-ordinates
$S_m(x, y) = x \dfrac{J'_m(x)Y_m(y) - J_m(y)Y'_m(x)}{J_m(x)Y_m(y) - J_m(y)Y_m(x)}$
$x_1 = Kr_1$
$x'_1, x'_0 = kr_1, kr_0$
y_0 = free-space wave admittance
$y_1 = \omega^2\epsilon_1\mu_0 - \beta^2$
$Y_m(x)$ = Bessel function of 2nd kind and order m
z = longitudinal co-ordinate
z_0 = free-space wave impedance
$\beta, \bar{\beta}$ = phase-change coefficient and normalised phase-change coefficient, respectively
η = antenna efficiency
θ = angular co-ordinate
$\bar{\Lambda} = \dfrac{j}{y_0}\dfrac{H_z}{E_z}$
ψ = azimuthal co-ordinate
ω = angular frequency

1 Introduction

During the last decade, two independent approaches to the design of an optimum-feed horn have resulted in a feed which is now used in antennas for communication-satellite earth stations and for radio astronomy. In the USA, Kay[1,2] and his associates studied wide-flare horns, and, while investigating the effect of flanges on radiation-pattern symmetry, devised the feed shown in Fig. 1*a*. Because of

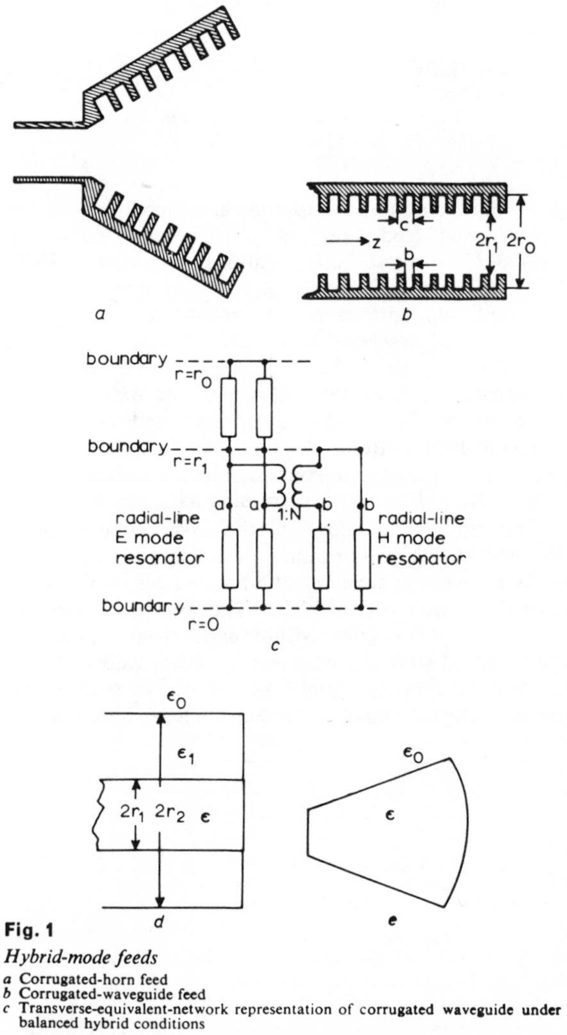

Fig. 1
Hybrid-mode feeds
a Corrugated-horn feed
b Corrugated-waveguide feed
c Transverse-equivalent-network representation of corrugated waveguide under balanced hybrid conditions

$\overleftarrow{Y}_{aa} = -\dfrac{j\omega\epsilon_0}{K^2} F_m(x_1)$, $\overrightarrow{Y}_{aa} = \dfrac{j\omega\epsilon_0}{k^2} S_m(x_1', x_0')$,
$\overrightarrow{Z}_{bb} = -\dfrac{j\omega\mu_0}{K^2} F_m(x_1)$, $N^2 = -m^2\beta^2/K^4$

d Dielectric cylinder
e Dielectric cone

Paper 6472 E, received 31st December 1970
Prof. Clarricoats is, and Dr. Saha was formerly, with the Department of Electrical & Electronic Engineering, Queen Mary College, University of London, Mile End Road, London E1, England. Dr. Saha is now with the Institute of Radio Physics & Electronics, Calcutta 9, India

Reprinted with permission from *Proc. Inst. Elec. Eng.*, vol. 118, pp. 1167–1176, Sept. 1971.

certain isotropic reflection characteristics associated with corrugated surfaces, Kay proposed the name scalar feed[2] for this class of horn. The horn exhibited pattern symmetry over almost an octave bandwidth and possessed negligible side lobes. In Australia, Minnett and Thomas[3] were the first to show that the field in the focal plane of a paraboloid reflector could be synthetised from cylindrical hybrid modes propagating along the reflector axis, and, following suggestions by Rumsey,[4] they proposed the corrugated waveguide[5] of Fig. 1*b* as a suitable guiding structure.

When the investigation described in this and the companion paper was begun in 1968, only a few theoretical and experimental results were available for the corrugated-waveguide feed horn, and only Kay's experimental results were available as a guide to the design of wide-angle corrugated horns. Subsequent to the publication of preliminary theoretical results by the authors,[6–8] it was discovered that parallel investigations had been in progress in several countries. In the USA, Viggh[9] had investigated theoretically some properties of modes which exist in corrugated conical horns, and had made an extensive experimental study of a monopulse corrugated horn. In Australia, Thomas[10] had made a spherical-mode analysis similar to that described in Part 2 and Vu[11] had studied the synthesis of focal-plane fields by a number of hybrid modes. In the Netherlands, Jeuken[12–14] and his associates investigated the radiation characteristics of narrow-flare-angle horns and scalar feeds. Recently, other workers[15–17] have discussed useful approximate design methods and we shall refer to these briefly. We confine our attention to horns of circular cross-section, although corrugated horns of square and rectangular cross-section have been investigated by Bryant[18–19] and others. The corrugated horn constitutes one suitable form of guidance structure for hybrid modes; the dielectric cylinder or cone of Figs. 1*d* and *e* constitutes another. Clarricoats[20] has pointed out a correspondence between the two structures and further reference to this feature will be made in Section 2.7.

In Pt. 1, we determine the propagation and radiation characteristics of the corrugated-waveguide feed of Fig. 1*b*, while in Pt. 2, we investigate the corrugated-conical-horn feed of Fig. 1*a* using spherical-mode analysis. However, when the horn flare angle is small, the properties of the conical horn can be deduced from cylindrical-mode theory, provided the phase variation over the radiating aperture is small. For larger flare angles, Narasimhan and Rao[15–16] have included the effect of phase error as a perturbation and have obtained good agreement with experimental results for horns with semiangles of up to 30°. Thus, although most corrugated horns used in dual-reflector antennas have dimensions which preclude them being considered as flared waveguides with constant-phase apertures, a study of the corrugated waveguide throws considerable light on many aspects of the design of conical corrugated horns.

For an antenna designer, the following properties of the feed are important:

(*a*) radiation pattern (especially symmetry and side-lobe level)
(*b*) input voltage standing-wave ratio (v.s.w.r.) at the junction between the feed and the connecting waveguide
(*c*) location of the phase centre
(*d*) frequency dependence of the above properties.

The following additional properties may be important in certain applications. In earth-station antennas, the feed-horn attenuation should be exceedingly small, and the actual attenuation over the operating band is a relevant property. When the primary feed is required to provide tracking information, the characteristics of higher modes need to be considered. In narrow-bandwidth feeds, such as those sometimes used in radioastronomy, several modes can be used to synthetise the focal-plane fields to improve the antenna efficiency. In dual-reflector antennas, a specially shaped subreflector can be used to achieve the same objective with a single mode in the feed.

To determine the above characteristics, it is first necessary to describe the fields within the feed and, in particular, in the feed aperture. The radiation pattern may then be determined either by a Kirchhoff–Huygen integration over the aperture or, in the case of the conical horn, by a spherical-modal expansion technique developed by the authors.[8] As far as it is known, an exact formulation of the problem of radiation from a corrugated circular waveguide has not been made. However, the excellent agreement obtained for the uniform circular waveguide[21] inspires confidence in aperture-field methods. This is especially so as the aperture field has a pronounced taper and fields at the waveguide edges are small.

2 Propagation and radiation behaviour of corrugated waveguides

2.1 Propagation characteristics

Propagation of electromagnetic waves in a corrugated waveguide was first considered in relation to linear accelerators,[22] although most attention was then given to the TM_{01} mode. Later, azimuthally dependent modes were considered when their presence was found to affect adversely the accelerator performance. In antenna applications, it is the unity azimuthally dependent modes which are of greatest importance, although the TM_{01} mode is relevant to antenna tracking.[23]

Clarricoats and Sobhy[24] investigated the properties of a wide range of corrugated structures of which that of Fig. 1*b* represents a special case. In their analysis, space harmonics were included in the region $0 < r < r_1$, while for $r_1 < r < r_0$, a *z* independent TM mode was assumed present. They found that, apart from when at frequencies near to the high-frequency cutoff of a mode, the influence of the space harmonics was slight and, for fast waves, neglecting space harmonics appeared entirely justified. In the following Sections, we neglect space harmonics and assume that $b/c \simeq 1$ corresponding to infinitely thin corrugations. The full characteristic equation for the propagation coefficient will also be quoted when the influence of the above ratio may be observed.

We assume a time dependence $e^{j\omega t}$ throughout. When $r < r_1$, the fields depend on z as $e^{-j\beta z}$, and when $r > r_1$, the fields are independent of z.

For $r < r_1$

$$E_z = a_m J_m(x) e^{jm\psi} \qquad (1)$$

$$H_z = -a_m j y_0 \bar{\Lambda} J_m(x) e^{jm\psi} \qquad (2)$$

$$E_r = -a_m j \frac{k}{K} \frac{J_m(x)}{x} \{\bar{\beta} F_m(x) + m\bar{\Lambda}\} e^{jm\psi} \qquad (3)$$

$$E_\psi = a_m \frac{k}{K} \frac{J_m(x)}{x} \{m\bar{\beta} + \bar{\Lambda} F_m(x)\} e^{jm\psi} \qquad (4)$$

$$H_r = -a_m \frac{k}{K} y_0 \frac{J_m(x)}{x} \{\bar{\beta}\bar{\Lambda} F_m(x) + m\} e^{jm\psi} \qquad (5)$$

$$H_\psi = -a_m j \frac{k}{K} y_0 \frac{J_m(x)}{x} \{m\bar{\beta}\bar{\Lambda} + F_m(x)\} e^{jm\psi} \qquad (6)$$

where $x = Kr,\ K^2 = k^2 - \beta^2,\ k^2 = \omega^2 \epsilon_0 \mu_0,\ k\bar{\beta} = \beta$

$$-jy_0\bar{\Lambda} = H_z/E_z,\ y_0 = (\epsilon_0/\mu_0)^{1/2}$$

For $r_0 > r > r_1$

$$E_z = \frac{a'_m}{Y_m(x'_0)} \{J_m(x') Y_m(x'_0) - Y_m(x') J_m(x'_0)\} \qquad (7)$$

$$H_\psi = -jy_0 \frac{a'_m}{Y_m(x'_0)} \{J'_m(x') Y_m(x'_0) - Y'_m(x') J_m(x'_0)\} \qquad (8)$$

$$x' = kr,\ x'_0 = kr_0$$

If the slotwidth is such that a radial-line TE mode cannot be supported, we assume that $E_\psi = 0$ at $r = r_1$.
Thus

$$m\bar{\beta} = -\bar{\Lambda} F_m(x_1) \qquad (9)$$

On matching the admittance H_ψ/E_z at $r = r_1$, the characteristic equation for $\bar{\beta}$ is obtained as

$$F_m(x_1) - \frac{(m\bar{\beta})^2}{F_m(x_1)} = \left(\frac{K}{k}\right)^2 S_m(x'_1, x'_0) \qquad (10)$$

where $x_1 = Kr_1,\ x'_1 = kr_1,\ x'_0 = kr_0$

Eqn. 10 is a special case of the more general equation derived by Clarricoats and Sobhy[24]:

$$\frac{b}{c}\sum_{N=-\infty}^{N=+\infty}\left\{F_m(x_{1N}) - \frac{(m\bar{\beta}_N)^2}{F_m(x_{1N})}\right\}\left(\frac{\sin\Delta}{\Delta}\right)^2 = \left(\frac{K_N}{k}\right)^2 S_m(x_1', x_0') \quad . \quad (11)$$

Here we assume $b/c = 1$, $\Delta = 0$, and only the fundamental mode of the series is included in the field expansion. A simple interpretation of eqn. 11 in terms of transverse-equivalent networks has been given by the above authors and the representation appropriate to eqn. 10 is shown in Fig. 1*c*.

Eqn. 10 has been solved for $\bar{\beta}$, with x_1' and r_1/r_0 as parameters and with $m = 0$ and $m = 1$. Typical dispersion curves for $m = 1$ modes are shown in Fig. 2*a–c*, and some computed

The cutoff frequencies of the first pair of modes move closer as r_1/r_0 decreases, and they meet when $r_1/r_0 \simeq 0{\cdot}48$ and $F(x_1') = S(x_1', x_0') = 0$. When r_1/r_0 is less than this value, the backward-wave mode possesses an Emode cutoff. Because of the neglect of space harmonics, the high-frequency cutoff of all modes corresponds to the condition $\bar{\beta} \rightarrow \infty$. This condition exists when $S_1(x_1', x_0') = 0$. However, at the value of x_1 which satisfies this condition for given r_1/r_0, the other propagating modes exhibit characteristics which are of special significance when the corrugated waveguide is used as a feed. Eqn. 10 shows that, when $S_m(x_1', x_0') = 0$

$$F_m(x_1) = \pm m\bar{\beta} \quad . \quad . \quad . \quad . \quad . \quad . \quad . \quad . \quad . \quad (12)$$

Thus $\bar{\Lambda} = \mp 1 \quad . \quad . \quad . \quad . \quad . \quad . \quad . \quad . \quad . \quad . \quad . \quad . \quad (13)$

$|\bar{\Lambda}|$ is the ratio of the longitudinal admittance to the freespace wave admittance. For this reason, the condition $|\bar{\Lambda}| = 1$ is

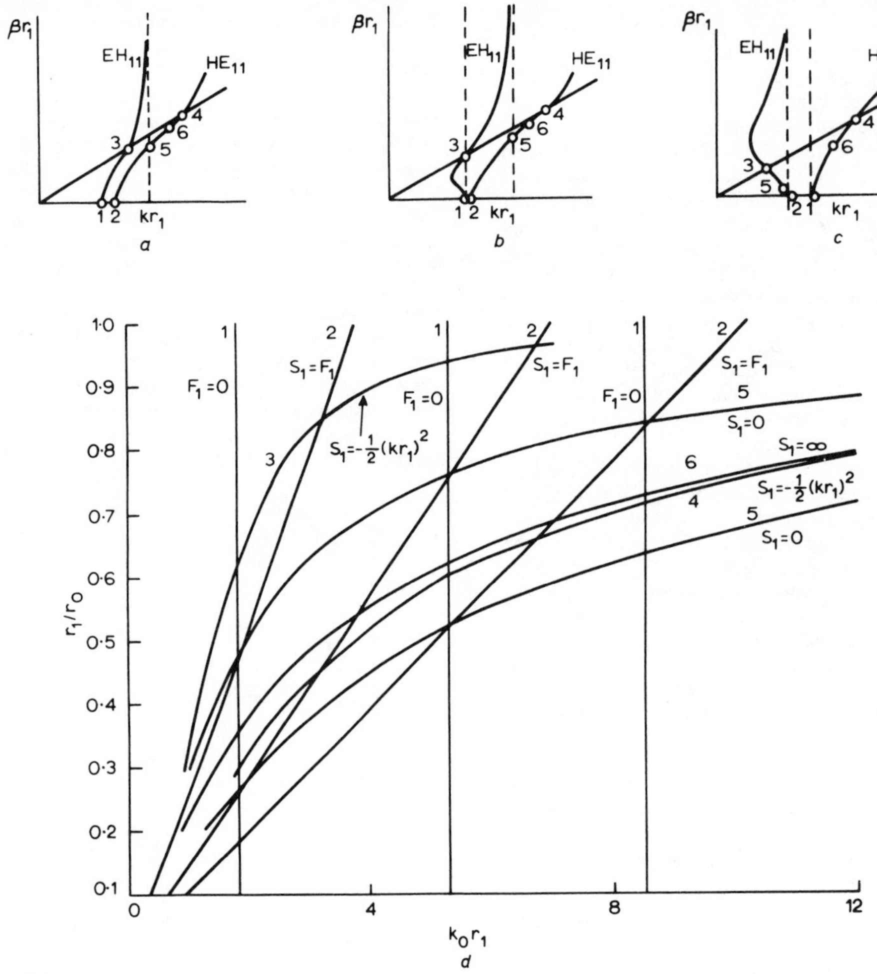

Fig. 2

Propagation characteristics corrugated waveguide

a–c dispersion diagrams for corrugated waveguide
a $r_1/r_0 = 0{\cdot}9$
b $r_1/r_0 = 0{\cdot}63$
c $r_1/r_0 = 0{\cdot}4$
d Parametric dependence of special points
Points 1 and 2 represent cutoff for modes with $E_z = 0$ and $H_z = 0$, respectively, at $\beta = 0$
Points 3 and 4 represent condition $\bar{\beta} = \beta/k = 1$, corresponding to $S_1(k, r_1, r_0) = -\frac{1}{2}(kr_1)^2$
Point 5 represents balanced hybrid or 'open-circuit' boundary condition corresponding to $S_1(k, r_1, r_0) = 0$
Point 6 represents short-circuit boundary condition corresponding to $S_1(k, r_1, r_0) = \infty$

curves are shown in Fig. 3. Comprehension will be aided if reference is made to the loci of special cases of eqn. 10 shown in Fig. 2*d*. When r_1/r_0 is near unity, the six lowest-order modes which we have investigated all exhibit forward-wave properties as in Fig. 3. As r_1/r_0 is decreased towards $0{\cdot}64$, the lowest-order mode which possess Hmode properties at cutoff also exhibits a backward-wave region.

called the balanced hybrid condition, and, in Section 2.4, we show that the radiation pattern is then symmetric. Modes with $\bar{\Lambda} = +1$ radiate with a maximum along the feed axis, while those with $\bar{\Lambda} = -1$ create a null.

Following the previous practice in uniform hybrid-mode structures,[25,26] the mode curves HE_{11}, EH_{11}, HE_{12} etc. would have been labelled from left to right across the dispersion diagram irrespective of their behaviour near cutoff. However, when we examine the radiation properties of the modes near the balanced hybrid condition, there appear grounds for labelling the first mode which exhibits $\bar{\Lambda} = +1$ (for finite β) the HE_{11} mode, and the first mode then becomes EH_{11}. This choice leads to agreement with the modes on a dielectric rod as revealed when their radiation characteristics

Thus, when the diameter of the waveguide aperture is large compared with a wavelength, the balanced hybrid condition is achieved when the slot depth approaches $\lambda/4$.

Other special conditions of Fig. 2*d* are summarised in Table 1. The condition $S_1 = \infty$ creates an apparent short circuit across the slots at $r = r_1$. Bryant[19] has proposed that this condition should be utilised at the transition between

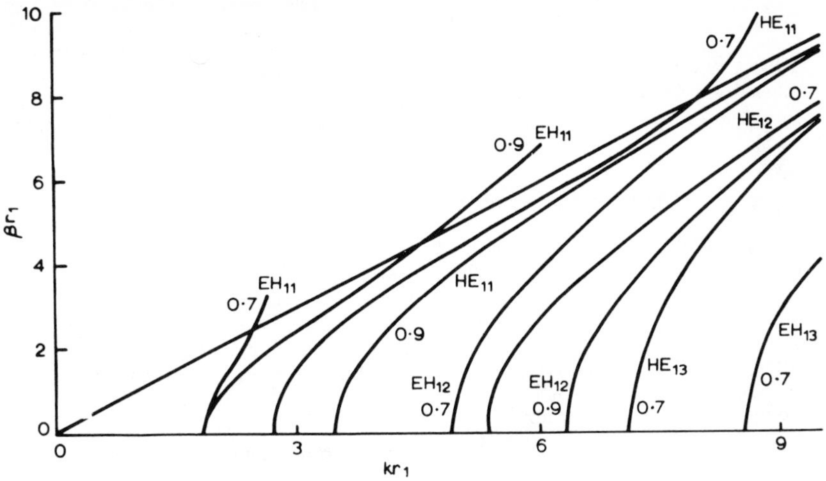

Fig. 3
Dispersion characteristics of hybrid modes in corrugated waveguide
Parameter $= r_1/r_0$

are compared with those of corrugated feeds in Section 2.7. The difficulties in the mode-nomenclature problem stem in part from the significant changes in field characteristics which can occur along a branch of a dispersion curve. For example, in Fig. 2*b*, the field pattern of the HE_{11} mode changes from being essentially similar to the E_{11} mode at cutoff to having a form more similar to a H_{11} mode at the balanced hybrid frequency. The case for calling a mode HE_{11} because it is alleged to resemble the H_{11} mode is hardly justified when, at certain frequencies, it has a pattern more like an E_{11} mode. We do not propose to resolve this nomenclature problem here, but will favour the latter convention because this is in more widespread use. Some difficulties could be removed by using the terminology 1st hybrid mode, 2nd hybrid mode etc., and, to distinguish azimuthal dependence, we could use the notation h_{11}, h_{12} mode etc., where the h denotes hybrid.

To design a corrugated-waveguide feed so that the balanced hybrid condition exists at the feed aperture, r_1/r_0 and x_1' must be chosen to satisfy the condition

$$S_m(x_1', x_0') = 0 \quad \ldots \quad (14)$$

A graph of this function is shown in Fig. 2*d*. For large values of x_1'

$$S_1 \frac{(x_1', x_0')}{x_1'} \simeq -\cot kd + \frac{1}{2x_1'} \quad \ldots \quad (15)$$

where $d = r_0 - r_1$

and, in the limit $x_1' \gg 1$, the slot input admittance is given by

$$\frac{H_\psi}{E_z} \simeq jy_0 \cot kd \quad \ldots \quad (16)$$

Table 1

SPECIAL CASES OF EQN. 10 CORRESPONDING TO SPECIAL POINTS IN FIG. 2*d*

Point	Equation determining x_1'
1	Cutoff with $E_z = 0$, $F_1(x_1') = 0$
2	Cutoff with $H_z = 0$, $F_1(x_1') = S_1(x_1', x_0')$
3, 4	$\bar{\beta} = 1$; $S_1(x_1', x_0') = -\frac{1}{2}(x_1')^2$
5	Balanced hybrid condition; $S_1(x_1', x_0') = 0$ [condition $\bar{\beta} = \infty$ also occurs when $S_1(x_1', x_0') = 0$]
6	'short-circuit' boundary condition $S_1(x_1', x_0') = \infty$

smooth and corrugated waveguide at the throat of a feed. The slot depth is then gradually reduced until balanced hybrid conditions are achieved at the feed aperture. We have used this technique, and the resulting feed exhibited a low input v.s.w.r. as discussed in Section 2.8.

2.2 Fields under balanced hybrid conditions

Under balanced hybrid conditions, eqns. 1–6 simplify as in eqns. 17–22 where the fields have been expressed in linearly polarised form:

$$E_z = \dot{a}_m J_m(x) \cos m\psi = \epsilon_z \cos m\psi \quad \ldots \quad (17)$$

$$H_z = \pm y_0 \epsilon_z \sin m\psi = h_z \sin m\psi \quad \ldots \quad (18)$$

$$E_r = -ja_m \frac{k}{K} \frac{J_m(x)}{x} \{\bar{\beta} F_m(x) \pm m\} \cos m\psi = \epsilon_r \cos m\psi \quad \ldots \quad (19)$$

$$E_\psi = ja_m \frac{k}{K} \frac{J_m(x)}{x} \{m\bar{\beta} \pm F_m(x)\} \sin m\psi = \epsilon_\psi \sin m\psi \quad \ldots \quad (20)$$

$$H_r = \pm y_0 \, \epsilon_r \sin m\psi = h_r \sin m\psi \quad \ldots \quad (21)$$

$$H_\psi = \pm y_0 \epsilon_\psi \cos m\psi = h_\psi \cos m\psi \quad \ldots \quad (22)$$

where the $\pm$ sign corresponds to $\bar{\Lambda} = \pm 1$.

We note that the condition

$$y_0 \boldsymbol{\epsilon}_t = \pm \boldsymbol{h}_t \quad \ldots \quad (23)$$

is satisfied.

Rumsey[4] has shown this to be a necessary condition for the transverse field in the aperture of the feed horn if the radiation pattern is to be circularly symmetric. Also, if the aperture field is linearly polarised on the axis, there is zero crosspolarised component of radiated field. It follows that, if the feed horn is excited by a circularly polarised input, the radiated field is perfectly circularly polarised: a feature of importance in radio-astronomy applications.

If the radius r_1 is large so that $kr_1 = x_1' \gg 1$, $\bar{\beta} \rightarrow 1$ under balanced hybrid conditions. On using the recurrence relationship

$$F_m(x) \pm m = \frac{xJ_{m\mp1}(x)}{J_m(x)} \quad \ldots \quad (24)$$

eqns. 19 and 20 become

$$E_r = -ja_m \frac{k}{K} J_{m\mp1}(x) \cos m\psi \quad \ldots \quad (25)$$

$$E_\psi = \pm j a_m \frac{k}{K} \mathrm{J}_{m\mp 1}(x) \sin m\psi \quad . \quad . \quad . \quad . \quad . \quad . \qquad (26)$$

A case of importance exists when $m = 1$, for which the HE_{11} axial radiation mode becomes

$$E_r = -j a_1 \frac{k}{K} \mathrm{J}_0(x) \cos \psi \quad . \quad . \quad . \quad . \quad . \quad . \quad . \qquad (27)$$

$$E_\psi = +j a_1 \frac{k}{K} \mathrm{J}_0(x) \sin \psi \quad . \quad . \quad . \quad . \quad . \quad . \quad . \qquad (28)$$

For a wave polarised in the x direction, $E_x = a_1(k/K)\mathrm{J}_0(x)$ and $E_y = 0$. If $\mathrm{J}_0(x)$ is expanded as a power series, the first three terms are

$$\mathrm{J}_0(x) = 1 - \frac{x^2}{4} + \frac{x^4}{32} \quad . \quad . \quad . \quad . \quad . \quad . \quad . \quad . \quad . \qquad (29)$$

Compare this expansion with that for the Gaussian function $\epsilon^{-(x/2)^2}$, where

$$\epsilon^{-(x/2)^2} = 1 - \frac{x^2}{4} + \frac{x^4}{16} \quad . \quad . \quad . \quad . \quad . \quad . \quad . \quad . \qquad (30)$$

The difference between the functions is only 1·7% when $x = 1$. As the maximum value of x_1 for the HE_{11} mode for an infinitely large aperture is only 2·4, the fields are nearly Gaussian over at least half the aperture. Subject to well known approximations, the radiation pattern of an antenna is the Fourier transform of the aperture distribution. Furthermore, as the Gaussian function transforms into itself, we may expect that the radiation pattern of a corrugated waveguide under balanced hybrid conditions will have a radiation pattern which is approximately Gaussian. This is confirmed in Section 2.4.

Computed transverse-field patterns for the first three balanced hybrid modes of unity azimuthal dependence are shown in Figs. 4*a–c*. As mentioned, for large apertures when $\bar{\beta} \to 1$ for the HE_{11} mode, the field under balanced hybrid conditions is nearly everywhere linearly polarised. Fig. 4*a* shows this to be the case when $kr_1 = 14{\cdot}47$. The ratio E_y/E_x is also shown in Fig. 4*d* for two values of kr_1, one of which corresponds to the balanced hybrid condition.

Further insight into the nature of the transverse field is provided by the Poynting vector $\boldsymbol{S}_z$:

$$\boldsymbol{S}_z = \frac{a_m'^2}{4} y_0 k^2 [\bar{\beta}(1 + \bar{\Lambda}^2)\{\mathrm{J}_0^2(x) + \mathrm{J}_2^2(x)\} + \bar{\Lambda}(1 + \bar{\beta}^2)\{\mathrm{J}_0^2(x) - \mathrm{J}_2^2(x)\} - 2\bar{\beta}(1 - \bar{\Lambda}^2)\mathrm{J}_0(x)\mathrm{J}_2(x) \cos 2\psi] \quad . \quad . \quad . \quad . \qquad (31)$$

Under balanced hybrid conditions $\bar{\Lambda} = \pm 1$, the second term vanishes and the power distribution is then circularly symmetric.

2.3 Attenuation

Since feed attenuation contributes to increased antenna-noise temperature, a calculation of the attenuation of the principal HE_{11} mode attenuation is relevant. In the following, we neglect losses at the surface $r = r_1$ and the power loss per groove, P_L, is then given by

$$P_L = \tfrac{1}{2} R_s \left\{ 4\pi \int_{r_1}^{r_0} (|H_r|^2 + |H_\psi|^2) r\,dr + 2\pi r_0 \left| H_\psi \right|^2_{r=r_0} \right\}$$
$$= P_{L1} + P_{L2} \quad . \quad . \quad . \quad . \qquad (32)$$

Since we have assumed a field dependence $e^{jm\psi}$, the components of power loss per groove for the mth azimuthal dependent mode are given by

$$P_{L1} = a_m^2 \frac{2\pi R_s}{k^2} y_0^2 \mathrm{J}_m^2(x_1) \left[\frac{1}{2}(m^2 - x_1'^2) + \frac{2}{\{\pi S_m^D(x_1', x_0')\}^2} - S_m(x_1', x_0') - \tfrac{1}{2}\{S_m(x_1', x_0')\}^2 \right] \qquad (33)$$

$$P_{L2} = a_m \frac{4 R_s b}{\pi k^2 r_0} y_0^2 \frac{\mathrm{J}_m^2(x_1)}{\{S_m^D(x_1', x_0')\}^2} \quad . \quad . \quad . \quad . \quad . \qquad (34)$$

while the total power is given by

$$P_T = a_m^2 \pi \frac{k^2}{K^4} y_0 \mathrm{J}_m^2(x_1) [\bar{\beta}(1 + \bar{\Lambda}^2)\{\tfrac{1}{2} F_m^2(x_1) + F_m(x_1) + \tfrac{1}{2}(x_1^2 - m^2)\} + m\bar{\Lambda}(1 + \bar{\beta}^2)] \quad . \qquad (35)$$

where $S_m^D(x_1', x_0')$ is the denominator of $S_m(x_1', x_0')$ and R_s is the surface resistance of the metal. The attenuation coefficient α is given by

$$\alpha = \frac{P_L}{2 P_T b} \quad . \quad . \quad . \quad . \quad . \quad . \quad . \quad . \quad . \quad . \qquad (36)$$

Fig. 5*a* shows the HE_{11} mode attenuation compared with that of the H_{11} mode in a circular waveguide of radius r_1 when the groove width b is chosen so that $\lambda/b \simeq 5$ under balanced hybrid conditions. Fig. 5*b* shows corresponding dispersion curves. Over at least an octave bandwidth, the corrugated waveguide exhibits lower attenuation. However, it must be recognised that the above calculation will lead to optimistically low attenuation for the HE_{11} mode. We have neglected surface roughness and have assumed that the surface resistance R_s is the same for all surfaces. The former assumption will raise the attenuation of both the HE_{11} and H_{11} modes, whereas the latter will raise the HE_{11} mode attenuation further, since it is unlikely that the surface finish of the corrugated waveguide can be as good as the drawn circular waveguide. Nevertheless, the predicted improvement is sufficient to warrant further investigations which are now in progress.

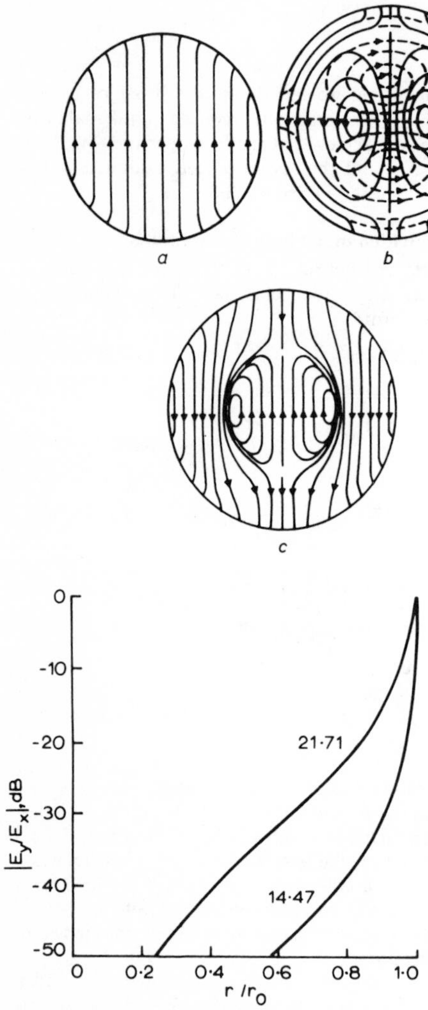

Fig. 4

Transverse field patterns for corrugated waveguides in region $r < r_1$

a Transverse electric-field pattern of HE_{11} mode under balanced hybrid conditions for $r_1/r_0 = 0{\cdot}9$
b Transverse electric- and magnetic-field pattern of $E\mathrm{H}_{12}$ mode under balanced hybrid conditions for $r_1/r_0 = 0{\cdot}9$
c Transverse electric-field pattern of HE_{12} mode under balanced hybrid conditions for $r_1/r_0 = 0{\cdot}9$
d Crosspolarised component of HE_{11} mode as a function of r/r_1 in corrugated circular waveguide for $r_1/r_0 = 0{\cdot}9$ and plane $\psi = 45^\circ$. Parameter x_1'

The explanation of the phenomena lies in the low value of H_r and H_ψ at $r = r_1$ for frequencies near the balanced hybrid frequency. At that frequency, $H_r = H_\psi = 0$ and the fields at

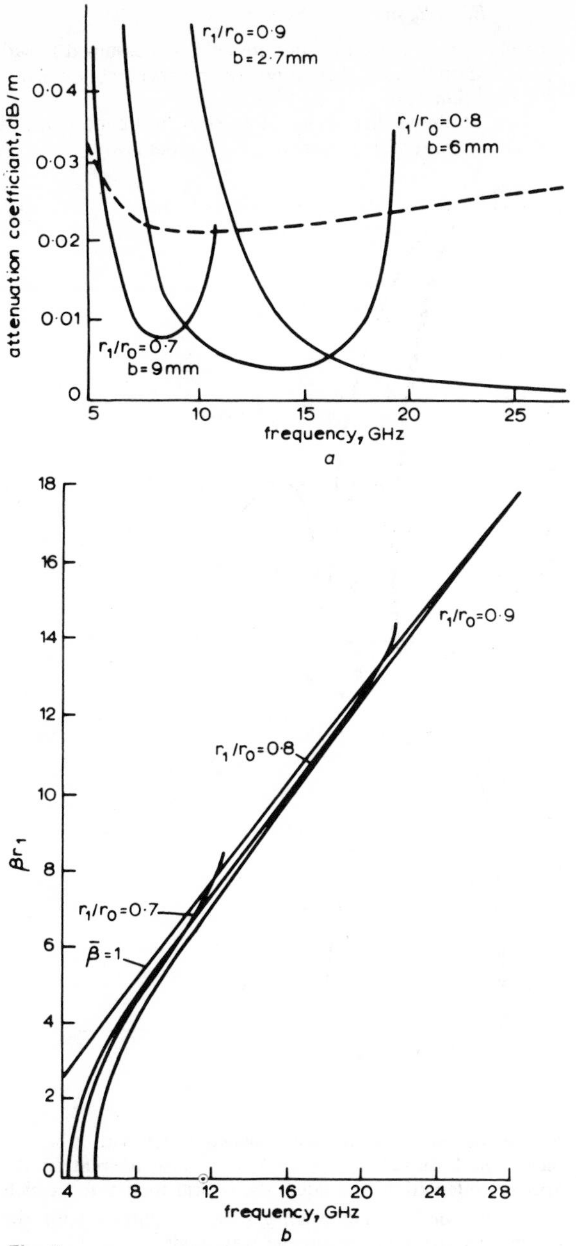

Fig. 5
Attenuation in corrugated circular waveguide
a Attenuation coefficient as function of frequency
b Normalised phase-change coefficient as function of frequency

$r = r_1$ are purely longitudinal. In addition, as the relative intensity of the longitudinal magnetic field decreases inversely with frequency, the minimum attenuation also decreases with frequency.

2.4 Radiation from corrugated waveguides

Radiation from a hybrid-mode guide under balanced hybrid conditions has been described by Minett and Thomas,[5] and we shall now derive general expressions for the radiation field. With reference to Fig. 6*a*, the electric field at a distant point P is

$$E_p = \frac{-jk}{4\pi R} e^{-jkR}\, \boldsymbol{i}_R \times \int_{aperture} \{\boldsymbol{i}_n \times \boldsymbol{E}_t - z_0 \boldsymbol{i}_R \times (\boldsymbol{i}_n \times \boldsymbol{H}_t)\} e^{jk\boldsymbol{r}\cdot\boldsymbol{i}_R} dS \quad (37)$$

If we may assume that $\boldsymbol{E}_t$ and $\boldsymbol{H}_t$ are the incident fields and that $\boldsymbol{E}_t$ and $\boldsymbol{H}_t$ vanish elsewhere in the plane $z = 0$, $r > r_1$, the evaluation of $\boldsymbol{E}_p$ merely involves a somewhat laborious integration over r and ψ. If the above assumption is not made, the determination of $\boldsymbol{E}_p$ involves the solution of integral equations by methods such as the Weiner–Hopf technique, and this analysis has only been undertaken for pure, rather than hybrid, modes.[21]

We may express the transverse fields by the following equations:

$$E_r = \boldsymbol{E}_r \cos m\psi \quad (38)$$

$$E_\psi = \boldsymbol{E}_\psi \sin m\psi \quad (39)$$

$$H_r = \boldsymbol{H}_r \sin m\psi \quad (40)$$

$$H_\psi = \boldsymbol{H}_\psi \cos m\psi \quad (41)$$

With some manipulation, we arrive at

$$E_{p\theta} = C\int_0^{2\pi}\int_0^{r_1}\{-(E_r + z_0\cos\theta H_\psi)\cos(\phi-\psi) - (E_\psi - z_0\cos\theta H_r)\sin(\phi-\psi)\}e^{jkr\sin\theta\cos(\phi-\psi)} r\,dr\,d\psi \quad (42)$$

$$E_{p\phi} = C\int_0^{2\pi}\int_0^{r_1}\{E_r\cos\theta + z_0 H_\psi)\sin(\phi-\psi) - (E_\psi\cos\theta - z_0 H_r)\cos(\phi-\psi)\}e^{jkr\sin\theta\cos(\phi-\psi)} r\,dr\,d\psi \quad (43)$$

where we have denoted the factor outside the integral in eqn. 37 by C. For $E_{p\theta}$, the quantity within brackets may be written as

$$[-\tfrac{1}{2}\sin\phi\{(E_r + E_\psi)\sin(m+1)\psi - (E_r - E_\psi)\sin(m-1)\psi - z_0\cos\theta(H_r - H_\psi)\sin(m+1)\psi - z_0\cos\theta(H_r + H_\psi)\sin(m-1)\psi\} - \tfrac{1}{2}\cos\phi\{(E_r + E_\psi)\cos(m+1)\psi + (E_r - E_\psi)\cos(m-1)\psi + z_0\cos\theta(H_r + H_\psi)\cos(m-1)\psi - z_0\cos\theta(H_r - H_\psi)\cos(m+1)\psi\}]$$

We use

$$\int_0^{2\pi} e^{jx\cos(\theta-\psi)} \begin{matrix}\cos\\ \sin\end{matrix}\, m\psi\, d\psi = 2\pi j^n \begin{matrix}\cos\\ \sin\end{matrix}\, n\phi J_n(x) \quad (44)$$

and note that

$$E_r + E_\psi = AJ_{m+1}(Kr) \quad (45)$$

$$E_r - E_\psi = BJ_{m-1}(Kr) \quad (46)$$

$$H_r + H_\psi = CJ_{m-1}(Kr) \quad (47)$$

$$H_r - H_\psi = DJ_{m+1}(Kr) \quad (48)$$

$$\begin{matrix}A\\ B\end{matrix} = \frac{ak}{K}[\bar{\Lambda} \mp \bar{\beta}] \quad (49)$$

$$\begin{matrix}C\\ D\end{matrix} = \frac{\pm ak}{z_0 K}[1 \pm \bar{\Lambda}\bar{\beta}] \quad (50)$$

where a is the amplitude of E_z in the feed aperture. For the r integration we are concerned with the Lommel integrals

$$\int_0^{r_1} rJ_{m\mp1}(Kr)J_{m\mp1}(kr\sin\theta)dr = \frac{kr_1\sin\theta J_{m\mp1}(Kr_1)J'_{m\mp1}(kr\sin\theta) - Kr_1 J_{m+1}(kr_1\sin\theta)J'_{m\mp1}(Kr_1)}{K^2 - k^2\sin^2\theta} \quad (51)$$

$$= \pm r_1^2\frac{J_m(x_1')J_m(x_1)}{x_1'x_1\sin\theta} + r_1^2\frac{\{x_1J_m(x_1)J_m'(x_1') - x_1'J_m(x_1')J_m'(x_1)\}}{x_1^2 - (x_1')^2\sin^2\theta} \quad (52)$$

$$= r_1^2\{\pm L(\theta) + Q(\theta)\} \quad (53)$$

Then,

$$E_{p\theta} = -\frac{akr_1}{2KR}e^{-jkR}(j)^{m+1}\cos m\phi\{L(\theta)\bar{\Lambda}(kr_1 + \bar{\beta}kr_1\cos\theta) + Q(\theta)(kr_1\cos\theta + kr_1\bar{\beta})\} \quad (54)$$

$$E_{p\phi} = \frac{akr_1}{2KR} e^{-jkR}(j)^{m+1} \sin m\phi \{L(\theta)(kr_1 + \bar{\beta} kr_1 \cos\theta) + Q(\theta)\bar{\Lambda}(kr_1 \cos\theta + kr_1\bar{\beta})\} \quad (55)$$

When $m = 1$ and $\bar{\Lambda} = \pm 1$,

$$E_{p\theta \atop \phi} = \begin{pmatrix}(+)\\(-)\end{pmatrix} F(\theta) \frac{akr_1}{2KR} e^{-jkR} \begin{pmatrix}\cos\\ \sin\end{pmatrix}\phi \quad . \quad . \quad . \quad . \quad (56)$$

$$F(\theta) = L(\theta)x_1'(1 + \bar{\beta}\cos\theta) \pm Q(\theta)x_1'(\cos\theta + \bar{\beta}) \quad . \quad . \quad . \quad . \quad (57)$$

Since $L(\theta) = Q(\theta)$ when $\theta = 0$ or π, $F(\theta) = 0$ when $\theta = 0$ and $\bar{\Lambda} = -1$ and when $\theta = \pi$ and $\bar{\Lambda} = +1$. Also, since

$$E_x = E_\theta \cos\phi - E\phi \sin\phi$$
$$E_y = E_\theta \sin\phi + E\phi \cos\phi$$

it follows that, since the aperture field was assumed linearly polarised on the axis, there is no crosspolarised component in the radiation field.

Eqn. 56 shows that, under balanced hybrid conditions, the radiation pattern is symmetric, and modes with $\bar{\Lambda} = +1$ have a maximum on the axis, whereas those with $\bar{\Lambda} = -1$ have a null. Subject to the approximations inherent in the aperture-integration technique, the hybrid modes for which $\bar{\Lambda} = +1$ exhibit a null when $\theta = \pi$, in contrast with the H_{11} mode radiating from circular waveguide.[21]

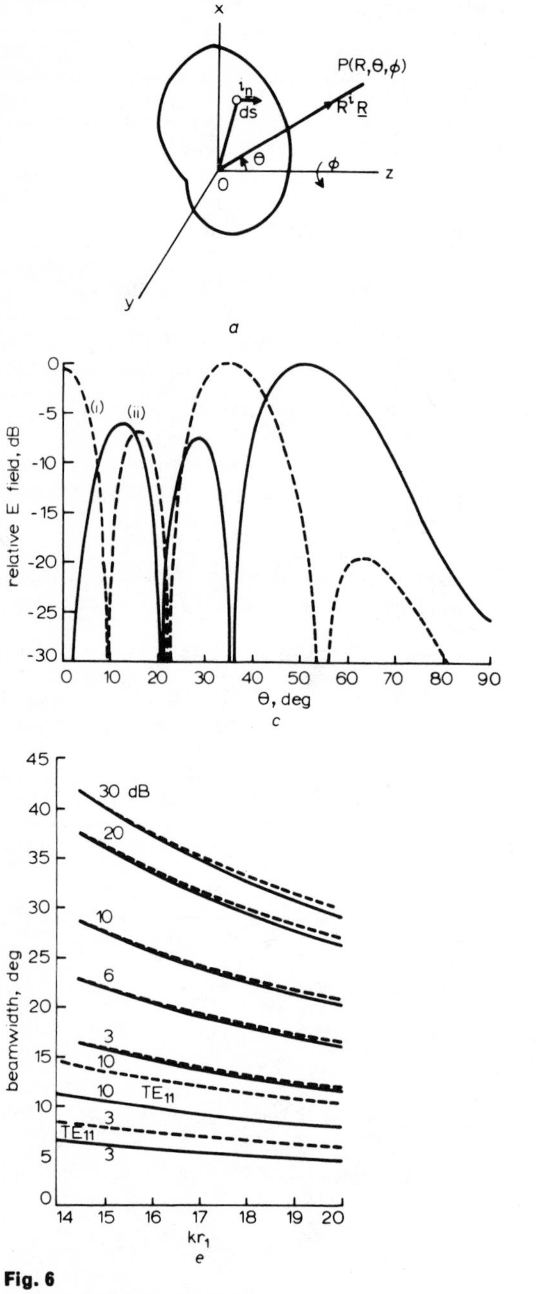

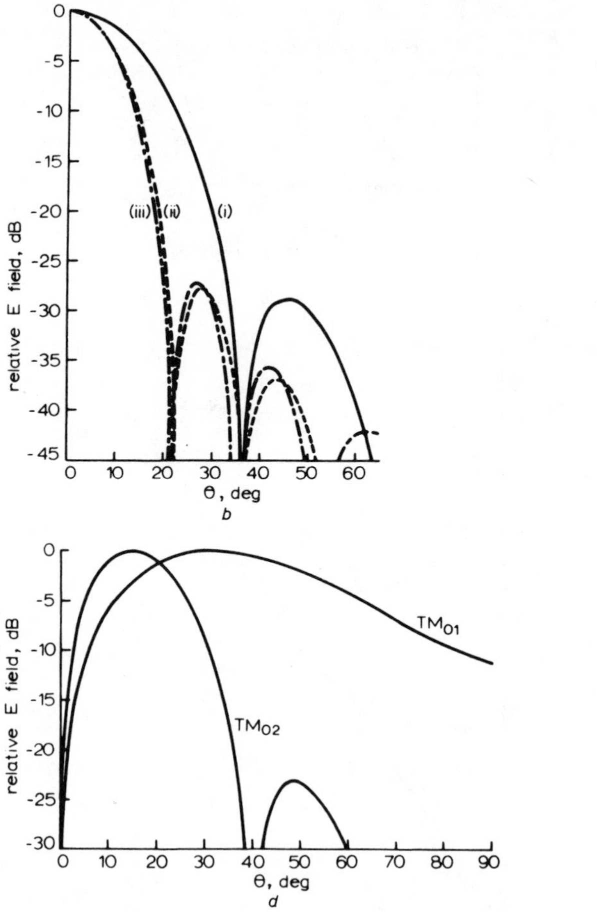

Fig. 6

Radiation from corrugated waveguide

a Co-ordinate system for plane aperture
b HE_{11} mode radiation patterns for $r_1/r_0 = 0{\cdot}85$
——— $kr_1 = 9{\cdot}245$ (balanced hybrid condition)
– – – $kr_1 = 13{\cdot}868$, $\bar{\Lambda} = 1{\cdot}27$ (E plane)
—·— $kr_1 = 13{\cdot}868$, $\bar{\Lambda} = 1{\cdot}27$ (H plane)
c Radiation patterns for HE_{12} and EH_{12} modes for $r_1/r_0 = 0{\cdot}9$, $kr_1 = 14{\cdot}47$
——— EH_{12} mode
– – – HE_{12} mode
d Radiation patterns of TM_{01} and TM_{02} modes
$r_1/r_0 = 0{\cdot}9$ and $kr_1 = 4{\cdot}0$ for TM_{01} mode
$r_1/r_0 = 0{\cdot}87$ and $kr_1 = 10{\cdot}85$ for TM_{02} mode
e Beamwidths of HE_{11} radiation pattern as a function of kr_1 for $r_1/r_0 = 0{\cdot}19$
——— E plane
-------- H plane

Fig. 6*b* and curves (i) and (ii) in Fig. 6*c* show radiation patterns at two values of kr_1 for the HE_{11} mode, and, under balanced hybrid conditions, for the HE_{12} and EH_{12} modes, respectively. Fig. 6*d* shows patterns for the TM_{01} and TM_{02} modes. Fig. 6*e* shows the beamwidth dependence on normalised frequency for the HE_{11} mode. The beamwidth is considerably broader than that for the dominant mode in a circular waveguide of radius r_1, because of a more pronounced aperture taper, especially in the Eplane. The symmetry of the radiation pattern of the corrugated waveguide is very good over at least a 2 : 1 bandwidth and, as Fig. 6*b* shows, the side-lobe level is very low.

For the azimuthally dependent higher modes, we observe that, while the HE_{12} mode exhibits a maximum along the feed axis, there is slightly stronger radiation in an off-axis lobe. For the EH_{12} mode, the pattern exhibits an axial null and the main lobe is substantially off axis. Higher-order modes are important when tracking information is required or when a prescribed radiation pattern is to be synthesised. An informative discussion of the problems of pattern synthesis has been presented by Vu.[11] The main disadvantage of the technique is that the pattern is highly frequency sensitive, since the higher modes must be present in the correct phase at the radiating aperture.

Experimental results for HE_{11} mode radiation from a horn with semiangle 12° are presented in Pt. 2 of the paper. Comparison with results calculated using the above theory shows that agreement is excellent over most of the main lobe, but that phase error fills in the first null. Provided the phase variation over the aperture ϕ is such that $\phi \ll \pi/2$, the above theory can be applied with confidence. The condition can be expressed as $kr_1 \tan \theta_1/2 \ll \pi/2$, where θ_1 is the semiangle of the horn. For small θ_1, we may rephrase the condition as $kr_1^2/2R_0 \ll \pi/2$, where R_0 is the horn length.

2.5 Gain factor of corrugated-waveguide feed

Under balanced hybrid conditions when the radiation pattern is symmetric, the feed gain is given by

$$G(\theta') = \frac{2|F(\theta')|^2}{\int_0^\pi |F(\theta)|^2 \sin\theta d\theta} \quad . \quad . \quad . \quad . \quad . \quad . \quad . \quad . \quad (58)$$

Table 2 shows the axial gain as a function of kr_1, with r_1/r_0 selected to maintain balanced hybrid conditions. The horn

Table 2

GAIN OF CORRUGATED CIRCULAR WAVEGUIDE WITH BALANCED HE_{11} MODE AT THE APERTURE

r_1/r_0	kr_1	Gain
		dB
0·70	4·0300	10·74
0·75	5·0728	12·68
0·80	6·6356	14·94
0·81	7·0473	15·44
0·82	7·5050	15·98
0·83	8·0167	16·55
0·84	8·5925	17·15
0·85	9·2453	17·77
0·86	9·9916	18·43
0·87	10·8530	19·15
0·88	11·8580	19·90
0·89	13·0470	20·75
0·90	14·4730	21·64
0·91	16·2160	22·65

gain factor lies between 65% and 70% over the range. This figure is less than that obtained for a paraboloid antenna when the waveguide is used as a prime feed. The explanation is that the focal-plane field of the paraboloid is more closely matched than a uniform field to the $J_0(x)$ distribution of the corrugated waveguide.

2.6 Gain factor of paraboloid reflector with corrugated-waveguide feed

When a corrugated waveguide is employed as a prime feed for a paraboloid reflector, the axial gain factor under balanced hybrid conditions is

$$G_f = \frac{2\cot^2 \Psi/2 \left| \int_0^\Psi F(\theta) \tan\frac{\theta}{2} d\theta \right|^2}{\int_0^\pi |F(\theta)|^2 \sin\theta d\theta} \quad . \quad . \quad . \quad . \quad . \quad (59)$$

where Ψ = semiangular aperture of paraboloid and $\cot \Psi/2 = 4f/D$. In Fig. 7, we show G_f as a function of Ψ for different kr_1 and r_1/r_0 chosen from Table 2. We note that the maximum value of G_f increases slightly with decreasing Ψ, and we recall[27] that the optimum angular aperture represents a compromise between spillover of the feed energy and aperture efficiency. At small angular aperture, it is possible to illuminate the aperture more uniformly, but, to avoid a long-focal-length system, a Cassegrain configuration must be used. However, diffraction by the subreflector and blockage will then deteriorate the gain, and a significant advantage is apparent only with shaped-reflector systems. The maximum gain factor for the paraboloid with a corrugated-waveguide feed is about 84%, and similar figures are also obtained with a wide-angle conical corrugated feed horn. An identical figure has been obtained by Phillips and Clarricoats[28] for spherical reflectors. The limitation is readily understood in terms of the focal-plane field distribution. Fig. 8[29] shows the focal-plane field due to a conventional and shaped Cassegrain antenna. Unless we employ higher-order hybrid modes to synthesise the second lobe in addition to the main lobe, the best compromise is obtained when the feed-horn diameter just encloses the central region of illumination. For the front-fed paraboloid or conventional Cassegrain antenna, the efficiency is then given by

$$\eta = 1 - J_0^2(x_1') \quad . \quad . \quad . \quad . \quad . \quad . \quad . \quad . \quad . \quad . \quad (60)$$

and, with $x_1' = 3\cdot83$, $\eta = 84\%$. By using a shaped subreflector, the energy contained in the central region is appreciably increased, as seen in Fig. 8.

We conclude this section by noting that the problem of optimising the gain factor of an antenna using a corrugated-waveguide feed is very similar to that of optimising the efficiency of excitation of the HE_{11} mode on a cored-fibre optical waveguide by means of a focusing lens. The problem was first considered by Snyder,[30] who obtained the same maximum excitation efficiency as above when the illumination was from a focused plane wave. More recently, Stern, Peace and Dyott[31] and Marcuse[32] have investigated the dependence

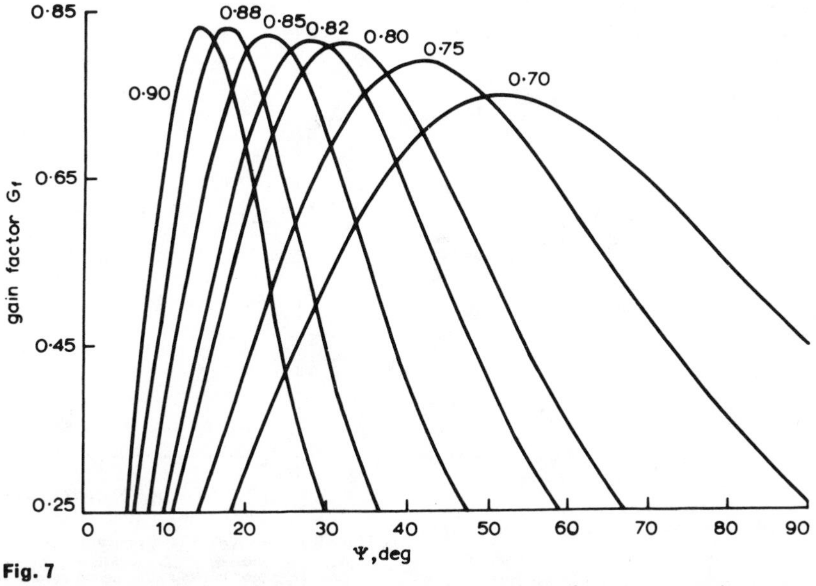

Fig. 7

Gain factor as function of semiangular aperture for parabolic reflector fed with corrugated-circular-waveguide feed

Parameter r_1/r_0

of angular aperture for both uniform and Gaussian beams. The optimum efficiency with a Gaussian amplitude distribution is approximately 98%, which compares with the efficiency of the shaped Cassegrain antenna. The main function of the shaped subreflector is as an amplitude-distribution transducer converting a focused uniform beam to one with approximately Gaussian distribution.

2.7 Similarities between corrugated feeds and optical waveguides

Considerable attention is being given to the use of a cylindrical dielectric waveguide of Fig. 1*d* for communication at optical frequencies. The relevance of this to a discussion of corrugated waveguides arises because of the close similarity in behaviour between the two structures. For example, insight into the behaviour of the radiation patterns of higher modes can be obtained by studying the visible patterns of an optical fibre.[33] Conversely, microwave modelling of certain optical-waveguide excitation problems can have economic advantages at the research phase.

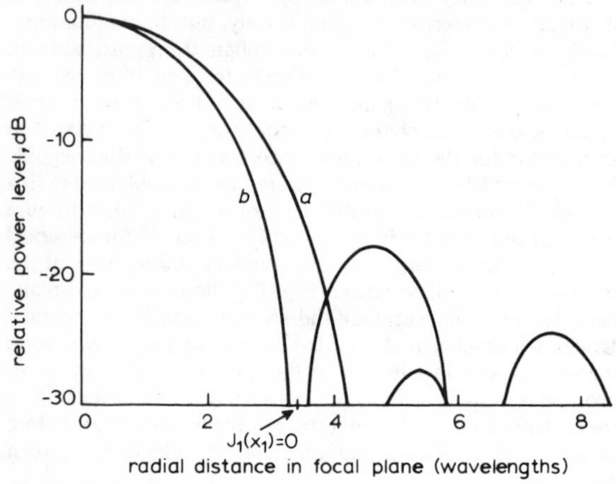

Fig. 8
Focal-plane field distribution of shaped and conventional Cassegrain antenna

For the purpose of comparison, we state the characteristic equation for the corrugated waveguide under balanced hybrid conditions in a form which permits ready comparison with the corresponding equation for the cored optical waveguide of Fig. 1*d*:

$$F_m^2(x_1) = m^2\bar{\beta}^2 \quad \ldots\ldots\ldots\ldots \quad (61)$$

The characteristic equation for the dielectric-rod structure is given by eqn. 62, provided $r_2/r_1 \gg 1$. In practice, the approximation is excellent when, typically, $r_2/r_1 > 10$. Also, $\delta = 0{\cdot}04$ where $\delta = (\epsilon - \epsilon_1)/\epsilon$.

$$\left\{\frac{\bar{\epsilon}F_m({}_1)}{x_1^2} + \frac{M_m(y_1)}{y_1^2}\right\}\left\{\frac{F_m(x_1)}{x_1^2} + \frac{M_m(y_1)}{y_1^2}\right\} = m^2\bar{\beta}^2\left(\frac{1}{x_1^2} + \frac{1}{y_1^2}\right)^2 \quad \ldots\ldots \quad (62)$$

In the dielectric waveguide, $\bar{\beta} = \beta k'$ and $k' = k\epsilon_1^{1/2}$. Under normal operating conditions, the energy is largely confined to $r < r_1$, and since $\delta \ll 1$ and $\bar{\beta} = \bar{\epsilon}^{1/2} \simeq 1$, eqn. 62 becomes

$$\{F_m(x_1) \mp m\} = -\frac{x_1^2}{y_1^2}\{M_m(y_1) \mp m\} \quad \ldots \quad (63)$$

By using a recurrence relationship for Bessel functions, eqn. 63 reduces to

$$\frac{x_1 J_{m\mp1}(x_1)}{J_m(x_1)} = \frac{x_1^2}{y_1}\frac{K_{m\mp1}(y_1)}{K_m(y_1)} \quad \ldots\ldots \quad (64)$$

If, in eqn. 61, $\bar{\beta} \simeq 1$, the corrugated-waveguide equation reduces to

$$\frac{x_1 J_{m\mp1}(x_1)}{J_m(x_1)} = 0 \quad \ldots\ldots\ldots\ldots \quad (65)$$

and evidently eqns. 64 and 65 tend to the same form when $y_1 \gg 1$. At high frequencies, $y_1 \to kr_1\delta^{1/2}$, and the characteristic equation for the eigenvaue x_1 has the same form for both corrugated waveguides and optical waveguides. Although, under normal operating conditions, y_1 is only about $2{\cdot}5$, the field in the core of the optical waveguide has a transverse dependence which closely approximates to $J_0(x)$. In contrast to the corrugated waveguide, E_ψ and H_ψ do not vanish at $r = r_1$, but their relative values are small, and tend to zero in the high-frequency limit. We stress that the analogue is valid only when the normalised dielectric difference δ is much less than unity. Under these conditions, $\bar{\Lambda} \simeq \pm 1$ for the dielectric waveguide. It is interesting to observe that, while the choice of a balanced-hybrid-mode feed system for microwave antennas was made only recently, the retinal receptors of vertebrates and insects have operated under these conditions for some millions of years!

Elsewhere,[33] one of the authors has shown that, under the above conditions, the radiation patterns of the two structures

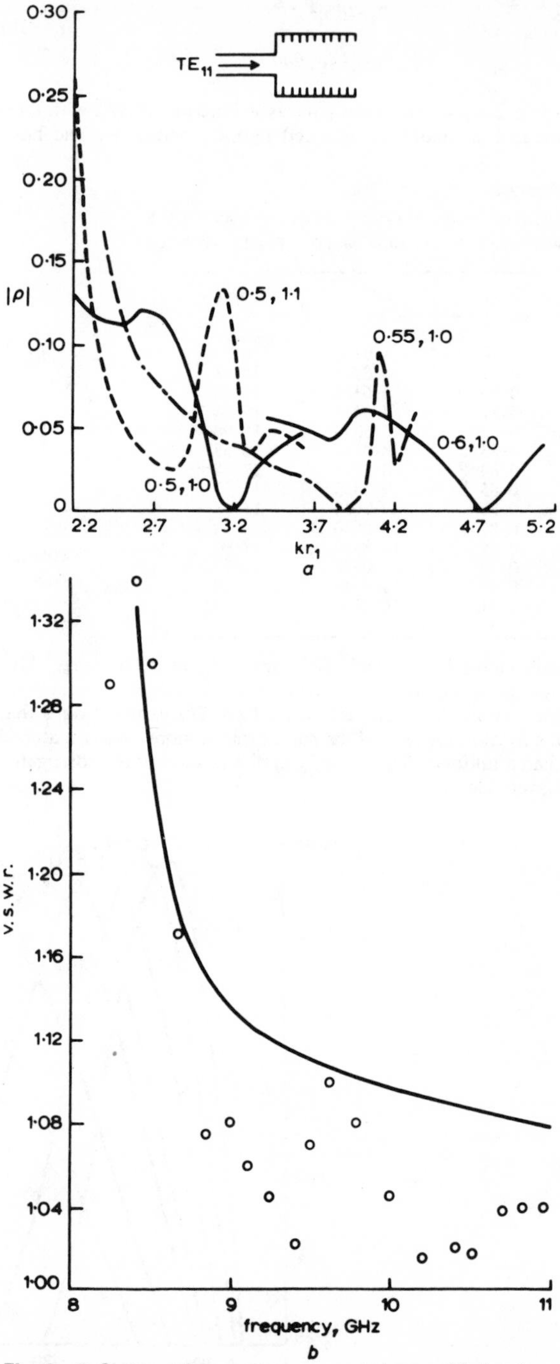

Fig. 9 *Reflection at homogeneous–corrugated-waveguide junction*
a Reflection coefficient of TE_{11} mode incident from a homogeneous circular waveguide on a junction with a corrugated circular waveguide. Parameters r_1/r_0, and r_1/r_h
b Experimental v.s.w.r. as a function of frequency measured at the throat of a narrow-flare-angle horn with $\theta_1 = 12°$ and theoretical curve for $r_1/r_0 = 0{\cdot}55$, $r_1/r_h = 1{\cdot}1$

are in close similarity. Thus, antenna-feed designers may gain insight by studying the excellent photographs of visual radiation patterns obtained by Kapany and his coworkers.[33,34] The above analysis also provides a basis for the design of 'dielguide' feeds[35] which can be viewed as 'optical waveguides at microwave frequencies'. Clarricoats and Salema[36] have predicted a 98% efficiency under optimum conditions for the excitation of the HE_{11} mode on a foam dielectric cylinder fed from a corrugated waveguide.

2.8 Excitation of modes in corrugated waveguide

Fig. 9*a* (insert) shows a junction between homogeneous and corrugated waveguides as at the feed input. In a high-efficiency antenna, the feed-input reflection coefficient must be low over the operating bandwidth, and in Section 2.8, we report on a theoretical and experimental study.

The reflection coefficient has been determined by means of a modal-analysis procedure developed by one of the authors[37,38] which has been fully described elsewhere. Briefly, the electric and magnetic fields in the aperture transverse plane are expanded in terms of the normal modes of both waveguides. The expansions are truncated after a finite number of terms, and, by applying orthogonality relationships, the complex excitation coefficients of the modes are determined. In particular, the excitation coefficient of the reflected dominant mode is obtained and the input v.s.w.r deduced. Further details are contained in Reference 39.

In our investigation of the junction of Fig. 9*a*, we have chosen 12 modes in each waveguide of which only the input TE_{11} mode and the output HE_{11} mode propagate. Fig. 9*a* shows the computed TE_{11} mode reflection coefficients as a function of normalised frequency for three values of r_1/r_0. The influence of varying the ratio r_h/r_0 is also shown. When the input waveguide and corrugated waveguide radii are the same, $r_1/r_h = 1$, then $\rho = 0$ when the normalised frequency is such that the slot input impedance is zero. We recall that, under this condition, $S_1(x_1', x_0') = \infty$ and reference to Fig. 9*a* confirms the above result. In our practical design, we have arranged the slot configuration at the throat so that, averaged over the initial slots, $r_1/r_0 = 0{\cdot}55$, $r_1/r_h \simeq 1{\cdot}1$ and $kr_1 = 2{\cdot}7$ at 9GHz. The measured input v.s.w.r. is shown in Fig. 9*b*. As the v.s.w.r. of the rectangular waveguide to circular waveguide transition was 1·05, values of v.s.w.r. less than 1·1 could not be measured accurately. The agreement between experimental and theoretical results lies within the accuracy of measurement. We conclude that, by following the proposal made by Bryant,[19] whereby the slot depth at the throat is approximately $\lambda/2$, a low-input v.s.w.r. may be achieved.

The above method of analysis has been applied by Clarricoats and Masterman[40] to the design of multimode monopulse-feed horns with uniform walls. Very recently, Cooper[43] has used the method to design multimode hybrid-mode feed horns as originally investigated by Vu.[41] In radioastronomy, where an extremely narrow operating bandwidth is acceptable, focal-plane synthesis may be achieved by using higher-order modes, and Minnett, Thomas and Vu[3,42] have considered in some detail the synthesis of the excitation coefficients for both paraboloidal and spherical antennas.

3 Conclusions

The propagation and radiation characteristics of corrugated waveguides have been determined using a cylindrical-mode analysis. We have shown that the radiated field exhibits circular symmetry, and, if the aperture field of the waveguide is linearly polarised on axis, there are zero cross-polarised components of radiated field. Furthermore, these desirable properties exist without much degradation over at least a 1·5 : 1 bandwidth. We have observed strong similarities between the propagation characteristics of corrugated waveguides and those of dielectric cylinders with relative permittivity near unity. This makes certain of the numerous results obtained by workers in the field of optical waveguides and fibre optics available to the antenna designer. It also suggests a modal method for the design of dielguide feeds. Thus, although corrugated waveguides have found rather limited application as feeds for large reflector antennas, the method of cylindrical-mode analysis provides substantial insight into the design of corrugated conical horns and related structures. For example, for narrow-flare-angle horns, several workers have used approximate techniques in conjunction with cylindrical-mode analysis to obtain results of engineering value.

4 References

1 KAY, A. F.: 'A wide flare horn—a novel feed for low noise broadband and high aperture efficiency antennas'. US Air Force Cambridge Research Laboratory report 62-757, Oct. 1962

2 KAY, A. F.: 'The scalar feed'. US Air Force Cambridge Research Laboratory report 62-347, March 1964

3 MINNETT, H. C., and THOMAS, B. MACA.: 'Fields in the image space of symmetrical focusing reflectors', *Proc. IEE*, 1968, **115**, (10), pp. 1419–1430

4 RUMSEY, V. H.: 'Horn antennas with uniform power patterns around their axes', *IEEE Trans.*, 1966, **AP-14**, pp. 656–658

5 MINNETT, H. C., and THOMAS, B. MACA.: 'A method of synthesizing radiation patterns with axial symmetry', *ibid.*, 1966, **AP-14**, pp. 654–656

6 CLARRICOATS, P. J. B.: 'Analysis of spherical hybrid modes in a corrugated conical horn', *Electron. Lett.*, 1969, **5**, pp. 189–190

7 CLARRICOATS, P. J. B., and SAHA, P. K.: 'Theoretical analysis of cylindrical hybrid modes in a corrugated horn', *ibid.*, 1969, **5**, pp. 187–189

8 CLARRICOATS, P. J. B., and SAHA, P. K.: 'Radiation from wide-flare-angle scalar horns', *ibid.*, 1969, **5**, pp. 376–378

9 VIGGH, M.: 'Study of design procedures and limitations for monopulse scalar feeds'. Rome Air Development Centre report RADC-TR-69-303, Nov. 1969

10 THOMAS, B. MACA.: 'Bandwidth properties of corrugated conical horns', *Electron. Lett.*, 1969, **5**, pp. 561–563

11 VU, T. B.: 'Optimisation of efficiency of reflector antennas: approximate method', *Proc. IEE*, 1970, **117**, (1), pp. 30–34

12 JEUKEN, M. E. J., and KIKKERT, J. S.: 'A broadband aperture antenna with a narrow beam', *Alta Frequenza*, 1969, **38**, pp. 270–276

13 JANSEN, J. K. N., JEUKEN, M. E. J., and LAMBRECHTSE, C. W.: 'A scalar feed'. Eindhoven University of Technology technical report 70-E-12, Dec. 1969

14 JEUKEN, M. E. J.: 'Frequency independence and symmetry properties of corrugated conical horn antennas with small flare angles'. Thesis, Eindhoven University of Technology, 1970

15 NARASIMHAN, M. S., and RAO, B. V.: 'Hybrid modes in corrugated conical horns', *Electron. Lett.*, 1970, **6**, pp. 32–34

16 NARASIMHAN, M. S., and RAO, B. V.: 'Diffraction by wide-flare-angle corrugated conical horns', *ibid.*, 1970, **6**, pp. 469–471

17 AU, H. K.: 'Hybrid modes in corrugated conical horns with narrow flare angle and arbitrary length', *ibid.*, 1970, **6**, pp. 769–771

18 BRYANT, G. H.: 'Propagation in corrugated waveguides', *Proc. IEE*, 1969, **116**, (2), pp. 203–213

19 BRYANT, G. H.: 'Monopulse multimode feed for military terminals *in* 'Earth station technology'. *IEE Conf. Publ.* 72, 1970, pp. 245–249

20 CLARRICOATS, P. J. B.: 'Similarities in the electromagnetic behaviour of optical waveguides and corrugated feeds', *Electron. Lett.*, 1970, **6**, pp. 178–180

21 COLLIN, R. E.: 'Field theory of guided waves' (McGraw-Hill, 1960)

22 WALKINSHAW, W.: 'Theoretical design of linear accelerators for electrons', *Proc. Phys. Soc.*, 1948, **61**, pp. 246–254

23 COOK, J. S., and LOWELL, R.: 'The autotrack system', *Bell Syst. Tech. J.*, 1963, **42**, pp. 1283–1307

24 CLARRICOATS, P. J. B., and SOBHY, M. I.: 'Propagation behaviour of periodically loaded waveguides', *Proc. IEE*, 1968, **115**, (5), pp. 652–661

25 CLARRICOATS, P. J. B.: 'Circular-waveguide backward-wave structures', *ibid.*, 1963, **110**, (2), pp. 261–270

26 WALDRON, R. A.: 'The theory of waveguides and cavities' (Maclaren & Sons, 1967), chap. 4

27 SILVER, S.: 'Microwave antenna theory and design—Vol. 12' (McGraw-Hill, 1949)

28 PHILLIPS, C. J. E., and CLARRICOATS, P. J. B.: 'Optimum design of a Gregorian-corrected spherical-reflector antenna', *Proc. IEE*, 1970, **117**, (4), pp. 718–734

29 PRATT, T.: 'High-efficiency feeds with tracking capability' *in* 'Earth station technology'. *IEE Conf. Publ.* 72, 1970, pp. 250–256

30 SNYDER, A. W.: 'Surface waveguide modes along a semi-infinite dielectric fibre excited by a plane wave', *J. Opt. Soc. Am.*, 1966, **56**, p. 601

31 STERN, J. R., PEACE, M., and DYOTT, R. B.: 'Launching into optical-fibre waveguide', *Electron. Lett.*, 1970, **6**, pp. 160–162

32 MARCUSE, D.: 'Excitation of the dominant mode of a round fibre by a Gaussian beam', *Bell Syst. Tech. J.*, 1970, **49**, pp. 1695–1704

33 KAPANY, N.: 'Fibre optics' (Academic Press, 1967)

34 KAPANY, N. S., BURKE, J. J., and FRAME, K.: 'Radiation characteristics of circular dielectric waveguides', *Appl. Optics*, 1965, **4**, p. 1534

35 BARTLETT, H. E., and MOSELEY, R. E.: 'Dielguides—highly efficient low noise antenna feeds', *Microwave J.*, 1966, **9**, p. 53

36 CLARRICOATS, P. J. B., and SALEMA, C. E. R.: 'Design of dielectric cone feeds for microwave antennas'. Proceedings of the 1971 European microwave conference, Stockholm, 1971, section B5

37 CLARRICOATS, P. J. B., and SLINN, K. R.: 'Numerical solution of waveguide-discontinuity problems', *Proc. IEE*, 1967, **114**, (7), pp. 878–886

38 MASTERMAN, P. H., and CLARRICOATS, P. J. B.: 'Computer field-matching solution of waveguide transverse discontinuities', *ibid.*, 1971, **118**, (1), pp. 51–63

39 SAHA, P. K.: 'Propagation and radiation characteristics of corrugated waveguides'. Ph.D. thesis, University of Leeds, March 1970

40 CLARRICOATS, P. J. B., and MASTERMAN, P. H.: 'A multimode monopulse feed for a satellite tracking antenna' *in* '1969 European Microwave Conference'. *IEE Conf. Publ.* 58, 1969, pp. 357–362

41 VU, T. B., and VU, Q. H.: 'Optimum feed for large radiotelescopes: experimental results', *Electron. Lett.*, 1970, **6**, pp. 159–160

42 THOMAS, B.MACA., MINNETT, H. C., and VU, T. B.: 'Fields in the focal region of a spherical reflector', *IEEE Trans.*, 1969, **AP-17**, pp. 229–232

43 COOPER, D. N.: 'Complex propagation coefficients and the step discontinuity in corrugated cylindrical waveguide', *Electron. Lett.*, 1971, **7**, pp. 135–136

Propagation and radiation behaviour of corrugated feeds

Part 2—Corrugated-conical-horn feed

Prof. P. J. B. Clarricoats, D.Sc.(Eng.), F.Inst.P., Fel.I.E.E.E., C.Eng., F.I.E.E., and P. K. Saha, B.Sc., M.Tech., Ph.D.

Indexing terms: *Antenna feeders, Waveguides, Guided electromagnetic-wave propagation*

Abstract

A theoretical and experimental investigation of the radiation behaviour of conical corrugated horns is described. The horn-aperture field is determined using spherical-mode analysis, and the radiation pattern is obtained by two methods, one of which employs a Kirchhoff–Huygen integration over a constant-phase surface at the mouth of the horn, and the other of which employs an expansion of the aperture field in terms of TE and TM spherical modes of freespace. Excellent agreement is obtained between the two methods and with experimental results. A theoretical investigation is reported of the use of lenses to correct the phase of a conical corrugated horn. Finally, the performance of paraboloid antennas using corrugated horns as feeds is briefly discussed.

List of principal symbols

A = electric-field-amplitude coefficient
$a = kR_0 \cos\theta'$
B = magnetic-field-amplitude coefficient
b' = slot width
$b = kR_0 \sin\theta'$
C_n = coefficient defined by eqn. 40
d = slot depth
$F_{\underset{i}{r}}(\theta')$ = real and imaginary part of pattern function
$f_\nu^m(\theta)$ = balanced hybrid-mode aperture-field function $= \dfrac{P_\nu^m(\cos\theta)}{\sin\theta} + \dfrac{dP_\nu^m(\cos\theta)}{d\theta}$
$f_n^m(\theta)$ = spherical-mode field function
$G_{\underset{i}{r}}(\theta,\theta')$ = function defined in eqn. 37
$g^m(\theta) = m\bar{\Lambda}\dfrac{P_\nu^m(\cos\theta)}{\sin\theta} + \dfrac{dP_\nu^m(\cos\theta)}{d\nu}$ [in places, the superscript m is omitted from $g^m(\theta)$ for clarity]
$\hat{H}^{(2)}(x) = xh_\nu^{(2)}(x)$
$h_\nu^{(2)}(x)$ = spherical Hankel function of the 2nd kind and of order ν
$h^m(\theta) = \bar{\Lambda}\dfrac{dP_\nu^m(\cos\theta)}{d\theta} + \dfrac{mP_\nu^m(\cos\theta)}{\sin\theta}$ [in places, the superscript m is omitted from $h^m(\theta)$ for clarity]
$h_\nu(x) = \dfrac{\hat{H}'(x)}{\hat{H}(x)}$
$J_m(x)$ = Bessel function of the 1st kind and order m
k = free-space wavenumber
m = azimuthal wavenumber
n = order of spherical mode
$P_\nu^m(\cos\theta)$ = associated Legendre function of the first kind and of order ν
$p_\nu^m(\theta) = \dfrac{dP_\nu^m(\cos\theta)}{d\theta} \Big/ P_\nu^m(\cos\theta)$
$Q_\nu^m(\cos\theta)$ = associated Legendre function of the 2nd kind and of order ν
R, R_0, R' = radial spherical co-ordinate, radius of horn at aperture and radial distance to far-field point, respectively
r_1, r_2 = radii defining slot (see Fig. 1*a*)
$x_0' = kR_0$
Y = wave admittance of slot at $\theta = \theta_1$
$\bar{Y}$ = normalised wave admittance $= \dfrac{-jY}{y_0}\dfrac{\nu(\nu+1)}{kR}$
y_0 = free-space wave admittance
$\alpha = \{\nu(\nu+1)\}^{1/2}$
$\alpha' = \{n(n+1)\}^{1/2}$
ν = separation constant obtained from eqn. 12
$\theta, \theta', \theta_1, \theta_2$ = polar spherical co-ordinate of point in aperture of horn, in space, at boundary of corrugations and at base of corrugations, respectively
ϕ, ϕ' = azimuthal spherical co-ordinate of point in aperture of horn and at radiation-field point, respectively
$\bar{\Lambda}$ = normalised hybrid factor $= jy_0\dfrac{B}{A}$
η_0 = free-space wave impedance
ω = angular frequency

1 Introduction

The cylindrical-mode analysis of corrugated-waveguide feeds presented in Pt. 1[1] may be applied to corrugated conical horns (Fig. 1*a*) only if the horn flare angle and length are sufficiently small for phase variation across the aperture plane to be negligible. This consideration usually restricts the results to horns with flare semiangles not exceeding about 5° if accurate radiation patterns are required.* In this paper, we apply spherical-mode analysis to the conical corrugated horn. Results have been obtained which are in good agreement with measurements for flare semiangles in the range 9–70°. For angles smaller than about 5°, computational inaccuracies may occur, and, since the cylindrical-mode analysis is then valid, continuity of results is assured. At angles approaching 90°, the assumption that the horn-aperture field is a single hybrid spherical mode becomes invalid, and, for semiangles exceeding 90°, the radiation pattern will resemble that of an open-ended waveguide. However, most corrugated horns currently used as feeds for large reflector antennas employ flare semiangles in the range 10–70°, and, within this range, the present theory is accurate.

We first determine the aperture field and obtain the radiation field by two methods. One employs a Kirchhoff–Huygen integration over a spherical constant-phase surface at the mouth of the horn, and in the other the aperture field is expanded in terms of freespace spherical-mode functions. Both methods provide results in excellent agreement with each other and with our experiments. The latter method is simple to apply and is useful when near-field results are required. As in Pt. 1, we consider the horn gain and gain factor of a paraboloid antenna fed with a corrugated feed horn. We also investigate theoretically the radiation characteristics of a

Paper 6473 E, received 31st December 1970
Prof. Clarricoats is, and Dr. Saha was formerly, with the Department of Electrical & Electronic Engineering, Queen Mary College, University of London, Mile End Road, London E1, England. Dr. Saha is now with the Institute of Radio Physics & Electronics, Calcutta 9, India

* The range of flare angles may be extended if the far field is determined by integration over a spherical cap

Reprinted with permission from *Proc. Inst. Elec. Eng.*, vol. 118, pp. 1177–1186, Sept. 1971.

corrugated horn with a phase-correcting lens in the aperture. Experimental results in support of this theory have been presented elsewhere.[2] A preliminary discussion of some of the results of this paper has been given previously by the authors[3,4] and, as mentioned in Part 1, since the present research was initiated, the authors have become aware of similar investigations by Viggh,[5] Thomas[6] and Jansen, Jeuken and Lambrechtse.[7] Approximate methods of solution which avoid the use of Legendre functions have been described by Narasimhan and Rao.[8,9] Another complementary investigation with especially useful experimental results has been undertaken by Booker.[10]

2 Propagation and radiation characteristics of corrugated conical horns

2.1 Determination of horn-aperture fields

Fig. 1*a* shows a section through a conical horn with corrugated walls connected to a circular feed waveguide. We assume that the field within the horn may be described in terms of a single spherical hybrid mode analogous to the cylindrical-hybrid-mode analysis discussed in Part 1. However, in the cylindrical corrugated waveguide, the field representation could be made exact, whereas, for the corrugated conical horn, this does not seem possible with currently available techniques, except in special cases. One of these is when the corrugation depth is such that the wave impedance E_R/H_ϕ is infinite at the mouth of the slots as in the optimum operating condition for a corrugated feed horn. Although this condition is satisfied only at a single frequency, comparison with experiment shows the assumption to be valid over a wide range of frequencies provided the boundary $\theta = \theta_1$

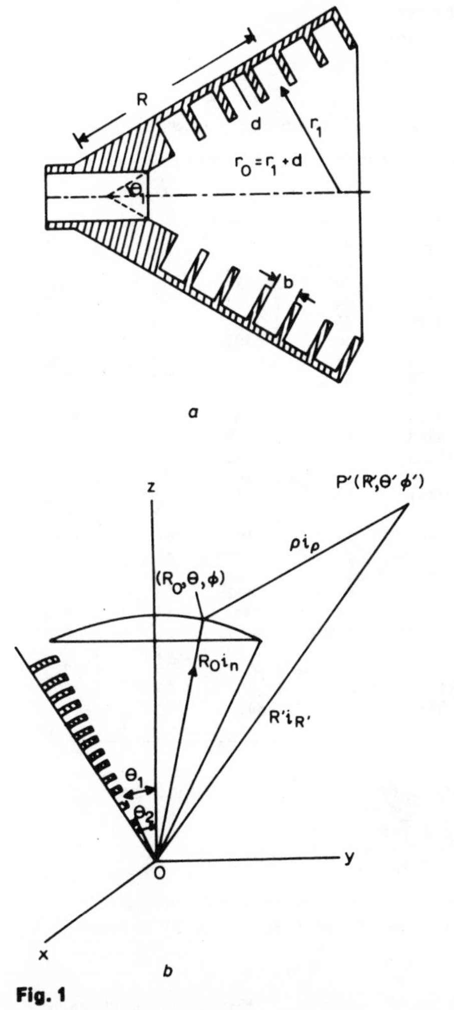

Fig. 1
Corrugated conical horn
a Section through corrugated conical horn
b Co-ordinate system for conical-horn analysis

does not support a surface wave. It is also necessary that the horn flare angle is not too large, otherwise the field near boresight will correspond more closely to the radiation field of the feed waveguide only slightly perturbed by the presence of the corrugated boundary

The modal field in the horn is derived from the electric and magnetic scalar potential functions A_R and F_R, where

$$A_R = A\hat{H}_\nu^{(2)}(kR)P_\nu^m(\cos\theta)\epsilon^{jm\phi} \quad . \quad . \quad . \quad . \quad . \quad (1)$$

$$F_R = B\hat{H}_\nu^{(2)}(kR)P_\nu^m(\cos\theta)\epsilon^{jm\phi} \quad . \quad . \quad . \quad . \quad . \quad (2)$$

The coefficients A and B depend on the excitation of the mode and are related through the equation

$$\frac{B}{A} = -j\eta_0\bar{\Lambda} \quad . \quad . \quad . \quad . \quad . \quad . \quad . \quad . \quad . \quad . \quad (3)$$

where $\eta_0 = (\mu_0/\epsilon_0)^{1/2}$ and the coefficient $\bar{\Lambda}$ depends on the boundary conditions. $\hat{H}_\nu^{(2)}(x) = kRh_\nu^{(2)}(kR)$, where $h_\nu^{(2)}(kR)$ is a spherical Hankel function of the 2nd kind, and henceforth the superscript (2) will be omitted.

$P_\nu^m(\cos\theta)$ is an associated Legendre function of order ν which, in general, is noninteger. $P_\nu^m(\cos\theta)$ is real provided $-1 < \cos\theta < +1$. This is always so in our investigation. The azimuthal dependence, $\epsilon^{jm\phi}$, corresponds to a circularly polarised form when $m = 1$ as in the present analysis. Later, we introduce a linearly polarised form to distinguish phase factors more clearly. A time dependence of the form $e^{j\omega t}$ is assumed throughout and is suppressed for convenience, so that the corresponding outward travelling spherical wave has a radial dependence e^{-jkR}. In general, $\hat{H}(x)$ is a complex function, although, when $x \gg 1$, $\hat{H}_\nu(x) \to j^{\nu+1}e^{+jx}$ and the radial dependence becomes that of a spherical wave. Eqns. 1 and 2 are the consequence of separating the variables in the spherical-wave equation: a procedure which is only justified if the boundary conditions on the surface $\theta = \theta_1$ are independent of R and ϕ. In practice, the boundary conditions depend on R_1, but, near the horn aperture, the dependence is slight and the assumption is well justified.

The field components in spherical co-ordinates are obtained from eqns. 1 and 2 as follows, where, for convenience, the functions $\hat{H}_\nu(kR)$ and $P_\nu^m(\cos\theta)$ are abbreviated and the factor $\epsilon^{jm\phi}$ omitted:

$$E_R = A\eta_0\nu\frac{(\nu+1)}{jkR^2}\hat{H}_\nu P_\nu^m \quad . \quad . \quad . \quad . \quad . \quad . \quad (4)$$

$$H_R = -A\bar{\Lambda}\nu\frac{(\nu+1)}{kR^2}\hat{H}_\nu P_\nu^m \quad . \quad . \quad . \quad . \quad . \quad . \quad (5)$$

$$E_\theta = -\eta_0 A\left(\frac{m\bar{\Lambda}}{R\sin\theta}\hat{H}_\nu P_\nu^m + \frac{j}{R}\hat{H}_\nu'\frac{dP_\nu^m}{d\theta}\right) \quad . \quad . \quad (6)$$

$$E_\phi = \eta_0 A\left(-\frac{j\bar{\Lambda}}{R}\hat{H}_\nu\frac{dP_\nu^m}{d\theta} + \frac{m}{R\sin\theta}\hat{H}_\nu' P_\nu^m\right) \quad . \quad (7)$$

$$H_\theta = A\left(\frac{jm\hat{H}_\nu}{R\sin\theta}P_\nu^m - \bar{\Lambda}\frac{\hat{H}_\nu'}{R}\frac{dP_\nu^m}{d\theta}\right) \quad . \quad . \quad . \quad (8)$$

$$H_\phi = -A\left(\frac{\hat{H}_\nu}{R}\frac{dP_\nu^m}{d\theta} + j\frac{\bar{\Lambda}m\hat{H}_\nu'}{R\sin\theta}P_\nu^m\right) \quad . \quad . \quad . \quad (9)$$

Let

$$p_\nu^m(\theta) = \frac{dP_\nu^m}{d\theta}(\cos\theta)/P_\nu^m(\cos\theta)$$

and

$$h_\nu(kr) = \frac{\hat{H}_\nu'(kr)}{\hat{H}_\nu(kr)}$$

Then

$$\frac{E_\phi}{H_R} = \frac{jkR\eta_0}{\nu(\nu+1)}\left(p_\nu^m(\theta) + \frac{jmh_\nu}{\bar{\Lambda}\sin\theta}\right) \quad . \quad . \quad . \quad . \quad (10)$$

and

$$\frac{H_\phi}{E_R} = \frac{-jkRy_0}{\nu(\nu+1)}\left(p_\nu^m(\theta) + \frac{j\bar{\Lambda}mh_\nu}{\sin\theta}\right) \quad . \quad . \quad . \quad . \quad (11)$$

Provided that $kb' < 2\pi$, no TE spherical mode can be supported within the slots[7]. Usually $kb' \simeq 1$, and we are then justified in placing $E_\phi/H_R = 0$ at $\theta = \theta_1$. If, in general, $H_\phi/E_R = Y$ at $\theta = \theta_1$, we obtain from eqns. 10 and 11, a characteristic equation for ν in terms of θ_1 and R:

$$p_\nu^m(\theta_1)\left\{Y + \frac{jkRy_0}{\nu(\nu+1)} y_0 p_\nu^m(\theta_1)\right\} = \frac{-jm^2kRy_0(h_\nu)^2}{\nu(\nu+1)\sin^2\theta_1} \quad . \; . \; . \; . \; (12)$$

If

$$\bar{Y} = \frac{-jY}{y_0}\frac{\nu(\nu+1)}{kR} \quad . \; . \; . \; . \; . \; . \; . \; . \; . \; (13)$$

eqn. 12 becomes

$$p_\nu^m(\theta_1)\{\bar{Y} + p_\nu^m(\theta_1)\} = \frac{-m^2}{\sin^2\theta_1}(h_\nu)^2 \quad . \; . \; . \; . \; (14)$$

provided $kR \gg 1$, $h_\nu \to -j$. Eqn. 14 is independent of R provided $\bar{Y}$ is independent of R, and strictly only then is the equation consistent with the initial 'separable-variable' assumption. The behaviour of $h_\nu(kR)$ has been studied by Jansen, Jeuken and Lambrechtse[7] who show that the above assumption is well satisfied for $\theta_1 > 30°$ provided $kR_0 > 20$, but as $\theta_1 \to 0$ the condition is only satisfied for $kR \to \infty$. For large x, an asymptotic form for h_ν is given by

$$h_\nu(x) = -j\{1 - \nu(\nu+1)/2x\} \quad . \; . \; . \; . \; . \; (15)$$

For slots formed on spherical surfaces as shown in Fig. 1*b*

$$Y = \frac{-jy_0}{kR}\,\frac{\frac{\partial}{\partial\theta}\{P_n^m(\cos\theta)Q_n^m(\cos\theta_2) - P_n^m(\cos\theta_2)Q_n^m(\cos\theta)\}_{\theta=\theta_1}}{P_n^m(\cos\theta_1)Q_n^m(\cos\theta_2) - P_n^m(\cos\theta_2)Q_n^m(\cos\theta_1)} \quad . \; . \; . \; . \; (16)$$

where $Q_n^m(\cos\theta)$ is an associated Legendre function of the 2nd kind. When $kR \gg 1$ and $kb' \ll 1$, Jansen *et al.*[7] have shown that $n \simeq kR$ and that the 'open-circuit' condition $Y = 0$ is satisfied when $kR_2(\theta_2 - \theta_1) = \pi(l + \frac{1}{2})$, where $l = 0, 1, 2, \ldots$ For the particular case $l = 0$, the slot depth $d = R(\theta_2 - \theta_1) = \lambda/4$, as for the corrugated waveguide. For small θ, eqn. 16 transforms to

$$Y = \frac{-jy_0}{kR\theta_1} S_m[\alpha\theta_1, \alpha\theta_2] \quad . \; . \; . \; . \; . \; . \; . \; . \; (17)$$

$$\text{where} \quad S_m(a,b) = -a\frac{\{J_m'(a)Y_m(b) - J_m(b)Y_m'(a)\}}{\{J_m(a)Y_m(b) - J_m(b)Y_m(a)\}}$$

$$\alpha' = \{n(n+1)\}^{1/2}$$

Since $\alpha' \simeq kR$, $\alpha'\theta_{1,2} \simeq kr_{1,2}$ and eqn. 17 is reduced to the form appropriate to a corrugated waveguide as given in Pt. 1. When $\alpha'\theta_1 \gg 1$, eqn. 16 becomes

$$Y \simeq jy_0\left(\cot kd + \frac{1}{2kr_1}\right) \quad . \; . \; . \; . \; . \; . \; . \; (18)$$

In our studies of the frequency dependence of corrugated horns, we have used eqn. 18 to determine Y but have neglected the second term.

When $Y \neq 0$, eqn. 14 depends on R as $1/R^2$ since

$$\bar{Y} \simeq \frac{\cot kd\nu(\nu+1)}{kR} \quad . \; . \; . \; . \; . \; . \; . \; . \; . \; (19)$$

In practice, $kR \gg 1$ at the mouth of a horn, and it is reasonable to assume that $\bar{Y}$ is independent of R when calculating aperture fields.

The particular case $\bar{Y} = 0$ is of special interest, since, under this condition, the radiation pattern of the feed horn is circularly symmetric and the crosspolarisation component is zero. When $\bar{Y} = 0$, eqn. 14 is reduced to

$$\sin^2\theta_1\{p_\nu^m(\theta_1)\}^2 = m^2 \quad . \; . \; . \; . \; . \; . \; . \; . \; (20)$$

where we have assumed $h_\nu(x) = -j$.

In Fig. 2, we show solutions of eqn. 20 for $m = 1$ in the range $0 < \theta_1 < 90°$ and $\nu < 12$. We have labelled the modes in accordance with the practice of Pt. 1, so that modes with a radiation pattern possessing a maximum on the axis $\theta = 0$, are called HE_{mn} and those with a null EH_{mn}. Since the lowest mode with $m = 1$ is of greatest importance in antenna applications, we provide, in Table 1, values of ν for this mode in the range $16° < \theta_1 < 90°$.

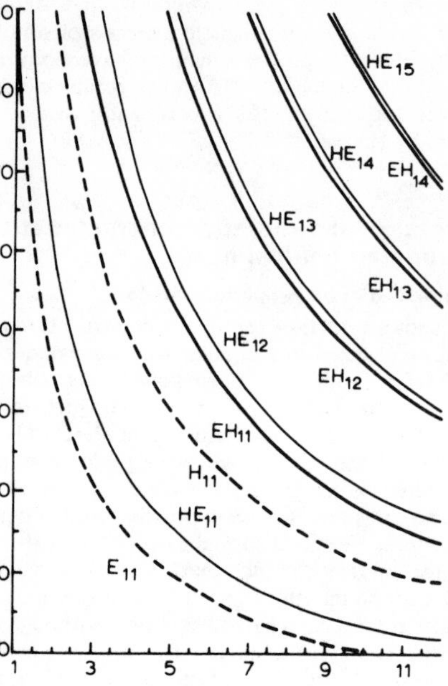

Fig. 2

Solutions of characteristic equation for HE_{1N} and HE_{1N} modes in corrugated conical horn

---- modes in uncorrugated horn

Table 1

FIRST ROOT ν OF $f_\nu^1(\theta_1) = 0$ FOR HE_{11} SPHERICAL MODE

$\theta_1°$	ν	$\theta_1°$	ν	$\theta_1°$	ν
16	8·1649	41	2·9982	66	1·8126
17	7·6617	42	2·9216	67	1·7851
18	7·2148	43	2·8487	68	1·7585
19	6·8152	44	2·7793	69	1·7327
20	6·4560	45	2·7132	70	1·7078
21	6·1313	46	2·6501	71	1·6837
22	5·8364	47	2·5898	72	1·6604
23	5·5674	48	2·5322	73	1·6379
24	5·3212	49	2·4770	74	1·6161
25	5·0949	50	2·4243	75	1·5949
26	4·8863	51	2·3737	76	1·5745
27	4·6933	52	2·3252	77	1·5546
28	4·5144	53	2·2787	78	1·5354
29	4·3481	54	2·2341	79	1·5168
30	4·1931	55	2·1912	80	1·4988
31	4·0483	56	2·1499	81	1·4813
32	3·9128	57	2·1103	82	1·4643
33	3·7857	58	2·0721	83	1·4479
34	3·6663	59	2·0354	84	1·4319
35	3·5539	60	2·0000	85	1·4164
36	3·4479	61	1·9659	86	1·4014
37	3·3479	62	1·9330	87	1·3869
38	3·2533	63	1·9013	88	1·3728
39	3·1637	64	1·8707	89	1·3591
40	3·0788	65	1·8412	90	1·3458

When θ_1 is small, $\sin\theta_1 \simeq \theta_1$ and eqn. 14 is reduced to

$$\left\{\alpha\theta_1\frac{J_m'(\alpha\theta_1)}{J_m(\alpha\theta_1)}\right\}^2 = m^2\left\{1 - \left(\frac{\alpha}{kR_1}\right)^2\right\} \quad . \; . \; . \; (21)$$

If we identify $\alpha = \sqrt{\nu(\nu+1)}$ with KR_1, where K is the transverse (to z) wavenumber of Pt. 1, eqn. 21 becomes

$$F_m^2(Kr_1) = m^2\bar{\beta}^2 \quad . \; . \; . \; . \; . \; . \; . \; . \; . \; (22)$$

where $\bar{\beta} = \beta/k$ and $K^2 = k^2 - \beta^2$. Eqn. 22 is the characteristic equation for the corrugated waveguide derived in Pt. 1 by means of a cylindrical-mode analysis.

Au[11] obtains eqn. 21 by using an additional boundary condition, namely continuity of H_θ and E_R at $\theta = \theta_1$. The equation may also be obtained directly from the asymptotic form of h_ν. Au has solved eqn. 21 for ν with θ_1 in the range 6–12° and with kR_1 between 30 and 110. At $\theta_1 = 6°$, where, for the above data, the difference in ν is greatest, $\nu = 21 \cdot 149$ when $kR_1 = 30$ and $\nu = 22 \cdot 477$ when $kR_1 = \infty$. When $\theta_1 > 12°$, the second term on the right-hand side of eqn. 21 has a negligible effect on ν. Au has also shown that, for larger values of θ_1, eqn. 21 yields values of ν in very close agreement with those obtained by the present authors from eqn. 20 As tabulated values of Bessel functions are more readily available than those of Legendre functions, this agreement may interest some workers.

From eqns. 10 and 11, we have, on making $h_\nu = -j$ and $\theta = \theta_1$,

$$\bar{\Lambda} = \frac{-m}{p_\nu(\theta_1)\sin\theta_1} \quad \ldots \quad (23)$$

$$\bar{\Lambda} = -(p_\nu^m(\theta_1) + \bar{Y})\frac{\sin\theta_1}{m} \quad \ldots \quad (24)$$

When $Y = 0$, we have $\bar{\Lambda} = \pm 1$ and we call this the balanced hybrid condition since the components E_R and H_R are then in the ratio of the free-space wave impedance. The positive sign corresponds to HE modes, the negative to EH modes.

From eqns. 6–9, we have, when $h_\nu = -j$,

$$E_\theta = -\eta_0 \frac{A\hat{H}_\nu}{R}\left(\frac{m\bar{\Lambda}P_\nu^m}{\sin\theta} + \frac{dP_\nu^m}{d\theta}\right)\cos m\phi = \frac{A\hat{H}_\nu}{R} e_\theta \cos m\phi \quad \ldots \quad (25)$$

$$E_\phi = \eta_0 \frac{A\hat{H}_\nu}{R}\left(\frac{\Lambda dP_\nu^m}{d\theta} + \frac{mP_\nu^m}{\sin\theta}\right)\sin m\phi = \frac{A\hat{H}_\nu}{R} e_\phi \sin m\phi \quad \ldots \quad (26)$$

In general,

$$H_\theta = -y_0 E_\phi \quad \ldots \quad (27)$$

$$H_\phi = y_0 E_\theta \quad \ldots \quad (28)$$

If $m = 1$, under balanced hybrid conditions with $\bar{\Lambda} = \pm 1$, $e_\theta = \mp e_\phi$, $h_\theta = \pm y_0 e_\theta$ and $h_\phi = \mp y_0 e_\phi$

In Fig. 3, we show the function $f^1_{\nu+}(\theta) = (P^1_\nu/\sin\theta) + (dP^1_\nu/d\theta)$ as a function of θ for four values of θ_1. We have normalised the curves by plotting $f^1_{\nu+}/\nu(\nu+1)$, since $f^1_{\nu+}(0) = \nu(\nu+1)$. For small θ, we may write $\sin\theta \simeq \theta$, and $P_\nu^m(\cos\theta) \simeq J_m(\alpha\theta)$. If this approximation is introduced into

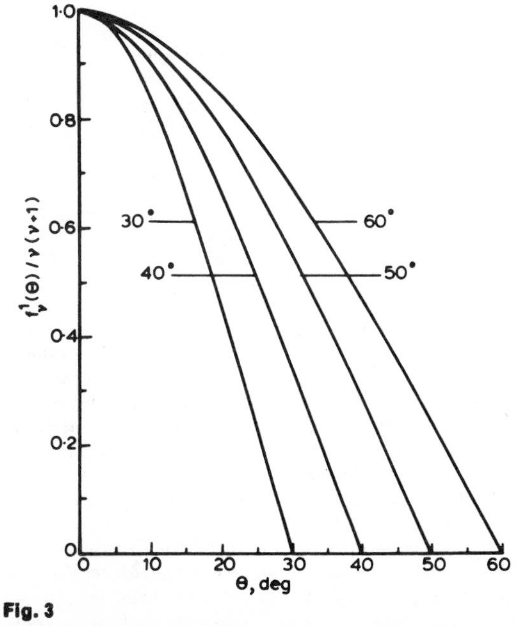

Fig. 3
Normalised aperture-field distribution for corrugated horn
Parameter denotes horn semiangle θ_1

eqn. 25 when $\bar{\Lambda} = \pm 1$, the use of a recurrence relationship for Bessel functions will give

$$e_\theta = J_{m\mp 1}(\alpha\theta) \quad \ldots \quad (29)$$

For $m = 1$ and $\bar{\Lambda} = +1$, eqn. 29 becomes $e_\theta = J_0(\alpha\theta)$, and in Pt. 1 we showed that this function approximates the Gaussian function $\exp\{-\alpha\theta/2)\}^2$ when $\alpha\theta$ is small. Because of the well known transform properties of Gaussian functions, we may anticipate that the radiation pattern of the HE_{11} mode will resemble the aperture distribution shown in Fig. 3. This comparison was first made by Clarricoats[12] using experimental results by Kay.

Thomas[13] has used eqn. 24 and 25 to study the dependence of the HE_{11} aperture distribution on $\bar{\Lambda}$ and the normalised surface admittance $\bar{Y}$. He concludes that the dependence is weak. This in accordance with the well known frequency-independent properties of the scalar feed as discussed in Section 2.2. We have also studied the frequency dependence of $\bar{\Lambda}$ and ν using eqns. 14 and 24 with Y as a function of kR_0 and kd from eqn. 19. Table 2 shows results for four values of θ_1; balanced hybrid conditions occur at the lowest value of kR_0.

Table 2

ROOTS OF CHARACTERISTIC EQN. 12 WITH $h_\nu = -j$ AND $Y = jy_0 \cot kd$ FOR DOMINANT HE_{11} MODE

kR_0	ν	$\bar{\Lambda}$	kR_0	ν	$\bar{\Lambda}$
15·0	2·4243	1·0000	20	2·4243	1·0000
16·5	2·4103	1·0307	22	2·4137	1·0230
18·0	2·3984	1·0579	24	2·4047	1·0434
19·5	2·3873	1·0842	26	2·3963	1·0629
21·0	2·3761	1·1119	28·	2·3876	1·0836
22·5	2·3634	1·1444	30	2·3777	1·1078
25·0	2·4243	1·0000	30	2·4243	1·0000
27·5	2·4158	1·0184	33	2·4172	1·0153
30·0	2·4085	1·0346	36	2·4111	1·0288
32·5	2·4017	1·0503	39	2·4054	1·0418
35·0	2·3947	1·0667	42	2·3994	1·0555
37·5	2·3866	1·0860	45	2·3926	1·0715
35·0	2·4243	1·0000	40	2·4243	1·0000
38·5	2·4182	1·0131	44	2·4190	1·0115
42·0	2·4130	1·0247	48	2·4144	1·0216
45·5	2·4080	1·0358	52	2·4100	1·0313
49·0	2·4029	1·0475	56	2·4055	1·0415
52·5	2·3970	1·0612	60	2·4003	1·0535

The mode is balanced at the lowest value of kR_0 and the hybrid factor $\bar{\Lambda}$ is calculated from eqn. 24. $\theta_1 = 50°$

2.2 Radiation from corrugated horn

2.2.1 Kirchhoff-Huygen method

Now that the aperture field at the surface $R = R_0$ of Fig. 1*b* is known, the radiation field E_p may be determined by a Kirchhoff-Huygen integration over the cap $R = R_0$, $-\theta_1 < \theta\,\theta_1$, $0 < \phi < 2\pi$. From Silver,[18]

$$E_p(R', \theta', \phi') = \frac{jk\exp(-jkR')}{4\pi R'} i_{R'} \times \int_s \{i_n \times E_{\tan g} - z_0 \times (i_n \times H_{\tan g})\}\exp(jkR_0 i_{R'} dS) \quad \ldots \quad (30)$$

$i_{R'}$, i_n are unit vectors and the fields $E_{\tan g} H_{\tan g}$ are tangential to the surface of the spherical cap. On replacing the factor outside the integral by c, we obtain, after some algebraic manipulation,[15]

$$E_{p\theta}(\theta', \phi') = c\int_0^{2\pi}\int_0^{\theta_1}[-E_\theta\cos(\phi'-\phi) - E_\phi\cos\theta\sin(\phi'-\phi) + z_0 H_\theta\cos\theta'\sin(\phi'-\phi) - z_0 H\phi\{\sin\theta\sin\theta' + \cos\theta\cos\theta'\cos(\phi'-\phi)\}]\exp[jkR_0\{\cos\theta\cos\theta' + \sin\theta\sin\theta'\cos(\phi'-\phi)\}]\sin\theta\, d\theta\, d\phi \quad . \quad . \quad (31)$$

$$E_{p\phi}(\theta', \phi') = c\int_0^{2\pi}\int_0^{\theta_1}[E_\theta \cos\theta' \sin(\phi' - \phi) - E_\phi\{\sin\theta\sin\theta' + \cos\theta\cos\theta'\cos(\phi' - \phi)\} + z_0 H_\theta \cos(\phi' - \phi) + z_0 H_\phi \cos\theta \sin(\phi' - \phi)] \exp[jkR_0\{\cos\theta\cos\theta' + \sin\theta\sin\theta'\cos(\phi' - \phi)\}] \sin\theta d\theta d\phi \quad . \quad . \quad (32)$$

Let $a = kR_0 \cos\theta'$ and $b = kR_0 \sin\theta'$, and, from eqns. 25 and 26, let

$$E_\theta(\theta, \phi) = -g(\theta) C \cos m\phi \quad . \quad . \quad . \quad . \quad . \quad . \quad (33)$$

$$E_\phi(\theta, \phi) = h(\theta) C \sin m\phi \quad . \quad . \quad . \quad . \quad . \quad . \quad . \quad (34)$$

where $g(\theta)$ and $h(\theta)$ are the functions within the brackets in eqns. 25 and 26, respectively. On substituting for E_θ and E_ϕ in eqn. 31 and using eqns. 27 and 28 to relate the magnetic- and electric-field components, we obtain, after performing the ϕ integration and combining the constants,

$$E_{p\theta}(\theta', \phi') = D \cos m\phi' \int_0^{\theta_1} [2jg(\theta) J_m(b \sin\theta) \sin\theta \sin\theta' + (j)^{m+1} J_{m+1}(b\sin\theta)\{g(\theta)(1 + \cos\theta\cos\theta') \mp h(\theta)(\cos\theta + \cos\theta')\} + j^{m-1} J_{m-1}(b \sin\theta) \{g(\theta)(1 + \cos\theta\cos\theta') \pm h(\theta)(\cos\theta + \cos\theta')\}] e^{(ja\cos\theta)} \sin\theta d\theta \quad . \quad . \quad . \quad . \quad . \quad (35)$$

The integral for $E_{p\phi}(\theta'\phi')$ is similar to that for $E_{p\theta}$ except that $g(\theta)$ and $h(\theta)$ are interchanged and $\cos m\phi'$ is replaced by $-\sin m\phi'$. When $\bar{\Lambda} = +1$, we have

$$g(\theta) = h(\theta) = f^m_{\nu+}(\theta) = \frac{mP^m_\nu}{\sin\theta} + \frac{dP^m_\nu}{d\theta}$$

and when $\bar{\Lambda} = 1$

$$g(\theta) = -h(\theta) = f^m_{\nu-}(\theta) = \frac{dP^m_\nu}{d\theta} - \frac{mP^m_\nu}{\sin\theta}$$

For the special case $m = 1$, $\bar{\Lambda} = +1$, we have

$$E_{p\theta}(\theta', \phi') = \{F_r(\theta') + jF_i(\theta')\} \cos\phi' \quad . \quad . \quad . \quad (36)$$

$$E_{p\phi}(\theta', \phi') = -\{F_r(\theta') + jF_i(\theta')\} \sin\phi' \quad . \quad . \quad (37)$$

where

$$F_{\substack{r\\i}}(\theta') = D \int_0^{\theta_1} f^1_{\nu+}(\theta) G_{\substack{r\\i}}(\theta, \theta') d\theta$$

and

$$G_{\substack{r\\i}}(\theta'\theta') = \{(1 + \cos\theta)(1 + \cos\theta')\sin\theta \, {}^{\cos}_{\sin}(a\cos\theta) J_0(b\sin\theta)\} - \{(1 - \cos\theta)(1 - \cos\theta')\sin\theta \, {}^{\cos}_{\sin}(a\cos\theta) J_2(b\sin\theta)\} \mp \{2\sin\theta' \sin^2\theta \, {}^{\sin}_{\cos}(a\cos\theta) J_1(b\sin\theta)\}$$

From eqns. 36 and 37, we observe that, under balanced hybrid conditions, pattern symmetry exists about the axis $\theta' = 0$. Examination of eqn. 38 reveals a maximum in the boresight direction $\theta' = 0$ for HE_{1n} modes, while for EH_{1n} modes there is a null on the boresight, and similarly for all modes with $m > 1$. As shown in Pt. 1, there is no cross-polarised component of radiated field if the aperture field is linearly polarised.

In passing, we draw attention to the close similarity between eqn. 38 and corresponding expressions derived by Rusch[5] for the far field scattered by a hyperboloid illuminated by a feed at its focus and which possesses a circularly symmetric radiation pattern. The correspondence might be expected, since the hyperboloid scatters a wave which, in a geometrical-optics approximation, has a phase centre at the complementary focus. We may therefore expect close similarities in the radiation patterns of wide-angle scalar feeds and hyperboloid subreflectors of the same angular aperture.

To compute the far-field pattern of a scalar horn using eqns. 36 and 37, specify m, θ_1, kd and kR_0 and then determine ν and $\bar{\Lambda}$ from which $g^m(\theta)$, $h^m(\theta)$ can be found. Finally, using eqn. 35 and a similar equation for E_ϕ, compute the E and Hplane patterns. In Fig. 4, we show results for the HE_{11} mode when $\theta_1 = 50°$, and the balanced hybrid condition occurs at a frequency such that $kR_0 = 20$. The patterns are typical of those observed for other corrugated horns with $20° < \theta_1 < 75°$, although the shape of the pattern near the boresight depends on the horn length. For certain combinations of horn flare angle and horn length, the axial gain may be slightly less

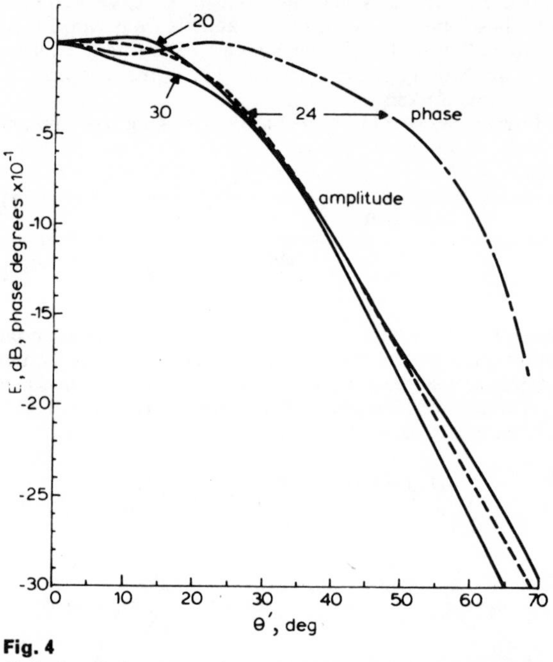

Fig. 4
Eplane radiation pattern for corrugated horn with semiangle 50°
Parameter denotes value of kR_0

than the off-axis gain, owing to destructive interference arising from the substantial phase variation over the horn-aperture plane. The phenomenon can be turned to advantage if a flat-topped beam is required. Although we have only shown the Eplane pattern, the Hplane patterns are almost identical over the 2 : 1 frequency band investigated. Fig. 4 also shows how the phase of the far field depends on θ; evidently there is a change of about $\pi/4$ when $\theta = \theta_1$. We have investigated the location of the phase centre following the method of Hu.[16] In Table 3, we show the deviation s, in

Table 3

DEVIATION OF PHASE CENTRE FROM HORN APEX

$\theta_1 = 30°$, $kR_0 = 30$		$\theta_1 = 50°$, $kR_0 = 30$	
Range of θ'	s/λ	Range of θ'	s/λ
$0 < \theta' \leqslant 4°$	0·60	$0° < \theta' \leqslant 6°$	0·20
$4° < \theta' \leqslant 8°$	0·44	$6° < \theta' \leqslant 15°$	0·11
$8° < \theta' \leqslant 10°$	0·35		

wavelengths, of the phase centre from the cone apex for $\theta_1 = 30°$ and $50°$ and for various angles from the boresight. For wide-angle horns, the phase centre is nearly coincident with the horn apex while, for very narrow-angle horns the phase centre lies nearly in the horn aperture. Computations made over a 1·5 :1 bandwidth reveal that, although s increases as frequency increases above the balanced hybrid value, the E and Hplane phase centres remain nearly coincidental.

Comparing Fig. 4 with the aperture-field distribution for $\theta_1 = 50°$ in Fig. 3, the similarity is evident. Generally, the field intensity decreases monotonically with θ and we observe that it falls to approximately -20dB when $\theta = \theta_1$. This characteristic is observed for horns with $\theta_1 > 35°$, while, for $\theta_1 < 35°$, the field intensity is slightly higher when $\theta = \theta_1$.

For $\theta_1 = 50°$, computations have shown a side-lobe structure in the angular range $100° > \theta > 180°$. However, the peak intensity when $kR_0 = 25$ is only -45dB, while for larger kR_0, the side-lobe level is even smaller. These results imply an exceedingly high beam efficiency, which has been substantiated experimentally by a number of workers with high-performance pattern-measuring facilities. In Section 3, we compare our own experimental results and computed results for horns with $\theta_1 = 12°$ and $\theta_1 = 30°$.

2.2.2 Modal-expansion method

In an alternative approach to the computation of the far field of a corrugated conical horn, we use an expansion of the horn-aperture electric field in terms of the spherical modes of free space.[17] To determine the excitation coefficients of these modes, we invoke the orthogonality properties of the Legendre functions over the spherical surface $R = R_0$ and assume that the field producing the excitation is zero outside the horn where $\theta > \theta_1$.

For convenience, we restrict our analysis to the case $m = 1$, $|\bar{\Lambda}| = 1$, for which the horn-aperture electric field is given by

$$E(R_0, \theta, \phi) = \frac{\exp(-jkR_0)}{R_0} f_\nu^1(\theta)(i_\theta \cos\phi - i_\phi \sin\phi) \quad . \quad (38)$$

We have set a multiplying constant equal to unity as we are concerned with radiation patterns rather than the absolute far-field intensity. The subscript $\pm$ has also been omitted from the $f_\nu^1(\theta)$ function, the choice of sign depending on the sign of $\bar{\Lambda}$. Let the electric far field be represented in terms of a combination of TE and TM spherical modes which exist in $R > R_0$. For $R = R_0$

$$E(R_0, \theta) = \sum_{n=1}^{N} C_n h_n^{(2)}(kR_0) f_n^1(\theta) \quad . \quad . \quad . \quad . \quad . \quad . \quad (39)$$

where $f_n^1(\theta) = (dP_n^1/d\theta) \pm (P_n^1/\sin\theta)$, the sign depending on the sign in $f_\nu^1(\theta)$. For $N > kR_0$, the coefficients C_n have negligible values and we may truncate the series at or near that value. On using well known orthogonality relationships, C_n is obtained as

$$C_n = \frac{\exp(-jkR_0)}{R_0} \frac{2n+1}{2n^2(n+1)^2 h_n^{(2)}(kR_0)} \int_0^{\theta_1} f_\nu^1(\theta) f_n^1(\theta) \sin\theta \, d\theta \quad . \quad . \quad . \quad . \quad (40)$$

Now that the intensity of excitation of the TE and TM spherical-mode combinations are known, the far field of the horn is obtained directly. On making use of the asymptotic expression for the spherical Hankel function, the normalised far-field pattern is given by

$$\left|\frac{E(\theta)}{E(0)}\right| = \left|\frac{\sum_{n=1}^{N} \frac{C_n j^{n+1}}{h_n^{(2)}(x_0')} f_n^1(\theta)}{\sum_{n=1}^{N} \frac{C_n j^{n+1}}{h_n^{(2)}(x_0')} f_n^1(0)}\right| \quad . \quad . \quad . \quad . \quad . \quad . \quad . \quad (41)$$

In Fig. 5, we compare radiation patterns predicted by the Kirchhoff–Huygen and modal-expansion methods for $\theta_1 = 50°$, 60° and 70°; the agreement is excellent. We have studied the convergence of the series and have found that for various observation angles, the pattern converges to within 1% when $N \simeq kR_0$. A good approximation to the final pattern is also obtained with only about six terms in the series, especially for wide-flare-angle horns. It is also possible to use the above

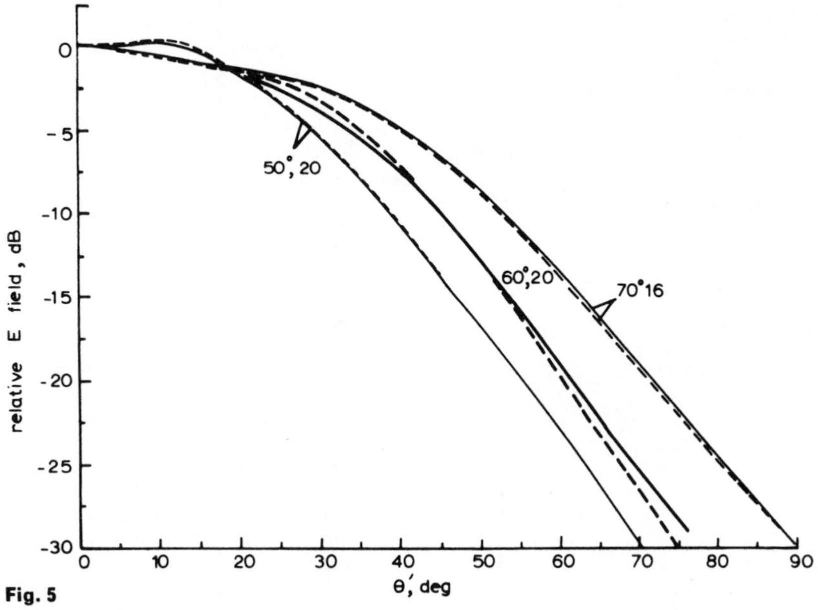

Fig. 5
E plane radiation pattern for corrugated horn
—— modal-expansion method
--- Kirchhoff–Huygen method, parameters θ_1, kR_0

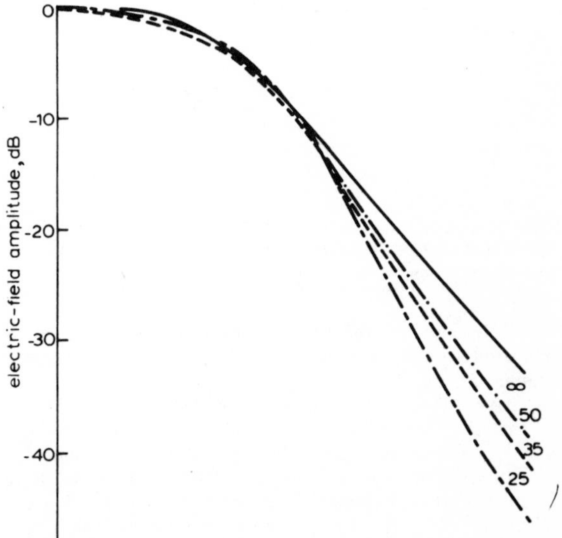

Fig. 6
Field in E plane of corrugated horn
Parameter denotes normalised distance kR from horn vertex
$kR_0 = 20$ for all values

method to determine the phase of the radiated field as in the Kirchhoff–Huygen aperture-integration method.

Although the modal-expansion method consumes more computer time than the aperture-integration method, it has the virtue of simplicity and it can be readily applied to the near-field region, where, as yet, the aperture-integration method has not been used owing to its complexity. As an example of near-field calculations, Fig. 6 shows, for $\theta_1 = 60°$, how the pattern changes with increasing distance from the horn aperture. Recently, we have made other near-field calculations and have obtained excellent agreement with experimental measurements of both amplitude and phase for horns with $\theta_1 = 12°$ and $\theta_1 = 70°$. This inspires confidence in the use of theoretically derived phase and amplitude data in the design of those dual-reflector antennas in which the subreflector lies in the horn near field.

2.3 Experimental observations of horn radiation pattern

Fig. 7 shows the two horns with $\theta_1 = 12°$ and 30°, respectively, the radiation patterns of which we have measured experimentally at frequencies between 8·5 and 11·0GHz. In both cases, balanced hybrid conditions occur at the aperture

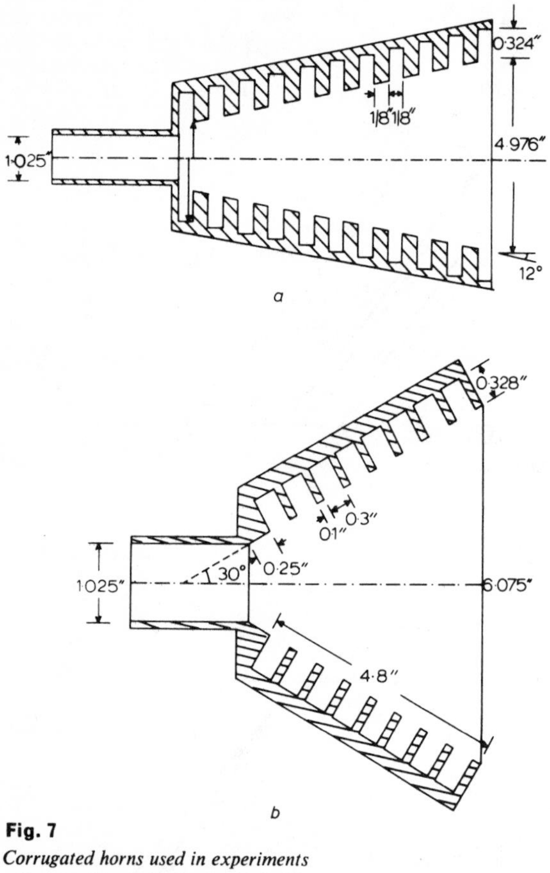

Fig. 7
Corrugated horns used in experiments
a Corrugated horn with flare semiangle 12°
b Corrugated horn with flare semiangle 30°

at 9GHz, and, for the narrow-flare horn, the slot depth is increased so that it approaches $\lambda/2$ in the throat, thereby minimising the input voltage standing-wave ratio (v.s.w.r.). We have arranged the dimensions of the slots at the throat so that $d < \lambda/2$ at 9GHz. A surface-wave condition (with $d > \lambda/2$) is not experienced at the maximum frequency of operation of our system. For the wide-flare horn, we have arranged that the slot depth is constant and that $d = \lambda/4$ at a frequency of 9GHz. Patterns were observed in both E and H planes at intervals of 0·5GHz over the above band, samples being given in Fig. 8. As the theoretical patterns were very similar in the two planes, even at the maximum frequency, the average of these has been plotted.

For the 12° horn, agreement between experimental patterns and those obtained by spherical-mode analysis is excellent up to $f = 10$GHz and lies within the accuracy of our measuring equipment. Owing to the $\lambda/5$ phase error over the plane aperture, the theoretical results from the cylindrical-mode analysis of Pt 1. agree only for observation angles near boresight and, as expected, the first null of the plane aperture pattern is filled in. At 11GHz, the agreement with theory is less satisfactory. In part, this may be accounted for by a lack of sensitivity of our apparatus at a frequency where the signal source emitted 10dB less power than at 9GHz.

For the 30° horn, agreement between predicted and measured patterns lies within experimental accuracy over the frequency bands. The v.s.w.r. has also been measured; it falls from 1·25 at 9GHz to 1·1 at 11GHz. Below 9GHz, there is a sharp increase in v.s.w.r., presumably caused by the onset of surface-wave excitation near the throat.

Since the above results were obtained, other workers have used our theory to design horns with flare angles from 9° to 70°, and, in all cases, agreement with experimental results has been uniformly satisfactory.

2.4 Lens-corrected horns

Our interest in lens-corrected corrugated horns initially stemmed from the desire to reduce the production cost of a horn to provide a narrow radiation pattern of high beam efficiency. To produce a narrow beam from a conventional radiating aperture, the aperture radius must contain many wavelengths, and the phase front should be nearly plane. These constraints imply a long narrow-flare-angle horn which, if made with corrugations throughout, proves expensive. Alternatively, one may employ a wide-angle horn with short flare length and correct the phase variations over the aperture plane; for example, by either a planoconvex lens or a meniscus lens.

The basic theory for lens-corrected horns without (corrugations) has been developed by Silver,[18] and an account of more recent techniques, including matching, has been given by Collin and Zucker.[19]

Fig. 9 shows planoconvex- and meniscus-lens-corrected horns where, for simplicity, we have omitted the horn corrugations from the diagram. From Silver[18], the following expressions are obtained relating the lens and horn parameters:

planoconvex lens

$$f = \frac{r(1 - n\cos\theta)}{1 - n} \qquad (42)$$

where $n^2 = \epsilon/\epsilon_0$ = relative permittivity of lens and f = focal length of lens.

meniscus lens

$$f = \frac{r(n - \cos\theta)}{n - 1} \qquad (43)$$

If the electric field in the horn aperture has a θ variation given by $f_v^1(\theta)$ corresponding to balanced hybrid conditions with $m = 1$, the field in the constant-phase plane is given by

$$f(\rho) = \frac{f_v^1(\theta) N_{1,2}(\theta)}{f(n-1)} \qquad (44)$$

where, for the planoconvex lens,

$$N_1(\theta) = \left\{\frac{(n\cos\theta - 1)^3}{n - \cos\theta}\right\}^{1/2} \qquad (45)$$

and, for the meniscus lens,

$$N_2(\theta) = \left\{\frac{(n - \cos\theta)^3}{n\cos\theta - 1}\right\}^{1/2} \qquad (46)$$

If $n\cos\theta - 1 = n_1(\theta)$ and $n - \cos\theta = n_2(\theta)$ and $n - \cos\theta = n_2(\theta)$, the far-field radiation pattern is obtained by integration over the aperture as follows:

$$g(\theta') = \int_0^{\theta_0} \frac{f_v^1(\theta)}{N_{1,2}(\theta)} J_0\left\{kR_0 \sin\theta' \sin\theta \frac{n_{1,2}(\theta_1)}{n_{1,2}(\theta)}\right\} \sin\theta d\theta \qquad (47)$$

where the subscripts refer to the planoconvex and meniscus lenses, respectively. Eqn. 47 is an approximate expression which is strictly valid for angles near the boresight and for apertures whose linear dimensions contain many wavelengths.

To assess the influence of lens correction, we have presented in Fig. 10 the patterns of a wide-angle corrugated horn with and without correcting lenses of the above types and a corrugated waveguide of the same aperture. All results have been obtained under balanced hybrid conditions. Evidently, the horn with a planoconvex lens does not produce a beamwidth much narrower than that of an uncorrected horn because, as Fig. 11 shows, the aperture distribution is heavily tapered. The meniscus lens has a narrower beam than an open corrugated waveguide, since the distribution is more nearly uniform.

We have investigated the dependence of the patterns on the horn flare angle as shown in Fig. 12. As the meniscus lens produces a nearly uniform aperture distribution, the pattern varies only slightly with flare angle, whereas, for the planoconvex lens, the width increases with horn flare angle. We conclude that, if a circularly symmetric radiation pattern with quite low side lobes is required, the corrugated horn with a meniscus lens provides a compact means for its realisation.

Both designs have been investigated by Green and Gill.[2] They measured the performance of a 40cm diameter planoconvex lens fed from a wide-angle corrugated horn at a frequency of 100GHz and a first side-lobe level below 30dB was observed.

For a meniscus lens of seven-wavelengths aperture, they observed a 93% main-beam efficiency at 60GHz. Sharp* constructed both types of lens-corrected horn for use in electron-scattering experiments at a frequency of 150GHz, the designs of which were based on the above theory. Results in general accordance with the theory have been observed.

We recognise that while, at centimetre wavelengths, lens-corrected corrugated horns are unlikely to find widespread application because of possible problems of matching, weight and power handling, at millimetre wavelengths, they generally have superior performance compared to reflectors.

2.5 Gain factor of corrugated-horn feed and front-fed paraboloid

An expression for the gain of a corrugated-waveguide feed was given in Pt. 1. The corresponding expression for the corrugated horn under balanced hybrid conditions is given by

$$G(\theta') = \frac{2\{F_r^2(\theta') + F_i^2(\theta')\}}{\int_0^{\pi} F_r^2(\theta) + F_i^2(\theta)|\sin\theta d\theta} \quad . \quad . \quad . \quad . \quad . \quad (48)$$

Table 4 shows, for the HE_{11} mode, the maximum gain computed from eqn. 48, using expressions for $F_{ri}(\theta)$ from eqn. 37 when θ_1 lies between 30° and 70°. Using an approximate expression for the horn-aperture field, Narasimhan and Rao[9] have investigated the dependence of axial gain on horn flare length and flare angle. Comparison with our results is only

* Private communication to authors

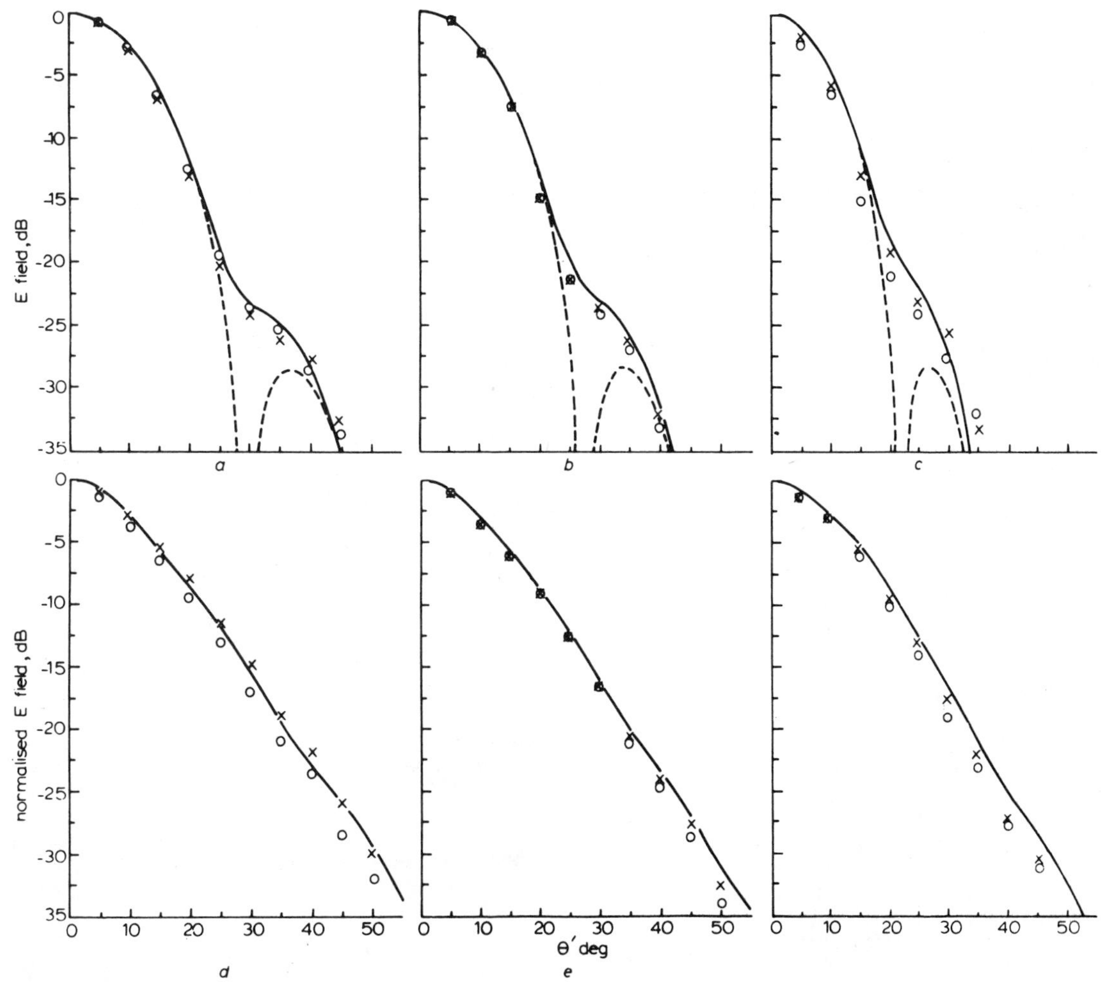

Fig. 8
Theoretical and experimentally measured radiation patterns

× *H* plane experimental points
○ *E* plane experimental points
—— theoretical average of *E* and *H* plane values obtained by spherical-mode analysis
- - - - obtained by cylindrical-mode analysis assuming constant phase over plane aperture

(*a*)–(*c*) $\theta_1 = 12°$
(*a*) $F = 8{\cdot}5$ GHz
(*b*) $F = 9{\cdot}0$ GHz
(*c*) $F = 11{\cdot}0$ GHz

(*d*)–(*f*) $\theta_1 = 30°$
(*d*) $F = 8{\cdot}5$ GHz
(*e*) $F = 9{\cdot}0$ GHz
(*f*) $F = 11{\cdot}0$ GHz

possible for the 30° horn, as the latter authors have studied mainly narrow-flare-angle horns, where their approximation $\sin \theta \simeq \theta$ is most valid. By interpolation, Narisimhan and Rao's predicted gain for $\theta_1 = 30°$ and $kR_0 = 30$ lies about

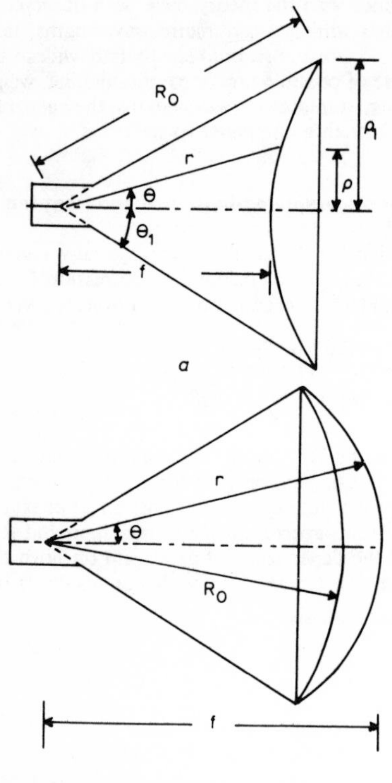

Fig. 9

Conical horns with planoconvex and meniscus lenses with corrugations omitted for clarity

a Planoconvex-lens-corrected horn
b Meniscus-lens-corrected horn

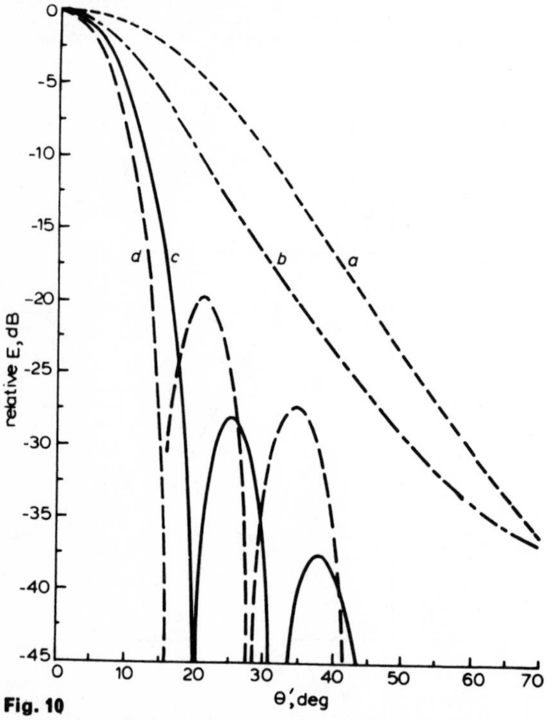

Fig. 10

Theoretical Eplane radiation pattern under balanced hybrid conditions

$\theta_1 = 40°$ uncorrected
---- $\theta_1 = 40°$ uncorrected
—·— $\theta_1 = 40°$, planoconvex lens, $n = 1{\cdot}6$
—— open-ended waveguide, $r_1/r_0 = 0{\cdot}91$
— — $\theta_1 = 40°$, meniscus lens, $n = 1{\cdot}6$

$\frac{2\pi r_i}{\lambda} = 16{\cdot}22$ in all cases

0·4dB below the value in Table 4. For most engineering purposes this accuracy is quite adequate.

Table 4

GAIN OF CORRUGATED HORNS UNDER BALANCED HYBRID

Flare semiangle θ_1	Gain
deg	dB
30°	18·4
40°	14·3
50°	13·4
60°	11·1
70°	9·8

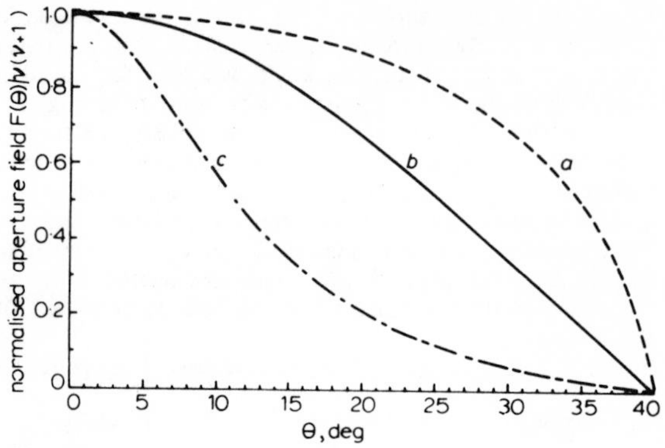

Fig. 11

Normalised aperture field as function of angle θ for corrugated horn with $\theta_1 = 40°$

— — — meniscus lens
——— uncorrected horn
— · — planoconvex lens

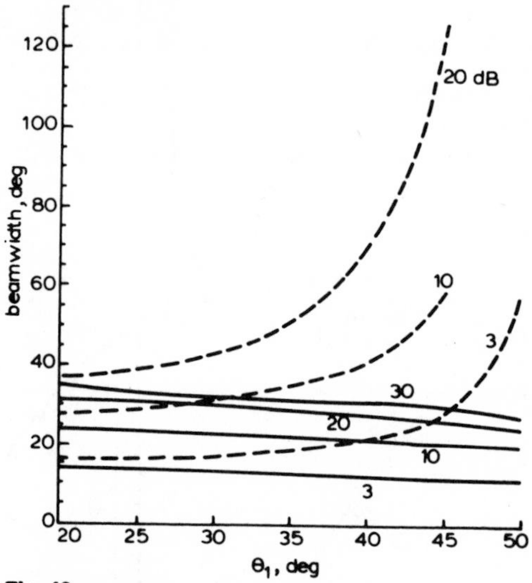

Fig. 12

Beamwidth as function of horn semiangle θ_1

——— meniscus lens, $n = 1{\cdot}6$
- - - - - planoconvex lens, $n = 1{\cdot}6$

When the horn is used as a primary feed for a parabolic-reflector antenna of semiangular aperture Ψ and with the horn phase centre at the focus, the antenna gain factor is given by

$$G_f(0) = \frac{2\cot^2\left(\frac{\Psi}{2}\right)\left|\int_0^{\Psi}\{F_r(0) + jF_i(\theta)\}\tan\frac{\theta}{2}d\theta\right|^2}{\int_0^{\pi}\{F_r^2(\theta) + F_i^2(\theta)\}\sin\theta d\theta} \qquad (49)$$

In Fig. 13 we show G_f as a function of Ψ for the five feeds of Table 4. As for the corrugated waveguide of Pt. I, the highest gain factor we have predicted is 84%. The corresponding angular aperture is 50°, and, from Fig. 4, the primary pattern taper, including space loss, is −9dB at the reflector edge. A discussion of the gain factor of a paraboloid fed from a circularly symmetric feed has been given by Silver,[19] and our results are consistent with his observations.

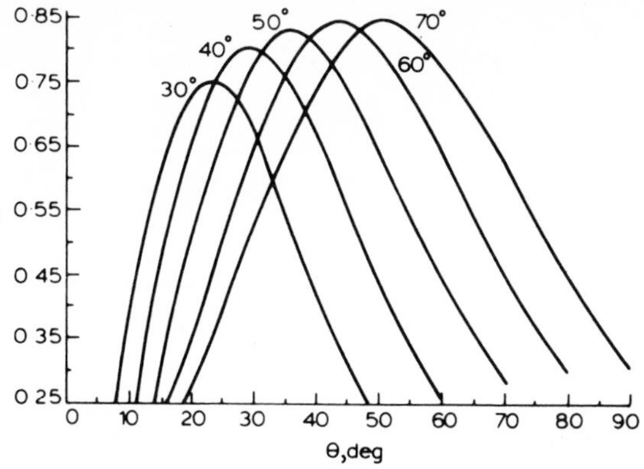

Fig. 13

Gain factor as function of observation angle θ′ for horns with θ_1 between 30° and 70°

Parameter θ_1
Corresponding values of horn gain shown in Table 4

3 Conclusions

We have determined the aperture field of corrugated conical horns from a solution of the spherical-wave equation. Radiation patterns have then been obtained by a Kirchhoff–Huygen aperture-integration method and a method which we have called modal expansion. The agreement between the theoretical patterns derived from the two methods and between theoretical and experimental results inspires considerable confidence in the accuracy of the methods. By using the above theory, corrugated horns with flare semiangles between 9° and 70° have been successfully designed. For horns with small flare angles, approximate methods of analysis[9] have provided results in substantial agreement with those obtained using the more exact spherical-mode analysis presented here. However, with the general availability of high-speed digital computers, the methods of spherical-mode analysis are simpler to apply.

Several areas of research remain open, one of which concerns the junction between a circular waveguide and corrugated horn. Although the modal-analysis methods previously developed by one of the authors[21,22] might be applied to this problem, there appear to exist substantial difficulties in providing an adequate description of the field in the throat region. The solution of this problem could yield an improved horn design with a very low input v.s.w.r. over a wide frequency bandwidth.

Another area of research concerns the design of multimode conical corrugated horns, where the additional modes are used to provide tracking information. An excellent preliminary study of this problem has been made by Viggh.[5]

Finally, we observe that corrugated horns are quite expensive to manufacture, and techniques aimed at reducing these costs justify study. We have proposed a method[14,22] whereby the slotted section of the horn is located only near the aperture. Provided the depth of the slots nearest to the throat are approximately λ/2, there then seems reason[14,22] to expect adequate performance, although it will be over a more limited frequency band. Further work on this and related topics is in progress

4 References

1 CLARRICOATS, P. J. B., and SAHA, P. K.: 'Propagation and radiation behaviour of corrugated feeds. Pt. 1—Corrugated-waveguide feed' (see p. 1167)
2 GREEN, K. A., and GILL, G. J.: 'Lens antennas for millimetre waves'. Proceedings of the Polytechnic Institute of Brooklyn symposium on submillimetre waves, March 1970, pp. 475–485
3 CLARRICOATS, P. J. B., and SAHA, P. K.: 'Radiation from wide-flare-angle scalar horns', *Electron. Lett.*, 1969, **5**, pp. 376–378
4 CLARRICOATS, P. J. B., and SAHA, P. K.: 'Radiation pattern of a lens-corrected conical scalar horn', *ibid.*, 1969, **5**, (23), pp. 592–593
5 VIGGH, M.: 'Study of design procedures and limitations for monopulse scalar feeds'. Rome Air Development Centre report RADC-TR-69-303, Nov. 1969
6 THOMAS, B. MACA.: 'Hybrid waveguide mode feeds for illumination of large focussing reflectors'. Proceedings of Radio Research Board symposium, Melbourne, Australia, Aug. 1968
7 JANSEN, J. K. N., JEUKEN, M. E. J., and LAMBRECHTSE, C. W.: 'A scalar feed'. Eindhoven University of Technology technical report 70-E-12, Dec. 1969
8 NARASIMHAN, M. S., and RAO, B. V.: 'Hybrid modes in corrugated conical horns', *Electron. Lett.*, 1970, **6**, pp. 32–34
9 NARASIMHAN, M. S., and RAO, B. V.: 'Diffraction by wide-flare-angle corrugated conical horns', *ibid.*, 1970, **6**, pp. 469–471
10 BOOKER, D.: 'A low noise feed for microwave antennas'. Ph.D. thesis, Sheffield University, Nov. 1970
11 AU, H. K.: 'Hybrid modes in corrugated conical horns with narrow flare angle and arbitrary length', *Electron. Lett.*, 1970, **6**, pp. 769–771
12 CLARRICOATS, P. J. B.: 'Similarities in the electromagnetic behaviour of optical waveguides and corrugated feeds', *ibid.*, 1970, **6**, pp. 168–180
13 THOMAS, B. MACA.: 'Bandwidth properties of corrugated conical horns', *ibid.*, 1969, **5**, pp. 561–563
14 SAHA, P. K.: 'Propagation and radiation characteristics of corrugated waveguides'. Ph.D. thesis, University of Leeds, March 1970
15 RUSCH, W. V. T.: 'Scattering from a hyperboloidal reflector in a Cassegrainian feed system', *IEEE Trans.*, 1963, **AP-11**, pp. 414–421
16 HU, Y. Y.: 'A method of determining phase centres and its application to electromagnetic horns', *J. Franklin Inst.*, 1961, pp. 31–39
17 HARRINGTON, R. F.: 'Time—harmonic electromagnetic fields' (McGraw-Hill, 1961)
18 SILVER, S.: 'Microwave antenna theory and design—Vol. 12' (McGraw-Hill, 1949)
19 COLLIN, R. E., and ZUCKER, F. J.: 'Antenna theory—Pt. 1' (McGraw-Hill, 1969)
20 CLARRICOATS, P. J. B., and SLINN, K. R.: 'Numerical solution of waveguide-discontinuity problems', *Proc. IEE*, 1967, **114**, (7), pp. 878–886
21 MASTERMAN, P. H., and CLARRICOATS, P. J. B.: 'Computer field-matching solution of waveguide transverse discontinuities', *ibid.*, 1971, **118**, (1), pp. 51–63
22 CLARRICOATS, P. J. B., and SAHA, P. K.: 'Scalar feeds for earth station antennas' *in* 'Earth station technology'. *IEE Conf. Publ.* 72, 1971, pp. 240–244

EXPERIMENTAL RADIATION PATTERN OF THE CORRUGATED CONICAL-HORN ANTENNA WITH SMALL FLARE ANGLE

An experimental study concerning the bandwidth of the conical horn antenna with small flare angle has been carried out. The conclusion is that such an antenna with small diameter has a symmetrical radiation pattern in a very small frequency range.

Recently,[1,2] the corrugated conical-horn antenna has been proposed as a feed for paraboloid-reflector antennas. The radiation pattern of this antenna is, under certain conditions, symmetrical with respect to the antenna axis. The investigation of this type of antenna is greatly facilitated by making a distinction between antennas with small and with large flare angles.[3] The theoretical radiation pattern of an antenna with a small flare angle can be found by treating it as an open circular waveguide radiator and, if necessary, with a quadratic-phase field distribution across the aperture. The radiation pattern of antennas with small flare angles and large diameters (10λ) has been studied already.[3] An important conclusion of this investigation is that these antennas possess a symmetrical radiation pattern in a frequency range of 1 : 1·3. These antennas can be used as a feed in a Cassegrain antenna, where the feed should have a small beam. Feeds in a paraboloid-reflector antenna with focal-point illumination should possess a radiation pattern with a large beamwidth, which implies that the diameter of this antenna should be much smaller than 10λ. To investigate the bandwidth of this type of antenna, we note that a symmetrical radiation pattern is obtained if $Z_z = \infty$ and $Z_\phi = 0$.[3] If we assume that there are many grooves per wavelength and that, in the grooves, only the dominant TM mode exists, then the condition for a symmetrical radiation pattern is given by (see Figs. 1A and 1B)

$$\mathscr{T}_n(kb)\,Y_n'(ka) - \mathscr{T}_n'(ka)\,Y_n(kb) = 0 \quad . \quad . \quad . \quad . \quad (1)$$

An asymptotic expansion of this expression for $n = 1$ shows that the depth of the grooves should be a quarter of a wavelength if $ka \gg 1$ and $kb \gg 1$, which is in good agreement with previous results.[3] In Fig. 1A the depth of the grooves has been plotted for small values of $2a/\lambda$ and for $n = 1$. From this curve, it is concluded that a broadband corrugated conical-horn antenna with a small flare angle can be designed only if the diameter of the aperture is large. In that case, the radiation pattern is symmetrical. However, the beamwidth is still a function of the frequency.

To verify this theory, two antennas have been constructed, one with a small diameter and the other with a large diameter. The radiation patterns have been measured. The results are given in Figs. 2A and 2B and are in agreement with expectations.

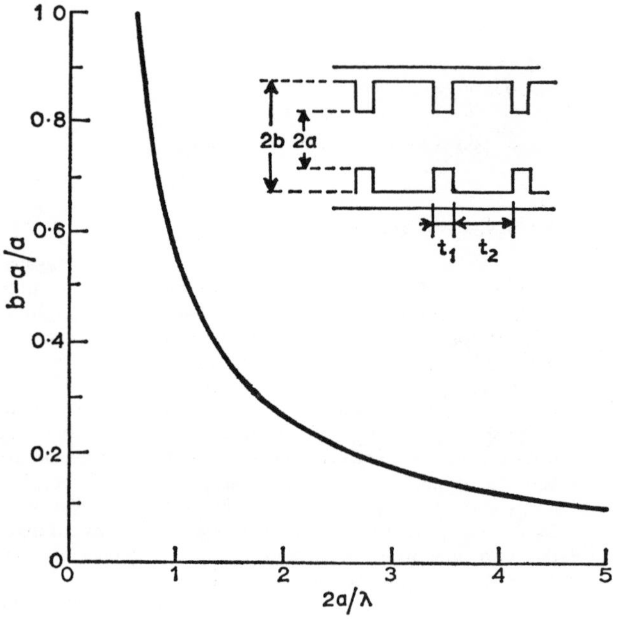

Fig. 1A *Depth of the groove against frequency; fixed diameter of waveguide*

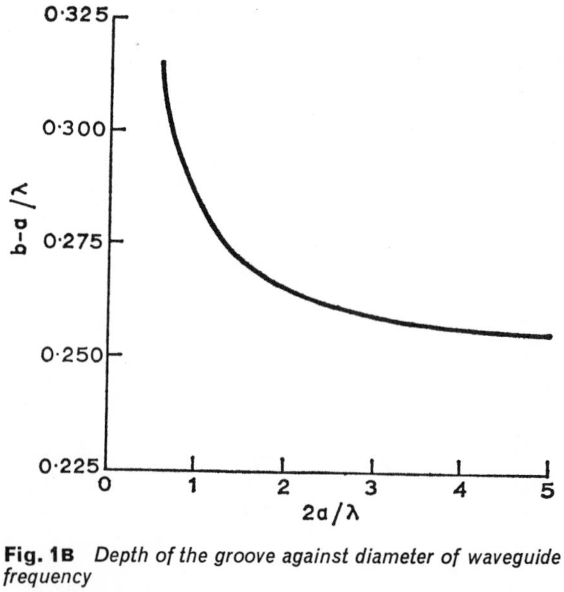

Fig. 1B *Depth of the groove against diameter of waveguide; fixed frequency*

Reprinted with permission from *Electron. Lett.*, vol. 5, pp. 484–485, Oct. 2, 1969.

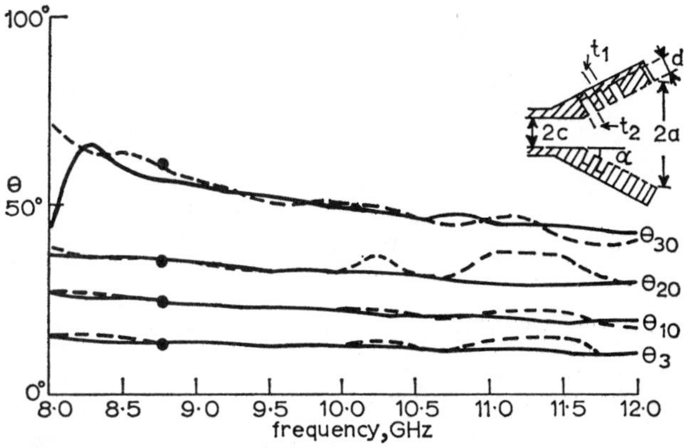

Fig. 2A *Beamwidth against frequency*

$t_1 = 2$ mm; $t_2 = 2$ mm; $2a = 91$ mm
$d = 9$ mm; $2c = 28$ mm; $\alpha = 15°$
34 grooves
○ computed, *E* plane and *H* plane
——— experimental, *H* plane
- - - - experimental, *E* plane

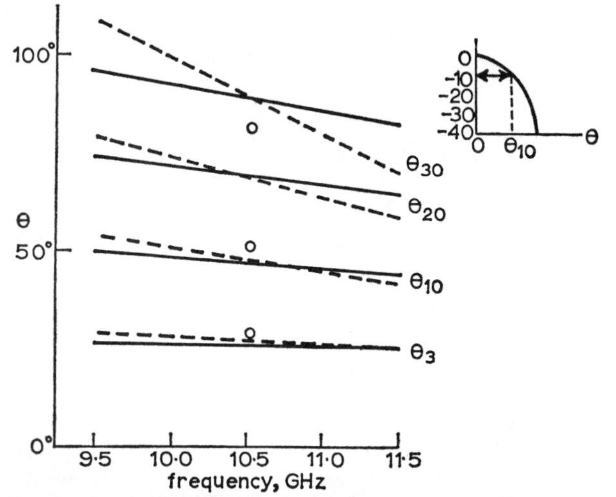

Fig. 2B *Beamwidth against frequency*

$t_1 = 1$ mm; $t_2 = 1 \cdot 5$ mm; $2a = 37$ mm
$d = 10 \cdot 5$ mm; $2c = 22$ mm; $\alpha = 12°$
4 grooves
○ computed, *E* plane and *H* plane
——— experimental, *H* plane
- - - - experimental, *E* plane

To obtain good matching, Bryant[4] proposed that the depth of the first groove at the throat of the horn should be half a wavelength. On the other hand, it is concluded from Fig. 1B that the depth of the grooves should decrease towards the aperture. In the two antennas discussed above, we have avoided the mechanical difficulties of constructing a horn antenna with variable depth of the grooves. In fact, the depth of the grooves was constant. For both antennas, the measured v.s.w.r. was lower than $1 \cdot 2$ in the frequency ranges indicated in Figs. 2A and 2B.

It is possible to compute the radiation pattern of these antennas with the theory developed in Reference 3, but only for the frequency which satisfied eqn. 1. The results of these computations are also plotted in Figs. 2A and 2B.

In conclusion, we see that the agreement between theoretical and experimental results is good only for the antenna with the large diameter. Finally, we note that, for frequencies other than the one mentioned above, the radiation pattern can be computed using the method proposed by Clarricoats and Saha.[5]

The author wishes to express his appreciation to I. C. Ongers for his help in computing the radiation pattern and to M. Knoben for the measurements carried out.

M. E. J. JEUKEN

2nd September 1969

Department of Electrical Engineering
Technological University
Insulindelaan 2, Eindhoven, Netherlands

References

1 MINETT, H. C., and THOMAS, MAC A.: 'A method of synthesizing radiation pattern with axial symmetry', *IEEE Trans.*, 1966, **AP-14**, pp. 654–656

2 SIMMONS, A. J., and KAY, A. F.: 'The scalar feed—a high performance feed for large paraboloid antenna', *IEE Conf. Publ.* 21, 1966, pp. 213–217

3 JEUKEN, M. E. J., and KIKKERT, J. S.: 'A broadband aperture antenna with a narrow beam', *Alta Frequenza*, 1969, **38**, Numero speciale, pp. 270–276

4 BRYANT, G. H.: 'Propagation in corrugated waveguides', *Proc. IEE*, 1969, **116**, pp. 203–213

5 CLARRICOATS, P. J. B., and SAHA, P. K.: 'Theoretical analysis of cylindrical hybrid modes in a corrugated horn', *Electron. Lett.*, 1969, **5**, pp. 187–189

SMALL CORRUGATED CONICAL-HORN ANTENNA WITH WIDE FLARE ANGLE

The radiation pattern of a small corrugated conical horn with a wide flare angle has been calculated by means of a Kirchhoff–Huygens integration. An assumption was made about the phase relation between the TE and the TM parts of the spherical hybrid mode in the horn. The solutions of the characteristic equation became dependent on the electrical length of the horn. Calculations and experiments showed a good agreement.

The radiation pattern of an open corrugated cylindrical waveguide is symmetrical in a small frequency range.[1] So this antenna cannot be used as a broadband feed in a paraboloid reflector with focal-point illumination. A good feed for this application has been proposed by Simmons and Kay.[2] They studied the properties of a conical-horn antenna with wide flare angle and fins perpendicular on the wall of the horn. They learnt by experiment that the radiation pattern of such an antenna is substantially constant in a frequency range of 1 : 1·6. The theoretical approach consists in replacing the wall of the antenna by an impedance plane with boundary conditions[3]

$$E_r = Z_r H_\phi \text{ and } E_\phi = Z_\phi H_r \quad . \quad . \quad . \quad . \quad . \quad . \quad (1)$$

Z_r and Z_ϕ are assumed to be frequency-independent.

The radiation pattern can be computed by means of a Kirchhoff–Huygens integration over the aperture S_A, the aperture being a segment of a sphere with radius a.

From the expressions of the far field it can be deduced that the radiation pattern will be symmetrical if the aperture fields satisfy the relations $E\phi = Z_0 H\phi$ and $E\theta = -Z_0 H\theta$. To investigate whether these conditions can be satisfied, we note that the electromagnetic field in a corrugated conical-

Reprinted with permission from *Electron. Lett.*, vol. 5, pp. 489–490, Oct. 2, 1969.

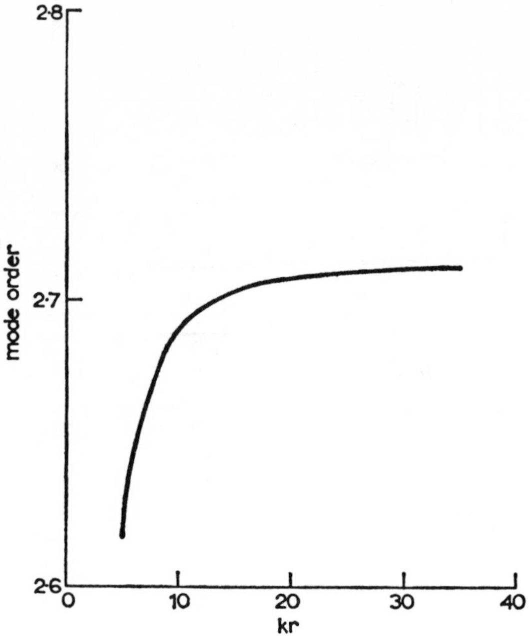

Fig. 1 *Mode order against kr*

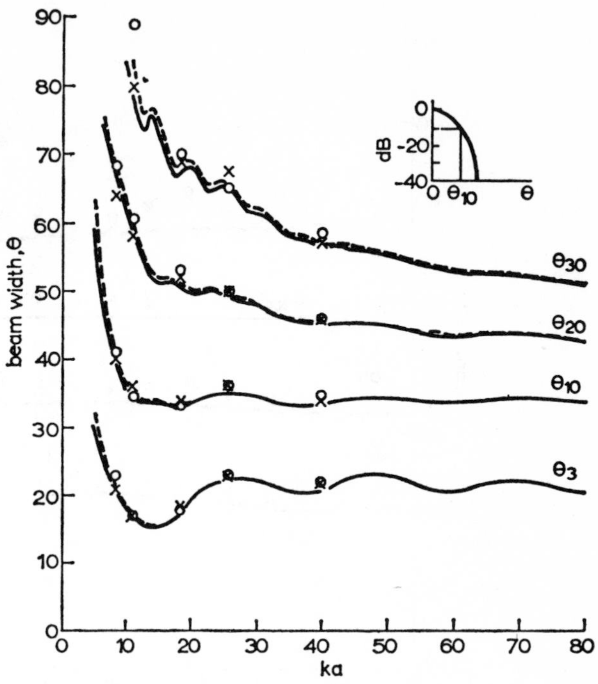

Fig. 2 *Beamwidth against ka*

——— computed, ○ experimental, *E* plane
– – – – computed, × experimental, *H* plane
For antennas A, B, C, D and E the values of *ka* are, respectively, 8·16, 10·9, 18·1, 25·4 and 39·8

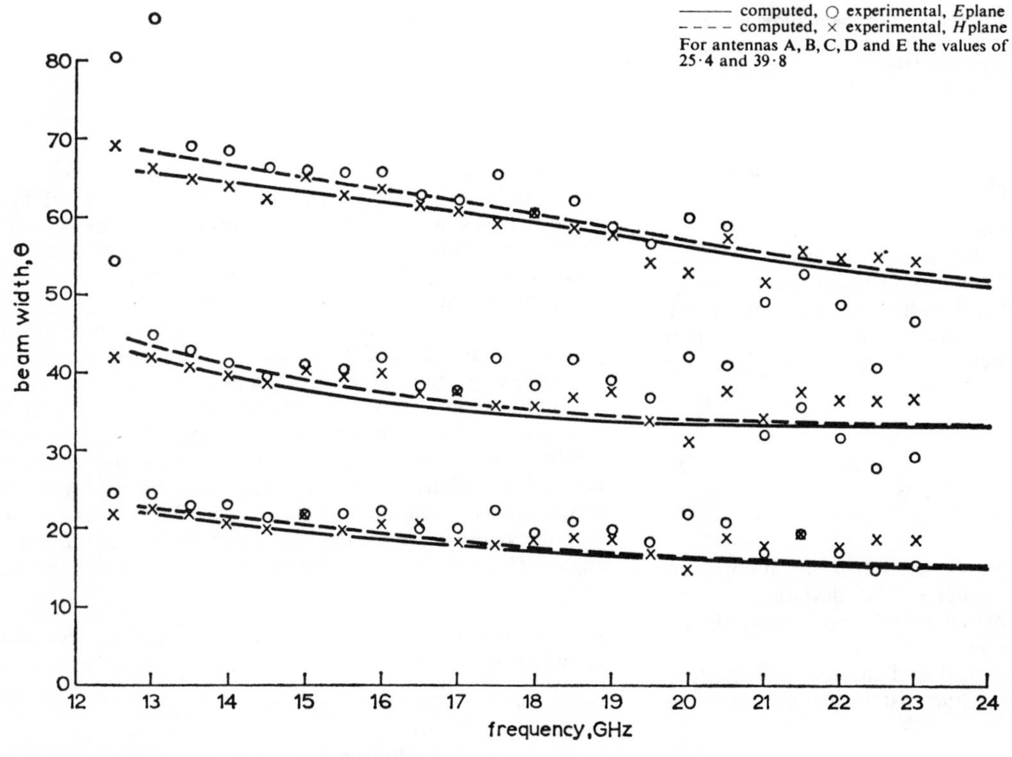

Fig. 3A *Antenna A, beamwidth against frequency*

$a = 2{\cdot}78$ cm, $d = 5{\cdot}35$ mm, $b = 2{\cdot}6$ mm
——— computed, ○ experimental, *E* plane
– – – – computed, × experimental, *H* plane

horn antenna is a spherical hybrid mode which can be derived from the potentials[4]

$$A_r = AP_\nu^1(\cos\theta)\cos\phi\hat{H}_\nu^{(2)}(kr) \quad . \quad . \quad . \quad . \quad . \quad (2)$$

$$F_r = FP_\nu^1(\cos\theta)\sin\phi\hat{H}_\nu^{(2)}(kr) \quad . \quad . \quad . \quad . \quad . \quad (3)$$

A symmetrical radiation pattern is obtained if $F/AZ_0 = 1$, provided that $Z_rZ_\phi + Z_0^2 = 0$.

Next we confine ourselves to the particular case $Z_r = \infty$, and find, for the characteristic equation,

$$\left\{\sin\theta\frac{dP_\nu^1(\cos\theta)}{d\theta} - \frac{F}{AZ_0}\frac{1}{jk\hat{H}_\nu^{(2)}(kr)}\frac{d\hat{H}_\nu^{(2)}(kr)}{dr}P_\nu^1(\cos\theta)\right\}_{\theta=\theta_0} = 0 \qquad (4)$$

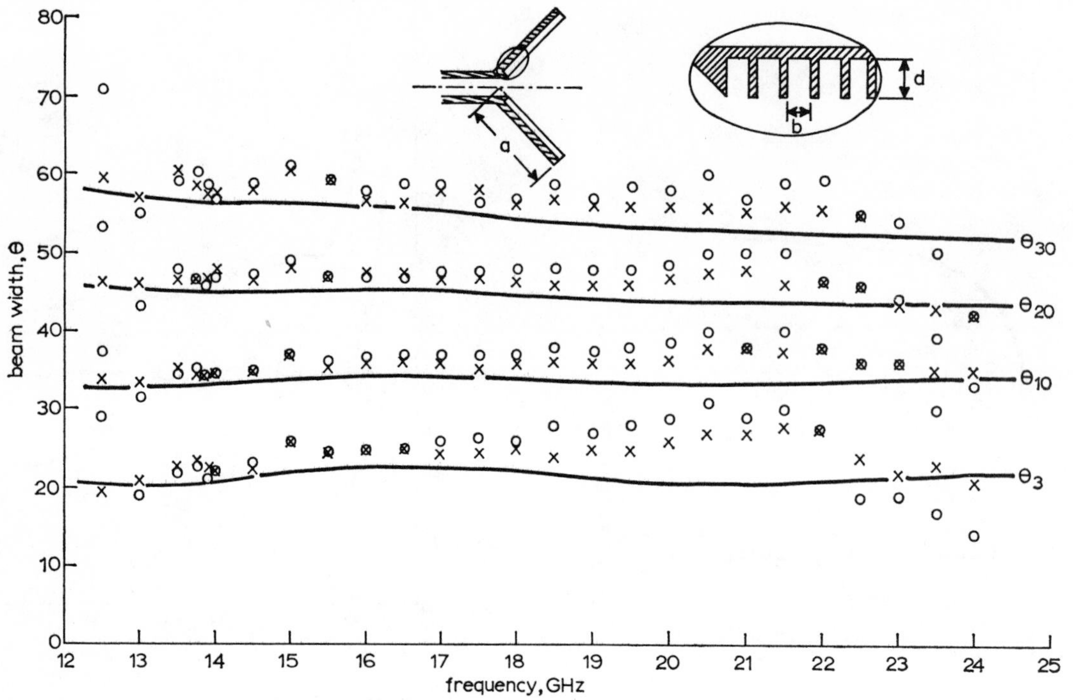

Fig. 3B *Antenna E, beamwidth against frequency*
$a = 13{\cdot}57$ cm, $d = 5{\cdot}35$ mm, $b = 2{\cdot}6$ mm
------ computed, *E*plane and *H*plane
○ experimental, *E*plane
× experimental, *H*plane

For large values of kr, $\dfrac{1}{jk\hat{H}_\nu^{(2)}(kr)}\dfrac{d\hat{H}_\nu^{(2)}(kr)}{dr}$ approaches -1 and eqn. 4 gives real values of ν.

The asymptotic expression for large kr has been dealt with by Clarricoats.[5] However, from a mechanical point of view, small antennas are desirable. Therefore we have given our attention to solutions of the characteristic equation for small kr. As these solutions will have to give real values for ν, we assume that

$$\frac{F}{AZ_0} = e^{-j(\psi-\pi)}$$

$$\psi = \arg\left\{\frac{1}{jk\hat{H}_\nu^{(2)}(kr)}\frac{d\hat{H}_\nu^{(2)}(kr)}{dr}\right\} \quad . \quad . \quad . \quad . \quad (5)$$

Although this assumption yields real values of ν, it implies a nonsymmetrical radiation pattern. The deviation of the symmetry, however, is so small that it does not deteriorate the performance of these radiators.

To calculate the aperture field and the radiation pattern of small antennas, the next characteristic equation should be solved:

$$\left\{\sin\theta\frac{dP_\nu^1(\cos\theta)}{d\theta} + \left|\frac{1}{jk\hat{H}_\nu^{(2)}(kr)}\frac{d\hat{H}_\nu^{(2)}(kr)}{dr}\right| P_\nu^1(\cos\theta)\right\}_{\theta=\theta_0} = 0 \quad . \quad . \quad . \quad . \quad (6)$$

The equation gives ν as a function of kr at a prescribed θ_0, as is shown in Fig. 2 for $\theta_0 = 45°$.

Once the equation has been solved, the radiation pattern follows after integration of the aperture fields over S_A. For comparison of computed results with experiments, five antennas have been constructed, all of which were of flare angle $\theta_0 = 45°$ but had varying length of horn. The measurements have been carried out at a frequency of 14 GHz. The height of the fins is then a quarter of a wavelength. The results are collected in Fig. 2 and are in good agreement with theoretical results. We have also measured the radiation pattern as a function of the frequency of the antennas A and E. The results are given in Figs. 3A and 3B.

From the agreement of theory and experiment, it may be concluded that the assumptions concerning both the boundary condition as well as the phase relation between the modes are justified, especially in the frequency range where the height of the fins is a quarter of a wavelength. The coincidence of theoretical and experimental results occurs also for other flare angles. This will be shown in a more extensive paper that will also contain details of the calculation.

M. E. J. JEUKEN
C. W. LAMBRECHTSE

2nd September 1969

Department of Electrical Engineering
Technological University
Insulindelaan 2, Eindhoven, Netherlands

References

1 JEUKEN, M. E. J.: 'Experimental radiation pattern of the corrugated conical-horn antenna with small flare angle' (see pp. 484–485)
2 SIMMONS, A. J., and KAY, A. F.: 'The scalar feed—a high performance feed for large paraboloid antenna', *IEE Conf. Publ.* 21, 1966, pp. 213–217
3 JEUKEN, M. E. J., and KIKKERT, J. S.: 'A broadband aperture antenna with a narrow beam', *Alta Frequenza*, 1969, **38**, Numero speciale, pp. 270–276
4 HARRINGTON, R. F.: 'Time-harmonic electromagnetic fields' (McGraw-Hill, 1961), pp. 264–269
5 CLARRICOATS, P. J. B.: 'Analysis of spherical hybrid modes in a corrugated conical horn', *Electron. Lett.*, 1969, **5**, pp. 189–190

The Scalar Feed

by JOZEF K. M. JANSEN, MARTIN E. J. JEUKEN and CEES W. LAMBRECHTSE *

The electromagnetic field in the grooves of a corrugated conical horn antenna has been investigated. The investigation starts by modifying the boundaries of the grooves in such a way that they coincide with the spherical coordinate system. Under the condition that the width of the grooves is small compared with the wavelength, the following results are obtained. The dominant mode in the grooves is a TM mode and the radiation pattern of the antenna is symmetrical with respect to the axis of the antenna, provided the depth of the grooves is a quarter of a wavelength and the right excitation has been applied. Experiments confirm the theory. The paper concludes with information concerning the design of the scalar feed.

Kegelhornantenne mit Rillen

Das elektromagnetische Feld in den Rillen einer Kegelhornantenne wird analysiert. Die Untersuchung beginnt mit der Anpassung der Wände der Rillen an ein Kugelkoordinatensystem. Unter der Voraussetzung, daß die Breite der Rillen klein gegen die Wellenlänge ist, werden folgende Ergebnisse gefunden: Die Grundwelle in den Rillen ist eine TM-Welle und die Strahlungscharakteristik der Antenne ist symmetrisch bezogen auf die Achse der Antenne, vorausgesetzt, daß die Tiefe der Rillen ein Viertel der Wellenlänge ist und die richtige Anregung angewendet wurde. Experimente bestätigen die Theorie. Der Beitrag schließt mit einer Betrachtung über den Entwurf von Kegelhornantennen mit Rillen.

1. Introduction

The illumination of a paraboloid reflector antenna depends on the properties of the feed used. In order to obtain a high efficiency it is necessary that the radiation pattern of the feed is as uniform as possible and produces little spillover energy. Besides, it is desirable that the radiation pattern of the feed is symmetrical. Finally, the feed should possess a well-defined phase centre. For some applications, for instance for an antenna for line-of-sight communications it is necessary that the feed possesses the above properties in a large frequency range. A feed having all these properties has been proposed by SIMMONS and KAY [1] and they called it "scalar feed". The scalar feed is a conical horn antenna with grooves, perpendicular to the wall of the horn. The flare angle of this feed can be small or large. The paper of SIMMONS and KAY gives only some experimental results without a theoretical explanation of the radiation pattern of the scalar feed. Moreover this paper does not contain useful design information concerning the scalar feed. This is mainly caused by the fact that a theoretical explanation of the radiation pattern of these feeds was not available at the moment of publication.

The investigation of the scalar feed is greatly facilitated by making a distinction between scalar feeds with a small and with a large flare angle. The radiation pattern of a scalar feed with small flare angle can be found by treating it as an open circular waveguide radiator and, if necessary, with a quadratic phase field distribution across the aperture. This has already been done by JEUKEN and KIKKERT [2]. They studied, both theoretically and experimentally, the radiation pattern of a conical horn antenna with small flare angle. The inner wall of the cone consisted of a corrugated boundary, composed of circumferential grooves. They found a good agreement between the experimental and theoretical radiation pattern for the frequency range where the depth of the grooves was approximately a quarter of a wavelength. In the paper [2] the effect of the corrugations has been described by means of an impedance boundary condition and the detailed behaviour of the electromagnetic fields in the grooves was not considered.

Especially the frequency-dependent behaviour of the electromagnetic field in the grooves has not been taken into account. Therefore it was not possible to find a theoretical explanation of the fact that the antenna has a symmetrical radiation pattern in a frequency range where the depth of the grooves is approximately a quarter of a wavelength. An explanation of this phenomenon can be found by considering a corrugated cylindrical waveguide with grooves perpendicular to the wall of the waveguide. Each groove can be considered as a short-circuited radial waveguide. The modes in a radial waveguide can be classified as TE-modes and TM-modes with respect to the z-axis which is perpendicular to the direction of propagation [3]. If the distance between the fins of a groove is smaller than half a wavelength then a TM-mode and the dominant mode can propagate in the radial waveguide. Owing to the excitation only the TM-mode is excited [4]

If the circular waveguide has a diameter which is large compared to the wavelength, then it can be proved that the depth of the grooves should be a quarter of a wavelength in order to obtain a symmetrical power radiation pattern [4]. Using the above model CLARRICOATS and SAHA [5] were able to calculate the power radiation pattern of an open

* Ir. J. K. M. JANSEN, c/o Department of Mathematics, Dr. M. E. J. JEUKEN and Ir. C. W. LAMBRECHTSE, c/o Department of Electrical Engineering, Technological University, Eindhoven, Netherlands.

Reprinted with permission from *Arch. Elek. Übertragung.*, vol. 26, pp. 22–30, Jan. 1972.

circular corrugated waveguide as a function of frequency. It should be noted that their results apply also to corrugated conical horn antennas with small flare angle [6].

Clarricoats [7] formulated the boundary conditions which should be applied in a corrugated conical horn antenna with large flare angle. He assumed that the grooves were perpendicular to the axis of the antenna. However, no information is available concerning the question whether this model can also be used for corrugated conical horn antennas with wide flare angles and grooves perpendicular to the wall of the antenna [8].

Summarising, we may say that there is a need of a better understanding of the effect of the corrugation, especially for antennas with wide flare angle. Moreover, it is desirable to compute the radiation pattern of the scalar feed with large flare angle in order to obtain useful design information concerning this feed. It is the purpose of the present paper to provide this information.

2. The Electromagnetic Field in the Groove

The scalar feed is a conical horn antenna with grooves perpendicular to the wall of the horn (Fig. 1).

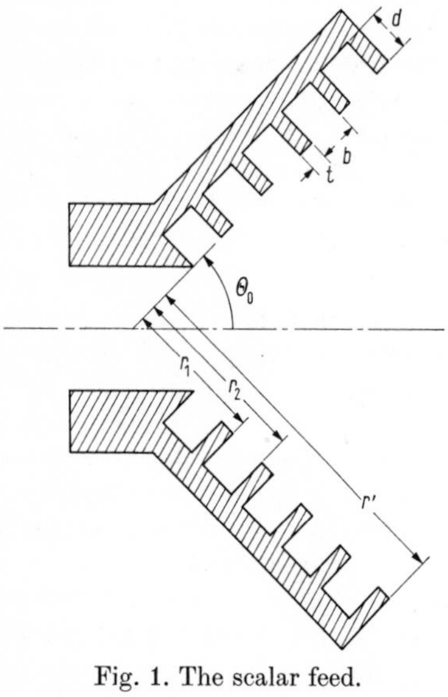

Fig. 1. The scalar feed.

The computation of the electromagnetic field in a groove is a difficult task, because the boundaries of the groove do not coincide with a coordinate system in which Maxwell's equations can be easily solved. Therefore, we change the boundaries of the groove in such a way that they coincide with the spherical coordinate system. For a groove not to close to the apex of the cone this is a good approximation.

One such groove is sketched in Fig. 2.

2.1. *The characteristic equation of the TM-mode*

In this section we shall study the conditions under which a TM-mode can propagate in a groove.

The TM-mode in the groove can be derived from the potential $A_r(r, \theta, \varphi)$ [9] by means of the following expressions

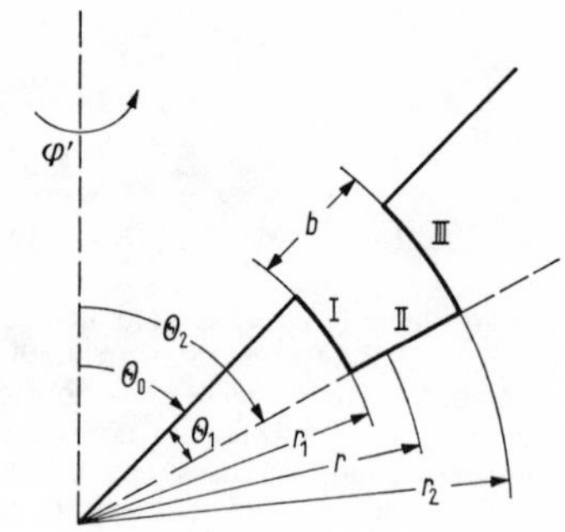

Fig. 2. Spherical groove and spherical coordinate system.

$$E_r = \frac{1}{\mathrm{j}\,\omega\,\varepsilon_0}\left(\frac{\partial^2}{\partial r^2} + k^2\right)A_r, \qquad H_r = 0, \tag{1}$$

$$E_\theta = \frac{1}{\mathrm{j}\,\omega\,\varepsilon_0}\,\frac{1}{r}\,\frac{\partial^2 A_r}{\partial r\,\partial\theta}, \qquad H_\theta = \frac{1}{r\sin\theta}\,\frac{\partial A_r}{\partial\varphi},$$

$$E_\varphi = \frac{1}{\mathrm{j}\,\omega\,\varepsilon_0}\,\frac{1}{r\sin\theta}\,\frac{\partial^2 A_r}{\partial r\,\partial\varphi}, \qquad H_\varphi = -\frac{1}{r}\,\frac{\partial A_r}{\partial\theta}.$$

The function $A_r(r, \theta, \varphi)$ has the form

$$\begin{aligned} A_r(r, \theta, \varphi) = {} & k\,r\,[a_n\,\mathrm{j}_n(k\,r) + b_n\,\mathrm{y}_n(k\,r)] \times \\ & \times [c_{nm}\,\mathrm{P}_n^m(\cos\theta) + d_{nm}\,\mathrm{Q}_n^m(\cos\theta)] \times \\ & \times (e_m\cos m\,\varphi + f_m\sin m\,\varphi)\,. \end{aligned} \tag{2}$$

In this expression the symbols used have the following meaning

$\mathrm{j}_n(k\,r)$, $\mathrm{y}_n(k\,r)$ are the spherical Bessel function and the spherical Neumann function, respectively.

$\mathrm{P}_n^m(\cos\theta)$, $\mathrm{Q}_n^m(\cos\theta)$ are the associated Legendre functions of the first kind and the second kind, respectively.

$a_n, b_n, c_{nm}, d_{nm}, e_m, f_m$ are constants which are determined by the boundary conditions and the strength of the electromagnetic field at the opening of the groove $\theta = \theta_0$.

The value of m depends on the way in which the electromagnetic field in the groove is excited. In most practical cases we have $m = 1$.

Application of the boundary condition $E_\varphi = 0$ for the boundaries I and III gives rise to the next equation

$$\begin{vmatrix} \mathrm{j}_n(k\,r_1) + k\,r_1\,\mathrm{j}_n'(k\,r_1) & \mathrm{y}_n(k\,r_1) + k\,r_1\,\mathrm{y}_n'(k\,r_1) \\ \mathrm{j}_n(k\,r_2) + k\,r_2\,\mathrm{j}_n'(k\,r_2) & \mathrm{y}_n(k\,r_2) + k\,r_2\,\mathrm{y}_n'(k\,r_2) \end{vmatrix} = 0\,. \tag{3}$$

A special solution exists if $k\,b = \pi$; then $n = 0$. If there is a solution of eq. (3), then $A_r(r, \theta, \varphi)$ has the form

$$\begin{aligned} A_r(r, \theta, \varphi) = {} & k\,r\{[\mathrm{y}_n(k\,r_1) + k\,r_1\,\mathrm{y}_n'(k\,r_1)]\,\mathrm{j}_n(k\,r) - \\ & - [\mathrm{j}_n(k\,r_1) + k\,r_1\,\mathrm{j}_n'(k\,r_1)]\,\mathrm{y}_n(k\,r)\} \times \\ & \times [\mathrm{Q}_n^m(\cos\theta_2)\,\mathrm{P}_n^m(\cos\theta) - \mathrm{P}_n^m(\cos\theta_2)\,\mathrm{Q}_n^m(\cos\theta)] \times \\ & \times (e_m\cos m\,\varphi + f_m\sin m\,\varphi)\,. \end{aligned} \tag{4}$$

In the derivation of eq. (4) use has been made of the boundary conditions $E_\varphi = 0$ for $\theta = \theta_2$ and $E_r = 0$ for $\theta = \theta_2$.

We see that eq. (4) represents two independent solutions; one with $f_m = 0$ and the other with $e_m = 0$. Next, we assume that the width of the groove is small compared with the wavelength, so $kb \ll 1$. We apply the recurrence formulas [10]

$$f_n'(x) = \frac{n}{x} f_n(x) - f_{n+1}(x)\,, \qquad f_n'(x) = f_{n-1}(x) - \frac{n+1}{x}\, f_n(x) \tag{5}$$

where $f_n(x)$ stands for $\mathrm{j}_n(x)$, $\mathrm{y}_n(x)$, respectively.

Next we define $k r_1 = x$, $k b = h$, and $k r_2 = x + h$. Using the expansions

$$\mathrm{j}_n(x+h) = \mathrm{j}_n(x) + h\,\mathrm{j}_n'(x) + 0(h^2)\,,$$
$$\mathrm{y}_n(x+h) = \mathrm{y}_n(x) + h\mathrm{y}_n'(x) + 0(h^2)$$

in eq. (3) we obtain the equation

$$(-hx)\left[\frac{n(n+1)}{x} - x\right] \begin{vmatrix} \mathrm{j}_{n+1}(x) & \mathrm{y}_{n+1}(x) \\ \mathrm{j}_n(x) & \mathrm{y}_n(x) \end{vmatrix} = = -\frac{h}{x^2}\,[n(n+1) - x^2] = 0\,. \tag{6}$$

So the solution of eq. (3) for small values of kb is given by

$$n(n+1) = (k r_1)^2 \tag{7}$$

or

$$n = -\frac{1}{2} \pm \left[\frac{1}{4} + (k r_1)^2\right]^{1/2}. \tag{8}$$

In the following considerations we shall omit the minus sign because it represents the same solution as the plus sign. From eq. (8) we now see that

$$n \approx k r_1 \quad \text{if} \quad k r_1 \gg 1 \quad \text{and} \quad kb \ll 1\,. \tag{9}$$

This result will be used in the following section. In conclusion, we see that a TM-mode can exist in the groove even if its width is small compared with the wavelength.

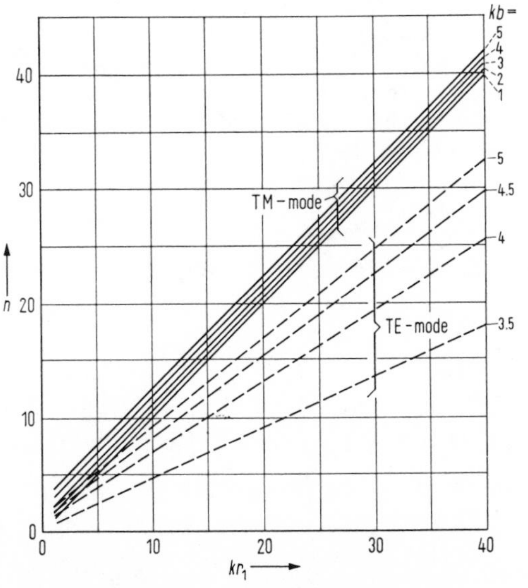

Fig. 3. n versus kr_1 with kb as parameter.

A numerical analysis of eq. (3), based on the method described in [11] gives n as a function of kr_1, for several values of kb. The results are collected in Fig. 3. Note that n is approximately a linear function of kr_1, which is in agreement with eq. (9).

A similar investigation can be carried out with the aim to find the conditions under which a TE-mode can propagate in a groove. The details of this investigation are given in [11]. The main conclusion is that a TE-mode cannot propagate in a groove, if the width of the groove is smaller than half a wavelength.

2.2. *The components of the electromagnetic field of the TM-mode*

From the preceding considerations we know that only a TM-mode can exist in the groove, provided the width of the groove is smaller than half a wavelength. So it is now interesting to investigate the components of the electromagnetic field of this mode in more detail.

In section 4 of the paper we shall prove that the boundary conditions $E_\varphi = 0$ and $Z_0 H_\varphi = 0$ give rise to a symmetrical radiation pattern. Therefore, we shall first investigate the conditions under which $Z_0 H_\varphi = 0$. From the general expression of A_r, eq. (4), we see that $Z_0 H_\varphi = 0$, if we can find a value of θ_0 which satisfies the equation

$$\mathrm{P}_n^{m\prime}(\cos\theta_0)\,\mathrm{Q}_n^m(\cos\theta_2) - \mathrm{P}_n^m(\cos\theta_2)\,\mathrm{Q}_n^{m\prime}(\cos\theta_0) = 0 \tag{10}$$

where the prime means differentiating with respect to the argument. Useful insight into the behaviour of the groove can be obtained if for the moment we restrict our considerations to the case that $kb \ll 1$ and $kr_1 \gg 1$. Then we know from eq. (9) that $n \gg 1$.

So an asymptotic expansion of $\mathrm{P}_n^m(\cos\theta)$ and $\mathrm{Q}_n^m(\cos\theta)$ can be substituted in eq. (10). These expansions are [12]

$$\mathrm{P}_n^m(\cos\theta) = \frac{\Gamma(m+n+1)}{\Gamma(n+3/2)}\left(\frac{\pi}{2}\sin\theta\right)^{-1/2} \times \times \cos\left[\left(n+\frac{1}{2}\right)\theta - \frac{\pi}{4} - \frac{m\pi}{2}\right] + 0\left(\frac{1}{n}\right), \tag{11}$$

$$\mathrm{Q}_n^m(\cos\theta) = \frac{\Gamma(m+n+1)}{\Gamma(n+3/2)}\left(\frac{\pi}{2\sin\theta}\right)^{1/2} \times \times \cos\left[\left(n+\frac{1}{2}\right)\theta + \frac{\pi}{4} + \frac{m\pi}{2}\right] + 0\left(\frac{1}{n}\right). \tag{12}$$

Substitution of eqs. (11) and (12) in eq. (10) and using the relation [13]

$$L_n^{m\prime}(u) = \frac{-mu}{1-u^2}\,L_n^m(u) - \frac{1}{(1-u^2)^{1/2}}\,L_n^{m+1}(u) \tag{13}$$

where $L_n^m(u)$ stands for $\mathrm{P}_n^m(u)$ or $\mathrm{Q}_n^m(u)$, we find after several algebraical manipulations

$$\tan\left(n+\frac{1}{2}\right)(\theta_2 - \theta_0) = \tan\left(n+\frac{1}{2}\right)\theta_1 = = (n+2)\tan\theta_0\,. \tag{14}$$

The solution of this equation is

$$\theta_1 = \frac{\arctan[(n+2)\tan\theta_0] + l\pi}{n+\frac{1}{2}}; \quad (15)$$

$$l = 0, 1, 2, \ldots$$

and for large values of n and θ_0 the approximation $\theta_1 \equiv \frac{\pi(2l+1)}{2n}$ is valid. We know that $n \approx kr_1$, so

$$\theta_1 = \frac{\pi(2l+1)}{2kr_1}. \quad (16)$$

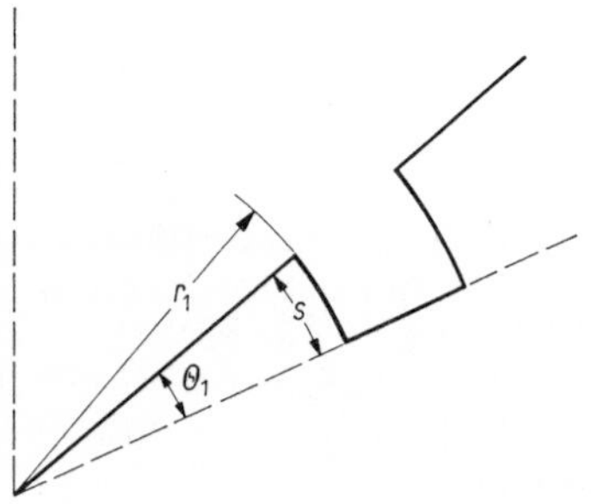

Fig. 4. Spherical groove with definition of s.

The depth of the groove s (Fig. 4) is now given by

$$s = r_1\theta_1 = \frac{\pi(2l+1)}{2k} = \frac{\lambda}{4}(2l+1) \quad (17)$$

and the important conclusion can be drawn that the depth of the groove should be the same for all grooves that are far enough from the apex of the cone.

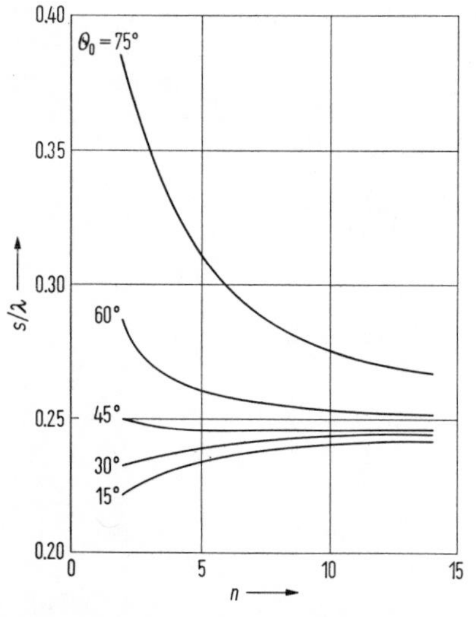

Fig. 5. s/λ versus n with flare angle θ_0 as parameter.

In the proof of eq. (17) we have assumed that the flare angle θ_0 is large enough. So there is need for an exact computation of the depth of the groove under the condition that $Z_0 H_\varphi = 0$ at the opening of the groove. Such a computation can be carried out starting from the Runge-Kutta method and is described in some detail in [11]. The results are given in Fig. 5 and we may draw the following conclusions:

i) for grooves for which $n > 15$, the depth of the grooves can be found using eq. (17);
ii) for grooves for which $5 < n < 15$, the depth of the grooves is virtually independent of θ_0 if $\theta_0 > 30°$;
iii) for grooves characterized by a low value of n and a low value of θ_0 we see that the depth of the grooves is a function of both n and θ_0.

So it is always possible to design the grooves in such a way that $Z_0 H_\varphi = 0$ at the opening of the grooves. Let us now study the electric field at the opening of the grooves. First we note that $E_\theta = 0$ if $Z_0 H_\varphi = 0$. For the case of $kb \ll 1$ some useful results can be derived from the general expressions (1) and (4). After a large amount of algebra we find

$$\frac{\mathrm{d}A_r}{\mathrm{d}(kr)} = \frac{(r-r_1)^2}{(kr_1)^2}[n(n+1) - (kr_1)^2]. \quad (18)$$

Using eqs. (1) and (6) we see that E_φ is zero in the groove. In the proof of eq. (18) use has been made of the same Taylor expansion, which has also been used in the derivation of eq. (6). This expansion is not valid for low values of kr_1. So, for grooves in the vicinity of the apex of the cone E_φ cannot be neglected.

However, extensive calculations, which are not included, show that $E_\varphi/E_r < 10^{-3}$ for $kr < 10$ and $kb \approx 1$.

2.3. *The boundary conditions at the wall of the corrugated horn*

The electromagnetic field at the opening of a narrow groove consists of the dominant TM-mode and evanescent modes. Experience teaches us that calculations concerning corrugated boundaries give useful results if the evanescent modes are neglected [14]. Suppose that there are many grooves per wavelength. Then we may formulate the boundary conditions at $\theta = \theta_0$ in terms of two impedances Z_φ and Z_r, defined by the relations

$$E_\varphi = Z_\varphi H_r, \quad E_r = Z_r H_\varphi. \quad (19)$$

We know that E_φ is zero at the opening of the grooves and at the dams, while currents in the φ-direction are possible. Hence $H_r \neq 0$ and $Z_\varphi = 0$. If we assume that the width of the dams is negligible, then we may write

$$Z_r = \frac{E_r}{H_\varphi} = -\frac{1}{\mathrm{j}\omega\varepsilon_0}\frac{n(n+1)}{r}A_r\left(\frac{\partial A_r}{\partial\theta}\right)^{-1} \quad (20)$$

with A_r given in eq. (4). Using $k^2r^2 \sim n(n+1)$ we find

$$Z_r = \frac{k^2 r}{\mathrm{j}\omega\varepsilon_0} \times \quad (21)$$
$$\times \frac{\mathrm{Q}_n^1(\cos\theta_2)\,\mathrm{P}_n^1(\cos\theta_0) - \mathrm{P}_n^1(\cos\theta_2)\mathrm{Q}_n^1(\cos\theta_0)}{\sin\theta_0[\mathrm{Q}_n^1(\cos\theta_2)\,\mathrm{P}_n^{1\prime}(\cos\theta_0) - \mathrm{P}_n^1(\cos\theta_2)\mathrm{Q}_n^{1\prime}(\cos\theta_0)]}.$$

Substitution of the expressions (11) and (12) in eq. (21) gives

$$Z_r \approx -\mathrm{j}Z_0\tan ks. \quad (22)$$

For the special case where the depth of the groove is a quarter of a wavelength we find $Z_r = \infty$.

3. The Electromagnetic Field in the Corrugated Conical Horn

Up till now we have studied the boundary conditions which should be applied at the boundary $\theta' = \theta_0$ for the calculation of the electromagnetic field in the region bounded by $\theta' < \theta_0$. Next we shall investigate which modes can exist in the corrugated horn. We observe that the boundary conditions can be satisfied with φ-independent TM-modes and TE-modes. However, these modes give rise to a dip in the radiation pattern in the forward direction and are not often used for antenna applications. In general, the electromagnetic field in the region $\theta' < \theta_0$ is a spherical hybrid mode. This mode can be understood as the sum of a TE-mode and a TM-mode. The components of this hybrid mode can be found from the potentials [9]

$$A_r(r', \theta', \varphi') = A_1 \mathrm{P}_\nu^1(\cos\theta') \cos\varphi' \,\hat{\mathrm{H}}_\nu^{(2)}(kr'), \qquad (23)$$
$$F_r(r', \theta', \varphi') = A_2 \mathrm{P}_\nu^1(\cos\theta') \sin\varphi' \,\hat{\mathrm{H}}_\nu^{(2)}(kr')$$

and summing the TE-part and TM-part. In eqs. (23) $\hat{\mathrm{H}}_\nu^{(2)}(kr')$ represents the spherical Hankel function of the second kind. It should be noted that primed coordinates are used for the description of the electromagnetic field in the horn. For the electromagnetic field in the grooves we have used unprimed coordinates. Finally, the coordinates of a point outside the horn antenna will be unprimed again. For the components of the spherical hybrid mode we now find

$$E_{r'} = \alpha(kr') \frac{\nu(\nu+1)}{\mathrm{j}kr'} \mathrm{P}_\nu^1(\cos\theta') \cos\varphi', \qquad (24)$$

$$E_{\theta'} = \alpha(kr') \left[\frac{\mathrm{dP}_\nu^1(\cos\theta')}{\mathrm{d}\theta'} \xi_\nu(kr') - \delta \frac{\mathrm{P}_\nu^1(\cos\theta')}{\sin\theta'}\right] \cos\varphi', \qquad (25)$$

$$E_{\varphi'} = \alpha(kr') \left[\frac{\mathrm{P}_\nu^1(\cos\theta')}{\sin\theta'} \xi_\nu(kr') + \delta \frac{\mathrm{dP}_\nu^1(\cos\theta')}{\mathrm{d}\theta'}\right] \sin\varphi', \qquad (26)$$

$$Z_0 H_{r'} = \alpha(kr')\, \delta \frac{\nu(\nu+1)}{\mathrm{j}kr'} \mathrm{P}_\nu^1(\cos\theta') \sin\varphi', \qquad (27)$$

$$Z_0 H_{\theta'} = \alpha(kr') \left[\delta \frac{\mathrm{dP}_\nu^1(\cos\theta')}{\mathrm{d}\theta'} \xi_\nu(kr') - \frac{\mathrm{P}_\nu^1(\cos\theta')}{\sin\theta'}\right] \sin\varphi', \qquad (28)$$

$$Z_0 H_{\varphi'} = \alpha(kr') \left[\frac{\mathrm{dP}_\nu^1(\cos\theta')}{\mathrm{d}\theta} + \delta\, \xi_\nu(kr') \frac{\mathrm{P}_\nu^1(\cos\theta')}{\sin\theta}\right] \cos\varphi' \qquad (29)$$

with the abbreviations

$$\alpha(kr') = \frac{A_1 Z_0 \hat{\mathrm{H}}_\nu^{(2)}(kr')}{r'},$$
$$\xi_\nu(kr') = \frac{\mathrm{d}\hat{\mathrm{H}}_\nu^{(2)}(kr')}{\mathrm{j}k\,\mathrm{d}r'} \frac{1}{\hat{\mathrm{H}}_\nu^{(2)}(kr')}, \qquad (30)$$
$$\delta = A_2 / A_1 Z_0 .$$

In the expressions (24) to (29) the unknown quantities are δ and ν. Using the asymptotic expansion of $\hat{\mathrm{H}}_\nu^{(2)}(kr')$ we see that $\lim_{kr' \to \infty} \xi_\nu(kr') = -1$. For a point not too close to the apex of the cone we assume that $\xi_\nu(kr') \approx -1$.

The boundary condition $Z_\varphi = 0$ gives the relation

$$\left.\frac{\mathrm{P}_\nu^1(\cos\theta)}{\sin\theta} + \delta \frac{\mathrm{dP}_\nu^1(\cos\theta)}{\mathrm{d}\theta}\right|_{\theta = \theta_0} = 0 . \qquad (31)$$

The boundary condition $E_{r'} = Z_r H_{\varphi'}$ gives rise to the equation for ν

$$\left.\frac{-\nu(\nu+1)}{\mathrm{j}kr'} \frac{Z_0}{Z_r} \mathrm{P}_\nu^1(\cos\theta) \frac{\mathrm{dP}_\nu^1(\cos\theta)}{\mathrm{d}\theta} - \left[\frac{\mathrm{dP}_\nu^1(\cos\theta)}{\mathrm{d}\theta}\right]^2 + \left[\frac{\mathrm{P}_\nu^1(\cos\theta)}{\sin\theta}\right]^2\right|_{\theta = \theta_0} = 0 . \qquad (32)$$

This equation contains the variable r' which implies that ν is a function of r'. However, this is not possible because in eq. (23) the assumption has been made that the method of separation of variables can be applied. Hence eq. (32) can be solved only if we assume that $Z_r = \infty$. This assumption implies that the depth of the grooves is a quarter of a wavelength. It should be emphasised that up till now no solutions of Maxwell's equations for a corrugated conical horn with a boundary condition given by eqs. (19) and (21) has been found. For the special case $Z_r = \infty$ we find $A_2 = \pm Z_0 A_1$. So two classes of modes can propagated in the corrugated conical horn. The modes for which $A_2 = Z_0 A_1$ are called $HE_{1\nu}^{(1)}$-modes, while the other modes are $HE_{1\nu}^{(2)}$-modes.

Finally we find for the characteristic equation

$$\left.\frac{\mathrm{dP}_\nu^1(\cos\theta')}{\mathrm{d}\theta'} \pm \frac{\mathrm{P}_\nu^1(\cos\theta')}{\sin\theta'}\right|_{\theta = \theta_0} = 0 . \qquad (33)$$

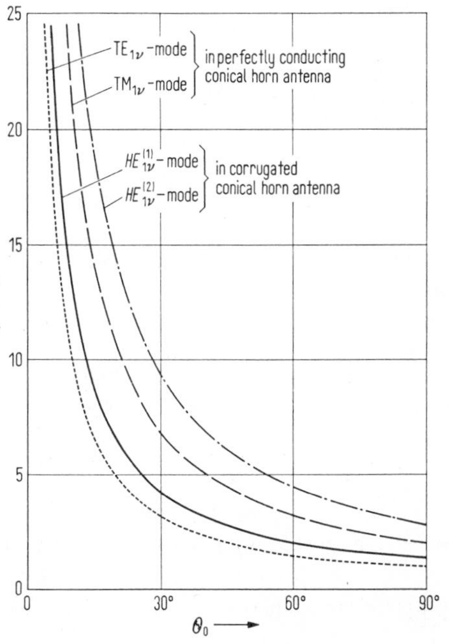

Fig. 6. ν versus flare angle θ_0 for several modes.

We have solved eq. (33) for the lowest value ν. The results are plotted in Fig. 6. For purposes of comparison we have also plotted the value of ν of the $TE_{1\nu}$-mode and the $TM_{1\nu}$-mode in a perfectly conducting conical horn. The function $\xi_\nu(kr')$ has also been computed for finite values of kr' and for those values of ν which occur for the $HE_{1\nu}^{(1)}$-mode in a very large horn and with flare angles $\theta_0 = 15°$, $30°$, $45°$, $60°$, and $75°$. The results are plotted in Fig. 7 and show that the approximation $\xi_\nu(kr') \approx -1$ is valid even for rather low values of kr'.

Let us now calculate the transverse electric and magnetic field components of the $HE_{1\nu}^{(1)}$-mode. Substitution of $A_1 Z_0 = A_2$ in eqs. (25), (26), (28), and (29) gives

$$E_{\theta'} = g_{1\nu}^{(1)}(r', \theta') \cos\varphi', \quad E_{\varphi'} = -\, g_{1\nu}^{(1)}(r', \theta') \sin\varphi',$$
$$Z_0 H_{\theta'} = -\, E_{\varphi'}, \qquad Z_0 H_{\varphi'} = E_{\theta'} \tag{34}$$

with $g_{1\nu}^{(1)}(r', \theta') = -\, \alpha(kr')\, f_{1\nu}^{(1)}(\theta')$,

$$f_{1\nu}^{(1)}(\theta') = \frac{\mathrm{d}P_\nu^1(\cos\theta')}{\mathrm{d}\theta'} + \frac{P_\nu^1(\cos\theta')}{\sin\theta'}.$$

Comparing eq. (33) with eq. (34) we see that all the transverse electric and magnetic components are zero for $\theta' = \theta_0$.

For the sake of completeness we also give the transverse electric and magnetic field components of the $HE_{1\nu}^{(2)}$-mode:

$$E_{\theta'} = g_{1\nu}^{(2)}(r', \theta') \cos\varphi', \quad E_{\varphi'} = g_{1\nu}^{(2)}(r', \theta') \sin\varphi',$$
$$Z_0 H_{\theta'} = -\, E_{\varphi'}, \qquad Z_0 H_{\varphi'} = E_{\theta'} \tag{35}$$

with $g_{1\nu}^{(2)}(r', \theta') = -\, \alpha(kr')\, f_{1\nu}^{(2)}(\theta')$,

$$f_{1\nu}^{(2)}(\theta') = \frac{\mathrm{d}P_\nu^1(\cos\theta')}{\mathrm{d}\theta'} - \frac{P_\nu^1(\cos\theta')}{\sin\theta'}.$$

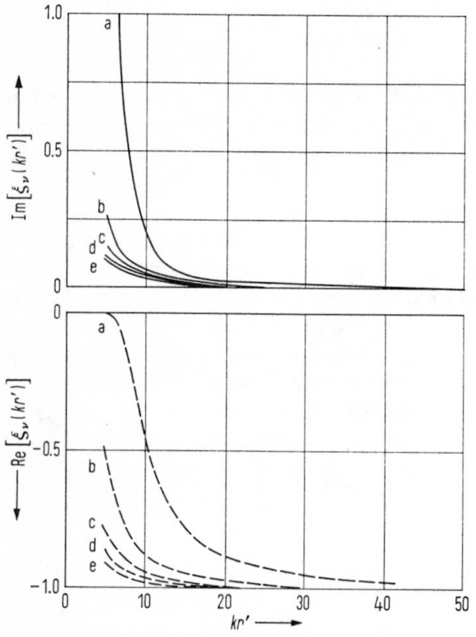

Fig. 7. $\mathrm{Re}[\xi_\nu(kr')]$ and $\mathrm{Im}[\xi_\nu(kr')]$ versus kr' with ν as parameter;
a) $\theta_0 = 15°$; $\nu = 8.74$,
b) $\theta_0 = 30°$; $\nu = 4.19$,
c) $\theta_0 = 45°$; $\nu = 2.71$,
d) $\theta_0 = 60°$; $\nu = 2.00$,
e) $\theta_0 = 75°$; $\nu = 1.59$.

4. The Radiation Pattern of the Corrugated Conical Horn Antenna

4.1. Computation of the radiation pattern

The electromagnetic field of a radiating conical horn antenna can be found from the following representation theorem [15]:

$$\underline{E}(\underline{r}) = \mathrm{curl}_p \int\limits_{S_A} [\underline{n}' \times \underline{E}(\underline{r}')]\, G(\underline{r}, \underline{r}')\, \mathrm{d}S + \tag{36}$$
$$+ \frac{1}{\mathrm{j}\,\omega\,\varepsilon_0} \mathrm{curl}_p\, \mathrm{curl}_p \int\limits_{S_A} [\underline{n}' \times \underline{H}(\underline{r}')]\, G(\underline{r}, \underline{r}')\, \mathrm{d}S,$$

$$\underline{H}(\underline{r}) = \mathrm{curl}_p \int\limits_{S_A} [\underline{n}' \times \underline{H}(\underline{r}')]\, G(\underline{r}, \underline{r}')\, \mathrm{d}S - \tag{37}$$
$$- \frac{1}{\mathrm{j}\,\omega\,\mu_0} \mathrm{curl}_p\, \mathrm{curl}_p \int\limits_{S_A} [\underline{n}' \times \underline{E}(\underline{r}')]\, G(\underline{r}, \underline{r}')\, \mathrm{d}S$$

with $G(\underline{r}, \underline{r}') = \dfrac{1}{4\pi} \dfrac{\mathrm{e}^{-\mathrm{j}k|\underline{r}-\underline{r}'|}}{|\underline{r}-\underline{r}'|}$.

In these expressions we have assumed that the outside of the horn antenna is perfectly conducting and no currents flow on the outside of the antenna. The aperture S_A is part of a sphere with radius r' (Fig. 8).

The far field approximation gives

$$E_\theta(r, \theta, \varphi) = \frac{\mathrm{e}^{-\mathrm{j}kr}}{r} \frac{\mathrm{j}k}{4\pi} \int\limits_{S_A} [(E_{\varphi'} \cos\theta' - Z_0 H_{\theta'} \cos\theta) \sin(\varphi - \varphi') + (E_{\theta'} + Z_0 H_{\varphi'} \cos\theta' \cos\theta) \cos(\varphi - \varphi') +$$
$$+ Z_0 H_{\varphi'} \sin\theta \sin\theta'] \exp\{\mathrm{j}\,kr'[\cos\theta\cos\theta' + \sin\theta\sin\theta'\cos(\varphi - \varphi')]\}\, (r')^2 \sin\theta'\, \mathrm{d}\theta'\, \mathrm{d}\varphi', \tag{38}$$

$$E_\varphi(r, \theta, \varphi) = \frac{\mathrm{e}^{-\mathrm{j}kr}}{r} \frac{\mathrm{j}k}{4\pi} \int\limits_{S_A} [-\, (E_{\theta'} \cos\theta + Z_0 H_{\varphi'} \cos\theta') \sin(\varphi - \varphi') + (-\, Z_0 H_{\theta'} +$$
$$+ E_{\varphi'} \cos\theta' \cos\theta) \cos(\varphi - \varphi') + E_{\varphi'} \sin\theta \sin\theta'] \exp\{\mathrm{j}\,kr'[\cos\theta\cos\theta' + \tag{39}$$
$$+ \sin\theta\sin\theta'\cos(\varphi - \varphi')]\}\, (r')^2 \sin\theta\, \mathrm{d}\theta'\, \mathrm{d}\varphi'.$$

Substituting eq. (34) in eqs. (38) and (39) and usings the relation

$$\exp[\mathrm{j}\,kr' \sin\theta \sin\theta' \cos(\varphi - \varphi')] = \mathrm{J}_0(kr' \sin\theta \sin\theta') + \sum_{n=1}^{\infty} 2\,\mathrm{j}^n \mathrm{J}_n(kr' \sin\theta\sin\theta') \cos n(\varphi - \varphi') \tag{40}$$

we obtain

$$E_\theta = -\frac{\mathrm{j}\,k}{4}\,\frac{\mathrm{e}^{-\mathrm{j}kr}}{r}\,A_1 Z_0\,\frac{\hat{\mathrm{H}}_\nu^{(2)}(k\,r')}{r'}\,(r')^2\cos\varphi\,F(\theta,\theta_0,k\,r')\,, \tag{41}$$

$$E_\varphi = \frac{\mathrm{j}\,k}{4}\,\frac{\mathrm{e}^{-\mathrm{j}kr}}{r}\,A_1 Z_0\,\frac{\hat{\mathrm{H}}_\nu^{(2)}(k\,r')}{r'}\,(r')^2\sin\varphi\,F(\theta,\theta_0,k\,r') \tag{42}$$

with

$$\begin{aligned} F(\theta,\theta_0,k\,r') = \int_0^{\theta_0} \{&(\cos\theta+\cos\theta')\,[\mathrm{J}_0(k\,r'\sin\theta\sin\theta') + \mathrm{J}_2(k\,r'\sin\theta\sin\theta')] + (1+\cos\theta\cos\theta')\,\times \\ &\times [\mathrm{J}_0(k\,r'\sin\theta\sin\theta') - \mathrm{J}_2(k\,r'\sin\theta\sin\theta')] + 2\,\mathrm{j}\sin\theta\sin\theta'\,\mathrm{J}_1(k\,r'\sin\theta\sin\theta')\}\,\times \\ &\times f_{1\nu}^{(1)}(\theta')\exp(\mathrm{j}\,k\,r'\cos\theta\cos\theta')\sin\theta'\,\mathrm{d}\theta'\,. \end{aligned} \tag{43}$$

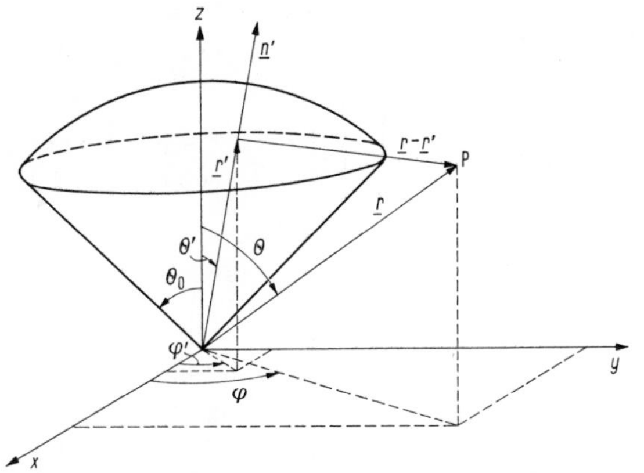

Fig. 8. Conical horn antenna with coordinate system.

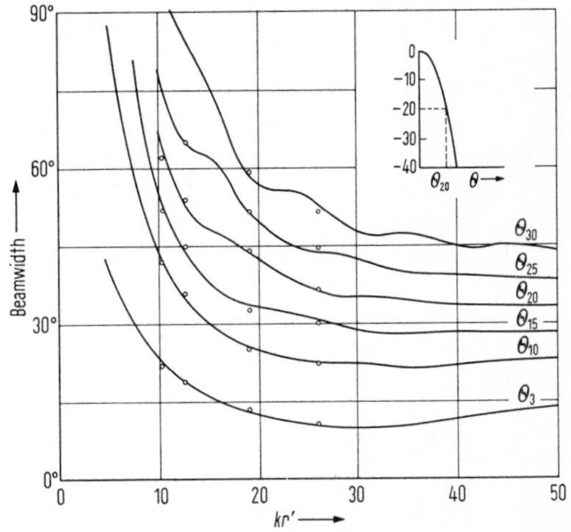

Fig. 9. Beamwidth versus $k\,r'$ for $\theta_0 = 30°$; dots indicate experimental results obtained with several antennas at a frequency of 14 GHz.

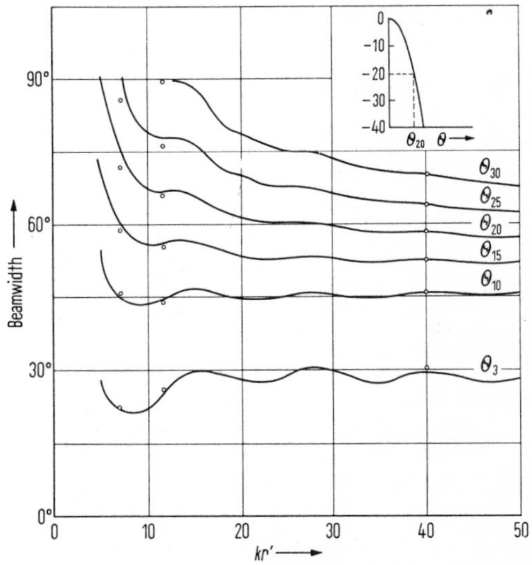

Fig. 10. Beamwidth versus $k\,r'$ for $\theta_0 = 60°$; dots indicate experimental results obtained with several antennas at a frequency of 14 GHz.

From the eqs. (41) and (42) we derive that $|E_\theta|^2 + |E_\varphi|^2$ is independent of φ. It should be noted that the same result has already been found in [2] for the case that the flare angle was small. So the radiation pattern of a corrugated conical horn antenna is symmetrical, provided the depth of the grooves is a quarter of a wavelength, because in that case $Z_r = \infty$.

Substitution of eq. (35) in eqs. (38) and (39) shows that the $HE_{1\nu}^{(2)}$-mode has also a symmetrical radiation pattern, but with a dip for $\theta = 0$. This type of radiation pattern is not studied in this paper. From eqs. (41) and (42) we derive that

$$\left|\frac{E_\theta(\theta,\theta_0 k\,r')}{E_\theta(0,\theta_0 k\,r')}\right| = \left|\frac{E_\varphi(\theta,\theta_0,k\,r')}{E_\varphi(0,\theta_0,k\,r')}\right| = \left|\frac{F(\theta,\theta_0,k\,r')}{F(0,\theta_0,k\,r')}\right|. \tag{44}$$

The function

$$20\,{}^{10}\!\log\left|\frac{F(\theta,\theta_0,k\,r')}{F(0,\theta_0,k\,r')}\right|$$

has been calculated for several values of θ_0 and $k\,r'$. From these calculations the beamwidth has been derived as a function of $k\,r'$ for $\theta_0 = 15°$, 30°, 45°, 60°, and 75°. The results are collected in [11]. Some results are plotted in Figs. 9 and 10. It should be noted that these results are found under the assumption that the function $\xi_\nu(k\,r') = -1$ and under the assumption that $E_{\varphi'} = 0$ and $Z_0 H_{\varphi'} = 0$ at the boundary $\theta' = \theta_0$.

4.2. Experimental investigation of the corrugated conical horn antenna

4.2.1. $\lambda/4$-grooves

A comparison of the theory of Section 4.1 with experimental results is possible, provided the depth of the grooves is a quarter of a wavelength, because only in that case the boundary condition $Z_0 H_{\varphi'} = 0$ is satisfied. For that purpose several antennas have been constructed in such a way that a wide variation in both the flare angle θ_0 and the length r' of the antennas was obtained. All the grooves were of the same depth and this was a quarter of a wavelength at the frequency 14 GHz [11].

The radiation pattern of these antennas has been measured for 14 GHz and some results are plotted in Figs. 9 and 10. The conclusion is that the experimental results are in good agreement with the theoretical predictions.

It is very interesting to investigate the effect of the length r' of the antenna on the radiation pattern. For this purpose the radiation patterns of two antennas with the same flare angle but different lengths have been given in Fig. 11. To hold the picture clear we have not plotted the theoretical patterns in Fig. 11, but the agreement is good, especially for the large antenna. We see that a large antenna has a flat radiation pattern and is very suitable as a feed in a paraboloid reflector antenna. It seems that the greatest length that can be used is not determined by electrical requirements but merely by mechanical ones, such as weight and space.

For the application of corrugated conical horn antennas it is mostly necessary that they can be used also for other frequencies than for which the grooves have a depth of a quarter of a wavelength. This question is discussed in Section 4.2.2.

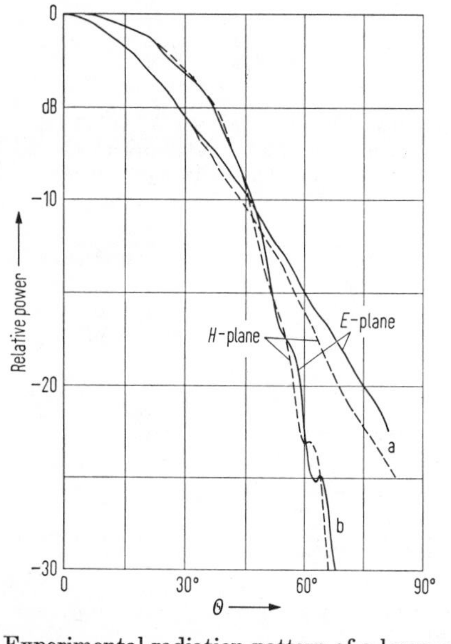

Fig. 11. Experimental radiation pattern of a large antenna and a short antenna with the same flare angle; frequency 14 GHz; a) antenna with $\theta_0 = 60°$, $r' = 2.80$ cm, b) antenna with $\theta_0 = 60°$, $r' = 13.64$ cm.

4.2.2. The bandwidth of the corrugated conical horn antenna

The bandwidths of the antennas, discussed in Section 4.2.1, have been studied by measuring the radiation pattern of each of them as a function of the frequency. The diameter of the circular waveguide, which is coupled to the cone, was so chosen that the cut-off frequency of the dominant TE_{11}-mode was approximately 10 GHz. The diameter of the waveguide is 18 mm. The depth of the grooves was a quarter of a wavelength at 14 GHz.

For conveniently constructing the antennas the depth of all the grooves was chosen equal and the boundaries of the grooves as straight lines. The purpose of the measurements which have been carried out can be formulated as follows:

i) to study surface wave phenomena, if any;

ii) to prove that a symmetrical radiation pattern is obtained if the depth of the grooves is a quarter of a wavelength. These measurements have already been discussed in the previous section;

iii) to investigate the deviation between the experimental and the theoretical results of Fig. 9 and 10, which are based on the assumption that $Z_0 H_{\varphi'}$ and $E_{\varphi'}$ are zero, independent of the frequency.

Two typical results of these measurements are plotted in Fig. 12 and 13. The solid line indicates

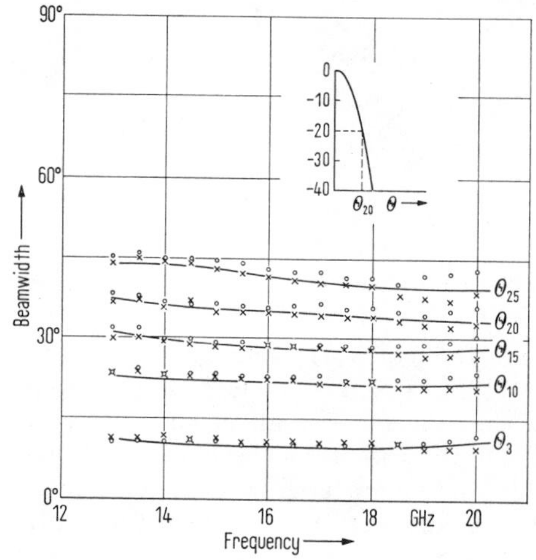

Fig. 12. Beamwidth versus frequency; antenna with $\theta_0 = 30°$ and $r' = 9.00$ cm;
— calculated, E-plane and H-plane,
○ experiment, E-plane,
× experiment, H-plane.

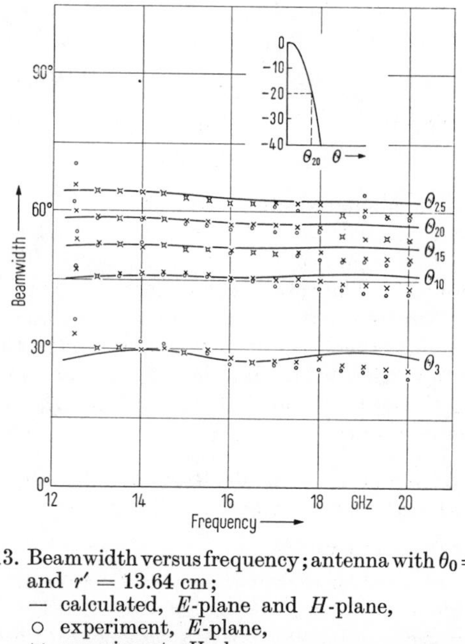

Fig. 13. Beamwidth versus frequency; antenna with $\theta_0 = 60°$ and $r' = 13.64$ cm;
— calculated, E-plane and H-plane,
○ experiment, E-plane,
× experiment, H-plane.

the theoretical beamwidth, based on the assumption that $Z_0 H_{\varphi'}$ and $E_{\varphi'}$ are zero. The main conclusion is that the scalar feed is indeed a broadband feed. On closer examination we observe that for frequencies for which the depth of the grooves is smaller than a quarter of a wavelength, a sudden change occurs in the shape of the radiation pattern.

Probably this is caused by a surface wave, as discussed by Kay [16], and it is clear that for the moment this phenomenon determines the lower limit of the frequency band for which the scalar feed can be used. For frequencies between 14 GHz and 20 GHz we observe a good agreement between the experimental results and the theoretical ones represented by the solid line. Apparently we may conclude that the boundary conditions $Z_0 H_{\varphi'} = 0$ and $E_{\varphi'} = 0$ are valid in a rather large frequency range. This fact gives us the opportunity to use Figs. 9 and 10 as design charts.

We have also investigated the V.S.W.R. of the antennas as a function of the frequency. One typical example is given in Fig. 14. Unfortunately, there is a large mismatch at the frequency for which the depth of the grooves is a quarter of a wavelength. However, we have also seen that for frequencies higher than the one mentioned above good radiation patterns are obtained. So it is recommendable to choose the depth of the grooves a little larger than a quarter of a wavelength for the lowest frequency for which the antenna will be used. In that case, a good matching and a good pattern are obtained in a rather large frequency band.

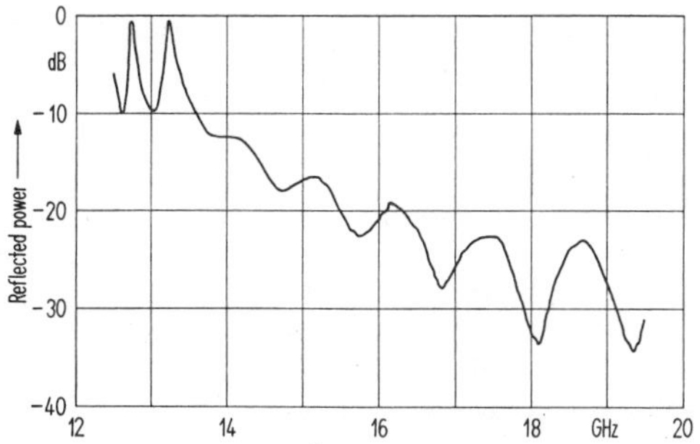

Fig. 14. Measured reflected power versus frequency; antenna with $\theta_0 = 45°$ and $r' = 3.71$ cm.

5. Conclusions

The electromagnetic field in the conical corrugated horn antenna and its radiation pattern have been studied theoretically. The main conclusion of this investigation is that the conical corrugated horn antenna has a symmetrical radiation pattern, provided the depth of the grooves is a quarter of a wavelength. The theory of the scalar feed has been formulated for this case. An experimental investigation shows that there is a good agreement between the experimental results and the theoretical calculations if the depth of the grooves is a quarter of a wavelength. Many measurements have been carried out at frequencies of 14 GHz to 20 GHz. From these measurements we can draw the following conclusions. For large antennas with a flare angle θ_0 smaller than 75° there is a good agreement between experimental results and calculations based on the assumption that $E_{\varphi'}$ and $Z_0 H_{\varphi'}$ are zero at the boundary $\theta' = \theta_0$, even at frequencies for which the depth of the grooves is not equal to a quarter of a wavelength. In case the flare angle is smaller than 75° and the antennas are short, again resonable agreement between theory and experiment has been found. The measurement of the V.S.W.R. shows that one should choose the depth of the grooves a little larger than a quarter of a wavelength for the lowest frequency for which the antenna will be used. The highest frequency which can be used is determined by the fact that the excitation of higher modes has to be prevented. An improvement of the bandwidth of the waveguide coupled to the cone will probably result in improvement of the bandwidth of the antenna.

Acknowledgements

The authors wish to thank Prof. Dr. ir. A. v. Trier for given them the opportunity to carry out the research described in this paper. The discussions with Prof. ir. C. A. Muller concerning the application of the scalar feed in antennas for radio-astronomical investigations are greatly appreciated. The authors appreciated the assistance of Mr. Knoben for the measurements carried out.

(Received July 1st, 1971.)

References

[1] Simmons, A. J and Kay, A. F., The scalar feed — a high performance feed for large paraboloid reflectors. Instn. Elect. Engrs. Conference Publication **21** [1966], 213–217.

[2] Jeuken, M. E. J. and Kikkert, J. S., A broadband aperture antenna with a narrow beam. Alta Frequenza **38** [1969], 270–276.

[3] Marcuvitz, N., Waveguide Handbook. McGraw-Hill Book Co., New York 1951.

[4] Jeuken, M. E. J., Experimental radiation pattern of the corrugated conical horn antenna with small flare angle. Electron. Letters **5** [1969], 484–485.

[5] Clarricoats, P. J. B. and Saha, P. K., Theoretical analysis of cylincrical hybrid modes in a corrugated horn. Electron. Letters **5** [1969], 187–189.

[6] Jeuken, M. E. J., Frequency-independence and symmetry properties of corrugated conical horn antennas with small flare angles. Ph. D. Thesis 1970, Eindhoven University of Technology, Netherlands.

[7] Clarricoats, P. J. B., Analysis of spherical hybrid modes in a corrugated conical horn. Electron. Letters **5** [1969], 189–190.

[8] Saha, P. K., Propagation and radiation characteristics of corrugated waveguides. Ph. D. Thesis, University of Leeds, England, 1970.

[9] Harrington, R. F., Time-harmonic electromagnetic fields; Chapter 6. McGraw-Hill Book Co., New York 1961.

[10] Abramowitz, M. and Stegun, I. A., Handbook of mathematical functions; p. 439. Dover Publications, New York 1965.

[11] Jansen, J. K. M., Jeuken, M. E. J. and Lambrechtse, C. W., The scalar feed. T. H. Report 70-E-12, Eindhoven University of Technology, Netherlands. (Copies of this report may be obtained on application to the second author.)

[12] Abramowitz [10], p. 336.

[13] Harrington [9], p. 469.

[14] Saxon, G., Jarvis, T. R., and White, I., Angular-dependent modes in circular corrugated waveguide. Proc. Instn. Elect. Engrs. **110** [1963], 1365–1373.

[15] Flügge, S., Handbuch der Physik; Bd. 25, S. 238–240. Springer-Verlag, Berlin 1961.

[16] Kay, A. F., The scalar feed. TRG Report, Contract AF 19 (604)-8057, March 1964.

The following article, which appeared after the completion of the present paper, is relevant to the material presented herein:

Clarricoats, P. J. B. and Saha, P. K., Propagation and radiation behaviour of corrugated feeds. Proc. Instn. Elect. Engrs. **118** [1971], 1167–1186.

HYBRID MODES IN CORRUGATED CONICAL HORNS

Indexing terms: Antenna radiation patterns, Antenna feeders

A simpler solution for spherical hybrid modes in corrugated conical horns has been shown to have a deviation from the rigorous solution of less than 0·7 dB for the case considered by Clarricoats. Expressions for the radiation pattern and gain of such a horn with small flare angle have been obtained under balanced hybrid conditions.

The importance of corrugated conical horns as low-noise feeds for large reflector antennas has been discussed by several authors.[1-3] Recently Clarricoats[4] has outlined an approximate analysis for spherical hybrid modes in a corrugated conical horn. For the same problem a simpler solution is presented here which facilitates study of other properties of corrugated-conical-horn antennas.

The flare (semivertical) angle of the corrugated conical horn is taken as α_0 (Fig. 1) and the corrugations are assumed

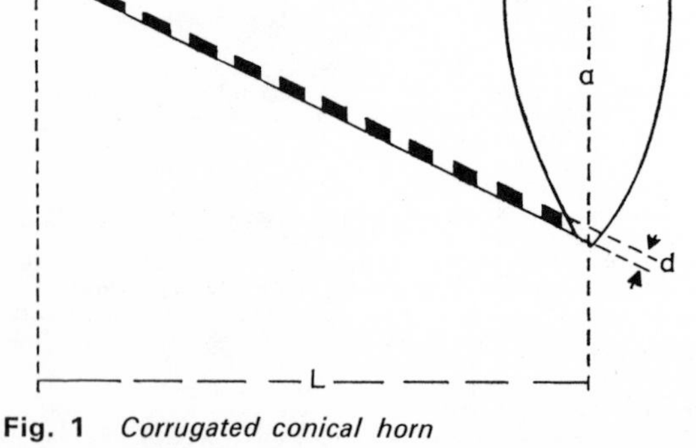

Fig. 1 *Corrugated conical horn*

to be very thin and closely packed, so that only a cutoff cylindrical E type mode exists within the slot when $\theta = \alpha_0$. In order to satisfy the boundary conditions, both E and H modes should be present in the horn region. The modes in a conical horn are derived from the vector potentials $\boldsymbol{A}$ and $\boldsymbol{F}$ given by $\boldsymbol{A} = \boldsymbol{a}_r A_r$ and $\boldsymbol{F} = \boldsymbol{a}_r F_r$, where $\boldsymbol{a}_r$ is the unit vector and A_r, F_r are given by[5]

$$A_r = a_{mn}\,\widehat{B_n(kr)}\,P_n{}^m(\cos\theta)\,e^{jm\Phi}$$

$$F_r = b_{mn}\,\widehat{B_n(kr)}\,P_n{}^m(\cos\theta)\,e^{jm\Phi} \quad . \quad . \quad . \quad . \quad . \quad (1)$$

corresponding to H and E modes, respectively. We have

$$\widehat{B_n(kr)} = \frac{\sqrt{(nkr)}}{2}\,H^2{}_{n+\frac{1}{2}}(kr)$$

and $H_n{}^2(x)$ is the Hankel function of the second kind. In eqn. 1, m is an integer and n is real and positive. The time convention e^{jwt} is implicit throughout. In order to obtain the simpler solution for spherical hybrid modes in the corrugated conical horn, the Θ part of the Helmholtz equation in spherical polar co-ordinates after separating the variables given by

$$\frac{1}{\Theta\sin\theta}\frac{\partial}{\partial\theta}\left(\sin\theta\frac{\partial\Theta}{\partial\theta}\right)+n(n+1)-\frac{m^2}{\sin^2\theta}=0 \quad . \quad (2)$$

is modified by replacing $\sin\theta$ by θ, resulting in

$$\frac{\partial^2\Theta}{\partial v^2}+\frac{1}{v}\frac{\partial\Theta}{\partial v}+\left(1-\frac{m^2}{v^2}\right)\Theta=0 \quad . \quad . \quad . \quad . \quad (3)$$

In eqn. 3, which is Bessel's differential equation, the solution is

$$\Theta = D_m\,J_m(v) \quad . \quad . \quad . \quad . \quad . \quad . \quad . \quad . \quad . \quad . \quad (4)$$

where $v = q\theta$ and $q = \sqrt{\{n(n+1)\}}$, D_m being an arbitrary constant. Since Θ is finite at $\theta = 0$, the Bessel function of the second kind is inadmissible. Using eqns. 1 and 4, the following expressions for A_r and F_r may be obtained:

$$\begin{Bmatrix} A_r \\ F_r \end{Bmatrix} = \begin{Bmatrix} a_{mn} \\ b_{mn} \end{Bmatrix}\widehat{B_n(kr)}\,J_m(q\theta)\,e^{jm\Phi} \quad . \quad . \quad . \quad . \quad (5)$$

Reprinted with permission from *Electron. Lett.*, vol. 6, pp. 32–34, Jan. 22, 1970.

The field vectors are obtained from eqn. 2 with the aid of the relations

$$\boldsymbol{E} = -\nabla \times \boldsymbol{F} + \frac{1}{jw\varepsilon_0} \nabla \times \nabla \times \boldsymbol{A}$$

$$\boldsymbol{H} = \nabla \times \boldsymbol{A} + \frac{1}{jw\mu_0} \nabla \times \nabla \times \boldsymbol{F} \quad . \quad . \quad . \quad . \quad . \quad . \quad (6)$$

Matching the boundary conditions at $\theta = \alpha_0$, under the far-field approximations, subject to the condition that $y = 0$, where

$$y = \frac{n(n+1)\cos\alpha_0 \cot kd}{kr}$$

as indicated by Clarricoats,[4] the characteristic equation is obtained as

$$\{F_m(\alpha_0)\}^2 = m^2$$

where

$$F_m(\alpha_0) = \frac{q\alpha_0 J_m'(q\alpha_0)}{J_m(q\alpha_0)}$$

where the prime denotes differentiation w.r.t. argument. Therefore

$$\left.\begin{aligned} & J_m'(q\alpha_0) \pm m\frac{J_m(q\alpha_0)}{q\alpha_0} = 0 \\ & J_{m\mp 1}(q\alpha_0) = 0 \\ & q = \frac{S_{m\mp 1,p}}{\alpha_0} \qquad n = -0{\cdot}5 + \sqrt{(0{\cdot}25 + q^2)} \end{aligned}\right\} \quad (7)$$

where $S_{m\mp 1,p}$ is the pth nonvanishing root of $J_{m\mp 1}(x) = 0$. The transverse electric field over the aperture, subject to the conditions stated above, can be represented by a simpler relation on substituting eqn. 5 into eqn. 6; namely

$$\boldsymbol{E}_t = \frac{-a_{mn}}{r} Z_0 B_n(kr) J_{m\mp 1}\left(\frac{S_{m\mp 1,p}\theta}{\alpha_0}\right) e^{jm\Phi} \quad (\pm \boldsymbol{a}_\theta + j\boldsymbol{a}_\Phi) \quad (8)$$

It would appear that the modified solution is valid only for small values of α_0. Actually this is not so because application of the boundary condition minimises the error that would otherwise be present at the boundary defined by $\theta = \alpha_0$.[6] For instance, for a horn with $\alpha_0 = 60°$ (the case discussed by Clarricoats), the θ variation of $\boldsymbol{E}_t$ in terms of spherical functions is given by

$$F_1(\theta) = \frac{d}{d\theta}\{P_1{}^2(\cos\theta)\} + \frac{P_1{}^2(\cos\theta)}{\sin\theta} \quad . \quad . \quad . \quad (9)$$

under balanced hybrid conditions. The solution for this particular case was obtained by equating the r.h.s. of eqn. 9 with zero, since $F_1(\theta) = 0$ for $\theta = \alpha_0$, and solving the resulting quadratic in $\cos\theta$ rather than solving the characteristic equation numerically. The θ variation for the same case according to eqn. 8 is given by

$$F_2(\theta) = J_0\left(\frac{S_{0,1}}{\alpha_0}\theta\right) \quad . \quad . \quad . \quad . \quad . \quad . \quad . \quad . \quad (10)$$

$F_1(\theta)$ and $F_2(\theta)$ are compared in Fig. 2 for $0 \leqslant \theta < \pi/3$. The values of $F_1(\theta)$ (in decibels) against θ are plotted as they are, whereas those of $F_2(\theta)$ (in decibels) are displaced -5 dB from their computed values to facilitate comparison. The maximum deviation of $F_2(\theta)$ from $F_1(\theta)$ is $0{\cdot}7$ dB {when $E(\theta)/E(0)$ is 32 dB}. Hence there is not much loss of accuracy in replacing the rigorous solution expressed in terms of spherical functions by the simpler or modified solution expressed in terms of Bessel functions.

For each value of m, there are two types of hybrids corresponding to the lower and upper signs in eqn. 8. For instance, when $m = 1$, for upper and lower signs, the θ variation of $\boldsymbol{E}_t$ is given by $J_0\{(S_{0,1}/\alpha_0)\theta\}$ and $J_2\{(S_{2,1}/\alpha_0)\theta\}$, respectively. Only the former expression is valid, since the latter predicts zero intensity along the polar axis. Also it is evident from eqn. 8 that the electric field over the aperture has the same taper along any radius independent of Φ. Therefore one obtains identical E and H plane patterns when the horn is used as a radiator.

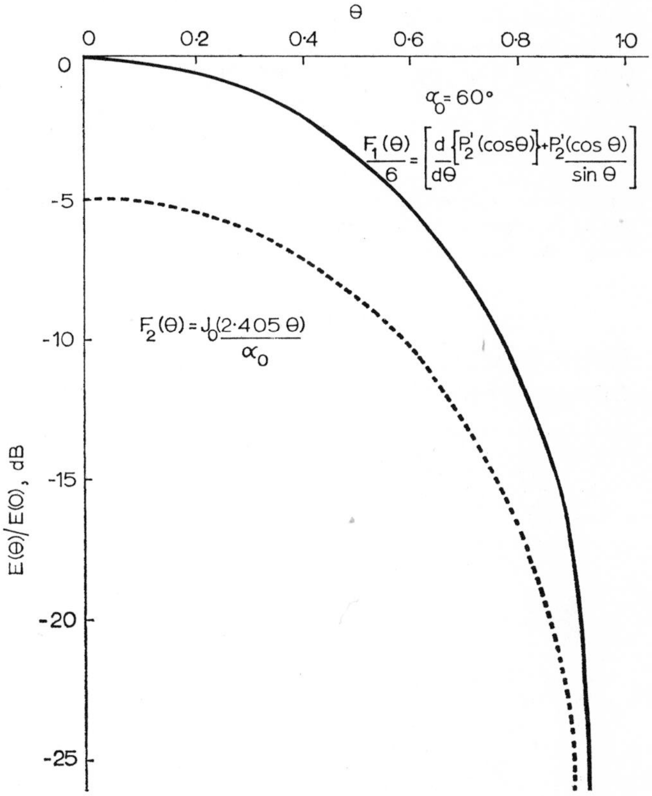

Fig. 2 *Comparison of F_1 (θ) and F_2 (θ)*

$F_2(\theta)$ is displaced by -5 dB from its actual values

The simpler expression for $\boldsymbol{E}_t$ given by eqn. 8 facilitates calculation of the diffracted far field and gain of the corrugated horn radiator. Using a vector diffraction formula,[7] the electric field over the aperture is integrated to obtain an expression for the diffracted far field. For this calculation, the flare angle α_0 is assumed to be so small that the phase variation of $\boldsymbol{E}_t$ over S may be neglected.[8] The diffracted far field for EH_{mn} or HE_{nm} modes (corresponding to the upper and lower signs in eqn. 8), respectively, is then given by

$$\boldsymbol{E}_p(R, \theta, \Phi) = C_{mn}\left(\frac{1+\cos\theta}{2}\right)\frac{\exp(-jkR)}{R}$$

$$\times \frac{J_{m\pm 1}\{(2\pi/\lambda_0)\, a \sin\theta\}}{\{S^2_{m\pm 1,p} - (4\pi^2 a^2/\lambda_0)\sin^2\theta\}}(\pm \boldsymbol{a}_\theta + j\boldsymbol{a}_\Phi)\, e^{jm\Phi} \quad (11)$$

where C_{mn} is independent of R, θ and Φ.

The total power crossing a spherical cap of radius L in the cone region is given by

$$P_t = \frac{\pi Z_0\, a_{mn}{}^2\, \alpha_0{}^2}{2} J'_{m\pm 1}(S_{m\pm 1,p})$$

The axial gain

$$G = \frac{4\pi P(0, 0)}{P_t}$$

$$= \frac{16\pi^2 (a/\lambda_0)^2 \, J'_{m\pm 1}(S_{m\pm 1, p})}{S^2_{m\pm 1, p}} \quad . \quad . \quad . \quad . \quad . \quad (12)$$

The range of validity of the radiation pattern and gain formulas given by eqns. 11 and 12 depend on both α_0 and a. If the upper limit for the maximum allowable phase error is taken as[9] $\pi/4$, eqns. 11 and 12 will give accurate results, when $\alpha_0 \leqslant 10°$ and $a \leqslant 1{\cdot}4\,\lambda_0$. But these formulas are useful even when $10° < \alpha_0 \leqslant 20°$ as a first approximation in predicting the radiation pattern and gain. When α_0 is sufficiently large ($\alpha_0 > 20°$), one cannot neglect the phase variation of $\boldsymbol{E}_t$ over S. Further work is in progress.

M. S. NARASIMHAN
B. V. RAO

Department of Electrical Engineering
Indian Institute of Technology
Powai, Bombay 76, India

22nd December 1969

References

1 SIMMONS, A. J., and KAY, A. F.: 'The scalar feed—a high performance feed for large paraboloidal reflectors', *IEE Conf. Publ.* 21, 1968, pp. 213–217
2 MINNET, H., and THOMAS, B. MAC.A.: 'Synthesis of improved feeds for large circular paraboloids', *ibid.*, 1968, pp. 262–266
3 MINNET, H., and THOMAS, B. MAC.A.: 'A method of synthesising radiation patterns with axial symmetry', *IEEE Trans.*, 1966, **AP-14**, pp. 654–656
4 CLARRICOATS, P. J. B.: 'Analysis of spherical hybrid modes in corrugated conical horn', *Electron. Lett.*, 1969, **5**, pp. 189–190
5 HARRINGTON, R. F.: 'Time harmonic electromagnetic fields' (McGraw-Hill, 1961), chap. 6, pp. 264–311
6 PIEFKE, G.: 'Reflexion und transmission beim einfall einer H_{on}-Welle auf einen kegelformigen Ubergang zwisehen Hohlleitern', *Arch. Elekt. Ubertragung*, 1961, **15**, pp. 444–454
7 SCHELKUNOFF, S. A.: 'On diffraction and radiation of electromagnetic waves', *Phys. Rev.*, 1939, **56**, pp. 308–316
8 WEEKS, W. L.: 'Antenna engineering' (McGraw-Hill, 1968), chap. 6, pp. 229–262
9 SILVER, S.: 'Microwave antenna theory and design' (McGraw-Hill, 1949), chap. 10, pp. 363–365

DIFFRACTION BY WIDE-FLARE-ANGLE CORRUGATED CONICAL HORNS

Indexing term: Antenna radiation patterns

Expressions for the diffracted far field of a wide-flare-angle corrugated conical horn (operating on the HE_{11} mode) have been obtained making use of a simpler expression for the aperture field. Expressions for the radiation pattern and gain reduce to a closed form when the flare (semivertical) angle is less than 30°. The theoretical results are in close agreement with experiment.

In a previous communication[1] by the authors, a simpler solution for spherical hybrid modes in corrugated conical horns was given, and it was used to obtain the radiation pattern and gain of a corrugated circular horn. The treatment is restricted to horns with small flare angles ($\alpha_0 \leqslant 10°$, $a \leqslant 1{\cdot}4\lambda_0$), in which case the phase variation of the electric field over the aperture may be neglected. When the flare angle is not small, phase variation of the aperture field must also be taken into account to obtain satisfactory agreement between theory and experiment. Expressions for the diffracted far field of a wide-flare-angle corrugated conical horn are derived here with the aid of a vector diffraction formula.[4] When the flare (semivertical) angle is less than 30°, these expressions reduce to a closed form in terms of Lommel's function and its derivatives. The theoretical results are in close agreement with the experimental results of Jeuken.[2, 3]

The aperture field of a corrugated conical horn, whose corrugations are assumed to be very thin and close packed, with a flare angle α_0 under balanced hybrid conditions, is given by[1]

$$\bar{E}_t = -\frac{a_{mp}}{r} Z_0 B_n(kr) J_{m\mp 1}\left(\frac{s_{m\mp 1,p}\,\theta}{\alpha_0}\right) \theta^{jm\phi}(\pm \bar{a}_\theta + j\bar{a}_\phi) \qquad (1)$$

where $B_n(x) = \sqrt{(\pi x/2)}\, H^2_{n+\frac{1}{2}}(x)$ where $H_y{}^2(x)$ is the Hankel function of second kind, Z_0 is the intrinsic impedance of free space, $s_{m\mp 1,p}$ is the pth nonvanishing root of $J_{m\mp 1}(x) = 0$ and a_{mp} is an arbitrary constant. When $\alpha_0 < 30°$, $\bar{E}_t$ can be expressed in a simpler form for the HE_{11} mode of excitation as

$$\bar{E}_t \simeq b_{11} J_0\left(\frac{2{\cdot}405}{a}\rho\right) \exp(-ju\rho^2)\, e^{j\psi}(\bar{a}_\rho + j\bar{a}_\psi) \qquad (2)$$

where $\bar{a}_\rho$ and $\bar{a}_\psi$ are the unit vectors at a point $P'(\rho', \psi')$ on the circular aperture of the horn expressed in polar coordinates, $u = \pi/\lambda_0 L$, and L is the axial length of the horn. Eqn. 2 follows from eqn. 1.

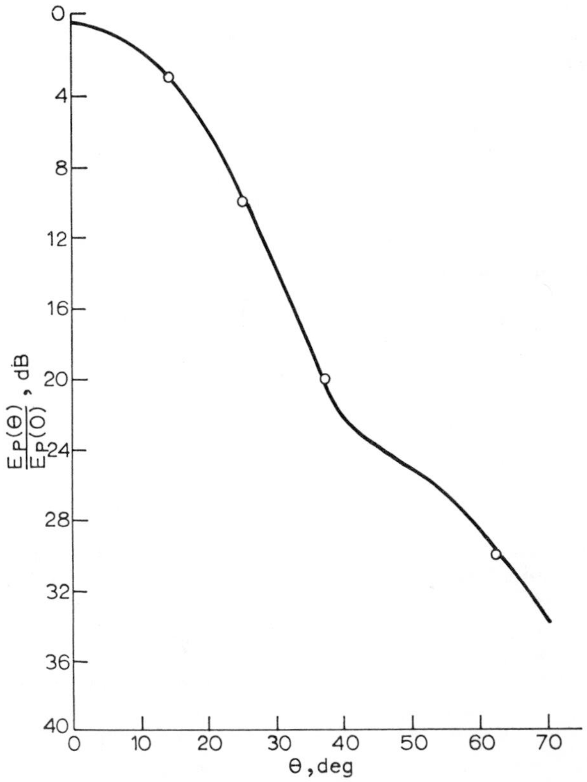

Fig. 1 *Radiation pattern of small-flare-angle horn*

○ experimental (Jeuken)
$\alpha_0 = 15°$, $a = 1{\cdot}33$, $\lambda_0 = 4{\cdot}05$ cm

The diffracted far field at an observation point $P(R, \theta, \phi)$ is calculated with the aid of the vector diffraction formula[4]

$$\bar{E}_s(P) = \frac{-jke^{-jkR}}{4\pi R} \bar{R}_1 \times [\{\bar{n} + \alpha\sqrt{(\mu/\varepsilon)}\,\bar{R}_1\} \times \bar{N}] \qquad (3)$$

In eqn. 3, $\alpha = \sqrt{(\varepsilon/\mu)}$, assuming a match between the radiator and free space. For a horn with $\alpha_0 < 30°$, one obtains, with the aid of eqns. 2 and 3, after a few manipulations,

$$\bar{E}_s(P) = C_{11}(1+\cos\theta)(\bar{a}_\theta + j\bar{a}_\phi) M e^{j\phi} \quad . \quad . \quad . \quad (4)$$

where

$$M = \int_0^1 J_0(p_{01} r) J_0(\alpha_1 r) \exp(-jvr^2) r dr \quad . \quad . \quad (5)$$

and C_{11} is a normalisation constant.

Reprinted with permission from *Electron. Lett.*, vol. 6, pp. 469–471, July 23, 1970.

In eqn. 5, $\alpha_1 = 2\pi a \sin\theta/\lambda_0$, $r = \rho/a$, $v = \pi a^2/(\lambda_0 L)$ and $p_{01} = 2{\cdot}405$. To facilitate evaluation of the radiation integral M in a closed form in terms of Lommel's function and its derivatives,[5] $J_0(p_{01} r)$ is approximated to by a polynomial of the form

$$J_0(p_{01} r) \simeq P(x) = b_3 x^3 + b_2 x^2 + b_1 x + b_0 \ldots \qquad (6)$$

where $b_0 = -0{\cdot}007259$, $b_1 = 0{\cdot}6525$, $b_2 = 0{\cdot}2708$, $b_3 = 0{\cdot}08399$, and $x = 1 - r^2$. It was verified that the deviation of the approximate expression from $J_0(p_{01} r)$ is very small within the range of integration. With the aid of eqns. 5 and 6 and the relationships[5]

$$W_0{}^n(\gamma, p) = \int_0^1 (1-\eta^2)^n J_0(p\eta)\, e^{j(\gamma/2)(1-\gamma^2)}\, \eta\, d\eta$$

$$= (2/j)^n \frac{\partial^n}{\partial \gamma^n} \frac{U_1(\gamma, p)}{\gamma} + i \frac{\partial^n}{\partial \gamma^n} \frac{U_2(\gamma, p)}{\gamma} \qquad (7)$$

$$U_1(\gamma, p) = \gamma \frac{J_1(p)}{p} - \gamma^3 \frac{J_3(p)}{p^3} + \gamma^5 \frac{J_5(p)}{p^5} \quad . \quad . \qquad (8)$$

$$U_2(\gamma, p) = \gamma^2 \frac{J_2(p)}{p^2} - \gamma^4 \frac{J_4(p)}{p^4} + \ldots \quad . \quad . \quad . \qquad (9)$$

one obtains

$$M = b_3 W_0{}^3(2v, \alpha_1) + b_2 W_0{}^2(2v, \alpha_1) + b_1 W_0{}^1(2v, \alpha_1) + b_0 W_0{}^0(2v, \alpha_1) \qquad (10)$$

Hence

$$\bar{E}_s(P) = \frac{C_{11} \exp(-jkR)}{R} \frac{(1+\cos\theta)}{2} \times (b_3 W_0{}^3 + b_2 W_0{}^2 + b_1 W_0{}^1 + b_0 W_0{}^0)(\bar{a}_\theta + j\bar{a}_\phi) \qquad (11)$$

To check the validity of the radiation formula (eqn. 11), a normalised radiation pattern of a corrugated conical horn with $\alpha_0 = 15°$, and $a = 1{\cdot}33\lambda_0$ (4·05 cm) was drawn (Fig. 1). This shows close agreement with the experimental values of Jeuken.[2]

It is also possible to obtain an expression for the axial gain of the horn in a closed form similar to the expression for radiation pattern given by eqn. 12. Axial gain is defined by[4]

$$G(0, 0) = \frac{4\pi P(0, 0)}{P_t} \quad . \quad . \quad . \quad . \quad . \quad . \quad . \quad . \quad . \qquad (12)$$

where P_t is the total power radiated and $P(0, 0)$ is the power along the polar axis, both being measured at the same observation point.

$$P_t = \tfrac{1}{2} \mathrm{Re} \int_{S'} (\bar{E}_t \times \bar{H}_t{}^*)\, dS' = \frac{\pi}{2} a_{11}{}^2 Z_0 \alpha_0{}^2 J_1{}^2(p_{01}) \qquad (13)$$

$$P(0, 0) = (a_{11}{}^2 Z_0/2)\{U_1{}^2(2v, p) + U_2{}^2(2v, p)\} \qquad (14)$$

where $p = 2{\cdot}405$. Hence, from eqns. 12, 13 and 14,

$$G = \frac{(4L^2/a^2)\{U_1{}^2(2v, p) + U_2{}^2(2v, p)\}}{J_1{}^2(p)} \quad . \quad . \quad . \qquad (15)$$

The radiation and gain formulas given by eqns. 11 and 15 can be used as a first approximation to the accurate formulas even when $30° < \alpha_0 < 45°$.

To calculate accurately the radiation pattern of a horn with a wide flare angle, the expression for $\bar{E}_t$ (eqn. 1) should be used without any approximation in Silver's formula for diffracted far field given by

$$\bar{E}_s(P) = \frac{-jk}{4\pi R} \bar{R}_1 \times \int_A \{\bar{n} \times \bar{E}_r - \sqrt{(\mu/\varepsilon)}\, \bar{R}_1 \times (\bar{n} \times \bar{H}_r)\} \times \exp(jk\bar{\rho}\bar{R}_1)\, dS \qquad (16)$$

The integral in eqn. 16 should be evaluated over a spherical cap of radius r_0, where $r_0 = L \sec\alpha_0$. After a lengthy derivation, one obtains the following expressions for the diffracted far field at an observation point $P(R, \theta, \phi)$ for a wide-flare-angle horn excited in the HE_{11} mode:

$$\bar{E}_s(P) = C_{11}(\bar{a}_\theta + j\bar{a}_\phi)\, F(\theta, \alpha_0, r_0)\, e^{j\phi} \quad . \quad . \quad . \quad . \qquad (17)$$

where C_{11} is a normalisation constant, and

$$F(\theta, \alpha_0, r_0) = \int_0^{\alpha_0} J_0(h\theta')\{(1+\cos\theta)(1+\cos\theta')\, J_0(f) - (1-\cos\theta)(1-\cos\theta')\, J_2(f) + 2j \sin\theta \sin\theta'\, J_1(f)\} \times \exp(jw\cos\theta') \sin\theta'\, d\theta' \quad . \quad . \quad . \quad . \quad . \qquad (18)$$

In eqn. 18, $h = 2{\cdot}405/\alpha_0$, $w = kr_0 \cos\theta$ and $f = kr_0 \sin\theta \sin\theta'$. It is evident from eqn. 17 that the far-field radiation pattern is circularly symmetric, with zero crosspolarisation response, when the aperture field is linearly polarised.

Normalised radiation patterns calculated according to eqn. 17 for horns with $\alpha_0 = 45°$ and $kr_0 = 18{\cdot}1$ and $39{\cdot}8$ are shown in Fig. 2. The integrals in eqn. 18 were calculated

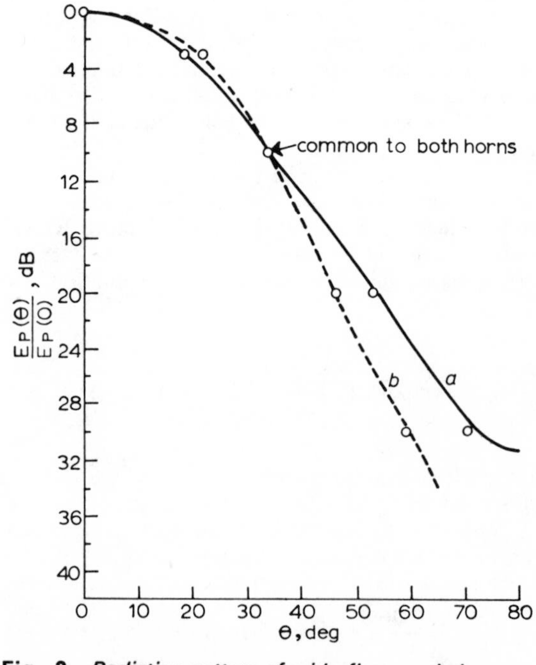

Fig. 2 *Radiation pattern of wide-flare-angle horn*
○ experimental (Jeuken)
a Horn with $\alpha_0 = 45°$, $2\pi a/\lambda_0 = 12{\cdot}8$
b Horn with $\alpha_0 = 45°$, $2\pi a/\lambda_0 = 28{\cdot}15$

numerically for this specific case with the aid of a digital computer. The theoretical plots are in good agreement with the experimental results of Jeuken.[3] This shows the correctness of the expressions used to represent the aperture field of a corrugated conical horn excited in the HE_{11} mode. The advantage in employing a simpler expression for the aperture field is that it enables one to obtain a closed-form expression for the radiation pattern and gain when $\alpha_0 < 30°$. The expression for gain facilitates study of the variation in gain with the significant dimensions of the horn. For wide-flare-angle horns, evaluation of the integrals is simplified, since one has to deal only with the Bessel function of the first kind, instead of both spherical and Bessel functions.

M. S. NARASIMHAN
B. V. RAO

Department of Electrical Engineering
Indian Institute of Technology
Bombay, India

19th June 1970

References

1 NARASIMHAN, M. S., and RAO, B. V.: 'Hybrid modes in corrugated conical horns', *Electron. Lett.*, 1970, **6**, pp. 32–34
2 JEUKEN, M. E. J.: 'Experimental radiation pattern of the corrugated conical-horn antenna with small flare angle', *ibid.*, 1969, **5**, pp. 484–485
3 JEUKEN, M. E. J., and LAMBRECHTSE, C. W.: 'Small corrugated conical-horn antenna with wide flare angle', *ibid.*, 1969, **5**, pp. 489–490
4 SILVER, S.: 'Microwave antenna theory and design' (McGraw-Hill, 1949), chap. 1, pp. 2–3 and chap. 5, pp. 161–162
5 MING-KUEI HU: Fresnel region field distributions of circular aperture antennas', *IRE Trans.*, 1960, **AP-8**, pp. 344–346

Corrugated conical horns with arbitrary corrugation depth

M. S. NARASIMHAN, Ph.D.*

Based on a paper presented at the 1971 European Microwave Conference in Stockholm.

SUMMARY

The form of fields in a conical horn with uniform circumferential corrugations, when the corrugation depth assumes arbitrary values in the interval $0{\cdot}25 \leqq (h/\lambda_0) \leqq 0{\cdot}5$ is investigated in this paper. Assuming the corrugations to be infinitely thin and sufficiently close-packed, an impedance boundary condition is imposed on the fields in the axial region. Subject to a far-field approximation, accurate expressions are derived for the aperture field through a hybrid-mode formalism, which are subsequently used to calculate numerically the diffracted far-field of the horn supporting the HE_{11} mode, using Silver's formula. Satisfactory agreement between calculated and measured values of the far-field pattern for a wide-flare horn having arbitrary values of h/λ_0 supports the validity of the theory presented. When the half-flare angle (α_0) is less than 30°, a closed form expression is derived for the on-axis gain of the horn.

* *Department of Electrical Engineering, Indian Institute of Technology, Madras 36. India.*

List of Principal Symbols

α_0, α_1	half-flare angle of the horn measured at the boundary of the corrugations and at the base of the corrugations respectively.
r_0	flare-length of the horn
L	axial length of the horn
a	aperture radius of the horn
t	thickness of the fins forming the corrugated boundary
w	spacing between any two adjacent fins
h	depth of the corrugations
r, θ, ϕ	spherical polar coordinates of a point at which electromagnetic fields are considered
$\mathbf{a}_r, \mathbf{a}_\theta, \mathbf{a}_\phi$	unit vectors associated with (r, θ, ϕ)
$\mathbf{E}_t, \mathbf{H}_t$	aperture fields tangential to the spherical cap defined by $r = r_0$ and $\theta = \alpha_0$
$\boldsymbol{E}^i, \boldsymbol{H}^i$	fields within a corrugation close to the aperture
$\mathrm{J}_n(x)$	Bessel function of first kind and nth order
$U_n(w, z)$	$\sum_{m=0}^{\infty} (-1)^m \left(\frac{w}{z}\right)^{n+2m} \mathrm{J}_{n+2m}(z)$
$b_n(x)$	spherical Hankel function of second kind
$B_n(x)$	$xb_n(x)$
$P_n^1(\cos\theta)$, $Q_n^1(\cos\theta)$	associated Legendre function of first and second kinds, respectively, of order n
$L_n^1(\cos\theta)$	$P_n^1(\cos\theta) - B_{11}\, Q_n^1(\cos\theta)$
B_{11}	constant associated with function $L_n^1(\cos\theta)$
C_{11}	normalization constant associated with the far-field
b_{11}, a_{11}	amplitudes of the potentials associated with the H_{11} and E_{11} modes, respectively, in the axial region of the horn
λ_0	free-space wavelength
k	$2\pi/\lambda_0$
Z_0	impedance of free space
Y_0	$1/Z_0$
μ_0, ε_0	permeability and permittivity of free-space
P_t	total power radiated by the horn
$P(\theta, \phi)$	power radiated per unit solid angle in the direction (θ, ϕ)
$G(0, 0)$	on-axis gain

1 Introduction

The corrugated conical horn has been the subject of study for many workers in recent years, because of its attractive features as a primary feed in large paraboloidal reflectors for communication-satellite earth stations and for radio astronomical research. Most of the workers who have significantly contributed to the analytical study of corrugated conical horn[1-5] have focused their attention on the balanced HE modes of

Reprinted with permission from *Radio Electron. Eng.*, vol. 43, pp. 188–192, Mar. 1973.

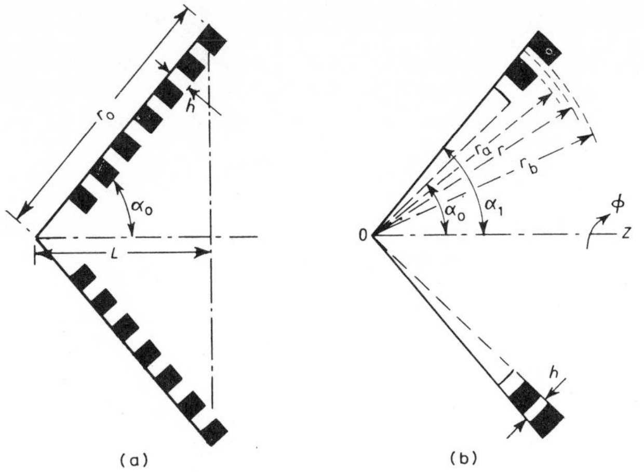

Fig. 1. Geometry of the corrugated conical horn.

excitation of the corrugated feed which correspond to a corrugation depth of one-fourth of the operating wavelength at the aperture edge. Thomas[6] has presented a limited theoretical analysis of the effect of varying the corrugation depth, by varying the operating frequency over an octave bandwidth. In this paper a more general analysis of spherical hybrid modes in corrugated conical horns than that by Jenken[1] is considered when the corrugation depth assumes arbitrary values in the interval ($\lambda_0/4 \leqq h \leqq \lambda_0/2$). Furthermore, an analytical study of the radiation properties (supported by experimental observations) of conical horns with circumferential corrugations of arbitrary depth is also presented.

2 Solution for Spherical Hybrid Modes

Analysis of fields in the axial region of a corrugated conical horn shown in Fig. 1(a), when the corrugation depth assumes arbitrary values in the interval $\lambda_0/4 \leqq h \leqq \lambda_0/2$ is based on a number of approximations. It is assumed first that the horn is excited by a circular waveguide proportioned to carry the dominant TE_{11} mode, and secondly that the thickness of the fins forming the corrugated boundary is very small when compared with the spacing between any two adjacent fins ($t \ll w$). Further, the number of corrugations within one wavelength of the operating frequency is assumed to be large (i.e. $t+w \ll \lambda_0$), so that the space harmonics may be ignored and fields in the axial region may be represented by a single spherical hybrid mode. This can be realized in practice by choosing $\lambda_0/(t+w) \geqq 10$ and $t \leqq w$.

The corrugated boundary shown in Fig. 1(a) does not coincide with any one of the three independent orthogonal surfaces of a coordinate system in which Maxwell's equation can be easily solved and the labour involved in deriving an exact solution of Maxwell's equation for this geometry is not commensurate with the results that can be expected. Therefore the boundary of the corrugations is slightly modified, as shown in Fig. 1(b), in order to facilitate solution of fields within the corrugations and in the axial region as well, without significant loss of accuracy.

The electromagnetic fields (E^i, H^i) within a corrugation (which is close to the aperture edge) can be derived from the vector potential $\mathbf{G} = \mathbf{a}_r u_r^i$, where

$$u_r^i = A_{11} B_n(kr) L_n^1(\cos\theta)\, e^{j\phi}. \tag{1}$$

The time convention $e^{j\omega t}$ is implicit throughout.

When there is a large number of corrugations within one wavelength, the TE modes cannot exist within the corrugations and only TM modes are possible. The reason for this is that for TE modes of excitation ($E_r = 0$) the closely spaced corrugations would force both E_θ and E_ϕ to vanish within the slot, when

$$\left(\frac{t+w}{\lambda_0}\right) \to 0.$$

The TM fields ($\mathbf{E}^i$, $\mathbf{H}^i$) within the corrugations may be obtained from equation (1) and when α_0 is small ($\alpha_0 < 30°$) a quasi-cylindrical approximation of the spherical wave function indicated by the author in previous papers[7,8] may be used in order to facilitate the analysis. This implies that for field representation within the corrugations, cylindrical wave functions corresponding to the spherical wave function $L_n'(\cos\theta)$ may be used. Such a procedure, after considerable algebraic manipulations, leads to the following expression for the admittance of a corrugation (sufficiently away from the horn-apex and close to the aperture) at its open end:

$$Y_r \simeq Y_z = \frac{H_\phi^i}{E_z^i} = \frac{jY_0[J_1'(k_0a)N_1(k_0p) - J_1(k_0p)N_1'(k_0a)]}{J_1(k_0p)N_1(k_0a) - J_1(k_0a)N_1(k_0p)}$$

$$\simeq jY_0 \cot\left(\frac{2\pi}{\lambda_0} h\right) \tag{2a}$$

where $ka \gg 1$ and $p = a+h$.

For large values of $\alpha_0(\sim 90°)$, an analytically simple and sufficiently accurate asymptotic solution[9] for the spherical wave function $L_n^1(\cos\theta)$, may be used to obtain expressions for H_ϕ and E_r^i. Subsequently these expressions also lead to the result

$$Y_r = H_\phi^i / E_r^i = jY_0 \cot\left(\frac{2\pi}{\lambda_0} h\right). \tag{2b}$$

Identity of equations (2a) and (2b) indicates the validity of using a single expression for Y_r for both small and wide-flare horns.

In the axial region when the corrugation depth is arbitrary, unbalanced spherical hybrid modes of the form HE_{11} is present, which can be decomposed into TE_{11} and TM_{11} modes. The potentials associated with the TE_{11} and TM_{11} modes are given by

$$\begin{bmatrix} u^m \\ u^e \end{bmatrix} = \begin{bmatrix} b_{11} \\ a_{11} \end{bmatrix} B_s(kr) P_s^1(\cos\theta)\, e^{j\phi} \tag{3}$$

respectively.

Subject to a far-field approximation, the components of the aperture field are given by

$$E_r = -ja_{11}\left(\frac{\mu_0}{\varepsilon_0}\right)^{\frac{1}{2}} \frac{B_s(kr)}{r} \frac{s(s+1)}{kr} P_s^1(\cos\theta)\, e^{j\phi} \tag{4}$$

$$E_\theta = -jb_{11}\frac{B_s(kr)}{r}\left[\frac{P_s^1(\cos\theta)}{\sin\theta} + \gamma\frac{dP_s^1(\cos\theta)}{d\theta}\right] e^{j\phi} \tag{5}$$

$$E_\phi = b_{11} \frac{B_s(kr)}{r} \left[\frac{\mathrm{d}P_s^1(\cos\theta)}{\mathrm{d}\theta} + \gamma \frac{P_s^1(\cos\theta)}{\sin\theta} \right] \mathrm{e}^{\mathrm{j}\phi} \tag{6}$$

where

$$\gamma = -\mathrm{j}(a_{11}/b_{11})\sqrt{\mu_0/\varepsilon_0}. \tag{7}$$

It follows from equation (7) that γ is the ratio of the E-field to that of the H-field present in the axial region. On applying the boundary condition, $E_\phi = 0$ at $\theta = \alpha_0$, one obtains

$$\left[\frac{\mathrm{d}P_s^1(\cos\theta)}{\mathrm{d}\theta} + \gamma \frac{P_s^1(\cos\theta)}{\sin\theta} \right]_{\theta=\alpha_0} = 0. \tag{8}$$

The following equation results on matching the fields within the corrugations with those in the axial region

$$\frac{s(s+1)\alpha_0}{kr_0(\gamma - 1/\gamma)} = \tan(kh). \tag{9}$$

For prescribed values of α_0 and γ (where $0 \leqq \gamma \leqq 1$), the values of s appearing in equation (8) were computed numerically using a digital-computer based iterative algorithm. Details relating to this have been treated elsewhere.[8] Values of s computed as function of α_0 with γ as a parameter are shown in Fig. 2. From known values of γ and kr_0, the normalized corrugation depth (h/λ_0) can be calculated from equation (9). Alternatively, one can read the value of γ for any arbitrary value of $h(\lambda_0/4 \leqq h \leqq \lambda_0/2)$ from a graph plotted between γ and h/λ_0. Once γ is known for a prescribed value of h/λ_0, the aperture field is also known.†

3 Calculation of the Far-Field Radiation Patterns

Different techniques are available for calculating accurately the radiation patterns of flared circular horns from a knowledge of the aperture field distribution. The classical multipole expansion technique, first used by Potter[10] and subsequently by others,[2] appears to be one of the most accurate methods of calculating the radiation patterns of circular aperture antennas. Another method of computation of far-field uses Silver's formula.[11] James and Longdon[12] have established that the modal function (or multipole) expansion method and Silver's formula are mathematically equivalent, when the observation point lies in the far-field. However, Silver's formula involves fewer special functions and integrations than the other method for calculating the radiated far-field. Therefore Silver's formula is used for the analysis of far-field patterns.

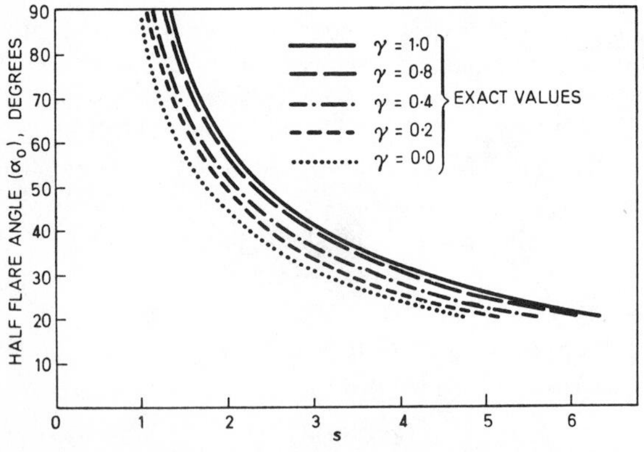

Fig. 2. Variation of the eigenvalue s with α_0 for different values of γ.

† It may be noted that when $\gamma = 0$, the horn supports the TE_{11} mode and for $\gamma = 1$, it supports a balanced HE_{11} mode.

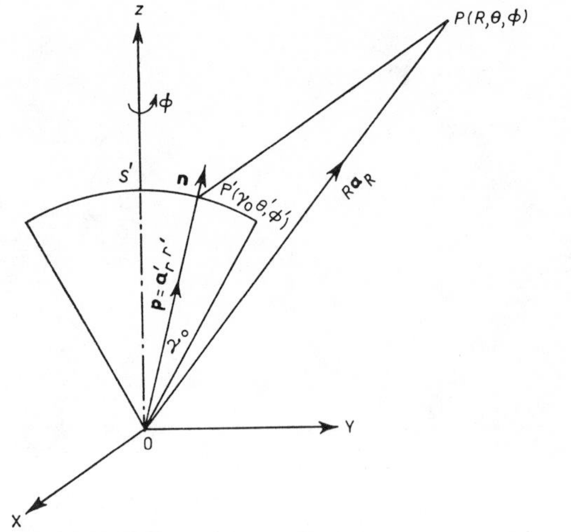

Fig, 3. Coordinate system for radiation formula.

Figure 3 shows the coordinate system for the radiation formula given by[10]

$$\mathbf{E}_P = \frac{-\mathrm{j}k}{4\pi R} \mathrm{e}^{-\mathrm{j}kR} \mathbf{a}_R \times \int_{S'} [\mathbf{n} \times \mathbf{E}'_t - Z_0 \mathbf{a}_R \times (\mathbf{n} \times \mathbf{H}'_t)] \times \times \mathrm{e}^{\mathrm{j}k\mathbf{P}\cdot\mathbf{a}_R} \mathrm{d}S' \tag{10}$$

In equation (10), variables relating to the aperture are primed and those of the far-field are unprimed. Assuming that $\mathbf{E}'_t$ and $\mathbf{H}'_t$ obey a far-field approximation $kr_o \gg s \gg 1$ so that[13]

$$\frac{E'_\theta}{H'_\phi} = -\frac{E'_\phi}{H'_\theta} = Z_0 \text{ over } S'. \tag{11}$$

The following expression is obtained for the far-field radiation patterns from equation (10) after extensive manipulations[9]:

$$\mathbf{E}_P = C_{11} \left(\frac{\mathrm{e}^{-\mathrm{j}kR}}{R} \right) (\mathbf{a}_\theta N_\theta^F \sin\phi + \mathbf{a}_\phi N_\phi^F \cos\phi) \tag{12}$$

where

$$N_\theta^F = N_\theta^{F_r} + \mathrm{j}N_\theta^{F_i}, \quad N_\phi^F = N_\phi^{F_r} + \mathrm{j}N_\phi^{F_i}$$

$$N_\theta^{F_r, F_i} = \int_0^{\alpha_0} \left[(p_1 + p_2) \frac{\cos}{\sin}(u) \mp p_3 \frac{\sin}{\cos}(u) \right] \mathrm{d}\theta'$$

$$N_\phi^{F_r, F_i} = \int_0^{\alpha_0} \left[(p_1 + p_2) \frac{\cos}{\sin}(u) \mp q_3 \frac{\sin}{\cos}(u) \right] \mathrm{d}\theta'$$

$$p_1 = F_1(\theta')(\cos\theta \cos\theta' + 1)[\mathrm{J}_0(u_1) - \mathrm{J}_2\, u_1)] \sin\theta'$$

$$p_2 = F_2(\theta')(\cos\theta + \cos\theta')[\mathrm{J}_0(u_1) + \mathrm{J}_2(u_1)] \sin\theta'$$

$$p_3 = 2F_1(\theta') \sin\theta \sin^2\theta' \,\mathrm{J}_1(u_1)$$

$$q_3 = 2F_2(\theta') \sin\theta \sin^2\theta' \,\mathrm{J}_1(u_1)$$

$$u = kr_0 \cos\theta \cos\theta' \text{ and } u_1 = kr_0 \sin\theta \sin\theta'$$

$$F_1(\theta) = \frac{P_s^1(\cos\theta)}{\sin\theta} + \gamma \frac{\mathrm{d}P_s^1(\cos\theta)}{\mathrm{d}\theta}$$

$$F_2(\theta) = \frac{\mathrm{d}P_s^1(\cos\theta)}{\mathrm{d}\theta} + \gamma \frac{P_s^1(\cos\theta)}{\sin\theta}$$

(a) E-plane,

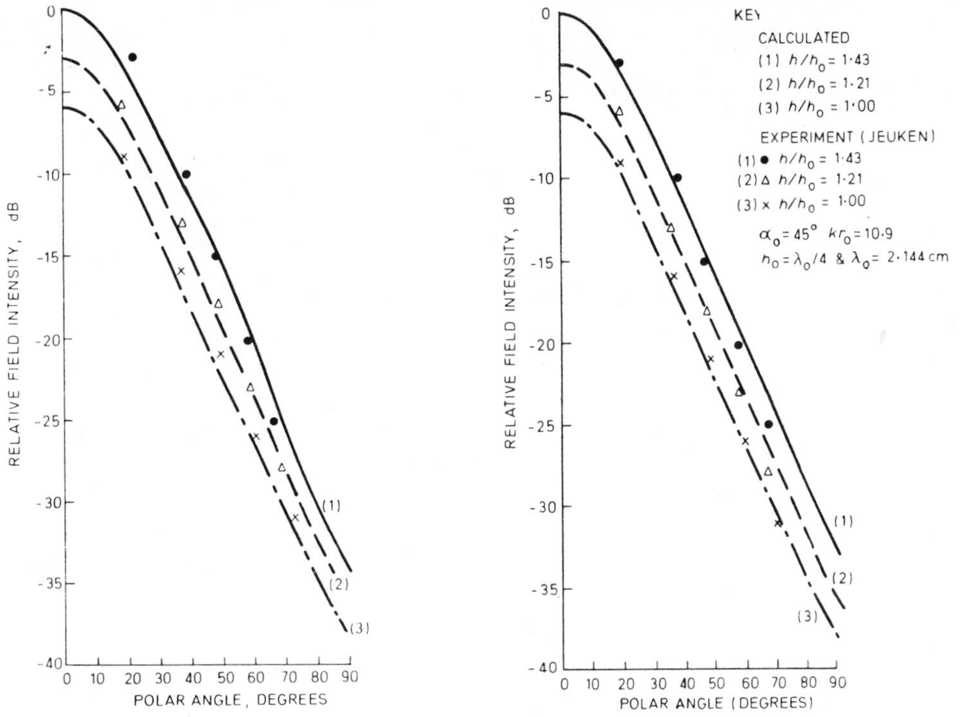

(b) H-plane.

Fig. 4. Far-field radiation patterns of a corrugated conical horn for arbitrary value of h/λ_0. To facilitate comparison, patterns (2) and (3) have been displaced from pattern (1) by 3 dB and 6 dB respectively.

Far-field radiation patterns of a wide-flare-corrugated conical horn with $\alpha_0 = 45°$ and $kr_0 = 10{\cdot}9$ obtained by calculation using equation (12), as well as by experiment, for three different values of 'h' are compared in Figs. 4(a) and 4(b) and a satisfactory agreement is noticed between the calculated and experimental results. Similar comparisons were made for several other horns with different values of α_0, r_0 and h and good agreement was noticed between calculated and experimental results. Figure 5 indicates how the far-field pattern is affected when h assumes several values† in the interval $(0{\cdot}25 \leqq h/\lambda_0 \leqq 0{\cdot}5)$ for a typical conical corrugated feed with $\alpha_0 = 45°$ and $kr_0 = 15$.

It is of interest to obtain an expression for the on-axis gain. Here the attention is focused on horns with $\alpha_0 < 30°$, since in this case a closed form expression can be obtained for on-axis gain in terms of the significant dimensions of the horn. Furthermore, given the axial length, the value of a_0 in order to realize an optimum value for G_a is generally found to be less than 30°, unless L is too short. In order to arrive at a closed form expression for the on-axis gain, it is necessary to express the transverse E-field components over the aperture in a form simpler than the one given by equations (5) and (6). For doing so, an analytically simple and sufficiently accurate solution used by the author in previous papers,[4,5,7] for studying modes in conical and conical scalar horns with small and wide flare angles is employed. With some algebra, one obtains the following expressions for $\mathbf{E}_t = \mathbf{a}_\theta E_\theta + \mathbf{a}_\phi E_\phi$, where

† In this case it is assumed that the variation in h is effected by varying the excitation frequency in the interval $1{\cdot}0 \leqq (f/f_0) \leqq 2$ where $\lambda_0 f_0 = c$.

$$E_\theta = \mathrm{j} b_{11} v_{11} B_s(kr)(1/r)\left[\frac{J_1(x)}{x} + \gamma J_1'(x)\right] e^{\mathrm{j}\phi} \tag{13}$$

$$E_\phi = b_{11} v_{11} B_s(kr)(1/r)\left[J_1'(x) + \gamma \frac{J_1(x)}{x}\right] e^{\mathrm{j}\phi} \tag{14}$$

and where $x = v_{11}\theta/\alpha_0$ and v_{11} is the first non-vanishing root of

$$(1-\gamma)\frac{J_1(p)}{p} = J_0(p). \tag{15}$$

Roots of equation (15) have been tabulated[14] for a few discrete values of γ in the interval $0 \leqq \gamma \leqq 1$. It has

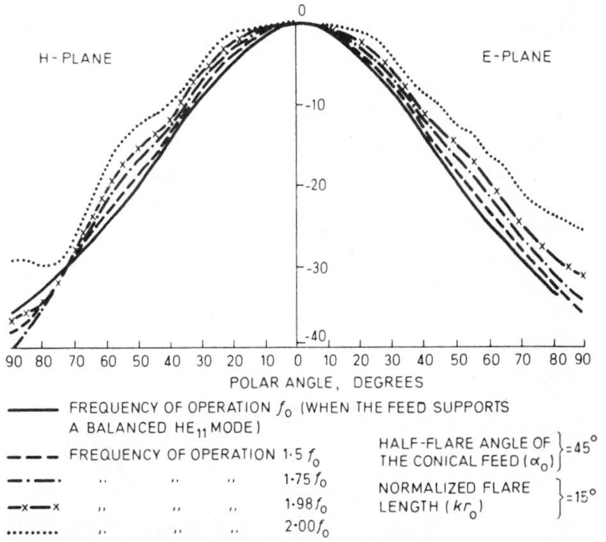

Fig. 5. Variation of E- and H-plane radiation patterns of the horn for changes in the operating frequency.

been verified that the transverse electric field components over the aperture given by equations (14) and (15) are close to the exact solution for E_θ and E_ϕ (given by equations (5) and (6)) even for large values of α_0.

The expression for on-axis gain is given by

$$G_a = G(0, 0) = \frac{4\pi P(0, 0)}{P_t}. \tag{16}$$

One obtains the following expressions for $P(0, 0)$ and P_t (appearing in equation (16)) from equations (14) and (15) after extensive algebraic manipulations and by assuming that $\sin \alpha_0 \simeq \alpha_0$ and $\alpha_0 \simeq a/L$,

$$P(0, 0) = \frac{b_{11}^2 L^2 (1+\gamma)^2 [U_1^2(2q, v_{11}) + U_2^2(2q, v_{11})]}{8Z_0} \tag{17}$$

$$P_t = \frac{\pi b_{11}^2 a^2}{8Z_0} \left[(1+\gamma)^2 \{J_0'^2(v_{11}) + J_0^2(v_{11})\} + \right.$$
$$\left. +(1-\gamma)^2 \left\{ J_2'^2(v_{11}) + \left(1 - \frac{4}{v_{11}^2}\right) J_2^2(v_{11}) \right\} \right] \tag{18}$$

$$G_a = \left(\frac{4L^2}{a^2}\right) \left[\frac{U_1^2(2q, v_{11}) + U_2^2(2q, v_{11})}{J_0'^2(v_{11}) + J_0^2(v_{11}) + \left(\frac{1-\gamma}{1+\gamma}\right)^2 \left\{ J_2'^2(v_{11}) + J_2^2(v_{11}) \left(1 - \frac{4}{v_{11}^2}\right) \right\}} \right] \tag{19}$$

It is of interest to note that when $\gamma = 1$, the expression for on-axis gain (equation (19)) reduces to that of a scalar horn supporting the balanced HE_{11} mode[6] and when $\gamma = 1$, with some algebraic manipulation the expression for G_a may be shown to reduce to the on-axis gain of a conical horn supporting a TE_{11} mode.[7] Clarricoats and Saha[15] have reported that the expression for G_a for the balanced HE_{11} mode (given by equation (19) with $\gamma = 1$) deviates from the more accurate form of G_a, based on the exact solution for E_θ and E_ϕ, only to the extent of 2·2% even when $\alpha_0 = 30°$. Observations stated above bear testimony to the validity of the expression for G_a given by equation (19).

4 Conclusions

A solution has been obtained for spherical hybrid modes in corrugated conical horns with arbitrary corrugation depth and the corrugated surface treated as an impedance boundary. When the circumferential corrugations have a depth equal to one-half of the operating wavelength, the hybrid-mode solution degenerates to the solution for the TE_{11} mode in a conical waveguide, thereby implying that for this particular choice of the corrugation depth, the corrugated surface appears to be a perfectly conducting metallic boundary for fields in the axial region. Satisfactory agreement between computed and measured far-field patterns of corrugated conical horns for a set of values of h and α_0 indicate the validity of the hybrid-mode formalism used as well as several assumptions made in the study of fields in the axial region of the horn. From a study of on-axis gain of horns with $\alpha_0 < 30°$, one observes that given h, α_0 and L, the upper and lower limits for the on-axis gain are given by the axial gains of conical and conical scalar horns of identical dimensions respectively.

5 Acknowledgments

The work reported here has been supported by the Centre for Systems and Devices, Department of Electrical Engineering, Indian Institute of Technology, Madras.

The author is thankful to Mr. R. V. Sitaram of the Microwave Engineering Group, Tata Institute of Fundamental Research, Bombay, for helpful discussions in the initial stages of the work. Thanks are also due to Dr. M. Jeuken of the Department of Electrical Engineering, Technological University, Eindhoven, for providing the experimental data on the far-field patterns of corrugated conical horns.

Computing facilities at the Computer Centre of the Tata Institute of Fundamental Research, Bombay, were made use of for the numerical computation of far-field patterns.

6 References

1. Clarricoats, P. J. B., 'Analysis of spherical hybrid modes in corrugated conical horn', *Electronics Letters*, **5**, pp. 189–90, 1st May 1969.
2. Clarricoats, P. J. B. and Saha, P. K., 'Radiation from wide-flare-angle scalar horns', *ibid*, **5**, pp. 376–8, 7th August 1969.
3. Jeuken, M. E. J. and Lambrechtse, C. W., 'Small corrugated conical-horn antenna with wide flare angle', *ibid*, **5**, pp. 489–90, 2nd October 1969.
4. Narasimhan, M. S. and Rao, B. V., 'Hybrid modes in corrugated conical horns', *ibid*, **6**, pp. 32–4, 22nd January 1970.
5. Narasimhan, M. S. and Rao, B. V., 'Diffraction by wide-flare-angle corrugated conical horns', *ibid*, **6**, pp. 469–71, 23rd July 1970.
6. Thomas, B. MacA., 'Bandwidth properties of corrugated conical horns', *ibid*, **5**, pp. 561–3, 30th October 1969.
7. Narasimhan, M. S. and Rao, B. V., 'Modes in a conical horn: new approach', *Proc. IEE* **118**, pp. 287–92, February 1971.
8. Narasimhan, M. S. 'Eigenvalues of a class of spherical wave functions', I.E.E.E. International Symposium Digest on Antennas and Propagation, Los Angeles, Cal. September 1971.
9. Narasimhan, M. S., 'Radiation properties of a class of microwave horn antennas', Ph.D. Thesis, Indian Institute of Technology, Bombay, September 1970.
10. Potter, P. D., 'Application of spherical wave theory to Cassegrainian-fed paraboloids', *IEEE Trans. on Antennas and Propagation*, **AP-15**, pp. 727–35, November 1967.
11. Silver, S., 'Microwave Antenna Theory and Design', Chapter 5. (McGraw-Hill, New York, 1949).
12. James, J. R. and Longdon, L. W., 'Calculation of radiation patterns', *Electronics Letters*, **5**, pp. 567–9, 30th October 1969.
13. Narasimhan, M. S. and Rao, B. V., 'Transmission properties of electromagnetic waves in conical waveguides', *Intl J. Electronics*, **27**, pp. 119–39, August 1969.
14. Abramovitz, M. and Stegun, I. A., 'Handbook of Mathematical Functions', pp. 355–433. (Dover, New York, 1965).
15. Clarricoats, P. J. B. and Saha, P. K., 'Propagation and radiation behaviour of corrugated feeds: Part 2', *Proc. IEE*, **118**, pp. 1177–86, September 1971.

Manuscript first received by the Institution on 23rd May 1972 and in final form on 3rd August 1972. (Paper No. 1509/CC 161).

Corrugated Conical Horn as a Space Feed for Phased-Array Illumination

M. S. NARASIMHAN

***Abstract*—The importance of corrugated conical horns in space-fed illumination of phased arrays is indicated. Design details pertaining to corrugated conical horns of optimum proportions for uniform illumination of a phased array with a prescribed area are also presented.**

This paper is concerned with the design of optimally flared corrugated conical horns for illumination of phased arrays. Flared horns are commonly employed for optical illumination of phased arrays as discussed in [1]. In an appropriately designed corrugated conical horn most of the radiated power is distributed over the main beam with very low sidelobe and backlobe. This, in essence, means that the percentage of overspilled energy radiated at angles greater than HPBW from the beam maximum is significantly smaller than what is observed in a horn with plane conducting walls. This feature makes it attractive for space-fed illumination of phased arrays.

Given the aperture area (as for instance a square with total area L_1^2/λ^2), illumination of the phased array for obtaining a desired amplitude and phase tapers at the periphery of a circle with diameter D_1/λ where $D_1 = \sqrt{2}L_1$, is possible by a judicious choice

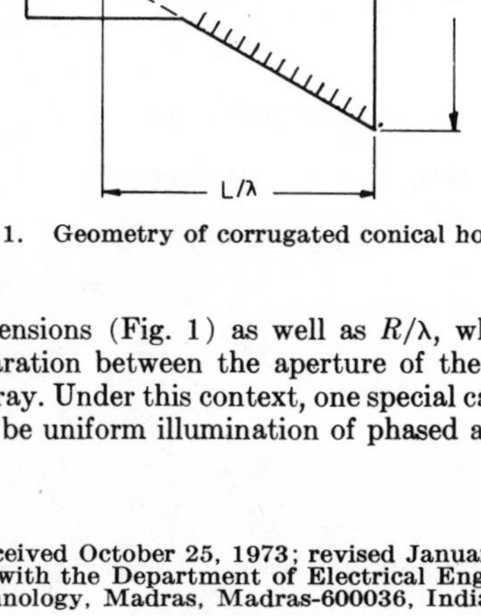

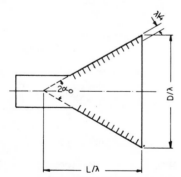

Fig. 1. Geometry of corrugated conical horns.

of the feed dimensions (Fig. 1) as well as R/λ, where R/λ is the distance of separation between the aperture of the horn and that of the phased array. Under this context, one special case of particular importance will be uniform illumination of phased arrays. A nearly uniform illumination of the array, without excessive spillover from the feed, is realized by suitably designing the feed so that the amplitude and phase tapers, from the center to the periphery of the circle of diameter D_1/λ, are made equal to 3 dB and $\pi/8$ radians, respectively. This stipulation results in the following expressions:

$$\frac{R}{\lambda} = 2\left(\frac{D_1}{\lambda}\right)^2 \tag{1}$$

$$\theta_f{}^3 = \tan^{-1}\left(\frac{\lambda}{2R}\right)^{1/2} = \tan^{-1}\left(\frac{0.25\lambda}{D_1}\right) \tag{2}$$

where $\theta_f{}^3$ is the 3-dB beamwidth of the corrugated feed measured from the boresight axis.

Design details concerning optimally flared corrugated conical horns[1] are needed for suitably selecting its dimensions so that the desired beamwidth (2) and a maximum on-axis gain are realized. For this purpose the following expression for the horn radiation pattern at a far-field point $P(r,\theta,\phi)$ will be employed [2]

$$\bar{E}(\theta) = C_{11}(1 + \cos\theta)M \exp(j\phi)(\bar{a}_\theta + j\bar{a}_\phi) \tag{3}$$

where

$$M = b_3 w_0{}^3(2v,\alpha_1) + b_2 w_0{}^2(2v,\alpha_1) + b_1 w_0{}^1(2v,\alpha_1) + b_0 w_0{}^0(2v,\alpha_1) \tag{4}$$

$$w_0{}^n(x,p) = \left(\frac{2}{j}\right)^n \left\{\frac{\partial^n}{\partial x^n}\left[\frac{U_1(x,p)}{x}\right] + j\frac{\partial^n}{\partial x^n}\left[\frac{U_2(x,p)}{x}\right]\right\} \tag{5}$$

$$U_1(x,p) = x\frac{J_1(p)}{p} - x^3\frac{J_3(p)}{p^3} + x^5\frac{J_5(p)}{p^5} \tag{6}$$

$$U_2(x,p) = x^2\frac{J_2(p)}{p^2} - x^4\frac{J_4(p)}{p^4} + \cdots \tag{7}$$

$$v = \frac{\pi a^2}{\lambda L}$$

$$\alpha_1 = ka\sin\theta$$

$$k = 2\pi/\lambda$$

(a,L) represent the aperture radius and axial length of the primary feed, $b_0 = -0.007259$, $b_1 = 0.6525$, $b_2 = 0.2708$, $b_3 = 0.08399$, and C_{11} is a normalization constant.

The on-axis gain of the horn is given by

$$G(0,0) = \frac{(4L^2/a^2)\left[U_1{}^2(2v,p_1) + U_2{}^2(2v,p_1)\right]}{J_1{}^2(p_1)} \tag{8}$$

where $p_1 = 2.405$.

[1] It may be pointed out that only horns with small flare angles ($2\alpha_0 < 60°$) are considered here, since even for an array with $D_1/\lambda = 20$, the horn flare is found to be approximately 30° so that (2) is satisfied. Furthermore, given the flare length ($L > 2\lambda$), flare angles of optimally flared horns are invariably found to be <60°.

Manuscript received October 25, 1973; revised January 15, 1974.
The author is with the Department of Electrical Engineering, Indian Institute of Technology, Madras, Madras-600036, India.

Reprinted from *IEEE Trans. Antennas Propagat.*, vol. AP-22, pp. 720–722, Sept. 1974.

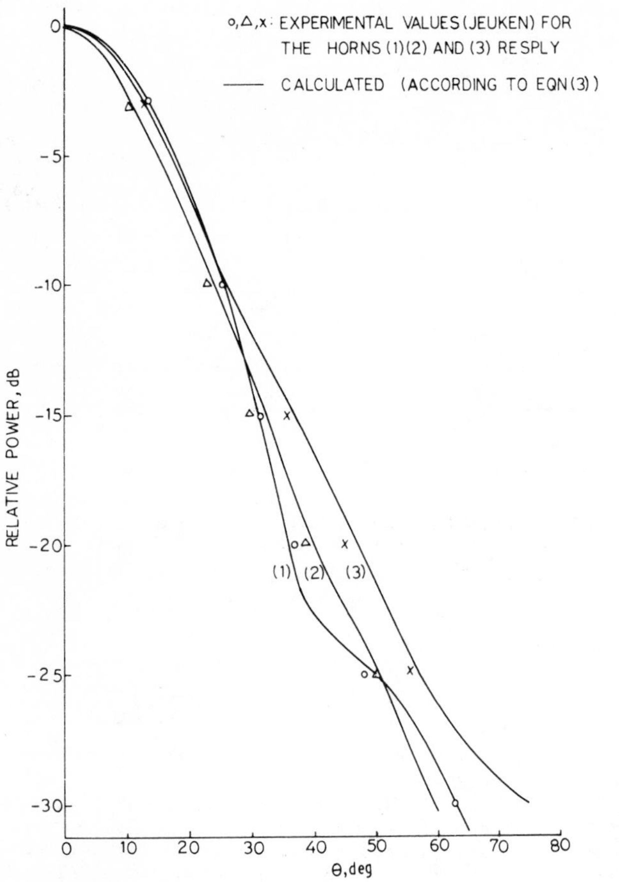

Fig. 2. Radiation patterns of corrugated conical horns. (a) $\alpha_0 = 15°$; $a = 1.3\lambda$. (b) $\alpha_0 = 30°$; $a = 2.1\lambda$. (c) $\alpha_0 = 30°$; $a = 2.67\lambda$.

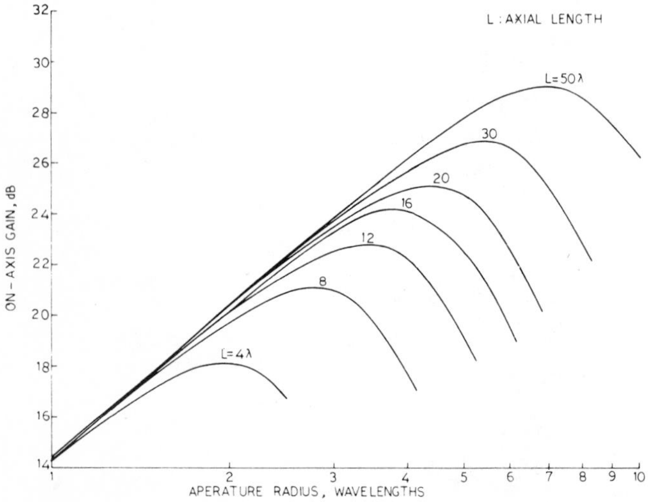

Fig. 3. Variation of on-axis gain with aperture radius.

The radiation formula (3) and the expression for on-axis gain (8) have been found to be accurate enough for all practical purposes when $2\alpha_0 < 60°$. In order to support this contention computed radiation patterns based on (3) have been compared with measured data in Fig. 2. for a few horns ($2\alpha_0 < 60°$). Furthermore Clarricoats and Saha [3] have compared the accuracy of the expression for on-axis gain (8) with more accurate expressions based on the spherical wave expansion technique and observed that the closed form expression for $G(0,0)$ as given by (8) is accurate enough for most engineering purposes when $2\alpha_0 < 60°$.

Based on (7), variation of on-axis gain as a function of a/λ with L/λ as a parameter has been studied (Fig. 3) and subsequently for a set of values of L/λ, the corresponding values of a/λ which

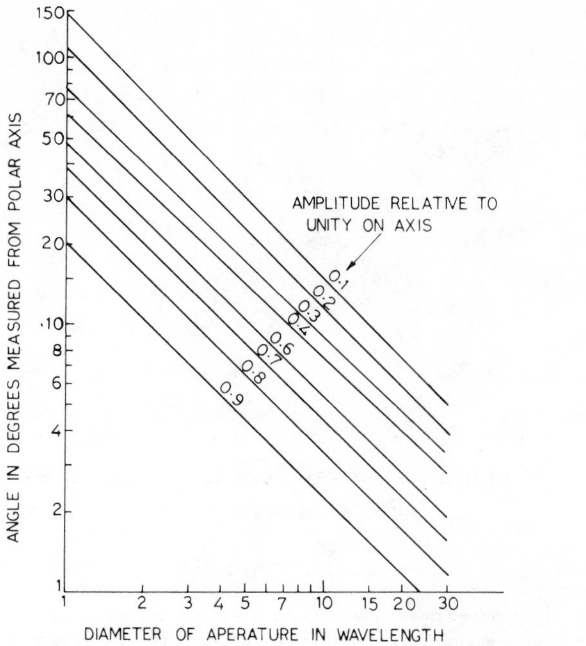

Fig 4. Data for plotting radiation patterns of optimum conical scalar horns.

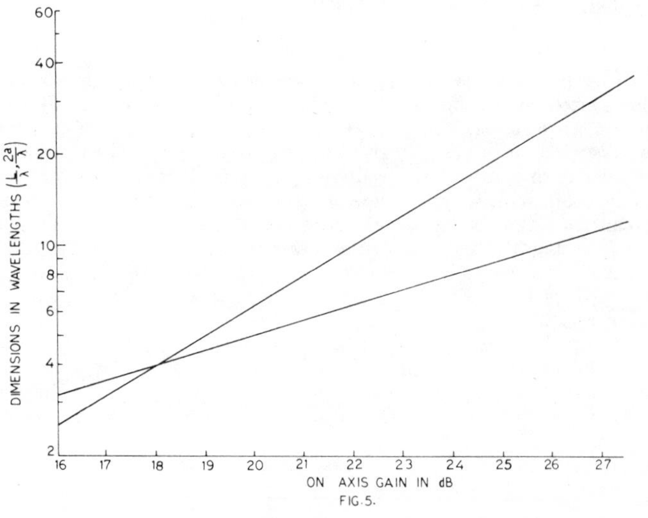

Fig. 5. On-axis gain of conical scalar horns of optimum proportions.

would result in maximum $G(0,0)$ have been determined with the aid of a digital computer based algorithm. Furthermore, a digital computer based curve fitting procedure was adopted to derive an expression for α_0 for an optimum horn with a prescribed L/λ, which is given by

$$\tan \alpha_0 = a_2 x^2 + a_1 x + a_0 \tag{9}$$

where $x = (\lambda/L)^{1/2}$; $a_2 = 1.3649 \times 10^{-3}$; $a_1 = 9.877 \times 10^{-1}$; $a_0 = 6.680 \times 10^{-5}$; and $0 < L < 50\lambda$.

From (9), one also obtains the following relation for an optimum horn

$$L/\lambda = \frac{(D/2\lambda - a_2)^2}{a_1^2} \tag{10}$$

where $D = 2a$.

In order to facilitate computation of radiation pattern and on-axis gain of an optimum scalar horn, two more useful plots have been presented through Figs. 4 and 5. Fig. 4 enables one to select the aperture width for a prescribed 3-dB beamwidth (which is very nearly equal to a relative amplitude level of 0.7) and Fig. 5 enables one to compute the corresponding on-axis gain and the axial length.

The author is thankful to Dr. M. Jeuken, Department of Electrical Engineering, Technological University, Eindhoven, The Netherlands, for having supplied the measured data on radiation patterns of corrugated conical horns.

ACKNOWLEDGMENT

The computing facilities of the Computer Center at Tata Institute of Fundamental Research, Colaba, Bombay-400005 have been made use of for several numerical computations involved in this paper.

REFERENCES

[1] M. I. Skolnik, *Radar Handbook.* New York: McGraw-Hill, 1970, ch. 11.

[2] M. S. Narasimhan and B. V. Rao, "Diffraction by wide-flare-angle corrugated conical horns," *Electron. Lett.*, vol. 6, no. 15, July 1970, pp. 469–471.

[3] P. J. B. Clarricoats and P. K. Saha, "Propagation and radiation behaviour of corrugated feeds: Part I," *Proc. Inst. Elec. Eng.*, vol. 118, pp. 1177–1186, Sept. 1971.

Part VII
Dielectric-Loaded Horns

Dielectric rod and tube antennas are relatively old [1], [2], but the first combination of a dielectric cone and a horn seems to have occurred in the mid-1960's as the first paper in this part, by Bartlett and Moseley, reveals. Not surprisingly, the motivation was to improve the performance of large satellite tracking antennas. Their dielectric cone, of light foamed plastic, extended beyond the horn and all the way to the subreflector of their Cassegrain system. An aperture efficiency of about 75 percent was claimed.

The second paper, by Tsandoulas and Fitzgerald, describes the use of dielectric wedges inside the walls of rectangular and pyramidal horns to create a dominant longitudinal section electric (LSE) mode. Their object is to increase the aperture efficiency of the radiator from the usual 81 percent to a value close to 100 percent. Such radiators would presumably be more useful in array applications than as feed horns. The following two short papers are concerned with the use of a dielectric plug in the end of round waveguide (Hamid *et al.*) and a dielectric band inside the aperture of a conical horn (Satoh). The former technique appears to narrow the radiation pattern and increases the gain. The latter technique has the opposite effect; the beam is broadened in the *E* plane. The reason for this is that the dielectric band acts as a mode converter for the TM_{11} mode so that the device becomes, in effect, a multimode horn.

The fifth paper in this part, by James, is a practical account of dielectric rod, tube, and horn antennas based on a semiempirical design approach. Next is a short contribution of Brooking, Clarricoats, and Olver in which predicted and experimental patterns are compared for a pyramidal dielectric excited by a pyramidal horn.

The last, a lengthy two-part paper by Clarricoats and Salema, is the most definitive treatment extant of conical dielectric horn radiators. In Part 1, the authors develop a theory of propagation and radiation by dielectric cones. In Part 2, they present a design theory for Cassegrain reflectors employing dielectric cone feeds. They emphasize the similarity between the hybrid modes that propagate on a dielectric cone and those in a corrugated horn.

Further papers and articles relating to dielectric horns and the use of dielectric radiators in general are found in [3]–[17].

References

[1] G. E. Mueller and W. A. Tyrell, "Polyrod antennas," *Bell Syst. Tech. J.*, vol. 26, pp. 837–851, Oct. 1947.

[2] D. G. Kiely, *Dielectric Aerials.* London: Methuen, 1953.

[3] M. A. Quddus and J. P. German, "Phase correction by dielectric slabs in sectoral horn antennas," *IEEE Trans. Antennas Propagat.*, vol. AP-9, pp. 413–415, July 1961.

[4] B. L. Lewis, "Large diameter dielectric rod end-fire antennas," *IEEE Trans. Antennas Propagat.*, vol. AP-14, pp. 239–240, Mar. 1966.

[5] J. R. James, "Theoretical investigation of cylindrical dielectric-rod antennas," *Proc. Inst. Elec. Eng.*, vol. 114, pp. 309–319, Mar. 1967.

[6] ——, "Leaky waves on a dielectric rod," *Electron. Lett.*, vol. 5, pp. 252–254, May 29, 1969.

[7] M. A. K. Hamid and A. Mohsen, "Diffraction by dielectric-loaded horns and corner reflectors," *IEEE Trans. Antennas Propagat.*, vol. AP-17, pp. 660–662, Sept. 1969.

[8] M. A. K. Hamid, R. J. Boulanger, N. J. Mostowy, and A. Mohsen, "Radiation characteristics of dielectric-loaded horn antennas," *Electron. Lett.*, vol. 6, pp. 20–21, Jan. 8, 1970.

[9] L. L. Oh, S. Y. Peng, and C. D. Lunden, "Effects of dielectrics on the radiation patterns of an electromagnetic horn," *IEEE Trans. Antennas Propagat.*, vol. AP-18, pp. 553–556, July 1970.

[10] R. J. Boulanger and M. A. K. Hamid, "A new type of dielectric-loaded waveguide antenna," *Microwave J.*, vol. 13, pp. 67–68, Dec. 1970.

[11] P. J. B. Clarricoats and C. E. R. C. Salema, "Propagation and radiation characteristics of low-permittivity dielectric cones," *Electron. Lett.*, vol. 7, pp. 483–485, Aug. 1971.

[12] ——, "Influence of launching horn on radiation characteristics of a dielectric cone feed," *Electron. Lett.*, vol. 8, pp. 200–202, Apr. 20, 1972.

[13] C. E. R. C. Salema and P. J. B. Clarricoats, "Radiation characteristics of dielectric cones," *Electron. Lett.*, vol. 8, pp. 414–416, Aug. 10, 1972.

[14] P. J. B. Clarricoats, C. E. R. C. Salema, and S. H. Lim, "Design of Cassegrain antennas employing dielectric cone feeds," *Electron. Lett.*, vol. 8, pp. 384–385, July 25, 1972.

[15] R. Baldwin and P. A. McInnes, "Radiation patterns of dielectric loaded rectangular horns," *IEEE Trans. Antennas Propagat.*, vol. AP-21, pp. 375–376, May 1973.

[16] J. Arnbak, "Leaky waves on a dielectric rod," *Electron. Lett.*, vol. 5, pp. 41–42, Feb. 6, 1969.

[17] R. Ashton and R. Baldwin, "Rectangular horn with dielectric-slab insert," *Electron. Lett.*, vol. 9, pp. 26–27, Jan. 25, 1973.

TECHNICAL SECTION

DIELGUIDES* — HIGHLY EFFICIENT LOW NOISE ANTENNA FEEDS

H. E. Bartlett
R. E. Moseley
Radiation Incorporated
Melbourne, Florida

INTRODUCTION

Designers of aperture antennas continually strive to increase antenna efficiency or, since the advent of extremely low noise receivers, to maximize the antenna gain-to-noise ratio—the ultimate goal being, of course, the uniformly illuminated aperture with no spillover. Past efforts[1,2] toward this goal have met with some success, but unfortunately the resulting primary feeds have been quite complex, difficult to practically implement and narrow band.

Using conventional techniques, aperture antenna design involves a compromise between illumination uniformity and the amount of energy lost in spillover. This compromise is required because the radiation pattern of all conventional feeds varies with angle in a manner which is governed by diffraction theory. A technique which virtually negates the requirement for compromise between illumination efficiency and spillover efficiency is required if one is to significantly improve the antenna efficiency above that attainable with conventional techniques ($\eta \approx 55$ per cent).

A new approach has been developed which tends to eliminate the requirement for compromise and which is conceptually simple, easily implemented and broadband. Dielectric guiding structures (Dielguides) are placed between primary feed and reflector or subreflector. These guiding structures utilize the phenomenon of total internal reflection[3] (TIR), which is a property of the boundary between dielectric media, to reduce spillover and provide a more uniform reflector illumination. The technique is applicable to both single and multiple reflector systems and it is compatible with any auto-track error signal generation method.

THEORY

As previously mentioned, the reduction of spillover radiation is accomplished through the phenomenon of total internal reflection. If an electromagnetic wave passing from a more dense to a less dense medium is incident on the boundary at an angle (measured from the normal to the boundary) greater than the critical angle, the wave is totally reflected. When the lower density medium is air, the critical angle is arc sin $1/\sqrt{\varepsilon}$. Referring to Figure 1(a), an exemplary Cassegrain Dielguide diagram, ray OAX represents energy that would be lost in spillover lobes in the absence of the guiding structure. With the addition of a properly designed Dielguide, the ray intersects the boundary at an angle Φ_1, greater than critical, and is redirected to the subreflector. Energy reflected from the subreflector impinges on the boundary at an angle less than critical and passes across the boundary to the main reflector.

Figure 1(b) further illustrates the effect of the Dielguide on the primary feed radiation pattern. θ_F represents the flare angle of the guiding structure, and θ_{CR} the critical angle of the dielectric. Without the Dielguide, all radiation past θ_F would be lost in spillover. With the Dielguide, energy between θ_F and $\theta_F + \pi/2 - \theta_{CR}$ is redirected to the subreflector. The additional energy incident on the subreflector is that contained in a conical sector $\pi/2 - \theta_{CR}$ wide. With properly chosen parameters, the redirected energy can be "folded" into the angular region subtended by the subreflector in a manner which results in a more uniform illumination, thereby providing improved illumination efficiency. It is noteworthy that the relationship for the critical angle does not contain frequency — the bandwidth of these devices being dependent only on the bandwidth of the primary feed and the requirement for sufficient electrical boundary length to effect TIR.

Dielguides are also applicable to prime-focus systems and their operation in such applications is similarly explained.

EXPERIMENTAL RESULTS

Dielguide models have been fabricated and evaluated employing both prime focus and Cassegrain aperture formation techniques. In addition, models employing both amplitude and phase monopulse error signal generation techniques have been constructed and evaluated. The results obtained from these models are presented in the following paragraphs. It is significant that both feeds can be made self-supporting, thus requiring no spars with their attendant aperture block. Further, as will be explained later, the Dielguide Cassegrain feed allows the use of much smaller subreflectors than can be employed with conventional feeds, thereby also considerably reducing aperture block.

Dielguide materials used have all been polystyrene based plastic foam. The relative dielectric constant has ranged from 1.08 to 1.5 and the loss tangent has been 0.0004 or less in all cases. In all experimental models fabricated to date, the loss incurred from the Dielguide material has been less than 0.1 dB. This loss represents

---

* *Patent Pending, S/N 413,819.*

Reprinted with permission from *Microwave J.*, vol. 9, pp. 53–58, Dec. 1966.

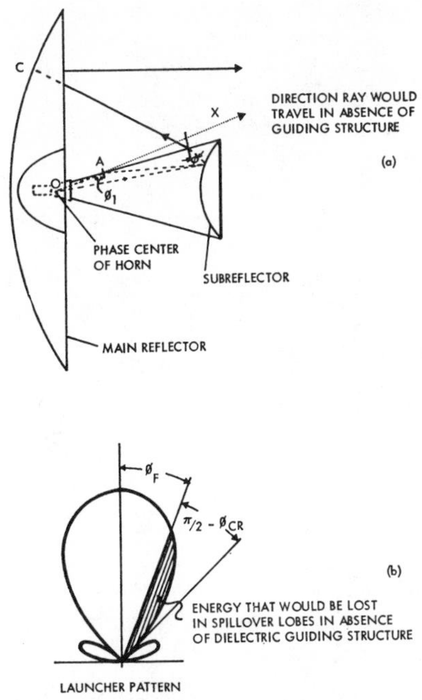

Figure 1 — Dielguide operation.

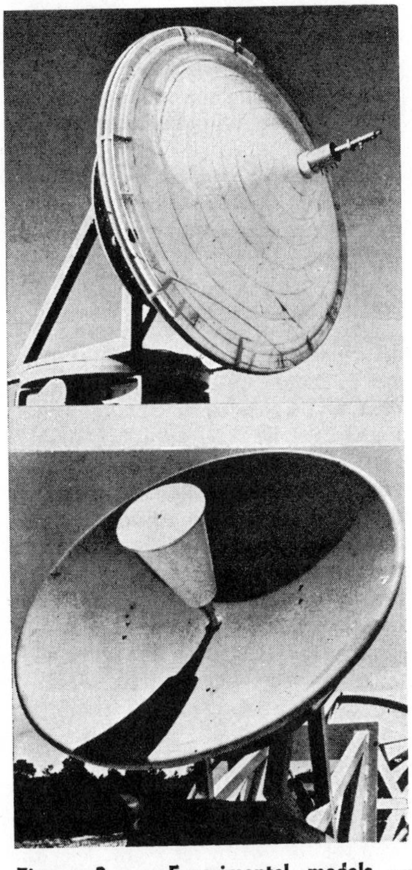

Figure 2 — Experimental models — a. prime focus, b. Cassegrain.

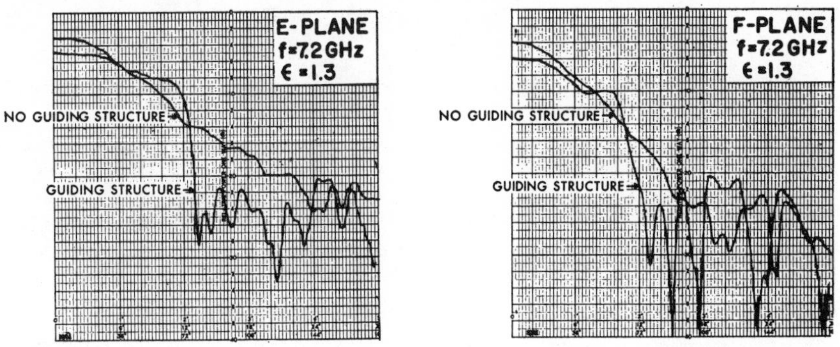

PRIMARY PATTERNS

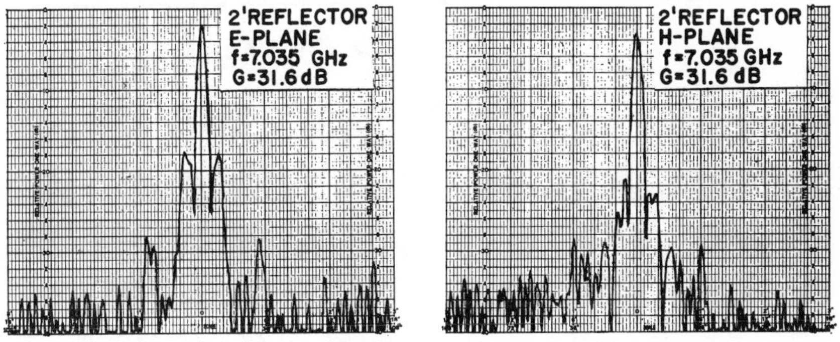

SECONDARY PATTERNS

Figure 3 — Prime focus model — typical primary and secondary patterns.

a noise temperature contribution of 7°K maximum which is offset several times over by the noise temperature reduction attributable to reduced spillover energy.

Prime Focus Model

Figure 2 includes a photograph of a prime focus Dielguide feed. Typical E- and H-plane primary feed patterns, with and without the Dielguide, and typical E- and H-plane secondary patterns are shown in Figure 3. The effect of the Dielguide boundary is apparent in the primary patterns. The spillover has been significantly reduced and the redirected energy has been utilized to provide a more uniform illumination. The secondary patterns are quite representative of a heavily illuminated circular aperture. The measured gain was 31.6 dB (2 foot reflector at 7.03 GHz), corresponding to a total antenna efficiency from measured gain of 72 per cent.

Cassegrain Model

A photograph of a Cassegrain Dielguide is also shown in Figure 2. The subreflector is fabricated of metalized plastic foam and it is attached directly to the large end of the Dielguide.

There is one important difference in the design of a conventional Cassegrain feed and a Dielguide Cassegrain feed. With a conventional Cassegrain feed the subreflector illumination is commonly tapered to −10 dB to −12 dB at the edges and subreflector electrical size is utilized to control the slope of the scatter pattern skirts.

The Dielguide feed guides energy to the subreflector and TIR provides

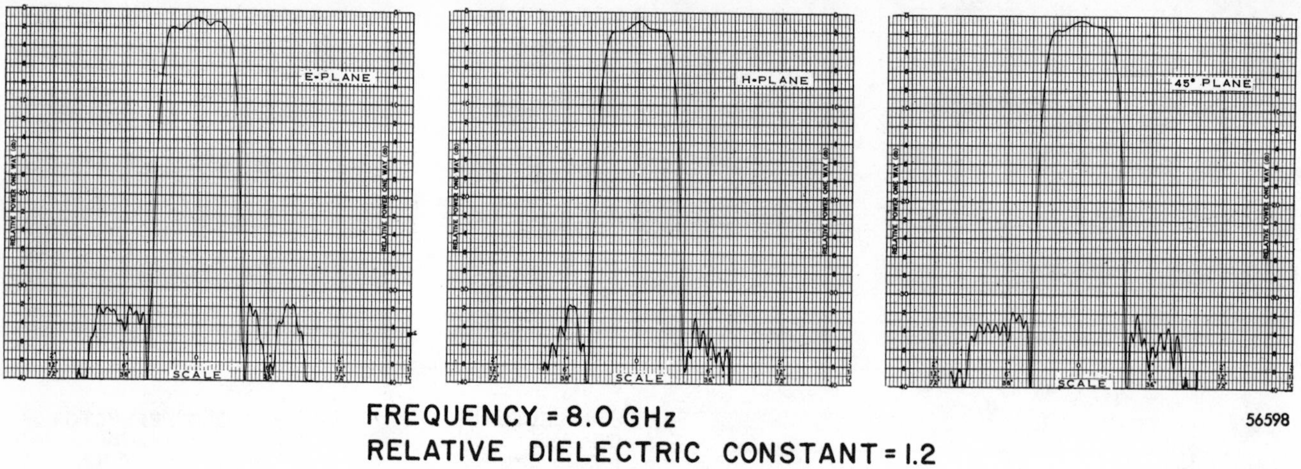

Figure 4 — Typical primary patterns — Cassegrain Dielguide feed.

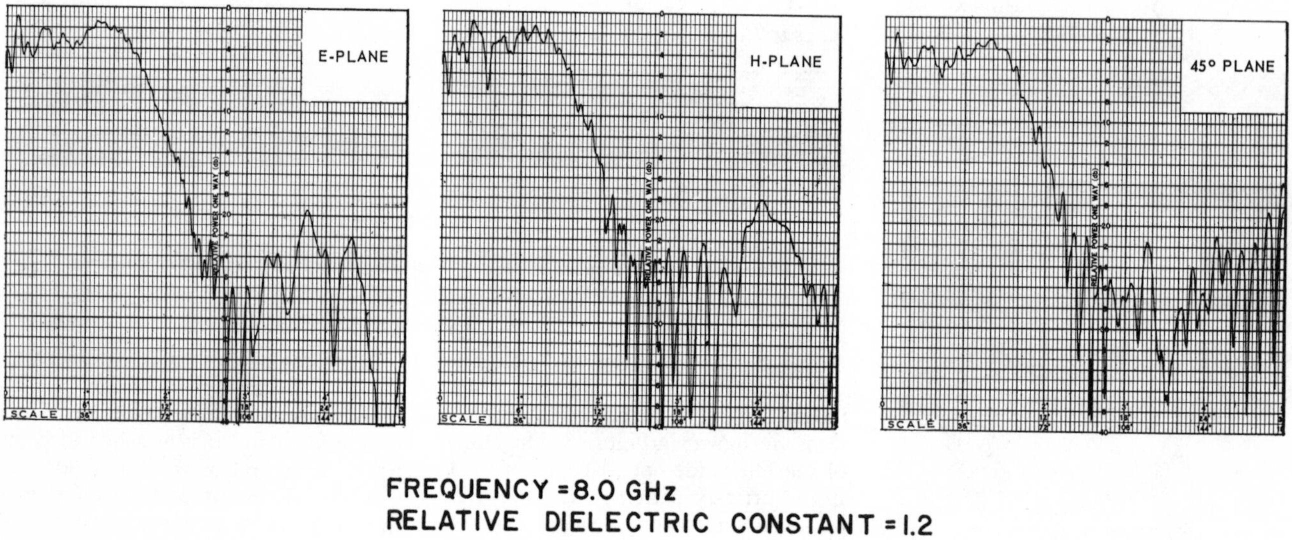

Figure 5 — Typical scatter patterns — Cassegrain Dielguide feed.

very steep primary pattern skirts such that the subreflector can be extended into the first nulls of the primary pattern (and still be quite small — 10λ or less). When the subreflector is extended into the first nulls of the primary pattern, the steep primary skirts transform into correspondingly steep scatter pattern skirts.

Typical E-, H- and 45° plane patterns for a Cassegrain Dielguide feed are shown in Figure 4. These patterns were probed across the base of the Dielguide and therefore represent the illumination on the subreflector. The very steep skirts caused by TIR are apparent, as is the "flat-topped" main lobe resulting from proper control of redirected energy. In addition, the three cuts show that the primary pattern is virtually circularly symmetric, another requirement for high antenna efficiency.

The resulting E-, H- and 45° plane scatter patterns are shown in Figure 5. Here again, the circular symmetry, uniform illumination, steep skirts and the low spillover past both the subreflector and the main reflector are apparent. A scatter pattern obtained from a 40λ subreflector and conventional feed is shown in Figure 6. A comparison of this scatter pattern and those obtained from the 10λ subreflector and Dielguide feed in Figure 5 clearly demonstrates the superiority of the Dielguide technique.

Table I

PREDICTED APERTURE EFFICIENCY

Frequency	η_{sp}	η_{at}	$\eta_{sp}\,\eta_{at}$
7.2 GHz	91.0 %	96.0 %	87.3 %
7.8 GHz	94.5 %	93.5 %	88.2 %
8.4 GHz	95.3 %	94.2 %	89.7 %

η_{sp} is spillover efficiency
η_{at} is illumination efficiency

A typical phase scatter pattern is shown in Figure 7. Calculated phase efficiency for Cassegrain Dielguide feeds is commonly 99 per cent or greater.

Predicted aperture efficiency (illumination efficiency times spillover efficiency — $\eta_{at}\,\eta_{sp}$) is tabulated in Table I over the 7.2 - 8.4 GHz frequency range. These efficiencies were calculated from scatter pattern data obtained from a Cassegrain Dielguide feed which was ultimately employed in an 8.5-foot diameter main reflector. Note that the spillover efficiency (η_{sp}) is very high; at 7.8 GHz, for example, only 5.5 per cent of the total energy radiated from the primary feed is spilled over, either past the subreflector or the main reflector. This is particularly significant in consideration of the fact that spillover energy is the major contributor to antenna noise temperature. Further, the product of illumination efficiency and spillover efficiency is in excess of 87 per

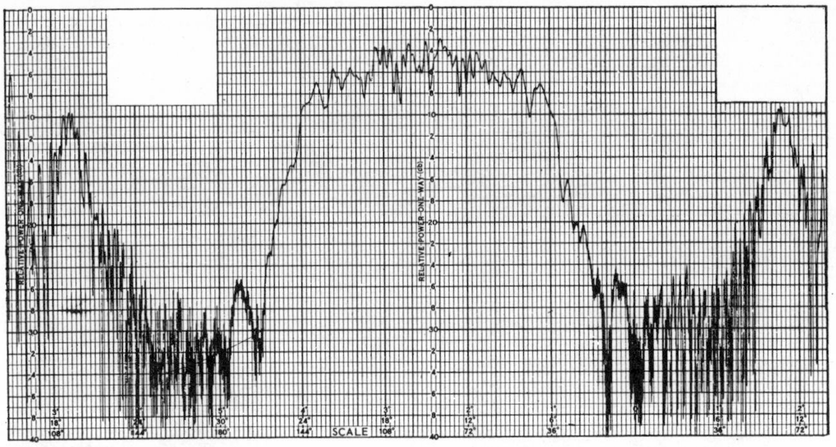

Figure 6 — Typical scatter pattern with conventional feed — subreflector diameter = 5 feet; frequency = 8.85 GHz; H-plane.

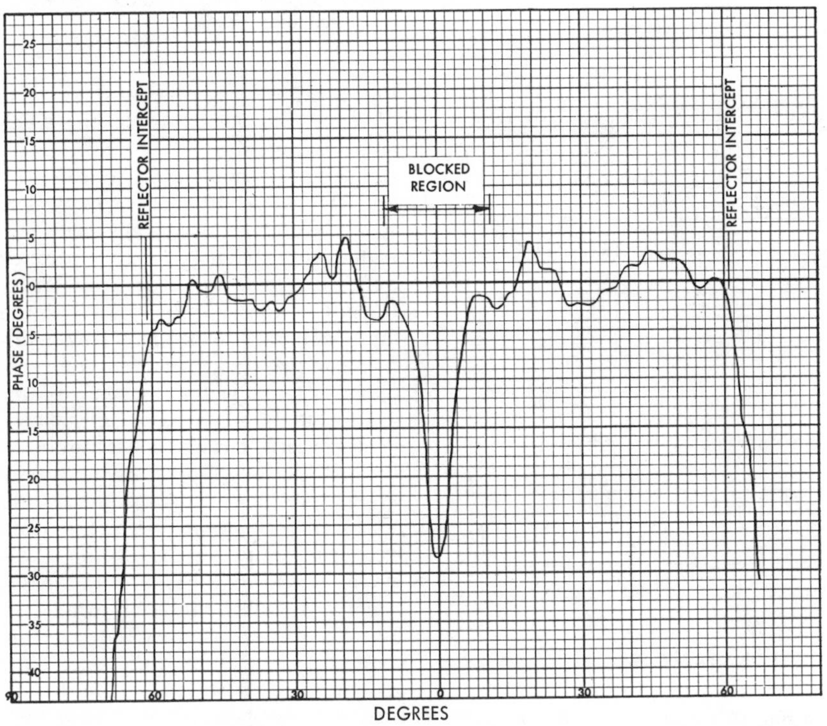

Figure 7 — Typical phase scatter pattern.

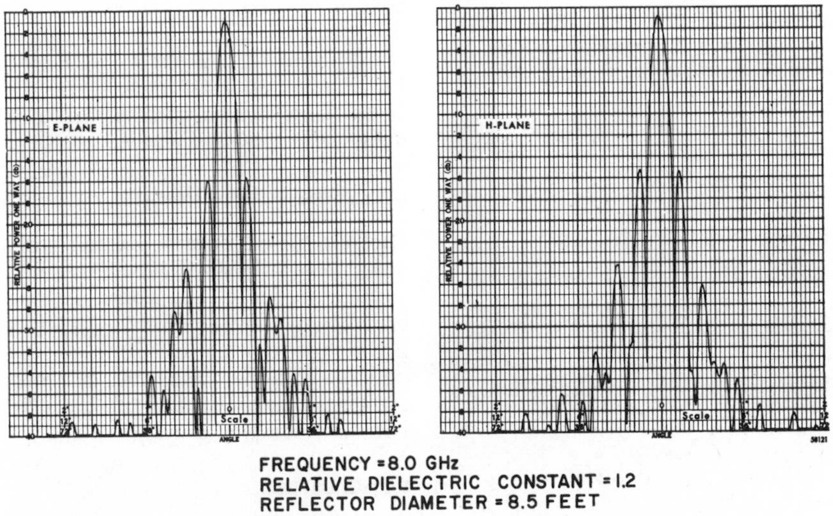

Figure 8 — Typical secondary patterns — Cassegrain dielguide feed.

cent over the entire frequency range. This product is commonly 55 to 65 per cent with conventional feeds, which results in total antenna efficiencies of 45 to 55 per cent.

Measured secondary patterns obtained from the previously mentioned 8.5-foot diameter antenna are shown in Figure 8. These patterns are quite representative of heavily illuminated circular apertures. The measured gain was 45.4 dB at 7.8 GHz, which corresponds to a total antenna efficiency of 75 per cent. The measured antenna efficiency over the entire 7.2 to 8.4 GHz band was greater than 75 per cent.

SMALLER SUBREFLECTORS

Electrically small subreflectors are currently being investigated and the results are quite encouraging. A typical scatter pattern obtained from a Dielguide feed and a 3.7λ subreflector is shown in Figure 9. Integration of sets of such patterns indicates realizable total antenna efficiencies of 65 to 70 per cent. This facet of the Dielguide technique is particularly significant in that it allows Cassegrain aperture formation with much smaller main reflectors than has been heretofore practical. It now appears that Cassegrain Dielguide feeds are usable, with good results, in main reflectors as small as 10λ in diameter.

AMPLITUDE MONOPULSE DIELGUIDE FEED

The common four-horn monopulse feed is conceptually quite simple, but good overall antenna performance is precluded by a basic problem. Stated simply, the problem is that the primary illumination function is too narrow in the sum mode and too wide in the two difference modes. These facts necessitate an illumination compromise which results in rather poor antenna performance in all three modes of operation.

An ideal monopulse feed would have both the sum and difference patterns contained in the same envelope. Several types of primary feeds have been developed which approach this ideal excitation to varying degrees.

The twelve-horn feed[4] provides good performance in all three modes of operation, but it suffers from two drawbacks: (a) the complexity and the attendant loss in the circuitry required to connect the twelve horns, and (b) an inefficient H-plane feed excitation.

The multimode monopulse feed[5] employs higher-order waveguide modes in a common aperture for error signal generation and illumination shaping. This type of feed provides

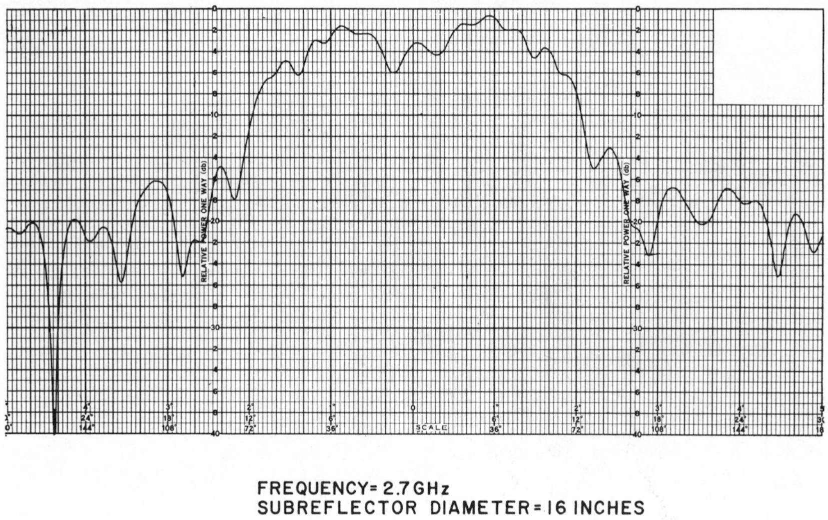

Figure 9 — Typical scatter pattern — 3.7λ subreflector.

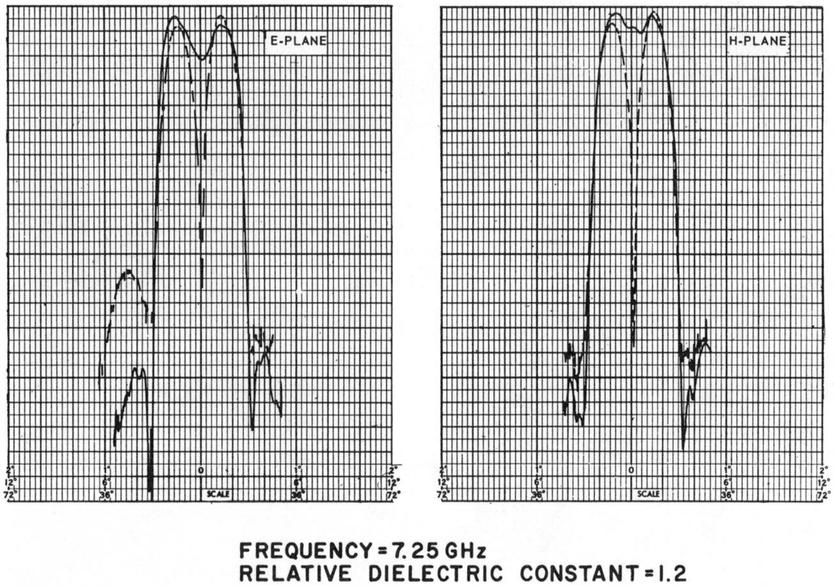

Figure 10 — Typical primary patterns — Cassegrain Dielguide monopulse feed.

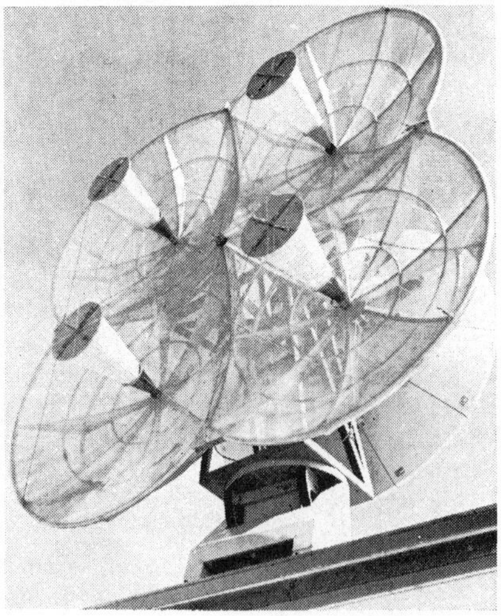

Figure 11 — Four reflector array — Dielguide feeds.

improved performance, but the technique is very complex and it suffers from extreme frequency sensitivity due to phase dispersion between the various higher-order modes employed.

The multimode-multihorn feed[6] employs a combination of multiple-horn excitation in one plane and multimode excitation in the other, and it substantially provides the ideal illumination. However, as one would expect, it suffers from a combination of the deficiencies discussed previously.

The Dielguide monopulse feed provides a near ideal excitation without any of the previously described drawbacks.

Typical E- and H-plane Cassegrain Dielguide monopulse primary patterns are shown in Figure 10. The very efficient sum mode excitation is obvious and the sum and difference patterns are constrained by TIR to the same envelope. The bounded horn Dielguide exciter is conceptually almost as simple as the four-horn feed, and the bandwidth is limited only by the bandwidth of the exciter and the requirement for sufficient electrical boundary length to effect TIR.

FOUR-REFLECTOR ARRAY

A four-reflector, phase monopulse array with Cassegrain Dielguide feeds has been constructed and evaluated for a specific military application requiring gain-to-noise maximization.

A photograph of the array is shown in Figure 11. It consists of four 10-foot diameter paraboloidal reflectors which have been cut square and joined on their common sides, and four Cassegrain Dielguide feeds. The resulting asymmetrical reflectors serve to illustrate the versatility of the Dielguide techniques.

The subject antenna has a low noise temperature requirement ($T_A = 38°K$ at 7° elevation). If conventional feeds with symmetrical primary patterns were used, there would be a significant amount of energy spilled over into the three adjacent reflectors. This spillover energy would result in comparatively high sidelobes several beamwidths off the main beam axis. These sidelobes are serious contributors to antenna noise temperature and they would preclude satisfaction of the noise temperature requirement. Flats were cut on two sides of the Dielguide, as shown in Figure 12, in an attempt to tailor the feed pattern to conform to the asymmetrical reflector contour. The results were successful and they are shown in Figure 13. If such shaping were possible with conventional bounded horns, the required technology would be extremely complex and difficult to practically implement.

Typical sum and difference patterns for this antenna are shown in Figure 14. The measured gain was 47.5 dB at 4.6 GHz, which corresponds to a total antenna efficiency of 80 per cent.

DIELGUIDE POWER CAPACITY

Dielguides have been tested to a peak power level of 3.0 MW and 4.0 kW average at 5.6 GHz. There was no breakdown or detectable heating. Earlier models, fabricated of slightly different material than that currently used, have been tested to 20 kW CW without excessive heating.

CONCLUSIONS

A new technique for providing highly efficient, low noise antenna feeds has

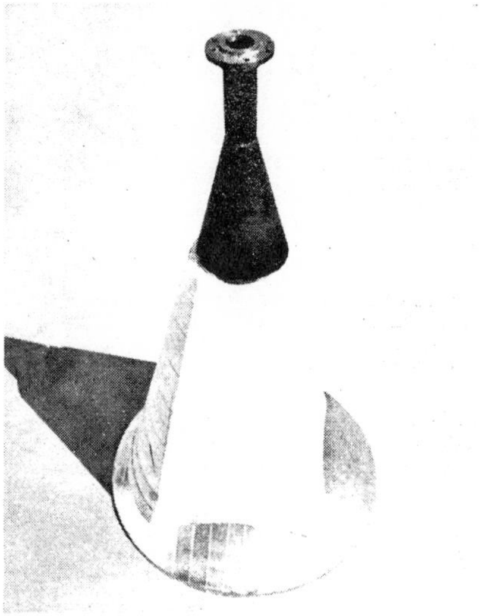

Figure 12 — Shaped Dielguide feed.

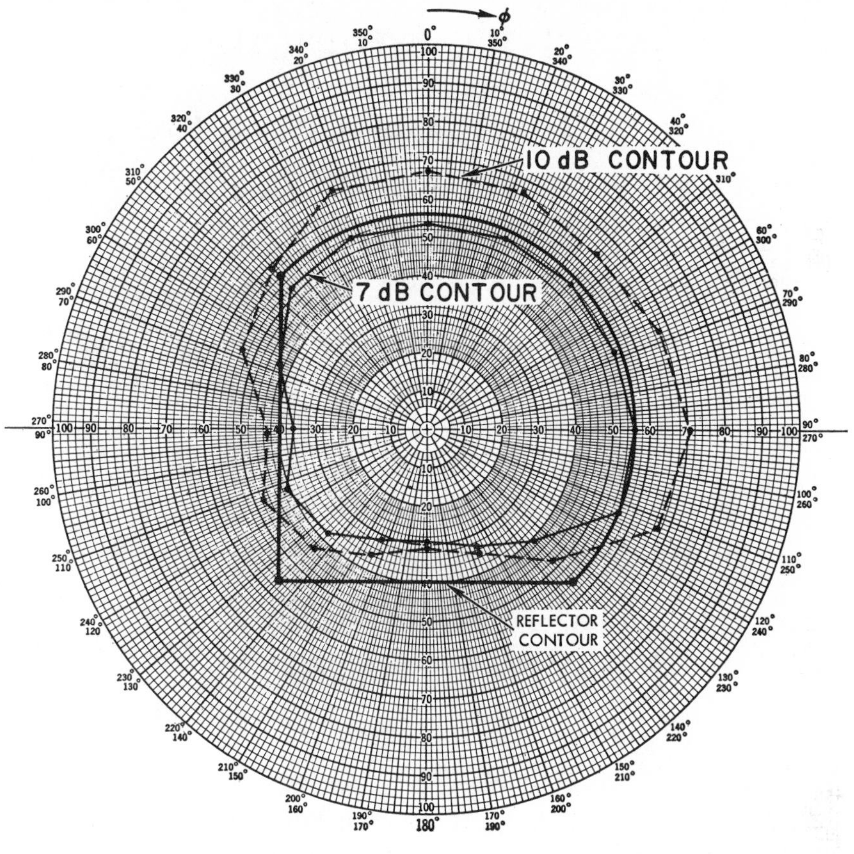

Figure 13 — Scatter pattern contour plot — shaped Dielguide feed.

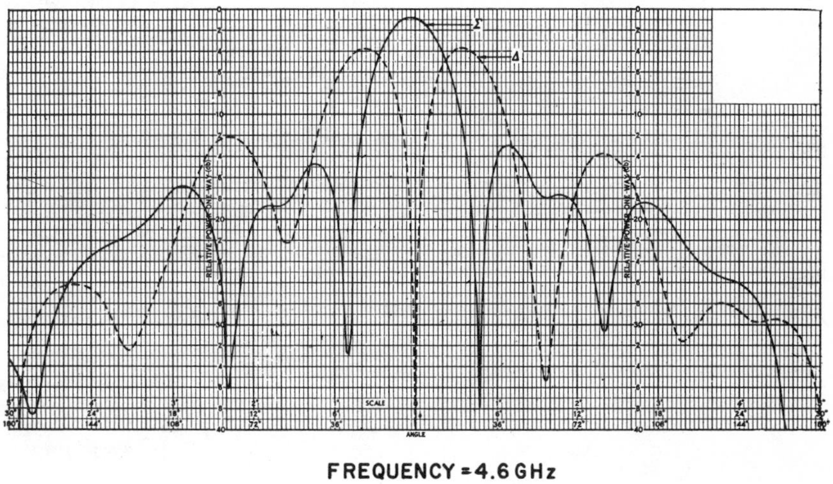

Figure 14 — Typical sum and difference patterns — four reflector array.

been developed. The technique has been successfully demonstrated in both prime focus and Cassegrain configurations as well as in amplitude and phase monopulse tracking antennas. Primary feeds which utilize this technique are conceptually simple, easily implemented, broadband and have high power capacity.

Total antenna efficiencies ranging from 75 to 80 per cent have been repeatedly measured during the course of the past year. Very simple, such efficiencies mean a 1.5 - 2.0 dB gain improvement over conventional state-of-the-art feeds in the same reflector. The system figure of merit is improved even more because of the noise temperature reduction.

Because of the extreme control of primary pattern shape offered by the Dielguide, it appears that the technique may afford solutions to other antenna problems, i.e., other than gain/noise maximization.

Finally, the Dielguide technique is based on the phenomenon of total internal reflection, a phenomenon widely used by optical people, but to the writers' knowledge this work represents its first application by antenna engineers.

ACKNOWLEDGMENTS

This work would not have been possible without the support of the U. S. Army Satellite Communications Agency under Contracts DA 36-039 AMC-03310(E) and DA 28-043 AMC-00389(S). A special note of appreciation is due W. Hoffmann of that agency for his faith and many helpful suggestions. The authors are also indebted to Dr. L. Pietsch and G. W. Collins of Radiation Incorporated for many stimulating discussions and countless experimental data.

REFERENCES

1. Potter, P. D., "A New Horn With Suppressed Sidelobes and Equal Beamwidths," the *microwave journal,* June 1963, pp. 71-78.

2. Schuster, D., et al., "The Determination of Noise Temperatures of Large Paraboloidal Antennas," *IRE Trans.-PGAP,* May 1962, pp. 286-291.

3. Ramos, S. and J. R. Whinnery, *Fields and Waves In Modern Ratio,* John Wiley & Sons, Inc., New York, N. Y., 1953, pp. 302-303.

4. Ricardi, L. J. and L. Niro, "Design of a Twelve-Horn Monopulse Feed," *IRE Int'l. Conv. Rec.,* Pt. I, 1961, pp. 93-102.

5. Jensen, P. A., "A Low-Noise Multimode Cassegrain Monopulse Feed with Polarization Diversity," *Nerem Rec.,* 1963, pp. 94-95.

6. Hannan, P. W., "Optimum Feed for All Three Modes of a Monopulse Antenna II: Practice, *IRE Trans.-AP,* Vol. AP-9, September 1961, pp. 454-461.

Aperture Efficiency Enhancement in Dielectrically Loaded Horns

G. N. TSANDOULAS, MEMBER, IEEE, AND W. D. FITZGERALD, MEMBER, IEEE

Abstract—The effect of symmetrically loading a horn aperture with E-plane dielectric slabs is examined both theoretically and experimentally. It is shown that aperture efficiencies of the order of 92–96 percent may be obtained easily and inexpensively. The technique, which was demonstrated experimentally for a small horn aperture, might find application in limited scan arrays.

Introduction

IN THIS WORK attention is directed to the dominant LSE_{10} mode field distribution and to the radiation characteristics of dielectrically loaded rectangular waveguides radiating directly into free space. The efficiency with which a horn radiator concentrates energy inside the main beam depends on the "flatness" of the aperture electric-field distribution. It is expected therefore that the dielectric loading arrangement shown in Fig. 1(c) will enhance the aperture efficiency under proper parameter selection.

The proposed loading method has already been mentioned as a valid way to equalize the radiation patterns of the two principal planes (E and H) for use as a paraboloid feed [1]. More recently, Quddus and German [2] introduced triangular dielectric wedges as phase correction elements in H-plane sectoral horns. Using variously shaped dielectric inserts Hamid *et al.* [3], [4] have shown experimentally that beneficial effects on beamwidth and directivity can occur. On the other hand, unloaded but multimode apertures such as the "box" horn [5] have yielded essentially similar results.

Our purpose is to present a systematic investigation of the efficiency increasing and pattern shaping capabilities of the symmetrically loaded horn in the single dominant mode regime. In this way the need for a box horn design is obviated with the effect that the required structure is very simple to implement. The technique may be used to advantage as a more efficient four-horn feed in a Cassegrainian system. A more interesting application would be in complete phased arrays which use electrically large ($>1.0\lambda$) elements to reduce the number needed in limited scan applications [6].

Schematically outlined in Fig. 1 are aperture-field distributions for three feed horn configurations showing the relative efficiencies of a standard horn, a box horn design, and a dielectrically loaded horn. In all cases it is assumed that the actual horns have flare angles shallow enough to make phase errors negligible.

Manuscript received March 10, 1971; revised June 14, 1971. This work was supported by the U. S. Department of the Army.
The authors are with M.I.T. Lincoln Laboratory, Lexington, Mass. 02173.

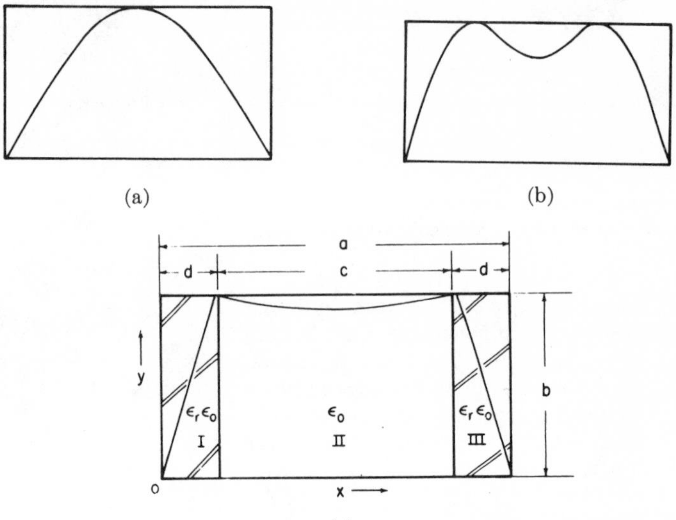

Fig. 1. (a) Dominant TE_{10} mode field distribution (empty horn). Maximum aperture efficiency ≈ 81 percent. (b) Dominant TE_{10} and TE_{30} mode superposition, (box horn design). Maximum aperture efficiency ≈ 90 percent. (c) Dielectrically loaded horn, dominant LSE_{10} mode only. Maximum theoretical aperture efficiency approaches 100 percent.

Field Expressions

Fig. 1(c) shows a transverse cut of the structure under investigation. The complete modal spectrum may be obtained in a number of ways as shown by Gardiol [7] and Tsandoulas *et al.* [8]. The last reference [8] examines the configuration obtained by interchanging the air and dielectric regions. Since the two problems are conceptually identical, the same analysis may be utilized. Thus, for the symmetric $LSE_{(m=\text{odd},0)}$ propagating modes, the electric-field components in the three regions are given by:

$$E_{y\text{I}} = E_0 \exp(j\gamma z) \sin \beta_1 \frac{x}{d} \tag{1}$$

$$E_{y\text{II}} = E_0 \frac{\sin \beta_1}{\cos \beta_2} \exp(j\gamma z) \cos \frac{2\beta_2}{c}\left(\frac{a}{2} - x\right) \tag{2}$$

$$E_{y\text{III}} = E_0 \exp(j\gamma z) \sin \beta_1 \left(\frac{x-a}{d}\right) \tag{3}$$

where E_0 is some arbitrary level of electric field, $\gamma = 2\pi/\lambda_g$ is the longitudinal propagation constant, and β_1/d and $2\beta_2/c$ are transverse propagation constants in dielectric and air, respectively. Relations between γ, β_1, and β_2 may

Reprinted from *IEEE Trans. Antennas Propagat.*, vol. AP-21, pp. 69–74, Jan. 1972.

be obtained from the wave equation:

$$\epsilon_r k_0^2 - \frac{\beta_1^2}{d^2} - \gamma^2 = 0 \tag{4}$$

$$k_0^2 - \frac{4\beta_2^2}{c^2} - \gamma^2 = 0 \tag{5}$$

where

$$k_0 = \frac{2\pi}{\lambda_0} = \omega(\mu_0\epsilon_0)^{1/2}.$$

An additional relation between β_1 and β_2 results upon the imposition of continuity on the magnetic fields across the air–dielectric interface. Consequently,

$$P \cot\left[2\frac{d}{a}sP\right] = \beta_2 \tan \beta_2 \tag{6}$$

where

$$P = \left[\beta_2^2 + (\epsilon_r - 1)\left(\frac{\pi a}{s\lambda}\right)^2\right]^{1/2} \tag{7}$$

and

$$s = \frac{1}{1 - 2(d/a)} \tag{8}$$

is the characteristic equation for β_2, while β_1 is given by

$$\beta_1 = 2\frac{d}{a}sP. \tag{9}$$

The ranges of the numbers β_1 (always real) and β_2 (either real or pure imaginary) are

$$0 \le \beta_1 \le \infty$$

$$0 \le \beta_2 \le \frac{\pi}{2}, \qquad \beta_2 \text{ real}$$

$$0 \le |\beta_2| \le \infty, \qquad \beta_2 \text{ imaginary}.$$

The transverse propagation constants determine the shape of the field distribution in each region and will be needed in the efficiency expressions to be derived shortly. The dominant LSE_{10} mode is described by the first root of the transcendental (6).

Analytical Expressions

The aperture efficiency η is defined as the ratio of the actual gain to that of a uniformly illuminated aperture [5]. Thus

$$\eta = \frac{G}{4\pi(ab/\lambda^2)} = \frac{\lambda^2 P(0,0)}{abP_T} \tag{10}$$

where $P(0,0)$ is the power radiated in the direction of the normal to the aperture plane ($\phi = 0$, $\theta = 0$ in a spherical coordinate system) and P_T is the total radiated power.

The derivation of the expression for η depends on certain simplifying assumptions regarding the nature of the electromagnetic wave at the aperture. In this work we assume that: 1) the electric-field distribution just outside the aperture is the same as that existing at any cross section inside; 2) only the dominant LSE_{10} mode is present; 3) there is negligible back reflection at the aperture. As we shall see later on in connection with our experimental results, the most crucial of these assumptions, the one about higher order modes, is valid.

Then, proceeding as in Silver [5], we have

$$P(0,0) = \frac{1}{2}R^2\left[\frac{\epsilon_0}{\mu_0}\right]^{1/2}|E_{AP}|^2$$

$$= \frac{[\epsilon_0/\mu_0]^{1/2}}{8\lambda^2}\left[1 + \left[\frac{\mu_0}{\epsilon_0}\right]^{1/2}\frac{\gamma}{\omega\mu_0}\right]^2 |N_y|^2 \tag{11}$$

where

$$N_y = \int_{\text{aperture}} E_y\, dA = b\int_x E_y\, dx \tag{12}$$

$$P_T = \frac{1}{2}\mathrm{Re}\int_{\text{aperture}} E_t \times H_t\, dA = \frac{b\gamma}{2\omega\mu_0}\int_x |E_y|^2\, dx \tag{13}$$

where we used the relation

$$H_x = \frac{\gamma}{\omega\mu_0}E_y \tag{14}$$

between the transverse electric and magnetic fields.

Substituting in (10) and carrying out the indicated integrations over each region of Fig. 1(c) separately, we finally obtain

$$\eta = \frac{\left[1 + \frac{\lambda}{\lambda_g}\right]^2}{4\left(\frac{\lambda}{\lambda_g}\right)} \cdot \frac{\left(4\frac{d}{a}\right)\left[\frac{1 - \cos\beta_1}{\beta_1} + \left(\frac{a}{2d} - 1\right)\frac{\sin\beta_2}{\beta_2}\frac{\sin\beta_1}{\cos\beta_2}\right]^2}{1 - \frac{\sin\beta_1}{\beta_1}\cos\beta_1 + \left(\frac{a}{2d} - 1\right)\left(\frac{\sin\beta_1}{\cos\beta_2}\right)^2\left[1 + \frac{\sin\beta_2}{\beta_2}\cos\beta_2\right]}. \tag{15}$$

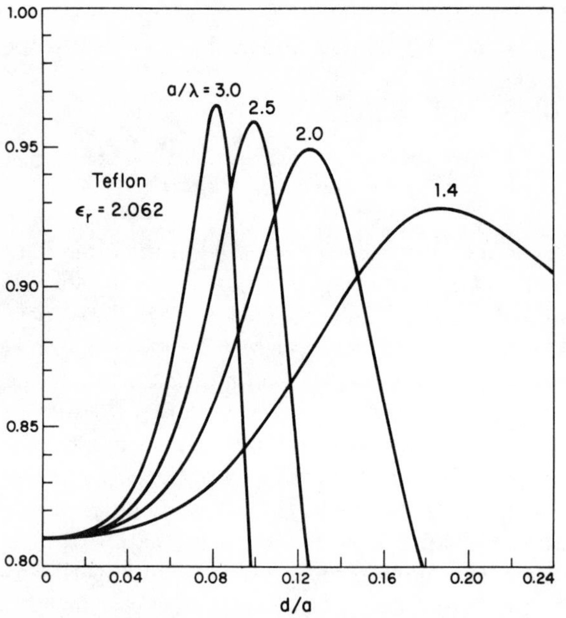

Fig. 2. Aperture efficiency versus dielectric filling factor. Material is Teflon, $\epsilon_r = 2.062$.

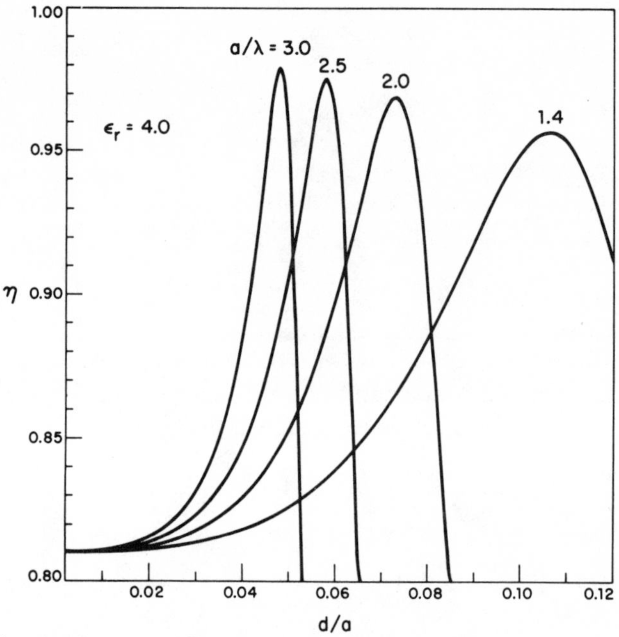

Fig. 3. Aperture efficiency versus dielectric filling factor. Commercially available material, $\epsilon_r = 4.0$.

The details of the calculation are omitted for brevity. The preceding reduces correctly to the value $(8/\pi^2)[1 + \lambda/\lambda_g]^2/(4\lambda/\lambda_g)$ for the fully filled and empty guide cases, but the approach to the limit must be made carefully. In connection with this, note that

$$\lim_{d\to 0} \beta_1 = 0 \qquad \lim_{d\to 0} \beta_2 = \frac{\pi}{2}$$

$$\lim_{d\to a/2} \beta_1 = \frac{\pi}{2} \qquad \lim_{d\to a/2} \beta_2 = j0.$$

The far-field pattern may be obtained by Fourier-transforming the aperture-field distribution. The results for E plane and H plane are, respectively,

$$P_E(\theta) = \frac{\sin(\pi(b/\lambda)\sin\theta)}{\pi(b/\lambda)\sin\theta} \tag{16}$$

$$\begin{aligned} P_H(\theta) = {} & \frac{d/a}{\beta_1^2 - u^2} \\ & \cdot [u \sin\beta_1 \sin v - \beta_1 \cos\beta_1 \cos v + \beta_1 \cos sv] \\ & + \frac{\sin\beta_1}{2s\cos\beta_2[\beta_2^2 - v^2]} \\ & \cdot [\beta_2 \sin\beta_2 \cos v - v \cos\beta_2 \sin v] \end{aligned} \tag{17}$$

where

$$u = 2\pi \frac{d}{\lambda} \sin\theta$$

$$v = \pi \frac{a}{\lambda s} \sin\theta$$

with s given by (8).

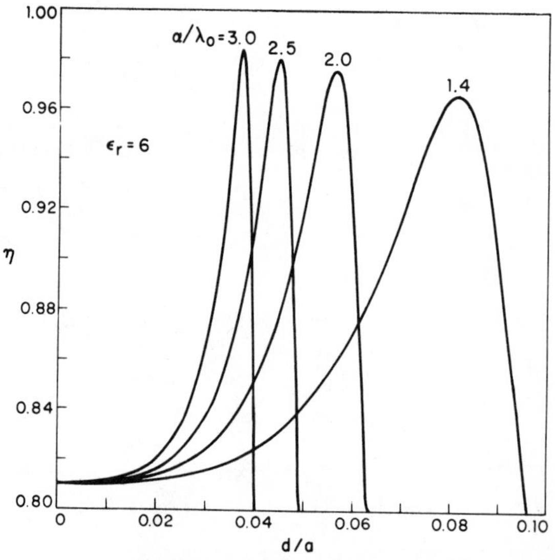

Fig. 4. Aperture efficiency versus dielectric filling factor. Commercially available material, $\epsilon_r = 6.0$.

Plots of η versus the dielectric filling factor d/a are given in Figs. 2, 3, and 4 for Teflon ($\epsilon_r = 2.062$), $\epsilon_r = 4.0$, and $\epsilon_r = 6.0$ for four aperture sizes. The efficiency exhibits, typically, a somewhat steep maximum, showing the improvement over the unloaded aperture case and then falls off rather rapidly to a minimum (0.6 to 0.5 is not unusual) before it starts climbing toward the fully filled guide value. These gyrations are connected intimately with the shape of the field across the aperture. Maximum efficiency occurs for a distribution slightly concave downward in the air region (β_2 slightly imaginary), much as shown in Fig. 1(c). A completely flat air region distribution is obtained when $\beta_2 = 0$ which occurs when

$$\frac{d}{a} = \frac{1}{4(a/\lambda)[\epsilon_r - 1]^{1/2}}. \tag{18}$$

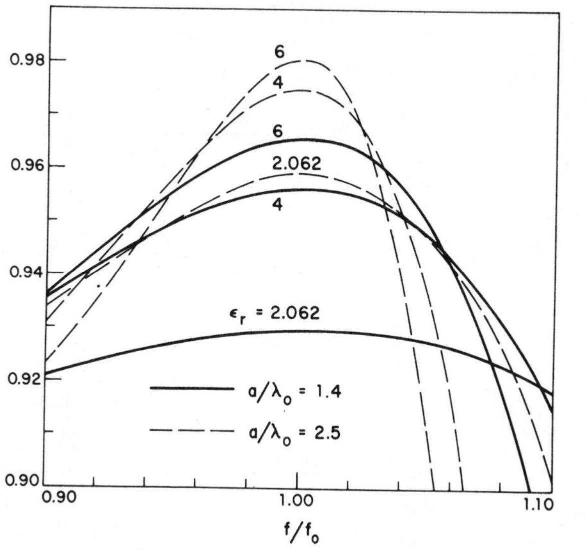

Fig. 5. Frequency dependence of aperture efficiency illustrating good bandwidth characteristics.

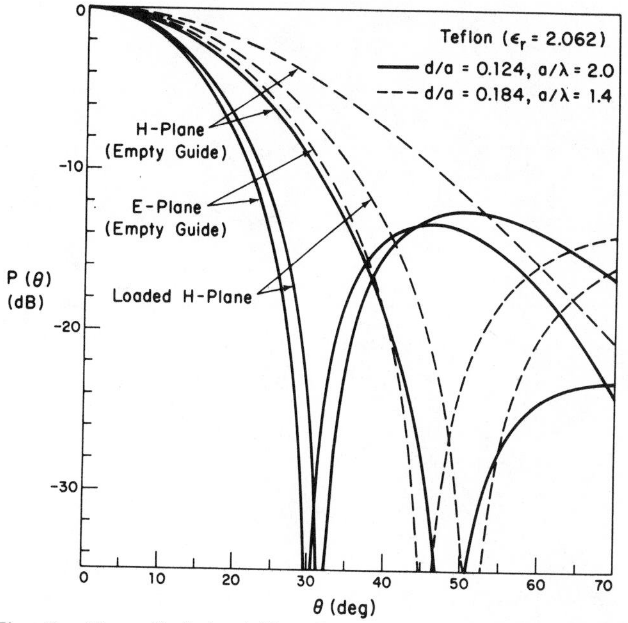

Fig. 7. Theoretical far-field patterns for loaded and unloaded apertures illustrating beamwidth reduction and sidelobe formation.

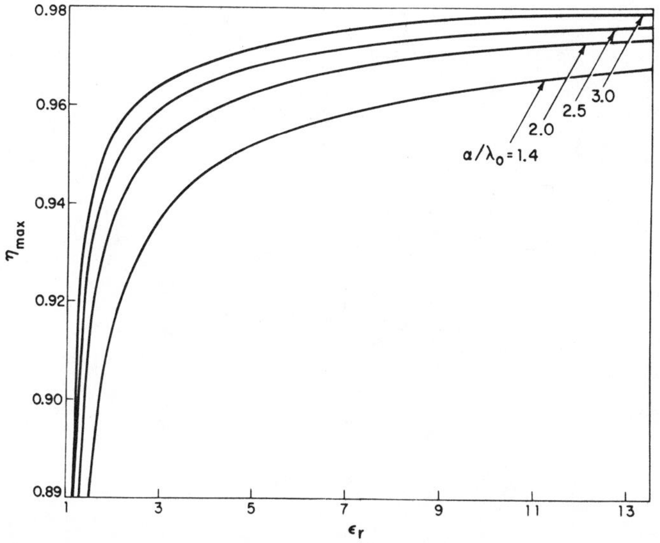

Fig. 6. Maximum theoretical aperture efficiency obtained by dielectric loading versus dielectric constant.

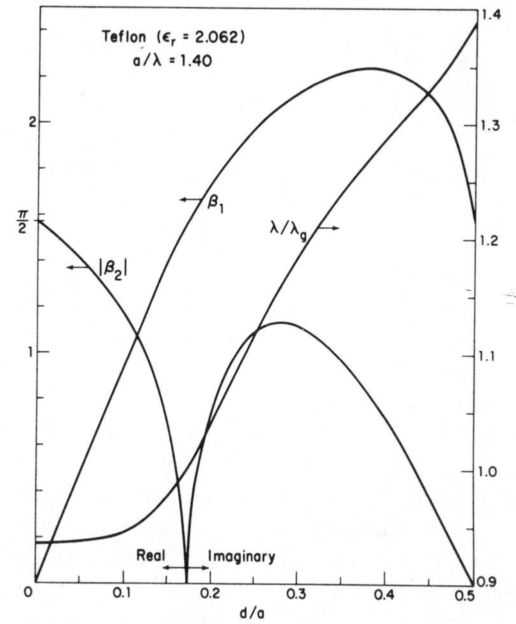

Fig. 8. Typical variation of transverse propagation numbers β_1 and $|\beta_2|$, and of normalized propagation constant λ/λ_g versus dielectric filling factor. Material is Teflon.

This will result in an efficiency slightly to the left of the peaks in Figs. 2, 3, and 4. Therefore, (18) may be used as an approximate criterion especially for the lower dielectric constants ($\epsilon_r < 4.0$) and for the small apertures ($a/\lambda < 2.0$).

The dependence of η on frequency is shown in Fig. 5. Good wide-band characteristics are obtained with narrowing frequency performance resulting with an increase in dielectric constant and/or aperture size.

From the figures it can be inferred that as the dielectric constant is increased the curves become steeper. Also, the frequency dependence is more critical. For these reasons, it is not advantageous to use materials with a dielectric constant greater than about 6. Fig. 6 shows the maximum possible theoretical efficiency as a function of ϵ_r. A knee is rapidly established so that diminishing returns are obtained after the value of 5 or 6 and at the expense of frequency response.

Fig. 7 shows how loading makes the H-plane pattern approach the sin x/x behavior of the E-plane pattern with the concomitant decreases in beamwidth. The ideal case (100 percent efficiency), results when the H-plane pattern is exactly like the E-plane pattern implying a completely flat-field distribution across the aperture in both dimensions.

The detailed variation of $\eta, \beta_1, \beta_2, \lambda_g$ and beamwidth over the entire range of filling factor is shown in Figs. 8 and 9

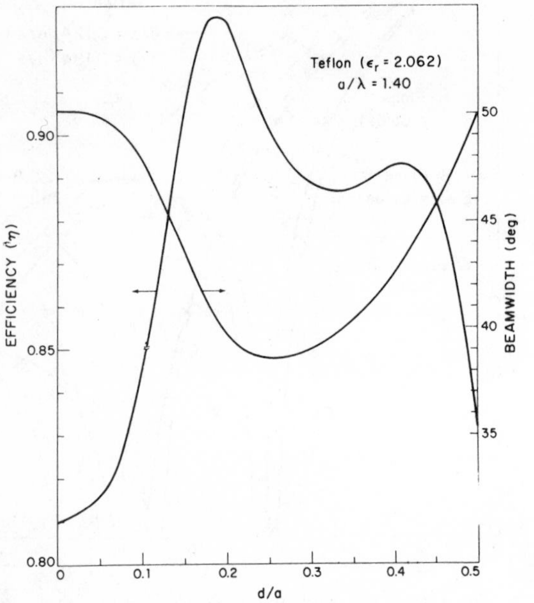

Fig. 9. Aperture efficiency and beamwidth dependence on d/a for Teflon-loaded aperture.

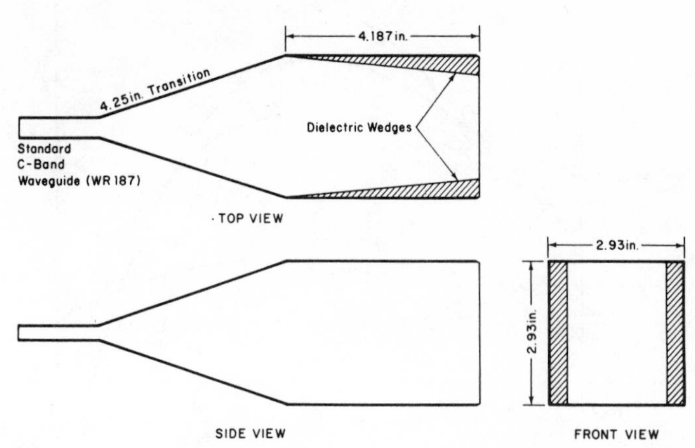

Fig. 10. One of experimental horns. It was used in obtaining results of Figs. 11, 12, and 13.

for Teflon and for $a/\lambda = 1.4$. This case is of interest since it was extensively investigated experimentally. Note that maximum efficiency and minimum beamwidth do not occur simultaneously. This means that although the beamwidth is decreasing, power begins to be transferred to the sidelobes, reducing the efficiency.

Experimental Results

Extensive measurements were made on a square aperture 1.4λ wide, for a frequency band centered at 5.65 GHz and for three dielectric materials with $\epsilon_r = 2.062$ (Teflon), 4.0, and 6.0.

Fig. 10 shows the details of the horn design for the 1.4 wavelength aperture. A box-like transition was added to the ends of the flared region for convenience in changing the dielectric wedges.

Fig. 11 shows experimental far-field patterns for three different materials. The expected beamwidth reduction as compared with the unloaded horn is evident. Table I shows −3 and −10 dB beamwidths.

The measured −3 dB beamwidth of 38° for Teflon compares well with the theoretical value of 40° from Fig. 9. Also the approach to the E plane is obvious in all cases.

Fig. 12 is a frequency run for Teflon. The pattern holds fairly constant for a 10 percent variation as implied by the corresponding efficiency curve in Fig. 5.

Fig. 13 shows the effect of operating away from the peak efficiency point of Fig. 2. Again, no significant deterioration is evident. On the contrary the beamwidths appear to decrease just as predicted in Fig. 9.

The very clean nature of all the patterns and the reasonable agreement with the theoretical results indicates the absence of serious higher order mode effects, a central assumption in our analysis.

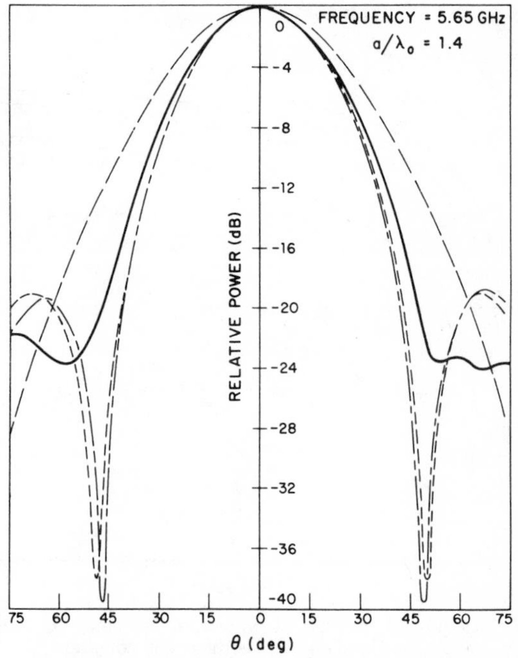

Fig. 11. Far-field H-plane patterns of C-band experimental horn showing effect of various dielectrics. Chosen values of d/a correspond to peaks of curves in Figs. 2, 3, and 4. — — — unloaded H plane. ——— Teflon loading ($\epsilon_r = 2.062$, $d/a = 0.184$). -------- $\epsilon_r = 4.0$ loading, ($d/a = 0.106$). — - — $\epsilon_r = 6.0$ loading, ($d/a = 0.0814$).

TABLE I
EXPERIMENTAL BEAMWIDTHS FOR THREE DIELECTRICS

	−3 dB Beamwidth	−10 dB Beamwidth
E plane	36°	64°
Unloaded H plane	46°	85°
Teflon loaded H plane	38°	68°
$\epsilon_r = 4.0$ loaded H plane	36°	64°
$\epsilon_r = 6.0$ loaded H plane	36°	63°

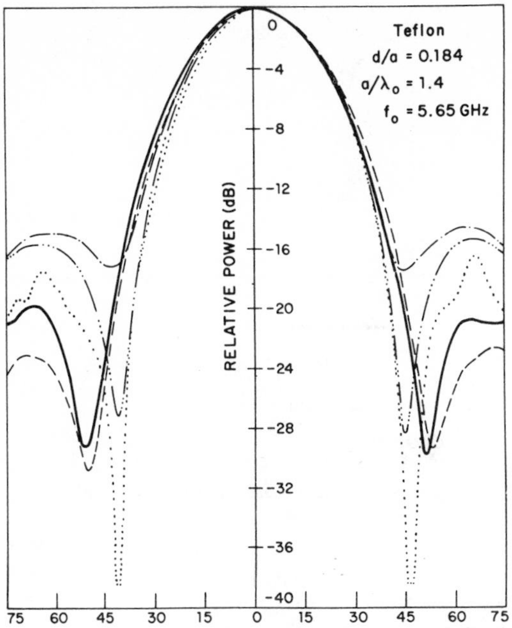

Fig. 12. Frequency pattern run for Teflon loading showing H-plane pattern behavior. —•••—•••— $f = 5.40$ GHz. —•—•— $f = 5.50$ GHz. ———— $f = 5.65$ GHz. - - - - - $f = 5.80$ GHz. •••••••• $f = 5.90$ GHz.

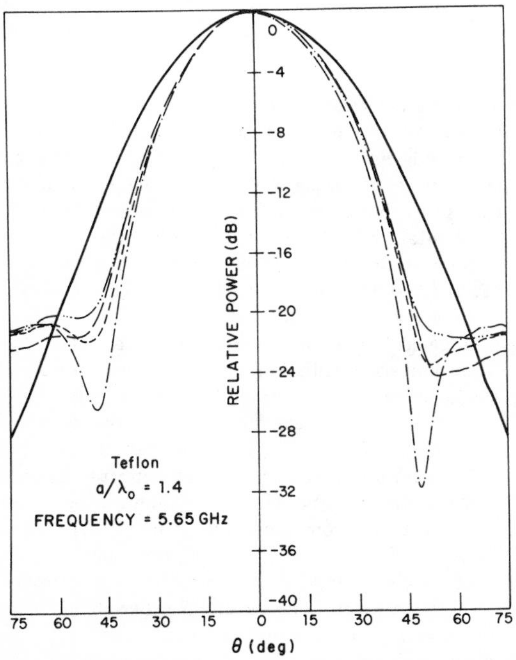

Fig. 13. Far-field H-plane patterns showing effect of dielectric slab thickness (d/a) variation for Teflon. ———— unloaded H plane. — — — — $d/a = 0.184$. —•••—•••— $d/a = 0.195$. - - - - - - $d/a = 0.205$. —•—•— $d/a = 0.215$.

On-axis gain measurements were also made, and in all cases substantial improvements were noticed. The predicted efficiency increase of about 0.55 dB for the Teflon case to about 0.75 dB for $\epsilon_r = 6$, was verified by repeated measurements of the peak intensity with and without the dielectric wedges. The average of a number of readings was within about 0.15 dB of the predicted value for all cases.

Conclusions

The efficacy of symmetric dielectric loading of horn apertures as a means of increasing the aperture efficiency has been demonstrated. The method provides a simple and inexpensive means of realizing high efficiency with small horns which find application in limited scan arrays for which a typical horn size might be the 1.4λ aperture that was experimentally investigated. For such sizes, computations of infinite array active element patterns and impedance showed little deviation from the isolated horn behavior for limited scan $(<15°)$ conditions.

Although the analysis was carried out assuming lossless dielectrics, the use of low loss commercially available materials $(\tan \delta \sim 2 \times 10^{-4})$ will introduce negligible loss.

By lining all four sides of a square horn with dielectric, a circularly polarized feed is obtained. However, this scheme must be carefully investigated separately since the fields are no longer purely TE but hybrid (HE).

References

[1] H. Jasik, *Antenna Engineering Handbook.* New York, McGraw-Hill, 1961.
[2] M. A. Quddus and J. P. German, "Phase correction by dielectric slabs in sectoral horn antennas," *IRE Trans. Antennas Propagat.* (Commun.), vol. AP-9, pp. 413–415, July 1961.
[3] M. A. K. Hamid and A. Mohsen, "Diffraction by dielectric-loaded horns and corner reflectors," *IEEE Trans. Antennas Propagat.* (Commun.), vol. AP-17, pp. 660–662, Sept. 1969.
[4] M. A. K. Hamid, R. J. Boulanger, N. J. Mostowy, and A. Mohsen, "Radiation characteristics of dielectric-loaded horn antennas," *Electron. Lett.*, vol. 6, no. 1, pp. 20–21, Jan. 1970.
[5] S. Silver, *Microwave Antenna Theory and Design*, M.I.T. Radiation Laboratory Series, vol. 12. New York: McGraw-Hill, 1949.
[6] W. D. Fitzgerald, "Limited electronic scanning with a near field Cassegrainian system," to be published.
[7] F. E. Gardiol, "Higher order modes in dielectrically loaded rectangular waveguides," *IEEE Trans. Microwave Theory Tech.*, vol. MTT-16, pp. 919–924, Nov. 1968.
[8] G. N. Tsandoulas, D. H. Temme, and F. G. Willwerth, "Longitudinal section mode analysis of dielectrically loaded rectangular waveguides with application to phase shifter design," *IEEE Trans. Microwave Theory Tech.*, vol. MTT-18, pp. 88–95, Feb. 1970.

A Dielectric-Loaded Circular Waveguide Antenna

M. A. K. HAMID, S. J. TOWAIJ, AND G. O. MARTENS

***Abstract*—A highly directive antenna of simple and lightweight structure is designed and tested experimentally. It consists of a dielectric rod with conical hole loading an open-ended circular waveguide. The test has shown that three different radiation patterns can be obtained depending on the depth of penetration of the rod inside the waveguide. Also an improvement on the axial gain can be obtained when the flare angles are smaller than 30°. The optimum design consists of a rod of conical flare angle of 7.5° which results in an improvement of 5 dB over the unloaded waveguide accompanied with a beamwidth which is half that of the unloaded structure. One practical application of the proposed design is its use as a feeder for parabolic reflectors, the advantage being the sharp nulls on both sides of the main lobe which will result in minimizing edge diffraction.**

The use of dielectric materials for increasing the axial directivity of rectangular waveguide antennas was recently reported by Boulanger and Hamid [1] who developed a lightweight small size highly directive probe for accurate null measurements of diffraction and scattering patterns, while the unloaded open-ended rectangular waveguide was reported by Beam *et al.* [2] who showed the broadening effect on the radiation pattern due to the change in the geometrical shape of the opening. The purpose of this investigation is to extend the method of Boulanger and Hamid for the rectangular structure to a circular waveguide loaded by a dielectric rod with a conical hole and to optimize the design experimentally. The applications of this antenna are similar to those of the rectangular waveguide antenna structure, particularly as a directive feed for parabolic reflectors as well as for radar detection of small objects, although such applications are not discussed here.

TABLE I

DEPTH OF PENETRATION d VERSUS VSWR

d (cm)	VSWR
0.5	1.05
1.0	1.5
2.0	1.7
2.5	2.0
3.0	1.7
4.0	1.62
5.0	1.60
5.1	1.35
6.3	2.2

Frequency = 10.1 GHz; VSWR for unloaded case = 1.065.

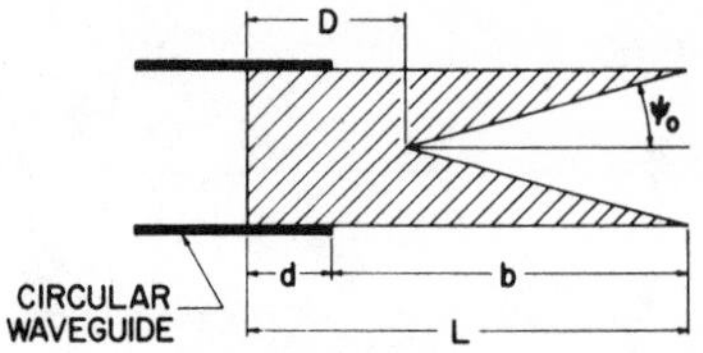

Fig. 1. Dielectric-loaded circular waveguide antenna.

TABLE II

CASE 1

L (cm)	D (cm)	d (cm)	Beam-width (degrees)	Main Lobe Level (dB)	Sidelobe Level (dB)
13.0	3.0	1	30.0	+4.2	−30.0
12.0	2.0	1	34.0	+4.3	−25.0
11.0	1.0	0.97	31.4	+4.5	−30.0

The experimental arrangement consists of a plexiglass dielectric rod of 2.54 relative dielectric constant and with a conical hole of flare angle ψ_0 inserted into the mouth of an open-ended 3-cm circular waveguide operating in the TM_{11} mode, as shown in Fig. 1. The resulting arrangement was tuned and tested as a radiating system at 10.1 GHz, and the radiation characteristics were compared with the tuned unloaded case. Several values of flare angles were used, and the radiation pattern for each case was obtained with the geometrical factors L, D, and d held constant. It was found that for $\psi_0 > 30°$, no improvement in the pattern was obtained. For $\psi_0 > 50°$, some decrease in the relative maximum level of the main lobe was observed and accompanied by increase in the beamwidth and sidelobe levels. For $\psi_0 < 30°$, some improvement was obtained, being reflected in an increase in the main beam amplitude and a decrease in the beamwidth. The optimum experimental value was found to be $\psi_0 = 7.5°$ approximately, and accordingly this case was chosen to evaluate the effect of the penetration depth on the pattern while simultaneously attempting to obtain a relation between the total length of the rod, penetration depth, and frequency. It was found that the distance D between the apex of the conical hole and the flat side of the rod should not be larger than 3 cm (one wavelength) as this would cause a decrease in the amplitude of the main lobe level. The effect of penetration depth d on the VSWR is given in Table I.

Manuscript received June 3, 1971. This work was supported in part by the National Research Council of Canada under Grant A-3326 and in part by the Defence Research Board of Canada under Grant 3801-42.
The authors are with the Department of Electrical Engineering, University of Manitoba, Winnipeg, Man., Canada.

Reprinted from *IEEE Trans. Antennas Propagat.*, vol. AP-20, pp. 96–97, Jan. 1972.

TABLE III
CASE 2: PLATEAU TYPE SIDELOBE

L (cm)	D (cm)	d (cm)	b (cm)	Beam-width (degrees)	Main Lobe Level (dB)	Sidelobe Level (dB)	Sidelobe Variation (dB)	Plateau Width (degrees)	Starting Location of Plateau (degrees)
12.0	2.0	4.0	8.0	26.2	+4.6	−16.0	∓1	28.0	29.0
11.0	1.0	3.0	8.0	27.0	+5.0	−17.5	∓1	30.0	30.0
9.0	—	1.0	8.0	27.6	+4.6	−16.0	∓1	30.8	29.0

TABLE IV
CASE 3

L (cm)	D (cm)	d (cm)	b (cm)	Beam-width (degrees)	Main Lobe Level (dB)	Sidelobe Level (dB)
12.0	2.0	5.0	7.0	29.0	+4.2	−17
11.0	1.0	4.0	7.0	25.6	+4.5	−17
9.0	—	1.9	6.9	28.2	+4.3	−17

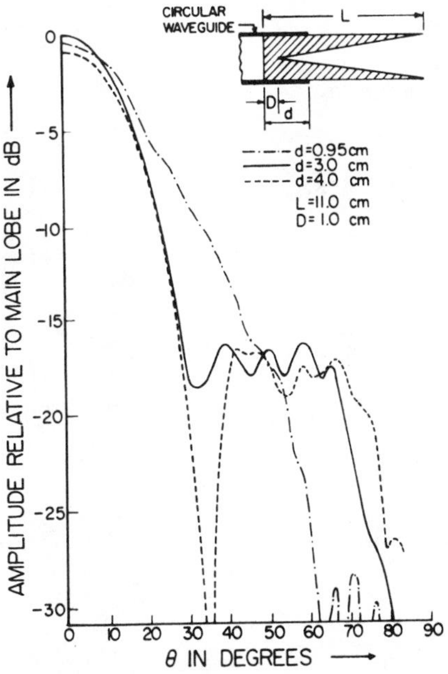

Fig. 2. Dielectric-loaded circular waveguide antenna patterns for different depths of penetration.

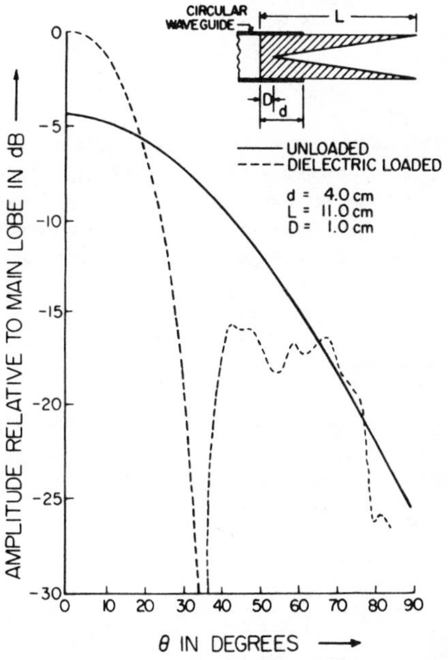

Fig. 3. Comparison of the antenna pattern with unloaded waveguide.

Tables II–IV show three different radiation characteristics obtained with variations in the penetration depth d. The first characteristic (Table II) was obtained with $d = 1$ cm for which 4 to 4.5 dB increase in the relative main lobe amplitude was observed, while the sidelobe level was found to be below −25 dB, and the beamwidth was found to be in the region of 30°. The second characteristic (Table III) was identified by a narrow beamwidth with approximately 4.5 to 5 dB increase in the main lobe amplitude as shown in Fig. 2. The main feature of this case is the presence of a plateau type sidelobe diagram with ±1 dB variation in the amplitude and about 30° in width starting from around $\theta = \pm 30°$. The beamwidth and average plateau level for this case were found to be 27° and −17 dB, respectively, corresponding to $b = 8$ cm. The third characteristic (Table IV) was identified by deep nulls on both sides of the main beam and −16 dB first sidelobe level as shown in Fig. 3. The pattern for this case showed a beamwidth of about 28° and a much steeper decline with θ. This pattern was obtained using $b = 7$ cm and was maintained until the total length L was made less than 9 cm.

REFERENCES

[1] R. J. Boulanger and M. A. K. Hamid, "A new type of dielectric-loaded waveguide antenna," *Microwave J.*, Dec. 1970.
[2] R. E. Beam, M. M. Astrahan, and H. F. Mathis, "Open-ended waveguide radiators," in *Proc. Nat. Electronics Conf.*, vol. 4, pp. 472–486, 1948.

Dielectric-Loaded Horn Antenna

TOSHIO SATOH

Abstract—A wide-band dual-mode horn, which has a rotationally symmetric beam and extremely low sidelobe levels, can be obtained by loading a dielectric band inside the horn antenna. Measured radiation characteristics of such antennas, including the so-called shaped-beam antenna, are shown.

I. Introduction

Many studies have been made on the dual-mode horn [1], corrugated horn [2], and other types of horns [3], [4] in an attempt to achieve a rotationally symmetric beam and extremely low sidelobe levels. The dual-mode horn with an abrupt waveguide junction at its throat, however, is strongly frequency dependent. The corrugated horn can maintain good radiation patterns over a wide frequency range, but it is massive and difficult to fabricate. Other approaches are either structurally complicated or large.

The author found that a wide-band dual-mode horn antenna could be realized [5] by simply loading a thin dielectric band inside a horn. This paper describes the principle of this horn antenna, its structure and measured radiation patterns. A few comments will be made on a shaped-beam horn [3], [6], which is one of the applications of a dielectric-loaded horn antenna.

II. Excitation of TM_{11} Mode by Dielectric Loading

Fig. 1 is a sketch of the dielectric-loaded conical horn antenna. A thin dielectric band, or tube, is loaded inside the horn to excite a series of higher modes, whose predominant component is the TM_{11} mode. This is because, when the horn is excited by the TE_{11} mode, the excitation of antiphase component of the electric field in the dielectric band results in a field distribution similar to that of TM_{11} mode across the cross section of the horn.

Measurements were made of the standing waves caused by an interaction of the modes excited by a dielectric band loaded in a circular waveguide. Fig. 2 shows the half-wavelengths of the standing waves, as well as the guided wavelengths for the TE_{11} and TM_{11} modes.

The dielectric material used throughout is Teflon, and its dielectric constant is 2.0. The measured values are a good fit to the computed curve of $L = (\lambda_{gTM_{11}} \cdot \lambda_{gTE_{11}})/(\lambda_{gTM_{11}} - \lambda_{gTE_{11}})$, indicating clearly the excitation of the TM_{11} mode by the dielectric loading. The mode conversion coefficient has been obtained from this measurement.

III. Bandwidth of Dual-Mode Horn

Phase progression of waves propagating in a horn can be calculated approximately by regarding the horn as a waveguide which is continuously changing its diameter. Fig. 3 shows the calculated curves for the phase difference between TE_{11} and TM_{11} modes within a conical horn; the two modes are set in phase at the horn aperture. It is of interest to note that a condition such as $\Delta\phi = 2n\pi$ (n = integer) is satisfied even in a horn. A dielectric band, or a mode generator, can thus be loaded inside the horn at the point where the curve gives $\Delta\phi = 2n\pi$ to make both modes in phase at

Manuscript received February 2, 1971; revised August 17, 1971. This work was supported by the International Telecommunications Satellite (INTELSAT) Consortium.

The author was with the KDD Research and Development Laboratory, Tokyo, Japan. He is now with COMSAT Laboratories, Clarksburg, Md. 20734.

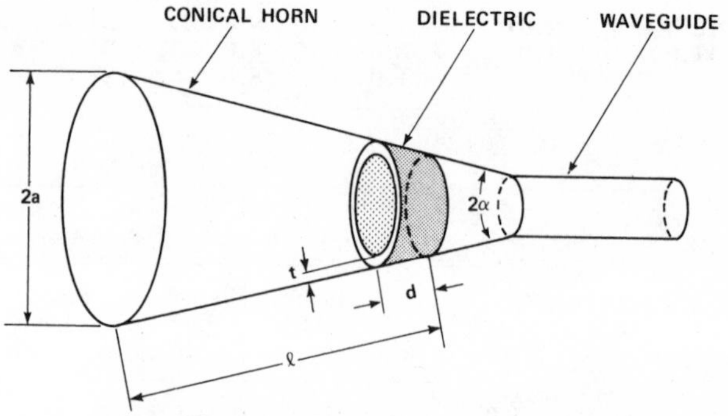

Fig. 1. Structure of dielectric-loaded horn antenna.

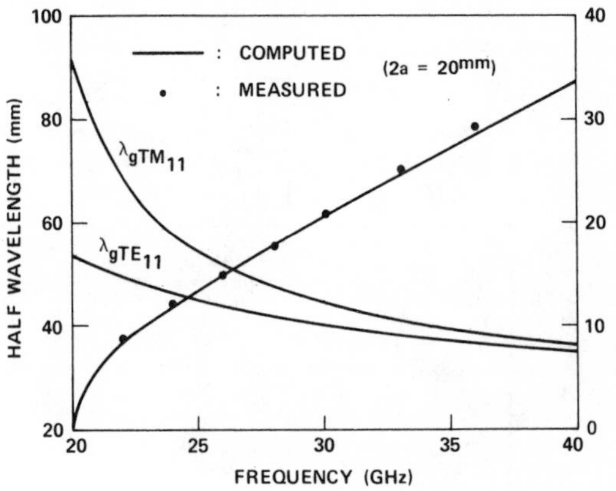

Fig. 2. Measured result of standing wavelength caused by dual-mode interaction.

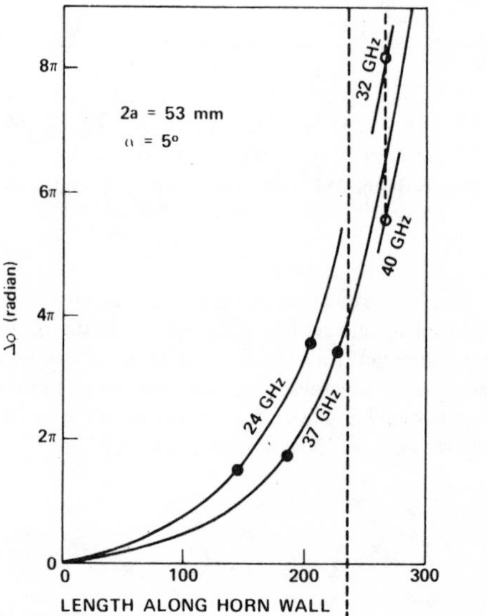

Fig. 3. Phase difference between TE_{11} and TM_{11} modes along horn wall.

Reprinted from *IEEE Trans. Antennas Propagat.*, vol. AP-20, pp. 199–201, Mar. 1972.

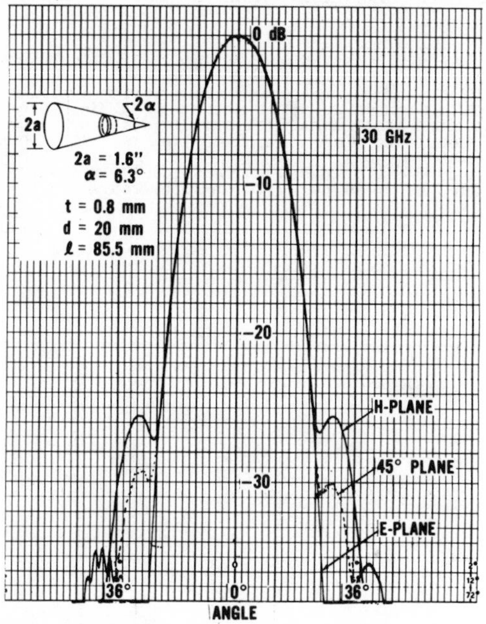

Fig. 4. Radiation patterns of dielectric-loaded horn antenna.

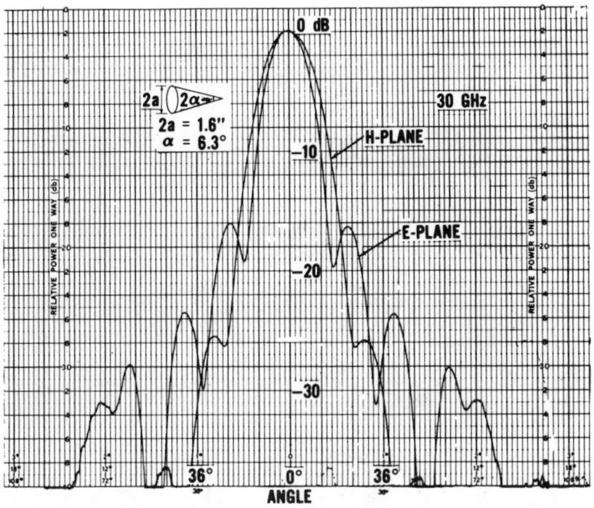

Fig. 5. Radiation patterns of unloaded horn antenna.

the horn aperture. The curve has a small gradient near the aperture and, therefore, the loading of a mode converter inside the horn, rather than in the waveguide, gives less frequency dependence in the phase difference of both modes. Points plotted on the calculated curves in Fig. 3 indicate the positions of dielectric bands which have minimum sidelobes in the experiments.

A single dielectric band can satisfy the condition of $2n\pi$ at several frequencies, for example, at 32 and 40 GHz, as shown experimentally by the circles in Fig. 3. The technique of modifying the length and flare angle of the dielectric-loaded horn to give necessary phase conditions at two or more arbitrarily selected frequencies will be interesting.

IV. Radiation Patterns of Dielectric-Loaded Horn

Fig. 4 shows radiation patterns of a dielectric-loaded horn antenna. The beam is completely symmetrical down to the −26-dB level and the sidelobes are extremely low in the E plane. Fig. 5 shows patterns for the same horn without the dielectric band. Sidelobe levels are as high as −16.5 dB in the E plane and the beamwidth difference in E and H planes at the −10-dB level is about 30 percent in this case. It was experimentally found that a bandwidth of more than 25 percent can maintain the beamwidth difference of less than ±5 percent and all sidelobe levels below −20 dB. The measured cross-polarization level of the dielectric-loaded conical horn was found to be lower by almost 20 dB than that of the conventional conical horn.

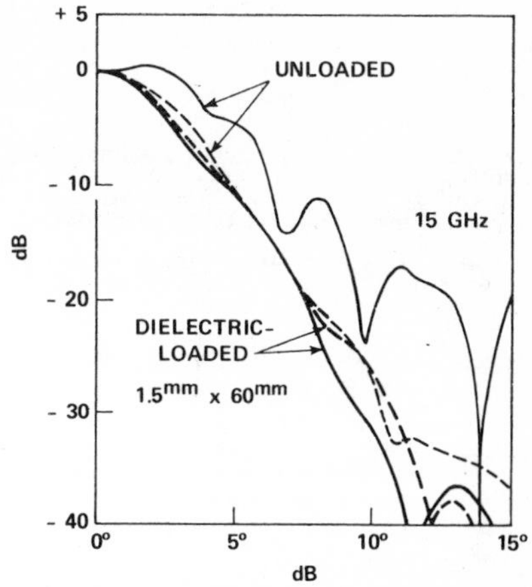

Fig. 6. Radiation patterns of dielectric-loaded horn reflector antenna (near-field pattern)

Phase patterns were also measured and, as expected, good results were obtained. For example, the phase difference in E and H planes of the horn shown in Fig. 4 was almost zero down to the −10-dB point in amplitude. This can be compared with the difference of 35° at the same angle for the unloaded horn.

The input VSWR, measured at various frequencies, was found to increase slightly when a dielectric band was loaded in the horn. For example, the worst case over the 28- to 35-GHz frequency range for the horn in Fig. 4 showed an increase from 1.09 to 1.12.

The dielectric-loading technique can also be applied to a horn reflector antenna by loading a dielectric band inside the horn which consists of the horn reflector antenna. Experiments were made on a horn-reflector antenna having a diameter of 500 mm and a flare angle of 16.5°; satisfactory patterns were obtained, as shown in Fig. 6.

V. Satellite-Borne Shaped-Beam Antenna

As an application of the dielectric-loaded horn, a so-called shaped-beam horn antenna will be discussed here. A shaped beam having an amplitude dip at the beam center and rotational symmetry can be obtained by a dielectric-loaded horn antenna with a dielectric "cap" or "tube" at the horn aperture. The value of the dip can be adjusted by changing the thickness and width of the dielectric cap. Experiments made in the 24-GHz band showed that this method could give a shaped-beam horn with a rotationally symmetric beam and sidelobes below −15 dB over a bandwidth of 20 percent, although the decrease at the beam center varied 1 to 4 dB in the band.

VI. Conclusion

Based on the new concept of higher mode generation, a dielectric-loaded horn antenna has been developed. It has a rotationally symmetric beam and extremely low sidelobes over a bandwidth of more than 25 percent. Some techniques to obtain wider frequency response are now under investigation.

This antenna can be used as a primary feed for a reflector-type antenna or a terrestrial microwave or millimeter-wave relay station antenna. This horn is considered to be suitable for a satellite-borne antenna because of its structural simplicity, light weight, and good radiation patterns.

Acknowledgment

The author wishes to express his thanks to M. Yamada and Dr. H. Yokoi of KDD Research and Development Laboratory, Tokyo, Japan, who gave many useful suggestions.

REFERENCES

[1] P. D. Potter, "A new horn antenna with suppressed sidelobes and equal beamwidth," *Microwave J.*, vol. 6, no. 6, p. 71, June 1963.
[2] R. E. Lawrie and L. Peters, Jr., "Modifications of horn antennas for low sidelobe levels," *IEEE Trans. Antennas Propagat.*, vol. AP-14, pp. 605–610, Sept. 1966.
[3] J. A. Ajioka and H. E. Harry, Jr., "Shaped beam antenna for earth coverage from a stabilized satellite," *IEEE Trans. Antennas Propagat.*, vol. AP-18, pp. 323–327, May 1970.
[4] S. B. Cohn, "Flare-angle changes in a horn as a means of pattern control," *Microwave J.*, vol. 13, no. 10, p. 41, Oct. 1970.
[5] T. Satoh and M. Yamada, "Dielectric-loaded conical horn antenna," Joint Conv. Rec. Four Elec. Inst. Jap., no. 1418, Mar. 1969 (in Japanese).
[6] T. Satoh, "Dielectric-loaded horn antenna," Inst. Electron. Commun. Eng. Jap., AP 70-46, Oct. 1970 (in Japanese).

Engineering Approach to the Design of Tapered Dielectric-rod and Horn Antennas

J. R. JAMES,
B.Sc., Ph.D., A.F.I.M.A., C.Eng., M.I.E.R.E.*

SUMMARY

The taper profile of optimized dielectric-rod and horn antennas is synthesized as a series of non-interacting planar radiating apertures. The method is semi-empirical, straightforward to apply, enables the dielectric-rod antenna to be satisfactorily optimized and provides a means of evaluating and optimizing a dielectric-horn antenna with variable wall thickness. The optimum profiles are taken as those which smoothly transform the surface-wave power from the launcher to the radiating aperture. The optimization of the dielectric-rod antenna considerably improves the radiation pattern while computations supported by measurements confirm earlier reports that a dielectric-horn can have a higher gain than a metal horn of similar dimension but side-lobe level is seen to be an important issue. Wide flare-angle horns give ideal E-plane patterns at the expense of a high side-lobe level in the H-plane; for small flare angles the dielectric horn gives similar patterns to the tapered rod antenna and thus preserves rotational symmetry. Calculations throughout are restricted to cylindrical geometry but other geometries and variations on the dielectric-horn principles are described. Useful engineering design data have been compiled for both the dielectric-horn and rod antennas and curves are given which determine near-optimum parameters for gains up to about 20 dB which is seen to be a practical operating limit for these surface wave devices. A unified impression of dielectric antennas emerges with the important conclusion that, when optimized, dielectric-rod and horn antennas are in fact competitive wth small metal horns for some applications; furthermore the dielectric-horn antenna, used singly or in arrays, is an ideal device for producing a low side-lobe level in the E-plane.

* *Department of Electrical and Electronic Engineering, Royal Military College of Science, Shrivenham, Swindon, Wiltshire.*

1. Introduction

The dielectric-rod antenna (Fig. 1(a)) has been extensively studied in recent years[1–5] and has proved to be a useful device in certain specialized applications; the dielectric-tube antenna has also received some attention[1,6] and is found to be similar in performance to the uniform dielectric-rod antenna. The dielectric-horn antenna also shown in Fig. 1(a) is perhaps the least known of all dielectric antennas and little has been established about it apart from the early reports[1,7] that its gain appears to exceed that of a metal horn of similar dimensions and this could be a significant property. Dielectric antennas bring about some saving in weight, have good sealing and corrosion properties and are now attracting renewed interest in view of the ease with which dielectrics can be manufactured with present-day techniques. The theoretical solution of these antennas is difficult because the radiation does not emanate from a simple plane aperture as in the metallic horn case; many isolated aspects of the problem have been successfully analysed[26] but until the overall radiating system can be treated as a whole the optimization of these antennas rests largely with the experimenter. In this paper an engineering approach to this problem is adopted whereby theoretical techniques are supplemented by experimental information. Optimized versions of these antennas are then compared with one another and also with the conventional metal horn.

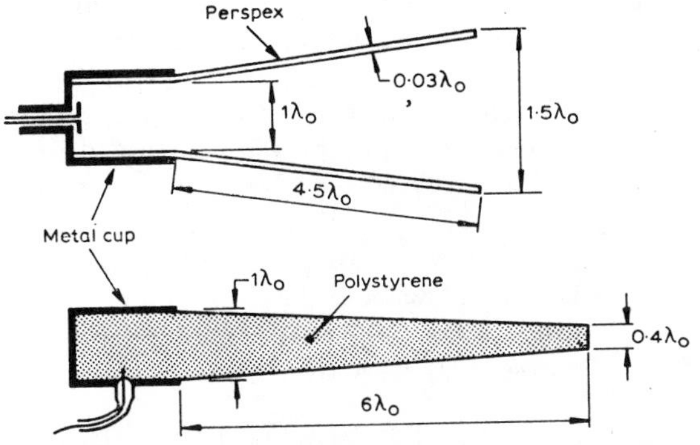

(a) Dielectric-horn antenna with uniform wall thickness (Kiely[1]) and dielectric-rod antenna with linear taper.

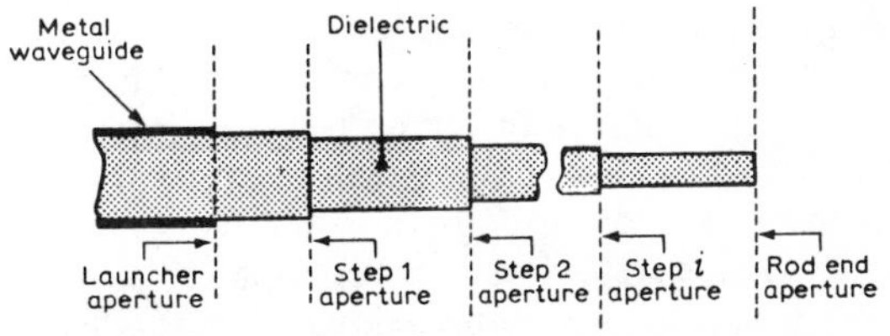

(b) Approximating the dielectric-rod profile by a series of steps, each one assumed to produce a planar aperture of infinite extent.

Fig. 1.

The investigation concentrates on tapered dielectric-rod and horn antennas and as little is known about the latter the paper is concerned with their evaluation. The dielectric-horn antenna is certainly no less involved a device than the tapered dielectric-rod antenna for which no accurate design data exists; the difficulty lies in

Reprinted with permission from *Radio Electron. Eng.*, vol. 42, pp. 251–259, June 1972.

calculating the radiation from the tapered structure to a sufficient accuracy and much the same problem occurs for dielectric-horn antennas. We describe a semi-empirical approach which assists in the selection of an optimum taper profile for the dielectric-rod antenna and useful design curves are obtained as a consequence. The dielectric-horn antenna may be calculated in a similar manner by synthesizing its profile by a system of short concentric dielectric tubes; the predominant radiation characteristics are, however, exhibited by the radiation from the end aperture alone and we evaluate the dielectric-horn on this simpler basis. Suitable applications for the antenna are pointed out and the essential design parameters identified. Calculations are confined to cylindrical geometry for simplicity and the treatment of other cross-sectional shapes follows in a similar manner but is computationally involved.

2. Semi-empirical Approach to Tapered Dielectric-rod Antennas

The diameter of the dielectric-rod is tapered along the antenna length to obtain a large efficient launching aperture in conjunction with a large radiating aperture at the rod end.[4] Unfortunately radiation leaks out along the taper and it is shown below that this radiation does not contribute usefully to the radiation pattern. The main design problem is therefore to select a taper profile which radiates least power and no exact means of calculation appears to exist. The writer has previously outlined[9] the following step-synthesis procedure whereby a step discontinuity on the rod is regarded as a radiating planar aperture of infinite extent in the plane of the discontinuity; with this approximation a tapered dielectric-rod antenna whose profile is assumed to be a series of m small non-interacting steps, may be treated as a system of m radiating planar apertures (Fig. 1(b)). The radiated E-field is given by the sum of the radiation from each aperture, thus

$$\mathbf{E} = -\frac{jk\,\mathrm{e}^{-jkR}}{4\pi R}\,\mathbf{R}_1 \times \sum_{i=0}^{m} K_i \int_A \left[(\mathbf{n}\times\mathbf{E}_i) - (\mu_0/\varepsilon_0)^{\frac{1}{2}}\mathbf{R}_1 \times (\mathbf{n}\times\mathbf{H}_i)\right] \mathrm{e}^{jk\rho_i\cdot\mathbf{R}_1}\,da \qquad (1)$$

where the far-field vector Kirchhoff integral is employed with the notation of Silver[12] and $(\mathbf{E}_i, \mathbf{H}_i)$ is the aperture field of the ith aperture. The aperture field is taken as the unperturbed surface wave on each rod segment and for the diameters and dielectric constant of interest only the dominant HE_{11} wave exists (see, for instance, Fig. 8.6 on page 72 of ref. 13). K_i for $i = 1, 2, 3, \ldots, m$, is a factor which defines the proportion of incident power radiated at each step. The launcher radiation corresponding to $i = 0$ is obtained approximately from a chopped-surface-wave-distribution as described in ref. 4. The radiation lost at each step can be estimated by the Lorentz reciprocity theorem[13] but in the present author's experience the resulting radiation pattern predictions are still too inaccurate to be useful; this is attributed to the fact that reflected waves at each step are neglected as is the interstep radiation coupling.[9] It was thought that a better approximation would result by taking the aperture field as the difference between the unperturbed fields on either side of the step but poor results were again obtained. Eventually experiments indicated that the leakage of radiation along a smooth monotonically decreasing taper was to a large extent governed by the rate of change of power flow ratios along the taper and the following empirical formula

$$P_i^{\mathrm{RAD}} = (P_i^{\mathrm{I}} + P_i^{\mathrm{O}})\left[1 - \frac{\gamma_{i+1}}{\gamma_i}\right]^W \qquad (2)$$

where

$$\gamma_i = P_i^{\mathrm{I}}/(P_i^{\mathrm{I}} + P_i^{\mathrm{O}}),$$

was found to give some approximate functional description of the radiating process. P_i^{RAD} is the power lost at the ith step and P_i^{I} and P_i^{O} are respectively the surface wave power flowing in the interior and exterior regions of the ith segment, $i = 1, 2, 3, \ldots, m$; W is an empirical constant which depends on rod geometry and dielectric constant and is to be determined by curve fitting the computed to the measured radiation patterns. From a physical standpoint W may be interpreted as a parameter embodying the complex effects which arise when the small steps are spaced closer together.

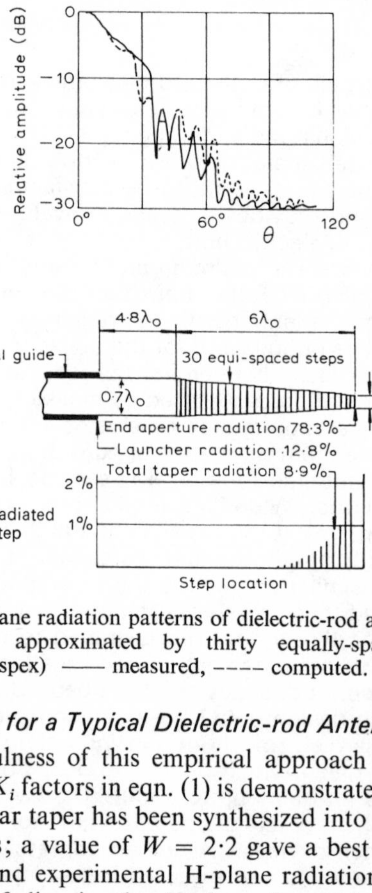

Fig. 2. H-plane radiation patterns of dielectric-rod antenna with linear taper, approximated by thirty equally-spaced steps. $\varepsilon_r = 2{\cdot}56$ (perspex) —— measured, ---- computed. $\phi = 0°$.

2.1. *Results for a Typical Dielectric-rod Antenna*

The usefulness of this empirical approach for determining the K_i factors in eqn. (1) is demonstrated in Fig. 2 where a linear taper has been synthesized into 30 equally spaced steps; a value of $W = 2{\cdot}2$ gave a best fit for the calculated and experimental H-plane radiation patterns. The angle θ lies in the H-plane for which $\phi = 0°$; θ and ϕ are spherical angular co-ordinates. Many other cases have been examined and a notable feature is that for smooth tapers both the experimental and computed patterns begin to converge for as little as three equally-spaced steps. A similar situation occurs for E-plane computations. The radiation from the taper increases the side-lobe level, is undesirable from an operational standpoint and is characteristic of a typical interference

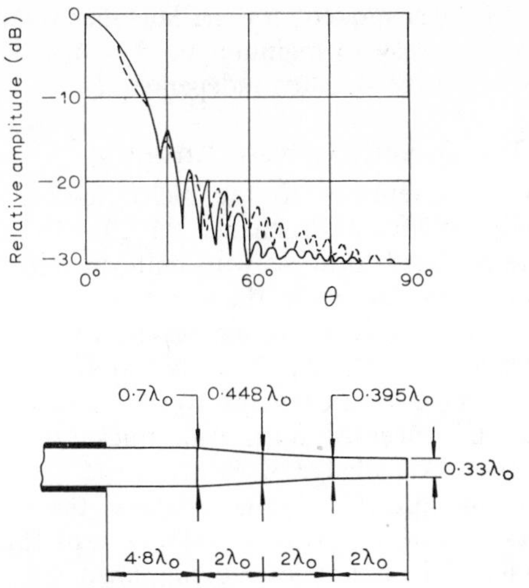

Fig. 3. H-plane radiation patterns of dielectric-rod antenna with optimized taper profile. $\varepsilon_r = 2{\cdot}56$ (perspex) —— measured, ---- computed. $\phi = 0°$.

pattern; that is to say there is little evidence that leaky wave radiation[2,24] is occurring at distinct angles. In the case shown the curve-fitted-computations show that the taper radiates near the end with a loss of 8·9% of its available surface wave power. It is evident from Fig. 2 that a concave profile would provide a more gradual taper near the rod end and hence reduce this premature loss of radiation at the expense of encouraging the taper to radiate nearer to the launcher region. Several profiles were computed and fitted to the measured radiation patterns to see if a compromise could be reached whereby the taper radiated uniformly along its length but at a negligible level; the concave profile in Fig. 3 gave best results and consists of three linearly tapered portions rather than a gradual curve, in order to ease machining difficulties. The curve fitting procedure indicated that negligible surface wave power was radiated along this taper and as such this is a well optimized dielectric-rod antenna; the computed gain was 19·6 dB but the measured gains were 2 dB less mainly due to the use of perspex. In these experiments the tapered section was separated from the launcher by a section of uniform diameter rod to isolate the various sources of radiation; in practice the antenna would consist of the tapered section only.

Marcuse[10] has recently calculated the radiated power from a tapered cylindrical dielectric-rod using a similar step synthesis approach. A particular case that he has treated (Fig. 8 in reference 10) is not too dissimilar to that in Fig. 2 and some comparison is permitted. Taking the same taper length as in Fig. 2 Marcuse calculates that a linear and an exponential taper lose 8% and 6% respectively of the incident power which is of the same order as the results given in Figs. 2 and 3. The percentage of radiation from the taper must be accurately known to within about 1% if the side-lobe level of the antenna is to be calculated within acceptable engineering limits; since Marcuse's mathematical model neglects radiation coupling effects[9,11] between the step apertures, doubts must be raised as to whether it is sufficiently accurate for the purposes of designing the dielectric-rod antenna without some recourse to measured data.

To increase the gain of the dielectric-rod antenna it is necessary to taper a longer rod to a smaller terminal diameter. Marcuse's results do not indicate that this will present difficulties and neither do any assessments based on the Lorentz reciprocity theorem,[13] yet in practice it has not been possible so far to increase readily the gain beyond about 20 dB; the reason seems to be that the taper dimensions are critical for small diameter rods and the rod lengths are excessive for a small increase in gain and are greater than $10\lambda_0$. An estimation by Snyder[14] for a very gentle linear taper shows that as the cut-off frequency is approached the taper radiation increases steeply thus supporting the above observation. This view is also compatible with other analytical results for a surface-wave structure.[26] The dielectric materials such as perspex are very convenient for experimental work but materials of lower loss such as polystyrene or polythene are necessary for operational devices. Whatever material is used the loss will increase with taper length but even for perspex this does not significantly contribute to the threshold effect.

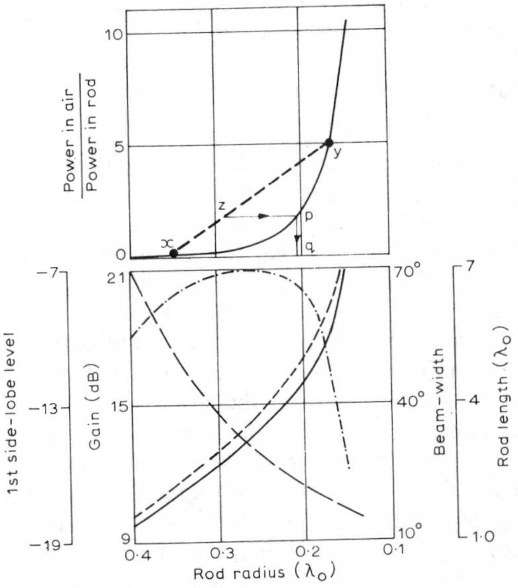

Fig. 4. Computed curves for tapered dielectric-rod antenna. $\varepsilon_r = 2{\cdot}5$ and launcher aperture radius $= 0{\cdot}4\lambda_0$; the following details refer to lower graph: —— antenna gain, ---- rod length, — — — 3 dB beamwidth, -·-·-·- 1st side-lobe level.

There is therefore substantial evidence that the tapered dielectric-rod antenna and also other surface-wave types, have a threshold performance beyond which they cease to be viable practical antennas. For the simple monotonically tapered short rod under consideration here we find that this threshold is in the vicinity of 20 dB gain. For longer rods it may be necessary to modulate the diameter periodically as in the 'cigar' antenna[15] in order to obtain higher gains but the antenna would then be several orders longer.

2.2. *Design Curves for Tapered Dielectric-rod Antennas*

The curves in Fig. 4 are based on the radiating properties established above and it is assumed that the optimum taper profile is one for which the ratio γ_{i+1}/γ_i in equation (2) is constant from step to step. With this criterion the taper profile is immediately defined once the terminal rod diameters are stated. The curves embrace a useful range of antenna performances up to the above mentioned gain threshold of 20 dB below which we have been able to optimize the tapers. The launcher radius is taken as $0{\cdot}4\lambda_0$ and we assume that the rod will fill the latter in which case the launcher radiation is known to be about 10% of the incident metal guide power;[4] the curves are based on this figure and the remaining power is assumed to emanate from the end aperture. The side-lobe can be improved by launching from a larger aperture or alternatively utilizing a ring source launcher.[13] There are many other techniques for increasing the launching efficiency such as placing a flange or choke[17] around the metal waveguide aperture but all improvements necessitate additional metallic components, increase the space occupied by the launcher and in some cases narrow the operating bandwidth. Practical system constraints will determine whether or not the launcher efficiency is to be optimized beyond that of the simple metal cup arrangement considered here (Fig. 1(a)); antenna gain and beamwidth will not vary appreciably with more efficient launching but the performance figures for side-lobe level in Fig. 4 are to be regarded as a conservative assessment of what can be achieved.

To demonstrate the use of Fig. 4 suppose that an antenna gain of 15 dB is required. A rod terminal radius of $0{\cdot}223\lambda_0$, 1st side-lobe level of $-7{\cdot}3$ dB, beamwidth 24° and rod length of $4{\cdot}4\lambda_0$ are given by the lower set of curves. To obtain the taper profile mark the power ratio curve at points x and y that correspond to the launcher and terminal radii of $0{\cdot}4\lambda_0$ and $0{\cdot}223\lambda_0$. Intermediate radii along the taper are then defined by projecting the line xy on to the abscissa via the power ratio curve (solid line in upper graph). To demonstrate this further the line xy already drawn in Fig. 4 corresponds to the terminal radii of the antenna in Fig. 3 and the point z when projected to q via p predicts an optimum radius of $0{\cdot}21\lambda_0$ at a distance of λ_0 along the taper as opposed to the value of $0{\cdot}224\lambda_0$ obtained by curve fitting. This is in good agreement considering the dielectric constant and launcher radius do not correspond exactly to the conditions of Fig. 4; similar agreement is obtained for other points along this taper.

Since the dielectric-rod antenna possesses radiation patterns with rotational symmetry,[4] the 1st side-lobe level quoted may be taken with good approximation as the value for either the E or H plane. It is believed that the curves are accurate enough for most design purposes and certainly much more informative than existing data based on a simplified sin x/x calculation.[2] A complete antenna design must embody the bandwidth and matching aspects of the launcher feed but our experiments have shown[27] that the radiation patterns are not sensitive to conditions within the launcher provided the latter is not heavily over-moded; for the launcher radius considered here it is easy to maintain the H_{11} mode and the feed design can be pursued independently.

3. The Dielectric-horn Antenna

Early references to the dielectric-horn antenna are Kiely[1] (1953) and Prochazka[7] (1959). These experiments were confined to horns with uniform wall thickness and calculations based on the assumed simplified radiation mechanism gave some agreement with measurements[7] but were generally insufficiently representative; as far as is known no attempt has previously been made to investigate the effect of horn wall thickness. The present improved knowledge of dielectric-rod and also dielectric tube antennas[6,17] now enables the dielectric-horn antenna with or without varying wall thickness to be evaluated in the following simplified way: the horn is regarded as a system of short concentric non-overlapping dielectric tubes with various external and internal radii b and a respectively, which approximate to the actual horn dimensions in a similar fashion to the synthesis of the stepped dielectric-rod profile (Fig. 1(b)). Experiments show that the horn could be justifiably represented in this way and furthermore the radiating system closely parallels the situation for the tapered rod antenna in that low side-lobe patterns corresponded to negligible radiation from the horn conical surface. From an evaluation standpoint it is therefore sufficient to consider only the radiation from the launcher and horn mouth and the subsequent computations carry this simplifica-

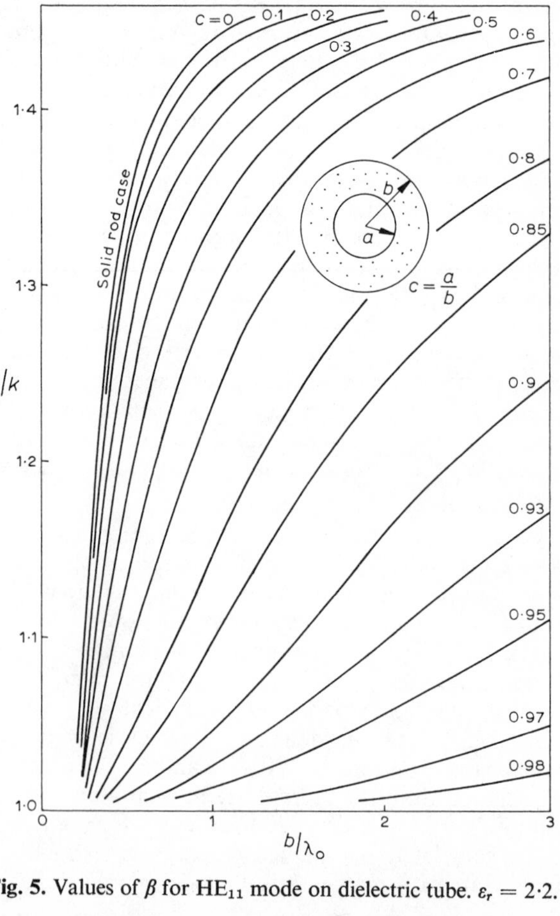

Fig. 5. Values of β for HE_{11} mode on dielectric tube. $\varepsilon_r = 2{\cdot}2$.

tion. The horn mouth is taken as a radiating dielectric tube and since a detailed study of the dielectric-tube antenna has already been described elsewhere[1,6,16] we emphasize only those details that are relevant to the horn situation.

3.1. *Surface-wave Modes on a Dielectric Tube*

One physical interpretation of the tapered dielectric-rod antenna is that the launcher field is progressively transformed along the taper until the surface-wave wavelength approximately matches that of free space. This view may be extended to the dielectric-horn antenna and to illustrate this further we have computed a range of wavelengths for the dominant hybrid mode on dielectric tubes whose dimensions are relevant to the horn situation. In Fig. 5 values of the phase constant β normalized by k, are plotted as a function of tube radius and thickness for $\varepsilon_r = 2{\cdot}2$ since most of our experiments use paraffin wax. $\beta/k = \lambda_0/\lambda$ where λ_0 and λ are the free-space and surface-wave wavelengths respectively. Taking the simplified stepped-tube model for the horn we see that the horn wall thickness must taper to a very small value at its mouth if the terminal radius is to be large whereas at the launcher end the wall needs to be very thick for good launching. In the designs described below we take $c(=a/b) = 0$ at the launcher in which case the launching efficiency from a metal cup as in Fig. 1(a) should be at least as good as for the dielectric rod case. It was conjectured that the efficiency would be higher since some rays emanating from the launcher would be diffracted forward by a wide flare angle dielectric horn and evidence of this effect is apparent in the experimental results below.

A second point of interest is whether it is reasonably valid to assume that only the HE_{11} mode need be considered on each elemental tube in this simplified model. To examine this, the cut-off dimensions for the next four higher modes on a dielectric-tube are plotted as a function of tube radius and thickness in Fig. 6; also superimposed in this figure is a horn profile which is typical of those used in the subsequent experiments. We see that only the symmetric modes and in particular the H_{01}, can exist on any of the elemental tubes in addition to the HE_{11} mode but with careful launching from the H_{11} mode in the dielectric-filled waveguide these symmetric modes should not be excited. For the cases considered below there is no evidence that symmetric modes are being excited and the assumption that only the HE_{11} mode need be considered is justified.

3.2. *Theoretical Evaluation of the Dielectric-horn Antenna*

The radiation calculation is carried out in a similar manner to that for the dielectric-rod antenna but the manipulations are necessarily more extensive due to the additional boundary condition; the salient details are summarized as follows. The launcher radiation is calculated from the unperturbed H_{11} mode in the latter, as was done in equation (1), and the launching efficiency is again based on a chopped-surface-wave distribution.[4] The horn mouth is regarded as a dielectric tube aperture for the purposes of calculating the radiation pattern; the relevant β is given in Fig. 5 and the unperturbed HE_{11} mode is taken as the aperture field. Using equation (1) but with $m = 0$ and 1 only, since we are assuming that an optimum non-radiating taper profile exists, the radiation pattern resolves into functions of Lommel integrals as in the rod case;[4] these equations are given in detail elsewhere.[17] As the antenna has a pencil-type beam, the gain can be readily calculated from E- and H-plane radiation patterns.[18]

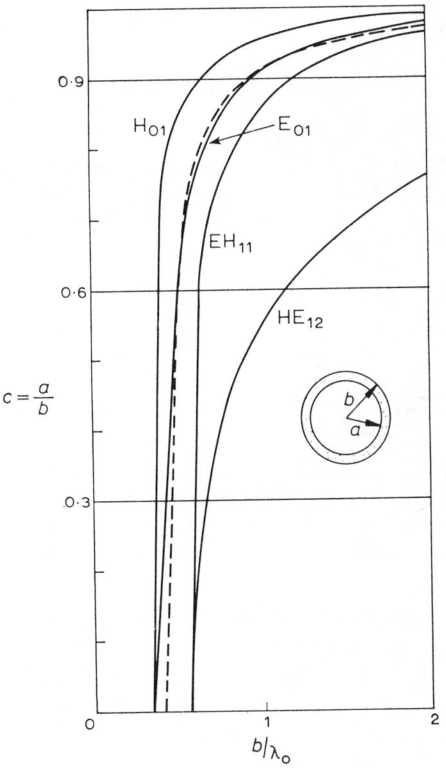

Fig. 6. Cut-off conditions of the next four modes above the HE_{11} mode. $\varepsilon_r = 2{\cdot}26$, ---- profile of typical dielectric horn.

Since the dielectric-horn antenna would appear to be a natural replacement for metal horns we will use the latter for the purposes of comparison. The radiation patterns of the metal horn have been obtained by applying the vector Kirchhoff integral[12] to the unperturbed H_{11} mode in the horn mouth; other modes have been neglected but the results agree well with measurements and geometric optics calculations[19] in the main lobe region which is of interest here.

In Fig. 7 the gain of an optimized dielectric-horn antenna is plotted as a function of the radius and wall thickness of the horn mouth; also given is the gain of a metal horn of identical mouth radius b. If a horn taper profile can be selected which is optimum, i.e. radiation is emitted solely from the launcher and horn mouth, then these curves show that the dielectric horn can always be arranged to have a higher gain than a metal horn of identical mouth dimensions by tapering the wall thickness to a very small value. This is in agreement with the earlier observations.[1]

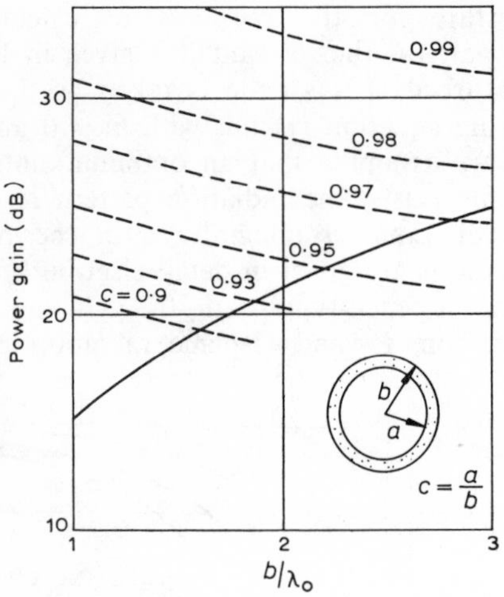

Fig. 7. Antenna power gain computed using the vector Kirchhoff integral. —— cylindrical metal horn aperture radius b;---- dielectric horn, $\varepsilon_r = 2{\cdot}2$, launcher radius $= 0{\cdot}4\lambda_o$, launcher loss $=$ 10%.

Unfortunately antenna gain is not the only system parameter of interest and the computations of the first side-lobe level (Fig. 8) show that the dielectric-horn is superior to the metal horn in the E-plane but considerably inferior in the H-plane; the high side-lobe level in the H-plane is not due to interference with the launcher since radiation from the latter is deliberately omitted in these curves. The explanation is that the E-field is concentrated in the dielectric walls, thus the field distribution tends to resemble two vertical line sources and creates an interference pattern in the H-plane; however this field distribution appears to be ideal as regards the E-plane. The inference from Figs. 7 and 8 is that a superior antenna to the metal horn can be obtained if the dielectric horn terminal radius is large and the wall very thin but this depends on whether a non-radiating taper profile can be found.

3.3. *Experimental Substantiation of Dielectric-horn Antenna Design*

After much experimenting it was found that the situation showed little departure from the dielectric rod case discussed above: that is, horn profiles that produced negligible radiation along their length could be found for antenna gains below about 20 dB while gains in excess of this figure are difficult to achieve. Similarly, radiation emanating from the taper increased the overall side-lobe level and did not contribute usefully to the radiation patterns. This immediately constrains the wall thickness in Fig. 7 to values of $c < 0{\cdot}93$ that produce very high H-plane side-lobe levels in Fig. 8 although the E-plane pattern continues to have a low side-lobe level. The H-plane side-lobe level can be improved by reducing the dielectric horn terminal diameter until the horn has zero flare angle.

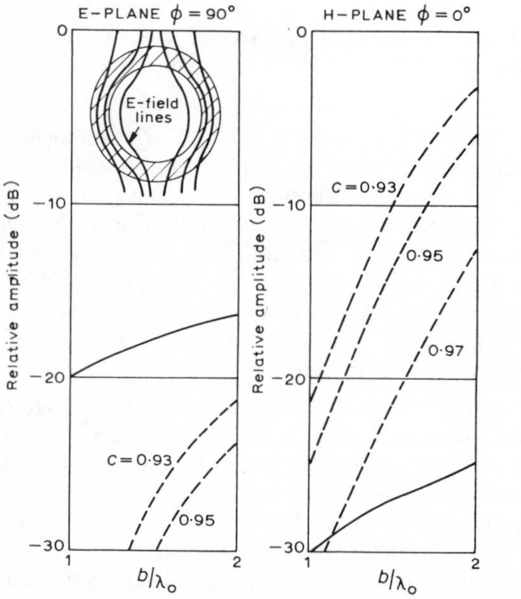

Fig. 8. First side-lobe level relative to main-lobe amplitude computed using the vector Kirchhoff formula. —— metal horn aperture radius b, ---- dielectric horn aperture, $\varepsilon_r = 2{\cdot}2$. Inset sketch shows concentration of E field in the dielectric tube walls.

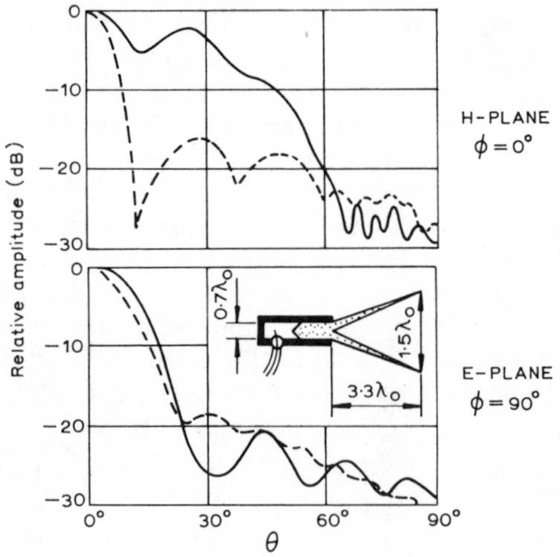

Fig. 9. Radiation patterns of wide flare angle dielectric horn. $\varepsilon_r = 2{\cdot}2$ (paraffin wax), $\lambda_o = 3{\cdot}2$ cm, $c = 0{\cdot}95$; —— measured, ---- computed assuming zero taper radiation loss and 12·8% launcher loss.

Several dielectric horns have been tested[23] which bear out these theoretical predictions and it is sufficient here to show three cases. In Fig. 9 the horn was too short for the given terminal wall diameter and thickness; it is considered that appreciable radiation occurs along the horn taper and this is responsible for the disagreement between the measured and computed patterns. Of particular interest here is the high side-lobe level in the H-plane as opposed to the low level in the E-plane and the fact that the contribution from the taper spoils the radiation characteristics in both planes. On reducing the flare angle and thickening the horn walls (Fig. 10), less radiation is lost along the horn taper and the measured results tend more to the computed values. Finally, Fig. 11(a) shows the patterns of a zero flare angle dielectric horn; the radiation along the horn taper has been considerably reduced and there is a low H-plane side-lobe level. The E-plane pattern was very similar thus exhibiting rotational symmetry of the beam. In fact this zero flare angle horn gives similar results to the linearly-tapered dielectric-rod antenna

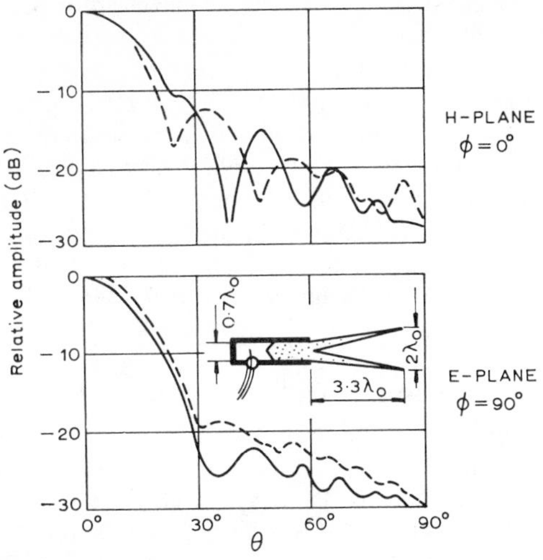

Fig. 10. Radiation patterns of moderate flare angle dielectric horn. $\varepsilon_r = 2{\cdot}2$ (paraffin wax), $\lambda_o = 3{\cdot}2$ cm, $c = 0{\cdot}9$; —— measured, ---- computed assuming zero taper radiation loss and 12·8% launcher loss.

(Fig. 2). The radiation along the horn taper could be reduced further by optimizing the profile but this presented machining difficulties and was not attempted.

The dielectric-horn antenna may therefore be summed up as follows: if equal beamwidths and low side-lobe levels are required in both the E and H-planes then the dielectric horn must have zero flare angle and is similar in length and performance to the tapered dielectric-rod antenna. Since the latter is slightly easier to manufacture it is a natural choice but the additional physical strength of the dielectric-horn should not be overlooked. There may be many applications where an optimized dielectric-rod or zero flare angle horn antenna may be preferred to a conventional cylindrical metal horn and comparison of Fig. 11(b) with Fig. 3 emphasizes the competitive performance of these dielectric antennas which can be brought about by optimizing the various taper profiles. If however a narrow beam with low side-lobe level is required in the E-plane only, the dielectric horn is without doubt more suitable than either the dielectric-rod or cylindrical metal horn antenna. From the experiments shown here it appears that a dielectric antenna will generally be 50% longer than a metal horn of similar performance; the physical diameter will of course be much less. Similar results hold for dielectric antennas and metal horns in rectangular geometry.

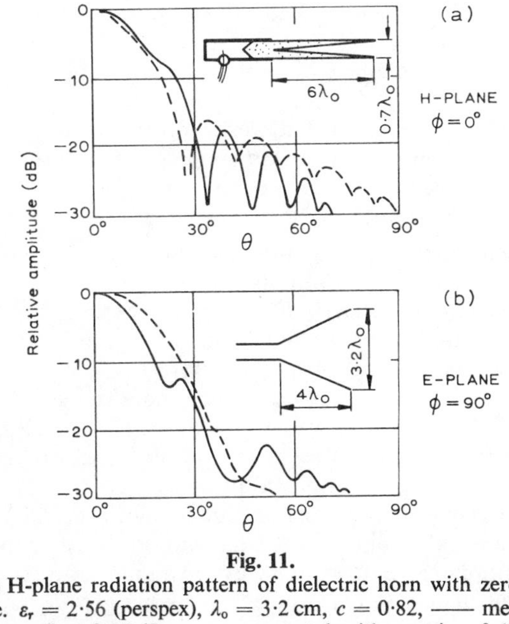

Fig. 11.

(a) H-plane radiation pattern of dielectric horn with zero flare angle. $\varepsilon_r = 2{\cdot}56$ (perspex), $\lambda_o = 3{\cdot}2$ cm, $c = 0{\cdot}82$, —— measured with a gain of 17 dB, ---- computed with a gain of 19·2 dB assuming no radiation from or dissipative losses in the taper and launcher loss of 12·8%. $\phi = 0°$.

(b) Measured radiation patterns of cylindrical metal horn. Measured gain = 18·5 dB; —— E-plane, ---- H-plane.

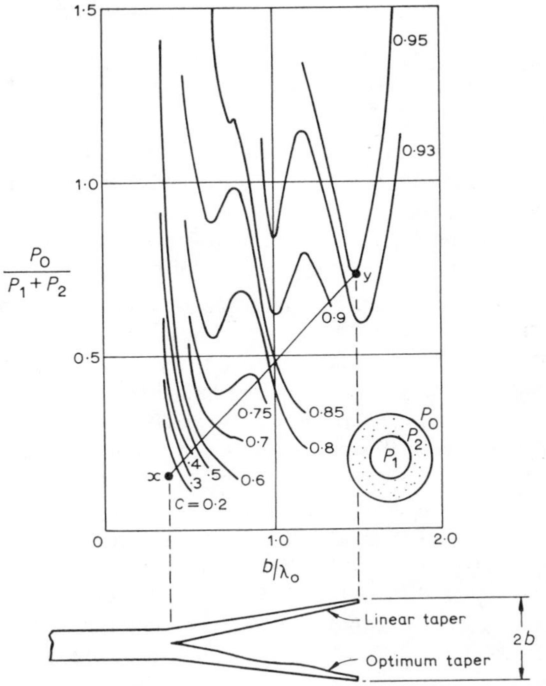

Fig. 12. Fraction of surface wave power within horn boundary based on step model approximation. Launcher and horn mouth radii correspond to point x and y; c values on line xy as a function of radius b define the near optimum profile, $\varepsilon_r = 2{\cdot}2$.

3.4 *Optimization of the Dielectric-horn Taper*

In principle the dielectric horn could be flared out in a variety of ways but here we have confined our study to flares with linear exterior walls in which case only the interior wall profile can be optimized to minimize the taper radiation losses. Tests have shown that as for the dielectric rod case, the fraction of surface wave power within the horn antenna exterior boundary wall as a function of radius b gives some indication as to how to choose the inside wall profile; these curves are given in Fig. 12, and define the inner wall profile as follows: the values of b and c that correspond to the horn dimensions at the launcher and mouth are marked on the curves at x and y; c values on the line xy then define the inner wall radius since b varies linearly along the horn length. We find however that the profile differs little from a straight line as the sketch in Fig. 12 shows and since a linear wall flare is easier to construct it has been adopted in most of our designs; the radiation along

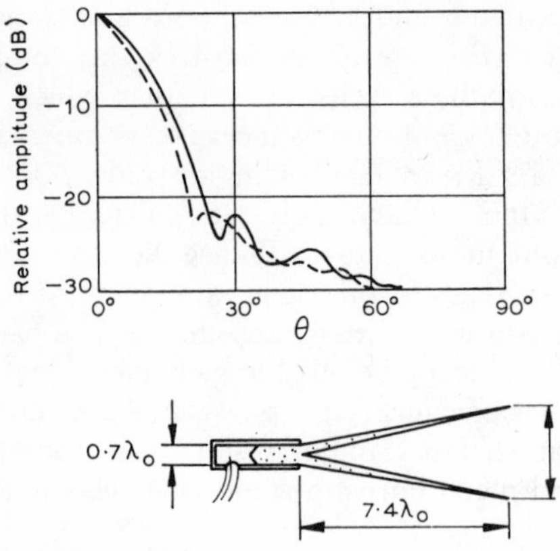

Fig. 13. E-plane radiation patterns of long wide flare angle horn. $\varepsilon_r = 2{\cdot}2$ (paraffin wax), $\lambda_o = 3{\cdot}2$ cm, $c = 0{\cdot}96$; —— measured, ---- computed with gain 24 dB assuming no radiation from or dissipative losses in the taper and 12·8% launcher loss. $\phi = 90°$.

the horn taper is then controlled by the terminal wall thickness and horn length. To design a zero flare angle horn profile the line xy becomes parallel to the ordinate axis and the c values vary in a smoother monotonic fashion giving a concave profile as in the rod case.

An example of the type of E-plane pattern that can be obtained from a long horn with linear walls is shown in Fig. 13. The radiation along the length is not negligible but is reduced to well below the launcher radiation level and computations agree well with measurements; further optimization of this horn was not attempted because of machining difficulties. The possibility of using an array of such horns suggests itself but grating lobe constraints need to be considered. It was anticipated that a wide flare-angle horn would collect some of the launcher radiation and for the wide flare angles used here some weak evidence exists in this respect since the computed side-lobe levels away from the main beam are generally higher than those actually measured. This is particularly so for the E-plane patterns of Figs. 9 and 10.

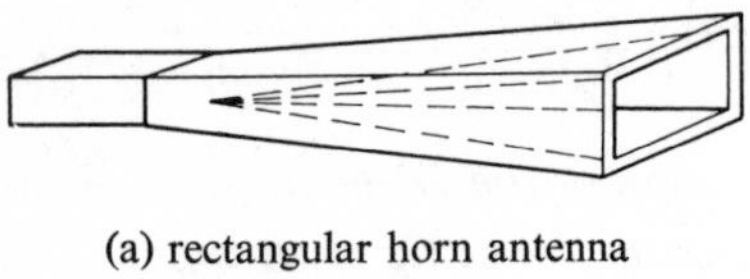

(a) rectangular horn antenna

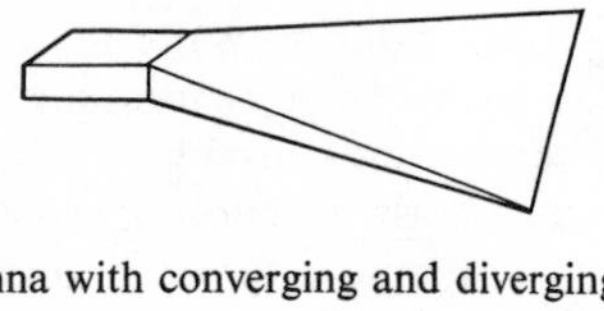

(b) wedge antenna with converging and diverging taper profiles

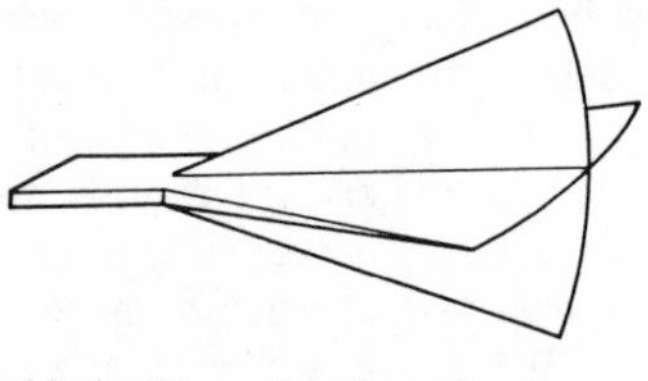

(c) double wedge-shaped antenna

Fig. 14. Various types of rectangular dielectric antenna suitable for rectangular waveguide launchers.

Another possibility is to maintain a constant value of c along the flare so that the internal and external walls diverge in a radial manner. It is evident from the curves above that it is not possible to choose c to satisfy both good radiation pattern and efficient launching conditions. To develop this principle further it is necessary to increase the size of the launcher and length of the antenna; a practical realization of this idea is the infra-red detection antenna found in moths which is tens of wavelengths long and has a relatively large diameter launcher.

4. Variations on the Dielectric Horn

Rectangular waveguide is more common than circular and it is possible to develop the above antennas for rectangular launchers. In fact a large variety of surface wave antennas may be developed using rectangular, elliptical, triangular and other cross-sectional shapes of rods and tubes. Unfortunately the trapped surface waves cannot be expressed in analytic form and recourse must be made to point-matching calculations.[20] Aperture fields are then obtained as a series and radiation patterns

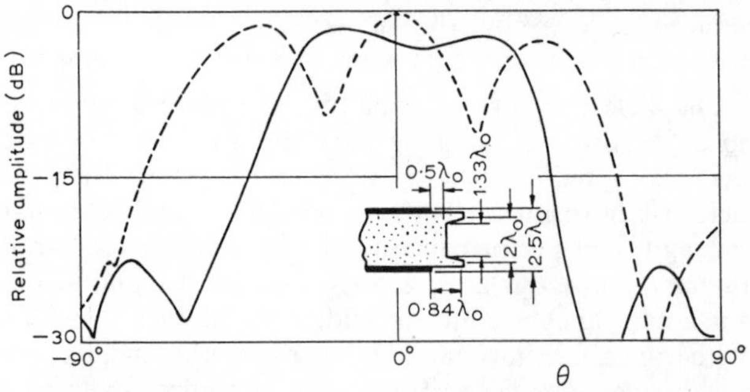

Fig. 15. Measured H-plane radiation patterns of dielectric filled overmoded cylindrical waveguide. $\varepsilon_r = 2{\cdot}2$ (paraffin wax), $\lambda_o = 3$ cm; ---- dielectric-filled waveguide aperture, —— with dielectric filling extended to form a short horn as sketched. $\phi = 0°$.

can only be obtained by numerical integration. Some examples of variations on the cylindrical dielectric horn are shown in Fig. 14 and we have tested them experimentally: these antennas are interesting but show no marked advantages over conventional forms although they may have specialized applications.

Much attention has been focused on the use of dielectric inserts in the mouth of the metal horns in order to reduce side-lobe level. For instance a recently reported dielectric wedge-shaped antenna[21,28] is very similar to the zero flare-angle horn (Fig. 11(a)). The insertion of dielectric strips into metal horn mouths[22] condenses the E-field in a similar way to the dielectric tube (Fig. 8). Another interesting effect is shown in Fig. 15 whereby a short thick dielectric horn protrudes from an overmoded cylindrical waveguide and enables a broad beam pattern to be obtained from what was previously a multi-lobed radiation pattern. One explanation[25] of this mode filtering action is that radiation coupling between the launcher and the horn adjusts itself to minimum for a certain set of modes in the metal launcher and a given geometry of the dielectric insert; another explanation is that the dielectric extension forms a resonant open cavity for these dimensions. Many other dielectric insert configurations are possible but their mechanism, as in the above case, is generally involved and much reliance is necessarily placed on actual measurements.

5. Discussion and Conclusions

The optimization of the taper profile of dielectric antennas is seen to present considerable theoretical difficulties; the approach developed here is to supplement theoretical considerations based on a simplified model with actual measured data and a high degree of optimization has been found possible. A conclusion of practical importance is that the optimization of the taper profile is well worthwhile and places both the dielectric-rod and zero flare-angle dielectric-horn antennas on a competitive footing with conventional metal horns of moderate gain. Design curves have been presented for commonly occurring values of dielectric constant but details of the general computer programs are available from the author. It is not envisaged that these dielectric devices will generally be alternatives to metal horns because robustness and power handling requirements obviously favour the metal antenna. However there are many applications where the low cost and weight, ease of manufacture and good corrosion and sealing properties associated with dielectric antennas will be an advantage; one such application is in large arrays.

Evaluation of the dielectric-horn antenna has shown that it could be particularly useful when directional properties in one plane only are required as is so often the case. An array of these devices is an interesting possibility.

When the flare angle is reduced to zero the dielectric-horn has similar patterns to the tapered rod antenna and exhibits rotational symmetry. The bandwidth of the dielectric-horn antenna is comparable to that of the tapered dielectric-rod antenna and is typically 1 GHz at X band, but this is more often than not constrained by the bandwidth of the feed system. An alternative launcher design has not been considered since the method used here seems to be widely applicable in practice to both horn and rod antennas.

An interesting fact has emerged that the dielectric-rod and horn antennas have similar actions despite their widely differing geometries; in essence the principle is to transform the launcher aperture into a larger one having an acceptable aperture distribution. The transformation may also be carried out by any one of a variety of open dielectric structures which are suitably tapered along their length. From a practical point of view there seems little to choose between the performance of these various forms of surface-wave antenna and the final choice rests with the overall system constraints; in particular the gain limitation experienced for the dielectric-rod and horn antennas seems to be a general feature.

6. Acknowledgments

Thanks are due to Mr. I. N. L. Gallett and Mr. E. Sigee for assistance with computations and measurements respectively, and to Professor M. H. N. Potok for his continued interest and advice.

7. References

1. Kiely, D. G., 'Dielectric Aerials' (Methuen Monograph, London, 1953).
2. Zucker, F. J., 'Surface and leaky-wave antennas', in Jasik, H. (Ed.), 'Antenna Engineering Handbook', Chap. 16. (McGraw-Hill, New York, 1961.)
3. Brown, J. and Spector, J. O., 'The radiating properties of end-fire aerials', *Proc. Instn Elect. Engrs*, **104B**, pp. 27–34, 1957.
4. James, J. R., 'Theoretical investigation of cylindrical dielectric-rod antennas', *Proc. Instn Elect. Engrs*, **114**, pp. 309–19, 1967.
5. Bach Andersen, J., 'Metallic and Dielectric Antennas' (Polyteknisk Forlag, Denmark, 1970).
6. Gallett, I. N. L., 'Radiation patterns of tubular dielectric structures'. European Microwave Conference, London, September 1969.
7. Prochazka, M., 'Die dielektrische hornantenna', *Hochfrequenztechnik u. Electroak.*, **68**, pp. 93–103, 1959.
8. James, J. R., 'Studies of cylindrical dielectric-rod antennas' Tech. Note RT41, Royal Military College of Science, June 1968.
9. James, J. R., 'Aperture coupling in cylindrical dielectric-rod antennas', *Electronics Letters*, **4**, pp. 39–41, 1968.
10. Marcuse, D., 'Radiation losses of the dominant mode in round dielectric waveguides', *Bell Syst. Tech. J.*, **49**, pp. 1665–93, 1970.
11. James, J. R., 'Some further properties of cylindrical dielectric-rod antennas', Tech. Note RT37, Royal Military College of Science, July 1967.
12. Silver, S., 'Microwave Antenna Theory and Design', p. 161 (McGraw-Hill, New York, 1949).
13. Barlow, H. M. and Brown, J., 'Radio Surface Waves', (Clarendon Press, Oxford, 1962).
14. Snyder, A. W., 'Radiation losses due to variations of radius on dielectric or optical fibres', *I.E.E.E. Trans. on Microwave Theory and Techniques*, **MTT-18**, No. 9, pp. 608–15, September 1970.
15. Barlow, H. M. and Brown, J. *loc. cit.*, p. 164.
16. Kharadly, M. M. Z. and Lewis, J. E., 'Properties of dielectric-tube waveguides', *Proc. I.E.E.*, **116**, No. 2, pp. 214–24, February 1969.
17. Potok, M. H. N., James, J. R. and Gallett, I. N. L., 'Dielectric antennas' 2nd Annual Research Report ELS/PR/No. 18, R.M.C.S. February 1970.
18. Silver, S., *loc. cit.*, p. 581.
19. Hamid, M. A. K., 'Diffraction by a conical horn', *I.E.E.E. Trans. on Antennas and Propagation*, **AP-16**, No. 5, pp. 520–8, September 1968.
20. James, J. R. and Gallett, I. N. L., 'Point-matched solutions for propagating modes on arbitrarily shaped dielectric-rods', *The Radio and Electronic Engineer*, **42**, No. 3, pp. 103–13, March 1972.
21. Boulanger, R. J. and Hamid, M. A. K., 'A new type of dielectric-loaded waveguide antenna', *Microwave J.*, December 1970, pp. 67–8.
22. Hamid, M. A. K. *et al.*, 'Radiation characteristics of dielectric-loaded horn antennas', *Electronics Letters*, **6**, pp. 20–1, 1970.
23. James, J. R., Gallett, I. N. L. and Sigee, E., 'New ideas and results on dielectric horns', Proceedings of the European Microwave Conference, Stockholm, August 1971.
24. James, J. R., 'Leaky waves on a dielectric rod', *Electronics Letters*, **5**, No. 11, pp. 252–4, May 1969.
25. James, J. R., 'Aperture coupling in surface wave antennas', Tech. Note RT33, Royal Military College of Science, February 1967.
26. Collin, R. E. and Zucker, F. J., 'Antenna Theory', Parts I and II. Inter-University Electronics Series (McGraw-Hill, New York, 1969).
27. Potok, M. H. N., James, J. R. and Gallett, I. N. L., 'Dielectric antennas' 1st Annual Research Report ELS/PR/ No. 16, R.M.C.S., November 1968.
28. Hamid, M. A. K. *et al.*, 'A dielectric loaded circular waveguide antenna', *I.E.E.E. Trans.*, **AP-20**, 1, pp. 96–97 January 1972.

Manuscript first received by the Institution on 29th February 1972 and in final form on 27th March 1972. (Paper No. 1451/CC130).

RADIATION PATTERNS OF PYRAMIDAL DIELECTRIC WAVEGUIDES

Indexing terms: Antenna radiation patterns, Dielectric devices, Reflector antennas, Waveguide antennas

The radiation patterns of pyramidal dielectric waveguides excited by pyramidal metallic horns are predicted and compared with patterns measured at 9 GHz. Satisfactory agreement is obtained, especially in the region of the main beam. At wide angles, the pattern corresponds quite closely to that of the launcher alone.

The use of dielectric waveguides to improve the performance of microwave reflector antennas was described qualitatively in 1966 by Bartlett and Moseley.[1] Recently, Clarricoats and Salema[2] proposed a theory that enables the radiation patterns of dielectric cones to be predicted with accuracy, and they also established a design procedure for Cassegrain antennas employing dielectric cones to support the subreflector. Our purpose is to describe an extension of the theory to pyramidal dielectric waveguides, as shown in the inset to Fig. 1, and to compare predicted radiation patterns with those obtained experimentally. Twenty-four configurations of dielectric waveguide and launcher have been examined; here, we shall discuss two representative results.

Following the procedure used with conical dielectric waveguides,[2] our first step is to determine the field distribution over the aperture of the dielectric radiator. We choose, in the present case, a plane aperture at slant distance L from the pyramidal-horn launcher, in contrast with a spherical aperture in the previous analysis. The plane contains the dielectric pyramid of maximum dimensions A and B. To obtain the field distribution over the aperture, associated with the dominant dielectric-waveguide mode, we use an approximate method proposed by Marcateli.[3] This method has since been substantiated by Ozkan[4] for rectangular dielectric waveguides with aspect ratios similar to those we have used. In this method, the transverse wavenumbers K_x and K_y inside a dielectric of rectangular cross-section $A' \times B'$, and the corresponding wavenumbers outside, are assumed to be those associated with two semi-infinite dielectric-slab waveguides of thicknesses A' and B', respectively, and supporting, respectively, the lowest-order TM and TE modes. Further, the longitudinal propagation coefficient β is assumed to satisfy the equation

$$K_x^2 + K_y^2 = \omega^2 \varepsilon \mu_0 - \beta^2$$

where ε is the permittivity of the dielectric. Since, in the above model, K_x and K_y depend on the transverse dimensions of the dielectric waveguide, β is a slowly varying function of z, if the waveguide is pyramidal. To obtain the phase variation at a point in the radiating aperture, β is evaluated as a function of z, and the component of β along the direction from the origin to the point in the aperture integrated to obtain the phase. The amplitude variation over the aperture is also readily obtained by following Marcateli,[3] once the wavenumbers have been computed.

The radiation patterns in H and E planes associated with the dielectric-waveguide aperture distributions have been computed using a Kirchhoff–Huygens integration program.[5] The results are shown by the crosses in Figs. 1 and 2. Also shown are the measured patterns (broken curves) obtained at a frequency of 9 GHz for two different pyramidal dielectric waveguides excited by the same launcher (Figs. 1 and 2, respectively). Following the studies of conical dielectric waveguides,[2] we observe close agreement between predicted and measured patterns over the main-beam region. Also

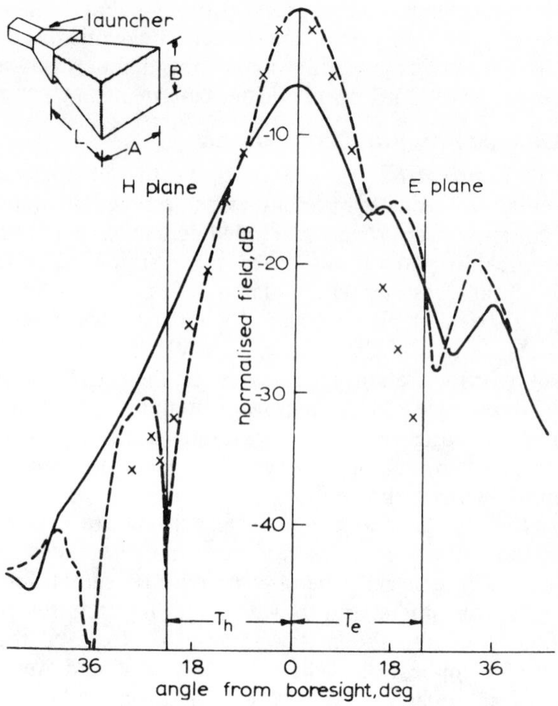

Fig. 1 *Radiation patterns of pyramidal dielectric waveguides*

Inset shows configuration
$\varepsilon = 1{\cdot}045$; $A = B = 22{\cdot}5$ cm, $L = 60$ cm
Trapping angles $T_L = T_e = 20°$
Launcher has aperture dimensions in the E plane of 14·3 cm and, in the H plane, of 19·4 cm
Slot length from apex = 36·0 cm
——— launcher
- - - - launcher and dielectric waveguide
× theoretical points

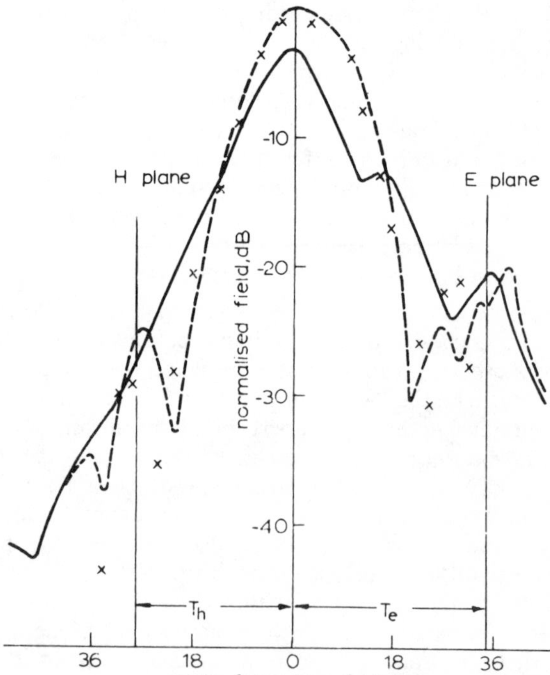

Fig. 2 *Radiation patterns of pyramidal dielectric waveguides*

$\varepsilon = 1{\cdot}108$; $A = 20$ cm, $B = 30$ cm, $L = 40$ cm
Trapping angles: $T_L = 28°$
$T_e = 35°$
Other parameters and notation as Fig. 1

Reprinted with permission from *Electron. Lett.*, vol. 10, pp. 33–34, Feb. 7, 1974.

shown in the Figures are measured patterns for the pyramidal-horn launcher (solid line), theoretical patterns having been omitted, as it has been shown previously[2] that they are in excellent agreement with those obtained experimentally. Again, as with conical dielectric waveguides, at angles greater than those producing total internal reflection of rays from the phase centres of the launcher, there is reasonable agreement between patterns of the composite structure and those of the launcher alone. In other words, beyond the so-called trapping angle, the pattern of the composite structure is essentially the pattern of the launcher only, slightly perturbed by the presence of the dielectric. Within the trapping region, the pattern is essentially that of the dielectric waveguide. Similar results have been obtained for other launcher and pyramidal- and sectoral-dielectric-waveguide configurations. However, we have found that agreement between measured and predicted patterns deteriorates when the aspect ratio a/b of the launcher differs significantly from that of the dielectric waveguide, A/B.

Pyramidal dielectric waveguides can be fabricated easily,[6] by the use of hot-wire methods. They provide an inexpensive means of raising the gain of an existing metallic horn by several decibels, and provide a means of exerting a measure of independent control over the H and E plane patterns of the composite feed, as is required in shaped-beam applications.

Acknowledgment: The authors gratefully acknowledge many valuable discussions with G. A. Hockham, and the use of the program prepared by C. E. R. C. Salema and S. H. Lim for the computation of radiation patterns. The experimental work described was supported, in part, by means of a grant from the UK Science Research Council. One of the authors (N.B.) is on leave from the Federal University of Rio de Janeiro, and is indebted to the National Research Council of Brazil for a research fellowship.

N. BROOKING
P. J. B. CLARRICOATS
A. D. OLVER

27th December 1973

Department of Electrical Engineering
Queen Mary College
Mile End Road, London E1 4NS, England

References

1 BARLETT, H. E., and MOSELEY, R. E.: 'Dielguides—highly efficient low-noise antenna feeds', *Microwave J.*, 1966, **9**, pp. 53–58

2 CLARRICOATS, P. J. B., and SALEMA, C. E. R. C.: 'Antennas employing conical dielectric horns. Pt. 1—Propagation and radiation characteristics of dielectric cones' *and* Pt. 2—Cassegrain antenna', *Proc. IEE*, 1972, **120**, (7), pp. 741–756

3 MARCATELI, E. A. J.: 'Dielectric rectangular waveguides and directional coupler for integrated optics', *Bell Syst. Tech. J.*, 1969, **48**, pp. 2071–2102

4 CULLEN, A. L., OZKAN, O., and JACKSON, L. A.: 'Point-matching technique for rectangular-cross-section dielectric rod', *Electron. Lett.*, 1971, **7**, pp. 497–499

5 SALEMA, C. E. R. C.: 'The calculation of radiation patterns of aperture antennas using the Kirchoff–Huygens formula'. Queen Mary College, London, Report CERCS/72/5

6 HONOUR, J., and MORRIS, J.: 'The fabrication of dielectric cones from expanded polystyrene foam'. Queen Mary College, London, Report JH/73/4

Antennas employing conical dielectric horns

Part 1—Propagation and radiation characteristics of dielectric cones

Prof. P. J. B. Clarricoats, D.Sc (Eng.), F.Inst.P., Fel.I.E.E.E., C.Eng., F.I.E.E., and C. E. R. C. Salema, Eng.º, Ph.D.

Indexing terms: Waveguide antennas, Antenna radiation Patterns, Dielectric devices, Antenna feeders

ABSTRACT

An approximate theory for the propagation and radiation characteristics of dielectric cones is developed. A formulation in terms of spherical modes is used in the interior of the cone, and boundary conditions are applied so that the field exterior to the cone has surface-wave properties. The propagation and radiation characteristics are found to resemble closely those for corrugated horns, and experimental results support the theoretical predictions.

LIST OF SYMBOLS

F = focal distance of a parabolic reflector
$F_m(x)$ = $x J_m'(x)/J_m(x)$
f = frequency
f_ν^m = $\{\sin\theta / P_\nu^m(\cos\theta)\}\{d P_\nu^m(\cos\theta)/d\theta\}$
$H_\nu(x) = x h_\nu^{(2)}(x)$ = Schelkunoff's spherical Bessel function
$h_\nu^{(2)}(x)$ = spherical Hankel function of the second kind and real order ν
$J_m(x)$ = Bessel function of the first kind and integer order m
j = $\sqrt{-1}$
$K_m(x)$ = modified Bessel function of the second kind and integer order m
k = $2\pi/\lambda = k_0 = \omega\sqrt{(\epsilon_0\mu_0)}$ free-space wave number
$M_m(x)$ = $x\, K_m'(x)/K_m(x)$
$P_\nu^m(\cos\theta)$ = associated Legendre function of the first kind and of order ν
$Y_m(x)$ = Bessel function of the second kind and integer order m
β = $2\pi/\lambda_g$, where λ_g is the wavelength inside a guiding structure
$\bar{\beta}$ = β/k_2
ϵ = dielectric permittivity
$\bar{\epsilon}$ = normalised dielectric permittivity
η = power efficiency
θ_T = trapping angle
θ_c = $\sin^{-1}(1/\sqrt{\epsilon_1})$ = critical angle
λ = free-space wavelength
μ = permeability
$\bar{\mu}$ = normalised permeability
ϕ = phase angle
$\omega = 2\pi f$ = angular frequency

1 INTRODUCTION

The ingenious use of a dielectric cone of low relative permittivity as a means to improve the efficiency of microwave reflector antennas was proposed in a patent application filed in 1964[1] by Bartlett and Mosely, details of which were subsequently published in 1966.[2] These authors described in qualitative terms the behaviour of both the prime-focus and Cassegrain configurations of Figs. 1a and 1b. They explained, using ray-optic concepts (see Fig. 1c) how some of the radiation from the feedhorn which misses the reflector S in the absence of the dielectric cone arrives there in its presence owing to total internal reflection at the dielectric-air boundary. After reflection at S, the rays pass through the dielectric-air boundary almost without effect, as the angle of incidence is then less than the critical angle. Experimental results showed that the secondary radiation patterns of the antennas employing the dielectric cones exhibited greater symmetry than hitherto, and antenna efficiencies between 75 and 80% were reported. Also, because of the guiding action of the dielectric, it was possible to use a smaller-diameter subreflector in the Cassegrain antenna and so reduce aperture blockage.

Although interest in these so-called 'dielguide' antennas has persisted since the announcements by Bartlett and his associates,[1-4] as far as we are aware no design theory has hitherto been proposed outside of the present study. Some preliminary reports on this study have been given previously.[5-10,16]

Our interest in dielectric-cone antennas arose from two sources. First, the need for a design for an antenna employing a dielectric cone to reduce spillover beyond a subreflector of small diameter. Secondly, the recognition[11] by one of us of the similarity between the dielectric-

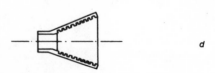

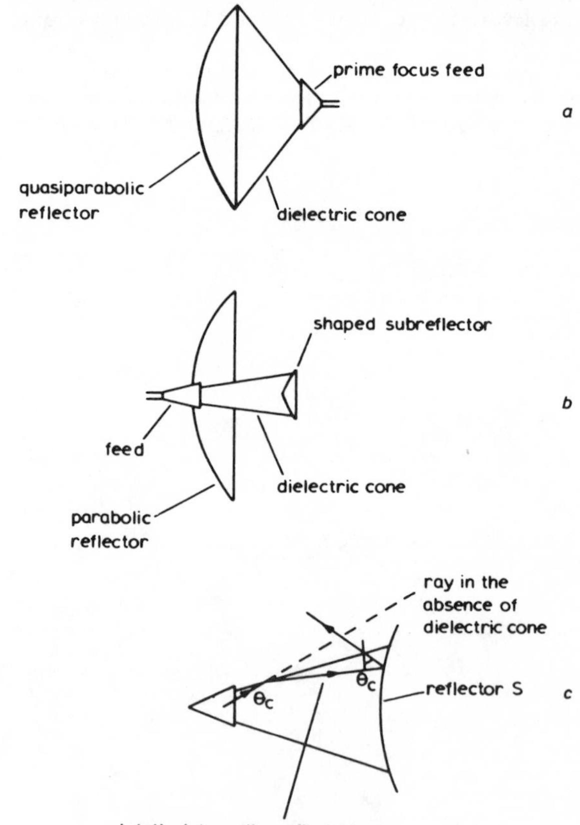

Fig. 1

Reflector antennas employing dielectric-cone feeds and corrugated horn

a Reflector with dielectric-cone and prime-focus feed
b Reflector with dielectric-cone and Cassegrain feed
c Ray diagram for dielectric-cone feed
d Corrugated horn

Paper 6960E, first received 18th January and in revised form 26th March 1973

Prof. Clarricoats is, and Dr. Salema was formerly, with the Department of Electrical & Electronic Engineering, Queen Mary College, University of London, Mile End Road, London E1 4NS, England. Dr. Salema is now with the Institute Superior Technico (Technical University of Lisbon), Portugal

Reprinted with permission from *Proc. Inst. Elec. Eng.*, vol. 120, pp. 741–749, July 1973.

cone antenna and the corrugated horn shown in Fig. 1d, leading to the possible development of an inexpensive replacement for the latter in certain applications.

In Part 1, we describe an approximate theory to account for radiation from a dielectric cone fed from a metallic horn. Part 2 describes the design of a Cassegrain antenna employing a dielectric cone to support the subreflector.

Our approach to a theory for the propagation and radiation properties of dielectric cones has been considerably influenced by earlier studies of corrugated waveguides and corrugated horns.[12,13] Although the propagation behaviour of the corrugated waveguide can be predicted exactly, the behaviour of the corrugated horn is necessarily approximate. Because of its relevance to the dielectric cone, we mention briefly the method of solution for the corrugated horn.

In the interior of the horn, $\theta < \theta_1$ solutions of Maxwell's equations in spherical co-ordinates are found using the method of separation of the variables, as for a cone with a continuous metallic boundary at $\theta = \theta_1$. In the simple theory, the fields in the slots are assumed to arise only from the lowest-order TM_m mode possessing the same azimuthal dependence m as the field in $\theta < \theta_1$. If $m > 0$ the fields in $\theta < \theta_1$ must possess both E_r and H_r components to satisfy the boundary conditions at $\theta = \theta_1$, and we call the resulting mode 'spherical hybrid'. Subject to the above assumptions, $E_\phi = 0$ at $\theta = \theta_1$ and the value of H_ϕ/E_r is determined by the slot depth. When the boundary conditions are matched at $\theta = \theta_1$, we obtain a characteristic equation for the separation constant ν which describes the θ dependence of the field through factors containing the associated Legendre function $P_\nu{}^m(\cos\theta)$ or its derivatives with respect to θ. However, unless we are concerned with fields well removed from the apex of the cone, so that the radial dependence is described only by a phase term e^{-jkr}, the resulting characteristic equation depends weakly upon r, thus contravening the initial assumption of separation of variables. Furthermore, unless the slot depth is adjusted with r so that H_ϕ/E_r is independent of r, the variation in boundary admittance will also contribute to make ν r-dependent. However, it has been found that experimental and theoretical radiation patterns, arising from the dominant HE_{11} mode in the horn, are in very good agreement provided $\theta_1 < 80°$. This observation inspired our present approach to the dielectric-cone problem.

In the present theory, we use the same approach as for the corrugated horn, only we chose our boundary conditions at $\theta = \theta_1, r = r_1$ appropriate to those for a dielectric rod of radius $r_1\theta_1$. This seems reasonable, since, in the limit $\theta_1 \to 0$, the field should reduce to that of a surface-wave mode propagating along a dielectric rod. As is well known, the field outside a dielectric rod decays almost exponentially and the field is quite tightly bound to the surface when the rod radius is large.

There is one important difference between the theory for the cone and for the corrugated horn. For the corrugated horn, the spherical hybrid HE_{11} mode is usually excited by an incident H_{11} mode in the input circular waveguide. Provided $\theta_1 < 80°$, experiment shows that nearly all the incident energy is converted to the HE_{11} mode at the horn aperture and none is observed to radiate directly from the discontinuity at the horn throat. By contrast, when a cone and feed horn are joined as in Fig. 1c some radiation will inevitably occur at the junction between the two.

Finally, we must conclude that the representation of the field of the dielectric cone in terms of a mode is inexact. The justification for the modal formulation rests on the satisfactory agreement demonstrated between experiment and theory.

2 PROPAGATION AND RADIATION CHARACTERISTICS OF DIELECTRIC CONES

2.1 Propagation characteristics of dielectric cones

Fig. 2 shows the dielectric cone of permittivity ϵ_1 surrounded by a medium of permittivity ϵ_2. Although, in practice, the cone is truncated at a finite value of r, we analyse the case where the cone extends indefinitely. In our approximate analysis, we assume that, within the dielectric region $\theta < \theta_1$, the field of the mth azimuthal dependent mode may be expressed as a spherical hybrid wave. In the region $\theta > \theta_1$, we assume that, provided $k_1 r_1 \gg 1$, the field decays with distance along the normal to the dielectric boundary, in the same way as if the dielectric was a uniform cylinder of radius r_1, θ_1. In this way, it is possible to ensure that the field experiences the same increase in phase with increasing radial distance, through $e^{-j\beta r}$, on both sides of the boundary $\theta = \theta_1$.

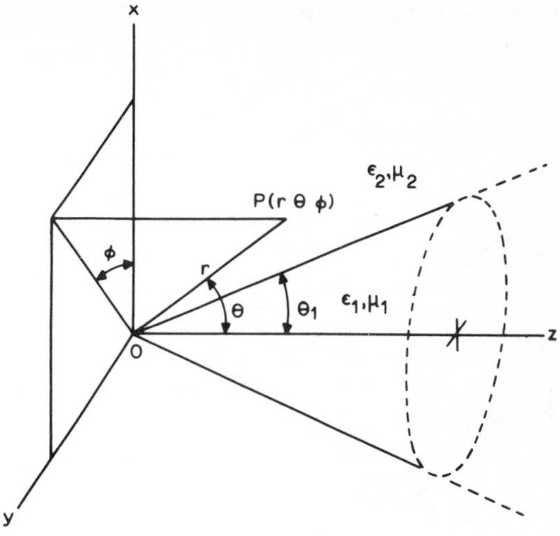

Fig. 2

System of co-ordinates for the dielectric cone

Subject to these assumptions, we obtain at $r = r_1$ the following characteristic equation for the separation constant $\kappa_1 = \{\nu(\nu+1)\}^{1/2}/r_1$, which is related to the interior transverse wavenumber in the corresponding propagation problem for a cylindrical-dielectric rod:

$$\left(\frac{\bar{\epsilon}_1 f_\nu{}^m(\cos\theta_1)}{\kappa_1{}^2}+\frac{M_m(\kappa_2 r_1)}{\kappa_2{}^2}\right)\left(\frac{f_\nu{}^m(\cos\theta_1)}{\kappa_1{}^2}+\frac{M_m(\kappa_2 r_1)}{\kappa_2{}^2}\right) = m^2\bar{\beta}^2\left(\frac{1}{\kappa_1{}^2}+\frac{1}{\kappa_2{}^2}\right)^2 \qquad (1)$$

where

$$\bar{\epsilon}_1 = \epsilon_1/\epsilon_2$$

$$\kappa_1{}^2 = \nu(\nu+1)/r_1{}^2$$

$$f_\nu{}^m(\cos\theta_1) = \sin\theta_1\left(\frac{\dfrac{dP_\nu{}^m(\cos\theta)}{d\theta}}{P_\nu{}^m(\cos\theta)}\right)_{\theta=\theta_1}$$

$$M_m(\kappa_2 r_1) = \kappa_2 r_1\frac{K'_m(\kappa_2 r_1)}{K_m(\kappa_2 r_1)}\left(\frac{\sin\theta}{\theta}\right)$$

$$\kappa_1{}^2 = k_1{}^2 - \beta^2$$

$$\kappa_2{}^2 = \beta^2 - k_2{}^2$$

$$\bar{\beta} = \beta/k_2$$

$$k_1{}^2 = \omega^2\epsilon_1\mu_0$$

$$k_2{}^2 = \omega^2\epsilon_2\mu_0$$

When $\theta_1 \to 0$, the above equation reduces the form of the characteristic equation for a dielectric rod of radius r_1, θ_1. A derivation of eqn. 1 based on approximate solutions of the spherical wave equation is to be found elsewhere.[16]

As in the analysis of corrugated horns, the characteristic equation is dependent on r_1, thus violating the initial assumption of separation of variables. However, it can be demonstrated numerically that, provided we restrict ourselves to large values of $k_1 r_1$, ν varies only slowly with r_1.

If, in eqn. 1, r_1 tends to infinity,

$$f_\nu{}^m(\cos\theta_1) = \pm m \qquad (2)$$

which is the characteristic equation for a corrugated horn operated under balanced hybrid conditions.*

Computed values of ν as a function of θ_1 are represented in Fig. 3, for the first hybrid mode of unity azimuthal dependence, designated HE_{11}, and for different normalised cone length. The values for the EH_{11} and HE_{12} modes with $k_2r = 500$ are also given for comparison. As the performance of

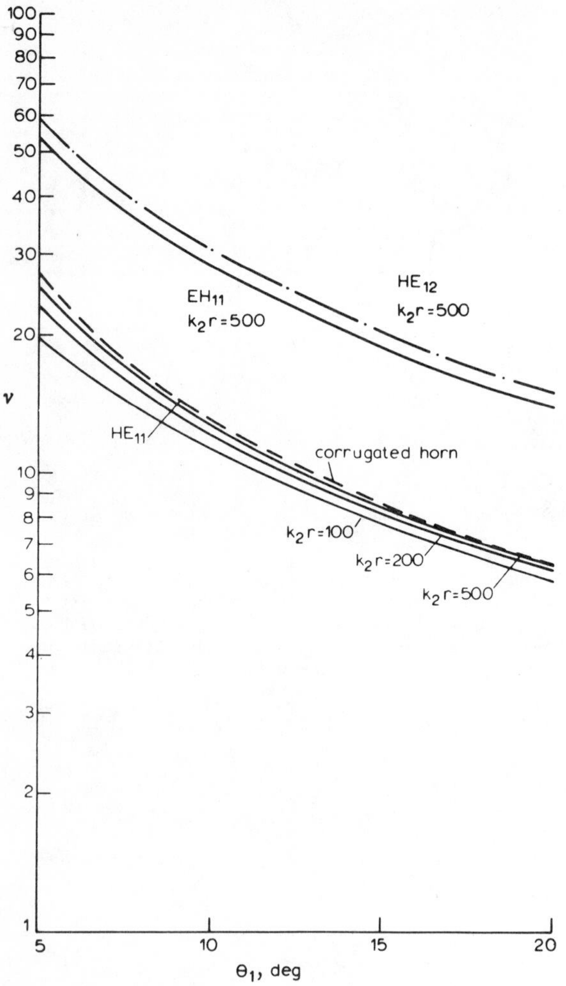

Fig. 3

Root of the characteristic equation of a dielectric cone against cone semiflare angle. Also shown is the root of the characteristic equation of a corrugated horn for the HE_{11} mode $\bar{\epsilon}_1 = 1{\cdot}10$

a dielectric-cone antenna can easily be predicted by comparison with the corrugated horn of the same slant length and the same value of ν, solutions of the corrugated-horn characteristic equation for the HE_{11} mode are also included.

It is interesting to remark that, for the majority of cases of practical importance ($\theta_1 < 15°$), the following approximations:

$$P_\nu{}^m(\cos\theta) \simeq J_m[\sqrt{\{\nu(\nu+1)\}}\theta] = J_m(\kappa_1 r\theta) \tag{3}$$

$$\frac{dP_\nu{}^m(\cos\theta)}{d\theta} \simeq \sqrt{\{\nu(\nu+1)\}}\, J'_m[\sqrt{\{\nu(\nu+1)\}}\theta] \simeq \kappa_1 r J'_m(\kappa_1 r\theta) \tag{4}$$

give almost exactly the same value for ν as can be obtained using the associated Legendre functions. Physically this is equivalent to treating the cone as a gradually expanding cylinder whose radius ρ at distance r from the apex is given by $\rho = r\theta_1$. Likewise, the values of the fields appropriate to the cylinder problem can also be used as a good approximation to the fields in the dielectric-cone problem. However, it must be borne in mind that, in the dielectric cone, the equiphase surfaces are spheres, centred on the apex of the cone, whereas, in the cylinder, the equiphase surfaces are planes normal to the axis. For values of θ_1 larger than 15°, we believe that the method presented above will give more accurate results, especially when radiation patterns are determined.

However, the dielectric-rod analogy is helpful in establishing the limiting condition for propagation of higher-order modes ($\bar{\beta} = 1$). Table 1 gives values of the normalised radius $V = (2\pi\rho_1/\lambda)(\bar{\epsilon}_1 - \bar{\epsilon}_2)^{1/2}$ under the condition, and for the first 21 modes of a cylinder for which $\epsilon_1 \approx \epsilon_2$ and with m = 1, 2, or 3.

TABLE 1

VALUES OF V UNDER THE CONDITION $\bar{\beta} = 1$

mode	V	mode	V	mode	V
HE_{11}	0	HE_{21}	2·41	HE_{31}	3·83
EH_{11}	3·83	EH_{21}	5·14	EH_{31}	6·38
HE_{12}	3·83	HE_{22}	5·52	HE_{32}	7·02
EH_{12}	7·02	EH_{22}	8·45	EH_{32}	9·76
HE_{13}	7·02	HE_{23}	8·65	HE_{33}	10·17
EH_{13}	10·18	EH_{23}	11·62	EH_{33}	13·02
HE_{14}	10·18	HE_{24}	11·79	HE_{34}	13·32

$V = \frac{2\pi\rho}{\lambda}\{\bar{\epsilon}_1 - \bar{\epsilon}_2\}^{1/2}$

2.2 The HE_{11}-mode aperture fields

We now examine in more detail the dominant HE_{11} mode of the dielectric cone, as this mode is of greatest importance in antenna applications. Figs. 4a-c present, respectively, the variation of the normalised magnetic field of a dielectric cone with the slant length r_1, semiflare angle θ_1 and the relative permittivity $\bar{\epsilon}_1$. The electric-field patterns are similar, but a discontinuity in the normal component occurs at $\theta = \theta_1$.

In Fig. 4b, we also depict the fields of the HE_{11} mode, under balanced-hybrid conditions, in a corrugated horn with $\theta_1 = 20°$ and 22·8°, respectively, and with k_2r_1 the same as for the dielectric cone. The latter value of θ_1 was chosen as it gives the same value for ν as for the 20° dielectric cone. The striking resemblance between the fields immediately suggests that the electromagnetic behaviour of dielectric cones and corrugated horns is similar. This similarity increases when the fields become more concentrated inside the cone.

As in the corrugated horn, the HE_{11} fields in the dielectric cone are nearly linearly polarised, and we have found this to be so even for cones with relative permittivities as high as 2·5.

2.3 Mode excitation

In practice, the approximate modal fields described above are excited when the dielectric cone is joined to a horn, the cross-section of which is usually either circular or rectangular. We shall now calculate the excitation coefficient of the modes using an approximate modal matching method which has been applied previously in optical waveguides.[14,15]

Consider a conical horn exciting the cone. At the interface S shown in the insert to Fig. 5, we expand the dominant-mode transverse (to r) field of the horn, shown on the left of eqns. 5 and 6, in terms of (a) spherical modes of the cone, possessing the same azimuthal dependence, and (b) the radiation fields E_R and H_R, which are orthogonal to the modal fields.

$$(1 + a_1)E_1 + \sum_{n=2}^{\infty} a_n E_n = \sum_{1}^{\infty} A_N E_N + E_R \tag{5}$$

$$(1 - a_1)H_1 - \sum_{n=2}^{\infty} a_n H_n = \sum_{1}^{\infty} A_N H_N + H_R \tag{6}$$

* *When balanced hybrid conditions occur, $H_\phi = E_\phi = 0$ at $\theta = \theta_1$*

In our approximation, we neglect the higher-order modes of the horn, and by the use of the orthogonality properties of the spherical modes obtain directly the excitation coefficients A_N:

$$\frac{A_N}{1 + a_1} = \frac{\int_S \mathbf{E}_1 \times \mathbf{H}_N^* \cdot d\mathbf{S}}{\int_S \mathbf{E}_M \times \mathbf{H}_N^* \cdot d\mathbf{S}} \qquad (7)$$

or

$$\frac{A_N^*}{1 - a_1^*} = \frac{\int_S \mathbf{E}_N \times \mathbf{H}_1^* \cdot d\mathbf{S}}{\int_S \mathbf{E}_N \times \mathbf{H}_N^* \cdot d\mathbf{S}} \qquad (8)$$

Fig. 5 shows the excitation efficiency of the first three modes of a dielectric cone, with $\theta_1 = 5{\cdot}9°$, $\bar{\epsilon}_1 = 1{\cdot}10$ and $k_2 r_1 = 140$, joined to a conical horn of semiflare angle θ_2.

In the junction of Fig. 5, the conical horn is assumed to touch the cone at the horn aperture. Although a slight improvement in efficiency occurs when there is an optimum gap between the horn and cone, the above represents a useful practical configuration. If required, the influence of a gap can be determined to a good approximation by considering a junction between a cylindrical waveguide and a cylindrical-dielectric rod.[16] Fig. 5 shows that, when the horn and cone semiangles coincide, there is negligible excitation of higher-order modes. However, we have practically investigated the above configuration with $\theta_2 = 14°$, and then the

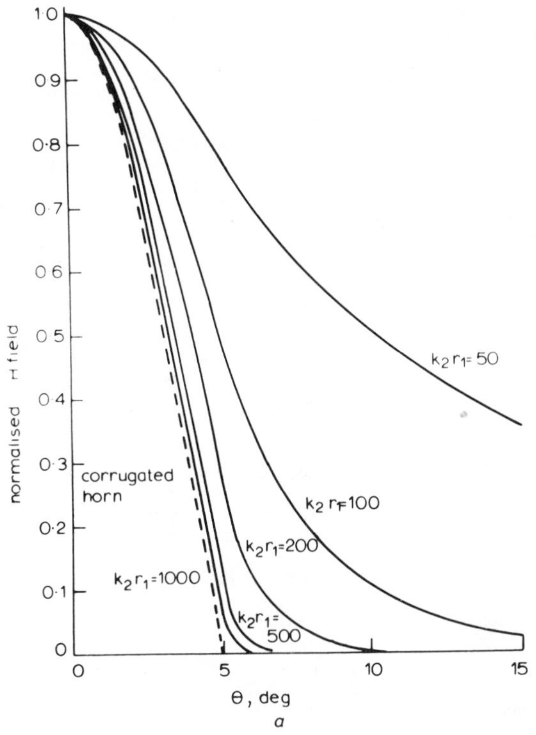

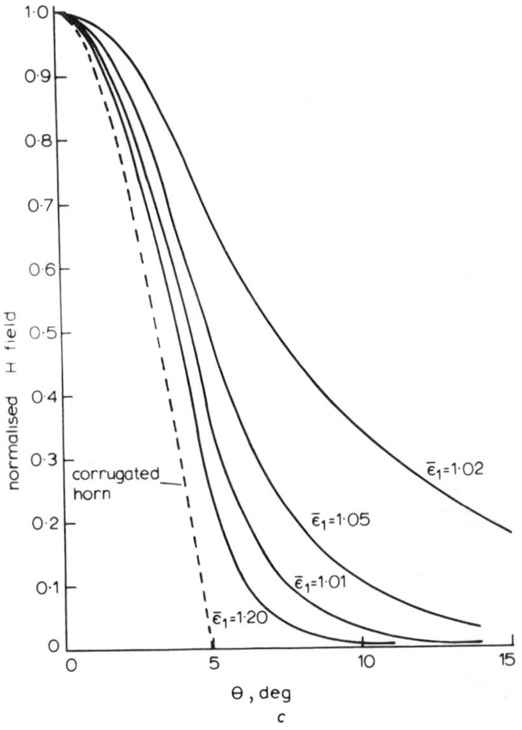

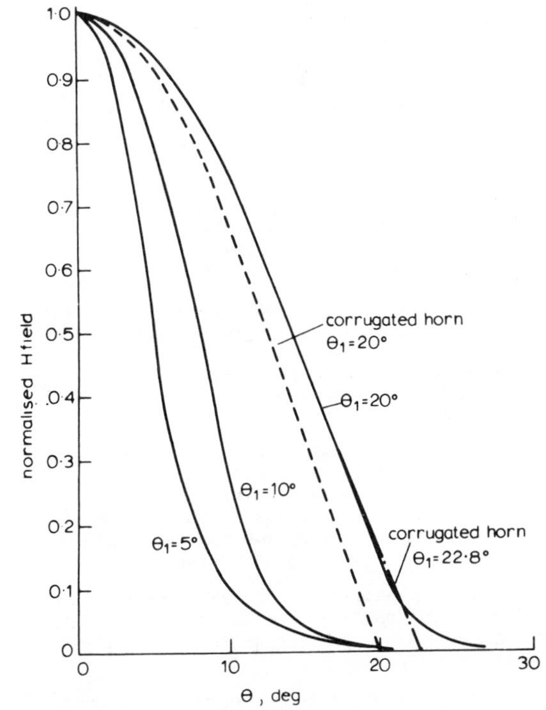

Fig. 4

Magnetic-field pattern over aperture of dielectric cone

a *Aperture field patterns for the* HE_{11} *mode of dielectric cones of different slant length. Also shown is the aperture field pattern of a corrugated horn of the same semiflare angle*

$\bar{\epsilon}_1 = 1{\cdot}05$

$\theta_1 = 5°$

b *Aperture field patterns for the* HE_{11} *mode of dielectric cones of different semiflare angle. Also shown are the aperture field patterns of two corrugated horns: one with* $\theta_1 = 22{\cdot}8°$ *so that the root of the characteristic equation is the same as a dielectric cone of* $\theta_1 = 20°$

$\bar{\epsilon}_1 = 1{\cdot}05$

$k_2 r_1 = 100$

c *Aperture field patterns for the* HE_{11} *mode of dielectric cones of different dielectric permittivity. Also shown is the aperture field pattern of a corrugated horn with the same semiflare angle*

$k_2 r_1 = 100$

$\theta_1 = 5°$

next two higher modes are excited with an efficiency of between 6 and 9%. The aperture distribution for the configuration is shown in Fig. 6c, and its behaviour will be discussed in the next Section.

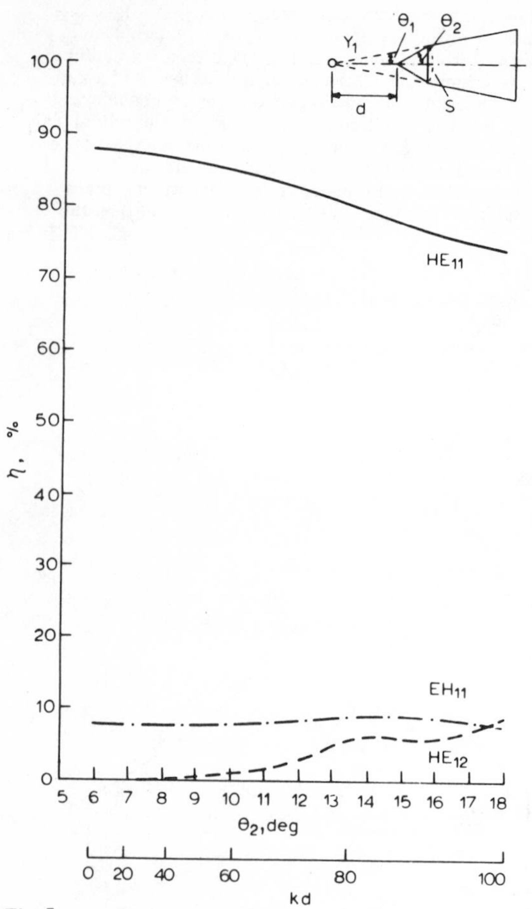

Fig. 5

Excitation efficiency of dielectric cone fed from conical-horn launcher
Cone parameters: $\theta_1 = 5{\cdot}9°, \bar{\epsilon}_1 = 1{\cdot}10, k_2 r_1 = 140$

2.4 Comparison of predicted and measured aperture fields

A number of dielectric cones have been constructed and their aperture fields measured using a small dipole probe. Although our theory has been developed on the assumption that the cone is of infinite extent in the r direction, the practical cones were about 30 wavelengths long. However, when the excitation of the higher-order modes is low and that of the HE_{11} mode sufficiently high, the measured aperture fields are in excellent agreement with the theoretical results, as Fig. 6a shows. For this case, the HE_{11} mode of the dielectric cone is excited by an HE_{11} mode in the corrugated waveguide with an efficiency of about 90%.

Elsewhere[16] we have shown that, when the excitation efficiency is not as high, the agreement between the measured aperture fields and the HE_{11}-mode fields deteriorates. Before examining a case where higher-order modes are excited, we show in Fig. 6b the aperture magnetic field for the first five modes of a dielectric cone with $\theta_1 = 10°$, $\bar{\epsilon}_1 = 1{\cdot}10$ and $k_2 r_1 = 200$. In this Figure the fields are normalised so that the maximum value for each mode is unity. Fig. 6c shows a dielectric cone excited by a conical horn. Evidently, the HE_{11} modal fields alone do not account for the measured aperture fields, but inclusion of the next two modes (EH_{11} and HE_{12}) produces a much better agreement between the predicted and measured fields. The relative excitation amplitude and phases of the three modes were computed numerically, as was the relative phase difference due to the different velocity of propagation of each mode along the cone. This was obtained by using a value of $\bar{\beta}$ for each mode which was an average between that at the horn aperture and that at the cone aperture.

2.5 Radiation patterns of the HE_{11} mode

The observed radiation of the composite cone-horn structure apparently comprises a contribution due to the mode or modes of the cone, together with radiation arising at the horn-cone discontinuity. From our discussion of the excitation problem in Section 2.3, it is evident that the amount of radiation at the discontinuity cannot be rigorously calculated, nor have we the means to evaluate the discontinuity pattern. However, from a knowledge of the radiation pattern of the horn alone and the modal excitation efficiencies, we shall later show how the discontinuity pattern can be estimated.

As a first stage in the prediction of the overall pattern, we compute the pattern due to the HE_{11} mode of the cone. This is obtained by a vector Kirchhoff-Huygens integration of the aperture fields of the mode, performed over the spherical cap $r = r_1$ that constitutes the equiphase surface. We assume that the aperture fields are the unperturbed incident fields, which is a very good approximation provided $\bar{\epsilon}_1$ is near unity.

The computed far-field radiation patterns are given in Figs. 7a–c for a set of dielectric cones. For convenience of comparison, all patterns are shown normalised to boresight, the normalising factor (the boresight gain) being indicated separately.

The frequency dependence is equivalent to a change in normalised cone length. Although not apparent from Fig. 7c, it is in fact possible, by an appropriate choice of parameters, to design dielectric cones whose performance is virtually frequency independent over a relatively large bandwidth.

To interpret these Figures, some general remarks are now made concerning the aperture fields from which they were computed. Fig. 4 shows that the HE_{11}-mode fields are Gaussian in appearance, and, in consequence, the corresponding radiation patterns are virtually free from sidelobes. For a given θ_1, the aperture pattern narrows with increasing ϵ_1 and the radiation pattern consequently broadens. With increasing length, the angular extent of the aperture pattern decreases, as shown in Fig. 4a, but, as the aperture diameter increases more rapidly, the radiation pattern at first narrows. However, as the equiphase surface for a cone is in the form of a spherical cap, the effect of phase deviation over a plane aperture at the mouth of the cone eventually dominates. Then the angular width of the radiation pattern and the gain both become oscillatory functions of length. In Fig. 7a the radiation pattern of the cone with $\theta_1 = 10°$ is narrower than that for $\theta_1 = 5°$. However, owing to the effects of phase error and field compression discussed above, there is only a 1·4 dB difference in gain instead of 6 dB.

In Fig. 4b we have shown a similarity between the aperture fields of a corrugated horn and those of a dielectric cone of comparable flare angle. When the radiation patterns and gain are compared they are also found to be very similar; thus we may use existing design curves for corrugated horns as a preliminary guide to the design of dielectric-cone antennas.

In corrugated horns, the effects of higher-order modes are not noticeable except where these modes are deliberately excited or where $\theta_1 > 80°$. However, in dielectric cones these modes are usually unavoidably excited, and in some cases their presence contributes significantly to modify both the aperture pattern and the radiation pattern.

The presence of higher-order modes in the radiation pattern of a dielectric cone has a number of practical consequences:

(a) The boresight gain is usually slightly increased and the main lobewidth decreased, owing to increased aperture efficiency, as is apparent in Fig. 6c.

(b) The sidelobe level may be increased.

(c) The antenna performance becomes more frequency dependent because the modes have different phase velocities. For cones of low permittivity this effect is slight, as these velocities are very close.

(d) For a similar reason, the equiphase surface is no longer a sphere centred on the apex of the cone, but, in practice, phase variations over the spherical cap of less than ±15° are observed.

(e) The crosspolarisation level may increase significantly if modes such as the EH_{11} are excited.

2.6 Radiation patterns of dielectric-cone antennas

As previously mentioned, when a dielectric cone is excited by a horn, the observed radiation pattern comprises contributions both from the cone aperture and the horn. For low-permittivity dielectric materials, the following method for predicting the overall radiation pattern is found to give satisfactory results:

Consider the far-field radiation pattern of the horn in the absence of the dielectric cone (see Fig. 8a) and, with the aid of Fig. 8b, identify the region, henceforth called the trapping region, limited by θ_T, where $\theta_T = \theta_{cc} + \theta_1$, and θ_{cc} = complement of the critical angle for total internal reflection at the dielectric-cone boundary. We now assume that the energy contained in the trapping region of the horn radiation pattern will be transferred to modes of the dielectric cone. The radiation pattern of these modes can be predicted by the method described in Section 2.5. The remaining portion of the radiation pattern of the horn is assumed to be unaffected by the cone apart from some slight angular displacement, which can be explained qualitatively as arising from the effects of refraction at the dielectric boundary.

It should be pointed out that there will remain an ill-defined region, for the values of θ close to θ_T, where the resultant radiation pattern cannot be predicted by this simple theory. The resultant predicted pattern, together with the measured pattern, is shown in Fig. 8c for a dielectric cone excited by a pyramidal horn. The agreement between the predicted and measured results is very good.

Experiments performed with other horns, for example Fig. 8d, lend further support to the method proposed. For all these, the computed patterns for the dielectric cone assume that only the HE_{11} mode is present, because all other modes, according to Table 1, cannot propagate at the horn aperture. It is obvious from these measurements that the resultant

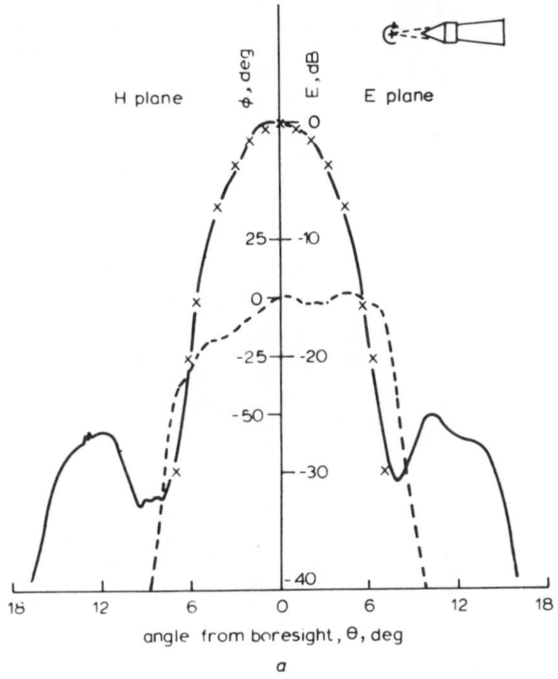

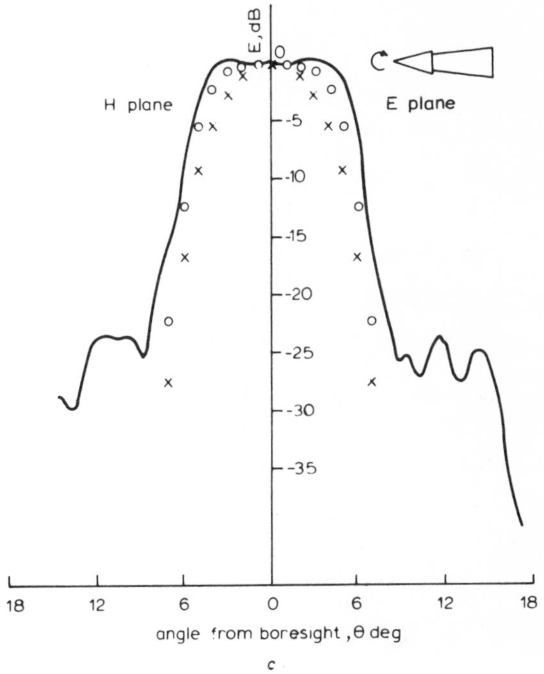

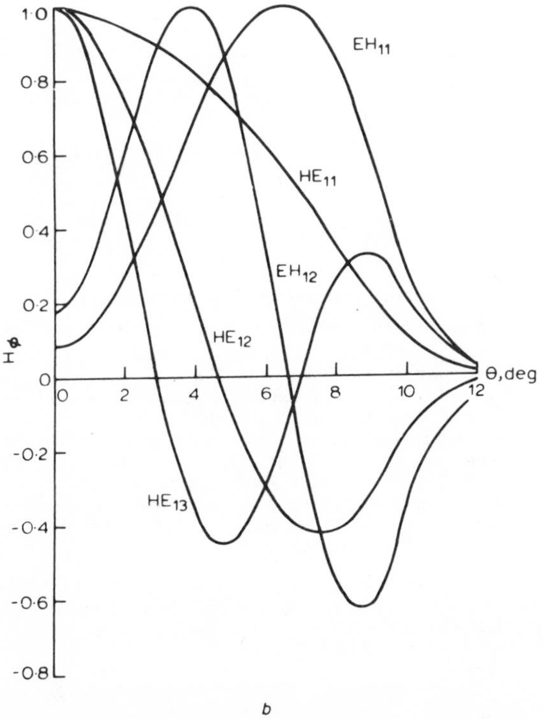

Fig. 6

Aperture field patterns of dielectric cones

a *Aperture electric-field pattern of a dielectric cone (Dc2)* excited by a corrugated waveguide operated in the HE_{11} mode. Frequency 9·0 GHz*
——— *amplitude (measured)*
- - - - *phase (measured)*
× × × *HE_{11}-mode amplitude (computed)*

b *Theoretical E plane aperture field patterns for the first five modes of unity azimuthal dependence of a dielectric cone with $\theta_1 = 10°$, $\epsilon_1 = 1{\cdot}10$ and $k_2 r_1 = 200$. Fields of the different modes are normalised to yield the same maximum value for each mode*

c *Aperture electric-field pattern of a dielectric cone (Dc3) excited by a conical horn (C3) operated in the TE_{11} mode. Frequency 11·2 GHz*
——— *measured*
× × × *HE_{11} mode (computed)*
○ ○ ○ *HE_{11} + EH_{11} + HE_{12} modes (computed)*

* *See Table 2 for nomenclature*

antenna has increased gain and the pattern improved symmetry. Also, because of the overall increase in gain and because the radiation pattern of the HE_{11} mode has virtually no sidelobes, the relative level of the sidelobes of the resultant antenna is lower than for the horn alone.

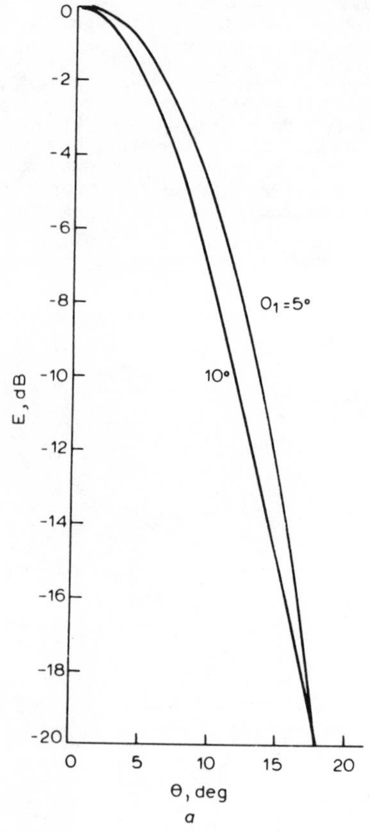

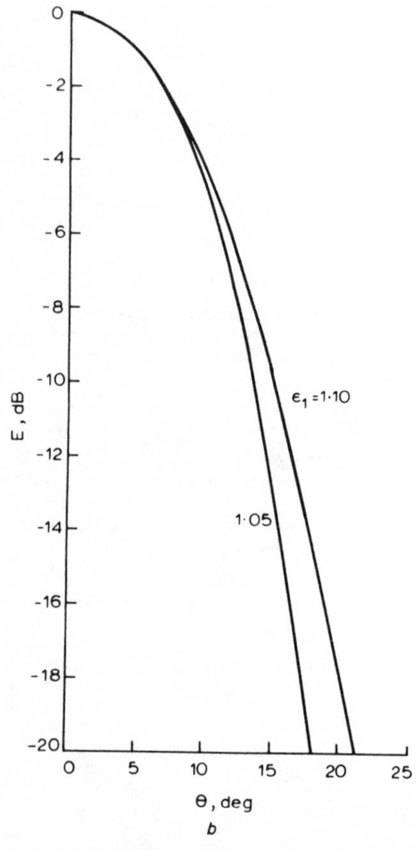

Although we envisage that the dielectric cone antenna should serve as a replacement for the corrugated horn in many situations, where a pattern is required with a narrow beamwidth and very low sidelobes, the combination of a dielectric cone and corrugated horn can provide the best design. Fig. 9a shows typical patterns, while Fig. 9b shows that the combined antenna has improved frequency characteristics.

3 CONCLUSIONS

We have demonstrated that, by means of an approximate theory, the radiation pattern of a dielectric cone excited by a horn can be predicted with sufficient accuracy for most antenna design purposes. The results also show that the radiation pattern of the dominant HE_{11} mode of the dielectric

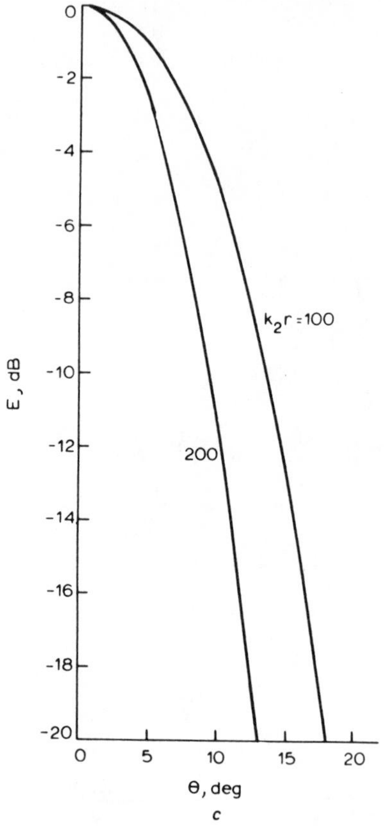

Fig. 7

Far-field radiation patterns of dielectric cones

a *E plane far-field radiation pattern of two dielectric cones with $\bar{\epsilon}_1 = 1{\cdot}05, k_2r_1 = 100, \theta_1 = 5$ and $10°$*
Gain on boresight (dBi) $\theta_1 = 5°$: $21{\cdot}93$, $\theta_1 = 10°$: $23{\cdot}32$

b *E plane far-field radiation pattern of two dielectric cones with $\theta_1 = 5°, k_2r_1 = 100, \bar{\epsilon}_1 = 1{\cdot}05$ and $1{\cdot}10$*
Gain on boresight (dBi) $\bar{\epsilon}_1 = 1{\cdot}05$: $21{\cdot}93$, $\bar{\epsilon}_1 = 1{\cdot}10$: $21{\cdot}18$

c *E plane far-field radiation pattern of two dielectric cones with $\bar{\epsilon}_1 = 1{\cdot}05, \theta_1 = 5°, k_2r_1 = 100$ and 200*
Gain on boresight (dBi) $k_2r_1 = 100$: $21{\cdot}93$, $k_2r_1 = 200$: $25{\cdot}26$

cone is very similar to that of the HE_{11} mode of the corrugated horn. The pattern is highly symmetrical, and, even with an inexpensive launching horn, the first sidlobe level lies at least 16 dB below boresight. The cone possesses the advantage over the corrugated horn of greater frequency independence and lower cost. A possible disadvantage in certain applications lies in the effects upon the cone of atmospheric moisture. We believe that this problem can be solved by an appropriate choice of the low-permittivity dielectric; e.g. by the use of a closed cell material which has been expanded by physical rather than chemical means.

The cones used in our antennas have been made from foam blocks originally intended for use in the building industry.

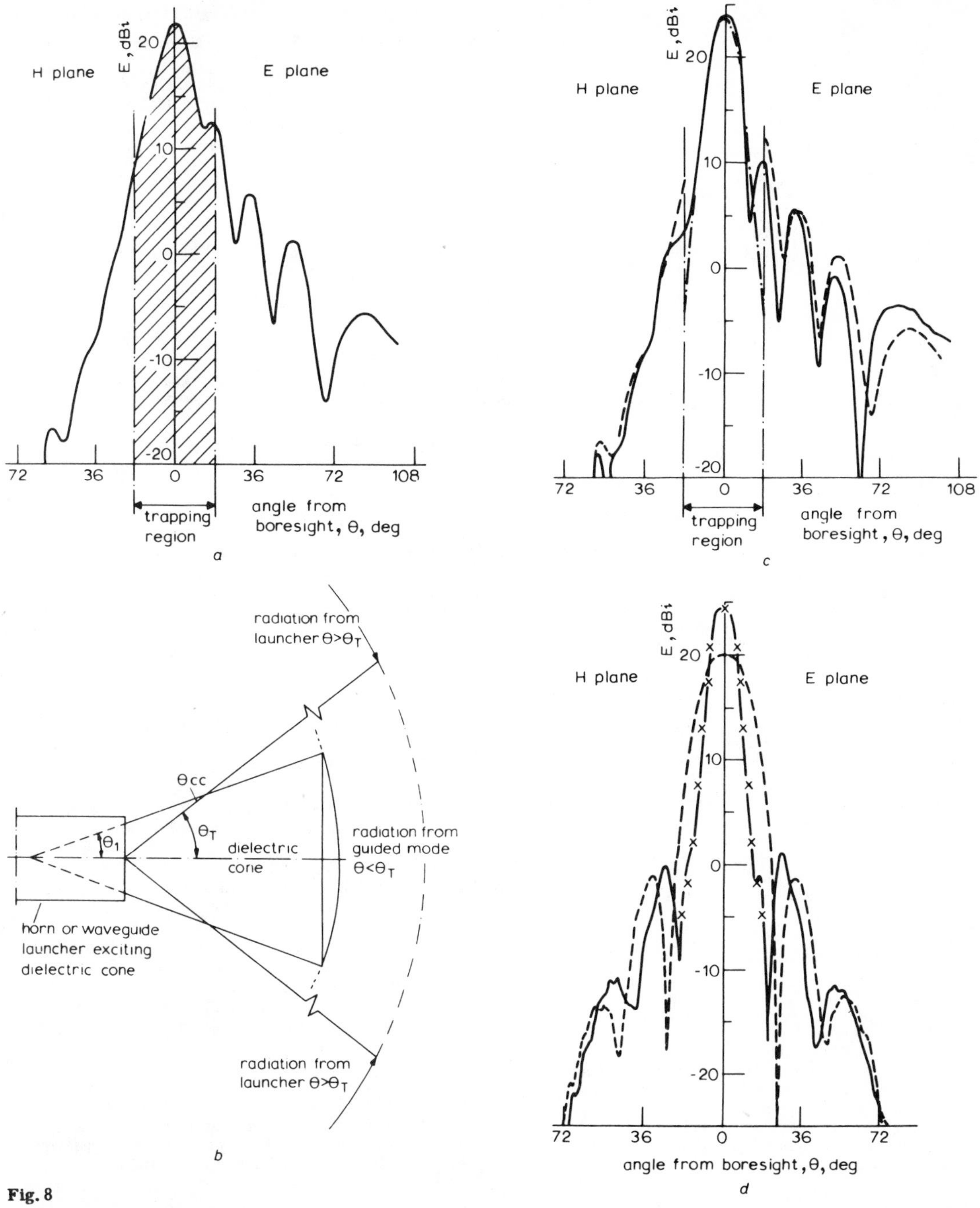

Fig. 8

Radiation patterns and their prediction

a *Computed far-field radiation pattern of pyramidal horn (P1) showing the trapping region for a dielectric cone with* $\theta_1 = 6°$ *and* $\bar{\epsilon}_1 = 1{\cdot}05$

b *Diagram describing the method used to include the effect of the launcher in the radiation pattern of a low-permittivity dielectric-cone antenna*

c *Far-field radiation pattern of a dielectric cone (Dc1) at 9·0 GHz*

- - - - *horn (computed)*

—·—· HE_{11} *mode (computed)*

——— *resultant pattern (measured)*

Launcher: pyramidal horn (P1)

d *Far-field radiation pattern of a dielectric cone at 9·0 GHz*

Launcher: corrugated waveguide, with the same mouth diameter as the corrugated horn C1, operated in the HE_{11} *mode*

- - - - *launcher only (measured)*

× × × HE_{11} *mode (computed)*

——— *resultant pattern (measured)*

In consequence, these high-performance antennas were of exceptionally low cost but were suitable only for laboratory use.

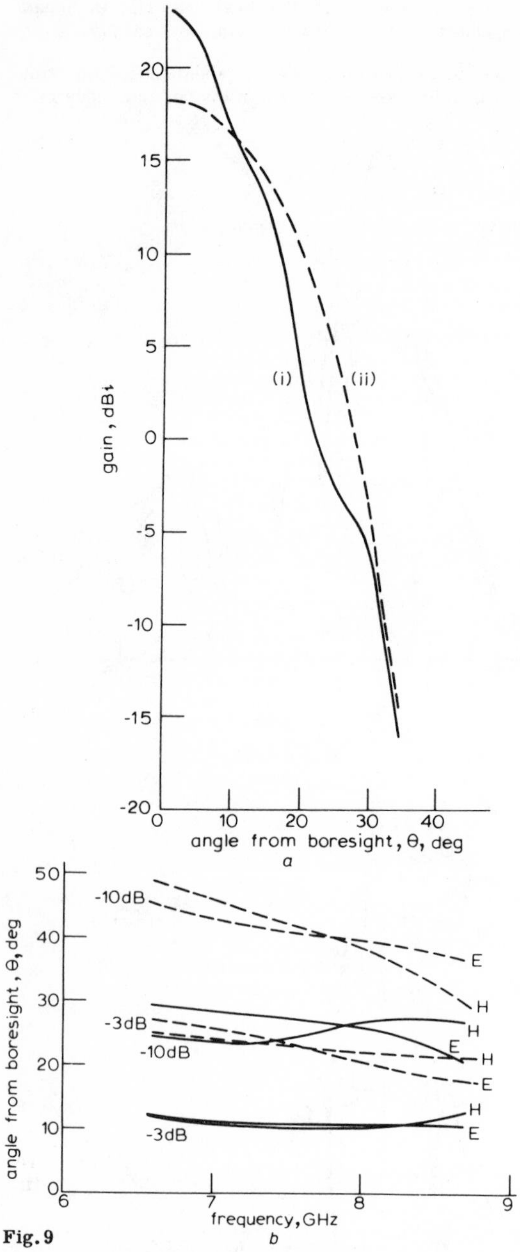

Fig. 9

Radiation pattern and beamwidth of corrugated horn and corrugated horn feeding a dielectric cone
a Measured E plane far-field radiation pattern at 7·3 GHz
(i) Dielectric cone (Dc5) excited by a corrugated horn (Cr1) operated in the HE_{11} mode
(ii) Corrugated horn (Cr1)
b Measured beamwidth as a function of frequency
---- *corrugated horn*
—— *dielectric cone (Dc6) excited by a corrugated horn (Cr1)*

4 ACKNOWLEDGMENTS

We gratefully acknowledge the assistance of our colleagues, K. B. Chan, S. H. Lim, A. D. Olver, G. T. Poulton, L. M. Seng and P. H. Masterman, and thank J. Honour and J. Morris for their significant contributions in the fabrication of the dielectric cones.

One of us (C.E.R.C.S.) is indebted to the Gulbenkian Foundation and the Instituto de Alta Cultura, Portugal, for a research fellowship.

The research described herein was sponsored, in part, by means of a grant from the UK Science Research Council, whose support we gratefully acknowledge.

TABLE 2

DIMENSIONS OF HORNS AND CONES USED IN EXPERIMENTS

Symbol	Antenna type	Dimensions
P1	Pyramidal horn	Aperture dimensions: E plane, 14·3 cm, H plane, 19·4 cm Slant length from apex: 36·0 cm
C1, 3	Conical horn	Aperture diameter: 11·3 cm, 12·7 cm Semiflare angle: 27·2°, 14° Feed-waveguide diameter: 2·54 cm, 2·59 cm
Cr1	Corrugated horn	Aperture diameter: 12·6 cm Semiflare angle: 6° Feed-waveguide diameter: 2·59 cm

Symbol	Antenna type	Aperture diameter	Length	Semi-flare-angle	$\bar{\epsilon}_1$
		cm	cm		
Dc1	Dielectric cone	17	43·2	6°	1·05
Dc2	Dielectric cone	17·2	44·2	6°	1·11
Dc3	Dielectric cone	18·3	30·5	6°	1·1
Dc4	Dielectric cone	21·3	65·5	5·2°	1·07
Dc5	Dielectric cone	23·6	50·8	6°	1·05

5 REFERENCES

1 BARTLETT, H. E., and MOSELEY, R. E.: United States Patent 3 430 244, Feb. 1969
2 BARTLETT, H. E., and MOSELEY, R. E.; 'Dielguides—highly efficient low noise antenna feeds', Microwave J., 1966, **9**, pp. 53-58
3 BARTLETT, H. E., and PIETSCH: United States Patent 3 414 903, Dec. 1968
4 BARTLETT, H. E.: United States Patent 3 611 391, Oct. 1971
5 CLARRICOATS, P. J. B., and SALEMA, C. E. R. C.: 'Propagation characteristics of low-permittivity cones', Electron. Lett. 1971, **7**, pp. 483-485
6 CLARRICOATS, P. J. B., and SALEMA. C. E. R. C.: 'Design of dieletric-cone feeds for microwave antennas', Proceedings of the 1971 European Microwave Conference, paper B5/4
7 CLARRICOATS, P. J. B., and SALEMA, C. E. R. C.: 'Influence of launching horn on radiation characteristics of a dielectric-cone feed', Electron. Lett. 1972, **8**, pp. 200-202
8 CLARRICOATS, P. J. B., SALEMA, C. E. R. C., and LIM, S. H.: 'Design of cassegrain antennas employing dielectric-cone fieeds', ibid., 1972, **8**, pp. 384-385
9 SALEMA, C. E. R. C., and CLARRICOATS, P. J. B.: 'Radiation characteristics of dielectric cones', ibid., 1972, **8**, pp. 414-416
10 CLARRICOATS, P. J. B.: 'Dielectric waveguides for microwave antennas', Proceedings of XVII General Assembly of URSI, Session VI-2, Warsaw, 1972
11 CLARRICOATS, P. J. B.: 'Similarities in the electromagnetic behaviour of optical waveguides and corrugated feeds', Electron. Lett., 1970, **6**, pp. 178-180
12 CLARRICOATS, P. J. B., and SAHA, P. K.: 'Propagation and radiation behaviour of corrugated feeds. Pt. 1—Corrugated waveguide feed', Proc. IEE, 1971, **118**, (9), pp. 1167-1176
13 CLARRICOATS, P. J. B., and SAHA, P. K.: Propagation and radiation behaviour of corrugated feeds. Pt. 2—Corrugated-conical-horn feed', ibid., 1971, **118**, (9), pp. 1177-1186
14 SNYDER, A. W.: 'Surface-waveguide modes along a semi-infinite dielectric fibre excited by a plane wave', J. Opt. Soc. Am., 1966, **56**, p. 601
15 CLARRICOATS, P. J. B., and CHAN, K. B.: 'Excitation and propagation of modes of a multilayer fibre', Electron. Lett. 1970, **6**, pp. 750-752
16 SALEMA, C. E. R. C.: 'Theory and design of dielectric cone antennas', Ph.D. Thesis, University of London, 1972

Antennas employing conical-dielectric horns
Part 2—The Cassegrain antenna

Prof. P. J. B. Clarricoats, D.Sc.(Eng.), F.Inst.P., Fel.I.E.E.E., C.Eng., F.I.E.E., and C. E. R. C. Salema, Eng.º, Ph.D.

Indexing terms: Reflector antennas, Antenna feeders, Antenna radiation patterns, Dielectric devices, Waveguide antennas

ABSTRACT

A design theory is presented for Cassegrain antennas employing dielectric-cone feeds. A modal approach is used to describe the aperture field over the subreflector, while a ray-optics method is employed to determine the subreflector profile and main-reflector aperture distribution. Experiments have been made with antennas designed for operation over bands centred near 11 and 18 GHz, and results are in generally good agreement with theory. These antennas are shown to have high efficiency, good main-beam symmetry and low mutual coupling.

1 INTRODUCTION

In our companion paper[1] (see p. 741), we have described an approximate theory for the propagation and radiation characteristics of the dielectric-cone waveguide. Here we consider the design of a Cassegrain antenna in which a dielectric-cone waveguide links the horn and subreflector, as in Fig. 1. The use of this configuration was first proposed by Bartlett and

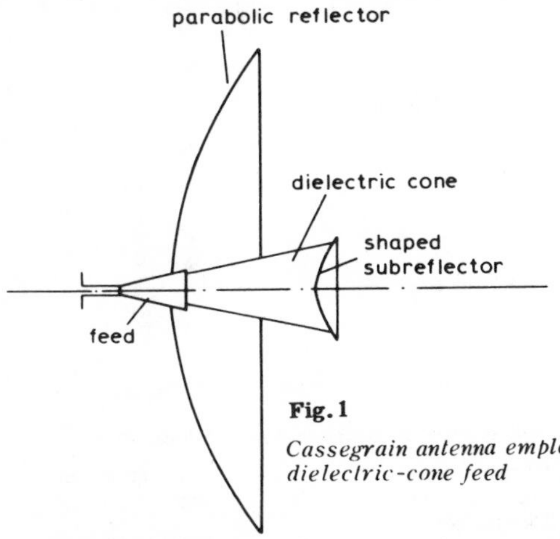

Fig. 1

Cassegrain antenna employing dielectric-cone feed

associates,[2-4] but, as far as we are aware, no design theory has been given outside of our preliminary communications.[5-10] The configuration leads to an increased antenna efficiency for the following reasons:

(a) In common with all Cassegrain antennas, there is an improved illumination of the main reflector, compared to a prime-focus feed, especially when F/D is small, e.g. 0·25-0·30. Also, the shaping of the subreflector which is now necessary for a constant-phase front across the main-reflector aperture fortuituously provides near optimum power distribution.

(b) When the main-reflector diameter is small, the subreflector diameter can be reduced to a level where blockage is tolerable without raising spillover to an unacceptable level. This improvement arises because energy is guided between the horn and the subreflector.

(c) The feed pattern has both a high degree of symmetry and low sidelobes, these properties being conveyed to the secondary pattern of the antenna.

In this paper we describe how a ray-optics formulation can be used to determine the shape of the subreflector, and a knowledge of the aperture field of the cone, based on the modal theory of Part 1, can be used to determine the antenna radiation pattern. We present experimental and theoretical results for two antennas designed to operate over bands centred near 11 and 18 GHz. This design procedure has also been used in the development of a feed system for a dual-subreflector spherical antenna, and an account of this will be presented elsewhere.

Paper 6961E, first received 18th January and in revised form 26th March 1973

Prof. Clarricoats is, and Dr. Salema was formerly, with the Department of Electrical & Electronic Engineering, Queen Mary College, University of London, Mile End Road, London E1 4NS, England. Dr. Salema is now with the Institute Superior Technico (Technical University of Lisbon), Portugal

2 DESIGN THEORY FOR A CASSEGRAIN ANTENNA EMPLOYING A DIELECTRIC-CONE WAVEGUIDE

2.1 General considerations

Fig. 2a shows the principal parameters of an antenna with a parabolic main reflector for which a dielectric-cone feed is to be designed for operation at a centre frequency f.

Our first objective is to determine the subreflector shape. To simplify the design procedure, we assume that all the energy which reaches the subreflector is in the form of the HE_{11} spherical hybrid mode of the dielectric cone, the properties of which have been discussed in some detail in Part 1. With this assumption, the equiphase surface is a sphere centred on the apex of the cone, and, in terms of geometric optics, all rays appear to originate at the apex of the cone.

The subreflector profile is calculated so that, after reflection at the subreflector, refraction at the dielectric-cone boundary and finally reflection at the main reflector, rays emerge parallel to the axis, thus transforming the equiphase surfaces from spheres, inside the cone, into planes at the reflector aperture. The assumption that all the energy that reaches the subreflector is in the form of the HE_{11} hybrid mode is clearly open to criticism. If higher-order modes exist and are excited, the resultant field distribution may be significantly different from that of the HE_{11} mode. However, our experience suggests that the equiphase surfaces are not modified substantially. Typical deviations from constant phase, over a sphere centred on the cone apex, are of the order of ±10° or less. While this observation justifies the method proposed to calculate the profile of the subreflector, the presence of higher modes may affect the aperture distribution and the edge taper, with consequent discrepancies between predicted and measured sidelobe levels.

By using the laws of reflection and refraction, eqns. 1-3 are obtained, from which the subreflector profile r, θ may be determined. The symbols are defined in Fig. 2a.

$$\frac{dr}{db} = \frac{d\theta}{db} r \tan^{-1} \frac{1}{2} (\theta + b + \delta) \tag{1}$$

$$\theta + b + \delta = \sin^{-1} \frac{s}{r} \times \frac{\tan b}{\sec (b + \delta)} \times \frac{\tan (b + \delta) + \tan \theta_D}{\tan b + \tan \theta_D} \tag{2}$$

$$\theta_D + b + \delta = \cos^{-1} \frac{\cos (\theta_D + b)}{\sqrt{\epsilon_1}} \tag{3}$$

By application of the law of conservation of energy, we obtain

$$f(\rho) = \frac{f(\theta) \sin \theta \sin^3 b}{(1-\cos b)^2} \frac{d\theta}{db} \tag{4}$$

where $f(\rho)$ and $f(\theta)$ are the field distributions across the aperture of the main reflector and subreflector, respectively.

Reprinted with permission from *Proc. Inst. Elec. Eng.*, vol. 120, pp. 750–756, July 1973.

Figs. 3 and 4 show, respectively, a typical subreflector profile and main-reflector aperture distribution obtained from a numerical solution of eqns. 1-3 and from eqn. 4. They exhibit considerable differences from those obtained without the dielectric cone, as in the classical Cassegrain antenna.

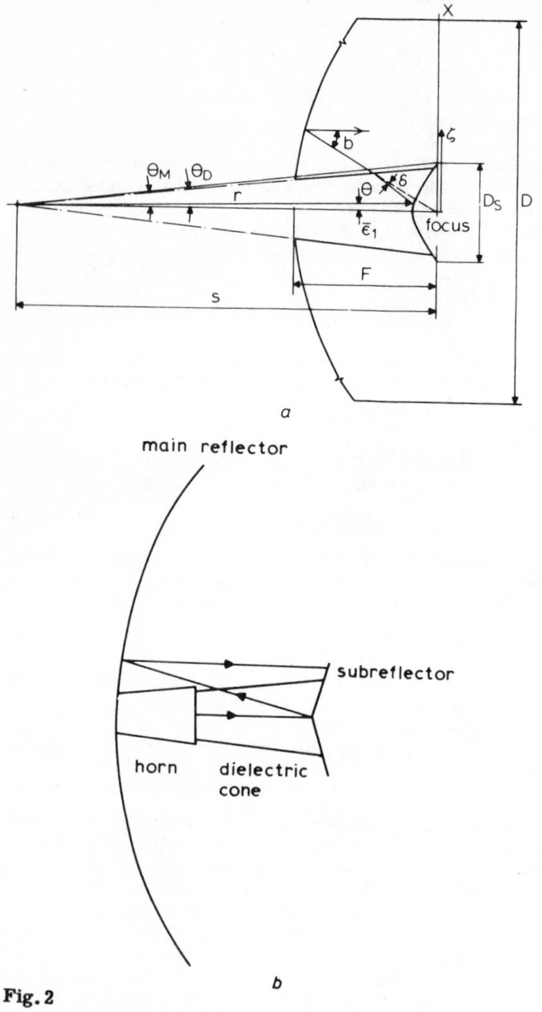

Fig. 2

a *Co-ordinate system and definition of parameters, for a Cassegrain reflector antenna*

b *Diagram explaining how to minimise the blocked diameter in a Cassegrain reflector antenna. For simplicity, refraction at the dielectric boundary is not shown on the drawing*

We note that in Fig. 3 the greatest departure from hyperboloidal shape occurs near the vertex of the reflector. As a consequence, energy is excluded from the blocked portion of the aperture as Fig. 4 shows, and we believe this to be one important reason for the increased efficiency obtained with a Cassegrain antenna with dielectric-cone feed. For comparison we also show the aperture distribution obtained in the absence of the dielectric cone but with the same HE_{11}-mode feed distribution. As θ_{max} is small, there is no discernible difference between a and b with the cone absent. With the cone present, the edge taper in the main-reflector distribution corresponds very closely to that at the subreflector, thus justifying an assumption made in the design procedure.

As previously noted, the rays that fall on the subreflector near the apex are deflected away from the feed horn, thus minimising the effect of the subreflector on the input v.s.w.r. By a proper choice of parameters, it is quite possible to arrange for these rays to pass just clear of the subreflector and so to fulfil the so-called 'optimum-blockage' condition. This was the basic design criterion for the first two experimental feeds which were built. Later, it was found that, as the power contribution per solid angle of emerging rays falls rapidly in the vicinity of the subreflector, systems designed on the above criterion give an effective blockage larger than the subreflector area. If this proves undesirable, the blockage may be reduced at the expense of a small increase in v.s.w.r. by allowing some of the innermost rays to be trapped again by the subreflector (see Fig. 2b).

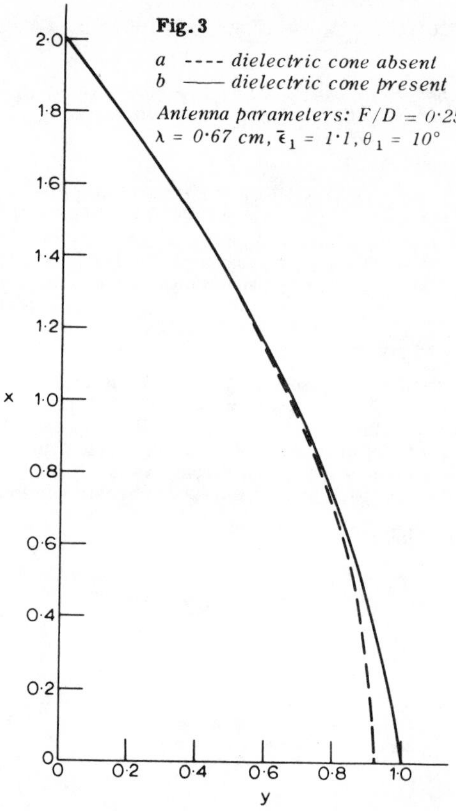

Fig. 3

a ---- *dielectric cone absent*

b —— *dielectric cone present*

Antenna parameters: $F/D = 0{\cdot}25$, $D = 24$ *cm*, $\lambda = 0{\cdot}67$ *cm*, $\bar{\epsilon}_1 = 1{\cdot}1$, $\theta_1 = 10°$

2.2 Choice of the antenna-system parameters

2.2.1 Subreflector diameter and edge illumination

The subreflector diameter D_s and the edge illumination E_g are determined by considering that for the same type of aperture illumination:

(a) A larger subreflector decreases aperture efficiency (by blockage) and increases relative first-sidelobe levels. However, it minimises spillover.

(b) For the same aperture blockage, a lower value of edge illumination yields lower relative-sidelobe levels but also lower aperture efficiency.

As the design of the subreflector is based on a geometric-optics procedure, a minimum diameter of about 7λ is considered a lower limit for the present design theory to perform well. For simplicity, we assume initially that the effective-blockage diameter D_B will be equal to the subreflector diameter D_s. By approximating the normalised aperture distributions as in Fig. 4 to linear distributions, as shown in Fig. 5c, it is possible to calculate the effect of blockage on the aperture efficiency and the first sidelobe level, as in Figs. 5a and 5b.

To determine the influence of the edge illumination on the front/back ratio, we use the analytic result due to Kritikos:[11]

$$G_{fb} = 20{\cdot}0 \log_{10}\left(\frac{D}{4F}\right) - E_g + G$$

where G_{fb} and E_g are expressed in dB, and G is expressed in dBi.

Note that F_g is the ratio between the fields at the edge and at the axis of the reflector (and is usually a negative number when expressed in dB).

We note that, to obtain a high front/back ratio, a deep reflector and a low edge illumination should be used. We also observe that a higher-gain antenna, irrespective of size, will exhibit a higher front/back ratio than a lower-gain antenna with the same F/D ratio and edge illumination.

2.2.2 Dielectric cone

Once the subreflector diameter D_S and the edge illumination E_g have been chosen, the next step is to select the cone semiflare angle θ_D and cone permittivity $\bar{\epsilon}_1$.

The cone semiflare angle θ_D is chosen with the considerations that:

(a) The cone semiflare angle must be smaller than θ_{cc}, the complement of the critical angle for the dielectric material:

$$\theta_{cc} = \cos^{-1}\left\{\frac{1}{(\bar{\epsilon}_1)^{1/2}}\right\}$$

(b) The smaller the semi-flare angle the longer the dielectric cone. Now, although a long dielectric-cone is not, in principle, undesirable, as losses can be kept very low, it forces the launcher horn to protrude from the back of the reflector, a situation which may not be acceptable from a mechanical point of view.

(c) The larger the semiflare angle, subject to the restriction in (a), the shorter the dielectric cone. However, as a consequence of the feed being brought nearer to the subreflector, rays reflected from the central region of the subreflector may be trapped and they will then convey energy back into the feed. Not only does this lower efficiency but it increases the input v.s.w.r. Our experience suggests that a starting point for the design should be within the range:

$$0{\cdot}5\theta_{cc} < \theta_D < 0{\cdot}7\theta_{cc}$$

The selection of the dielectric permittivity is obviously dependent on the value of the cone semiflare angle.

Apart from the critical angle, the following additional factors are relevant:

If all else is constant, a lower value of ϵ_1 will mean that the fields decay less rapidly outside the cone. As well as decreasing excitation efficiency, this also increases spillover past the subreflector. Subreflectors of smaller diameter therefore demand a higher permittivity, whereas, for larger subreflectors, the permittivity may be smaller. From our experience a minimum value of $\bar{\epsilon}_1 = 1{\cdot}10$ should be used for $D_S \simeq 8\lambda$. Values of $\bar{\epsilon}_1$ less than 1·04 are not likely to prove useful even for a much larger subreflector.

After $\bar{\epsilon}_1$ and θ_D have been selected, it is possible to determine the diameter of the dielectric cone where its periphery meets the subreflector D_D, to obtain the required edge illumination. Although, in principle, the result of the dielectric-cone theory should be used, in the absence of sufficient numerical results we have found it convenient and accurate enough to approximate the fields of the HE_{11} mode of the cone by the fields of the HE_{11} mode of a cylinder of diameter D_D. As an example, assume we have selected $\bar{\epsilon}_1 = 1{\cdot}1$; we then use Fig. 6 as follows:

(a) Choose a suitable value for the dielectric-cone diameter D_D, say D_{D1}

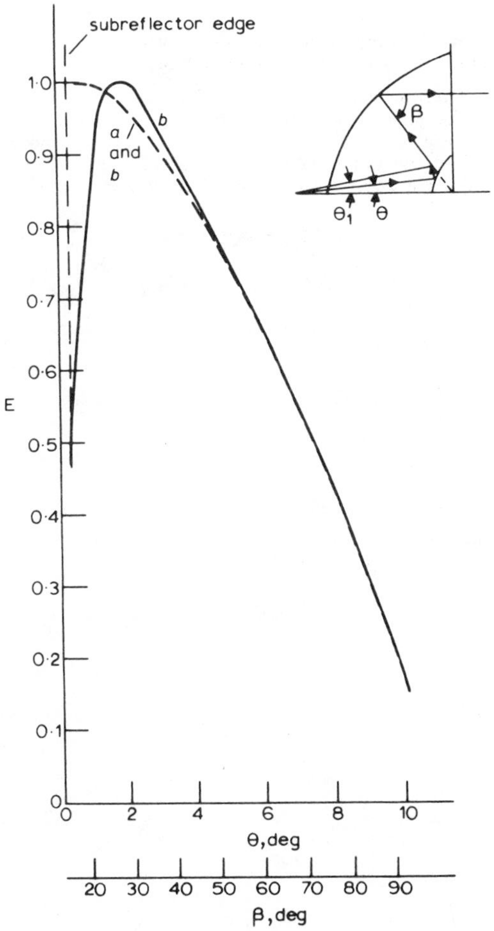

Fig. 4

Normalised electric-field distribution over

a Subreflector (θ scale)
b Main-reflector aperture (β scale)

(i) ---- dielectric cone absent
(ii) —— dielectric cone present

As θ_{max} is small, there is no discernible difference between a and b with cone absent. The distribution over the subreflector is assumed to correspond to the HE_{11} mode in both cases

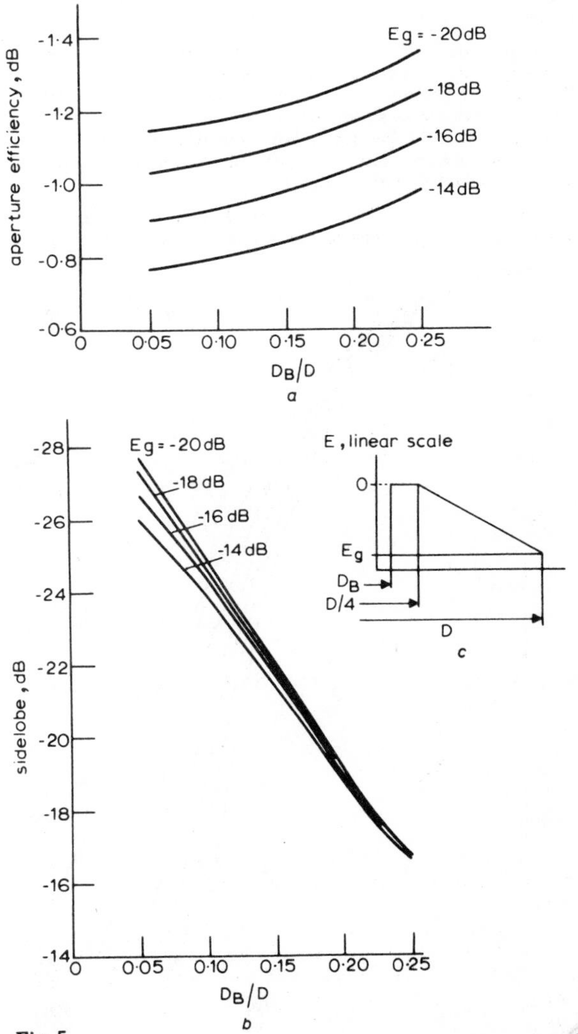

Fig. 5

a Aperture efficiency as a function of the blocked diameter for the aperture distribution described in inset c

b Level of the first sidelobe, in dB below boresight, as a function of the blocked diameter, for the aperture distribution given in Fig. 5a

(b) Calculate

$k_2\rho_1 = \pi D_{D1}/\lambda$

(c) Calculate the ratio

$D_S/D_{D1} = \rho/\rho_1$

(d) From the relevant curve find the value of the field at D_S relative to boresight. If no curve is given for the value of $k_2\rho_1$, interpolate. Use the knowledge that the value of the subreflector edge illumination is approximately the same as the main-reflector edge illumination.

(e) If D_{D1} yields the wrong edge illumination, select another value, say D_{D2}, and repeat the procedure. A linear interpolation between the calculated edge illumination for D_{D1} and D_{D2} will usually be found to be satisfactory.

Knowing the diameter of the dielectric cone, its permittivity and the diameter of the subreflector, it is possible to calculate the fraction of the spillover energy, due to the energy of the HE_{11} mode which lies beyond the subreflector. Again we have approximated the dielectric cone by a dielectric cylinder of diameter D_D and have used Fig. 7 to determine the value. For a low edge illumination (<-16dB) it is usually found that the spillover energy of the HE_{11} mode is a very small fraction of the total spillover and, in most cases, can be neglected.

Once the parameters that define the dielectric cone have been fixed it is necessary to perform a complete ray tracing, by solving eqns. 1-3 to obtain the subreflector profile $r(\theta)$. The extreme ray corresponding to $\theta \to 0$ in Fig. 2a establishes the effective blockage diameter D_B.

As mentioned before, it is possible to choose θ_D and $\bar{\epsilon}_1$ so that either the innermost ray emerges clear of the subreflector, thus minimising the effect of the feed v.s.w.r. (but increasing the blocked diameter above the subreflector diameter), or that the innermost rays are allowed to be trapped by the subreflector minimising the blocked diameter, at the cost of a slightly larger v.s.w.r.

In cases where the calculated blocked diameter is very different from the subreflector diameter, a new set of values of θ_D and $\bar{\epsilon}_1$ has to be used and the design procedure repeated, until the desired results are obtained.

After ray tracing has been completed, the remaining problem of the excitation of the dielectric cone can be considered.

2.3 Launching horn

The launching horn has to convert the energy from a waveguide mode into the dielectric-cone mode. Although the controlled use of the higher-order modes seems to provide a way of improving the aperture efficiency, in this design procedure we consider only the fundamental HE_{11} mode, and therefore the launcher will be chosen on the basis of maximum excitation for this mode.

The choice of the type of launcher is normally made on economic grounds. Two broadband types are suggested:

(a) corrugated horn

(b) conical horn

The corrugated horn[12] yields a higher HE_{11}-mode excitation, minimises higher-order-mode excitation and also, because of its extremely low sidelobe level, is an obvious first choice on performance grounds. However, in general, it is more expensive to manufacture. The conical horn, being simpler and therefore inexpensive, is an alternative.

From the point of view of the excitation of the dielectric cone, the launching horn should have:

(i) the apex coincident with the apex of the dielectric cone.

(ii) the diameter of the mouth somewhat larger than the diameter of the dielectric cone at the junction D_D.

For small semiflare angles (less than about 20°), the launching horn can be conveniently optimised using the curves given for the excitation of a dielectric rod by either a smooth or a corrugated circular waveguide[13], of which Fig. 8 is an example. For best accuracy, the equivalent-waveguide and

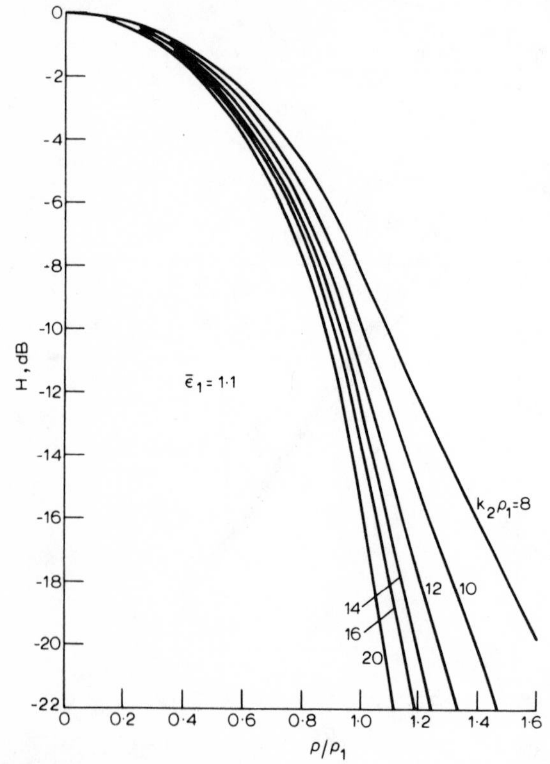

Fig. 6

Transverse magnetic fields of the HE_{11} mode in the aperture of a dielectric cylinder with $\bar{\epsilon}_1 = 1{\cdot}10$, as a function of ρ/ρ_1

Parameter $k_2 r_1$ = 8, 10, 12, 14, 16 and 20

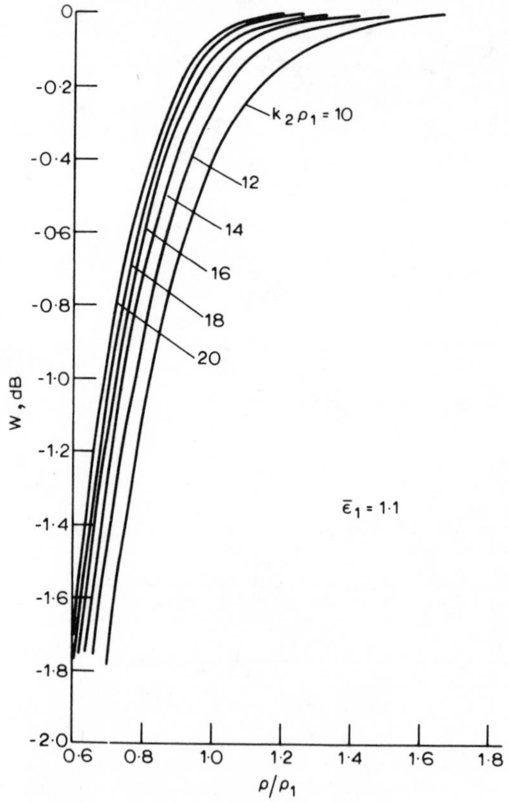

Fig. 7

$$W\left(\frac{\rho}{\rho_1}\right) = \frac{\int_0^{\rho} E \times H^{*}.n d\rho}{\int_0^{\infty} E \times H^{*}.n d\rho}$$ *for the HE_{11} mode*

of dielectric cylinders with $\bar{\epsilon}_1 = 1{\cdot}10$ and $k_2\rho_1$ = 10, 12, 14, 16, 18 and 20 dielectric-cylinder radius should be taken, respectively, (see Fig. 8b) as

$$\rho_{WG} = R_1\theta_H$$

$$\rho_{DC} = R_1\theta_D$$

When there is a limitation on the dimensions of the feed beyond the apex of the main reflector, it may be necessary to contemplate a launching horn whose apex is not coincident with the dielectric-cone apex and which results in a lower excitation efficiency. This effect may be evaluated and has been discussed in our companion paper.[1] It is found that, provided the phase error between the dielectric-cone fields and the exciting fields is less than about 45°, the reduction in efficiency is only marginal and can usually be tolerated.

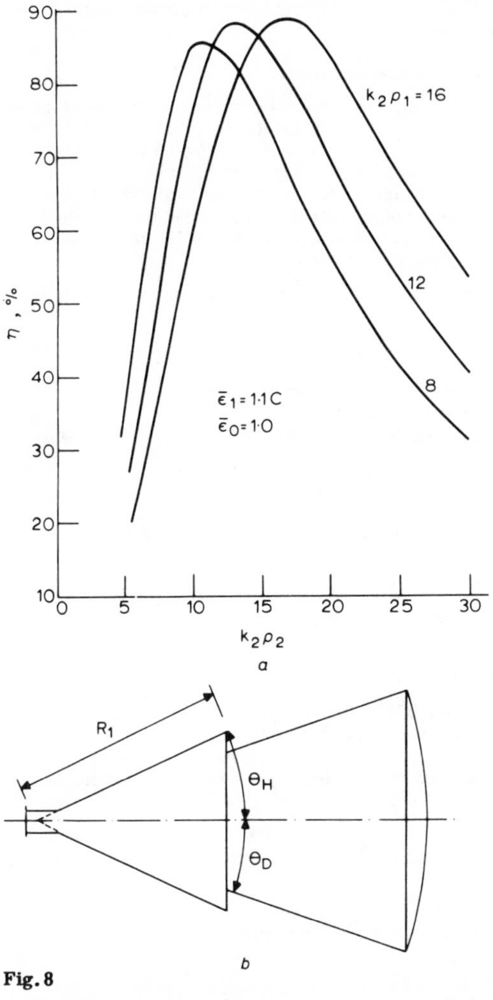

Fig. 8

a *Excitation efficiency of the HE_{11} mode of a dielectric cylinder with radius ρ_1*
Launcher: circular waveguide of internal radius ρ_2 operating in the TE_{11} mode

b *Radius of the equivalent waveguide and dielectric cylinder for the calculation of the excitation efficiency*

3 EXPERIMENTAL RESULTS FOR CASSEGRAIN ANTENNAS USING DIELECTRIC-CONE FEEDS

To verify the design procedure of Section 2, two different antennas were designed, built and tested. A detailed description of each antenna, and the predicted and achieved performance, are presented below.

3.1 A dielectric-cone feed for a 1·22 m-diameter focal-plane-reflector antenna for operation in the 10·5-11·5 GHz range

3.1.1 Specifications and design

The design of a suitable feed for a 1·22 m-diameter focal-plane reflector was approached to provide the following characteristics:

(a) Higher aperture efficiency than that normally achieved with an open-waveguide feed at the focus (43-48%)

(b) Very low far-out sidelobes (< −60 dB)

(c) Low coupling between closely spaced antennas

(d) Low crosspolarisation in principal planes (< − 30 dB)

(e) Low v.s.w.r. (preferably better than 1·10)

(f) Low cost.

The antenna parameters including those arising from our design are shown in column 1 of Table 1.

The design of the above antenna was accomplished before all of the factors discussed in Section 2 were fully appreciated, the main purpose being to ascertain that, using the technique, a plane phase front could be obtained at the reflector aperture.

Among the effects not considered were:

(i) the loss of excitation efficiency which results from phase errors across the horn/dielectric-cone interface

(ii) the effects resulting from the presence of higher-order modes.

For simplicity, the launcher horn was chosen to be a conical horn and was constructed from a sheet of copper, hammered around a wooden former. Its aperture was mounted flush with a plate supplied with the reflector. The subreflector was moulded in resin, reinforced with glass fibre and finished to provide a surface accuracy of better than 0·37 mm r.m.s. The subreflector was then sprayed with silver paint.

The dielectric material obtained is normally used in the building industry for thermal-insulation purposes. It was available in blocks with approximate dimensions 20·3 × 20·3 × 10·2 cm, which had to be glued together to achieve the

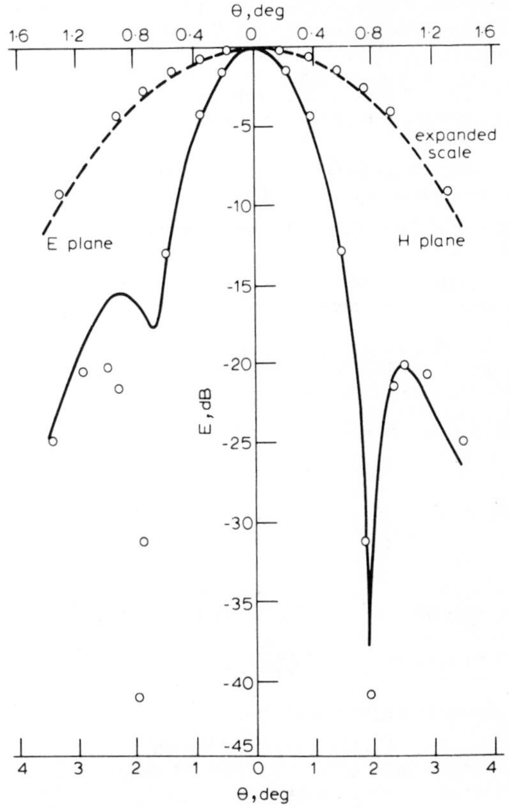

Fig. 9

Far-field radiation pattern of the 1·2 m-diameter Cassegrain reflector; frequency 11·2 GHz
—— measured
- - - - predicted, based on a linear aperture distribution as in Fig. 5a with −17 dB edge taper

TABLE 1

PARAMETERS OF ANTENNAS

Parameter	Antenna A	Antenna B
Main reflector diameter D	1·22 m	0·61 m
Main reflector focal length F	3·05 cm	17·8 cm
Design frequency f	11·2 GHz	17·7 GHz
Subreflector diameter D_S	20·3 cm	9·4 cm
Effective blocked diameter D_B	20·7 cm	10·6 cm
Dielectric material: expanded polystyrene with (appoximate) density	80 kg/m^3	80 kg/m^3
Relative dielectric permittivity ϵ_1	1·10-1·12	1·10-1·12
Dielectric-cone diameter at the subreflector D_D	18·3 cm	8·4 cm
Dielectric-cone semiflare angle θ_D	5·9°	9·5°
Semiflare angle subtended, at the dielectric-cone apex, by the subreflector θ_M	6·52°	10·6°
Dielectric-cone diameter at the mouth of the horn	11·9 cm	4.95 cm
Launching horn	Conical horn	Conical horn
Distance between launching-horn apex and dielectric-cone apex	34 cm	0
Launching-horn mouth diameter	12·7 cm	5·2 cm
Launching-horn semiflare angle	14°	12°

desired length of cone before turning on a lathe. Unfortunately it was found that, in some batches, the density of the material varied by as much as 50% from one block to another, and also some blocks had quite large pockets of air or very low-density material. Higher-quality dielectric materials are available, and their use is suggested where high performance must be guaranteed. The above materials were chosen because of their very low cost.

Initially, an edge illumination of −22·5 dB was selected to achieve very low sidelobes. However, a measurement of the dielectric-cone aperture fields at the subreflector position gave a value of −17 dB, and the discrepancy was shown to be due to the presence of higher-order modes, as discussed in Part 1.

In the design of the subreflector, and in the following calculations, the measured value of edge illumination was used.

At the design frequency (11·2 GHz) the aperture losses are predicted as follows:

Aperture illumination losses (obtained by integration over the aperture field as in Fig. 4)	−1·06 dB
HE_{11}-mode excitation efficiency (Fig. 8)	−0·78 dB
Spillover due to the HE_{11} mode (Fig. 7)	−0·02 dB
Main-reflector surface tolerance (−0·28 mm r.m.s.)	−0·02 dB
Subreflector surface tolerance	−0·02 dB
Total	−1·88 dB

The predicted performance of the antenna at 11·2 GHz is then

Gain	41·22 dB
Efficiency	65% (−1·88 dB)
First sidelobe	−20·6 dB (relative to boresight gain)
Front/back ratio	58 dB

3.1.2 Measured performance

The phase of the field in the aperture of the reflector was measured using a dipole probe and a network analyser. The maximum variation was found to be ±20°.

The direct measurement of the far-field radiation pattern was accomplished using a high-performance outdoor antenna measuring range. A prediction of the far-field pattern and gain was performed on the basis of a Kirchhoff-Huygens integration over the predicted aperture field, and the results are compared with measured patterns in Fig. 9.

The results of the far-field measurements are summarised in Table 2.

The crosspolarisation levels are given in Table 3; these were measured only in the principal planes both for reasons of convenience and for comparison with the specifications.

Two identical models of the antenna were produced so that coupling measurements could be obtained with them mounted adjacently on a tower. The maximum coupling level measured was −90 dB; this occurred when the antennas were mounted back-to-back and separated by about 1 m. Further details are given elsewhere.[13]

V.S.W.R. measured at the rectangular-waveguide input was better than 1·4 over the entire frequency range. A simple 3-screw tuning section made possible the reduction of this value to better than 1·2 over the range 10·5-11·7 GHz.

3.2 Dielectric-cone feed for a 0·61 m-diameter reflector for operation in the frequency range 17·7-19·7 GHz

3.2.1 Specifications and design

The design of an efficient dielectric-cone feed for an existing 0·61 m-diameter and 17·8 cm focal-length reflector, for microwave-relay applications in the 17·7-19·7 GHz frequency band was undertaken. The antenna parameters are given in col. 2 of Table 1. As experience has shown that dielectric-cone feeds operate well above their design frequency, but not so well below it, the lowest frequency was chosen as the design frequency.

At the design frequency, the aperture losses are predicted as follows:

Aperture illumination losses (including blockage)	−1·14 dB
HE_{11}-mode excitation efficiency	−0·65 dB
Spillover due to HE_{11} mode	−0·05 dB
Main-reflector surface tolerance (0·25 mm r.m.s.)	−0·04 dB
Total	−1·88 dB

The predicted performance of the antenna at 17·7 GHz is then

Gain	39·44 dBi
Aperture efficiency	65%(= −1·88 dB)

3.2.2 Measured performance

The measurement of the far-field radiation patterns was carried out on a second outdoor measuring range. Although the performance of this range is generally good, the presence of trees influenced the backlobe of the radiation pattern and raised the front/back ratio.

The performance of the antenna is summarised in Table 4.

4 CONCLUSIONS

The measurements presented support the following specific conclusions:

(a) Deep reflectors of a reasonably small aperture size (about 40λ) can be efficiently illuminated when a dielectric-cone feed is used in a Cassegrain configuration. This performance is obtained over a relatively large bandwidth.

(b) The control of the aperture edge illumination enables a very low level of far-out sidelobes and a high value of the front/back gain to be achieved. For the same reason, a low value of coupling between closely spaced antennas becomes possible.

(c) The v.s.w.r.s can be made reasonably low over the entire bandwidth, and with further study it is felt that the values observed could be further reduced.

(d) The average crosspolarisation level is slightly below the −30 dB specification. Some imperfections in the fabrication of both antennas could account for this observation. The presence of the EH_{11} mode may also contribute.

(e) The level of the first sidelobe is rather higher than was at first expected, especially in the E plane, and this is also attributed to the presence of higher-order modes.

(f) The control of the higher-order modes appears to offer a method to further improve the aperture efficiency, without an appreciable reduction in bandwidth.

TABLE 2

MEASURED PERFORMANCE OF A 1·22 M-DIAMETER CASSEGRAIN REFLECTOR

	E plane	H plane	Average	E plane	H plane	Average
Frequency, GHz		10·5			11·5	
Gain, dBi*	40·34	41·05	40·71	40·77	41·81	41·30
Efficiency, %	60·0	70·5	65·2	55·2	70·2	62·7
First sidelobe	15·8	21·0	—	14·0	17·0	—
Maximum value of sidelobes for angles larger than 110°, dB	−54	−62	—	−60	−65	—
Front/back ratio, dB	60	62	—	63	65	—

* Calculated by integration of the measured pattern

Generally, we have demonstrated that Cassegrain antennas employing dielectric-cone waveguides can be successfully designed using a theory which embraces both modal and ray-optic concepts. Features of these antennas are their high efficiency, low far-out sidelobes and low mutual coupling. As discussed in Part 1, it remains to be demonstrated that the dielectric-cone antenna can perform well over long periods in an all-weather environment. Where the design is used in conjunction with a radome, the principal problem is to ensure inhibition of moisture. If it is not possible to use a radome, it may prove advantageous to surround the cone with a dielectric cladding of larger diameter and of very low permittivity, the outer surface of which could be suitably protected. By using the cladding, the influence of the protective coating on antenna performance should be reduced.

TABLE 3

MAXIMUM CROSSPOLARISATION LEVELS OF THE RADIATION PATTERN MEASURED IN THE PRINCIPAL PLANES OF THE 1·22 M-DIAMETER REFLECTOR

Frequency, GHz	Maximum crosspolarisation (in dB below boresight)	
	E plane	H plane
10·7	−30·8	−23
11·2	−25·8	−24

TABLE 4

MEASURED PERFORMANCE OF A 0·61 M-DIAMETER CASSEGRAIN REFLECTOR

Frequency, GHz	17·7	19·4
Gain, dBi*	38·81	39·52
Efficiency, %	60·2	59·8
First sidelobe level in the E plane, dB	−14·2	−13·8
First sidelobe level in the H plane, dB	−19·5	−16·5
Maximum sidelobe level for $\theta > 110°$ in the E plane, dB	−50	−54
Maximum sidelobe level for $\theta > 110°$ in the H plane, dB	−50	−54
Gain, front/back, dB	50	54

* Calculated by pattern integration

In terms of future studies of electromagnetic performance, we shall be investigating further the influence of higher modes and especially seeking to determine how their excitation may be used to control the antenna patterns and crosspolarisation characteristics. We shall also study the performance of dielectric-cone Cassegrain antennas in which the main reflector is shaped, as in the well known Galindo-Williams design, using conventional feeds.

5 ACKNOWLEDGMENT

We gratefully acknowledge the assistance of our colleagues, K. B. Chan, S. H. Lim, A. D. Olver, G. T. Poulton and L. M. Seng, and thank J. Honour and J. Morris for their significant contributions in the fabrication of the dielectric cones.

We thank W. C. Morgan of Andrew Antenna Systems, Lochgelly, Scotland, for making available their antenna-range facilities, and K. Slinn for help in the production and testing of the 11 GHz antenna. Similarly, we acknowledge the assistance of the Post Office Research Department, Martlesham Heath, especially D. Knox, in the production and testing of the 18 GHz antenna.

One of us (C. E. R. C. S.) is indebted to the Gulbenkian Foundation and the Instituto de Alta Cultura, Portugal, for a research fellowship.

The research described herein was sponsored in part by means of a grant from the Science Research Council, whose support we gratefully acknowledge.

6 REFERENCES

1 CLARRICOATS, P. J. B., and SALEMA, C. E. R. C.: 'Antennas employing conical-dielectric horns. Pt. 1—Propagation and radiation characteristics of dielectric cones' (see pp. 741-749)

2 BARTLETT, H. E., and MOSELEY, R. E.: United States Patent 3430244, Feb. 1969

3 BARTLETT, H. E., and PIETSCH: United States Patent 3414903, Dec. 1968

4 BARTLETT, H. E.: United States Patent 3611391, Oct. 1971

5 CLARRICOATS, P. J. B., and SALEMA, C. E. R. C.: 'Propagation characteristics of low-permittivity cones', Electron. Lett., 1971, **7**, pp. 483-485

6 CLARRICOATS, P. J. B., and SALEMA, C. E. R. C.: 'Design of dielectric-cone feeds for microwave antennas'. Proceedings of the European Microwave Conference, 1971, paper B5/4

7 CLARRICOATS, P. J. B., and SALEMA, C. E. R. C.: 'Influence of launching horn on radiation characteristics of a dielectric-cone feed', Electron. Lett., 1972, **8**, pp. 200-202

8 CLARRICOATS, P. J. B., SALEMA, C. E. R. C., and LIM, S. H.: 'Design of cassegrain antennas employing dielectric-cone feeds', ibid., 1972, **8**, pp. 384-385

9 SALEMA, C. E. R. C., and CLARRICOATS, P. J. B.: 'Radiation characteristics of dielectric cones', ibid., 1972, **8**, pp. 414-416

10 CLARRICOATS, P. J. B.: 'Dielectric waveguides for microwave antennas'. Proceedings of XVII General Assembly of URSI, Warsaw, 1972, Session VI-2

11 KRITIKOS, H. N.: 'The extended-aperture method for the determination of the shadow region radiation of parabolic reflectors', IEEE Trans., 1963, **AP-11**, pp. 400-404

12 CLARRICOATS, P. J. B., and SAHA, P. K.: 'Propagation and radiation behaviour of corrugated feeds. Pt. 2—Corrugated-conical-horn feed', Proc. IEE, 1971, **118**, (9), pp. 1177-1186

13 SALEMA, C. E. R. C.: 'Theory and design of dielectric-cone antennas'. Ph.D. Thesis, University of London, 1972

Part VIII
Horn-Reflector Antennas

High directivity can be obtained from horn radiators only if the horn is very long, or if some means of correcting the phase error due to the spherical wave in the aperture is provided. An alternative to a lens for this purpose is the use of a reflecting surface that is part of a paraboloid of revolution whose focal point lies at the apex of the horn. A patent on such a combination of horn and reflector was obtained by Bell Laboratories' workers in 1941 [1], and these antennas have been used ever since in the Bell System's transcontinental microwave relay links. A similar antenna, called the hoghorn, was created in England in 1946 [2]; it was intended for fan beam applications.

Only two papers make up this part, but each is a comprehensive treatment of large, high gain versions of the horn reflector. The first, by Crawford, Hogg, and Hunt, describes a 43-dB gain (at 2390 MHz) pyramidal type designed for use in Project Echo. The second paper, by Hines, Li, and Turrin, describes the very large conical horn reflector of the satellite communication ground station at Andover, ME. Its measured gain of 58 dB at 4170 MHz corresponds to an aperture efficiency of very nearly 81 percent, a very high value indeed. Reference [3] contains an account of the precise measurement of the gain of the pyramidal version.

An interesting variant, obtained by triply folding a horn reflector, results in a more compact structure and is discussed in [4]. Japanese workers have investigated a diagonal horn-reflector antenna, and report on its performance in [5].

References

[1] H. T. Friis and A. C. Beck, U. S. Patent 2 236 393, Mar. 25, 1941.

[2] A. B. Pippard, "The hoghorn: An electromagnetic horn radiator of medium-sized aperture," *J. Inst. Elec. Eng.*, vol. 93, pt. III A, pp. 1528–1530, 1946.

[3] D. C. Hogg and R. W. Wilson, "A precise measurement of the gain of a large horn-reflector antenna," *Bell Syst. Tech. J.*, vol. 44, pp. 1019–1030, July 1965.

[4] A. J. Giger and R. H: Turrin, "The triply-folded horn reflector: A compact ground station antenna design for satellite communications," *Bell Syst. Tech. J.*, vol. 44, pp. 1229–1253, Sept. 1965.

[5] Y. Takeichi, M. Mizusawa, and T. Katagi, "The diagonal horn-reflector antenna," presented at the IEEE Int. Symp. on Antennas and Propagation, Austin, TX, Dec. 1969.

PROJECT ECHO

A Horn-Reflector Antenna for Space Communication

By A. B. CRAWFORD, D. C. HOGG and L. E. HUNT

(Manuscript received April 7, 1961)

This paper describes the mechanical features of the horn-reflector antenna used for receiving signals reflected from the Project Echo balloon satellite and presents in some detail the electrical characteristics (radiation patterns and gain) measured at a frequency of 2390 mc. Theoretically derived characteristics which agree very well with the measurements are also presented; details of the calculations are given in the appendices.

I. INTRODUCTION

The horn-reflector type of antenna was originated at Bell Telephone Laboratories, Holmdel, New Jersey, in the early 1940's[1] and is now in extensive use in the Bell System's transcontinental microwave relay network.[2] It is a combination of a square electromagnetic horn and a reflector that is a sector of a paraboloid of revolution, as illustrated in Fig. 1. The apex of the horn coincides with the focus of the paraboloid. Since the antenna design is based on geometrical optics and has no frequency-sensitive elements, it is extremely broadband; it is not polarization-sensitive and can be used in any linear or circular polarization. The antenna is essentially an offset paraboloidal antenna, so that very little of the energy incident on the reflector is reflected back into the feed to produce an impedance mismatch. Due to the shielding effect of the horn, the far side and back lobes are very small.

These features, together with high aperture efficiency, make the horn-reflector attractive for use in satellite communication systems. In particular, the low side and back lobes insure that when the antenna beam is pointed to the sky very little noise power is received from the ground;* the antenna is thus a low-noise transducer which permits exploitation

* A discussion of the noise properties of antennas is given in Ref. 3.

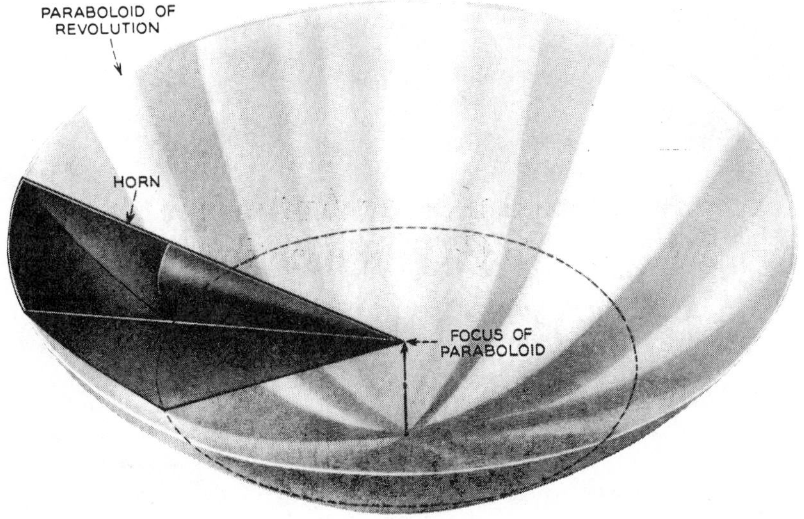

Fig. 1 — Sketch showing relationship of horn-reflector antenna to a paraboloid of revolution.

of the low-noise features of the maser amplifier. An effective noise temperature of about 2°K has been measured for the horn-reflector type of antenna.[4]

II. MECHANICAL DESCRIPTION OF THE ANTENNA

Fig. 2 is a photograph of the horn-reflector antenna erected on the Crawford Hill site of the Holmdel Laboratory and used in the Project Echo experiment.* To permit the antenna beam to be directed to any part of the sky, the antenna is mounted with the axis of the horn horizontal. Rotation about this axis affords tracking in elevation while the entire assembly is rotated about a vertical axis for tracking in azimuth. The antenna is about 50 feet in length, the radiating aperture is approximately 20 by 20 feet, and the weight is about 18 tons. The structure was designed to survive winds of 100 miles per hour.

The elevation structure, both horn and reflector, is constructed of aluminum. The elevation wheel, 30 feet in diameter, supports all radial loads and rotates on rollers mounted on the base frame. All axial or thrust loads are taken by a large ball bearing at the apex end of the

* Although this antenna was designed and constructed by the Bell System as part of its research and development program, it was operated in connection with Project Echo under Contract NASW-110 for the National Aeronautics and Space Administration.

horn. The horn proper continues through this bearing into the equipment cab. Here is located a tapered transition section from square to round waveguide, a rotating joint, and waveguide take-offs which provide for the simultaneous reception of either two orthogonal linearly polarized signals or two circularly polarized signals of opposite sense. The ability to locate the receiver equipment at the apex of the horn, thus eliminating the loss and noise contribution of a connecting line, is an important feature of this antenna.

The triangular base frame is constructed of structural steel shapes. It rotates on wheels about a center pintle ball bearing on a track 30 feet in diameter. The track consists of stress-relieved, planed steel plates which were individually adjusted to produce a track flat to about $\frac{1}{64}$ inch. The faces of the wheels are cone-shaped to minimize sliding friction. A tangential force of about 100 pounds is sufficient to start the antenna in motion.

The horn flares at an angle of 28°. As can be seen in Fig. 1, the antenna is generated by swinging the side projection through this angle. Thus the two sides of the horn are flat surfaces, while the front and back surfaces are sections of cones. There are several advantages to this type of construction: right-angle sections can be used for the corners of the horn; the reflector can be constructed of identical longitudinal sections;

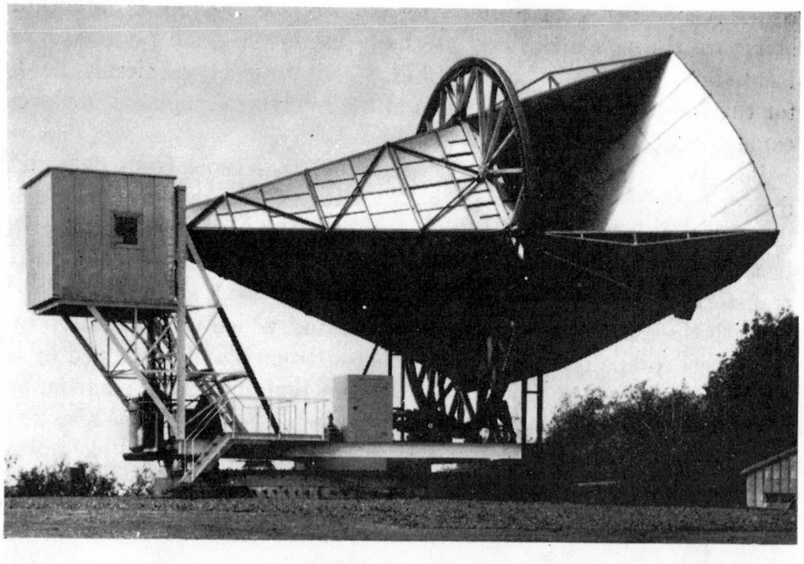

Fig. 2 — Horn-reflector antenna used in Project Echo experiment.

the intersections of the front and back conical surfaces with the paraboloid of revolution are circles in planes perpendicular to the axis of the paraboloid, thus providing accurate and readily available references for use in constructing the reflector. Nine accurately fabricated parabolic ribs were used for the reflector, one end of each being fastened to a curved (arc of a circle) beam at the wheel while the other end was fixed on a circle scribed on a temporary horizontal work table. The ribs were tied together by cross bracing and by a large triangular crossbeam, which in turn was tied by columns to the vertical wheel. The aluminum sheets that make up the reflecting surface were then fastened to the ribs; these have curved stiffeners to produce the small curvature required in the plane perpendicular to the ribs. It is believed that the reflector surface is accurately paraboloidal to $\pm\frac{1}{32}$ inch.

The antenna is driven in azimuth and elevation by 10 H.P. direct-current servo gear-motors.* Power is transmitted by sprockets (with teeth specially cut for rack operation) to roller chains which are fastened to the vertical wheel and to the plates forming the horizontal track. The roller chain proved to be a satisfactory substitute for a large bull gear; by the use of a radial arm and dial indicator, the rollers of the chains were adjusted to lie on 30-foot-diameter circles to an accuracy of about 0.005 inch. The maximum speed of rotation in both azimuth and elevation is 5° per second; the maximum acceleration for both axes is 5° per second per second. Power for the drives is brought to the rotating structure through a slip-ring assembly inside the small plywood house located over the center bearing (Fig. 2). All the electrical circuits needed for the operation of the antenna and the receiving equipment in the cab come through the slip-ring assembly.

Positional information for the antenna is derived from data units driven by large (48-inch) accurately cut and accurately aligned gears located on the bearings at the apex of the horn and at the center of the base frame. The data units contain synchro transmitters and control transformers operated in a two-speed, 1:1 and 36:1, system.

With the exception of the steel base frame, which was fabricated by a local steel company, the antenna was constructed and assembled by the Holmdel Laboratory shops under the direction of H. W. Anderson, who also collaborated in the design. Assistance in the design was also given by R. O'Regan, S. A. Darby and several members of the electro-mechanical development group at the Whippany Laboratory. The latter group also was instrumental in procuring special equipment such as data units, gears, and slip-ring assembly.

* This is more power than required, particularly for the elevation drive, but these motor and control packages were standard items and were readily available.

The antenna has performed well electrically and mechanically during the Project Echo experiment. It was subjected to winds of 80 mph during Hurricane Donna, September 12, 1960, without damage. It has been customary to disengage the azimuth sprocket drive when the antenna is not in use, thus permitting the structure to "weathervane" and seek a position of minimum wind resistance.

III. THEORETICAL DISCUSSION

The manner in which the spherical wave diverges from the apex of the horn is shown schematically in Fig. 3(a). This wave, for the greater

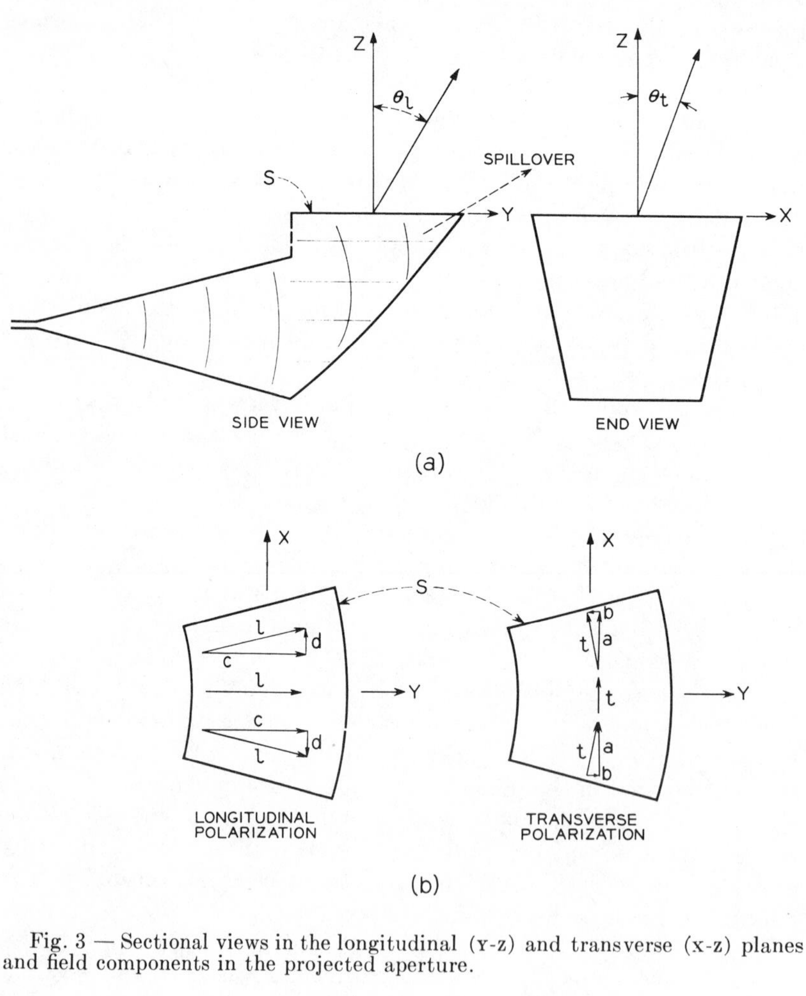

Fig. 3 — Sectional views in the longitudinal (Y-Z) and transverse (X-Z) planes and field components in the projected aperture.

part, maintains the characteristic amplitude distribution of the TE_{10} mode as it proceeds along the horn; nevertheless, it is a spherical wave and undergoes inverse distance attenuation up to the point where it is rendered equiphase by the paraboloidal reflector. Thus, over the surface of the projected aperture, s in Fig. 3(a), the field has an unsymmetrical amplitude taper in the direction of the horn axis due to inverse distance attenuation in addition to the symmetrical characteristic of the TE_{10} mode.

In Fig. 3(b), two sets of vectors, t and l, representing transverse and longitudinal polarization in the projected aperture, are shown. On the bisector of the aperture, t is parallel to the x-axis and l to the y-axis; however, at points removed from the bisector, t and l preserve the polarization established in the pyramidal horn, and therefore are inclined with respect to the principal axes. At these points, t and l are broken down into components a, b and c, d respectively, as indicated in Fig. 3(b); note that there is asymmetry about the bisector in the cross components b and d.

The aperture field being known, one can calculate the field at a large distance R in the region near the axis of the beam to good approximation by

$$E = \frac{j}{\lambda R} \int_S E_i \, e^{-j\beta(y \sin \theta_l + x \sin \theta_t)} \, ds, \tag{1}$$

where E_i represents any one of the components a, b, c, or d, and θ_l and θ_t are angles in the principal plane, which either contains or is transverse to the axis of the pyramidal horn. The longitudinal plane contains the horn and beam axes; the transverse plane contains the beam axis and is normal to the axis of the horn. Thus, in Fig. 3, θ_l lies in the yz plane and θ_t in the xz plane. Both the principal and cross-polarized radiation patterns* may be computed using (1), provided the appropriate aperture field component E_i is chosen. The computed patterns are shown in Figs. 4, 5, and 6 as dashed curves†; the experimental data are shown as solid lines and will be discussed later. The two cross-polarization patterns in the longitudinal plane are zero for all angles since the aperture field components b and d are antisymmetrical with respect to that plane.

The radiation patterns for circular polarization may be calculated by combining the appropriate principal and cross-polarized components of the far field. An example of the method is given in Appendix B. The

* Details are given in Appendix A.

† The computations were made for points separated 0.25° in θ; thus, although the dashed curves extend to the −50 db level, they do not represent the depths of the nulls for the case of longitudinal plane patterns, but rather only their positions.

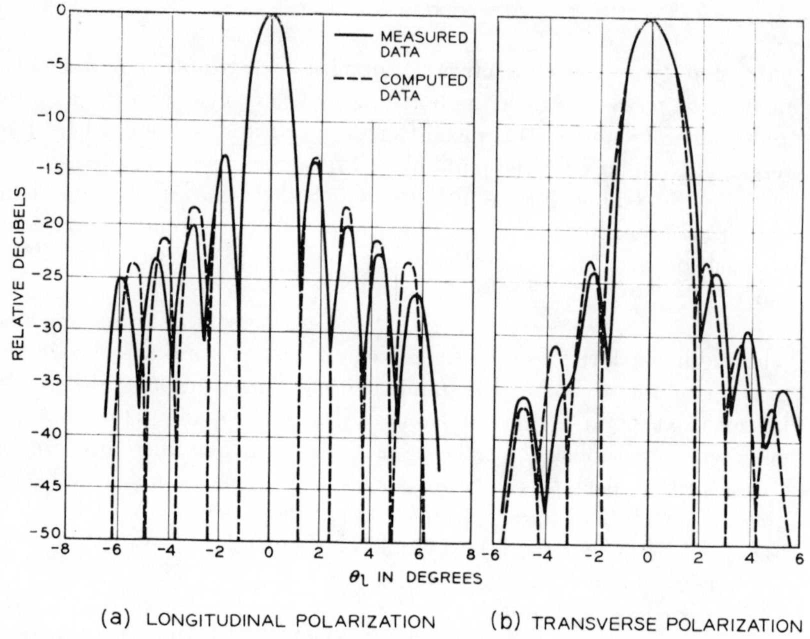

Fig. 4 — Principal radiation patterns in the longitudinal plane (2390 mc).

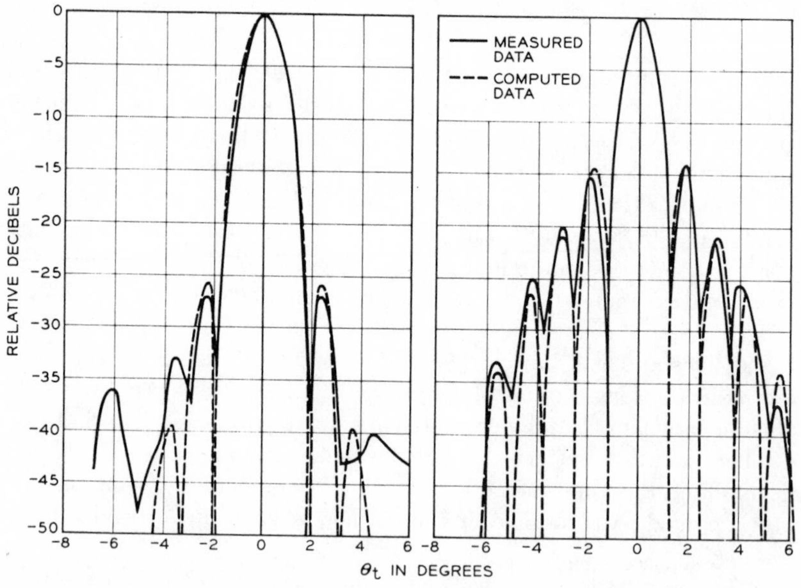

Fig. 5 — Principal radiation patterns in the transverse plane (2390 mc).

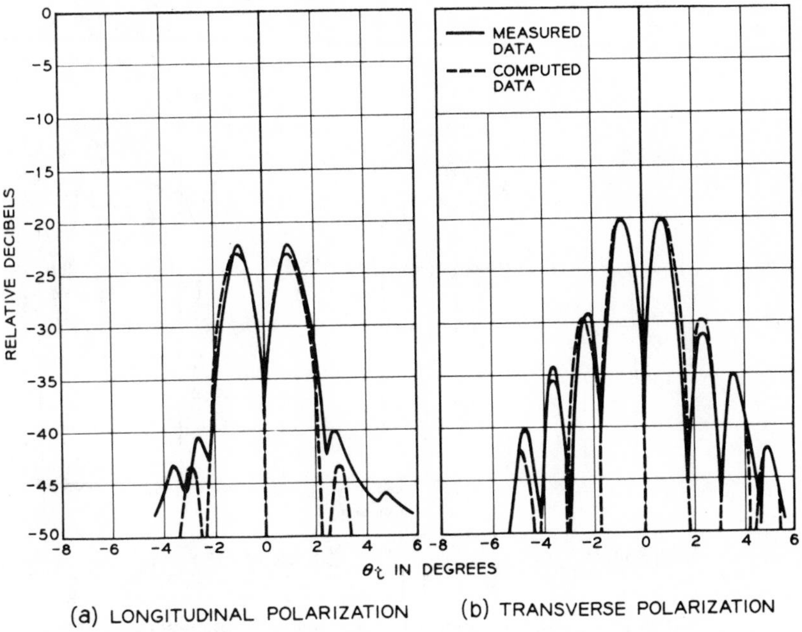

Fig. 6 — Cross-polarized radiation patterns in the transverse plane (2390 mc).

dashed lines of Figs. 7(a) and 8(a) show calculated radiation patterns where the antenna receives the desired (transmitted) sense of circular polarization, and Figs. 7(b) and 8(b) show the undesired sense. Note especially Figs. 8(a) and (b) for the transverse plane, in which the patterns are unsymmetrical with respect to the $\theta_t = 0$ axis; in Fig. 8(a), the maximum of the main beam is at $\theta_t = -0.1°$. This effect is more clearly demonstrated by assuming that the antenna receives both clockwise and counter-clockwise senses simultaneously, as would be the case for a linearly polarized incident wave; the beam, for one sense, shifts to $\theta_t = +0.1°$ and for the other to $\theta_t = -0.1°$; this effect is shown in Fig. 9. The slight tilting of the beam in circular polarization is a consequence of asymmetry in the phase of the cross-polarized components of the far field.

Unfortunately, all the energy which proceeds along the horn does not illuminate the paraboloidal reflecting surface; some of it is diffracted at the edge of the horn aperture. As indicated by the dashed line in Fig. 3(a), the wave is again diffracted by the edge of the reflector and produces perturbations in the far-field pattern. The lobes thus produced are referred to as spillover lobes; in Appendix D a method of calculating

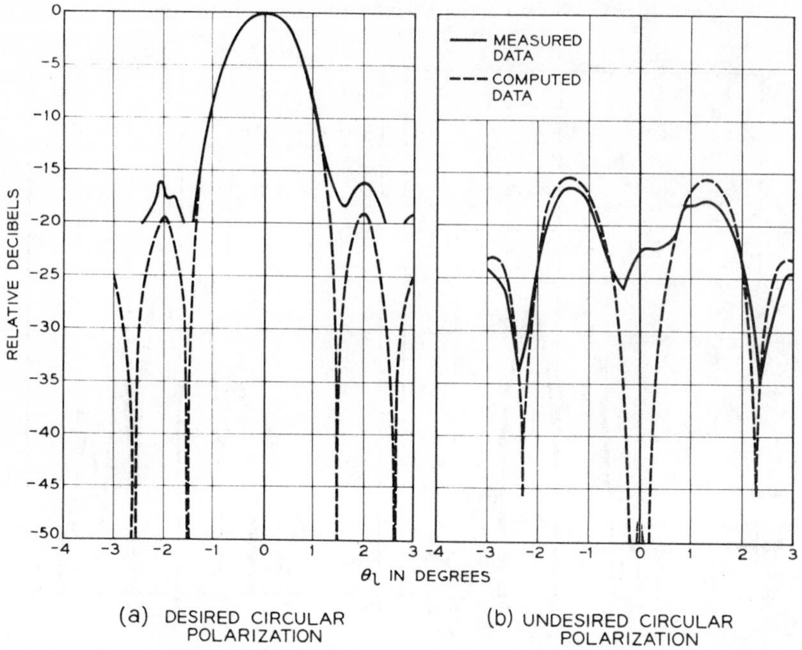

Fig. 7 — Circularly polarized radiation pattern in the longitudinal plane (2390 mc).

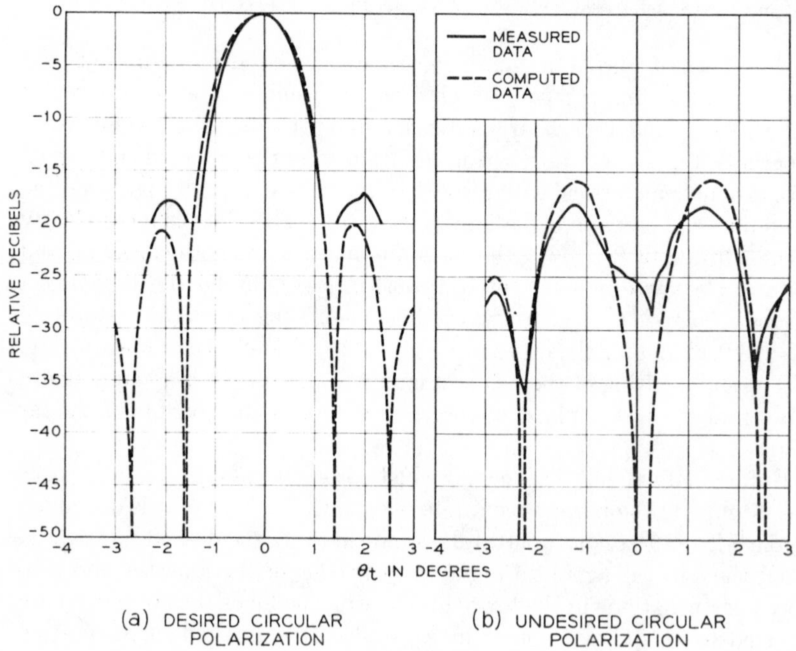

Fig. 8 — Circularly polarized radiation patterns in the transverse plane (2390 mc).

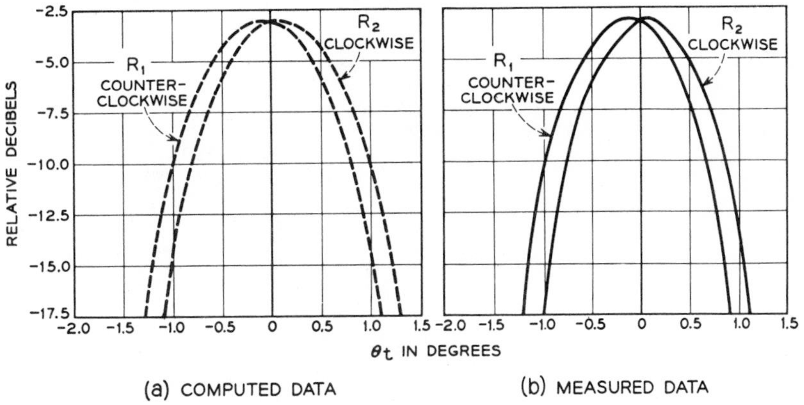

Fig. 9 — Circularly polarized radiation patterns in the transverse plane, showing dependence of beam displacement on sense of polarization.

them is discussed. The points in Fig. 10 show the spillover effect calculated for longitudinal polarization in the longitudinal plane. The maximum spillover energy is at an angle $\theta \simeq 70°$; as indicated in the insert in Fig. 11, this differs by 7° from the direction determined by the flare angle of the horn, namely, 77°. For transverse polarization, the spillover effect is much reduced because of the cosine distribution in the z direction in the horn for that polarization.

IV. TECHNIQUE OF MEASUREMENTS

The important electrical properties of the antenna to be measured are its gain and radiation patterns at the frequency of interest, in this case 2390 mc. To make such measurements, it is necessary to provide a

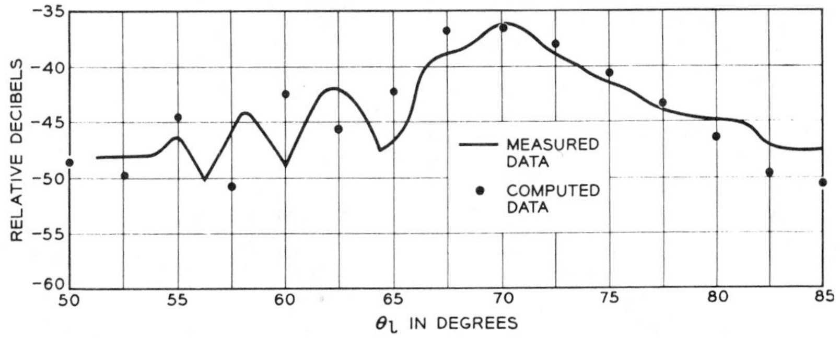

Fig. 10 — Calculated and measured spillover lobe; longitudinal plane, longitudinal polarization.

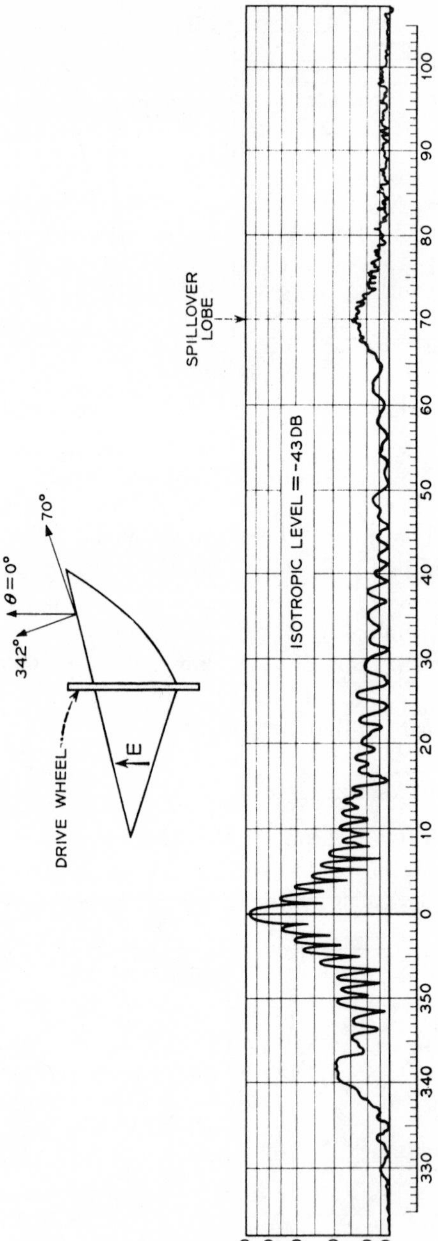

Fig. 11 — Extended radiation pattern; longitudinal plane, longitudinal polarization.

known incident field. In free space, ideally, the incident field would be uniform in amplitude and phase over the region occupied by the aperture of the antenna. In practice, this is accomplished by placing a source at a sufficient distance such that the wave incident at the antenna under test is essentially plane. The usual criterion is that the phase deviation over the aperture not exceed $\pi/8$. For the 20-foot aperture considered here, this criterion requires that a test transmitter operating at 2390 mc be at least one-third mile away; the distance used for these tests was about two miles. The antenna is not in free space, however, and environment such as trees and contours of the local terrain introduce reflections which distort the incident field. For these tests, nearby trees were removed and, both before and after the antenna was in place, the incident field was checked by exploring it with a probe consisting of a small horn. The horn was mounted on a motor-driven carriage that was drawn up and down a 55-foot vertical tower, the received output being continuously recorded. The tower was set at several horizontal positions so that the incident field over the area to be occupied by the antenna was mapped out. These height runs showed irregular variations in the incident field, but these did not exceed ± 1 db, and therefore were considered small enough to permit meaningful measurements. An analysis of the height runs indicated that, in addition to the direct space wave, a second wave, reflected from the intervening ground, was also present. The analysis fixed the reflection point at about midpath at an elevation corresponding to the tree-top level with an amplitude reflection coefficient of about 0.07.

V. GAIN MEASUREMENTS

The gain of the horn-reflector antenna was measured by comparing the strength of its received signal with that of a standard horn.* The latter was located in the plane of the aperture of the horn-reflector, but off to one side. The field at this particular location of the standard horn was equal to the average intensity of the field illuminating the horn reflector, as obtained from the height run data.

The measurement procedure consisted first of aiming the horn-reflector for optimum received signal strength and continuously recording the output. Because of scintillation of the signal, it was necessary to integrate for several seconds to obtain a dependable signal level. The coaxial line which fed the receiver was then shifted from the horn-reflector to the standard horn and the results recorded for a like period. A number of

* A pyramidal horn whose gain at 2390 mc, calculated from its physical dimensions, was 20.1 db.

such comparisons were made. The gain of the horn-reflector, referred to an isotropic radiator, was then obtained by adding the db difference between those two signal strengths to the db gain of the standard horn.

A double detection receiver was used in all the measurements. Signal-level differences were established by an attenuator in the intermediate frequency (65 mc) channel which was calibrated to an accuracy of ±0.05 db. The gain was measured using both longitudinal and transverse polarizations and the results averaged:

Calculated gain of standard horn:	20.1 db,
Measured gain of horn-reflector over standard horn:	23.2 db,
Gain of horn-reflector:	43.3 db.

The rms scatter of the gain measurements was 0.16 db, due principally to scintillation of the signal.

The theoretical value for the horn-reflector gain is calculated by the method discussed in Appendix C. Due to the asymmetrical geometry of the aperture, the gain depends slightly on polarization, namely 43.43 db for longitudinal and 43.35 db for transverse. The average theoretical gain is therefore 43.39 db, which is 1.12 db below full area gain (44.51 db).

If we compare the measured and calculated values, the gain is 0.09 db less than expected.* Part of this discrepancy is due to the irregularities in the incident field discussed above in connection with the height run data. If one assumes that the variations in the phase of the incident field are random over the aperture, the deviation of the phase variation being derived from the 0.07 db reflection coefficient discussed above, one can estimate the decrease in received signal† due to this effect; this turns out to be 0.02 db, so that the discrepancy between calculated and measured values is reduced slightly. The remainder is most likely due to spillover.

VI. PATTERN MEASUREMENTS

Radiation patterns were obtained by continuously recording the receiver output as the horn-reflector was rotated at a constant speed.

There are several directional patterns of interest; these include the principal and cross-polarized patterns for the two linear polarizations in the two principal planes, and patterns in circular polarization for the

* In other words, the measured effective area is 1.2 db below actual area, or the measured efficiency, 76 per cent.

† For a small random fluctuation, the decrease in signal is $e^{-\delta^2}$ where δ is the standard deviation of the fluctuations in phase.[5]

two planes. As discussed in Section II, the two cross-polarized patterns in the longitudinal plane are expected to be zero, due to the odd symmetry of the cross-polarized components of the aperture field.

Detailed patterns for the principal polarizations in the region of the main beam are shown in Figs. 4 and 5 for longitudinal and transverse planes respectively. Measured data are shown by full lines and theoretical data by dashed lines. In general, the measurements agree very well with the calculated patterns except for some relatively small departures which are considered to be due to reflections from the environment and to scintillation. The salient factors obtained from the principal linear polarization patterns are shown in Table I.

The cross-polarization patterns in the transverse plane are shown in Fig. 6; here also the agreement between experiment and theory is considered to be good. The levels of cross-polarization in the longitudinal plane which are theoretically zero were lower than −30 db in the region near $\theta_l = 0$ and fell rapidly to less than −45 db for other angles.

The response of the antenna to circularly polarized waves is shown by the patterns of Figs. 7 through 9. In general, the agreement between measurement and theory is not as satisfactory as for the linear polarization patterns; this disagreement is believed due in part to lack of sufficient measuring range in the receivers used for the two circular senses. When both the transmitting test antenna and the horn-reflector were adjusted for the same sense of polarization, the first side lobes in both the longitudinal and transverse planes, as seen in Figs. 7(a) and 8(a), measured about 3 db higher than predicted by theory; the main beamwidths, however, agreed well with calculations. When the horn-reflector was adjusted to receive the sense opposite to that transmitted, the response on the first side lobes, as shown in Figs. 7(b) and 8(b), was about 2 db lower than predicted, while the response in the direction of the principal axis was about −27 db. The discrepancy between this value and that predicted by theory is believed due partly to depolarization by

Table I

Plane	Polarization	Beamwidths (3-db points)		Level of first minor lobes	
		Measured	Calculated	Measured	Calculated
transverse	longitudinal	1.35°	1.30°	−27.0db	−26.5 db
longitudinal	longitudinal	1.10°	1.10°	−13.5	−13.5
transverse	transverse	1.00°	1.00°	−14.5	−14.5
longitudinal	transverse	1.55°	1.55°	−24.0	−23.0

the ground and partly to imperfect circular polarization from the transmitter.*

A test was made in which the horn-reflector received simultaneously both senses of circular polarization which were generated by a wave from the test transmitter that was linearly polarized. The results appear in Fig. 9; the slight beam tilt, as evidenced by the displacement in opposite directions from $\theta = 0$ depending on the sense of polarization, agrees well with theoretical values. A similar displacement between the two senses was observed while receiving noise from the moon and sun.

Fig. 11 shows an extended radiation pattern measured in the longitudinal plane using longitudinal polarization. Let us refer to this region as the spillover sector; it is shown here in preference to any other sector because the level of the far-side lobes is of the order of the isotropic level rather than 10 to 30 db or so below isotropic, as is the case for the other sectors.[2,4] The most prominent spurious lobe is the so-called spillover lobe at an angle of 70° from the main beam. A more detailed plot of the spillover lobe is shown in Fig. 10, the points being values calculated in Appendix D. The agreement in level and shape of the measured and calculated curves is fairly good; however, the calculated data appear to be translated about two degrees toward smaller values of θ_l. Pattern measurements using transverse polarization showed much lower levels for the far lobes in the spillover sector.

Also apparent in Fig. 11 is a prominent lobe at angle 342°. This lobe is apparently associated with the 30-foot-diameter drive wheel, which, as may be seen in the insert in Fig. 11, tends to shadow the aperture in that direction. Diffraction over the rim of the wheel might be the cause of this spurious lobe.

VII. CONCLUDING REMARKS

The performance characteristics of a relatively large horn-reflector type of antenna, measured at a frequency of 2390 mc, agree satisfactorily with calculated performance. The measured radiation patterns are readily identified with those calculated to at least the third side lobes, the antenna gain being about one-tenth decibel less than expected. This good performance, in conjunction with the low-noise properties of this type of antenna, place it in a favorable position, not only for use in space communications, but also for use as a standard for absolute flux measurements in radio astronomy. Of some concern is a small amount of spill-

* The circular polarization was produced by a quarter-wave plate placed in front of the transmitting horn; the axial ratio, measured by rotating a 20-db horn antenna at the receiving site, was about 0.8 db.

over which degrades the performance in one sector of the radiation pattern; fortunately, in the above applications, the spillover sector is directed skyward and therefore the noise contribution is small in the microwave band.

Assistance in the assembly and adjustment of electrical components and in the measurement of the electrical properties of the antenna was given by R. A. Semplak, H. A. Gorenflo, and R. A. Desmond. Computation of the theoretical data was made by Mrs. C. L. Beattie.

APPENDIX A

Calculation of Patterns for Linear Polarization

The radiation patterns for linear polarization in the region of the main beam of the antenna are calculated using

$$E = \frac{j}{\lambda R} \int_S E_i \, e^{-j\beta(y \sin \theta_l + x \sin \theta_t)} \, ds, \tag{2}$$

where E_i is a component of the aperture field and x, y are coordinates in the projected aperture, S; R is the distance from the antenna to the

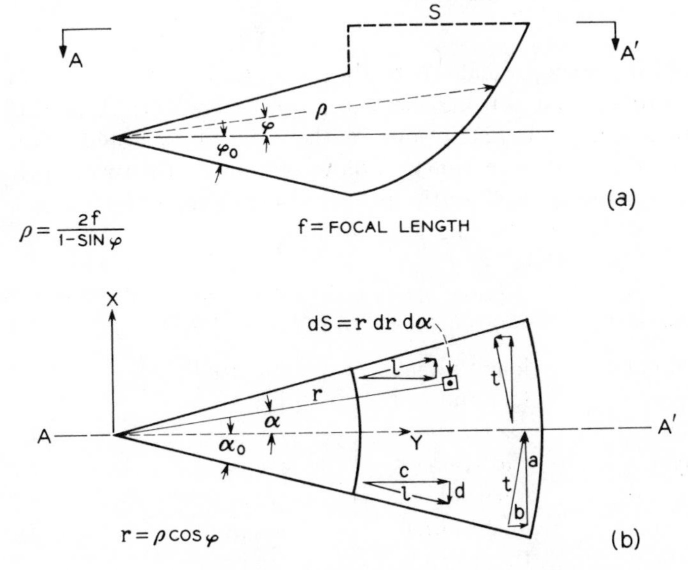

Fig. 12 — Coordinate system and projected aperture, S.

distant field point; θ_l and θ_t are angles in the principal planes; $\beta = 2\pi/\lambda$.

Since energy proceeds down the square horn in essentially a dominant waveguide mode, the field is constant along one coordinate and has a cosine distribution along the orthogonal coordinate. In addition, the field of the spherical wave decreases inversely with the distance ρ shown in Fig. 12(a), but, since the spherical phase front is corrected by the reflector, negligible attenuation occurs between the reflector and the projected aperture, S, in the plane AA′.

The total fields l and t, and the field components a, b, c, and d in the projected aperture, are shown in Fig. 12(b). Each of these can be expressed in terms of the symbols shown in the figure:

$$\begin{aligned} E_a &= E_0 \frac{\rho_0}{\rho} \cos \frac{\pi\varphi}{2\varphi_0} \cos \alpha, \\ E_b &= E_0 \frac{\rho_0}{\rho} \cos \frac{\pi\varphi}{2\varphi_0} \sin \alpha, \\ E_c &= E_0 \frac{\rho_0}{\rho} \cos \frac{\pi\alpha}{2\alpha_0} \cos \alpha, \\ E_d &= E_0 \frac{\rho_0}{\rho} \cos \frac{\pi\alpha}{2\alpha_0} \sin \alpha. \end{aligned} \tag{3}$$

The field has been normalized to the value E_0 at $\rho = \rho_0 = 2f$ (where $\varphi = \alpha = 0$), φ_0 and α_0 being the flare angles of the horn. Equation (3), substituted for E_i in (2), results in the far-field equations. However, for comparison with experimental data, one must specify the principal plane of interest as well as the polarization; therefore let us designate the far fields in the following way:

Polarization of Antenna	*Plane of Measurement*	*Polarization of Far Field*	*Designation of Far Field*
longitudinal	longitudinal	longitudinal	E_1
transverse	longitudinal	transverse	E_2
longitudinal	transverse	longitudinal	E_3
transverse	transverse	transverse	E_4
longitudinal	longitudinal	transverse	E_5
transverse	longitudinal	longitudinal	E_6
longitudinal	transverse	transverse	E_7
transverse	transverse	longitudinal	E_8

These designations are related to (2) and (3) as follows:

$$\begin{bmatrix} E_1 \\ E_2 \\ E_5 \\ E_6 \end{bmatrix} = j \frac{4f^2}{\lambda R} \int_{-\alpha_0}^{\alpha_0} d\alpha \int_{-\varphi_0}^{\varphi_0} d\varphi \begin{bmatrix} E_c \\ E_a \\ E_d \\ E_b \end{bmatrix} \frac{\rho}{\rho_0} \frac{\cos \varphi}{1 - \sin \varphi} e^{-j\beta\rho \cos \varphi \cos \alpha \sin \theta_l},$$

$$\begin{bmatrix} E_3 \\ E_4 \\ E_7 \\ E_8 \end{bmatrix} = j \frac{4f^2}{\lambda R} \int_{-\alpha_0}^{\alpha_0} d\alpha \int_{-\varphi_0}^{\varphi_0} d\varphi \begin{bmatrix} E_c \\ E_a \\ E_d \\ E_b \end{bmatrix} \frac{\rho}{\rho_0} \frac{\cos \varphi}{1 - \sin \varphi} e^{-j\beta\rho \cos \varphi \sin \alpha \sin \theta_t}.$$

Integration shows that E_5 and E_6 are zero. The remainder are computed by numerical integration, with E_1, E_2, E_3, E_4, E_7, and E_8 corresponding to the patterns in Figs. 4(a), 4(b), 5(a), 5(b), 6(a), and 6(b) respectively.

APPENDIX B

Calculation of Patterns for Circular Polarization

The far-field patterns for circular polarization may now be calculated using the designations discussed in Appendix A. As an example, consider Fig. 13, in which the horn is assumed to be fed at the throat with a clockwise circularly polarized wave $-i_x - ji_z$, i_x and i_z being vectors

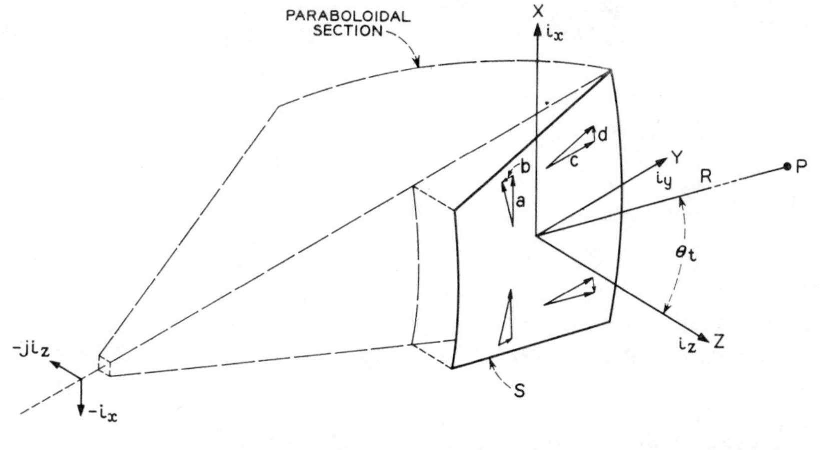

Fig. 13 — Aperture field components for calculation of circular polarization: distant point, P, is in the transverse plane.

in the x and z directions and $j = \sqrt{-1}$. Upon reflection by the paraboloidal section, this wave produces an aperture field

$$E_s = (i_x E_a - i_y E_b) + j(i_y E_c + i_x E_d), \tag{4}$$

i_y being in the y direction.* If we restrict the discussion to the transverse plane, E_a, E_b, E_c, and E_d are the aperture field components which produce the far fields E_4, E_8, E_3, and E_7 discussed above.† At a point P defined by a line R in the transverse plane making a small positive angle θ_t with respect to the z-axis, the field is

$$E_p = i_x E_4 - j i_y E_8 + j i_y E_3 - i_x E_7 . \tag{5}$$

In (5), account has been taken of the fact that the phase of the cross-polarized fields, E_7 and E_8, differs from that of the principal fields by 90°. Gathering together the x and y components, (5) becomes

$$E_p = i_x(E_4 - E_7) + j i_y(E_3 - E_8),$$

which can be broken down into two circularly polarized waves

$$E_{p_{\text{ccw}}} = \frac{i_x}{2}(E_3 + E_4 - E_7 - E_8) + j\frac{i_y}{2}(E_3 + E_4 - E_7 - E_8), \tag{6}$$

and

$$E_{p_{\text{cw}}} = \frac{i_x}{2}(E_3 - E_4 + E_7 - E_8) - j\frac{i_y}{2}(E_3 - E_4 + E_7 - E_8), \tag{7}$$

with (6) being the desired and (7) the undesired sense of rotation.

If the point P in Fig. 13 is below the z-axis such that θ_t is negative, the signs of the cross-polarized components E_7 and E_8 are reversed and the fields are

$$E_{p_{\text{ccw}}} = \frac{i_x}{2}(E_3 + E_4 + E_7 + E_8) + j\frac{i_y}{2}(E_3 + E_4 + E_7 + E_8) \tag{8}$$

and

$$E_{p_{\text{cw}}} = \frac{i_x}{2}(E_3 - E_4 - E_7 + E_8) - j\frac{i_y}{2}(E_3 - E_4 - E_7 + E_8). \tag{9}$$

Comparison of (6) with (8) and (7) with (9) shows that the radiation patterns in circular polarization will be somewhat unsymmetrical about the $\theta_t = 0$ axis.

* Note reversal in sense of polarization on reflection.

† Here, E_a, E_b, $\cdots$, E_4, E_8, $\cdots$ etc., are the amplitudes of the aperture and far fields.

In the longitudinal plane, since the cross-polarized fields are zero, the radiation patterns for circular polarization are symmetrical about $\theta_l = 0$.

APPENDIX C

Gain

The antenna gain may be calculated using

$$G = 4\pi R^2 \frac{F(0)}{P_s}, \tag{10}$$

where $F(0) = (1/\eta) \mid E(0)|^2$ is the density of power flow in the direction $\theta_t = \theta_l = 0$ as obtained from (2) by numerical integration ($\eta = 120\pi$); P_s, the total power radiated by the aperture is obtained by integration of either of the components l or t of Fig. 12. For example, since

$$E_l = E_0 \frac{\rho_0}{\rho} \cos \frac{\pi\varphi}{2\varphi_0}$$

and

$$ds = r\,dr\,d\theta = 4f^2 \frac{\cos\varphi}{(1 - \sin\phi)^2}\,d\varphi\,d\alpha,$$

$$P_s = \frac{E_0^2}{\eta} 4f^2 \int_{-\alpha_0}^{\alpha_0} d\alpha \int_{-\varphi_0}^{\varphi_0} d\varphi \cos^2 \frac{\pi\alpha}{2\alpha_0} \cos\varphi = \frac{E_0^2}{\eta} 8f^2\alpha_0 \sin\varphi_0 .$$

The efficiency of the antenna is given by A_e/S, where $A_e = \lambda^2 G/4\pi$ is the effective area and

$$S = \int_s r\,dr\,d\alpha = 16f^2\alpha_0 \frac{\sin\varphi_0}{\cos^2\varphi_0}$$

is the actual area of the projected aperture.

APPENDIX D

The Spillover Lobe

The spherical wave in the horn (shown in Fig. 14) is diffracted at edge A and part of the energy proceeds beyond the rim of the reflector, C. For the purpose of calculating the spillover lobe, the antenna configuration is idealized by replacing the curved reflector, shown dashed in Fig. 14, with a plane semi-infinite sheet, the edge of which is $c/2$ above the axis of the horn. The distant field of this horn-sheet combination can then be calculated by use of Fourier transforms, as discussed by Woonton.[6] Restricting the discussion to the plane of Fig. 14, one obtains for the distant field at a point R, θ not too far removed from the axis of the horn:

$$E' = \left(\frac{j}{2\pi\lambda R}\right)^{\frac{1}{2}} E_0 e^{j(\pi-1)\gamma^2 b\lambda} \left\{ \sqrt{\lambda l} e^{j\pi\gamma^2\lambda l} [C(v_2) - C(v_1) - jS(v_2) + jS(v_1)] - (1+j)\sqrt{\pi} \int_{-a/2}^{a/2} e^{-j\pi(h^2/\lambda l - 2\gamma h)} [C(v_0) - jS(v_0)]\, dh \right\}, \tag{11}$$

where E_0 is the field at the center of the horn aperture,

$$v_0 = \frac{1}{\sqrt{2b\lambda}} [c - 2(h - \gamma b\lambda)],$$

$$v_1 = \sqrt{\frac{2}{l\lambda}} [\gamma l\lambda - a/2],$$

$$v_2 = \sqrt{\frac{2}{l\lambda}} [\gamma l\lambda + a/2];$$

and $\gamma = -(1/\lambda)\sin(\pi/2 - \theta)$; a is the width of the horn aperture along the h coordinate; and b, c, l are the dimensions shown in Fig. 14, C and S being Fresnel integrals.

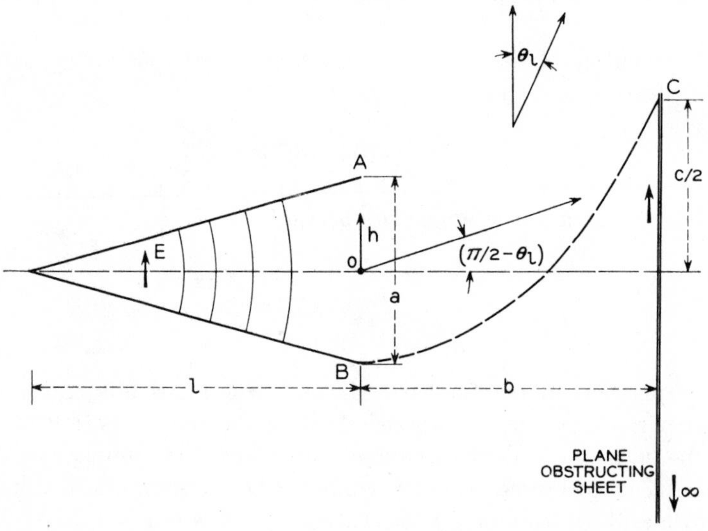

Fig. 14 — Two-dimensional geometry used for calculating the spillover lobe.

The two-dimensional solution, (11), predicts quite accurately the value of θ_l at which maximum spillover occurs, but it is in error in absolute value because in reality the diffracting edges A and C are of finite length and are curved. One can account approximately for the curvature of edge C by assuming that the diffraction effect in the plane of Fig. 14 and the effect in the plane AC, normal to the figure, are separable. In that case, (11) is multiplied by a factor

$$K = \frac{\int_{-d}^{d} e^{-j\pi(x^2/\lambda r)} \cos \frac{\pi x}{2d}\, dx}{\int_{-d}^{d} \cos \frac{\pi x}{2d}\, dx},$$

where x is the coordinate normal to the plane of Fig. 14 at C, $2d$ the extent of the edge along the x-axis, and r its radius of curvature.

The values plotted in Fig. 10 are KE'; K amounts to -10.5 db for the case under consideration.

REFERENCES

1. Friis, H. T., and Beck, A. C., U. S. Patent 2,236,393.
2. Friis, R. W., and May, A. S., A New Broad-Band Microwave Antenna System, A.I.E.E. Trans., Pt. I, **77,** 1958, p. 97.
3. Hogg, D. C., Problems in Low Noise Reception of Microwaves, I.R.E. Trans., Nat. Symp. on Space Electronics and Telemetry, 1960, p. 8-2.
4. DeGrasse, R. W., Hogg, D. C., Ohm, E. A., and Scovil, H. E. D., Ultra-Low-Noise Antenna and Receiver Combination for Satellite or Space Communication, Proc. Nat. Elect. Conf., **15,** 1959, p. 370.
5. Ruze, J., Nuovo Cimento, **9,** supp. 3, 1952, p. 364.
6. Woonton, G. A., The Effect of an Obstacle in the Fresnel Field on the Distant Field of a Linear Radiator, J. Appl. Phys., **21,** 1950, p. 577.

The Electrical Characteristics of the Conical Horn-Reflector Antenna

By J. N. HINES, TINGYE LI and R. H. TURRIN

(Manuscript received February 11, 1963)

The conical horn-reflector antenna was selected for the satellite communication ground station because of its broadband and low-noise properties. Prior to the construction of the full-size antenna, theoretical and model studies of its electrical characteristics were undertaken. These studies consisted of computing gain and radiation patterns for two modes of excitation, constructing of model antennas and measuring them. Results of these studies are presented in this paper together with results of the measurements of the full size antenna at Andover, Maine.

I. INTRODUCTION

The horn-reflector antenna was selected for the satellite communication ground station because of its broadband and low-noise properties along with certain operational advantages. Two forms of the horn-reflector antenna exist, the pyramidal and the conical. The *pyramidal* horn-reflector antenna has been widely used in the Bell System's microwave radio relay network since its inception at Bell Telephone Laboratories, Holmdel, New Jersey, over 20 years ago.[1] Recently, a large steerable version of this antenna with a 20 × 20-foot aperture[2] was built at Holmdel, New Jersey, and employed in both the Echo and Telstar communications satellite projects. More recently, a very large *conical* horn-reflector antenna was constructed at Andover, Maine, and an identical one at Pleumeur-Bodou, France, for the Telstar communications satellite project. Electrically, the two types of the horn-reflector antenna are very similar, but the conical form possesses certain structural advantages. The suitability and the performance of these antennas are amply reflected in the success of these projects.

Prior to construction of the full-size conical horn-reflector antenna, theoretical and model studies of the electrical characteristics of the antenna were undertaken. These studies consisted of computing gain and radiation patterns for two modes of excitation, constructing model antennas and measuring them. We present in this paper results of these studies together with results of the measurements of the full-size antenna at Andover, Maine.

II. DESCRIPTION OF ANTENNAS

2.1 *General*

The geometry of the horn reflector is shown in Fig. 1. The antenna consists of a paraboloidal reflecting section illuminated by a conical horn. The apex of the horn coincides with the focus of the paraboloid,

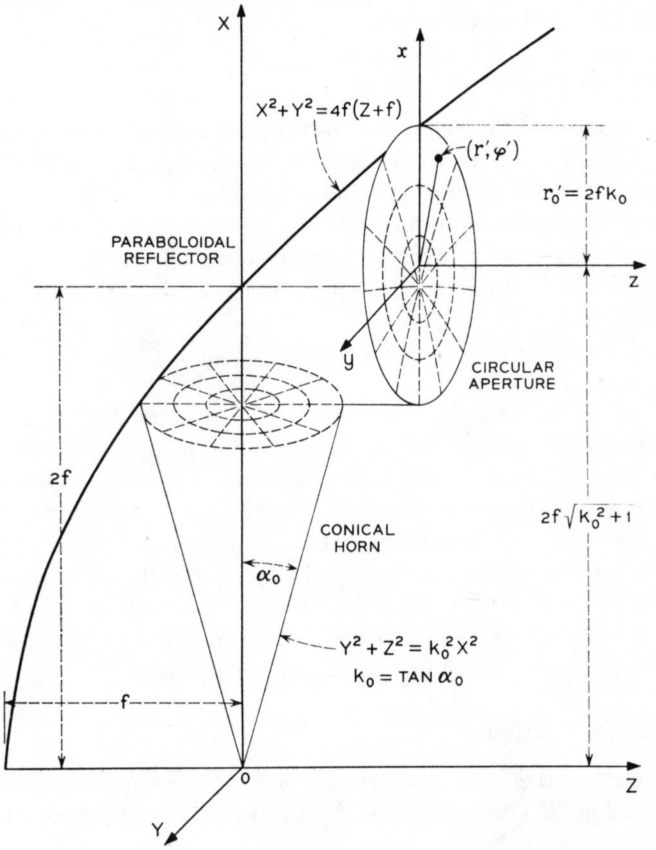

Fig. 1 — Geometry of the conical horn-reflector antenna.

and the axis of the horn is perpendicular to the axis of the paraboloid. The paraboloidal section acts as a combined right-angle reflector and phase corrector for the diverging spherical wave from the conical horn, so that the wave appearing at the circular aperture has a plane wavefront. A cylindrical section encircles the aperture and is attached to both the conical horn and the paraboloidal reflector. This cylindrical aperture shield contributes to the low-noise characteristic of this type of antenna.

The antenna can be excited in as many ways as there are modes in the conical horn.[3,4] For small flare angles the field configurations over the spherical equiphase surfaces are essentially the same as those of a circular waveguide. It is certainly true in this case, where the total flare angle is 31.5 degrees. Therefore, we refer to the dominant wave in the horn as the TE_{11} wave and the second propagating wave as the TM_{01} wave. The former is used for communication and the two are used together for automatic tracking.

2.2 *Model Antennas*

Two models of the conical horn-reflector antenna were constructed at the Holmdel and at the Whippany, N. J., Bell Laboratories. These are referred to as models one and two, respectively. Photographs of these model antennas are shown in Fig. 2. Model one was employed for extensive TE_{11} mode pattern measurements, while model two was employed primarily to investigate the TM_{01} mode radiation patterns. Neither model was measured to exact scale of the large antenna (in terms of wavelength). Pertinent dimensions and information about the models are given in Table I.

The reflector surface of model one was constructed of $\frac{1}{16}$-inch brass strips which form sectors of the paraboloid. The strips, approximately two inches wide, were bonded to a rigid ribbed frame with a resin cement. The surface accuracy was obtained with the aid of precision templates; the surface was then hand honed. The reflector surface of model two was constructed with the aid of a paraboloidal deep dish which was used as a mold. The dish surface tolerance, therefore, determined the tolerance of the reflector of the model antenna. Both models had aperture shields which were cut in a plane tangent to the cone surface.

2.3 *Full Size Antenna*

A sketch of the full-size antenna constructed at Andover, Maine, is shown in Fig. 3. The mechanical design of the antenna is reported else-

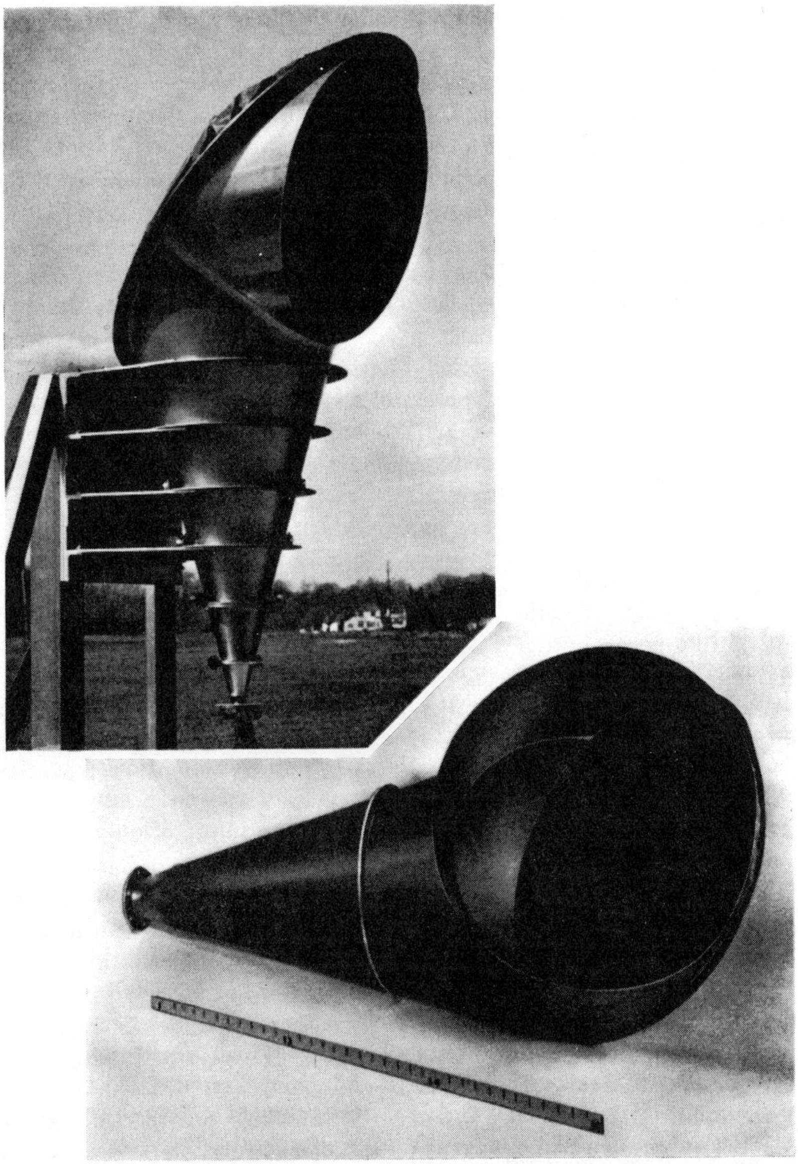

Fig. 2 — Photographs of the model antennas: upper, model one; lower, mode two.

TABLE I

	Model One	Model Two
Aperture diameter	27 inches	23 inches
Flare angle	31.5 degrees	27 degrees
Measuring frequency	11.2 kmc	10.0 kmc
Construction material	Brass sheet	Resin-impregnated Fiberglas coated with silver paint
Reflector surface tolerance	±0.010 inch	±0.060 inch

where.[5] Some of the important features of the antenna are given in Table II.

The antenna and support structure rotate about a central pintle bearing on two sets of tracks for azimuth motion. Elevation motion is accomplished by rotating the antenna about its cone axis. A rotary joint is located in the cone section approximately 6 feet from the apex. The entire antenna structure is enclosed in a 210-foot diameter radome.

III. THEORETICAL PATTERN COMPUTATION

The paraboloidal section of the antenna transforms the spherical wave in the conical horn into a plane wave. However, due to the curvature of the reflector and the differences of path length involved, the aperture field configuration is not the same as that in the horn but is somewhat distorted; the field lines tend to crowd toward that edge of the aperture closest to the apex of the horn. The amount of distortion depends upon the flare angle of the horn and becomes more pronounced as the angle increases.

Equations relating coordinates in the cone with coordinates in the aperture plane are derived in Appendix A. In essence, polar coordinates in the cone are transformed into bipolar coordinates in the aperture plane (see Fig. 1). The transformation is therefore conformal.

Once the equations of transformation are known, the linear (x and y) components of the aperture fields for the TE_{11} wave and the TM_{01} wave can be written; these are given in Appendix B. Since the principal electric vector of the TE_{11} wave can be arbitrarily oriented in the aperture plane, we have chosen two principal directions of polarization for our computation. One of these is designated longitudinal polarization, where the principal electric vector in the aperture plane is parallel to the axis of the cone; the other is designated transverse polarization, where the principal electric vector in the aperture plane is orthogonal to the axis

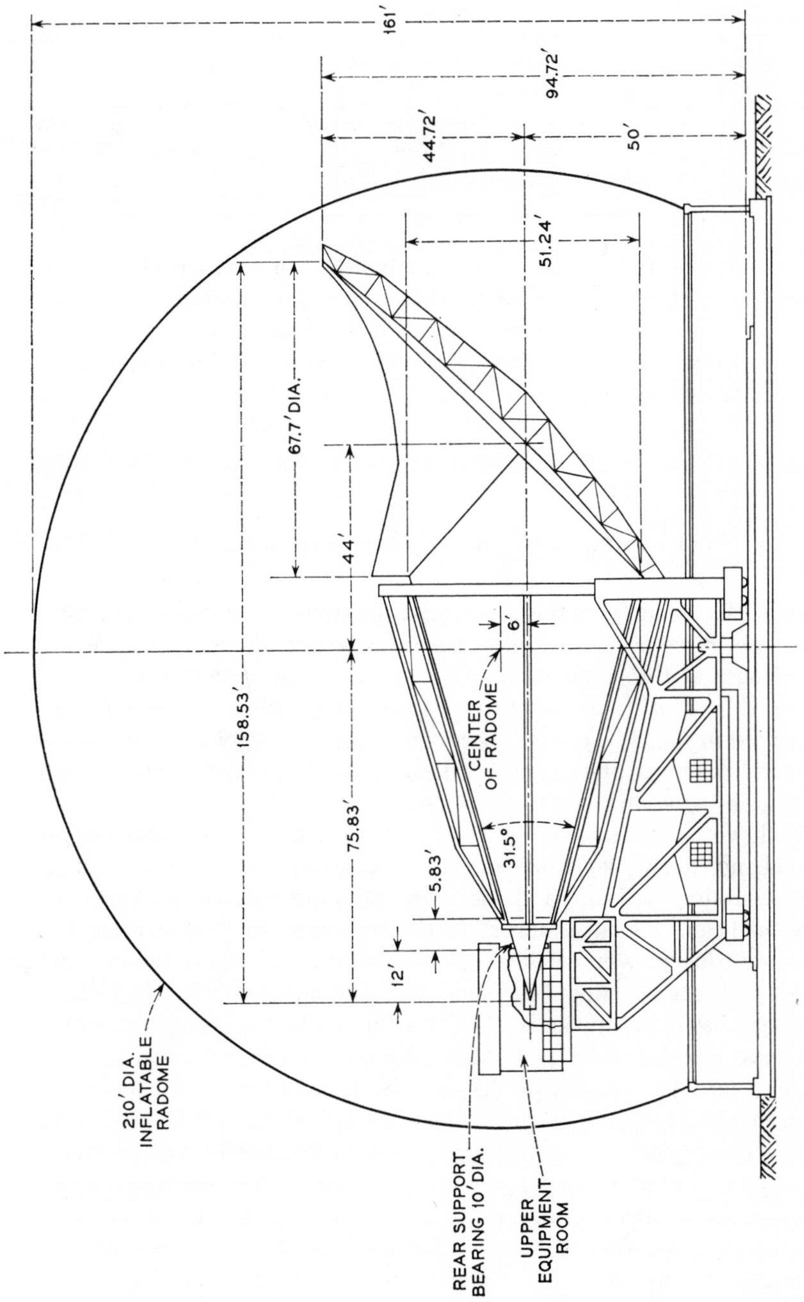

Fig. 3 — Sketch of the full-size conical horn-reflector antenna at Andover, Maine.

TABLE II

Total flare angle of conical horn	31.5 degrees
Focal length of paraboloid	60 feet
Diameter of aperture	67.7 feet = 280 wavelengths at the receiving frequency of 4079.73 mc and 440 wavelengths at the transmitting frequency of 6389.58 mc.
Aperture area	3600 square feet

of the cone. The TM_{01} wave, however, is axially symmetric in the conical horn and therefore has no principal direction of polarization.

The aperture fields being known, one can calculate the far-field patterns of the antenna near the axis of the beam to good approximation by using the integral[6]

$$\begin{aligned} g(\theta,\varphi) &= \frac{1}{4f^2}\int_0^{2\pi}\int_0^{r_0'} E(r',\varphi')\exp\,[j\beta r'\sin\theta\cos(\varphi-\varphi')]r'\,dr'\,d\varphi' \\ &= \int_0^{2\pi}\int_0^{k_0} E(s,\varphi')\exp\,[jus\cos(\varphi-\varphi')]s\,ds\,d\varphi' \end{aligned} \tag{1}$$

where $E(r',\varphi')$ represents the components of the aperture field under consideration, $\beta = 2\pi/\lambda$ is the propagation constant of free space, f is the focal length of the paraboloid, $k_0 = \tan\alpha_0 = \tan$ ($\frac{1}{2}$ flare angle of the cone), $r_0' = 2f\,k_0$ is the radius of the aperture, and $u = 2\beta f\sin\theta$. As illustrated in Fig. 1, the polar coordinates $r'(s = r'/2f)$ and φ' are in the aperture plane, and the angles θ and φ refer to the polar (z) axis through the center of the aperture plane.

We have computed the radiation patterns in two principal (longitudinal and transverse) planes and in a 45-degree plane. The longitudinal plane contains the beam and the horn axes; the transverse plane contains the beam axis but is normal to the horn axis (see Fig. 4). Since the aperture fields are symmetric about the longitudinal plane, the integral given by (1) can be reduced further. The reduced integrals for the various cases are listed in Appendix C. These integrals were programmed for numerical integration on an IBM 704 computer.

The computed patterns of the antenna excited by a TE_{11} wave are given in Figs. 5, 6 and 7, which show (as dashed curves) the principal and the cross-polarized patterns for longitudinal and transverse polarizations and in the two principal planes. Because the cross-polarized components of the aperture fields are antisymmetric about the longitudinal plane, the cross-polarized patterns for both polarizations are zero for all angles in that plane and therefore are not shown. Fig. 8 gives the

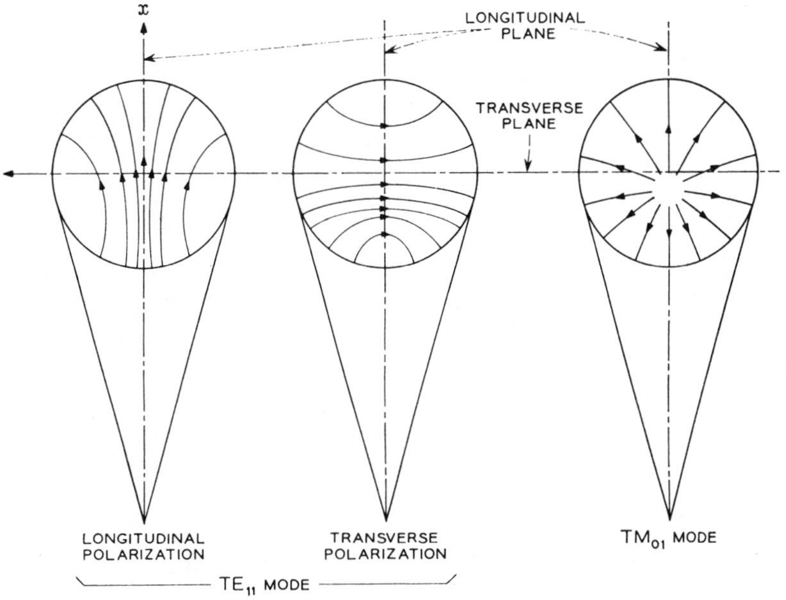

Fig. 4 — Sketch showing the electric field lines in the aperture plane of the antenna for the two modes of excitation. The principal planes in which radiation patterns are calculated and measured are also indicated.

computed radiation patterns of the antenna excited by a TM_{01} wave. Fig. 8(a) shows the pattern in the longitudinal plane for the longitudinal component of the field, and Fig. 8(b) shows the pattern in the transverse plane for the transverse component of the field. The pattern for the transverse component is zero for all angles in the longitudinal plane, and all the lobes of the pattern for the longitudinal component are more than 50 db down in the transverse plane; these patterns therefore are not shown.

The aperture efficiencies of the antenna excited by a TE_{11} wave are calculated to be 0.806 for the longitudinal polarization and 0.807 for the transverse polarization.

The radiation patterns for circular polarization may be calculated by combining the appropriate principal and cross-polarized components of the far field.[2] The computed patterns in the longitudinal and in the transverse planes are shown in Figs. 9 and 10. Due to the presence of the cross-polarized components of the far field in the transverse plane, the circularly polarized radiation patterns in the transverse plane are unsymmetrical; the maximum of the main beam is shifted by 0.97 u off the u = 0 axis, which is about one-thirteenth of the 3-db beamwidth. The direction of this shift is dependent upon the sense of the polarization, the shift being $+0.97\ u$ for one sense and $-0.97\ u$ for the other.

Certain salient features of the antenna are summarized in Table III for linear polarization and in Table IV for circular polarization. For example, at the receiver frequency of 4170 mc the power gain and the half-power beamwidth for circular polarization are 58.17 db and 0.228°, respectively, and at the transmitter frequency of 6390 mc they are 61.86 db and 0.149°, respectively.

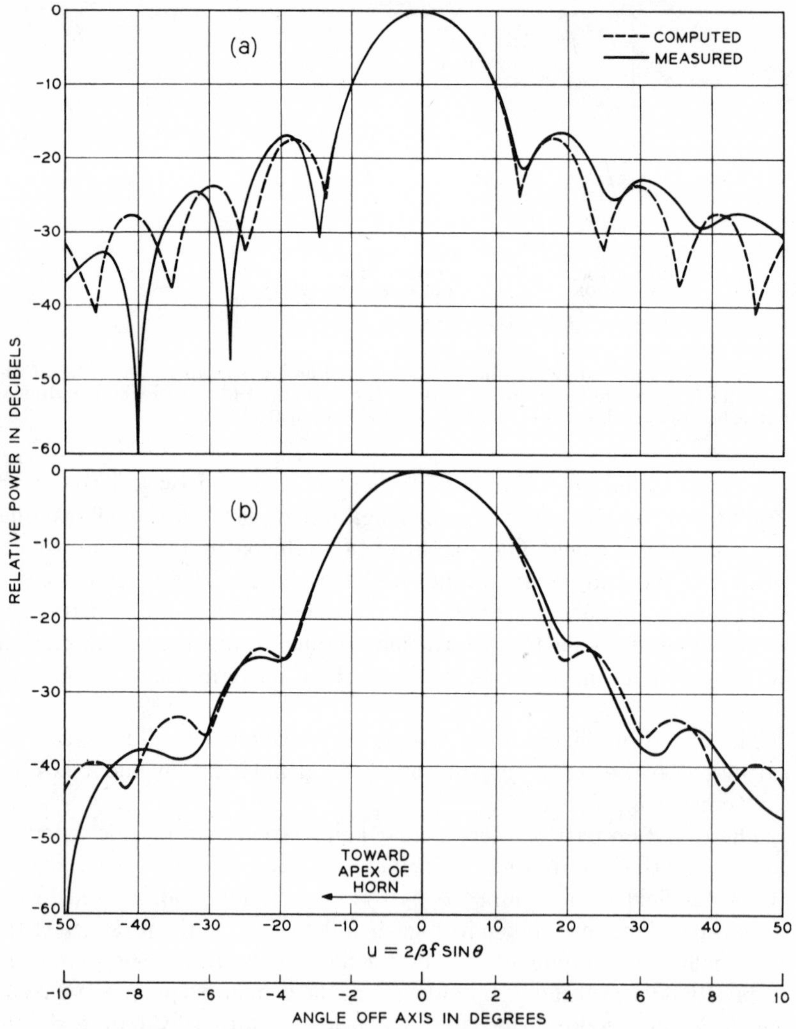

Fig. 5 — Radiation patterns for TE_{11} mode in the longitudinal plane (model one): (a) longitudinal polarization; (b) transverse polarization.

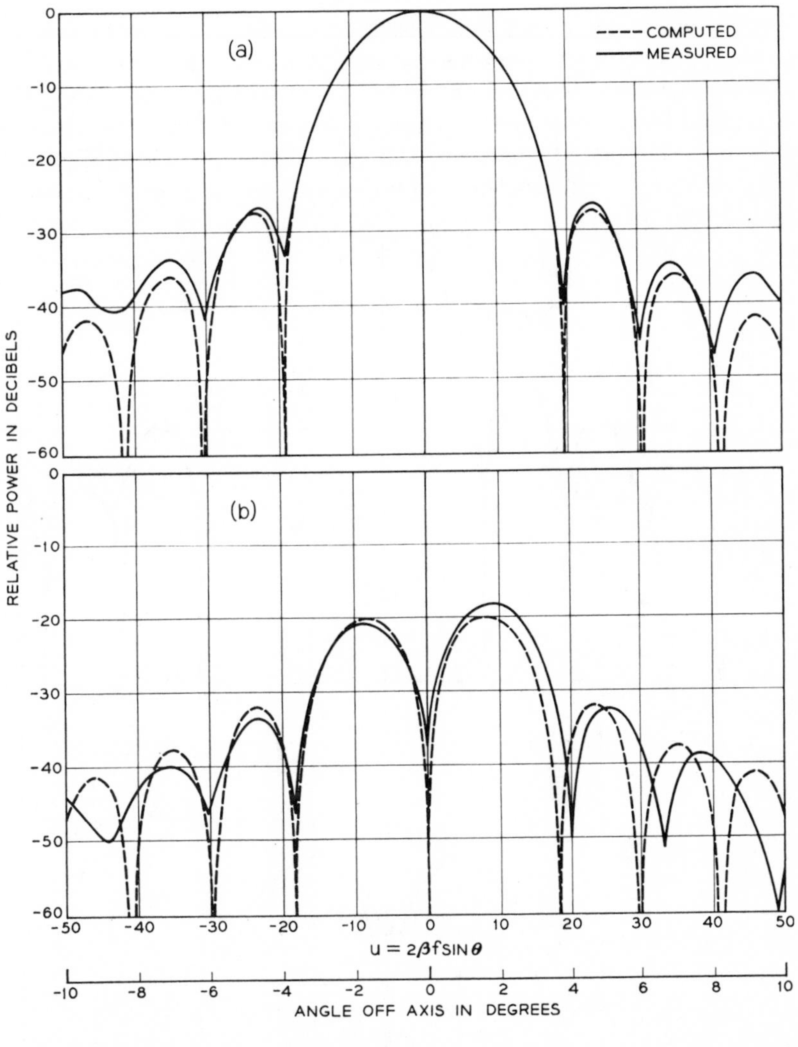

Fig. 6 — Radiation patterns for TE_{11} mode in the transverse plane (model one): (a) principal patterns for longitudinal polarization; (b) cross-polarized patterns for longitudinal polarization.

IV. MEASURED RESULTS

4.1 *Model Antennas*

Far-field radiation pattern measurements for linear polarization were made on both model antennas and showed good agreement with theoretically computed patterns. Both antennas were measured on outdoor ranges where standard antenna measuring procedure was employed. In particular, TE_{11} mode patterns for both longitudinal and transverse polarizations were measured on model one at 11.2 kmc. The measured patterns in longitudinal and transverse planes are shown as solid curves along with the computed patterns in Figs. 5 through 7. The TM_{01} mode patterns which were important to automatic tracking were measured

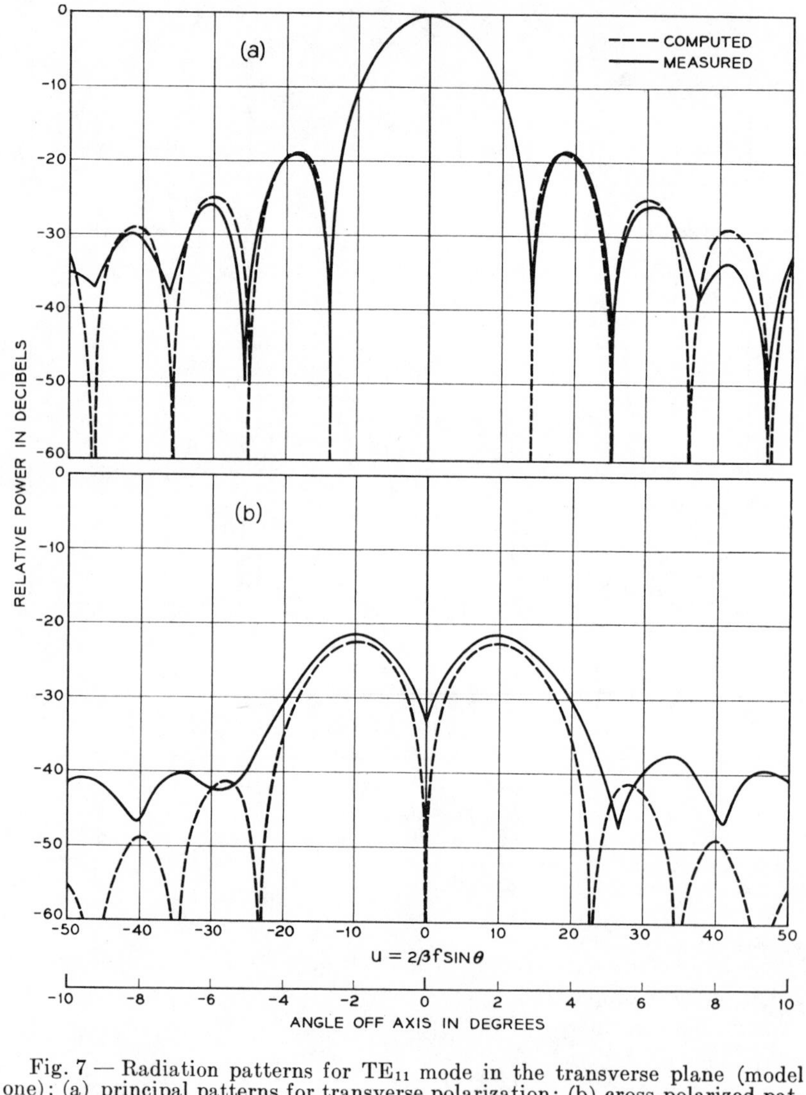

Fig. 7 — Radiation patterns for TE_{11} mode in the transverse plane (model one): (a) principal patterns for transverse polarization; (b) cross-polarized patterns for transverse polarization.

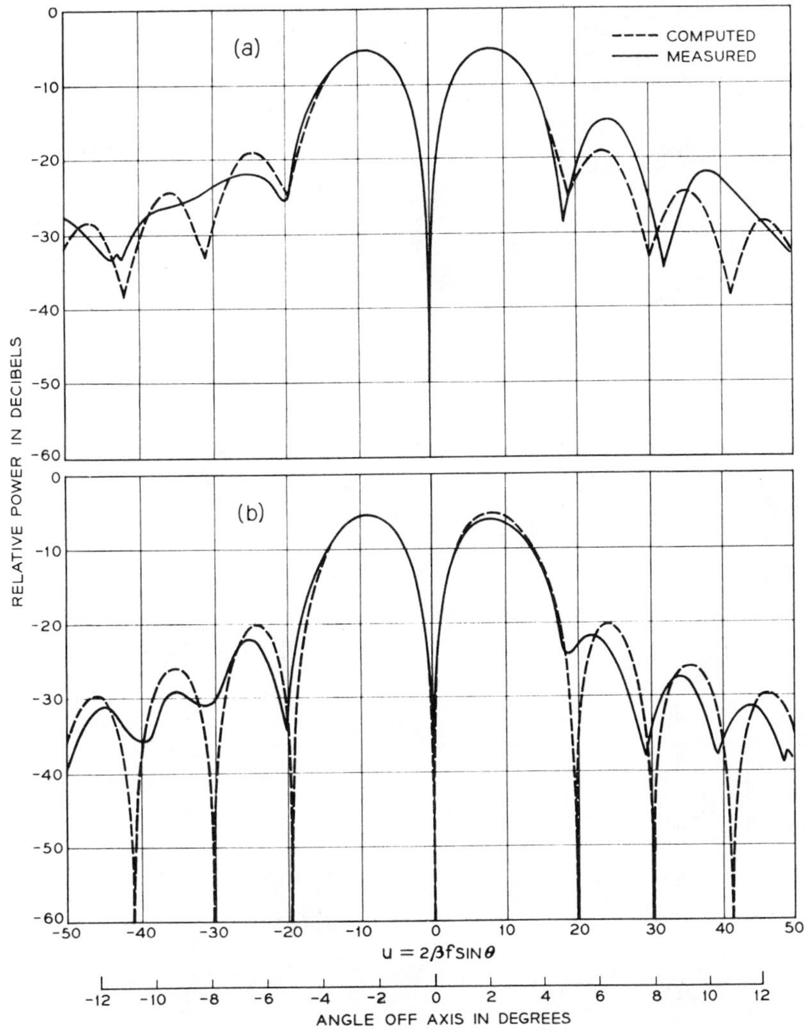

Fig. 8 — Radiation patterns for TM_{01} mode (model two): (a) in the longitudinal plane for the longitudinal component of the aperture field; (b) in the transverse plane for the transverse component of the aperture field.

on model two; these patterns are characterized by nulls in the direction of the TE_{11} beam maxima. The measured and computed patterns for the longitudinal component in the longitudinal plane and for the transverse component in the transverse plane are shown in Fig. 8, where the relative power scales are normalized to the TE_{11} mode beam maxima.

In general, the agreement between measured and computed patterns is good, especially in the region of the main beam and first side lobes. The agreement becomes poor for levels near and below the isotropic level. The discrepancies are probably due to a variety of factors which include higher-order modes, depolarization due to ground roughness, mechanical inaccuracies, and approximations involved in the theoretical analysis.

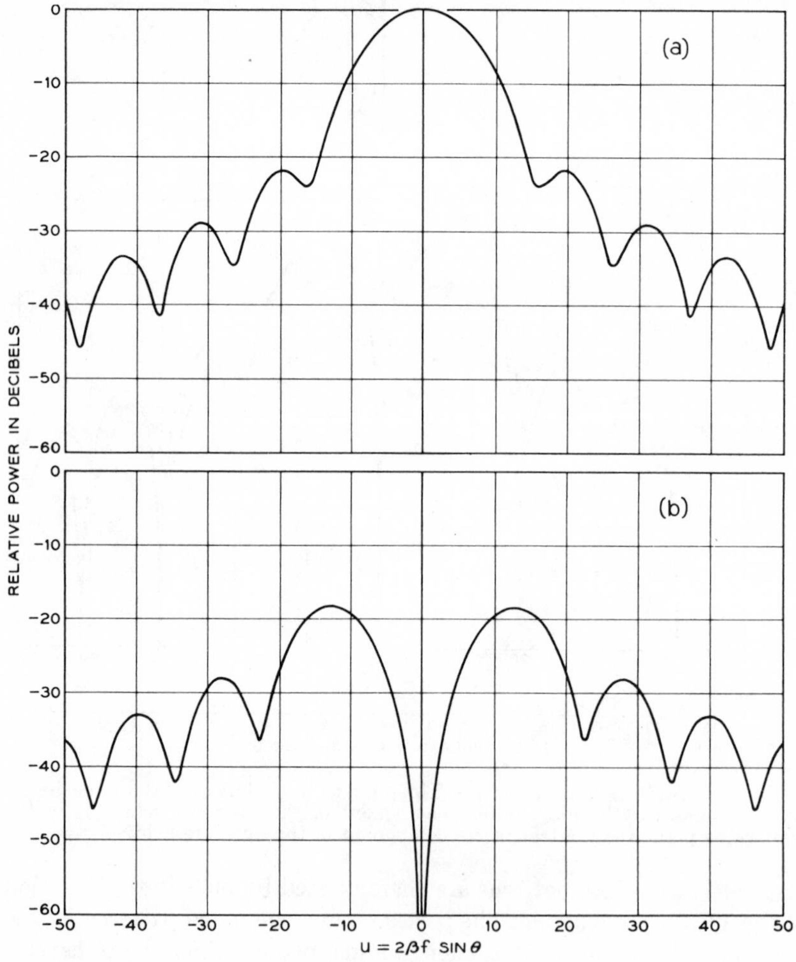

Fig. 9 — Computed circularly polarized radiation patterns for TE_{11} mode in the longitudinal plane: (a) desired sense; (b) undesired sense.

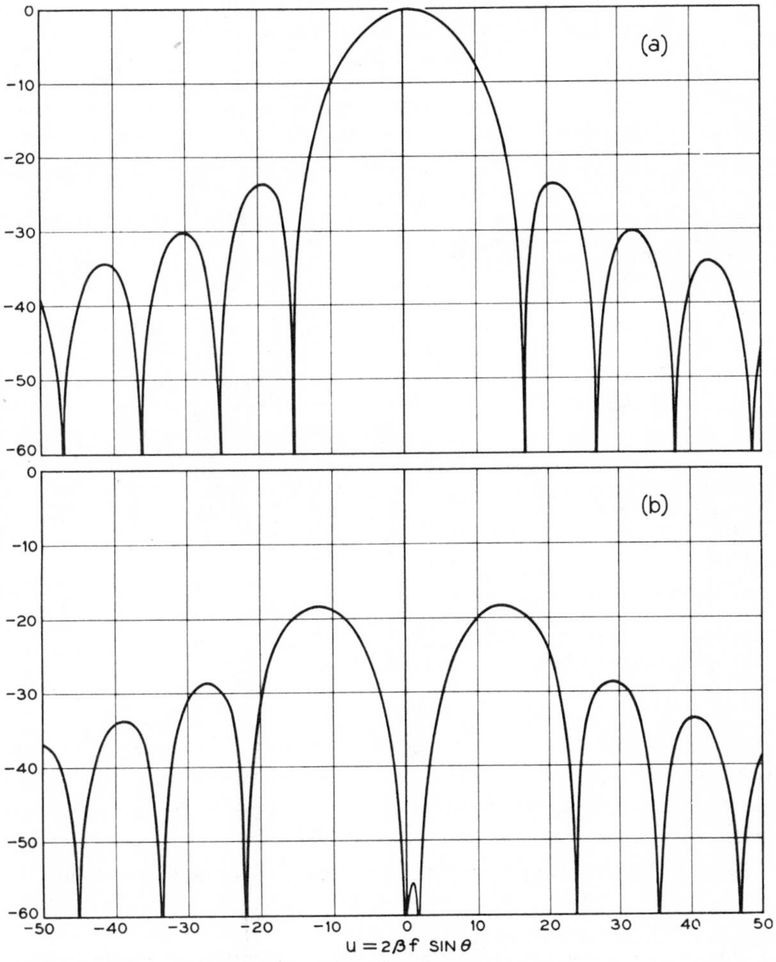

Fig. 10 — Computed circularly polarized radiation patterns for TE_{11} mode in the transverse plane: (a) desired sense; (b) undesired sense.

Gain measurements for both longitudinal and transverse polarization were made on model one, and the difference in gain between the two polarizations was less than the measurement error. The average of the measured gain corresponded to an effective area 1.3 ± 0.2 db less than the actual area. Theoretically the effective area should be 0.94 db less than the actual area.

A characteristic of the horn-reflector antenna is the spillover lobe in

TABLE III — COMPUTED RADIATION CHARACTERISTICS OF THE CONICAL HORN-REFLECTOR ANTENNA FOR LINEAR POLARIZATION (FLARE ANGLE = 31.5°)

TE_{11} Mode	Longitudinal Polarization			Transverse Polarization		
	Long. Plane	Trans. Plane	45° Plane	Long. Plane	Trans. Plane	45° Plane
3-db beamwidth ($u = 2\beta f \sin \theta$)	11.2	14.6	12.7	14.0	11.7	12.7
Null beamwidth ($u = 2\beta f \sin \theta$)	27.2	38.4	32.6	39.0	27.4	32.6
Maximum cross-polarization (db)	$-\infty$	−20.0	−17.7	$-\infty$	−22.3	−17.5
First side-lobe level (db)	−17.2	−27.0	−22.1	−24.1	−18.2	−23.1
2nd side-lobe level (db)	−23.5	−35.8	−29.6	−33.4	−24.5	−29.6
3rd side-lobe level (db)	−27.5	−41.8	−34.1	−39.4	−28.5	−33.6
TM_{01} Mode	Longitudinal Component			Transverse Component		
	Long. Plane	Trans. Plane	45° Plane	Long. Plane	Trans. Plane	45° Plane
Principal-lobe level* (db)	−5.5	−52.7	−8.5	$-\infty$	−5.7	−8.7
Null level* (db)	−52.7		−52.7		$-\infty$	$-\infty$
Width between principal lobes ($u = 2\beta f \sin \theta$)	17.0		17.0		17.0	17.0
Null width at 20 db below peak of principal lobe ($u = 2\beta f \sin \theta$)	1.1		1.1		1.1	1.1
First side-lobe level* (db)	−19.0		−22.6		−20.5	−22.9

* Relative to major-lobe level of TE_{11} mode.

the longitudinal plane with longitudinal polarization caused by diffraction over the edge of the reflector.[2] This spillover lobe in the radiation pattern was measured on model one and found to be at +68° with a level of −35 db from the main beam. The spillover does not occur for transverse polarization because of the taper in the aperture field.

TABLE IV — COMPUTED RADIATION CHARACTERISTICS OF THE CONICAL HORN-REFLECTOR ANTENNA FOR CIRCULAR POLARIZATION (FLARE ANGLE = 31.5°)

TE_{11} Mode	Longitudinal Plane	Transverse Plane
3-db beamwidth ($u = 2\beta f \sin \theta$)	12.7	12.8
Null beamwidth ($u = 2\beta f \sin \theta$)	33.6	32.4
Beam shift ($u = 2\beta f \sin \theta$)	0	0.97
Maximum level of undesired sense of polarization (db)	−18.3	−18.2
First side-lobe level (db)	−21.7	−23.6
2nd side-lobe level (db)	−28.9	−30.1
3rd side-lobe level (db)	−33.3	−34.3

4.2 *Full-Size Antenna*

4.2.1 *General*

A series of measurements and tests were conducted during February, March, and April, 1962, on the antenna at Andover, Maine. These consisted of boresight, gain, polarization and pattern measurements.

The boresight antenna,* located atop a 250-foot tower on Black Mountain 4.6 miles away, was used to illuminate the horn reflector during these measurements. The beamwidth of the boresight antenna and its height above ground were selected so that the maximum level of the ground reflected signal received by the horn reflector would be 45 db or more below the maximum direct signal when the horn reflector is on boresight. Actual measurements indicated that the reflected signal was more than 50 db below the direct signal. Evidence that the incident field was quite uniform in the azimuth plane was obtained when a comparison was made between patterns measured in the normal and plunged positions (i.e., both azimuth and elevation reversed from normal position). The comparison revealed that the two sets are nearly identical; that is, the patterns "turned over" with the antenna.

4.2.2 *Boresighting*

The electrical boresight axis is defined as the direction of the null in the center of the TM_{01} pattern used in the autotrack system. As the initial step in the calibration of antenna pointing, this axis was located and the angle data readouts were set to the boresight antenna coordinates.

The distance to the boresight antenna is approximately 24,000 feet, which is about 37 per cent shorter than that required for the conventional phase deviation of $\pi/8$ radian across the aperture. The effect of boresighting at a reduced range was investigated theoretically.[7] It was found that at this range the null in the TM_{01} pattern shifts in azimuth 0.007 degree away from the aperture normal toward the apex of the horn feed section.

By using a technique of plunging the antenna first in azimuth and then in elevation so as to again point at the boresight antenna, it is possible to determine the precise electrical pointing direction of the antenna with respect to the rotational axes. This was done, and the results of the tests

* The boresight antenna is a two-foot diameter paraboloidal reflector illuminated by a circularly polarized feed. It has a power gain of 25 db and an axial ratio of less than 2 db at 4080 mc.

can be summarized as follows. The magnitude of the parallax with respect to the azimuth axis obtained from the geometry of the ground station is 0.106 degree (the aperture is offset from the axis of azimuthal rotation). Boresighting at the reduced range decreases this angle by 0.007 degree so that the magnitude of the electric azimuth parallax should be 0.099 degree. However, the average measured electrical parallax was 0.123 $\pm$ 0.005 degree. This indicates that there is a slight outward pitch of the reflector surface which is equal to one-half this amount, or 0.012 degree, when the antenna is pointing at the boresight tower. The surveyed elevation angle to the boresight tower is 3.960 degrees and the average electrical elevation angle measured by plunging was 3.990 $\pm$ 0.005 degrees. The difference indicated an 0.030 $\pm$ 0.005 degree droop of the reflector at low elevation. These, along with more recent star-tracking measurements, generally corroborate the sag predicted by structural analysis.

4.2.3 *Gain Measurements*

Because time was at a premium, the usual technique of measuring the vertical distribution of the incident field with the standard gain horn to determine its average value was not employed in measuring the power gain of the horn-reflector antenna. Instead the standard horn was placed at a convenient point at the edge of the roof of the upper equipment room (see Fig. 3). The measured value of power gain was 57.8 $\pm$ 0.3 db. To lend support to this measurement, the directivity of the horn reflector was determined by integrating its measured radiation patterns. The value so obtained is 57.6 $\pm$ 0.2 db. These results are to be compared with the theoretical value of 57.97 db. The measurements were made at a frequency of 4080 mc.

4.2.4 *Radiation Pattern Measurements*

Radiation pattern measurements were made for the TE_{11} mode and the TM_{01} mode at 4080 mc with the antenna in the position in which it is normally operated. The horizontal and vertical components of the circularly polarized TE_{11} field excited in the circular feed section at the apex of the conical horn were measured. The patterns are called the $(TE_{11})_X$ and $(TE_{11})_Y$ patterns respectively, because they are measured at the horn apex, which does not rotate in elevation with the rest of the antenna. For small changes in elevation about this position, however, $(TE_{11})_X$ essentially corresponds to longitudinal polarization, and $(TE_{11})_Y$ to transverse polarization (see Fig. 4). The TM_{01} patterns were measured in the same manner. All of these measurements were repeated with the antenna in the plunged position. The normal position patterns are shown and compared with the computed patterns in Figs. 11 to 13. The dashed curves in the figures represent computed patterns of the far field for linear polarization with the exception of the one in Fig. 13(a), which represents the computed pattern in the longitudinal plane at the reduced range.[7]

Agreement between measured and predicted patterns over the sector of the major lobes is excellent and is fairly good in the side-lobe regions. Some discrepancy is to be expected in the side-lobe regions, however, since the measured patterns include the effect of the cross-polarized response of the antenna (the incident field was circularly polarized) while the computed points include only the linearly polarized response of the antenna. In addition, the patterns were measured at a reduced range.

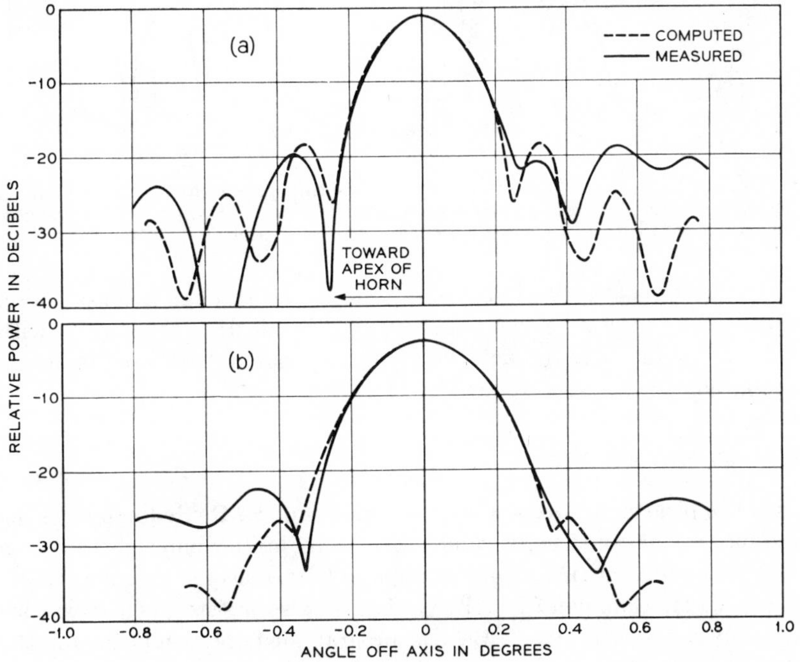

Fig. 11 — Principal radiation patterns of the full size antenna for TE_{11} mode in the longitudinal plane: (a) longitudinal polarization $(TE_{11})_X$; (b) transverse polarization $(TE_{11})_Y$. (The dashed curves are computed far-field patterns.)

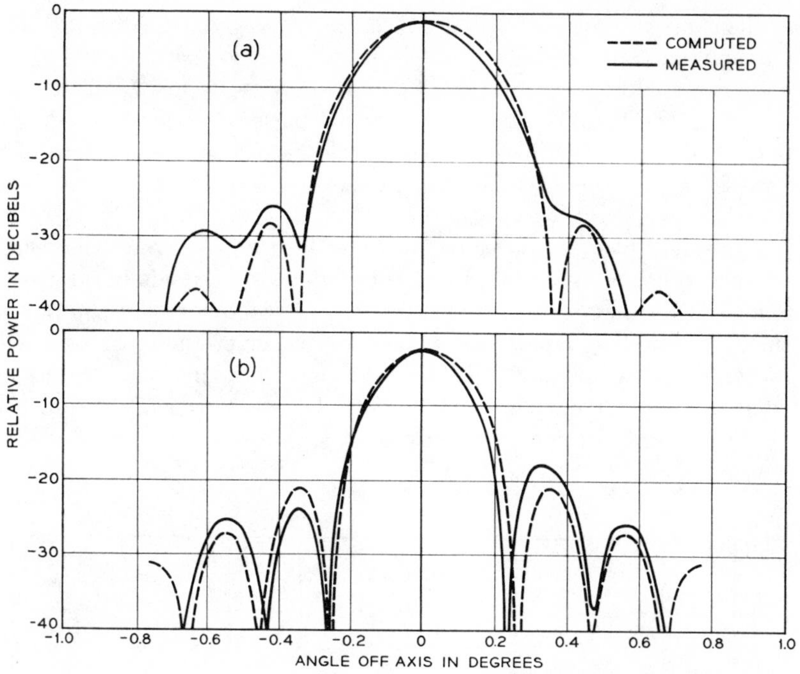

Fig. 12 — Principal radiation patterns of the full size antenna for TE_{11} mode in the transverse plane: (a) longitudinal polarization $(TE_{11})_X$; (b) transverse polarization $(TE_{11})_Y$. (The dashed curves are computed far-field patterns.)

The patterns described above were measured through a construction shelter before the permanent radome was installed. A comparison with those measured later through the permanent radome disclosed no measurable change in the patterns.

V. ACKNOWLEDGMENTS

It is a pleasure to acknowledge the efforts of R. R. Redington for assistance in the construction and adjustment of the boresight antenna and in the measurements on the full-size horn-reflector antenna. E. M. Elam, J. H. Hammond and E. C. Snyder also assisted in the various measurements. Mrs. C. L. Beattie programmed the computer for the pattern and gain computations. The aid and encouragement of A. B. Crawford, J. S. Cook and R. Lowell in these efforts are also acknowledged. In addition, the patience of the people in the servo-control group

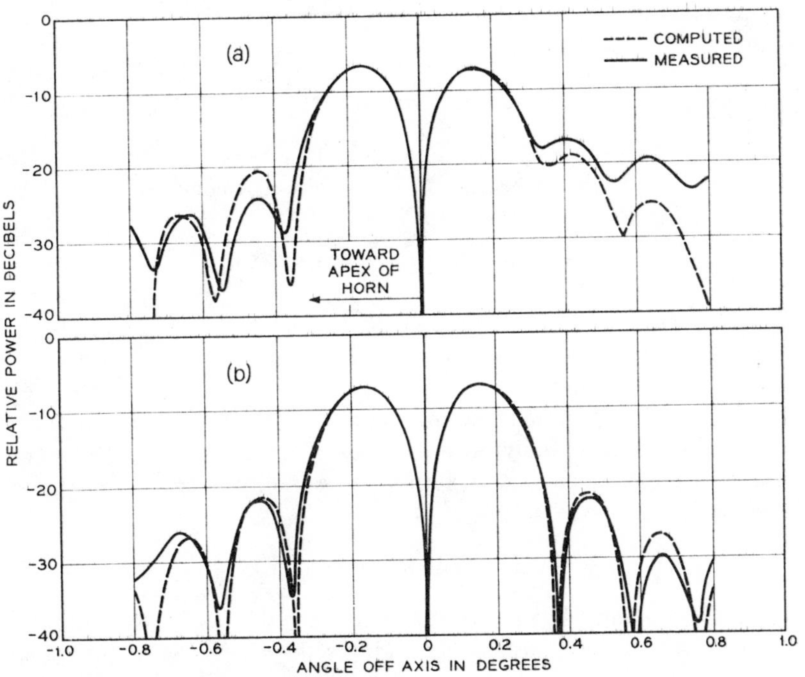

Fig. 13 — Radiation patterns of the full size antenna for TM_{01} mode: (a) in the longitudinal plane for the longitudinal component of the aperture field (the dashed curve is computed for the reduced range); (b) in the transverse plane for the transverse component of the aperture field (the dashed curve is the computed far-field pattern).

and their care exercised in moving the antenna during measurements are greatly appreciated.

APPENDIX A

The Geometry of the Antenna

The geometry of the conical horn-reflector antenna is given in Fig. 1. The apex of the conical section, which is also the focus of the paraboloidal section, is taken to be the origin of the coordinate system (X, Y, Z), and the axis of the cone is taken to be coincident with the X axis.

The equation of a cone coaxial with the conical horn is

$$Y^2 + Z^2 = k^2X^2, \tag{2}$$

where k = tan α and 2α = flare angle of the cone. The equation of the paraboloid is

$$X^2 + Y^2 = 4f(Z + f), \tag{3}$$

where f is the focal length. Eliminating Z between (2) and (3) gives the equation for the projection of intersection of cone and paraboloid in the X-Y plane. This equation is

$$(X - 2f\sqrt{k^2 + 1})^2 + Y^2 = 4f^2k^2, \tag{4}$$

which is a circle with center at $(2f\sqrt{k^2 + 1}, 0)$ and radius equal to $2fk$. Since (2) also represents circles in the Y-Z plane, we see that the paraboloidal reflector transforms a family of concentric circles in the Y-Z plane into a family of nonconcentric circles in the X-Y plane. Similarly, we can show that a family of radial lines in the Y-Z plane, after reflection from the paraboloid, transforms into a family of circles in the X-Y plane which are described by

$$X^2 + (Y - 2f \cot \eta)^2 = 4f^2 \operatorname{cosec}^2 \eta, \tag{5}$$

where $\eta = \arctan (Y/Z)$ = constant defines the family of radial lines in the Y-Z plane. Equations (4) and (5) describe a set of orthogonal coordinate systems in the X-Y plane. This is the familiar bipolar coordinate system.[8] Therefore, the transformation from the set of polar coordinates in the Y-Z plane into the set of bipolar coordinates in the X-Y plane is a conformal transformation.

APPENDIX B

The Aperture Field

The radial and the circular components of the field in the conical horn are given by

$$E_\rho = \frac{1}{\kappa\rho} J_1(\kappa\rho) \cos \eta \tag{6}$$

$$E_\eta = -\tfrac{1}{2}[J_0(\kappa\rho) - J_2(\kappa\rho)] \sin \eta \tag{7}$$

for TE_{11} mode, longitudinal polarization,

$$E_\rho = \frac{1}{\kappa\rho} J_1(\kappa\rho) \sin \eta \tag{8}$$

$$E_\eta = \tfrac{1}{2}[J_0(\kappa\rho) - J_2(\kappa\rho)] \cos \eta \tag{9}$$

for TE_{11} mode, transverse polarization, and

$$E_\rho = J_1(\gamma\rho) \tag{10}$$

$$E_\eta = 0 \tag{11}$$

for TM_{01} mode. In the above equations $\rho^2 = X^2 + Z^2$, $\tan \eta = Y/Z$ and J_n is a Bessel function of the first kind and nth order. The arguments of the Bessel function $\kappa\rho$ and $\gamma\rho$ are equal to 1.841184 (k/k_0) and 2.404826 (k/k_0), respectively, where $k_0 = \tan \alpha_0$ and $2\alpha_0$ is the total flare angle of the horn.

After reflection from the paraboloidal section, these polar components of the field transform conformally into the corresponding bipolar components in the aperture plane. E_η will lie along the family of circles given by (4) and E_ρ will lie along the orthogonal family of circles given by (5). Since the bipolar coordinate system is a curvilinear system, it is necessary to obtain the linear components of the field before radiation patterns can be computed.

For the purpose of computing radiation patterns, it is convenient to take the center of the aperture as the origin of the coordinate system. Now, the periphery of the aperture is a circle given by (4) with k replaced by k_0. Letting the center of the circular aperture be the origin of a new coordinate system in which

$$x = X - 2f\sqrt{k_0^2 + 1} \quad \text{and} \quad y = Y,$$

equation (4) becomes

$$(x + 2f\sqrt{k_0^2 + 1} - 2f\sqrt{k^2 + 1})^2 + y^2 = 4f^2k^2. \tag{12}$$

This equation gives the direction of E_η in the aperture plane. The angle, ψ_η, which E_η makes with the x axis is given by

$$\tan \psi_\eta = \frac{dy}{dx} = -(x + 2f\sqrt{k_0^2 + 1} - 2f\sqrt{k^2 + 1})/y. \tag{13}$$

Since E_ρ is perpendicular to E_η, the angle ψ_ρ between E_ρ and the x axis is given by

$$\tan \psi_\rho = -\left(\frac{dy}{dx}\right)^{-1} = -\cot \psi_\eta. \tag{14}$$

Knowing the angles ψ_η and ψ_ρ, we can now write expressions for the linear components of the aperture field; they are:

$$E_x = \frac{2f}{d}[E_\rho \cos \psi_\rho + E_\eta \cos \psi_\eta] \tag{15}$$

and

$$E_y = \frac{2f}{d}\,[E_\rho \sin \psi_\rho + E_\eta \sin \psi_\eta]\,. \tag{16}$$

where $d = f + (X^2 + Y^2)/4f$ is the distance from the apex of the horn to the reflector. The factor $2f/d$, therefore, takes into account the attenuation due to path-length difference for the spherical wave in the conical section of the antenna.

APPENDIX C

List of Integrals Used in Pattern Computation

C.1 TE_{11} *Mode*

(*i*) Longitudinal plane ($\varphi = 0°$ and $180°$)

(a) Principal patterns

$$\begin{matrix} g_L(u) \\ \\ g_T(u) \end{matrix} = \int_0^\pi \int_0^{k_0} \begin{matrix} {}_LE_x(s,\varphi') \\ \\ {}_TE_y(s,\varphi') \end{matrix} \exp\,(jus \cos \varphi')\,s\,ds\,d\varphi'$$

(b) Cross-polarized patterns

$$\begin{matrix} g_L(u) \\ \\ g_T(u) \end{matrix} = 0$$

(*ii*) Transverse plane ($\varphi = 90°$ and $270°$)

(a) Principal patterns

$$\begin{matrix} g_L(u) \\ \\ g_T(u) \end{matrix} = \int_0^\pi \int_0^{k_0} \begin{matrix} {}_LE_x(s,\varphi') \\ \\ {}_TE_y(s,\varphi') \end{matrix} \cos\,(us \sin \varphi')\,s\,ds\,d\varphi'$$

(b) Cross-polarized patterns

$$\begin{matrix} g_L(u) \\ \\ g_T(u) \end{matrix} = \int_0^\pi \int_0^{k_0} \begin{matrix} {}_LE_y(s,\varphi') \\ \\ {}_TE_x(s,\varphi') \end{matrix} \sin\,(us \sin \varphi')\,s\,ds\,d\varphi'$$

(*iii*) 45° plane ($\varphi = 45°$ and 225°)

(a) Principal patterns

$$\begin{matrix} g_L(u) \\ g_T(u) \end{matrix} = \int_0^{\pi} \int_0^{k_0} \begin{matrix} {}_LE_x(s,\varphi') \\ {}_TE_y(s,\varphi') \end{matrix} \cos\left(\frac{us}{\sqrt{2}} \sin \varphi'\right) \exp\left(j \frac{us}{\sqrt{2}} \cos \varphi'\right) s\, ds\, d\varphi'$$

(b) Cross-polarized patterns

$$\begin{matrix} g_L(u) \\ g_T(u) \end{matrix} = \int_0^{\pi} \int_0^{k_0} \begin{matrix} {}_LE_y(s,\varphi') \\ {}_TE_x(s,\varphi') \end{matrix} \sin\left(\frac{us}{\sqrt{2}} \sin \varphi'\right) \exp\left(j \frac{us}{\sqrt{2}} \cos \varphi'\right) s\, ds\, d\varphi'$$

In the above equations the subscripts L and T denote longitudinal and transverse polarizations, respectively.

C.2 *TM_{01} Mode*

(*i*) Longitudinal plane ($\varphi = 0°$ and 180°)

(a) Longitudinal component pattern

$$g_{TM}(u) = \int_0^{\pi} \int_0^{k_0} E_x(s,\varphi') \exp\,(jus \cos \varphi')s\, ds\, d\varphi'$$

(b) Transverse component pattern

$$g_{TM}(u) = 0$$

(*ii*) Transverse plane ($\varphi = 90°$ and 270°)

(a) Longitudinal component pattern

$$g_{TM}(u) = \int_0^{\pi} \int_0^{k_0} E_x(s,\varphi') \cos\,(us \sin \varphi')s\, ds\, d\varphi'$$

(b) Transverse component pattern

$$g_{TM}(u) = \int_0^{\pi} \int_0^{k_0} E_y(s,\varphi') \sin\,(us \sin \varphi')s\, ds\, d\varphi'$$

(*iii*) 45° plane ($\varphi = 45°$ and 225°)

(a) Longitudinal component pattern

$$g_{TM}(u) = \int_0^{\pi} \int_0^{k_0} E_x(s,\varphi') \cos\left(\frac{us}{\sqrt{2}} \sin \varphi'\right) \exp\left(j \frac{us}{\sqrt{2}} \cos \varphi'\right) s\, ds\, d\varphi'.$$

(b) Transverse component pattern

$$g_{\mathrm{TM}}(u) = \int_0^{\pi} \int_0^{k_0} E_y(s,\varphi') \sin\left(\frac{us}{\sqrt{2}} \sin \varphi'\right) \exp\left(j \frac{us}{\sqrt{2}} \cos \varphi'\right) s \, ds \, d\varphi'.$$

REFERENCES

1. Friis, H. T., and Beck, A. C., U. S. Patent 2,236,393, filed March 1, 1939, issued March 25, 1941.
2. Crawford, A. B., Hogg, D. C., and Hunt, L. E., A Horn-Reflector Antenna for Space Communication, B.S.T.J., **40,** July, 1961, pp. 1095–1116.
3. Buchholz, H., The Propagation of Electromagnetic Waves in a Conical Horn, Ann. d. Physik, **37,** February, 1940, pp. 173–225.
4. Schorr, M. G. and Beck, F. J., Jr., Electromagnetic Field of the Conical Horn, J. Appl. Phys., **21,** August, 1950, pp. 795–801.
5. Dolling, J. C., Blackmore, R. W., Kindermann, W. J., and Woodard, K. B., The Mechanical Design of the Conical Horn-Reflector Antenna and Radome, B.S.T.J., this issue, p. 1137.
6. Silver, S., *Microwave Antenna Theory and Design*, McGraw-Hill, New York, 1949, p. 192.
7. Lange, J., unpublished work.
8. Stratton, J. A., *Electromagnetic Theory*, McGraw-Hill, New York, 1941, p. 55.

Author Index

Subject Index

Editor's Biography

A. W. Love (M'58–SM'75) was born and educated in Toronto, Ont., Canada, receiving the B.A. degree in mathematics and physics in 1938, the M.A. in physics in 1939, and the Ph.D degree in physics in 1951, all from the University of Toronto. Following service as a Radar Officer in the U.K., the Middle East, and Australia in World War II, he then spent the years 1946–1948 as a Research Officer in the Commonwealth Scientific and Industrial Research Organization, Sydney, Australia. His work on noise standards in that organization's Radiophysics Laboratory led to interests in radio astronomy and microwave radiometry which he still maintains today.

Beginning in 1951 he spent six years in mining geophysical exploration activities with Newmont Exploration Limited, Jerome, AZ. He entered the aerospace field in 1957 with Wiley Electronics Company, Phoenix, AZ, where he developed the first successful airborne mapping radiometer, a passive sensor able to produce terrain images under all weather, day or night conditions. In 1963 he joined Rockwell International's Autonetics Division, Anaheim, CA, in charge of advanced antenna development. This was followed by two years in ECM and reentry systems work with National Engineering Science Company, Newport Beach, CA. Returning to Autonetics in late 1965, he engaged, for a time, in studies related to infrared and microwave emission processes in planetary atmospheres before he returned to the development of single and dual polarized line source feeds for large spherical reflectors. Since 1971 he has been with the Space Division of Rockwell International, Seal Beach, CA, pursuing the development of precision microwave radiometers and high beam efficiency antennas for the remote measurement of sea surface temperature from an orbiting satellite.

Dr. Love is listed in *American Men of Science*, has authored 15 papers in the above fields, and is the holder of five patents. He received the IEEE Antennas and Propagation Society's 1973 Best Paper Award for his paper, "Scale Model Development of a High Efficiency Dual Polarized Line Feed for the Arecibo Spherical Reflector," which appeared in the September 1973 issue of the Transactions.